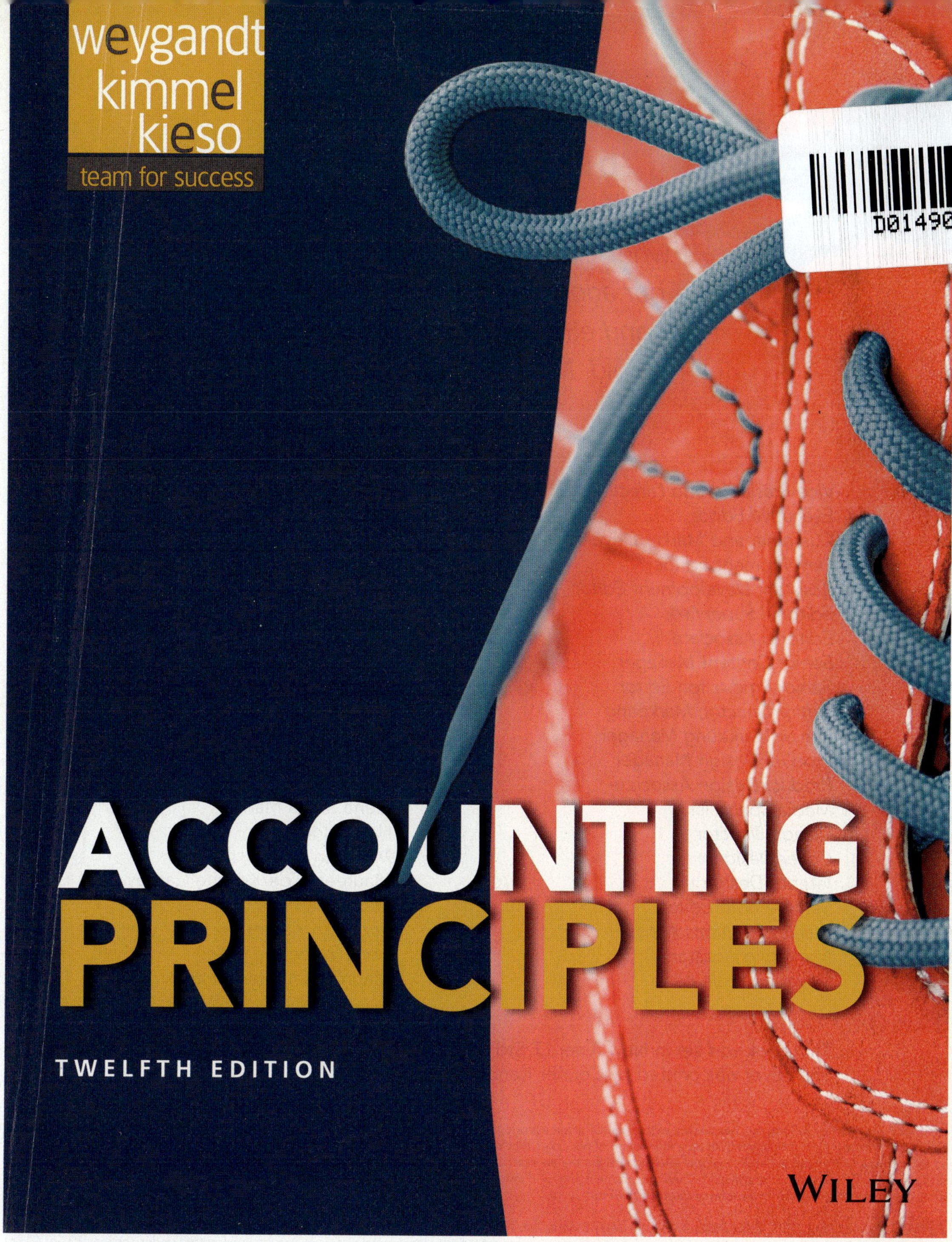

Chapters 1–18

Jerry J. Weygandt PhD, CPA
University of Wisconsin—Madison
Madison, Wisconsin

Paul D. Kimmel PhD, CPA
University of Wisconsin—Milwaukee
Milwaukee, Wisconsin

Donald E. Kieso PhD, CPA
Northern Illinois University
DeKalb, Illinois

WILEY

DEDICATED TO

*the **Wiley sales representatives** who sell our books and service our adopters in a professional and ethical manner, and to Enid, Merlynn, and Donna*

Vice President and Director	George Hoffman
Executive Editor	Michael McDonald
Customer and Market Development Manager	Christopher DeJohn
Development Editor	Ed Brislin
Assistant Development Editor	Rebecca Costantini
Editorial Supervisor	Terry Ann Tatro
Editorial Associate	Margaret Thompson
Senior Content Manager	Dorothy Sinclair
Senior Production Editor	Valerie A. Vargas
Senior Director, Marketing	Amy Scholz
Senior Marketing Manager	Karolina Zarychta Honsa
Product Design Manager	Allison Morris
Product Design Associate	Matt Origoni
Media Specialist	Elena Santa Maria
Design Director	Harry Nolan
Cover Design	Maureen Eide
Interior Design	Maureen Eide/Kristine Carney
Senior Photo Editor	Mary Ann Price
Market Solutions Assistant	Elizabeth Kearns
Marketing Assistant	Anna Wilhelm
Cover and title page	Marina Grau/Shutterstock

This book was set in New Aster LT Std by Aptara®, Inc. and printed and bound by Courier Kendallville. The cover was printed by Courier Kendallville.

Founded in 1807, John Wiley & Sons, Inc. has been a valued source of knowledge and understanding for more than 200 years, helping people around the world meet their needs and fulfill their aspirations. Our company is built on a foundation of principles that include responsibility to the communities we serve and where we live and work. In 2008, we launched a Corporate Citizenship Initiative, a global effort to address the environmental, social, economic, and ethical challenges we face in our business. Among the issues we are addressing are carbon impact, paper specifications and procurement, ethical conduct within our business and among our vendors, and community and charitable support. For more information, please visit our website: www.wiley.com/go/citizenship.

ISBN-13 978-1-118-97874-0

Binder-Ready Version ISBN 978-1-118-96990-8

Printed in the United States of America

10 9 8 7 6 5 4 3 2 1

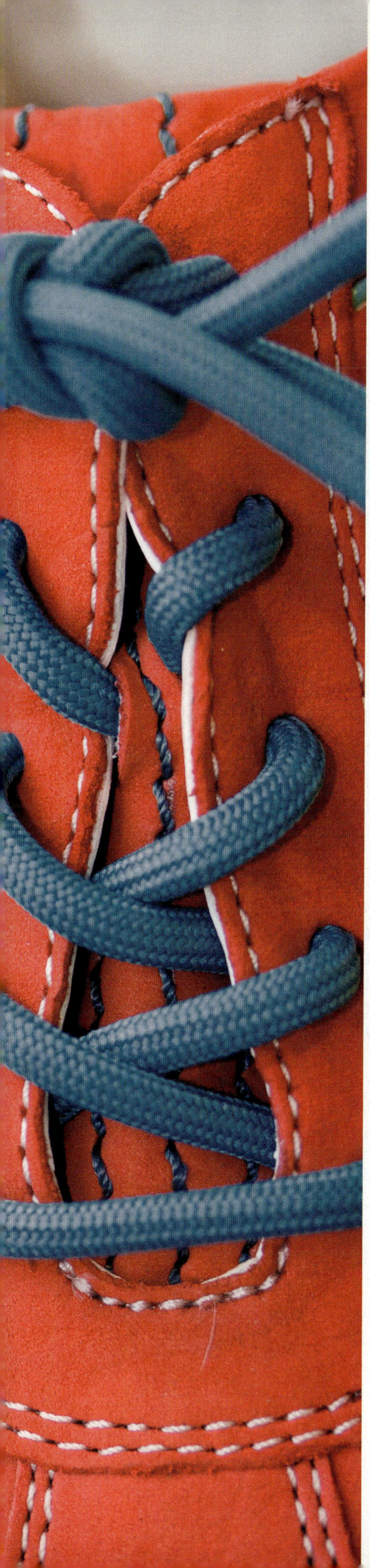

Brief Contents

*Available at the book's companion website, **www.wiley.com/college/weygandt**.

From the Authors

Dear Student,

Why This Course? *Remember your biology course in high school? Did you have one of those "invisible man" models (or maybe something more high-tech than that) that gave you the opportunity to look "inside" the human body? This accounting course offers something similar. To understand a business, you have to understand the financial insides of a business organization. An accounting course will help you understand the essential financial components of businesses. Whether you are looking at a large multinational company like* Apple *or* Starbucks *or a single-owner software consulting business or coffee shop, knowing the fundamentals of accounting will help you understand what is happening. As an employee, a manager, an investor,a business owner, or a director of your own personal finances—any of which roles you will have at some point in your life—you will make better decisions for having taken this course.*

"Whether you are looking at a large multinational company like Apple or Starbucks or a single-owner software consulting business or coffee shop, knowing the fundamentals of accounting will help you understand what is happening."

Why This Book? *Hundreds of thousands of students have used this textbook. Your instructor has chosen it for you because of its trusted reputation. The authors have worked hard to keep the book fresh, timely, and accurate.*

How to Succeed? *We've asked many students and many instructors whether there is a secret for success in this course. The nearly unanimous answer turns out to be not much of a secret: "Do the homework." This is one course where doing is learning. The more time you spend on the homework assignments—using the various tools that this textbook provides—the more likely you are to learn the essential concepts, techniques, and methods of accounting. Besides the textbook itself, WileyPLUS and the book's companion website also offers various support resources.*

Good luck in this course. We hope you enjoy the experience and that you put to good use throughout a lifetime of success the knowledge you obtain in this course. We are sure you will not be disappointed.

Jerry J. Weygandt
Paul D. Kimmel
Donald E. Kieso

Author Commitment

Jerry Weygandt

Jerry J. Weygandt, PhD, CPA, is Arthur Andersen Alumni Emeritus Professor of Accounting at the University of Wisconsin—Madison. He holds a Ph.D. in accounting from the University of Illinois. Articles by Professor Weygandt have appeared in the *Accounting Review, Journal of Accounting Research, Accounting Horizons, Journal of Accountancy*, and other academic and professional journals. These articles have examined such financial reporting issues as accounting for price-level adjustments, pensions, convertible securities, stock option contracts, and interim reports. Professor Weygandt is author of other accounting and financial reporting books and is a member of the American Accounting Association, the American Institute of Certified Public Accountants, and the Wisconsin Society of Certified Public Accountants. He has served on numerous committees of the American Accounting Association and as a member of the editorial board of the Accounting Review; he also has served as President and Secretary-Treasurer of the American Accounting Association. In addition, he has been actively involved with the American Institute of Certified Public Accountants and has been a member of the Accounting Standards Executive Committee (AcSEC) of that organization. He has served on the FASB task force that examined the reporting issues related to accounting for income taxes and served as a trustee of the Financial Accounting Foundation. Professor Weygandt has received the Chancellor's Award for Excellence in Teaching and the Beta Gamma Sigma Dean's Teaching Award. He is on the board of directors of M & I Bank of Southern Wisconsin. He is the recipient of the Wisconsin Institute of CPA's Outstanding Educator's Award and the Lifetime Achievement Award. In 2001 he received the American Accounting Association's Outstanding Educator Award.

Paul Kimmel

Paul D. Kimmel, PhD, CPA, received his bachelor's degree from the University of Minnesota and his doctorate in accounting from the University of Wisconsin. He is an Associate Professor at the University of Wisconsin—Milwaukee, and has public accounting experience with Deloitte & Touche (Minneapolis). He was the recipient of the UWM School of Business Advisory Council Teaching Award, the Reggie Taite Excellence in Teaching Award and a three-time winner of the Outstanding Teaching Assistant Award at the University of Wisconsin. He is also a recipient of the Elijah Watts Sells Award for Honorary Distinction for his results on the CPA exam. He is a member of the American Accounting Association and the Institute of Management Accountants and has published articles in *Accounting Review, Accounting Horizons, Advances in Management Accounting, Managerial Finance, Issues in Accounting Education, Journal of Accounting Education,* as well as other journals. His research interests include accounting for financial instruments and innovation in accounting education. He has published papers and given numerous talks on incorporating critical thinking into accounting education, and helped prepare a catalog of critical thinking resources for the Federated Schools of Accountancy.

Don Kieso

Donald E. Kieso, PhD, CPA, received his bachelor's degree from Aurora University and his doctorate in accounting from the University of Illinois. He has served as chairman of the Department of Accountancy and is currently the KPMG Emeritus Professor of Accountancy at Northern Illinois University. He has public accounting experience with Price Waterhouse & Co. (San Francisco and Chicago) and Arthur Andersen & Co. (Chicago) and research experience with the Research Division of the American Institute of Certified Public Accountants (New York). He has done post doctorate work as a Visiting Scholar at the University of California at Berkeley and is a recipient of NIU's Teaching Excellence Award and four Golden Apple Teaching Awards. Professor Kieso is the author of other accounting and business books and is a member of the American Accounting Association, the American Institute of Certified Public Accountants, and the Illinois CPA Society. He has served as a member of the Board of Directors of the Illinois CPA Society, then AACSB's Accounting Accreditation Committees, the State of Illinois Comptroller's Commission, as Secretary-Treasurer of the Federation of Schools of Accountancy, and as Secretary-Treasurer of the American Accounting Association. Professor Kieso is currently serving on the Board of Trustees and Executive Committee of Aurora University, as a member of the Board of Directors of Kishwaukee Community Hospital, and as Treasurer and Director of Valley West Community Hospital. From 1989 to 1993 he served as a charter member of the national Accounting Education Change Commission. He is the recipient of the Outstanding Accounting Educator Award from the Illinois CPA Society, the FSA's Joseph A. Silvoso Award of Merit, the NIU Foundation's Humanitarian Award for Service to Higher Education, a Distinguished Service Award from the Illinois CPA Society, and in 2003 an honorary doctorate from Aurora University.

Practice Made Simple

The Team for Success is focused on helping students get the most out of their accounting course by **making practice simple**. Both in the printed text and the online environment of *WileyPLUS*, new opportunities for self-guided practice allow students to check their knowledge of accounting concepts, skills, and problem-solving techniques as they receive individual feedback at the question, learning objective, and course level.

Personalized Practice

Based on cognitive science, **WileyPLUS with ORION** is a personalized, adaptive learning experience that gives students the practice they need to build proficiency on topics while using their study time most effectively. The adaptive engine is powered by hundreds of unique questions per chapter, giving students endless opportunities for practice throughout the course.

WILEY

Streamlined Learning Objectives

Newly streamlined learning objectives help students make the best use of their time outside of class. Each learning objective is addressed by reading content, answering a variety of practice and assessment questions, and watching educational videos, so that no matter where students begin their work, the relevant resources and practice are readily accessible.

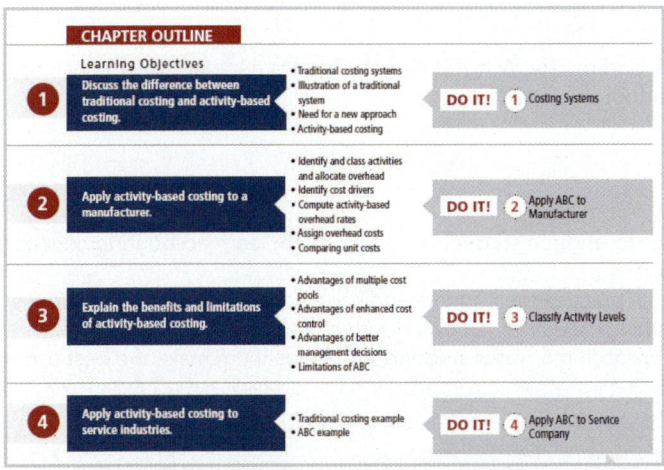

CHAPTER OUTLINE

Learning Objectives		
1 Discuss the difference between traditional costing and activity-based costing.	• Traditional costing systems • Illustration of a traditional system • Need for a new approach • Activity-based costing	DO IT! 1 Costing Systems
2 Apply activity-based costing to a manufacturer.	• Identify and class activities and allocate overhead • Identify cost drivers • Compute activity-based overhead rates • Assign overhead costs • Comparing unit costs	DO IT! 2 Apply ABC to Manufacturer
3 Explain the benefits and limitations of activity-based costing.	• Advantages of multiple cost pools • Advantages of enhanced cost control • Advantages of better management decisions • Limitations of ABC	DO IT! 3 Classify Activity Levels
4 Apply activity-based costing to service industries.	• Traditional costing example • ABC example	DO IT! 4 Apply ABC to Service Company

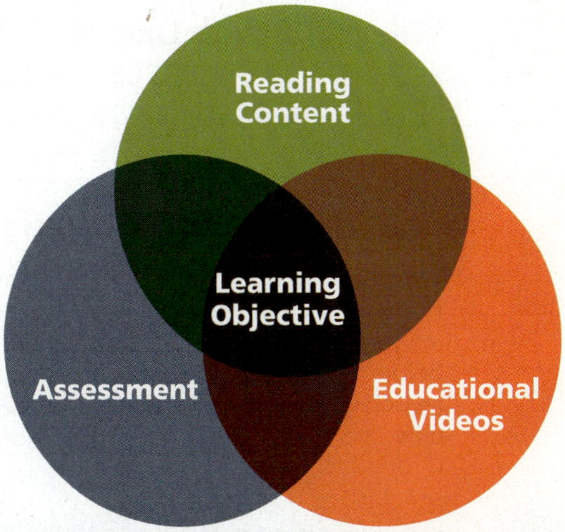

Review and Practice

A new section in the text and in **WileyPLUS** offers students more opportunities for self-guided practice.

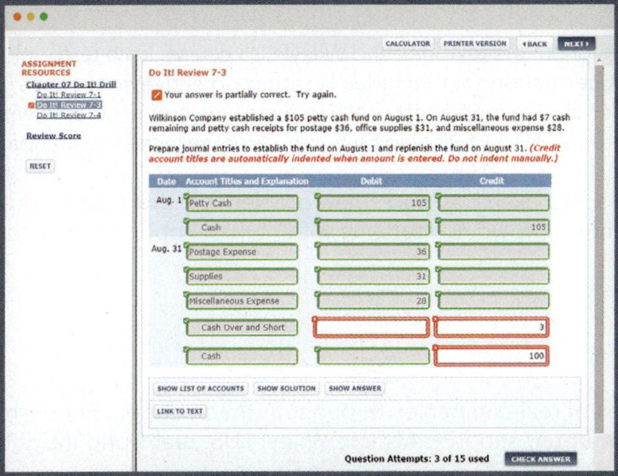

In the text, the new Review and Practice section includes:

- Learning Objectives Review
- Glossary Review
- Practice Multiple-Choice Questions and Solutions
- Practice Exercises and Solutions
- Practice Problem and Solution

In **WileyPLUS**, the new practice assignments include several Do ITs, Brief Exercises, Exercises, and Problems, giving students the opportunity to check their work or see the answer and solution after their final attempt.

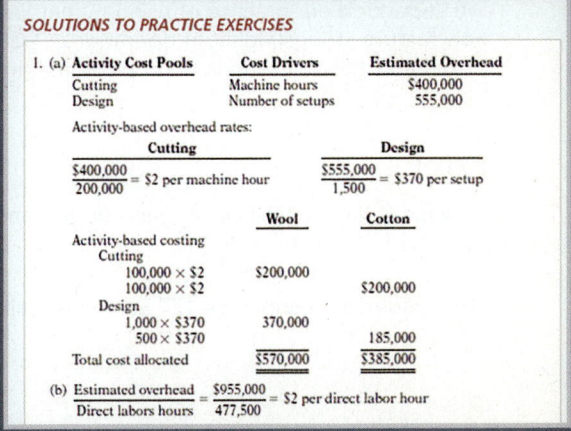

SOLUTIONS TO PRACTICE EXERCISES

1. (a)

Activity Cost Pools	Cost Drivers	Estimated Overhead
Cutting	Machine hours	$400,000
Design	Number of setups	555,000

Activity-based overhead rates:

Cutting: $\frac{\$400,000}{200,000} = \$2$ per machine hour

Design: $\frac{\$555,000}{1,500} = \$370$ per setup

	Wool	Cotton
Activity-based costing		
Cutting		
100,000 × $2	$200,000	
100,000 × $2		$200,000
Design		
1,000 × $370	370,000	
500 × $370		185,000
Total cost allocated	$570,000	$385,000

(b) $\frac{\text{Estimated overhead}}{\text{Direct labors hours}} = \frac{\$955,000}{477,500} = \$2$ per direct labor hour

WILEY

What's New?

WileyPLUS with ORION

Over 5,500 new questions are available for practice and review. WileyPLUS with Orion is an adaptive study and practice tool that helps students build proficiency in course topics.

Updated Content and Design

We scrutinized all chapter material to find new ways to engage students and help them learn accounting concepts. Homework problems were updated in all chapters.

A new learning objective structure helps students practice their understanding of concepts with DO IT! exercises before they move on to different topics in other learning objectives. Coupled with a new interior design and revised infographics, the new outcomes-oriented approach motivates students and helps them make the best use of their time.

WileyPLUS Videos

Over 300 videos are available in WileyPLUS. More than 150 of the videos are new to the 12th Edition. The videos walk students through relevant homework problems and solutions, review important concepts, provide overviews of Excel skills, and explore topics in a real-world context.

Student Practice and Solutions

New practice opportunities with solutions are integrated throughout the textbook and WileyPLUS course. Each textbook chapter now provides students with a **Review and Practice** section that includes learning objective summaries, multiple-choice questions with feedback for each answer choice, and both practice exercises and problems with solutions. Also, each learning objective module in the textbook is now followed by a DO IT! exercise with an accompanying solution.

In **WileyPLUS**, two brief exercises, two DO IT! exercises, two exercises, and a new problem are available for practice with each chapter. These practice questions are algorithmic, providing students with multiple opportunities for advanced practice.

Real World Context

We expanded our practice of using numerous examples of real companies throughout the textbook. For example, new feature stories highlight operations of Clif Bar, Groupon, and REI. Also, in WileyPLUS, real-world Insight boxes now have questions that can be assigned as homework.

Excel

New Excel skill videos help students understand Excel features they can apply in their accounting studies.

More information about the 12th Edition is available on the book's website at **www.wiley.com/college/weygandt**.

Table of Contents

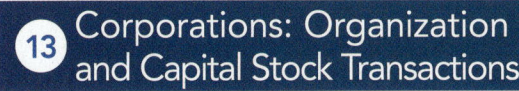

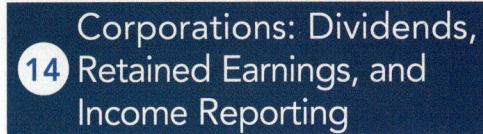

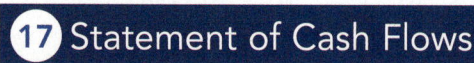

*Available online at **www.wiley.com/college/weygandt**.

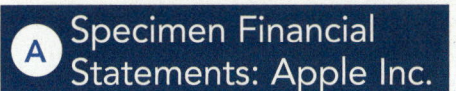

Acknowledgments

Accounting Principles has benefited greatly from the input of focus group participants, manuscript reviewers, those who have sent comments by letter or e-mail, ancillary authors, and proofers. We greatly appreciate the constructive suggestions and innovative ideas of reviewers and the creativity and accuracy of the ancillary authors and checkers.

Twelfth Edition

Karen Andrews
Lewis-Clark State College

Sandra Bailey
Oregon Institute of Technology

Shele Bannon
Queensborough Community College

Robert Barta
Suffolk County Community College

Quent Below
Roane State Community College

Lila Bergman
Hunter College

Glen Brauchle
Dowling College

Douglas Brown
Forsyth Technical Community College

Ronald Campbell
North Carolina A&T State University

Elizabeth Capener
Dominican University of California

Beth Carraway
Horry-Georgetown Technical College

Jackie Caseu
Cape Fear Community College

Kim Charland
Kansas State University

Suzanne Cory
St. Mary's University

Paul Cox
Medgar Evers College

Joseph Cunningham
Harford Community College

Kate Demarest
Carroll Community College

Richard Dugger
Kilgore College

Bill Elliott
Oral Roberts University

Cole Engel
Fort Hays State University

Gary Ford
Tompkins Cortland Community College

Alan Foster
J.S. Reynolds Community College

Dale Fowler
Ohio Christian University

George Gardner
Bemidji State University

Willard Garman
University of California, Los Angeles

Jospeh Jurkowski
D'youville College

Randy Kidd
Metropolitan Community College

Cindy Killian
Wilkes Community College

Shirly Kleiner
Johnson County Community College

David Krug
Johnson County Community College

Christy Land
Catawba Valley Community College

Anita Leslie
York Technical College

Lori Major
Luzerne County Community College

Charles Malone
North Carolina A&T State University

Ken Mark
Kansas City Kansas Community College

Barbara Michal
University of Rio Grande

Allison Moore
Los Angeles Southwest College

Brandis Phillips
North Carolina A&T State University

Mary Phillips
North Carolina Central University

La Vonda Ramey
Schoolcraft College

J. Ramos-Alexander
New Jersey City University

Michelle Randall
Schoolcraft College

Ruthie Reynolds
Tennessee State University

Kathie Rogers
Suffolk Community College

Kent Schneider
East Tennessee State University

Nadia Schwartz
Augustana College

Mehdi Sheikholeslami
Bemidji State University

Bradley Smith
Des Moines Area Community College

Emil Soriano
Contra Costa College

John Stancil
Florida Southern College

Linda Summey
Central Carolina Community College

Joan Van Hise
Fairfield University

Pat Wright
Long Island University

Judith Zander
Grossmont College

WileyPLUS Developers and Reviewers

Carole Brandt-Fink
Laura McNally
Melanie Yon

Ancillary Authors, Contributors, Proofers, and Accuracy Checkers

Bridget Anakwe
Delaware State University

Michael Barnes
Lansing Community College

Ellen Bartley
St. Joseph's College

LuAnn Bean
Florida Institute of Technology

Jack Borke
University of Wisconsin—Platteville

Sandee Cohen
Columbia College Chicago

Terry Elliott
Morehead State University

James Emig
Villanova University

Larry Falcetto
Emporia State University

Heidi Hansel
Kirkwood Community College

Coby Harmon
University of California—Santa Barbara

Karen Hern
Grossmont College

Derek Jackson
St. Mary's University of Minnesota

Laurie Larson
Valencia College

Jeanette Milius
Iowa Western Community College

Jill Misuraca
University of Tampa

Barbara Muller
Arizona State University

Yvonne Phang
Borough of Manhattan Community College

Laura Prosser
Black Hills State University

Alice Sineath
University of Maryland University College

Lakshmy Sivaratnam
Kansas City Kansas Community College

Teresa Speck
St. Mary's University of Minnesota

Lynn Stallworth
Appalachian State University

Calvin Tan
Kapiolani Community College

Mike Trebesh
Lansing Community College

Dick Wasson
Southwestern College

Lori Grady Zaher
Bucks County Community College

Advisory Board

Janice Akao
Butler Community College

Michael Barnes
Lansing Community College

Jackie Casey
Cape Fear Community College

Lisa Cole
Johnson County Community College

Susan Cordes
Johnson County Community College

Kim Gatzke
Delgado Community College

Drew Goodson
Central Carolina Community College

Thomas Kam
Hawaii Pacific University

Alfonso Maldonado
Laredo Community College

Lakshmy Sivaratnam
Kansas City Kansas Community College

Patricia Walczak
Lansing Community College

We appreciate the considerable support provided to us by the following people at Current Designs: Mike Cichanowski, Jim Brown, Diane Buswell, and Jake Greseth. We also benefited from the assistance and suggestions provided to us by Joan Van Hise in the preparation of materials related to sustainability.

We appreciate the exemplary support and commitment given to us by executive editor Michael McDonald, senior marketing manager Karolina Zarychta Honsa, customer and product development manager Christopher DeJohn, development editor Ed Brislin, assistant development editor Rebecca Costantini, market solutions assistant Elizabeth Kearns, marketing assistant Anna Wilhelm, editorial supervisor Terry Ann Tatro, editorial associate Margaret Thompson, product design manager Allie Morris, product design associate Matt Origoni, designers Maureen Eide and Kristine Carney, photo editor Mary Ann Price, indexer Steve Ingle, and Denise Showers at Aptara. All of these professionals provided innumerable services that helped the textbook take shape.

Finally, our thanks to Amy Scholz, Susan Elbe, George Hoffman, Tim Stookesberry, Douglas Reiner, Brent Gordon, Joe Heider, and Steve Smith for their support and leadership in Wiley's Global Education. We will appreciate suggestions and comments from users—instructors and students alike. You can send your thoughts and ideas about the textbook to us via email at: *AccountingAuthors@yahoo.com.*

Jerry J. Weygandt
Madison, Wisconsin

Paul D. Kimmel
Milwaukee, Wisconsin

Donald E. Kieso
DeKalb, Illinois

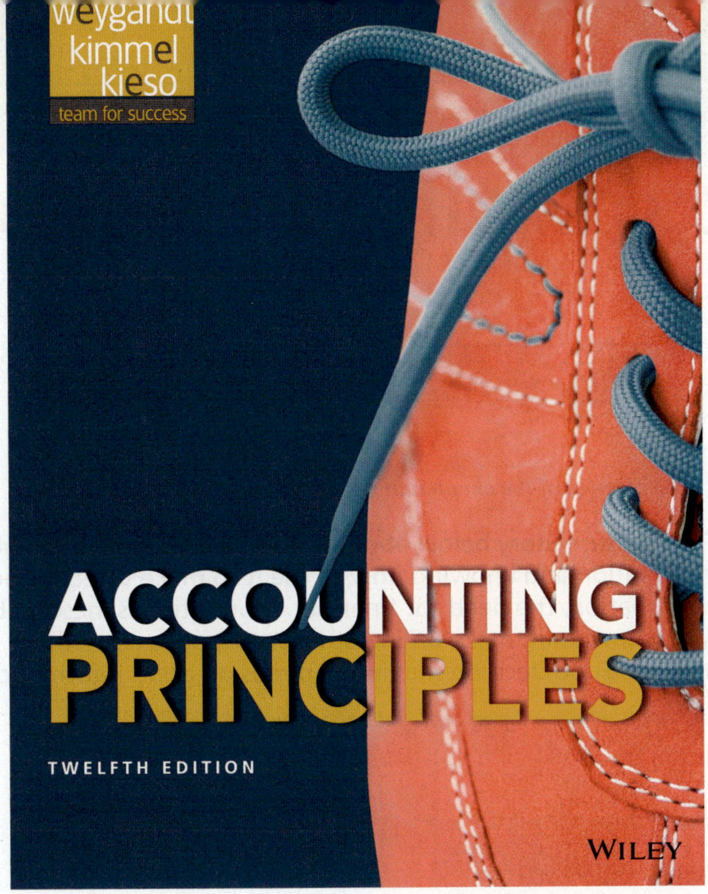
weygandt
kimmel
kieso
team for success
ACCOUNTING
PRINCIPLES
TWELFTH EDITION
WILEY

1 Accounting in Action

*The **Chapter Preview** describes the purpose of the chapter and highlights major topics.*

CHAPTER PREVIEW The Feature Story below about Clif Bar & Company highlights the importance of having good financial information and knowing how to use it to make effective business decisions. Whatever your pursuits or occupation, the need for financial information is inescapable. You cannot earn a living, spend money, buy on credit, make an investment, or pay taxes without receiving, using, or dispensing financial information. Good decision-making depends on good information.

*The **Feature Story** helps you picture how the chapter topic relates to the real world of accounting and business.*

FEATURE STORY

Knowing the Numbers

Many students who take this course do not plan to be accountants. If you are in that group, you might be thinking, "If I'm not going to be an accountant, why do I need to know accounting?" Well, consider this quote from Harold Geneen, the former chairman of IT&T: "To be good at your business, you have to know the numbers—cold." In business, accounting and financial statements are the means for communicating the numbers. If you don't know how to read financial statements, you can't really know your business.

Many businesses agree with this view. They see the value of their employees being able to read financial statements and understand how their actions affect the company's financial results. For example, consider Clif Bar & Company. The original Clif Bar® energy bar was created in 1990 by Gary Erickson and his mother in her kitchen. Today, the company has almost 300 employees.

Clif Bar is guided by what it calls its Five Aspirations—Sustaining Our Business, Our Brands, Our People, Our Community, and the Planet. Its website documents its efforts and accomplishments in these five areas. Just a few examples include the company's use of organic products to protect soil, water, and biodiversity; the "smart" solar array (the largest in North America), which provides nearly all the electrical needs for its 115,000-square foot building; and the incentives Clif Bar provides to employees to reduce their personal environmental impact, such as $6,500 toward the purchase of an efficient car or $1,000 per year for eco-friendly improvements toward their homes.

One of the company's proudest moments was the creation of an employee stock ownership plan (ESOP) in 2010. This plan gives its employees 20% ownership of the company (Gary and his wife Kit own the other 80%). The ESOP also resulted in Clif Bar enacting an open-book management program, including the commitment to educate all employee-owners about its finances. Armed with this basic financial knowledge, employees are more aware of the financial impact of their actions, which leads to better decisions.

Many other companies have adopted this open-book management approach. Even in companies that do not practice open-book management, employers generally assume that managers in all areas of the company are "financially literate."

Taking this course will go a long way to making you financially literate. In this textbook, you will learn how to read and prepare financial statements, and how to use basic tools to evaluate financial results. Throughout this textbook, we attempt to increase your familiarity with financial reporting by providing numerous references, questions, and exercises that encourage you to explore the financial statements of well-known companies.

© Dan Moore/iStockphoto

*The **Chapter Outline** presents the chapter's topics and subtopics, as well as practice opportunities.*

CHAPTER OUTLINE

Learning Objectives

	Learning Objective	Topics	Practice
1	Identify the activities and users associated with accounting.	• Three activities • Accounting data users	DO IT! 1 Basic Concepts
2	Explain the building blocks of accounting: ethics, principles, and assumptions.	• Ethics • GAAP • Measurement principles • Assumptions	DO IT! 2 Building Blocks of Accounting
3	State the accounting equation, and define its components.	• Assets • Liabilities • Owner's equity	DO IT! 3 Owner's Equity Effects
4	Analyze the effects of business transactions on the accounting equation.	• Transaction analysis • Summary of transactions	DO IT! 4 Tabular Analysis
5	Describe the four financial statements and how they are prepared.	• Income statement • Owner's equity statement • Balance sheet • Statement of cash flows	DO IT! 5 Financial Statement Items

Go to the ***REVIEW AND PRACTICE*** section at the end of the chapter for a review of key concepts and practice applications with solutions.

Visit **WileyPLUS with ORION** for additional tutorials and practice opportunities.

LEARNING OBJECTIVE 1

Identify the activities and users associated with accounting.

What consistently ranks as one of the top career opportunities in business? What frequently rates among the most popular majors on campus? What was the undergraduate degree chosen by **Nike** founder Phil Knight, **Home Depot** co-founder Arthur Blank, former acting director of the **Federal Bureau of Investigation (FBI)** Thomas Pickard, and numerous members of Congress? Accounting.[1] Why did these people choose accounting? They wanted to understand what was happening financially to their organizations. Accounting is the financial information system that provides these insights. In short, to understand your organization, you have to know the numbers.

Essential terms are printed in blue when they first appear, and are defined in the end-of-chapter Glossary Review.

Accounting consists of three basic activities—it **identifies**, **records**, and **communicates** the economic events of an organization to interested users. Let's take a closer look at these three activities.

Three Activities

As a starting point to the accounting process, a company **identifies** the **economic events relevant to its business**. Examples of economic events are the sale of snack chips by **PepsiCo**, the provision of cell phone services by **AT&T**, and the payment of wages by **Facebook**.

Once a company like PepsiCo identifies economic events, it **records** those events in order to provide a history of its financial activities. Recording consists of keeping a **systematic**, **chronological diary of events**, measured in dollars and cents. In recording, PepsiCo also classifies and summarizes economic events.

Finally, PepsiCo **communicates** the collected information to interested users by means of **accounting reports**. The most common of these reports are called **financial statements**. To make the reported financial information meaningful, PepsiCo reports the recorded data in a standardized way. It accumulates information resulting from similar transactions. For example, PepsiCo accumulates all sales transactions over a certain period of time and reports the data as one amount in the company's financial statements. Such data are said to be reported **in the aggregate**. By presenting the recorded data in the aggregate, the accounting process simplifies a multitude of transactions and makes a series of activities understandable and meaningful.

A vital element in communicating economic events is the accountant's ability to **analyze and interpret** the reported information. Analysis involves use of ratios, percentages, graphs, and charts to highlight significant financial trends and relationships. Interpretation involves **explaining the uses**, **meaning**, **and limitations of reported data**. Appendices A–E show the financial statements of **Apple Inc.**, **PepsiCo Inc.**, **The Coca-Cola Company**, **Amazon.com, Inc.**, and **Wal-Mart Stores, Inc.**, respectively. (In addition, in the *A Look at IFRS* section at the end of each chapter, the French company **Louis Vuitton Moët Hennessy** is analyzed.) We refer to these statements at various places throughout the textbook. At this point, these financial statements probably strike you as complex and confusing. By the end of this course, you'll be surprised at your ability to understand, analyze, and interpret them.

Illustration 1-1 summarizes the activities of the accounting process.

[1]The appendix to this chapter describes job opportunities for accounting majors and explains why accounting is such a popular major.

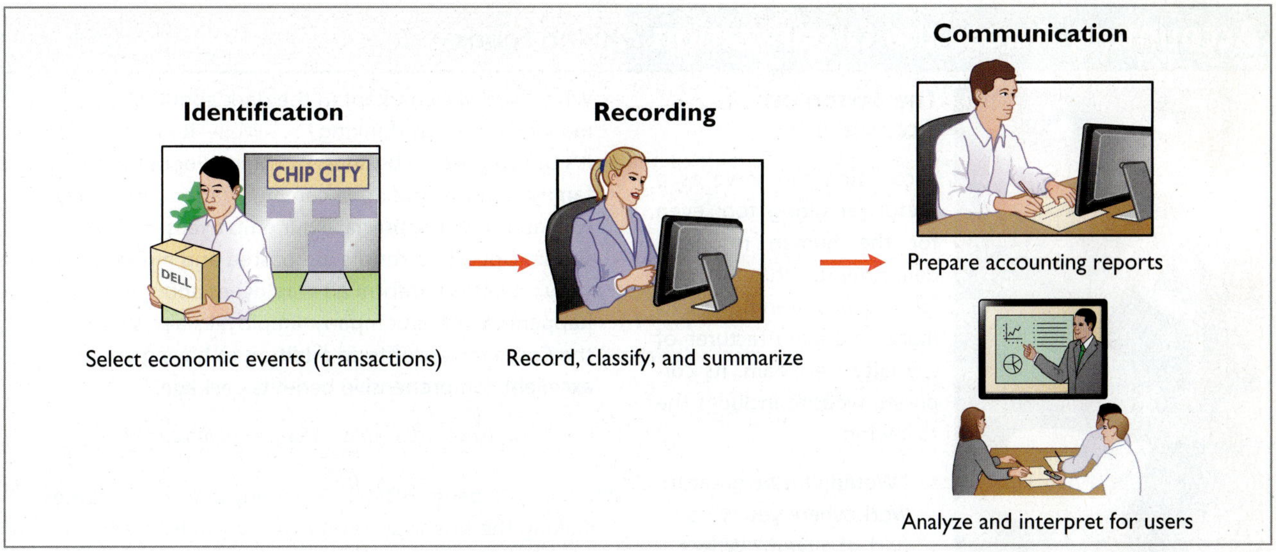

Illustration 1-1
The activities of the accounting process

You should understand that the accounting process **includes** the bookkeeping function. **Bookkeeping** usually involves **only** the recording of economic events. It is therefore just one part of the accounting process. In total, accounting involves **the entire process of identifying, recording, and communicating economic events.**[2]

Who Uses Accounting Data

The financial information that users need depends upon the kinds of decisions they make. There are two broad groups of users of financial information: internal users and external users.

INTERNAL USERS

Internal users of accounting information are managers who plan, organize, and run the business. These include marketing managers, production supervisors, finance directors, and company officers. In running a business, internal users must answer many important questions, as shown in Illustration 1-2.

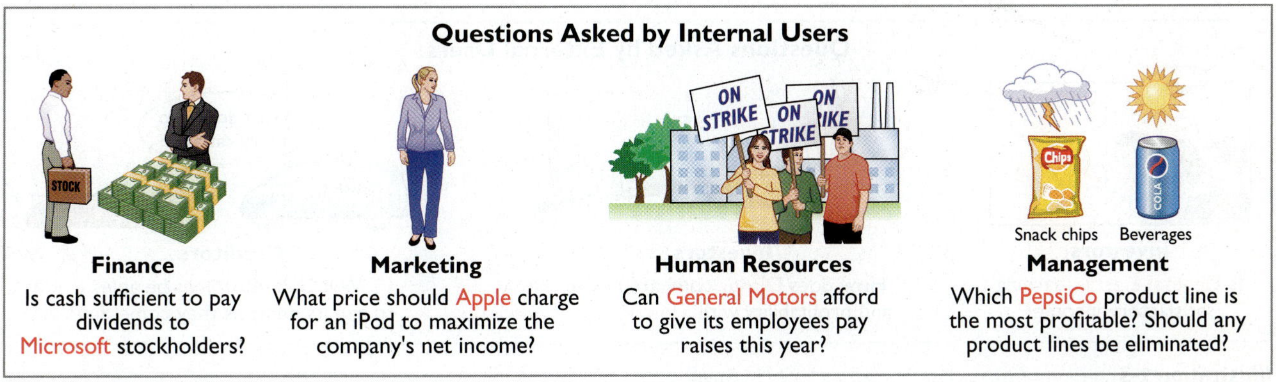
Questions Asked by Internal Users
STOCK
ON STRIKE
ON STRIKE
Chips
COLA
Snack chips
Beverages
Finance
Is cash sufficient to pay dividends to Microsoft stockholders?
Marketing
What price should Apple charge for an iPod to maximize the company's net income?
Human Resources
Can General Motors afford to give its employees pay raises this year?
Management
Which PepsiCo product line is the most profitable? Should any product lines be eliminated?

Illustration 1-2
Questions that internal users ask

To answer these and other questions, internal users need detailed information on a timely basis. **Managerial accounting** provides internal reports to help users make decisions about their companies. Examples are financial comparisons of operating alternatives, projections of income from new sales campaigns, and forecasts of cash needs for the next year.

---

[2]The origins of accounting are generally attributed to the work of Luca Pacioli, an Italian Renaissance mathematician. Pacioli was a close friend and tutor to Leonardo da Vinci and a contemporary of Christopher Columbus. In his 1494 text *Summa de Arithmetica, Geometria, Proportione et Proportionalite*, Pacioli described a system to ensure that financial information was recorded efficiently and accurately.

Accounting Across the Organization — Rhino Foods

© Agnieszka Pastuszak-Maksim/iStockphoto

The Scoop on Accounting

Accounting can serve as a useful recruiting tool even for the human resources department. Rhino Foods, located in Burlington, Vermont, is a manufacturer of specialty ice cream. Its corporate website includes the following:

"Wouldn't it be great to work where you were part of a team? Where your input and hard work made a difference? Where you weren't kept in the dark about what management was thinking? . . . Well—it's not a dream! It's the way we do business . . . Rhino Foods believes in family, honesty and open communication—we really care about and appreciate our employees—and it shows. Operating results are posted and monthly group meetings inform all employees about what's happening in the Company. Employees also share in the Company's profits, in addition to having an excellent comprehensive benefits package."

Source: www.rhinofoods.com/workforus/workforus.html.

What are the benefits to the company and its employees of making the financial statements available to all employees? (Go to **WileyPLUS** for this answer and additional questions.)

Accounting Across the Organization boxes demonstrate applications of accounting information in various business functions.

EXTERNAL USERS

External users are individuals and organizations outside a company who want financial information about the company. The two most common types of external users are investors and creditors. **Investors** (owners) use accounting information to decide whether to buy, hold, or sell ownership shares of a company. **Creditors** (such as suppliers and bankers) use accounting information to evaluate the risks of granting credit or lending money. Illustration 1-3 shows some questions that investors and creditors may ask.

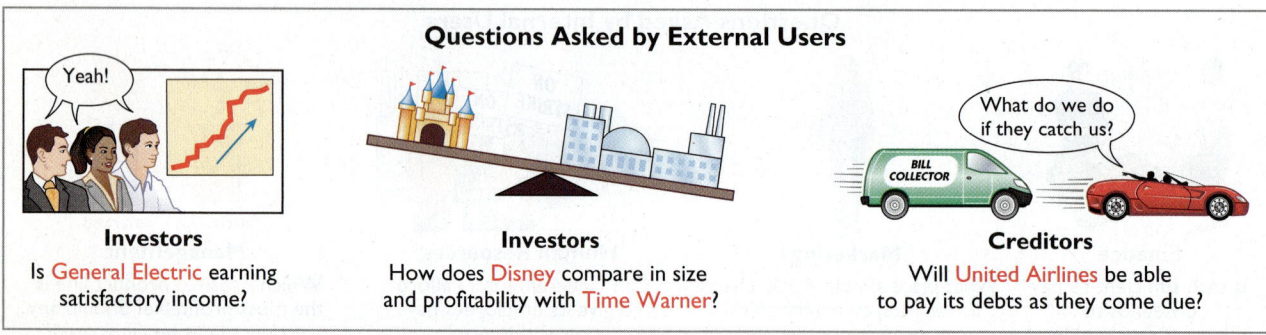

Questions Asked by External Users

Investors	Investors	Creditors
Is General Electric earning satisfactory income?	How does Disney compare in size and profitability with Time Warner?	Will United Airlines be able to pay its debts as they come due?

Illustration 1-3
Questions that external users ask

Financial accounting answers these questions. It provides economic and financial information for investors, creditors, and other external users. The information needs of external users vary considerably. **Taxing authorities**, such as the Internal Revenue Service, want to know whether the company complies with tax laws. **Regulatory agencies**, such as the Securities and Exchange Commission or the Federal Trade Commission, want to know whether the company is operating within prescribed rules. **Customers** are interested in whether a company like Telsa will continue to honor product warranties and support its product lines. **Labor unions** such as the Major League Baseball Players Association want to know whether the owners have the ability to pay increased wages and benefits.

DO IT! 1 Basic Concepts

Indicate whether each of the five statements presented below is true or false.

1. The three steps in the accounting process are identification, recording, and communication.
2. Bookkeeping encompasses all steps in the accounting process.
3. Accountants prepare, but do not interpret, financial reports.
4. The two most common types of external users are investors and company officers.
5. Managerial accounting activities focus on reports for internal users.

*The **DO IT!** exercises ask you to put newly acquired knowledge to work. They outline the **Action Plan** necessary to complete the exercise, and they show a **Solution**.*

Solution

1. True **2.** False. Bookkeeping involves only the recording step. **3.** False. Accountants analyze and interpret information in reports as part of the communication step. **4.** False. The two most common types of external users are investors and creditors. **5.** True.

Related exercise material: **E1-1, E1-2, and DO IT! 1-1.**

Action Plan

✔ Review the basic concepts discussed.

✔ Develop an understanding of the key terms used.

LEARNING OBJECTIVE 2 Explain the building blocks of accounting: ethics, principles, and assumptions.

A doctor follows certain protocols in treating a patient's illness. An architect follows certain structural guidelines in designing a building. Similarly, an accountant follows certain standards in reporting financial information. These standards are based on specific principles and assumptions. For these standards to work, however, a fundamental business concept must be present—ethical behavior.

Ethics in Financial Reporting

People won't gamble in a casino if they think it is "rigged." Similarly, people won't play the stock market if they think stock prices are rigged. In recent years, the financial press has been full of articles about financial scandals at **Enron**, **WorldCom**, **HealthSouth**, **AIG**, and other companies. As the scandals came to light, mistrust of financial reporting in general grew. One article in the *Wall Street Journal* noted that "repeated disclosures about questionable accounting practices have bruised investors' faith in the reliability of earnings reports, which in turn has sent stock prices tumbling." Imagine trying to carry on a business or invest money if you could not depend on the financial statements to be honestly prepared. Information would have no credibility. There is no doubt that a sound, well-functioning economy depends on accurate and dependable financial reporting.

United States regulators and lawmakers were very concerned that the economy would suffer if investors lost confidence in corporate accounting because of unethical financial reporting. In response, Congress passed the **Sarbanes-Oxley Act (SOX)**. Its intent is to reduce unethical corporate behavior and decrease the likelihood of future corporate scandals. As a result of SOX, top management must now certify the accuracy of financial information. In addition, penalties for fraudulent financial activity are much more severe. Also, SOX increased the independence requirements of the outside auditors who review the accuracy of corporate financial statements and increased the oversight role of boards of directors.

ETHICS NOTE

Circus-founder P.T. Barnum is alleged to have said, "Trust everyone, but cut the deck." What Sarbanes-Oxley does is to provide measures that (like cutting the deck of playing cards) help ensure that fraud will not occur.

Ethics Notes help sensitize you to some of the ethical issues in accounting.

The standards of conduct by which actions are judged as right or wrong, honest or dishonest, fair or not fair, are **ethics**. Effective financial reporting depends on sound ethical behavior. To sensitize you to ethical situations in business and to give you practice at solving ethical dilemmas, we address ethics in a number of ways in this textbook:

1. A number of the *Feature Stories* and other parts of the textbook discuss the central importance of ethical behavior to financial reporting.
2. *Ethics Insight* boxes and marginal *Ethics Notes* highlight ethics situations and issues in actual business settings.
3. Many of the *People, Planet, and Profit Insight* boxes focus on ethical issues that companies face in measuring and reporting social and environmental issues.
4. At the end of the chapter, an *Ethics Case* simulates a business situation and asks you to put yourself in the position of a decision-maker in that case.

When analyzing these various ethics cases, as well as experiences in your own life, it is useful to apply the three steps outlined in Illustration 1-4.

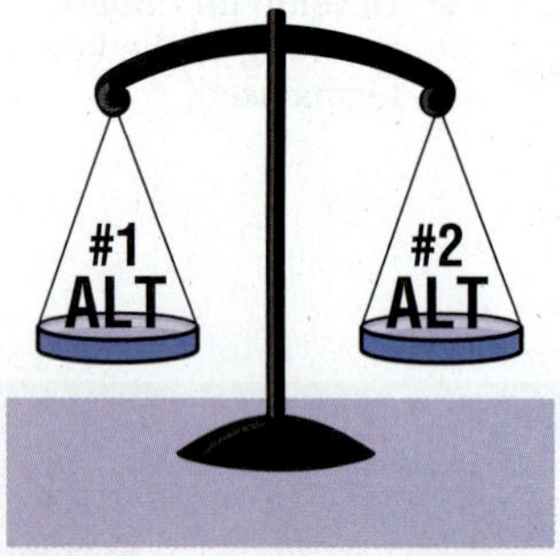

1. Recognize an ethical situation and the ethical issues involved.
Use your personal ethics to identify ethical situations and issues. Some businesses and professional organizations provide written codes of ethics for guidance in some business situations.

2. Identify and analyze the principal elements in the situation.
Identify the **stakeholders**—persons or groups who may be harmed or benefited. Ask the question: What are the responsibilities and obligations of the parties involved?

3. Identify the alternatives, and weigh the impact of each alternative on various stakeholders.
Select the most ethical alternative, considering all the consequences. Sometimes there will be one right answer. Other situations involve more than one right solution; these situations require an evaluation of each and a selection of the best alternative.

Illustration 1-4
Steps in analyzing ethics cases and situations

***Insight** boxes provide examples of business situations from various perspectives—ethics, investor, international, and corporate social responsibility. Guideline answers to the critical thinking questions are available in **WileyPLUS** and at **www.wiley.com/college/weygandt**. Additional questions are offered in **WileyPLUS**.*

Ethics Insight Dewey & LeBoeuf LLP

© Alliance/Shutterstock

I Felt the Pressure—Would You?

"I felt the pressure." That's what some of the employees of the now-defunct law firm of Dewey & LeBoeuf LLP indicated when they helped to overstate revenue and use accounting tricks to hide losses and cover up cash shortages. These employees worked for the former finance director and former chief financial officer (CFO) of the firm. Here are some of their comments:

- "I was instructed by the CFO to create invoices, knowing they would not be sent to clients. When I created these invoices, I knew that it was inappropriate."
- "I intentionally gave the auditors incorrect information in the course of the audit."

What happened here is that a small group of lower-level employees over a period of years carried out the instructions of their bosses. Their bosses, however, seemed to have no concern as evidenced by various e-mails with one another in which they referred to their financial manipulations as accounting tricks, cooking the books, and fake income.

Source: Ashby Jones, "Guilty Pleas of Dewey Staff Detail the Alleged Fraud," *Wall Street Journal* (March 28, 2014).

Why did these employees lie, and what do you believe should be their penalty for these lies? (Go to **WileyPLUS** for this answer and additional questions.)

Generally Accepted Accounting Principles

The accounting profession has developed standards that are generally accepted and universally practiced. This common set of standards is called **generally accepted accounting principles (GAAP)**. These standards indicate how to report economic events.

The primary accounting standard-setting body in the United States is the **Financial Accounting Standards Board (FASB)**. The **Securities and Exchange Commission (SEC)** is the agency of the U.S. government that oversees U.S. financial markets and accounting standard-setting bodies. The SEC relies on the FASB to develop accounting standards, which public companies must follow. Many countries outside of the United States have adopted the accounting standards issued by the **International Accounting Standards Board (IASB)**. These standards are called **International Financial Reporting Standards (IFRS)**.

As markets become more global, it is often desirable to compare the results of companies from different countries that report using different accounting standards. In order to increase comparability, in recent years the two standard-setting bodies have made efforts to reduce the differences between U.S. GAAP and IFRS. This process is referred to as **convergence**. As a result of these convergence efforts, it is likely that someday there will be a single set of high-quality accounting standards that are used by companies around the world. Because convergence is such an important issue, we highlight any major differences between GAAP and IFRS in *International Notes* (as shown in the margin here) and provide a more in-depth discussion in the *A Look at IRFS* section at the end of each chapter.

International Note

Over 100 countries use International Financial Reporting Standards (called IFRS). For example, all companies in the European Union follow international standards. The differences between U.S. and international standards are not generally significant.

***International Notes** highlight differences between U.S. and international accounting standards.*

Measurement Principles

GAAP generally uses one of two measurement principles, the historical cost principle or the fair value principle. Selection of which principle to follow generally relates to trade-offs between relevance and faithful representation. **Relevance** means that financial information is capable of making a difference in a decision. **Faithful representation** means that the numbers and descriptions match what really existed or happened—they are factual.

Helpful Hint
Relevance and *faithful representation* are two primary qualities that make accounting information useful for decision-making.

***Helpful Hints** further clarify concepts being discussed.*

HISTORICAL COST PRINCIPLE

The **historical cost principle** (or cost principle) dictates that companies record assets at their cost. This is true not only at the time the asset is purchased, but also over the time the asset is held. For example, if **Best Buy** purchases land for \$300,000, the company initially reports it in its accounting records at \$300,000. But what does Best Buy do if, by the end of the next year, the fair value of the land has increased to \$400,000? Under the historical cost principle, it continues to report the land at \$300,000.

FAIR VALUE PRINCIPLE

The **fair value principle** states that assets and liabilities should be reported at fair value (the price received to sell an asset or settle a liability). Fair value information may be more useful than historical cost for certain types of assets and liabilities. For example, certain investment securities are reported at fair value because market price information is usually readily available for these types of assets. In determining which measurement principle to use, companies weigh the factual nature of cost figures versus the relevance of fair value. In general, most companies choose to use cost. Only in situations where assets are actively traded, such as investment securities, do companies apply the fair value principle extensively.

Assumptions

Assumptions provide a foundation for the accounting process. Two main assumptions are the **monetary unit assumption** and the **economic entity assumption**.

MONETARY UNIT ASSUMPTION

The **monetary unit assumption** requires that companies include in the accounting records only transaction data that can be expressed in money terms. This assumption enables accounting to quantify (measure) economic events. The monetary unit assumption is vital to applying the historical cost principle.

This assumption prevents the inclusion of some relevant information in the accounting records. For example, the health of a company's owner, the quality of service, and the morale of employees are not included. The reason: Companies cannot quantify this information in money terms. Though this information is important, companies record only events that can be measured in money.

ECONOMIC ENTITY ASSUMPTION

ETHICS NOTE

The importance of the economic entity assumption is illustrated by scandals involving Adelphia. In this case, senior company employees entered into transactions that blurred the line between the employees' financial interests and those of the company. For example, Adelphia guaranteed over $2 billion of loans to the founding family.

An economic entity can be any organization or unit in society. It may be a company (such as Crocs, Inc.), a governmental unit (the state of Ohio), a municipality (Seattle), a school district (St. Louis District 48), or a church (Southern Baptist). The **economic entity assumption** requires that the activities of the entity be kept separate and distinct from the activities of its owner and all other economic entities. To illustrate, Sally Rider, owner of Sally's Boutique, must keep her personal living costs separate from the expenses of the business. Similarly, J. Crew and Gap Inc. are segregated into separate economic entities for accounting purposes.

PROPRIETORSHIP A business owned by one person is generally a **proprietorship**. The owner is often the manager/operator of the business. Small service-type businesses (plumbing companies, beauty salons, and auto repair shops), farms, and small retail stores (antique shops, clothing stores, and used-book stores) are often proprietorships. **Usually, only a relatively small amount of money (capital) is necessary to start in business as a proprietorship. The owner (proprietor) receives any profits, suffers any losses, and is personally liable for all debts of the business.** There is no legal distinction between the business as an economic unit and the owner, but the accounting records of the business activities are kept separate from the personal records and activities of the owner.

PARTNERSHIP A business owned by two or more persons associated as partners is a **partnership**. In most respects a partnership is like a proprietorship except that more than one owner is involved. Typically, a partnership agreement (written or oral) sets forth such terms as initial investment, duties of each partner, division of net income (or net loss), and settlement to be made upon death or withdrawal of a partner. Each partner generally has unlimited personal liability for the debts of the partnership. **Like a proprietorship, for accounting purposes the partnership transactions must be kept separate from the personal activities of the partners.** Partnerships are often used to organize retail and service-type businesses, including professional practices (lawyers, doctors, architects, and certified public accountants).

CORPORATION A business organized as a separate legal entity under state corporation law and having ownership divided into transferable shares of stock is a **corporation**. The holders of the shares (stockholders) **enjoy limited liability**; that is, they are not personally liable for the debts of the corporate entity. Stockholders **may transfer all or part of their ownership shares to other investors at any time** (i.e., sell their shares). The ease with which ownership can change adds to the attractiveness of investing in a corporation. Because ownership can be transferred without dissolving the corporation, the corporation **enjoys an unlimited life**.

Although the combined number of proprietorships and partnerships in the United States is more than five times the number of corporations, the revenue produced by corporations is eight times greater. Most of the largest companies in the United States—for example, **ExxonMobil**, **Ford**, **Wal-Mart Stores, Inc.**, **Citigroup**, and **Apple**—are corporations.

Accounting Across the Organization

Josef Volavka/iStockphoto

Spinning the Career Wheel

How will the study of accounting help you? A working knowledge of accounting is desirable for virtually every field of business. Some examples of how accounting is used in business careers include:

General management: Managers at Ford Motors, Massachusetts General Hospital, California State University—Fullerton, a McDonald's franchise, and a Trek bike shop all need to understand accounting data in order to make wise business decisions.

Marketing: Marketing specialists at Procter & Gamble must be sensitive to costs and benefits, which accounting helps them quantify and understand. Making a sale is meaningless unless it is a profitable sale.

Finance: Do you want to be a banker for Citicorp, an investment analyst for Goldman Sachs, or a stock broker for Merrill Lynch? These fields rely heavily on accounting knowledge to analyze financial statements. In fact, it is difficult to get a good job in a finance function without two or three courses in accounting.

Real estate: Are you interested in being a real estate broker for Prudential Real Estate? Because a third party—the bank—is almost always involved in financing a real estate transaction, brokers must understand the numbers involved: Can the buyer afford to make the payments to the bank? Does the cash flow from an industrial property justify the purchase price? What are the tax benefits of the purchase?

How might accounting help you? (Go to **WileyPLUS** for this answer and additional questions.)

DO IT! 2 Building Blocks of Accounting

Indicate whether each of the five statements presented below is true or false.

1. Congress passed the Sarbanes-Oxley Act to reduce unethical behavior and decrease the likelihood of future corporate scandals.
2. The primary accounting standard-setting body in the United States is the Financial Accounting Standards Board (FASB).
3. The historical cost principle dictates that companies record assets at their cost. In later periods, however, the fair value of the asset must be used if fair value is higher than its cost.
4. Relevance means that financial information matches what really happened; the information is factual.
5. A business owner's personal expenses must be separated from expenses of the business to comply with accounting's economic entity assumption.

Solution

1. True. **2.** True. **3.** False. The historical cost principle dictates that companies record assets at their cost. Under the historical cost principle, the company must also use cost in later periods. **4.** False. Faithful representation, not relevance, means that financial information matches what really happened; the information is factual. **5.** True.

Related exercise material: **E1-3, E1-4, and DO IT! 1-2.**

Action Plan

✔ Review the discussion of ethics and financial reporting standards.

✔ Develop an understanding of the key terms used.

LEARNING OBJECTIVE 3

State the accounting equation, and define its components.

The two basic elements of a business are what it owns and what it owes. **Assets** are the resources a business owns. For example, Google has total assets of approximately $93.8 billion. Liabilities and owner's equity are the rights or claims against these resources. Thus, Google has $93.8 billion of claims against its $93.8 billion of assets. Claims of those to whom the company owes money (creditors) are called **liabilities**. Claims of owners are called **owner's equity**. Google has liabilities of $22.1 billion and owners' equity of $71.7 billion.

We can express the relationship of assets, liabilities, and owner's equity as an equation, as shown in Illustration 1-5.

Illustration 1-5
The basic accounting equation

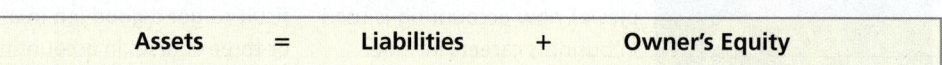

Assets	=	Liabilities	+	Owner's Equity

This relationship is the **basic accounting equation**. Assets must equal the sum of liabilities and owner's equity. Liabilities appear before owner's equity in the basic accounting equation because they are paid first if a business is liquidated.

The accounting equation applies to all **economic entities** regardless of size, nature of business, or form of business organization. It applies to a small proprietorship such as a corner grocery store as well as to a giant corporation such as PepsiCo. The equation provides the **underlying framework** for recording and summarizing economic events.

Let's look in more detail at the categories in the basic accounting equation.

Assets

As noted above, **assets** are resources a business owns. The business uses its assets in carrying out such activities as production and sales. The common characteristic possessed by all assets is **the capacity to provide future services or benefits**. In a business, that service potential or future economic benefit eventually results in cash inflows (receipts). For example, consider Campus Pizza, a local restaurant. It owns a delivery truck that provides economic benefits from delivering pizzas. Other assets of Campus Pizza are tables, chairs, jukebox, cash register, oven, tableware, and, of course, cash.

Liabilities

Liabilities are claims against assets—that is, existing debts and obligations. Businesses of all sizes usually borrow money and purchase merchandise on credit. These economic activities result in payables of various sorts:

- Campus Pizza, for instance, purchases cheese, sausage, flour, and beverages on credit from suppliers. These obligations are called **accounts payable**.
- Campus Pizza also has a **note payable** to First National Bank for the money borrowed to purchase the delivery truck.
- Campus Pizza may also have **salaries and wages payable** to employees and **sales and real estate taxes payable** to the local government.

All of these persons or entities to whom Campus Pizza owes money are its **creditors**.

Creditors may legally force the liquidation of a business that does not pay its debts. In that case, the law requires that creditor claims be paid **before** ownership claims.

Owner's Equity

The ownership claim on total assets is **owner's equity**. It is equal to total assets minus total liabilities. Here is why: The assets of a business are claimed by either creditors or owners. To find out what belongs to owners, we subtract the creditors' claims (the liabilities) from assets. The remainder is the owner's claim on the assets—the owner's equity. Since the claims of creditors must be paid **before** ownership claims, owner's equity is often referred to as **residual equity**.

Helpful Hint
In some places, we use the term "owner's equity" and in others we use "owners' equity." *Owner's* (singular, possessive) refers to one owner (the case with a sole proprietorship). *Owners'* (plural, possessive) refers to multiple owners (the case with partnerships or corporations).

INCREASES IN OWNER'S EQUITY

In a proprietorship, owner's investments and revenues increase owner's equity.

INVESTMENTS BY OWNER **Investments by owner** are the assets the owner puts into the business. These investments increase owner's equity. They are recorded in a category called **owner's capital**.

REVENUES **Revenues** are the **gross increase in owner's equity resulting from business activities entered into for the purpose of earning income**. Generally, revenues result from selling merchandise, performing services, renting property, and lending money. Common sources of revenue are sales, fees, services, commissions, interest, dividends, royalties, and rent.

Revenues usually result in an increase in an asset. They may arise from different sources and are called various names depending on the nature of the business. Campus Pizza, for instance, has two categories of sales revenues—pizza sales and beverage sales.

DECREASES IN OWNER'S EQUITY

In a proprietorship, owner's drawings and expenses decrease owner's equity.

DRAWINGS An owner may withdraw cash or other assets for personal use. We use a separate classification called **drawings** to determine the total withdrawals for each accounting period. **Drawings decrease owner's equity.** They are recorded in a category called owner's drawings.

EXPENSES **Expenses** are the cost of assets consumed or services used in the process of earning revenue. They are **decreases in owner's equity that result from operating the business**. For example, Campus Pizza recognizes the following expenses: cost of ingredients (meat, flour, cheese, tomato paste, mushrooms, etc.); cost of beverages; salaries and wages expense; utilities expense (electric, gas, and water expense); delivery expense (gasoline, repairs, licenses, etc.); supplies expense (napkins, detergents, aprons, etc.); rent expense; interest expense; and property tax expense.

In summary, owner's equity is increased by an owner's investments and by revenues from business operations. Owner's equity is decreased by an owner's withdrawals of assets and by expenses. Illustration 1-6 expands the basic accounting equation by showing the items that comprise owner's equity. This format is referred to as the **expanded accounting equation**.

Illustration 1-6
Expanded accounting equation

Basic Equation	Assets	=	Liabilities	+	Owner's Equity							
Expanded Equation	Assets	=	Liabilities	+	Owner's Capital	−	Owner's Drawings	+	Revenues	−	Expenses	

DO IT! 3 Owner's Equity Effects

Action Plan

✔ Understand the sources of revenue.

✔ Understand what causes expenses.

✔ Review the rules for changes in owner's equity.

✔ Recognize that drawings are withdrawals of cash or other assets from the business for personal use.

Classify the following items as investment by owner (I), owner's drawings (D), revenues (R), or expenses (E). Then indicate whether each item increases or decreases owner's equity.

1. Rent Expense. **3.** Drawings.
2. Service Revenue. **4.** Salaries and Wages Expense.

Solution

1. Rent Expense is an expense (E); it decreases owner's equity. **2.** Service Revenue is revenue (R); it increases owner's equity. **3.** Drawings is owner's drawings (D); it decreases owner's equity. **4.** Salaries and Wages Expense is an expense (E); it decreases owner's equity.

Related exercise material: **BE1-1, BE1-2, BE1-3, BE1-4, BE1-5, BE1-8, E1-5, and DO IT! 1-3.**

LEARNING OBJECTIVE 4 Analyze the effects of business transactions on the accounting equation.

Transactions (**business transactions**) are a business's economic events recorded by accountants. Transactions may be external or internal. **External transactions** involve economic events between the company and some outside enterprise. For example, Campus Pizza's purchase of cooking equipment from a supplier, payment of monthly rent to the landlord, and sale of pizzas to customers are external transactions. **Internal transactions** are economic events that occur entirely within one company. The use of cooking and cleaning supplies are internal transactions for Campus Pizza.

Companies carry on many activities that do not represent business transactions. Examples are hiring employees, responding to e-mails, talking with customers, and placing merchandise orders. Some of these activities may lead to business transactions. Employees will earn wages, and suppliers will deliver ordered merchandise. The company must analyze each event to find out if it affects the components of the accounting equation. If it does, the company will record the transaction. Illustration 1-7 demonstrates the transaction identification process.

Illustration 1-7
Transaction identification process

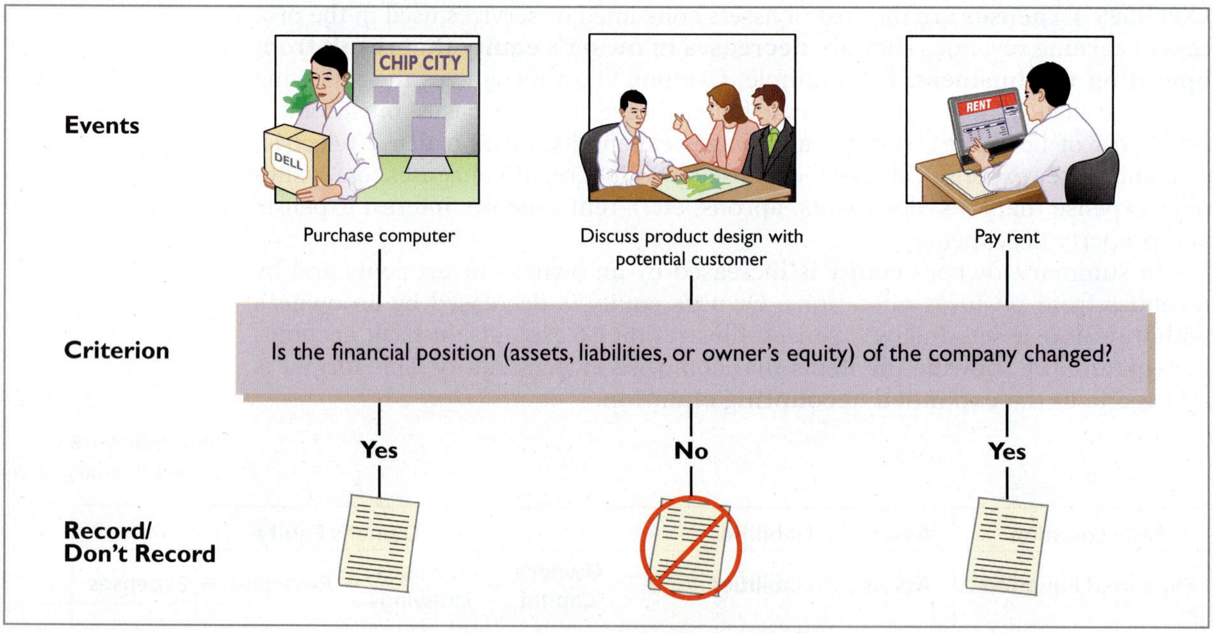

Each transaction must have a dual effect on the accounting equation. For example, if an asset is increased, there must be a corresponding (1) decrease in another asset, (2) increase in a specific liability, or (3) increase in owner's equity.

Two or more items could be affected. For example, as one asset is increased $10,000, another asset could decrease $6,000 and a liability could increase $4,000. Any change in a liability or ownership claim is subject to similar analysis.

Transaction Analysis

To demonstrate how to analyze transactions in terms of the accounting equation, we will review the business activities of Softbyte, a smartphone app development company. Softbyte is the creation of Ray Neal, an entrepreneur who wants to create focused apps that inspire and engage users of all ages. Ray was encouraged to start his own business after the success of "FoodAlert," a customizable app he developed that tracks the daily location of local food trucks. The following business transactions occur during Softbyte's first month of operations.

Helpful Hint
Study these transactions until you are sure you understand them. They are not difficult, but understanding them is important to your success in this course. The ability to analyze transactions in terms of the basic accounting equation is essential in accounting.

TRANSACTION (1). INVESTMENT BY OWNER Ray Neal starts a smartphone app development company which he names Softbyte. On September 1, 2017, he invests $15,000 cash in the business. This transaction results in an equal increase in assets and owner's equity.

Basic Analysis	The asset Cash increases $15,000, and owner's equity (identified as Owner's Capital) increases $15,000.

Equation Analysis

	Assets	=	Liabilities	+	Owner's Equity	
	Cash	=			Owner's Capital	
(1)	**+$15,000**	=			**+$15,000**	**Initial investment**

Observe that the equality of the accounting equation has been maintained. Note that the investments by the owner do not represent revenues, and they are excluded in determining net income. Therefore, it is necessary to make clear that the increase is an investment (increasing Owner's Capital) rather than revenue.

TRANSACTION (2). PURCHASE OF EQUIPMENT FOR CASH Softbyte purchases computer equipment for $7,000 cash. This transaction results in an equal increase and decrease in total assets, though the composition of assets changes.

Basic Analysis	The asset Cash decreases $7,000, and the asset Equipment increases $7,000.

Equation Analysis

	Assets			=	Liabilities	+	Owner's Equity
	Cash	+	Equipment	=			Owner's Capital
	$15,000						$15,000
(2)	**−7,000**		**+$7,000**				
	$ 8,000	+	$7,000	=			$15,000
	$15,000						

Observe that total assets are still $15,000. Owner's equity also remains at $15,000, the amount of Ray Neal's original investment.

TRANSACTION (3). PURCHASE OF SUPPLIES ON CREDIT Softbyte purchases for $1,600 from Mobile Solutions headsets and other computer accessories expected to last several months. Mobile Solutions agrees to allow Softbyte to pay this bill in October. This transaction is a purchase on account (a credit purchase). Assets increase because of the expected future benefits of using the headsets and computer accessories, and liabilities increase by the amount due to Mobile Solutions.

Basic Analysis: The asset Supplies increases $1,600, and the liability Accounts Payable increases $1,600.

Equation Analysis

	Assets					=	Liabilities	+	Owner's Equity
	Cash	+	Supplies	+	Equipment	=	Accounts Payable	+	Owner's Capital
	$8,000				$7,000				$15,000
(3)			+$1,600				+$1,600		
	$8,000	+	$1,600	+	$7,000	=	$1,600	+	$15,000
			$16,600					$16,600	

Total assets are now $16,600. This total is matched by a $1,600 creditor's claim and a $15,000 ownership claim.

TRANSACTION (4). SERVICES PERFORMED FOR CASH Softbyte receives $1,200 cash from customers for app development services it has performed. This transaction represents Softbyte's principal revenue-producing activity. Recall that **revenue increases owner's equity**.

Basic Analysis: The asset Cash increases $1,200, and owner's equity increases $1,200 due to Service Revenue.

Equation Analysis

	Assets					=	Liabilities	+	Owner's Equity			
	Cash	+	Supplies	+	Equipment	=	Accounts Payable	+	Owner's Capital	+	Revenues	
	$8,000		$1,600		$7,000		$1,600		$15,000			
(4)	+1,200										+$1,200	Service Revenue
	$9,200	+	$1,600	+	$7,000	=	$1,600	+	$15,000	+	$1,200	
			$17,800						$17,800			

The two sides of the equation balance at $17,800. Service Revenue is included in determining Softbyte's net income.

Note that we do not have room to give details for each individual revenue and expense account in this illustration. Thus, revenues (and expenses when we get to them) are summarized under one column heading for Revenues and one for Expenses. However, it is important to keep track of the category (account) titles affected (e.g., Service Revenue) as they will be needed when we prepare financial statements later in the chapter.

TRANSACTION (5). PURCHASE OF ADVERTISING ON CREDIT Softbyte receives a bill for $250 from the *Daily News* for advertising on its online website but postpones payment until a later date. This transaction results in an increase in liabilities and a decrease in owner's equity.

Basic Analysis	The liability Accounts Payable increases $250, and owner's equity decreases $250 due to Advertising Expense.

Equation Analysis

	Assets			= Liabilities +	Owner's Equity			
	Cash	+ Supplies	+ Equipment	= Accounts Payable	+ Owner's Capital	+ Revenues	− Expenses	
	$9,200	$1,600	$7,000	$1,600	$15,000	$1,200		
(5)				+250			−$250	Advertising Expense
	$9,200 +	$1,600 +	$7,000	= $1,850	+ $15,000	+ $1,200	− $ 250	
	$17,800			$17,800				

The two sides of the equation still balance at $17,800. Owner's equity decreases when Softbyte incurs the expense. Expenses are not always paid in cash at the time they are incurred. When Softbyte pays at a later date, the liability Accounts Payable will decrease, and the asset Cash will decrease [see Transaction (8)]. The cost of advertising is an expense (rather than an asset) because the company has **used** the benefits. Advertising Expense is included in determining net income.

TRANSACTION (6). SERVICES PERFORMED FOR CASH AND CREDIT Softbyte performs $3,500 of app development services for customers. The company receives cash of $1,500 from customers, and it bills the balance of $2,000 on account. This transaction results in an equal increase in assets and owner's equity.

Basic Analysis	Three specific items are affected: The asset Cash increases $1,500, the asset Accounts Receivable increases $2,000, and owner's equity increases $3,500 due to Service Revenue.

Equation Analysis

	Assets				= Liabilities +	Owner's Equity			
	Cash	+ Accounts Receivable	+ Supplies	+ Equipment	= Accounts Payable	+ Owner's Capital	+ Revenues	− Expenses	
	$9,200		$1,600	$7,000	$1,850	$15,000	$1,200	$250	
(6)	+1,500	+$2,000					+3,500		Service Revenue
	$10,700 +	$ 2,000 +	$1,600 +	$7,000	= $1,850	+ $15,000	+ $4,700	− $250	
	$21,300				$21,300				

Softbyte recognizes $3,500 in revenue when it performs the service. In exchange for this service, it received $1,500 in Cash and Accounts Receivable of $2,000. This Accounts Receivable represents customers' promises to pay $2,000 to Softbyte in the future. When it later receives collections on account, Softbyte will increase Cash and will decrease Accounts Receivable [see Transaction (9)].

TRANSACTION (7). PAYMENT OF EXPENSES Softbyte pays the following expenses in cash for September: office rent $600, salaries and wages of employees $900, and utilities $200. These payments result in an equal decrease in assets and owner's equity.

Basic Analysis	The asset Cash decreases $1,700, and owner's equity decreases $1,700 due to the specific expense categories (Rent Expense, Salaries and Wages Expense, and Utilities Expense).

Equation Analysis

	Assets				= Liabilities +	Owner's Equity		
	Cash	+ Accounts Receivable	+ Supplies	+ Equipment	= Accounts Payable	+ Owner's Capital	+ Revenues	− Expenses
	$10,700	$2,000	$1,600	$7,000	$1,850	$15,000	$4,700	$ 250
(7)	−1,700							−600 Rent Expense −900 Sal. and Wages Exp. −200 Utilities Exp.
	$9,000 +	$2,000 +	$1,600 +	$7,000 =	$1,850 +	$15,000 +	$4,700 −	$1,950
	$19,600				$19,600			

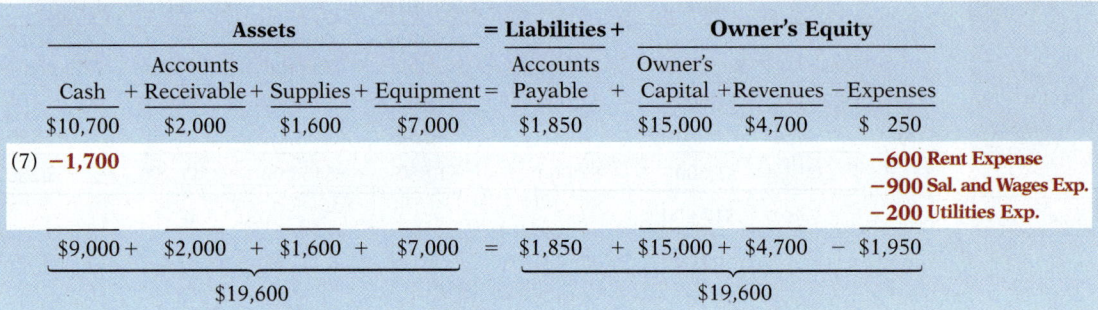

The two sides of the equation now balance at $19,600. Three lines in the analysis indicate the different types of expenses that have been incurred.

TRANSACTION (8). PAYMENT OF ACCOUNTS PAYABLE Softbyte pays its $250 *Daily News* bill in cash. The company previously [in Transaction (5)] recorded the bill as an increase in Accounts Payable and a decrease in owner's equity.

Basic Analysis	This cash payment "on account" decreases the asset Cash by $250 and also decreases the liability Accounts Payable by $250.

Equation Analysis

	Assets				= Liabilities +	Owner's Equity		
	Cash	+ Accounts Receivable	+ Supplies	+ Equipment	= Accounts Payable	+ Owner's Capital	+ Revenues	− Expenses
	$9,000	$2,000	$1,600	$7,000	$1,850	$15,000	$4,700	$1,950
(8)	−250				−250			
	$8,750 +	$2,000 +	$1,600 +	$7,000 =	$1,600 +	$15,000 +	$4,700 −	$1,950
	$19,350				$19,350			

Observe that the payment of a liability related to an expense that has previously been recorded does not affect owner's equity. The company recorded this expense in Transaction (5) and should not record it again.

TRANSACTION (9). RECEIPT OF CASH ON ACCOUNT Softbyte receives $600 in cash from customers who had been billed for services [in Transaction (6)]. Transaction (9) does not change total assets, but it changes the composition of those assets.

Basic Analysis	The asset Cash increases $600, and the asset Accounts Receivable decreases $600.

Equation Analysis

	Assets							=	Liabilities	+	Owner's Equity				
	Cash	+	Accounts Receivable	+	Supplies	+	Equipment	=	Accounts Payable	+	Owner's Capital	+	Revenues	−	Expenses
	$8,750		$2,000		$1,600		$7,000		$1,600		$15,000		$4,700		$1,950
(9)	**+600**		**−600**												
	$9,350	+	$1,400	+	$1,600	+	$7,000	=	$1,600	+	$15,000	+	$4,700	−	$1,950
	$19,350								$19,350						

Note that the collection of an account receivable for services previously billed and recorded does not affect owner's equity. Softbyte already recorded this revenue in Transaction (6) and should not record it again.

TRANSACTION (10). WITHDRAWAL OF CASH BY OWNER Ray Neal withdraws $1,300 in cash from the business for his personal use. This transaction results in an equal decrease in assets and owner's equity.

Basic Analysis	The asset Cash decreases $1,300, and owner's equity decreases $1,300 due to owner's withdrawal (Owner's Drawings).

Equation Analysis

	Assets							=	Liabilities	+	Owner's Equity							
	Cash	+	Accounts Receivable	+	Supplies	+	Equipment	=	Accounts Payable	+	Owner's Capital	−	Owner's Drawings	+	Revenues	−	Expenses	
	$9,350		$1,400		$1,600		$7,000		$1,600		$15,000				$4,700		$1,950	
(10)	**−1,300**												**−$1,300**					**Drawings**
	$8,050	+	$1,400	+	$1,600	+	$7,000	=	$1,600	+	$15,000	−	$1,300	+	$4,700	−	$1,950	
	$18,050								$18,050									

Observe that the effect of a cash withdrawal by the owner is the opposite of the effect of an investment by the owner. **Owner's drawings are not expenses.** Expenses are incurred for the purpose of earning revenue. Drawings do not generate revenue. They are a **disinvestment**. Like owner's investment, the company excludes owner's drawings in determining net income.

Summary of Transactions

Illustration 1-8 (page 20) summarizes the September transactions of Softbyte to show their cumulative effect on the basic accounting equation. It also indicates the transaction number and the specific effects of each transaction.

Illustration 1-8 demonstrates some significant facts:

1. Each transaction is analyzed in terms of its effect on:
   (a) The three components of the basic accounting equation.
   (b) Specific items within each component.
2. The two sides of the equation must always be equal.

	Assets				= Liabilities +	Owner's Equity				
Transaction	Cash	+ Accounts Receivable	+ Supplies	+ Equipment	= Accounts Payable	+ Owner's Capital	− Owner's Drawings	+ Rev.	− Exp.	
(1)	+$15,000					+$15,000				**Initial invest.**
(2)	−7,000			+$7,000						
(3)			+$1,600		+$1,600					
(4)	+1,200							+$1,200		**Service Revenue**
(5)					+250				−$250	**Adver. Expense**
(6)	+1,500	+$2,000						+3,500		**Service Revenue**
(7)	−600								−600	**Rent Expense**
	−900								−900	**Sal./Wages Exp.**
	−200								−200	**Utilities Expense**
(8)	−250				−250					
(9)	+600	−600								
(10)	−1,300						−$1,300			**Drawings**
	$ 8,050 +	$1,400 +	$1,600 +	$7,000	= $1,600	+ $15,000	− $1,300	+ $4,700	− $1,950	
	$18,050				**$18,050**					

Illustration 1-8
Tabular summary of Softbyte transactions

There! You made it through your first transaction analysis. If you feel a bit shaky on any of the transactions, it might be a good idea at this point to get up, take a short break, and come back again for a 10- to 15-minute review of the transactions, to make sure you understand them before you go on to the next section.

DO IT! 4 Tabular Analysis

Action Plan

- ✔ Analyze the effects of each transaction on the accounting equation.
- ✔ Use appropriate category names (not descriptions).
- ✔ Keep the accounting equation in balance.

Transactions made by Virmari & Co., a public accounting firm, for the month of August are shown below. Prepare a tabular analysis which shows the effects of these transactions on the expanded accounting equation, similar to that shown in Illustration 1-8.

1. The owner invested $25,000 cash in the business.
2. The company purchased $7,000 of office equipment on credit.
3. The company received $8,000 cash in exchange for services performed.
4. The company paid $850 for this month's rent.
5. The owner withdrew $1,000 cash for personal use.

Solution

	Assets		= Liabilities +	Owner's Equity				
Transaction	Cash	+ Equipment	= Accounts Payable	+ Owner's Capital	− Owner's Drawings	+ Revenues	− Expenses	
(1)	+$25,000			+$25,000				
(2)		+$7,000	+$7,000					
(3)	+8,000					+$8,000		**Service Revenue**
(4)	−850						−$850	**Rent Expense**
(5)	−1,000				−$1,000			**Drawings**
	$31,150 +	$7,000	= $7,000	+ $25,000	− $1,000	+ $8,000	− $850	
	$38,150		$38,150					

Related exercise material: **BE1-6, BE1-7, BE1-9, E1-6, E1-7, E1-8, and DO IT! 1-4.**

LEARNING OBJECTIVE 5

Describe the four financial statements and how they are prepared.

Companies prepare four financial statements from the summarized accounting data:

1. An **income statement** presents the revenues and expenses and resulting net income or net loss for a specific period of time.
2. An **owner's equity statement** summarizes the changes in owner's equity for a specific period of time.
3. A **balance sheet** reports the assets, liabilities, and owner's equity at a specific date.
4. A **statement of cash flows** summarizes information about the cash inflows (receipts) and outflows (payments) for a specific period of time.

International Note

The primary types of financial statements required by GAAP and IFRS are the same. In practice, some format differences do exist in presentations commonly employed by GAAP companies compared to IFRS companies.

These statements provide relevant financial data for internal and external users. Illustration 1-9 (page 22) shows the financial statements of Softbyte.

Note that the statements shown in Illustration 1-9 are interrelated:

1. Net income of $2,750 on the **income statement** is added to the beginning balance of owner's capital in the **owner's equity statement**.
2. Owner's capital of $16,450 at the end of the reporting period shown in the **owner's equity statement** is reported on the **balance sheet**.
3. Cash of $8,050 on the **balance sheet** is reported on the **statement of cash flows**.

Helpful Hint
The income statement, owner's equity statement, and statement of cash flows are all for a *period* of time, whereas the balance sheet is for a *point* in time.

Also, explanatory notes and supporting schedules are an integral part of every set of financial statements. We illustrate these notes and schedules in later chapters of this textbook.

Be sure to carefully examine the format and content of each statement in Illustration 1-9. We describe the essential features of each in the following sections.

Income Statement

The income statement reports the revenues and expenses for a specific period of time. (In Softbyte's case, this is "For the Month Ended September 30, 2017.") Softbyte's income statement is prepared from the data appearing in the owner's equity columns of Illustration 1-8 (page 20).

Alternative Terminology
The income statement is sometimes referred to as the *statement of operations, earnings statement,* or *profit and loss statement.*

Alternative Terminology *notes introduce other terms you might hear or read.*

The income statement lists revenues first, followed by expenses. Finally the statement shows net income (or net loss). **Net income** results when revenues exceed expenses. A **net loss** occurs when expenses exceed revenues.

Although practice varies, we have chosen in our illustrations and homework solutions to list expenses in order of magnitude. (We will consider alternative formats for the income statement in later chapters.)

Note that the income statement does **not** include investment and withdrawal transactions between the owner and the business in measuring net income. For example, as explained earlier, Ray Neal's withdrawal of cash from Softbyte was not regarded as a business expense.

Owner's Equity Statement

The owner's equity statement reports the changes in owner's equity for a specific period of time. The time period is the same as that covered by the income statement. Data for the preparation of the owner's equity statement come from the owner's equity columns of the tabular summary (Illustration 1-8) and from the income statement. The first line of the statement shows the beginning owner's equity amount (which was zero at the start of the business). Then come the owner's investments, net income (or loss), and the owner's drawings. This statement indicates **why** owner's equity has increased or decreased during the period.

Illustration 1-9
Financial statements and their interrelationships

Helpful Hint
The heading of each statement identifies the company, the type of statement, and the specific date or time period covered by the statement.

SOFTBYTE
Income Statement
For the Month Ended September 30, 2017

Revenues		
Service revenue		$ 4,700
Expenses		
Salaries and wages expense	$900	
Rent expense	600	
Advertising expense	250	
Utilities expense	200	
Total expenses		1,950
Net income		$ 2,750

(1)

SOFTBYTE
Owner's Equity Statement
For the Month Ended September 30, 2017

Owner's capital, September 1		$ –0–
Add: Investments	$15,000	
Net income	2,750	17,750
		17,750
Less: Drawings		1,300
Owner's capital, September 30		$16,450

Helpful Hint
Note that final sums are double-underlined, and negative amounts (in the statement of cash flows) are presented in parentheses.

SOFTBYTE
Balance Sheet
September 30, 2017

Assets

Cash	$ 8,050
Accounts receivable	1,400
Supplies	1,600
Equipment	7,000
Total assets	$ 18,050

(2)

Liabilities and Owner's Equity

Liabilities	
Accounts payable	$ 1,600
Owner's equity	
Owner's capital	16,450
Total liabilities and owner's equity	$ 18,050

(3)

SOFTBYTE
Statement of Cash Flows
For the Month Ended September 30, 2017

Cash flows from operating activities		
Cash receipts from revenues		$ 3,300
Cash payments for expenses		(1,950)
Net cash provided by operating activities		1,350
Cash flows from investing activities		
Purchase of equipment		(7,000)
Cash flows from financing activities		
Investments by owner	$15,000	
Drawings by owner	(1,300)	13,700
Net increase in cash		8,050
Cash at the beginning of the period		0
Cash at the end of the period		$ 8,050

Helpful Hint
The arrows in this illustration show the interrelationships of the four financial statements.

1. Net income is computed first and is needed to determine the ending balance in owner's equity.
2. The ending balance in owner's equity is needed in preparing the balance sheet.
3. The cash shown on the balance sheet is needed in preparing the statement of cash flows.

What if Softbyte had reported a net loss in its first month? Let's assume that during the month of September 2017, Softbyte lost $10,000. Illustration 1-10 shows the presentation of a net loss in the owner's equity statement.

Illustration 1-10
Presentation of net loss

SOFTBYTE
Owner's Equity Statement
For the Month Ended September 30, 2017

Owner's capital, September 1		$ -0-
Add: Investments		15,000
		15,000
Less: Drawings	$ 1,300	
Net loss	**10,000**	11,300
Owner's capital, September 30		$ 3,700

If the owner makes any additional investments, the company reports them in the owner's equity statement as investments.

Balance Sheet

Softbyte's balance sheet reports the assets, liabilities, and owner's equity at a specific date (in Softbyte's case, September 30, 2017). The company prepares the balance sheet from the column headings of the tabular summary (Illustration 1-8) and the month-end data shown in its last line.

Observe that the balance sheet lists assets at the top, followed by liabilities and owner's equity. Total assets must equal total liabilities and owner's equity. Softbyte reports only one liability—accounts payable—in its balance sheet. In most cases, there will be more than one liability. When two or more liabilities are involved, a customary way of listing is as follows.

Illustration 1-11
Presentation of liabilities

Liabilities	
Notes payable	$ 10,000
Accounts payable	63,000
Salaries and wages payable	18,000
Total liabilities	**$91,000**

The balance sheet is a snapshot of the company's financial condition at a specific moment in time (usually the month-end or year-end).

Statement of Cash Flows

The statement of cash flows provides information on the cash receipts and payments for a specific period of time. The statement of cash flows reports (1) the cash effects of a company's operations during a period, (2) its investing activities, (3) its financing activities, (4) the net increase or decrease in cash during the period, and (5) the cash amount at the end of the period.

Reporting the sources, uses, and change in cash is useful because investors, creditors, and others want to know what is happening to a company's most liquid resource. The statement of cash flows provides answers to the following simple but important questions.

1. Where did cash come from during the period?
2. What was cash used for during the period?
3. What was the change in the cash balance during the period?

As shown in Softbyte's statement of cash flows, cash increased $8,050 during the period. Net cash provided by operating activities increased cash $1,350. Cash flow from investing activities decreased cash $7,000. And cash flow from financing activities increased cash $13,700. At this time, you need not be concerned with how these amounts are determined. Chapter 17 will examine the statement of cash flows in detail.

People, Planet, and Profit Insight

Beyond Financial Statements

Should we expand our financial statements beyond the income statement, owner's equity statement, balance sheet, and statement of cash flows? Some believe we should take into account ecological and social performance, in addition to financial results, in evaluating a company. The argument is that a company's responsibility lies with anyone who is influenced by its actions. In other words, a company should be interested in benefiting many different parties, instead of only maximizing stockholders' interests.

A socially responsible business does not exploit or endanger any group of individuals. It follows fair trade practices, provides safe environments for workers, and bears responsibility for environmental damage. Granted, measurement of these factors is difficult. How to report this information is also controversial. But many interesting and useful efforts are underway. Throughout this textbook, we provide additional insights into how companies are attempting to meet the challenge of measuring and reporting their contributions to society, as well as their financial results, to stockholders.

Why might a company's stockholders be interested in its environmental and social performance? (Go to **WileyPLUS** for this answer and additional questions.)

DO IT! 5 Financial Statement Items

Presented below is selected information related to Flanagan Company at December 31, 2017. Flanagan reports financial information monthly.

Equipment	$10,000	Utilities Expense	$ 4,000
Cash	8,000	Accounts Receivable	9,000
Service Revenue	36,000	Salaries and Wages Expense	7,000
Rent Expense	11,000	Notes Payable	16,500
Accounts Payable	2,000	Owner's Drawings	5,000

(a) Determine the total assets of Flanagan Company at December 31, 2017.

(b) Determine the net income that Flanagan Company reported for December 2017.

(c) Determine the owner's equity of Flanagan Company at December 31, 2017.

Action Plan

✔ Remember the basic accounting equation: assets must equal liabilities plus owner's equity.

✔ Review previous financial statements to determine how total assets, net income, and owner's equity are computed.

Solution

(a) The total assets are $27,000, comprised of Cash $8,000, Accounts Receivable $9,000, and Equipment $10,000.

(b) Net income is $14,000, computed as follows.

Revenues		
Service revenue		$36,000
Expenses		
Rent expense	$11,000	
Salaries and wages expense	7,000	
Utilities expense	4,000	
Total expenses		22,000
Net income		$14,000

(c) The ending owner's equity of Flanagan Company is $8,500. By rewriting the accounting equation, we can compute owner's equity as assets minus liabilities, as follows.

Total assets [as computed in (a)]		$27,000
Less: Liabilities		
Notes payable	$16,500	
Accounts payable	2,000	18,500
Owner's equity		$ 8,500

Note that it is not possible to determine the company's owner's equity in any other way because the beginning total for owner's equity is not provided.

Related exercise material: **BE1-10, BE1-11, E1-9, E1-10, E1-11, E1-12, E1-13, E1-14, E1-15, E1-16, and DO IT! 1-5.**

LEARNING OBJECTIVE *6

APPENDIX 1A: Explain the career opportunities in accounting.

Why is accounting such a popular major and career choice? First, there are a lot of jobs. In many cities in recent years, the demand for accountants exceeded the supply. Not only are there a lot of jobs, but there are a wide array of opportunities. As one accounting organization observed, "accounting is one degree with 360 degrees of opportunity."

Accounting is also hot because it is obvious that accounting matters. Interest in accounting has increased, ironically, because of the attention caused by the accounting failures of companies such as Enron and WorldCom. These widely publicized scandals revealed the important role that accounting plays in society. Most people want to make a difference, and an accounting career provides many opportunities to contribute to society. Finally, the Sarbanes-Oxley Act (SOX) (see page 7) significantly increased the accounting and internal control requirements for corporations. This dramatically increased demand for professionals with accounting training.

Accountants are in such demand that it is not uncommon for accounting students to have accepted a job offer a year before graduation. As the following discussion reveals, the job options of people with accounting degrees are virtually unlimited.

Public Accounting

Individuals in **public accounting** offer expert service to the general public, in much the same way that doctors serve patients and lawyers serve clients. A major portion of public accounting involves **auditing**. In auditing, a certified public accountant (CPA) examines company financial statements and provides an opinion as to how accurately the financial statements present the company's results and financial position. Analysts, investors, and creditors rely heavily on these "audit opinions," which CPAs have the exclusive authority to issue.

Taxation is another major area of public accounting. The work that tax specialists perform includes tax advice and planning, preparing tax returns, and representing clients before governmental agencies such as the Internal Revenue Service.

A third area in public accounting is **management consulting**. It ranges from installing basic accounting software or highly complex enterprise resource planning systems, to performing support services for major marketing projects and merger and acquisition activities.

Many CPAs are entrepreneurs. They form small- or medium-sized practices that frequently specialize in tax or consulting services.

Private Accounting

Instead of working in public accounting, you might choose to be an employee of a for-profit company such as Starbucks, Google, or PepsiCo. In **private** (or **managerial) accounting**, you would be involved in activities such as cost accounting (finding the cost of producing specific products), budgeting, accounting information system design and support, and tax planning and preparation. You might also be a member of your company's internal audit team. In response to SOX, the internal auditors' job of reviewing the company's operations to ensure compliance with company policies and to increase efficiency has taken on increased importance.

Alternatively, many accountants work for not-for-profit organizations such as the Red Cross or the Bill and Melinda Gates Foundation, or for museums, libraries, or performing arts organizations.

Governmental Accounting

Another option is to pursue one of the many accounting opportunities in governmental agencies. For example, the Internal Revenue Service (IRS), Federal Bureau of Investigation (FBI), and the Securities and Exchange Commission (SEC) all employ accountants. The FBI has a stated goal that at least 15 percent of its new agents should be CPAs. There is also a very high demand for accounting educators at public colleges and universities and in state and local governments.

Forensic Accounting

Forensic accounting uses accounting, auditing, and investigative skills to conduct investigations into theft and fraud. It is listed among the top 20 career paths of the future. The job of forensic accountants is to catch the perpetrators of the estimated $600 billion per year of theft and fraud occurring at U.S. companies. This includes tracing money-laundering and identity-theft activities as well as tax evasion. Insurance companies hire forensic accountants to detect frauds such as arson, and law offices employ forensic accountants to identify marital assets in divorces. Forensic accountants often have FBI, IRS, or similar government experience.

"Show Me the Money"

How much can a new accountant make? Take a look at the average salaries for college graduates in public and private accounting. Keep in mind if you also have a CPA license, you'll make 10–15% more when you start out.

Illustration 1A-1
Salary estimates for jobs in public and corporate accounting

Employer	Jr. Level (0–3 yrs.)	Sr. Level (4–6 yrs.)
Public accounting (large firm)	$51,500–$74,250	$71,000–$92,250
Public accounting (small firm)	$42,500–$60,500	$57,000–$74,000
Corporate accounting (large company)	$41,750–$68,500	$67,000–$86,500
Corporate accounting (small company)	$37,000–$56,750	$52,750–$68,500

Helpful Hint
For up-to-date salary estimates, check out **www.startheregoplaces.com**.

Serious earning potential over time gives CPAs great job security. Here are some examples of upper-level salaries for managers in corporate accounting. Note that geographic region, experience, education, CPA certification, and company size each play a role in determining salary.

Illustration 1A-2
Upper-level management salaries in corporate accounting

Position	Large Company	Small to Medium Company
Chief financial officer	$189,750–$411,000	$96,750–$190,500
Corporate controller	$128,000–$199,000	$82,750–$144,750
Tax manager	$100,250–$142,500	$79,500–$110,750

The Review and Practice section provides opportunities for students to review key concepts and terms as well as complete multiple-choice questions, exercises, and a comprehensive problem. Detailed solutions are also included.

REVIEW AND PRACTICE

LEARNING OBJECTIVES REVIEW

1 Identify the activities and users associated with accounting. Accounting is an information system that identifies, records, and communicates the economic events of an organization to interested users. The major users and uses of accounting are as follows. (a) Management uses accounting information to plan, organize, and run the business. (b) Investors (owners) decide whether to buy, hold, or sell their financial interests on the basis of accounting data. (c) Creditors (suppliers and bankers) evaluate the risks of granting credit or lending money on the basis of accounting information. Other groups that use accounting information are taxing authorities, regulatory agencies, customers, and labor unions.

2 Explain the building blocks of accounting: ethics, principles, and assumptions. Ethics are the standards of conduct by which actions are judged as right or wrong. Effective financial reporting depends on sound ethical behavior.

Generally accepted accounting principles are a common set of standards used by accountants. The primary accounting standard-setting body in the United States is the Financial Accounting Standards Board. The monetary unit assumption requires that companies include in the accounting records only transaction data that can be expressed in terms of money. The economic entity assumption requires that the activities of each economic entity be kept separate from the activities of its owner(s) and other economic entities.

3 State the accounting equation, and define its components. The basic accounting equation is:

Assets = Liabilities + Owner's Equity

Assets are resources a business owns. Liabilities are creditorship claims on total assets. Owner's equity is the ownership claim on total assets.

The expanded accounting equation is:

Assets = Liabilities + Owner's Capital − Owner's Drawings + Revenues − Expenses

Owner's capital is assets the owner puts into the business. Owner's drawings are the assets the owner withdraws for personal use. Revenues are increases in assets resulting from income-earning activities. Expenses are the costs of assets consumed or services used in the process of earning revenue.

4 Analyze the effects of business transactions on the accounting equation. Each business transaction must have a dual effect on the accounting equation. For example, if an individual asset increases, there must be a corresponding (1) decrease in another asset, (2) increase in a specific liability, or (3) increase in owner's equity.

5 Describe the four financial statements and how they are prepared. An income statement presents the revenues and expenses, and resulting net income or net loss, for a specific period of time. An owner's equity statement summarizes the changes in owner's equity for a specific period of time. A balance sheet reports the assets, liabilities, and owner's equity at a specific date. A statement of cash flows summarizes information about the cash inflows (receipts) and outflows (payments) for a specific period of time.

***6 Explain the career opportunities in accounting.** Accounting offers many different jobs in fields such as public and private accounting, governmental, and forensic accounting. Accounting is a popular major because there are many different types of jobs, with unlimited potential for career advancement.

GLOSSARY REVIEW

Accounting The information system that identifies, records, and communicates the economic events of an organization to interested users. (p. 4).

Assets Resources a business owns. (p. 12).

***Auditing** The examination of financial statements by a certified public accountant in order to express an opinion as to the fairness of presentation. (p. 25).

Balance sheet A financial statement that reports the assets, liabilities, and owner's equity at a specific date. (p. 2).

Basic accounting equation Assets = Liabilities + Owner's equity. (p. 21).

Bookkeeping A part of the accounting process that involves only the recording of economic events. (p. 5).

Convergence The process of reducing the differences between U.S. GAAP and IFRS. (p. 9).

Corporation A business organized as a separate legal entity under state corporation law, having ownership divided into transferable shares of stock. (p. 10).

Drawings Withdrawal of cash or other assets from an unincorporated business for the personal use of the owner(s). (p. 13).

Economic entity assumption An assumption that requires that the activities of the entity be kept separate and distinct from the activities of its owner and all other economic entities. (p. 10).

Ethics The standards of conduct by which actions are judged as right or wrong, honest or dishonest, fair or not fair. (p. 7).

Expanded accounting equation Assets = Liabilities + Owner's capital − Owner's drawings + Revenues − Expenses. (p. 13).

Expenses The cost of assets consumed or services used in the process of earning revenue. (p. 13).

Fair value principle An accounting principle stating that assets and liabilities should be reported at fair value (the price received to sell an asset or settle a liability). (p. 9).

Faithful representation Numbers and descriptions match what really existed or happened—they are factual. (p. 9).

Financial accounting The field of accounting that provides economic and financial information for investors, creditors, and other external users. (p. 6).

Financial Accounting Standards Board (FASB) A private organization that establishes generally accepted accounting principles in the United States (GAAP). (p. 9).

***Forensic accounting** An area of accounting that uses accounting, auditing, and investigative skills to conduct investigations into theft and fraud. (p. 26).

Generally accepted accounting principles (GAAP) Common standards that indicate how to report economic events. (p. 8).

Historical cost principle An accounting principle that states that companies should record assets at their cost. (p. 9).

Income statement A financial statement that presents the revenues and expenses and resulting net income or net loss of a company for a specific period of time. (p. 21).

International Accounting Standards Board (IASB) An accounting standard-setting body that issues standards adopted by many countries outside of the United States. (p. 9).

International Financial Reporting Standards (IFRS) International accounting standards set by the International Accounting Standards Board (IASB). (p. 9).

Investments by owner The assets an owner puts into the business. (p. 13).

Liabilities Creditor claims against total assets. (p. 12).

***Management consulting** An area of public accounting ranging from development of accounting and computer systems to support services for marketing projects and merger and acquisition activities. (p. 25).

Managerial accounting The field of accounting that provides internal reports to help users make decisions about their companies. (p. 5).

Monetary unit assumption An assumption stating that companies include in the accounting records only transaction data that can be expressed in terms of money. (p. 9).

Net income The amount by which revenues exceed expenses. (p. 21).

Net loss The amount by which expenses exceed revenues. (p. 21).

Owner's equity The ownership claim on total assets. (p. 13).

Owner's equity statement A financial statement that summarizes the changes in owner's equity for a specific period of time. (p. 21).

Partnership A business owned by two or more persons associated as partners. (p. 10).

***Private (or managerial) accounting** An area of accounting within a company that involves such activities as cost accounting, budgeting, design and support of accounting information systems, and tax planning and preparation. (p. 26).

Proprietorship A business owned by one person. (p. 10).

***Public accounting** An area of accounting in which the accountant offers expert service to the general public. (p. 25).

Relevance Financial information that is capable of making a difference in a decision. (p. 9).

Revenues The gross increase in owner's equity resulting from business activities entered into for the purpose of earning income. (p. 13).

Sarbanes-Oxley Act (SOX) Law passed by Congress intended to reduce unethical corporate behavior. (p. 7).

Securities and Exchange Commission (SEC) A governmental agency that oversees U.S. financial markets and accounting standard-setting bodies. (p. 9).

Statement of cash flows A financial statement that summarizes information about the cash inflows (receipts) and cash outflows (payments) for a specific period of time. (p. 21).

***Taxation** An area of public accounting involving tax advice, tax planning, preparing tax returns, and representing clients before governmental agencies. (p. 25).

Transactions The economic events of a business that are recorded by accountants. (p. 14).

PRACTICE MULTIPLE-CHOICE QUESTIONS

(LO 1) 1. Which of the following is **not** a step in the accounting process?
(a) Identification. (c) Recording.
(b) Economic entity. (d) Communication.

2. Which of the following statements about users of accounting information is **incorrect**? (LO 1)
(a) Management is an internal user.
(b) Taxing authorities are external users.

(c) Present creditors are external users.
(d) Regulatory authorities are internal users.

(LO 2) **3.** The historical cost principle states that:
(a) assets should be initially recorded at cost and adjusted when the fair value changes.
(b) activities of an entity are to be kept separate and distinct from its owner.
(c) assets should be recorded at their cost.
(d) only transaction data capable of being expressed in terms of money be included in the accounting records.

(LO 2) **4.** Which of the following statements about basic assumptions is **correct**?
(a) Basic assumptions are the same as accounting principles.
(b) The economic entity assumption states that there should be a particular unit of accountability.
(c) The monetary unit assumption enables accounting to measure employee morale.
(d) Partnerships are not economic entities.

(LO 2) **5.** The three types of business entities are:
(a) proprietorships, small businesses, and partnerships.
(b) proprietorships, partnerships, and corporations.
(c) proprietorships, partnerships, and large businesses.
(d) financial, manufacturing, and service companies.

(LO 3) **6.** Net income will result during a time period when:
(a) assets exceed liabilities.
(b) assets exceed revenues.
(c) expenses exceed revenues.
(d) revenues exceed expenses.

(LO 3) **7.** As of December 31, 2017, Kent Company has assets of $3,500 and owner's equity of $2,000. What are the liabilities for Kent Company as of December 31, 2017?
(a) $1,500. (c) $2,500.
(b) $1,000. (d) $2,000.

(LO 4) **8.** Performing services on account will have the following effects on the components of the basic accounting equation:
(a) increase assets and decrease owner's equity.
(b) increase assets and increase owner's equity.
(c) increase assets and increase liabilities.
(d) increase liabilities and increase owner's equity.

(LO 4) **9.** Which of the following events is **not** recorded in the accounting records?
(a) Equipment is purchased on account.
(b) An employee is terminated.
(c) A cash investment is made into the business.
(d) The owner withdraws cash for personal use.

10. During 2017, Bruske Company's assets decreased $50,000 and its liabilities decreased $50,000. Its owner's equity therefore: (LO 4)
(a) increased $50,000. (c) decreased $100,000.
(b) decreased $50,000. (d) did not change.

11. Payment of an account payable affects the components of the accounting equation in the following way. (LO 4)
(a) Decreases owner's equity and decreases liabilities.
(b) Increases assets and decreases liabilities.
(c) Decreases assets and increases owner's equity.
(d) Decreases assets and decreases liabilities.

12. Which of the following statements is **false**? (LO 5)
(a) A statement of cash flows summarizes information about the cash inflows (receipts) and outflows (payments) for a specific period of time.
(b) A balance sheet reports the assets, liabilities, and owner's equity at a specific date.
(c) An income statement presents the revenues, expenses, changes in owner's equity, and resulting net income or net loss for a specific period of time.
(d) An owner's equity statement summarizes the changes in owner's equity for a specific period of time.

13. On the last day of the period, Alan Cesska Company buys a $900 machine on credit. This transaction will affect the: (LO 5)
(a) income statement only.
(b) balance sheet only.
(c) income statement and owner's equity statement only.
(d) income statement, owner's equity statement, and balance sheet.

14. The financial statement that reports assets, liabilities, and owner's equity is the: (LO 5)
(a) income statement.
(b) owner's equity statement.
(c) balance sheet.
(d) statement of cash flows.

***15.** Services performed by a public accountant include: (LO 6)
(a) auditing, taxation, and management consulting.
(b) auditing, budgeting, and management consulting.
(c) auditing, budgeting, and cost accounting.
(d) auditing, budgeting, and management consulting.

Solutions

1. (b) Economic entity is not one of the steps in the accounting process. The other choices are true because (a) identification is the first step in the accounting process, (c) recording is the second step in the accounting process, and (d) communication is the third and final step in the accounting process.

2. (d) Regulatory authorities are external, not internal, users of accounting information. The other choices are true statements.

3. (c) The historical cost principle states that assets should be recorded at their cost. The other choices are incorrect because (a) the historical cost principle does not say that assets should be adjusted for changes in fair value, (b) describes the economic entity assumption, and (d) describes the monetary unit assumption.

4. (b) The economic entity assumption states that there should be a particular unit of accountability. The other choices are incorrect because (a) basic assumptions are not the same as accounting principles, (c) the monetary unit assumption allows accounting to measure economic events, and (d) partnerships are economic entities.

5. (b) Proprietorships, partnerships, and corporations are the three types of business entities. Choices (a) and (c) are incorrect because small and large businesses only denote the sizes of businesses. Choice (d) is incorrect because financial, manufacturing, and service companies are types of businesses, not business entities.

6. (d) Net income results when revenues exceed expenses. The other choices are incorrect because (a) assets and liabilities are not used in the computation of net income; (b) revenues, not assets, are included in the computation of net income; and (c) when expenses exceed revenues, a net loss results.

7. (a) Using a variation of the basic accounting equation, Assets − Owner's equity = Liabilities, $3,500 − $2,000 = $1,500. Therefore, choices (b) $1,000, (c) $2,500, and (d) $2,000 are incorrect.

8. (b) When services are performed on account, assets are increased and owner's equity is increased. The other choices are incorrect because when services are performed on account (a) owner's equity is increased, not decreased; (c) liabilities are not affected; and (d) owner's equity is increased and liabilities are not affected.

9. (b) If an employee is terminated, this represents an activity of a company, not a business transaction. Assets, liabilities, and owner's equity are not affected. Thus, there is no effect on the accounting equation. The other choices are incorrect because they are all recorded: (a) when equipment is purchased on account, both assets and liabilities increase; (c) when a cash investment is made into a business, both assets and owner's equity increase; and (d) when an owner withdraws cash for personal use, both assets and owner's equity decrease.

10. (d) In this situation, owner's equity does not change because only assets and liabilities decreased $50,000. Therefore, the other choices are incorrect.

11. (d) Payment of an account payable results in an equal decrease of assets (cash) and liabilities (accounts payable). The other choices are incorrect because payment of an account payable (a) does not affect owner's equity, (b) does not increase assets, and (c) does not affect owner's equity.

12. (c) An income statement represents the revenues, expenses, and the resulting net income or net loss for a specific period of time but not the changes in owner's equity. The other choices are true statements.

13. (b) This transaction will cause assets to increase by $900 and liabilities to increase by $900. The other choices are incorrect because this transaction (a) will have no effect on the income statement, (c) will have no effect on the income statement or the owner's equity statement, and (d) will affect the balance sheet but not the income statement or the owner's equity statement.

14. (c) The balance sheet is the statement that reports assets, liabilities and owner's equity. The other choices are incorrect because (a) the income statement reports revenues and expenses, (b) the owner's equity statement reports details about owner's equity, and (d) the statement of cash flows reports inflows and outflows of cash.

***15. (a)** Auditing, taxation, and management consulting are all services performed by public accountants. The other choices are incorrect because public accountants do not perform budgeting or cost accounting.

PRACTICE EXERCISES

Analyze the effect of transactions.

(LO 3, 4)

1. Selected transactions for Fabulous Flora Company are listed below.

1. Made cash investment to start business.
2. Purchased equipment on account.
3. Paid salaries.
4. Billed customers for services performed.
5. Received cash from customers billed in (4).
6. Withdrew cash for owner's personal use.
7. Incurred advertising expense on account.
8. Purchased additional equipment for cash.
9. Received cash from customers when service was performed.

Instructions

List the numbers of the above transactions and describe the effect of each transaction on assets, liabilities, and owner's equity. For example, the first answer is: (1) Increase in assets and increase in owner's equity.

Solution

1. 1. Increase in assets and increase in owner's equity.
   2. Increase in assets and increase in liabilities.
   3. Decrease in assets and decrease in owner's equity.
   4. Increase in assets and increase in owner's equity.

5. Increase in assets and decrease in assets.
6. Decrease in assets and decrease in owner's equity.
7. Increase in liabilities and decrease in owner's equity.
8. Increase in assets and decrease in assets.
9. Increase in assets and increase in owner's equity.

Analyze the effect of transactions on assets, liabilities, and owner's equity.

(LO 3, 4)

2. Alma's Payroll Services Company entered into the following transactions during May 2017.

1. Purchased computers for $15,000 from Bytes of Data on account.
2. Paid $3,000 cash for May rent on storage space.
3. Received $12,000 cash from customers for contracts billed in April.
4. Performed payroll services for Magic Construction Company for $2,500 cash.
5. Paid Northern Ohio Power Co. $7,000 cash for energy usage in May.
6. Alma invested an additional $25,000 in the business.
7. Paid Bytes of Data for the computers purchased in (1) above.
8. Incurred advertising expense for May of $900 on account.

Instructions

Indicate with the appropriate letter whether each of the transactions above results in:

(a) an increase in assets and a decrease in assets.
(b) an increase in assets and an increase in owner's equity.
(c) an increase in assets and an increase in liabilities.
(d) a decrease in assets and a decrease in owner's equity.
(e) a decrease in assets and a decrease in liabilities.
(f) an increase in liabilities and a decrease in owner's equity.
(g) an increase in owner's equity and a decrease in liabilities.

Solution

2. 1. (c)	3. (a)	5. (d)	7. (e)
2. (d)	4. (b)	6. (b)	8. (f)

PRACTICE PROBLEM

Prepare a tabular presentation and financial statements.

(LO 4, 5)

Joan Robinson opens her own law office on July 1, 2017. During the first month of operations, the following transactions occurred.

1. Joan invested $11,000 in cash in the law practice.
2. Paid $800 for July rent on office space.
3. Purchased equipment on account $3,000.
4. Performed legal services to clients for cash $1,500.
5. Borrowed $700 cash from a bank on a note payable.
6. Performed legal services for client on account $2,000.
7. Paid monthly expenses: salaries and wages $500, utilities $300, and advertising $100.
8. Joan withdrew $1,000 cash for personal use.

Instructions

(a) Prepare a tabular summary of the transactions.

(b) Prepare the income statement, owner's equity statement, and balance sheet at July 31, 2017, for Joan Robinson, Attorney.

Solution

(a)

	Assets			= Liabilities		+ Owner's Equity			
Trans-action	Cash	+ Accounts Receivable	+ Equipment	= Notes Payable	+ Accounts Payable	+ Owner's Capital	− Owner's Drawings	+ Revenues	− Expenses
(1)	+$11,000					+$11,000			
(2)	−800								−$800
(3)			+$3,000		+$3,000				
(4)	+1,500							+$1,500	
(5)	+700			+$700					
(6)		+$2,000						+2,000	
(7)	−500								−500
	−300								−300
	−100								−100
(8)	−1,000						−$1,000		
	$10,500	+ $2,000	+ $3,000	= $700	+ $3,000	+ $11,000	− $1,000	+ $3,500	− $1,700
	$15,500			$15,500					

(b)

JOAN ROBINSON, ATTORNEY
Income Statement
For the Month Ended July 31, 2017

Revenues		
Service revenue		$3,500
Expenses		
Rent expense	$800	
Salaries and wages expense	500	
Utilities expense	300	
Advertising expense	100	
Total expenses		1,700
Net income		$1,800

JOAN ROBINSON, ATTORNEY
Owner's Equity Statement
For the Month Ended July 31, 2017

Owner's capital, July 1		$ 0
Add: Investments	$11,000	
Net income	1,800	12,800
		12,800
Less: Drawings		1,000
Owner's capital, July 31		$11,800

JOAN ROBINSON, ATTORNEY
Balance Sheet
July 31, 2017

Assets

Cash	$10,500
Accounts receivable	2,000
Equipment	3,000
Total assets	$15,500

Liabilities and Owner's Equity

Liabilities	
Notes payable	$ 700
Accounts payable	3,000
Total liabilities	3,700
Owner's equity	
Owner's capital	11,800
Total liabilities and owner's equity	$15,500

WileyPLUS Brief Exercises, Exercises, DO IT! Exercises, and Problems and many additional resources are available for practice in WileyPLUS

NOTE: All asterisked Questions, Exercises, and Problems relate to material in the appendix to the chapter.

QUESTIONS

1. "Accounting is ingrained in our society and it is vital to our economic system." Do you agree? Explain.
2. Identify and describe the steps in the accounting process.
3. (a) Who are internal users of accounting data? (b) How does accounting provide relevant data to these users?
4. What uses of financial accounting information are made by (a) investors and (b) creditors?
5. "Bookkeeping and accounting are the same." Do you agree? Explain.
6. Trenton Travel Agency purchased land for $90,000 cash on December 10, 2017. At December 31, 2017, the land's value has increased to $93,000. What amount should be reported for land on Trenton's balance sheet at December 31, 2017? Explain.
7. What is the monetary unit assumption?
8. What is the economic entity assumption?
9. What are the three basic forms of business organizations for profit-oriented enterprises?
10. Rachel Hipp is the owner of a successful printing shop. Recently, her business has been increasing, and Rachel has been thinking about changing the organization of her business from a proprietorship to a corporation. Discuss some of the advantages Rachel would enjoy if she were to incorporate her business.
11. What is the basic accounting equation?
12. (a) Define the terms assets, liabilities, and owner's equity.
    (b) What items affect owner's equity?
13. Which of the following items are liabilities of Siebers Jewelry Stores?
    (a) Cash.
    (b) Accounts payable.
    (c) Owner's drawings.
    (d) Accounts receivable.
    (e) Supplies.
    (f) Equipment.
    (g) Salaries and wages payable.
    (h) Service revenue.
    (i) Rent expense.
14. Can a business enter into a transaction in which only the left side of the basic accounting equation is affected? If so, give an example.
15. Are the following events recorded in the accounting records? Explain your answer in each case.
    (a) The owner of the company dies.
    (b) Supplies are purchased on account.
    (c) An employee is fired.
    (d) The owner of the business withdraws cash from the business for personal use.
16. Indicate how the following business transactions affect the basic accounting equation.
    (a) Paid cash for janitorial services.
    (b) Purchased equipment for cash.
    (c) Invested cash in the business.
    (d) Paid accounts payable in full.
17. Listed below are some items found in the financial statements of Tony Gruber Co. Indicate in which financial statement(s) the following items would appear.
    (a) Service revenue.
    (b) Equipment.
    (c) Advertising expense.
    (d) Accounts receivable.
    (e) Owner's capital.
    (f) Salaries and wages payable.
18. In February 2017, Maria Osgood invested an additional $10,000 in her business, Osgood's Pharmacy, which is organized as a proprietorship. Osgood's accountant, Carl Sota, recorded this receipt as an increase in cash and revenues. Is this treatment appropriate? Why or why not?
19. "A company's net income appears directly on the income statement and the owner's equity statement, and it is included indirectly in the company's balance sheet." Do you agree? Explain.
20. Saylor Enterprises had a capital balance of $168,000 at the beginning of the period. At the end of the accounting period, the capital balance was $198,000.
    (a) Assuming no additional investment or withdrawals during the period, what is the net income for the period?
    (b) Assuming an additional investment of $13,000 but no withdrawals during the period, what is the net income for the period?
21. Summarized operations for Bayles Co. for the month of July are as follows.

    Revenues recognized: for cash $20,000; on account $70,000.

    Expenses incurred: for cash $26,000; on account $40,000.

    Indicate for Bayles Co. (a) the total revenues, (b) the total expenses, and (c) net income for the month of July.
22. The basic accounting equation is Assets = Liabilities + Owner's equity. Replacing the words in that equation with dollar amounts, what is Apple's accounting equation at September 24, 2013? (*Hint:* Owner's equity is equivalent to shareholders' equity.)

BRIEF EXERCISES

Use basic accounting equation.
(LO 3)

BE1-1 Presented below is the basic accounting equation. Determine the missing amounts.

	Assets	=	Liabilities	+	Owner's Equity
(a)	$90,000		$50,000		?
(b)	?		$44,000		$70,000
(c)	$94,000		?		$53,000

Use basic accounting equation.
(LO 3)

BE1-2 Given the accounting equation, answer each of the following questions.

(a) The liabilities of Weber Company are $120,000 and the owner's equity is $232,000. What is the amount of Weber Company's total assets?
(b) The total assets of Weber Company are $190,000 and its owner's equity is $91,000. What is the amount of its total liabilities?
(c) The total assets of Weber Company are $800,000 and its liabilities are equal to one-half of its total assets. What is the amount of Weber Company's owner's equity?

Use basic accounting equation.
(LO 3)

BE1-3 At the beginning of the year, Gilles Company had total assets of $800,000 and total liabilities of $300,000. Answer the following questions.

(a) If total assets increased $150,000 during the year and total liabilities decreased $60,000, what is the amount of owner's equity at the end of the year?
(b) During the year, total liabilities increased $100,000 and owner's equity decreased $70,000. What is the amount of total assets at the end of the year?
(c) If total assets decreased $80,000 and owner's equity increased $120,000 during the year, what is the amount of total liabilities at the end of the year?

Solve expanded accounting equation.
(LO 3)

BE1-4 Use the expanded accounting equation to answer each of the following questions.

(a) The liabilities of Kafka Company are $90,000. Owner's capital is $150,000; drawings are $40,000; revenues, $450,000; and expenses, $320,000. What is the amount of Kafka Company's total assets?
(b) The total assets of Rivera Company are $57,000. Owner's capital is $25,000; drawings are $7,000; revenues, $52,000; and expenses, $35,000. What is the amount of the company's total liabilities?
(c) The total assets of Alcorn Co. are $600,000 and its liabilities are equal to two-thirds of its total assets. What is the amount of Alcorn Co.'s owner's equity?

Identify assets, liabilities, and owner's equity.
(LO 3)

BE1-5 Indicate whether each of the following items is an asset (A), liability (L), or part of owner's equity (OE).

_______	(a) Accounts receivable	_______	(d) Supplies
_______	(b) Salaries and wages payable	_______	(e) Owner's capital
_______	(c) Equipment	_______	(f) Notes payable

Determine effect of transactions on basic accounting equation.
(LO 4)

BE1-6 Presented below are three business transactions. On a sheet of paper, list the letters (a), (b), and (c) with columns for assets, liabilities, and owner's equity. For each column, indicate whether the transactions increased (+), decreased (−), or had no effect (NE) on assets, liabilities, and owner's equity.

(a) Purchased supplies on account.
(b) Received cash for performing a service.
(c) Paid expenses in cash.

Determine effect of transactions on basic accounting equation.
(LO 4)

BE1-7 Follow the same format as in BE1-6. Determine the effect on assets, liabilities, and owner's equity of the following three transactions.

(a) Invested cash in the business.
(b) Withdrawal of cash by owner.
(c) Received cash from a customer who had previously been billed for services performed.

Classify items affecting owner's equity.
(LO 3)

BE1-8 Classify each of the following items as owner's drawings (D), revenue (R), or expense (E).

_______ (a) Advertising expense
_______ (b) Service revenue
_______ (c) Insurance expense
_______ (d) Salaries and wages expense
_______ (e) Owner's drawings
_______ (f) Rent revenue
_______ (g) Utilities expense

BE1-9 Presented below are three transactions. Mark each transaction as affecting owner's investment (I), owner's drawings (D), revenue (R), expense (E), or not affecting owner's equity (NOE).

Determine effect of transactions on basic owner's equity.

(LO 4)

_______ (a) Received cash for services performed
_______ (b) Paid cash to purchase equipment
_______ (c) Paid employee salaries

BE1-10 In alphabetical order below are balance sheet items for Mendoza Company at December 31, 2017. Kathy Mendoza is the owner of Mendoza Company. Prepare a balance sheet, following the format of Illustration 1-9.

Prepare a balance sheet.

(LO 5)

Accounts payable	$90,000
Accounts receivable	72,500
Cash	49,000
Owner's capital	31,500

BE1-11 Indicate whether the following items would appear on the income statement (IS), balance sheet (BS), or owner's equity statement (OE).

Determine where items appear on financial statements.

(LO 5)

_______ (a) Notes payable
_______ (b) Advertising expense
_______ (c) Owner's capital
_______ (d) Cash
_______ (e) Service revenue

DO IT! Exercises

DO IT! 1-1 Indicate whether each of the five statements presented below is true or false.

Review basic concepts.

(LO 1)

1. The three steps in the accounting process are identification, recording, and examination.
2. The accounting process includes the bookkeeping function.
3. Managerial accounting provides reports to help investors and creditors evaluate a company.
4. The two most common types of external users are investors and creditors.
5. Internal users include human resources managers.

DO IT! 1-2 Indicate whether each of the five statements presented below is true or false.

Identify building blocks of accounting.

(LO 2)

1. Congress passed the Sarbanes-Oxley Act to ensure that investors invest only in companies that will be profitable.
2. The standards of conduct by which actions are judged as loyal or disloyal are ethics.
3. The primary accounting standard-setting body in the United States is the Securities and Exchange Commission (SEC).
4. The historical cost principle dictates that companies record assets at their cost and continue to report them at their cost over the time the assets are held.
5. The monetary unit assumption requires that companies record only transactions that can be measured in money.

DO IT! 1-3 Classify the following items as investment by owner (I), owner's drawings (D), revenues (R), or expenses (E). Then indicate whether each item increases or decreases owner's equity.

Evaluate effects of transactions on owner's equity.

(LO 3)

(1) Drawings.
(2) Rent revenue.
(3) Advertising expense.
(4) Owner puts personal assets into the business.

DO IT! 1-4 Transactions made by M. Alberti and Co., a law firm, for the month of March are shown below and on the next page. Prepare a tabular analysis which shows the effects of these transactions on the expanded accounting equation, similar to that shown in Illustration 1-8.

Prepare tabular analysis.

(LO 4)

1. The company performed $20,000 of services for customers, on credit.
2. The company received $20,000 in cash from customers who had been billed for services (in transaction 1).

3. The company received a bill for $2,300 of advertising but will not pay it until a later date.
4. M. Alberti withdrew $3,600 cash from the business for personal use.

Determine specific amounts on the financial statements.

(LO 5)

DO IT! 1-5 Presented below is selected information related to Kirby Company at December 31, 2017. Kirby reports financial information monthly.

Accounts Payable	$ 3,000	Salaries and Wages Expense	$16,500
Cash	6,500	Notes Payable	25,000
Advertising Expense	6,000	Rent Expense	10,500
Service Revenue	53,500	Accounts Receivable	13,500
Equipment	29,000	Owner's Drawings	7,500

(a) Determine the total assets of Kirby Company at December 31, 2017.
(b) Determine the net income that Kirby Company reported for December 2017.
(c) Determine the owner's equity of Kirby Company at December 31, 2017.

EXERCISES

Classify the three activities of accounting.

(LO 1)

E1-1 Genesis Company performs the following accounting tasks during the year.

________Analyzing and interpreting information.
________Classifying economic events.
________Explaining uses, meaning, and limitations of data.
________Keeping a systematic chronological diary of events.
________Measuring events in dollars and cents.
________Preparing accounting reports.
________Reporting information in a standard format.
________Selecting economic activities relevant to the company.
________Summarizing economic events.

Accounting is "an information system that **identifies**, **records**, and **communicates** the economic events of an organization to interested users."

Instructions
Categorize the accounting tasks performed by Genesis as relating to either the identification (I), recording (R), or communication (C) aspects of accounting.

Identify users of accounting information.

(LO 1)

E1-2 (a) The following are users of financial statements.

________Customers	________Securities and Exchange Commission
________Internal Revenue Service	________Store manager
________Labor unions	________Suppliers
________Marketing manager	________Vice president of finance
________Production supervisor	

Instructions
Identify the users as being either **external users** or **internal users**.

(b) The following questions could be asked by an internal user or an external user.

________Can we afford to give our employees a pay raise?
________Did the company earn a satisfactory income?
________Do we need to borrow in the near future?
________How does the company's profitability compare to other companies?
________What does it cost us to manufacture each unit produced?
________Which product should we emphasize?
________Will the company be able to pay its short-term debts?

Instructions
Identify each of the questions as being more likely asked by an **internal user** or an **external user**.

Discuss ethics and the historical cost principle.

(LO 2)

E1-3 Angela Duffy, president of Duffy Company, has instructed Jana Barth, the head of the accounting department for Duffy Company, to report the company's land in the company's accounting reports at its fair value of $170,000 instead of its cost of $100,000. Duffy says, "Showing the land at $170,000 will make our company look like a better investment when we try to attract new investors next month."

Instructions
Explain the ethical situation involved for Jana Barth, identifying the stakeholders and the alternatives.

E1-4 The following situations involve accounting principles and assumptions.

Use accounting concepts.
(LO 2)

1. Tisinai Company owns buildings that are worth substantially more than they originally cost. In an effort to provide more relevant information, Tisinai reports the buildings at fair value in its accounting reports.
2. Kingston Company includes in its accounting records only transaction data that can be expressed in terms of money.
3. Roger Holloway, owner of Roger's Photography, records his personal living costs as expenses of the business.

Instructions
For each of the three situations, say if the accounting method used is correct or incorrect. If correct, identify which principle or assumption supports the method used. If incorrect, identify which principle or assumption has been violated.

E1-5 Diehl Cleaners has the following balance sheet items.

Classify accounts as assets, liabilities, and owner's equity.
(LO 3)

Accounts payable	Accounts receivable
Cash	Notes payable
Equipment	Salaries and wages payable
Supplies	Owner's capital

Instructions
Classify each item as an asset, liability, or owner's equity.

E1-6 Selected transactions for Green Valley Lawn Care Company are listed below.

Analyze the effect of transactions.
(LO 4)

1. Made cash investment to start business.
2. Paid monthly rent.
3. Purchased equipment on account.
4. Billed customers for services performed.
5. Withdrew cash for owner's personal use.
6. Received cash from customers billed in (4).
7. Incurred advertising expense on account.
8. Purchased additional equipment for cash.
9. Received cash from customers when service was performed.

Instructions
List the numbers of the above transactions and describe the effect of each transaction on assets, liabilities, and owner's equity. For example, the first answer is: (1) Increase in assets and increase in owner's equity.

E1-7 Falske Computer Timeshare Company entered into the following transactions during May 2017.

Analyze the effect of transactions on assets, liabilities, and owner's equity.
(LO 4)

1. Purchased computers for $20,000 from Digital Equipment on account.
2. Paid $4,000 cash for May rent on storage space.
3. Received $17,000 cash from customers for contracts billed in April.
4. Performed computer services for Viking Construction Company for $4,000 cash.
5. Paid Tri-State Power Co. $11,000 cash for energy usage in May.
6. Falske invested an additional $29,000 in the business.
7. Paid Digital Equipment for the computers purchased in (1) above.
8. Incurred advertising expense for May of $1,200 on account.

Instructions
Indicate with the appropriate letter whether each of the transactions above results in:

(a) An increase in assets and a decrease in assets.
(b) An increase in assets and an increase in owner's equity.
(c) An increase in assets and an increase in liabilities.

(d) A decrease in assets and a decrease in owner's equity.
(e) A decrease in assets and a decrease in liabilities.
(f) An increase in liabilities and a decrease in owner's equity.
(g) An increase in owner's equity and a decrease in liabilities.

Analyze transactions and compute net income.
(LO 4)

E1-8 An analysis of the transactions made by Arthur Cooper & Co., a certified public accounting firm, for the month of August is shown below. The expenses were $650 for rent, $4,800 for salaries and wages, and $400 for utilities.

	Cash	+ Accounts Receivable	+ Supplies	+ Equipment	= Accounts Payable	+ Owner's Capital	− Owner's Drawings	+ Revenues	− Expenses
1.	+$15,000					+$15,000			
2.	−2,000			+$5,000	+$3,000				
3.	−750		+$750						
4.	+4,600	+$3,900						+$8,500	
5.	−1,500				−1,500				
6.	−2,000						−$2,000		
7.	−650								−$650
8.	+450	−450							
9.	−4,800								−4,800
10.					+400				−400

Instructions
(a) Describe each transaction that occurred for the month.
(b) Determine how much owner's equity increased for the month.
(c) Compute the amount of net income for the month.

Prepare financial statements.
(LO 5)

E1-9 An analysis of transactions for Arthur Cooper & Co. was presented in E1–8.

Instructions
Prepare an income statement and an owner's equity statement for August and a balance sheet at August 31, 2017. Assume that August is the company's first month of business.

Determine net income (or loss).
(LO 5)

E1-10 Finch Company had the following assets and liabilities on the dates indicated.

December 31	Total Assets	Total Liabilities
2016	$400,000	$250,000
2017	$460,000	$300,000
2018	$590,000	$400,000

Finch began business on January 1, 2016, with an investment of $100,000.

Instructions
From an analysis of the change in owner's equity during the year, compute the net income (or loss) for:
(a) 2016, assuming Finch's drawings were $15,000 for the year.
(b) 2017, assuming Finch made an additional investment of $45,000 and had no drawings in 2017.
(c) 2018, assuming Finch made an additional investment of $15,000 and had drawings of $25,000 in 2018.

Analyze financial statements items.
(LO 5)

E1-11 Two items are omitted from each of the following summaries of balance sheet and income statement data for two proprietorships for the year 2017, Greene's Goods and Solar Enterprises.

	Greene's Goods	Solar Enterprises
Beginning of year:		
Total assets	$110,000	$129,000
Total liabilities	85,000	(c)
Total owner's equity	(a)	80,000

End of year:		
Total assets	160,000	180,000
Total liabilities	120,000	50,000
Total owner's equity	40,000	130,000
Changes during year in owner's equity:		
Additional investment	(b)	25,000
Drawings	37,000	(d)
Total revenues	220,000	100,000
Total expenses	175,000	60,000

Instructions
Determine the missing amounts.

E1-12 The following information relates to Armanda Co. for the year 2017.

Prepare income statement and owner's equity statement.

(LO 5)

Owner's capital, January 1, 2017	$48,000	Advertising expense	$ 1,800
Owner's drawings during 2017	6,000	Rent expense	10,400
Service revenue	63,600	Utilities expense	3,100
Salaries and wages expense	29,500		

Instructions
After analyzing the data, prepare an income statement and an owner's equity statement for the year ending December 31, 2017.

E1-13 Abby Roland is the bookkeeper for Cheng Company. Abby has been trying to determine the correct balance sheet for Cheng Company. Cheng's balance sheet is shown below.

Correct an incorrectly prepared balance sheet.

(LO 5)

CHENG COMPANY
Balance Sheet
December 31, 2017

Assets		**Liabilities**	
Cash	$15,000	Accounts payable	$21,000
Supplies	8,000	Accounts receivable	(6,500)
Equipment	46,000	Owner's capital	67,500
Owner's drawings	13,000	Total liabilities and	
Total assets	$82,000	owner's equity	$82,000

Instructions
Prepare a correct balance sheet.

E1-14 Loren Satina is the sole owner of Clear View Park, a public camping ground near the Lake Mead National Recreation Area. Loren has compiled the following financial information as of December 31, 2017.

Compute net income and prepare a balance sheet.

(LO 5)

Revenues during 2017—camping fees	$140,000	Fair value of equipment	$140,000
Revenues during 2017—general store	65,000	Notes payable	60,000
Accounts payable	11,000	Expenses during 2017	150,000
Cash on hand	23,000	Accounts receivable	17,500
Original cost of equipment	105,500		

Instructions
(a) Determine Loren Satina's net income from Clear View Park for 2017.
(b) Prepare a balance sheet for Clear View Park as of December 31, 2017.

E1-15 Presented below is financial information related to the 2017 operations of Sea Legs Cruise Company.

Prepare an income statement.

(LO 5)

Maintenance and repairs expense	$ 95,000
Utilities expense	13,000
Salaries and wages expense	142,000
Advertising expense	24,500
Ticket revenue	410,000

Instructions
Prepare the 2017 income statement for Sea Legs Cruise Company.

Prepare an owner's equity statement.
(LO 5)

E1-16 Presented below is information related to the sole proprietorship of Alice Henning, attorney.

Legal service revenue—2017	$335,000
Total expenses—2017	211,000
Assets, January 1, 2017	96,000
Liabilities, January 1, 2017	62,000
Assets, December 31, 2017	168,000
Liabilities, December 31, 2017	100,000
Drawings—2017	?

Instructions
Prepare the 2017 owner's equity statement for Alice Henning's legal practice.

EXERCISES: SET B AND CHALLENGE EXERCISES

Visit the book's companion website, at **www.wiley.com/college/weygandt**, and choose the Student Companion site to access Exercises: Set B and Challenge Exercises.

PROBLEMS: SET A

Analyze transactions and compute net income.
(LO 3, 4)

P1-1A On April 1, Julie Spengel established Spengel's Travel Agency. The following transactions were completed during the month.

1. Invested $15,000 cash to start the agency.
2. Paid $600 cash for April office rent.
3. Purchased equipment for $3,000 cash.
4. Incurred $700 of advertising costs in the *Chicago Tribune*, on account.
5. Paid $900 cash for office supplies.
6. Performed services worth $10,000: $3,000 cash is received from customers, and the balance of $7,000 is billed to customers on account.
7. Withdrew $600 cash for personal use.
8. Paid *Chicago Tribune* $500 of the amount due in transaction (4).
9. Paid employees' salaries $2,500.
10. Received $4,000 in cash from customers who have previously been billed in transaction (6).

Check figures provide a key number to let you know you are on the right track.

(a) Total assets $20,800

(b) Net income $6,200

Instructions
(a) Prepare a tabular analysis of the transactions using the following column headings: Cash, Accounts Receivable, Supplies, Equipment, Accounts Payable, Owner's Capital, Owner's Drawings, Revenues, and Expenses.
(b) From an analysis of the owner's equity columns, compute the net income or net loss for April.

Analyze transactions and prepare income statement, owner's equity statement, and balance sheet.
(LO 3, 4, 5)

P1-2A Judi Salem opened a law office on July 1, 2017. On July 31, the balance sheet showed Cash $5,000, Accounts Receivable $1,500, Supplies $500, Equipment $6,000, Accounts Payable $4,200, and Owner's Capital $8,800. During August, the following transactions occurred.

1. Collected $1,200 of accounts receivable.
2. Paid $2,800 cash on accounts payable.
3. Recognized revenue of $7,500 of which $3,000 is collected in cash and the balance is due in September.
4. Purchased additional equipment for $2,000, paying $400 in cash and the balance on account.
5. Paid salaries $2,500, rent for August $900, and advertising expenses $400.

6. Withdrew $700 in cash for personal use.
7. Received $2,000 from Standard Federal Bank—money borrowed on a note payable.
8. Incurred utility expenses for month on account $270.

Instructions

(a) Prepare a tabular analysis of the August transactions beginning with July 31 balances. The column headings should be as follows: Cash + Accounts Receivable + Supplies + Equipment = Notes Payable + Accounts Payable + Owner's Capital − Owner's Drawings + Revenues − Expenses.

(b) Prepare an income statement for August, an owner's equity statement for August, and a balance sheet at August 31.

(a) Total assets $16,800

(b) Net income $3,430
Ending capital $11,530

P1-3A On June 1, Cindy Godfrey started Divine Designs Co., a company that provides craft opportunities, by investing $12,000 cash in the business. Following are the assets and liabilities of the company at June 30 and the revenues and expenses for the month of June.

Prepare income statement, owner's equity statement, and balance sheet.

(LO 5)

Cash	$10,150	Service Revenue	$6,500
Accounts Receivable	2,800	Advertising Expense	500
Supplies	2,000	Rent Expense	1,600
Equipment	10,000	Gasoline Expense	200
Notes Payable	9,000	Utilities Expense	150
Accounts Payable	1,200		

Cindy made no additional investment in June but withdrew $1,300 in cash for personal use during the month.

Instructions

(a) Prepare an income statement and owner's equity statement for the month of June and a balance sheet at June 30, 2017.

(b) Prepare an income statement and owner's equity statement for June assuming the following data are not included above: (1) $900 of services were performed and billed but not collected at June 30, and (2) $150 of gasoline expense was incurred but not paid.

(a) Net income $4,050
Owner's equity $14,750
Total assets $24,950

(b) Owner's equity $15,500

P1-4A Trixie Maye started her own consulting firm, Matrix Consulting, on May 1, 2017. The following transactions occurred during the month of May.

Analyze transactions and prepare financial statements.

(LO 3, 4, 5)

May	1	Trixie invested $7,000 cash in the business.
	2	Paid $900 for office rent for the month.
	3	Purchased $600 of supplies on account.
	5	Paid $125 to advertise in the *County News*.
	9	Received $4,000 cash for services performed.
	12	Withdrew $1,000 cash for personal use.
	15	Performed $5,400 of services on account.
	17	Paid $2,500 for employee salaries.
	20	Paid for the supplies purchased on account on May 3.
	23	Received a cash payment of $4,000 for services performed on account on May 15.
	26	Borrowed $5,000 from the bank on a note payable.
	29	Purchased equipment for $4,200 on account.
	30	Paid $275 for utilities.

Instructions

(a) Show the effects of the previous transactions on the accounting equation using the following format.

(a) Total assets $20,800

	Assets				=	Liabilities		Owner's Equity			
Date	Cash +	Accounts Receivable +	Supplies +	Equipment	=	Notes Payable +	Accounts Payable +	Owner's Capital −	Owner's Drawings +	Revenues −	Expenses

(b) Prepare an income statement for the month of May.

(c) Prepare a balance sheet at May 31, 2017.

(b) Net income $5,600

(c) Cash $14,600

Determine financial statement amounts and prepare owner's equity statement.

(LO 4, 5)

P1-5A Financial statement information about four different companies is as follows.

	Alpha Company	Beta Company	Psi Company	Omega Company
January 1, 2017				
Assets	$ 80,000	$ 90,000	(g)	$150,000
Liabilities	41,000	(d)	80,000	(j)
Owner's equity	(a)	40,000	49,000	90,000
December 31, 2017				
Assets	(b)	112,000	170,000	(k)
Liabilities	60,000	72,000	(h)	100,000
Owner's equity	50,000	(e)	82,000	151,000
Owner's equity changes in year				
Additional investment	(c)	8,000	10,000	15,000
Drawings	15,000	(f)	12,000	10,000
Total revenues	350,000	410,000	(i)	500,000
Total expenses	333,000	385,000	350,000	(l)

Instructions

(a) Determine the missing amounts. (*Hint:* For example, to solve for (a), Assets − Liabilities = Owner's equity = $39,000.)

(b) Prepare the owner's equity statement for Alpha Company.

(c) Write a memorandum explaining the sequence for preparing financial statements and the interrelationship of the owner's equity statement to the income statement and balance sheet.

PROBLEMS: SET B AND SET C

Visit the book's companion website, at **www.wiley.com/college/weygandt**, and choose the Student Companion site to access Problems: Set B and Set C.

CONTINUING PROBLEM

The ***Cookie Creations*** *problem starts in this chapter and continues through Chapter 18. The business begins as a sole proprietorship and then evolves into a partnership and finally a corporation. You also can find this problem at the book's companion website.*

COOKIE CREATIONS: AN ENTREPRENEURIAL JOURNEY

© leungchopan/ Shutterstock

CC1 Natalie Koebel spent much of her childhood learning the art of cookie-making from her grandmother. They passed many happy hours mastering every type of cookie imaginable and later creating new recipes that were both healthy and delicious. Now at the start of her second year in college, Natalie is investigating various possibilities for starting her own business as part of the requirements of the entrepreneurship program in which she is enrolled.

A long-time friend insists that Natalie has to somehow include cookies in her business plan. After a series of brainstorming sessions, Natalie settles on the idea of operating a cookie-making school. She will start on a part-time basis and offer her services in people's homes. Now that she has started thinking about it, the possibilities seem endless. During the fall, she will concentrate on holiday cookies. She will offer individual lessons and group sessions (which will probably be more entertainment than education for the participants). Natalie also decides to include children in her target market.

The first difficult decision is coming up with the perfect name for her business. In the end, she settles on "Cookie Creations" and then moves on to more important issues.

Instructions

(a) What form of business organization—proprietorship, partnership, or corporation—do you recommend that Natalie use for her business? Discuss the benefits and weaknesses of each form and give the reasons for your choice.

(b) Will Natalie need accounting information? If yes, what information will she need and why? How often will she need this information?

(c) Identify specific asset, liability, and owner's equity accounts that Cookie Creations will likely use to record its business transactions.

(d) Should Natalie open a separate bank account for the business? Why or why not?

BROADENING YOUR PERSPECTIVE

FINANCIAL REPORTING AND ANALYSIS

Financial Reporting Problem: Apple Inc.

BYP1-1 The financial statements of Apple Inc. for 2013 are presented in Appendix A. Instructions for accessing and using the company's complete annual report, including the notes to the financial statements, are also provided in Appendix A.

Instructions

Refer to Apple's financial statements and answer the following questions.

(a) What were Apple's total assets at September 28, 2013? At September 29, 2012?
(b) How much cash (and cash equivalents) did Apple have on September 28, 2013?
(c) What amount of accounts payable did Apple report on September 28, 2013? On September 29, 2012?
(d) What were Apple's net sales in 2011? In 2012? In 2013?
(e) What is the amount of the change in Apple's net income from 2012 to 2013?

Comparative Analysis Problem: PepsiCo, Inc. vs. The Coca-Cola Company

BYP1-2 PepsiCo, Inc.'s financial statements are presented in Appendix B. Financial statements of The Coca-Cola Company are presented in Appendix C. Instructions for accessing and using the complete annual reports of PepsiCo and Coca-Cola, including the notes to the financial statements, are also provided in Appendices B and C, respectively.

Instructions

(a) Based on the information contained in these financial statements, determine the following for each company.
  (1) Total assets at December 28, 2013, for PepsiCo and for Coca-Cola at December 31, 2013.
  (2) Accounts (notes) receivable, net at December 28, 2013, for PepsiCo and at December 31, 2013, for Coca-Cola.
  (3) Net revenues for year ended in 2013.
  (4) Net income for year ended in 2013.
(b) What conclusions concerning the two companies can be drawn from these data?

Comparative Analysis Problem: Amazon.com, Inc. vs. Wal-Mart Stores, Inc.

BYP1-3 Amazon.com, Inc.'s financial statements are presented in Appendix D. Financial statements of Wal-Mart Stores, Inc. are presented in Appendix E. Instructions for accessing and using the complete annual reports of Amazon and Wal-Mart, including the notes to the financial statements, are also provided in Appendices D and E, respectively.

Instructions

(a) Based on the information contained in these financial statements, determine the following for each company.
  (1) Total assets at December 31, 2013, for Amazon and for Wal-Mart at January 31, 2014.
  (2) Receivables (net) at December 31, 2013, for Amazon and for Wal-Mart at January 31, 2014.
  (3) Net sales (product only) for year ended in 2013 (2014 for Wal-Mart).
  (4) Net income for the year ended in 2013 (2014 for Wal-Mart).
(b) What conclusions concerning these two companies can be drawn from these data?

Real-World Focus

BYP1-4 This exercise will familiarize you with skill requirements, job descriptions, and salaries for accounting careers.

Address: **www.careers-in-accounting.com**, or go to **www.wiley.com/college/weygandt**

Instructions

Go to the site shown above. Answer the following questions.

(a) What are the three broad areas of accounting (from "Skills and Talents")?
(b) List eight skills required in accounting.
(c) How do the three accounting areas differ in terms of these eight required skills?
(d) Explain one of the key job options in accounting.
(e) What is the overall salary range for a junior staff accountant?

CRITICAL THINKING

Decision-Making Across the Organization

BYP1-5 Anya and Nick Ramon, local golf stars, opened the Chip-Shot Driving Range on March 1, 2017, by investing $25,000 of their cash savings in the business. A caddy shack was constructed for cash at a cost of $8,000, and $800 was spent on golf balls and golf clubs. The Ramons leased five acres of land at a cost of $1,000 per month and paid the first month's rent. During the first month, advertising costs totaled $750, of which $100 was unpaid at March 31, and $500 was paid to members of the high-school golf team for retrieving golf balls. All revenues from customers were deposited in the company's bank account. On March 15, Anya and Nick withdrew a total of $1,000 in cash for personal living expenses. A $120 utility bill was received on March 31 but was not paid. On March 31, the balance in the company's bank account was $18,900.

Anya and Nick thought they had a pretty good first month of operations. But, their estimates of profitability ranged from a loss of $6,100 to net income of $2,480.

Instructions

With the class divided into groups, answer the following.

(a) How could the Ramons have concluded that the business operated at a loss of $6,100? Was this a valid basis on which to determine net income?
(b) How could the Ramons have concluded that the business operated at a net income of $2,480? (*Hint:* Prepare a balance sheet at March 31.) Was this a valid basis on which to determine net income?
(c) Without preparing an income statement, determine the actual net income for March.
(d) What was the revenue recognized in March?

Communication Activity

BYP1-6 Sandi Alcon, the bookkeeper for New York Company, has been trying to determine the correct balance sheet for the company. The company's balance sheet is shown below.

NEW YORK COMPANY
Balance Sheet
For the Month Ended December 31, 2017

Assets		Liabilities	
Equipment	$25,500	Owner's capital	$26,000
Cash	9,000	Accounts receivable	(6,000)
Supplies	2,000	Owner's drawings	(2,000)
Accounts payable	(8,000)	Notes payable	10,500
	$28,500		$28,500

Instructions

Explain to Sandi Alcon in a memo why the original balance sheet is incorrect, and what should be done to correct it.

Ethics Case

BYP1-7 After numerous campus interviews, Travis Chase, a senior at Great Northern College, received two office interview invitations from the Baltimore offices of two large firms. Both firms offered to cover his out-of-pocket expenses (travel, hotel, and meals). He scheduled the interviews for both firms on the same day, one in the morning and one in the afternoon. At the conclusion of each interview, he submitted to both firms his total out-of-pocket expenses for the trip to Baltimore: mileage $112 (280 miles at $0.40), hotel $130, meals $36, and parking and tolls $18, for a total of $296. He believes this approach is appropriate. If he had made two trips, his cost would have been two times $296. He is also certain that neither firm knew he had visited the other on that same trip. Within 10 days, Travis received two checks in the mail, each in the amount of $296.

Instructions
(a) Who are the stakeholders (affected parties) in this situation?
(b) What are the ethical issues in this case?
(c) What would you do in this situation?

All About You

BYP1-8 Some people are tempted to make their finances look worse to get financial aid. Companies sometimes also manage their financial numbers in order to accomplish certain goals. Earnings management is the planned timing of revenues, expenses, gains, and losses to smooth out bumps in net income. In managing earnings, companies' actions vary from being within the range of ethical activity to being both unethical and illegal attempts to mislead investors and creditors.

Instructions
Provide responses for each of the following questions.

(a) Discuss whether you think each of the following actions (adapted from **www.finaid.org/fafsa/maximize.phtml**) to increase the chances of receiving financial aid is ethical.
   (1) Spend the student's assets and income first, before spending parents' assets and income.
   (2) Accelerate necessary expenses to reduce available cash. For example, if you need a new car, buy it before applying for financial aid.
   (3) State that a truly financially dependent child is independent.
   (4) Have a parent take an unpaid leave of absence for long enough to get below the "threshold" level of income.
(b) What are some reasons why a **company** might want to overstate its earnings?
(c) What are some reasons why a **company** might want to understate its earnings?
(d) Under what circumstances might an otherwise ethical person decide to illegally overstate or understate earnings?

FASB Codification Activity

BYP1-9 The FASB has developed the Financial Accounting Standards Board Accounting Standards Codification (or more simply "the Codification"). The FASB's primary goal in developing the Codification is to provide in one place all the authoritative literature related to a particular topic. To provide easy access to the Codification, the FASB also developed the Financial Accounting Standards Board Codification Research System (CRS). CRS is an online, real-time database that provides easy access to the Codification. The Codification and the related CRS provide a topically organized structure, subdivided into topic, subtopics, sections, and paragraphs, using a numerical index system.

You may find this system useful in your present and future studies, and so we have provided an opportunity to use this online system as part of the *Broadening Your Perspective* section.

Instructions
Academic access to the FASB Codification is available through university subscriptions, obtained from the American Accounting Association (at **http://aaahq.org/FASB/Access.cfm**), for an annual fee of $150. This subscription covers an unlimited number of students within a single institution. Once this access has been obtained by your school, you should log in (at **http://aaahq.org/ascLogin.cfm**) and familiarize yourself with the resources that are accessible at the FASB Codification site.

Considering People, Planet, and Profit

BYP1-10 This chapter's Feature Story discusses the fact that although Clif Bar & Company is not a public company, it does share its financial information with its employees as part of its open-book management approach. Further, although it does not publicly share its financial information, it does provide a different form of an annual report to external users. In this report, the company provides information regarding its sustainability efforts.

Address: **www.issuu.com/clifbar/docs/clif_all_aspirations_2012**

Instructions

Access the 2010 annual report of Clif Bar & Company at the site shown above and then answer the following questions.

(a) What are the Five Aspirations?

(b) What was the company 10-year compounded annual growth rate? What is the amount of 10-year organic purchases made by the company?

A Look at IFRS

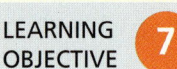

LEARNING OBJECTIVE 7

Describe the impact of international accounting standards on U.S. financial reporting.

Most agree that there is a need for one set of international accounting standards. Here is why:

Multinational corporations. Today's companies view the entire world as their market. For example, Coca-Cola, Intel, and McDonald's generate more than 50% of their sales outside the United States. Many foreign companies, such as Toyota, Nestlé, and Sony, find their largest market to be the United States.

Mergers and acquisitions. The mergers between Fiat/Chrysler and Vodafone/Mannesmann suggest that we will see even more such business combinations of companies from different countries in the future.

Information technology. As communication barriers continue to topple through advances in technology, companies and individuals in different countries and markets are becoming more comfortable buying and selling goods and services from one another.

Financial markets. Financial markets are of international significance today. Whether it is currency, equity securities (stocks), bonds, or derivatives, there are active markets throughout the world trading these types of instruments.

Key Points

Following are the key similarities and differences between GAAP and IFRS as related to accounting fundamentals.

Similarities

- The basic techniques for recording business transactions are the same for U.S. and international companies.
- Both international and U. S. accounting standards emphasize transparency in financial reporting. Both sets of standards are primarily driven by meeting the needs of investors and creditors.
- The three most common forms of business organizations, proprietorships, partnerships, and corporations, are also found in countries that use international accounting standards

Differences

- International standards are referred to as International Financial Reporting Standards (IFRS), developed by the International Accounting Standards Board. Accounting standards in the United States are referred to as generally accepted accounting principles (GAAP) and are developed by the Financial Accounting Standards Board.
- IFRS tends to be simpler in its accounting and disclosure requirements; some people say it is more "principles-based." GAAP is more detailed; some people say it is more "rules-based."
- The internal control standards applicable to Sarbanes-Oxley (SOX) apply only to large public companies listed on U.S. exchanges. There is continuing debate as to whether non-U.S. companies should have to comply with this extra layer of regulation.

Looking to the Future

Both the IASB and the FASB are hard at work developing standards that will lead to the elimination of major differences in the way certain transactions are accounted for and reported.

IFRS Practice

IFRS Self-Test Questions

1. Which of the following is **not** a reason why a single set of high-quality international accounting standards would be beneficial?
   (a) Mergers and acquisition activity.
   (b) Financial markets.
   (c) Multinational corporations.
   (d) GAAP is widely considered to be a superior reporting system.
2. The Sarbanes-Oxley Act determines:
   (a) international tax regulations.
   (b) internal control standards as enforced by the IASB.
   (c) internal control standards of U.S. publicly traded companies.
   (d) U.S. tax regulations.
3. IFRS is considered to be more:
   (a) principles-based and less rules-based than GAAP.
   (b) rules-based and less principles-based than GAAP.
   (c) detailed than GAAP.
   (d) None of the above.

IFRS Exercises

IFRS1-1 Who are the two key international players in the development of international accounting standards? Explain their role.

IFRS1-2 What is the benefit of a single set of high-quality accounting standards?

International Financial Reporting Problem: Louis Vuitton

IFRS1-3 The financial statements of Louis Vuitton are presented in Appendix F. Instructions for accessing and using the company's complete annual report, including the notes to its financial statements, are also provided in Appendix F.

Instructions

Visit Louis Vuitton's corporate website and answer the following questions from the company's 2013 annual report.

(a) What accounting firm performed the audit of Louis Vuitton's financial statements?
(b) What is the address of the company's corporate headquarters?
(c) What is the company's reporting currency?

Answers to IFRS Self-Test Questions

1. d **2.** c **3.** a

2 The Recording Process

CHAPTER PREVIEW In Chapter 1, we analyzed business transactions in terms of the accounting equation, and we presented the cumulative effects of these transactions in tabular form. Imagine a company like MF Global (as in the Feature Story below) using the same tabular format as Softbyte to keep track of its transactions. In a single day, MF Global engaged in thousands of business transactions. To record each transaction this way would be impractical, expensive, and unnecessary. Instead, companies use a set of procedures and records to keep track of transaction data more easily. This chapter introduces and illustrates these basic procedures and records.

FEATURE STORY

Accidents Happen

How organized are you financially? Take a short quiz. Answer yes or no to each question:

- Does your wallet contain so many cash machine receipts that you've been declared a walking fire hazard?
- Do you wait until your debit card is denied before checking the status of your funds?
- Was Aaron Rodgers (the quarterback for the Green Bay Packers) playing high school football the last time you verified the accuracy of your bank account?

If you think it is hard to keep track of the many transactions that make up your life, imagine how difficult it is for a big corporation to do so. Not only that, but now consider how important it is for a large company to have good accounting records, especially if it has control of your life savings. MF Global Holdings Ltd is such a company. As a big investment broker, it held billions of dollars of investments for clients. If you had your life savings invested at MF Global, you might be slightly displeased if you heard this from one of its representatives: "You know, I kind of remember an account for someone with a name like yours—now what did we do with that?"

Unfortunately, that is almost exactly what happened to MF Global's clients shortly before it filed for bankruptcy. During the days immediately following the bankruptcy filing, regulators and auditors struggled to piece things together. In the words of one regulator, "Their books are a disaster . . . we're trying to figure out what numbers are real numbers." One company that considered buying an interest in MF Global walked away from the deal because it "couldn't get a sense of what was on the balance sheet." That company said the information that should have been instantly available instead took days to produce.

It now appears that MF Global did not properly segregate customer accounts from company accounts. And, because of its sloppy recordkeeping, customers were not protected when the company had financial troubles. Total customer losses were approximately $1 billion. As you can see, accounting matters!

Source: S. Patterson and A. Lucchetti, "Inside the Hunt for MF Global Cash," *Wall Street Journal Online* (November 11, 2011).

Nick Laham/Getty Images, Inc.

CHAPTER OUTLINE

Learning Objectives

	Learning Objective	Topics	DO IT!
1	Describe how accounts, debits, and credits are used to record business transactions.	• The account • Debits and credits • Summary of debit/credit rules	DO IT! 1 Normal Account Balances
2	Indicate how a journal is used in the recording process.	• Steps in the recording process • The journal	DO IT! 2 Recording Business Activities
3	Explain how a ledger and posting help in the recording process.	• The ledger • Posting • The recording process illustrated • Summary illustration of journalizing and posting	DO IT! 3 Posting
4	Prepare a trial balance.	• Limitations of a trial balance • Locating errors • Dollar signs and underlining	DO IT! 4 Trial Balance

Go to the ***REVIEW AND PRACTICE*** section at the end of the chapter for a review of key concepts and practice applications with solutions.

Visit **WileyPLUS with ORION** for additional tutorials and practice opportunities.

LEARNING OBJECTIVE **1**

Describe how accounts, debits, and credits are used to record business transactions.

The Account

An **account** is an individual accounting record of increases and decreases in a specific asset, liability, or owner's equity item. For example, Softbyte (the company discussed in Chapter 1) would have separate accounts for Cash, Accounts Receivable, Accounts Payable, Service Revenue, Salaries and Wages Expense, and so on. (Note that whenever we are referring to a specific account, we capitalize the name.)

In its simplest form, an account consists of three parts: (1) a title, (2) a left or debit side, and (3) a right or credit side. Because the format of an account resembles the letter T, we refer to it as a **T-account**. Illustration 2-1 shows the basic form of an account.

Illustration 2-1
Basic form of account

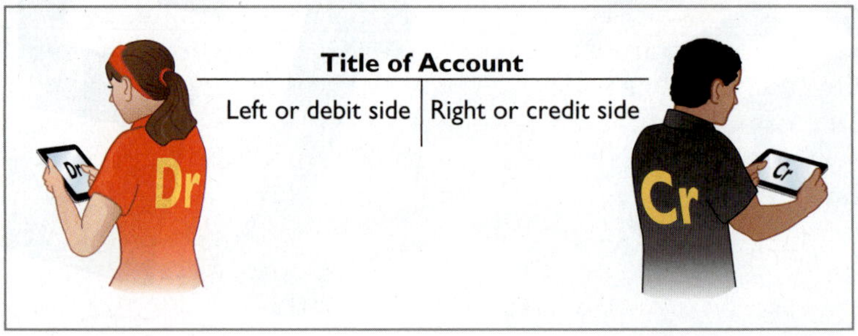

We use this form often throughout this book to explain basic accounting relationships.

Debits and Credits

The term **debit** indicates the left side of an account, and **credit** indicates the right side. They are commonly abbreviated as **Dr.** for debit and **Cr.** for credit. They **do not** mean increase or decrease, as is commonly thought. We use the terms **debit** and **credit** repeatedly in the recording process to describe **where** entries are made in accounts. For example, the act of entering an amount on the left side of an account is called **debiting** the account. Making an entry on the right side is **crediting** the account.

When comparing the totals of the two sides, an account shows a **debit balance** if the total of the debit amounts exceeds the credits. An account shows a **credit balance** if the credit amounts exceed the debits. Note the position of the debit side and credit side in Illustration 2-1.

The procedure of recording debits and credits in an account is shown in Illustration 2-2 for the transactions affecting the Cash account of Softbyte. The data are taken from the Cash column of the tabular summary in Illustration 1-8 (page 20).

Illustration 2-2
Tabular summary and account form for Softbyte's Cash account

Tabular Summary

Cash
$15,000
−7,000
1,200
1,500
−1,700
−250
600
−1,300
$ 8,050

Account Form

Cash			
(Debits)	15,000	(Credits)	7,000
	1,200		1,700
	1,500		250
	600		1,300
Balance (Debit)	8,050		

Every positive item in the tabular summary represents a receipt of cash. Every negative amount represents a payment of cash. **Notice that in the account form, we record the increases in cash as debits and the decreases in cash as credits.** For example, the $15,000 receipt of cash (in red) is debited to Cash, and the −$7,000 payment of cash (in blue) is credited to Cash.

Having increases on one side and decreases on the other reduces recording errors and helps in determining the totals of each side of the account as well as the account balance. The balance is determined by netting the two sides (subtracting one amount from the other). The account balance, a debit of $8,050, indicates that Softbyte had $8,050 more increases than decreases in cash. In other words, Softbyte started with a balance of zero and now has $8,050 in its Cash account.

DEBIT AND CREDIT PROCEDURE

In Chapter 1, you learned the effect of a transaction on the basic accounting equation. Remember that each transaction must affect two or more accounts to keep the basic accounting equation in balance. In other words, for each transaction, debits must equal credits. The equality of debits and credits provides the basis for the **double-entry system** of recording transactions.

Under the double-entry system, the dual (two-sided) effect of each transaction is recorded in appropriate accounts. This system provides a logical method for recording transactions and also helps ensure the accuracy of the recorded amounts as well as the detection of errors. If every transaction is recorded with equal debits and credits, the sum of all the debits to the accounts must equal the sum of all the credits.

The double-entry system for determining the equality of the accounting equation is much more efficient than the plus/minus procedure used in Chapter 1. The following discussion illustrates debit and credit procedures in the double-entry system.

International Note

Rules for accounting for specific events sometimes differ across countries. Despite the differences, the double-entry accounting system is the basis of accounting systems worldwide.

DR./CR. PROCEDURES FOR ASSETS AND LIABILITIES

In Illustration 2-2 for Softbyte, increases in Cash—an asset—were entered on the left side, and decreases in Cash were entered on the right side. We know that both sides of the basic equation (Assets = Liabilities + Owner's Equity) must be equal. It therefore follows that increases and decreases in liabilities will have to be recorded **opposite from** increases and decreases in assets. Thus, increases in liabilities must be entered on the right or credit side, and decreases in liabilities must be entered on the left or debit side. The effects that debits and credits have on assets and liabilities are summarized in Illustration 2-3.

Illustration 2-3
Debit and credit effects—assets and liabilities

Debits	Credits
Increase assets	Decrease assets
Decrease liabilities	Increase liabilities

Asset accounts normally show debit balances. That is, debits to a specific asset account should exceed credits to that account. Likewise, **liability accounts normally show credit balances**. That is, credits to a liability account should exceed debits to that account. The **normal balance** of an account is on the side where an increase in the account is recorded. Illustration 2-4 shows the normal balances for assets and liabilities.

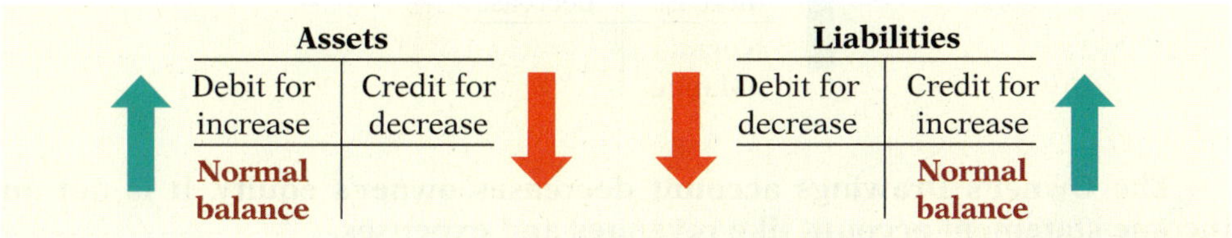

Illustration 2-4
Normal balances—assets and liabilities

Knowing the normal balance in an account may help you trace errors. For example, a credit balance in an asset account such as Land or a debit balance in a liability account such as Salaries and Wages Payable usually indicates an error. Occasionally, though, an abnormal balance may be correct. The Cash account, for example, will have a credit balance when a company has overdrawn its bank balance (i.e., written a check that "bounced").

DR./CR. PROCEDURES FOR OWNER'S EQUITY

As Chapter 1 indicated, owner's investments and revenues increase owner's equity. Owner's drawings and expenses decrease owner's equity. Companies keep accounts for each of these types of transactions.

OWNER'S CAPITAL Investments by owners are credited to the Owner's Capital account. Credits increase this account, and debits decrease it. When an owner invests cash in the business, the company debits (increases) Cash and credits (increases) Owner's Capital. When the owner's investment in the business is reduced, Owner's Capital is debited (decreased).

Illustration 2-5 shows the rules of debit and credit for the Owner's Capital account.

Illustration 2-5
Debit and credit effects—Owner's Capital

Debits	Credits
Decrease Owner's Capital	Increase Owner's Capital

We can diagram the normal balance in Owner's Capital as follows.

Illustration 2-6
Normal balance—Owner's Capital

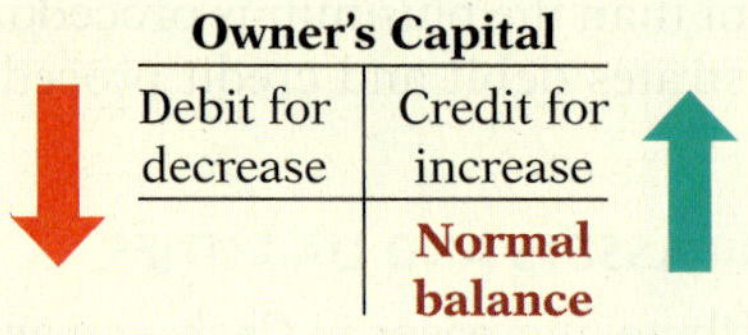

OWNER'S DRAWINGS An owner may withdraw cash or other assets for personal use. Withdrawals could be debited directly to Owner's Capital to indicate a decrease in owner's equity. However, it is preferable to use a separate account, called Owner's Drawings. This separate account makes it easier to determine total withdrawals for each accounting period. Owner's Drawings is increased by debits and decreased by credits. Normally, the drawings account will have a debit balance.

Illustration 2-7 shows the rules of debit and credit for the Owner's Drawings account.

Illustration 2-7
Debit and credit effects—Owner's Drawings

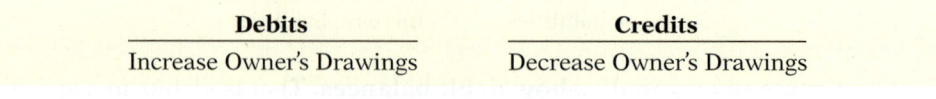

Debits	Credits
Increase Owner's Drawings	Decrease Owner's Drawings

We can diagram the normal balance as follows.

Illustration 2-8
Normal balance—Owner's Drawings

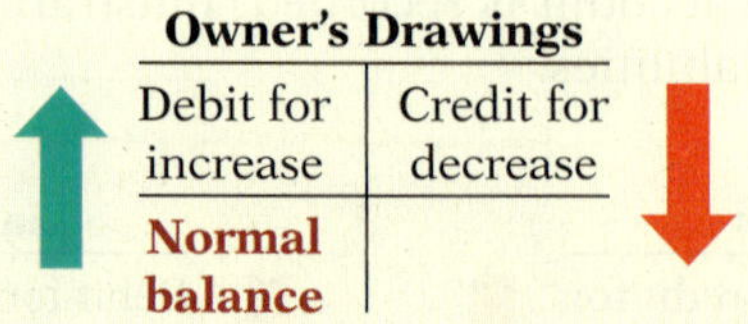

The Owner's Drawings account decreases owner's equity. It is not an income statement account like revenues and expenses.

Investor Insight Chicago Cubs

Jonathan Daniel/Getty Images, Inc.

Keeping Score

The Chicago Cubs baseball team probably has these major revenue and expense accounts:

Revenues	Expenses
Admissions (ticket sales)	Players' salaries
Concessions	Administrative salaries
Television and radio	Travel
Advertising	Ballpark maintenance

Do you think that the Chicago Bears football team would be likely to have the same major revenue and expense accounts as the Cubs? (Go to **WileyPLUS** for this answer and additional questions.)

REVENUES AND EXPENSES The purpose of earning revenues is to benefit the owner(s) of the business. When a company recognizes revenues, owner's equity increases. Therefore, **the effect of debits and credits on revenue accounts is the same as their effect on Owner's Capital**. That is, revenue accounts are increased by credits and decreased by debits.

Helpful Hint
Because revenues increase owner's equity, a revenue account has the same debit/credit rules as the Owner's Capital account. Expenses have the opposite effect.

Expenses have the opposite effect. Expenses decrease owner's equity. Since expenses decrease net income and revenues increase it, it is logical that the increase and decrease sides of expense accounts should be the opposite of revenue accounts. Thus, expense accounts are increased by debits and decreased by credits. Illustration 2-9 shows the rules of debits and credits for revenues and expenses.

Illustration 2-9
Debit and credit effects—revenues and expenses

Debits	Credits
Decrease revenues	Increase revenues
Increase expenses	Decrease expenses

Credits to revenue accounts should exceed debits. Debits to expense accounts should exceed credits. Thus, revenue accounts normally show credit balances, and expense accounts normally show debit balances. Illustration 2-10 shows the normal balances for revenues and expenses.

Illustration 2-10
Normal balances—revenues and expenses

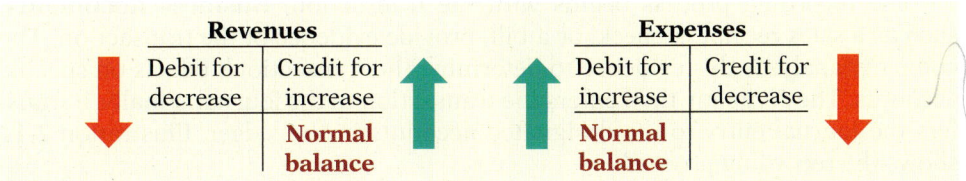

Revenues		Expenses	
Debit for decrease	Credit for increase	Debit for increase	Credit for decrease
	Normal balance	**Normal balance**	

Helpful Hint
You may want to bookmark Illustration 2-11. You probably will refer to it often.

Summary of Debit/Credit Rules

Illustration 2-11 shows a summary of the debit/credit rules and effects on each type of account. Study this diagram carefully. It will help you understand the fundamentals of the double-entry system.

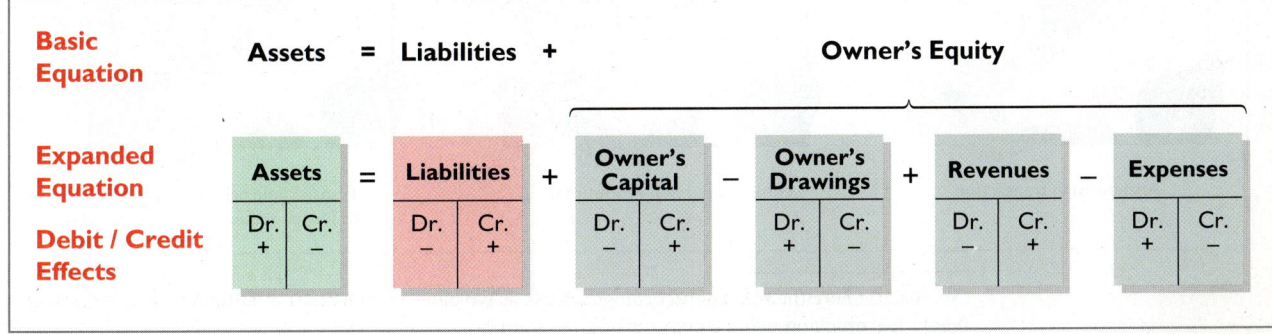

Illustration 2-11
Summary of debit/credit rules

Basic Equation	**Assets**	=	**Liabilities**	+	**Owner's Equity**						
Expanded Equation	**Assets**	=	**Liabilities**	+	**Owner's Capital**	−	**Owner's Drawings**	+	**Revenues**	−	**Expenses**
Debit / Credit Effects	Dr. + / Cr. −		Dr. − / Cr. +		Dr. − / Cr. +		Dr. + / Cr. −		Dr. − / Cr. +		Dr. + / Cr. −

DO IT! 1 Normal Account Balances

Action Plan

✔ Determine the types of accounts needed. Kate will need asset accounts for each different type of asset she invests in the business and liability accounts for any debts she incurs.

✔ Understand the types of owner's equity accounts. Only Owner's Capital will be needed when Kate begins the business. Other owner's equity accounts will be needed later.

Kate Browne has just rented space in a shopping mall. In this space, she will open a hair salon to be called "Hair It Is." A friend has advised Kate to set up a double-entry set of accounting records in which to record all of her business transactions.

Identify the balance sheet accounts that Kate will likely need to record the transactions needed to open her business. Indicate whether the normal balance of each account is a debit or a credit.

Solution

Kate would likely need the following accounts in which to record the transactions necessary to ready her hair salon for opening day:

Cash (debit balance)	If she borrows money: Notes Payable (credit balance)
Equipment (debit balance)	
Supplies (debit balance)	Owner's Capital (credit balance)
Accounts Payable (credit balance)	

Related exercise material: **BE2-1, BE2-2, E2-1, E2-2, E2-4, and DO IT! 2-1.**

LEARNING OBJECTIVE 2 Indicate how a journal is used in the recording process.

ETHICS NOTE

International Outsourcing Services, LLC was accused of submitting fraudulent store coupons to companies for reimbursement of as much as $250 million. Use of proper business documents reduces the likelihood of fraudulent activity.

Steps in the Recording Process

Although it is possible to enter transaction information directly into the accounts without using a journal, few businesses do so. Practically every business uses three basic steps in the recording process:

1. Analyze each transaction for its effects on the accounts.
2. Enter the transaction information in a **journal**.
3. Transfer the journal information to the appropriate accounts in the **ledger**.[1]

The recording process begins with the transaction. **Business documents**, such as a sales receipt, a check, or a bill, provide evidence of the transaction. The company analyzes this evidence to determine the transaction's effects on specific accounts. The company then enters the transaction in the journal. Finally, it transfers the journal entry to the designated accounts in the ledger. Illustration 2-12 shows the recording process.

Illustration 2-12
The recording process

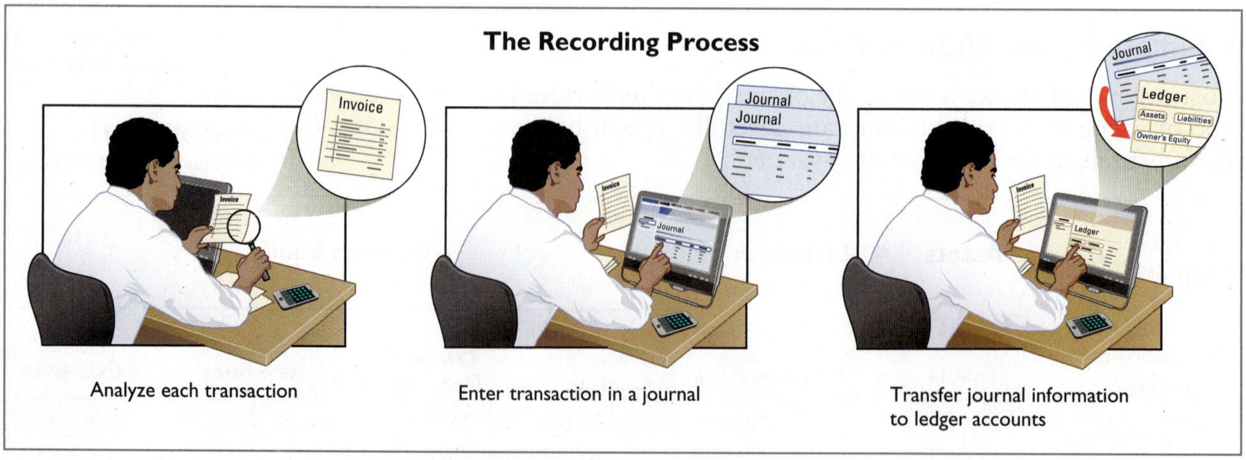

[1]We discuss here the manual recording process as we believe students should understand it first before learning and using a computerized system.

The steps in the recording process occur repeatedly. In Chapter 1, we illustrated the first step, the analysis of transactions, and will give further examples in this and later chapters. The other two steps in the recording process are explained in the next sections.

The Journal

Companies initially record transactions in chronological order (the order in which they occur). Thus, the **journal** is referred to as the book of original entry. For each transaction, the journal shows the debit and credit effects on specific accounts.

Companies may use various kinds of journals, but every company has the most basic form of journal, a **general journal**. Typically, a general journal has spaces for dates, account titles and explanations, references, and two amount columns. See the format of the journal in Illustration 2-13 (below). *Whenever we use the term "journal" in this textbook, we mean the general journal unless we specify otherwise.*

The journal makes several significant contributions to the recording process:

1. It discloses in one place the **complete effects of a transaction**.
2. It provides a **chronological record** of transactions.
3. It helps to **prevent or locate errors** because the debit and credit amounts for each entry can be easily compared.

JOURNALIZING

Entering transaction data in the journal is known as **journalizing**. Companies make separate journal entries for each transaction. A complete entry consists of (1) the date of the transaction, (2) the accounts and amounts to be debited and credited, and (3) a brief explanation of the transaction.

Illustration 2-13 shows the technique of journalizing, using the first two transactions of Softbyte. Recall that on September 1, Ray Neal invested $15,000 cash in the business, and Softbyte purchased computer equipment for $7,000 cash. The number J1 indicates that these two entries are recorded on the first page of the journal. Illustration 2-13 shows the standard form of journal entries for these two transactions. (The boxed numbers correspond to explanations in the list below the illustration.)

Illustration 2-13
Technique of journalizing

GENERAL JOURNAL **J1**

Date	Account Titles and Explanation	Ref.	Debit	Credit
2017		[5]		
Sept. 1 [2]	Cash		15,000	
[1] [3]	Owner's Capital			15,000
[4]	(Owner's investment of cash in business)			
1	Equipment		7,000	
	Cash			7,000
	(Purchase of equipment for cash)			

[1] The date of the transaction is entered in the Date column.

[2] The debit account title (that is, the account to be debited) is entered first at the extreme left margin of the column headed "Account Titles and Explanation," and the amount of the debit is recorded in the Debit column.

[3] The credit account title (that is, the account to be credited) is indented and entered on the next line in the column headed "Account Titles and Explanation," and the amount of the credit is recorded in the Credit column.

[4] A brief explanation of the transaction appears on the line below the credit account title. A space is left between journal entries. The blank space separates individual journal entries and makes the entire journal easier to read.

[5] The column titled Ref. (which stands for Reference) is left blank when the journal entry is made. This column is used later when the journal entries are transferred to the ledger accounts.

It is important to use correct and specific account titles in journalizing. Erroneous account titles lead to incorrect financial statements. However, some flexibility exists initially in selecting account titles. The main criterion is that each title must appropriately describe the content of the account. Once a company chooses the specific title to use, it should record under that account title all later transactions involving the account.[2]

SIMPLE AND COMPOUND ENTRIES

Some entries involve only two accounts, one debit and one credit. (See, for example, the entries in Illustration 2-13.) This type of entry is called a **simple entry**. Some transactions, however, require more than two accounts in journalizing. An entry that requires three or more accounts is a **compound entry**. To illustrate, assume that on July 1, Butler Company purchases a delivery truck costing $14,000. It pays $8,000 cash now and agrees to pay the remaining $6,000 on account (to be paid later). The compound entry is as follows.

Illustration 2-14
Compound journal entry

GENERAL JOURNAL — J1

Date	Account Titles and Explanation	Ref.	Debit	Credit
2017				
July 1	Equipment		14,000	
	Cash			8,000
	Accounts Payable			6,000
	(Purchased truck for cash with balance on account)			

In a compound entry, the standard format requires that all debits be listed before the credits.

Accounting Across the Organization — Microsoft

© flyfloor/iStockphoto

Boosting Microsoft's Profits

Microsoft originally designed the Xbox 360 to have 256 megabytes of memory. But the design department said that amount of memory wouldn't support the best special effects. The purchasing department said that adding more memory would cost $30—which was 10% of the estimated selling price of $300. The marketing department, however, "determined that adding the memory would let Microsoft reduce marketing costs and attract more game developers, boosting royalty revenue. It would also extend the life of the console, generating more sales."

As a result of these changes, Xbox enjoyed great success. But, it does have competitors. Its newest video game console, Xbox One, is now in a battle with Sony's Playstation4 for market share. How to compete? First, Microsoft bundled the critically acclaimed *Titanfall* with its Xbox One. By including the game most Xbox One buyers were going to purchase anyway, Microsoft was making its console more attractive. In addition, retailers are also discounting the Xbox, which should get the momentum going for increased sales. What Microsoft is doing is making sure that Xbox One is the center of the home entertainment system in the long run, even if it suffers a bit of a hardware loss today.

Sources: Robert A. Guth, "New Xbox Aim for Microsoft: Profitability," *Wall Street Journal* (May 24, 2005), p. C1; and David Thier, "Will Microsoft Give the Xbox One a $50 Price Cut?," *www.Forbes.com* (March 26, 2014).

In what ways is this Microsoft division using accounting to assist in its effort to become more profitable? (Go to **WileyPLUS** for this answer and additional questions.)

[2]*In homework problems, you should use specific account titles when they are given.* When account titles are not given, you may select account titles that identify the nature and content of each account. The account titles used in journalizing should not contain explanations such as Cash Paid or Cash Received.

DO IT! 2 Recording Business Activities

Kate Browne engaged in the following activities in establishing her salon, Hair It Is:

1. Opened a bank account in the name of Hair It Is and deposited $20,000 of her own money in this account as her initial investment.
2. Purchased equipment on account (to be paid in 30 days) for a total cost of $4,800.
3. Interviewed three people for the position of hair stylist.

Prepare the entries to record the transactions.

Solution

The three activities would be recorded as follows.

1. Cash	20,000	
Owner's Capital		20,000
(Owner's investment of cash in business)		
2. Equipment	4,800	
Accounts Payable		4,800
(Purchase of equipment on account)		

3. No entry because no transaction has occurred.

Related exercise material: **BE2-3, BE2-4, BE2-5, BE2-6, E2-3, E2-5, E2-6, E2-7, and DO IT! 2-2.**

Action Plan

✔ Understand which activities need to be recorded and which do not. Any that affect assets, liabilities, or owner's equity should be recorded in a journal.

✔ Analyze the effects of transactions on asset, liability, and owner's equity accounts.

LEARNING OBJECTIVE 3 **Explain how a ledger and posting help in the recording process.**

The Ledger

The entire group of accounts maintained by a company is the **ledger**. The ledger provides the balance in each of the accounts as well as keeps track of changes in these balances.

Companies may use various kinds of ledgers, but every company has a general ledger. A **general ledger** contains all the asset, liability, and owner's equity accounts, as shown in Illustration 2-15 for J. Lind Company. *Whenever we use the term "ledger" in this textbook, we are referring to the general ledger unless we specify otherwise.*

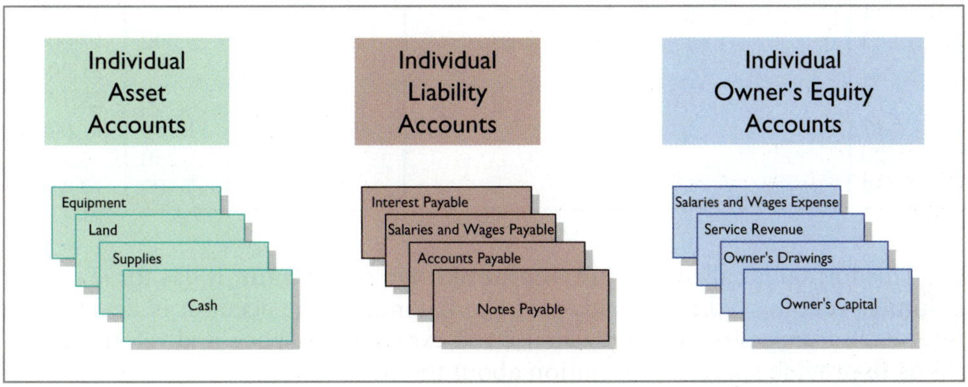

Illustration 2-15
The general ledger, which contains all of a company's accounts

Companies arrange the ledger in the sequence in which they present the accounts in the financial statements, beginning with the balance sheet accounts. First in order are the asset accounts, followed by liability accounts, owner's capital, owner's drawings, revenues, and expenses. Each account is numbered for easier identification.

The ledger provides the balance in each of the accounts. For example, the Cash account shows the amount of cash available to meet current obligations. The Accounts Receivable account shows amounts due from customers. Accounts Payable shows amounts owed to creditors.

Ethics Insight Credit Suisse Group

© Nuno Silva/iStockphoto

A Convenient Overstatement

Sometimes a company's investment securities suffer a permanent decline in value below their original cost. When this occurs, the company is supposed to reduce the recorded value of the securities on its balance sheet ("write-them down" in common financial lingo) and record a loss. It appears, however, that during the financial crisis of 2008, employees at some financial institutions chose to look the other way as the value of their investments skidded.

A number of Wall Street traders that worked for the investment bank Credit Suisse Group were charged with intentionally overstating the value of securities that had suffered declines of approximately $2.85 billion. One reason that they may have been reluctant to record the losses is out of fear that the company's shareholders and clients would panic if they saw the magnitude of the losses. However, personal self-interest might have been equally to blame—the bonuses of the traders were tied to the value of the investment securities.

Source: S. Pulliam, J. Eaglesham, and M. Siconolfi, "U.S. Plans Changes on Bond Fraud," *Wall Street Journal Online* (February 1, 2012).

What incentives might employees have had to overstate the value of these investment securities on the company's financial statements? (Go to **WileyPLUS** for this answer and additional questions.)

STANDARD FORM OF ACCOUNT

The simple T-account form used in accounting textbooks is often very useful for illustration purposes. However, in practice, the account forms used in ledgers are much more structured. Illustration 2-16 shows a typical form, using assumed data from a cash account.

Illustration 2-16
Three-column form of account

CASH					NO. 101
Date	**Explanation**	**Ref.**	**Debit**	**Credit**	**Balance**
2017					
June 1			25,000		25,000
2				8,000	17,000
3			4,200		21,200
9			7,500		28,700
17				11,700	17,000
20				250	16,750
30				7,300	9,450

This format is called the **three-column form of account**. It has three money columns—debit, credit, and balance. The balance in the account is determined after each transaction. Companies use the explanation space and reference columns to provide special information about the transaction.

Posting

Transferring journal entries to the ledger accounts is called **posting**. This phase of the recording process accumulates the effects of journalized transactions into the individual accounts. Posting involves the following steps.

1. In the **ledger**, in the appropriate columns of the account(s) debited, enter the date, journal page, and debit amount shown in the journal.
2. In the reference column of the **journal**, write the account number to which the debit amount was posted.
3. In the **ledger**, in the appropriate columns of the account(s) credited, enter the date, journal page, and credit amount shown in the journal.
4. In the reference column of the **journal**, write the account number to which the credit amount was posted.

Illustration 2-17 shows these four steps using Softbyte's first journal entry. The boxed numbers indicate the sequence of the steps.

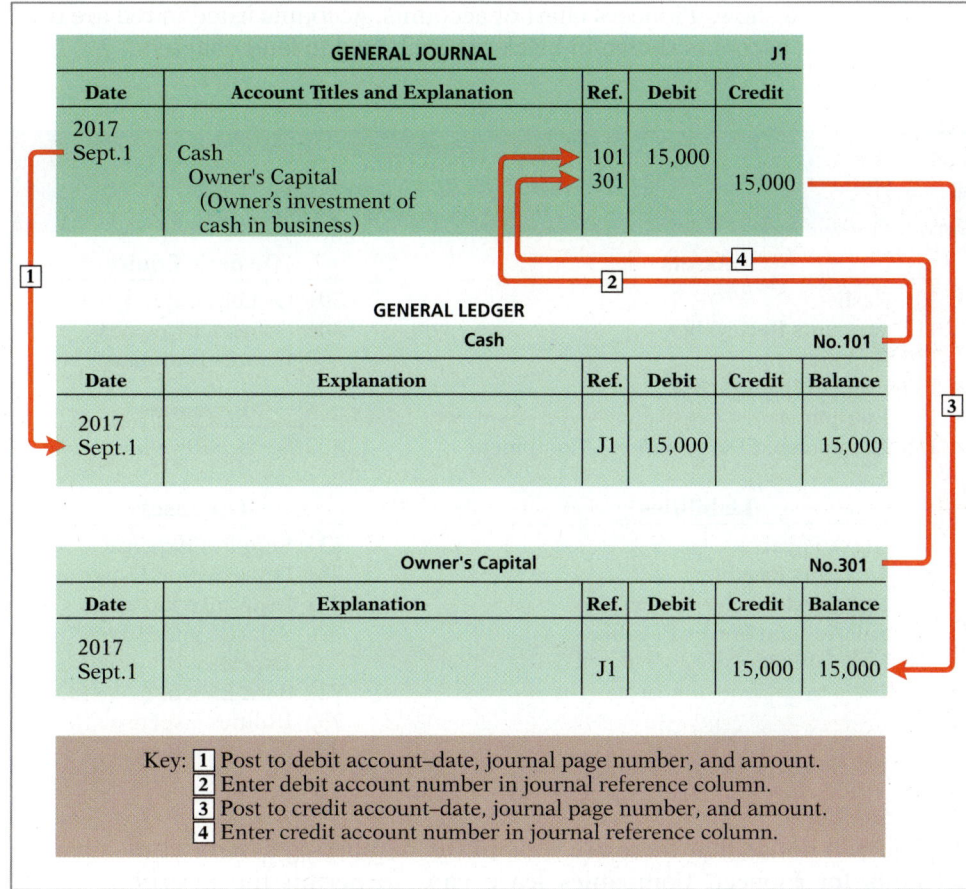

Illustration 2-17
Posting a journal entry

GENERAL JOURNAL — J1

Date	Account Titles and Explanation	Ref.	Debit	Credit
2017 Sept. 1	Cash	101	15,000	
	Owner's Capital	301		15,000
	(Owner's investment of cash in business)			

GENERAL LEDGER

Cash — No. 101

Date	Explanation	Ref.	Debit	Credit	Balance
2017 Sept. 1		J1	15,000		15,000

Owner's Capital — No. 301

Date	Explanation	Ref.	Debit	Credit	Balance
2017 Sept. 1		J1		15,000	15,000

Key:
1 Post to debit account–date, journal page number, and amount.
2 Enter debit account number in journal reference column.
3 Post to credit account–date, journal page number, and amount.
4 Enter credit account number in journal reference column.

Posting should be performed in chronological order. That is, the company should post all the debits and credits of one journal entry before proceeding to the next journal entry. Postings should be made on a timely basis to ensure that the ledger is up-to-date.[3]

The reference column of a ledger account indicates the journal page from which the transaction was posted.[4] The explanation space of the ledger account is used infrequently because an explanation already appears in the journal.

---

[3]*In homework problems, you can journalize all transactions before posting any of the journal entries.*

[4]After the last entry has been posted, the accountant should scan the reference column **in the journal**, to confirm that all postings have been made.

CHART OF ACCOUNTS

The number and type of accounts differ for each company. The number of accounts depends on the amount of detail management desires. For example, the management of one company may want a single account for all types of utility expense. Another may keep separate expense accounts for each type of utility, such as gas, electricity, and water. Similarly, a small company like Softbyte will have fewer accounts than a corporate giant like Dell. Softbyte may be able to manage and report its activities in 20 to 30 accounts, while Dell may require thousands of accounts to keep track of its worldwide activities.

Most companies have a **chart of accounts**. This chart lists the accounts and the account numbers that identify their location in the ledger. The numbering system that identifies the accounts usually starts with the balance sheet accounts and follows with the income statement accounts.

Helpful Hint
On the textbook's front endpapers, you also will find an expanded chart of accounts.

In this and the next two chapters, we will be explaining the accounting for Pioneer Advertising (a service company). Accounts 101–199 indicate asset accounts; 200–299 indicate liabilities; 301–350 indicate owner's equity accounts; 400–499, revenues; 601–799, expenses; 800–899, other revenues; and 900–999, other expenses. Illustration 2-18 shows Pioneer's chart of accounts. Accounts listed in red are used in this chapter; accounts shown in black are explained in later chapters.

Illustration 2-18
Chart of accounts

PIONEER ADVERTISING
Chart of Accounts

Assets	Owner's Equity
101 Cash	301 Owner's Capital
112 Accounts Receivable	306 Owner's Drawings
126 Supplies	350 Income Summary
130 Prepaid Insurance	**Revenues**
157 Equipment	400 Service Revenue
158 Accumulated Depreciation—Equipment	
Liabilities	**Expenses**
200 Notes Payable	631 Supplies Expense
201 Accounts Payable	711 Depreciation Expense
209 Unearned Service Revenue	722 Insurance Expense
212 Salaries and Wages Payable	726 Salaries and Wages Expense
230 Interest Payable	729 Rent Expense
	732 Utilities Expense
	905 Interest Expense

You will notice that there are gaps in the numbering system of the chart of accounts for Pioneer. Companies leave gaps to permit the insertion of new accounts as needed during the life of the business.

The Recording Process Illustrated

Helpful Hint
The Accounting Cycle Tutorial in *WileyPLUS* provides an interactive presentation of the accounting cycle using these transaction analyses.

Illustrations 2-19 through 2-28 (pages 61–65) show the basic steps in the recording process, using the October transactions of Pioneer Advertising. Pioneer's accounting period is a month. In these illustrations, a basic analysis, an equation analysis, and a debit-credit analysis precede the journal entry and posting of each transaction. For simplicity, we use the T-account form to show the posting instead of the standard account form.

Study these transaction analyses carefully. **The purpose of transaction analysis is first to identify the type of account involved, and then to determine whether to make a debit or a credit to the account.** You should always perform this type of analysis before preparing a journal entry. Doing so will help you understand the journal entries discussed in this chapter as well as more complex journal entries in later chapters.

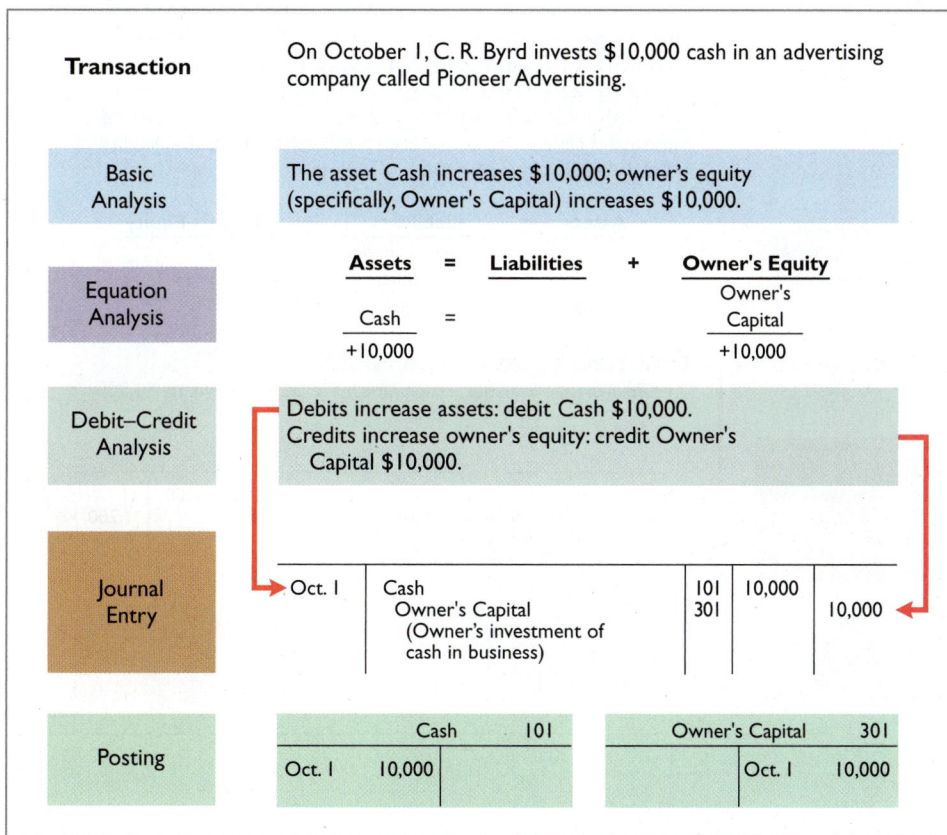

Illustration 2-19
Investment of cash by owner

Transaction
On October 1, C. R. Byrd invests $10,000 cash in an advertising company called Pioneer Advertising.

Basic Analysis
The asset Cash increases $10,000; owner's equity (specifically, Owner's Capital) increases $10,000.

Equation Analysis

Assets	=	Liabilities	+	Owner's Equity
Cash	=			Owner's Capital
+10,000				+10,000

Debit–Credit Analysis
Debits increase assets: debit Cash $10,000.
Credits increase owner's equity: credit Owner's Capital $10,000.

Journal Entry

Oct. 1	Cash	101	10,000	
	Owner's Capital	301		10,000
	(Owner's investment of cash in business)			

Posting

Cash	101	Owner's Capital	301
Oct. 1 10,000			Oct. 1 10,000

Cash Flows
+10,000

Helpful Hint
Follow these steps:
1. Determine what type of account is involved.
2. Determine what items increased or decreased and by how much.
3. Translate the increases and decreases into debits and credits.

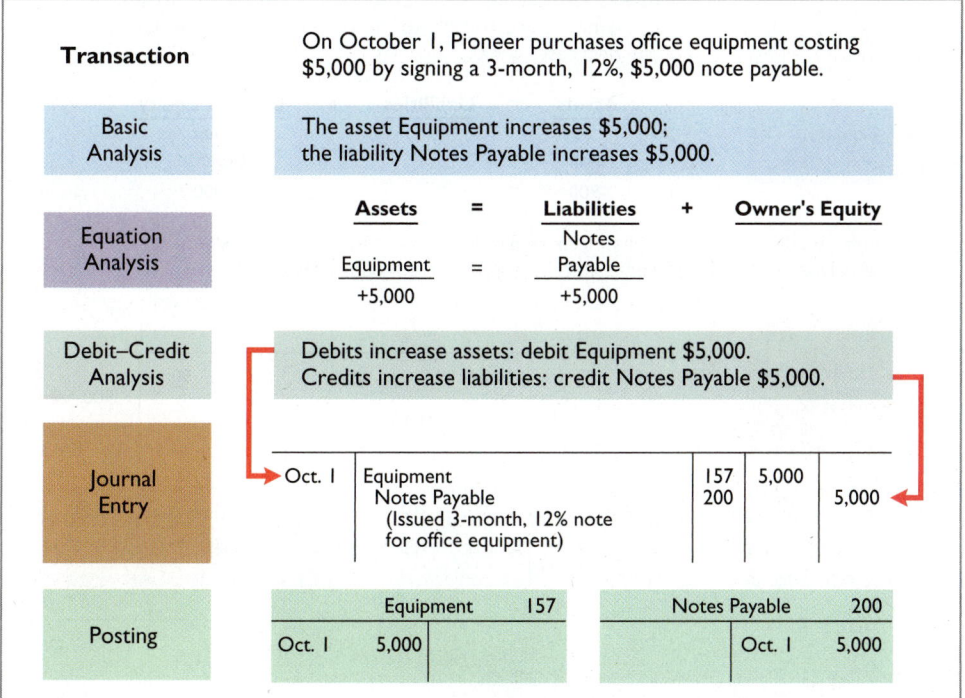

Illustration 2-20
Purchase of office equipment

Transaction
On October 1, Pioneer purchases office equipment costing $5,000 by signing a 3-month, 12%, $5,000 note payable.

Basic Analysis
The asset Equipment increases $5,000; the liability Notes Payable increases $5,000.

Equation Analysis

Assets	=	Liabilities	+	Owner's Equity
Equipment	=	Notes Payable		
+5,000		+5,000		

Debit–Credit Analysis
Debits increase assets: debit Equipment $5,000.
Credits increase liabilities: credit Notes Payable $5,000.

Journal Entry

Oct. 1	Equipment	157	5,000	
	Notes Payable	200		5,000
	(Issued 3-month, 12% note for office equipment)			

Posting

Equipment	157	Notes Payable	200
Oct. 1 5,000			Oct. 1 5,000

Cash Flows
no effect

Illustration 2-21
Receipt of cash for future service

Transaction

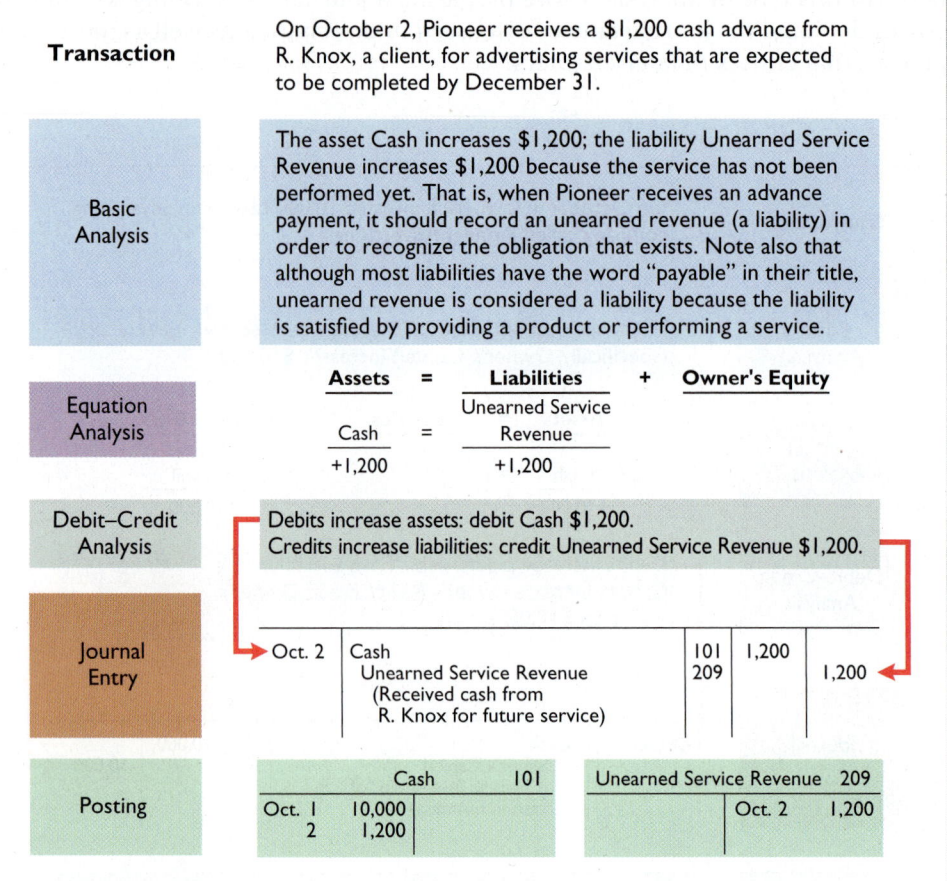

On October 2, Pioneer receives a $1,200 cash advance from R. Knox, a client, for advertising services that are expected to be completed by December 31.

Basic Analysis

The asset Cash increases $1,200; the liability Unearned Service Revenue increases $1,200 because the service has not been performed yet. That is, when Pioneer receives an advance payment, it should record an unearned revenue (a liability) in order to recognize the obligation that exists. Note also that although most liabilities have the word "payable" in their title, unearned revenue is considered a liability because the liability is satisfied by providing a product or performing a service.

Equation Analysis

Assets	=	**Liabilities**	+	**Owner's Equity**
Cash	=	Unearned Service Revenue		
+1,200		+1,200		

Cash Flows
+1,200

Debit–Credit Analysis

Debits increase assets: debit Cash $1,200.
Credits increase liabilities: credit Unearned Service Revenue $1,200.

Journal Entry

Oct. 2	Cash	101	1,200	
	Unearned Service Revenue	209		1,200
	(Received cash from R. Knox for future service)			

Posting

Cash			101
Oct. 1	10,000		
2	1,200		

Unearned Service Revenue			209
		Oct. 2	1,200

Illustration 2-22
Payment of monthly rent

Transaction

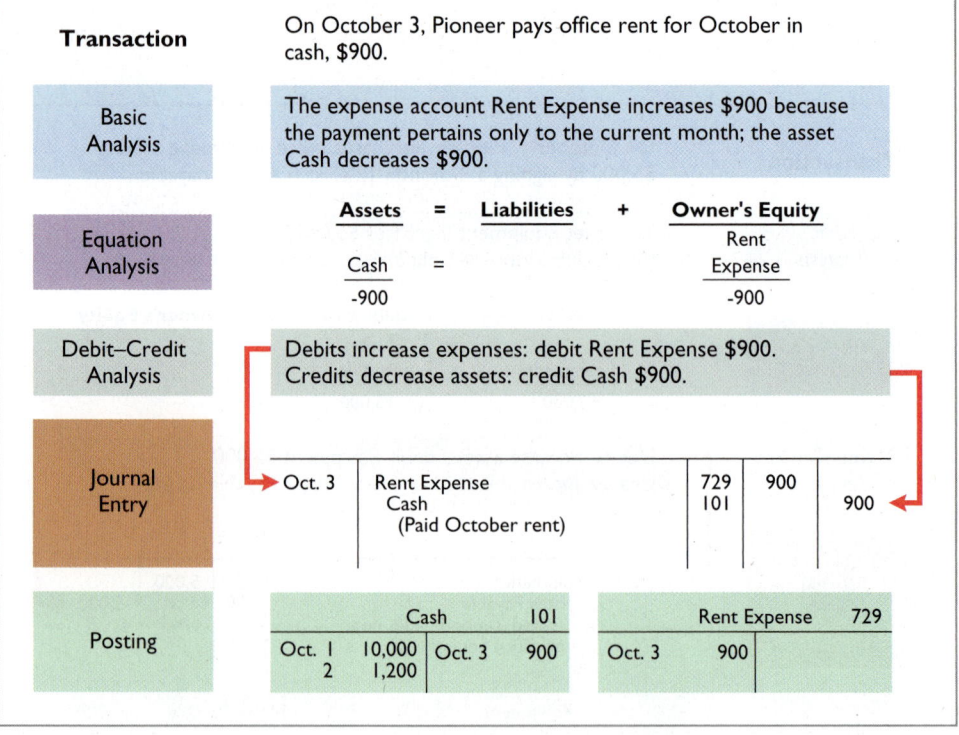

On October 3, Pioneer pays office rent for October in cash, $900.

Basic Analysis

The expense account Rent Expense increases $900 because the payment pertains only to the current month; the asset Cash decreases $900.

Equation Analysis

Assets	=	**Liabilities**	+	**Owner's Equity**
Cash	=			Rent Expense
-900				-900

Cash Flows
−900

Debit–Credit Analysis

Debits increase expenses: debit Rent Expense $900.
Credits decrease assets: credit Cash $900.

Journal Entry

Oct. 3	Rent Expense	729	900	
	Cash	101		900
	(Paid October rent)			

Posting

Cash			101
Oct. 1	10,000	Oct. 3	900
2	1,200		

Rent Expense			729
Oct. 3	900		

Illustration 2-23
Payment for insurance

Transaction

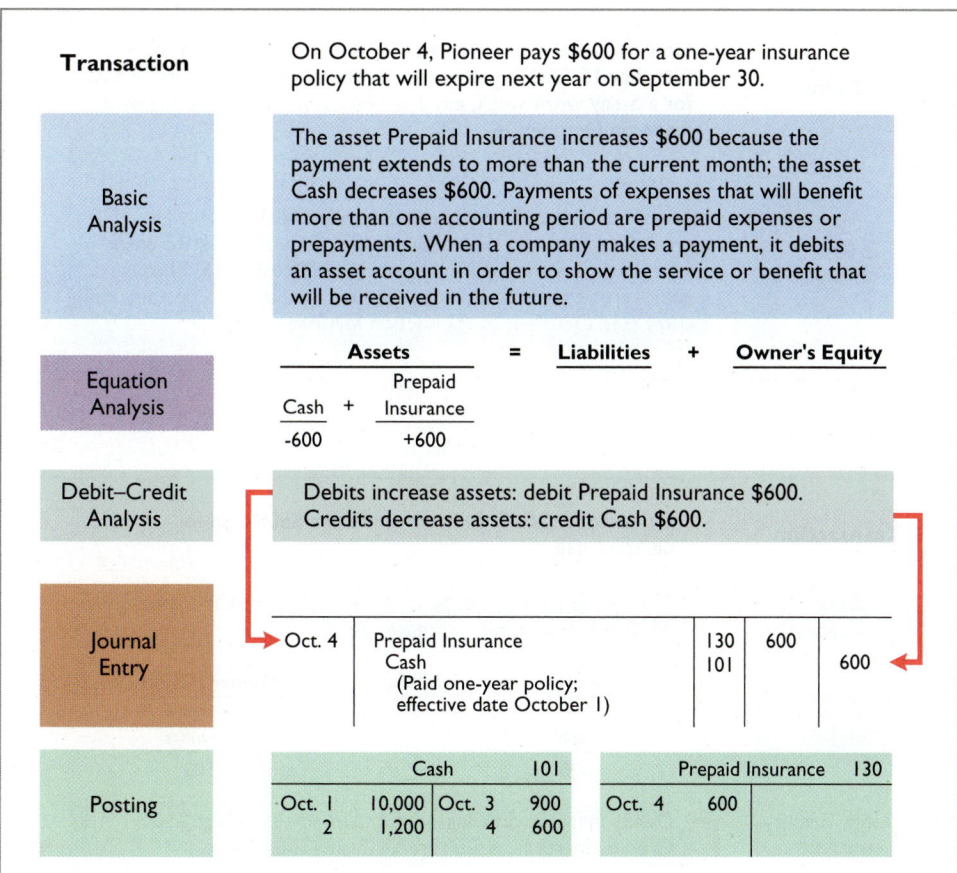

On October 4, Pioneer pays $600 for a one-year insurance policy that will expire next year on September 30.

Basic Analysis

The asset Prepaid Insurance increases $600 because the payment extends to more than the current month; the asset Cash decreases $600. Payments of expenses that will benefit more than one accounting period are prepaid expenses or prepayments. When a company makes a payment, it debits an asset account in order to show the service or benefit that will be received in the future.

Equation Analysis

Assets			=	Liabilities	+	Owner's Equity
Cash	+	Prepaid Insurance				
-600		+600				

Debit–Credit Analysis

Debits increase assets: debit Prepaid Insurance $600.
Credits decrease assets: credit Cash $600.

Journal Entry

Oct. 4	Prepaid Insurance	130	600	
	Cash	101		600
	(Paid one-year policy; effective date October 1)			

Posting

Cash			101
Oct. 1	10,000	Oct. 3	900
2	1,200	4	600

Prepaid Insurance			130
Oct. 4	600		

Cash Flows
−600

Illustration 2-24
Purchase of supplies on credit

Transaction

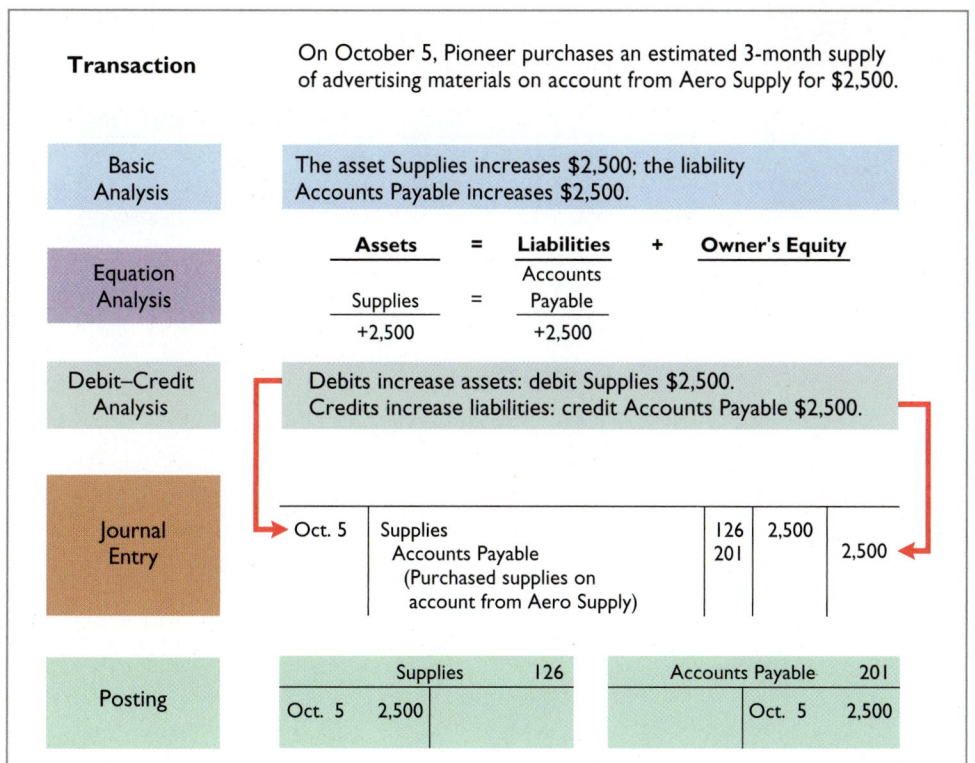

On October 5, Pioneer purchases an estimated 3-month supply of advertising materials on account from Aero Supply for $2,500.

Basic Analysis

The asset Supplies increases $2,500; the liability Accounts Payable increases $2,500.

Equation Analysis

Assets	=	Liabilities	+	Owner's Equity
Supplies	=	Accounts Payable		
+2,500		+2,500		

Debit–Credit Analysis

Debits increase assets: debit Supplies $2,500.
Credits increase liabilities: credit Accounts Payable $2,500.

Journal Entry

Oct. 5	Supplies	126	2,500	
	Accounts Payable	201		2,500
	(Purchased supplies on account from Aero Supply)			

Posting

Supplies			126
Oct. 5	2,500		

Accounts Payable			201
		Oct. 5	2,500

Cash Flows
no effect

Illustration 2-25
Hiring of employees

Cash Flows
no effect

Event	On October 9, Pioneer hires four employees to begin work on October 15. Each employee is to receive a weekly salary of $500 for a 5-day work week, payable every 2 weeks—first payment made on October 26.
Basic Analysis	A business transaction has not occurred. There is only an agreement between the employer and the employees to enter into a business transaction beginning on October 15. Thus, a debit–credit analysis is not needed because there is no accounting entry (see October 26 transaction for first entry).

Illustration 2-26
Withdrawal of cash by owner

Cash Flows
−500

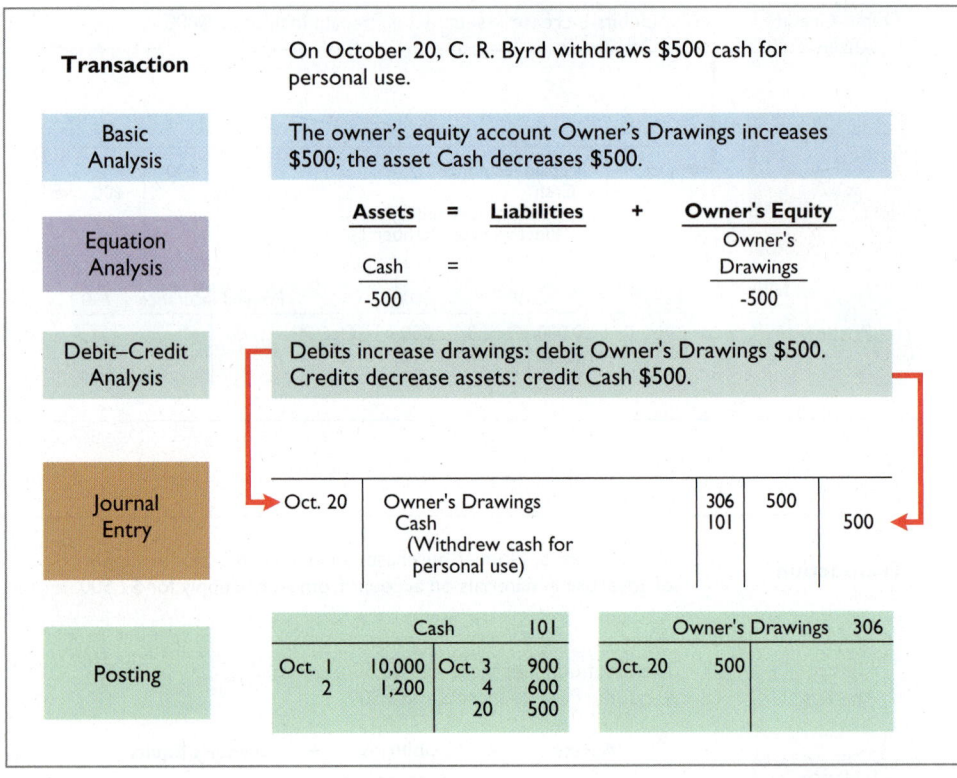

Transaction	On October 20, C. R. Byrd withdraws $500 cash for personal use.
Basic Analysis	The owner's equity account Owner's Drawings increases $500; the asset Cash decreases $500.

Equation Analysis

Assets	=	**Liabilities**	+	**Owner's Equity**
Cash	=			Owner's Drawings
-500				-500

Debit–Credit Analysis: Debits increase drawings: debit Owner's Drawings $500.
Credits decrease assets: credit Cash $500.

Journal Entry

Oct. 20	Owner's Drawings	306	500	
	Cash	101		500
	(Withdrew cash for personal use)			

Posting

Cash			101
Oct. 1	10,000	Oct. 3	900
2	1,200	4	600
		20	500

Owner's Drawings			306
Oct. 20	500		

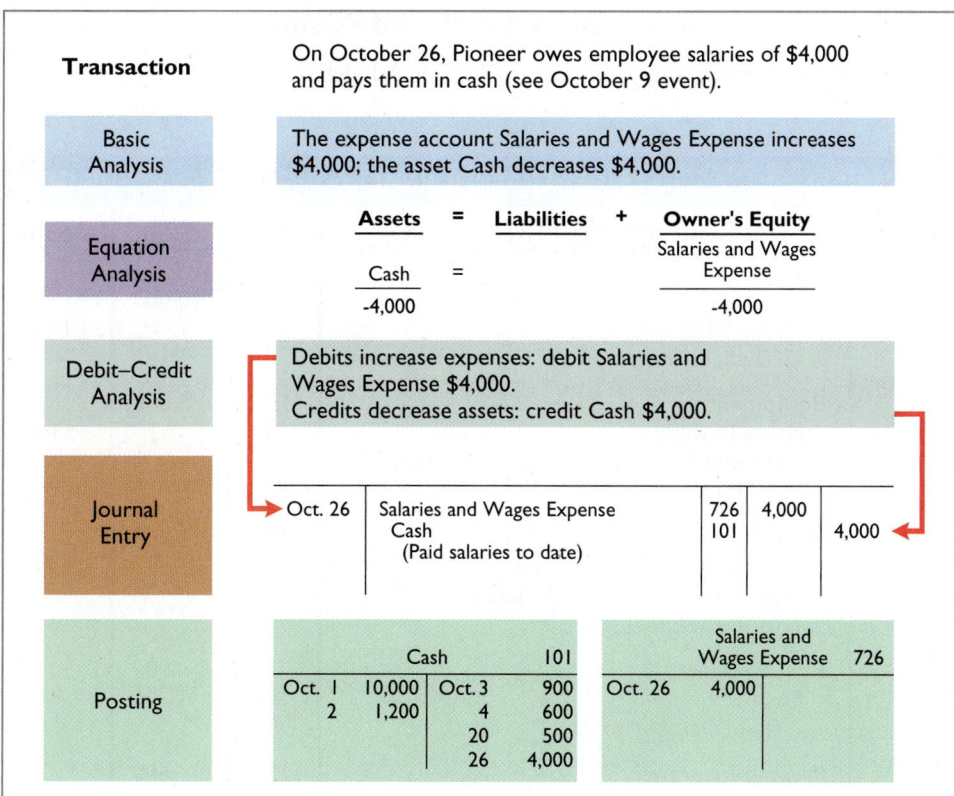

Illustration 2-27
Payment of salaries

Transaction
On October 26, Pioneer owes employee salaries of $4,000 and pays them in cash (see October 9 event).

Basic Analysis
The expense account Salaries and Wages Expense increases $4,000; the asset Cash decreases $4,000.

Equation Analysis

Assets	=	Liabilities	+	Owner's Equity
Cash	=			Salaries and Wages Expense
-4,000				-4,000

Cash Flows
−4,000

Debit–Credit Analysis
Debits increase expenses: debit Salaries and Wages Expense $4,000.
Credits decrease assets: credit Cash $4,000.

Journal Entry

Oct. 26	Salaries and Wages Expense	726	4,000	
	Cash	101		4,000
	(Paid salaries to date)			

Posting

Cash			101
Oct. 1	10,000	Oct. 3	900
2	1,200	4	600
		20	500
		26	4,000

Salaries and Wages Expense			726
Oct. 26	4,000		

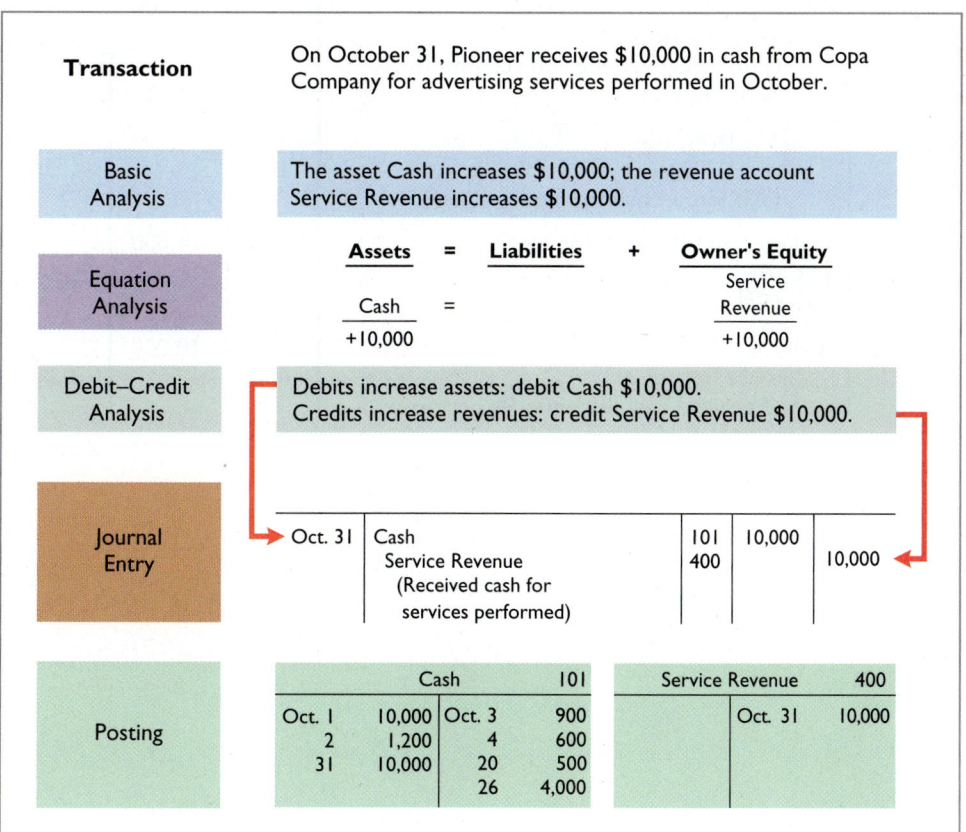

Illustration 2-28
Receipt of cash for services performed

Transaction
On October 31, Pioneer receives $10,000 in cash from Copa Company for advertising services performed in October.

Basic Analysis
The asset Cash increases $10,000; the revenue account Service Revenue increases $10,000.

Equation Analysis

Assets	=	Liabilities	+	Owner's Equity
Cash	=			Service Revenue
+10,000				+10,000

Cash Flows
+10,000

Debit–Credit Analysis
Debits increase assets: debit Cash $10,000.
Credits increase revenues: credit Service Revenue $10,000.

Journal Entry

Oct. 31	Cash	101	10,000	
	Service Revenue	400		10,000
	(Received cash for services performed)			

Posting

Cash			101
Oct. 1	10,000	Oct. 3	900
2	1,200	4	600
31	10,000	20	500
		26	4,000

Service Revenue			400
		Oct. 31	10,000

Summary Illustration of Journalizing and Posting

Illustration 2-29 shows the journal for Pioneer Advertising for October.

Illustration 2-29
General journal entries

GENERAL JOURNAL — **PAGE J1**

Date	Account Titles and Explanation	Ref.	Debit	Credit
2017				
Oct. 1	Cash	101	10,000	
	Owner's Capital	301		10,000
	(Owner's investment of cash in business)			
1	Equipment	157	5,000	
	Notes Payable	200		5,000
	(Issued 3-month, 12% note for office equipment)			
2	Cash	101	1,200	
	Unearned Service Revenue	209		1,200
	(Received cash from R. Knox for future service)			
3	Rent Expense	729	900	
	Cash	101		900
	(Paid October rent)			
4	Prepaid Insurance	130	600	
	Cash	101		600
	(Paid one-year policy; effective date October 1)			
5	Supplies	126	2,500	
	Accounts Payable	201		2,500
	(Purchased supplies on account from Aero Supply)			
20	Owner's Drawings	306	500	
	Cash	101		500
	(Withdrew cash for personal use)			
26	Salaries and Wages Expense	726	4,000	
	Cash	101		4,000
	(Paid salaries to date)			
31	Cash	101	10,000	
	Service Revenue	400		10,000
	(Received cash for services performed)			

Illustration 2-30 shows the ledger, with all balances in red.

Illustration 2-30
General ledger

GENERAL LEDGER

Cash — No. 101

Date	Explanation	Ref.	Debit	Credit	Balance
2017					
Oct. 1		J1	10,000		10,000
2		J1	1,200		11,200
3		J1		900	10,300
4		J1		600	9,700
20		J1		500	9,200
26		J1		4,000	5,200
31		J1	10,000		15,200

Supplies — No. 126

Date	Explanation	Ref.	Debit	Credit	Balance
2017					
Oct. 5		J1	2,500		2,500

Prepaid Insurance — No. 130

Date	Explanation	Ref.	Debit	Credit	Balance
2017					
Oct. 4		J1	600		600

Equipment — No. 157

Date	Explanation	Ref.	Debit	Credit	Balance
2017					
Oct. 1		J1	5,000		5,000

Notes Payable — No. 200

Date	Explanation	Ref.	Debit	Credit	Balance
2017					
Oct. 1		J1		5,000	5,000

Accounts Payable — No. 201

Date	Explanation	Ref.	Debit	Credit	Balance
2017					
Oct. 5		J1		2,500	2,500

Unearned Service Revenue — No. 209

Date	Explanation	Ref.	Debit	Credit	Balance
2017					
Oct. 2		J1		1,200	1,200

Owner's Capital — No. 301

Date	Explanation	Ref.	Debit	Credit	Balance
2017					
Oct. 1		J1		10,000	10,000

Owner's Drawings — No. 306

Date	Explanation	Ref.	Debit	Credit	Balance
2017					
Oct. 20		J1	500		500

Service Revenue — No. 400

Date	Explanation	Ref.	Debit	Credit	Balance
2017					
Oct. 31		J1		10,000	10,000

Salaries and Wages Expense — No. 726

Date	Explanation	Ref.	Debit	Credit	Balance
2017					
Oct. 26		J1	4,000		4,000

Rent Expense — No. 729

Date	Explanation	Ref.	Debit	Credit	Balance
2017					
Oct. 3		J1	900		900

DO IT! 3 Posting

Kate Browne recorded the following transactions in a general journal during the month of March.

Mar. 4	Cash	2,280	
	Service Revenue		2,280
15	Salaries and Wages Expense	400	
	Cash		400
19	Utilities Expense	92	
	Cash		92

Post these entries to the Cash account of the general ledger to determine its ending balance. The beginning balance of Cash on March 1 was $600.

Action Plan

✔ Recall that posting involves transferring the journalized debits and credits to specific accounts in the ledger.

✔ Determine the ending balance by netting the total debits and credits.

Solution

Cash

3/1 Bal.	600	3/15	400
3/4	2,280	3/19	92
3/31 Bal.	2,388		

Related exercise material: **BE2-7, BE2-8, E2-8, E2-12, and DO IT! 2-3.**

LEARNING OBJECTIVE **4**

Prepare a trial balance.

A **trial balance** is a list of accounts and their balances at a given time. Customarily, companies prepare a trial balance at the end of an accounting period. They list accounts in the order in which they appear in the ledger. Debit balances appear in the left column and credit balances in the right column.

The trial balance proves the mathematical equality of debits and credits after posting. Under the double-entry system, this equality occurs when the sum of the debit account balances equals the sum of the credit account balances. **A trial balance may also uncover errors in journalizing and posting.** For example, a trial balance may well have detected the error at MF Global discussed in the Feature Story. **In addition, a trial balance is useful in the preparation of financial statements**, as we will explain in the next two chapters.

The steps for preparing a trial balance are:

1. List the account titles and their balances in the appropriate debit or credit column.
2. Total the debit and credit columns.
3. Prove the equality of the two columns.

Illustration 2-31 shows the trial balance prepared from Pioneer Advertising's ledger. Note that the total debits equal the total credits.

Illustration 2-31
A trial balance

Helpful Hint
Note that the order of presentation in the trial balance is:
Assets
Liabilities
Owner's equity
Revenues
Expenses

PIONEER ADVERTISING
Trial Balance
October 31, 2017

	Debit	Credit
Cash	$ 15,200	
Supplies	2,500	
Prepaid Insurance	600	
Equipment	5,000	
Notes Payable		$ 5,000
Accounts Payable		2,500
Unearned Service Revenue		1,200
Owner's Capital		10,000
Owner's Drawings	500	
Service Revenue		10,000
Salaries and Wages Expense	4,000	
Rent Expense	900	
	$28,700	**$28,700**

A trial balance is a necessary checkpoint for uncovering certain types of errors. For example, if only the debit portion of a journal entry has been posted, the trial balance would bring this error to light.

ETHICS NOTE

An *error* is the result of an unintentional mistake; it is neither ethical nor unethical. An *irregularity* is an intentional misstatement, which *is* viewed as unethical.

Limitations of a Trial Balance

A trial balance does not guarantee freedom from recording errors, however. Numerous errors may exist even though the totals of the trial balance columns agree. For example, the trial balance may balance even when:

1. A transaction is not journalized.
2. A correct journal entry is not posted.
3. A journal entry is posted twice.

4. Incorrect accounts are used in journalizing or posting.
5. Offsetting errors are made in recording the amount of a transaction.

As long as equal debits and credits are posted, even to the wrong account or in the wrong amount, the total debits will equal the total credits. **The trial balance does not prove that the company has recorded all transactions or that the ledger is correct.**

Locating Errors

Errors in a trial balance generally result from mathematical mistakes, incorrect postings, or simply transcribing data incorrectly. What do you do if you are faced with a trial balance that does not balance? First, determine the amount of the difference between the two columns of the trial balance. After this amount is known, the following steps are often helpful:

1. If the error is $1, $10, $100, or $1,000, re-add the trial balance columns and recompute the account balances.
2. If the error is divisible by 2, scan the trial balance to see whether a balance equal to half the error has been entered in the wrong column.
3. If the error is divisible by 9, retrace the account balances on the trial balance to see whether they are incorrectly copied from the ledger. For example, if a balance was $12 and it was listed as $21, a $9 error has been made. Reversing the order of numbers is called a **transposition error**.
4. If the error is not divisible by 2 or 9, scan the ledger to see whether an account balance in the amount of the error has been omitted from the trial balance, and scan the journal to see whether a posting of that amount has been omitted.

Dollar Signs and Underlining

Note that dollar signs do not appear in journals or ledgers. Dollar signs are typically used only in the trial balance and the financial statements. Generally, a dollar sign is shown only for the first item in the column and for the total of that column. A single line (a totaling rule) is placed under the column of figures to be added or subtracted. Total amounts are double-underlined to indicate they are final sums.

Investor Insight Fannie Mae

Enviromatic/iStockphoto

Why Accuracy Matters

While most companies record transactions very carefully, the reality is that mistakes still happen. For example, bank regulators fined Bank One Corporation (now Chase) $1.8 million because they felt that the unreliability of the bank's accounting system caused it to violate regulatory requirements.

Also, in recent years Fannie Mae, the government-chartered mortgage association, announced a series of large accounting errors. These announcements caused alarm among investors, regulators, and politicians because they fear that the errors may suggest larger, undetected problems. This is important because the home-mortgage market depends on Fannie Mae to buy hundreds of billions of dollars of mortgages each year from banks, thus enabling the banks to issue new mortgages.

Finally, before a major overhaul of its accounting system, the financial records of Waste Management Inc. were in such disarray that of the company's 57,000 employees, 10,000 were receiving pay slips that were in error.

The Sarbanes-Oxley Act was created to minimize the occurrence of errors like these by increasing every employee's responsibility for accurate financial reporting.

In order for these companies to prepare and issue financial statements, their accounting equations (debits and credits) must have been in balance at year-end. How could these errors or misstatements have occurred? (Go to **WileyPLUS** for this answer and additional questions.)

DO IT! 4 Trial Balance

The following accounts come from the ledger of SnowGo Company at December 31, 2017.

157	Equipment	$88,000	301	Owner's Capital	$20,000
306	Owner's Drawings	8,000	212	Salaries and Wages Payable	2,000
201	Accounts Payable	22,000	200	Notes Payable (due in 3 months)	19,000
726	Salaries and Wages Expense	42,000	732	Utilities Expense	3,000
112	Accounts Receivable	4,000	130	Prepaid Insurance	6,000
400	Service Revenue	95,000	101	Cash	7,000

Prepare a trial balance in good form.

Action Plan

- ✔ Determine normal balances and list accounts in the order they appear in the ledger.
- ✔ Accounts with debit balances appear in the left column, and those with credit balances in the right column.
- ✔ Total the debit and credit columns to prove equality.

Solution

SNOWGO COMPANY
Trial Balance
December 31, 2017

	Debit	Credit
Cash	$ 7,000	
Accounts Receivable	4,000	
Prepaid Insurance	6,000	
Equipment	88,000	
Notes Payable		$ 19,000
Accounts Payable		22,000
Salaries and Wages Payable		2,000
Owner's Capital		20,000
Owner's Drawings	8,000	
Service Revenue		95,000
Utilities Expense	3,000	
Salaries and Wages Expense	42,000	
	$158,000	$158,000

Related exercise material: **BE2-9, BE2-10, E2-9, E2-10, E2-11, E2-13, E2-14, and DO IT! 2-4.**

REVIEW AND PRACTICE

LEARNING OBJECTIVES REVIEW

1 Describe how accounts, debits, and credits are used to record business transactions. An account is a record of increases and decreases in specific asset, liability, and owner's equity items. The terms debit and credit are synonymous with left and right. Assets, drawings, and expenses are increased by debits and decreased by credits. Liabilities, owner's capital, and revenues are increased by credits and decreased by debits.

2 Indicate how a journal is used in the recording process. The basic steps in the recording process are (a) analyze each transaction for its effects on the accounts, (b) enter the transaction information in a journal, and (c) transfer the journal information to the appropriate accounts in the ledger.

The initial accounting record of a transaction is entered in a journal before the data are entered in the accounts. A journal (a) discloses in one place the complete effects of a transaction, (b) provides a chronological record of transactions, and (c) prevents or locates errors because the debit and credit amounts for each entry can be easily compared.

3 Explain how a ledger and posting help in the recording process. The ledger is the entire group of accounts maintained by a company. The ledger provides the balance in each of the accounts as well as keeps track of changes in these balances. Posting is the transfer of journal entries to the ledger accounts. This phase of the recording process accumulates the effects of journalized transactions in the individual accounts.

4 **Prepare a trial balance.** A trial balance is a list of accounts and their balances at a given time. Its primary purpose is to prove the equality of debits and credits after posting. A trial balance also uncovers errors in journalizing and posting and is useful in preparing financial statements.

GLOSSARY REVIEW

Account A record of increases and decreases in specific asset, liability, or owner's equity items. (p. 50).

Chart of accounts A list of accounts and the account numbers that identify their location in the ledger. (p. 60).

Compound entry A journal entry that involves three or more accounts. (p. 56).

Credit The right side of an account. (p. 50).

Debit The left side of an account. (p. 50).

Double-entry system A system that records in appropriate accounts the dual effect of each transaction. (p. 51).

General journal The most basic form of journal. (p. 55).

General ledger A ledger that contains all asset, liability, and owner's equity accounts. (p. 57).

Journal An accounting record in which transactions are initially recorded in chronological order. (p. 55).

Journalizing The entering of transaction data in the journal. (p. 55).

Ledger The entire group of accounts maintained by a company. (p. 57).

Normal balance An account balance on the side where an increase in the account is recorded. (p. 51).

Posting The procedure of transferring journal entries to the ledger accounts. (p. 59).

Simple entry A journal entry that involves only two accounts. (p. 56).

T-account The basic form of an account. (p. 50).

Three-column form of account A form with columns for debit, credit, and balance amounts in an account. (p. 58).

Trial balance A list of accounts and their balances at a given time. (p. 68).

PRACTICE MULTIPLE-CHOICE QUESTIONS

(LO 1) **1.** Which of the following statements about an account is **true**?
(a) The right side of an account is the debit or increase side.
(b) An account is an individual accounting record of increases and decreases in specific asset, liability, and owner's equity items.
(c) There are separate accounts for specific assets and liabilities but only one account for owner's equity items.
(d) The left side of an account is the credit or decrease side.

(LO 1) **2.** Debits:
(a) increase both assets and liabilities.
(b) decrease both assets and liabilities.
(c) increase assets and decrease liabilities.
(d) decrease assets and increase liabilities.

(LO 1) **3.** A revenue account:
(a) is increased by debits.
(b) is decreased by credits.
(c) has a normal balance of a debit.
(d) is increased by credits.

(LO 1) **4.** Accounts that normally have debit balances are:
(a) assets, expenses, and revenues.
(b) assets, expenses, and owner's capital.
(c) assets, liabilities, and owner's drawings.
(d) assets, owner's drawings, and expenses.

5. The expanded accounting equation is: (LO 1)
(a) Assets + Liabilities = Owner's Capital + Owner's Drawings + Revenues + Expenses.
(b) Assets = Liabilities + Owner's Capital + Owner's Drawings + Revenues − Expenses.
(c) Assets = Liabilities − Owner's Capital − Owner's Drawings − Revenues − Expenses.
(d) Assets = Liabilities + Owner's Capital − Owner's Drawings + Revenues − Expenses.

6. Which of the following is **not** part of the recording process? (LO 2)
(a) Analyzing transactions.
(b) Preparing a trial balance.
(c) Entering transactions in a journal.
(d) Posting transactions.

7. Which of the following statements about a journal is **false**? (LO 2)
(a) It is not a book of original entry.
(b) It provides a chronological record of transactions.
(c) It helps to locate errors because the debit and credit amounts for each entry can be readily compared.
(d) It discloses in one place the complete effect of a transaction.

8. The purchase of supplies on account should result in: (LO 2)
(a) a debit to Supplies Expense and a credit to Cash.
(b) a debit to Supplies Expense and a credit to Accounts Payable.

(c) a debit to Supplies and a credit to Accounts Payable.
(d) a debit to Supplies and a credit to Accounts Receivable.

(LO 3) **9.** The order of the accounts in the ledger is:
(a) assets, revenues, expenses, liabilities, owner's capital, owner's drawings.
(b) assets, liabilities, owner's capital, owner's drawings, revenues, expenses.
(c) owner's capital, assets, revenues, expenses, liabilities, owner's drawings.
(d) revenues, assets, expenses, liabilities, owner's capital, owner's drawings.

(LO 3) **10.** A ledger:
(a) contains only asset and liability accounts.
(b) should show accounts in alphabetical order.
(c) is a collection of the entire group of accounts maintained by a company.
(d) is a book of original entry.

(LO 3) **11.** Posting:
(a) normally occurs before journalizing.
(b) transfers ledger transaction data to the journal.
(c) is an optional step in the recording process.
(d) transfers journal entries to ledger accounts.

(LO 3) **12.** Before posting a payment of $5,000, the Accounts Payable of Senator Company had a normal balance of $16,000. The balance after posting this transaction was:
(a) $21,000. (c) $11,000.
(b) $5,000. (d) Cannot be determined.

13. A trial balance: (LO 4)
(a) is a list of accounts with their balances at a given time.
(b) proves the journalized transactions are correct.
(c) will not balance if a correct journal entry is posted twice.
(d) proves that all transactions have been recorded.

14. A trial balance will not balance if: (LO 4)
(a) a correct journal entry is posted twice.
(b) the purchase of supplies on account is debited to Supplies and credited to Cash.
(c) a $100 cash drawing by the owner is debited to Owner's Drawings for $1,000 and credited to Cash for $100.
(d) a $450 payment on account is debited to Accounts Payable for $45 and credited to Cash for $45.

15. The trial balance of Jeong Company had accounts with the following normal balances: Cash $5,000, Service Revenue $85,000, Salaries and Wages Payable $4,000, Salaries and Wages Expense $40,000, Rent Expense $10,000, Owner's Capital $42,000, Owner's Drawings $15,000, and Equipment $61,000. In preparing a trial balance, the total in the debit column is: (LO 4)
(a) $131,000. (c) $91,000.
(b) $216,000. (d) $116,000.

Solutions

1. (b) An account is an individual accounting record of increases and decreases in specific asset, liability, and owner's equity items. The other choices are incorrect because (a) the right side of the account is the credit side, not the debit side, and can be the increase or the decrease side, depending on the specific classification account; (c) there are also separate accounts for different owner's equity items; and (d) the left side of the account is the debit side, not the credit side, and can be either the decrease or the increase side, depending on the specific classification account.

2. (c) Debits increase assets but they decrease liabilities. The other choices are incorrect because debits (a) decrease, not increase, liabilities; (b) increase, not decrease, assets; and (d) increase, not decrease, assets and decrease, not increase, liabilities.

3. (d) A revenue account is increased by credits. The other choices are incorrect because a revenue account (a) is increased by credits, not debits; (b) is decreased by debits, not credits; and (c) has a normal balance of a credit, not a debit.

4. (d) Assets, owner's drawings, and expenses all have normal debit balances. The other choices are incorrect because (a) revenues have normal credit balances, (b) owner's capital has a normal credit balance, and (c) liabilities have normal credit balances.

5. (d) The expanded accounting equation is Assets = Liabilities + Owner's Capital − Owner's Drawings + Revenue − Expenses. The other choices are incorrect because (a) both Owner's Drawings and Expenses must be subtracted, not added, and Liabilities should be added to the right side of equation, not to the left side; (b) Owner's Drawings must be subtracted, not added; and (c) Owner's Capital and Revenues must be added, not subtracted.

6. (b) Preparing the trial balance is not part of the recording process. Choices (a) analyzing transactions, (b) preparing a trial balance, and (c) entering transactions in a journal are all part of the recording process.

7. (a) The journal is a book of original entry. The other choices are all true statements.

8. (c) The purchase of supplies on account results in a debit to Supplies and a credit to Accounts Payable. The other choices are incorrect because the purchase of supplies on account results in (a) a debit to Supplies, not Supplies Expense, and a credit to Accounts Payable, not Cash; (b) a debit to Supplies, not Supplies Expense; and (d) a credit to Accounts Payable, not Accounts Receivable.

9. (b) The correct order of the accounts in the ledger is assets, liabilities, owner's capital, owner's drawing, revenues, expenses. The other choices are incorrect because they do not reflect this order. The order of the accounts in the ledger is (1) balance sheet accounts: assets, liabilities, and owner's equity accounts (owner's capital and owner's drawings); and then (2) income statement accounts: revenues and expenses.

10. (c) A ledger is a collection of all the accounts maintained by a company. The other choices are incorrect because a ledger (a) contains all account types—assets, liabilities, owner's equity, revenue, and expense accounts—not just assets and liability accounts; (b) usually shows accounts in account number order, not alphabetical order; and (d) is not a book of original entry because entries made in the ledger come from the journals (the books of original entry).

11. (d) Posting transfers journal entries to ledger accounts. The other choices are incorrect because posting (a) occurs after journalizing, (b) transfers journal transaction data to the ledger; and (c) is not an optional step in the recording process.

12. (c) The balance is $11,000 ($16,000 normal balance − $5,000 payment), not (a) $21,000 or (b) $5,000. Choice (d) is incorrect because the balance can be determined.

13. (a) A trial balance is a list of accounts with their balances at a given time. The other choices are incorrect because (b) the trial balance does not prove that journalized transactions are correct; (c) if a journal entry is posted twice, the trial balance will still balance; and (d) the trial balance does not prove that all transactions have been recorded.

14. (c) The trial balance will not balance in this case because the debit of $1,000 to Owner's Drawings is not equal to the credit of $100 to Cash. The other choices are incorrect because (a) if a correct journal entry is posted twice, the trial balance will still balance; (b) if the purchase of supplies on account is debited to Supplies and credited to Cash, Cash and Accounts Payable will be understated but the trial balance will still balance; and (d) since the debit and credit amounts are the same, the trial balance will still balance but both Accounts Payable and Cash will be overstated.

15. (a) The total debit column = $5,000 (Cash) + $40,000 (Salaries and Wages Expense) + $10,000 (Rent Expense) + $15,000 (Owner's Drawings) + $61,000 (Equipment) = $131,000. The normal balance for Assets, Expenses, and Owner's Drawings is a debit. The other choices are incorrect because (b) revenue of $85,000 should not be included in the total of $216,000 and its normal balance is a credit; (c) the total of $91,000 is missing the Salaries and Wages Expense of $40,000, which has a normal balance of a debit; and (d) the total of $116,000 is missing the Owner's Drawings of $15,000, which has a normal balance of a debit.

PRACTICE EXERCISES

Analyze transactions and determine their effect on accounts.

(LO 1)

1. Presented below is information related to Hammond Real Estate Agency.

Oct.	1	Lia Berge begins business as a real estate agent with a cash investment of $30,000
	2	Paid rent, $700, on office space.
	3	Purchases office equipment for $2,800, on account.
	6	Sells a house and lot for Hal Smith; bills Hal Smith $4,400 for realty services performed.
	27	Pays $1,100 on the balance related to the transaction of October 3.
	30	Receives bill for October utilities, $130 (not paid at this time).

Instructions

Journalize the transactions. (You may omit explanations)

Solution

1.

GENERAL JOURNAL

Date	Account Titles and Explanation	Ref.	Debit	Credit
Oct. 1	Cash		30,000	
	Owner's Capital			30,000
2	Rent Expense		700	
	Cash			700
3	Equipment		2,800	
	Accounts Payable			2,800
6	Accounts Receivable		4,400	
	Service Revenue			4,400
27	Accounts Payable		1,100	
	Cash			1,100
30	Utilities Expense		130	
	Accounts Payable			130

Journalize transactions from account data and prepare a trial balance.

(LO 2, 4)

2. The T-accounts below summarize the ledger of Depot Company at the end of the first month of operations.

Cash No. 101

4/1	16,000	4/15	700
4/12	1,200	4/25	1,600
4/29	900		
4/30	1,600		

Unearned Service Revenue No. 209

		4/30	1,600

Accounts Receivable			No. 112
4/7	2,900	4/29	900

Supplies			No. 126
4/4	1,900		

Accounts Payable			No. 201
4/25	1,600	4/4	1,900

Owner's Capital			No. 301
		4/1	16,000

Service Revenue			No. 400
		4/7	2,900
		4/12	1,200

Salaries and Wages Expense			No. 726
4/15	700		

Instructions

(a) Prepare the complete general journal (including explanations) from which the postings to Cash were made.

(b) Prepare a trial balance at April 30, 2017.

Solution

2. (a)

GENERAL JOURNAL

Date	Account Titles and Explanation	Ref.	Debit	Credit
Apr. 1	Cash		16,000	
	Owner's Capital			16,000
	(Owner's investment of cash in business)			
12	Cash		1,200	
	Service Revenue			1,200
	(Received cash for services performed)			
15	Salaries and Wages Expense		700	
	Cash			700
	(Paid salaries to date)			
25	Accounts payable		1,600	
	Cash			1,600
	(Paid creditors on account)			
29	Cash		900	
	Accounts Receivable			900
	(Received cash in payment of account)			
30	Cash		1,600	
	Unearned Service Revenue			1,600
	(Received cash for future services)			

(b)

DEPOT COMPANY
Trial Balance
April 30, 2017

	Debit	Credit
Cash	$17,400	
Accounts Receivable	2,000	
Supplies	1,900	
Accounts Payable		$ 300
Unearned Service Revenue		1,600
Owner's Capital		16,000
Service Revenue		4,100
Salaries and Wages Expense	700	
	$22,000	$22,000

PRACTICE PROBLEM

Journalize transactions, post, and prepare a trial balance.

(LO 1, 2, 3, 4)

Bob Sample opened the Campus Laundromat on September 1, 2017. During the first month of operations, the following transactions occurred.

Sept.	1	Bob invested $20,000 cash in the business.
	2	The company paid $1,000 cash for store rent for September.
	3	Purchased washers and dryers for $25,000, paying $10,000 in cash and signing a $15,000, 6-month, 12% note payable.
	4	Paid $1,200 for a one-year accident insurance policy.
	10	Received a bill from the *Daily News* for online advertising of the opening of the laundromat $200.
	20	Bob withdrew $700 cash for personal use.
	30	The company determined that cash receipts for laundry services for the month were $6,200.

The chart of accounts for the company is the same as that for Pioneer Advertising plus No. 610 Advertising Expense.

Instructions

(a) Journalize the September transactions. (Use J1 for the journal page number.)

(b) Open ledger accounts and post the September transactions.

(c) Prepare a trial balance at September 30, 2017.

Solution

(a) **GENERAL JOURNAL** J1

Date	Account Titles and Explanation	Ref.	Debit	Credit
2017				
Sept. 1	Cash	101	20,000	
	Owner's Capital	301		20,000
	(Owner's investment of cash in business)			
2	Rent Expense	729	1,000	
	Cash	101		1,000
	(Paid September rent)			
3	Equipment	157	25,000	
	Cash	101		10,000
	Notes Payable	200		15,000
	(Purchased laundry equipment for cash and 6-month, 12% note payable)			
4	Prepaid Insurance	130	1,200	
	Cash	101		1,200
	(Paid one-year insurance policy)			
10	Advertising Expense	610	200	
	Accounts Payable	201		200
	(Received bill from *Daily News* for advertising)			
20	Owner's Drawings	306	700	
	Cash	101		700
	(Withdrew cash for personal use)			
30	Cash	101	6,200	
	Service Revenue	400		6,200
	(Received cash for services performed)			

(b)

GENERAL LEDGER

Cash **No. 101**

Date	Explanation	Ref.	Debit	Credit	Balance
2017					
Sept. 1		J1	20,000		20,000
2		J1		1,000	19,000
3		J1		10,000	9,000
4		J1		1,200	7,800
20		J1		700	7,100
30		J1	6,200		13,300

Prepaid Insurance **No. 130**

Date	Explanation	Ref.	Debit	Credit	Balance
2017					
Sept. 4		J1	1,200		1,200

Equipment **No. 157**

Date	Explanation	Ref.	Debit	Credit	Balance
2017					
Sept. 3		J1	25,000		25,000

Notes Payable **No. 200**

Date	Explanation	Ref.	Debit	Credit	Balance
2017					
Sept. 3		J1		15,000	15,000

Accounts Payable **No. 201**

Date	Explanation	Ref.	Debit	Credit	Balance
2017					
Sept. 10		J1		200	200

Owner's Capital **No. 301**

Date	Explanation	Ref.	Debit	Credit	Balance
2017					
Sept. 1		J1		20,000	20,000

Owner's Drawings **No. 306**

Date	Explanation	Ref.	Debit	Credit	Balance
2017					
Sept. 20		J1	700		700

Service Revenue **No. 400**

Date	Explanation	Ref.	Debit	Credit	Balance
2017					
Sept. 30		J1		6,200	6,200

Advertising Expense **No. 610**

Date	Explanation	Ref.	Debit	Credit	Balance
2017					
Sept. 10		J1	200		200

Rent Expense **No. 729**

Date	Explanation	Ref.	Debit	Credit	Balance
2017					
Sept. 2		J1	1,000		1,000

(c)

CAMPUS LAUNDROMAT
Trial Balance
September 30, 2017

	Debit	Credit
Cash	$13,300	
Prepaid Insurance	1,200	
Equipment	25,000	
Notes Payable		$15,000
Accounts Payable		200
Owner's Capital		20,000
Owner's Drawings	700	
Service Revenue		6,200
Advertising Expense	200	
Rent Expense	1,000	
	$41,400	$41,400

WileyPLUS Brief Exercises, Exercises, DO IT! Exercises, and Problems and many additional resources are available for practice in WileyPLUS

QUESTIONS

1. Describe the parts of a T-account.
2. "The terms debit and credit mean increase and decrease, respectively." Do you agree? Explain.
3. Heath Precourt, a fellow student, contends that the double-entry system means each transaction must be recorded twice. Is Heath correct? Explain.

4. Erica Mendez, a beginning accounting student, believes debit balances are favorable and credit balances are unfavorable. Is Erica correct? Discuss.
5. State the rules of debit and credit as applied to (a) asset accounts, (b) liability accounts, and (c) the owner's equity accounts (revenue, expenses, owner's drawings, and owner's capital).
6. What is the normal balance for each of the following accounts? (a) Accounts Receivable. (b) Cash. (c) Owner's Drawings. (d) Accounts Payable. (e) Service Revenue. (f) Salaries and Wages Expense. (g) Owner's Capital.
7. Indicate whether each of the following accounts is an asset, a liability, or an owner's equity account and whether it has a normal debit or credit balance: (a) Accounts Receivable, (b) Accounts Payable, (c) Equipment, (d) Owner's Drawings, and (e) Supplies.
8. For the following transactions, indicate the account debited and the account credited.
   (a) Supplies are purchased on account.
   (b) Cash is received on signing a note payable.
   (c) Employees are paid salaries in cash.
9. Indicate whether the following accounts generally will have (a) debit entries only, (b) credit entries only, or (c) both debit and credit entries.
   (1) Cash.
   (2) Accounts Receivable.
   (3) Owner's Drawings.
   (4) Accounts Payable.
   (5) Salaries and Wages Expense.
   (6) Service Revenue.
10. What are the basic steps in the recording process?
11. What are the advantages of using a journal in the recording process?
12. (a) When entering a transaction in the journal, should the debit or credit be written first?
    (b) Which should be indented, the debit or credit?
13. Describe a compound entry, and provide an example.
14. (a) Should business transaction debits and credits be recorded directly in the ledger accounts?
    (b) What are the advantages of first recording transactions in the journal and then posting to the ledger?
15. The account number is entered as the last step in posting the amounts from the journal to the ledger. What is the advantage of this step?
16. Journalize the following business transactions.
    (a) Qing Wei invests $9,000 cash in the business.
    (b) Insurance of $800 is paid for the year.
    (c) Supplies of $2,000 are purchased on account.
    (d) Cash of $7,500 is received for services performed.
17. (a) What is a ledger?
    (b) What is a chart of accounts and why is it important?
18. What is a trial balance and what are its purposes?
19. Victor Grimm is confused about how accounting information flows through the accounting system. He believes the flow of information is as follows.
    (a) Debits and credits posted to the ledger.
    (b) Business transaction occurs.
    (c) Information entered in the journal.
    (d) Financial statements are prepared.
    (e) Trial balance is prepared.

    Is Victor correct? If not, indicate to Victor the proper flow of the information.
20. Two students are discussing the use of a trial balance. They wonder whether the following errors, each considered separately, would prevent the trial balance from balancing.
    (a) The bookkeeper debited Cash for $600 and credited Salaries and Wages Expense for $600 for payment of wages.
    (b) Cash collected on account was debited to Cash for $900 and Service Revenue was credited for $90.

    What would you tell them?
21. What are the normal balances for Apple's Cash, Accounts Payable, and Interest Expense accounts?

BRIEF EXERCISES

Indicate debit and credit effects and normal balance. (LO 1)

BE2-1 For each of the following accounts, indicate the effects of (a) a debit and (b) a credit on the accounts and (c) the normal balance of the account.

1. Accounts Payable.
2. Advertising Expense.
3. Service Revenue.
4. Accounts Receivable.
5. Owner's Capital.
6. Owner's Drawings.

Identify accounts to be debited and credited. (LO 1)

BE2-2 Transactions for the Tage Oslo Company for the month of June are presented below. Identify the accounts to be debited and credited for each transaction.

June 1 Tage Oslo invests $5,000 cash in a small welding business of which he is the sole proprietor.
2 Purchases equipment on account for $2,400.
3 $800 cash is paid to landlord for June rent.
12 Sends a bill to J. Kronsnoble for $300 for welding work performed on account.

Journalize transactions. (LO 2)

BE2-3 Using the data in BE2-2, journalize the transactions. (You may omit explanations.)

Identify and explain steps in recording process. (LO 2)

BE2-4 Jen Shumway, a fellow student, is unclear about the basic steps in the recording process. Identify and briefly explain the steps in the order in which they occur.

Indicate basic and debit-credit analysis.
(LO 2)

BE2-5 M. Gonzales has the following transactions during August of the current year. Indicate (a) the effect on the accounting equation and (b) the debit-credit analysis illustrated on pages 61–65 of the textbook.

Aug.	1	Opens an office as a financial advisor, investing $8,000 in cash.
	4	Pays insurance in advance for 6 months, $1,800 cash.
	16	Receives $3,600 from clients for services performed.
	27	Pays secretary $1,000 salary.

Journalize transactions.
(LO 2)

BE2-6 Using the data in BE2-5, journalize the transactions. (You may omit explanations.)

Post journal entries to T-accounts.
(LO 3)

BE2-7 Selected transactions for the Brook Wang Company are presented in journal form below. Post the transactions to T-accounts. Make one T-account for each item and determine each account's ending balance.

J1

Date	Account Titles and Explanation	Ref.	Debit	Credit
May 5	Accounts Receivable		4,400	
	Service Revenue			4,400
	(Billed for services performed)			
12	Cash		2,400	
	Accounts Receivable			2,400
	(Received cash in payment of account)			
15	Cash		3,000	
	Service Revenue			3,000
	(Received cash for services performed)			

Post journal entries to standard form of account.
(LO 3)

BE2-8 Selected journal entries for the Brook Wang Company are presented in BE2-7. Post the transactions using the standard form of account.

Prepare a trial balance.
(LO 4)

BE2-9 From the ledger balances given below, prepare a trial balance for the Amaro Company at June 30, 2017. List the accounts in the order shown on page 58 of the textbook. All account balances are normal.

Accounts Payable $8,100, Cash $5,800, Owner's Capital $15,000, Owner's Drawings $1,200, Equipment $17,000, Service Revenue $10,000, Accounts Receivable $3,000, Salaries and Wages Expense $5,100, and Rent Expense $1,000.

Prepare a correct trial balance.
(LO 4)

BE2-10 An inexperienced bookkeeper prepared the following trial balance. Prepare a correct trial balance, assuming all account balances are normal.

CAPPSHAW COMPANY
Trial Balance
December 31, 2017

	Debit	Credit
Cash	$10,800	
Prepaid Insurance		$ 3,500
Accounts Payable		3,000
Unearned Service Revenue	2,200	
Owner's Capital		9,000
Owner's Drawings		4,500
Service Revenue		25,600
Salaries and Wages Expense	18,600	
Rent Expense		2,400
	$31,600	$48,000

DO IT! Exercises

DO IT! 2-1 Tom Rast has just rented space in a strip mall. In this space, he will open a photography studio, to be called "Picture This!" A friend has advised Tom to set up a double-entry set of accounting records in which to record all of his business transactions.

Identify normal balances. (LO 1)

Identify the balance sheet accounts that Tom will likely need to record the transactions needed to open his business. Indicate whether the normal balance of each account is a debit or credit.

DO IT! 2-2 Tom Rast engaged in the following activities in establishing his photography studio, Picture This!:

Record business activities. (LO 2)

1. Opened a bank account in the name of Picture This! and deposited $6,300 of his own money into this account as his initial investment.
2. Purchased photography supplies at a total cost of $1,100. The business paid $400 in cash and the balance is on account.
3. Obtained estimates on the cost of photography equipment from three different manufacturers.

In what form (type of record) should Tom record these three activities? Prepare the entries to record the transactions.

DO IT! 2-3 Tom Rast recorded the following transactions during the month of April.

Post transactions. (LO 3)

April 3	Cash	3,400	
	Service Revenue		3,400
April 16	Rent Expense	700	
	Cash		700
April 20	Salaries and Wages Expense	250	
	Cash		250

Post these entries to the Cash T-account of the general ledger to determine the ending balance in cash. The beginning balance in cash on April 1 was $1,600.

DO IT! 2-4 The following accounts are taken from the ledger of Carland Company at December 31, 2017.

Prepare a trial balance. (LO 4)

200	Notes Payable	$20,000	101	Cash	$ 6,000
301	Owner's Capital	28,000	126	Supplies	6,000
157	Equipment	80,000	729	Rent Expense	4,000
306	Owner's Drawings	8,000	212	Salaries and Wages Payable	3,000
726	Salaries and Wages Expense	38,000	201	Accounts Payable	11,000
400	Service Revenue	88,000	112	Accounts Receivable	8,000

Prepare a trial balance in good form.

EXERCISES

E2-1 Kim Yi has prepared the following list of statements about accounts.

Analyze statements about accounting and the recording process. (LO 1)

1. An account is an accounting record of either a specific asset or a specific liability.
2. An account shows only increases, not decreases, in the item it relates to.
3. Some items, such as Cash and Accounts Receivable, are combined into one account.
4. An account has a left, or credit side, and a right, or debit side.
5. A simple form of an account consisting of just the account title, the left side, and the right side, is called a T-account.

Instructions

Identify each statement as true or false. If false, indicate how to correct the statement.

E2-2 Selected transactions for A. Mane, an interior decorator, in her first month of business, are as follows.

Identify debits, credits, and normal balances. (LO 1)

Jan. 2 Invested $10,000 cash in business.

3 Purchased used car for $3,000 cash for use in business.

9 Purchased supplies on account for $500.
11 Billed customers $2,400 for services performed.
16 Paid $350 cash for advertising.
20 Received $700 cash from customers billed on January 11.
23 Paid creditor $300 cash on balance owed.
28 Withdrew $1,000 cash for personal use by owner.

Instructions
For each transaction, indicate the following.

(a) The basic type of account debited and credited (asset, liability, owner's equity).
(b) The specific account debited and credited (Cash, Rent Expense, Service Revenue, etc.).
(c) Whether the specific account is increased or decreased.
(d) The normal balance of the specific account.

Use the following format, in which the January 2 transaction is given as an example.

	Account Debited				Account Credited			
Date	**(a) Basic Type**	**(b) Specific Account**	**(c) Effect**	**(d) Normal Balance**	**(a) Basic Type**	**(b) Specific Account**	**(c) Effect**	**(d) Normal Balance**
Jan. 2	Asset	Cash	Increase	Debit	Owner's Equity	Owner's Capital	Increase	Credit

Journalize transactions.
(LO 2)

E2-3 Data for A. Mane, interior decorator, are presented in E2-2.

Instructions
Journalize the transactions using journal page J1. (You may omit explanations.)

Analyze transactions and determine their effect on accounts.
(LO 1)

E2-4 The following information relates to Sanculi Real Estate Agency.

Oct. 1 Alan Sanculi begins business as a real estate agent with a cash investment of $15,000.
2 Hires an administrative assistant.
3 Purchases office furniture for $1,900, on account.
6 Sells a house and lot for R. Craig; bills R. Craig $3,800 for realty services performed.
27 Pays $1,100 on the balance related to the transaction of October 3.
30 Pays the administrative assistant $2,500 in salary for October.

Instructions
Prepare the debit-credit analysis for each transaction as illustrated on pages 61–65.

Journalize transactions.
(LO 2)

E2-5 Transaction data for Sanculi Real Estate Agency are presented in E2-4.

Instructions
Journalize the transactions. (You may omit explanations.)

Analyze transactions and journalize.
(LO 1, 2)

E2-6 Marx Industries had the following transactions.

1. Borrowed $5,000 from the bank by signing a note.
2. Paid $3,100 cash for a computer.
3. Purchased $850 of supplies on account.

Instructions
(a) Indicate what accounts are increased and decreased by each transaction.
(b) Journalize each transaction. (Omit explanations.)

Analyze transactions and journalize.
(LO 1, 2)

E2-7 Halladay Enterprises had the following selected transactions.

1. Bo Halladay invested $4,000 cash in the business.
2. Paid office rent of $840.
3. Performed consulting services and billed a client $5,200.
4. Bo Halladay withdrew $750 cash for personal use.

Instructions
(a) Indicate the effect each transaction has on the accounting equation (Assets = Liabilities + Owner's Equity), using plus and minus signs.
(b) Journalize each transaction. (Omit explanations.)

Analyze statements about the ledger.

(LO 3)

E2-8 Teresa Alvarez has prepared the following list of statements about the general ledger.

1. The general ledger contains all the asset and liability accounts but no owner's equity accounts.
2. The general ledger is sometimes referred to as simply the ledger.
3. The accounts in the general ledger are arranged in alphabetical order.
4. Each account in the general ledger is numbered for easier identification.
5. The general ledger is a book of original entry.

Instructions

Identify each statement as true or false. If false, indicate how to correct the statement.

Post journal entries and prepare a trial balance.

(LO 3, 4)

E2-9 Selected transactions from the journal of June Feldman, investment broker, are presented below.

Date	Account Titles and Explanation	Ref.	Debit	Credit
Aug. 1	Cash		5,000	
	Owner's Capital			5,000
	(Owner's investment of cash in business)			
10	Cash		2,600	
	Service Revenue			2,600
	(Received cash for services performed)			
12	Equipment		5,000	
	Cash			2,300
	Notes Payable			2,700
	(Purchased equipment for cash and notes payable)			
25	Accounts Receivable		1,700	
	Service Revenue			1,700
	(Billed clients for services performed)			
31	Cash		900	
	Accounts Receivable			900
	(Receipt of cash on account)			

Instructions

(a) Post the transactions to T-accounts.
(b) Prepare a trial balance at August 31, 2017.

Journalize transactions from account data and prepare a trial balance.

(LO 2, 4)

E2-10 The T-accounts below summarize the ledger of Daggett Landscaping Company at the end of the first month of operations.

Cash No. 101

4/1	12,000	4/15	1,300
4/12	900	4/25	1,500
4/29	400		
4/30	1,000		

Accounts Receivable No. 112

4/7	3,200	4/29	400

Supplies No. 126

4/4	1,800		

Accounts Payable No. 201

4/25	1,500	4/4	1,800

Unearned Service Revenue No. 209

		4/30	1,000

Owner's Capital No. 301

		4/1	12,000

Service Revenue No. 400

		4/7	3,200
		4/12	900

Salaries and Wages Expense No. 726

4/15	1,300		

Instructions

(a) Prepare the complete general journal (including explanations) from which the postings to Cash were made.
(b) Prepare a trial balance at April 30, 2017.

Journalize transactions from account data and prepare a trial balance.

(LO 2, 4)

E2-11 Presented below is the ledger for Shumway Co.

Cash			**No. 101**
10/1	3,000	10/4	400
10/10	750	10/12	1,500
10/10	4,000	10/15	350
10/20	500	10/30	300
10/25	2,000	10/31	500

Accounts Receivable			**No. 112**
10/6	800	10/20	500
10/20	940		

Supplies			**No. 126**
10/4	400		

Equipment			**No. 157**
10/3	2,000		

Notes Payable			**No. 200**
		10/10	4,000

Accounts Payable			**No. 201**
10/12	1,500	10/3	2,000

Owner's Capital			**No. 301**
		10/1	3,000
		10/25	2,000

Owner's Drawings			**No. 306**
10/30	300		

Service Revenue			**No. 400**
		10/6	800
		10/10	750
		10/20	940

Salaries and Wages Expense			**No. 726**
10/31	500		

Rent Expense			**No. 729**
10/15	350		

Instructions

(a) Reproduce the journal entries for the transactions that occurred on October 1, 10, and 20, and provide explanations for each.
(b) Determine the October 31 balance for each of the accounts above, and prepare a trial balance at October 31, 2017.

Prepare journal entries and post using standard account form.

(LO 2, 3)

E2-12 Selected transactions for Dianne Burke Company during its first month in business are presented below.

Sept.	1	Invested $10,000 cash in the business.
	5	Purchased equipment for $12,000 paying $4,000 in cash and the balance on account.
	25	Paid $3,000 cash on balance owed for equipment.
	30	Withdrew $700 cash for personal use.

Burke's chart of accounts shows: No. 101 Cash, No. 157 Equipment, No. 201 Accounts Payable, No. 301 Owner's Capital, and No. 306 Owner's Drawings.

Instructions

(a) Journalize the transactions on page J1 of the journal. (Omit explanations.)
(b) Post the transactions using the standard account form.

Analyze errors and their effects on trial balance.

(LO 4)

E2-13 The bookkeeper for J.L. Kang Equipment Repair made a number of errors in journalizing and posting, as described below.

1. A credit posting of $525 to Accounts Receivable was omitted.
2. A debit posting of $750 for Prepaid Insurance was debited to Insurance Expense.
3. A collection from a customer of $100 in payment of its account owed was journalized and posted as a debit to Cash $100 and a credit to Service Revenue $100.
4. A credit posting of $415 to Property Taxes Payable was made twice.

5. A cash purchase of supplies for $250 was journalized and posted as a debit to Supplies $25 and a credit to Cash $25.
6. A debit of $625 to Advertising Expense was posted as $652.

Instructions

For each error:

(a) Indicate whether the trial balance will balance.
(b) If the trial balance will not balance, indicate the amount of the difference.
(c) Indicate the trial balance column that will have the larger total.

Consider each error separately. Use the following form, in which error (1) is given as an example.

Error	(a) In Balance	(b) Difference	(c) Larger Column
(1)	No	$525	debit

E2-14 The accounts in the ledger of Overnite Delivery Service contain the following balances on July 31, 2017.

Prepare a trial balance.

(LO 4)

Accounts Receivable	$ 7,642	Prepaid Insurance	$ 1,968
Accounts Payable	8,396	Maintenance and Repairs Expense	961
Cash	?	Service Revenue	10,610
Equipment	49,360	Owner's Drawings	700
Gasoline Expense	758	Owner's Capital	42,000
Utilities Expense	523	Salaries and Wages Expense	4,428
Notes Payable	17,000	Salaries and Wages Payable	815

Instructions

Prepare a trial balance with the accounts arranged as illustrated in the chapter and fill in the missing amount for Cash.

EXERCISES: SET B AND CHALLENGE EXERCISES

Visit the book's companion website, at **www.wiley.com/college/weygandt**, and choose the Student Companion site to access Exercises: Set B and Challenge Exercises.

PROBLEMS: SET A

P2-1A Holz Disc Golf Course was opened on March 1 by Ian Holz. The following selected events and transactions occurred during March.

Journalize a series of transactions.

(LO 1, 2)

GLS

Mar.	1	Invested $20,000 cash in the business.
	3	Purchased Rainbow Golf Land for $15,000 cash. The price consists of land $12,000, shed $2,000, and equipment $1,000. (Make one compound entry.)
	5	Paid advertising expenses of $900.
	6	Paid cash $600 for a one-year insurance policy.
	10	Purchased golf discs and other equipment for $1,050 from Stevenson Company payable in 30 days.
	18	Received $1,100 in cash for golf fees (Holz records golf fees as service revenue).
	19	Sold 150 coupon books for $10 each. Each book contains 4 coupons that enable the holder to play one round of disc golf.
	25	Withdrew $800 cash for personal use.
	30	Paid salaries of $250.
	30	Paid Stevenson Company in full.
	31	Received $2,700 cash for golf fees.

Holz Disc Golf uses the following accounts: Cash, Prepaid Insurance, Land, Buildings, Equipment, Accounts Payable, Unearned Service Revenue, Owner's Capital, Owner's Drawings, Service Revenue, Advertising Expense, and Salaries and Wages Expense.

Instructions

Journalize the March transactions.

Journalize transactions, post, and prepare a trial balance.

(LO 1, 2, 3, 4)

GLS

P2-2A Emily Valley is a licensed dentist. During the first month of the operation of her business, the following events and transactions occurred.

April	1	Invested $20,000 cash in her business.
	1	Hired a secretary-receptionist at a salary of $700 per week payable monthly.
	2	Paid office rent for the month $1,100.
	3	Purchased dental supplies on account from Dazzle Company $4,000.
	10	Performed dental services and billed insurance companies $5,100.
	11	Received $1,000 cash advance from Leah Mataruka for an implant.
	20	Received $2,100 cash for services performed from Michael Santos.
	30	Paid secretary-receptionist for the month $2,800.
	30	Paid $2,400 to Dazzle for accounts payable due.

Emily uses the following chart of accounts: No. 101 Cash, No. 112 Accounts Receivable, No. 126 Supplies, No. 201 Accounts Payable, No. 209 Unearned Service Revenue, No. 301 Owner's Capital, No. 400 Service Revenue, No. 726 Salaries and Wages Expense, and No. 729 Rent Expense.

Instructions

(a) Journalize the transactions.

(b) Post to the ledger accounts.

(c) Prepare a trial balance on April 30, 2017.

(c) Trial balance totals $29,800

Journalize transactions, post, and prepare a trial balance.

(LO 1, 2, 3, 4)

P2-3A Maquoketa Services was formed on May 1, 2017. The following transactions took place during the first month.

Transactions on May 1:

1. Jay Bradford invested $40,000 cash in the company, as its sole owner.
2. Hired two employees to work in the warehouse. They will each be paid a salary of $3,050 per month.
3. Signed a 2-year rental agreement on a warehouse; paid $24,000 cash in advance for the first year.
4. Purchased furniture and equipment costing $30,000. A cash payment of $10,000 was made immediately; the remainder will be paid in 6 months.
5. Paid $1,800 cash for a one-year insurance policy on the furniture and equipment.

Transactions during the remainder of the month:

6. Purchased basic office supplies for $420 cash.
7. Purchased more office supplies for $1,500 on account.
8. Total revenues earned were $20,000—$8,000 cash and $12,000 on account.
9. Paid $400 to suppliers for accounts payable due.
10. Received $3,000 from customers in payment of accounts receivable.
11. Received utility bills in the amount of $380, to be paid next month.
12. Paid the monthly salaries of the two employees, totaling $6,100.

Instructions

(a) Prepare journal entries to record each of the events listed. (Omit explanations.)

(b) Post the journal entries to T-accounts.

(c) Prepare a trial balance as of May 31, 2017.

(c) Trial balance totals $81,480

Prepare a correct trial balance.

(LO 4)

XLS

P2-4A The trial balance of Avtar Sandhu Co. shown below does not balance.

AVTAR SANDHU CO.
Trial Balance
June 30, 2017

	Debit	Credit
Cash		$ 3,340
Accounts Receivable	$ 2,812	
Supplies	1,200	
Equipment	2,600	
Accounts Payable		3,666
Unearned Service Revenue	1,100	
Owner's Capital		8,000
Owner's Drawings	800	
Service Revenue		2,480
Salaries and Wages Expense	3,200	
Utilities Expense	810	
	$12,522	$17,486

Each of the listed accounts has a normal balance per the general ledger. An examination of the ledger and journal reveals the following errors.

1. Cash received from a customer in payment of its account was debited for $580, and Accounts Receivable was credited for the same amount. The actual collection was for $850.
2. The purchase of a computer on account for $710 was recorded as a debit to Supplies for $710 and a credit to Accounts Payable for $710.
3. Services were performed on account for a client for $980. Accounts Receivable was debited for $980, and Service Revenue was credited for $98.
4. A debit posting to Salaries and Wages Expense of $700 was omitted.
5. A payment of a balance due for $306 was credited to Cash for $306 and credited to Accounts Payable for $360.
6. The withdrawal of $600 cash for Sandhu's personal use was debited to Salaries and Wages Expense for $600 and credited to Cash for $600.

Instructions

Prepare a correct trial balance. (*Hint:* It helps to prepare the correct journal entry for the transaction described and compare it to the mistake made.)

Trial balance totals $15,462

P2-5A The Starr Theater, owned by Meg Vargo, will begin operations in March. The Starr will be unique in that it will show only triple features of sequential theme movies. As of March 1, the ledger of Starr showed: No. 101 Cash $3,000, No. 140 Land $24,000, No. 145 Buildings (concession stand, projection room, ticket booth, and screen) $10,000, No. 157 Equipment $10,000, No. 201 Accounts Payable $7,000, and No. 301 Owner's Capital $40,000. During the month of March, the following events and transactions occurred.

Journalize transactions, post, and prepare a trial balance.

(LO 1, 2, 3, 4)

GLS

Mar. 2 Rented the three *Indiana Jones* movies to be shown for the first 3 weeks of March. The film rental was $3,500; $1,500 was paid in cash and $2,000 will be paid on March 10.

3 Ordered the *Lord of the Rings* movies to be shown the last 10 days of March. It will cost $200 per night.

9 Received $4,300 cash from admissions.

10 Paid balance due on *Indiana Jones* movies rental and $2,100 on March 1 accounts payable.

11 Starr Theater contracted with Adam Ladd to operate the concession stand. Ladd is to pay 15% of gross concession receipts, payable monthly, for the rental of the concession stand.

12 Paid advertising expenses $900.

20 Received $5,000 cash from customers for admissions.

20 Received the *Lord of the Rings* movies and paid the rental fee of $2,000.

31 Paid salaries of $3,100.

31 Received statement from Adam Ladd showing gross receipts from concessions of $6,000 and the balance due to Starr Theater of $900 ($6,000 × 15%) for March. Ladd paid one-half the balance due and will remit the remainder on April 5.

31 Received $9,000 cash from customers for admissions.

In addition to the accounts identified above, the chart of accounts includes: No. 112 Accounts Receivable, No. 400 Service Revenue, No. 429 Rent Revenue, No. 610 Advertising Expense, No. 726 Salaries and Wages Expense, and No. 729 Rent Expense.

Instructions

(a) Enter the beginning balances in the ledger. Insert a check mark (✓) in the reference column of the ledger for the beginning balance.

(b) Journalize the March transactions. Starr records admission revenue as service revenue, rental of the concession stand as rent revenue, and film rental expense as rent expense.

(c) Post the March journal entries to the ledger. Assume that all entries are posted from page 1 of the journal.

(d) Prepare a trial balance on March 31, 2017.

(d) Trial balance totals $64,100

PROBLEMS: SET B AND SET C

Visit the book's companion website, at **www.wiley.com/college/weygandt**, and choose the Student Companion site to access Problems: Set B and Set C.

CONTINUING PROBLEM

COOKIE CREATIONS: AN ENTREPRENEURIAL JOURNEY

(*Note:* This is a continuation of the Cookie Creations problem from Chapter 1.)

© leungchopan/ Shutterstock

CC2 After researching the different forms of business organization. Natalie Koebel decides to operate "Cookie Creations" as a proprietorship. She then starts the process of getting the business running. In November 2016, the following activities take place.

Nov. 8 Natalie cashes her U.S. Savings Bonds and receives $520, which she deposits in her personal bank account.

8 She opens a bank account under the name "Cookie Creations" and transfers $500 from her personal account to the new account.

11 Natalie pays $65 for advertising.

13 She buys baking supplies, such as flour, sugar, butter, and chocolate chips, for $125 cash. (*Hint:* Use Supplies account.)

14 Natalie starts to gather some baking equipment to take with her when teaching the cookie classes. She has an excellent top-of-the-line food processor and mixer that originally cost her $750. Natalie decides to start using it only in her new business. She estimates that the equipment is currently worth $300. She invests the equipment in the business.

16 Natalie realizes that her initial cash investment is not enough. Her grandmother lends her $2,000 cash, for which Natalie signs a note payable in the name of the business. Natalie deposits the money in the business bank account. (*Hint:* The note does not have to be repaid for 24 months. As a result, the note payable should be reported in the accounts as the last liability and also on the balance sheet as the last liability.)

17 She buys more baking equipment for $900 cash.

20 She teaches her first class and collects $125 cash.

25 Natalie books a second class for December 4 for $150. She receives $30 cash in advance as a down payment.

30 Natalie pays $1,320 for a one-year insurance policy that will expire on December 1, 2017.

Instructions

(a) Prepare journal entries to record the November transactions.
(b) Post the journal entries to general ledger accounts.
(c) Prepare a trial balance at November 30.

BROADENING YOUR PERSPECTIVE

FINANCIAL REPORTING AND ANALYSIS

Financial Reporting Problem: Apple Inc.

BYP2-1 The financial statements of Apple Inc. are presented in Appendix A. Instructions for accessing and using the company's complete annual report, including the notes to the financial statements, are also provided in Appendix A.

Apple's financial statements contain the following selected accounts, stated in millions of dollars.

Accounts Payable	Cash and Cash Equivalents
Accounts Receivable	Research and Development Expense
Property, Plant, and Equipment	Inventories

Instructions

(a) Answer the following questions.
(1) What is the increase and decrease side for each account?
(2) What is the normal balance for each account?

(b) Identify the probable other account in the transaction and the effect on that account when:
   (1) Accounts Receivable is decreased.
   (2) Accounts Payable is decreased.
   (3) Inventories are increased.

(c) Identify the other account(s) that ordinarily would be involved when:
   (1) Research and Development Expense is increased.
   (2) Property, Plant, and Equipment is increased.

Comparative Analysis Problem: PepsiCo, Inc. vs. The Coca-Cola Company

BYP2-2 PepsiCo, Inc.'s financial statements are presented in Appendix B. Financial statement of The Coca-Cola Company are presented in Appendix C. Instructions for accessing and using the complete annual reports of PepsiCo and Coca-Cola, including the notes to the financial statements, are also provided in Appendices B and C, respectively.

Instructions

(a) Based on the information contained in the financial statements, determine the normal balance of the listed accounts for each company.

PepsiCo	Coca-Cola
1. Inventory	1. Accounts Receivable
2. Property, Plant, and Equipment	2. Cash and Cash Equivalents
3. Accounts Payable	3. Cost of Goods Sold (expense)
4. Interest Expense	4. Sales (revenue)

(b) Identify the other account ordinarily involved when:
   (1) Accounts Receivable is increased.
   (2) Salaries and Wages Payable is decreased.
   (3) Property, Plant, and Equipment is increased.
   (4) Interest Expense is increased.

Comparative Analysis Problem: Amazon.com, Inc. vs. Wal-Mart Stores, Inc.

BYP2-3 Amazon.com, Inc.'s financial statements are presented in Appendix D. Financial statements of Wal-Mart Stores, Inc. are presented in Appendix E. Instructions for accessing and using the complete annual reports of Amazon and Wal-Mart, including the notes to the financial statements, are also provided in Appendices D and E, respectively.

Instructions

(a) Based on the information contained in the financial statements, determine the normal balance of the listed accounts for each company.

Amazon	Wal-Mart
1. Interest Expense	1. Net Product Revenues
2. Cash and Cash Equivalents	2. Inventories
3. Accounts Payable	3. Cost of Sales

(b) Identify the other account ordinarily involved when:
   (1) Accounts Receivable is increased.
   (2) Interest Expense is increased.
   (3) Salaries and Wages Payable is decreased.
   (4) Service Revenue is increased.

Real-World Focus

BYP2-4 Much information about specific companies is available on the Internet. Such information includes basic descriptions of the company's location, activities, industry, financial health, and financial performance.

Address: **biz.yahoo.com/i**, or go to **www.wiley.com/college/weygandt**

Steps

1. Type in a company name, or use index to find company name.
2. Choose **Profile**. Perform instructions (a)–(c) below.
3. Click on the company's specific industry to identify competitors. Perform instructions (d)–(g) below.

Instructions

Answer the following questions.

(a) What is the company's industry?
(b) What is the company's total sales?
(c) What is the company's net income?
(d) What are the names of four of the company's competitors?
(e) Choose one of these competitors.
(f) What is this competitor's name? What are its sales? What is its net income?
(g) Which of these two companies is larger by size of sales? Which one reported higher net income?

BYP2-5 The January 27, 2011, edition of the *New York Times* contains an article by Richard Sandomir entitled "N.F.L. Finances, as Seen Through Packers' Records." The article discusses the fact that the Green Bay Packers are the only NFL team that publicly publishes its annual report.

Instructions

Read the article and answer the following questions.

(a) Why are the Green Bay Packers the only professional football team to publish and distribute an annual report?
(b) Why is the football players' labor union particularly interested in the Packers' annual report?
(c) In addition to the players' labor union, what other outside party might be interested in the annual report?
(d) Even though the Packers' revenue increased in recent years, the company's operating profit fell significantly. How does the article explain this decline?

CRITICAL THINKING

Communication Activity

BYP2-6 Amelia's Maid Company offers home-cleaning service. Two recurring transactions for the company are billing customers for services performed and paying employee salaries. For example, on March 15, bills totaling $6,000 were sent to customers and $2,000 was paid in salaries to employees.

Instructions

Write a memo to your instructor that explains and illustrates the steps in the recording process for each of the March 15 transactions. Use the format illustrated in the text under the heading, "The Recording Process Illustrated" (p. 61).

Ethics Cases

BYP2-7 Ellynn Kole is the assistant chief accountant at Doman Company, a manufacturer of computer chips and cellular phones. The company presently has total sales of $20 million. It is the end of the first quarter. Ellynn is hurriedly trying to prepare a trial balance so that quarterly financial statements can be prepared and released to management and the regulatory agencies. The total credits on the trial balance exceed the debits by $1,000. In order to meet the 4 p.m. deadline, Ellynn decides to force the debits and credits into balance by adding the amount of the difference to the Equipment account. She chooses Equipment because it is one of the larger account balances; percentage-wise, it will be the least misstated. Ellynn "plugs" the difference! She believes that the difference will not affect anyone's decisions. She wishes that she had another few days to find the error but realizes that the financial statements are already late.

Instructions

(a) Who are the stakeholders in this situation?
(b) What are the ethical issues involved in this case?
(c) What are Ellynn's alternatives?

BYP2-8 If you haven't already done so, in the not-too-distant future you will prepare a résumé. In some ways, your résumé is like a company's annual report. Its purpose is to enable others to evaluate your past, in an effort to predict your future.

A résumé is your opportunity to create a positive first impression. It is important that it be impressive—but it should also be accurate. In order to increase their job prospects, some people are tempted to "inflate" their résumés by overstating the importance of some past accomplishments or positions. In fact, you might even think that "everybody does it" and that if you don't do it, you will be at a disadvantage.

David Edmondson, the president and CEO of well-known electronics retailer Radio Shack, overstated his accomplishments by claiming that he had earned a bachelor's of science degree, when in fact he had not. Apparently, his employer had not done a background check to ensure the accuracy of his résumé. Should Radio Shack have fired him?

YES: Radio Shack is a publicly traded company. Investors, creditors, employees, and others doing business with the company will not trust it if its leader is known to have poor integrity. The "tone at the top" is vital to creating an ethical organization.

NO: Mr. Edmondson had been a Radio Shack employee for 11 years. He had served the company in a wide variety of positions, and had earned the position of CEO through exceptional performance. While the fact that he lied 11 years earlier on his résumé was unfortunate, his service since then made this past transgression irrelevant. In addition, the company was in the midst of a massive restructuring, which included closing 700 of its 7,000 stores. It could not afford additional upheaval at this time.

Instructions

Write a response indicating your position regarding this situation. Provide support for your view.

All About You

BYP2-9 Every company needs to plan in order to move forward. Its top management must consider where it wants the company to be in three to five years. Like a company, you need to think about where you want to be three to five years from now, and you need to start taking steps now in order to get there.

Instructions

Provide responses to each of the following items.

(a) Where would you like to be working in three to five years? Describe your plan for getting there by identifying between five and 10 specific steps that you need to take.

(b) In order to get the job you want, you will need a résumé. Your résumé is the equivalent of a company's annual report. It needs to provide relevant and reliable information about your past accomplishments so that employers can decide whether to "invest" in you. Do a search on the Internet to find a good résumé format. What are the basic elements of a résumé?

(c) A company's annual report provides information about a company's accomplishments. In order for investors to use the annual report, the information must be reliable; that is, users must have faith that the information is accurate and believable. How can you provide assurance that the information on your résumé is reliable?

(d) Prepare a résumé assuming that you have accomplished the five to 10 specific steps you identified in part (a). Also, provide evidence that would give assurance that the information is reliable.

Considering People, Planet, and Profit

BYP2-10 Auditors provide a type of certification of corporate financial statements. Certification is used in many other aspects of business as well. For example, it plays a critical role in the sustainability movement. The February 7, 2012, issue of the *New York Times* contained an article by S. Amanda Caudill entitled "Better Lives in Better Coffee," which discusses the role of certification in the coffee business.

Address: **http://scientistatwork.blogs.nytimes.com/2012/02/07/better-lives-in-better-coffee**

Instructions

Read the article and answer the following questions.

(a) The article mentions three different certification types that coffee growers can obtain from three different certification bodies. Using financial reporting as an example, what potential problems might the existence of multiple certification types present to coffee purchasers?

(b) According to the author, which certification is most common among coffee growers? What are the possible reasons for this?

(c) What social and environmental benefits are coffee certifications trying to achieve? Are there also potential financial benefits to the parties involved?

A Look at IFRS

LEARNING OBJECTIVE 5

Compare the procedures for the accounting process under GAAP and IFRS.

International companies use the same set of procedures and records to keep track of transaction data. Thus, the material in Chapter 2 dealing with the account, general rules of debit and credit, and steps in the recording process—the journal, ledger, and chart of accounts—is the same under both GAAP and IFRS.

Key Points

Following are the key similarities and differences between GAAP and IFRS as related to the recording process.

Similarities

- Transaction analysis is the same under IFRS and GAAP.
- Both the IASB and the FASB go beyond the basic definitions provided in the textbook for the key elements of financial statements, that is assets, liabilities, equity, revenue, and expenses. The implications of the expanded definitions are discussed in more advanced accounting courses.
- As shown in the textbook, dollar signs are typically used only in the trial balance and the financial statements. The same practice is followed under IFRS, using the currency of the country where the reporting company is headquartered.
- A trial balance under IFRS follows the same format as shown in the textbook.

Differences

- IFRS relies less on historical cost and more on fair value than do FASB standards.
- Internal controls are a system of checks and balances designed to prevent and detect fraud and errors. While most public U.S. companies have these systems in place, many non-U.S. companies have never completely documented the controls nor had an independent auditors attest to their effectiveness.

Looking to the Future

The basic recording process shown in this textbook is followed by companies across the globe. It is unlikely to change in the future. The definitional structure of assets, liabilities, equity, revenues, and expenses may change over time as the IASB and FASB evaluate their overall conceptual framework for establishing accounting standards.

IFRS Practice

IFRS Self-Test Questions

1. Which statement is **correct** regarding IFRS?
   (a) IFRS reverses the rules of debits and credits, that is, debits are on the right and credits are on the left.
   (b) IFRS uses the same process for recording transactions as GAAP.
   (c) The chart of accounts under IFRS is different because revenues follow assets.
   (d) None of the above statements are correct.
2. The expanded accounting equation under IFRS is as follows:
   (a) Assets = Liabilities + Owner's Capital + Owner's Drawings + Revenues − Expenses.
   (b) Assets + Liabilities = Owner's Capital + Owner's Drawings + Revenues − Expenses.
   (c) Assets = Liabilities + Owner's Capital − Owner's Drawings + Revenues − Expenses.
   (d) Assets = Liabilities + Owner's Capital + Owner's Drawings − Revenues − Expenses.
3. A trial balance:
   (a) is the same under IFRS and GAAP.
   (b) proves that transactions are recorded correctly.

(c) proves that all transactions have been recorded.
(d) will not balance if a correct journal entry is posted twice.

4. One difference between IFRS and GAAP is that:
   (a) GAAP uses accrual-accounting concepts and IFRS uses primarily the cash basis of accounting.
   (b) IFRS uses a different posting process than GAAP.
   (c) IFRS uses more fair value measurements than GAAP.
   (d) the limitations of a trial balance are different between IFRS and GAAP.
5. The general policy for using proper currency signs (dollar, yen, pound, etc.) is the same for both IFRS and this textbook. This policy is as follows:
   (a) Currency signs only appear in ledgers and journal entries.
   (b) Currency signs are only shown in the trial balance.
   (c) Currency signs are shown for all compound journal entries.
   (d) Currency signs are shown in trial balances and financial statements.

International Financial Reporting Problem: Louis Vuitton

IFRS2-1 The financial statements of Louis Vuitton are presented in Appendix F. Instructions for accessing and using the company's complete annual report, including the notes to its financial statements, are also provided in Appendix F.

Instructions

Describe in which statement each of the following items is reported, and the position in the statement (e.g., current asset).

(a) Other operating income and expense.
(b) Cash and cash equivalents.
(c) Trade accounts payable.
(d) Cost of net financial debt.

Answers to IFRS Self-Test Questions

1. b **2.** c **3.** a **4.** c **5.** d

3 Adjusting the Accounts

CHAPTER PREVIEW **In Chapter 1, you learned a neat little formula: Net income = Revenues − Expenses. In Chapter 2, you learned some rules for recording revenue and expense transactions. Guess what? Things are not really that nice and neat. In fact, it is often difficult for companies to determine in what time period they should report some revenues and expenses. In other words, in measuring net income, timing is everything.**

FEATURE STORY

Keeping Track of Groupons

Who doesn't like buying things at a discount? That's why it's not surprising that three years after it started as a company, Groupon was estimated to be worth $16 billion. This translates into an average increase in value of almost $15 million per day.

Now consider that Groupon had previously been estimated to be worth even more than that. What happened? Well, accounting regulators and investors began to question the way that Groupon had accounted for some of its transactions. But if Groupon sells only coupons ("groupons"), how hard can it be to accurately account for that? It turns out that accounting for coupons is not as easy as you might think.

First, consider what happens when Groupon makes a sale. Suppose it sells a groupon for $30 for Highrise Hamburgers. When it receives the $30 from the customer, it must turn over half of that amount ($15) to Highrise Hamburgers. So should Groupon record revenue for the full $30 or just $15? Until recently, Groupon recorded the full $30. But, in response to an SEC ruling on the issue, Groupon now records revenue of $15 instead.

A second issue is a matter of timing. When should Groupon record this $15 revenue? Should it record the revenue when it sells the groupon, or must it wait until the customer uses the groupon at Highrise Hamburgers? You can find the answer to this question in the notes to Groupon's financial statements. It recognizes the revenue once "the number of customers who purchase the daily deal exceeds the predetermined threshold, the Groupon has been electronically delivered to the purchaser and a listing of Groupons sold has been made available to the merchant."

The accounting becomes even more complicated when you consider the company's loyalty programs. Groupon offers free or discounted groupons to its subscribers for doing things such as referring new customers or participating in promotions. These groupons are to be used for future purchases, yet the company must record the expense at the time the customer receives the groupon. The cost of these programs is huge for Groupon, so the timing of this expense can definitely affect its reported income.

The final kicker is that Groupon, like all other companies, must rely on many estimates in its financial reporting. For example, Groupon reports that "estimates are utilized for, but not limited to, stock-based compensation, income taxes, valuation of acquired goodwill and intangible assets, customer refunds, contingent liabilities and the depreciable lives of fixed assets." It concludes by saying that "actual results could differ materially from those estimates." So, next time you use a coupon, think about what that means for the company's accountants!.

Rudy Archuleta/Redux Pictures

CHAPTER OUTLINE

Learning Objectives

1 Explain the accrual basis of accounting and the reasons for adjusting entries.

- Fiscal and calendar years
- Accrual- vs. cash-basis accounting
- Recognizing revenues and expenses
- Need for adjusting entries
- Types of adjusting entries

DO IT! 1 Timing Concepts

2 Prepare adjusting entries for deferrals.

- Prepaid expenses
- Unearned revenues

DO IT! 2 Adjusting Entries for Deferrals

3 Prepare adjusting entries for accruals.

- Accrued revenues
- Accrued expenses
- Summary of basic relationships

DO IT! 3 Adjusting Entries for Accruals

4 Describe the nature and purpose of an adjusted trial balance.

- Preparing the adjusted trial balance
- Preparing financial statements

DO IT! 4 Trial Balance

Go to the ***REVIEW AND PRACTICE*** section at the end of the chapter for a review of key concepts and practice applications with solutions.

Visit **WileyPLUS with ORION** for additional tutorials and practice opportunities.

LEARNING OBJECTIVE 1

Explain the accrual basis of accounting and the reasons for adjusting entries.

If we could wait to prepare financial statements until a company ended its operations, no adjustments would be needed. At that point, we could easily determine its final balance sheet and the amount of lifetime income it earned.

However, most companies need immediate feedback about how well they are doing. For example, management usually wants monthly financial statements. The Internal Revenue Service requires all businesses to file annual tax returns. Therefore, **accountants divide the economic life of a business into artificial time periods**. This convenient assumption is referred to as the **time period assumption**.

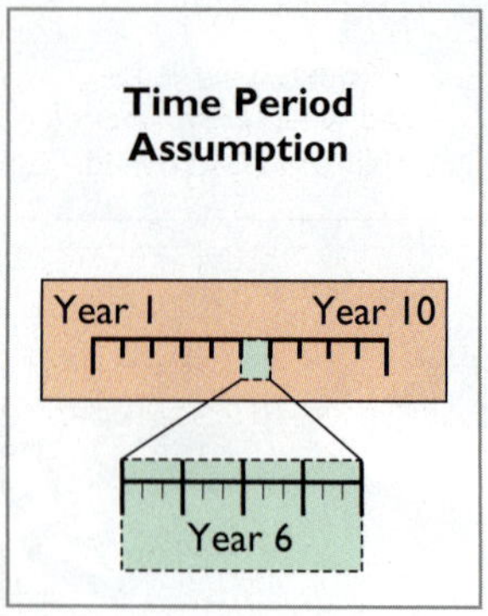

Alternative Terminology
The time period assumption is also called the *periodicity assumption*.

Many business transactions affect more than one of these arbitrary time periods. For example, the airplanes purchased by **Southwest Airlines** five years ago are still in use today. We must determine the relevance of each business transaction to specific accounting periods. (How much of the cost of an airplane contributed to operations this year?)

Fiscal and Calendar Years

Both small and large companies prepare financial statements periodically in order to assess their financial condition and results of operations. **Accounting time periods are generally a month, a quarter, or a year.** Monthly and quarterly time periods are called **interim periods**. Most large companies must prepare both quarterly and annual financial statements.

An accounting time period that is one year in length is a **fiscal year**. A fiscal year usually begins with the first day of a month and ends 12 months later on the last day of a month. Many businesses use the **calendar year** (January 1 to December 31) as their accounting period. Some do not. Companies whose fiscal year differs from the calendar year include **Delta Air Lines**, June 30, and **The Walt Disney Company**, September 30. Sometimes a company's year-end will vary from year to year. For example, **PepsiCo**'s fiscal year ends on the Friday closest to December 31, which was December 29 in 2012 and December 28 in 2013.

Accrual- versus Cash-Basis Accounting

What you will learn in this chapter is **accrual-basis accounting**. Under the accrual basis, companies record transactions that change a company's financial statements **in the periods in which the events occur**. For example, using the accrual basis to determine net income means companies recognize revenues when they perform services (rather than when they receive cash). It also means recognizing expenses when incurred (rather than when paid).

An alternative to the accrual basis is the cash basis. Under **cash-basis accounting**, companies record revenue when they receive cash. They record an expense when they pay out cash. The cash basis seems appealing due to its simplicity, but it often produces misleading financial statements. It fails to record revenue for a company that has performed services but for which the company has not received the cash. As a result, the cash basis does not match expenses with revenues.

Accrual-basis accounting is therefore in accordance with generally accepted accounting principles (GAAP). Individuals and some small companies, however, do use cash-basis accounting. The cash basis is justified for small businesses because they often have few receivables and payables. Medium and large companies use accrual-basis accounting.

Recognizing Revenues and Expenses

It can be difficult to determine when to report revenues and expenses. The revenue recognition principle and the expense recognition principle help in this task.

REVENUE RECOGNITION PRINCIPLE

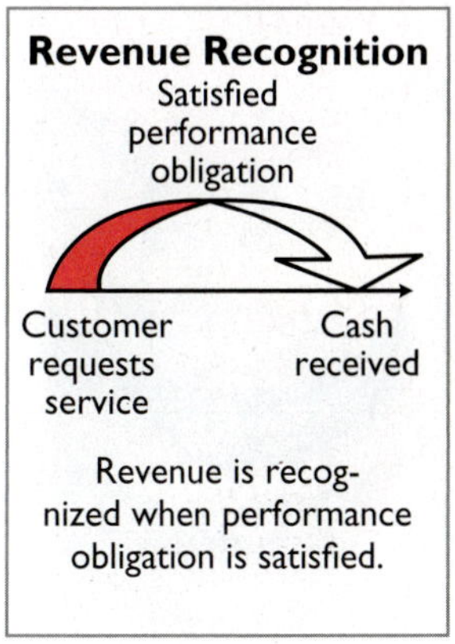

When a company agrees to perform a service or sell a product to a customer, it has a **performance obligation**. When the company meets this performance obligation, it recognizes revenue. The **revenue recognition principle** therefore requires that companies recognize revenue in the accounting period in which the performance obligation is satisfied. To illustrate, assume that Dave's Dry Cleaning cleans clothing on June 30 but customers do not claim and pay for their clothes until the first week of July. Dave's should record revenue in June when it performed the service (satisfied the performance obligation) rather than in July when it received the cash. At June 30, Dave's would report a receivable on its balance sheet and revenue in its income statement for the service performed.

EXPENSE RECOGNITION PRINCIPLE

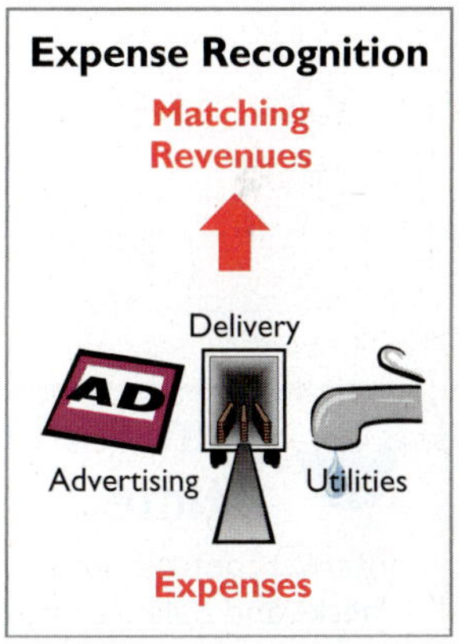

Accountants follow a simple rule in recognizing expenses: "Let the expenses follow the revenues." Thus, expense recognition is tied to revenue recognition. In the dry cleaning example, this means that Dave's should report the salary expense incurred in performing the June 30 cleaning service in the same period in which it recognizes the service revenue. The critical issue in expense recognition is when the expense makes its contribution to revenue. This may or may not be the same period in which the expense is paid. If Dave's does not pay the salary incurred on June 30 until July, it would report salaries payable on its June 30 balance sheet.

This practice of expense recognition is referred to as the **expense recognition principle** (often referred to as the **matching principle**). It dictates that efforts (expenses) be matched with results (revenues). Illustration 3-1 summarizes the revenue and expense recognition principles.

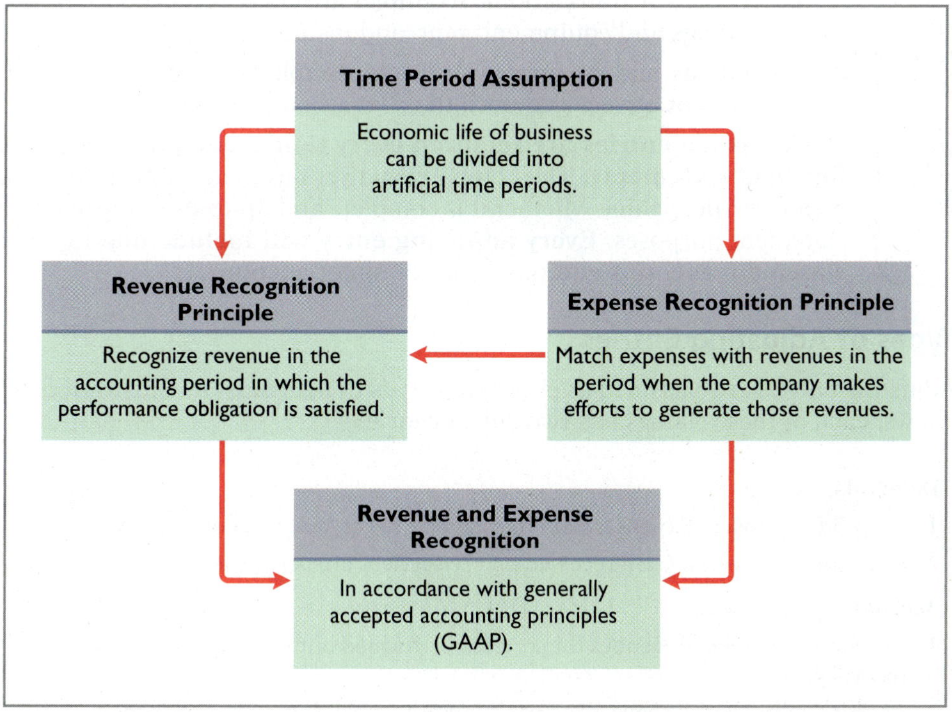

Illustration 3-1
GAAP relationships in revenue and expense recognition

Ethics Insight Krispy Kreme

© Dean Turner/iStockphoto

Cooking the Books?

Allegations of abuse of the revenue recognition principle have become all too common in recent years. For example, it was alleged that Krispy Kreme sometimes doubled the number of doughnuts shipped to wholesale customers at the end of a quarter to boost quarterly results. The customers shipped the unsold doughnuts back after the beginning of the next quarter for a refund. Conversely, Computer Associates International was accused of backdating sales—that is, reporting a sale in one period that did not actually occur until the next period in order to achieve the earlier period's sales targets.

What motivates sales executives and finance and accounting executives to participate in activities that result in inaccurate reporting of revenues? (Go to **WileyPLUS** for this answer and additional questions.)

The Need for Adjusting Entries

In order for revenues to be recorded in the period in which services are performed and for expenses to be recognized in the period in which they are incurred, companies make adjusting entries. **Adjusting entries ensure that the revenue recognition and expense recognition principles are followed.**

Adjusting entries are necessary because the **trial balance**—the first pulling together of the transaction data—may not contain up-to-date and complete data. This is true for several reasons:

1. Some events are not recorded daily because it is not efficient to do so. Examples are the use of supplies and the earning of wages by employees.
2. Some costs are not recorded during the accounting period because these costs expire with the passage of time rather than as a result of recurring daily transactions. Examples are charges related to the use of buildings and equipment, rent, and insurance.
3. Some items may be unrecorded. An example is a utility service bill that will not be received until the next accounting period.

Adjusting entries are required every time a company prepares financial statements. The company analyzes each account in the trial balance to determine whether it is complete and up-to-date for financial statement purposes. **Every adjusting entry will include one income statement account and one balance sheet account.**

International Note

Internal controls are a system of checks and balances designed to detect and prevent fraud and errors. The Sarbanes-Oxley Act requires U.S. companies to enhance their systems of internal control. However, many foreign companies do not have to meet strict internal control requirements. Some U.S. companies believe that this gives foreign firms an unfair advantage because developing and maintaining internal controls can be very expensive.

Types of Adjusting Entries

Adjusting entries are classified as either **deferrals** or **accruals**. As Illustration 3-2 shows, each of these classes has two subcategories.

Illustration 3-2
Categories of adjusting entries

Deferrals:

1. **Prepaid expenses**: Expenses paid in cash before they are used or consumed.
2. **Unearned revenues**: Cash received before services are performed.

Accruals:

1. **Accrued revenues**: Revenues for services performed but not yet received in cash or recorded.
2. **Accrued expenses**: Expenses incurred but not yet paid in cash or recorded.

Subsequent sections give examples of each type of adjustment. Each example is based on the October 31 trial balance of Pioneer Advertising from Chapter 2, reproduced in Illustration 3-3.

Illustration 3-3
Trial balance

PIONEER ADVERTISING
Trial Balance
October 31, 2017

	Debit	Credit
Cash	$ 15,200	
Supplies	2,500	
Prepaid Insurance	600	
Equipment	5,000	
Notes Payable		$ 5,000
Accounts Payable		2,500
Unearned Service Revenue		1,200
Owner's Capital		10,000
Owner's Drawings	500	
Service Revenue		10,000
Salaries and Wages Expense	4,000	
Rent Expense	900	
	$28,700	$28,700

We assume that Pioneer uses an accounting period of one month. Thus, monthly adjusting entries are made. The entries are dated October 31.

DO IT! 1 Timing Concepts

Several timing concepts are discussed on pages 94–95. A list of concepts is provided in the left column below, with a description of the concept in the right column below. There are more descriptions provided than concepts. Match the description of the concept to the concept.

1. ____Accrual-basis accounting.
2. ____Calendar year.
3. ____Time period assumption.
4. ____Expense recognition principle.

(a) Monthly and quarterly time periods.
(b) Efforts (expenses) should be matched with results (revenues).
(c) Accountants divide the economic life of a business into artificial time periods.
(d) Companies record revenues when they receive cash and record expenses when they pay out cash.
(e) An accounting time period that starts on January 1 and ends on December 31.
(f) Companies record transactions in the period in which the events occur.

Action Plan
✔ Review the glossary terms identified on pages 122–123.
✔ Study carefully the revenue recognition principle, the expense recognition principle, and the time period assumption.

Solution

1. f **2.** e **3.** c **4.** b

Related exercise material: **BE3-1, BE3-2, E3-1, E3-2, E3-3, and DO IT! 3-1.**

LEARNING OBJECTIVE 2

Prepare adjusting entries for deferrals.

To defer means to postpone or delay. **Deferrals** are expenses or revenues that are recognized at a date later than the point when cash was originally exchanged. The two types of deferrals are prepaid expenses and unearned revenues.

Prepaid Expenses

When companies record payments of expenses that will benefit more than one accounting period, they record an asset called **prepaid expenses** or **prepayments**. When expenses are prepaid, an asset account is increased (debited) to show the service or benefit that the company will receive in the future. Examples of common prepayments are insurance, supplies, advertising, and rent. In addition, companies make prepayments when they purchase buildings and equipment.

Prepaid expenses are costs that expire either with the passage of time (e.g., rent and insurance) **or through use** (e.g., supplies). The expiration of these costs does not require daily entries, which would be impractical and unnecessary. Accordingly, companies postpone the recognition of such cost expirations until they prepare financial statements. At each statement date, they make adjusting entries to record the expenses applicable to the current accounting period and to show the remaining amounts in the asset accounts.

Prior to adjustment, assets are overstated and expenses are understated. Therefore, as shown in Illustration 3-4, **an adjusting entry for prepaid expenses results in an increase (a debit) to an expense account and a decrease (a credit) to an asset account**.

Illustration 3-4
Adjusting entries for prepaid expenses

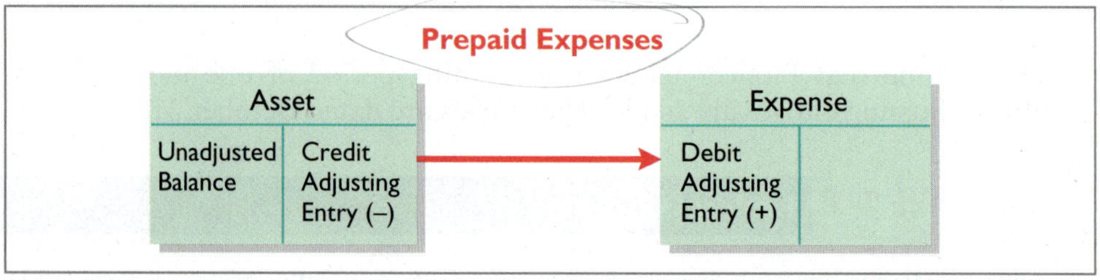

Let's look in more detail at some specific types of prepaid expenses, beginning with supplies.

SUPPLIES

The purchase of supplies, such as paper and envelopes, results in an increase (a debit) to an asset account. During the accounting period, the company uses supplies. Rather than record supplies expense as the supplies are used, companies recognize supplies expense at the **end** of the accounting period. At the end of the accounting period, the company counts the remaining supplies. As shown in Illustration 3-5, the difference between the unadjusted balance in the Supplies (asset) account and the actual cost of supplies on hand represents the supplies used (an expense) for that period.

Recall from Chapter 2 that Pioneer Advertising purchased supplies costing \$2,500 on October 5. Pioneer recorded the purchase by increasing (debiting) the asset Supplies. This account shows a balance of \$2,500 in the October 31 trial balance. An inventory count at the close of business on October 31 reveals that \$1,000 of supplies are still on hand. Thus, the cost of supplies used is \$1,500 (\$2,500 − \$1,000). This use of supplies decreases an asset, Supplies. It also decreases owner's equity by increasing an expense account, Supplies Expense. This is shown in Illustration 3-5.

After adjustment, the asset account Supplies shows a balance of \$1,000, which is equal to the cost of supplies on hand at the statement date. In addition, Supplies Expense shows a balance of \$1,500, which equals the cost of supplies used in October. **If Pioneer does not make the adjusting entry, October expenses are understated and net income is overstated by \$1,500. Moreover, both assets and owner's equity will be overstated by \$1,500 on the October 31 balance sheet.**

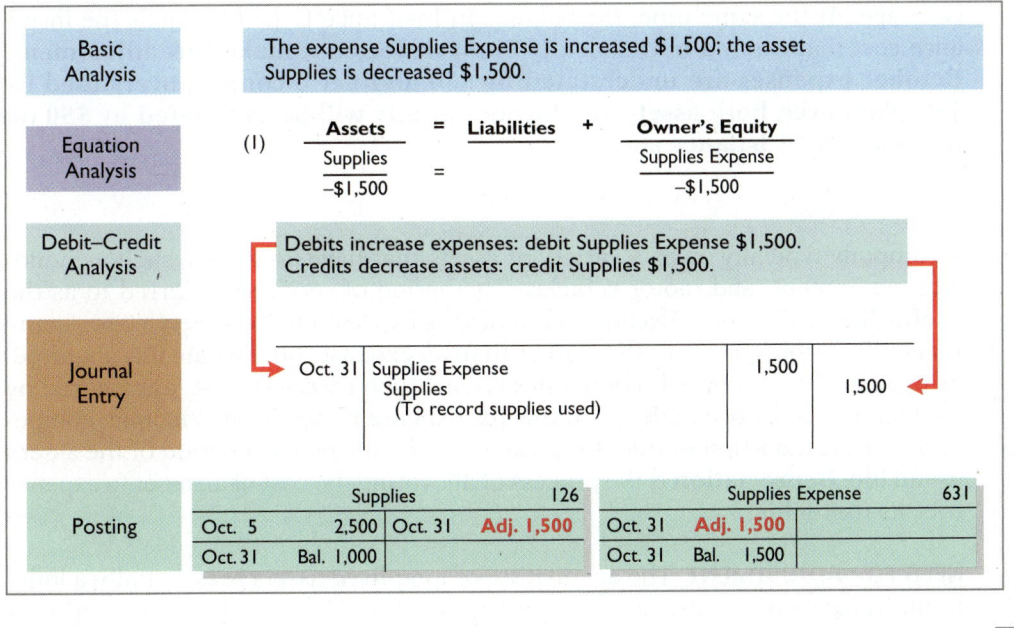

Illustration 3-5
Adjustment for supplies

Basic Analysis

The expense Supplies Expense is increased $1,500; the asset Supplies is decreased $1,500.

Equation Analysis

	Assets	=	Liabilities	+	Owner's Equity
(1)	Supplies	=			Supplies Expense
	−$1,500				−$1,500

Debit–Credit Analysis

Debits increase expenses: debit Supplies Expense $1,500.
Credits decrease assets: credit Supplies $1,500.

Journal Entry

Oct. 31	Supplies Expense	1,500	
	Supplies		1,500
	(To record supplies used)		

Posting

Supplies			126
Oct. 5	2,500	Oct. 31	**Adj. 1,500**
Oct. 31	Bal. 1,000		

Supplies Expense			631
Oct. 31	**Adj. 1,500**		
Oct. 31	Bal. 1,500		

INSURANCE

Companies purchase insurance to protect themselves from losses due to fire, theft, and unforeseen events. Insurance must be paid in advance, often for more than one year. The cost of insurance (premiums) paid in advance is recorded as an increase (debit) in the asset account Prepaid Insurance. At the financial statement date, companies increase (debit) Insurance Expense and decrease (credit) Prepaid Insurance for the cost of insurance that has expired during the period.

On October 4, Pioneer Advertising paid $600 for a one-year fire insurance policy. Coverage began on October 1. Pioneer recorded the payment by increasing (debiting) Prepaid Insurance. This account shows a balance of $600 in the October 31 trial balance. Insurance of $50 ($600 ÷ 12) expires each month. The expiration of prepaid insurance decreases an asset, Prepaid Insurance. It also decreases owner's equity by increasing an expense account, Insurance Expense.

As shown in Illustration 3-6, the asset Prepaid Insurance shows a balance of $550, which represents the unexpired cost for the remaining 11 months of

Insurance

Oct. 4

Insurance purchased; record asset

Insurance Policy			
Oct $50	Nov $50	Dec $50	Jan $50
Feb $50	March $50	April $50	May $50
June $50	July $50	Aug $50	Sept $50
1 YEAR $600			

Oct. 31
Insurance expired; record insurance expense

Illustration 3-6
Adjustment for insurance

Basic Analysis

The expense Insurance Expense is increased $50; the asset Prepaid Insurance is decreased $50.

Equation Analysis

	Assets	=	Liabilities	+	Owner's Equity
(2)	Prepaid Insurance	=			Insurance Expense
	−$50				−$50

Debit–Credit Analysis

Debits increase expenses: debit Insurance Expense $50.
Credits decrease assets: credit Prepaid Insurance $50.

Journal Entry

Oct. 31	Insurance Expense	50	
	Prepaid Insurance		50
	(To record insurance expired)		

Posting

Prepaid Insurance			130
Oct. 4	600	Oct. 31	**Adj. 50**
Oct. 31	Bal. 550		

Insurance Expense			722
Oct. 31	**Adj. 50**		
Oct. 31	Bal. 50		

coverage. At the same time, the balance in Insurance Expense equals the insurance cost that expired in October. **If Pioneer does not make this adjustment, October expenses are understated by $50 and net income is overstated by $50. Moreover, both assets and owner's equity will be overstated by $50 on the October 31 balance sheet.**

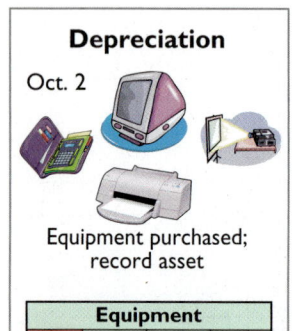

DEPRECIATION

A company typically owns a variety of assets that have long lives, such as buildings, equipment, and motor vehicles. The period of service is referred to as the **useful life** of the asset. Because a building is expected to be of service for many years, it is recorded as an asset, rather than an expense, on the date it is acquired. As explained in Chapter 1, companies record such assets **at cost**, as required by the historical cost principle. To follow the expense recognition principle, companies allocate a portion of this cost as an expense during each period of the asset's useful life. **Depreciation** is the process of allocating the cost of an asset to expense over its useful life.

Depreciation

Oct. 2

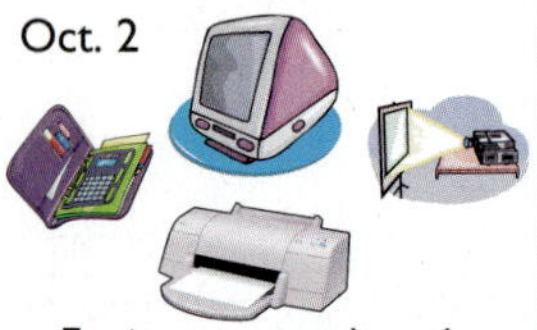

Equipment purchased; record asset

Equipment			
Oct $40	Nov $40	Dec $40	Jan $40
Feb $40	March $40	April $40	May $40
June $40	July $40	Aug $40	Sept $40
Depreciation = $480/year			

Oct. 31
Depreciation recognized; record depreciation expense

NEED FOR ADJUSTMENT The acquisition of long-lived assets is essentially a long-term prepayment for the use of an asset. An adjusting entry for depreciation is needed to recognize the cost that has been used (an expense) during the period and to report the unused cost (an asset) at the end of the period. One very important point to understand: **Depreciation is an allocation concept, not a valuation concept.** That is, depreciation **allocates an asset's cost to the periods in which it is used. Depreciation does not attempt to report the actual change in the value of the asset.**

For Pioneer Advertising, assume that depreciation on the equipment is $480 a year, or $40 per month. As shown in Illustration 3-7, rather than decrease (credit) the asset account directly, Pioneer instead credits Accumulated Depreciation—Equipment. Accumulated Depreciation is called a **contra asset account**. Such

Illustration 3-7
Adjustment for depreciation

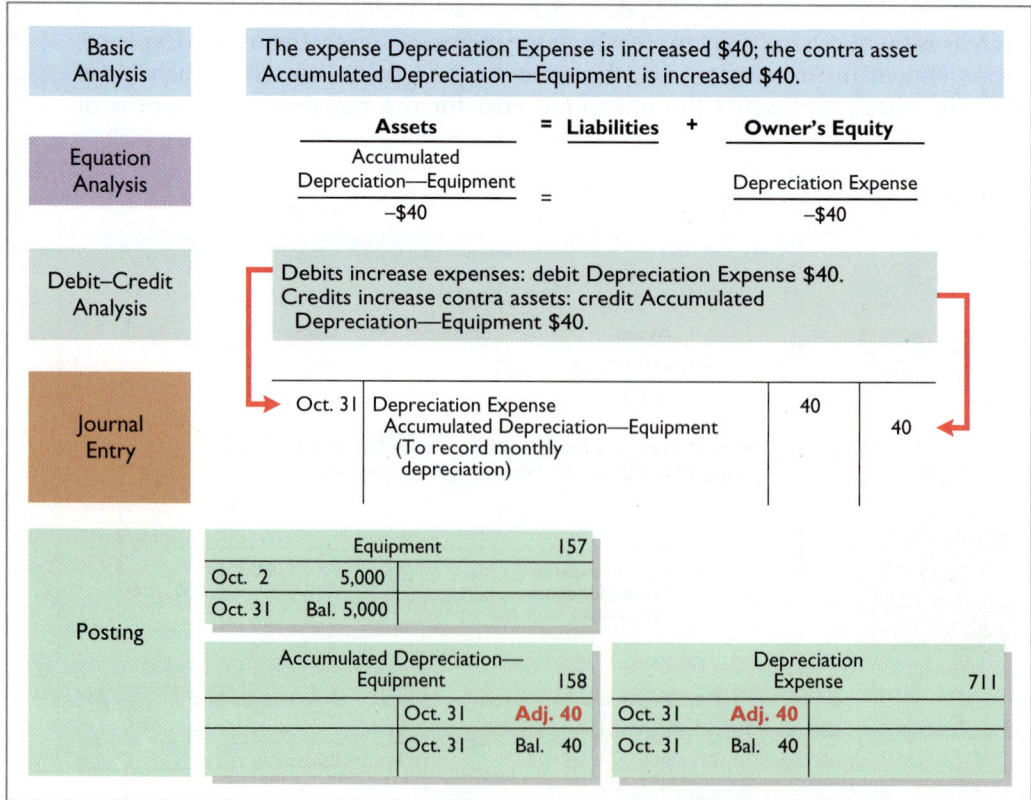

Basic Analysis: The expense Depreciation Expense is increased $40; the contra asset Accumulated Depreciation—Equipment is increased $40.

Equation Analysis:

Assets	=	Liabilities	+	Owner's Equity
Accumulated Depreciation—Equipment	=			Depreciation Expense
−$40				−$40

Debit–Credit Analysis: Debits increase expenses: debit Depreciation Expense $40. Credits increase contra assets: credit Accumulated Depreciation—Equipment $40.

Journal Entry:

Date	Account	Debit	Credit
Oct. 31	Depreciation Expense	40	
	Accumulated Depreciation—Equipment		40
	(To record monthly depreciation)		

Posting:

Equipment 157			
Oct. 2	5,000		
Oct. 31	Bal. 5,000		

Accumulated Depreciation—Equipment 158			
		Oct. 31	Adj. 40
		Oct. 31	Bal. 40

Depreciation Expense 711			
Oct. 31	Adj. 40		
Oct. 31	Bal. 40		

an account is offset against an asset account on the balance sheet. Thus, the Accumulated Depreciation—Equipment account offsets the asset Equipment. **This account keeps track of the total amount of depreciation expense taken over the life of the asset.** To keep the accounting equation in balance, Pioneer decreases owner's equity by increasing an expense account, Depreciation Expense.

The balance in the Accumulated Depreciation—Equipment account will increase $40 each month, and the balance in Equipment remains $5,000.

Helpful Hint
All contra accounts have increases, decreases, and normal balances opposite to the account to which they relate.

STATEMENT PRESENTATION As indicated, Accumulated Depreciation—Equipment is a contra asset account. It is offset against Equipment on the balance sheet. The normal balance of a contra asset account is a credit. A theoretical alternative to using a contra asset account would be to decrease (credit) the asset account by the amount of depreciation each period. But using the contra account is preferable for a simple reason: It discloses **both** the original cost of the equipment **and** the total cost that has been expensed to date. Thus, in the balance sheet, Pioneer deducts Accumulated Depreciation—Equipment from the related asset account, as shown in Illustration 3-8.

Illustration 3-8
Balance sheet presentation of accumulated depreciation

Equipment	$ 5,000
Less: Accumulated depreciation—equipment	40
	$4,960

Book value is the difference between the cost of any depreciable asset and its related accumulated depreciation. In Illustration 3-8, the book value of the equipment at the balance sheet date is $4,960. The book value and the fair value of the asset are generally two different values. As noted earlier, **the purpose of depreciation is not valuation but a means of cost allocation.**

Alternative Terminology
Book value is also referred to as *carrying value.*

Depreciation expense identifies the portion of an asset's cost that expired during the period (in this case, in October). The accounting equation shows that **without this adjusting entry, total assets, total owner's equity, and net income are overstated by $40 and depreciation expense is understated by $40.**

Illustration 3-9 summarizes the accounting for prepaid expenses.

Illustration 3-9
Accounting for prepaid expenses

ACCOUNTING FOR PREPAID EXPENSES

Examples	Reason for Adjustment	Accounts Before Adjustment	Adjusting Entry
Insurance, supplies, advertising, rent, depreciation	Prepaid expenses recorded in asset accounts have been used.	Assets overstated. Expenses understated.	Dr. Expenses Cr. Assets or Contra Assets

Unearned Revenues

When companies receive cash before services are performed, they record a liability by increasing (crediting) a liability account called **unearned revenues**. In other words, a company now has a performance obligation (liability) to transfer a service to one of its customers. Items like rent, magazine subscriptions, and customer deposits for future service may result in unearned revenues. Airlines such as **United**, **Southwest**, and **Delta**, for instance, treat receipts from the sale of tickets as unearned revenue until the flight service is provided.

Unearned revenues are the opposite of prepaid expenses. Indeed, unearned revenue on the books of one company is likely to be a prepaid expense on the books of the company that has made the advance payment. For example, if identical accounting periods are assumed, a landlord will have unearned rent revenue when a tenant has prepaid rent.

Unearned Revenues
Oct. 2
Thank you in advance for your work
I will finish by Dec. 31
$1,200
Cash is received in advance; liability is recorded
Oct. 31
Some service has been performed; some revenue is recorded

When a company receives payment for services to be performed in a future accounting period, it increases (credits) an unearned revenue (a liability) account to recognize the liability that exists. The company subsequently recognizes revenues when it performs the service. During the accounting period, it is not practical to make daily entries as the company performs services. Instead, the company delays recognition of revenue until the adjustment process. Then, the company makes an adjusting entry to record the revenue for services performed during the period and to show the liability that remains at the end of the accounting period. Typically, prior to adjustment, liabilities are overstated and revenues are understated. Therefore, as shown in Illustration 3-10, **the adjusting entry for unearned revenues results in a decrease (a debit) to a liability account and an increase (a credit) to a revenue account.**

Illustration 3-10
Adjusting entries for unearned revenues

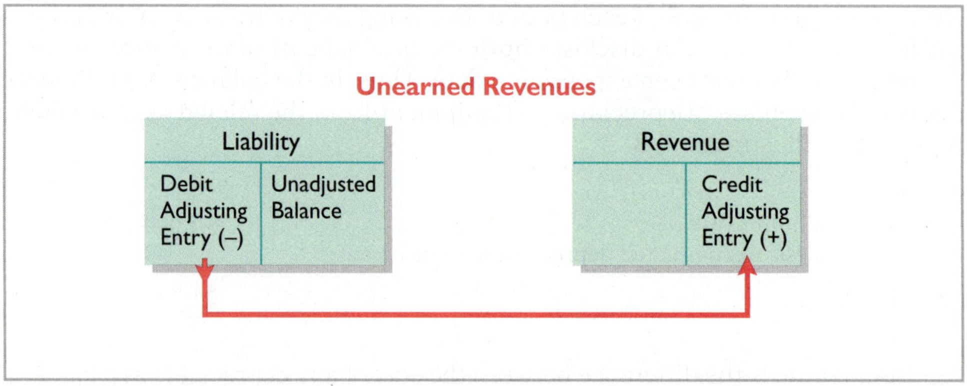

Pioneer Advertising received $1,200 on October 2 from R. Knox for advertising services expected to be completed by December 31. Pioneer credited the payment to Unearned Service Revenue. This liability account shows a balance of $1,200 in the October 31 trial balance. From an evaluation of the services Pioneer performed for Knox during October, the company determines that it should recognize $400 of revenue in October. The liability (Unearned Service Revenue) is therefore decreased, and owner's equity (Service Revenue) is increased.

As shown in Illustration 3-11, the liability Unearned Service Revenue now shows a balance of $800. That amount represents the remaining advertising services expected to be performed in the future. At the same time, Service Revenue shows

Illustration 3-11
Service revenue accounts after adjustment

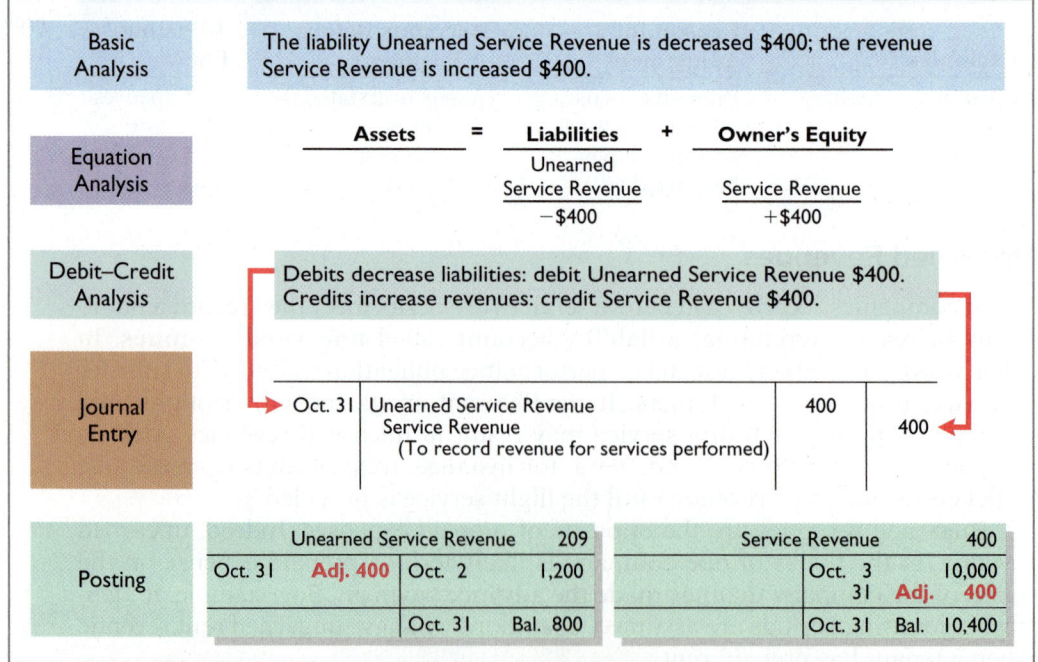

Basic Analysis

The liability Unearned Service Revenue is decreased $400; the revenue Service Revenue is increased $400.

Equation Analysis

Assets	=	Liabilities	+	Owner's Equity
		Unearned Service Revenue		Service Revenue
		−$400		+$400

Debit–Credit Analysis

Debits decrease liabilities: debit Unearned Service Revenue $400.
Credits increase revenues: credit Service Revenue $400.

Journal Entry

Oct. 31	Unearned Service Revenue	400	
	Service Revenue		400
	(To record revenue for services performed)		

Posting

Unearned Service Revenue			209
Oct. 31 Adj. 400		Oct. 2	1,200
		Oct. 31 Bal.	800

Service Revenue			400
		Oct. 3	10,000
		31 Adj.	400
		Oct. 31 Bal.	10,400

total revenue recognized in October of $10,400. **Without this adjustment, revenues and net income are understated by $400 in the income statement. Moreover, liabilities will be overstated and owner's equity will be understated by $400 on the October 31 balance sheet.**

Illustration 3-12 summarizes the accounting for unearned revenues.

Illustration 3-12
Accounting for unearned revenues

ACCOUNTING FOR UNEARNED REVENUES

Examples	Reason for Adjustment	Accounts Before Adjustment	Adjusting Entry
Rent, magazine subscriptions, customer deposits for future service	Unearned revenues recorded in liability accounts are now recognized as revenue for services performed.	Liabilities overstated. Revenues understated.	Dr. Liabilities Cr. Revenues

Accounting Across the Organization — Best Buy

© Skip ODonnell/iStockphoto

Turning Gift Cards into Revenue

Those of you who are marketing majors (and even most of you who are not) know that gift cards are among the hottest marketing tools in merchandising today. Customers purchase gift cards and give them to someone for later use. In a recent year, gift-card sales topped $95 billion.

Although these programs are popular with marketing executives, they create accounting questions. Should revenue be recorded at the time the gift card is sold, or when it is exercised? How should expired gift cards be accounted for? In a recent balance sheet, Best Buy reported unearned revenue related to gift cards of $428 million.

Source: Robert Berner, "Gift Cards: No Gift to Investors," *BusinessWeek* (March 14, 2005), p. 86.

Suppose that Robert Jones purchases a $100 gift card at Best Buy on December 24, 2016, and gives it to his wife, Mary Jones, on December 25, 2016. On January 3, 2017, Mary uses the card to purchase $100 worth of CDs. When do you think Best Buy should recognize revenue and why? (Go to **WileyPLUS** for this answer and additional questions.)

DO IT! 2 Adjusting Entries for Deferrals

The ledger of Hammond Company, on March 31, 2017, includes these selected accounts before adjusting entries are prepared.

	Debit	Credit
Prepaid Insurance	$ 3,600	
Supplies	2,800	
Equipment	25,000	
Accumulated Depreciation—Equipment		$5,000
Unearned Service Revenue		9,200

An analysis of the accounts shows the following.

1. Insurance expires at the rate of $100 per month.
2. Supplies on hand total $800.
3. The equipment depreciates $200 a month.
4. During March, services were performed for one-half of the unearned service revenue.

Prepare the adjusting entries for the month of March.

Action Plan

- ✔ Make adjusting entries at the end of the period for revenues recognized and expenses incurred in the period.
- ✔ Don't forget to make adjusting entries for deferrals. Failure to adjust for deferrals leads to overstatement of the asset or liability and understatement of the related expense or revenue.

Solution

1. Insurance Expense	100	
Prepaid Insurance		100
(To record insurance expired)		
2. Supplies Expense	2,000	
Supplies		2,000
(To record supplies used)		
3. Depreciation Expense	200	
Accumulated Depreciation—Equipment		200
(To record monthly depreciation)		
4. Unearned Service Revenue	4,600	
Service Revenue		4,600
(To record revenue for services performed)		

Related exercise material: **BE3-2, BE3-3, BE3-4, BE3-5, BE3-6, and DO IT! 3-2.**

LEARNING OBJECTIVE 3

Prepare adjusting entries for accruals.

The second category of adjusting entries is **accruals**. Prior to an accrual adjustment, the revenue account (and the related asset account) or the expense account (and the related liability account) are understated. Thus, the adjusting entry for accruals will **increase both a balance sheet and an income statement account**.

Accrued Revenues

Accrued Revenues

Revenue and receivable are recorded for unbilled services

Revenues for services performed but not yet recorded at the statement date are **accrued revenues**. Accrued revenues may accumulate (accrue) with the passing of time, as in the case of interest revenue. These are unrecorded because the earning of interest does not involve daily transactions. Companies do not record interest revenue on a daily basis because it is often impractical to do so. Accrued revenues also may result from services that have been performed but not yet billed nor collected, as in the case of commissions and fees. These may be unrecorded because only a portion of the total service has been performed and the clients will not be billed until the service has been completed.

An adjusting entry records the receivable that exists at the balance sheet date and the revenue for the services performed during the period. Prior to adjustment, both assets and revenues are understated. As shown in Illustration 3-13, **an adjusting entry for accrued revenues results in an increase (a debit) to an asset account and an increase (a credit) to a revenue account**.

Illustration 3-13
Adjusting entries for accrued revenues

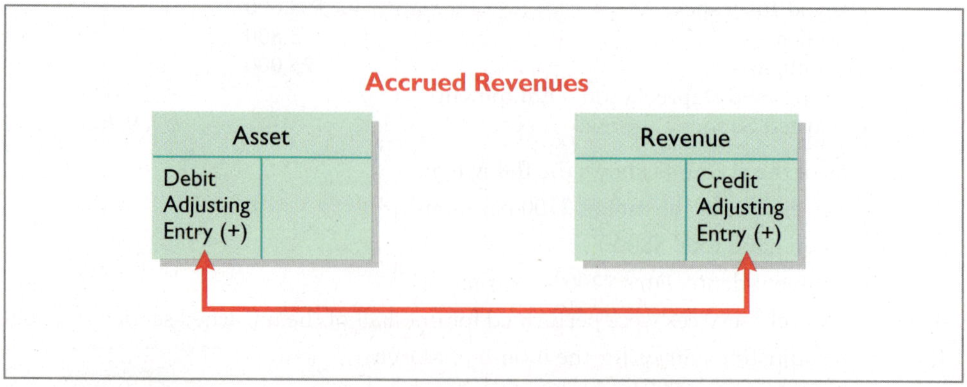

In October, Pioneer Advertising performed services worth $200 that were not billed to clients on or before October 31. Because these services are not billed, they are not recorded. The accrual of unrecorded service revenue increases an asset account, Accounts Receivable. It also increases owner's equity by increasing a revenue account, Service Revenue, as shown in Illustration 3-14.

Illustration 3-14
Adjustment for accrued revenue

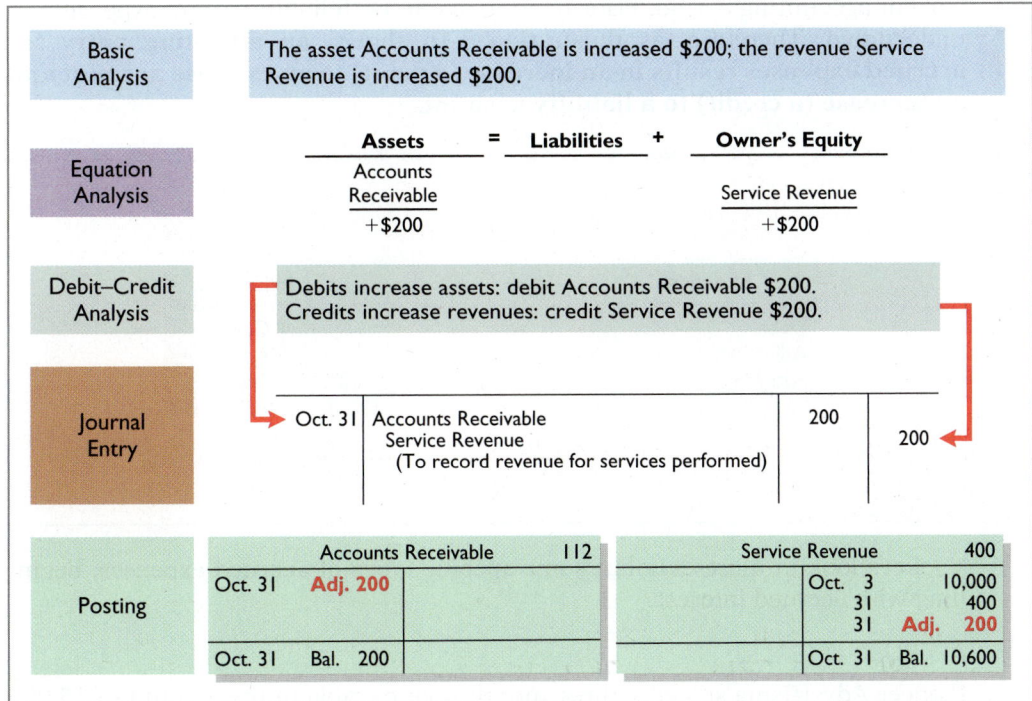

Basic Analysis	The asset Accounts Receivable is increased $200; the revenue Service Revenue is increased $200.
Equation Analysis	**Assets** = **Liabilities** + **Owner's Equity** Accounts Receivable +$200 = Service Revenue +$200
Debit–Credit Analysis	Debits increase assets: debit Accounts Receivable $200. Credits increase revenues: credit Service Revenue $200.
Journal Entry	Oct. 31 Accounts Receivable 200 Service Revenue 200 (To record revenue for services performed)
Posting	see T-accounts below

Accounts Receivable	112		Service Revenue	400
Oct. 31 **Adj. 200**				Oct. 3 10,000
				31 400
				31 **Adj. 200**
Oct. 31 Bal. 200				Oct. 31 Bal. 10,600

The asset Accounts Receivable shows that clients owe Pioneer $200 at the balance sheet date. The balance of $10,600 in Service Revenue represents the total revenue for services performed by Pioneer during the month ($10,000 + $400 + $200). **Without the adjusting entry, assets and owner's equity on the balance sheet and revenues and net income on the income statement are understated.**

On November 10, Pioneer receives cash of $200 for the services performed in October and makes the following entry.

Nov. 10	Cash	200	
	Accounts Receivable		200
	(To record cash collected on account)		

A	=	L	+	OE
+200				
−200				

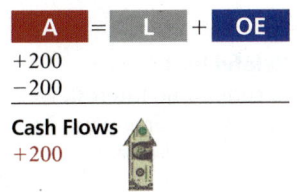

Cash Flows
+200

The company records the collection of the receivables by a debit (increase) to Cash and a credit (decrease) to Accounts Receivable.

Illustration 3-15 summarizes the accounting for accrued revenues.

Equation analyses *summarize the effects of transactions on the three elements of the accounting equation, as well as the effect on cash flows.*

ACCOUNTING FOR ACCRUED REVENUES

Examples	Reason for Adjustment	Accounts Before Adjustment	Adjusting Entry
Interest, rent, services	Services performed but not yet received in cash or recorded.	Assets understated. Revenues understated.	Dr. Assets Cr. Revenues

Illustration 3-15
Accounting for accrued revenues

ETHICS NOTE

A report released by Fannie Mae's board of directors stated that improper adjusting entries at the mortgage-finance company resulted in delayed recognition of expenses caused by interest rate changes. The motivation for such accounting apparently was the desire to hit earnings estimates.

Accrued Expenses

Expenses incurred but not yet paid or recorded at the statement date are called **accrued expenses**. Interest, taxes, and salaries are common examples of accrued expenses.

Companies make adjustments for accrued expenses to record the obligations that exist at the balance sheet date and to recognize the expenses that apply to the current accounting period. Prior to adjustment, both liabilities and expenses are understated. Therefore, as Illustration 3-16 shows, **an adjusting entry for accrued expenses results in an increase (a debit) to an expense account and an increase (a credit) to a liability account.**

Illustration 3-16
Adjusting entries for accrued expenses

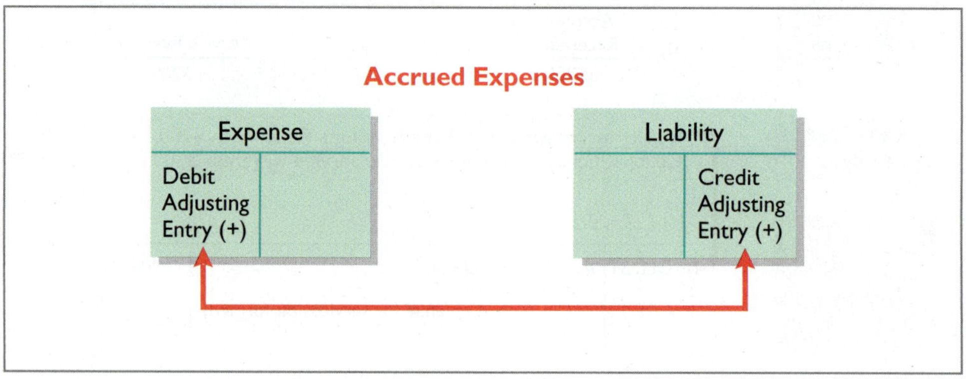

Let's look in more detail at some specific types of accrued expenses, beginning with accrued interest.

ACCRUED INTEREST

Pioneer Advertising signed a three-month note payable in the amount of $5,000 on October 1. The note requires Pioneer to pay interest at an annual rate of 12%.

The amount of the interest recorded is determined by three factors: (1) the face value of the note; (2) the interest rate, which is always expressed as an annual rate; and (3) the length of time the note is outstanding. For Pioneer, the total interest due on the $5,000 note at its maturity date three months in the future is $150 ($\$5{,}000 \times 12\% \times \frac{3}{12}$), or $50 for one month. Illustration 3-17 shows the formula for computing interest and its application to Pioneer for the month of October.

Illustration 3-17
Formula for computing interest

Face Value of Note	×	Annual Interest Rate	×	Time in Terms of One Year	=	Interest
$5,000	×	12%	×	$\frac{1}{12}$	=	$50

Helpful Hint
In computing interest, we express the time period as a fraction of a year.

As Illustration 3-18 shows, the accrual of interest at October 31 increases a liability account, Interest Payable. It also decreases owner's equity by increasing an expense account, Interest Expense.

Interest Expense shows the interest charges for the month of October. Interest Payable shows the amount of interest the company owes at the statement date. Pioneer will not pay the interest until the note comes due at the end of three months. Companies use the Interest Payable account, instead of crediting Notes Payable, to disclose the two different types of obligations—interest and principal—in the accounts and statements. **Without this adjusting entry, liabilities and interest expense are understated, and net income and owner's equity are overstated.**

ACCRUED SALARIES AND WAGES

Companies pay for some types of expenses, such as employee salaries and wages, after the services have been performed. Pioneer Advertising paid salaries and wages on October 26 for its employees' first two weeks of work. The next payment

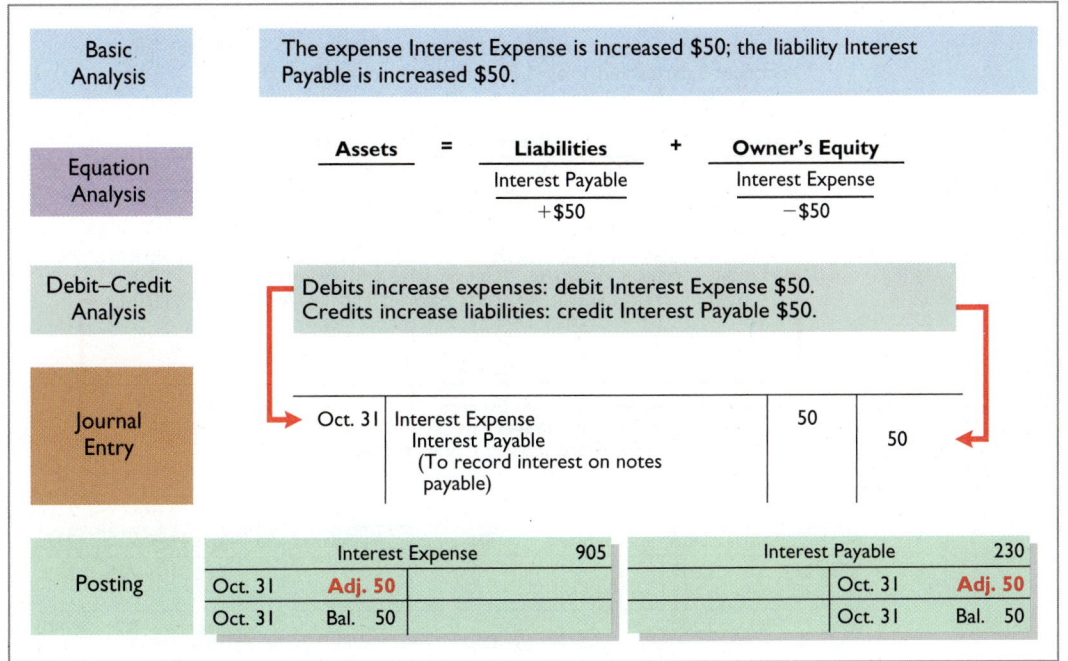

Basic Analysis

The expense Interest Expense is increased $50; the liability Interest Payable is increased $50.

Equation Analysis

Assets	=	Liabilities	+	Owner's Equity
		Interest Payable		Interest Expense
		+$50		−$50

Debit–Credit Analysis

Debits increase expenses: debit Interest Expense $50.
Credits increase liabilities: credit Interest Payable $50.

Journal Entry

Oct. 31	Interest Expense	50	
	Interest Payable		50
	(To record interest on notes payable)		

Posting

Interest Expense			905
Oct. 31	Adj. 50		
Oct. 31	Bal. 50		

Interest Payable			230
		Oct. 31	Adj. 50
		Oct. 31	Bal. 50

Illustration 3-18
Adjustment for accrued interest

of salaries will not occur until November 9. As Illustration 3-19 shows, three working days remain in October (October 29–31).

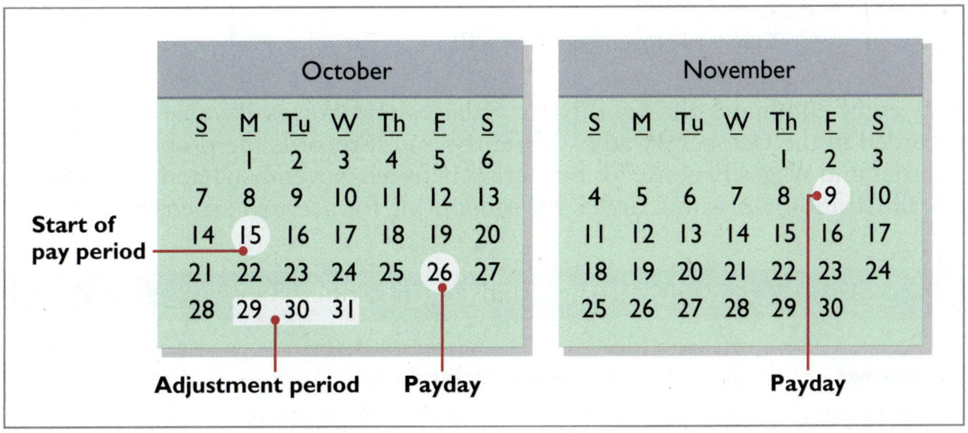

Illustration 3-19
Calendar showing Pioneer's pay periods

At October 31, the salaries and wages for these three days represent an accrued expense and a related liability to Pioneer. The employees receive total salaries and wages of $2,000 for a five-day work week, or $400 per day. Thus, accrued salaries and wages at October 31 are $1,200 ($400 × 3). This accrual increases a liability, Salaries and Wages Payable. It also decreases owner's equity by increasing an expense account, Salaries and Wages Expense, as shown in Illustration 3-20 (page 108).

After this adjustment, the balance in Salaries and Wages Expense of $5,200 (13 days × $400) is the actual salary and wages expense for October. The balance in Salaries and Wages Payable of $1,200 is the amount of the liability for salaries and wages Pioneer owes as of October 31. **Without the $1,200 adjustment for salaries and wages, Pioneer's expenses are understated $1,200 and its liabilities are understated $1,200.**

Pioneer pays salaries and wages every two weeks. Consequently, the next payday is November 9, when the company will again pay total salaries and wages of $4,000. The payment consists of $1,200 of salaries and wages payable at October 31 plus $2,800 of salaries and wages expense for November (7 working days, as shown in the November calendar × $400). Therefore, Pioneer makes the following entry on November 9.

Basic Analysis
The expense Salaries and Wages Expense is increased $1,200; the liability account Salaries and Wages Payable is increased $1,200.

Equation Analysis

Assets	=	Liabilities	+	Owner's Equity
		Salaries and Wages Payable		Salaries and Wages Expense
		+$1,200		−$1,200

Debit–Credit Analysis
Debits increase expenses: debit Salaries and Wages Expense $1,200.
Credits increase liabilities: credit Salaries and Wages Payable $1,200.

Journal Entry

Oct. 31	Salaries and Wages Expense	1,200	
	Salaries and Wages Payable		1,200
	(To record accrued salaries and wages)		

Posting

Salaries and Wages Expense	726		
Oct. 26	4,000		
31 Adj.	1,200		
Oct. 31 Bal.	5,200		

Salaries and Wages Payable			212
		Oct. 31 Adj.	1,200
		Oct. 31 Bal.	1,200

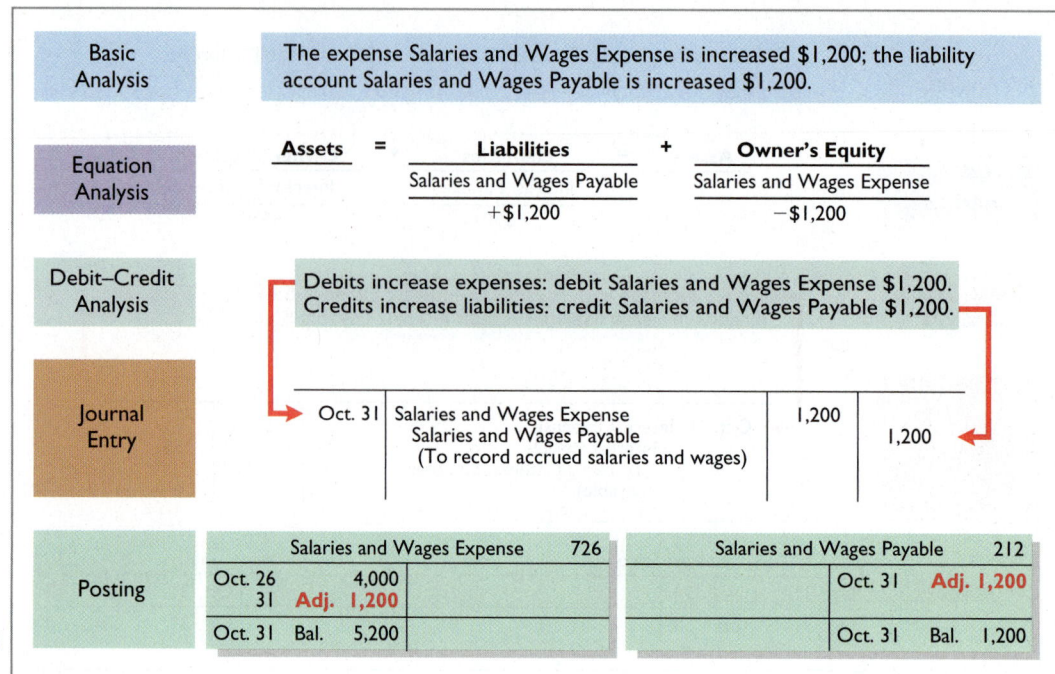

Illustration 3-20
Adjustment for accrued salaries and wages

A	=	L	+	OE
		−1,200		
				−2,800
−4,000				

Cash Flows
−4,000

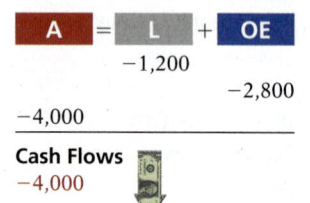

Nov. 9	Salaries and Wages Payable	1,200	
	Salaries and Wages Expense	2,800	
	Cash		4,000
	(To record November 9 payroll)		

This entry eliminates the liability for Salaries and Wages Payable that Pioneer recorded in the October 31 adjusting entry, and it records the proper amount of Salaries and Wages Expense for the period between November 1 and November 9.

Illustration 3-21 summarizes the accounting for accrued expenses.

Illustration 3-21
Accounting for accrued expenses

ACCOUNTING FOR ACCRUED EXPENSES

Examples	Reason for Adjustment	Accounts Before Adjustment	Adjusting Entry
Interest, rent, salaries	Expenses have been incurred but not yet paid in cash or recorded.	Expenses understated. Liabilities understated.	Dr. Expenses Cr. Liabilities

People, Planet, and Profit Insight

© Nathan Gleave/iStockphoto

Got Junk?

Do you have an old computer or two that you no longer use? How about an old TV that needs replacing? Many people do. Approximately 163,000 computers and televisions become obsolete each day. Yet, in a recent year, only 11% of computers were recycled. It is estimated that 75% of all computers ever sold are sitting in storage somewhere, waiting to be disposed of. Each of these old TVs and computers is loaded with lead, cadmium, mercury, and other toxic chemicals. If you have one of these electronic gadgets, you have a responsibility, and a probable cost, for disposing of it. Companies have the same problem, but their discarded materials may include lead paint, asbestos, and other toxic chemicals.

What accounting issue might this cause for companies? (Go to **WileyPLUS** for this answer and additional questions.)

Summary of Basic Relationships

Illustration 3-22 summarizes the four basic types of adjusting entries. Take some time to study and analyze the adjusting entries. Be sure to note that **each adjusting entry affects one balance sheet account and one income statement account**.

Illustration 3-22
Summary of adjusting entries

Type of Adjustment	Accounts Before Adjustment	Adjusting Entry
Prepaid expenses	Assets overstated. Expenses understated.	Dr. Expenses Cr. Assets or Contra Assets
Unearned revenues	Liabilities overstated. Revenues understated.	Dr. Liabilities Cr. Revenues
Accrued revenues	Assets understated. Revenues understated.	Dr. Assets Cr. Revenues
Accrued expenses	Expenses understated. Liabilities understated.	Dr. Expenses Cr. Liabilities

Illustrations 3-23 (below) and 3-24 (on page 110) show the journalizing and posting of adjusting entries for Pioneer Advertising on October 31. The ledger identifies all adjustments by the reference J2 because they have been recorded on page 2 of the general journal. The company may insert a center caption "Adjusting Entries" between the last transaction entry and the first adjusting entry in the journal. When you review the general ledger in Illustration 3-24, note that the entries highlighted in color are the adjustments.

Illustration 3-23
General journal showing adjusting entries

GENERAL JOURNAL J2

Date	Account Titles and Explanation	Ref.	Debit	Credit
2017	Adjusting Entries			
Oct. 31	Supplies Expense	631	1,500	
	Supplies	126		1,500
	(To record supplies used)			
31	Insurance Expense	722	50	
	Prepaid Insurance	130		50
	(To record insurance expired)			
31	Depreciation Expense	711	40	
	Accumulated Depreciation—Equipment	158		40
	(To record monthly depreciation)			
31	Unearned Service Revenue	209	400	
	Service Revenue	400		400
	(To record revenue for services performed)			
31	Accounts Receivable	112	200	
	Service Revenue	400		200
	(To record revenue for services performed)			
31	Interest Expense	905	50	
	Interest Payable	230		50
	(To record interest on notes payable)			
31	Salaries and Wages Expense	726	1,200	
	Salaries and Wages Payable	212		1,200
	(To record accrued salaries and wages)			

Helpful Hint
(1) Adjusting entries should not involve debits or credits to Cash.
(2) Evaluate whether the adjustment makes sense. For example, an adjustment to recognize supplies used should increase Supplies Expense.
(3) Double-check all computations.
(4) Each adjusting entry affects one balance sheet account and one income statement account.

Illustration 3-24
General ledger after adjustment

GENERAL LEDGER

Cash — No. 101

Date	Explanation	Ref.	Debit	Credit	Balance
2017					
Oct. 1		J1	10,000		10,000
2		J1	1,200		11,200
3		J1		900	10,300
4		J1		600	9,700
20		J1		500	9,200
26		J1		4,000	5,200
31		J1	10,000		15,200

Accounts Receivable — No. 112

Date	Explanation	Ref.	Debit	Credit	Balance
2017					
Oct. 31	**Adj. entry**	**J2**	**200**		**200**

Supplies — No. 126

Date	Explanation	Ref.	Debit	Credit	Balance
2017					
Oct. 5		J1	2,500		2,500
31	**Adj. entry**	**J2**		**1,500**	**1,000**

Prepaid Insurance — No. 130

Date	Explanation	Ref.	Debit	Credit	Balance
2017					
Oct. 4		J1	600		600
31	**Adj. entry**	**J2**		**50**	**550**

Equipment — No. 157

Date	Explanation	Ref.	Debit	Credit	Balance
2017					
Oct. 1		J1	5,000		5,000

Accumulated Depreciation—Equipment — No. 158

Date	Explanation	Ref.	Debit	Credit	Balance
2017					
Oct. 31	**Adj. entry**	**J2**		**40**	**40**

Notes Payable — No. 200

Date	Explanation	Ref.	Debit	Credit	Balance
2017					
Oct. 1		J1		5,000	5,000

Accounts Payable — No. 201

Date	Explanation	Ref.	Debit	Credit	Balance
2017					
Oct. 5		J1		2,500	2,500

Unearned Service Revenue — No. 209

Date	Explanation	Ref.	Debit	Credit	Balance
2017					
Oct. 2		J1		1,200	1,200
31	**Adj. entry**	**J2**	**400**		**800**

Salaries and Wages Payable — No. 212

Date	Explanation	Ref.	Debit	Credit	Balance
2017					
Oct. 31	**Adj. entry**	**J2**		**1,200**	**1,200**

Interest Payable — No. 230

Date	Explanation	Ref.	Debit	Credit	Balance
2017					
Oct. 31	**Adj. entry**	**J2**		**50**	**50**

Owner's Capital — No. 301

Date	Explanation	Ref.	Debit	Credit	Balance
2017					
Oct. 1		J1		10,000	10,000

Owner's Drawings — No. 306

Date	Explanation	Ref.	Debit	Credit	Balance
2017					
Oct. 20		J1	500		500

Service Revenue — No. 400

Date	Explanation	Ref.	Debit	Credit	Balance
2017					
Oct. 31		J1		10,000	10,000
31	**Adj. entry**	**J2**		**400**	**10,400**
31	**Adj. entry**	**J2**		**200**	**10,600**

Supplies Expense — No. 631

Date	Explanation	Ref.	Debit	Credit	Balance
2017					
Oct. 31	**Adj. entry**	**J2**	**1,500**		**1,500**

Depreciation Expense — No. 711

Date	Explanation	Ref.	Debit	Credit	Balance
2017					
Oct. 31	**Adj. entry**	**J2**	**40**		**40**

Insurance Expense — No. 722

Date	Explanation	Ref.	Debit	Credit	Balance
2017					
Oct. 31	**Adj. entry**	**J2**	**50**		**50**

Salaries and Wages Expense — No. 726

Date	Explanation	Ref.	Debit	Credit	Balance
2017					
Oct. 26		J1	4,000		4,000
31	**Adj. entry**	**J2**	**1,200**		**5,200**

Rent Expense — No. 729

Date	Explanation	Ref.	Debit	Credit	Balance
2017					
Oct. 3		J1	900		900

Interest Expense — No. 905

Date	Explanation	Ref.	Debit	Credit	Balance
2017					
Oct. 31	**Adj. entry**	**J2**	**50**		**50**

DO IT! 3 Adjusting Entries for Accruals

Micro Computer Services began operations on August 1, 2017. At the end of August 2017, management prepares monthly financial statements. The following information relates to August.

1. At August 31, the company owed its employees $800 in salaries and wages that will be paid on September 1.
2. On August 1, the company borrowed $30,000 from a local bank on a 15-year mortgage. The annual interest rate is 10%.
3. Revenue for services performed but unrecorded for August totaled $1,100.

Prepare the adjusting entries needed at August 31, 2017.

Solution

1. Salaries and Wages Expense	800	
Salaries and Wages Payable		800
(To record accrued salaries)		
2. Interest Expense	250	
Interest Payable		250
(To record accrued interest: $\$30,000 \times 10\% \times \frac{1}{12} = \$250$)		
3. Accounts Receivable	1,100	
Service Revenue		1,100
(To record revenue for services performed)		

Related exercise material: **BE3-7, E3-5, E3-6, E3-7, E3-8, E3-9, and DO IT! 3-3.**

Action Plan

✔ Make adjusting entries at the end of the period to recognize revenues for services performed and for expenses incurred.

✔ Don't forget to make adjusting entries for accruals. Adjusting entries for accruals will increase both a balance sheet and an income statement account.

LEARNING OBJECTIVE 4 Describe the nature and purpose of an adjusted trial balance.

After a company has journalized and posted all adjusting entries, it prepares another trial balance from the ledger accounts. This trial balance is called an **adjusted trial balance**. It shows the balances of all accounts, including those adjusted, at the end of the accounting period. The purpose of an adjusted trial balance is to **prove the equality** of the total debit balances and the total credit balances in the ledger after all adjustments. Because the accounts contain all data needed for financial statements, the adjusted trial balance is the **primary basis for the preparation of financial statements**.

Preparing the Adjusted Trial Balance

Illustration 3-25 (page 112) presents the adjusted trial balance for Pioneer Advertising prepared from the ledger accounts in Illustration 3-24. The amounts affected by the adjusting entries are highlighted in color. Compare these amounts to those in the unadjusted trial balance in Illustration 3-3 (page 97). In this comparison, you will see that there are more accounts in the adjusted trial balance as a result of the adjusting entries made at the end of the month.

Illustration 3-25
Adjusted trial balance

PIONEER ADVERTISING
Adjusted Trial Balance
October 31, 2017

	Debit	Credit
Cash	$ 15,200	
Accounts Receivable	**200**	
Supplies	**1,000**	
Prepaid Insurance	**550**	
Equipment	5,000	
Accumulated Depreciation—Equipment		**$ 40**
Notes Payable		5,000
Accounts Payable		2,500
Interest Payable		**50**
Unearned Service Revenue		**800**
Salaries and Wages Payable		**1,200**
Owner's Capital		10,000
Owner's Drawings	500	
Service Revenue		10,600
Salaries and Wages Expense	**5,200**	
Supplies Expense	**1,500**	
Rent Expense	900	
Insurance Expense	**50**	
Interest Expense	**50**	
Depreciation Expense	**40**	
	$30,190	**$30,190**

Preparing Financial Statements

Companies can prepare financial statements directly from the adjusted trial balance. Illustrations 3-26 (page 113) and 3-27 (page 114) present the interrelationships of data in the adjusted trial balance and the financial statements.

As Illustration 3-26 shows, companies prepare the income statement from the revenue and expense accounts. Next, they use the owner's capital and drawings accounts and the net income (or net loss) from the income statement to prepare the owner's equity statement.

PIONEER ADVERTISING
Adjusted Trial Balance
October 31, 2017

Account	Debit	Credit
Cash	$15,200	
Accounts Receivable	200	
Supplies	1,000	
Prepaid Insurance	550	
Equipment	5,000	
Accumulated Depreciation—Equipment		$ 40
Notes Payable		5,000
Accounts Payable		2,500
Unearned Service Revenue		800
Salaries and Wages Payable		1,200
Interest Payable		50
Owner's Capital		10,000
Owner's Drawings	500	
Service Revenue		10,600
Salaries and Wages Expense	5,200	
Supplies Expense	1,500	
Rent Expense	900	
Insurance Expense	50	
Interest Expense	50	
Depreciation Expense	40	
	$30,190	$30,190

PIONEER ADVERTISING
Income Statement
For the Month Ended October 31, 2017

Revenues		
Service revenue		$10,600
Expenses		
Salaries and wages expense	$5,200	
Supplies expense	1,500	
Rent expense	900	
Insurance expense	50	
Interest expense	50	
Depreciation expense	40	
Total expenses		7,740
Net income		$ 2,860

PIONEER ADVERTISING
Owner's Equity Statement
For the Month Ended October 31, 2017

Owner's capital, October 1	$ -0-
Add: Investments	10,000
	10,000
Net income	2,860
	12,860
Owner's drawings	500
Owner's capital, October 31	$12,360

To balance sheet

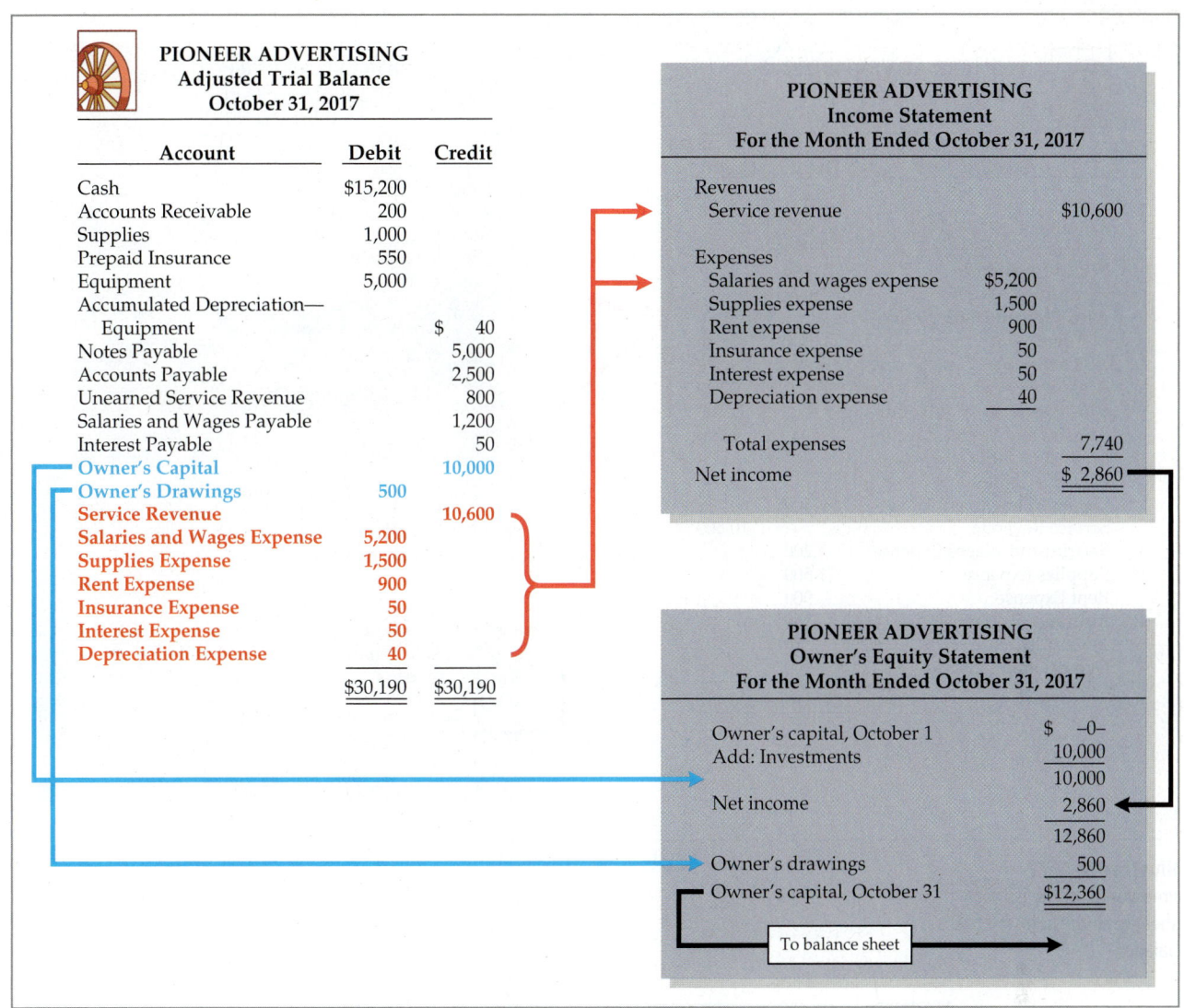

Illustration 3-26
Preparation of the income statement and owner's equity statement from the adjusted trial balance

As Illustration 3-27 (page 114) shows, companies then prepare the balance sheet from the asset and liability accounts and the ending owner's capital balance as reported in the owner's equity statement.

PIONEER ADVERTISING
Adjusted Trial Balance
October 31, 2017

Account	Debit	Credit
Cash	$15,200	
Accounts Receivable	200	
Supplies	1,000	
Prepaid Insurance	550	
Equipment	5,000	
Accumulated Depreciation—Equipment		$ 40
Notes Payable		5,000
Accounts Payable		2,500
Unearned Service Revenue		800
Salaries and Wages Payable		1,200
Interest Payable		50
Owner's Capital		10,000
Owner's Drawings	500	
Service Revenue		10,600
Salaries and Wages Expense	5,200	
Supplies Expense	1,500	
Rent Expense	900	
Insurance Expense	50	
Interest Expense	50	
Depreciation Expense	40	
	$30,190	$30,190

PIONEER ADVERTISING
Balance Sheet
October 31, 2017

Assets		
Cash		$15,200
Accounts receivable		200
Supplies		1,000
Prepaid insurance		550
Equipment	$5,000	
Less: Accumulated depreciation—equip.	40	4,960
Total assets		$21,910
Liabilities and Owner's Equity		
Liabilities		
Notes payable		$ 5,000
Accounts payable		2,500
Unearned service revenue		800
Salaries and wages payable		1,200
Interest payable		50
Total liabilities		9,550
Owner's equity		
Owner's capital		12,360
Total liabilities and owner's equity		$21,910

Capital balance at Oct. 31 from owner's equity statement in Illustration 3-26

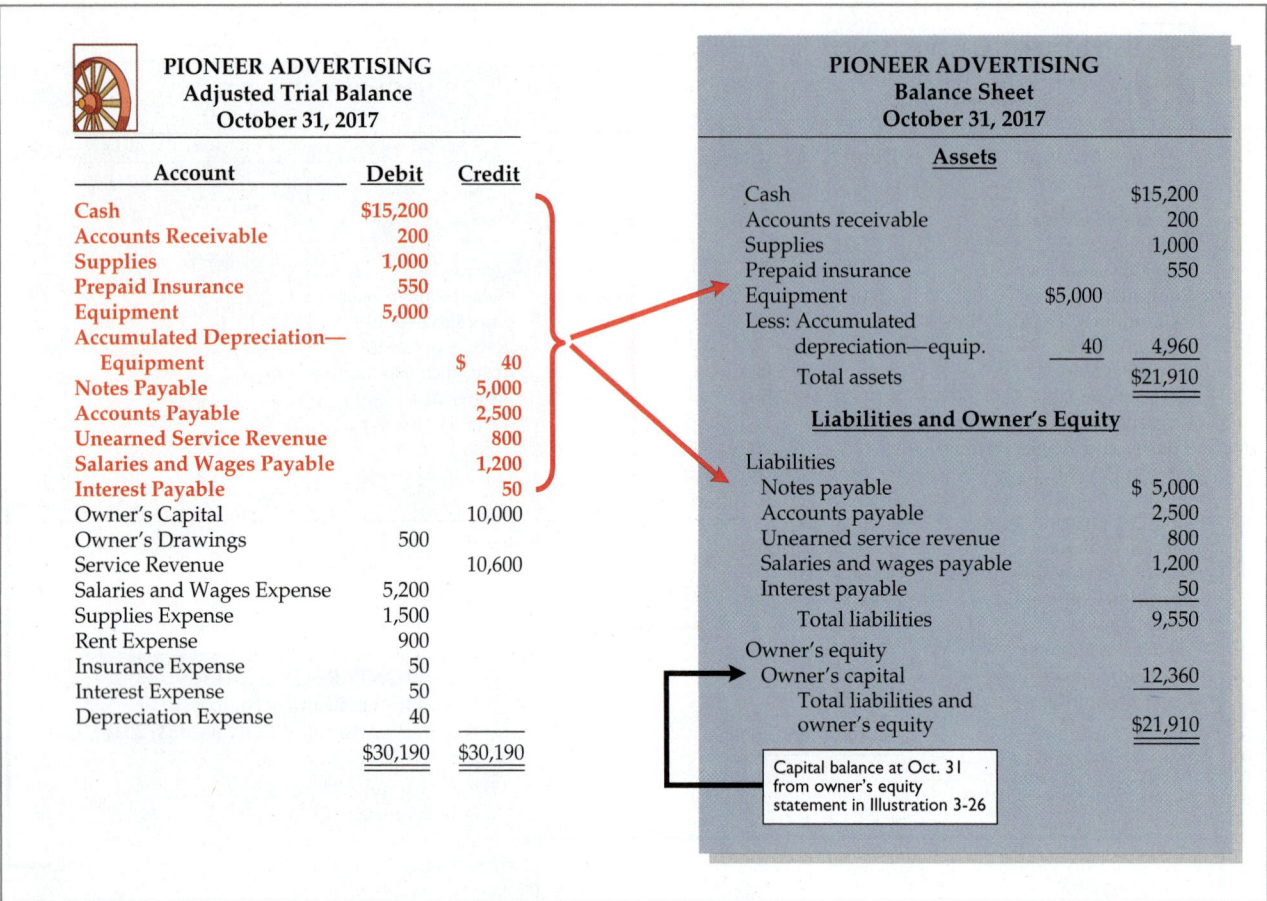

Illustration 3-27
Preparation of the balance sheet from the adjusted trial balance

DO IT! 4 Trial Balance

Skolnick Co. was organized on April 1, 2017. The company prepares quarterly financial statements. The adjusted trial balance amounts at June 30 are shown below.

	Debit		Credit
Cash	$ 6,700	Accumulated Depreciation—Equipment	$ 850
Accounts Receivable	600	Notes Payable	5,000
Prepaid Rent	900	Accounts Payable	1,510
Supplies	1,000	Salaries and Wages Payable	400
Equipment	15,000	Interest Payable	50
Owner's Drawings	600	Unearned Rent Revenue	500
Salaries and Wages Expense	9,400	Owner's Capital	14,000
Rent Expense	1,500	Service Revenue	14,200
Depreciation Expense	850	Rent Revenue	800
Supplies Expense	200		
Utilities Expense	510		
Interest Expense	50		
	$37,310		$37,310

(a) Determine the net income for the quarter April 1 to June 30.

(b) Determine the total assets and total liabilities at June 30, 2017, for Skolnick Co.

(c) Determine the amount of owner's capital at June 30, 2017.

Solution

(a) The net income is determined by adding revenues and subtracting expenses. The net income is computed as follows.

Revenues		
Service revenue	$14,200	
Rent revenue	800	
Total revenues		$15,000
Expenses		
Salaries and wages expense	9,400	
Rent expense	1,500	
Depreciation expense	850	
Utilities expense	510	
Supplies expense	200	
Interest expense	50	
Total expenses		12,510
Net income		$ 2,490

(b) Total assets and liabilities are computed as follows.

Assets			Liabilities	
Cash		$ 6,700	Notes payable	$5,000
Accounts receivable		600	Accounts payable	1,510
Supplies		1,000	Unearned rent revenue	500
Prepaid rent		900	Salaries and wages payable	400
Equipment	$15,000		Interest payable	50
Less: Accumulated depreciation—equipment	850	14,150		
Total assets		$23,350	Total liabilities	$7,460

(c)

Owner's capital, April 1	$ 0
Add: Investments	14,000
Net income	2,490
Less: Owner's drawings	600
Owner's capital, June 30	$15,890

Related exercise material: **BE3-9, BE3-10, E3-11, E3-12, E3-13, and DO IT! 3-4.**

Action Plan

- ✔ In an adjusted trial balance, all asset, liability, revenue, and expense accounts are properly stated.
- ✔ To determine the ending balance in Owner's Capital, add net income and subtract dividends.

LEARNING OBJECTIVE *5

APPENDIX 3A: Prepare adjusting entries for the alternative treatment of deferrals.

In discussing adjusting entries for prepaid expenses and unearned revenues, we illustrated transactions for which companies made the initial entries to balance sheet accounts. In the case of prepaid expenses, the company debited the prepayment to an asset account. In the case of unearned revenue, the company credited a liability account to record the cash received.

Some companies use an alternative treatment. (1) When a company prepays an expense, it debits that amount to an expense account. (2) When it receives payment for future services, it credits the amount to a revenue account. In this appendix, we describe the circumstances that justify such entries and the different adjusting entries that may be required. This alternative treatment of prepaid expenses and unearned revenues has the same effect on the financial statements as the procedures described in the chapter.

Prepaid Expenses

Prepaid expenses become expired costs either through the passage of time (e.g., insurance) or through consumption (e.g., advertising supplies). If at the time of purchase the company expects to consume the supplies before the next financial statement date, **it may choose to debit (increase) an expense account rather than an asset account. This alternative treatment is simply more convenient.**

Assume that Pioneer Advertising expects that it will use before the end of the month all of the supplies purchased on October 5. A debit of $2,500 to Supplies Expense (rather than to the asset account Supplies) on October 5 will eliminate the need for an adjusting entry on October 31. At October 31, the Supplies Expense account will show a balance of $2,500, which is the cost of supplies used between October 5 and October 31.

But what if the company does not use all the supplies? For example, what if an inventory of $1,000 of advertising supplies remains on October 31? Obviously, the company would need to make an adjusting entry. Prior to adjustment, the expense account Supplies Expense is overstated $1,000, and the asset account Supplies is understated $1,000. Thus, Pioneer makes the following adjusting entry.

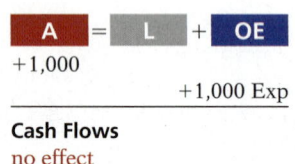

A	= L	+ OE
+1,000		
		+1,000 Exp

Cash Flows
no effect

Oct. 31	Supplies	1,000	
	Supplies Expense		1,000
	(To record supplies inventory)		

After the company posts the adjusting entry, the accounts show the following.

Illustration 3A-1
Prepaid expenses accounts after adjustment

Supplies

10/31	**Adj.**	**1,000**		

Supplies Expense

10/5		2,500	10/31	**Adj.**	**1,000**
10/31	**Bal.**	**1,500**			

After adjustment, the asset account Supplies shows a balance of $1,000, which is equal to the cost of supplies on hand at October 31. In addition, Supplies Expense shows a balance of $1,500. This is equal to the cost of supplies used between October 5 and October 31. Without the adjusting entry, expenses are overstated and net income is understated by $1,000 in the October income statement. Also, both assets and owner's equity are understated by $1,000 on the October 31 balance sheet.

Illustration 3A-2 compares the entries and accounts for advertising supplies in the two adjustment approaches.

Illustration 3A-2
Adjustment approaches—a comparison

Prepayment Initially Debited to Asset Account (per chapter)				Prepayment Initially Debited to Expense Account (per appendix)			
Oct. 5	Supplies	2,500		Oct. 5	Supplies Expense	2,500	
	Accounts Payable		2,500		Accounts Payable		2,500
Oct. 31	Supplies Expense	1,500		Oct. 31	Supplies	1,000	
	Supplies		1,500		Supplies Expense		1,000

After Pioneer posts the entries, the accounts appear as follows.

Illustration 3A-3
Comparison of accounts

(per chapter)

Supplies

10/5	2,500	10/31 **Adj.**	**1,500**
10/31 **Bal.**	**1,000**		

Supplies Expense

10/31 **Adj.**	**1,500**		

(per appendix)

Supplies

10/31 **Adj.**	**1,000**		

Supplies Expense

10/5	2,500	10/31 **Adj.**	**1,000**
10/31 **Bal.**	**1,500**		

Note that the account balances under each alternative are the same at October 31: Supplies $1,000 and Supplies Expense $1,500.

Unearned Revenues

Unearned revenues are recognized as revenue at the time services are performed. Similar to the case for prepaid expenses, companies may credit (increase) a revenue account when they receive cash for future services.

To illustrate, assume that Pioneer Advertising received $1,200 for future services on October 2. Pioneer expects to perform the services before October 31.[1] In such a case, the company credits Service Revenue. If Pioneer in fact performs the service before October 31, no adjustment is needed.

However, if at the statement date Pioneer has not performed $800 of the services, it would make an adjusting entry. Without the entry, the revenue account Service Revenue is overstated $800, and the liability account Unearned Service Revenue is understated $800. Thus, Pioneer makes the following adjusting entry.

Helpful Hint
The required adjusted balances here are Service Revenue $400 and Unearned Service Revenue $800.

Oct. 31	Service Revenue	800	
	Unearned Service Revenue		800
	(To record unearned service revenue)		

A	=	L	+	OE
				−800 Rev
		+800		

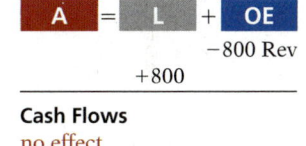

Cash Flows
no effect

After Pioneer posts the adjusting entry, the accounts show the following.

Illustration 3A-4
Unearned service revenue accounts after adjustment

Unearned Service Revenue

		10/31 **Adj.**	**800**

Service Revenue

10/31 **Adj.**	**800**	10/2	1,200
		10/31 **Bal.**	**400**

The liability account Unearned Service Revenue shows a balance of $800. This equals the services that will be performed in the future. In addition, the balance in Service Revenue equals the services performed in October. Without the adjusting entry, both revenues and net income are overstated by $800 in the October income statement. Also, liabilities are understated by $800 and owner's equity is overstated by $800 on the October 31 balance sheet.

[1]This example focuses only on the alternative treatment of unearned revenues. For simplicity, we have ignored the entries to Service Revenue pertaining to the immediate recognition of revenue ($10,000) and the adjusting entry for accrued revenue ($200).

Illustration 3A-5 compares the entries and accounts for initially recording unearned service revenue in (1) a liability account or (2) a revenue account.

Illustration 3A-5
Adjustment approaches—a comparison

Unearned Service Revenue Initially Credited to Liability Account (per chapter)				Unearned Service Revenue Initially Credited to Revenue Account (per appendix)			
Oct. 2	Cash	1,200		Oct. 2	Cash	1,200	
	Unearned Service Revenue		1,200		Service Revenue		1,200
Oct. 31	Unearned Service Revenue	400		Oct. 31	Service Revenue	800	
	Service Revenue		400		Unearned Service Revenue		800

After Pioneer posts the entries, the accounts appear as follows.

Illustration 3A-6
Comparison of accounts

(per chapter)

Unearned Service Revenue

Debit		Credit	
10/31 **Adj.**	**400**	10/2	1,200
		10/31 **Bal.**	**800**

Service Revenue

Debit		Credit	
		10/31 **Adj.**	**400**

(per appendix)

Unearned Service Revenue

Debit		Credit	
		10/31 **Adj.**	**800**

Service Revenue

Debit		Credit	
10/31 **Adj.**	**800**	10/2	1,200
		10/31 **Bal.**	**400**

Note that the balances in the accounts are the same under the two alternatives: Unearned Service Revenue $800 and Service Revenue $400.

Summary of Additional Adjustment Relationships

Illustration 3A-7
Summary of basic relationships for deferrals

Illustration 3A-7 provides a summary of basic relationships for deferrals.

Type of Adjustment	Reason for Adjustment	Account Balances before Adjustment	Adjusting Entry
1. Prepaid expenses	(a) Prepaid expenses initially recorded in asset accounts have been used.	Assets overstated. Expenses understated.	Dr. Expenses Cr. Assets
	(b) **Prepaid expenses initially recorded in expense accounts have not been used.**	**Assets understated.** **Expenses overstated.**	**Dr. Assets** **Cr. Expenses**
2. Unearned revenues	(a) Unearned revenues initially recorded in liability accounts are now recognized as revenue.	Liabilities overstated. Revenues understated.	Dr. Liabilities Cr. Revenues
	(b) **Unearned revenues initially recorded in revenue accounts are still unearned.**	**Liabilities understated.** **Revenues overstated.**	**Dr. Revenues** **Cr. Liabilities**

Alternative adjusting entries **do not apply** to accrued revenues and accrued expenses because **no entries occur before companies make these types of adjusting entries**.

LEARNING OBJECTIVE *6

APPENDIX 3B: Discuss financial reporting concepts.

This appendix provides a summary of the concepts in action used in this textbook. In addition, it provides other useful concepts which accountants use as a basis for recording and reporting financial information.

Qualities of Useful Information

Recently, the FASB completed the first phase of a project in which it developed a conceptual framework to serve as the basis for future accounting standards. The framework begins by stating that the primary objective of financial reporting is to provide financial information that is **useful** to investors and creditors for making decisions about providing capital. Useful information should possess two fundamental qualities, relevance and faithful representation, as shown in Illustration 3B-1.

Illustration 3B-1
Fundamental qualities of useful information

Relevance Accounting information has **relevance** if it would make a difference in a business decision. Information is considered relevant if it provides information that has **predictive value**, that is, helps provide accurate expectations about the future, and has **confirmatory value**, that is, confirms or corrects prior expectations. **Materiality** is a company-specific aspect of relevance. An item is material when its **size** makes it likely to influence the decision of an investor or creditor.

Faithful Representation **Faithful representation** means that information accurately depicts what really happened. To provide a faithful representation, information must be **complete** (nothing important has been omitted), **neutral** (is not biased toward one position or another), and **free from error**.

ENHANCING QUALITIES

In addition to the two fundamental qualities, the FASB also describes a number of enhancing qualities of useful information. These include **comparability**, **consistency**, **verifiability**, **timeliness**, and **understandability**. In accounting, **comparability** results when different companies use the same accounting principles. Another characteristic that enhances comparability is consistency. **Consistency** means that a company uses the same accounting principles and methods from year to year. Information is **verifiable** if independent observers, using the same methods, obtain similar results. For accounting information to have relevance, it must be **timely**. That is, it must be available to decision-makers before it loses its capacity to influence decisions. For example, public companies like Google or Best Buy provide their annual reports to investors within 60 days of their year-end. Information has the quality of **understandability** if it is presented in a clear and concise fashion, so that reasonably informed users of that information can interpret it and comprehend its meaning.

Assumptions in Financial Reporting

To develop accounting standards, the FASB relies on some key assumptions, as shown in Illustration 3B-2 (page 120). These include assumptions about the monetary unit, economic entity, time period, and going concern.

Illustration 3B-2
Key assumptions in financial reporting

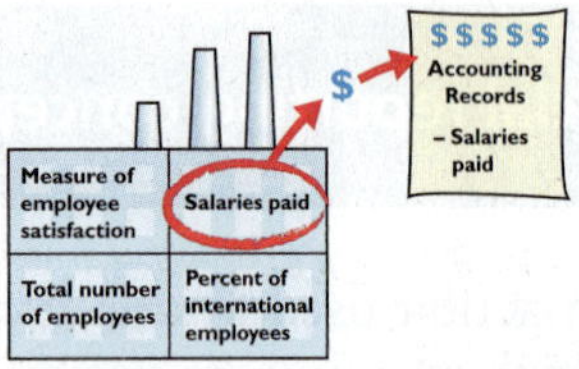

Monetary Unit Assumption The **monetary unit assumption** requires that only those things that can be expressed in money are included in the accounting records. This means that certain important information needed by investors, creditors, and managers, such as customer satisfaction, is not reported in the financial statements.

Economic Entity Assumption The **economic entity assumption** states that every economic entity can be separately identified and accounted for. In order to assess a company's performance and financial position accurately, it is important to not blur company transactions with personal transactions (especially those of its managers) or transactions of other companies.

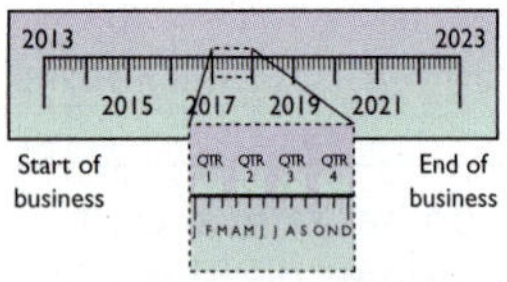

Time Period Assumption Notice that the income statement, retained earnings statement, and statement of cash flows all cover periods of one year, and the balance sheet is prepared at the end of each year. The **time period assumption** states that the life of a business can be divided into artificial time periods and that useful reports covering those periods can be prepared for the business.

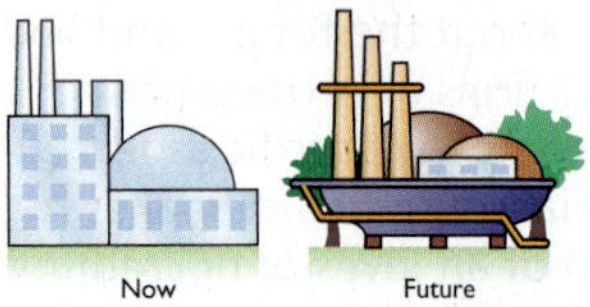

Going Concern Assumption The **going concern assumption** states that the business will remain in operation for the foreseeable future. Of course, many businesses do fail, but in general it is reasonable to assume that the business will continue operating.

Principles in Financial Reporting

MEASUREMENT PRINCIPLES

GAAP generally uses one of two measurement principles, the historical cost principle or the fair value principle. Selection of which principle to follow generally relates to trade-offs between relevance and faithful representation.

HISTORICAL COST PRINCIPLE The **historical cost principle** (or cost principle, discussed in Chapter 1) dictates that companies record assets at their cost. This is true not only at the time the asset is purchased but also over the time the asset is held. For example, if land that was purchased for $30,000 increases in value to $40,000, it continues to be reported at $30,000.

FAIR VALUE PRINCIPLE The **fair value principle** (discussed in Chapter 1) indicates that assets and liabilities should be reported at fair value (the price received to sell an asset or settle a liability). Fair value information may be more useful than historical cost for certain types of assets and liabilities. For example, certain investment securities are reported at fair value because market price information is often readily available for these types of assets. In choosing between cost and fair value, two qualities that make accounting information useful for decision-making are used—relevance and faithful representation. In determining which measurement principle to use, the factual nature of cost figures are weighed versus the relevance of fair value. In general, most assets follow the historical cost principle because fair values may not be representationally faithful. Only in situations where assets are actively traded, such as investment securities, is the fair value principle applied.

Prepaid expenses (prepayments) Expenses paid in cash before they are used or consumed. (p. 98).

***Relevance** The quality of information that indicates the information makes a difference in a decision. (p. 119).

Revenue recognition principle The principle that companies recognize revenue in the accounting period in which the performance obligation is satisfied. (pp. 95, 121).

***Timely** Information that is available to decision-makers before it loses its capacity to influence decisions. (p. 119).

Time period assumption An assumption that accountants can divide the economic life of a business into artificial time periods. (pp. 94, 120).

***Understandability** Information presented in a clear and concise fashion so that users can interpret it and comprehend its meaning. (p. 119).

Unearned revenues A liability recorded for cash received before services are performed. (p. 101).

Useful life The length of service of a long-lived asset. (p. 100).

***Verifiable** The quality of information that occurs when independent observers, using the same methods, obtain similar results. (p. 119).

PRACTICE MULTIPLE-CHOICE QUESTIONS

(LO 1) 1. The revenue recognition principle states that:
   (a) revenue should be recognized in the accounting period in which a performance obligation is satisfied.
   (b) expenses should be matched with revenues.
   (c) the economic life of a business can be divided into artificial time periods.
   (d) the fiscal year should correspond with the calendar year.

(LO 1) 2. The time period assumption states that:
   (a) companies must wait until the calendar year is completed to prepare financial statements.
   (b) companies use the fiscal year to report financial information.
   (c) the economic life of a business can be divided into artificial time periods.
   (d) companies record information in the time period in which the events occur.

(LO 1) 3. Which of the following statements about the accrual basis of accounting is **false**?
   (a) Events that change a company's financial statements are recorded in the periods in which the events occur.
   (b) Revenue is recognized in the period in which services are performed.
   (c) This basis is in accord with generally accepted accounting principles.
   (d) Revenue is recorded only when cash is received, and expense is recorded only when cash is paid.

(LO 1) 4. The principle or assumption dictating that efforts (expenses) be matched with accomplishments (revenues) is the:
   (a) expense recognition principle.
   (b) cost assumption.
   (c) time period assumption.
   (d) revenue recognition principle.

(LO 1) 5. Adjusting entries are made to ensure that:
   (a) expenses are recognized in the period in which they are incurred.
   (b) revenues are recorded in the period in which services are performed.
   (c) balance sheet and income statement accounts have correct balances at the end of an accounting period.
   (d) All the responses above are correct.

6. Each of the following is a major type (or category) of adjusting entries **except**: (LO 1)
   (a) prepaid expenses.
   (b) accrued revenues.
   (c) accrued expenses.
   (d) recognized revenues.

7. The trial balance shows Supplies $1,350 and Supplies Expense $0. If $600 of supplies are on hand at the end of the period, the adjusting entry is: (LO 2)

(a) Supplies	600	
Supplies Expense		600
(b) Supplies	750	
Supplies Expense		750
(c) Supplies Expense	750	
Supplies		750
(d) Supplies Expense	600	
Supplies		600

8. Adjustments for prepaid expenses: (LO 2)
   (a) decrease assets and increase revenues.
   (b) decrease expenses and increase assets.
   (c) decrease assets and increase expenses.
   (d) decrease revenues and increase assets.

9. Accumulated Depreciation is: (LO 2)
   (a) a contra asset account.
   (b) an expense account.
   (c) an owner's equity account.
   (d) a liability account.

10. Rivera Company computes depreciation on delivery equipment at $1,000 for the month of June. The adjusting entry to record this depreciation is as follows. (LO 2)

(a) Depreciation Expense	1,000	
Accumulated Depreciation—Rivera Company		1,000
(b) Depreciation Expense	1,000	
Equipment		1,000
(c) Depreciation Expense	1,000	
Accumulated Depreciation—Equipment		1,000
(d) Equipment Expense	1,000	
Accumulated Depreciation—Equipment		1,000

11. Adjustments for unearned revenues: (LO 2)
   (a) decrease liabilities and increase revenues.
   (b) have an assets-and-revenues-account relationship.

(c) increase assets and increase revenues.
(d) decrease revenues and decrease assets.

(LO 3) **12.** Adjustments for accrued revenues:
(a) have a liabilities-and-revenues-account relationship.
(b) have an assets-and-revenues-account relationship.
(c) decrease assets and revenues.
(d) decrease liabilities and increase revenues.

(LO 3) **13.** Anika Wilson earned a salary of $400 for the last week of September. She will be paid on October 1. The adjusting entry for Anika's employer at September 30 is:

(a) No entry is required.

(b) Salaries and Wages Expense	400	
Salaries and Wages Payable		400
(c) Salaries and Wages Expense	400	
Cash		400
(d) Salaries and Wages Payable	400	
Cash		400

(LO 4) **14.** Which of the following statements is **incorrect** concerning the adjusted trial balance?
(a) An adjusted trial balance proves the equality of the total debit balances and the total credit balances in the ledger after all adjustments are made.
(b) The adjusted trial balance provides the primary basis for the preparation of financial statements.
(c) The adjusted trial balance lists the account balances segregated by assets and liabilities.
(d) The adjusted trial balance is prepared after the adjusting entries have been journalized and posted.

***15.** The trial balance shows Supplies $0 and Supplies Expense $1,500. If $800 of supplies are on hand at the end of the period, the adjusting entry is: (LO 5)
(a) debit Supplies $800 and credit Supplies Expense $800.
(b) debit Supplies Expense $800 and credit Supplies $800.
(c) debit Supplies $700 and credit Supplies Expense $700.
(d) debit Supplies Expense $700 and credit Supplies $700.

***16.** Neutrality is an ingredient of: (LO 6)

	Faithful Representation	Relevance
(a)	Yes	Yes
(b)	No	No
(c)	Yes	No
(d)	No	Yes

***17.** Which item is a constraint in financial accounting? (LO 6)
(a) Comparability.
(b) Materiality.
(c) Cost.
(d) Consistency.

Solutions

1. (a) Revenue should be recognized in the accounting period in which a performance obligation is satisfied. The other choices are incorrect because (b) defines the expense recognition principle, (c) describes the time period assumption, and (d) a company's fiscal year does not need to correspond with the calendar year.

2. (c) The economic life of a business can be divided into artificial time periods. The other choices are incorrect because (a) companies report their activities on a more frequent basis and not necessarily based on a calendar year; (b) companies report financial information more frequently than annually, such as monthly or quarterly, in order to evaluate results of operations; and (d) describes accrual-basis accounting.

3. (d) Under the accrual basis of accounting, revenue is recognized when the performance obligation is satisfied, not when cash is received, and expense is recognized when incurred, not when cash is paid. The other choices are all true statements.

4. (a) The expense recognition principle dictates that expenses be matched with revenues. The other choices are incorrect because (b) there is no cost assumption, but the historical cost principle states that assets should be recorded at their cost; (c) the time period assumption states that the economic life of a business can be divided into artificial time periods; and (d) the revenue recognition principle indicates that revenue should be recognized in the accounting period in which a performance obligation is satisfied.

5. (d) Adjusting entries are made for the reasons noted in choices (a), (b), and (c). The other choices are true statements, but (d) is the better answer.

6. (d) Unearned revenues, not recognized revenues, are one of the major categories of adjusting entries. The other choices all list one of the major categories of adjusting entries.

7. (c) Debiting Supplies Expense for $750 and crediting Supplies for $750 will decrease Supplies and increase Supplies Expense. The other choices are incorrect because (a) will increase Supplies and decrease Supplies Expense and also for the wrong amounts, (b) will increase Supplies and decrease Supplies Expense, and (d) will cause Supplies to have an incorrect balance of $750 ($1,350 − $600) and Supplies Expense to have an incorrect balance of $600 ($0 + $600).

8. (c) Adjustments for prepaid expenses decrease assets and increase expenses. The other choices are incorrect because an adjusting entry for prepaid expenses (a) increases expenses, not revenues; (b) increases, not decreases, expenses and decreases, not increases, assets; and (d) increases expenses, not decreases, revenues and decreases, not increases, assets.

9. (a) Accumulated Depreciation is a contra asset account; it is offset against an asset account on the balance sheet. The other choices are incorrect because Accumulated Depreciation is not (b) an expense account nor located on the income statement, (c) an owner's equity account, or (d) a liability account.

10. (c) The adjusting entry is to debit Depreciation Expense and credit Accumulated Depreciation—Equipment. The other choices are incorrect because (a) the contra asset account title includes the asset being depreciated, not the company name; (b) the credit should be to the contra asset account, not directly to the asset; and (d) the debit for this entry should be Depreciation Expense, not Equipment Expense.

11. (a) Adjustments for unearned revenues will consist of a debit (decrease) to unearned revenues (a liability) and a credit (increase) to a revenue account. Choices (b), (c), and (d) are incorrect because adjustments for unearned revenues will increase revenues but will have no effect on assets.

12. (b) Adjustments for accrued revenues will have an assets-and-revenues-account relationship. Choices (a) and (d) are incorrect because adjustments for accrued revenues have no effect on liabilities. Choice (c) is incorrect because these adjustments will increase, not decrease, both assets and revenues.

13. (b) The adjusting entry should be to debit Salaries and Wages Expense for $400 and credit Salaries and Wages Payable for $400. The other choices are incorrect because (a) if an adjusting entry is not made, the amount of money owed (liability) that is shown on the balance sheet will be understated and the amount of salaries and wages expense will also be understated; (c) the credit account is incorrect as adjusting entries never affect cash; and (d) the debit account should be Salaries and Wages Expense and the credit account should be Salaries and Wages Payable. Adjusting entries never affect cash.

14. (c) The accounts on the trial balance can be segregated by the balance in the account—either debit or credit—not whether they are assets or liabilities. All accounts in the ledger are included in the adjusted trial balance, not just assets and liabilities. The other choices are all true statements.

***15. (a)** This adjusting entry correctly states the Supplies account at $800 ($0 + $800) and the Supplies Expense account at $700 ($1,500 − $800). The other choices are incorrect because (b) will cause the Supplies account to have a credit balance (assets have a normal debit balance) and the Supplies Expense account to be stated at $2,300, which is too high; (c) will result in a $700 balance in the Supplies account ($100 too low) and an $800 balance in the Supplies Expense account ($100 too high); and (d) will cause the Supplies account to have a credit balance (assets have a normal debit balance) and the Supplies Expense account to be stated at $2,200, which is too high.

***16. (c)** Neutrality is one of the enhancing qualities that makes information more representationally faithful, not relevant. Therefore, choices (a), (b), and (d) are incorrect.

***17. (c)** Cost is a constraint in financial accounting. The other choices are all enhancing qualities of useful information.

PRACTICE EXERCISES

Prepare adjusting entries. (LO 2, 3)

1. Evan Watts, D.D.S., opened a dental practice on January 1, 2017. During the first month of operations, the following transactions occurred.

1. Watts performed services for patients totaling $2,400. These services have not yet been recorded.
2. Utility expenses incurred but not paid prior to January 31 totaled $400.
3. Purchased dental equipment on January 1 for $80,000, paying $20,000 in cash and signing a $60,000, 3-year note payable. The equipment depreciates $500 per month. Interest is $600 per month.
4. Purchased a one-year malpractice insurance policy on January 1 for $12,000.
5. Purchased $2,600 of dental supplies. On January 31, determined that $900 of supplies were on hand.

Instructions

Prepare the adjusting entries on January 31. Account titles are Accumulated Depreciation—Equipment, Depreciation Expense, Service Revenue, Accounts Receivable, Insurance Expense, Interest Expense, Interest Payable, Prepaid Insurance, Supplies, Supplies Expense, Utilities Expense, and Utilities Payable.

Solution

1.	JANUARY 31		
Jan. 31	Accounts Receivable	2,400	
	Service Revenue		2,400
	Utilities Expense	400	
	Utilities Payable		400
	Depreciation Expense	500	
	Accumulated Depreciation—Equipment		500
	Interest Expense	600	
	Interest Payable		600
	Insurance Expense ($12,000 ÷ 12)	1,000	
	Prepaid Insurance		1,000
	Supplies Expense ($2,600 − $900)	1,700	
	Supplies		1,700

Prepare correct income statement.

(LO 2, 3, 4)

2. The income statement of Venden Co. for the month of July shows net income of $4,000 based on Service Revenue $8,700, Salaries and Wages Expense $2,500, Supplies Expense $1,700, and Utilities Expense $500. In reviewing the statement, you discover the following.

1. Insurance expired during July of $700 was omitted.
2. Supplies expense includes $250 of supplies that are still on hand at July 31.
3. Depreciation on equipment of $300 was omitted.
4. Accrued but unpaid wages at July 31 of $400 were not included.
5. Services performed but unrecorded totaled $650.

Instructions

Prepare a correct income statement for July 2017.

Solution

2.

VENDEN CO.
Income Statement
For the Month Ended July 31, 2017

Revenues		
Service revenue ($8,700 + $650)		$9,350
Expenses		
Salaries and wages expense ($2,500 + $400)	$2,900	
Supplies expense ($1,700 − $250)	1,450	
Utilities expense	500	
Insurance expense	700	
Depreciation expense	300	
Total expenses		5,850
Net income		$3,500

PRACTICE PROBLEM

Prepare adjusting entries from selected data.

(LO 2, 3)

The Green Thumb Lawn Care Company began operations on April 1. At April 30, the trial balance shows the following balances for selected accounts.

Prepaid Insurance	$ 3,600
Equipment	28,000
Notes Payable	20,000
Unearned Service Revenue	4,200
Service Revenue	1,800

Analysis reveals the following additional data.

1. Prepaid insurance is the cost of a 2-year insurance policy, effective April 1.
2. Depreciation on the equipment is $500 per month.
3. The note payable is dated April 1. It is a 6-month, 12% note.
4. Seven customers paid for the company's 6-month lawn service package of $600 beginning in April. The company performed services for these customers in April.
5. Lawn services performed for other customers but not recorded at April 30 totaled $1,500.

Instructions

Prepare the adjusting entries for the month of April. Show computations.

Solution

GENERAL JOURNAL					J1
Date	**Account Titles and Explanation**	**Ref.**	**Debit**	**Credit**
	Adjusting Entries			
Apr. 30	Insurance Expense		150	
	Prepaid Insurance			150
	(To record insurance expired: $3,600 ÷ 24 = $150 per month)			
30	Depreciation Expense		500	
	Accumulated Depreciation—Equipment			500
	(To record monthly depreciation)			
30	Interest Expense		200	
	Interest Payable			200
	(To record interest on notes payable: $20,000 × 12% × 1/12 = $200)			
30	Unearned Service Revenue		700	
	Service Revenue			700
	(To record revenue for services performed: $600 ÷ 6 = $100; $100 per month × 7 = $700)			
30	Accounts Receivable		1,500	
	Service Revenue			1,500
	(To record revenue for services performed)			

WileyPLUS Brief Exercises, Exercises, DO IT! Exercises, and Problems and many additional resources are available for practice in WileyPLUS

NOTE: All asterisked Questions, Exercises, and Problems relate to material in the appendices to the chapter.

QUESTIONS

1. (a) How does the time period assumption affect an accountant's analysis of business transactions?
   (b) Explain the terms fiscal year, calendar year, and interim periods.
2. Define two generally accepted accounting principles that relate to adjusting the accounts.
3. Susan Hardy, a lawyer, accepts a legal engagement in March, performs the work in April, and is paid in May. If Hardy's law firm prepares monthly financial statements, when should it recognize revenue from this engagement? Why?
4. Why do accrual-basis financial statements provide more useful information than cash-basis statements?
5. In completing the engagement in Question 3, Hardy pays no costs in March, $2,000 in April, and $2,500 in May (incurred in April). How much expense should the firm deduct from revenues in the month when it recognizes the revenue? Why?
6. "Adjusting entries are required by the historical cost principle of accounting." Do you agree? Explain.
7. Why may a trial balance not contain up-to-date and complete financial information?
8. Distinguish between the two categories of adjusting entries, and identify the types of adjustments applicable to each category.
9. What is the debit/credit effect of a prepaid expense adjusting entry?
10. "Depreciation is a valuation process that results in the reporting of the fair value of the asset." Do you agree? Explain.
11. Explain the differences between depreciation expense and accumulated depreciation.
12. G. Phillips Company purchased equipment for $18,000. By the current balance sheet date, $6,000 had been depreciated. Indicate the balance sheet presentation of the data.
13. What is the debit/credit effect of an unearned revenue adjusting entry?
14. A company fails to recognize revenue for services performed but not yet received in cash or recorded. Which of the following accounts are involved in the adjusting entry: (a) asset, (b) liability, (c) revenue, or (d) expense? For the accounts selected, indicate whether they would be debited or credited in the entry.
15. A company fails to recognize an expense incurred but not paid. Indicate which of the following accounts is debited and which is credited in the adjusting entry: (a) asset, (b) liability, (c) revenue, or (d) expense.
16. A company makes an accrued revenue adjusting entry for $900 and an accrued expense adjusting entry for

$700. How much was net income understated prior to these entries? Explain.

17. On January 9, a company pays $5,000 for salaries and wages of which $2,000 was reported as Salaries and Wages Payable on December 31. Give the entry to record the payment.

18. For each of the following items before adjustment, indicate the type of adjusting entry (prepaid expense, unearned revenue, accrued revenue, or accrued expense) that is needed to correct the misstatement. If an item could result in more than one type of adjusting entry, indicate each of the types.
    (a) Assets are understated.
    (b) Liabilities are overstated.
    (c) Liabilities are understated.
    (d) Expenses are understated.
    (e) Assets are overstated.
    (f) Revenue is understated.

19. One-half of the adjusting entry is given below. Indicate the account title for the other half of the entry.
    (a) Salaries and Wages Expense is debited.
    (b) Depreciation Expense is debited.
    (c) Interest Payable is credited.
    (d) Supplies is credited.
    (e) Accounts Receivable is debited.
    (f) Unearned Service Revenue is debited.

20. "An adjusting entry may affect more than one balance sheet or income statement account." Do you agree? Why or why not?

21. Why is it possible to prepare financial statements directly from an adjusted trial balance?

*22. Dashan Company debits Supplies Expense for all purchases of supplies and credits Rent Revenue for all advanced rentals. For each type of adjustment, give the adjusting entry.

*23. (a) What is the primary objective of financial reporting?
    (b) Identify the characteristics of useful accounting information.

*24. Dan Fineman, the president of King Company, is pleased. King substantially increased its net income in 2017 while keeping its unit inventory relatively the same. Howard Gross, chief accountant, cautions Dan, however. Gross says that since King changed its method of inventory valuation, there is a consistency problem and it is difficult to determine whether King is better off. Is Gross correct? Why or why not?

*25. What is the distinction between comparability and consistency?

*26. Describe the constraint inherent in the presentation of accounting information.

*27. Quinn Becker is president of Better Books. She has no accounting background. Becker cannot understand why fair value is not used as the basis for all accounting measurement and reporting. Discuss.

*28. What is the economic entity assumption? Give an example of its violation.

BRIEF EXERCISES

Indicate why adjusting entries are needed.
(LO 1)

BE3-1 The ledger of Althukair Company includes the following accounts. Explain why each account may require adjustment.

(a) Prepaid Insurance.
(b) Depreciation Expense.
(c) Unearned Service Revenue.
(d) Interest Payable.

Identify the major types of adjusting entries.
(LO 1, 2)

BE3-2 Kee Company accumulates the following adjustment data at December 31. Indicate (a) the type of adjustment (prepaid expense, accrued revenue, and so on), and (b) the status of accounts before adjustment (overstated or understated).

1. Supplies of $100 are on hand.
2. Services performed but not recorded total $900.
3. Interest of $200 has accumulated on a note payable.
4. Rent collected in advance totaling $650 has been earned.

Prepare adjusting entry for supplies.
(LO 2)

BE3-3 Schramel Advertising Company's trial balance at December 31 shows Supplies $6,700 and Supplies Expense $0. On December 31, there are $2,100 of supplies on hand. Prepare the adjusting entry at December 31, and using T-accounts, enter the balances in the accounts, post the adjusting entry, and indicate the adjusted balance in each account.

Prepare adjusting entry for depreciation.
(LO 2)

BE3-4 At the end of its first year, the trial balance of Bronowski Company shows Equipment $30,000 and zero balances in Accumulated Depreciation—Equipment and Depreciation Expense. Depreciation for the year is estimated to be $4,000. Prepare the adjusting entry for depreciation at December 31, post the adjustments to T-accounts, and indicate the balance sheet presentation of the equipment at December 31.

Prepare adjusting entry for prepaid expense.
(LO 2)

BE3-5 On July 1, 2017, Major Co. pays $15,120 to Cruz Insurance Co. for a 3-year insurance contract. Both companies have fiscal years ending December 31. For Major Co., journalize and post the entry on July 1 and the adjusting entry on December 31.

Prepare adjusting entry for unearned revenue.

(LO 2)

BE3-6 Using the data in BE3-5, journalize and post the entry on July 1 and the adjusting entry on December 31 for Cruz Insurance Co. Cruz uses the accounts Unearned Service Revenue and Service Revenue.

Prepare adjusting entries for accruals.

(LO 3)

BE3-7 The bookkeeper for Abduli Company asks you to prepare the following accrued adjusting entries at December 31.

1. Interest on notes payable of $400 is accrued.
2. Services performed but not recorded total $2,300.
3. Salaries earned by employees of $900 have not been recorded.

Use the following account titles: Service Revenue, Accounts Receivable, Interest Expense, Interest Payable, Salaries and Wages Expense, and Salaries and Wages Payable.

Analyze accounts in an unadjusted trial balance.

(LO 1, 2, 3)

BE3-8 The trial balance of Obenauf Company includes the following balance sheet accounts, which may require adjustment. For each account that requires adjustment, indicate (a) the type of adjusting entry (prepaid expense, unearned revenue, accrued revenue, or accrued expense) and (b) the related account in the adjusting entry.

Accounts Receivable	Interest Payable
Prepaid Insurance	Unearned Service Revenue
Accumulated Depreciation—Equipment	

Prepare an income statement from an adjusted trial balance.

(LO 4)

BE3-9 The adjusted trial balance of Wilder Company at December 31, 2017, includes the following accounts: Owner's Capital $15,600, Owner's Drawings $7,000, Service Revenue $39,000, Salaries and Wages Expense $16,000, Insurance Expense $2,000, Rent Expense $4,000, Supplies Expense $1,500, and Depreciation Expense $1,300. Prepare an income statement for the year.

Prepare an owner's equity statement from an adjusted trial balance.

(LO 4)

BE3-10 Partial adjusted trial balance data for Wilder Company is presented in BE3-9. The balance in Owner's Capital is the balance as of January 1. Prepare an owner's equity statement for the year assuming net income is $14,200 for the year.

Prepare adjusting entries under alternative treatment of deferrals.

(LO 5)

***BE3-11** Eckholm Company records all prepayments in income statement accounts. At April 30, the trial balance shows Supplies Expense $2,800, Service Revenue $9,200, and zero balances in related balance sheet accounts. Prepare the adjusting entries at April 30 assuming (a) $400 of supplies on hand and (b) $3,000 of service revenue should be reported as unearned.

Identify characteristics of useful information.

(LO 6)

***BE3-12** The accompanying chart shows the qualitative characteristics of useful accounting information. Fill in the blanks.

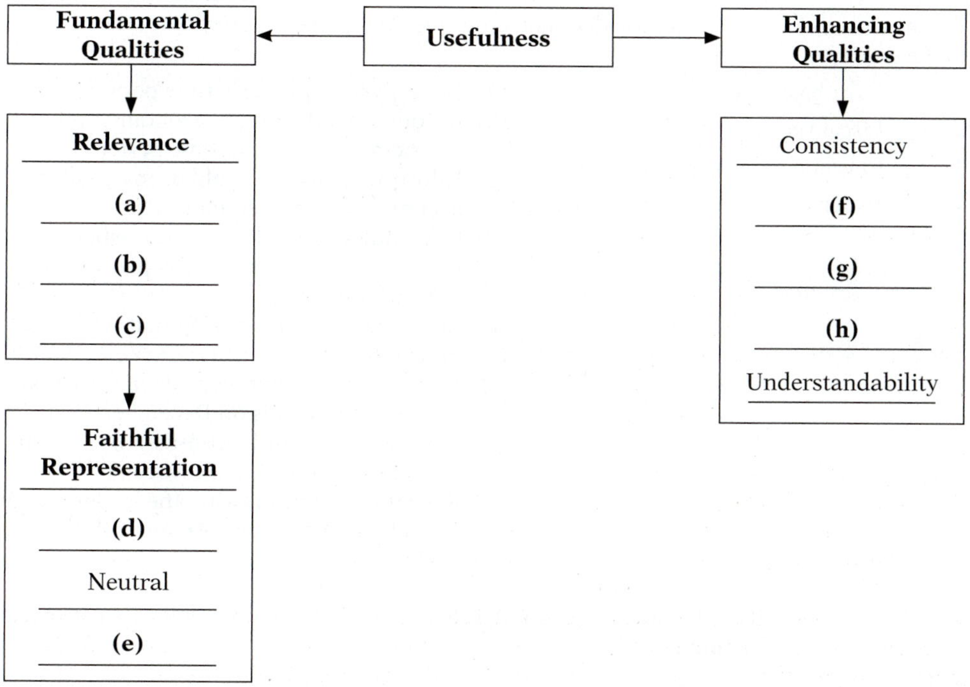

Identify characteristics of useful information.

(LO 6)

***BE3-13** Given the characteristics of useful accounting information, complete each of the following statements.

(a) For information to be _____, it should have predictive value, confirmatory value, and be material.

(b) _____ is the quality of information that gives assurance that the information accurately depicts what really happened.

(c) _____ means using the same accounting principles and methods from year to year within a company.

Identify characteristics of useful information.

(LO 6)

***BE3-14** Here are some qualitative characteristics of useful accounting information:

1. Predictive value.
2. Neutral.
3. Verifiable.
4. Timely.

Match each qualitative characteristic to one of the following statements.

_______ (a) Accounting information should help provide accurate expectations about future events.

_______ (b) Accounting information cannot be selected, prepared, or presented to favor one set of interested users over another.

_______ (c) The quality of information that occurs when independent observers, using the same methods, obtain similar results.

_______ (d) Accounting information must be available to decision-makers before it loses its capacity to influence their decisions.

Define full disclosure principle.

(LO 6)

***BE3-15** Select the response that completes the following statement correctly. The full disclosure principle dictates that:

(a) financial statements should disclose all assets at their cost.

(b) financial statements should disclose only those events that can be measured in currency.

(c) financial statements should disclose all events and circumstances that would matter to users of financial statements.

(d) financial statements should not be relied on unless an auditor has expressed an unqualified opinion on them.

DO IT! Exercises

Identify timing concepts.

(LO 1)

DO IT! 3-1 Several timing concepts are discussed on pages 94–95. A list of concepts is provided below in the left column, with a description of the concept in the right column. There are more descriptions provided than concepts. Match the description of the concept to the concept.

1. ____ Cash-basis accounting.
2. ____ Fiscal year.
3. ____ Revenue recognition principle.
4. ____ Expense recognition principle.

(a) Monthly and quarterly time periods.

(b) Accountants divide the economic life of a business into artificial time periods.

(c) Efforts (expenses) should be matched with accomplishments (revenues).

(d) Companies record revenues when they receive cash and record expenses when they pay out cash.

(e) An accounting time period that is one year in length.

(f) An accounting time period that starts on January 1 and ends on December 31.

(g) Companies record transactions in the period in which the events occur.

(h) Recognize revenue in the accounting period in which a performance obligation is satisfied.

Prepare adjusting entries for deferrals.

(LO 2)

DO IT! 3-2 The ledger of Jahnke, Inc. on March 31, 2017, includes the following selected accounts before adjusting entries.

	Debit	Credit
Prepaid Insurance	2,400	
Supplies	2,500	
Equipment	30,000	
Unearned Service Revenue		9,000

An analysis of the accounts shows the following.

1. Insurance expires at the rate of $300 per month.
2. Supplies on hand total $1,100.
3. The equipment depreciates $480 per month.
4. During March, services were performed for two-fifths of the unearned service revenue.

Prepare the adjusting entries for the month of March.

DO IT! 3-3 Fiske Computer Services began operations in July 2017. At the end of the month, the company prepares monthly financial statements. It has the following information for the month.

Prepare adjusting entries for accruals.

(LO 3)

1. At July 31, the company owed employees $1,300 in salaries that the company will pay in August.
2. On July 1, the company borrowed $20,000 from a local bank on a 10-year note. The annual interest rate is 6%.
3. Service revenue unrecorded in July totaled $2,400.

Prepare the adjusting entries needed at July 31, 2017.

DO IT! 3-4 Yang Co. was organized on April 1, 2017. The company prepares quarterly financial statements. The adjusted trial balance amounts at June 30 are shown below.

Calculate amounts from trial balance.

(LO 4)

	Debit		Credit
Cash	$ 5,360	Accumulated Depreciation— Equipment	$ 700
Accounts Receivable	480	Notes Payable	4,000
Prepaid Rent	720	Accounts Payable	790
Supplies	920	Salaries and Wages Payable	300
Equipment	12,000	Interest Payable	40
Owner's Drawings	500	Unearned Rent Revenue	400
Salaries and Wages Expense	7,400	Owner's Capital	11,200
Rent Expense	1,200	Service Revenue	11,360
Depreciation Expense	700	Rent Revenue	1,100
Supplies Expense	160		$29,890
Utilities Expense	410		
Interest Expense	40		
	$29,890		

(a) Determine the net income for the quarter April 1 to June 30.
(b) Determine the total assets and total liabilities at June 30, 2017, for Yang Company.
(c) Determine the amount that appears for Owner's Capital at June 30, 2017.

EXERCISES

E3-1 Chloe Davis has prepared the following list of statements about the time period assumption.

Explain the time period assumption.

(LO 1)

1. Adjusting entries would not be necessary if a company's life were not divided into artificial time periods.
2. The IRS requires companies to file annual tax returns.
3. Accountants divide the economic life of a business into artificial time periods, but each transaction affects only one of these periods.
4. Accounting time periods are generally a month, a quarter, or a year.
5. A time period lasting one year is called an interim period.
6. All fiscal years are calendar years, but not all calendar years are fiscal years.

Instructions
Identify each statement as true or false. If false, indicate how to correct the statement.

Distinguish between cash and accrual basis of accounting.
(LO 1)

E3-2 On numerous occasions, proposals have surfaced to put the federal government on the accrual basis of accounting. This is no small issue. If this basis were used, it would mean that billions in unrecorded liabilities would have to be booked, and the federal deficit would increase substantially.

Instructions
(a) What is the difference between accrual-basis accounting and cash-basis accounting?
(b) Why would politicians prefer the cash basis over the accrual basis?
(c) Write a letter to your senator explaining why the federal government should adopt the accrual basis of accounting.

Compute cash and accrual accounting income.
(LO 1)

E3-3 Carillo Industries collected $108,000 from customers in 2017. Of the amount collected, $25,000 was for services performed in 2016. In addition, Carillo performed services worth $36,000 in 2017, which will not be collected until 2018.

Carillo Industries also paid $72,000 for expenses in 2017. Of the amount paid, $30,000 was for expenses incurred on account in 2016. In addition, Carillo incurred $42,000 of expenses in 2017, which will not be paid until 2018.

Instructions
(a) Compute 2017 cash-basis net income.
(b) Compute 2017 accrual-basis net income.

Identify the type of adjusting entry needed.
(LO 1, 2, 3)

E3-4 Hong Corporation encounters the following situations:

1. Hong collects $1,300 from a customer in 2017 for services to be performed in 2018.
2. Hong incurs utility expense which is not yet paid in cash or recorded.
3. Hong's employees worked 3 days in 2017 but will not be paid until 2018.
4. Hong performs services for customers but has not yet received cash or recorded the transaction.
5. Hong paid $2,400 rent on December 1 for the 4 months starting December 1.
6. Hong received cash for future services and recorded a liability until the service was performed.
7. Hong performed consulting services for a client in December 2017. On December 31, it had not billed the client for services provided of $1,200.
8. Hong paid cash for an expense and recorded an asset until the item was used up.
9. Hong purchased $900 of supplies in 2017; at year-end, $400 of supplies remain unused.
10. Hong purchased equipment on January 1, 2017; the equipment will be used for 5 years.
11. Hong borrowed $10,000 on October 1, 2017, signing an 8% one-year note payable.

Instructions
Identify what type of adjusting entry (prepaid expense, unearned revenue, accrued expense, or accrued revenue) is needed in each situation at December 31, 2017.

Prepare adjusting entries from selected data.
(LO 2, 3)

E3-5 Devin Wolf Company has the following balances in selected accounts on December 31, 2017.

Accounts Receivable	$ –0–
Accumulated Depreciation—Equipment	–0–
Equipment	7,000
Interest Payable	–0–
Notes Payable	10,000
Prepaid Insurance	2,100
Salaries and Wages Payable	–0–
Supplies	2,450
Unearned Service Revenue	30,000

All the accounts have normal balances. The information below has been gathered at December 31, 2017.

1. Devin Wolf Company borrowed $10,000 by signing a 9%, one-year note on September 1, 2017.

2. A count of supplies on December 31, 2017, indicates that supplies of $900 are on hand.
3. Depreciation on the equipment for 2017 is $1,000.
4. Devin Wolf Company paid $2,100 for 12 months of insurance coverage on June 1, 2017.
5. On December 1, 2017, Devin Wolf collected $32,000 for consulting services to be performed from December 1, 2017, through March 31, 2018.
6. Devin Wolf performed consulting services for a client in December 2017. The client will be billed $4,200.
7. Devin Wolf Company pays its employees total salaries of $9,000 every Monday for the preceding 5-day week (Monday through Friday). On Monday, December 29, employees were paid for the week ending December 26. All employees worked the last 3 days of 2017.

Instructions

Prepare adjusting entries for the seven items described above.

Identify types of adjustments and account relationships.

(LO 2, 3, 4)

E3-6 Zaragoza Company accumulates the following adjustment data at December 31.

1. Services performed but not recorded total $1,000.
2. Supplies of $300 have been used.
3. Utility expenses of $225 are unpaid.
4. Services related to unearned service revenue of $260 were performed.
5. Salaries of $800 are unpaid.
6. Prepaid insurance totaling $350 has expired.

Instructions

For each of the above items indicate the following.

(a) The type of adjustment (prepaid expense, unearned revenue, accrued revenue, or accrued expense).
(b) The status of accounts before adjustment (overstatement or understatement).

Prepare adjusting entries from selected account data.

(LO 2, 3)

E3-7 The ledger of Passehl Rental Agency on March 31 of the current year includes the selected accounts, shown below, before adjusting entries have been prepared.

	Debit	Credit
Prepaid Insurance	$ 3,600	
Supplies	2,800	
Equipment	25,000	
Accumulated Depreciation—Equipment		$ 8,400
Notes Payable		20,000
Unearned Rent Revenue		10,200
Rent Revenue		60,000
Interest Expense	–0–	
Salaries and Wages Expense	14,000	

An analysis of the accounts shows the following.

1. The equipment depreciates $400 per month.
2. One-third of the unearned rent revenue was earned during the quarter.
3. Interest of $500 is accrued on the notes payable.
4. Supplies on hand total $750.
5. Insurance expires at the rate of $300 per month.

Instructions

Prepare the adjusting entries at March 31, assuming that adjusting entries are made **quarterly**. Additional accounts are Depreciation Expense, Insurance Expense, Interest Payable, and Supplies Expense.

Prepare adjusting entries.

(LO 2, 3)

E3-8 Meghan Lindh, D.D.S., opened a dental practice on January 1, 2017. During the first month of operations, the following transactions occurred.

1. Performed services for patients who had dental plan insurance. At January 31, $875 of such services were performed but not yet recorded.
2. Utility expenses incurred but not paid prior to January 31 totaled $650.

3. Purchased dental equipment on January 1 for $80,000, paying $20,000 in cash and signing a $60,000, 3-year note payable. The equipment depreciates $400 per month. Interest is $500 per month.
4. Purchased a one-year malpractice insurance policy on January 1 for $24,000.
5. Purchased $1,600 of dental supplies. On January 31, determined that $400 of supplies were on hand.

Instructions

Prepare the adjusting entries on January 31. Account titles are Accumulated Depreciation—Equipment, Depreciation Expense, Service Revenue, Accounts Receivable, Insurance Expense, Interest Expense, Interest Payable, Prepaid Insurance, Supplies, Supplies Expense, Utilities Expense, and Utilities Payable.

Prepare adjusting entries.
(LO 2, 3)

E3-9 The trial balance for Pioneer Advertising is shown in Illustration 3-3 (page 97). Instead of the adjusting entries shown in the textbook at October 31, assume the following adjustment data.

1. Supplies on hand at October 31 total $500.
2. Expired insurance for the month is $120.
3. Depreciation for the month is $50.
4. Services related to unearned service revenue in October worth $600 were performed.
5. Services performed but not recorded at October 31 are $360.
6. Interest accrued at October 31 is $95.
7. Accrued salaries at October 31 are $1,625.

Instructions

Prepare the adjusting entries for the items above.

Prepare correct income statement.
(LO 1, 2, 3)

XLS

E3-10 The income statement of Montee Co. for the month of July shows net income of $1,400 based on Service Revenue $5,500, Salaries and Wages Expense $2,300, Supplies Expense $1,200, and Utilities Expense $600. In reviewing the statement, you discover the following.

1. Insurance expired during July of $400 was omitted.
2. Supplies expense includes $250 of supplies that are still on hand at July 31.
3. Depreciation on equipment of $150 was omitted.
4. Accrued but unpaid salaries and wages at July 31 of $300 were not included.
5. Services performed but unrecorded totaled $650.

Instructions

Prepare a correct income statement for July 2017.

Analyze adjusted data.
(LO 1, 2, 3, 4)

XLS

E3-11 A partial adjusted trial balance of Frangesch Company at January 31, 2017, shows the following.

FRANGESCH COMPANY
Adjusted Trial Balance
January 31, 2017

	Debit	Credit
Supplies	$ 850	
Prepaid Insurance	2,400	
Salaries and Wages Payable		$ 920
Unearned Service Revenue		750
Supplies Expense	950	
Insurance Expense	400	
Salaries and Wages Expense	2,900	
Service Revenue		2,000

Instructions

Answer the following questions, assuming the year begins January 1.

(a) If the amount in Supplies Expense is the January 31 adjusting entry, and $1,000 of supplies was purchased in January, what was the balance in Supplies on January 1?

(b) If the amount in Insurance Expense is the January 31 adjusting entry, and the original insurance premium was for one year, what was the total premium and when was the policy purchased?

(c) If $3,800 of salaries was paid in January, what was the balance in Salaries and Wages Payable at December 31, 2016?

E3-12 Selected accounts of Holly Company are shown as follows.

Journalize basic transactions and adjusting entries.

(LO 2, 3)

Supplies Expense

7/31	800		

Supplies

7/1 Bal.	1,100	7/31	800
7/10	650		

Salaries and Wages Payable

		7/31	1,200

Accounts Receivable

7/31	500		

Unearned Service Revenue

7/31	1,150	7/1 Bal.	1,500
		7/20	1,000

Salaries and Wages Expense

7/15	1,200		
7/31	1,200		

Service Revenue

		7/14	2,000
		7/31	1,150
		7/31	500

Instructions

After analyzing the accounts, journalize (a) the July transactions and (b) the adjusting entries that were made on July 31. (*Hint:* July transactions were for cash.)

E3-13 The trial balances before and after adjustment for Turnquist Company at the end of its fiscal year are presented below.

Prepare adjusting entries from analysis of trial balances.

(LO 2, 3, 4)

TURNQUIST COMPANY
Trial Balance
August 31, 2017

	Before Adjustment		After Adjustment	
	Dr.	**Cr.**	**Dr.**	**Cr.**
Cash	$10,400		$10,400	
Accounts Receivable	8,800		11,400	
Supplies	2,300		900	
Prepaid Insurance	4,000		2,500	
Equipment	14,000		14,000	
Accumulated Depreciation—Equipment		$ 3,600		$ 4,500
Accounts Payable		5,800		5,800
Salaries and Wages Payable		–0–		1,100
Unearned Rent Revenue		1,500		400
Owner's Capital		15,600		15,600
Service Revenue		34,000		36,600
Rent Revenue		11,000		12,100
Salaries and Wages Expense	17,000		18,100	
Supplies Expense	–0–		1,400	
Rent Expense	15,000		15,000	
Insurance Expense	–0–		1,500	
Depreciation Expense	–0–		900	
	$71,500	$71,500	$76,100	$76,100

Instructions

Prepare the adjusting entries that were made.

Prepare financial statements from adjusted trial balance.
(LO 4)

E3-14 The adjusted trial balance for Turnquist Company is given in E3-13.

Instructions

Prepare the income and owner's equity statements for the year and the balance sheet at August 31.

Record transactions on accrual basis; convert revenue to cash receipts.
(LO 2, 3)

E3-15 The following data are taken from the comparative balance sheets of Bundies Billiards Club, which prepares its financial statements using the accrual basis of accounting.

December 31	2017	2016
Accounts receivable from members	$16,000	$ 8,000
Unearned service revenue	17,000	25,000

Members are billed based upon their use of the club's facilities. Unearned service revenues arise from the sale of gift certificates, which members can apply to their future use of club facilities. The 2017 income statement for the club showed that service revenue of $161,000 was earned during the year.

Instructions

(*Hint:* You will probably find it helpful to use T-accounts to analyze these data.)

(a) Prepare journal entries for each of the following events that took place during 2017.
 (1) Accounts receivable from 2016 were all collected.
 (2) Gift certificates outstanding at the end of 2016 were all redeemed.
 (3) An additional $38,000 worth of gift certificates were sold during 2017. A portion of these was used by the recipients during the year; the remainder was still outstanding at the end of 2017.
 (4) Services performed for members for 2017 were billed to members.
 (5) Accounts receivable for 2017 (i.e., those billed in item [4] above) were partially collected.

(b) Determine the amount of cash received by the club, with respect to member services, during 2017.

Journalize adjusting entries.
(LO 5)

***E3-16** Zac Brown Company has the following balances in selected accounts on December 31, 2017.

Service Revenue	$40,000
Insurance Expense	2,700
Supplies Expense	2,450

All the accounts have normal balances. Zac Brown Company debits prepayments to expense accounts when paid, and credits unearned revenues to revenue accounts when received. The following information below has been gathered at December 31, 2017.

1. Zac Brown Company paid $2,700 for 12 months of insurance coverage on June 1, 2017.
2. On December 1, 2017, Zac Brown Company collected $40,000 for consulting services to be performed from December 1, 2017, through March 31, 2018.
3. A count of supplies on December 31, 2017, indicates that supplies of $900 are on hand.

Instructions

Prepare the adjusting entries needed at December 31, 2017.

Journalize transactions and adjusting entries.
(LO 5)

***E3-17** At Sekon Company, prepayments are debited to expense when paid, and unearned revenues are credited to revenue when cash is received. During January of the current year, the following transactions occurred.

Jan.	2	Paid $1,920 for fire insurance protection for the year.
	10	Paid $1,700 for supplies.
	15	Received $6,100 for services to be performed in the future.

On January 31, it is determined that $2,100 of the services were performed and that there are $650 of supplies on hand.

Instructions

(a) Journalize and post the January transactions. (Use T-accounts.)
(b) Journalize and post the adjusting entries at January 31.
(c) Determine the ending balance in each of the accounts.

***E3-18** Presented below are the assumptions and principles discussed in this chapter.

Identify accounting assumptions and principles.

(LO 6)

1. Full disclosure principle.
2. Going concern assumption.
3. Monetary unit assumption.
4. Time period assumption.
5. Historical cost principle.
6. Economic entity assumption.

Instructions

Identify by number the accounting assumption or principle that is described below. Do not use a number more than once.

_______ (a) Is the rationale for why plant assets are not reported at liquidation value. (*Note:* Do not use the historical cost principle.)
_______ (b) Indicates that personal and business recordkeeping should be separately maintained.
_______ (c) Assumes that the monetary unit is the "measuring stick" used to report on financial performance.
_______ (d) Separates financial information into time periods for reporting purposes.
_______ (e) Measurement basis used when a reliable estimate of fair value is not available.
_______ (f) Dictates that companies should disclose all circumstances and events that make a difference to financial statement users.

***E3-19** Weber Co. had three major business transactions during 2017.

Identify the assumption or principle that has been violated.

(LO 6)

(a) Reported at its fair value of $260,000 merchandise inventory with a cost of $208,000.
(b) The president of Weber Co., Austin Weber, purchased a truck for personal use and charged it to his expense account.
(c) Weber Co. wanted to make its 2017 income look better, so it added 2 more weeks to the year (a 54-week year). Previous years were 52 weeks.

Instructions

In each situation, identify the assumption or principle that has been violated, if any, and discuss what the company should have done.

***E3-20** The following characteristics, assumptions, principles, or constraint guide the FASB when it creates accounting standards.

Identity financial accounting concepts and principles.

(LO 6)

Relevance	Expense recognition principle
Faithful representation	Time period assumption
Comparability	Going concern assumption
Consistency	Historical cost principle
Monetary unit assumption	Full disclosure principle
Economic entity assumption	Materiality

Match each item above with a description below.

1. _______ Ability to easily evaluate one company's results relative to another's.
2. _______ Belief that a company will continue to operate for the foreseeable future.
3. _______ The judgment concerning whether an item's size is large enough to matter to decision-makers.
4. _______ The reporting of all information that would make a difference to financial statement users.
5. _______ The practice of preparing financial statements at regular intervals.
6. _______ The quality of information that indicates the information makes a difference in a decision.
7. _______ A belief that items should be reported on the balance sheet at the price that was paid to acquire them.
8. _______ A company's use of the same accounting principles and methods from year to year.
9. _______ Tracing accounting events to particular companies.
10. _______ The desire to minimize bias in financial statements.
11. _______ Reporting only those things that can be measured in monetary units.
12. _______ Dictates that efforts (expenses) be matched with results (revenues).

***E3-21** Speyeware International Inc., headquartered in Vancouver, Canada, specializes in Internet safety and computer security products for both the home and commercial markets. In a recent balance sheet, it reported a deficit of US$5,678,288. It has reported only net losses since its inception. In spite of these losses, Speyeware's shares of stock have traded anywhere from a high of $3.70 to a low of $0.32 on the Canadian Venture Exchange.

Comment on the objective and qualitative characteristics of accounting information.

(LO 6)

Speyeware's financial statements have historically been prepared in Canadian dollars. Recently, the company adopted the U.S. dollar as its reporting currency.

Instructions

(a) What is the objective of financial reporting? How does this objective meet or not meet Speyeware's investors' needs?
(b) Why would investors want to buy Speyeware's shares if the company has consistently reported losses over the last few years? Include in your answer an assessment of the relevance of the information reported on Speyeware's financial statements.
(c) Comment on how the change in reporting information from Canadian dollars to U.S. dollars likely affected the readers of Speyeware's financial statements. Include in your answer an assessment of the comparability of the information.

Comment on the objective and qualitative characteristics of financial reporting.

(LO 6)

***E3-22** A friend of yours, Gina Moore, recently completed an undergraduate degree in science and has just started working with a biotechnology company. Gina tells you that the owners of the business are trying to secure new sources of financing which are needed in order for the company to proceed with development of a new healthcare product. Gina said that her boss told her that the company must put together a report to present to potential investors.

Gina thought that the company should include in this package the detailed scientific findings related to the Phase I clinical trials for this product. She said, "I know that the biotech industry sometimes has only a 10% success rate with new products, but if we report all the scientific findings, everyone will see what a sure success this is going to be! The president was talking about the importance of following some set of accounting principles. Why do we need to look at some accounting rules? What they need to realize is that we have scientific results that are quite encouraging, some of the most talented employees around, and the start of some really great customer relationships. We haven't made any sales yet, but we will. We just need the funds to get through all the clinical testing and get government approval for our product. Then these investors will be quite happy that they bought in to our company early!"

Instructions

(a) What is accounting information?
(b) Comment on how Gina's suggestions for what should be reported to prospective investors conforms to the qualitative characteristics of accounting information. Do you think that the things that Gina wants to include in the information for investors will conform to financial reporting guidelines?

EXERCISES: SET B AND CHALLENGE EXERCISES

Visit the book's companion website, at **www.wiley.com/college/weygandt**, and choose the Student Companion site to access Exercises: Set B and Challenge Exercises.

PROBLEMS: SET A

Prepare adjusting entries, post to ledger accounts, and prepare an adjusted trial balance.

(LO 2, 3, 4)

P3-1A Logan Krause started her own consulting firm, Krause Consulting, on May 1, 2017. The trial balance at May 31 is as follows.

KRAUSE CONSULTING
Trial Balance
May 31, 2017

Account Number		Debit	Credit
101	Cash	$ 4,500	
112	Accounts Receivable	6,000	
126	Supplies	1,900	
130	Prepaid Insurance	3,600	
149	Equipment	11,400	
201	Accounts Payable		$ 4,500
209	Unearned Service Revenue		2,000
301	Owner's Capital		18,700
400	Service Revenue		9,500
726	Salaries and Wages Expense	6,400	
729	Rent Expense	900	
		$34,700	$34,700

In addition to those accounts listed on the trial balance, the chart of accounts for Krause Consulting also contains the following accounts and account numbers: No. 150 Accumulated Depreciation—Equipment, No. 212 Salaries and Wages Payable, No. 631 Supplies Expense, No. 717 Depreciation Expense, No. 722 Insurance Expense, and No. 732 Utilities Expense.

Other data:

1. $900 of supplies have been used during the month.
2. Utilities expense incurred but not paid on May 31, 2017, $250.
3. The insurance policy is for 2 years.
4. $400 of the balance in the unearned service revenue account remains unearned at the end of the month.
5. May 31 is a Wednesday, and employees are paid on Fridays. Krause Consulting has two employees, who are paid $920 each for a 5-day work week.
6. The office furniture has a 5-year life with no salvage value. It is being depreciated at $190 per month for 60 months.
7. Invoices representing $1,700 of services performed during the month have not been recorded as of May 31.

Instructions

(a) Prepare the adjusting entries for the month of May. Use J4 as the page number for your journal.
(b) Post the adjusting entries to the ledger accounts. Enter the totals from the trial balance as beginning account balances and place a check mark in the posting reference column.
(c) Prepare an adjusted trial balance at May 31, 2017. (c) Adj. trial balance $37,944

Prepare adjusting entries, post, and prepare adjusted trial balance and financial statements.

(LO 2, 3, 4)

P3-2A Mac's Motel opened for business on May 1, 2017. Its trial balance before adjustment on May 31 is as follows.

MAC'S MOTEL
Trial Balance
May 31, 2017

Account Number		Debit	Credit
101	Cash	$ 3,500	
126	Supplies	2,080	
130	Prepaid Insurance	2,400	
140	Land	12,000	
141	Buildings	60,000	
149	Equipment	15,000	
201	Accounts Payable		$ 4,800
208	Unearned Rent Revenue		3,300
275	Mortgage Payable		40,000
301	Owner's Capital		41,380
429	Rent Revenue		10,300
610	Advertising Expense	600	
726	Salaries and Wages Expense	3,300	
732	Utilities Expense	900	
		$99,780	$99,780

In addition to those accounts listed on the trial balance, the chart of accounts for Mac's Motel also contains the following accounts and account numbers: No. 142 Accumulated Depreciation—Buildings, No. 150 Accumulated Depreciation—Equipment, No. 212 Salaries and Wages Payable, No. 230 Interest Payable, No. 619 Depreciation Expense, No. 631 Supplies Expense, No. 718 Interest Expense, and No. 722 Insurance Expense.

Other data:

1. Prepaid insurance is a 1-year policy starting May 1, 2017.
2. A count of supplies shows $750 of unused supplies on May 31.
3. Annual depreciation is $3,000 on the buildings and $1,500 on equipment.
4. The mortgage interest rate is 12%. (The mortgage was taken out on May 1.)
5. Two-thirds of the unearned rent revenue has been earned.
6. Salaries of $750 are accrued and unpaid at May 31.

(c) Adj. trial balance $101,305
(d) Net income $4,645
Ending capital $46,025
Total assets $93,075

Instructions

(a) Journalize the adjusting entries on May 31.
(b) Prepare a ledger using the three-column form of account. Enter the trial balance amounts and post the adjusting entries. (Use J1 as the posting reference.)
(c) Prepare an adjusted trial balance on May 31.
(d) Prepare an income statement and an owner's equity statement for the month of May and a balance sheet at May 31.

Prepare adjusting entries and financial statements.

(LO 2, 3, 4)

P3-3A Alena Co. was organized on July 1, 2017. Quarterly financial statements are prepared. The unadjusted and adjusted trial balances as of September 30 are shown below.

ALENA CO.
Trial Balance
September 30, 2017

	Unadjusted		Adjusted	
	Dr.	**Cr.**	**Dr.**	**Cr.**
Cash	$ 8,700		$ 8,700	
Accounts Receivable	10,400		11,500	
Supplies	1,500		650	
Prepaid Rent	2,200		500	
Equipment	18,000		18,000	
Accumulated Depreciation—Equipment		$ –0–		$ 700
Notes Payable		10,000		10,000
Accounts Payable		2,500		2,500
Salaries and Wages Payable		–0–		725
Interest Payable		–0–		100
Unearned Rent Revenue		1,900		450
Owner's Capital		22,000		22,000
Owner's Drawings	1,600		1,600	
Service Revenue		16,000		17,100
Rent Revenue		1,410		2,860
Salaries and Wages Expense	8,000		8,725	
Rent Expense	1,900		3,600	
Depreciation Expense			700	
Supplies Expense			850	
Utilities Expense	1,510		1,510	
Interest Expense			100	
	$53,810	$53,810	$56,435	$56,435

(b) Net income $4,475
Ending capital $24,875
Total assets $38,650

Instructions

(a) Journalize the adjusting entries that were made.
(b) Prepare an income statement and an owner's equity statement for the 3 months ending September 30 and a balance sheet at September 30.
(c) If the note bears interest at 12%, how many months has it been outstanding?

Prepare adjusting entries.

(LO 2, 3)

P3-4A A review of the ledger of Remina Company at December 31, 2017, produces the following data pertaining to the preparation of annual adjusting entries.

1. Insurance expense $4,890

1. Prepaid Insurance $10,440. The company has separate insurance policies on its buildings and its motor vehicles. Policy B4564 on the building was purchased on April 1, 2016, for $7,920. The policy has a term of 3 years. Policy A2958 on the vehicles was purchased on January 1, 2017, for $4,500. This policy has a term of 2 years.

2. Rent revenue $84,000

2. Unearned Rent Revenue $429,000. The company began subleasing office space in its new building on November 1. At December 31, the company had the following rental contracts that are paid in full for the entire term of the lease.

Date	Term (in months)	Monthly Rent	Number of Leases
Nov. 1	9	$5,000	5
Dec. 1	6	$8,500	4

3. Notes Payable $120,000. This balance consists of a note for 9 months at an annual interest rate of 9%, dated November 1.
4. Salaries and Wages Payable $0. There are eight salaried employees. Salaries are paid every Friday for the current week. Five employees receive a salary of $700 each per week, and three employees earn $500 each per week. Assume December 31 is a Tuesday. Employees do not work weekends. All employees worked the last 2 days of December.

3. Interest expense $1,800

4. Salaries and wages expense $2,000

Instructions

Prepare the adjusting entries at December 31, 2017.

P3-5A On November 1, 2017, the account balances of Hamm Equipment Repair were as follows.

Journalize transactions and follow through accounting cycle to preparation of financial statements.

(LO 2, 3, 4)

GLS

No.		Debit	No.		Credit
101	Cash	$ 2,400	154	Accumulated Depreciation—Equipment	$ 2,000
112	Accounts Receivable	4,250	201	Accounts Payable	2,600
126	Supplies	1,800	209	Unearned Service Revenue	1,200
153	Equipment	12,000	212	Salaries and Wages Payable	700
			301	Owner's Capital	13,950
		$20,450			$20,450

During November, the following summary transactions were completed.

Nov.	8	Paid $1,700 for salaries due employees, of which $700 is for October salaries.
	10	Received $3,620 cash from customers on account.
	12	Received $3,100 cash for services performed in November.
	15	Purchased equipment on account $2,000.
	17	Purchased supplies on account $700.
	20	Paid creditors on account $2,700.
	22	Paid November rent $400.
	25	Paid salaries $1,700.
	27	Performed services on account and billed customers for these services $2,200.
	29	Received $600 from customers for future service.

Adjustment data consist of:

1. Supplies on hand $1,400.
2. Accrued salaries payable $350.
3. Depreciation for the month is $200.
4. Services related to unearned service revenue of $1,220 were performed.

Instructions

(a) Enter the November 1 balances in the ledger accounts.
(b) Journalize the November transactions.
(c) Post to the ledger accounts. Use J1 for the posting reference. Use the following additional accounts: No. 407 Service Revenue, No. 615 Depreciation Expense, No. 631 Supplies Expense, No. 726 Salaries and Wages Expense, and No. 729 Rent Expense.
(d) Prepare a trial balance at November 30.
(e) Journalize and post adjusting entries.
(f) Prepare an adjusted trial balance.
(g) Prepare an income statement and an owner's equity statement for November and a balance sheet at November 30.

(d) Trial balance $25,650
(f) Adj. trial balance $26,200
(g) Net income $1,770; Ending capital $15,720 Total assets $19,250

***P3-6A** Johnson Graphics Company was organized on January 1, 2017, by Cameron Johnson. At the end of the first 6 months of operations, the trial balance contained the accounts shown on page 142.

Prepare adjusting entries, adjusted trial balance, and financial statements using appendix.

(LO 2, 3, 4, 5)

	Debit		Credit
Cash	$ 8,600	Notes Payable	$ 20,000
Accounts Receivable	14,000	Accounts Payable	9,000
Equipment	45,000	Owner's Capital	22,000
Insurance Expense	2,700	Sales Revenue	52,100
Salaries and Wages Expense	30,000	Service Revenue	6,000
Supplies Expense	3,700		
Advertising Expense	1,900		
Rent Expense	1,500		
Utilities Expense	1,700		
	$109,100		$109,100

Analysis reveals the following additional data.

1. The $3,700 balance in Supplies Expense represents supplies purchased in January. At June 30, $1,500 of supplies are on hand.
2. The note payable was issued on February 1. It is a 9%, 6-month note.
3. The balance in Insurance Expense is the premium on a one-year policy, dated March 1, 2017.
4. Service revenues are credited to revenue when received. At June 30, services revenue of $1,300 are unearned.
5. Revenue for services performed but unrecorded at June 30 totals $2,000.
6. Depreciation is $2,250 per year.

Instructions

(a) Journalize the adjusting entries at June 30. (Assume adjustments are recorded every 6 months.)

(b) Prepare an adjusted trial balance.

(c) Prepare an income statement and owner's equity statement for the 6 months ended June 30 and a balance sheet at June 30.

(b) Adj. trial balance $112,975
(c) Net income $18,725
Ending capital $40,725
Total assets $71,775

PROBLEMS: SET B AND SET C

Visit the book's companion website, at **www.wiley.com/college/weygandt**, and choose the Student Companion site to access Problems: Set B and Set C.

CONTINUING PROBLEM

COOKIE CREATIONS: AN ENTREPRENEURIAL JOURNEY

(*Note:* This is a continuation of the Cookie Creations problem from Chapters 1 and 2. Use the information from the previous chapters and follow the instructions below using the general ledger accounts you have already prepared.)

© leungchopan/ Shutterstock

CC3 It is the end of November and Natalie has been in touch with her grandmother. Her grandmother asked Natalie how well things went in her first month of business. Natalie, too, would like to know if she has been profitable or not during November. Natalie realizes that in order to determine Cookie Creations' income, she must first make adjustments.

Natalie puts together the following additional information.

1. A count reveals that $35 of baking supplies were used during November.
2. Natalie estimates that all of her baking equipment will have a useful life of 5 years or 60 months. (Assume Natalie decides to record a full month's worth of depreciation, regardless of when the equipment was obtained by the business.)
3. Natalie's grandmother has decided to charge interest of 6% on the note payable extended on November 16. The loan plus interest is to be repaid in 24 months. (Assume that half a month of interest accrued during November.)
4. On November 30, a friend of Natalie's asks her to teach a class at the neighborhood school. Natalie agrees and teaches a group of 35 first-grade students how to make gingerbread cookies. The next day, Natalie prepares an invoice for $300 and leaves it with the school principal. The principal says that he will pass the invoice along to the head office, and it will be paid sometime in December.

5. Natalie receives a utilities bill for $45. The bill is for utilities consumed by Natalie's business during November and is due December 15.

Instructions

Using the information that you have gathered through Chapter 2, and based on the new information above, do the following.

(a) Prepare and post the adjusting journal entries.
(b) Prepare an adjusted trial balance.
(c) Using the adjusted trial balance, calculate Cookie Creations' net income or net loss for the month of November. Do not prepare an income statement.

BROADENING YOUR PERSPECTIVE

FINANCIAL REPORTING AND ANALYSIS

Financial Reporting Problem: Apple Inc.

BYP3-1 The financial statements of Apple Inc. are presented in Appendix A at the end of this textbook. Instructions for accessing and using the company's complete annual report, including the notes to the financial statements, are also provided in Appendix A.

Instructions

(a) Using the consolidated financial statements and related information, identify items that may result in adjusting entries for prepayments.
(b) Using the consolidated financial statements and related information, identify items that may result in adjusting entries for accruals.
(c) What has been the trend since 2011 for net income?

Comparative Analysis Problem: PepsiCo, Inc. vs. The Coca-Cola Company

BYP3-2 PepsiCo, Inc.'s financial statements are presented in Appendix B. Financial statements of The Coca-Cola Company are presented in Appendix C. Instructions for accessing and using the complete annual reports of PepsiCo and Coca-Cola, including the notes to the financial statements, are also provided in Appendices B and C, respectively.

Instructions

Based on information contained in these financial statements, determine the following for each company.

(a) Net increase (decrease) in property, plant, and equipment (net) from 2012 to 2013.
(b) Increase (decrease) in selling, general, and administrative expenses from 2012 to 2013.
(c) Increase (decrease) in long-term debt (obligations) from 2012 to 2013.
(d) Increase (decrease) in net income from 2012 to 2013.
(e) Increase (decrease) in cash and cash equivalents from 2012 to 2013.

Comparative Analysis Problem: Amazon.com, Inc. vs. Wal-Mart Stores, Inc.

BYP3-3 Amazon.com, Inc.'s financial statements are presented in Appendix D. Financial statements of Wal-Mart Stores, Inc. are presented in Appendix E. Instructions for accessing and using the complete annual reports of Amazon and Wal-Mart, including the notes to the financial statements, are also provided in Appendices D and E, respectively.

Instructions

Based on information contained in these financial statements, determine the following for each company.

1. (a) Increase (decrease) in interest expense from 2012 to 2013.
   (b) Increase (decrease) in net income from 2012 to 2013.
   (c) Increase (decrease) in cash flow from operations from 2012 to 2013.
2. Cash flow from operations and net income for each company is different. What are some possible reasons for these differences?

Real-World Focus

BYP3-4 No financial decision-maker should ever rely solely on the financial information reported in the annual report to make decisions. It is important to keep abreast of financial news. This activity demonstrates how to search for financial news on the Internet.

Address: **http://biz.yahoo.com/i**, or go to **www.wiley.com/college/weygandt**

Steps:

1. Type in either Wal-Mart, Target Corp., or Kmart.
2. Choose **News**.
3. Select an article that sounds interesting to you and that would be relevant to an investor in these companies.

Instructions

(a) What was the source of the article (e.g., Reuters, Businesswire, Prnewswire)?

(b) Assume that you are a personal financial planner and that one of your clients owns stock in the company. Write a brief memo to your client summarizing the article and explaining the implications of the article for his or her investment.

CRITICAL THINKING

Decision-Making Across the Organization

BYP3-5 Happy Camper Park was organized on April 1, 2016, by Erica Hatt. Erica is a good manager but a poor accountant. From the trial balance prepared by a part-time bookkeeper, Erica prepared the following income statement for the quarter that ended March 31, 2017.

HAPPY CAMPER PARK
Income Statement
For the Quarter Ended March 31, 2017

Revenues		
Rent revenue		$90,000
Operating expenses		
Advertising	$ 5,200	
Salaries and wages	29,800	
Utilities	900	
Depreciation	800	
Maintenance and repairs	4,000	
Total operating expenses		40,700
Net income		$49,300

Erica thought that something was wrong with the statement because net income had never exceeded $20,000 in any one quarter. Knowing that you are an experienced accountant, she asks you to review the income statement and other data.

You first look at the trial balance. In addition to the account balances reported above in the income statement, the ledger contains the following additional selected balances at March 31, 2017.

Supplies	$ 6,200
Prepaid Insurance	7,200
Notes Payable	12,000

You then make inquiries and discover the following.

1. Rent revenues include advanced rentals for summer occupancy $15,000.
2. There were $1,700 of supplies on hand at March 31.
3. Prepaid insurance resulted from the payment of a one-year policy on January 1, 2017.
4. The mail on April 1, 2017, brought the following bills: advertising for week of March 24, $110; repairs made March 10, $260; and utilities, $180.
5. There are four employees who receive wages totaling $300 per day. At March 31, 2 days' salaries and wages have been incurred but not paid.
6. The note payable is a 3-month, 10% note dated January 1, 2017.

Instructions

With the class divided into groups, answer the following.

(a) Prepare a correct income statement for the quarter ended March 31, 2017.

(b) Explain to Erica the generally accepted accounting principles that she did not recognize in preparing her income statement and their effect on her results.

Communication Activity

BYP3-6 In reviewing the accounts of Kelli Taylor Co. at the end of the year, you discover that adjusting entries have not been made.

Instructions
Write a memo to Kelli Taylor, the owner of Kelli Taylor Co., that explains the following: the nature and purpose of adjusting entries, why adjusting entries are needed, and the types of adjusting entries that may be made.

Ethics Case

BYP3-7 Russell Company is a pesticide manufacturer. Its sales declined greatly this year due to the passage of legislation outlawing the sale of several of Russell's chemical pesticides. In the coming year, Russell will have environmentally safe and competitive chemicals to replace these discontinued products. Sales in the next year are expected to greatly exceed any prior year's. The decline in sales and profits appears to be a one-year aberration. But even so, the company president fears a large dip in the current year's profits. He believes that such a dip could cause a significant drop in the market price of Russell's stock and make the company a takeover target.

To avoid this possibility, the company president calls in Zoe Baas, controller, to discuss this period's year-end adjusting entries. He urges her to accrue every possible revenue and to defer as many expenses as possible. He says to Zoe, "We need the revenues this year, and next year can easily absorb expenses deferred from this year. We can't let our stock price be hammered down!" Zoe didn't get around to recording the adjusting entries until January 17, but she dated the entries December 31 as if they were recorded then. Zoe also made every effort to comply with the president's request.

Instructions
(a) Who are the stakeholders in this situation?
(b) What are the ethical considerations of (1) the president's request and (2) Zoe dating the adjusting entries December 31?
(c) Can Zoe accrue revenues and defer expenses and still be ethical?

All About You

BYP3-8 Companies must report or disclose in their financial statement information about all liabilities, including potential liabilities related to environmental cleanup. There are many situations in which you will be asked to provide personal financial information about your assets, liabilities, revenue, and expenses. Sometimes you will face difficult decisions regarding what to disclose and how to disclose it.

Instructions
Suppose that you are putting together a loan application to purchase a home. Based on your income and assets, you qualify for the mortgage loan, but just barely. How would you address each of the following situations in reporting your financial position for the loan application? Provide responses for each of the following situations.

(a) You signed a guarantee for a bank loan that a friend took out for $20,000. If your friend doesn't pay, you will have to pay. Your friend has made all of the payments so far, and it appears he will be able to pay in the future.
(b) You were involved in an auto accident in which you were at fault. There is the possibility that you may have to pay as much as $50,000 as part of a settlement. The issue will not be resolved before the bank processes your mortgage request.
(c) The company for which you work isn't doing very well, and it has recently laid off employees. You are still employed, but it is quite possible that you will lose your job in the next few months.

Considering People, Planet, and Profit

BYP3-9 Many companies have potential pollution or environmental-disposal problems—not only for electronic gadgets, but also for the lead paint or asbestos they sold. How do we fit these issues into the accounting equation? Are these costs and related liabilities that companies should report?

> **YES:** As more states impose laws holding companies responsible, and as more courts levy pollution-related fines, it becomes increasingly likely that companies will have to pay large amounts in the future.
>
> **NO:** The amounts still are too difficult to estimate. Putting inaccurate estimates on the financial statements reduces their usefulness. Instead, why not charge the costs later, when the actual environmental cleanup or disposal occurs, at which time the company knows the actual cost?

Instructions
Write a response indicating your position regarding this situation. Provide support for your view.

FASB Codification Activity

BYP3-10 If your school has a subscription to the FASB Codification, go to **http://aaahq.org/asclogin.cfm** to log in and prepare responses to the following.

Instructions
Access the glossary ("Master Glossary") to answer the following.

(a) What is the definition of revenue?
(b) What is the definition of compensation?

A Look at IFRS

LEARNING OBJECTIVE 7 **Compare the procedures for adjusting entries under GAAP and IFRS.**

It is often difficult for companies to determine in what time period they should report particular revenues and expenses. Both the IASB and FASB are working on a joint project to develop a common conceptual framework that will enable companies to better use the same principles to record transactions consistently over time.

Key Points

Following are the key similarities and differences between GAAP and IFRS as related to accrual accounting.

Similarities

- In this chapter, you learned accrual-basis accounting applied under GAAP. Companies applying IFRS also use accrual-basis accounting to ensure that they record transactions that change a company's financial statements in the period in which events occur.
- Similar to GAAP, cash-basis accounting is not in accordance with IFRS.
- IFRS also divides the economic life of companies into artificial time periods. Under both GAAP and IFRS, this is referred to as the **time period assumption**.
- The **general** revenue recognition principle required by GAAP that is used in this textbook is similar to that used under IFRS.
- Revenue recognition fraud is a major issue in U.S. financial reporting. The same situation occurs in other countries, as evidenced by revenue recognition breakdowns at Dutch software company Baan NV, Japanese electronics giant NEC, and Dutch grocer Ahold NV.

Differences

- Under IFRS, revaluation (using fair value) of items such as land and buildings is permitted. IFRS allows depreciation based on revaluation of assets, which is not permitted under GAAP.
- The terminology used for revenues and gains, and expenses and losses, differs somewhat between IFRS and GAAP. For example, income under IFRS includes both revenues, which arise during the normal course of operating activities, and gains, which arise from activities outside of the normal sales of goods and services. The term income is not used this way under GAAP. Instead, under GAAP income refers to the net difference between revenues and expenses.
- Under IFRS, expenses include both those costs incurred in the normal course of operations as well as losses that are not part of normal operations. This is in contrast to GAAP, which defines each separately.

Looking to the Future

The IASB and FASB are completing a joint project on revenue recognition. The purpose of this project is to develop comprehensive guidance on when to recognize revenue. It is hoped that this approach will lead to more consistent accounting in this area. For more on this topic, see **www.fasb.org/project/revenue_recognition.shtml**.

IFRS Practice

IFRS Self-Test Questions

1. IFRS:
   (a) uses accrual accounting.
   (b) uses cash-basis accounting.
   (c) allows revenue to be recognized when a customer makes an order.
   (d) requires that revenue not be recognized until cash is received.
2. Which of the following statements is **false**?
   (a) IFRS employs the time period assumption.
   (b) IFRS employs accrual accounting.
   (c) IFRS requires that revenues and costs must be capable of being measured reliably.
   (d) IFRS uses the cash basis of accounting.
3. As a result of the revenue recognition project by the FASB and IASB:
   (a) revenue recognition places more emphasis on when the performance obligation is satisfied.
   (b) revenue recognition places more emphasis on when revenue is realized.
   (c) revenue recognition places more emphasis on when expenses are incurred.
   (d) revenue is no longer recorded unless cash has been received.
4. Which of the following is **false**?
   (a) Under IFRS, the term income describes both revenues and gains.
   (b) Under IFRS, the term expenses includes losses.
   (c) Under IFRS, companies do not engage in the adjusting process.
   (d) Under IFRS, revenue recognition fraud is a major issue.
5. Accrual-basis accounting:
   (a) is optional under IFRS.
   (b) results in companies recording transactions that change a company's financial statements in the period in which events occur.
   (c) has been eliminated as a result of the IASB/FASB joint project on revenue recognition.
   (d) is not consistent with the IASB conceptual framework.

International Financial Reporting Problem: Louis Vuitton

IFRS3-1 The financial statements of Louis Vuitton are presented in Appendix F. Instructions for accessing and using the company's complete annual report, including the notes to its financial statements, are also provided in Appendix F.

Instructions
Visit Louis Vuitton's corporate website and answer the following questions from Louis Vuitton's 2013 annual report.

(a) From the notes to the financial statements, how does the company determine the amount of revenue to record at the time of a sale?
(b) From the notes to the financial statements, how does the company determine the provision for product returns?
(c) Using the consolidated income statement and consolidated statement of financial position, identify items that may result in adjusting entries for deferrals.
(d) Using the consolidated income statement, identify two items that may result in adjusting entries for accruals.

Answers to IFRS Self-Test Questions

1. a **2.** d **3.** a **4.** c **5.** b

4 Completing the Accounting Cycle

CHAPTER PREVIEW As the Feature Story below highlights, at Rhino Foods, Inc., financial statements help employees understand what is happening in the business. In Chapter 3, we prepared financial statements directly from the adjusted trial balance. However, with so many details involved in the end-of-period accounting procedures, it is easy to make errors. One way to minimize errors in the records and to simplify the end-of-period procedures is to use a worksheet.

In this chapter, we will explain the role of the worksheet in accounting. We also will study the remaining steps in the accounting cycle, especially the closing process, again using Pioneer Advertising as an example. Then, we will consider correcting entries and classified balance sheets.

FEATURE STORY

Everyone Likes to Win

When Ted Castle was a hockey coach at the University of Vermont, his players were self-motivated by their desire to win. Hockey was a game you usually either won or lost. But at Rhino Foods, Inc., a bakery-foods company he founded in Burlington, Vermont, he discovered that manufacturing-line workers were not so self-motivated. Ted thought, what if he turned the food-making business into a game, with rules, strategies, and trophies?

In a game, knowing the score is all-important. Ted felt that only if the employees know the score—know exactly how the business is doing daily, weekly, monthly—could he turn food-making into a game. But Rhino is a closely held, family-owned business, and its financial statements and profits were confidential. Ted wondered, should he open Rhino's books to the employees?

A consultant put Ted's concerns in perspective when he said, "Imagine you're playing touch football. You play for an hour or two, and the whole time I'm sitting there with a book, keeping score. All of a sudden I blow the whistle, and I say, 'OK, that's it. Everybody go home.' I close my book and walk away. How would you feel?" Ted opened his books and revealed the financial statements to his employees.

The next step was to teach employees the rules and strategies of how to "win" at making food. The first lesson: "Your opponent at Rhino is expenses. You must cut and control expenses." Ted and his staff distilled those lessons into daily scorecards—production reports and income statements—that keep Rhino's employees up-to-date on the game. At noon each day, Ted posts the previous day's results at the entrance to the production room. Everyone checks whether they made or lost money on what they produced the day before. And it's not just an academic exercise: There's a bonus check for each employee at the end of every four-week "game" that meets profitability guidelines.

Rhino has flourished since the first game. Employment has increased from 20 to 130 people, while both revenues and profits have grown dramatically.

Comstock/Getty Images, Inc.

CHAPTER OUTLINE

Learning Objectives

Learning Objective	Topics	DO IT!
1 Prepare a worksheet.	• Steps in preparing a worksheet • Preparing financial statements from a worksheet • Preparing adjusting entries from a worksheet	DO IT! 1 Worksheet
2 Prepare closing entries and a post-closing trial balance.	• Preparing closing entries • Posting closing entries • Preparing a post-closing trial balance	DO IT! 2 Closing Entries
3 Explain the steps in the accounting cycle and how to prepare correcting entries.	• Summary of the accounting cycle • Reversing entries • Correcting entries	DO IT! 3 Correcting Entries
4 Identify the sections of a classified balance sheet.	• Current assets • Long-term investments • Property, plant, and equipment • Intangible assets • Current liabilities • Long-term liabilities • Owner's equity	DO IT! 4 Balance Sheet Classifications

Go to the ***REVIEW AND PRACTICE*** section at the end of the chapter for a review of key concepts and practice applications with solutions.

Visit **WileyPLUS with ORION** for additional tutorials and practice opportunities.

LEARNING OBJECTIVE 1

Prepare a worksheet.

A **worksheet** is a multiple-column form used in the adjustment process and in preparing financial statements. As its name suggests, the worksheet is a working tool. **It is not a permanent accounting record.** It is neither a journal nor a part of the general ledger. The worksheet is merely a device used in preparing adjusting entries and the financial statements. Companies generally computerize worksheets using an electronic spreadsheet program such as Excel.

Illustration 4-1 shows the basic form of a worksheet and the five steps for preparing it. Each step is performed in sequence. **The use of a worksheet is optional.** When a company chooses to use one, it prepares financial statements directly from the worksheet. It enters the adjustments in the worksheet columns and then journalizes and posts the adjustments after it has prepared the financial statements. Thus, worksheets make it possible to provide the financial statements to management and other interested parties at an earlier date.

Steps in Preparing a Worksheet

We will use the October 31 trial balance and adjustment data of Pioneer Advertising from Chapter 3 to illustrate how to prepare a worksheet. In the following pages, we describe and then demonstrate each step of the process.

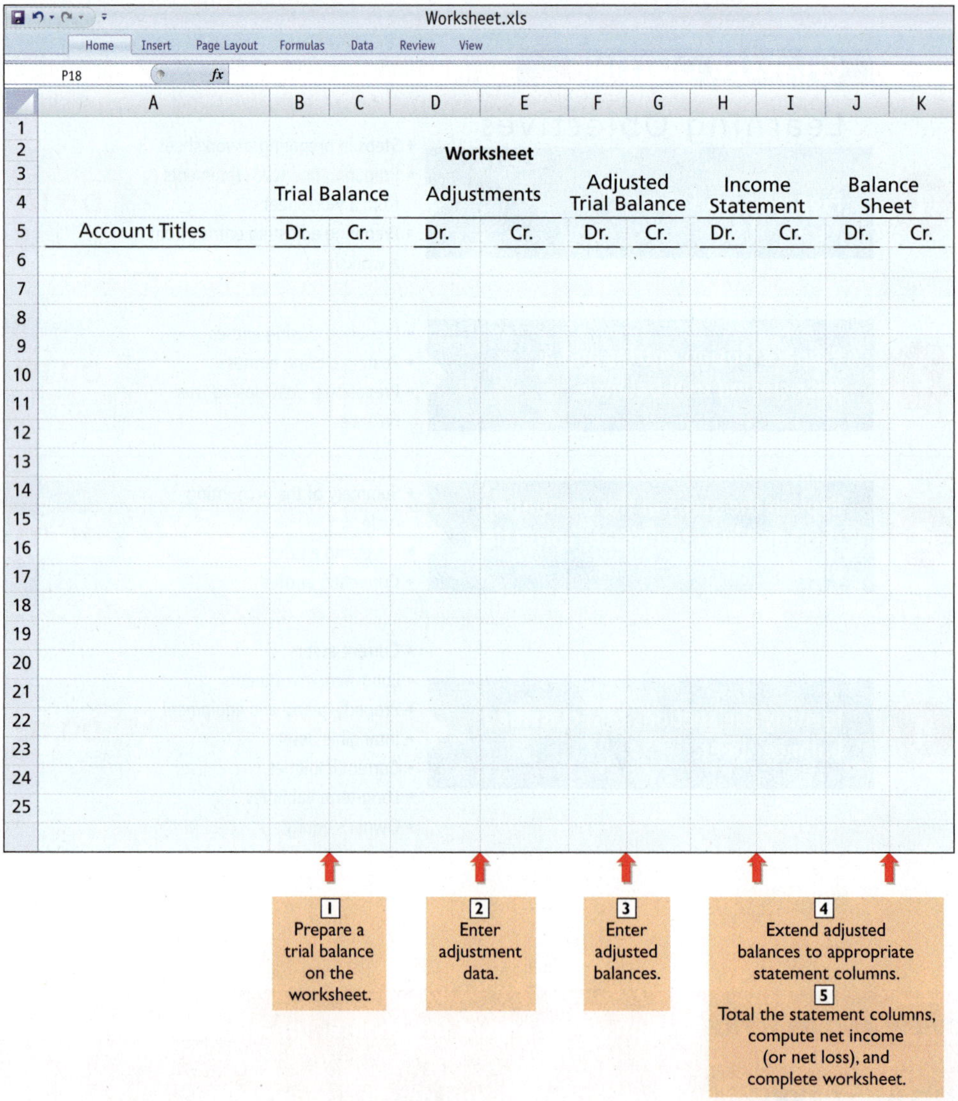

Illustration 4-1
Form and procedure for a worksheet

STEP 1: PREPARE A TRIAL BALANCE ON THE WORKSHEET

The first step in preparing a worksheet is to enter all ledger accounts with balances in the account titles column and then enter debit and credit amounts from the ledger in the trial balance columns. Illustration 4-2 shows the worksheet trial balance for Pioneer Advertising. This trial balance is the same one that appears in Illustration 2-31 (page 68) and Illustration 3-3 (page 97).

Illustration 4-2
Preparing a trial balance

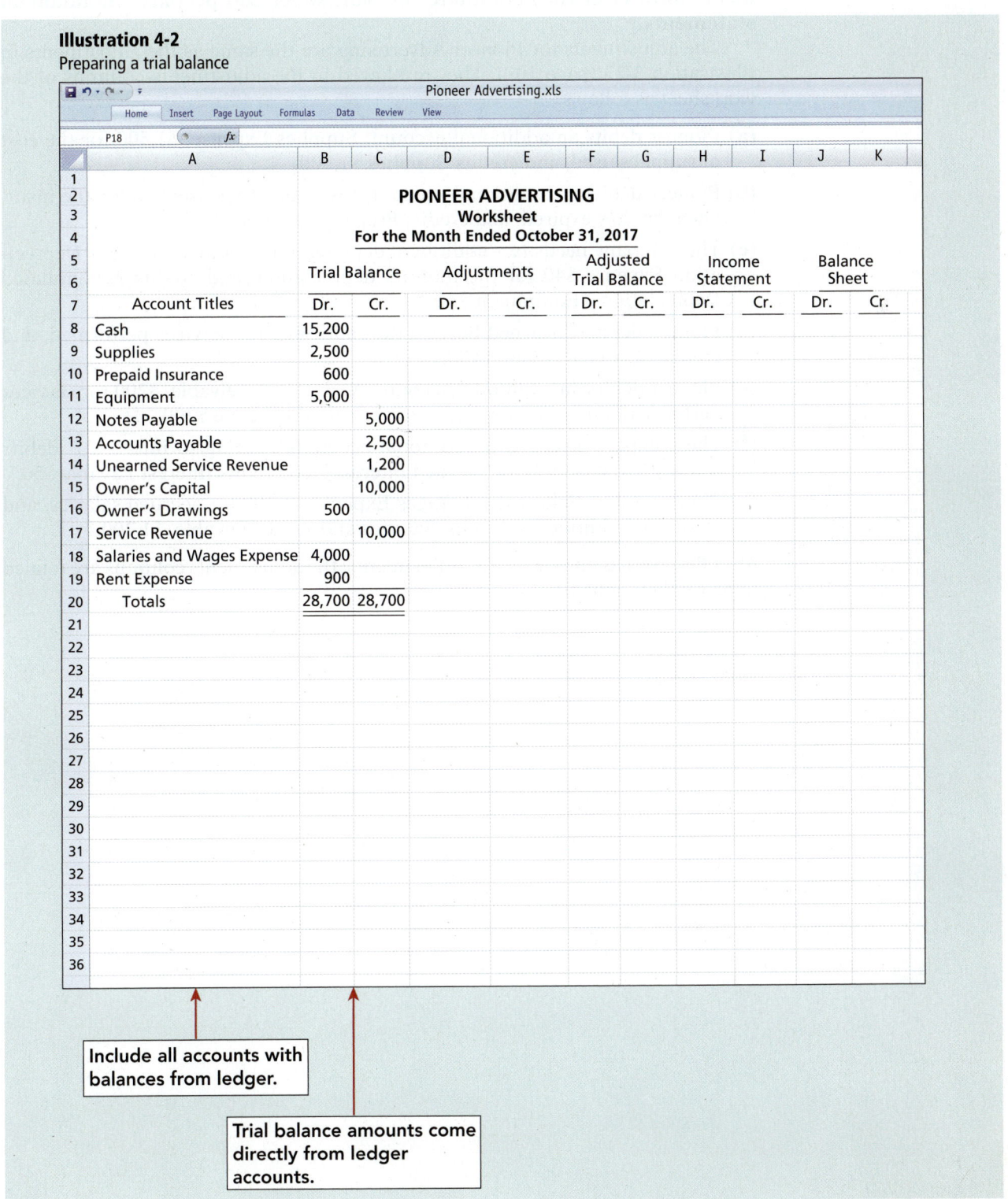

Pioneer Advertising.xls

Home | Insert | Page Layout | Formulas | Data | Review | View

P18 *fx*

PIONEER ADVERTISING
Worksheet
For the Month Ended October 31, 2017

Account Titles	Trial Balance Dr.	Trial Balance Cr.	Adjustments Dr.	Adjustments Cr.	Adjusted Trial Balance Dr.	Adjusted Trial Balance Cr.	Income Statement Dr.	Income Statement Cr.	Balance Sheet Dr.	Balance Sheet Cr.
Cash	15,200									
Supplies	2,500									
Prepaid Insurance	600									
Equipment	5,000									
Notes Payable		5,000								
Accounts Payable		2,500								
Unearned Service Revenue		1,200								
Owner's Capital		10,000								
Owner's Drawings	500									
Service Revenue		10,000								
Salaries and Wages Expense	4,000									
Rent Expense	900									
Totals	28,700	28,700								

Include all accounts with balances from ledger.

Trial balance amounts come directly from ledger accounts.

STEP 2: ENTER THE ADJUSTMENTS IN THE ADJUSTMENTS COLUMNS

As shown in Illustration 4-3, the second step when using a worksheet is to enter all adjustments in the adjustments columns. In entering the adjustments, use applicable trial balance accounts. If additional accounts are needed, insert them on the lines immediately below the trial balance totals. A different letter identifies the debit and credit for each adjusting entry. The term used to describe this process is **keying. Companies do not journalize the adjustments until after they complete the worksheet and prepare the financial statements.**

The adjustments for Pioneer Advertising are the same as the adjustments in Illustration 3-23 (page 109). They are keyed in the adjustments columns of the worksheet as follows.

(a) Pioneer debits an additional account, Supplies Expense, $1,500 for the cost of supplies used, and credits Supplies $1,500.

(b) Pioneer debits an additional account, Insurance Expense, $50 for the insurance that has expired, and credits Prepaid Insurance $50.

(c) The company needs two additional depreciation accounts. It debits Depreciation Expense $40 for the month's depreciation, and credits Accumulated Depreciation—Equipment $40.

(d) Pioneer debits Unearned Service Revenue $400 for services performed, and credits Service Revenue $400.

(e) Pioneer debits an additional account, Accounts Receivable, $200 for services performed but not billed, and credits Service Revenue $200.

(f) The company needs two additional accounts relating to interest. It debits Interest Expense $50 for accrued interest, and credits Interest Payable $50.

(g) Pioneer debits Salaries and Wages Expense $1,200 for accrued salaries, and credits an additional account, Salaries and Wages Payable, $1,200.

After Pioneer has entered all the adjustments, the adjustments columns are totaled to prove their equality.

Illustration 4-3A

Entering the adjustments in the adjustments columns

Pioneer Advertising.xls

Home Insert Page Layout Formulas Data Review View

P18 fx

PIONEER ADVERTISING
Worksheet
For the Month Ended October 31, 2017

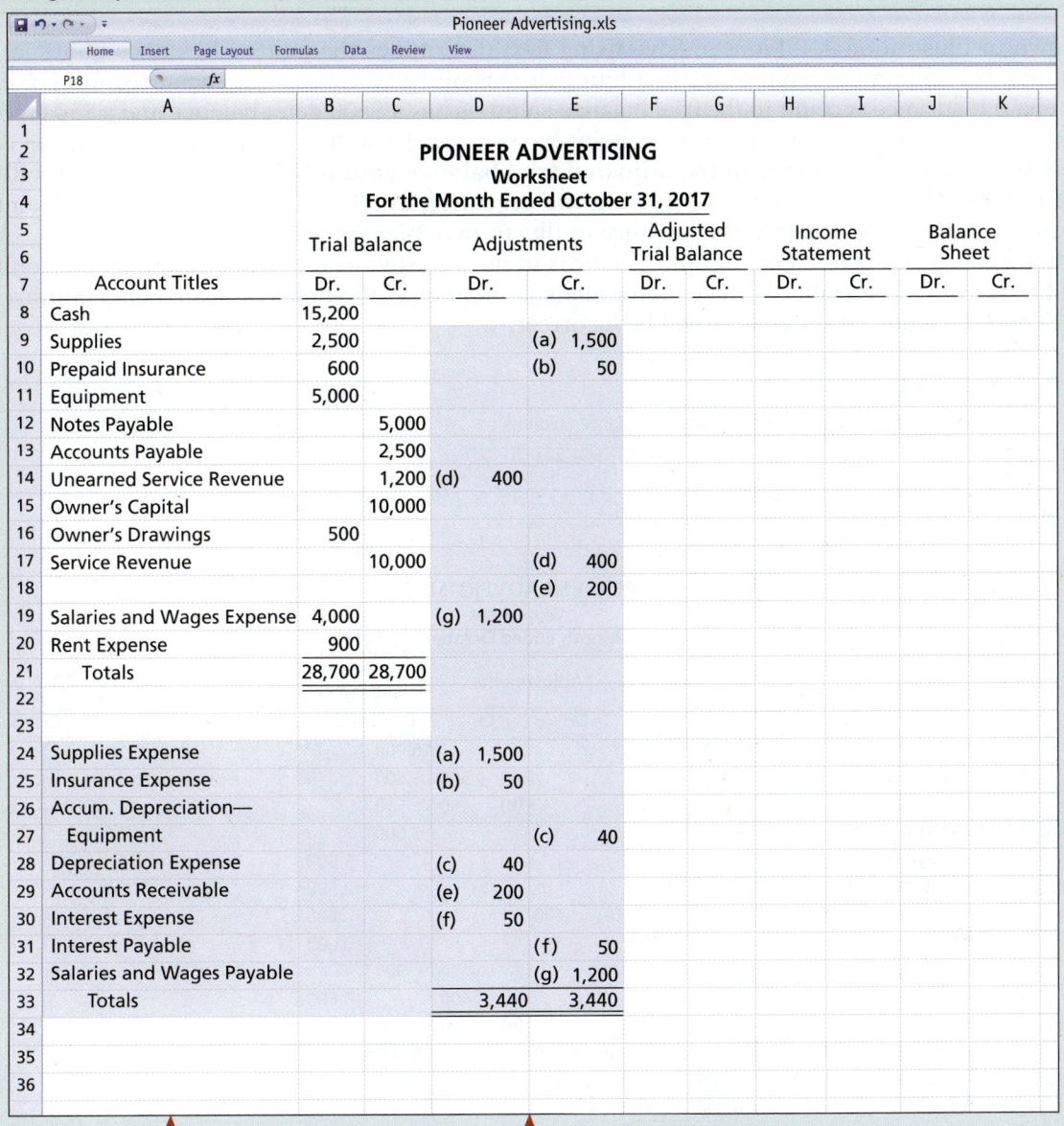

	A	B	C	D	E	F	G	H	I	J	K
5–6		Trial Balance		Adjustments		Adjusted Trial Balance		Income Statement		Balance Sheet	
7	Account Titles	Dr.	Cr.	Dr.	Cr.	Dr.	Cr.	Dr.	Cr.	Dr.	Cr.
8	Cash	15,200									
9	Supplies	2,500			(a) 1,500						
10	Prepaid Insurance	600			(b) 50						
11	Equipment	5,000									
12	Notes Payable		5,000								
13	Accounts Payable		2,500								
14	Unearned Service Revenue		1,200	(d) 400							
15	Owner's Capital		10,000								
16	Owner's Drawings	500									
17	Service Revenue		10,000		(d) 400						
18					(e) 200						
19	Salaries and Wages Expense	4,000		(g) 1,200							
20	Rent Expense	900									
21	Totals	28,700	28,700								
22											
23											
24	Supplies Expense			(a) 1,500							
25	Insurance Expense			(b) 50							
26	Accum. Depreciation—										
27	Equipment				(c) 40						
28	Depreciation Expense			(c) 40							
29	Accounts Receivable			(e) 200							
30	Interest Expense			(f) 50							
31	Interest Payable				(f) 50						
32	Salaries and Wages Payable				(g) 1,200						
33	Totals			3,440	3,440						
34											
35											
36											

Add additional accounts as needed to complete the adjustments:
(a) Supplies Used.
(b) Insurance Expired.
(c) Depreciation Expensed.
(d) Service Revenue Recognized.
(e) Service Revenue Accrued.
(f) Interest Accrued.
(g) Salaries Accrued.

Enter adjustment amounts in appropriate columns, and use letters to cross-reference the debit and credit adjustments.

Total adjustments columns and check for equality.

STEP 3: ENTER ADJUSTED BALANCES IN THE ADJUSTED TRIAL BALANCE COLUMNS

As shown in Illustration 4-4, Pioneer Advertising next determines the adjusted balance of an account by combining the amounts entered in the first four columns of the worksheet for each account. For example, the Prepaid Insurance account in the trial balance columns has a $600 debit balance and a $50 credit in the adjustments columns. The result is a $550 debit balance recorded in the adjusted trial balance columns. **For each account, the amount in the adjusted trial balance columns is the balance that will appear in the ledger after journalizing and posting the adjusting entries.** The balances in these columns are the same as those in the adjusted trial balance in Illustration 3-25 (page 112).

After Pioneer has entered all account balances in the adjusted trial balance columns, the columns are totaled to prove their equality. If the column totals do not agree, the financial statement columns will not balance and the financial statements will be incorrect.

Illustration 4-4
Entering adjusted balances in the adjusted trial balance columns

Pioneer Advertising.xls

Home | Insert | Page Layout | Formulas | Data | Review | View

P18 | fx

PIONEER ADVERTISING
Worksheet
For the Month Ended October 31, 2017

	A	B	C	D	E	F	G	H	I	J	K
5–6		Trial Balance		Adjustments		Adjusted Trial Balance		Income Statement		Balance Sheet	
7	Account Titles	Dr.	Cr.	Dr.	Cr.	Dr.	Cr.	Dr.	Cr.	Dr.	Cr.
8	Cash	15,200				15,200					
9	Supplies	2,500			(a) 1,500	1,000					
10	Prepaid Insurance	600			(b) 50	550					
11	Equipment	5,000				5,000					
12	Notes Payable		5,000				5,000				
13	Accounts Payable		2,500				2,500				
14	Unearned Service Revenue		1,200	(d) 400			800				
15	Owner's Capital		10,000				10,000				
16	Owner's Drawings	500				500					
17	Service Revenue		10,000		(d) 400		10,600				
18					(e) 200						
19	Salaries and Wages Expense	4,000		(g) 1,200		5,200					
20	Rent Expense	900				900					
21	Totals	28,700	28,700								
22											
23											
24	Supplies Expense			(a) 1,500		1,500					
25	Insurance Expense			(b) 50		50					
26	Accum. Depreciation—										
27	Equipment				(c) 40		40				
28	Depreciation Expense			(c) 40		40					
29	Accounts Receivable			(e) 200		200					
30	Interest Expense			(f) 50		50					
31	Interest Payable				(f) 50		50				
32	Salaries and Wages Payable				(g) 1,200		1,200				
33	Totals			3,440	3,440	30,190	30,190				
34											
35											
36											

Combine trial balance amounts with adjustment amounts to obtain the adjusted trial balance.

Total adjusted trial balance columns and check for equality.

STEP 4: EXTEND ADJUSTED TRIAL BALANCE AMOUNTS TO APPROPRIATE FINANCIAL STATEMENT COLUMNS

As shown in Illustration 4-5, the fourth step is to extend adjusted trial balance amounts to the income statement and balance sheet columns of the worksheet. Pioneer Advertising enters balance sheet accounts in the appropriate balance sheet debit and credit columns. For instance, it enters Cash in the balance sheet debit column, and Notes Payable in the balance sheet credit column. Pioneer extends Accumulated Depreciation—Equipment to the balance sheet credit column. The reason is that accumulated depreciation is a contra asset account with a credit balance.

Helpful Hint Every adjusted trial balance amount must be extended to one of the four statement columns.

Because the worksheet does not have columns for the owner's equity statement, Pioneer extends the balance in owner's capital to the balance sheet credit column. In addition, it extends the balance in owner's drawings to the balance sheet debit column because it is an owner's equity account with a debit balance.

The company enters the expense and revenue accounts such as Salaries and Wages Expense and Service Revenue in the appropriate income statement columns.

Illustration 4-5
Extending the adjusted trial balance amounts to appropriate financial statement columns

Pioneer Advertising.xls

Home Insert Page Layout Formulas Data Review View

P18 fx

PIONEER ADVERTISING
Worksheet
For the Month Ended October 31, 2017

	A	B	C	D	E	F	G	H	I	J	K
5–6		Trial Balance		Adjustments		Adjusted Trial Balance		Income Statement		Balance Sheet	
7	Account Titles	Dr.	Cr.	Dr.	Cr.	Dr.	Cr.	Dr.	Cr.	Dr.	Cr.
8	Cash	15,200				15,200				15,200	
9	Supplies	2,500			(a) 1,500	1,000				1,000	
10	Prepaid Insurance	600			(b) 50	550				550	
11	Equipment	5,000				5,000				5,000	
12	Notes Payable		5,000				5,000				5,000
13	Accounts Payable		2,500				2,500				2,500
14	Unearned Service Revenue		1,200	(d) 400			800				800
15	Owner's Capital		10,000				10,000				10,000
16	Owner's Drawings	500				500				500	
17	Service Revenue		10,000		(d) 400		10,600		10,600		
18					(e) 200						
19	Salaries and Wages Expense	4,000		(g) 1,200		5,200		5,200			
20	Rent Expense	900				900		900			
21	Totals	28,700	28,700								
22											
23											
24	Supplies Expense			(a) 1,500		1,500		1,500			
25	Insurance Expense			(b) 50		50		50			
26	Accum. Depreciation—										
27	Equipment				(c) 40		40				40
28	Depreciation Expense			(c) 40		40		40			
29	Accounts Receivable			(e) 200		200				200	
30	Interest Expense			(f) 50		50		50			
31	Interest Payable				(f) 50		50				50
32	Salaries and Wages Payable				(g) 1,200		1,200				1,200
33	Totals			3,440	3,440	30,190	30,190				
34											
35											
36											

Extend all revenue and expense account balances to the income statement columns.

Extend all asset and liability account balances, as well as owner's capital and drawings account balances, to the balance sheet columns.

STEP 5: TOTAL THE STATEMENT COLUMNS, COMPUTE THE NET INCOME (OR NET LOSS), AND COMPLETE THE WORKSHEET

As shown in Illustration 4-6, Pioneer Advertising must now total each of the financial statement columns. The net income or loss for the period is the difference between the totals of the two income statement columns. If total credits exceed total debits, the result is net income. In such a case, the company inserts the words "Net Income" in the account titles space. It then enters the amount in the income statement debit column and the balance sheet credit column. **The debit amount balances the income statement columns; the credit amount balances the balance sheet columns.** In addition, the credit in the balance sheet column indicates the increase in owner's equity resulting from net income.

What if total debits in the income statement columns exceed total credits? In that case, Pioneer has a net loss. It enters the amount of the net loss in the income statement credit column and the balance sheet debit column.

After entering the net income or net loss, Pioneer determines new column totals. The totals shown in the debit and credit income statement columns will match. So will the totals shown in the debit and credit balance sheet columns. If either the income statement columns or the balance sheet columns are not equal after the net income or net loss has been entered, there is an error in the worksheet.

Illustration 4-6 Computing net income or net loss and completing the worksheet

Home Insert Page Layout Formulas Data Review View

	A	B	C	D	E	F	G	H	I	J	K
1											
2				**PIONEER ADVERTISING**							
3				**Worksheet**							
4				**For the Month Ended October 31, 2017**							
5		Trial Balance		Adjustments		Adjusted Trial Balance		Income Statement		Balance Sheet	
6											
7	Account Titles	Dr.	Cr.	Dr.	Cr.	Dr.	Cr.	Dr.	Cr.	Dr.	Cr.
8	Cash	15,200				15,200				15,200	
9	Supplies	2,500			(a) 1,500	1,000				1,000	
10	Prepaid Insurance	600			(b) 50	550				550	
11	Equipment	5,000				5,000				5,000	
12	Notes Payable		5,000				5,000				5,000
13	Accounts Payable		2,500				2,500				2,500
14	Unearned Service Revenue		1,200	(d) 400			800				800
15	Owner's Capital		10,000				10,000				10,000
16	Owner's Drawings	500				500				500	
17	Service Revenue		10,000		(d) 400		10,600		10,600		
18					(e) 200						
19	Salaries and Wages Expense	4,000		(g) 1,200		5,200		5,200			
20	Rent Expense	900				900		900			
21	Totals	28,700	28,700								
22											
23											
24	Supplies Expense			(a) 1,500		1,500		1,500			
25	Insurance Expense			(b) 50		50		50			
26	Accum. Depreciation—										
27	Equipment				(c) 40		40				40
28	Depreciation Expense			(c) 40		40		40			
29	Accounts Receivable			(e) 200		200				200	
30	Interest Expense			(f) 50		50		50			
31	Interest Payable				(f) 50		50				50
32	Salaries and Wages Payable				(g) 1,200		1,200				1,200
33	Totals			3,440	3,440	30,190	30,190	7,740	10,600	22,450	19,590
34											
35	Net Income							2,860			2,860
36	Totals							10,600	10,600	22,450	22,450

The difference between the totals of the two income statement columns determines net income or net loss.

Net income is extended to the credit column of the balance sheet columns. (Net loss would be extended to the debit column.)

Preparing Financial Statements from a Worksheet

After a company has completed a worksheet, it has at hand all the data required for preparation of financial statements. The income statement is prepared from the income statement columns. The balance sheet and owner's equity statement are prepared from the balance sheet columns. Illustration 4-7 shows the financial

Illustration 4-7
Financial statements from a worksheet

PIONEER ADVERTISING
Income Statement
For the Month Ended October 31, 2017

Revenues		
Service revenue		$10,600
Expenses		
Salaries and wages expense	$5,200	
Supplies expense	1,500	
Rent expense	900	
Insurance expense	50	
Interest expense	50	
Depreciation expense	40	
Total expenses		7,740
Net income		$ 2,860

PIONEER ADVERTISING
Owner's Equity Statement
For the Month Ended October 31, 2017

Owner's capital, October 1		$ -0-
Add: Investments	$10,000	
Net income	2,860	12,860
		12,860
Less: Drawings		500
Owner's capital, October 31		$12,360

PIONEER ADVERTISING
Balance Sheet
October 31, 2017

Assets		
Cash		$15,200
Accounts receivable		200
Supplies		1,000
Prepaid insurance		550
Equipment	$5,000	
Less: Accumulated depreciation—equipment	40	4,960
Total assets		$21,910
Liabilities and Owner's Equity		
Liabilities		
Notes payable	$5,000	
Accounts payable	2,500	
Interest payable	50	
Unearned service revenue	800	
Salaries and wages payable	1,200	
Total liabilities		$ 9,550
Owner's equity		
Owner's capital		12,360
Total liabilities and owner's equity		$21,910

statements prepared from Pioneer Advertising's worksheet. At this point, the company has not journalized or posted adjusting entries. Therefore, ledger balances for some accounts are not the same as the financial statement amounts.

The amount shown for owner's capital on the worksheet is the account balance **before considering drawings and net income (or loss)**. When the owner has made no additional investments of capital during the period, this worksheet amount for owner's capital is the balance at the beginning of the period.

Using a worksheet, companies can prepare financial statements before they journalize and post adjusting entries. **However, the completed worksheet is not a substitute for formal financial statements.** The format of the data in the financial statement columns of the worksheet is not the same as the format of the financial statements. **A worksheet is essentially a working tool of the accountant**; companies do not distribute it to management and other parties.

Preparing Adjusting Entries from a Worksheet

A worksheet is not a journal, and it cannot be used as a basis for posting to ledger accounts. To adjust the accounts, the company must journalize the adjustments and post them to the ledger. **The adjusting entries are prepared from the adjustments columns of the worksheet.** The reference letters in the adjustments columns and the explanations of the adjustments at the bottom of the worksheet help identify the adjusting entries. The journalizing and posting of adjusting entries **follows** the preparation of financial statements when a worksheet is used. The adjusting entries on October 31 for Pioneer Advertising are the same as those shown in Illustration 3-23 (page 109).

Helpful Hint
Note that writing the explanation to the adjustment at the bottom of the worksheet is not required.

DO IT! 1 Worksheet

Susan Elbe is preparing a worksheet. Explain to Susan how she should extend the following adjusted trial balance accounts to the financial statement columns of the worksheet.

Cash	Owner's Drawings
Accumulated Depreciation—Equipment	Service Revenue
Accounts Payable	Salaries and Wages Expense

Solution

Income statement debit column—Salaries and Wages Expense
Income statement credit column—Service Revenue
Balance sheet debit column—Cash; Owner's Drawings
Balance sheet credit column—Accumulated Depreciation—Equipment; Accounts Payable

Related exercise material: **BE4-1, BE4-2, BE4-3, E4-1, E4-2, E4-5, E4-6, and DO IT! 4-1.**

Action Plan
- ✔ Balance sheet: Extend assets to debit column. Extend liabilities to credit column. Extend contra assets to credit column. Extend drawings account to debit column.
- ✔ Income statement: Extend expenses to debit column. Extend revenues to credit column.

LEARNING OBJECTIVE 2 Prepare closing entries and a post-closing trial balance.

At the end of the accounting period, the company makes the accounts ready for the next period. This is called **closing the books**. In closing the books, the company distinguishes between temporary and permanent accounts.

Temporary accounts relate only to a given accounting period. They include all income statement accounts and the owner's drawings account. **The company closes all temporary accounts at the end of the period.**

In contrast, **permanent accounts** relate to one or more future accounting periods. They consist of all balance sheet accounts, including the owner's capital account. **Permanent accounts are not closed from period to period.** Instead, the company carries forward the balances of permanent accounts into the next accounting period. Illustration 4-8 identifies the accounts in each category.

Alternative Terminology
Temporary accounts are sometimes called *nominal accounts*, and permanent accounts are sometimes called *real accounts*.

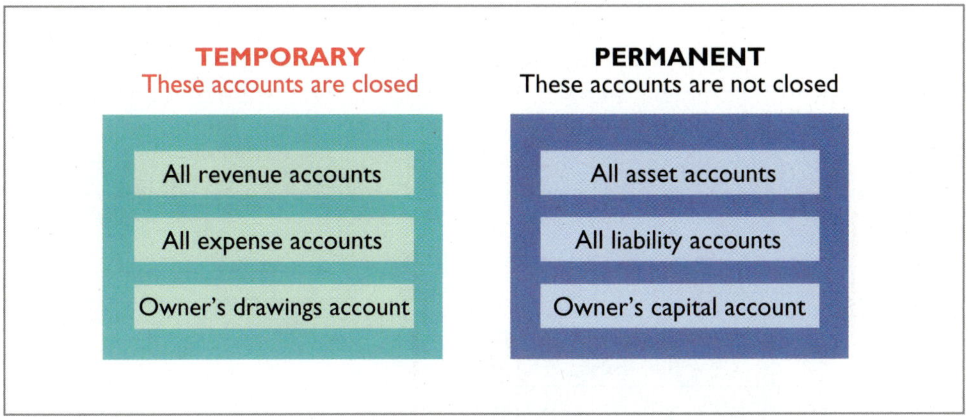

TEMPORARY
These accounts are closed
All revenue accounts
All expense accounts
Owner's drawings account
PERMANENT
These accounts are not closed
All asset accounts
All liability accounts
Owner's capital account

Illustration 4-8
Temporary versus permanent accounts

Preparing Closing Entries

At the end of the accounting period, the company transfers temporary account balances to the permanent owner's equity account, Owner's Capital, by means of closing entries.[1]

Closing entries formally recognize in the ledger the transfer of net income (or net loss) and owner's drawings to owner's capital. The owner's equity statement shows the results of these entries. **Closing entries also produce a zero balance in each temporary account.** The temporary accounts are then ready to accumulate data in the next accounting period separate from the data of prior periods. Permanent accounts are not closed.

Journalizing and posting closing entries is a required step in the accounting cycle. (See Illustration 4-15 on page 166.) The company performs this step after it has prepared financial statements. In contrast to the steps in the cycle that you have already studied, companies generally journalize and post closing entries **only at the end of the annual accounting period**. Thus, all temporary accounts will contain data for the entire year.

In preparing closing entries, companies could close each income statement account directly to owner's capital. However, to do so would result in excessive detail in the permanent Owner's Capital account. Instead, companies close the revenue and expense accounts to another temporary account, **Income Summary**, and they transfer the resulting net income or net loss from this account to owner's capital.

Companies **record closing entries in the general journal**. A center caption, Closing Entries, inserted in the journal between the last adjusting entry and the first closing entry, identifies these entries. Then the company posts the closing entries to the ledger accounts.

Companies generally prepare closing entries directly from the adjusted balances in the ledger. They could prepare separate closing entries for each nominal account, but the following four entries accomplish the desired result more efficiently:

1. Debit each revenue account for its balance, and credit Income Summary for total revenues.
2. Debit Income Summary for total expenses, and credit each expense account for its balance.

[1]We explain closing entries for a partnership and for a corporation in Chapters 12 and 13, respectively.

Helpful Hint
Owner's Drawings is closed directly to Owner's Capital and not to Income Summary. Owner's Drawings is not an expense.

3. Debit Income Summary and credit Owner's Capital for the amount of net income.
4. Debit Owner's Capital for the balance in the Owner's Drawings account, and credit Owner's Drawings for the same amount.

Illustration 4-9 presents a diagram of the closing process. In it, the boxed numbers refer to the four entries required in the closing process.

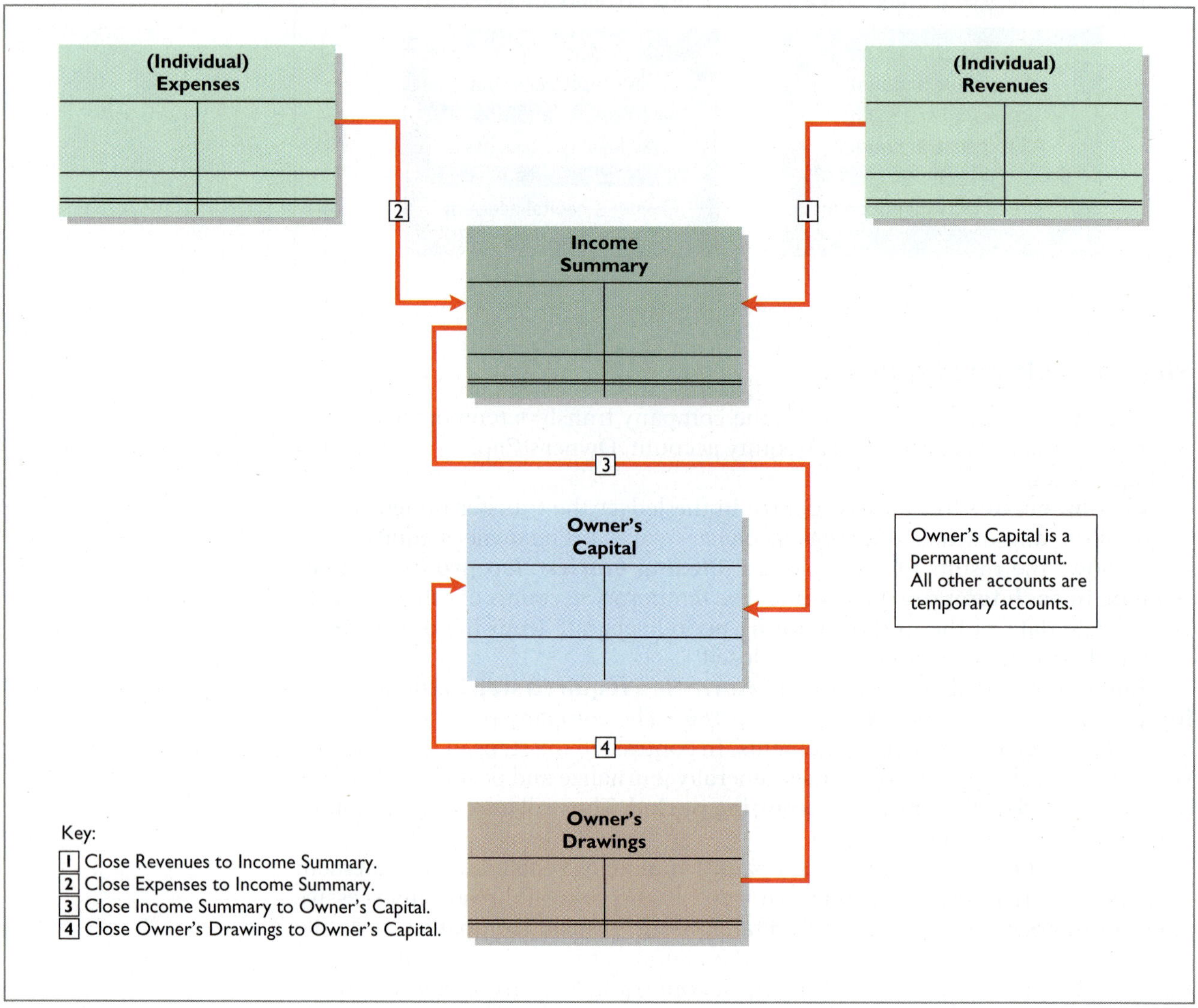

Illustration 4-9
Diagram of closing process—proprietorship

If there were a net loss (because expenses exceeded revenues), entry 3 in Illustration 4-9 would be reversed: there would be a credit to Income Summary and a debit to Owner's Capital.

CLOSING ENTRIES ILLUSTRATED

In practice, companies generally prepare closing entries only at the end of the annual accounting period. However, to illustrate the journalizing and posting of closing entries, we will assume that Pioneer Advertising closes its books monthly. Illustration 4-10 shows the closing entries at October 31. (The numbers in parentheses before each entry correspond to the four entries diagrammed in Illustration 4-9.)

Illustration 4-10
Closing entries journalized

GENERAL JOURNAL J3

Date	Account Titles and Explanation	Ref.	Debit	Credit
	Closing Entries			
2017	(1)			
Oct. 31	Service Revenue	400	10,600	
	Income Summary	350		10,600
	(To close revenue account)			
	(2)			
31	Income Summary	350	7,740	
	Supplies Expense	631		1,500
	Depreciation Expense	711		40
	Insurance Expense	722		50
	Salaries and Wages Expense	726		5,200
	Rent Expense	729		900
	Interest Expense	905		50
	(To close expense accounts)			
	(3)			
31	Income Summary	350	2,860	
	Owner's Capital	301		2,860
	(To close net income to capital)			
	(4)			
31	Owner's Capital	301	500	
	Owner's Drawings	306		500
	(To close drawings to capital)			

Note that the amounts for Income Summary in entries (1) and (2) are the totals of the income statement credit and debit columns, respectively, in the worksheet.

A couple of cautions in preparing closing entries. (1) Avoid unintentionally doubling the revenue and expense balances rather than zeroing them. (2) Do not close Owner's Drawings through the Income Summary account. **Owner's Drawings is not an expense, and it is not a factor in determining net income.**

Posting Closing Entries

Illustration 4-11 shows the posting of the closing entries and the underlining (ruling) of the accounts. Note that all temporary accounts have zero balances after posting the closing entries. In addition, notice that the balance in owner's capital (Owner's Capital) represents the total equity of the owner at the end of the accounting period. This balance is shown on the balance sheet and is the ending capital reported on the owner's equity statement, as shown in Illustration 4-7 (page 157). Pioneer Advertising uses the Income Summary account only in closing. It does not journalize and post entries to this account during the year.

Helpful Hint
The balance in Income Summary before it is closed must equal the net income or net loss for the period.

As part of the closing process, Pioneer totals, balances, and double-underlines its temporary accounts—revenues, expenses, and Owner's Drawings, as shown in T-account form in Illustration 4-11 (page 162). It does not close its permanent accounts—assets, liabilities, and Owner's Capital. Instead, Pioneer draws a single underline beneath the current-period entries for the permanent accounts. The account balance is then entered below the single underline and is carried forward to the next period (for example, see Owner's Capital).

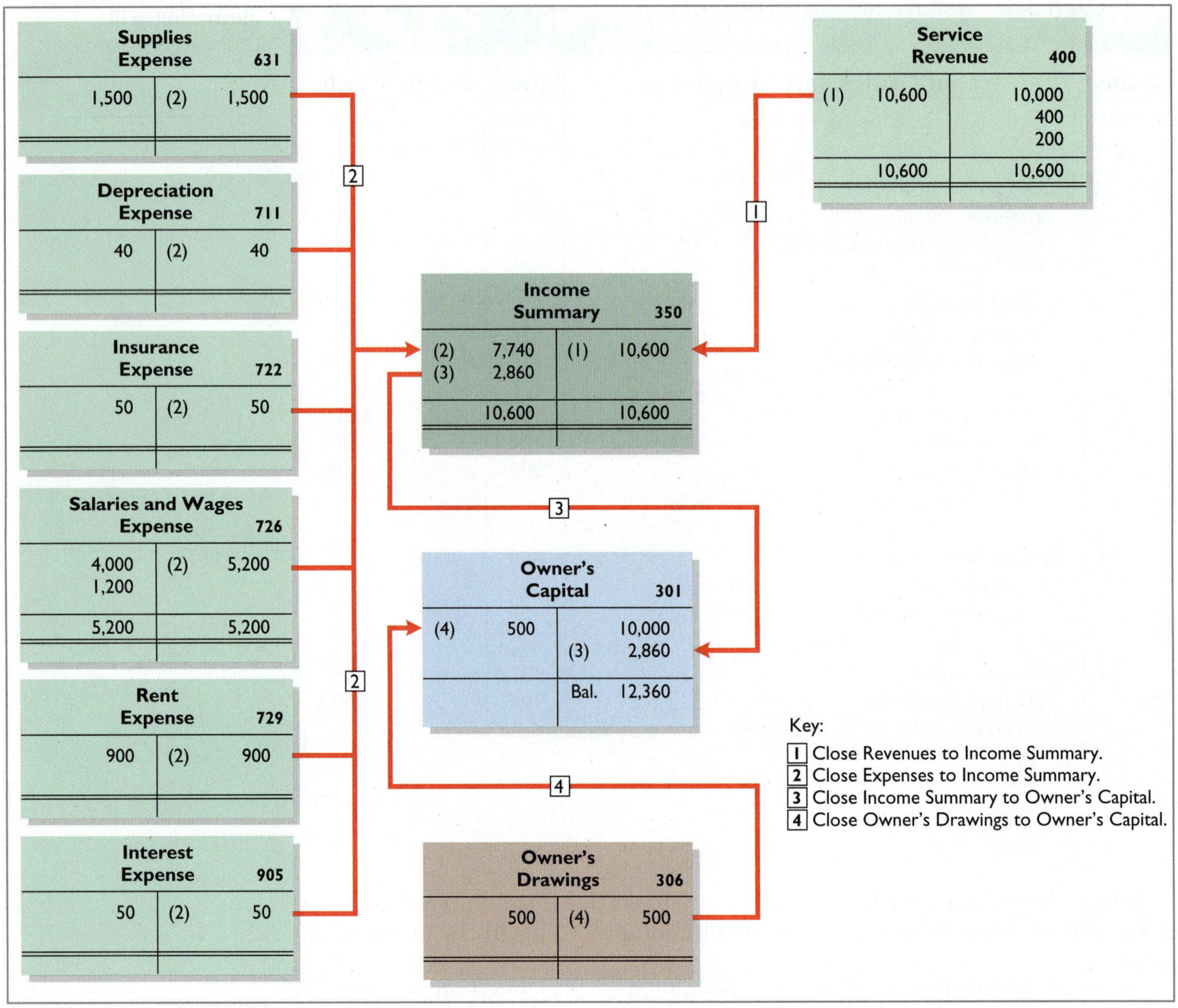

Illustration 4-11
Posting of closing entries

Accounting Across the Organization — Cisco Systems

© Steve Cole/iStockphoto

Cisco Performs the Virtual Close

Technology has dramatically shortened the closing process. Recent surveys have reported that the average company now takes only six to seven days to close, rather than the previous 20 days. But a few companies do much better. Cisco Systems can perform a "virtual close"—closing within 24 hours on any day in the quarter. The same is true at Lockheed Martin Corp., which improved its closing time by 85% in just the last few years. Not very long ago, it took 14 to 16 days. Managers at these companies emphasize that this increased speed has not reduced the accuracy and completeness of the data.

This is not just showing off. Knowing exactly where you are financially all of the time allows the company to respond faster than its competitors. It also means that the hundreds of people who used to spend 10 to 20 days a quarter tracking transactions can now be more usefully employed on things such as mining data for business intelligence to find new business opportunities.

Source: "Reporting Practices: Few Do It All," *Financial Executive* (November 2003), p. 11.

Who else benefits from a shorter closing process? (Go to **WileyPLUS** for this answer and additional questions.)

Preparing a Post-Closing Trial Balance

After Pioneer Advertising has journalized and posted all closing entries, it prepares another trial balance, called a **post-closing trial balance**, from the ledger. The post-closing trial balance lists permanent accounts and their balances after the journalizing and posting of closing entries. The purpose of the post-closing trial balance is **to prove the equality of the permanent account balances carried forward into the next accounting period**. Since all temporary accounts will have zero balances, **the post-closing trial balance will contain only permanent—balance sheet—accounts**.

Illustration 4-12 shows the post-closing trial balance for Pioneer Advertising.

Illustration 4-12
Post-closing trial balance

PIONEER ADVERTISING
Post-Closing Trial Balance
October 31, 2017

	Debit	Credit
Cash	$ 15,200	
Accounts Receivable	200	
Supplies	1,000	
Prepaid Insurance	550	
Equipment	5,000	
Accumulated Depreciation—Equipment		$ 40
Notes Payable		5,000
Accounts Payable		2,500
Unearned Service Revenue		800
Salaries and Wages Payable		1,200
Interest Payable		50
Owner's Capital		12,360
	$21,950	$21,950

Pioneer prepares the post-closing trial balance from the permanent accounts in the ledger. Illustration 4-13 (page 164) shows the permanent accounts in Pioneer's general ledger.

(Permanent Accounts Only)

GENERAL LEDGER

Cash — No. 101

Date	Explanation	Ref.	Debit	Credit	Balance
2017					
Oct. 1		J1	10,000		10,000
2		J1	1,200		11,200
3		J1		900	10,300
4		J1		600	9,700
20		J1		500	9,200
26		J1		4,000	5,200
31		J1	10,000		**15,200**

Accounts Receivable — No. 112

Date	Explanation	Ref.	Debit	Credit	Balance
2017					
Oct. 31	Adj. entry	J2	**200**		**200**

Supplies — No. 126

Date	Explanation	Ref.	Debit	Credit	Balance
2017					
Oct. 5		J1	2,500		2,500
31	Adj. entry	J2		**1,500**	**1,000**

Prepaid Insurance — No. 130

Date	Explanation	Ref.	Debit	Credit	Balance
2017					
Oct. 4		J1	600		600
31	Adj. entry	J2		**50**	**550**

Equipment — No. 157

Date	Explanation	Ref.	Debit	Credit	Balance
2017					
Oct. 1		J1	5,000		**5,000**

Accumulated Depreciation—Equipment — No. 158

Date	Explanation	Ref.	Debit	Credit	Balance
2017					
Oct. 31	Adj. entry	J2		**40**	**40**

Notes Payable — No. 200

Date	Explanation	Ref.	Debit	Credit	Balance
2017					
Oct. 1		J1		5,000	**5,000**

Accounts Payable — No. 201

Date	Explanation	Ref.	Debit	Credit	Balance
2017					
Oct. 5		J1		2,500	**2,500**

Unearned Service Revenue — No. 209

Date	Explanation	Ref.	Debit	Credit	Balance
2017					
Oct. 2		J1		1,200	1,200
31	Adj. entry	J2	400		**800**

Salaries and Wages Payable — No. 212

Date	Explanation	Ref.	Debit	Credit	Balance
2017					
Oct. 31	Adj. entry	J2		**1,200**	**1,200**

Interest Payable — No. 230

Date	Explanation	Ref.	Debit	Credit	Balance
2017					
Oct. 31	Adj. entry	J2		**50**	**50**

Owner's Capital — No. 301

Date	Explanation	Ref.	Debit	Credit	Balance
2017					
Oct. 1		J1		10,000	10,000
31	**Closing entry**	**J3**		**2,860**	**12,860**
31	**Closing entry**	**J3**	**500**		**12,360**

Note: The permanent accounts for Pioneer Advertising are shown here. Illustration 4-14 (page 165) shows the temporary accounts. Both permanent and temporary accounts are part of the general ledger. They are segregated here to aid in learning.

Illustration 4-13
General ledger, permanent accounts

A post-closing trial balance provides evidence that the company has properly journalized and posted the closing entries. It also shows that the accounting equation is in balance at the end of the accounting period. However, like the trial balance, it does not prove that Pioneer has recorded all transactions or that the ledger is correct. For example, the post-closing trial balance still will balance even if a transaction is not journalized and posted or if a transaction is journalized and posted twice.

The remaining accounts in the general ledger are temporary accounts, shown in Illustration 4-14. After Pioneer correctly posts the closing entries, each temporary account has a zero balance. These accounts are double-underlined to finalize the closing process.

(Temporary Accounts Only)

GENERAL LEDGER

Owner's Drawings — No. 306

Date	Explanation	Ref.	Debit	Credit	Balance
2017					
Oct. 20		J1	500		500
31	**Closing entry**	**J3**		**500**	**–0–**

Income Summary — No. 350

Date	Explanation	Ref.	Debit	Credit	Balance
2017					
Oct. 31	**Closing entry**	**J3**		**10,600**	**10,600**
31	**Closing entry**	**J3**	**7,740**		**2,860**
31	**Closing entry**	**J3**	**2,860**		**–0–**

Service Revenue — No. 400

Date	Explanation	Ref.	Debit	Credit	Balance
2017					
Oct. 31		J1		10,000	10,000
31	Adj. entry	J2		400	10,400
31	Adj. entry	J2		200	10,600
31	**Closing entry**	**J3**	**10,600**		**–0–**

Supplies Expense — No. 631

Date	Explanation	Ref.	Debit	Credit	Balance
2017					
Oct. 31	Adj. entry	J2	1,500		1,500
31	**Closing entry**	**J3**		**1,500**	**–0–**

Depreciation Expense — No. 711

Date	Explanation	Ref.	Debit	Credit	Balance
2017					
Oct. 31	Adj. entry	J2	**40**		40
31	**Closing entry**	**J3**		**40**	**–0–**

Insurance Expense — No. 722

Date	Explanation	Ref.	Debit	Credit	Balance
2017					
Oct. 31	Adj. entry	J2	**50**		50
31	**Closing entry**	**J3**		**50**	**–0–**

Salaries and Wages Expense — No. 726

Date	Explanation	Ref.	Debit	Credit	Balance
2017					
Oct. 26		J1	4,000		4,000
31	Adj. entry	J2	**1,200**		5,200
31	**Closing entry**	**J3**		**5,200**	**–0–**

Rent Expense — No. 729

Date	Explanation	Ref.	Debit	Credit	Balance
2017					
Oct. 3		J1	900		900
31	**Closing entry**	**J3**		**900**	**–0–**

Interest Expense — No. 905

Date	Explanation	Ref.	Debit	Credit	Balance
2017					
Oct. 31	Adj. entry	J2	**50**		50
31	**Closing entry**	**J3**		**50**	**–0–**

Note: The temporary accounts for Pioneer Advertising are shown here. Illustration 4-13 (page 164) shows the permanent accounts. Both permanent and temporary accounts are part of the general ledger. They are segregated here to aid in learning.

Illustration 4-14
General ledger, temporary accounts

DO IT! 2 Closing Entries

The worksheet for Hancock Company shows the following in the financial statement columns:

Owner's drawings $15,000
Owner's capital $42,000
Net income $18,000

Prepare the closing entries at December 31 that affect owner's capital.

Solution

Dec. 31	Income Summary	18,000	
	Owner's Capital		18,000
	(To close net income to capital)		
31	Owner's Capital	15,000	
	Owner's Drawings		15,000
	(To close drawings to capital)		

Action Plan

✔ Close Income Summary to Owner's Capital.

✔ Close Owner's Drawings to Owner's Capital.

Related exercise material: **BE4-4, BE4-5, BE4-6, E4-4, E4-7, E4-8, E4-11, and DO IT! 4-2.**

LEARNING OBJECTIVE 3

Explain the steps in the accounting cycle and how to prepare correcting entries.

Summary of the Accounting Cycle

Illustration 4-15 summarizes the steps in the accounting cycle. You can see that the cycle begins with the analysis of business transactions and ends with the preparation of a post-closing trial balance.

Illustration 4-15
Steps in the accounting cycle

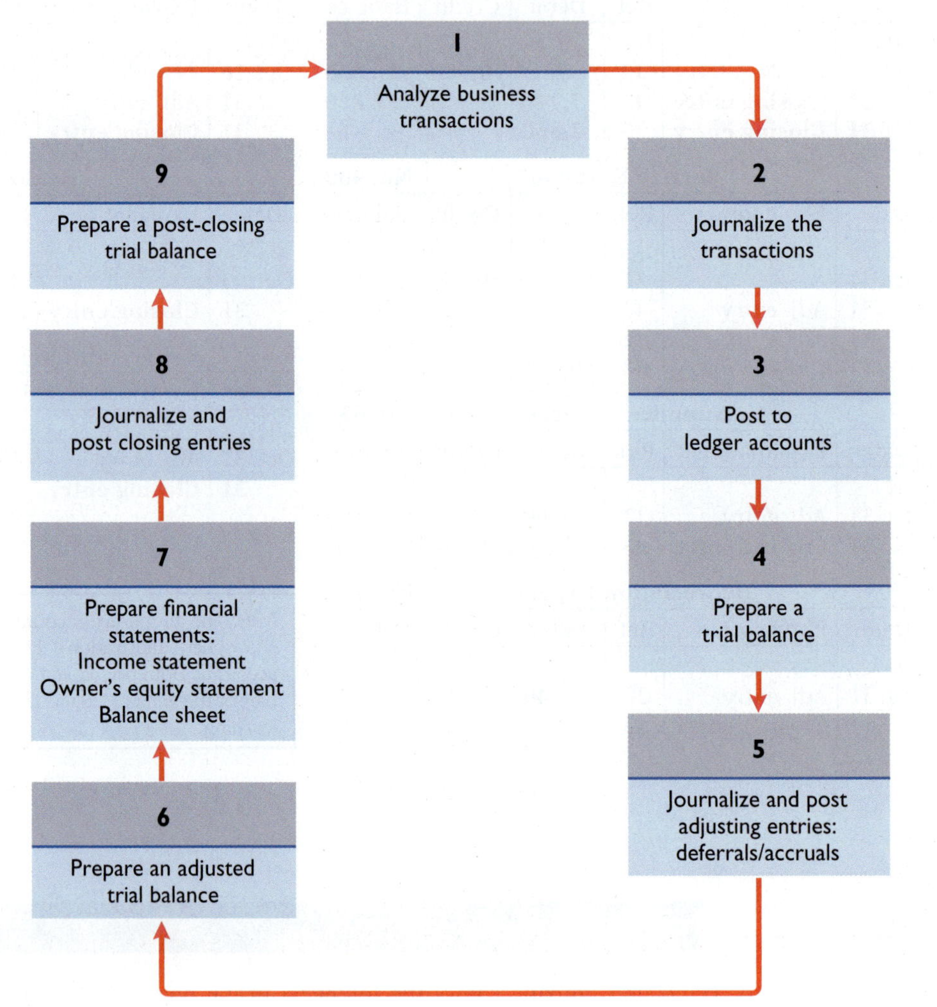

Optional steps: If a worksheet is prepared, Steps 4, 5, and 6 are incorporated in the worksheet. If reversing entries are prepared, they occur between Steps 9 and 1 as discussed below.

Steps 1–3 may occur daily during the accounting period. Companies perform Steps 4–7 on a periodic basis, such as monthly, quarterly, or annually. Steps 8 and 9—closing entries and a post-closing trial balance—usually take place only at the end of a company's **annual** accounting period.

There are also two **optional steps** in the accounting cycle. As you have seen, companies may use a worksheet in preparing adjusting entries and financial statements. In addition, they may use reversing entries, as explained below.

Reversing Entries—An Optional Step

Some accountants prefer to reverse certain adjusting entries by making a **reversing entry** at the beginning of the next accounting period. A reversing entry is the exact opposite of the adjusting entry made in the previous period. **Use of reversing**

entries is an optional bookkeeping procedure; it is not a required step in the accounting cycle. Accordingly, we have chosen to cover this topic in an appendix at the end of the chapter.

Correcting Entries—An Avoidable Step

Unfortunately, errors may occur in the recording process. Companies should correct errors, **as soon as they discover them**, by journalizing and posting **correcting entries.** If the accounting records are free of errors, no correcting entries are needed.

You should recognize several differences between correcting entries and adjusting entries. First, adjusting entries are an integral part of the accounting cycle. Correcting entries, on the other hand, are unnecessary if the records are error-free. Second, companies journalize and post adjustments **only at the end of an accounting period**. In contrast, companies make correcting entries **whenever they discover an error**. Finally, adjusting entries always affect at least one balance sheet account and one income statement account. In contrast, correcting entries may involve any combination of accounts in need of correction. **Correcting entries must be posted before closing entries.**

To determine the correcting entry, it is useful to compare the incorrect entry with the correct entry. Doing so helps identify the accounts and amounts that should—and should not—be corrected. After comparison, the accountant makes an entry to correct the accounts. The following two cases for Mercato Co. illustrate this approach.

ETHICS NOTE

When companies find errors in previously released income statements, they restate those numbers. Perhaps because of the increased scrutiny caused by Sarbanes-Oxley, in a recent year companies filed a record 1,195 restatements.

CASE 1

On May 10, Mercato Co. journalized and posted a $50 cash collection on account from a customer as a debit to Cash $50 and a credit to Service Revenue $50. The company discovered the error on May 20, when the customer paid the remaining balance in full.

Illustration 4-16
Comparison of entries

Incorrect Entry (May 10)			Correct Entry (May 10)		
Cash	50		Cash	50	
Service Revenue		50	Accounts Receivable		50

Comparison of the incorrect entry with the correct entry reveals that the debit to Cash $50 is correct. However, the $50 credit to Service Revenue should have been credited to Accounts Receivable. As a result, both Service Revenue and Accounts Receivable are overstated in the ledger. Mercato makes the following correcting entry.

Illustration 4-17
Correcting entry

Correcting Entry

May 20	Service Revenue	50	
	Accounts Receivable		50
	(To correct entry of May 10)		

A	=	L	+	OE
				−50 Rev
−50				

Cash Flows
no effect

CASE 2

On May 18, Mercato purchased on account equipment costing $450. The transaction was journalized and posted as a debit to Equipment $45 and a credit to Accounts Payable $45. The error was discovered on June 3, when Mercato received the monthly statement for May from the creditor.

Illustration 4-18
Comparison of entries

Incorrect Entry (May 18)			Correct Entry (May 18)		
Equipment	45		Equipment	450	
Accounts Payable		45	Accounts Payable		450

Comparison of the two entries shows that two accounts are incorrect. Equipment is understated $405, and Accounts Payable is understated $405. Mercato makes the correcting entry shown in Illustration 4-19 (page 168).

A	=	L	+	OE
+405				
		+405		

Cash Flows
no effect

Illustration 4-19
Correcting entry

Correcting Entry

June 3	Equipment	405	
	Accounts Payable		405
	(To correct entry of May 18)		

Instead of preparing a correcting entry, **it is possible to reverse the incorrect entry and then prepare the correct entry**. This approach will result in more entries and postings than a correcting entry, but it will accomplish the desired result.

Accounting Across the Organization — Yale Express

© Christian Lagereek/iStockphoto

Lost in Transportation

Yale Express, a short-haul trucking firm, turned over much of its cargo to local truckers to complete deliveries. Yale collected the entire delivery charge. When billed by the local trucker, Yale sent payment for the final phase to the local trucker. Yale used a cutoff period of 20 days into the next accounting period in making its adjusting entries for accrued liabilities. That is, it waited 20 days to receive the local truckers' bills to determine the amount of the unpaid but incurred delivery charges as of the balance sheet date.

On the other hand, Republic Carloading, a nationwide, long-distance freight forwarder, frequently did not receive transportation bills from truckers to whom it passed on cargo until months after the year-end. In making its year-end adjusting entries, Republic waited for months in order to include all of these outstanding transportation bills.

When Yale Express merged with Republic Carloading, Yale's vice president employed the 20-day cutoff procedure for both firms. As a result, millions of dollars of Republic's accrued transportation bills went unrecorded. When the company detected the error and made correcting entries, these and other errors changed a reported profit of $1.14 million into a loss of $1.88 million!

What might Yale Express's vice president have done to produce more accurate financial statements without waiting months for Republic's outstanding transportation bills? (Go to **WileyPLUS** for this answer and additional questions.)

DO IT! 3 Correcting Entries

Sanchez Company discovered the following errors made in January 2017.

1. A payment of Salaries and Wages Expense of $600 was debited to Supplies and credited to Cash, both for $600.
2. A collection of $3,000 from a client on account was debited to Cash $200 and credited to Service Revenue $200.
3. The purchase of supplies on account for $860 was debited to Supplies $680 and credited to Accounts Payable $680.

Correct the errors without reversing the incorrect entry.

Action Plan

✔ Compare the incorrect entry with correct entry.

✔ After comparison, make an entry to correct the accounts.

Solution

1. Salaries and Wages Expense	600	
Supplies		600
2. Service Revenue	200	
Cash	2,800	
Accounts Receivable		3,000
3. Supplies ($860 − $680)	180	
Accounts Payable		180

Related exercise material: **BE4-9, E4-12, E4-13, and DO IT! 4-3.**

LEARNING OBJECTIVE 4

Identify the sections of a classified balance sheet.

The balance sheet presents a snapshot of a company's financial position at a point in time. To improve users' understanding of a company's financial position, companies often use a classified balance sheet. A **classified balance sheet** groups together similar assets and similar liabilities, using a number of standard classifications and sections. This is useful because items within a group have similar economic characteristics. A classified balance sheet generally contains the standard classifications listed in Illustration 4-20.

Assets	Liabilities and Owner's Equity
Current assets	Current liabilities
Long-term investments	Long-term liabilities
Property, plant, and equipment	Owner's (Stockholders') equity
Intangible assets	

Illustration 4-20
Standard balance sheet classifications

These groupings help financial statement readers determine such things as (1) whether the company has enough assets to pay its debts as they come due, and (2) the claims of short- and long-term creditors on the company's total assets. Many of these groupings can be seen in the balance sheet of Franklin Company shown in Illustration 4-21 below and on the next page. In the sections that follow, we explain each of these groupings.

Illustration 4-21
Classified balance sheet

FRANKLIN COMPANY
Balance Sheet
October 31, 2017

Assets			
Current assets			
Cash		$ 6,600	
Debt investments		2,000	
Accounts receivable		7,000	
Notes receivable		1,000	
Inventory		3,000	
Supplies		2,100	
Prepaid insurance		400	
Total current assets			$22,100
Long-term investments			
Stock investments		5,200	
Investment in real estate		2,000	7,200
Property, plant, and equipment			
Land		10,000	
Equipment	$24,000		
Less: Accumulated depreciation—equipment	5,000	19,000	29,000
Intangible assets			
Patents			3,100
Total assets			$61,400

Illustration 4-21
(continued)

Helpful Hint
Recall that the basic accounting equation is Assets = Liabilities + Owner's Equity.

Liabilities and Owner's Equity

Current liabilities		
Notes payable	$11,000	
Accounts payable	2,100	
Unearned service revenue	900	
Salaries and wages payable	1,600	
Interest payable	450	
Total current liabilities		$16,050
Long-term liabilities		
Mortgage payable	10,000	
Notes payable	1,300	
Total long-term liabilities		11,300
Total liabilities		27,350
Owner's equity		
Owner's capital		34,050
Total liabilities and owner's equity		$61,400

Current Assets

Current assets are assets that a company expects to convert to cash or use up within one year or its operating cycle, whichever is longer. In Illustration 4-21, Franklin Company had current assets of $22,100. For most businesses, the cutoff for classification as current assets is one year from the balance sheet date. For example, accounts receivable are current assets because the company will collect them and convert them to cash within one year. Supplies is a current asset because the company expects to use them up in operations within one year.

Some companies use a period longer than one year to classify assets and liabilities as current because they have an operating cycle longer than one year. The **operating cycle** of a company is the average time that it takes to purchase inventory, sell it on account, and then collect cash from customers. For most businesses, this cycle takes less than a year so they use a one-year cutoff. But for some businesses, such as vineyards or airplane manufacturers, this period may be longer than a year. **Except where noted, we will assume that companies use one year to determine whether an asset or liability is current or long-term.**

Common types of current assets are (1) cash, (2) investments (such as short-term U.S. government securities), (3) receivables (notes receivable, accounts receivable, and interest receivable), (4) inventories, and (5) prepaid expenses (supplies and insurance). **On the balance sheet, companies usually list these items in the order in which they expect to convert them into cash.**

Illustration 4-22 presents the current assets of Southwest Airlines Co.

Illustration 4-22
Current assets section

Real World

SOUTHWEST AIRLINES CO.
Balance Sheet (partial)
(in millions)

Current assets	
Cash and cash equivalents	$1,390
Short-term investments	369
Accounts receivable	241
Inventories	181
Prepaid expenses and other current assets	420
Total current assets	$2,601

As we explain later in the chapter, a company's current assets are important in assessing its short-term debt-paying ability.

Long-Term Investments

Long-term investments are generally (1) investments in stocks and bonds of other companies that are normally held for many years, (2) long-term assets such as land or buildings that a company is not currently using in its operating activities, and (3) long-term notes receivable. In Illustration 4-21, Franklin Company reported total long-term investments of $7,200 on its balance sheet.

Alternative Terminology
Long-term investments are often referred to simply as *investments*.

Yahoo! Inc. reported long-term investments in its balance sheet, as shown in Illustration 4-23.

Real World

YAHOO! INC.
Balance Sheet (partial)
(in thousands)

Long-term investments	
Investments in securities	$90,266

Illustration 4-23
Long-term investments section

Property, Plant, and Equipment

Alternative Terminology
Property, plant, and equipment is sometimes called *fixed assets* or *plant assets*.

Property, plant, and equipment are assets with relatively long useful lives that a company is currently using in operating the business. This category includes land, buildings, machinery and equipment, delivery equipment, and furniture. In Illustration 4-21, Franklin Company reported property, plant, and equipment of $29,000.

Depreciation is the practice of allocating the cost of assets to a number of years. Companies do this by systematically assigning a portion of an asset's cost as an expense each year (rather than expensing the full purchase price in the year of purchase). The assets that the company depreciates are reported on the balance sheet at cost less accumulated depreciation. The **accumulated depreciation** account shows the total amount of depreciation that the company has expensed thus far in the asset's life. In Illustration 4-21, Franklin Company reported accumulated depreciation of $5,000.

Illustration 4-24 presents the property, plant, and equipment of Cooper Tire & Rubber Company.

International Note

Recently, China adopted International Financial Reporting Standards (IFRS). This was done in an effort to reduce fraud and increase investor confidence in financial reports. Under these standards, many items, such as property, plant, and equipment, may be reported at current fair values rather than historical cost.

Real World

COOPER TIRE & RUBBER COMPANY
Balance Sheet (partial)
(in thousands)

Property, plant, and equipment		
Land and land improvements	$ 41,553	
Buildings	298,706	
Machinery and equipment	1,636,091	
Molds, cores, and rings	268,158	$2,244,508
Less: Accumulated depreciation		1,252,692
		$ 991,816

Illustration 4-24
Property, plant, and equipment section

Intangible Assets

Many companies have long-lived assets that do not have physical substance yet often are very valuable. We call these assets **intangible assets**. One significant intangible asset is goodwill. Others include patents, copyrights, and trademarks

Helpful Hint
Sometimes intangible assets are reported under a broader heading called *"Other assets."*

or trade names that give the company **exclusive right** of use for a specified period of time. In Illustration 4-21, Franklin Company reported intangible assets of $3,100.

Illustration 4-25 shows the intangible assets of media giant **Time Warner, Inc.**

Illustration 4-25
Intangible assets section

Real World

TIME WARNER, INC.
Balance Sheet (partial)
(in millions)

Intangible assets	
Goodwill	$40,953
Film library	2,690
Customer lists	2,540
Cable television franchises	38,048
Sports franchises	262
Brands, trademarks, and other intangible assets	8,313
	$92,806

People, Planet, and Profit Insight

© Gehringi/iStockphoto

Regaining Goodwill

After falling to unforeseen lows amidst scandals, recalls, and economic crises, the American public's positive perception of the reputation of corporate America is on the rise. Overall corporate reputation is experiencing rehabilitation as the American public gives high marks overall to corporate America, specific industries, and the largest number of individual companies in a dozen years. This is according to the findings of the *2011 Harris Interactive RQ Study,* which measures the reputations of the 60 most visible companies in the United States.

The survey focuses on six reputational dimensions that influence reputation and consumer behavior. Four of these dimensions, along with the five corporations that ranked highest within each, are as follows.

- **Social Responsibility**: (1) Whole Foods Market, (2) Johnson & Johnson, (3) Google, (4) The Walt Disney Company, (5) Procter & Gamble Co.
- **Emotional Appeal**: (1) Johnson & Johnson, (2) Amazon.com, (3) UPS, (4) General Mills, (5) Kraft Foods
- **Financial Performance**: (1) Google, (2) Berkshire Hathaway, (3) Apple, (4) Intel, (5) The Walt Disney Company
- **Products and Services**: (1) Intel Corporation, (2) 3M Company, (3) Johnson & Johnson, (4) Google, (5) Procter & Gamble Co.

Source: www.harrisinteractive.com.

Name two industries today which are probably rated low on the reputational characteristics of "being trusted" and "having high ethical standards." (Go to **WileyPLUS** for this answer and additional questions.)

ETHICS NOTE

A company that has more current assets than current liabilities can increase the ratio of current assets to current liabilities by using cash to pay off some current liabilities. This gives the appearance of being more liquid. Do you think this move is ethical?

Current Liabilities

In the liabilities and owner's equity section of the balance sheet, the first grouping is current liabilities. **Current liabilities** are obligations that the company is to pay within the coming year or its operating cycle, whichever is longer. Common examples are accounts payable, salaries and wages payable, notes payable, interest payable, and income taxes payable. Also included as current liabilities are current maturities of long-term obligations—payments to be made within the next year on long-term obligations. In Illustration 4-21, Franklin Company reported five different types of current liabilities, for a total of $16,050.

Illustration 4-26 shows the current liabilities section adapted from the balance sheet of Marcus Corporation.

Illustration 4-26
Current liabilities section

Real World

MARCUS CORPORATION
Balance Sheet (partial)
(in thousands)

Current liabilities	
Notes payable	$ 239
Accounts payable	24,242
Current maturities of long-term debt	57,250
Other current liabilities	27,477
Income taxes payable	11,215
Salaries and wages payable	6,720
Total current liabilities	$127,143

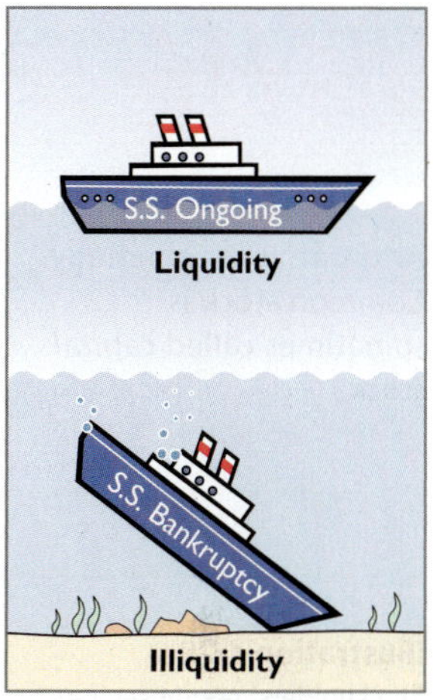

Users of financial statements look closely at the relationship between current assets and current liabilities. This relationship is important in evaluating a company's **liquidity**—its ability to pay obligations expected to be due within the next year. When current assets exceed current liabilities, the likelihood for paying the liabilities is favorable. When the reverse is true, short-term creditors may not be paid, and the company may ultimately be forced into bankruptcy.

Accounting Across the Organization — REL Consultancy Group

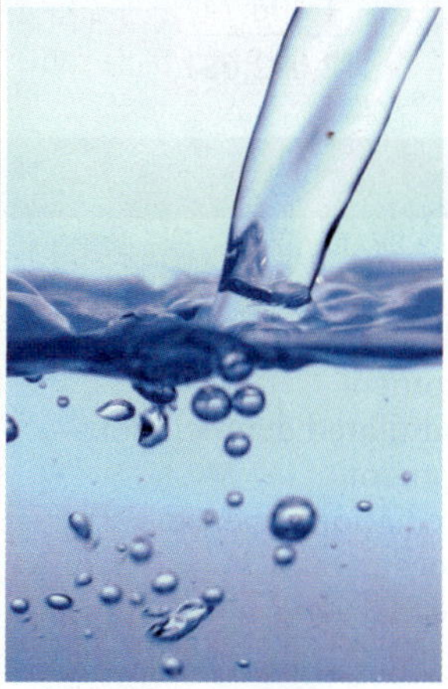
© Jorge Salcedo/iStockphoto

Can a Company Be Too Liquid?

There actually is a point where a company can be too liquid—that is, it can have too much working capital (current assets less current liabilities). While it is important to be liquid enough to be able to pay short-term bills as they come due, a company does not want to tie up its cash in extra inventory or receivables that are not earning the company money.

By one estimate from the REL Consultancy Group, the thousand largest U.S. companies have on their books cumulative excess working capital of $764 billion. Based on this figure, companies could have reduced debt by 36% or increased net income by 9%. Given that managers throughout a company are interested in improving profitability, it is clear that they should have an eye toward managing working capital. They need to aim for a "Goldilocks solution"—not too much, not too little, but just right.

Source: K. Richardson, "Companies Fall Behind in Cash Management," *Wall Street Journal* (June 19, 2007).

What can various company managers do to ensure that working capital is managed efficiently to maximize net income? (Go to **WileyPLUS** for this answer and additional questions.)

Long-Term Liabilities

Long-term liabilities are obligations that a company expects to pay **after** one year. Liabilities in this category include bonds payable, mortgages payable, long-term notes payable, lease liabilities, and pension liabilities. Many companies report long-term debt maturing after one year as a single amount in the balance sheet and show the details of the debt in notes that accompany the financial statements. Others list the various types of long-term liabilities. In Illustration 4-21, Franklin Company reported long-term liabilities of $11,300.

Illustration 4-27 (page 174) shows the long-term liabilities that The Procter & Gamble Company reported in its balance sheet.

Illustration 4-27
Long-term liabilities section

Real World

THE PROCTER & GAMBLE COMPANY
Balance Sheet (partial)
(in millions)

Long-term liabilities	
Long-term debt	$23,375
Deferred income taxes	12,015
Other noncurrent liabilities	5,147
Total long-term liabilities	$40,537

Owner's Equity

Alternative Terminology
Common stock is sometimes called *capital stock*.

The content of the owner's equity section varies with the form of business organization. In a proprietorship, there is one capital account. In a partnership, there is a capital account for each partner. Corporations divide owners' equity into two accounts—Common Stock (sometimes referred to as Capital Stock) and Retained Earnings. Corporations record stockholders' investments in the company by debiting an asset account and crediting the Common Stock account. They record in the Retained Earnings account income retained for use in the business. Corporations combine the Common Stock and Retained Earnings accounts and report them on the balance sheet as **stockholders' equity**. (We discuss these corporation accounts in later chapters.) Nordstrom, Inc. recently reported its stockholders' equity section as follows.

Illustration 4-28
Stockholders' equity section

Real World

NORDSTROM, INC.
Balance Sheet (partial)
(in thousands)

Stockholders' equity	
Common stock, 271,331 shares	$ 685,934
Retained earnings	1,406,747
Total stockholders' equity	$2,092,681

DO IT! 4 Balance Sheet Classifications

The following accounts were taken from the financial statements of Callahan Company.

_______ Salaries and wages payable	_______ Stock investments (long-term)
_______ Service revenue	_______ Equipment
_______ Interest payable	_______ Accumulated depreciation—equipment
_______ Goodwill	_______ Depreciation expense
_______ Debt investments (short-term)	_______ Owner's capital
_______ Mortgage payable (due in 3 years)	_______ Unearned service revenue

Match each of the following to its proper balance sheet classification, shown below. If the item would not appear on a balance sheet, use "NA."

Current assets (CA)	Current liabilities (CL)
Long-term investments (LTI)	Long-term liabilities (LTL)
Property, plant, and equipment (PPE)	Owner's equity (OE)
Intangible assets (IA)	

Action Plan

✔ Analyze whether each financial statement item is an asset, liability, or owner's equity.

✔ Determine if asset and liability items are short-term or long-term.

Solution

__CL__	Salaries and wages payable	__LTI__	Stock investments (long-term)
__NA__	Service revenue	__PPE__	Equipment
__CL__	Interest payable	__PPE__	Accumulated depreciation—equipment
__IA__	Goodwill	__NA__	Depreciation expense
__CA__	Debt investments (short-term)	__OE__	Owner's capital
__LTL__	Mortgage payable (due in 3 years)	__CL__	Unearned service revenue

Related exercise material: **BE4-11, E4-14, E4-15, E4-16, E4-17, and DO IT! 4-4.**

LEARNING OBJECTIVE *5

APPENDIX 4A: Prepare reversing entries.

After preparing the financial statements and closing the books, it is often helpful to reverse some of the adjusting entries before recording the regular transactions of the next period. Such entries are **reversing entries**. Companies make **a reversing entry at the beginning of the next accounting period**. Each reversing entry **is the exact opposite of the adjusting entry made in the previous period**. The recording of reversing entries is an **optional step** in the accounting cycle.

The purpose of reversing entries is to simplify the recording of a subsequent transaction related to an adjusting entry. For example, in Chapter 3 (page 108), the payment of salaries after an adjusting entry resulted in two debits: one to Salaries and Wages Payable and the other to Salaries and Wages Expense. With reversing entries, the company can debit the entire subsequent payment to Salaries and Wages Expense. **The use of reversing entries does not change the amounts reported in the financial statements.** What it does is simplify the recording of subsequent transactions.

Reversing Entries Example

Companies most often use reversing entries to reverse two types of adjusting entries: accrued revenues and accrued expenses. To illustrate the optional use of reversing entries for accrued expenses, we will use the salaries expense transactions for Pioneer Advertising as illustrated in Chapters 2, 3, and 4. The transaction and adjustment data are as follows.

1. October 26 (initial salary entry): Pioneer pays $4,000 of salaries and wages earned between October 15 and October 26.
2. October 31 (adjusting entry): Salaries and wages earned between October 29 and October 31 are $1,200. The company will pay these in the November 9 payroll.
3. November 9 (subsequent salary entry): Salaries and wages paid are $4,000. Of this amount, $1,200 applied to accrued salaries and wages payable and $2,800 was earned between November 1 and November 9.

Illustration 4A-1 shows the entries with and without reversing entries.

Illustration 4A-1
Comparative entries—not reversing vs. reversing

Without Reversing Entries (per chapter)				With Reversing Entries (per appendix)			
	Initial Salary Entry				Initial Salary Entry		
Oct. 26	Salaries and Wages Expense	4,000		Oct. 26	(Same entry)		
	Cash		4,000				
	Adjusting Entry				Adjusting Entry		
Oct. 31	Salaries and Wages Expense	1,200		Oct. 31	(Same entry)		
	Salaries and Wages Payable		1,200				
	Closing Entry				Closing Entry		
Oct. 31	Income Summary	5,200		Oct. 31	(Same entry)		
	Salaries and Wages Expense		5,200				
	Reversing Entry				Reversing Entry		
Nov. 1	No reversing entry is made.			Nov. 1	**Salaries and Wages Payable**	**1,200**	
					Salaries and Wages Expense		**1,200**
	Subsequent Salary Entry				Subsequent Salary Entry		
Nov. 9	Salaries and Wages Payable	1,200		Nov. 9	**Salaries and Wages Expense**	**4,000**	
	Salaries and Wages Expense	2,800			**Cash**		**4,000**
	Cash		4,000				

The first three entries are the same whether or not Pioneer uses reversing entries. The last two entries are different. The November 1 **reversing entry** eliminates the $1,200 balance in Salaries and Wages Payable created by the October 31 adjusting entry. The reversing entry also creates a $1,200 credit balance in the Salaries and Wages Expense account. As you know, it is unusual for an expense account to have a credit balance. The balance is correct in this instance, though, because it anticipates that the entire amount of the first salaries and wages payment in the new accounting period will be debited to Salaries and Wages Expense. This debit will eliminate the credit balance. The resulting debit balance in the expense account will equal the salaries and wages expense incurred in the new accounting period ($2,800 in this example).

If Pioneer makes reversing entries, it can debit all cash payments of expenses to the expense account. This means that on November 9 (and every payday) Pioneer can debit Salaries and Wages Expense for the amount paid, without regard to any accrued salaries and wages payable. Being able to make the **same entry each time** simplifies the recording process. The company can record subsequent transactions as if the related adjusting entry had never been made.

Illustration 4A-2 shows the posting of the entries with reversing entries.

Salaries and Wages Expense

10/26 Paid	4,000	10/31 Closing	5,200
31 Adjusting	1,200		
	5,200		5,200
11/9 Paid	4,000	**11/1 Reversing**	**1,200**

Salaries and Wages Payable

11/1 Reversing	**1,200**	10/31 Adjusting	1,200

Illustration 4A-2
Postings with reversing entries

A company can also use reversing entries for accrued revenue adjusting entries. For Pioneer, the adjusting entry was Accounts Receivable (Dr.) $200 and Service Revenue (Cr.) $200. Thus, the reversing entry on November 1 is:

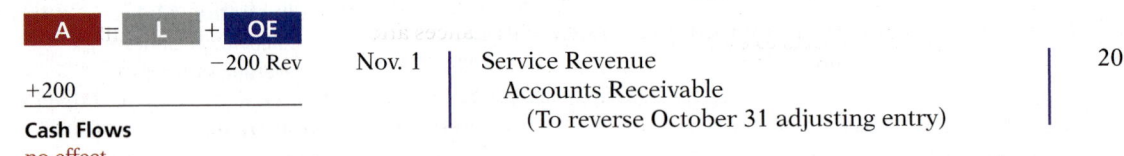

A	=	L	+	OE
				−200 Rev
+200				

Cash Flows
no effect

Nov. 1	Service Revenue	200	
	Accounts Receivable		200
	(To reverse October 31 adjusting entry)		

When Pioneer collects the accrued service revenue, it debits Cash and credits Service Revenue.

REVIEW AND PRACTICE

LEARNING OBJECTIVES REVIEW

1 Prepare a worksheet. The steps in preparing a worksheet are as follows. (a) Prepare a trial balance on the worksheet. (b) Enter the adjustments in the adjustments columns. (c) Enter adjusted balances in the adjusted trial balance columns. (d) Extend adjusted trial balance amounts to appropriate financial statement columns. (e) Total the statement columns, compute net income (or net loss), and complete the worksheet.

2 Prepare closing entries and a post-closing trial balance. Closing the books occurs at the end of an accounting period. The process is to journalize and post closing entries and then underline and balance all accounts. In closing the books, companies make separate entries to close revenues and expenses to Income Summary, Income Summary to Owner's Capital, and Owner's Drawings to Owner's Capital. Only temporary accounts are closed. A post-closing trial balance contains the balances in permanent accounts that are carried forward to the next accounting period. The purpose of this trial balance is to prove the equality of these balances.

3 Explain the steps in the accounting cycle and how to prepare correcting entries. The required steps in the accounting cycle are (1) analyze business transactions, (2) journalize the transactions, (3) post to ledger accounts, (4) prepare a trial balance, (5) journalize and post adjusting entries, (6) prepare an adjusted trial balance, (7) prepare financial statements, (8) journalize and post closing entries, and (9) prepare a post-closing trial balance.

One way to determine the correcting entry is to compare the incorrect entry with the correct entry. After comparison, the company makes a correcting entry to correct the accounts. An alternative to a correcting entry is to reverse the incorrect entry and then prepare the correct entry.

4 Identify the sections of a classified balance sheet. A classified balance sheet categorizes assets as current assets; long-term investments; property, plant, and equipment; and intangibles. Liabilities are classified as either current or long-term. There is also an owner's (owners') equity section, which varies with the form of business organization.

***5 Prepare reversing entries.** Reversing entries are the opposite of the adjusting entries made in the preceding period. Some companies choose to make reversing entries at the beginning of a new accounting period to simplify the recording of later transactions related to the adjusting entries. In most cases, only accrued adjusting entries are reversed.

GLOSSARY REVIEW

Classified balance sheet A balance sheet that contains standard classifications or sections. (p. 169).

Closing entries Entries made at the end of an accounting period to transfer the balances of temporary accounts to a permanent owner's equity account, Owner's Capital. (p. 159).

Correcting entries Entries to correct errors made in recording transactions. (p. 167).

Current assets Assets that a company expects to convert to cash or use up within one year. (p. 170).

Current liabilities Obligations that a company expects to pay within the coming year or its operating cycle, whichever is longer. (p. 172).

Income Summary A temporary account used in closing revenue and expense accounts. (p. 159).

Intangible assets Noncurrent assets that do not have physical substance. (p. 171).

Liquidity The ability of a company to pay obligations expected to be due within the next year. (p. 173).

Long-term investments Generally, (1) investments in stocks and bonds of other companies that companies normally hold for many years, and (2) long-term assets, such as land and buildings, not currently being used in operations. (p. 171).

Long-term liabilities Obligations that a company expects to pay after one year. (p. 173).

Operating cycle The average time that it takes to purchase inventory, sell it on account, and then collect cash from customers. (p. 170).

Permanent (real) accounts Accounts that relate to one or more future accounting periods. Consist of all balance sheet accounts. Balances are carried forward to the next accounting period. (p. 159).

Post-closing trial balance A list of permanent accounts and their balances after a company has journalized and posted closing entries. (p. 163).

Property, plant, and equipment Assets with relatively long useful lives and currently being used in operations. (p. 171).

Reversing entry An entry, made at the beginning of the next accounting period that is the exact opposite of the adjusting entry made in the previous period. (p. 166).

Stockholders' equity The ownership claim of shareholders on total assets. It is to a corporation what owner's equity is to a proprietorship. (p. 174).

Temporary (nominal) accounts Accounts that relate only to a given accounting period. Consist of all income statement accounts and owner's drawings account. All temporary accounts are closed at end of the accounting period. (p. 158).

Worksheet A multiple-column form that may be used in making adjusting entries and in preparing financial statements. (p. 150).

PRACTICE MULTIPLE-CHOICE QUESTIONS

(LO 1) 1. Which of the following statements is **incorrect** concerning the worksheet?
(a) The worksheet is essentially a working tool of the accountant.
(b) The worksheet is distributed to management and other interested parties.
(c) The worksheet cannot be used as a basis for posting to ledger accounts.
(d) Financial statements can be prepared directly from the worksheet before journalizing and posting the adjusting entries.

(LO 1) 2. In a worksheet, net income is entered in the following columns:
(a) income statement (Dr) and balance sheet (Dr).
(b) income statement (Cr) and balance sheet (Dr).
(c) income statement (Dr) and balance sheet (Cr).
(d) income statement (Cr) and balance sheet (Cr).

(LO 1) 3. In the unadjusted trial balance of its worksheet for the year ended December 31, 2017, Knox Company reported Equipment of $120,000. The year-end adjusting entries require an adjustment of $15,000 for depreciation expense for the equipment. After the adjusted trial balance is completed, what amount should be shown in the financial statement columns?
(a) A debit of $105,000 for Equipment in the balance sheet column.
(b) A credit of $15,000 for Depreciation Expense—Equipment in the income statement column.
(c) A debit of $120,000 for Equipment in the balance sheet column.
(d) A debit of $15,000 for Accumulated Depreciation—Equipment in the balance sheet column.

(LO 2) 4. An account that will have a zero balance after closing entries have been journalized and posted is:
(a) Service Revenue.
(b) Supplies.
(c) Prepaid Insurance.
(d) Accumulated Depreciation—Equipment.

(LO 2) 5. When a net loss has occurred, Income Summary is:
(a) debited and Owner's Capital is credited.
(b) credited and Owner's Capital is debited.
(c) debited and Owner's Drawings is credited.
(d) credited and Owner's Drawings is debited.

(LO 2) 6. The closing process involves separate entries to close (1) expenses, (2) drawings, (3) revenues, and (4) income summary. The correct sequencing of the entries is:
(a) (4), (3), (2), (1).
(b) (1), (2), (3), (4).
(c) (3), (1), (4), (2).
(d) (3), (2), (1), (4).

(LO 2) 7. Which types of accounts will appear in the post-closing trial balance?
(a) Permanent (real) accounts.
(b) Temporary (nominal) accounts.
(c) Accounts shown in the income statement columns of a worksheet.
(d) None of these answer choices is correct.

(LO 3) 8. All of the following are required steps in the accounting cycle **except**:
(a) journalizing and posting closing entries.
(b) preparing financial statements.
(c) journalizing the transactions.
(d) preparing a worksheet.

9. The proper order of the following steps in the accounting cycle is: (LO 3)
(a) prepare unadjusted trial balance, journalize transactions, post to ledger accounts, journalize and post adjusting entries.
(b) journalize transactions, prepare unadjusted trial balance, post to ledger accounts, journalize and post adjusting entries.
(c) journalize transactions, post to ledger accounts, prepare unadjusted trial balance, journalize and post adjusting entries.
(d) prepare unadjusted trial balance, journalize and post adjusting entries, journalize transactions, post to ledger accounts.

10. When Ramirez Company purchased supplies worth $500, it incorrectly recorded a credit to Supplies for $5,000 and a debit to Cash for $5,000. Before correcting this error: (LO 3)
(a) Cash is overstated and Supplies is overstated.
(b) Cash is understated and Supplies is understated.
(c) Cash is understated and Supplies is overstated.
(d) Cash is overstated and Supplies is understated.

11. Cash of $100 received at the time the service was performed was journalized and posted as a debit to Cash $100 and a credit to Accounts Receivable $100. Assuming the incorrect entry is not reversed, the correcting entry is: (LO 3)
(a) debit Service Revenue $100 and credit Accounts Receivable $100.
(b) debit Accounts Receivable $100 and credit Service Revenue $100.
(c) debit Cash $100 and credit Service Revenue $100.
(d) debit Accounts Receivable $100 and credit Cash $100.

12. The correct order of presentation in a classified balance sheet for the following current assets is: (LO 4)
(a) accounts receivable, cash, prepaid insurance, inventory.
(b) cash, inventory, accounts receivable, prepaid insurance.
(c) cash, accounts receivable, inventory, prepaid insurance.
(d) inventory, cash, accounts receivable, prepaid insurance.

13. A company has purchased a tract of land. It expects to build a production plant on the land in approximately 5 years. During the 5 years before construction, the land will be idle. The land should be reported as: (LO 4)
(a) property, plant, and equipment.
(b) land expense.
(c) a long-term investment.
(d) an intangible asset.

14. In a classified balance sheet, assets are usually classified using the following categories: (LO 4)
(a) current assets; long-term assets; property, plant, and equipment; and intangible assets.
(b) current assets; long-term investments; property, plant, and equipment; and tangible assets.

(c) current assets; long-term investments; tangible assets; and intangible assets.
(d) current assets; long-term investments; property, plant, and equipment; and intangible assets.

(LO 4) **15.** Current assets are listed:
(a) by expected conversion to cash.
(b) by importance.
(c) by longevity.
(d) alphabetically.

(LO 5)***16.** On December 31, Kevin Hartman Company correctly made an adjusting entry to recognize $2,000 of accrued salaries payable. On January 8 of the next year, total salaries of $3,400 were paid. Assuming the correct reversing entry was made on January 1, the entry on January 8 will result in a credit to Cash $3,400 and the following debit(s):
(a) Salaries and Wages Payable $1,400 and Salaries and Wages Expense $2,000.
(b) Salaries and Wages Payable $2,000 and Salaries and Wages Expense $1,400.
(c) Salaries and Wages Expense $3,400.
(d) Salaries and Wages Payable $3,400.

Solutions

1. (b) The worksheet is a working tool of the accountant; it is not distributed to management and other interested parties. The other choices are all true statements.

2. (c) Net income is entered in the Dr column of the income statement and the Cr column of the balance sheet. The other choices are incorrect because net income is entered in the (a) Cr (not Dr) column of the balance sheet, (b) Dr (not Cr) column of the income statement and in the Cr (not Dr) column of the balance sheet, and (d) Dr (not Cr) column of the income statement.

3. (c) A debit of $120,000 for Equipment would appear in the balance sheet column. The other choices are incorrect because (a) Equipment, less accumulated depreciation of $15,000, would total $105,000 under assets on the balance sheet, not on the worksheet; (b) a debit, not credit, for Depreciation Expense would appear in the income statement column; and (d) a credit, not debit, of $15,000 for Accumulated Depreciation—Equipment would appear in the balance sheet column.

4. (a) The Service Revenue account will have a zero balance after closing entries have been journalized and posted because it is a temporary account. The other choices are incorrect because (b) Supplies, (c) Prepaid Insurance, and (d) Accumulation Depreciation—Equipment are all permanent accounts and therefore not closed in the closing process.

5. (b) The effect of a net loss is a credit to Income Summary and a debit to Owner's Capital. The other choices are incorrect because (a) Income Summary is credited, not debited, and Owner's Capital is debited, not credited; (c) Income Summary is credited, not debited, and Owner's Drawings is not affected; and (d) Owner's Capital, not Owner's Drawings, is debited.

6. (c) The correct order is (3) revenues, (1) expenses, (4) income summary, and (2) drawings. Therefore, choices (a), (b), and (d) are incorrect.

7. (a) Permanent accounts appear in the post-closing trial balance. The other choices are incorrect because (b) temporary accounts and (c) income statement accounts are closed to a zero balance and are therefore not included in the post-closing trial balance. Choice (d) is wrong as there is only one correct answer for this question.

8. (d) Preparing a worksheet is not a required step in the accounting cycle. The other choices are all required steps in the accounting cycle.

9. (c) The proper order of the steps in the accounting cycle is (1) journalize transactions, (2) post to ledger accounts, (3) prepare unadjusted trial balance, and (4) journalize and post adjusting entries. Therefore, choices (a), (b), and (d) are incorrect.

10. (d) This entry causes Cash to be overstated and Supplies to be understated. Supplies should have been debited (increasing supplies) and Cash should have been credited (decreasing cash). The other choices are incorrect because (a) Supplies is understated, not overstated; (b) Cash is overstated, not understated; and (c) Cash is overstated, not understated, and Supplies is understated, not overstated.

11. (b) The correcting entry is to debit Accounts Receivable $100 and credit Service Revenue $100. The other choices are incorrect because (a) Service Revenue should be credited, not debited, and Accounts Receivable should be debited, not credited; (c) Service Revenue should be credited for $100, and Cash should not be included in the correcting entry as it was recorded properly; and (d) Accounts Receivable should be debited for $100 and Cash should not be included in the correcting entry as it was recorded properly.

12. (c) Companies list current assets on balance sheet in the order of liquidity: cash, accounts receivable, inventory, and prepaid insurance. Therefore, choices (a), (b), and (d) are incorrect.

13. (c) Long-term investments include long-term assets such as land that a company is not currently using in its operating activities. The other choices are incorrect because (a) land would be reported as property, plant, and equipment only if it is being currently used in the business; (b) land is an asset, not an expense; and (d) land has physical substance and thus is a tangible property.

14. (d) These are the categories usually used in a classified balance sheet. The other choices are incorrect because the categories (a) "long-term assets" and (b) and (c) "tangible assets" are generally not used.

15. (a) Current assets are listed in order of their liquidity, not (b) by importance, (c) by longevity, or (d) alphabetically.

***16. (c)** The use of reversing entries simplifies the recording of the first payroll following the end of the year by eliminating the need to make an entry to the Salaries and Wages Payable account. The other choices are incorrect because (a) Salaries and Wages Payable is not part of the payroll entry on January 8, and the debit to Salaries and Wages Expense should be for $3,400, not $2,000; and (b) and (d) the Salaries and Wages Expense account, not the Salaries and Wages Payable account, should be debited.

PRACTICE EXERCISES

Journalize and post closing entries, and prepare a post-closing trial balance.

(LO 2)

1. Hercules Company ended its fiscal year on August 31, 2017. The company's adjusted trial balance as of the end of its fiscal year is as shown below.

HERCULES COMPANY
Adjusted Trial Balance
August 31, 2017

No.	Account Titles	Debit	Credit
101	Cash	$10,900	
112	Accounts Receivable	6,200	
157	Equipment	10,600	
167	Accumulated Depr.—Equip.		$ 5,400
201	Accounts Payable		2,800
208	Unearned Rent Revenue		1,200
301	Owner's Capital		31,700
306	Owner's Drawings	12,000	
404	Service Revenue		42,400
429	Rent Revenue		6,100
711	Depreciation Expense	2,700	
720	Salaries and Wages Expense	37,100	
732	Utilities Expense	10,100	
		$89,600	$89,600

Instructions

(a) Prepare the closing entries using page J15 in a general journal.

(b) Post to Owner's Capital and No. 350 Income Summary accounts. (Use the three-column form.)

(c) Prepare a post-closing trial balance at August 31, 2017.

Solution

1. (a)

GENERAL JOURNAL J15

Date	Account Titles	Ref.	Debit	Credit
Aug. 31	Service Revenue	404	42,400	
	Rent Revenue	429	6,100	
	Income Summary	350		48,500
	(To close revenue accounts)			
31	Income Summary	350	49,900	
	Salaries and Wages Expense	720		37,100
	Utilities Expense	732		10,100
	Depreciation Expense	711		2,700
	(To close expense accounts)			
31	Owner's Capital	301	1,400	
	Income Summary	350		1,400
	(To close net loss to capital)			
31	Owner's Capital	301	12,000	
	Owner's Drawings	306		12,000
	(To close drawings to capital)			

(b)

Owner's Capital No. 301

Date	Explanation	Ref.	Debit	Credit	Balance
Aug. 31	Balance				31,700
31	Close net loss	J15	1,400		30,300
31	Close drawings	J15	12,000		18,300

Income Summary No. 350

Date	Explanation	Ref.	Debit	Credit	Balance
Aug. 31	Close revenue	J15		48,500	48,500
31	Close expenses	J15	49,000		(1,400)
31	Close net loss	J15		1,400	0

(c)

HERCULES COMPANY
Post-Closing Trial Balance
August 31, 2017

	Debit	Credit
Cash	$10,900	
Accounts Receivable	6,200	
Equipment	10,600	
Accumulated Depreciation—Equipment		$ 5,400
Accounts Payable		2,800
Unearned Rent Revenue		1,200
Owner's Capital		18,300
	$27,700	$27,700

2. The adjusted trial balance for Hercules Company is presented in Practice Exercise 1.

Prepare financial statements.
(LO 4)

Instructions

(a) Prepare an income statement and an owner's equity statement for the year ended August 31, 2017. Hercules did not make any capital investments during the year.

(b) Prepare a classified balance sheet at August 31, 2017.

Solution

2. (a)

HERCULES COMPANY
Income Statement
For the Year Ended August 31, 2017

Revenues		
Service revenue	$42,400	
Rent revenue	6,100	
Total revenues		$48,500
Expenses		
Salaries and wages expense	37,100	
Utilities expense	10,100	
Depreciation expense	2,700	
Total expenses		49,900
Net loss		$ (1,400)

HERCULES COMPANY
Owner's Equity Statement
For the Year Ended August 31, 2017

Owner's capital, September 1, 2016		$31,700
Less: Net loss	$ 1,400	
Owner's drawings	12,000	13,400
Owner's capital, August 31, 2017		$18,300

(b)

HERCULES COMPANY Balance Sheet August 31, 2017		
Assets		
Current assets		
Cash	$10,900	
Accounts receivable	6,200	
Total current assets		$17,100
Property, plant, and equipment		
Equipment	10,600	
Less: Accumulated depreciation—equip.	5,400	5,200
Total assets		$22,300
Liabilities and Owner's Equity		
Current liabilities		
Accounts payable	$2,800	
Unearned rent revenue	1,200	
Total current liabilities		$ 4,000
Owner's equity		
Owner's capital		18,300
Total liabilities and owner's equity		$22,300

PRACTICE PROBLEM

Prepare worksheet and classified balance sheet, and journalize closing entries.

(LO 1, 2, 4)

At the end of its first month of operations, Pampered Pet Service has the following unadjusted trial balance.

PAMPERED PET SERVICE
August 31, 2017
Trial Balance

	Debit	Credit
Cash	$ 5,400	
Accounts Receivable	2,800	
Supplies	1,300	
Prepaid Insurance	2,400	
Equipment	60,000	
Notes Payable		$40,000
Accounts Payable		2,400
Owner's Capital		30,000
Owner's Drawings	1,000	
Service Revenue		4,900
Salaries and Wages Expense	3,200	
Utilities Expense	800	
Advertising Expense	400	
	$77,300	$77,300

Other data:

1. Insurance expires at the rate of $200 per month.
2. $1,000 of supplies are on hand at August 31.
3. Monthly depreciation on the equipment is $900.
4. Interest of $500 on the notes payable has accrued during August.

Instructions

(a) Prepare a worksheet.

(b) Prepare a classified balance sheet assuming $35,000 of the notes payable are long-term.

(c) Journalize the closing entries.

Solution

(a)

PAMPERED PET SERVICE
Worksheet for the Month Ended August 31, 2017

Account Titles	Trial Balance Dr.	Trial Balance Cr.	Adjustments Dr.	Adjustments Cr.	Adjusted Trial Balance Dr.	Adjusted Trial Balance Cr.	Income Statement Dr.	Income Statement Cr.	Balance Sheet Dr.	Balance Sheet Cr.
Cash	5,400				5,400				5,400	
Accounts Receivable	2,800				2,800				2,800	
Supplies	1,300			(b) 300	1,000				1,000	
Prepaid Insurance	2,400			(a) 200	2,200				2,200	
Equipment	60,000				60,000				60,000	
Notes Payable		40,000				40,000				40,000
Accounts Payable		2,400				2,400				2,400
Owner's Capital		30,000				30,000				30,000
Owner's Drawings	1,000				1,000				1,000	
Service Revenue		4,900				4,900		4,900		
Salaries and Wages Expense	3,200				3,200		3,200			
Utilities Expense	800				800		800			
Advertising Expense	400				400		400			
Totals	77,300	77,300								
Insurance Expense			(a) 200		200		200			
Supplies Expense			(b) 300		300		300			
Depreciation Expense			(c) 900		900		900			
Accumulated Depreciation—Equipment				(c) 900		900				900
Interest Expense			(d) 500		500		500			
Interest Payable				(d) 500		500				500
Totals			1,900	1,900	78,700	78,700	6,300	4,900	72,400	73,800
Net Loss								1,400	1,400	
Totals							6,300	6,300	73,800	73,800

Explanation: (a) insurance expired, (b) supplies used, (c) depreciation expensed, and (d) interest accrued.

(b)

PAMPERED PET SERVICE
Balance Sheet
August 31, 2017

Assets		
Current assets		
Cash	$ 5,400	
Accounts receivable	2,800	
Supplies	1,000	
Prepaid insurance	2,200	
Total current assets		$11,400
Property, plant, and equipment		
Equipment	60,000	
Less: Accumulated depreciation—equipment	900	59,100
Total assets		$70,500
Liabilities and Owner's Equity		
Current liabilities		
Notes payable	$ 5,000	
Accounts payable	2,400	
Interest payable	500	
Total current liabilities		$ 7,900
Long-term liabilities		
Notes payable		35,000
Total liabilities		42,900
Owner's equity		
Owner's capital		27,600*
Total liabilities and owner's equity		$70,500

*Owner's capital $30,000 less drawings $1,000 and net loss $1,400.

(c)

Aug. 31	Service Revenue	4,900	
	Income Summary		4,900
	(To close revenue account)		
31	Income Summary	6,300	
	Salaries and Wages Expense		3,200
	Depreciation Expense		900
	Utilities Expense		800
	Interest Expense		500
	Advertising Expense		400
	Supplies Expense		300
	Insurance Expense		200
	(To close expense accounts)		
31	Owner's Capital	1,400	
	Income Summary		1,400
	(To close net loss to capital)		
31	Owner's Capital	1,000	
	Owner's Drawings		1,000
	(To close drawings to capital)		

WileyPLUS Brief Exercises, Exercises, DO IT! Exercises, and Problems and many additional resources are available for practice in WileyPLUS

NOTE: All asterisked Questions, Exercises, and Problems relate to material in the appendix to the chapter.

QUESTIONS

1. "A worksheet is a permanent accounting record and its use is required in the accounting cycle." Do you agree? Explain.
2. Explain the purpose of the worksheet.
3. What is the relationship, if any, between the amount shown in the adjusted trial balance column for an account and that account's ledger balance?
4. If a company's revenues are $125,000 and its expenses are $113,000, in which financial statement columns of the worksheet will the net income of $12,000 appear? When expenses exceed revenues, in which columns will the difference appear?
5. Why is it necessary to prepare formal financial statements if all of the data are in the statement columns of the worksheet?
6. Identify the account(s) debited and credited in each of the four closing entries, assuming the company has net income for the year.
7. Describe the nature of the Income Summary account and identify the types of summary data that may be posted to this account.
8. What are the content and purpose of a post-closing trial balance?
9. Which of the following accounts would not appear in the post-closing trial balance? Interest Payable, Equipment, Depreciation Expense, Owner's Drawings, Unearned Service Revenue, Accumulated Depreciation—Equipment, and Service Revenue.
10. Distinguish between a reversing entry and an adjusting entry. Are reversing entries required?
11. Indicate, in the sequence in which they are made, the three required steps in the accounting cycle that involve journalizing.
12. Identify, in the sequence in which they are prepared, the three trial balances that are often used to report financial information about a company.
13. How do correcting entries differ from adjusting entries?
14. What standard classifications are used in preparing a classified balance sheet?
15. What is meant by the term "operating cycle?"
16. Define current assets. What basis is used for arranging individual items within the current assets section?
17. Distinguish between long-term investments and property, plant, and equipment.
18. (a) What is the term used to describe the owner's equity section of a corporation? (b) Identify the two owners' equity accounts in a corporation and indicate the purpose of each.
19. Using Apple's annual report, determine its current liabilities at September 29, 2012, and September 28, 2013. Were current liabilities higher or lower than current assets in these two years?

*20. Cigale Company prepares reversing entries. If the adjusting entry for interest payable is reversed, what type of an account balance, if any, will there be in Interest Payable and Interest Expense after the reversing entry is posted?

*21. At December 31, accrued salaries payable totaled $3,500. On January 10, total salaries of $8,000 are paid. (a) Assume that reversing entries are made at January 1. Give the January 10 entry, and indicate the Salaries and Wages Expense account balance after the entry is posted. (b) Repeat part (a) assuming reversing entries are not made.

BRIEF EXERCISES

List the steps in preparing a worksheet. (LO 1)

BE4-1 The steps in using a worksheet are presented in random order below. List the steps in the proper order by placing numbers 1–5 in the blank spaces.

(a) _____ Prepare a trial balance on the worksheet.
(b) _____ Enter adjusted balances.
(c) _____ Extend adjusted balances to appropriate statement columns.
(d) _____ Total the statement columns, compute net income (loss), and complete the worksheet.
(e) _____ Enter adjustment data.

Prepare partial worksheet. (LO 1)

BE4-2 The ledger of Lentz Company includes the following unadjusted balances: Prepaid Insurance $3,000, Service Revenue $58,000, and Salaries and Wages Expense $25,000. Adjusting entries are required for (a) expired insurance $1,800; (b) services performed $1,100, but unbilled and uncollected; and (c) accrued salaries payable $800. Enter the unadjusted balances and adjustments into a worksheet and complete the worksheet for all accounts. (*Note:* You will need to add the following accounts: Accounts Receivable, Salaries and Wages Payable, and Insurance Expense.)

Identify worksheet columns for selected accounts.
(LO 1)

BE4-3 The following selected accounts appear in the adjusted trial balance columns of the worksheet for Ashram Company: Accumulated Depreciation, Depreciation Expense, Owner's Capital, Owner's Drawings, Service Revenue, Supplies, and Accounts Payable. Indicate the financial statement column (income statement Dr., balance sheet Cr., etc.) to which each balance should be extended.

Prepare closing entries from ledger balances.
(LO 2)

BE4-4 The ledger of Duston Company contains the following balances: Owner's Capital $30,000, Owner's Drawings $2,000, Service Revenue $50,000, Salaries and Wages Expense $29,000, and Supplies Expense $7,000. Prepare the closing entries at December 31.

Post closing entries; underline and balance T-accounts.
(LO 2)

BE4-5 Using the data in BE4-4, enter the balances in T-accounts, post the closing entries, and underline and balance the accounts.

Journalize and post closing entries using the three-column form of account.
(LO 2)

BE4-6 The income statement for Arbor Vitae Golf Club for the month ending July 31 shows Service Revenue $16,400, Salaries and Wages Expense $8,400, Maintenance and Repairs Expense $2,500, and Net Income $5,700. Prepare the entries to close the revenue and expense accounts. Post the entries to the revenue and expense accounts, and complete the closing process for these accounts using the three-column form of account.

Identify post-closing trial balance accounts.
(LO 2)

BE4-7 Using the data in BE4-3, identify the accounts that would be included in a post-closing trial balance.

List the required steps in the accounting cycle in sequence.
(LO 3)

BE4-8 The steps in the accounting cycle are listed in random order below. List the steps in proper sequence, assuming no worksheet is prepared, by placing numbers 1–9 in the blank spaces.

(a) __4__ Prepare a trial balance.
(b) __2__ Journalize the transactions.
(c) __8__ Journalize and post closing entries.
(d) __7__ Prepare financial statements.
(e) __5__ Journalize and post adjusting entries.
(f) __3__ Post to ledger accounts.
(g) __9__ Prepare a post-closing trial balance.
(h) __6__ Prepare an adjusted trial balance.
(i) __1__ Analyze business transactions.

Prepare correcting entries.
(LO 3)

BE4-9 At Raymond Company, the following errors were discovered after the transactions had been journalized and posted. Prepare the correcting entries.

1. A collection on account from a customer for $870 was recorded as a debit to Cash $870 and a credit to Service Revenue $870.
2. The purchase of store supplies on account for $1,510 was recorded as a debit to Supplies $1,150 and a credit to Accounts Payable $1,150.

Prepare the current assets section of a balance sheet.
(LO 4)

BE4-10 The balance sheet debit column of the worksheet for Mrotet Company includes the following accounts: Accounts Receivable $12,500, Prepaid Insurance $3,600, Cash $4,100, Supplies $5,200, and Debt Investments (short-term) $6,700. Prepare the current assets section of the balance sheet, listing the accounts in proper sequence.

Classify accounts on balance sheet.
(LO 4)

BE4-11 The following are the major balance sheet classifications:

Current assets (CA)
Long-term investments (LTI)
Property, plant, and equipment (PPE)
Intangible assets (IA)
Current liabilities (CL)
Long-term liabilities (LTL)
Owner's equity (OE)

Match each of the following accounts to its proper balance sheet classification.

__CL__ Accounts payable
__CA__ Accounts receivable
__PPE__ Accumulated depreciation—buildings
__PPE__ Buildings
__CA__ Cash
__IA__ Copyrights
__CL__ Income taxes payable
__LTI__ Debt investments (long-term)
__PPE__ Land
__CA__ Inventory
__IA__ Patents
__CA__ Supplies

***BE4-12** At October 31, Zanskas Company made an accrued expense adjusting entry of $2,100 for salaries. Prepare the reversing entry on November 1, and indicate the balances in Salaries and Wages Payable and Salaries and Wages Expense after posting the reversing entry.

Prepare reversing entries. (LO 5)

DO IT! Exercises

DO IT! 4-1 Jordan Carr is preparing a worksheet. Explain to Jordan how he should extend the following adjusted trial balance accounts to the financial statement columns of the worksheet.

Prepare a worksheet. (LO 1)

Service Revenue	Accounts Receivable
Notes Payable	Accumulated Depreciation
Owner's Capital	Utilities Expense

DO IT! 4-2 The worksheet for Ajeeb Company shows the following in the financial statement columns.

Prepare closing entries. (LO 2)

Owner's drawings	$22,000
Owner's capital	70,000
Net income	41,000

Prepare the closing entries at December 31 that affect owner's capital.

DO IT! 4-3 Hanson Company has an inexperienced accountant. During the first month on the job, the accountant made the following errors in journalizing transactions. All entries were posted as made.

Prepare correcting entries. (LO 3)

1. The purchase of supplies for $650 cash was debited to Equipment $210 and credited to Cash $210.
2. A $500 withdrawal of cash for B. Hanson's personal use was debited to Salaries and Wages Expense $900 and credited to Cash $900.
3. A payment on account of $820 to a creditor was debited to Accounts Payable $280 and credited to Cash $280.

Prepare the correcting entries.

DO IT! 4-4 The following accounts were taken from the financial statements of Giles Company.

Match accounts to balance sheet classifications. (LO 4)

__NA__ Interest revenue	__OE__ Owner's capital
__CL__ Utilities payable	__PPE__ Accumulated depreciation—equipment
__CL__ Accounts payable	__PPE__ Equipment
__CA__ Supplies	__NA__ Salaries and wages expense
__LTL__ Bonds payable	__LTI__ Debt investments (long-term)
__IA__ Goodwill	__CL__ Unearned rent revenue

Match each of the accounts to its proper balance sheet classification, as shown below. If the item would not appear on a balance sheet, use "NA."

Current assets (CA)	Current liabilities (CL)
Long-term investments (LTI)	Long-term liabilities (LTL)
Property, plant, and equipment (PPE)	Owner's equity (OE)
Intangible assets (IA)	

EXERCISES

E4-1 The trial balance columns of the worksheet for Dixon Company at June 30, 2017, are as follows.

Complete the worksheet. (LO 1)

DIXON COMPANY
Worksheet
For the Month Ended June 30, 2017

	Trial Balance	
Account Titles	**Dr.**	**Cr.**
Cash	2,320	
Accounts Receivable	2,440	
Supplies	1,880	
Accounts Payable		1,120
Unearned Service Revenue		240
Owner's Capital		3,600
Service Revenue		2,400
Salaries and Wages Expense	560	
Miscellaneous Expense	160	
	7,360	7,360

Other data:

1. A physical count reveals $500 of supplies on hand.
2. $100 of the unearned revenue is still unearned at month-end.
3. Accrued salaries are $210.

Instructions

Enter the trial balance on a worksheet and complete the worksheet.

Complete the worksheet.

(LO 1)

E4-2 The adjusted trial balance columns of the worksheet for Savaglia Company are as follows.

SAVAGLIA COMPANY
Worksheet (partial)
For the Month Ended April 30, 2017

	Adjusted Trial Balance		Income Statement		Balance Sheet	
Account Titles	**Dr.**	**Cr.**	**Dr.**	**Cr.**	**Dr.**	**Cr.**
Cash	10,000					
Accounts Receivable	7,840					
Prepaid Rent	2,280					
Equipment	23,050					
Accumulated Depreciation—Equip.		4,900				
Notes Payable		5,700				
Accounts Payable		4,920				
Owner's Capital		27,960				
Owner's Drawings	3,650					
Service Revenue		15,590				
Salaries and Wages Expense	10,840					
Rent Expense	760					
Depreciation Expense	650					
Interest Expense	57					
Interest Payable		57				
Totals	59,127	59,127				

Instructions

Complete the worksheet.

Prepare financial statements from worksheet.

(LO 1, 4)

E4-3 Worksheet data for Savaglia Company are presented in E4-2. The owner did not make any additional investments in the business in April.

Instructions
Prepare an income statement, an owner's equity statement, and a classified balance sheet.

E4-4 Worksheet data for Savaglia Company are presented in E4-2.

Journalize and post closing entries and prepare a post-closing trial balance.

(LO 2)

Instructions
(a) Journalize the closing entries at April 30.
(b) Post the closing entries to Income Summary and Owner's Capital. Use T-accounts.
(c) Prepare a post-closing trial balance at April 30.

E4-5 The adjustments columns of the worksheet for Becker Company are shown below.

Prepare adjusting entries from a worksheet, and extend balances to worksheet columns.

(LO 1)

	Adjustments	
Account Titles	**Debit**	**Credit**
Accounts Receivable	1,100	
Prepaid Insurance		300
Accumulated Depreciation—Equipment		900
Salaries and Wages Payable		500
Service Revenue		1,100
Salaries and Wages Expense	500	
Insurance Expense	300	
Depreciation Expense	900	
	2,800	2,800

Instructions
(a) Prepare the adjusting entries.
(b) Assuming the adjusted trial balance amount for each account is normal, indicate the financial statement column to which each balance should be extended.

E4-6 Selected worksheet data for Rosa Company are presented below.

Derive adjusting entries from worksheet data.

(LO 1)

Account Titles	Trial Balance		Adjusted Trial Balance	
	Dr.	**Cr.**	**Dr.**	**Cr.**
Accounts Receivable	?		34,000	
Prepaid Insurance	26,000		20,000	
Supplies	7,000		?	
Accumulated Depreciation—Equipment		12,000		?
Salaries and Wages Payable		?		5,600
Service Revenue		88,000		97,000
Insurance Expense			?	
Depreciation Expense			10,000	
Supplies Expense			4,500	
Salaries and Wages Expense	?		49,000	

Instructions
(a) Fill in the missing amounts.
(b) Prepare the adjusting entries that were made.

E4-7 Victoria Lee Company had the following adjusted trial balance.

Prepare closing entries, and prepare a post-closing trial balance.

(LO 2)

VICTORIA LEE COMPANY
Adjusted Trial Balance
For the Month Ended June 30, 2017

Account Titles	Adjusted Trial Balance Debit	Adjusted Trial Balance Credit
Cash	$ 3,712	
Accounts Receivable	3,904	
Supplies	480	
Accounts Payable		$ 1,382
Unearned Service Revenue		160
Owner's Capital		5,760
Owner's Drawings	550	
Service Revenue		4,300
Salaries and Wages Expense	1,260	
Miscellaneous Expense	256	
Supplies Expense	1,900	
Salaries and Wages Payable		460
	$12,062	$12,062

Instructions

(a) Prepare closing entries at June 30, 2017.
(b) Prepare a post-closing trial balance.

Journalize and post closing entries, and prepare a post-closing trial balance.

(LO 2)

E4-8 Okabe Company ended its fiscal year on July 31, 2017. The company's adjusted trial balance as of the end of its fiscal year is shown below.

OKABE COMPANY
Adjusted Trial Balance
July 31, 2017

No.	Account Titles	Debit	Credit
101	Cash	$ 9,840	
112	Accounts Receivable	8,780	
157	Equipment	15,900	
158	Accumulated Depreciation—Equip.		$ 7,400
201	Accounts Payable		4,220
208	Unearned Rent Revenue		1,800
301	Owner's Capital		45,200
306	Owner's Drawings	16,000	
400	Service Revenue		64,000
429	Rent Revenue		6,500
711	Depreciation Expense	8,000	
726	Salaries and Wages Expense	55,700	
732	Utilities Expense	14,900	
		$129,120	$129,120

Instructions

(a) Prepare the closing entries using page J15.
(b) Post to Owner's Capital and No. 350 Income Summary accounts. (Use the three-column form.)
(c) Prepare a post-closing trial balance at July 31.

Prepare financial statements.

(LO 4)

E4-9 The adjusted trial balance for Okabe Company is presented in E4-8.

Instructions

(a) Prepare an income statement and an owner's equity statement for the year. Okabe did not make any capital investments during the year.
(b) Prepare a classified balance sheet at July 31.

Answer questions related to the accounting cycle.
(LO 3)

E4-10 Renee Davis has prepared the following list of statements about the accounting cycle.

1. "Journalize the transactions" is the first step in the accounting cycle.
2. Reversing entries are a required step in the accounting cycle.
3. Correcting entries do not have to be part of the accounting cycle.
4. If a worksheet is prepared, some steps of the accounting cycle are incorporated into the worksheet.
5. The accounting cycle begins with the analysis of business transactions and ends with the preparation of a post-closing trial balance.
6. All steps of the accounting cycle occur daily during the accounting period.
7. The step of "post to the ledger accounts" occurs before the step of "journalize the transactions."
8. Closing entries must be prepared before financial statements can be prepared.

Instructions

Identify each statement as true or false. If false, indicate how to correct the statement.

Prepare closing entries.
(LO 2)

E4-11 Selected accounts for Tamora's Salon are presented below. All June 30 postings are from closing entries.

Salaries and Wages Expense

6/10	3,200	6/30	8,800
6/28	5,600		

Service Revenue

6/30	18,100	6/15	9,700
		6/24	8,400

Owner's Capital

6/30	2,100	6/1	12,000
		6/30	5,000
		Bal.	14,900

Supplies Expense

6/12	600	6/30	1,300
6/24	700		

Rent Expense

6/1	3,000	6/30	3,000

Owner's Drawings

6/13	1,000	6/30	2,100
6/25	1,100		

Instructions

(a) Prepare the closing entries that were made.
(b) Post the closing entries to Income Summary.

Prepare correcting entries.
(LO 3)

E4-12 Noah Bahr Company discovered the following errors made in January 2017.

1. A payment of Salaries and Wages Expense of $700 was debited to Equipment and credited to Cash, both for $700.
2. A collection of $1,000 from a client on account was debited to Cash $100 and credited to Service Revenue $100.
3. The purchase of equipment on account for $760 was debited to Equipment $670 and credited to Accounts Payable $670.

Instructions

(a) Correct the errors by reversing the incorrect entry and preparing the correct entry.
(b) Correct the errors without reversing the incorrect entry.

Prepare correcting entries.
(LO 3)

E4-13 Patel Company has an inexperienced accountant. During the first 2 weeks on the job, the accountant made the following errors in journalizing transactions. All entries were posted as made.

1. A payment on account of $750 to a creditor was debited to Accounts Payable $570 and credited to Cash $570.
2. The purchase of supplies on account for $560 was debited to Equipment $56 and credited to Accounts Payable $56.
3. A $500 withdrawal of cash for N. Patel's personal use was debited to Salaries and Wages Expense $500 and credited to Cash $500.

Instructions

Prepare the correcting entries.

Prepare a classified balance sheet.
(LO 4)

E4-14 The adjusted trial balance for McCoy Bowling Alley at December 31, 2017, contains the following accounts.

	Debit		Credit
Buildings	$128,800	Owner's Capital	$115,000
Accounts Receivable	14,520	Accumulated Depreciation—Buildings	42,600
Prepaid Insurance	4,680	Accounts Payable	12,300
Cash	18,040	Notes Payable	97,780
Equipment	62,400	Accumulated Depreciation—Equipment	18,720
Land	67,000	Interest Payable	3,800
Insurance Expense	780	Service Revenue	17,180
Depreciation Expense	7,360		$307,380
Interest Expense	3,800		
	$307,380		

Instructions

(a) Prepare a classified balance sheet; assume that $20,000 of the note payable will be paid in 2018.

(b) Comment on the liquidity of the company.

Classify accounts on balance sheet.

(LO 4)

E4-15 The following are the major balance sheet classifications.

Current assets (CA)	Current liabilities (CL)
Long-term investments (LTI)	Long-term liabilities (LTL)
Property, plant, and equipment (PPE)	Owner's equity (OE)
Intangible assets (IA)	

Instructions

Classify each of the following accounts taken from Faust Company's balance sheet.

CL	Accounts payable	PPE	Accumulated depreciation—equipment
CA	Accounts receivable	PPE	Buildings
CA	Cash	PPE	Land (in use)
OE	Owner's capital	LTL	Notes payable (due in 2 years)
IA	Patents	CA	Supplies
CL	Salaries and wages payable	PPE	Equipment – PPE
CA	Inventory	CA	Prepaid expenses
CA	Stock investments (to be sold in 7 months)		

Prepare a classified balance sheet.

(LO 4)

E4-16 The following items were taken from the financial statements of J. Pineda Company. (All amounts are in thousands.)

Long-term debt	$ 1,000	Accumulated depreciation—equipment	$ 5,655
Prepaid insurance	880	Accounts payable	1,444
Equipment	11,500	Notes payable (due after 2018)	400
Stock investments (long-term)	264	Owner's capital	12,955
Debt investments (short-term)	3,690	Accounts receivable	1,696
Notes payable (due in 2018)	500	Inventory	1,256
Cash	2,668		

Instructions

Prepare a classified balance sheet in good form as of December 31, 2017.

Prepare financial statements.

(LO 4)

E4-17 These financial statement items are for Basten Company at year-end, July 31, 2017.

Salaries and wages payable	$ 2,080	Notes payable (long-term)	$ 1,800
Salaries and wages expense	48,700	Cash	14,200
Utilities expense	22,600	Accounts receivable	9,780
Equipment	34,400	Accumulated depreciation—equipment	6,000
Accounts payable	4,100	Owner's drawings	3,000
Service revenue	63,000	Depreciation expense	4,000
Rent revenue	8,500	Owner's capital (beginning of the year)	51,200

Instructions

(a) Prepare an income statement and an owner's equity statement for the year. The owner did not make any new investments during the year.

(b) Prepare a classified balance sheet at July 31.

***E4-18** Lovrek Company pays salaries of $12,000 every Monday for the preceding 5-day week (Monday through Friday). Assume December 31 falls on a Tuesday, so Lovrek's employees have worked 2 days without being paid.

Use reversing entries.

(LO 5)

Instructions

(a) Assume the company does not use reversing entries. Prepare the December 31 adjusting entry and the entry on Monday, January 6, when Lovrek pays the payroll.

(b) Assume the company does use reversing entries. Prepare the December 31 adjusting entry, the January 1 reversing entry, and the entry on Monday, January 6, when Lovrek pays the payroll.

***E4-19** On December 31, the adjusted trial balance of Shihata Employment Agency shows the following selected data.

Prepare closing and reversing entries.

(LO 2, 5)

Accounts Receivable	$24,500	Service Revenue	$92,500
Interest Expense	7,700	Interest Payable	2,200

Analysis shows that adjusting entries were made to (1) accrue $5,000 of service revenue and (2) accrue $2,200 interest expense.

Instructions

(a) Prepare the closing entries for the temporary accounts shown above at December 31.

(b) Prepare the reversing entries on January 1.

(c) Post the entries in (a) and (b). Underline and balance the accounts. (Use T-accounts.)

(d) Prepare the entries to record (1) the collection of the accrued revenue on January 10 and (2) the payment of all interest due ($3,000) on January 15.

(e) Post the entries in (d) to the temporary accounts.

EXERCISES: SET B AND CHALLENGE EXERCISES

Visit the book's companion website, at **www.wiley.com/college/weygandt**, and choose the Student Companion site to access Exercises: Set B and Challenge Exercises.

PROBLEMS: SET A

P4-1A The trial balance columns of the worksheet for Warren Roofing at March 31, 2017, are as follows.

Prepare a worksheet, financial statements, and adjusting and closing entries.

(LO 1, 2, 4)

WARREN ROOFING
Worksheet
For the Month Ended March 31, 2017

	Trial Balance	
Account Titles	**Dr.**	**Cr.**
Cash	4,500	
Accounts Receivable	3,200	
Supplies	2,000	
Equipment	11,000	
Accumulated Depreciation—Equipment		1,250
Accounts Payable		2,500
Unearned Service Revenue		550
Owner's Capital		12,900
Owner's Drawings	1,100	
Service Revenue		6,300
Salaries and Wages Expense	1,300	
Miscellaneous Expense	400	
	23,500	23,500

Other data:

1. A physical count reveals only $480 of roofing supplies on hand.
2. Depreciation for March is $250.
3. Unearned revenue amounted to $260 at March 31.
4. Accrued salaries are $700.

(a) Adjusted trial balance $24,450
(b) Net income $2,420
Total assets $17,680

Instructions

(a) Enter the trial balance on a worksheet and complete the worksheet.
(b) Prepare an income statement and owner's equity statement for the month of March and a classified balance sheet at March 31. T. Warren made an additional investment in the business of $10,000 in March.
(c) Journalize the adjusting entries from the adjustments columns of the worksheet.
(d) Journalize the closing entries from the financial statement columns of the worksheet.

Complete worksheet; prepare financial statements, closing entries, and post-closing trial balance.

(LO 1, 2, 4)

GLS

P4-2A The adjusted trial balance columns of the worksheet for Thao Company, owned by D. Thao, are as follows.

THAO COMPANY
Worksheet
For the Year Ended December 31, 2017

Account No.	Account Titles	Adjusted Trial Balance Dr.	Adjusted Trial Balance Cr.
101	Cash	5,300	
112	Accounts Receivable	10,800	
126	Supplies	1,500	
130	Prepaid Insurance	2,000	
157	Equipment	27,000	
158	Accumulated Depreciation—Equipment		5,600
200	Notes Payable		15,000
201	Accounts Payable		6,100
212	Salaries and Wages Payable		2,400
230	Interest Payable		600
301	Owner's Capital		13,000
306	Owner's Drawings	7,000	
400	Service Revenue		61,000
610	Advertising Expense	8,400	
631	Supplies Expense	4,000	
711	Depreciation Expense	5,600	
722	Insurance Expense	3,500	
726	Salaries and Wages Expense	28,000	
905	Interest Expense	600	
	Totals	103,700	103,700

(a) Net income $10,900

(b) Current assets $19,600
Current liabilities $14,100

(e) Post-closing trial balance $46,600

Instructions

(a) Complete the worksheet by extending the balances to the financial statement columns.
(b) Prepare an income statement, owner's equity statement, and a classified balance sheet. (*Note:* $5,000 of the notes payable become due in 2018.) D. Thao did not make any additional investments in the business during the year.
(c) Prepare the closing entries. Use J14 for the journal page.
(d) Post the closing entries. Use the three-column form of account. Income Summary is No. 350.
(e) Prepare a post-closing trial balance.

Prepare financial statements, closing entries, and post-closing trial balance.

(LO 1, 2, 4)

P4-3A The completed financial statement columns of the worksheet for Bray Company are shown as follows.

BRAY COMPANY
Worksheet
For the Year Ended December 31, 2017

Account No.	Account Titles	Income Statement Dr.	Income Statement Cr.	Balance Sheet Dr.	Balance Sheet Cr.
101	Cash			8,800	
112	Accounts Receivable			10,800	
130	Prepaid Insurance			2,800	
157	Equipment			24,000	
158	Accumulated Depreciation—Equip.				4,200
201	Accounts Payable				9,000
212	Salaries and Wages Payable				2,400
301	Owner's Capital				19,500
306	Owner's Drawings			11,000	
400	Service Revenue		60,000		
622	Maintenance and Repairs Expense	1,700			
711	Depreciation Expense	2,800			
722	Insurance Expense	1,800			
726	Salaries and Wages Expense	30,000			
732	Utilities Expense	1,400			
	Totals	37,700	60,000	57,400	35,100
	Net Income	22,300			22,300
		60,000	60,000	57,400	57,400

Instructions

(a) Prepare an income statement, an owner's equity statement, and a classified balance sheet.

(b) Prepare the closing entries. L. Bray did not make any additional investments during the year.

(c) Post the closing entries and underline and balance the accounts. (Use T-accounts.) Income Summary is account No. 350.

(d) Prepare a post-closing trial balance.

(a) Ending capital $30,800
Total current assets $22,400

(d) Post-closing trial balance $46,400

P4-4A Vang Management Services began business on January 1, 2017, with a capital investment of $120,000. The company manages condominiums for owners (Service Revenue) and rents space in its own office building (Rent Revenue). The trial balance and adjusted trial balance columns of the worksheet at the end of the first year are as follows.

Complete worksheet; prepare classified balance sheet, entries, and post-closing trial balance.

(LO 1, 2, 4)

VANG MANAGEMENT SERVICES
Worksheet
For the Year Ended December 31, 2017

Account Titles	Trial Balance Dr.	Trial Balance Cr.	Adjusted Trial Balance Dr.	Adjusted Trial Balance Cr.
Cash	13,800		13,800	
Accounts Receivable	28,300		28,300	
Prepaid Insurance	3,600		2,400	
Land	67,000		67,000	
Buildings	127,000		127,000	
Equipment	59,000		59,000	
Accounts Payable		12,500		12,500
Unearned Rent Revenue		6,000		1,500
Mortgage Payable		120,000		120,000
Owner's Capital		144,000		144,000
Owner's Drawings	22,000		22,000	
Service Revenue		90,700		90,700
Rent Revenue		29,000		33,500
Salaries and Wages Expense	42,000		42,000	
Advertising Expense	20,500		20,500	
Utilities Expense	19,000		19,000	
Totals	402,200	402,200		

Account Titles	Trial Balance Dr.	Trial Balance Cr.	Adjusted Trial Balance Dr.	Adjusted Trial Balance Cr.
Insurance Expense			1,200	
Depreciation Expense			6,600	
Accumulated Depreciation—Buildings				3,000
Accumulated Depreciation—Equipment				3,600
Interest Expense			10,000	
Interest Payable				10,000
Totals			418,800	418,800

(a) Net income $24,900
(b) Total current assets $44,500
(e) Post-closing trial balance $297,500

Instructions

(a) Prepare a complete worksheet.
(b) Prepare a classified balance sheet. (*Note:* $30,000 of the mortgage note payable is due for payment next year.)
(c) Journalize the adjusting entries.
(d) Journalize the closing entries.
(e) Prepare a post-closing trial balance.

Complete all steps in accounting cycle.

(LO 1, 2, 4)

GLS

P4-5A Anya Clark opened Anya's Cleaning Service on July 1, 2017. During July, the following transactions were completed.

July	1	Anya invested $20,000 cash in the business.
	1	Purchased used truck for $12,000, paying $4,000 cash and the balance on account.
	3	Purchased cleaning supplies for $2,100 on account.
	5	Paid $1,800 cash on a 1-year insurance policy effective July 1.
	12	Billed customers $4,500 for cleaning services.
	18	Paid $1,500 cash on amount owed on truck and $1,400 on amount owed on cleaning supplies.
	20	Paid $2,800 cash for employee salaries.
	21	Collected $3,400 cash from customers billed on July 12.
	25	Billed customers $6,000 for cleaning services.
	31	Paid $350 for the monthly gasoline bill for the truck.
	31	Withdraw $5,600 cash for personal use.

The chart of accounts for Anya's Cleaning Service contains the following accounts: No. 101 Cash, No. 112 Accounts Receivable, No. 126 Supplies, No. 130 Prepaid Insurance, No. 157 Equipment, No. 158 Accumulated Depreciation—Equipment, No. 201 Accounts Payable, No. 212 Salaries and Wages Payable, No. 301 Owner's Capital, No. 306 Owner's Drawings, No. 350 Income Summary, No. 400 Service Revenue, No. 631 Supplies Expense, No. 633 Gasoline Expense, No. 711 Depreciation Expense, No. 722 Insurance Expense, and No. 726 Salaries and Wages Expense.

(b) Trial balance $37,700
(c) Adjusted trial balance $41,900
(d) Net income $6,900
Total assets $29,500
(g) Post-closing trial balance $30,000

Instructions

(a) Journalize and post the July transactions. Use page J1 for the journal and the three-column form of account.
(b) Prepare a trial balance at July 31 on a worksheet.
(c) Enter the following adjustments on the worksheet and complete the worksheet.
    (1) Unbilled and uncollected revenue for services performed at July 31 were $2,700.
    (2) Depreciation on equipment for the month was $500.
    (3) One-twelfth of the insurance expired.
    (4) An inventory count shows $600 of cleaning supplies on hand at July 31.
    (5) Accrued but unpaid employee salaries were $1,000.
(d) Prepare the income statement and owner's equity statement for July and a classified balance sheet at July 31.
(e) Journalize and post adjusting entries. Use page J2 for the journal.
(f) Journalize and post closing entries and complete the closing process. Use page J3 for the journal.
(g) Prepare a post-closing trial balance at July 31.

P4-6A Casey Hartwig, CPA, was retained by Global Cable to prepare financial statements for April 2017. Hartwig accumulated all the ledger balances per Global's records and found the following.

Analyze errors and prepare correcting entries and trial balance.

(LO 3)

GLOBAL CABLE
Trial Balance
April 30, 2017

	Debit	Credit
Cash	$ 4,100	
Accounts Receivable	3,200	
Supplies	800	
Equipment	10,600	
Accumulated Depreciation—Equip.		$ 1,350
Accounts Payable		2,100
Salaries and Wages Payable		700
Unearned Service Revenue		890
Owner's Capital		12,900
Service Revenue		5,450
Salaries and Wages Expense	3,300	
Advertising Expense	600	
Miscellaneous Expense	290	
Depreciation Expense	500	
	$23,390	$23,390

Casey Hartwig reviewed the records and found the following errors.

1. Cash received from a customer on account was recorded as $950 instead of $590.
2. A payment of $75 for advertising expense was entered as a debit to Miscellaneous Expense $75 and a credit to Cash $75.
3. The first salary payment this month was for $1,900, which included $700 of salaries payable on March 31. The payment was recorded as a debit to Salaries and Wages Expense $1,900 and a credit to Cash $1,900. (No reversing entries were made on April 1.)
4. The purchase on account of a printer costing $310 was recorded as a debit to Supplies and a credit to Accounts Payable for $310.
5. A cash payment of repair expense on equipment for $96 was recorded as a debit to Equipment $69 and a credit to Cash $69.

Instructions

(a) Prepare an analysis of each error showing (1) the incorrect entry, (2) the correct entry, and (3) the correcting entry. Items 4 and 5 occurred on April 30, 2017.

(b) Prepare a correct trial balance.

(b) Trial balance $22,690

PROBLEMS: SET B AND SET C

Visit the book's companion website, at **www.wiley.com/college/weygandt**, and choose the Student Companion site to access Problems: Set B and Set C.

COMPREHENSIVE PROBLEM: CHAPTERS 2 TO 4

CP4 Ashley Williams opened Ashley's Maids Cleaning Service on July 1, 2017. During July, the company completed the following transactions.

July	1	Invested $14,000 cash in the business.
	1	Purchased a used truck for $10,000, paying $3,000 cash and the balance on account.
	3	Purchased cleaning supplies for $800 on account.
	5	Paid $2,160 on a 1-year insurance policy, effective July 1.
	12	Billed customers $3,800 for cleaning services.
	18	Paid $1,000 of amount owed on truck, and $400 of amount owed on cleaning supplies.
	20	Paid $1,600 for employee salaries.
	21	Collected $1,400 from customers billed on July 12.
	25	Billed customers $1,900 for cleaning services.

31 Paid gasoline for the month on the truck, $400.
31 Withdrew $700 cash for personal use.

The chart of accounts for Ashley's Maids Cleaning Service contains the following accounts: No. 101 Cash, No. 112 Accounts Receivable, No. 126 Supplies, No. 130 Prepaid Insurance, No. 157 Equipment, No. 158 Accumulated Depreciation—Equipment, No. 201 Accounts Payable, No. 212 Salaries and Wages Payable, No. 301 Owner's Capital, No. 306 Owner's Drawings, No. 350 Income Summary, No. 400 Service Revenue, No. 631 Supplies Expense, No. 633 Gasoline Expense, No. 711 Depreciation Expense, No. 722 Insurance Expense, and No. 726 Salaries and Wages Expense.

Instructions

(a) Journalize and post the July transactions. Use page J1 for the journal.

(b) Trial balance totals $26,100

(b) Prepare a trial balance at July 31 on a worksheet.

(c) Enter the following adjustments on the worksheet, and complete the worksheet.
   (1) Unbilled fees for services performed at July 31 were $1,300.
   (2) Depreciation on equipment for the month was $200.
   (3) One-twelfth of the insurance expired.
   (4) An inventory count shows $100 of cleaning supplies on hand at July 31.
   (5) Accrued but unpaid employee salaries were $500.

(d) Net income $3,420 Total assets $23,620

(d) Prepare the income statement and owner's equity statement for July, and a classified balance sheet at July 31, 2017.

(e) Journalize and post the adjusting entries. Use page J2 for the journal.

(f) Journalize and post the closing entries, and complete the closing process. Use page J3 for the journal.

(g) Trial balance totals $23,820

(g) Prepare a post-closing trial balance at July 31.

CONTINUING PROBLEM

© leungchopan/ Shutterstock

COOKIE CREATIONS: AN ENTREPRENEURIAL JOURNEY

(*Note:* This is a continuation of the Cookie Creations problem from Chapters 1 through 3.)

CC4 Natalie had a very busy December. At the end of the month, after journalizing and posting the December transactions and adjusting entries, Natalie prepared the following adjusted trial balance.

COOKIE CREATIONS
Adjusted Trial Balance
December 31, 2016

	Debit	**Credit**
Cash	$1,180	
Accounts Receivable	875	
Supplies	350	
Prepaid Insurance	1,210	
Equipment	1,200	
Accumulated Depreciation—Equipment		$ 40
Accounts Payable		75
Salaries and Wages Payable		56
Interest Payable		15
Unearned Service Revenue		300
Notes Payable		2,000
Owner's Capital		800
Owner's Drawings	500	
Service Revenue		4,515
Salaries and Wages Expense	1,006	
Utilities Expense	125	
Advertising Expense	165	
Supplies Expense	1,025	
Depreciation Expense	40	
Insurance Expense	110	
Interest Expense	15	
	$7,801	$7,801

Instructions

Using the information in the adjusted trial balance, do the following.

(a) Prepare an income statement and an owner's equity statement for the 2 months ended December 31, 2016, and a classified balance sheet at December 31, 2016. The note payable has a stated interest rate of 6%, and the principal and interest are due on November 16, 2018.

(b) Natalie has decided that her year-end will be December 31, 2016. Prepare and post closing entries as of December 31, 2016.

(c) Prepare a post-closing trial balance.

BROADENING YOUR PERSPECTIVE

FINANCIAL REPORTING AND ANALYSIS

Financial Reporting Problem: Apple Inc.

BYP4-1 The financial statements of Apple Inc. are presented in Appendix A at the end of this textbook. Instructions for accessing and using the company's complete annual report, including the notes to the financial statements, are also provided in Appendix A.

Instructions

Answer the questions below using Apple's Consolidated Balance Sheets.

(a) What were Apple's total current assets at September 28, 2013, and September 29, 2012?

(b) Are assets that Apple included under current assets listed in proper order? Explain.

(c) How are Apple's assets classified?

(d) What was Apple's "Cash and cash equivalents" at September 28, 2013?

(e) What were Apple's total current liabilities at September 28, 2013, and September 29, 2012?

Comparative Analysis Problem: PepsiCo, Inc. vs. The Coca-Cola Company

BYP4-2 PepsiCo, Inc.'s financial statements are presented in Appendix B. Financial statements of The Coca-Cola Company are presented in Appendix C. Instructions for accessing and using the complete annual reports of PepsiCo and Coca-Cola, including the notes to the financial statements, are also provided in Appendices B and C, respectively.

Instructions

(a) Based on the information contained in these financial statements, determine each of the following for PepsiCo at December 31, 2013, and for Coca-Cola at December 31, 2013.
  (1) Total current assets.
  (2) Net amount of property, plant, and equipment (land, buildings, and equipment).
  (3) Total current liabilities.
  (4) Total equity.

(b) What conclusions concerning the companies' respective financial positions can be drawn?

Comparative Analysis Problem: Amazon.com, Inc. vs. Wal-Mart Stores, Inc.

BYP4-3 Amazon.com, Inc.'s financial statements are presented in Appendix D. Financial statements of Wal-Mart Stores, Inc. are presented in Appendix E. Instructions for accessing and using the complete annual reports of Amazon and Wal-Mart, including the notes to the financial statements, are also provided in Appendices D and E, respectively.

Instructions

(a) Based on the information contained in these financial statements, determine the following for Amazon at December 31, 2013, and Wal-Mart at January 31, 2014.
  (1) Total current assets.
  (2) Net amount of property and equipment (fixed assets), net.
  (3) Total current liabilities.
  (4) Total equity.

(b) What conclusions concerning these two companies can be drawn from these data?

Real-World Focus

BYP4-4 Numerous companies have established home pages on the Internet, e.g., the soda companies Capt'n Eli Root Beer Company **(www.captneli.com/rootbeer.php)** and Cheerwine **(www.cheerwine.com)**.

Instructions

Examine the home pages of any two companies and answer the following questions.

(a) What type of information is available?
(b) Is any accounting-related information presented?
(c) Would you describe the home page as informative, promotional, or both? Why?

CRITICAL THINKING

Decision-Making Across the Organization

BYP4-5 Whitegloves Janitorial Service was started 2 years ago by Jenna Olson. Because business has been exceptionally good, Jenna decided on July 1, 2017, to expand operations by acquiring an additional truck and hiring two more assistants. To finance the expansion, Jenna obtained on July 1, 2017, a $25,000, 10% bank loan, payable $10,000 on July 1, 2018, and the balance on July 1, 2019. The terms of the loan require the borrower to have $10,000 more current assets than current liabilities at December 31, 2017. If these terms are not met, the bank loan will be refinanced at 15% interest. At December 31, 2017, the accountant for Whitegloves Janitorial Service Inc. prepared the balance sheet shown below.

WHITEGLOVES JANITORIAL SERVICE
Balance Sheet
December 31, 2017

Assets		**Liabilities and Owner's Equity**	
Current assets		Current liabilities	
Cash	$ 6,500	Notes payable	$10,000
Accounts receivable	9,000	Accounts payable	2,500
Supplies	5,200	Total current liabilities	12,500
Prepaid insurance	4,800	Long-term liability	
Total current assets	25,500	Notes payable	15,000
Property, plant, and equipment		Total liabilities	27,500
Equipment (net)	22,000	Owner's equity	
Delivery trucks (net)	34,000	Owner's capital	54,000
Total property, plant, and equipment	56,000		
Total assets	$81,500	Total liabilities and owner's equity	$81,500

Jenna presented the balance sheet to the bank's loan officer on January 2, 2018, confident that the company had met the terms of the loan. The loan officer was not impressed. She said, "We need financial statements audited by a CPA." A CPA was hired and immediately realized that the balance sheet had been prepared from a trial balance and not from an adjusted trial balance. The adjustment data at the balance sheet date consisted of the following.

1. Unbilled janitorial services performed were $3,700.
2. Janitorial supplies on hand were $2,500.
3. Prepaid insurance was a 3-year policy dated January 1, 2017.
4. December expenses incurred but unpaid at December 31, $500.
5. Interest on the bank loan was not recorded.
6. The amounts for property, plant, and equipment presented in the balance sheet were reported net of accumulated depreciation (cost less accumulated depreciation). These amounts were $4,000 for cleaning equipment and $5,000 for delivery trucks as of January 1, 2017. Depreciation for 2017 was $2,000 for cleaning equipment and $5,000 for delivery trucks.

Instructions

With the class divided into groups, answer the following.

(a) Prepare a correct balance sheet.
(b) Were the terms of the bank loan met? Explain.

Communication Activity

BYP4-6 The accounting cycle is important in understanding the accounting process.

Instructions

Write a memo to your instructor that lists the steps of the accounting cycle in the order they should be completed. End with a paragraph that explains the optional steps in the cycle.

Ethics Case

BYP4-7 As the controller of Take No Prisoners Perfume Company, you discover a misstatement that overstated net income in the prior year's financial statements. The misleading financial statements appear in the company's annual report which was issued to banks and other creditors less than a month ago. After much thought about the consequences of telling the president, Mike Flanary, about this misstatement, you gather your courage to inform him. Mike says, "Hey! What they don't know won't hurt them. But, just so we set the record straight, we'll adjust this year's financial statements for last year's misstatement. We can absorb that misstatement better in this year than in last year anyway! Just don't make such a mistake again."

Instructions

(a) Who are the stakeholders in this situation?
(b) What are the ethical issues in this situation?
(c) What would you do as a controller in this situation?

All About You

BYP4-8 Companies prepare balance sheets in order to know their financial position at a specific point in time. This enables them to make a comparison to their position at previous points in time, and gives them a basis for planning for the future. In order to evaluate your financial position, you need to prepare a personal balance sheet. Assume that you have compiled the following information regarding your finances. (*Note:* Some of the items might not be used in your personal balance sheet.)

Amount owed on student loan balance (long-term)	$ 5,000
Balance in checking account	1,200
Certificate of deposit (6-month)	3,000
Annual earnings from part-time job	11,300
Automobile	7,000
Balance on automobile loan (current portion)	1,500
Balance on automobile loan (long-term portion)	4,000
Home computer	800
Amount owed to you by younger brother	300
Balance in money market account	1,800
Annual tuition	6,400
Video and stereo equipment	1,250
Balance owed on credit card (current portion)	150
Balance owed on credit card (long-term portion)	1,650

Instructions

Prepare a personal balance sheet using the format you have learned for a classified balance sheet for a company. For the capital account, use Owner's Capital.

FASB Codification Activity

BYP4-9 If your school has a subscription to the FASB Codification, go to **http://aaahq.org/ascLogin.cfm** to log in and prepare responses to the following.

Instructions

(a) Access the glossary ("Master Glossary") at the FASB Codification website to answer the following.
 (1) What is the definition of current assets?
 (2) What is the definition of current liabilities?
(b) A company wants to offset its accounts payable against its cash account and show a cash amount net of accounts payable on its balance sheet. Identify the criteria (found in the FASB Codification) under which a company has the right of set off. Does the company have the right to offset accounts payable against the cash account?

A Look at IFRS

LEARNING OBJECTIVE 6 **Compare the procedures for the closing process under GAAP and IFRS.**

The classified balance sheet, although generally required internationally, contains certain variations in format when reporting under IFRS.

Key Points

Following are the key similarities and differences between GAAP and IFRS related to the closing process and the financial statements.

Similarities

- The procedures of the closing process are applicable to all companies, whether they are using IFRS or GAAP.
- IFRS generally requires a classified statement of financial position similar to the classified balance sheet under GAAP.
- IFRS follows the same guidelines as this textbook for distinguishing between current and noncurrent assets and liabilities.

Differences

- IFRS recommends but does not require the use of the title "statement of financial position" rather than balance sheet.
- The format of statement of financial position information is often presented differently under IFRS. Although no specific format is required, many companies that follow IFRS present statement of financial position information in this order:
  - ♦ Non-current assets
  - ♦ Current assets
  - ♦ Equity
  - ♦ Non-current liabilities
  - ♦ Current liabilities
- Under IFRS, current assets are usually listed in the reverse order of liquidity. For example, under GAAP cash is listed first, but under IFRS it is listed last.
- IFRS has many differences in terminology from what are shown in your textbook. For example, in the following sample statement of financial position, notice in the investment category that stock is called shares.

FRANKLIN COMPANY Statement of Financial Position October 31, 2017			
Assets			
Intangible assets			
Patents			$ 3,100
Property, plant, and equipment			
Land		$10,000	
Equipment	$24,000		
Less: Accumulated depreciation	5,000	19,000	29,000
Long-term investments			
Share investments		5,200	
Investment in real estate		2,000	7,200
Current assets			
Prepaid insurance		400	
Supplies		2,100	
Inventory		3,000	
Notes receivable		1,000	
Accounts receivable		7,000	
Debt investments		2,000	
Cash		6,600	22,100
Total assets			$61,400
Equity and Liabilities			
Equity			
Owner's capital			$34,050
Non-current liabilities			
Mortgage payable		$10,000	
Notes payable		1,300	11,300
Current liabilities			
Notes payable		11,000	
Accounts payable		2,100	
Salaries and wages payable		1,600	
Unearned service revenue		900	
Interest payable		450	16,050
Total equity and liabilities			$61,400

- Both GAAP and IFRS are increasing the use of fair value to report assets. However, at this point IFRS has adopted it more broadly. As examples, under IFRS, companies can apply fair value to property, plant, and equipment, and in some cases intangible assets.

Looking to the Future

The IASB and the FASB are working on a project to converge their standards related to financial statement presentation. A key feature of the proposed framework is that each of the statements will be organized in the same format, to separate an entity's financing activities from its operating and investing activities and, further, to separate financing activities into transactions with owners and creditors. Thus, the same classifications used in the statement of financial position would also be used in the income statement and the statement of cash flows. The project has three phases. You can follow the joint financial presentation project at the following link: **http://www.fasb.org/project/financial_statement_presentation.shtml**.

IFRS Practice

IFRS Self-Test Questions

1. A company has purchased a tract of land and expects to build a production plant on the land in approximately 5 years. During the 5 years before construction, the land will be idle. Under IFRS, the land should be reported as:
   (a) land expense.
   (b) property, plant, and equipment.
   (c) an intangible asset.
   (d) a long-term investment.
2. Current assets under IFRS are listed generally:
   (a) by importance.
   (b) in the reverse order of their expected conversion to cash.
   (c) by longevity.
   (d) alphabetically.
3. Companies that use IFRS:
   (a) may report all their assets on the statement of financial position at fair value.
   (b) may offset assets against liabilities and show net assets and net liabilities on their statements of financial position, rather than the underlying detailed line items.
   (c) may report noncurrent assets before current assets on the statement of financial position.
   (d) do not have any guidelines as to what should be reported on the statement of financial position.
4. Companies that follow IFRS to prepare a statement of financial position generally use the following order of classification:
   (a) current assets, current liabilities, noncurrent assets, noncurrent liabilities, equity.
   (b) noncurrent assets, noncurrent liabilities, current assets, current liabilities, equity.
   (c) noncurrent assets, current assets, equity, noncurrent liabilities, current liabilities.
   (d) equity, noncurrent assets, current assets, noncurrent liabilities, current liabilities.

IFRS Exercises

IFRS4-1 In what ways does the format of a statement of financial of position under IFRS often differ from a balance sheet presented under GAAP?

IFRS4-2 What term is commonly used under IFRS in reference to the balance sheet?

IFRS4-3 The statement of financial position for Wallby Company includes the following accounts (in British pounds): Accounts Receivable £12,500, Prepaid Insurance £3,600, Cash £15,400, Supplies £5,200, and Debt Investments (short-term) £6,700. Prepare the current assets section of the statement of financial position, listing the accounts in proper sequence.

IFRS4-4 The following information is available for Sutter Bowling Alley at December 31, 2017.

Buildings	$128,800	Owner's Capital	$115,000
Accounts Receivable	14,520	Accumulated Depreciation—Buildings	42,600
Prepaid Insurance	4,680	Accounts Payable	12,300
Cash	18,040	Notes Payable	97,780
Equipment	62,400	Accumulated Depreciation—Equipment	18,720
Land	64,000	Interest Payable	2,600
Insurance Expense	780	Bowling Revenues	14,180
Depreciation Expense	7,360		
Interest Expense	2,600		

Prepare a classified statement of financial position. Assume that $13,900 of the notes payable will be paid in 2018.

International Comparative Analysis Problem: Apple vs. Louis Vuitton

IFRS4-5 The financial statements of Louis Vuitton are presented in Appendix F. Instructions for accessing and using the company's complete annual report, including the notes to its financial statements, are also provided in Appendix F.

Instructions

Identify five differences in the format of the statement of financial position used by Louis Vuitton compared to a company, such as Apple, that follows GAAP. (Apple's financial statements are available in Appendix A.)

Answers to IFRS Self-Test Questions

1. d **2.** b **3.** c **4.** c

5 Accounting for Merchandising Operations

CHAPTER PREVIEW Merchandising is one of the largest and most influential industries in the United States. It is likely that a number of you will work for a merchandiser. Therefore, understanding the financial statements of merchandising companies is important. In this chapter, you will learn the basics about reporting merchandising transactions. In addition, you will learn how to prepare and analyze a commonly used form of the income statement—the multiple-step income statement.

FEATURE STORY

Buy Now, Vote Later

Have you ever shopped for outdoor gear at an REI (Recreational Equipment Incorporated) store? If so, you might have been surprised if a salesclerk asked if you were a member. A member? What do you mean a member? You soon realize that REI might not be your typical store. In fact, there's a lot about REI that makes it different.

REI is a consumer cooperative, or "co-op" for short. To figure out what that means, consider this quote from the company's annual stewardship report:

> As a cooperative, the Company is owned by its members. Each member is entitled to one vote in the election of the Company's Board of Directors. Since January 1, 2008, the nonrefundable, nontransferable, one-time membership fee has been 20 dollars. As of December 31, 2010, there were approximately 10.8 million members.

Voting rights? Now that's something you don't get from shopping at Wal-Mart. REI members get other benefits as well, including sharing in the company's profits through a dividend at the end of the year, which can be used for purchases at REI stores during the next two years. The more you spend, the bigger your dividend.

Since REI is a co-op, you might also wonder whether management's incentives might be a little different than at other stores. For example, is management still concerned about making a profit? The answer is yes, as it ensures the long-term viability of the company. At the same time, REI's members want the company to be run efficiently, so that prices remain low. In order for its members to evaluate just how well management is doing, REI publishes an audited annual report, just like publicly traded companies do. So, while profit maximization might not be the ultimate goal for REI, the accounting and reporting issues are similar to those of a typical corporation.

How well is this business model working for REI? Well, it has consistently been rated as one of the best places to work in the United States by *Fortune* magazine. It is one of only five companies named each year since the list was created in 1998. Also, REI had sustainable business practices long before social responsibility became popular at other companies. The CEO's stewardship report states "we reduced the absolute amount of energy we use despite opening four new stores and growing our business; we grew the amount of FSC-certified paper we use to 58.4 percent of our total paper footprint—including our cash register receipt paper; we facilitated 2.2 million volunteer hours and we provided $3.7 million to more than 330 conservation and recreation nonprofits."

So, while REI, like other retailers, closely monitors its financial results, it also strives to succeed in other areas. And, with over 10 million votes at stake, REI's management knows that it has to deliver.

© omgimages/iStockphoto

CHAPTER OUTLINE

Learning Objectives

Learning Objective	Topics	DO IT!
1 Describe merchandising operations and inventory systems.	• Operating cycles • Flow of costs	DO IT! 1 Merchandising Operations and Inventory Systems
2 Record purchases under a perpetual inventory system.	• Freight costs • Purchase returns and allowances • Purchase discounts • Summary of purchasing transactions	DO IT! 2 Purchase Transactions
3 Record sales under a perpetual inventory system.	• Sales returns and allowances • Sales discounts	DO IT! 3 Sales Transactions
4 Apply the steps in the accounting cycle to a merchandising company.	• Adjusting entries • Closing entries • Summary of merchandising entries	DO IT! 4 Closing Entries
5 Compare a multiple-step with a single-step income statement.	• Multiple-step income statement • Single-step income statement • Classified balance sheet	DO IT! 5 Financial Statement Classifications

Go to the ***REVIEW AND PRACTICE*** section at the end of the chapter for a review of key concepts and practice applications with solutions.

Visit **WileyPLUS with ORION** for additional tutorials and practice opportunities.

LEARNING OBJECTIVE 1

Describe merchandising operations and inventory systems.

REI, **Wal-Mart**, and **Amazon.com** are called merchandising companies because they buy and sell merchandise rather than perform services as their primary source of revenue. Merchandising companies that purchase and sell directly to consumers are called **retailers**. Merchandising companies that sell to retailers are known as **wholesalers**. For example, retailer **Walgreens** might buy goods from wholesaler **McKesson**. Retailer **Office Depot** might buy office supplies from wholesaler **United Stationers**. The primary source of revenues for merchandising companies is the sale of merchandise, often referred to simply as **sales revenue** or **sales**. A merchandising company has two categories of expenses: cost of goods sold and operating expenses.

Cost of goods sold is the total cost of merchandise sold during the period. This expense is directly related to the revenue recognized from the sale of goods. Illustration 5-1 shows the income measurement process for a merchandising company. The items in the two blue boxes are unique to a merchandising company; they are not used by a service company.

Illustration 5-1
Income measurement process for a merchandising company

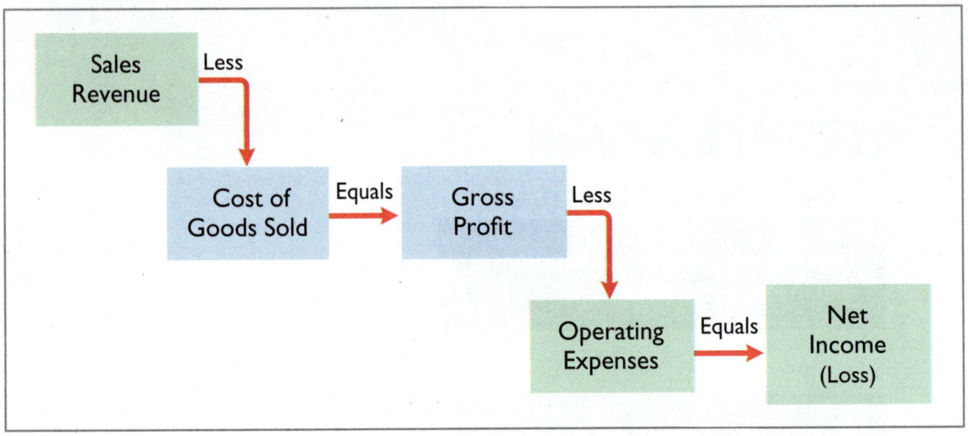

Operating Cycles

The operating cycle of a merchandising company ordinarily is longer than that of a service company. The purchase of merchandise inventory and its eventual sale lengthen the cycle. Illustration 5-2 shows the operating cycle of a service company.

Illustration 5-2
Operating cycle for a service company

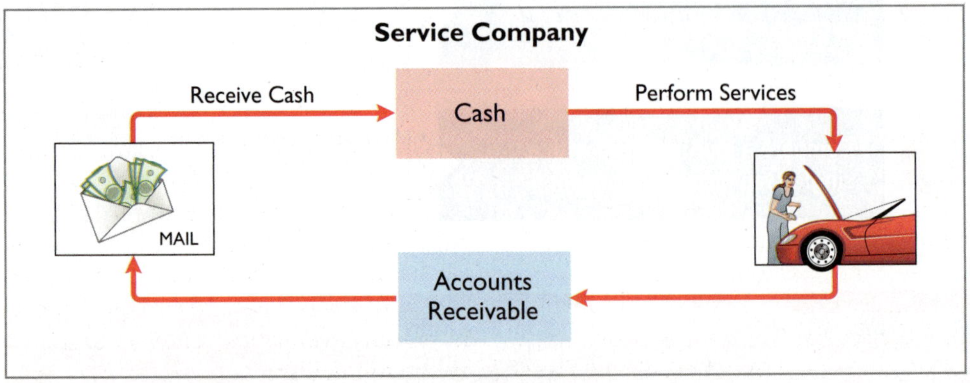

Illustration 5-3 shows the operating cycle of a merchandising company.

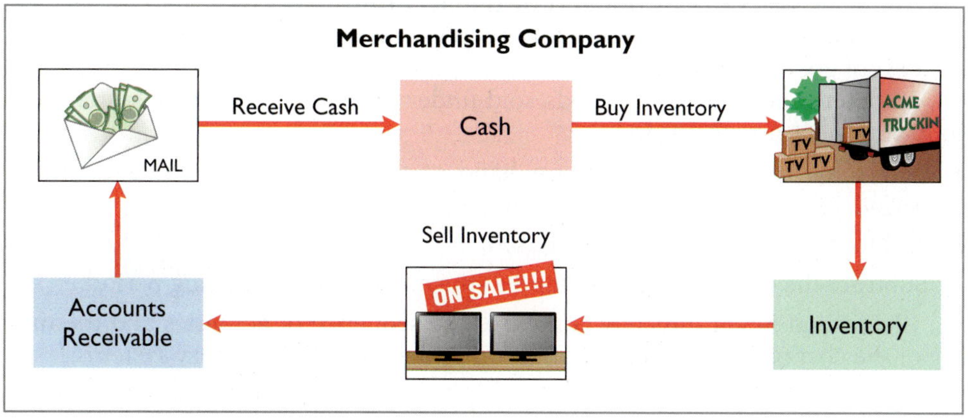

Illustration 5-3
Operating cycle for a merchandising company

Note that the added asset account for a merchandising company is the Inventory account. Companies report inventory as a current asset on the balance sheet.

Flow of Costs

The flow of costs for a merchandising company is as follows. Beginning inventory plus the cost of goods purchased is the cost of goods available for sale. As goods are sold, they are assigned to cost of goods sold. Those goods that are not sold by the end of the accounting period represent ending inventory. Illustration 5-4 describes these relationships. Companies use one of two systems to account for inventory: a **perpetual inventory system** or a **periodic inventory system**.

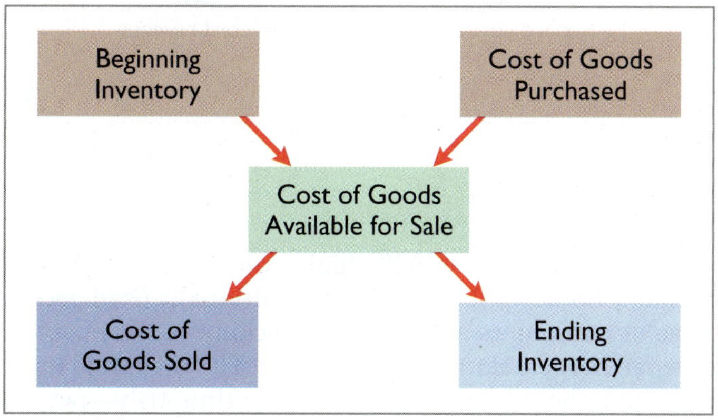

Illustration 5-4
Flow of costs

PERPETUAL SYSTEM

In a **perpetual inventory system**, companies keep detailed records of the cost of each inventory purchase and sale. These records continuously—perpetually—show the inventory that should be on hand for every item. For example, a Ford dealership has separate inventory records for each automobile, truck, and van on its lot and showroom floor. Similarly, a Kroger grocery store uses bar codes and optical scanners to keep a daily running record of every box of cereal and every jar of jelly that it buys and sells. Under a perpetual inventory system, a company determines the cost of goods sold **each time a sale occurs**.

Helpful Hint
For control purposes, companies take a physical inventory count under the perpetual system, even though it is not needed to determine cost of goods sold.

PERIODIC SYSTEM

In a **periodic inventory system**, companies do not keep detailed inventory records of the goods on hand throughout the period. Instead, they determine the cost of goods sold **only at the end of the accounting period**—that is, periodically. At that point, the company takes a physical inventory count to determine the cost of goods on hand.

To determine the cost of goods sold under a periodic inventory system, the following steps are necessary:

1. Determine the cost of goods on hand at the beginning of the accounting period.
2. Add to it the cost of goods purchased.
3. Subtract the cost of goods on hand at the end of the accounting period.

Illustration 5-5 graphically compares the sequence of activities and the timing of the cost of goods sold computation under the two inventory systems.

Illustration 5-5
Comparing perpetual and periodic inventory systems

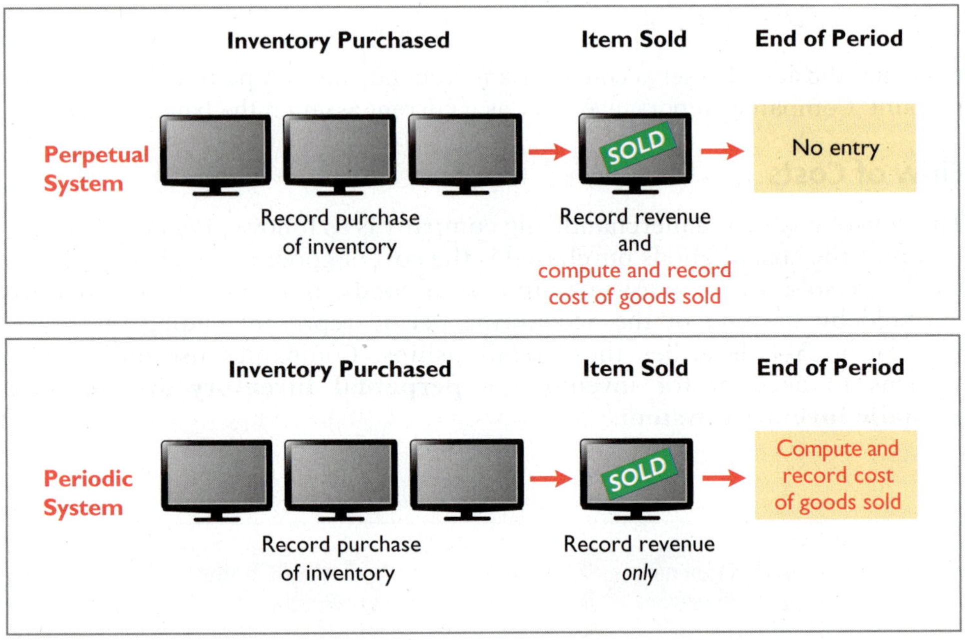

ADVANTAGES OF THE PERPETUAL SYSTEM

Companies that sell merchandise with high unit values, such as automobiles, furniture, and major home appliances, have traditionally used perpetual systems. The growing use of computers and electronic scanners has enabled many more companies to install perpetual inventory systems. The perpetual inventory system is so named because the accounting records continuously—perpetually—show the quantity and cost of the inventory that should be on hand at any time.

A perpetual inventory system provides better control over inventories than a periodic system. Since the inventory records show the quantities that should be on hand, the company can count the goods at any time to see whether the amount of goods actually on hand agrees with the inventory records. If shortages are uncovered, the company can investigate immediately. Although a perpetual inventory system requires both additional clerical work and expense to maintain the subsidiary records, a computerized system can minimize this cost. Much of Amazon.com's success is attributed to its sophisticated inventory system.

Some businesses find it either unnecessary or uneconomical to invest in a sophisticated, computerized perpetual inventory system such as Amazon's. Many small merchandising businesses find that basic accounting software provides some of the essential benefits of a perpetual inventory system. Also, managers of some small businesses still find that they can control their merchandise and manage day-to-day operations using a periodic inventory system.

Because of the widespread use of the perpetual inventory system, we illustrate it in this chapter. We discuss and illustrate the periodic system in Appendix 5B.

Investor Insight Morrow Snowboards, Inc.

© Ben Blankenburg/iStockphoto

Morrow Snowboards Improves Its Stock Appeal

Investors are often eager to invest in a company that has a hot new product. However, when snowboard-maker Morrow Snowboards, Inc. issued shares of stock to the public for the first time, some investors expressed reluctance to invest in Morrow because of a number of accounting control problems. To reduce investor concerns, Morrow implemented a perpetual inventory system to improve its control over inventory. In addition, the company stated that it would perform a physical inventory count every quarter until it felt that its perpetual inventory system was reliable.

If a perpetual system keeps track of inventory on a daily basis, why do companies ever need to do a physical count? (Go to **WileyPLUS** for this answer and additional questions.)

DO IT! 1 Merchandising Operations and Inventory Systems

Indicate whether the following statements are true or false.

1. The primary source of revenue for a merchandising company results from performing services for customers.
2. The operating cycle of a service company is usually shorter than that of a merchandising company.
3. Sales revenue less cost of goods sold equals gross profit.
4. Ending inventory plus the cost of goods purchased equals cost of goods available for sale.

Solution

1. False. The primary source of revenue for a service company results from performing services for customers. **2.** True. **3.** True. **4.** False. Beginning inventory plus the cost of goods purchased equals cost of goods available for sale.

Related exercise material: **BE5-1, BE5-2, E5-1, and DO IT! 5-1.**

Action Plan

✔ Review merchandising concepts.

✔ Understand the flow of costs in a merchandising company.

LEARNING OBJECTIVE 2 Record purchases under a perpetual inventory system.

Companies purchase inventory using cash or credit (on account). They normally record purchases when they receive the goods from the seller. Every purchase should be supported by business documents that provide written evidence of the transaction. Each cash purchase should be supported by a canceled check or a cash register receipt indicating the items purchased and amounts paid. Companies record cash purchases by an increase in Inventory and a decrease in Cash.

A **purchase invoice** should support each credit purchase. This invoice indicates the total purchase price and other relevant information. However, the purchaser does not prepare a separate purchase invoice. Instead, the purchaser uses as a purchase invoice a copy of the sales invoice sent by the seller. In Illustration 5-6, for example, Sauk Stereo (the buyer) uses as a purchase invoice the sales invoice prepared by PW Audio Supply (the seller).

Illustration 5-6
Sales invoice used as purchase invoice by Sauk Stereo

INVOICE NO. 731

PW AUDIO SUPPLY
27 CIRCLE DRIVE
HARDING, MICHIGAN 48281

SOLD TO
Firm Name: Sauk Stereo
Attention of: James Hoover, Purchasing Agent
Address: 125 Main Street
City: Chelsea State: Illinois Zip: 60915

Date 5/4/17	Salesperson Malone	Terms 2/10, n/30	FOB Shipping Point		
Catalog No.	**Description**	**Quantity**	**Price**	**Amount**	
X572Y9820	Printed Circuit Board-prototype	1	2,300	$2,300	
A2547Z45	Production Model Circuits	5	300	1,500	

IMPORTANT: ALL RETURNS MUST BE MADE WITHIN 10 DAYS — **TOTAL** $3,800

Helpful Hint
To better understand the contents of this invoice, identify these items:
1. Seller
2. Invoice date
3. Purchaser
4. Salesperson
5. Credit terms
6. Freight terms
7. Goods sold: catalog number, description, quantity, price per unit
8. Total invoice amount

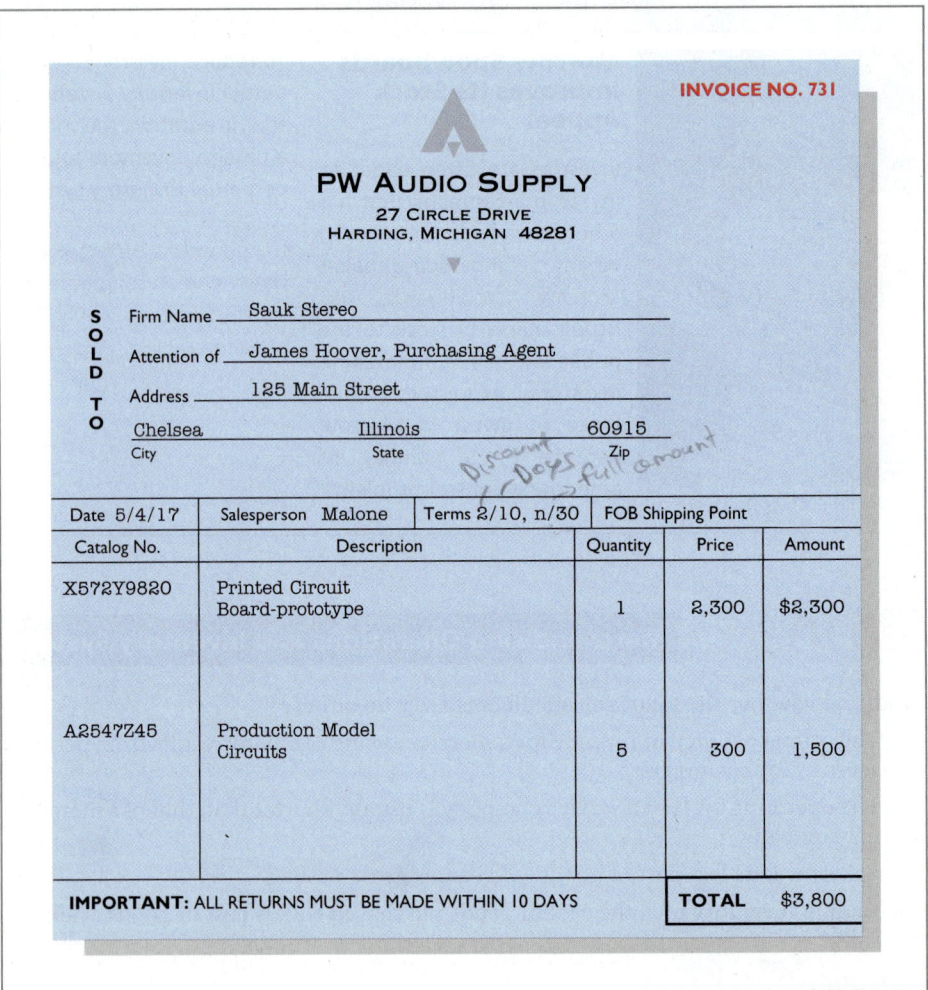

Sauk Stereo makes the following journal entry to record its purchase from PW Audio Supply. The entry increases (debits) Inventory and increases (credits) Accounts Payable.

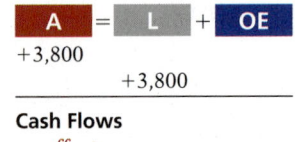

A	=	L	+	OE
+3,800				
		+3,800		

Cash Flows
no effect

May 4	Inventory	3,800	
	Accounts Payable		3,800
	(To record goods purchased on account from PW Audio Supply)		

Under the perpetual inventory system, companies record purchases of merchandise for sale in the Inventory account. Thus, **REI** would increase (debit) Inventory for clothing, sporting goods, and anything else purchased for resale to customers.

Not all purchases are debited to Inventory, however. Companies record purchases of assets acquired for use and not for resale, such as supplies, equipment, and similar items, as increases to specific asset accounts rather than to Inventory.

For example, to record the purchase of materials used to make shelf signs or for cash register receipt paper, REI would increase (debit) Supplies.

Freight Costs

The sales agreement should indicate who—the seller or the buyer—is to pay for transporting the goods to the buyer's place of business. When a common carrier such as a railroad, trucking company, or airline transports the goods, the carrier prepares a freight bill in accord with the sales agreement.

Freight terms are expressed as either FOB shipping point or FOB destination. The letters FOB mean **free on board**. Thus, **FOB shipping point** means that the seller places the goods free on board the carrier, and the buyer pays the freight costs. Conversely, **FOB destination** means that the seller places the goods free on board to the buyer's place of business, and the seller pays the freight. For example, the sales invoice in Illustration 5-6 indicates FOB shipping point. Thus, the buyer (Sauk Stereo) pays the freight charges. Illustration 5-7 illustrates these shipping terms.

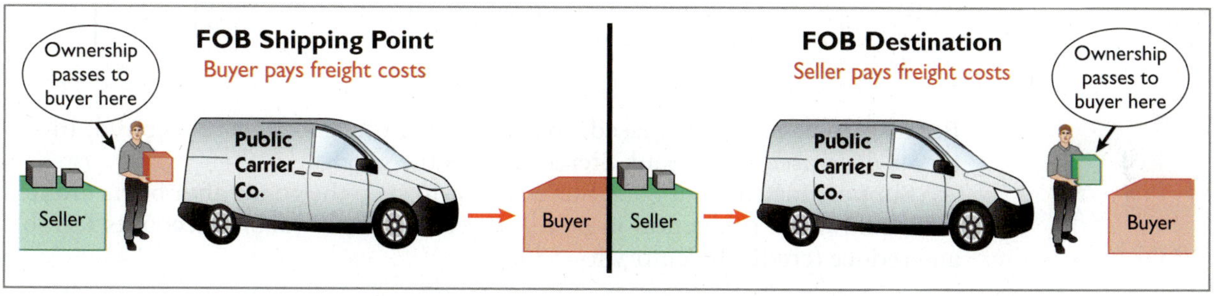

Illustration 5-7
Shipping terms

FREIGHT COSTS INCURRED BY THE BUYER

When the buyer incurs the transportation costs, these costs are considered part of the cost of purchasing inventory. Therefore, the buyer debits (increases) the Inventory account. For example, if Sauk Stereo (the buyer) pays Public Carrier Co. $150 for freight charges on May 6, the entry on Sauk Stereo's books is:

May 6	Inventory	150	
	Cash		150
	(To record payment of freight on goods purchased)		

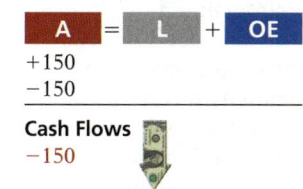

A = L + OE
+150
−150

Cash Flows
−150

Thus, any freight costs incurred by the buyer are part of the cost of merchandise purchased. The reason: Inventory cost should include all costs to acquire the inventory, including freight necessary to deliver the goods to the buyer. Companies recognize these costs as cost of goods sold when inventory is sold.

FREIGHT COSTS INCURRED BY THE SELLER

In contrast, **freight costs incurred by the seller on outgoing merchandise are an operating expense to the seller**. These costs increase an expense account titled Freight-Out (sometimes called Delivery Expense). For example, if the freight terms on the invoice in Illustration 5-6 had required PW Audio Supply (the seller) to pay the freight charges, the entry by PW Audio Supply would be:

May 4	Freight-Out (or Delivery Expense)	150	
	Cash		150
	(To record payment of freight on goods sold)		

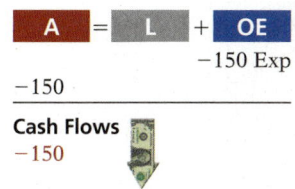

A = L + OE
−150 Exp
−150

Cash Flows
−150

When the seller pays the freight charges, the seller will usually establish a higher invoice price for the goods to cover the shipping expense.

Purchase Returns and Allowances

A purchaser may be dissatisfied with the merchandise received because the goods are damaged or defective, of inferior quality, or do not meet the purchaser's specifications. In such cases, the purchaser may return the goods to the seller for credit if the sale was made on credit, or for a cash refund if the purchase was for cash. This transaction is known as a **purchase return**. Alternatively, the purchaser may choose to keep the merchandise if the seller is willing to grant an allowance (deduction) from the purchase price. This transaction is known as a **purchase allowance**.

Assume that Sauk Stereo returned goods costing $300 to PW Audio Supply on May 8. The following entry by Sauk Stereo for the returned merchandise decreases (debits) Accounts Payable and decreases (credits) Inventory.

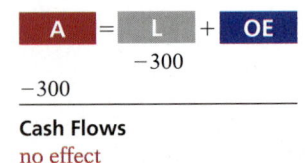

A	=	L	+	OE
		−300		
−300				

Cash Flows
no effect

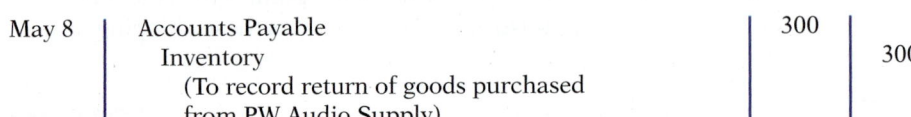

May 8	Accounts Payable	300	
	Inventory		300
	(To record return of goods purchased from PW Audio Supply)		

Because Sauk Stereo increased Inventory when the goods were received, Inventory is decreased when Sauk Stereo returns the goods.

Suppose instead that Sauk Stereo chose to keep the goods after being granted a $50 allowance (reduction in price). It would reduce (debit) Accounts Payable and reduce (credit) Inventory for $50.

Purchase Discounts

The credit terms of a purchase on account may permit the buyer to claim a cash discount for prompt payment. The buyer calls this cash discount a **purchase discount**. This incentive offers advantages to both parties. The purchaser saves money, and the seller is able to shorten the operating cycle by converting the accounts receivable into cash.

Helpful Hint
The term *net* in "net 30" means the remaining amount due after subtracting any sales returns and allowances and partial payments.

Credit terms specify the amount of the cash discount and time period in which it is offered. They also indicate the time period in which the purchaser is expected to pay the full invoice price. In the sales invoice in Illustration 5-6 (page 212), credit terms are 2/10, n/30, which is read "two-ten, net thirty." This means that the buyer may take a 2% cash discount on the invoice price, less ("net of") any returns or allowances, if payment is made within 10 days of the invoice date (the **discount period**). Otherwise, the invoice price, less any returns or allowances, is due 30 days from the invoice date.

Alternatively, the discount period may extend to a specified number of days following the month in which the sale occurs. For example, 1/10 EOM (end of month) means that a 1% discount is available if the invoice is paid within the first 10 days of the next month.

When the seller elects not to offer a cash discount for prompt payment, credit terms will specify only the maximum time period for paying the balance due. For example, the invoice may state the time period as n/30, n/60, or n/10 EOM. This means, respectively, that the buyer must pay the net amount in 30 days, 60 days, or within the first 10 days of the next month.

When the buyer pays an invoice within the discount period, the amount of the discount decreases Inventory. Why? Because companies record inventory at cost and, by paying within the discount period, the buyer has reduced its cost. To illustrate, assume Sauk Stereo pays the balance due of $3,500 (gross invoice price of $3,800 less purchase returns and allowances of $300) on May 14, the last day of the discount period. The cash discount is $70 ($3,500 × 2%), and Sauk Stereo pays $3,430 ($3,500 − $70). The entry Sauk Stereo makes to record its May 14 payment decreases (debits) Accounts Payable by the amount of the gross invoice price, reduces (credits) Inventory by the $70 discount, and reduces (credits) Cash by the net amount owed.

May 14	Accounts Payable	3,500	
	Cash		3,430
	Inventory		70
	(To record payment within discount period)		

A	=	L	+	OE
		−3,500		
−3,430				
−70				

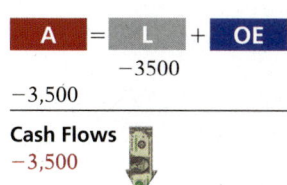

Cash Flows
−3,430

If Sauk Stereo failed to take the discount and instead made full payment of $3,500 on June 3, it would debit Accounts Payable and credit Cash for $3,500 each.

June 3	Accounts Payable	3,500	
	Cash		3,500
	(To record payment with no discount taken)		

A	=	L	+	OE
		−3500		
−3,500				

Cash Flows
−3,500

A merchandising company usually should take all available discounts. Passing up the discount may be viewed as **paying interest** for use of the money. For example, passing up the discount offered by PW Audio Supply would be comparable to Sauk Stereo paying an interest rate of 2% for the use of $3,500 for 20 days. This is the equivalent of an annual interest rate of approximately 36.5% (2% × 365/20). Obviously, it would be better for Sauk Stereo to borrow at prevailing bank interest rates of 6% to 10% than to lose the discount.

Summary of Purchasing Transactions

The following T-account (with transaction descriptions in red) provides a summary of the effect of the previous transactions on Inventory. Sauk Stereo originally purchased $3,800 worth of inventory for resale. It then returned $300 of goods. It paid $150 in freight charges, and finally, it received a $70 discount off the balance owed because it paid within the discount period. This results in a balance in Inventory of $3,580.

	Inventory				
Purchase	May 4	3,800	May 8	300	**Purchase return**
Freight-in	6	150	14	70	**Purchase discount**
Balance		3,580			

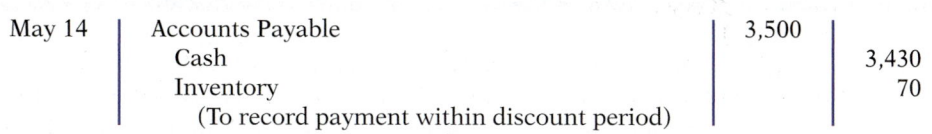

DO IT! 2 Purchase Transactions

On September 5, De La Hoya Company buys merchandise on account from Junot Diaz Company. The selling price of the goods is $1,500, and the cost to Diaz Company was $800. On September 8, De La Hoya returns defective goods with a selling price of $200. Record the transactions on the books of De La Hoya Company.

Solution

Sept. 5	Inventory	1,500	
	Accounts Payable		1,500
	(To record goods purchased on account)		
8	Accounts Payable	200	
	Inventory		200
	(To record return of defective goods)		

Action Plan

- ✔ Purchaser records goods at cost.
- ✔ When goods are returned, purchaser reduces Inventory.

Related exercise material: **BE5-3, BE5-5, E5-2, E5-3, E5-4, and DO IT! 5-2.**

LEARNING OBJECTIVE 3

Record sales under a perpetual inventory system.

In accordance with the revenue recognition principle, companies record sales revenue when the performance obligation is satisfied. Typically, the performance obligation is satisfied when the goods transfer from the seller to the buyer. At this point, the sales transaction is complete and the sales price established.

Sales may be made on credit or for cash. A **business document** should support every sales transaction, to provide written evidence of the sale. **Cash register documents** provide evidence of cash sales. A **sales invoice**, like the one shown in Illustration 5-6 (page 212), provides support for a credit sale. The original copy of the invoice goes to the customer, and the seller keeps a copy for use in recording the sale. The invoice shows the date of sale, customer name, total sales price, and other relevant information.

The seller makes two entries for each sale. **The first entry records the sale**: The seller increases (debits) Cash (or Accounts Receivable if a credit sale) and also increases (credits) Sales Revenue. **The second entry records the cost of the merchandise sold**: The seller increases (debits) Cost of Goods Sold and also decreases (credits) Inventory for the cost of those goods. As a result, the Inventory account will show at all times the amount of inventory that should be on hand.

To illustrate a credit sales transaction, PW Audio Supply records its May 4 sale of $3,800 to Sauk Stereo (see Illustration 5-6) as follows (assume the merchandise cost PW Audio Supply $2,400).

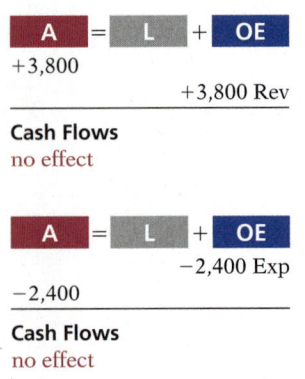

A	=	L	+	OE
+3,800				
				+3,800 Rev

Cash Flows
no effect

May 4	Accounts Receivable	3,800	
	Sales Revenue		3,800
	(To record credit sale to Sauk Stereo per invoice #731)		

A	=	L	+	OE
				−2,400 Exp
−2,400				

Cash Flows
no effect

4	Cost of Goods Sold	2,400	
	Inventory		2,400
	(To record cost of merchandise sold on invoice #731 to Sauk Stereo)		

For internal decision-making purposes, merchandising companies may use more than one sales account. For example, PW Audio Supply may decide to keep separate sales accounts for its sales of TVs, Blu-ray players, and headsets. REI might use separate accounts for camping gear, children's clothing, and ski equipment—or it might have even more narrowly defined accounts. By using separate sales accounts for major product lines, rather than a single combined sales account, company management can more closely monitor sales trends and respond more strategically to changes in sales patterns. For example, if TV sales are increasing while Blu-ray player sales are decreasing, PW Audio Supply might reevaluate both its advertising and pricing policies on these items to ensure they are optimal.

On its income statement presented to outside investors, a merchandising company normally would provide only a single sales figure—the sum of all of its individual sales accounts. This is done for two reasons. First, providing detail on all of its individual sales accounts would add considerable length to its income statement. Second, companies do not want their competitors to know the details of their operating results. However, Microsoft recently expanded its disclosure of revenue from three to five types. The reason: The additional categories enabled financial statement users to better evaluate the growth of the company's consumer and Internet businesses.

ETHICS NOTE

Many companies are trying to improve the quality of their financial reporting. For example, General Electric now provides more detail on its revenues and operating profits.

At the end of "Anatomy of a Fraud" stories, which describe some recent real-world frauds, we discuss the missing control activities that would likely have prevented or uncovered the fraud.

ANATOMY OF A FRAUD[1]

Holly Harmon was a cashier at a national superstore for only a short while when she began stealing merchandise using three methods. Under the first method, her husband or friends took UPC labels from cheaper items and put them on more expensive items. Holly then scanned the goods at the register. Using the second method, Holly scanned an item at the register but then voided the sale and left the merchandise in the shopping cart. A third approach was to put goods into large plastic containers. She scanned the plastic containers but not the goods within them. One day, Holly did not call in sick or show up for work. In such instances, the company reviews past surveillance tapes to look for suspicious activity by employees. This enabled the store to observe the thefts and to identify the participants.

Total take: $12,000

THE MISSING CONTROLS

Human resource controls. A background check would have revealed Holly's previous criminal record. She would not have been hired as a cashier.

Physical controls. Software can flag high numbers of voided transactions or a high number of sales of low-priced goods. Random comparisons of video records with cash register records can ensure that the goods reported as sold on the register are the same goods that are shown being purchased on the video recording. Finally, employees should be aware that they are being monitored.

Source: Adapted from Wells, *Fraud Casebook* (2007), pp. 251–259.

Sales Returns and Allowances

We now look at the "flip side" of purchase returns and allowances, which the seller records as **sales returns and allowances**. These are transactions where the seller either accepts goods back from the buyer (a return) or grants a reduction in the purchase price (an allowance) so the buyer will keep the goods. PW Audio Supply's entries to record credit for returned goods involve (1) an increase (debit) in Sales Returns and Allowances (a contra account to Sales Revenue) and a decrease (credit) in Accounts Receivable at the $300 selling price, and (2) an increase (debit) in Inventory (assume a $140 cost) and a decrease (credit) in Cost of Goods Sold, as shown below (assuming that the goods were not defective).

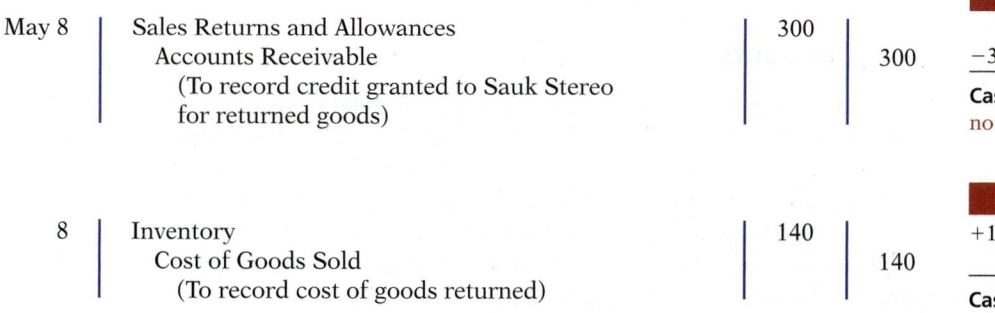

May 8	Sales Returns and Allowances	300	
	Accounts Receivable		300
	(To record credit granted to Sauk Stereo for returned goods)		

A	=	L	+	OE
				−300 Rev
−300				

Cash Flows
no effect

8	Inventory	140	
	Cost of Goods Sold		140
	(To record cost of goods returned)		

A	=	L	+	OE
+140				
				+140 Exp

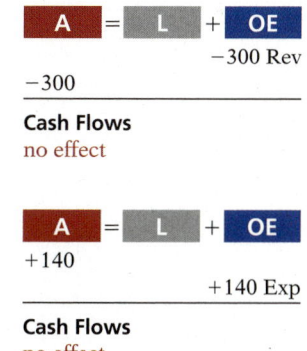

Cash Flows
no effect

If Sauk Stereo returns goods because they are damaged or defective, then PW Audio Supply's entry to Inventory and Cost of Goods Sold should be for the fair value of the returned goods, rather than their cost. For example, if the returned

[1]The "Anatomy of a Fraud" stories in this textbook are adapted from *Fraud Casebook: Lessons from the Bad Side of Business,* edited by Joseph T. Wells (Hoboken, NJ: John Wiley & Sons, Inc., 2007). Used by permission. The names of some of the people and organizations in the stories are fictitious, but the facts in the stories are true.

goods were defective and had a fair value of $50, PW Audio Supply would debit Inventory for $50 and credit Cost of Goods Sold for $50.

What happens if the goods are not returned but the seller grants the buyer an allowance by reducing the purchase price? In this case, the seller debits Sales Returns and Allowances and credits Accounts Receivable for the amount of the allowance. An allowance has no impact on Inventory or Cost of Goods Sold.

Sales Returns and Allowances is a **contra revenue account** to Sales Revenue. This means that it is offset against a revenue account on the income statement. The normal balance of Sales Returns and Allowances is a debit. Companies use a contra account, instead of debiting Sales Revenue, to disclose in the accounts and in the income statement the amount of sales returns and allowances. Disclosure of this information is important to management. Excessive returns and allowances may suggest problems—inferior merchandise, inefficiencies in filling orders, errors in billing customers, or delivery or shipment mistakes. Moreover, a decrease (debit) recorded directly to Sales Revenue would obscure the relative importance of sales returns and allowances as a percentage of sales. It also could distort comparisons between total sales in different accounting periods.

Accounting Across the Organization — Costco Wholesale Corp.

© Jacob Wackerhausen/iStockphoto

Should Costco Change Its Return Policy?

In most industries, sales returns are relatively minor. But returns of consumer electronics can really take a bite out of profits. Recently, the marketing executives at Costco Wholesale Corp. faced a difficult decision. Costco has always prided itself on its generous return policy. Most goods have had an unlimited grace period for returns. However, a new policy requires that certain electronics must be returned within 90 days of their purchase. The reason? The cost of returned products such as high-definition TVs, computers, and iPods cut an estimated 8¢ per share off Costco's earnings per share, which was $2.30.

Source: Kris Hudson, "Costco Tightens Policy on Returning Electronics," *Wall Street Journal* (February 27, 2007), p. B4.

If a company expects significant returns, what are the implications for revenue recognition? (Go to **WileyPLUS** for this answer and additional questions.)

Sales Discounts

As mentioned in our discussion of purchase transactions, the seller may offer the customer a cash discount—called by the seller a **sales discount**—for the prompt payment of the balance due. Like a purchase discount, a sales discount is based on the invoice price less returns and allowances, if any. The seller increases (debits) the Sales Discounts account for discounts that are taken. For example, PW Audio Supply makes the following entry to record the cash receipt on May 14 from Sauk Stereo within the discount period.

A	=	L	+	OE
+3,430				
				−70 Rev
−3,500				

Cash Flows
+3,430

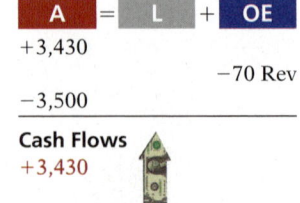

May 14	Cash	3,430	
	Sales Discounts	70	
	Accounts Receivable		3,500
	(To record collection within 2/10, n/30 discount period from Sauk Stereo)		

Like Sales Returns and Allowances, Sales Discounts is a **contra revenue account** to Sales Revenue. Its normal balance is a debit. PW Audio Supply uses this account, instead of debiting Sales Revenue, to disclose the amount of cash discounts taken by customers. If Sauk Stereo does not take the discount, PW Audio Supply increases (debits) Cash for $3,500 and decreases (credits) Accounts Receivable for the same amount at the date of collection.

The following T-accounts summarize the three sales-related transactions and show their combined effect on net sales.

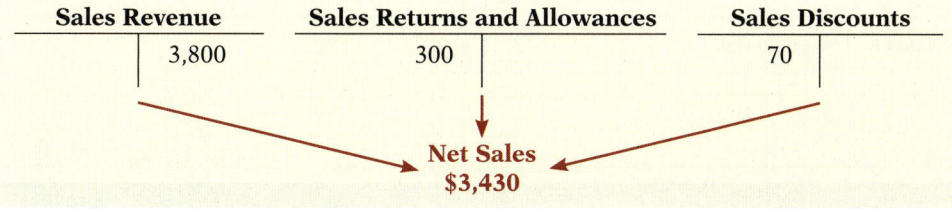

Sales Revenue		Sales Returns and Allowances		Sales Discounts	
	3,800	300		70	

Net Sales
$3,430

People, Planet, and Profit Insight — PepsiCo

Helen Sessions/Alamy

Selling Green

Here is a question an executive of PepsiCo was asked: Should PepsiCo market green? The executive indicated that the company should, as he believes it's the No. 1 thing consumers all over the world care about. Here are some of his thoughts on this issue:

"Sun Chips are part of the food business I run. It's a 'healthy snack.' We decided that Sun Chips, if it's a healthy snack, should be made in facilities that have a net-zero footprint. In other words, I want off the electric grid everywhere we make Sun Chips. We did that. Sun Chips should be made in a facility that puts back more water than it uses. It does that. And we partnered with our suppliers and came out with the world's first compostable chip package.

Now, there was an issue with this package: It was louder than the New York subway, louder than jet engines taking off. What would a company that's committed to green do: walk away or stay committed? If your people are passionate, they're going to fix it for you as long as you stay committed. Six months later, the compostable bag has half the noise of our current package.

So the view today is: we should market green, we should be proud to do it . . . it has to be a 360-degree process, both internal and external. And if you do that, you can monetize environmental sustainability for the shareholders."

Source: "Four Problems—and Solutions," *Wall Street Journal* (March 7, 2011), p. R2.

What is meant by "monetize environmental sustainability" for shareholders? (Go to **WileyPLUS** for this answer and additional questions.)

DO IT! 3 Sales Transactions

On September 5, De La Hoya Company buys merchandise on account from Junot Diaz Company. The selling price of the goods is $1,500, and the cost to Diaz Company was $800. On September 8, De La Hoya returns defective goods with a selling price of $200 and a fair value of $30. Record the transactions on the books of Junot Diaz Company.

Action Plan

✔ Seller records both the sale and the cost of goods sold at the time of the sale.

✔ When goods are returned, the seller records the return in a contra account, Sales Returns and Allowances, and reduces Accounts Receivable.

Solution

Sept. 5	Accounts Receivable	1,500	
	Sales Revenue		1,500
	(To record credit sale)		
5	Cost of Goods Sold	800	
	Inventory		800
	(To record cost of goods sold on account)		

Action Plan (cont'd)

✔ Any goods returned increase Inventory and reduce Cost of Goods Sold. Defective or damaged inventory is recorded at fair value (scrap value).

8	Sales Returns and Allowances	200	
	Accounts Receivable		200
	(To record credit granted for receipt of returned goods)		
8	Inventory	30	
	Cost of Goods Sold		30
	(To record fair value of goods returned)		

Related exercise material: **BE5-3, BE5-4, E5-3, E5-4, E5-5, and DO IT! 5-3.**

LEARNING OBJECTIVE 4

Apply the steps in the accounting cycle to a merchandising company.

Up to this point, we have illustrated the basic entries for transactions relating to purchases and sales in a perpetual inventory system. Now we consider the remaining steps in the accounting cycle for a merchandising company. Each of the required steps described in Chapter 4 for service companies apply to merchandising companies. Appendix 5A to this chapter shows use of a worksheet by a merchandiser (an optional step).

Adjusting Entries

A merchandising company generally has the same types of adjusting entries as a service company. However, a merchandiser using a perpetual system will require one additional adjustment to make the records agree with the actual inventory on hand. Here's why. At the end of each period, for control purposes, a merchandising company that uses a perpetual system will take a physical count of its goods on hand. The company's unadjusted balance in Inventory usually does not agree with the actual amount of inventory on hand. The perpetual inventory records may be incorrect due to recording errors, theft, or waste. Thus, the company needs to adjust the perpetual records to make the recorded inventory amount agree with the inventory on hand. **This involves adjusting Inventory and Cost of Goods Sold.**

For example, suppose that PW Audio Supply has an unadjusted balance of $40,500 in Inventory. Through a physical count, PW Audio Supply determines that its actual merchandise inventory at December 31 is $40,000. The company would make an adjusting entry as follows.

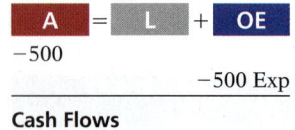

A	=	L	+	OE
−500				−500 Exp

Cash Flows
no effect

Dec. 31	Cost of Goods Sold	500	
	Inventory		500
	(To adjust inventory to physical count)		

Closing Entries

A merchandising company, like a service company, closes to Income Summary all accounts that affect net income. In journalizing, the company credits all temporary accounts with debit balances, and debits all temporary accounts with credit balances, as shown below for PW Audio Supply. Note that PW Audio Supply closes Cost of Goods Sold to Income Summary.

Helpful Hint
The easiest way to prepare the first two closing entries is to identify the temporary accounts by their balances and then prepare one entry for the credits and one for the debits.

Dec. 31	Sales Revenue	480,000	
	Income Summary		480,000
	(To close income statement accounts with credit balances)		

31	Income Summary	450,000	
	Sales Returns and Allowances		12,000
	Sales Discounts		8,000
	Cost of Goods Sold		316,000
	Salaries and Wages Expense		64,000
	Freight-Out		7,000
	Advertising Expense		16,000
	Utilities Expense		17,000
	Depreciation Expense		8,000
	Insurance Expense		2,000
	(To close income statement accounts with debit balances)		
31	Income Summary	30,000	
	Owner's Capital		30,000
	(To close net income to capital)		
31	Owner's Capital	15,000	
	Owner's Drawings		15,000
	(To close drawings to capital)		

After PW Audio Supply has posted the closing entries, all temporary accounts have zero balances. Also, Owner's Capital has a balance that is carried over to the next period.

Summary of Merchandising Entries

Illustration 5-8 summarizes the entries for the merchandising accounts using a perpetual inventory system.

Illustration 5-8
Daily recurring and adjusting and closing entries

	Transactions	Daily Recurring Entries	Dr.	Cr.
Sales Transactions	Selling merchandise to customers.	Cash or Accounts Receivable	XX	
		Sales Revenue		XX
		Cost of Goods Sold	XX	
		Inventory		XX
	Granting sales returns or allowances to customers.	Sales Returns and Allowances	XX	
		Cash or Accounts Receivable		XX
		Inventory	XX	
		Cost of Goods Sold		XX
	Paying freight costs on sales; FOB destination.	Freight-Out	XX	
		Cash		XX
	Receiving payment from customers within discount period.	Cash	XX	
		Sales Discounts	XX	
		Accounts Receivable		XX
Purchase Transactions	Purchasing merchandise for resale.	Inventory	XX	
		Cash or Accounts Payable		XX
	Paying freight costs on merchandise purchased; FOB shipping point.	Inventory	XX	
		Cash		XX
	Receiving purchase returns or allowances from suppliers.	Cash or Accounts Payable	XX	
		Inventory		XX
	Paying suppliers within discount period.	Accounts Payable	XX	
		Inventory		XX
		Cash		XX

Events	Adjusting and Closing Entries		
Adjust because book amount is higher than the inventory amount determined to be on hand.	Cost of Goods Sold	XX	
	Inventory		XX
Closing temporary accounts with credit balances.	Sales Revenue	XX	
	Income Summary		XX
Closing temporary accounts with debit balances.	Income Summary	XX	
	Sales Returns and Allowances		XX
	Sales Discounts		XX
	Cost of Goods Sold		XX
	Freight-Out		XX
	Expenses		XX

Illustration 5-8
(continued)

DO IT! 4 Closing Entries

The trial balance of Celine's Sports Wear Shop at December 31 shows Inventory $25,000, Sales Revenue $162,400, Sales Returns and Allowances $4,800, Sales Discounts $3,600, Cost of Goods Sold $110,000, Rent Revenue $6,000, Freight-Out $1,800, Rent Expense $8,800, and Salaries and Wages Expense $22,000. Prepare the closing entries for the above accounts.

Action Plan

- ✔ Close all temporary accounts with credit balances to Income Summary by debiting these accounts.
- ✔ Close all temporary accounts with debit balances, except drawings, to Income Summary by crediting these accounts.

Solution

The two closing entries are:

Date	Account	Debit	Credit
Dec. 31	Sales Revenue	162,400	
	Rent Revenue	6,000	
	Income Summary		168,400
	(To close accounts with credit balances)		
31	Income Summary	151,000	
	Cost of Goods Sold		110,000
	Sales Returns and Allowances		4,800
	Sales Discounts		3,600
	Freight-Out		1,800
	Rent Expense		8,800
	Salaries and Wages Expense		22,000
	(To close accounts with debit balances)		

Related exercise material: **BE5-6, BE5-7, E5-6, E5-7, E5-8, and DO IT! 5-4.**

LEARNING OBJECTIVE 5 Compare a multiple-step with a single-step income statement.

Merchandising companies widely use the classified balance sheet introduced in Chapter 4 and one of two forms for the income statement. This section explains the use of these financial statements by merchandisers.

Multiple-Step Income Statement

The **multiple-step income statement** is so named because it shows several steps in determining net income. Two of these steps relate to the company's principal operating activities. A multiple-step statement also distinguishes between

operating and **nonoperating activities**. Finally, the statement highlights intermediate components of income and shows subgroupings of expenses.

INCOME STATEMENT PRESENTATION OF SALES

The multiple-step income statement begins by presenting **sales revenue**. It then deducts contra revenue accounts—sales returns and allowances, and sales discounts—from sales revenue to arrive at **net sales**. Illustration 5-9 presents the sales section for PW Audio Supply, using assumed data.

Illustration 5-9
Computation of net sales

PW AUDIO SUPPLY
Income Statement (partial)

Sales		
Sales revenue		$ 480,000
Less: Sales returns and allowances	$12,000	
Sales discounts	8,000	20,000
Net sales		**$460,000**

GROSS PROFIT

From Illustration 5-1, you learned that companies deduct cost of goods sold from sales revenue to determine **gross profit**. For this computation, companies use **net sales** (which takes into consideration Sales Returns and Allowances and Sales Discounts) as the amount of sales revenue. On the basis of the sales data in Illustration 5-9 (net sales of $460,000) and cost of goods sold under the perpetual inventory system (assume $316,000), PW Audio Supply's gross profit is $144,000, computed as follows.

Alternative Terminology
Gross profit is sometimes referred to as *gross margin*.

Illustration 5-10
Computation of gross profit

Net sales	$ 460,000
Cost of goods sold	316,000
Gross profit	**$144,000**

We also can express a company's gross profit as a percentage, called the **gross profit rate**. To do so, we divide the amount of gross profit by net sales. For PW Audio Supply, the **gross profit rate** is 31.3%, computed as follows.

Illustration 5-11
Gross profit rate formula and computation

Gross Profit	÷	Net Sales	=	Gross Profit Rate
$144,000	÷	$460,000	=	31.3%

Analysts generally consider the gross profit **rate** to be more useful than the gross profit **amount**. The rate expresses a more meaningful (qualitative) relationship between net sales and gross profit. For example, a gross profit of $1,000,000 may sound impressive. But if it is the result of a gross profit rate of only 7%, it is not so impressive. The gross profit rate tells how many cents of each sales dollar go to gross profit.

Gross profit represents the **merchandising profit** of a company. It is not a measure of the overall profitability because operating expenses are not yet deducted. But managers and other interested parties closely watch the amount and trend of gross profit. They compare current gross profit with amounts reported in past periods. They also compare the company's gross profit rate with rates of competitors and with industry averages. Such comparisons provide information about the effectiveness of a company's purchasing function and the soundness of its pricing policies.

OPERATING EXPENSES AND NET INCOME

Operating expenses are the next component in measuring net income for a merchandising company. They are the expenses incurred in the process of earning sales revenue. These expenses are similar in merchandising and service companies. At PW Audio Supply, operating expenses were $114,000. The company determines its net income by subtracting operating expenses from gross profit. Thus, net income is $30,000, as shown below.

Illustration 5-12
Operating expenses in computing net income

Gross profit	$144,000
Operating expenses	**114,000**
Net income	$ 30,000

The net income amount is the so-called "bottom line" of a company's income statement.

NONOPERATING ACTIVITIES

Nonoperating activities consist of various revenues and expenses and gains and losses that are unrelated to the company's main line of operations. When nonoperating items are included, the label "**Income from operations**" (or "Operating income") precedes them. This label clearly identifies the results of the company's normal operations, an amount determined by subtracting cost of goods sold and operating expenses from net sales. The results of nonoperating activities are shown in the categories "**Other revenues and gains**" and "**Other expenses and losses**." Illustration 5-13 lists examples of each.

Illustration 5-13
Other items of nonoperating activities

Other Revenues and Gains
Interest revenue from notes receivable and marketable securities.
Dividend revenue from investments in common stock.
Rent revenue from subleasing a portion of the store.
Gain from the sale of property, plant, and equipment.
Other Expenses and Losses
Interest expense on notes and loans payable.
Casualty losses from recurring causes, such as vandalism and accidents.
Loss from the sale or abandonment of property, plant, and equipment.
Loss from strikes by employees and suppliers.

ETHICS NOTE

Companies manage earnings in various ways. ConAgra Foods recorded a non-recurring gain for $186 million from the sale of Pilgrim's Pride stock to help meet an earnings projection for the quarter.

Merchandising companies report the nonoperating activities in the income statement immediately after the company's operating activities. Illustration 5-14 shows these sections for PW Audio Supply, using assumed data.

The distinction between operating and nonoperating activities is crucial to many external users of financial data. These users view operating income as sustainable and many nonoperating activities as non-recurring. Therefore, when forecasting next year's income, analysts put the most weight on this year's operating income and less weight on this year's nonoperating activities.

Illustration 5-14
Multiple-step income statement

PW AUDIO SUPPLY
Income Statement
For the Year Ended December 31, 2017

Calculation of gross profit	**Sales**		
	Sales revenue		$480,000
	Less: Sales returns and allowances	$12,000	
	Sales discounts	8,000	20,000
	Net sales		460,000
	Cost of goods sold		316,000
	Gross profit		144,000
Calculation of income from operations	**Operating expenses**		
	Salaries and wages expense	64,000	
	Utilities expense	17,000	
	Advertising expense	16,000	
	Depreciation expense	8,000	
	Freight-out	7,000	
	Insurance expense	2,000	
	Total operating expenses		114,000
	Income from operations		30,000
Results of nonoperating activities	**Other revenues and gains**		
	Interest revenue	3,000	
	Gain on disposal of plant assets	600	3,600
	Other expenses and losses		
	Interest expense	1,800	
	Casualty loss from vandalism	200	2,000
	Net income		$ 31,600

Ethics Insight IBM

ImageRite/Getty Images, Inc.

Disclosing More Details

After Enron, increased investor criticism and regulator scrutiny forced many companies to improve the clarity of their financial disclosures. For example, IBM began providing more detail regarding its "Other gains and losses." It had previously included these items in its selling, general, and administrative expenses, with little disclosure. For example, previously if IBM sold off one of its buildings at a gain, it would include this gain in the selling, general and administrative expense line item, thus reducing that expense. This made it appear that the company had done a better job of controlling operating expenses than it actually had.

As another example, when eBay sold the remainder of its investment in Skype to Microsoft, it reported a gain in "Other revenues and gains" of $1.7 billion. Since eBay's total income from operations was $2.4 billion, it was very important that the gain from the Skype sale not be buried in operating income.

Why have investors and analysts demanded more accuracy in isolating "Other gains and losses" from operating items? (Go to **WileyPLUS** for this answer and additional questions.)

Single-Step Income Statement

Another income statement format is the **single-step income statement**. The statement is so named because only one step—subtracting total expenses from total revenues—is required in determining net income.

In a single-step statement, all data are classified into two categories: (1) **revenues**, which include both operating revenues and other revenues and gains; and (2) **expenses**, which include cost of goods sold, operating expenses, and other expenses and losses. Illustration 5-15 shows a single-step statement for PW Audio Supply.

Illustration 5-15
Single-step income statement

PW AUDIO SUPPLY Income Statement For the Year Ended December 31, 2017		
Revenues		
Net sales		$460,000
Interest revenue		3,000
Gain on disposal of plant assets		600
Total revenues		463,600
Expenses		
Cost of goods sold	$316,000	
Operating expenses	114,000	
Interest expense	1,800	
Casualty loss from vandalism	200	
Total expenses		432,000
Net income		$ 31,600

There are two primary reasons for using the single-step format. (1) A company does not realize any type of profit or income until total revenues exceed total expenses, so it makes sense to divide the statement into these two categories. (2) The format is simpler and easier to read. *For homework problems, however, you should use the single-step format only when specifically instructed to do so.*

Classified Balance Sheet

In the balance sheet, merchandising companies report inventory as a current asset immediately below accounts receivable. Recall from Chapter 4 that companies generally list current asset items in the order of their closeness to cash (liquidity). Inventory is less close to cash than accounts receivable because the goods must first be sold and then collection made from the customer. Illustration 5-16 presents the assets section of a classified balance sheet for PW Audio Supply.

Illustration 5-16
Assets section of a classified balance sheet

PW AUDIO SUPPLY Balance Sheet (Partial) December 31, 2017		
Assets		
Current assets		
Cash		$ 9,500
Accounts receivable		16,100
Inventory		40,000
Prepaid insurance		1,800
Total current assets		67,400
Property, plant, and equipment		
Equipment	$80,000	
Less: Accumulated depreciation—equipment	24,000	56,000
Total assets		$123,400

Helpful Hint
The $40,000 is the cost of the inventory on hand, not its expected selling price.

DO IT! 5 Financial Statement Classifications

You are presented with the following list of accounts from the adjusted trial balance for merchandiser Gorman Company. Indicate in which financial statement and under what classification each of the following would be reported.

Accounts Payable
Accounts Receivable
Accumulated Depreciation—Buildings
Accumulated Depreciation—Equipment
Advertising Expense
Buildings
Cash
Depreciation Expense
Equipment
Freight-Out
Gain on Disposal of Plant Assets
Insurance Expense
Interest Expense
Interest Payable
Inventory
Land
Notes Payable (due in 3 years)
Owner's Capital (beginning balance)
Owner's Drawings
Property Taxes Payable
Salaries and Wages Expense
Salaries and Wages Payable
Sales Returns and Allowances
Sales Revenue
Utilities Expense

Solution

Account	Financial Statement	Classification
Accounts Payable	Balance sheet	Current liabilities
Accounts Receivable	Balance sheet	Current assets
Accumulated Depreciation—Buildings	Balance sheet	Property, plant, and equipment
Accumulated Depreciation—Equipment	Balance sheet	Property, plant, and equipment
Advertising Expense	Income statement	Operating expenses
Buildings	Balance sheet	Property, plant, and equipment
Cash	Balance sheet	Current assets
Depreciation Expense	Income statement	Operating expenses
Equipment	Balance sheet	Property, plant, and equipment
Freight-Out	Income statement	Operating expenses
Gain on Disposal of Plant Assets	Income statement	Other revenues and gains
Insurance Expense	Income statement	Operating expenses
Interest Expense	Income statement	Other expenses and losses
Interest Payable	Balance sheet	Current liabilities
Inventory	Balance sheet	Current assets
Land	Balance sheet	Property, plant, and equipment
Notes Payable (due in 3 years)	Balance sheet	Long-term liabilities
Owner's Capital	Owner's equity statement	Beginning balance
Owner's Drawings	Owner's equity statement	Deduction section
Property Taxes Payable	Balance sheet	Current liabilities
Salaries and Wages Expense	Income statement	Operating expenses
Salaries and Wages Payable	Balance sheet	Current liabilities
Sales Returns and Allowances	Income statement	Sales
Sales Revenue	Income statement	Sales
Utilities Expense	Income statement	Operating expenses

Action Plan

- ✔ **Review the major sections of the income statement: sales, cost of goods sold, operating expenses, other revenues and gains, and other expenses and losses.**
- ✔ **Add net income and investments to beginning capital and deduct drawings to arrive at ending capital in the owner's equity statement.**
- ✔ **Review the major sections of the balance sheet, income statement, and owner's equity statement.**

Related exercise material: **BE5-8, BE5-9, E5-9, E5-10, E5-12, E5-13, E5-14, and DO IT! 5-5.**

LEARNING OBJECTIVE *6

APPENDIX 5A: Prepare a worksheet for a merchandising company.

Using a Worksheet

As indicated in Chapter 4, a worksheet enables companies to prepare financial statements before they journalize and post adjusting entries. The steps in preparing a worksheet for a merchandising company are the same as for a service company (see pages 150–156). Illustration 5A-1 shows the worksheet for PW Audio Supply (excluding nonoperating items). The unique accounts for a merchandiser using a **perpetual inventory system** are in red.

PW Audio Supply.xls

PW AUDIO SUPPLY
Worksheet
For the Year Ended December 31, 2017

	Accounts	Trial Balance Dr.	Trial Balance Cr.	Adjustments Dr.	Adjustments Cr.	Adjusted Trial Balance Dr.	Adjusted Trial Balance Cr.	Income Statement Dr.	Income Statement Cr.	Balance Sheet Dr.	Balance Sheet Cr.
8	Cash	9,500				9,500				9,500	
9	Accounts Receivable	16,100				16,100				16,100	
10	Inventory	40,500			(a) 500	40,000				40,000	
11	Prepaid Insurance	3,800			(b) 2,000	1,800				1,800	
12	Equipment	80,000				80,000				80,000	
13	Accumulated Depreciation—Equipment		16,000		(c) 8,000		24,000				24,000
14	Accounts Payable		20,400				20,400				20,400
15	Owner's Capital		83,000				83,000				83,000
16	Owner's Drawings	15,000				15,000				15,000	
17	Sales Revenue		480,000				480,000		480,000		
18	Sales Returns and Allowances	12,000				12,000		12,000			
19	Sales Discounts	8,000				8,000		8,000			
20	Cost of Goods Sold	315,500		(a) 500		316,000		316,000			
21	Freight-Out	7,000				7,000		7,000			
22	Advertising Expense	16,000				16,000		16,000			
23	Salaries and Wages Expense	59,000		(d) 5,000		64,000		64,000			
24	Utilities Expense	17,000				17,000		17,000			
25	Totals	599,400	599,400								
26	Insurance Expense			(b) 2,000		2,000		2,000			
27	Depreciation Expense			(c) 8,000		8,000		8,000			
28	Salaries and Wages Payable				(d) 5,000		5,000				5,000
29	Totals			15,500	15,500	612,400	612,400	450,000	480,000	162,400	132,400
30	Net Income							30,000			30,000
31	Totals							480,000	480,000	162,400	162,400

Key: (a) Adjustment to inventory on hand. (b) Insurance expired. (c) Depreciation expense. (d) Salaries and wages accrued.

Illustration 5A-1
Worksheet for merchandising company—perpetual inventory system

TRIAL BALANCE COLUMNS

Data for the trial balance come from the ledger balances of PW Audio Supply at December 31. The amount shown for Inventory, $40,500, is the year-end inventory amount from the perpetual inventory system.

ADJUSTMENTS COLUMNS

A merchandising company generally has the same types of adjustments as a service company. As you see in the worksheet, adjustments (b), (c), and (d) are for insurance, depreciation, and salaries. Pioneer Advertising, as illustrated in Chapters 3 and 4, also had these adjustments. Adjustment (a) was required to adjust the perpetual inventory carrying amount to the actual count.

After PW Audio Supply enters all adjustments data on the worksheet, it establishes the equality of the adjustments column totals. It then extends the balances in all accounts to the adjusted trial balance columns.

ADJUSTED TRIAL BALANCE

The adjusted trial balance shows the balance of all accounts after adjustment at the end of the accounting period.

INCOME STATEMENT COLUMNS

Next, the merchandising company transfers the accounts and balances that affect the income statement from the adjusted trial balance columns to the income statement columns. PW Audio Supply shows Sales Revenue of $480,000 in the credit column. It shows the contra revenue accounts Sales Returns and Allowances $12,000 and Sales Discounts $8,000 in the debit column. The difference of $460,000 is the net sales shown on the income statement (Illustration 5-14, page 225).

Finally, the company totals all the credits in the income statement column and compares those totals to the total of the debits in the income statement column. If the credits exceed the debits, the company has net income. PW Audio Supply has net income of $30,000. If the debits exceed the credits, the company would report a net loss.

BALANCE SHEET COLUMNS

The major difference between the balance sheets of a service company and a merchandiser is inventory. PW Audio Supply shows the ending inventory amount of $40,000 in the balance sheet debit column. The information to prepare the owner's equity statement is also found in these columns. That is, the Owner's Capital account is $83,000. Owner's Drawings are $15,000. Net income results when the total of the debit column exceeds the total of the credit column in the balance sheet columns. A net loss results when the total of the credits exceeds the total of the debit balances.

LEARNING OBJECTIVE *7

APPENDIX 5B: Record purchases and sales under a periodic inventory system.

As described in this chapter, companies may use one of two basic systems of accounting for inventories: (1) the perpetual inventory system or (2) the periodic inventory system. In the chapter, we focused on the characteristics of the perpetual inventory system. In this appendix, we discuss and illustrate the **periodic inventory system**. One key difference between the two systems is the point at which the company computes cost of goods sold. For a visual reminder of this difference, refer back to Illustration 5-5 (on page 210).

Determining Cost of Goods Sold Under a Periodic System

Determining cost of goods sold is different when a periodic inventory system is used rather than a perpetual system. As you have seen, a company using a **perpetual system** makes an entry to record cost of goods sold and to reduce inventory each time a sale is made. A company using a **periodic system** does not determine cost of goods sold until the end of the period. At the end of the period, the company performs a count to determine the ending balance of inventory. It then **calculates cost of goods sold by subtracting ending inventory from the cost of goods available for sale**. Goods available for sale is the sum of beginning inventory plus purchases, as shown in Illustration 5B-1.

Illustration 5B-1
Basic formula for cost of goods sold using the periodic system

	Beginning Inventory
+	Cost of Goods Purchased
	Cost of Goods Available for Sale
−	Ending Inventory
	Cost of Goods Sold

Another difference between the two approaches is that the perpetual system directly adjusts the Inventory account for any transaction that affects inventory (such as freight costs, returns, and discounts). The periodic system does not do this. Instead, it creates different accounts for purchases, freight costs, returns, and discounts. These various accounts are shown in Illustration 5B-2, which presents the calculation of cost of goods sold for PW Audio Supply using the periodic approach.

Illustration 5B-2
Cost of goods sold for a merchandiser using a periodic inventory system

Helpful Hint
The far right column identifies the primary items that make up cost of goods sold of $316,000. The middle column explains cost of goods purchased of $320,000. The left column reports contra purchase items of $17,200.

PW AUDIO SUPPLY
Cost of Goods Sold
For the Year Ended December 31, 2017

Cost of goods sold			
Inventory, January 1			**$ 36,000**
Purchases		$325,000	
Less: Purchase returns and allowances	$10,400		
Purchase discounts	6,800	17,200	
Net purchases		307,800	
Add: Freight-in		12,200	
Cost of goods purchased			**320,000**
Cost of goods available for sale			356,000
Less: Inventory, December 31			**40,000**
Cost of goods sold			**$316,000**

Note that the basic elements from Illustration 5B-1 are highlighted in Illustration 5B-2. You will learn more in Chapter 6 about how to determine cost of goods sold using the periodic system.

The use of the periodic inventory system does not affect the form of presentation in the balance sheet. As under the perpetual system, a company reports inventory in the current assets section.

Recording Merchandise Transactions

In a **periodic inventory system**, companies record revenues from the sale of merchandise when sales are made, just as in a perpetual system. Unlike the perpetual system, however, companies **do not attempt on the date of sale to**

record the cost of the merchandise sold. Instead, they take a physical inventory count at the **end of the period** to determine (1) the cost of the merchandise then on hand and (2) the cost of the goods sold during the period. And, **under a periodic system, companies record purchases of merchandise in the Purchases account rather than in the Inventory account**. Also, in a periodic system, purchase returns and allowances, purchase discounts, and freight costs on purchases are recorded in separate accounts.

To illustrate the recording of merchandise transactions under a periodic inventory system, we will use purchase/sales transactions between PW Audio Supply and Sauk Stereo, as illustrated for the perpetual inventory system in this chapter.

Recording Purchases of Merchandise

On the basis of the sales invoice (Illustration 5-6, shown on page 212) and receipt of the merchandise ordered from PW Audio Supply, Sauk Stereo records the $3,800 purchase as follows.

Helpful Hint
Be careful not to debit purchases of equipment or supplies to a Purchases account.

May 4	Purchases	3,800	
	Accounts Payable		3,800
	(To record goods purchased on account from PW Audio Supply)		

Purchases is a temporary account whose normal balance is a debit.

FREIGHT COSTS

When the purchaser directly incurs the freight costs, it debits the account Freight-In (or Transportation-In). For example, if Sauk Stereo pays Public Carrier Co. $150 for freight charges on its purchase from PW Audio Supply on May 6, the entry on Sauk Stereo's books is:

Alternative Terminology
Freight-In is also called *Transportation-In.*

May 6	Freight-In (Transportation-In)	150	
	Cash		150
	(To record payment of freight on goods purchased)		

Like Purchases, Freight-In is a temporary account whose normal balance is a debit. **Freight-In is part of cost of goods purchased.** The reason is that cost of goods purchased should include any freight charges necessary to bring the goods to the purchaser. Freight costs are not subject to a purchase discount. Purchase discounts apply only to the invoice cost of the merchandise.

PURCHASE RETURNS AND ALLOWANCES

Sauk Stereo returns $300 of goods to PW Audio Supply and prepares the following entry to recognize the return.

May 8	Accounts Payable	300	
	Purchase Returns and Allowances		300
	(To record return of goods purchased from PW Audio Supply)		

Purchase Returns and Allowances is a temporary account whose normal balance is a credit.

PURCHASE DISCOUNTS

On May 14, Sauk Stereo pays the balance due on account to PW Audio Supply, taking the 2% cash discount allowed by PW Audio Supply for payment within 10 days. Sauk Stereo records the payment and discount as follows.

May 14	Accounts Payable ($3,800 − $300)	3,500	
	Purchase Discounts ($3,500 × .02)		70
	Cash		3,430
	(To record payment within the discount period)		

Purchase Discounts is a temporary account whose normal balance is a credit.

Recording Sales of Merchandise

The seller, PW Audio Supply, records the sale of $3,800 of merchandise to Sauk Stereo on May 4 (sales invoice No. 731, Illustration 5-6, page 212) as follows.

May 4	Accounts Receivable	3,800	
	Sales Revenue		3,800
	(To record credit sales per invoice #731 to Sauk Stereo)		

SALES RETURNS AND ALLOWANCES

To record the returned goods received from Sauk Stereo on May 8, PW Audio Supply records the $300 sales return as follows.

May 8	Sales Returns and Allowances	300	
	Accounts Receivable		300
	(To record credit granted to Sauk Stereo for returned goods)		

SALES DISCOUNTS

On May 14, PW Audio Supply receives payment of $3,430 on account from Sauk Stereo. PW Audio Supply honors the 2% cash discount and records the payment of Sauk Stereo's account receivable in full as follows.

May 14	Cash	3,430	
	Sales Discounts ($3,500 × .02)	70	
	Accounts Receivable ($3,800 − $300)		3,500
	(To record collection within 2/10, n/30 discount period from Sauk Stereo)		

COMPARISON OF ENTRIES—PERPETUAL VS. PERIODIC

Illustration 5B-3 summarizes the periodic inventory entries shown in this appendix and compares them to the perpetual system entries from the chapter. Entries that differ in the two systems are shown in color.

ENTRIES ON SAUK STEREO'S BOOKS							
	Transaction	**Perpetual Inventory System**			**Periodic Inventory System**		
May 4	Purchase of merchandise on credit.	**Inventory**	**3,800**		**Purchases**	**3,800**	
		Accounts Payable		3,800	Accounts Payable		3,800
6	Freight costs on purchases.	**Inventory**	**150**		**Freight-In**	**150**	
		Cash		150	Cash		150
8	Purchase returns and allowances.	Accounts Payable	300		Accounts Payable	300	
		Inventory		**300**	**Purchase Returns and Allowances**		**300**
14	Payment on account with a discount.	Accounts Payable	3,500		Accounts Payable	3,500	
		Cash		3,430	Cash		3,430
		Inventory		**70**	**Purchase Discounts**		**70**

ENTRIES ON PW AUDIO SUPPLY'S BOOKS							
	Transaction	**Perpetual Inventory System**			**Periodic Inventory System**		
May 4	Sale of merchandise on credit.	Accounts Receivable	3,800		Accounts Receivable	3,800	
		Sales Revenue		3,800	Sales Revenue		3,800
		Cost of Goods Sold	**2,400**		**No entry for cost of goods sold**		
		Inventory		**2,400**			
8	Return of merchandise sold.	Sales Returns and Allowances	300		Sales Returns and Allowances	300	
		Accounts Receivable		300	Accounts Receivable		300
		Inventory	**140**		**No entry**		
		Cost of Goods Sold		**140**			
14	Cash received on account with a discount.	Cash	3,430		Cash	3,430	
		Sales Discounts	70		Sales Discounts	70	
		Accounts Receivable		3,500	Accounts Receivable		3,500

Illustration 5B-3
Comparison of entries for perpetual and periodic inventory systems

Journalizing and Posting Closing Entries

For a merchandising company, like a service company, all accounts that affect the determination of net income are closed to Income Summary. Data for the preparation of closing entries may be obtained from the income statement columns of the worksheet. In journalizing, all debit column amounts are credited, and all credit columns amounts are debited. To close the merchandise inventory in a periodic inventory system:

1. The beginning inventory balance is debited to Income Summary and credited to Inventory.
2. The ending inventory balance is debited to Inventory and credited to Income Summary.

The two entries for PW Audio Supply are as follows.

	(1)		
Dec. 31	Income Summary	36,000	
	Inventory		36,000
	(To close beginning inventory)		
	(2)		
31	Inventory	40,000	
	Income Summary		40,000
	(To record ending inventory)		

After posting, the Inventory and Income Summary accounts will show the following.

Illustration 5B-4
Posting closing entries for merchandise inventory

Inventory		Income Summary	
1/1 Bal. 36,000	12/31 Close **36,000**	12/31 Close **36,000**	12/31 Close **40,000**
12/31 Close **40,000**			
12/31 Bal. 40,000			

Often, the closing of inventory is included with other closing entries, as shown below for PW Audio Supply. (*Close inventory with other accounts in homework problems unless stated otherwise.*)

Helpful Hint
Except for merchandise inventory, the easiest way to prepare the first two closing entries is to identify the temporary accounts by their balances and then prepare one entry for the credits and one for the debits.

Dec. 31	**Inventory (Dec. 31)**	**40,000**	
	Sales Revenue	480,000	
	Purchase Returns and Allowances	10,400	
	Purchase Discounts	6,800	
	Income Summary		537,200
	(To record ending inventory and close accounts with credit balances)		
31	Income Summary	507,200	
	Inventory (Jan. 1)		**36,000**
	Sales Returns and Allowances		12,000
	Sales Discounts		8,000
	Purchases		325,000
	Freight-In		12,200
	Salaries and Wages Expense		64,000
	Freight-Out		7,000
	Advertising Expense		16,000
	Utilities Expense		17,000
	Depreciation Expense		8,000
	Insurance Expense		2,000
	(To close beginning inventory and other income statement accounts with debit balances)		
31	Income Summary	30,000	
	Owner's Capital		30,000
	(To transfer net income to capital)		
31	Owner's Capital	15,000	
	Owner's Drawings		15,000
	(To close drawings to capital)		

After the closing entries are posted, all temporary accounts have zero balances. In addition, Owner's Capital has a credit balance of $98,000: beginning balance + net income − drawings ($83,000 + $30,000 − $15,000).

Using a Worksheet

As indicated in Chapter 4, a worksheet enables companies to prepare financial statements before journalizing and posting adjusting entries. The steps in preparing a worksheet for a merchandising company are the same as they are for a service company (see pages 150–156).

TRIAL BALANCE COLUMNS

Data for the trial balance come from the ledger balances of PW Audio Supply at December 31. The amount shown for Inventory, $36,000, is the beginning inventory amount from the periodic inventory system.

ADJUSTMENTS COLUMNS

A merchandising company generally has the same types of adjustments as a service company. As you see in the worksheet in Illustration 5B-5, adjustments (a), (b), and (c) are for insurance, depreciation, and salaries and wages. These adjustments were also required for Pioneer Advertising, as illustrated in Chapters 3 and 4. The unique accounts for a merchandiser using a **periodic inventory system** are shown in capital red letters. Note, however, that the worksheet excludes nonoperating items.

After all adjustment data are entered on the worksheet, the equality of the adjustment column totals is established. The balances in all accounts are then extended to the adjusted trial balance columns.

Illustration 5B-5
Worksheet for merchandising company—periodic inventory system

PW Audio Supply.xls

Home Insert Page Layout Formulas Data Review View

P18 fx

PW AUDIO SUPPLY
Worksheet
For the Year Ended December 31, 2017

	A	B	C	D	E	F	G	H	I	J	K
5–6		Trial Balance		Adjustments		Adjusted Trial Balance		Income Statement		Balance Sheet	
7	Accounts	Dr.	Cr.	Dr.	Cr.	Dr.	Cr.	Dr.	Cr.	Dr.	Cr.
8	Cash	9,500				9,500				9,500	
9	Accounts Receivable	16,100				16,100				16,100	
10	INVENTORY	36,000				36,000		36,000	40,000	40,000	
11	Prepaid Insurance	3,800			(a) 2,000	1,800				1,800	
12	Equipment	80,000				80,000				80,000	
13	Accumulated Depreciation—Equipment		16,000		(b) 8,000		24,000				24,000
14	Accounts Payable		20,400				20,400				20,400
15	Owner's Capital		83,000				83,000				83,000
16	Owner's Drawings	15,000				15,000				15,000	
17	SALES REVENUE		480,000				480,000		480,000		
18	SALES RETURNS AND ALLOWANCES	12,000				12,000		12,000			
19	SALES DISCOUNTS	8,000				8,000		8,000			
20	PURCHASES	325,000				325,000		325,000			
21	PURCHASE RETURNS AND ALLOWANCES		10,400				10,400		10,400		
22	PURCHASE DISCOUNTS		6,800				6,800		6,800		
23	FREIGHT-IN	12,200				12,200		12,200			
24	Freight-Out	7,000				7,000		7,000			
25	Advertising Expense	16,000				16,000		16,000			
26	Salaries and Wages Expense	59,000		(c) 5,000		64,000		64,000			
27	Utilities Expense	17,000				17,000		17,000			
28	Totals	616,600	616,600								
29	Insurance Expense			(a) 2,000		2,000		2,000			
30	Depreciation Expense			(b) 8,000		8,000		8,000			
31	Salaries and Wages Payable				(c) 5,000		5,000				5,000
32	Totals			15,000	15,000	629,600	629,600	507,200	537,200	162,400	132,400
33	Net Income							30,000			30,000
34	Totals							537,200	537,200	162,400	162,400

Key: (a) Insurance expired. (b) Depreciation expense. (c) Salaries and wages accrued.

INCOME STATEMENT COLUMNS

Next, PW Audio Supply transfers the accounts and balances that affect the income statement from the adjusted trial balance columns to the income statement columns. The company shows Sales Revenue of $480,000 in the credit column. It shows the contra revenue accounts, Sales Returns and Allowances of $12,000 and Sales Discounts of $8,000 in the debit column. The difference of $460,000 is the net sales shown on the income statement (Illustration 5-9, page 223). Similarly, Purchases of $325,000 and Freight-In of $12,200 are extended to the debit column. The contra purchase accounts, Purchase Returns and Allowances of $10,400 and Purchase Discounts of $6,800, are extended to the credit columns.

The worksheet procedures for the Inventory account merit specific comment. The procedures are:

1. The beginning balance, $36,000, is extended from the adjusted trial balance column to the **income statement debit column**. From there, it can be added in reporting cost of goods available for sale in the income statement.
2. The ending inventory, $40,000, is added to the worksheet by an **income statement credit and a balance sheet debit**. The credit makes it possible to deduct ending inventory from the cost of goods available for sale in the income statement to determine cost of goods sold. The debit means the ending inventory can be reported as an asset on the balance sheet.

These two procedures are specifically illustrated below:

Illustration 5B-6
Worksheet procedures for inventories

	Income Statement			Balance Sheet	
	Dr.	Cr.		Dr.	Cr.
Inventory	(1) 36,000	40,000 ←	(2)	→ 40,000	

The computation for cost of goods sold, taken from the income statement column in Illustration 5B-5, is as follows.

Illustration 5B-7
Computation of cost of goods sold from worksheet columns

Debit Column		Credit Column	
Beginning inventory	$ 36,000	Ending inventory	$40,000
Purchases	325,000	Purchase returns and allowances	10,400
Freight-in	12,200	Purchase discounts	6,800
Total debits	373,200	Total credits	$57,200
Less: Total credits	57,200		
Cost of goods sold	**$316,000**		

Helpful Hint
In a periodic system, cost of goods sold is a computation—it is not a separate account with a balance.

Finally, PW Audio Supply totals all the credits in the income statement column and compares these totals to the total of the debits in the income statement column. If the credits exceed the debits, the company has net income. PW Audio Supply has net income of $30,000. If the debits exceed the credits, the company would report a net loss.

BALANCE SHEET COLUMNS

The major difference between the balance sheets of a service company and a merchandising company is inventory. PW Audio Supply shows ending inventory of $40,000 in the balance sheet debit column. The information to prepare the owner's equity statement is also found in these columns. That is, the Owner's Capital account is $83,000. Owner's Drawings are $15,000. Net income results when the total of the debit column exceeds the total of the credit column in the balance sheet columns. A net loss results when the total of the credits exceeds the total of the debit balances.

REVIEW AND PRACTICE

LEARNING OBJECTIVES REVIEW

1 Describe merchandising operations and inventory systems. Because of inventory, a merchandising company has sales revenue, cost of goods sold, and gross profit. To account for inventory, a merchandising company must choose between a perpetual and a periodic inventory system.

2 Record purchases under a perpetual inventory system. The company debits the Inventory account for all purchases of merchandise and freight-in, and credits it for purchase discounts and purchase returns and allowances.

3 Record sales under a perpetual inventory system. When a merchandising company sells inventory, it debits Accounts Receivable (or Cash) and credits Sales Revenue for the **selling price** of the merchandise. At the same time, it debits Cost of Goods Sold and credits Inventory for the **cost** of the inventory items sold. Sales Returns and Allowances and Sales Discounts are debited and are contra revenue accounts.

4 Apply the steps in the accounting cycle to a merchandising company. Each of the required steps in the accounting cycle for a service company applies to a merchandising company. A worksheet is again an optional step. Under a perpetual inventory system, the company must adjust the Inventory account to agree with the physical count.

5 Compare a multiple-step with a single-step income statement. A multiple-step income statement shows numerous steps in determining net income, including nonoperating activities sections. A single-step income statement classifies all data under two categories, revenues or expenses, and determines net income in one step.

***6 Prepare a worksheet for a merchandising company.** The steps in preparing a worksheet for a merchandising company are the same as for a service company. The unique accounts for a merchandiser are Inventory, Sales Revenue, Sales Returns and Allowances, Sales Discounts, and Cost of Goods Sold.

***7 Record purchases and sales under a periodic inventory system.** In recording purchases under a periodic system, companies must make entries for (a) cash and credit purchases, (b) purchase returns and allowances, (c) purchase discounts, and (d) freight costs. In recording sales, companies must make entries for (a) cash and credit sales, (b) sales returns and allowances, and (c) sales discounts.

GLOSSARY REVIEW

Contra revenue account An account that is offset against a revenue account on the income statement. (p. 218).

Cost of goods sold The total cost of merchandise sold during the period. (p. 208).

FOB destination Freight terms indicating that the seller places the goods free on board to the buyer's place of business, and the seller pays the freight. (p. 213).

FOB shipping point Freight terms indicating that the seller places goods free on board the carrier, and the buyer pays the freight costs. (p. 213).

Gross profit The excess of net sales over the cost of goods sold. (p. 223).

Gross profit rate Gross profit expressed as a percentage, by dividing the amount of gross profit by net sales. (p. 223).

Income from operations Income from a company's principal operating activity; determined by subtracting cost of goods sold and operating expenses from net sales. (p. 224).

Multiple-step income statement An income statement that shows several steps in determining net income. (p. 222).

Net sales Sales revenue less sales returns and allowances and less sales discounts. (p. 223).

Nonoperating activities Various revenues, expenses, gains, and losses that are unrelated to a company's main line of operations. (p. 224).

Operating expenses Expenses incurred in the process of earning sales revenue. (p. 224).

Other expenses and losses A nonoperating-activities section of the income statement that shows expenses and losses unrelated to the company's main line of operations. (p. 224).

Other revenues and gains A nonoperating-activities section of the income statement that shows revenues and gains unrelated to the company's main line of operations. (p. 224).

Periodic inventory system An inventory system under which the company does not keep detailed inventory records throughout the accounting period but determines the cost of goods sold only at the end of an accounting period. (p. 210).

Perpetual inventory system An inventory system under which the company keeps detailed records of the cost of each inventory purchase and sale, and the records continuously show the inventory that should be on hand. (p. 209).

Purchase allowance A deduction made to the selling price of merchandise, granted by the seller so that the buyer will keep the merchandise. (p. 214).

Purchase discount A cash discount claimed by a buyer for prompt payment of a balance due. (p. 214).

Purchase invoice A document that supports each credit purchase. (p. 212).

Purchase return A return of goods from the buyer to the seller for a cash or credit refund. (p. 214).

Sales discount A reduction given by a seller for prompt payment of a credit sale. (p. 218).

Sales invoice A document that supports each credit sale. (p. 216).

Sales returns and allowances Purchase returns and allowances from the seller's perspective. See *Purchase return* and *Purchase allowance,* above. (p. 217).

Sales revenue (Sales) The primary source of revenue in a merchandising company. (p. 208).

Single-step income statement An income statement that shows only one step in determining net income. (p. 226).

PRACTICE MULTIPLE-CHOICE QUESTIONS

(LO 1) **1.** Gross profit will result if:
(a) operating expenses are less than net income.
(b) sales revenues are greater than operating expenses.
(c) sales revenues are greater than cost of goods sold.
(d) operating expenses are greater than cost of goods sold.

(LO 2) **2.** Under a perpetual inventory system, when goods are purchased for resale by a company:
(a) purchases on account are debited to Inventory.
(b) purchases on account are debited to Purchases.
(c) purchase returns are debited to Purchase Returns and Allowances.
(d) freight costs are debited to Freight-Out.

(LO 3) **3.** The sales accounts that normally have a debit balance are:
(a) Sales Discounts.
(b) Sales Returns and Allowances.
(c) Both (a) and (b).
(d) Neither (a) nor (b).

(LO 3) **4.** A credit sale of $750 is made on June 13, terms 2/10, net/30. A return of $50 is granted on June 16. The amount received as payment in full on June 23 is:
(a) $700. (c) $685.
(b) $686. (d) $650.

(LO 2) **5.** Which of the following accounts will normally appear in the ledger of a merchandising company that uses a perpetual inventory system?
(a) Purchases. (c) Cost of Goods Sold.
(b) Freight-In. (d) Purchase Discounts.

(LO 3) **6.** To record the sale of goods for cash in a perpetual inventory system:
(a) only one journal entry is necessary to record cost of goods sold and reduction of inventory.
(b) only one journal entry is necessary to record the receipt of cash and the sales revenue.
(c) two journal entries are necessary: one to record the receipt of cash and sales revenue, and one to record the cost of goods sold and reduction of inventory.
(d) two journal entries are necessary: one to record the receipt of cash and reduction of inventory, and one to record the cost of goods sold and sales revenue.

7. The steps in the accounting cycle for a merchandising company are the same as those in a service company **except**: (LO 4)
(a) an additional adjusting journal entry for inventory may be needed in a merchandising company.
(b) closing journal entries are not required for a merchandising company.
(c) a post-closing trial balance is not required for a merchandising company.
(d) a multiple-step income statement is required for a merchandising company.

8. The multiple-step income statement for a merchandising company shows each of the following features **except**: (LO 5)
(a) gross profit.
(b) cost of goods sold.
(c) a sales section.
(d) an investing activities section.

9. If sales revenues are $400,000, cost of goods sold is $310,000, and operating expenses are $60,000, the gross profit is: (LO 5)
(a) $30,000. **(c)** $340,000.
(b) $90,000. **(d)** $400,000.

10. A single-step income statement: (LO 5)
(a) reports gross profit.
(b) does not report cost of goods sold.
(c) reports sales revenue and "Other revenues and gains" in the revenues section of the income statement.
(d) reports operating income separately.

11. Which of the following appears on both a single-step and a multiple-step income statement? (LO 5)
(a) Inventory.
(b) Gross profit.
(c) Income from operations.
(d) Cost of goods sold.

***12.** In a worksheet using a perpetual inventory system, Inventory is shown in the following columns: (LO 6)
(a) adjusted trial balance debit and balance sheet debit.
(b) income statement debit and balance sheet debit.
(c) income statement credit and balance sheet debit.
(d) income statement credit and adjusted trial balance debit.

(LO 7) *13. In determining cost of goods sold in a periodic system:
(a) purchase discounts are deducted from net purchases.
(b) freight-out is added to net purchases.
(c) purchase returns and allowances are deducted from net purchases.
(d) freight-in is added to net purchases.

(LO 7) *14. If beginning inventory is $60,000, cost of goods purchased is $380,000, and ending inventory is $50,000, cost of goods sold is:
(a) $390,000.
(b) $370,000.
(c) $330,000.
(d) $420,000.

*15. When goods are purchased for resale by a company using a periodic inventory system: (LO 7)
(a) purchases on account are debited to Inventory.
(b) purchases on account are debited to Purchases.
(c) purchase returns are debited to Purchase Returns and Allowances.
(d) freight costs are debited to Purchases.

Solutions

1. (c) Gross profit will result if sales revenues are greater than cost of goods sold. The other choices are incorrect because (a) operating expenses and net income are not used in the computation of gross profit; (b) gross profit results when sales revenues are greater than cost of goods sold, not operating expenses; and (d) gross profit results when sales revenues, not operating expenses, are greater than cost of goods sold.

2. (a) Under a perpetual inventory system, when a company purchases goods for resale, purchases on account are debited to the Inventory account, not (b) Purchases or (c) Purchase Returns and Allowances. Choice (d) is incorrect because freight costs are also debited to the Inventory account, not the Freight-Out account.

3. (c) Both Sales Discounts and Sales Returns and Allowances normally have a debit balance. Choices (a) and (b) are both correct, but (c) is the better answer. Choice (d) is incorrect as both (a) and (b) are correct.

4. (b) The full amount of $686 is paid within 10 days of the purchase ($750 − $50) − [($750 − $50) × 2%]. The other choices are incorrect because (a) does not consider the discount of $14; (c) the amount of the discount is based upon the amount after the return is granted ($700 × 2%), not the amount before the return of merchandise ($750 × 2%); and (d) does not constitute payment in full on June 23.

5. (c) The Cost of Goods Sold account normally appears in the ledger of a merchandising company using a perpetual inventory system. The other choices are incorrect because (a) the Purchases account, (b) the Freight-In account, and (d) the Purchase Discounts account all appear in the ledger of a merchandising company that uses a periodic inventory system.

6. (c) Two journal entries are necessary: one to record the receipt of cash and sales revenue, and one to record the cost of goods sold and reduction of inventory. The other choices are incorrect because (a) only considers the recognition of the expense and ignores the revenue, (b) only considers the recognition of revenue and leaves out the expense or cost of merchandise sold, and (d) the receipt of cash and sales revenue, not reduction of inventory, are paired together, and the cost of goods sold and reduction of inventory, not sales revenue, are paired together.

7. (a) An additional adjusting journal entry for inventory may be needed in a merchandising company to adjust for a physical inventory count, but it is not needed for a service company. The other choices are incorrect because (b) closing journal entries and (c) a post-closing trial balance are required for both types of companies, Choice (d) is incorrect because while a multiple-step income statement is not required for a merchandising company, it is useful to distinguish income generated from operating the business versus income or loss from nonrecurring, nonoperating items.

8. (d) An investing activities section appears on the statement of cash flows, not on a multiple-step income statement. Choices (a) gross profit, (b) cost of goods sold, and (c) a sales section are all features of a multiple-step income statement.

9. (b) Gross profit = Sales revenue ($400,000) − Cost of goods sold ($310,000) = $90,000, not (a) $30,000, (c) $340,000, or (d) $400,000.

10. (c) Both sales revenue and "Other revenues and gains" are reported in the revenues section of a single-step income statement. The other choices are incorrect because (a) gross profit is not reported on a single-step income statement, (b) cost of goods sold is included in the expenses section of a single-step income statement, and (d) income from operations is not shown separately on a single-step income statement.

11. (d) Cost of goods sold appears on both a single-step and a multiple-step income statement. The other choices are incorrect because (a) inventory does not appear on either a single-step or a multiple-step income statement and (b) gross profit and (c) income from operations appear on a multiple-step income statement but not on a single-step income statement.

12. (a) In a worksheet using a perpetual inventory system, inventory is shown in the adjusted trial balance debit column and in the balance sheet debit column. The other choices are incorrect because the Inventory account is not shown in the income statement columns.

***13. (d)** In determining cost of goods sold in a periodic system, freight-in is added to net purchases. The other choices are incorrect because (a) purchase discounts are deducted from purchases, not net purchases; (b) freight-out is a cost of sales, not a cost of purchases; and (c) purchase returns and allowances are deducted from purchases, not net purchases.

***14. (a)** Beginning inventory ($60,000) + Cost of goods purchased ($380,000) − Ending inventory ($50,000) = Cost of goods sold ($390,000), not (b) $370,000, (c) $330,000, or (d) $420,000.

***15. (b)** Purchases for resale are debited to the Purchases account. The other choices are incorrect because (a) purchases on account are debited to Purchases, not Inventory; (c) Purchase Returns and Allowances are always credited; and (d) freight costs are debited to Freight-In, not Purchases.

PRACTICE EXERCISES

Prepare purchase and sales entries.

(LO 2, 3)

1. On June 10, Spinner Company purchased $10,000 of merchandise from Lawrence Company, FOB shipping point, terms 2/10, n/30. Spinner pays the freight costs of $600 on June 11. Damaged goods totaling $700 are returned to Lawrence for credit on June 12. The fair value of these goods is $300. On June 19, Spinner pays Lawrence in full, less the purchase discount. Both companies use a perpetual inventory system.

Instructions

(a) Prepare separate entries for each transaction on the books of Spinner Company.

(b) Prepare separate entries for each transaction for Lawrence Company. The merchandise purchased by Spinner on June 10 had cost Lawrence $6,400.

Solution

1. (a)

June 10	Inventory	10,000	
	Accounts Payable		10,000
11	Inventory	600	
	Cash		600
12	Accounts Payable	700	
	Inventory		700
19	Accounts Payable ($10,000 − $700)	9,300	
	Inventory ($9,300 × 2%)		186
	Cash ($9,300 − $186)		9,114

(b)

June 10	Accounts Receivable	10,000	
	Sales Revenue		10,000
	Cost of Goods Sold	6,400	
	Inventory		6,400
12	Sales Returns and Allowances	700	
	Accounts Receivable		700
	Inventory	300	
	Cost of Goods Sold		300
19	Cash ($9,300 − $186)	9,114	
	Sales Discounts ($9,300 × 2%)	186	
	Accounts Receivable ($10,000 − $700)		9,300

Prepare multiple-step and single-step income statements.

(LO 5)

2. In its income statement for the year ended December 31, 2017, Sale Company reported the following condensed data.

Interest expense	$ 50,000	Net sales	$1,650,000
Operating expenses	590,000	Interest revenue	20,000
Cost of goods sold	902,000	Loss on disposal of equipment	7,000

Instructions

(a) Prepare a multiple-step income statement.

(b) Prepare a single-step income statement.

Solution

2. (a)

SALE COMPANY Income Statement For the Year Ended December 31, 2017			
Net sales			$1,650,000
Cost of goods sold			902,000
Gross profit			748,000
Operating expenses			590,000
Income from operations			158,000
Other revenues and gains			
Interest revenue		$20,000	
Other expenses and losses			
Interest expense	$50,000		
Loss on disposal of equipment	7,000	57,000	(37,000)
Net income			$ 121,000

(b)

SALE COMPANY Income Statement For the Year Ended December 31, 2017		
Revenues		
Net sales	$1,650,000	
Interest revenue	20,000	
Total revenues		$1,670,000
Expenses		
Cost of goods sold	902,000	
Operating expenses	590,000	
Interest expenses	50,000	
Loss on sale of equipment	7,000	
Total expenses		1,549,000
Net income		$ 121,000

PRACTICE PROBLEM

Prepare a multiple-step income statement.

(LO 5)

The adjusted trial balance columns of Falcetto Company's worksheet for the year ended December 31, 2017, are as follows.

	Debit		Credit
Cash	14,500	Accumulated Depreciation— Equipment	18,000
Accounts Receivable	11,100	Notes Payable	25,000
Inventory	29,000	Accounts Payable	10,600
Prepaid Insurance	2,500	Owner's Capital	81,000
Equipment	95,000	Sales Revenue	536,800
Owner's Drawings	12,000	Interest Revenue	2,500
Sales Returns and Allowances	6,700		673,900
Sales Discounts	5,000		
Cost of Goods Sold	363,400		
Freight-Out	7,600		
Advertising Expense	12,000		
Salaries and Wages Expense	56,000		
Utilities Expense	18,000		
Rent Expense	24,000		
Depreciation Expense	9,000		
Insurance Expense	4,500		
Interest Expense	3,600		
	673,900		

Instructions

Prepare a multiple-step income statement for Falcetto Company.

Solution

FALCETTO COMPANY Income Statement For the Year Ended December 31, 2017		
Sales		
Sales revenue		$536,800
Less: Sales returns and allowances	$ 6,700	
Sales discounts	5,000	11,700
Net sales		525,100
Cost of goods sold		363,400
Gross profit		161,700
Operating expenses		
Salaries and wages expense	56,000	
Rent expense	24,000	
Utilities expense	18,000	
Advertising expense	12,000	
Depreciation expense	9,000	
Freight-out	7,600	
Insurance expense	4,500	
Total operating expenses		131,100
Income from operations		30,600
Other revenues and gains		
Interest revenue	2,500	
Other expenses and losses		
Interest expense	3,600	1,100
Net income		$ 29,500

WileyPLUS Brief Exercises, Exercises, DO IT! Exercises, and Problems and many additional resources are available for practice in WileyPLUS

NOTE: All asterisked Questions, Exercises, and Problems relate to material in the appendices to the chapter.

QUESTIONS

1. (a) "The steps in the accounting cycle for a merchandising company are different from the accounting cycle for a service company." Do you agree or disagree? (b) Is the measurement of net income for a merchandising company conceptually the same as for a service company? Explain.
2. Why is the normal operating cycle for a merchandising company likely to be longer than for a service company?
3. What components of revenues and expenses are different between merchandising and service companies?
4. How does income measurement differ between a merchandising and a service company?
5. When is cost of goods sold determined in a perpetual inventory system?
6. Distinguish between FOB shipping point and FOB destination. Identify the freight terms that will result in a debit to Inventory by the buyer and a debit to Freight-Out by the seller.
7. Explain the meaning of the credit terms 2/10, n/30.
8. Goods costing $2,000 are purchased on account on July 15 with credit terms of 2/10, n/30. On July 18, a $200 credit memo is received from the supplier for damaged goods. Give the journal entry on July 24 to record payment of the balance due within the discount period using a perpetual inventory system.
9. Celina Harris believes revenues from credit sales may be recorded before they are collected in cash. Do you agree? Explain.
10. (a) What is the primary source document for recording (1) cash sales and (2) credit sales? (b) Using XXs for amounts, give the journal entry for each of the transactions in part (a).
11. A credit sale is made on July 10 for $900, terms 2/10, n/30. On July 12, $100 of goods are returned for credit. Give the journal entry on July 19 to record the receipt of the balance due within the discount period.

12. Explain why the Inventory account will usually require adjustment at year-end.
13. Prepare the closing entries for the Sales Revenue account, assuming a balance of $200,000 and the Cost of Goods Sold account with a $145,000 balance.
14. What merchandising account(s) will appear in the post-closing trial balance?
15. Cupery Co. has sales revenue of $105,000, cost of goods sold of $70,000, and operating expenses of $20,000. What is its gross profit and its gross profit rate?
16. Stefan Page Company reports net sales of $800,000, gross profit of $370,000, and net income of $240,000. What are its operating expenses?
17. Identify the distinguishing features of an income statement for a merchandising company.
18. Identify the sections of a multiple-step income statement that relate to (a) operating activities, and (b) nonoperating activities.
19. How does the single-step form of income statement differ from the multiple-step form?
20. Determine Apple's gross profit rate for 2013 and 2012. Indicate whether it increased or decreased from 2012 to 2013.
*21. Indicate the columns of the worksheet in a perpetual system in which (a) inventory and (b) cost of goods sold will be shown.
*22. Identify the accounts that are added to or deducted from Purchases in a periodic system to determine the cost of goods purchased. For each account, indicate whether it is added or deducted.
*23. Goods costing $3,000 are purchased on account on July 15 with credit terms of 2/10, n/30. On July 18, a $200 credit was received from the supplier for damaged goods. Give the journal entry on July 24 to record payment of the balance due within the discount period, assuming a periodic inventory system.

BRIEF EXERCISES

Compute missing amounts in determining cost of goods sold. (LO 1)

BE5-1 Presented below are the components in determining cost of goods sold. Determine the missing amounts.

	Beginning Inventory	Purchases	Cost of Goods Available for Sale	Ending Inventory	Cost of Goods Sold
(a)	$80,000	$100,000	?	?	$120,000
(b)	$50,000	?	$115,000	$35,000	?
(c)	?	$110,000	$160,000	$29,000	?

Compute missing amounts in determining net income. (LO 1)

BE5-2 Presented below are the components in Veasy Company's income statement. Determine the missing amounts.

	Sales Revenue	Cost of Goods Sold	Gross Profit	Operating Expenses	Net Income
(a)	$ 75,000	?	$28,000	?	$ 9,800
(b)	$108,000	$70,000	?	?	$29,500
(c)	?	$83,900	$79,600	$39,500	?

Journalize perpetual inventory entries. (LO 2, 3)

BE5-3 Cha Company buys merchandise on account from Wirtz Company. The selling price of the goods is $780, and the cost of the goods is $470. Both companies use perpetual inventory systems. Journalize the transaction on the books of both companies.

Journalize sales transactions. (LO 3)

BE5-4 Prepare the journal entries to record the following transactions on Novy Company's books using a perpetual inventory system.

(a) On March 2, Novy Company sold $900,000 of merchandise to Opps Company, terms 2/10, n/30. The cost of the merchandise sold was $590,000.
(b) On March 6, Opps Company returned $90,000 of the merchandise purchased on March 2. The cost of the returned merchandise was $62,000.
(c) On March 12, Novy Company received the balance due from Opps Company.

Journalize purchase transactions. (LO 2)

BE5-5 From the information in BE5-4, prepare the journal entries to record these transactions on Opps Company's books under a perpetual inventory system.

Prepare adjusting entry for inventory. (LO 4)

BE5-6 At year-end, the perpetual inventory records of Gutierrez Company showed merchandise inventory of $98,000. The company determined, however, that its actual inventory on hand was $96,100. Record the necessary adjusting entry.

Prepare closing entries for accounts. (LO 4)

BE5-7 Brueser Company has the following account balances: Sales Revenue $195,000, Sales Discounts $2,000, Cost of Goods Sold $117,000, and Inventory $40,000. Prepare the entries to record the closing of these items to Income Summary.

Prepare sales section of income statement.
(LO 5)

BE5-8 Nelson Company provides the following information for the month ended October 31, 2017: sales on credit $280,000, cash sales $95,000, sales discounts $5,000, and sales returns and allowances $11,000. Prepare the sales section of the income statement based on this information.

Contrast presentation in multiple-step and single-step income statements.
(LO 5)

BE5-9 Explain where each of the following items would appear on (1) a multiple-step income statement, and on (2) a single-step income statement: (a) gain on sale of equipment, (b) interest expense, (c) casualty loss from vandalism, and (d) cost of goods sold.

Compute net sales, gross profit, income from operations, and gross profit rate.
(LO 5)

BE5-10 Assume Kupfer Company has the following reported amounts: Sales revenue $510,000, Sales returns and allowances $15,000, Cost of goods sold $330,000, and Operating expenses $90,000. Compute the following: (a) net sales, (b) gross profit, (c) income from operations, and (d) gross profit rate. (Round to one decimal place.)

Identify worksheet columns for selected accounts.
(LO 6)

***BE5-11** Presented below is the format of the worksheet using the perpetual inventory system presented in Appendix 5A.

Trial Balance		Adjustments		Adjusted Trial Balance		Income Statement		Balance Sheet	
Dr.	Cr.	Dr.	Cr.	Dr.	Cr.	Dr.	Cr.	Dr.	Cr.

Indicate where the following items will appear on the worksheet: (a) Cash, (b) Inventory, (c) Sales revenue, and (d) Cost of goods sold.

Example:
Cash: Trial balance debit column; Adjusted trial balance debit column; and Balance sheet debit column.

Compute net purchases and cost of goods purchased.
(LO 7)

***BE5-12** Assume that Morgan Company uses a periodic inventory system and has these account balances: Purchases $450,000, Purchase Returns and Allowances $13,000, Purchase Discounts $9,000, and Freight-In $18,000. Determine net purchases and cost of goods purchased.

Compute cost of goods sold and gross profit.
(LO 7)

***BE5-13** Assume the same information as in BE5-12 and also that Morgan Company has beginning inventory of $60,000, ending inventory of $90,000, and net sales of $730,000. Determine the amounts to be reported for cost of goods sold and gross profit.

Journalize purchase transactions.
(LO 7)

***BE5-14** Prepare the journal entries to record these transactions on Shabani Company's books using a periodic inventory system.

(a) On March 2, Shabani Company purchased $900,000 of merchandise from Ballas Company, terms 2/10, n/30.
(b) On March 6, Shabani Company returned $110,000 of the merchandise purchased on March 2.
(c) On March 12, Shabani Company paid the balance due to Ballas Company.

Prepare closing entries for merchandise accounts.
(LO 7)

***BE5-15** T. Corlett Company has the following merchandise account balances: Sales Revenue $180,000, Sales Discounts $2,000, Purchases $120,000, and Purchases Returns and Allowances $30,000. In addition, it has a beginning inventory of $40,000 and an ending inventory of $30,000. Prepare the entries to record the closing of these items to Income Summary using the periodic inventory system.

Identify worksheet columns for selected accounts
(LO 7)

***BE5-16** Presented below is the format of the worksheet using the periodic inventory system presented in Appendix 5B.

Trial Balance		Adjustments		Adjusted Trial Balance		Income Statement		Balance Sheet	
Dr.	Cr.	Dr.	Cr.	Dr.	Cr.	Dr.	Cr.	Dr.	Cr.

Indicate where the following items will appear on the worksheet: (a) Cash, (b) Beginning inventory, (c) Accounts payable, and (d) Ending inventory.

Example
Cash: Trial balance debit column; Adjustment trial balance debit column; and Balance sheet debit column.

DO IT! Exercises

DO IT! 5-1 Indicate whether the following statements are true or false.

Answer general questions about merchandisers. (LO 1)

1. A merchandising company reports gross profit but a service company does not.
2. Under a periodic inventory system, a company determines the cost of goods sold each time a sale occurs.
3. A service company is likely to use accounts receivable but a merchandising company is not likely to do so.
4. Under a periodic inventory system, the cost of goods on hand at the beginning of the accounting period plus the cost of goods purchased less the cost of goods on hand at the end of the accounting period equals cost of goods sold.

DO IT! 5-2 On October 5, Wang Company buys merchandise on account from Davis Company. The selling price of the goods is $4,800, and the cost to Davis Company is $3,100. On October 8, Wang returns defective goods with a selling price of $650 and a fair value of $100. Record the transactions on the books of Wang Company.

Record transactions of purchasing company. (LO 2)

DO IT! 5-3 Assume information similar to that in **DO IT! 5-2**: On October 5, Wang Company buys merchandise on account from Davis Company. The selling price of the goods is $4,800, and the cost to Davis Company is $3,100. On October 8, Wang returns defective goods with a selling price of $650 and a fair value of $100. Record the transactions on the books of Davis Company.

Record transactions of selling company. (LO 3)

DO IT! 5-4 The trial balance of Beads and Bangles at December 31 shows Inventory $21,000, Sales Revenue $156,000, Sales Returns and Allowances $4,000, Sales Discounts $3,000, Cost of Goods Sold $92,400, Interest Revenue $5,000, Freight-Out $1,800, Utilities Expense $7,700, and Salaries and Wages Expense $19,500. Prepare the closing entries for Beads and Bangles for these accounts.

Prepare closing entries for a merchandising company. (LO 4)

DO IT! 5-5 Pfannes Company is preparing its multiple-step income statement, owner's equity statement, and classified balance sheet. Using the column headings **Account**, **Financial Statement**, and **Classification**, indicate in which financial statement and under what classification each of the following would be reported.

Classify financial statement accounts. (LO 5)

Account	Financial Statement	Classification
Accounts Payable		
Accounts Receivable		
Accumulated Depreciation—Buildings		
Cash		
Casualty Loss from Vandalism		
Cost of Goods Sold		
Depreciation Expense		
Equipment		
Freight-Out		
Insurance Expense		
Interest Payable		
Inventory		
Land		
Notes Payable (due in 5 years)		
Owner's Capital (beginning balance)		
Owner's Drawings		
Property Taxes Payable		
Salaries and Wages Expense		
Salaries and Wages Payable		
Sales Returns and Allowances		
Sales Revenue		
Unearned Rent Revenue		
Utilities Expense		

EXERCISES

Answer general questions about merchandisers.

(LO 1)

E5-1 Mr. McKenzie has prepared the following list of statements about service companies and merchandisers.

1. Measuring net income for a merchandiser is conceptually the same as for a service company.
2. For a merchandiser, sales less operating expenses is called gross profit.
3. For a merchandiser, the primary source of revenues is the sale of inventory.
4. Sales salaries and wages is an example of an operating expense.
5. The operating cycle of a merchandiser is the same as that of a service company.
6. In a perpetual inventory system, no detailed inventory records of goods on hand are maintained.
7. In a periodic inventory system, the cost of goods sold is determined only at the end of the accounting period.
8. A periodic inventory system provides better control over inventories than a perpetual system.

Instructions

Identify each statement as true or false. If false, indicate how to correct the statement.

Journalize purchase transactions.

(LO 2)

E5-2 Information related to Kerber Co. is presented below.

1. On April 5, purchased merchandise from Wilkes Company for $23,000, terms 2/10, net/30, FOB shipping point.
2. On April 6, paid freight costs of $900 on merchandise purchased from Wilkes.
3. On April 7, purchased equipment on account for $26,000.
4. On April 8, returned damaged merchandise to Wilkes Company and was granted a $3,000 credit for returned merchandise.
5. On April 15, paid the amount due to Wilkes Company in full.

Instructions

(a) Prepare the journal entries to record these transactions on the books of Kerber Co. under a perpetual inventory system.

(b) Assume that Kerber Co. paid the balance due to Wilkes Company on May 4 instead of April 15. Prepare the journal entry to record this payment.

Journalize perpetual inventory entries.

(LO 2, 3)

E5-3 On September 1, Nixa Office Supply had an inventory of 30 calculators at a cost of $18 each. The company uses a perpetual inventory system. During September, the following transactions occurred.

Sept.	6	Purchased 90 calculators at $22 each from York, terms net/30.
	9	Paid freight of $90 on calculators purchased from York Co.
	10	Returned 3 calculators to York Co. for $69 credit (including freight) because they did not meet specifications.
	12	Sold 26 calculators costing $23 (including freight) for $31 each to Sura Book Store, terms n/30.
	14	Granted credit of $31 to Sura Book Store for the return of one calculator that was not ordered.
	20	Sold 30 calculators costing $23 for $32 each to Davis Card Shop, terms n/30.

Instructions

Journalize the September transactions.

Prepare purchase and sales entries.

(LO 2, 3)

E5-4 On June 10, Diaz Company purchased $8,000 of merchandise from Taylor Company, FOB shipping point, terms 2/10, n/30. Diaz pays the freight costs of $400 on June 11. Damaged goods totaling $300 are returned to Taylor for credit on June 12. The fair value of these goods is $70. On June 19, Diaz pays Taylor Company in full, less the purchase discount. Both companies use a perpetual inventory system.

Instructions

(a) Prepare separate entries for each transaction on the books of Diaz Company.

(b) Prepare separate entries for each transaction for Taylor Company. The merchandise purchased by Diaz on June 10 had cost Taylor $4,800.

Journalize sales transactions.

(LO 3)

E5-5 Presented below are transactions related to R. Humphrey Company.

1. On December 3, R. Humphrey Company sold $570,000 of merchandise to Frazier Co., terms 1/10, n/30, FOB destination. R. Humphrey paid $400 for freight charges. The cost of the merchandise sold was $350,000.
2. On December 8, Frazier Co. was granted an allowance of $20,000 for merchandise purchased on December 3.
3. On December 13, R. Humphrey Company received the balance due from Frazier Co.

Instructions

(a) Prepare the journal entries to record these transactions on the books of R. Humphrey Company using a perpetual inventory system.

(b) Assume that R. Humphrey Company received the balance due from Frazier Co. on January 2 of the following year instead of December 13. Prepare the journal entry to record the receipt of payment on January 2.

Prepare sales section and closing entries.

(LO 4, 5)

E5-6 The adjusted trial balance of Sang Company shows the following data pertaining to sales at the end of its fiscal year October 31, 2017: Sales Revenue $820,000, Freight-Out $16,000, Sales Returns and Allowances $25,000, and Sales Discounts $13,000.

Instructions

(a) Prepare the sales section of the income statement.

(b) Prepare separate closing entries for (1) sales revenue, and (2) the contra accounts to sales revenue.

Prepare adjusting and closing entries.

(LO 4)

E5-7 Tim Jarosz Company had the following account balances at year-end: Cost of Goods Sold $60,000, Inventory $15,000, Operating Expenses $29,000, Sales Revenue $115,000, Sales Discounts $1,200, and Sales Returns and Allowances $1,700. A physical count of inventory determines that merchandise inventory on hand is $13,600.

Instructions

(a) Prepare the adjusting entry necessary as a result of the physical count.

(b) Prepare closing entries.

Prepare adjusting and closing entries.

(LO 4)

E5-8 Presented below is information related to Hoerl Co. for the month of January 2017.

Ending inventory per perpetual records	$ 21,600	Insurance expense	$ 12,000
		Rent expense	20,000
Ending inventory actually on hand	21,000	Salaries and wages expense	55,000
		Sales discounts	10,000
Cost of goods sold	218,000	Sales returns and allowances	13,000
Freight-out	7,000	Sales revenue	380,000

Instructions

(a) Prepare the necessary adjusting entry for inventory.

(b) Prepare the necessary closing entries.

Prepare multiple-step income statement.

(LO 5)

E5-9 Presented below is information for Kaila Company for the month of March 2017.

Cost of goods sold	$215,000	Rent expense	$ 30,000
Freight-out	7,000	Sales discounts	8,000
Insurance expense	6,000	Sales returns and allowances	13,000
Salaries and wages expense	58,000	Sales revenue	380,000

Instructions

(a) Prepare a multiple-step income statement.

(b) Compute the gross profit rate.

Prepare multiple-step and single-step income statements.

(LO 5)

XLS

E5-10 In its income statement for the year ended December 31, 2017, Anhad Company reported the following condensed data.

Operating expenses	$ 725,000	Interest revenue	$ 28,000
Cost of goods sold	1,289,000	Loss on disposal of plant assets	17,000
Interest expense	70,000	Net sales	2,200,000

Instructions

(a) Prepare a multiple-step income statement.

(b) Prepare a single-step income statement.

Prepare correcting entries for sales and purchases.

(LO 2, 3)

E5-11 An inexperienced accountant for Stahr Company made the following errors in recording merchandising transactions.

1. A $210 refund to a customer for faulty merchandise was debited to Sales Revenue $210 and credited to Cash $210.
2. A $180 credit purchase of supplies was debited to Inventory $180 and credited to Cash $180.
3. A $215 sales discount was debited to Sales Revenue.
4. A cash payment of $20 for freight on merchandise purchases was debited to Freight-Out $200 and credited to Cash $200.

Instructions

Prepare separate correcting entries for each error, assuming that the incorrect entry is not reversed. (Omit explanations.)

Compute various income measures.

(LO 5)

E5-12 In 2017, Laquen Company had net sales of $900,000 and cost of goods sold of $522,000. Operating expenses were $225,000, and interest expense was $11,000. Laquen prepares a multiple-step income statement.

Instructions

(a) Compute Laquen's gross profit.
(b) Compute the gross profit rate. Why is this rate computed by financial statement users?
(c) What is Laquen's income from operations and net income?
(d) If Laquen prepared a single-step income statement, what amount would it report for net income?
(e) In what section of its classified balance sheet should Laquen report inventory?

Compute missing amounts and compute gross profit rate.

(LO 5)

E5-13 Presented below is financial information for two different companies.

	Summer Company	Winter Company
Sales revenue	$92,000	(d)
Sales returns	(a)	$ 5,000
Net sales	87,000	102,000
Cost of goods sold	56,000	(e)
Gross profit	(b)	41,500
Operating expenses	15,000	(f)
Net income	(c)	18,000

Instructions

(a) Determine the missing amounts.
(b) Determine the gross profit rates. (Round to one decimal place.)

Compute missing amounts.

(LO 5)

E5-14 Financial information is presented below for three different companies.

	Hardy Cosmetics	Yee Grocery	Wang Wholesalers
Sales revenue	$90,000	$ (e)	$122,000
Sales returns and allowances	(a)	5,000	12,000
Net sales	86,000	95,000	(i)
Cost of goods sold	56,000	(f)	(j)
Gross profit	(b)	38,000	24,000
Operating expenses	15,000	(g)	18,000
Income from operations	(c)	(h)	(k)
Other expenses and losses	4,000	7,000	(l)
Net income	(d)	11,000	5,000

Instructions

Determine the missing amounts.

Complete worksheet using a perpetual inventory system.

(LO 6)

***E5-15** Presented on the next page are selected accounts for McPhan Company as reported in the worksheet using a perpetual inventory system at the end of May 2017.

Accounts	Adjusted Trial Balance		Income Statement		Balance Sheet	
	Dr.	Cr.	Dr.	Cr.	Dr.	Cr.
Cash	11,000					
Inventory	76,000					
Sales Revenue		480,000				
Sales Returns and Allowances	10,000					
Sales Discounts	9,000					
Cost of Goods Sold	300,000					

Instructions
Complete the worksheet by extending amounts reported in the adjusted trial balance to the appropriate columns in the worksheet. Do not total individual columns.

***E5-16** The trial balance columns of the worksheet using a perpetual inventory system for Balistreri Company at June 30, 2017, are as follows.

Prepare a worksheet using a perpetual inventory system.

(LO 6)

BALISTRERI COMPANY
Worksheet
For the Month Ended June 30, 2017

Account Titles	Trial Balance Debit	Trial Balance Credit
Cash	1,920	
Accounts Receivable	2,440	
Inventory	11,640	
Accounts Payable		1,120
Owner's Capital		3,500
Sales Revenue		42,500
Cost of Goods Sold	20,560	
Operating Expenses	10,560	
	47,120	47,120

Other data:
Operating expenses incurred on account, but not yet recorded, total $1,500.

Instructions
Enter the trial balance on a worksheet and complete the worksheet.

***E5-17** The trial balance of A. Wiencek Company at the end of its fiscal year, August 31, 2017, includes these accounts: Inventory $19,500; Purchases $149,000; Sales Revenue $190,000; Freight-In $5,000; Sales Returns and Allowances $3,000; Freight-Out $1,000; and Purchase Returns and Allowances $2,000. The ending inventory is $23,000.

Prepare cost of goods sold section.

(LO 7)

Instructions
Prepare a cost of goods sold section for the year ending August 31 (periodic inventory).

***E5-18** On January 1, 2017, Brooke Hanson Corporation had inventory of $50,000. At December 31, 2017, Brooke Hanson had the following account balances.

Compute various income statement items.

(LO 7)

Freight-in	$ 4,000
Purchases	509,000
Purchase discounts	6,000
Purchase returns and allowances	2,000
Sales revenue	840,000
Sales discounts	5,000
Sales returns and allowances	10,000

At December 31, 2017, Brooke Hanson determines that its ending inventory is $60,000.

Instructions
(a) Compute Brooke Hanson's 2017 gross profit.
(b) Compute Brooke Hanson's 2017 operating expenses if net income is $130,000 and there are no nonoperating activities.

Prepare cost of goods sold section.

(LO 7)

***E5-19** Below is a series of cost of goods sold sections for companies B, F, L, and R.

	B	F	L	R
Beginning inventory	$ 180	$ 70	$1,000	$ (j)
Purchases	1,620	1,060	(g)	43,590
Purchase returns and allowances	40	(d)	290	(k)
Net purchases	(a)	1,030	6,210	41,090
Freight-in	110	(e)	(h)	2,240
Cost of goods purchased	(b)	1,280	7,940	(l)
Cost of goods available for sale	1,870	1,350	(i)	49,530
Ending inventory	250	(f)	1,450	6,230
Cost of goods sold	(c)	1,230	7,490	43,300

Instruction
Fill in the lettered blanks to complete the cost of goods sold sections.

Journalize purchase transactions.

(LO 7)

***E5-20** This information relates to Nandi Co.

1. On April 5, purchased merchandise from Dion Company for $25,000, terms 2/10, net/30, FOB shipping point.
2. On April 6, paid freight costs of $900 on merchandise purchased from Dion Company.
3. On April 7, purchased equipment on account for $30,000.
4. On April 8, returned some of April 5 merchandise, which cost $2,800, to Dion Company.
5. On April 15, paid the amount due to Dion Company in full.

Instructions
(a) Prepare the journal entries to record these transactions on the books of Nandi Co. using a periodic inventory system.
(b) Assume that Nandi Co. paid the balance due to Dion Company on May 4 instead of April 15. Prepare the journal entry to record this payment.

Journalize purchase transactions.

(LO 7)

***E5-21** Presented below is information related to Chung Co.

1. On April 5, purchased merchandise from Jose Company for $21,000, terms 2/10, net/30, FOB shipping point.
2. On April 6, paid freight costs of $800 on merchandise purchased from Jose.
3. On April 7, purchased equipment on account from Winker Mfg. Co. for $26,000.
4. On April 8, returned merchandise, which cost $4,000, to Jose Company.
5. On April 15, paid the amount due to Jose Company in full.

Instructions
(a) Prepare the journal entries to record these transactions on the books of Chung Co. using a periodic inventory system.
(b) Assume that Chung Co. paid the balance due to Jose Company on May 4 instead of April 15. Prepare the journal entry to record this payment.

Complete worksheet.

(LO 7)

***E5-22** Presented below are selected accounts for T. Swift Company as reported in the worksheet at the end of May 2017. Ending inventory is $75,000.

Accounts	Adjusted Trial Balance		Income Statement		Balance Sheet	
	Dr.	Cr.	Dr.	Cr.	Dr.	Cr.
Cash	9,000					
Inventory	80,000					
Purchases	240,000					
Purchase Returns and Allowances		30,000				
Sales Revenue		450,000				
Sales Returns and Allowances	10,000					
Sales Discounts	5,000					
Rent Expense	42,000					

Instructions
Complete the worksheet by extending amounts reported in the adjustment trial balance to the appropriate columns in the worksheet. The company uses the periodic inventory system.

EXERCISES: SET B AND CHALLENGE EXERCISES

Visit the book's companion website, at **www.wiley.com/college/weygandt**, and choose the Student Companion site to access Exercises: Set B and Challenge Exercises.

PROBLEMS: SET A

Journalize purchase and sales transactions under a perpetual inventory system.

(LO 2, 3)

P5-1A Kern's Book Warehouse distributes hardcover books to retail stores and extends credit terms of 2/10, n/30 to all of its customers. At the end of May, Kern's inventory consisted of books purchased for $1,800. During June, the following merchandising transactions occurred.

June	1	Purchased books on account for $1,600 from Binsfeld Publishers, FOB destination, terms 2/10, n/30. The appropriate party also made a cash payment of $50 for the freight on this date.
	3	Sold books on account to Reading Rainbow for $2,500. The cost of the books sold was $1,440.
	6	Received $100 credit for books returned to Binsfeld Publishers.
	9	Paid Binsfeld Publishers in full, less discount.
	15	Received payment in full from Reading Rainbow.
	17	Sold books on account to Rapp Books for $1,800. The cost of the books sold was $1,080.
	20	Purchased books on account for $1,800 from McGinn Publishers, FOB destination, terms 2/15, n/30. The appropriate party also made a cash payment of $60 for the freight on this date.
	24	Received payment in full from Rapp Books.
	26	Paid McGinn Publishers in full, less discount.
	28	Sold books on account to Baeten Bookstore for $1,600. The cost of the books sold was $970.
	30	Granted Baeten Bookstore $120 credit for books returned costing $72.

Kern's Book Warehouse's chart of accounts includes the following: No. 101 Cash, No. 112 Accounts Receivable, No. 120 Inventory, No. 201 Accounts Payable, No. 401 Sales Revenue, No. 412 Sales Returns and Allowances, No. 414 Sales Discounts, and No. 505 Cost of Goods Sold.

Instructions

Journalize the transactions for the month of June for Kern's Book Warehouse using a perpetual inventory system.

Journalize, post, and prepare a partial income statement.

(LO 2, 3, 5)

P5-2A Renner Hardware Store completed the following merchandising transactions in the month of May. At the beginning of May, the ledger of Renner showed Cash of $5,000 and Owner's Capital of $5,000.

May	1	Purchased merchandise on account from Braun's Wholesale Supply $4,200, terms 2/10, n/30.
	2	Sold merchandise on account $2,100, terms 1/10, n/30. The cost of the merchandise sold was $1,300.
	5	Received credit from Braun's Wholesale Supply for merchandise returned $300.
	9	Received collections in full, less discounts, from customers billed on sales of $2,100 on May 2.
	10	Paid Braun's Wholesale Supply in full, less discount.
	11	Purchased supplies for cash $400.
	12	Purchased merchandise for cash $1,400.
	15	Received refund for poor quality merchandise from supplier on cash purchase $150.
	17	Purchased merchandise from Valley Distributors $1,300, FOB shipping point, terms 2/10, n/30.
	19	Paid freight on May 17 purchase $130.
	24	Sold merchandise for cash $3,200. The merchandise sold had a cost of $2,000.
	25	Purchased merchandise from Lumley, Inc. $620, FOB destination, terms 2/10, n/30.

27 Paid Valley Distributors in full, less discount.
29 Made refunds to cash customers for defective merchandise $70. The returned merchandise had a fair value of $30.
31 Sold merchandise on account $1,000 terms n/30. The cost of the merchandise sold was $560.

Renner Hardware's chart of accounts includes the following: No. 101 Cash, No. 112 Accounts Receivable, No. 120 Inventory, No. 126 Supplies, No. 201 Accounts Payable, No. 301 Owner's Capital, No. 401 Sales Revenue, No. 412 Sales Returns and Allowances, No. 414 Sales Discounts, and No. 505 Cost of Goods Sold.

Instructions

(a) Journalize the transactions using a perpetual inventory system.

(b) Enter the beginning cash and capital balances and post the transactions. (Use J1 for the journal reference.)

(c) Gross profit $2,379

(c) Prepare an income statement through gross profit for the month of May 2017.

Prepare financial statements and adjusting and closing entries.

(LO 4, 5)

P5-3A Big Box Store is located in midtown Madison. During the past several years, net income has been declining because of suburban shopping centers. At the end of the company's fiscal year on November 30, 2017, the following accounts appeared in two of its trial balances.

	Unadjusted	Adjusted		Unadjusted	Adjusted
Accounts Payable	$ 25,200	$ 25,200	Notes Payable	$ 37,000	$ 37,000
Accounts Receivable	30,500	30,500	Owner's Capital	101,700	101,700
Accumulated Depr.—Equip.	34,000	45,000	Owner's Drawings	10,000	10,000
Cash	26,000	26,000	Prepaid Insurance	10,500	3,500
Cost of Goods Sold	518,000	518,000	Property Tax Expense		2,500
Freight-Out	6,500	6,500	Property Taxes Payable		2,500
Equipment	146,000	146,000	Rent Expense	15,000	15,000
Depreciation Expense		11,000	Salaries and Wages Expense	96,000	96,000
Insurance Expense		7,000	Sales Revenue	720,000	720,000
Interest Expense	6,400	6,400	Sales Commissions Expense	6,500	11,000
Interest Revenue	2,000	2,000	Sales Commissions Payable		4,500
Inventory	32,000	32,000	Sales Returns and Allowances	8,000	8,000
			Utilities Expense	8,500	8,500

Instructions

(a) Net income $32,100
Owner's capital $123,800
Total assets $193,000

(a) Prepare a multiple-step income statement, an owner's equity statement, and a classified balance sheet. Notes payable are due in 2020.

(b) Journalize the adjusting entries that were made.

(c) Journalize the closing entries that are necessary.

Journalize, post, and prepare a trial balance.

(LO 2, 3, 4)

GLS

P5-4A Yolanda Hagen, a former disc golf star, operates Yolanda's Discorama. At the beginning of the current season on April 1, the ledger of Yolanda's Discorama showed Cash $1,800, Inventory $2,500, and Owner's Capital $4,300. The following transactions were completed during April.

Apr. 5 Purchased golf discs, bags, and other inventory on account from Mumford Co. $1,200, FOB shipping point, terms 2/10, n/60.
7 Paid freight on the Mumford purchase $50.
9 Received credit from Mumford Co. for merchandise returned $100.
10 Sold merchandise on account for $900, terms n/30. The merchandise sold had a cost of $540.
12 Purchased disc golf shirts and other accessories on account from Saucer Sportswear $670, terms 1/10, n/30.
14 Paid Mumford Co. in full, less discount.
17 Received credit from Saucer Sportswear for merchandise returned $70.
20 Made sales on account for $610, terms n/30. The cost of the merchandise sold was $370.
21 Paid Saucer Sportswear in full, less discount.
27 Granted an allowance to customers for clothing that was flawed $20.
30 Received payments on account from customers $900.

Instructions

(a) Journalize the April transactions using a periodic inventory system.
(b) Using T-accounts, enter the beginning balances in the ledger accounts and post the April transactions.
(c) Prepare a trial balance on April 30, 2017.
(d) Prepare an income statement through gross profit, assuming merchandise inventory on hand at April 30 is $4,824.

(c) Tot. trial balance $8,376
Gross profit $465

PROBLEMS: SET B AND SET C

Visit the book's companion website, at **www.wiley.com/college/weygandt**, and choose the Student Companion site to access Problems: Set B and Set C.

COMPREHENSIVE PROBLEM

CP5 On December 1, 2017, Rodriguez Distributing Company had the following account balances.

	Debit		Credit
Cash	$ 7,200	Accumulated Depreciation—	
Accounts Receivable	4,600	Equipment	$ 2,200
Inventory	12,000	Accounts Payable	4,500
Supplies	1,200	Salaries and Wages Payable	1,000
Equipment	22,000	Owner's Capital	39,300
	$47,000		$47,000

During December, the company completed the following summary transactions.

Dec.	6	Paid $1,600 for salaries and wages due employees, of which $600 is for December and $1,000 is for November salaries and wages payable.
	8	Received $2,200 cash from customers in payment of account (no discount allowed).
	10	Sold merchandise for cash $6,300. The cost of the merchandise sold was $4,100.
	13	Purchased merchandise on account from Boehm Co. $9,000, terms 2/10, n/30.
	15	Purchased supplies for cash $2,000.
	18	Sold merchandise on account $15,000, terms 3/10, n/30. The cost of the merchandise sold was $10,000.
	20	Paid salaries and wages $1,800.
	23	Paid Boehm Co. in full, less discount.
	27	Received collections in full, less discounts, from customers billed on December 18.

Adjustment data:

1. Accrued salaries and wages payable $840.
2. Depreciation $200 per month.
3. Supplies on hand $1,500.

Instructions

(a) Journalize the December transactions using a perpetual inventory system.
(b) Enter the December 1 balances in the ledger T-accounts and post the December transactions. Use Cost of Goods Sold, Depreciation Expense, Salaries and Wages Expense, Sales Revenue, Sales Discounts, and Supplies Expense.
(c) Journalize and post adjusting entries.
(d) Prepare an adjusted trial balance.
(e) Prepare an income statement and an owner's equity statement for December and a classified balance sheet at December 31.

(d) Totals $68,340
(e) Net income $1,610

CONTINUING PROBLEM

COOKIE CREATIONS: AN ENTREPRENEURIAL JOURNEY

© leungchopan/ Shutterstock

(*Note:* This is a continuation of the Cookie Creations problem from Chapters 1 through 4.)

CC5 Because Natalie has had such a successful first few months, she is considering other opportunities to develop her business. One opportunity is the sale of fine European mixers. The owner of Kzinski Supply Company has approached Natalie to become the exclusive U.S. distributor of these fine mixers. The current cost of a mixer is approximately $525 (U.S.), and Natalie would sell each one for $1,050. Natalie comes to you for advice on how to account for these mixers.

Go to the book's companion website, **www.wiley.com/college/weygandt**, *to see the completion of this problem.*

BROADENING YOUR PERSPECTIVE

FINANCIAL REPORTING AND ANALYSIS

Financial Reporting Problem: Apple Inc.

BYP5-1 The financial statements of Apple Inc. are presented in Appendix A at the end of this textbook. Instructions for accessing and using the company's complete annual report, including the notes to the financial statements, are also provided in Appendix A.

Instructions
Answer the following questions using Apple's Consolidated Statement of Income.

(a) What was the percentage change in (1) sales and in (2) net income from 2011 to 2012 and from 2012 to 2013?
(b) What was the company's gross profit rate in 2011, 2012, and 2013?
(c) What was the company's percentage of net income to net sales in 2011, 2012, and 2013? Comment on any trend in this percentage.

Comparative Analysis Problem: PepsiCo, Inc. vs. The Coca-Cola Company

BYP5-2 PepsiCo's financial statements are presented in Appendix B. Financial statements of The Coca-Cola Company are presented in Appendix C. Instructions for accessing and using the complete annual reports of PepsiCo and Coca-Cola, including the notes to the financial statements, are also provided in Appendices B and C, respectively.

Instructions
(a) Based on the information contained in these financial statements, determine each of the following for each company.
   (1) Gross profit for 2013.
   (2) Gross profit rate for 2013.
   (3) Operating income for 2013.
   (4) Percentage change in operating income from 2012 to 2013.
(b) What conclusions concerning the relative profitability of the two companies can you draw from these data?

Comparative Analysis Problem: Amazon.com, Inc. vs. Wal-Mart Stores, Inc.

BYP5-3 Amazon.com, Inc.'s financial statements are presented in Appendix D. Financial statements of Wal-Mart Stores, Inc. are presented in Appendix E. (Use Wal-Mart's January 31, 2014, financial statements for comparative purposes.) Instructions for accessing and using the complete annual reports of Amazon and Wal-Mart, including the notes to the financial statements, are also provided in Appendices D and E, respectively.

Instructions

(a) Based on the information contained in these financial statements, determine each of the following for each company. Use Amazon's net product sales to compute gross profit information.
   (1) Gross profit for 2013.
   (2) Gross profit rate for 2013.
   (3) Operating income for 2013.
   (4) Percentage change in operating income from 2012 to 2013.

(b) What conclusions concerning the relative profitability of the two companies can you draw from these data?

Real-World Focus

BYP5-4 No financial decision-maker should ever rely solely on the financial information reported in the annual report to make decisions. It is important to keep abreast of financial news. This activity demonstrates how to search for financial news on the Web.

Address: **biz.yahoo.com/i**, or go to **www.wiley.com/college/weygandt**

Steps:

1. Type in either PepsiCo or Coca-Cola.
2. Choose **News**.
3. Select an article that sounds interesting to you.

Instructions

(a) What was the source of the article (e.g., Reuters, Businesswire, PR Newswire)?

(b) Assume that you are a personal financial planner and that one of your clients owns stock in the company. Write a brief memo to your client, summarizing the article and explaining the implications of the article for his or her investment.

CRITICAL THINKING

Decision-Making Across the Organization

BYP5-5 Three years ago, Amy Hessler and her brother-in-law Jacob Seelig opened Family Department Store. For the first two years, business was good, but the following condensed income results for 2016 were disappointing.

FAMILY DEPARTMENT STORE
Income Statement
For the Year Ended December 31, 2016

Net sales		$700,000
Cost of goods sold		553,000
Gross profit		147,000
Operating expenses		
Selling expenses	$100,000	
Administrative expenses	20,000	120,000
Net income		$ 27,000

Amy believes the problem lies in the relatively low gross profit rate (gross profit divided by net sales) of 21%. Jacob believes the problem is that operating expenses are too high.

Amy thinks the gross profit rate can be improved by making both of the following changes. She does not anticipate that these changes will have any effect on operating expenses.

1. Increase average selling prices by 17%. This increase is expected to lower sales volume so that total sales will increase only 6%.
2. Buy merchandise in larger quantities and take all purchase discounts. These changes are expected to increase the gross profit rate by 3 percentage points.

Jacob thinks expenses can be cut by making both of the following changes. He feels that these changes will not have any effect on net sales.

1. Cut sales salaries of $60,000 in half and give sales personnel a commission of 2% of net sales.
2. Reduce store deliveries to one day per week rather than twice a week. This change will reduce delivery expenses of $30,000 by 40%.

Amy and Jacob come to you for help in deciding the best way to improve net income.

Instructions

With the class divided into groups, answer the following.

(a) Prepare a condensed income statement for 2017, assuming (1) Amy's changes are implemented and (2) Jacob's ideas are adopted.

(b) What is your recommendation to Amy and Jacob?

(c) Prepare a condensed income statement for 2017, assuming both sets of proposed changes are made.

Communication Activity

BYP5-6 The following situation is in chronological order.

1. Parker decides to buy a surfboard.
2. He calls Surfing USA Co. to inquire about its surfboards.
3. Two days later, he requests Surfing USA Co. to make a surfboard.
4. Three days later, Surfing USA Co. sends him a purchase order to fill out.
5. He sends back the purchase order.
6. Surfing USA Co. receives the completed purchase order.
7. Surfing USA Co. completes the surfboard.
8. Parker picks up the surfboard.
9. Surfing USA Co. bills Parker.
10. Surfing USA Co. receives payment from Parker.

Instructions

In a memo to the president of Surfing USA Co., answer the following.

(a) When should Surfing USA Co. record the sale?

(b) Suppose that with his purchase order, Parker is required to make a down payment. Would that change your answer?

Ethics Case

BYP5-7 Tiffany Lyons was just hired as the assistant treasurer of Key West Stores. The company is a specialty chain store with nine retail stores concentrated in one metropolitan area. Among other things, the payment of all invoices is centralized in one of the departments Tiffany will manage. Her primary responsibility is to maintain the company's high credit rating by paying all bills when due and to take advantage of all cash discounts.

Jay Barnes, the former assistant treasurer who has been promoted to treasurer, is training Tiffany in her new duties. He instructs Tiffany that she is to continue the practice of preparing all checks "net of discount" and dating the checks the last day of the discount period. "But," Jay continues, "we always hold the checks at least 4 days beyond the discount period before mailing them. That way, we get another 4 days of interest on our money. Most of our creditors need our business and don't complain. And, if they scream about our missing the discount period, we blame it on the mail room or the post office. We've only lost one discount out of every hundred we take that way. I think everybody does it. By the way, welcome to our team!"

Instructions

(a) What are the ethical considerations in this case?

(b) Who are the stakeholders that are harmed or benefitted in this situation?

(c) Should Tiffany continue the practice started by Jay? Does she have any choice?

All About You

BYP5-8 There are many situations in business where it is difficult to determine the proper period in which to record revenue. Suppose that after graduation with a degree in finance, you take a job as a manager at a consumer electronics store called Impact Electronics. The company has expanded rapidly in order to compete with Best Buy. Impact has also begun selling gift cards for its electronic products. The cards are available in any dollar amount and allow the holder of the card to purchase an item for up to 2 years from the time the card is purchased. If the card is not used during that 2 years, it expires.

Instructions

Answer the following questions.

At what point should the revenue from the gift cards be recognized? Should the revenue be recognized at the time the card is sold, or should it be recorded when the card is redeemed? Explain the reasoning to support your answers.

FASB Codification Activity

BYP5-9 If your school has a subscription to the FASB Codification, go to **http://aaahq.org/ascLogin.cfm** to log in and prepare responses to the following.

Instructions

(a) Access the glossary ("Master Glossary") to answer the following:
   (1) What is the definition provided for inventory?
   (2) What is a customer?

(b) What guidance does the Codification provide concerning reporting inventories above cost?

A Look at IFRS

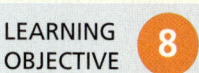

LEARNING OBJECTIVE 8 **Compare the accounting for merchandising under GAAP and IFRS.**

The basic accounting entries for merchandising are the same under both GAAP and IFRS. The income statement is a required statement under both sets of standards. The basic format is similar although some differences do exist.

Key Points

Following are the key similarities and differences between GAAP and IFRS related to inventories.

Similarities

- Under both GAAP and IFRS, a company can choose to use either a perpetual or periodic inventory systems.
- The definition of inventories is basically the same under GAAP and IFRS.
- As indicated above, the basic accounting entries for merchandising are the same under both GAAP and IFRS.
- Both GAAP and IFRS require that income statement information be presented for multiple years. For example, IFRS requires that 2 years of income statement information be presented, whereas GAAP requires 3 years.

Differences

- Under GAAP companies generally classify income statement items by function. Classification by function leads to descriptions like administration, distribution, and manufacturing. Under IFRS, companies must classify expenses either by nature or by function. Classification by nature leads to descriptions such as the following: salaries, depreciation expense, and utilities expense. If a company uses the functional-expense method on the income statement, disclosure by nature is required in the notes to the financial statements.
- Presentation of the income statement under GAAP follows either a single-step or multiple-step format. IFRS does not mention a single-step or multiple-step approach.
- Under IFRS revaluation of land, buildings, and intangible assets is permitted. The initial gains and losses resulting from this revaluation are reported as adjustments to equity, often referred to as **other comprehensive income**. The effect of this difference is that the use of IFRS results in more transactions affecting equity (other comprehensive income) but not net income.

Looking to the Future

The IASB and FASB are working on a project that would rework the structure of financial statements. Specifically, this project will address the issue of how to classify various items in the income statement. A main goal of this new approach is to provide information that better represents how businesses are run. In addition, this approach draws attention away from just one number—net income. It will adopt major groupings similar to those currently used by the statement of cash flows (operating, investing, and financing), so that numbers can be more readily traced across statements. For example, the amount of income that is generated by operations would be traceable to the assets and liabilities used to generate the income. Finally, this approach would also provide detail, beyond that currently seen in most statements (either GAAP or IFRS), by requiring that line items be presented both by function and by nature. The new financial statement format was heavily influenced by suggestions from financial statement analysts.

IFRS Practice

IFRS Self-Test Questions

1. Which of the following would **not** be included in the definition of inventory under IFRS?
   (a) Photocopy paper held for sale by an office-supply store.
   (b) Stereo equipment held for sale by an electronics store.
   (c) Used office equipment held for sale by the human relations department of a plastics company.
   (d) All of the above would meet the definition.
2. Which of the following would **not** be a line item of a company reporting costs by nature?
   (a) Depreciation expense.
   (b) Salaries expense.
   (c) Interest expense.
   (d) Manufacturing expense.
3. Which of the following would **not** be a line item of a company reporting costs by function?
   (a) Administration.
   (b) Manufacturing.
   (c) Utilities expense.
   (d) Distribution.
4. Which of the following statements is **false**?
   (a) IFRS specifically requires use of a multiple-step income statement.
   (b) Under IFRS, companies can use either a perpetual or periodic system.
   (c) The proposed new format for financial statements was heavily influenced by the suggestions of financial statement analysts.
   (d) The new income statement format will try to de-emphasize the focus on the "net income" line item.

IFRS Exercises

IFRS5-1 Explain the difference between the "nature-of-expense" and "function-of-expense" classifications.

IFRS5-2 For each of the following income statement line items, state whether the item is a "by nature" expense item or a "by function" expense item.

_______ Cost of goods sold
_______ Depreciation expense
_______ Salaries and wages expense
_______ Selling expenses
_______ Utilities expense
_______ Delivery expense
_______ General and administrative expenses

IFRS5-3 Matilda Company reported the following amounts (in euros) in 2017: Net income, €150,000; Unrealized gain related to revaluation of buildings, €10,000; and Unrealized loss on non-trading securities, €(35,000). Determine Matilda's total comprehensive income for 2017.

International Financial Reporting Problem: Louis Vuitton

IFRS5-4 The financial statements of Louis Vuitton are presented in Appendix F. Instructions for accessing and using the company's complete annual report, including the notes to its financial statements, are also provided in Appendix F.

Instructions

Use Louis Vuitton's annual report to answer the following questions.

(a) Does Louis Vuitton use a multiple-step or a single-step income statement format? Explain how you made your determination.

(b) Instead of "interest expense," what label does Louis Vuitton use for interest costs that it incurs?

(c) Using the notes to the company's financial statements, determine the following:

(1) Composition of the inventory.

(2) Amount of inventory (gross) before impairment.

Answers to IFRS Self-Test Questions

1. c **2.** d **3.** c **4.** a

6 Inventories

CHAPTER PREVIEW In the previous chapter, we discussed the accounting for merchandise inventory using a perpetual inventory system. In this chapter, we explain the methods used to calculate the cost of inventory on hand at the balance sheet date and the cost of goods sold.

FEATURE STORY

"Where Is That Spare Bulldozer Blade?"

Let's talk inventory—big, bulldozer-size inventory. Caterpillar Inc. is the world's largest manufacturer of construction and mining equipment, diesel and natural gas engines, and industrial gas turbines. It sells its products in over 200 countries, making it one of the most successful U.S. exporters. More than 70% of its productive assets are located domestically, and nearly 50% of its sales are foreign.

In the past, Caterpillar's profitability suffered, but today it is very successful. A big part of this turnaround can be attributed to effective management of its inventory. Imagine what it costs Caterpillar to have too many bulldozers sitting around in inventory—a situation the company definitely wants to avoid. Yet Caterpillar must also make sure it has enough inventory to meet demand.

At one time during a 7-year period, Caterpillar's sales increased by 100% while its inventory increased by only 50%. To achieve this dramatic reduction in the amount of resources tied up in inventory while continuing to meet customers' needs, Caterpillar used a two-pronged approach. First, it completed a factory modernization program, which greatly increased its production efficiency. The program reduced by 60% the amount of inventory the company processes at any one time. It also reduced by an incredible 75% the time it takes to manufacture a part.

Second, Caterpillar dramatically improved its parts distribution system. It ships more than 100,000 items daily from its 23 distribution centers strategically located around the world (10 million square feet of warehouse space—remember, we're talking bulldozers). The company can virtually guarantee that it can get any part to anywhere in the world within 24 hours.

These changes led to record exports, profits, and revenues for Caterpillar. It would seem that things couldn't be better. But industry analysts, as well as the company's managers, thought otherwise. In order to maintain Caterpillar's position as the industry leader, management began another major overhaul of inventory production and inventory management processes. The goal: to cut the number of repairs in half, increase productivity by 20%, and increase inventory turnover by 40%.

In short, Caterpillar's ability to manage its inventory has been a key reason for its past success and will very likely play a huge part in its future profitability as well.

James Porter/Workbook/Getty Images, Inc.

CHAPTER OUTLINE

Learning Objectives

Learning Objective	Topics	DO IT!
1 Discuss how to classify and determine inventory.	• Classifying inventory • Determining inventory quantities	DO IT! 1 Rules of Ownership
2 Apply inventory cost flow methods and discuss their financial effects.	• Specific identification • Cost flow assumptions • Financial statement and tax effects • Using cost flow methods consistently	DO IT! 2 Cost Flow Methods
3 Indicate the effects of inventory errors on the financial statements.	• Income statement effects • Balance sheet effects	DO IT! 3 Inventory Errors
4 Explain the statement presentation and analysis of inventory.	• Presentation • Lower-of-cost-or-market • Analysis	DO IT! 4 LCM and Inventory Turnover

Go to the ***REVIEW AND PRACTICE*** section at the end of the chapter for a review of key concepts and practice applications with solutions.

Visit **WileyPLUS with ORION** for additional tutorials and practice opportunities.

LEARNING OBJECTIVE 1

Discuss how to classify and determine inventory.

Two important steps in the reporting of inventory at the end of the accounting period are the classification of inventory based on its degree of completeness and the determination of inventory amounts.

Classifying Inventory

How a company classifies its inventory depends on whether the firm is a merchandiser or a manufacturer. In a **merchandising** company, such as those described in Chapter 5, inventory consists of many different items. For example, in a grocery store, canned goods, dairy products, meats, and produce are just a few of the inventory items on hand. These items have two common characteristics: (1) they are owned by the company, and (2) they are in a form ready for sale to customers in the ordinary course of business. Thus, merchandisers need only one inventory classification, **merchandise inventory**, to describe the many different items that make up the total inventory.

In a **manufacturing** company, some inventory may not yet be ready for sale. As a result, manufacturers usually classify inventory into three categories: finished goods, work in process, and raw materials. **Finished goods inventory** is manufactured items that are completed and ready for sale. **Work in process** is that portion of manufactured inventory that has been placed into the production process but is not yet complete. **Raw materials** are the basic goods that will be used in production but have not yet been placed into production.

Helpful Hint
Regardless of the classification, companies report all inventories under Current Assets on the balance sheet.

For example, Caterpillar classifies earth-moving tractors completed and ready for sale as **finished goods**. It classifies the tractors on the assembly line in various stages of production as **work in process**. The steel, glass, tires, and other components that are on hand waiting to be used in the production of tractors are identified as **raw materials**. Illustration 6-1 shows an adapted excerpt from Note 7 of Caterpillar's annual report.

Illustration 6-1
Composition of Caterpillar's inventory

	December 31		
(millions of dollars)	**2013**	**2012**	**2011**
Raw materials	$ 2,966	$ 3,573	$ 3,766
Work-in-process	2,589	2,920	2,959
Finished goods	6,785	8,767	7,562
Other	285	287	257
Total inventories	**$12,625**	**$15,547**	**$14,544**

By observing the levels and changes in the levels of these three inventory types, financial statement users can gain insight into management's production plans. For example, low levels of raw materials and high levels of finished goods suggest that management believes it has enough inventory on hand and production will be slowing down—perhaps in anticipation of a recession. Conversely, high levels of raw materials and low levels of finished goods probably signal that management is planning to step up production.

Many companies have significantly lowered inventory levels and costs using **just-in-time (JIT) inventory** methods. Under a just-in-time method, companies manufacture or purchase goods only when needed for use. Dell is famous for having developed a system for making computers in response to individual customer requests. Even though it makes each computer to meet each customer's particular specifications, Dell is able to assemble the computer and put it on a truck in less than 48 hours. The success of the JIT system depends on reliable suppliers. By integrating its information systems with those of its suppliers, Dell reduced its inventories to nearly zero. This is a huge advantage in an industry where products become obsolete nearly overnight.

The accounting concepts discussed in this chapter apply to the inventory classifications of both merchandising and manufacturing companies. Our focus here is on merchandise inventory. Additional issues specific to manufacturing companies are discussed later in the managerial section of this textbook (Chapters 19–26).

Accounting Across the Organization — Ford

© PeskyMonkey/iStockphoto

A Big Hiccup

JIT can save a company a lot of money, but it isn't without risk. An unexpected disruption in the supply chain can cost a company a lot of money. Japanese automakers experienced just such a disruption when a 6.8-magnitude earthquake caused major damage to the company that produces 50% of their piston rings. The rings themselves cost only $1.50, but you can't make a car without them. As a result, the automakers were forced to shut down production for a few days—a loss of tens of thousands of cars.

Similarly, a major snowstorm halted production at the Canadian plants of Ford. A Ford spokesperson said, "Because the plants run with just-in-time inventory, we don't have large stockpiles of parts sitting around. When you have a somewhat significant disruption, you can pretty quickly run out of parts."

Sources: Amy Chozick, "A Key Strategy of Japan's Car Makers Backfires," *Wall Street Journal* (July 20, 2007); and Kate Linebaugh, "Canada Military Evacuates Motorists Stranded by Snow," *Wall Street Journal* (December 15, 2010).

What steps might the companies take to avoid such a serious disruption in the future? (Go to **WileyPLUS** for this answer and additional questions.)

Determining Inventory Quantities

No matter whether they are using a periodic or perpetual inventory system, all companies need to determine inventory quantities at the end of the accounting period. If using a perpetual system, companies take a physical inventory for the following reasons:

1. To check the accuracy of their perpetual inventory records.
2. To determine the amount of inventory lost due to wasted raw materials, shoplifting, or employee theft.

Companies using a periodic inventory system take a physical inventory for **two different purposes**: to determine the inventory on hand at the balance sheet date, and to determine the cost of goods sold for the period.

Determining inventory quantities involves two steps: (1) taking a physical inventory of goods on hand and (2) determining the ownership of goods.

ETHICS NOTE

In a famous fraud, a salad oil company filled its storage tanks mostly with water. The oil rose to the top, so auditors thought the tanks were full of oil. The company also said it had more tanks than it really did: It repainted numbers on the tanks to confuse auditors.

TAKING A PHYSICAL INVENTORY

Companies take a physical inventory at the end of the accounting period. Taking a physical inventory involves actually counting, weighing, or measuring each kind of inventory on hand. In many companies, taking an inventory is a formidable task. Retailers such as Target, True Value Hardware, or Home Depot have thousands of different inventory items. An inventory count is generally more accurate when goods are not being sold or received during the counting. Consequently, companies often "take inventory" when the business is closed or when business is slow. Many retailers close early on a chosen day in January—after the holiday sales and returns, when inventories are at their lowest level—to count inventory. **Wal-Mart Stores, Inc.**, for example, has a year-end of January 31.

Ethics Insight Leslie Fay

© Greg Brookes/iStockphoto

Falsifying Inventory to Boost Income

Managers at women's apparel maker Leslie Fay were convicted of falsifying inventory records to boost net income—and consequently to boost management bonuses. In another case, executives at Craig Consumer Electronics were accused of defrauding lenders by manipulating inventory records. The indictment said the company classified "defective goods as new or refurbished" and claimed that it owned certain shipments "from overseas suppliers" when, in fact, Craig either did not own the shipments or the shipments did not exist.

What effect does an overstatement of inventory have on a company's financial statements? (Go to **WileyPLUS** for this answer and additional questions.)

DETERMINING OWNERSHIP OF GOODS

One challenge in computing inventory quantities is determining what inventory a company owns. To determine ownership of goods, two questions must be answered: Do all of the goods included in the count belong to the company? Does the company own any goods that were not included in the count?

GOODS IN TRANSIT A complication in determining ownership is **goods in transit** (on board a truck, train, ship, or plane) at the end of the period. The company may have purchased goods that have not yet been received, or it may have sold goods that have not yet been delivered. To arrive at an accurate count, the company must determine ownership of these goods.

Goods in transit should be included in the inventory of the company that has legal title to the goods. Legal title is determined by the terms of the sale, as shown in Illustration 6-2 and described below.

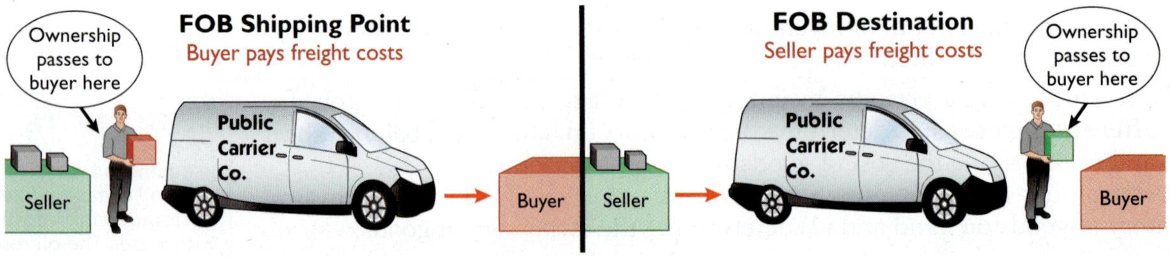

Illustration 6-2
Terms of sale

1. When the terms are **FOB (free on board) shipping point**, ownership of the goods passes to the buyer when the public carrier accepts the goods from the seller.

2. When the terms are **FOB destination**, ownership of the goods remains with the seller until the goods reach the buyer.

If goods in transit at the statement date are ignored, inventory quantities may be seriously miscounted. Assume, for example, that Hargrove Company has 20,000 units of inventory on hand on December 31. It also has the following goods in transit:

1. Sales of 1,500 units shipped December 31 FOB destination.
2. Purchases of 2,500 units shipped FOB shipping point by the seller on December 31.

Hargrove has legal title to both the 1,500 units sold and the 2,500 units purchased. If the company ignores the units in transit, it would understate inventory quantities by 4,000 units (1,500 + 2,500).

As we will see later in the chapter, inaccurate inventory counts affect not only the inventory amount shown on the balance sheet but also the cost of goods sold calculation on the income statement.

CONSIGNED GOODS In some lines of business, it is common to hold the goods of other parties and try to sell the goods for them for a fee, but without taking ownership of the goods. These are called **consigned goods**.

For example, you might have a used car that you would like to sell. If you take the item to a dealer, the dealer might be willing to put the car on its lot and charge you a commission if it is sold. Under this agreement, the dealer **would not take ownership** of the car, which would still belong to you. Therefore, if an inventory count were taken, the car would not be included in the dealer's inventory because the dealer does not own it.

Many car, boat, and antique dealers sell goods on consignment to keep their inventory costs down and to avoid the risk of purchasing an item that they will not be able to sell. Today, even some manufacturers are making consignment agreements with their suppliers in order to keep their inventory levels low.

ANATOMY OF A FRAUD

Ted Nickerson, CEO of clock manufacturer Dally Industries, was feared by all of his employees. Ted also had expensive tastes. To support this habit, Ted took out large loans, which he collateralized with his shares of Dally Industries stock. If the price of Dally's stock fell, he was required to provide the bank with more shares of stock. To achieve target net income figures and thus maintain the stock price, Ted coerced employees in the company to alter inventory figures. Inventory quantities were manipulated by changing the amounts on inventory control tags after the year-end physical inventory count. For example, if a tag said there were 20 units of a particular item, the tag was changed to 220. Similarly, the unit costs that were used to determine the value of ending inventory were increased from, for example, $125 per unit to $1,250. Both of these fraudulent changes had the effect of increasing the amount of reported ending inventory. This reduced cost of goods sold and increased net income.

Total take: $245,000

THE MISSING CONTROL

Independent internal verification. The company should have spot-checked its inventory records periodically, verifying that the number of units in the records agreed with the amount on hand and that the unit costs agreed with vendor price sheets.

Source: Adapted from Wells, *Fraud Casebook* (2007), pp. 502–509.

DO IT! 1 Rules of Ownership

Hasbeen Company completed its inventory count. It arrived at a total inventory value of $200,000. As a new member of Hasbeen's accounting department, you have been given the information listed below. Discuss how this information affects the reported cost of inventory.

1. Hasbeen included in the inventory goods held on consignment for Falls Co., costing $15,000.
2. The company did not include in the count purchased goods of $10,000 which were in transit (terms: FOB shipping point).
3. The company did not include in the count sold inventory with a cost of $12,000 which was in transit (terms: FOB shipping point).

Action Plan

- ✔ Apply the rules of ownership to goods held on consignment.
- ✔ Apply the rules of ownership to goods in transit.

Solution

The goods of $15,000 held on consignment should be deducted from the inventory count. The goods of $10,000 purchased FOB shipping point should be added to the inventory count. Sold goods of $12,000 which were in transit FOB shipping point should not be included in the ending inventory. Thus, inventory should be carried at $195,000 ($200,000 − $15,000 + $10,000).

Related exercise material: **BE6-1, BE6-2, E6-1, E6-2, and DO IT! 6-1.**

LEARNING OBJECTIVE 2 Apply inventory cost flow methods and discuss their financial effects.

Inventory is accounted for at cost. Cost includes all expenditures necessary to acquire goods and place them in a condition ready for sale. For example, freight costs incurred to acquire inventory are added to the cost of inventory, but the cost of shipping goods to a customer are a selling expense.

After a company has determined the quantity of units of inventory, it applies unit costs to the quantities to compute the total cost of the inventory and the cost of goods sold. This process can be complicated if a company has purchased inventory items at different times and at different prices.

For example, assume that Crivitz TV Company purchases three identical 50-inch TVs on different dates at costs of $720, $750, and $800. During the year, Crivitz sold two sets at $1,200 each. These facts are summarized in Illustration 6-3.

Illustration 6-3
Data for inventory costing example

Purchases			
February 3	1 TV	at	$720
March 5	1 TV	at	$750
May 22	1 TV	at	$800
Sales			
June 1	2 TVs	for	$2,400 ($1,200 × 2)

Cost of goods sold will differ depending on which two TVs the company sold. For example, it might be $1,470 ($720 + $750), or $1,520 ($720 + $800), or $1,550 ($750 + $800). In this section, we discuss alternative costing methods available to Crivitz.

Specific Identification

If Crivitz can positively identify which particular units it sold and which are still in ending inventory, it can use the **specific identification method** of inventory costing. For example, if Crivitz sold the TVs it purchased on February 3 and May 22, then its cost of goods sold is $1,520 ($720 + $800), and its ending inventory is $750 (see Illustration 6-4). Using this method, companies can accurately determine ending inventory and cost of goods sold.

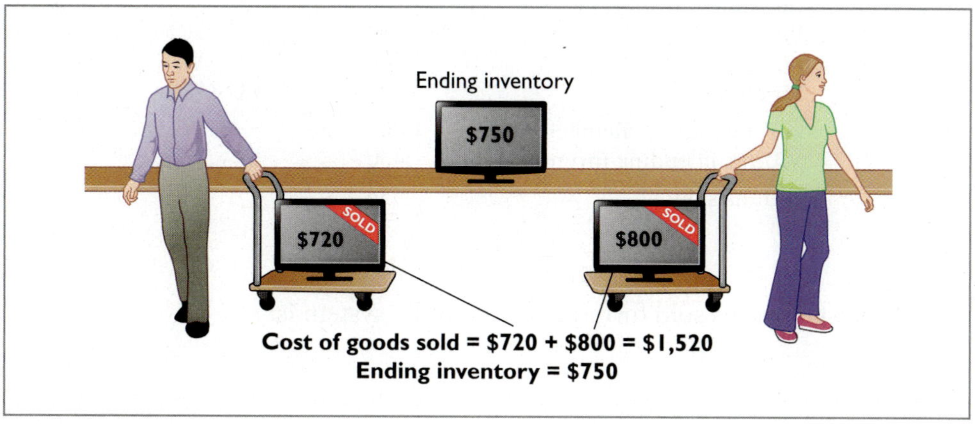

Illustration 6-4
Specific identification method

Specific identification requires that companies keep records of the original cost of each individual inventory item. Historically, specific identification was possible only when a company sold a limited variety of high-unit-cost items that could be identified clearly from the time of purchase through the time of sale. Examples of such products are cars, pianos, or expensive antiques.

Today, bar coding, electronic product codes, and radio frequency identification make it theoretically possible to do specific identification with nearly any type of product. The reality is, however, that this practice is still relatively rare. Instead, rather than keep track of the cost of each particular item sold, most companies make assumptions, called **cost flow assumptions**, about which units were sold.

ETHICS NOTE

A major disadvantage of the specific identification method is that management may be able to manipulate net income. For example, it can boost net income by selling units purchased at a low cost, or reduce net income by selling units purchased at a high cost.

Cost Flow Assumptions

Because specific identification is often impractical, other cost flow methods are permitted. These differ from specific identification in that they **assume** flows of costs that may be unrelated to the physical flow of goods. There are three assumed cost flow methods:

1. First-in, first-out (FIFO)
2. Last-in, first-out (LIFO)
3. Average-cost

There is no accounting requirement that the cost flow assumption be consistent with the physical movement of the goods. Company management selects the appropriate cost flow method.

To demonstrate the three cost flow methods, we will use a **periodic** inventory system. We assume a periodic system because **very few companies use perpetual LIFO, FIFO, or average-cost** to cost their inventory and related cost of goods sold. Instead, companies that use perpetual systems often use an assumed cost (called a standard cost) to record cost of goods sold at the time of sale. Then, at the end of the period when they count their inventory, they **recalculate cost**

of goods sold using periodic FIFO, LIFO, or average-cost as shown in this chapter and adjust cost of goods sold to this recalculated number.[1]

To illustrate the three inventory cost flow methods, we will use the data for Houston Electronics' Astro condensers, shown in Illustration 6-5.

Illustration 6-5
Data for Houston Electronics

HOUSTON ELECTRONICS
Astro Condensers

Date	Explanation	Units	Unit Cost	Total Cost
Jan. 1	Beginning inventory	100	$10	$ 1,000
Apr. 15	Purchase	200	11	2,200
Aug. 24	Purchase	300	12	3,600
Nov. 27	Purchase	400	13	5,200
	Total units available for sale	1,000		$12,000
	Units in ending inventory	450		
	Units sold	550		

The cost of goods sold formula in a periodic system is:

(Beginning Inventory + Purchases) − Ending Inventory = Cost of Goods Sold

Houston Electronics had a total of 1,000 units available to sell during the period (beginning inventory plus purchases). The total cost of these 1,000 units is $12,000, referred to as **cost of goods available for sale**. A physical inventory taken at December 31 determined that there were 450 units in ending inventory. Therefore, Houston sold 550 units (1,000 − 450) during the period. To determine the cost of the 550 units that were sold (the cost of goods sold), we assign a cost to the ending inventory and subtract that value from the cost of goods available for sale. The value assigned to the ending inventory **will depend on which cost flow method we use**. No matter which cost flow assumption we use, though, the sum of cost of goods sold plus the cost of the ending inventory must equal the cost of goods available for sale—in this case, $12,000.

FIRST-IN, FIRST-OUT (FIFO)

The **first-in, first-out (FIFO) method** assumes that the **earliest goods** purchased are the first to be sold. FIFO often parallels the actual physical flow of merchandise. That is, it generally is good business practice to sell the oldest units first. Under the FIFO method, therefore, the **costs** of the earliest goods purchased are the first to be recognized in determining cost of goods sold. (This does not necessarily mean that the oldest units **are** sold first, but that the costs of the oldest units are **recognized** first. In a bin of picture hangers at the hardware store, for example, no one really knows, nor would it matter, which hangers are sold first.) Illustration 6-6 shows the allocation of the cost of goods available for sale at Houston Electronics under FIFO.

[1]Also, some companies use a perpetual system to keep track of units, but they do not make an entry for perpetual cost of goods sold. In addition, firms that employ LIFO tend to use **dollar-value LIFO**, a method discussed in upper-level courses. FIFO periodic and FIFO perpetual give the same result. Therefore, companies should not incur the additional cost to use FIFO perpetual. Few companies use perpetual average-cost because of the added cost of recordkeeping. Finally, for instructional purposes, we believe it is easier to demonstrate the cost flow assumptions under the periodic system, which makes it more pedagogically appropriate.

Illustration 6-6
Allocation of costs—FIFO method

COST OF GOODS AVAILABLE FOR SALE

Date	Explanation	Units	Unit Cost	Total Cost
Jan. 1	Beginning inventory	100	$10	$ 1,000
Apr. 15	Purchase	200	11	2,200
Aug. 24	Purchase	300	12	3,600
Nov. 27	Purchase	400	13	5,200
	Total	1,000		**$12,000**

STEP 1: ENDING INVENTORY

Date	Units	Unit Cost	Total Cost
Nov. 27	400	$13	$ 5,200
Aug. 24	50	12	600
Total	450		**$5,800**

STEP 2: COST OF GOODS SOLD

Cost of goods available for sale	$12,000
Less: Ending inventory	5,800
Cost of goods sold	**$ 6,200**

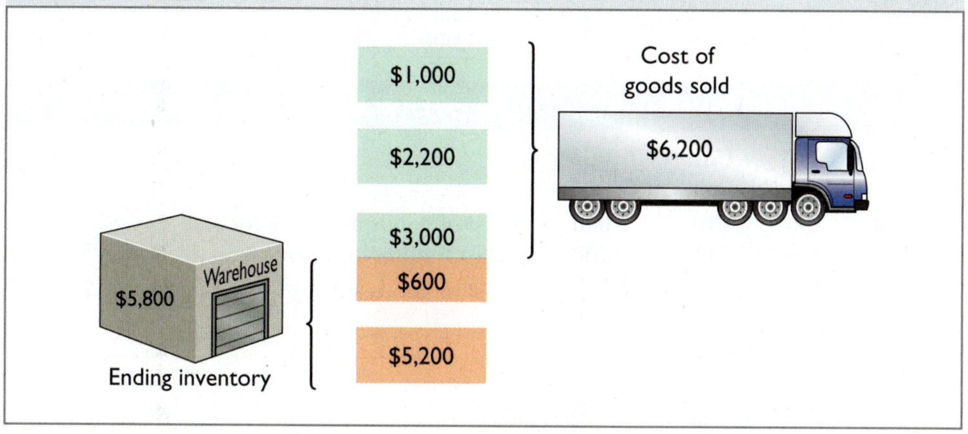

Helpful Hint
Note the sequencing of the allocation: (1) compute ending inventory, and (2) determine cost of goods sold.

Helpful Hint
Another way of thinking about the calculation of FIFO ending inventory is the **LISH assumption**—last in still here.

Under FIFO, since it is assumed that the first goods purchased were the first goods sold, ending inventory is based on the prices of the most recent units purchased. That is, **under FIFO, companies obtain the cost of the ending inventory by taking the unit cost of the most recent purchase and working backward until all units of inventory have been costed.** In this example, Houston Electronics prices the 450 units of ending inventory using the **most recent** prices. The last purchase was 400 units at $13 on November 27. The remaining 50 units are priced using the unit cost of the second most recent purchase, $12, on August 24. Next, Houston Electronics calculates cost of goods sold by subtracting the cost of the units **not sold** (ending inventory) from the cost of all goods available for sale.

Illustration 6-7 demonstrates that companies also can calculate cost of goods sold by pricing the 550 units sold using the prices of the first 550 units acquired. Note that of the 300 units purchased on August 24, only 250 units are assumed sold. This agrees with our calculation of the cost of ending inventory, where 50 of these units were assumed unsold and thus included in ending inventory.

Illustration 6-7
Proof of cost of goods sold

Date	Units	Unit Cost	Total Cost
Jan. 1	100	$10	$ 1,000
Apr. 15	200	11	2,200
Aug. 24	250	12	3,000
Total	550		**$6,200**

LAST-IN, FIRST-OUT (LIFO)

The **last-in, first-out (LIFO) method** assumes that the **latest goods** purchased are the first to be sold. LIFO seldom coincides with the actual physical flow of inventory. (Exceptions include goods stored in piles, such as coal or hay, where goods are removed from the top of the pile as they are sold.) Under the LIFO method, the **costs** of the latest goods purchased are the first to be recognized in determining cost of goods sold. Illustration 6-8 shows the allocation of the cost of goods available for sale at Houston Electronics under LIFO.

Illustration 6-8
Allocation of costs—LIFO method

COST OF GOODS AVAILABLE FOR SALE

Date	Explanation	Units	Unit Cost	Total Cost
Jan. 1	Beginning inventory	100	$10	$ 1,000
Apr. 15	Purchase	200	11	2,200
Aug. 24	Purchase	300	12	3,600
Nov. 27	Purchase	400	13	5,200
	Total	1,000		**$12,000**

STEP 1: ENDING INVENTORY

Date	Units	Unit Cost	Total Cost
Jan. 1	100	$10	$ 1,000
Apr. 15	200	11	2,200
Aug. 24	150	12	1,800
Total	450		**$5,000**

STEP 2: COST OF GOODS SOLD

Cost of goods available for sale	$12,000
Less: Ending inventory	5,000
Cost of goods sold	**$ 7,000**

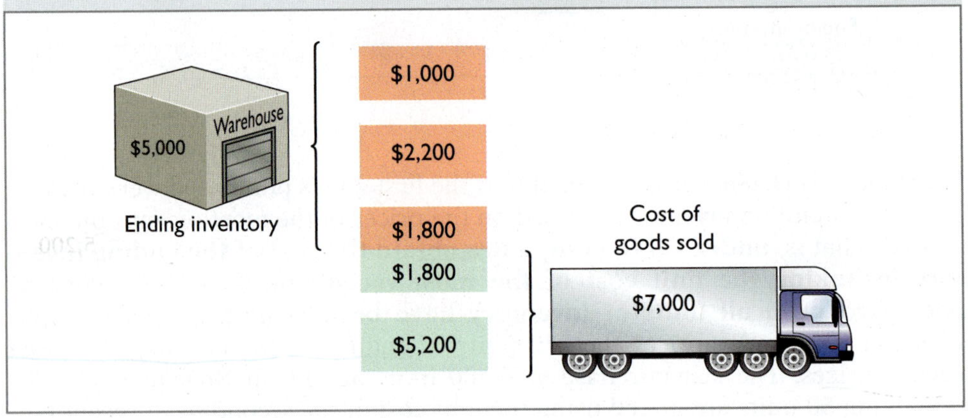

Helpful Hint
Another way of thinking about the calculation of LIFO ending inventory is the **FISH assumption**—first in still here.

Under LIFO, since it is assumed that the first goods sold were those that were most recently purchased, ending inventory is based on the prices of the oldest units purchased. That is, **under LIFO, companies obtain the cost of the ending inventory by taking the unit cost of the earliest goods available for sale and working forward until all units of inventory have been costed**. In this example, Houston Electronics prices the 450 units of ending inventory using the **earliest** prices. The first purchase was 100 units at $10 in the January 1 beginning inventory. Then, 200 units were purchased at $11. The remaining 150 units needed are priced at $12 per unit (August 24 purchase). Next, Houston Electronics calculates cost of goods sold by subtracting the cost of the units **not sold** (ending inventory) from the cost of all goods available for sale.

Illustration 6-9 demonstrates that companies also can calculate cost of goods sold by pricing the 550 units sold using the prices of the last 550 units acquired. Note that of the 300 units purchased on August 24, only 150 units are assumed sold. This agrees with our calculation of the cost of ending inventory, where 150 of these units were assumed unsold and thus included in ending inventory.

Date	Units	Unit Cost	Total Cost
Nov. 27	400	$13	$5,200
Aug. 24	150	12	1,800
Total	550		$7,000

Illustration 6-9
Proof of cost of goods sold

Under a periodic inventory system, which we are using here, **all goods purchased during the period are assumed to be available for the first sale, regardless of the date of purchase**.

AVERAGE-COST

The **average-cost method** allocates the cost of goods available for sale on the basis of the **weighted-average unit cost** incurred. The average-cost method assumes that goods are similar in nature. Illustration 6-10 presents the formula and a sample computation of the weighted-average unit cost.

Cost of Goods Available for Sale	÷	Total Units Available for Sale	=	Weighted-Average Unit Cost
$12,000	÷	1,000	=	$12

Illustration 6-10
Formula for weighted-average unit cost

The company then applies the weighted-average unit cost to the units on hand to determine the cost of the ending inventory. Illustration 6-11 shows the allocation of the cost of goods available for sale at Houston Electronics using average-cost.

Illustration 6-11
Allocation of costs—average-cost method

COST OF GOODS AVAILABLE FOR SALE

Date	Explanation	Units	Unit Cost	Total Cost
Jan. 1	Beginning inventory	100	$10	$ 1,000
Apr. 15	Purchase	200	11	2,200
Aug. 24	Purchase	300	12	3,600
Nov. 27	Purchase	400	13	5,200
	Total	1,000		$12,000

STEP 1: ENDING INVENTORY

$12,000 ÷ 1,000 = $12

Units	Unit Cost	Total Cost
450	$12	$5,400

STEP 2: COST OF GOODS SOLD

Cost of goods available for sale	$12,000
Less: Ending inventory	5,400
Cost of goods sold	$ 6,600

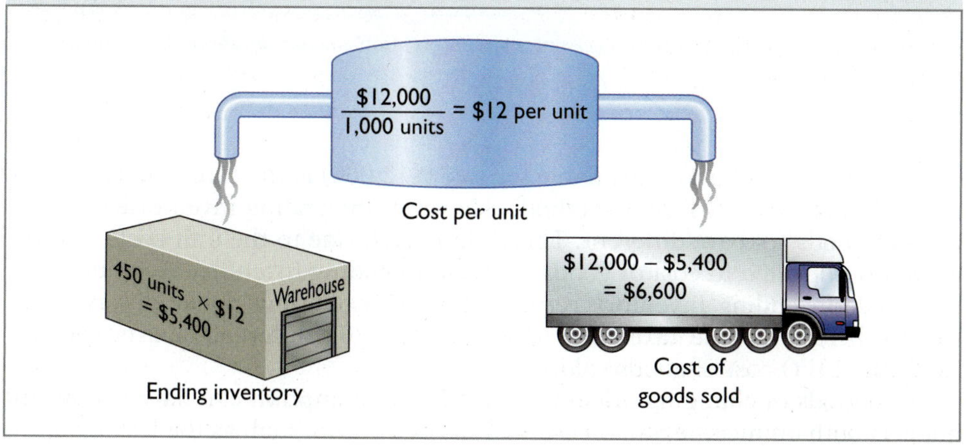

We can verify the cost of goods sold under this method by multiplying the units sold times the weighted-average unit cost (550 × $12 = $6,600). Note that this method does **not** use the average of the unit costs. That average is $11.50 ($10 + $11 + $12 + $13 = $46; $46 ÷ 4). The average-cost method instead uses the average **weighted by** the quantities purchased at each unit cost.

Financial Statement and Tax Effects of Cost Flow Methods

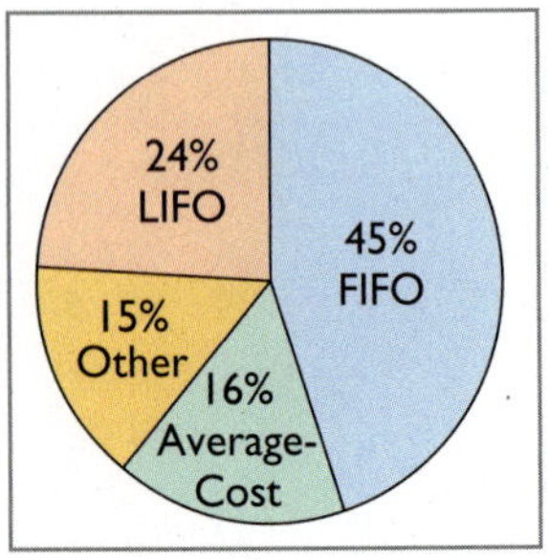

Illustration 6-12
Use of cost flow methods in major U.S. companies

Each of the three assumed cost flow methods is acceptable for use. For example, Reebok International Ltd. and Wendy's International currently use the FIFO method of inventory costing. Campbell Soup Company, Kroger, and Walgreen Drugs use LIFO for part or all of their inventory. Bristol-Myers Squibb, Starbucks, and Motorola use the average-cost method. In fact, a company may also use more than one cost flow method at the same time. Stanley Black & Decker Manufacturing Company, for example, uses LIFO for domestic inventories and FIFO for foreign inventories. Illustration 6-12 (in the margin) shows the use of the three cost flow methods in 500 large U.S. companies.

The reasons companies adopt different inventory cost flow methods are varied, but they usually involve one of three factors: (1) income statement effects, (2) balance sheet effects, or (3) tax effects.

INCOME STATEMENT EFFECTS

To understand why companies might choose a particular cost flow method, let's examine the effects of the different cost flow assumptions on the financial statements of Houston Electronics. The condensed income statements in Illustration 6-13 assume that Houston sold its 550 units for $18,500, had operating expenses of $9,000, and is subject to an income tax rate of 30%.

Illustration 6-13
Comparative effects of cost flow methods

HOUSTON ELECTRONICS
Condensed Income Statements

	FIFO	LIFO	Average-Cost
Sales revenue	$18,500	$18,500	$18,500
Beginning inventory	1,000	1,000	1,000
Purchases	11,000	11,000	11,000
Cost of goods available for sale	12,000	12,000	12,000
Ending inventory	**5,800**	**5,000**	**5,400**
Cost of goods sold	6,200	7,000	6,600
Gross profit	12,300	11,500	11,900
Operating expenses	9,000	9,000	9,000
Income before income taxes*	3,300	2,500	2,900
Income tax expense (30%)	990	750	870
Net income	**$ 2,310**	**$ 1,750**	**$ 2,030**

*We are assuming that Houston Electronics is a corporation, and corporations are required to pay income taxes.

Note the cost of goods available for sale ($12,000) is the same under each of the three inventory cost flow methods. However, the ending inventories and the costs of goods sold are different. This difference is due to the unit costs that the company allocated to cost of goods sold and to ending inventory. Each dollar of difference in ending inventory results in a corresponding dollar difference in income before income taxes. For Houston, an $800 difference exists between FIFO and LIFO cost of goods sold.

In periods of changing prices, the cost flow assumption can have significant impacts both on income and on evaluations of income, such as the following.

1. In a period of inflation, FIFO produces a higher net income because lower unit costs of the first units purchased are matched against revenue.
2. In a period of inflation, LIFO produces a lower net income because higher unit costs of the last goods purchased are matched against revenue.
3. If prices are falling, the results from the use of FIFO and LIFO are reversed. FIFO will report the lowest net income and LIFO the highest.
4. Regardless of whether prices are rising or falling, average-cost produces net income between FIFO and LIFO.

As shown in the Houston example (Illustration 6-13), in a period of rising prices FIFO reports the highest net income ($2,310) and LIFO the lowest ($1,750); average-cost falls between these two amounts ($2,030).

To management, higher net income is an advantage. It causes external users to view the company more favorably. In addition, management bonuses, if based on net income, will be higher. Therefore, when prices are rising (which is usually the case), companies tend to prefer FIFO because it results in higher net income.

Others believe that LIFO presents a more realistic net income number. That is, LIFO matches the more recent costs against current revenues to provide a better measure of net income. During periods of inflation, many challenge the quality of non-LIFO earnings, noting that failing to match current costs against current revenues leads to an understatement of cost of goods sold and an overstatement of net income. As some indicate, net income computed using FIFO creates **"paper or phantom profits"**—that is, earnings that do not really exist.

BALANCE SHEET EFFECTS

A major advantage of the FIFO method is that in a period of inflation, the costs allocated to ending inventory will approximate their current cost. For example, for Houston Electronics, 400 of the 450 units in the ending inventory are costed under FIFO at the higher November 27 unit cost of $13.

Conversely, a major shortcoming of the LIFO method is that in a period of inflation, the costs allocated to ending inventory may be significantly understated in terms of current cost. The understatement becomes greater over prolonged periods of inflation if the inventory includes goods purchased in one or more prior accounting periods. For example, Caterpillar has used LIFO for more than 50 years. Its balance sheet shows ending inventory of $12,625 million. But the inventory's actual current cost if FIFO had been used is $15,129 million.

TAX EFFECTS

We have seen that both inventory on the balance sheet and net income on the income statement are higher when companies use FIFO in a period of inflation. Yet, many companies have selected LIFO. Why? The reason is that LIFO results in the lowest income taxes (because of lower net income) during times of rising prices. For example, at Houston Electronics, income taxes are $750 under LIFO, compared to $990 under FIFO. The tax savings of $240 makes more cash available for use in the business.

Helpful Hint
A tax rule, often referred to as the **LIFO conformity rule**, requires that if companies use LIFO for tax purposes they must also use it for financial reporting purposes. This means that if a company chooses the LIFO method to reduce its tax bills, it will also have to report lower net income in its financial statements.

Using Inventory Cost Flow Methods Consistently

Whatever cost flow method a company chooses, it should use that method consistently from one accounting period to another. This approach is often referred to as the **consistency concept**, which means that a company uses the same accounting principles and methods from year to year. Consistent application enhances the comparability of financial statements over successive time periods. In contrast, using the FIFO method one year and the LIFO method the next year would make it difficult to compare the net incomes of the two years.

Although consistent application is preferred, it does not mean that a company may never change its inventory costing method. When a company adopts a different method, it should disclose in the financial statements the change and its effects on net income. Illustration 6-14 shows a typical disclosure, using information from recent financial statements of **Quaker Oats** (now a unit of **PepsiCo**).

Illustration 6-14
Disclosure of change in cost flow method

Real World

QUAKER OATS
Notes to the Financial Statements

Note 1: Effective July 1, the Company adopted the LIFO cost flow assumption for valuing the majority of U.S. Grocery Products inventories. The Company believes that the use of the LIFO method better matches current costs with current revenues. The effect of this change on the current year was to decrease net income by $16.0 million.

International Insight — ExxonMobil Corporation

Bloomberg/Getty Images

Is LIFO Fair?

ExxonMobil Corporation, like many U.S. companies, uses LIFO to value its inventory for financial reporting and tax purposes. In one recent year, this resulted in a cost of goods sold figure that was $5.6 billion higher than under FIFO. By increasing cost of goods sold, ExxonMobil reduces net income, which reduces taxes. Critics say that LIFO provides an unfair "tax dodge." As Congress looks for more sources of tax revenue, some lawmakers favor the elimination of LIFO. Supporters of LIFO argue that the method is conceptually sound because it matches current costs with current revenues. In addition, they point out that this matching provides protection against inflation.

International accounting standards do not allow the use of LIFO. Because of this, the net income of foreign oil companies such as BP and Royal Dutch Shell are not directly comparable to U.S. companies, which makes analysis difficult.

Source: David Reilly, "Big Oil's Accounting Methods Fuel Criticism," *Wall Street Journal* (August 8, 2006), p. C1.

What are the arguments for and against the use of LIFO? (Go to **WileyPLUS** for this answer and additional questions.)

DO IT! 2 Cost Flow Methods

The accounting records of Shumway Ag Implements show the following data.

Beginning inventory	4,000 units at $ 3
Purchases	6,000 units at $ 4
Sales	7,000 units at $12

Determine the cost of goods sold during the period under a periodic inventory system using (a) the FIFO method, (b) the LIFO method, and (c) the average-cost method.

Action Plan
- ✔ Understand the periodic inventory system.
- ✔ Allocate costs between goods sold and goods on hand (ending inventory) for each cost flow method.
- ✔ Compute cost of goods sold for each method.

Solution

Cost of goods available for sale = (4,000 × $3) + (6,000 × $4) = $36,000
Ending inventory = 10,000 − 7,000 = 3,000 units

(a) FIFO: $36,000 − (3,000 × $4) = $24,000

(b) LIFO: $36,000 − (3,000 × $3) = $27,000

(c) Average cost per unit: [(4,000 @ $3) + (6,000 @ $4)] ÷ 10,000 = $3.60
Average-cost: $36,000 − (3,000 × $3.60) = $25,200

Related exercise material: **BE6-3, BE6-4, BE6-5, E6-3, E6-4, E6-5, E6-6, E6-7, E6-8, and DO IT! 6-2.**

LEARNING OBJECTIVE 3

Indicate the effects of inventory errors on the financial statements.

Unfortunately, errors occasionally occur in accounting for inventory. In some cases, errors are caused by failure to count or price the inventory correctly. In other cases, errors occur because companies do not properly recognize the transfer of legal title to goods that are in transit. When errors occur, they affect both the income statement and the balance sheet.

Income Statement Effects

Under a periodic inventory system, both the beginning and ending inventories appear in the income statement. The ending inventory of one period automatically becomes the beginning inventory of the next period. Thus, inventory errors affect the computation of cost of goods sold and net income in two periods.

The effects on cost of goods sold can be computed by first entering incorrect data in the formula in Illustration 6-15 and then substituting the correct data.

Illustration 6-15
Formula for cost of goods sold

Beginning Inventory	+	Cost of Goods Purchased	−	Ending Inventory	=	Cost of Goods Sold

If the error understates **beginning** inventory, cost of goods sold will be understated. If the error understates **ending** inventory, cost of goods sold will be overstated. Illustration 6-16 shows the effects of inventory errors on the current year's income statement.

Illustration 6-16
Effects of inventory errors on current year's income statement

When Inventory Error:	Cost of Goods Sold Is:	Net Income Is:
Understates beginning inventory	Understated	Overstated
Overstates beginning inventory	Overstated	Understated
Understates ending inventory	Overstated	Understated
Overstates ending inventory	Understated	Overstated

So far, the effects of inventory errors are fairly straightforward. Now, though, comes the (at first) surprising part: An error in the ending inventory of the current period will have a **reverse effect on net income of the next accounting period**. Illustration 6-17 (page 278) shows this effect. As you study the illustration, you will see that the reverse effect comes from the fact that understating ending inventory in 2016 results in understating beginning inventory in 2017 and overstating net income in 2017.

Over the two years, though, total net income is correct because the errors **offset each other**. Notice that total income using incorrect data is $35,000 ($22,000 + $13,000), which is the same as the total income of $35,000 ($25,000 + $10,000) using correct data. Also note in this example that an error in the beginning inventory does not result in a corresponding error in the ending inventory for that period. The correctness of the ending inventory depends entirely on the accuracy of taking and costing the inventory at the balance sheet date under the periodic inventory system.

ETHICS NOTE

Inventory fraud increases during recessions. Such fraud includes pricing inventory at amounts in excess of its actual value, or claiming to have inventory when no inventory exists. Inventory fraud usually overstates ending inventory, thereby understating cost of goods sold and creating higher income.

SAMPLE COMPANY
Condensed Income Statements

	2016				2017			
	Incorrect		Correct		Incorrect		Correct	
Sales revenue		$80,000		$80,000		$90,000		$90,000
Beginning inventory	$20,000		$20,000		**$12,000**		**$15,000**	
Cost of goods purchased	40,000		40,000		68,000		68,000	
Cost of goods available for sale	60,000		60,000		80,000		83,000	
Ending inventory	**12,000**		**15,000**		23,000		23,000	
Cost of goods sold		48,000		45,000		57,000		60,000
Gross profit		32,000		35,000		33,000		30,000
Operating expenses		10,000		10,000		20,000		20,000
Net income		$22,000		$25,000		$13,000		$10,000

$(3,000) Net income understated (2016)

$3,000 Net income overstated (2017)

The errors cancel. Thus, the combined total income for the 2-year period is correct.

Illustration 6-17
Effects of inventory errors on two years' income statements

Balance Sheet Effects

Companies can determine the effect of ending inventory errors on the balance sheet by using the basic accounting equation: Assets = Liabilities + Owner's Equity. Errors in the ending inventory have the effects shown in Illustration 6-18.

Illustration 6-18
Effects of ending inventory errors on balance sheet

Ending Inventory Error	Assets	Liabilities	Owner's Equity
Overstated	Overstated	No effect	Overstated
Understated	Understated	No effect	Understated

The effect of an error in ending inventory on the subsequent period was shown in Illustration 6-17. Recall that if the error is not corrected, the combined total net income for the two periods would be correct. Thus, total owner's equity reported on the balance sheet at the end of 2017 will also be correct.

DO IT! 3 Inventory Errors

Action Plan

✔ An ending inventory error in one period will have an equal and opposite effect on cost of goods sold and net income in the next period.

✔ After two years, the errors have offset each other.

Visual Company overstated its 2016 ending inventory by $22,000. Determine the impact this error has on ending inventory, cost of goods sold, and owner's equity in 2016 and 2017.

Solution

	2016	2017
Ending inventory	$22,000 overstated	No effect
Cost of goods sold	$22,000 understated	$22,000 overstated
Owner's equity	$22,000 overstated	No effect

Related exercise material: **BE6-6, E6-9, E6-10, and DO IT! 6-3.**

LEARNING OBJECTIVE 4

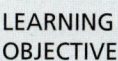

Explain the statement presentation and analysis of inventory.

Presentation

As indicated in Chapter 5, inventory is classified in the balance sheet as a current asset immediately below receivables. In a multiple-step income statement, cost of goods sold is subtracted from net sales. There also should be disclosure of (1) the major inventory classifications, (2) the basis of accounting (cost, or lower-of-cost-or-market), and (3) the cost method (FIFO, LIFO, or average-cost).

Wal-Mart Stores, Inc., for example, in its January 31, 2014, balance sheet reported inventories of $44,858 million under current assets. The accompanying notes to the financial statements, as shown in Illustration 6-19, disclosed the following information.

Real World

WAL-MART STORES, INC.
Notes to the Financial Statements

Note 1. Summary of Significant Accounting Policies

Inventories

The Company values inventories at the lower of cost or market as determined primarily by the retail method of accounting, using the last-in, first-out ("LIFO") method for substantially all of the WalMart U.S. segment's inventories. The WalMart International segment's inventories are primarily valued by the retail method of accounting, using the first-in, first-out ("FIFO") method. The retail method of accounting results in inventory being valued at the lower of cost or market since permanent markdowns are currently taken as a reduction of the retail value of inventory. The Sam's Club segment's inventories are valued based on the weighted-average cost using the LIFO method. At January 31, 2014 and 2013, the Company's inventories valued at LIFO approximate those inventories as if they were valued at FIFO.

Illustration 6-19
Inventory disclosures by Wal-Mart

As indicated in this note, Wal-Mart values its inventories at the lower-of-cost-or-market using LIFO and FIFO.

Lower-of-Cost-or-Market

The value of inventory for companies selling high-technology or fashion goods can drop very quickly due to continual changes in technology or fashions. These circumstances sometimes call for inventory valuation methods other than those presented so far. For example, at one time purchasing managers at Ford decided to make a large purchase of palladium, a precious metal used in vehicle emission devices. They made this purchase because they feared a future shortage. The shortage did not materialize, and by the end of the year the price of palladium had plummeted. Ford's inventory was then worth $1 billion less than its original cost. Do you think Ford's inventory should have been stated at cost, in accordance with the historical cost principle, or at its lower replacement cost?

As you probably reasoned, this situation requires a departure from the cost basis of accounting. This is done by valuing the inventory at the **lower-of-cost-or-market (LCM)** in the period in which the price decline occurs. LCM is a basis whereby inventory is stated at the lower of either its cost or market value as determined by current replacement cost. LCM is an example of the accounting convention of **conservatism**. Conservatism means that the approach adopted among accounting alternatives is the method that is least likely to overstate assets and net income.

International Note

Under U.S. GAAP, companies cannot reverse inventory write-downs if inventory increases in value in subsequent periods. IFRS permits companies to reverse write-downs in some circumstances.

Companies apply LCM to the items in inventory after they have used one of the cost flow methods (specific identification, FIFO, LIFO, or average-cost) to determine cost. Under the LCM basis, market is defined as **current replacement cost**, not selling price. For a merchandising company, current replacement cost is the cost of purchasing the same goods at the present time from the usual suppliers in the usual quantities. Current replacement cost is used because a decline in the replacement cost of an item usually leads to a decline in the selling price of the item.

To illustrate the application of LCM, assume that Ken Tuckie TV has the following lines of merchandise with costs and market values as indicated. LCM produces the results shown in Illustration 6-20. Note that the amounts shown in the final column are the lower-of-cost-or-market amounts for each item.

Illustration 6-20
Computation of lower-of-cost-or-market

	Units	Cost per Unit	Market per Unit	Lower-of-Cost-or-Market
Flat-screen TVs	100	$600	$550	$ 55,000 ($550 × 100)
Satellite radios	500	90	104	45,000 ($90 × 500)
Blu-ray players	850	50	48	40,800 ($48 × 850)
CDs	3,000	5	6	15,000 ($5 × 3,000)
Total inventory				$155,800

Analysis

The amount of inventory carried by a company has significant economic consequences. And inventory management is a double-edged sword that requires constant attention. On the one hand, management wants to have a great variety and quantity available so that customers have a wide selection and items are always in stock. But, such a policy may incur high carrying costs (e.g., investment, storage, insurance, obsolescence, and damage). On the other hand, low inventory levels lead to stock-outs and lost sales. Common ratios used to manage and evaluate inventory levels are inventory turnover and a related measure, days in inventory.

Inventory turnover measures the number of times on average the inventory is sold during the period. Its purpose is to measure the liquidity of the inventory. The inventory turnover is computed by dividing cost of goods sold by the average inventory during the period. Unless seasonal factors are significant, average inventory can be computed from the beginning and ending inventory balances. For example, Wal-Mart reported in its 2014 annual report a beginning inventory of $43,803 million, an ending inventory of $44,858 million, and cost of goods sold for the year ended January 31, 2014, of $358,069 million. The inventory turnover formula and computation for Wal-Mart are shown below.

Illustration 6-21
Inventory turnover formula and computation for Wal-Mart

Cost of Goods Sold	÷	Average Inventory	=	Inventory Turnover
$358,069	÷	$\frac{\$44,858 + \$43,803}{2}$	=	8.1 times

A variant of the inventory turnover is **days in inventory**. This measures the average number of days inventory is held. It is calculated as 365 divided by the inventory turnover. For example, Wal-Mart's inventory turnover of 8.1 times divided into 365 is approximately 45.1 days. This is the approximate time that it takes a company to sell the inventory once it arrives at the store.

There are typical levels of inventory in every industry. Companies that are able to keep their inventory at lower levels and higher turnovers and still satisfy customer needs are the most successful.

Accounting Across the Organization — Sony

© Dmitry Kutlayev/iStockphoto

Too Many TVs or Too Few?

Financial analysts closely monitored the inventory management practices of companies during the recent recession. For example, some analysts following Sony expressed concern because the company built up its inventory of televisions in an attempt to sell 25 million liquid crystal display (LCD) TVs—a 60% increase over the prior year. A year earlier, Sony had cut its inventory levels so that its quarterly days in inventory was down to 38 days, compared to 61 days for the same quarter a year before that. But now, as a result of its inventory build-up, days in inventory rose to 59 days. While management was saying that it didn't think that Sony's inventory levels were now too high, analysts were concerned that the company would have to engage in very heavy discounting in order to sell off its inventory. Analysts noted that the losses from discounting can be "punishing."

Source: Daisuke Wakabayashi, "Sony Pledges to Corral Inventory," *Wall Street Journal* Online (November 2, 2010).

For Sony, what are the advantages and disadvantages of having a low days in inventory measure? (Go to **WileyPLUS** for this answer and additional questions.)

DO IT! 4 LCM and Inventory Turnover

(a) Tracy Company sells three different types of home heating stoves (gas, wood, and pellet). The cost and market value of its inventory of stoves are as follows.

	Cost	Market
Gas	$ 84,000	$ 79,000
Wood	250,000	280,000
Pellet	112,000	101,000

Determine the value of the company's inventory under the lower-of-cost-or-market approach.

Solution

The lowest value for each inventory type is gas $79,000, wood $250,000, and pellet $101,000. The total inventory value is the sum of these amounts, $430,000.

Action Plan

- ✔ Determine whether cost or market value is lower for each inventory type.
- ✔ Sum the lowest value of each inventory type to determine the total value of inventory.

(b) Early in 2017, Westmoreland Company switched to a just-in-time inventory system. Its sales revenue, cost of goods sold, and inventory amounts for 2016 and 2017 are shown below.

	2016	2017
Sales revenue	$2,000,000	$1,800,000
Cost of goods sold	1,000,000	910,000
Beginning inventory	290,000	210,000
Ending inventory	210,000	50,000

Determine the inventory turnover and days in inventory for 2016 and 2017. Discuss the changes in the amount of inventory, the inventory turnover and days in inventory, and the amount of sales across the two years.

Solution

	2016	2017
Inventory turnover	$\frac{\$1,000,000}{(\$290,000 + \$210,000)/2} = 4$	$\frac{\$910,000}{(\$210,000 + \$50,000)/2} = 7$
Days in inventory	$365 \div 4 = 91.3$ days	$365 \div 7 = 52.1$ days

Action Plan

- ✔ To find the inventory turnover, divide cost of goods sold by average inventory.
- ✔ To determine days in inventory, divide 365 days by the inventory turnover.

Action Plan (cont'd)

✔ Just-in-time inventory reduces the amount of inventory on hand, which reduces carrying costs. Reducing inventory levels by too much has potential negative implications for sales.

The company experienced a very significant decline in its ending inventory as a result of the just-in-time inventory. This decline improved its inventory turnover and its days in inventory. However, its sales declined by 10%. It is possible that this decline was caused by the dramatic reduction in the amount of inventory that was on hand, which increased the likelihood of "stock-outs." To determine the optimal inventory level, management must weigh the benefits of reduced inventory against the potential lost sales caused by stock-outs.

Related exercise material: **BE6-7, BE6-8, E6-11, E6-12, E6-13, E6-14, and DO IT! 6-4.**

LEARNING OBJECTIVE *5

APPENDIX 6A: Apply the inventory cost flow methods to perpetual inventory records.

What inventory cost flow methods can companies employ if they use a perpetual inventory system? Simple—they can use any of the inventory cost flow methods described in the chapter. To illustrate the application of the three assumed cost flow methods (FIFO, LIFO, and average-cost), we will use the data shown in Illustration 6A-1 and in this chapter for Houston Electronics' Astro condensers.

Illustration 6A-1
Inventoriable units and costs

HOUSTON ELECTRONICS
Astro Condensers

Date	Explanation	Units	Unit Cost	Total Cost	Balance in Units
1/1	Beginning inventory	100	$10	$ 1,000	100
4/15	Purchases	200	11	2,200	300
8/24	Purchases	300	12	3,600	600
9/10	Sale	550			50
11/27	Purchases	400	13	5,200	450
				$12,000	

First-In, First-Out (FIFO)

Under perpetual FIFO, the company charges to cost of goods sold the cost of the earliest goods on hand **prior to each sale**. Therefore, the cost of goods sold on September 10 consists of the units on hand January 1 and the units purchased April 15 and August 24. Illustration 6A-2 shows the inventory under a FIFO method perpetual system.

Illustration 6A-2
Perpetual system—FIFO

Date	Purchases		Cost of Goods Sold	Balance (in units and cost)	
January 1				(100 @ $10)	$ 1,000
April 15	(200 @ $11)	$2,200		(100 @ $10) (200 @ $11)	$ 3,200
August 24	(300 @ $12)	$3,600		(100 @ $10) (200 @ $11) (300 @ $12)	$ 6,800
September 10			(100 @ $10) (200 @ $11) (250 @ $12) **$6,200**	(50 @ $12)	$ 600
November 27	(400 @ $13)	$5,200		(50 @ $12) (400 @ $13)	**$5,800**

Cost of goods sold → $6,200

Ending inventory → $5,800

The ending inventory in this situation is $5,800, and the cost of goods sold is $6,200 [(100 @ $10) + (200 @ $11) + (250 @ $12)].

Compare Illustrations 6-6 (page 271) and 6A-2. You can see that the results under FIFO in a perpetual system are the **same as in a periodic system**. In both cases, the ending inventory is $5,800 and cost of goods sold is $6,200. Regardless of the system, the first costs in are the costs assigned to cost of goods sold.

Last-In, First-Out (LIFO)

Under the LIFO method using a perpetual system, the company charges to cost of goods sold the cost of the most recent purchase prior to sale. Therefore, the cost of the goods sold on September 10 consists of all the units from the August 24 and April 15 purchases plus 50 of the units in beginning inventory. Illustration 6A-3 shows the computation of the ending inventory under the LIFO method.

Illustration 6A-3
Perpetual system—LIFO

Date	Purchases		Cost of Goods Sold	Balance (in units and cost)	
January 1				(100 @ $10)	$ 1,000
April 15	(200 @ $11)	$2,200		(100 @ $10) (200 @ $11)	$ 3,200
August 24	(300 @ $12)	$3,600		(100 @ $10) (200 @ $11) (300 @ $12)	$ 6,800
September 10			(300 @ $12) (200 @ $11) (50 @ $10) **$6,300** (Cost of goods sold)	(50 @ $10)	$ 500
November 27	(400 @ $13)	$5,200		(50 @ $10) (400 @ $13)	**$5,700** (Ending inventory)

The use of LIFO in a perpetual system will usually produce cost allocations that differ from those using LIFO in a periodic system. In a perpetual system, the company allocates the latest units purchased **prior to each sale** to cost of goods sold. In contrast, in a periodic system, the latest units purchased **during the period** are allocated to cost of goods sold. Thus, when a purchase is made after the last sale, the LIFO periodic system will apply this purchase to the previous sale. Compare Illustrations 6-8 (page 272) and 6A-3. Illustration 6-8 shows that the 400 units at $13 purchased on November 27 applied to the sale of 550 units on September 10. Under the LIFO perpetual system in Illustration 6A-3, the 400 units at $13 purchased on November 27 are all applied to the ending inventory.

The ending inventory in this LIFO perpetual illustration is $5,700, and cost of goods sold is $6,300, as compared to the LIFO periodic Illustration 6-8 (page 272) where the ending inventory is $5,000 and cost of goods sold is $7,000.

Average-Cost

The average-cost method in a perpetual inventory system is called the **moving-average method**. Under this method, the company computes a new average **after each purchase**, by dividing the cost of goods available for sale by the units on hand. The average cost is then applied to (1) the units sold, to determine the cost of goods sold, and (2) the remaining units on hand, to determine the ending inventory amount. Illustration 6A-4 (page 284) shows the application of the moving-average cost method by Houston Electronics (computations of the moving-average unit cost are shown after Illustration 6A-4).

Illustration 6A-4
Perpetual system—moving-average method

Date	Purchases	Cost of Goods Sold	Balance (in units and cost)
January 1			(100 @ $10) $ 1,000
April 15	(200 @ $11) $2,200		(300 @ $10.667) $ 3,200
August 24	(300 @ $12) $3,600		(600 @ $11.333) $ 6,800
September 10		(550 @ $11.333)	(50 @ $11.333) $ 567
		$6,233	
November 27	(400 @ $13) $5,200		(450 @ $12.816) **$5,767**

Cost of goods sold

Ending inventory

As indicated, Houston Electronics computes **a new average each time it makes a purchase**.

1. On April 15, after Houston buys 200 units for $2,200, a total of 300 units costing $3,200 ($1,000 + $2,200) are on hand. The average unit cost is $10.667 ($3,200 ÷ 300).
2. On August 24, after Houston buys 300 units for $3,600, a total of 600 units costing $6,800 ($1,000 + $2,200 + $3,600) are on hand. The average cost per unit is $11.333 ($6,800 ÷ 600).
3. On September 10, to compute cost of goods sold, Houston uses this unit cost of $11.333 until it makes another purchase, when the company computes a new unit cost. Accordingly, the unit cost of the 550 units sold on September 10 is $11.333, and the total cost of goods sold is $6,233.
4. On November 27, following the purchase of 400 units for $5,200, there are 450 units on hand costing $5,767 ($567 + $5,200) with a new average cost of $12.816 ($5,767 ÷ 450).

Compare this moving-average cost under the perpetual inventory system to Illustration 6-11 (page 273) showing the average-cost method under a periodic inventory system.

LEARNING OBJECTIVE *6

APPENDIX 6B: Describe the two methods of estimating inventories.

In the chapter, we assumed that a company would be able to physically count its inventory. What if it cannot? What if the inventory were destroyed by fire or flood, for example? In that case, the company would use an estimate.

Two circumstances explain why companies sometimes estimate inventories. First, a casualty such as fire, flood, or earthquake may make it impossible to take a physical inventory. Second, managers may want monthly or quarterly financial statements, but a physical inventory is taken only annually. The need for estimating inventories occurs primarily with a periodic inventory system because of the absence of perpetual inventory records.

There are two widely used methods of estimating inventories: (1) the gross profit method, and (2) the retail inventory method.

Gross Profit Method

The **gross profit method** estimates the cost of ending inventory by applying a gross profit rate to net sales. This method is relatively simple but effective. Accountants, auditors, and managers frequently use the gross profit method to test the reasonableness of the ending inventory amount. It will detect large errors.

To use this method, a company needs to know its net sales, cost of goods available for sale, and gross profit rate. The company then can estimate its gross profit for the period. Illustration 6B-1 shows the formulas for using the gross profit method.

Illustration 6B-1
Gross profit method formulas

Step 1:	**Net Sales**	**−**	**Estimated Gross Profit**	**=**	**Estimated Cost of Goods Sold**
Step 2:	**Cost of Goods Available for Sale**	**−**	**Estimated Cost of Goods Sold**	**=**	**Estimated Cost of Ending Inventory**

To illustrate, assume that Kishwaukee Company wishes to prepare an income statement for the month of January. Its records show net sales of $200,000, beginning inventory $40,000, and cost of goods purchased $120,000. In the preceding year, the company realized a 30% gross profit rate. It expects to earn the same rate this year. Given these facts and assumptions, Kishwaukee can compute the estimated cost of the ending inventory at January 31 under the gross profit method as follows.

Illustration 6B-2
Example of gross profit method

Step 1:	
Net sales	$ 200,000
Less: Estimated gross profit (30% × $200,000)	60,000
Estimated cost of goods sold	**$140,000**
Step 2:	
Beginning inventory	$ 40,000
Cost of goods purchased	120,000
Cost of goods available for sale	160,000
Less: Estimated cost of goods sold	140,000
Estimated cost of ending inventory	**$ 20,000**

The gross profit method is based on the assumption that the gross profit rate will remain constant. But, it may not remain constant, due to a change in merchandising policies or in market conditions. In such cases, the company should adjust the rate to reflect current operating conditions. In some cases, companies can obtain a more accurate estimate by applying this method on a department or product-line basis.

Note that companies should not use the gross profit method to prepare financial statements at the end of the year. These statements should be based on a physical inventory count.

Retail Inventory Method

A retail store such as Home Depot, Ace Hardware, or Walmart has thousands of different types of merchandise at low unit costs. In such cases, it is difficult and time-consuming to apply unit costs to inventory quantities. An alternative is to use the **retail inventory method** to estimate the cost of inventory. Most retail companies can establish a relationship between cost and sales price. The company then applies the cost-to-retail percentage to the ending inventory at retail prices to determine inventory at cost.

Under the retail inventory method, a company's records must show both the cost and retail value of the goods available for sale. Illustration 6B-3 (page 286) presents the formulas for using the retail inventory method.

We can demonstrate the logic of the retail method by using unit-cost data. Assume that Ortiz Inc. has marked 10 units purchased at $7 to sell for $10 per unit. Thus, the cost-to-retail ratio is 70% ($70 ÷ $100). If four units remain unsold, their retail value is $40 (4 × $10), and their cost is $28 ($40 × 70%). This amount agrees with the total cost of goods on hand on a per unit basis (4 × $7).

Illustration 6B-3
Retail inventory method formulas

Step 1:	Goods Available for Sale at Retail	−	Net Sales	=	Ending Inventory at Retail
Step 2:	Goods Available for Sale at Cost	÷	Goods Available for Sale at Retail	=	Cost-to-Retail Ratio
Step 3:	Ending Inventory at Retail	×	Cost-to-Retail Ratio	=	Estimated Cost of Ending Inventory

Illustration 6B-4 shows application of the retail method for Valley West. Note that it is not necessary to take a physical inventory to determine the estimated cost of goods on hand at any given time.

Illustration 6B-4
Application of retail inventory method

	At Cost	At Retail
Beginning inventory	$14,000	$ 21,500
Goods purchased	61,000	78,500
Goods available for sale	$75,000	100,000
Less: Net sales		70,000
Step (1) Ending inventory at retail =		**$ 30,000**

Step (2) Cost-to-retail ratio = $75,000 ÷ $100,000 = 75%
Step (3) Estimated cost of ending inventory = $30,000 × 75% = $22,500

Helpful Hint
In determining inventory at retail, companies use selling prices of the units.

The retail inventory method also facilitates taking a physical inventory at the end of the year. Valley West can value the goods on hand at the prices marked on the merchandise, and then apply the cost-to-retail ratio to the goods on hand at retail to determine the ending inventory at cost.

The major disadvantage of the retail method is that it is an averaging technique. Thus, it may produce an incorrect inventory valuation if the mix of the ending inventory is not representative of the mix in the goods available for sale. Assume, for example, that the cost-to-retail ratio of 75% for Valley West consists of equal proportions of inventory items that have cost-to-retail ratios of 70%, 75%, and 80%. If the ending inventory contains only items with a 70% ratio, an incorrect inventory cost will result. Companies can minimize this problem by applying the retail method on a department or product-line basis.

REVIEW AND PRACTICE

LEARNING OBJECTIVES REVIEW

1 Discuss how to classify and determine inventory. Merchandisers need only one inventory classification, merchandise inventory, to describe the different items that make up total inventory. Manufacturers, on the other hand, usually classify inventory into three categories: finished goods, work in process, and raw materials. To determine inventory quantities, manufacturers (1) take a physical inventory of goods on hand and (2) determine the ownership of goods in transit or on consignment.

2 Apply inventory cost flow methods and discuss their financial effects. The primary basis of accounting for inventories is cost. Cost of goods available for sale includes (a) cost of beginning inventory and (b) cost of goods purchased. The inventory cost flow methods are specific identification and three assumed cost flow methods—FIFO, LIFO, and average-cost.

When prices are rising, the first-in, first-out (FIFO) method results in lower cost of goods sold and higher net income than the other methods. The last-in, first-out

(LIFO) method results in the lowest income taxes. The reverse is true when prices are falling. In the balance sheet, FIFO results in an ending inventory that is closest to current value. Inventory under LIFO is the farthest from current value.

3 Indicate the effects of inventory errors on the financial statements. In the income statement of the current year: (a) If beginning inventory is understated, net income is overstated. The reverse occurs if beginning inventory is overstated. (b) If ending inventory is overstated, net income is overstated. If ending inventory is understated, net income is understated. In the following period, its effect on net income for that period is reversed, and total net income for the two years will be correct.

In the balance sheet: Ending inventory errors will have the same effect on total assets and total owner's equity and no effect on liabilities.

4 Explain the statement presentation and analysis of inventory. Inventory is classified in the balance sheet as a current asset immediately below receivables. There also should be disclosure of (1) the major inventory classifications, (2) the basis of accounting, and (3) the cost method.

Companies use the lower-of-cost-or-market (LCM) basis when the current replacement cost (market) is less than cost. Under LCM, companies recognize the loss in the period in which the price decline occurs.

The inventory turnover is cost of goods sold divided by average inventory. To convert it to average days in inventory, divide 365 days by the inventory turnover.

***5 Apply the inventory cost flow methods to perpetual inventory records.** Under FIFO and a perpetual inventory system, companies charge to cost of goods sold the cost of the earliest goods on hand prior to each sale. Under LIFO and a perpetual system, companies charge to cost of goods sold the cost of the most recent purchase prior to sale. Under the moving-average (average-cost) method and a perpetual system, companies compute a new average cost after each purchase.

***6 Describe the two methods of estimating inventories.** The two methods of estimating inventories are the gross profit method and the retail inventory method. Under the gross profit method, companies apply a gross profit rate to net sales to determine estimated gross profit and cost of goods sold. They then subtract estimated cost of goods sold from cost of goods available for sale to determine the estimated cost of the ending inventory.

Under the retail inventory method, companies compute a cost-to-retail ratio by dividing the cost of goods available for sale by the retail value of the goods available for sale. They then apply this ratio to the ending inventory at retail to determine the estimated cost of the ending inventory.

GLOSSARY REVIEW

Average-cost method Inventory costing method that uses the weighted-average unit cost to allocate to ending inventory and cost of goods sold the cost of goods available for sale. (p. 273).

Consigned goods Goods held for sale by one party although ownership of the goods is retained by another party. (p. 267).

Consistency concept Dictates that a company use the same accounting principles and methods from year to year. (p. 275).

Current replacement cost The current cost to replace an inventory item. (p. 280).

Days in inventory Measure of the average number of days inventory is held; calculated as 365 divided by inventory turnover. (p. 280).

Finished goods inventory Manufactured items that are completed and ready for sale. (p. 264).

First-in, first-out (FIFO) method Inventory costing method that assumes that the costs of the earliest goods purchased are the first to be recognized as cost of goods sold. (p. 270).

FOB (free on board) destination Freight terms indicating that ownership of the goods remains with the seller until the goods reach the buyer. (p. 267).

FOB (free on board) shipping point Freight terms indicating that ownership of the goods passes to the buyer when the public carrier accepts the goods from the seller. (p. 266).

***Gross profit method** A method for estimating the cost of the ending inventory by applying a gross profit rate to net sales and subtracting estimated cost of goods sold from cost of goods available for sale. (p. 284).

Inventory turnover A ratio that measures the number of times on average the inventory sold during the period; computed by dividing cost of goods sold by the average inventory during the period. (p. 280).

Just-in-time (JIT) inventory Inventory system in which companies manufacture or purchase goods only when needed for use. (p. 264).

Last-in, first-out (LIFO) method Inventory costing method that assumes the costs of the latest units purchased are the first to be allocated to cost of goods sold. (p. 272).

Lower-of-cost-or-market (LCM) A basis whereby inventory is stated at the lower of either its cost or its market value as determined by current replacement cost. (p. 279).

***Moving-average method** A new average is computed after each purchase, by dividing the cost of goods available for sale by the units on hand. (p. 283).

Raw materials Basic goods that will be used in production but have not yet been placed into production. (p. 264).

***Retail inventory method** A method for estimating the cost of the ending inventory by applying a cost-to-retail ratio to the ending inventory at retail. (p. 285).

Specific identification method An actual physical flow costing method in which items still in inventory are specifically costed to arrive at the total cost of the ending inventory. (p. 269).

Weighted-average unit cost Average cost that is weighted by the number of units purchased at each unit cost. (p. 273).

Work in process That portion of manufactured inventory that has been placed into the production process but is not yet complete. (p. 264).

PRACTICE MULTIPLE-CHOICE QUESTIONS

(LO 1) 1. Which of the following should **not** be included in the physical inventory of a company?
(a) Goods held on consignment from another company.
(b) Goods shipped on consignment to another company.
(c) Goods in transit from another company shipped FOB shipping point.
(d) None of the above.

(LO 1) 2. As a result of a thorough physical inventory, Railway Company determined that it had inventory worth $180,000 at December 31, 2017. This count did not take into consideration the following facts: Rogers Consignment store currently has goods worth $35,000 on its sales floor that belong to Railway but are being sold on consignment by Rogers. The selling price of these goods is $50,000. Railway purchased $13,000 of goods that were shipped on December 27, FOB destination, that will be received by Railway on January 3. Determine the correct amount of inventory that Railway should report.
(a) $230,000. (c) $228,000.
(b) $215,000. (d) $193,000.

(LO 2) 3. Cost of goods available for sale consists of two elements: beginning inventory and
(a) ending inventory.
(b) cost of goods purchased.
(c) cost of goods sold.
(d) All of the answer choices are correct.

(LO 2) 4. Poppins Company has the following:

	Units	Unit Cost
Inventory, Jan. 1	8,000	$11
Purchase, June 19	13,000	12
Purchase, Nov. 8	5,000	13

If Poppins has 9,000 units on hand at December 31, the cost of the ending inventory under FIFO is:
(a) $99,000. (c) $113,000.
(b) $108,000. (d) $117,000.

(LO 2) 5. Using the data in Question 4 above, the cost of the ending inventory under LIFO is:
(a) $113,000. (c) $99,000.
(b) $108,000. (d) $100,000.

(LO 2) 6. Hansel Electronics has the following:

	Units	Unit Cost
Inventory, Jan. 1	5,000	$ 8
Purchase, April 2	15,000	$10
Purchase, Aug. 28	20,000	$12

If Hansel has 7,000 units on hand at December 31, the cost of ending inventory under the average-cost method is:
(a) $84,000. (c) $56,000.
(b) $70,000. (d) $75,250.

7. In periods of rising prices, LIFO will produce: (LO 2)
(a) higher net income than FIFO.
(b) the same net income as FIFO.
(c) lower net income than FIFO.
(d) higher net income than average-cost.

8. Factors that affect the selection of an inventory costing method do **not** include: (LO 2)
(a) tax effects.
(b) balance sheet effects.
(c) income statement effects.
(d) perpetual vs. periodic inventory system.

9. Falk Company's ending inventory is understated $4,000. The effects of this error on the current year's cost of goods sold and net income, respectively, are: (LO 3)
(a) understated, overstated.
(b) overstated, understated.
(c) overstated, overstated.
(d) understated, understated.

10. Pauline Company overstated its inventory by $15,000 at December 31, 2016. It did not correct the error in 2016 or 2017. As a result, Pauline's owner's equity was: (LO 3)
(a) overstated at December 31, 2016, and understated at December 31, 2017.
(b) overstated at December 31, 2016, and properly stated at December 31, 2017.
(c) understated at December 31, 2016, and understated at December 31, 2017.
(d) overstated at December 31, 2016, and overstated at December 31, 2017.

11. Norton Company purchased 1,000 widgets and has 200 widgets in its ending inventory at a cost of $91 each and a current replacement cost of $80 each. The ending inventory under lower-of-cost-or-market is: (LO 4)
(a) $91,000. (c) $18,200.
(b) $80,000. (d) $16,000.

12. Santana Company had beginning inventory of $80,000, ending inventory of $110,000, cost of goods sold of $285,000, and sales of $475,000. Santana's days in inventory is: (LO 4)
(a) 73 days. (c) 102.5 days.
(b) 121.7 days. (d) 84.5 days.

13. Which of these would cause the inventory turnover to increase the most? (LO 4)
(a) Increasing the amount of inventory on hand.
(b) Keeping the amount of inventory on hand constant but increasing sales.
(c) Keeping the amount of inventory on hand constant but decreasing sales.
(d) Decreasing the amount of inventory on hand and increasing sales.

*14. In a perpetual inventory system: (LO 5)
(a) LIFO cost of goods sold will be the same as in a periodic inventory system.

(b) average costs are a simple average of unit costs incurred.
(c) a new average is computed under the average-cost method after each sale.
(d) FIFO cost of goods sold will be the same as in a periodic inventory system.

*15. King Company has sales of $150,000 and cost of goods available for sale of $135,000. If the gross profit rate is 30%, the estimated cost of the ending inventory under the gross profit method is: (LO 6)
(a) $15,000.
(b) $30,000.
(c) $45,000.
(d) $75,000.

Solutions

1. (a) Goods held on consignment should not be included because another company has title (ownership) to the goods. The other choices are incorrect because (b) goods shipped on consignment to another company and (c) goods in transit from another company shipped FOB shipping point should be included in a company's ending inventory. Choice (d) is incorrect as there is a correct answer for this question.

2. (b) The inventory held on consignment by Rogers should be included in Railway's inventory balance at cost ($35,000). The purchased goods of $13,000 should not be included in inventory until January 3 because the goods are shipped FOB destination. Therefore, the correct amount of inventory is $215,000 ($180,000 + $35,000), not (a) $230,000, (c) $228,000, or (d) $193,000.

3. (b) Cost of goods available for sale consists of beginning inventory and cost of goods purchased, not (a) ending inventory or (c) cost of goods sold. Therefore, choice (d) All of the above is also incorrect.

4. (c) Under FIFO, ending inventory will consist of 5,000 units from the Nov. 8 purchase and 4,000 units from the June 19 purchase. Therefore, ending inventory is (5,000 × $13) + (4,000 × $12) = $113,000, not (a) $99,000, (b) $108,000, or (d) $117,000.

5. (d) Under LIFO, ending inventory will consist of 8,000 units from the inventory at Jan. 1 and 1,000 units from the June 19 purchase. Therefore, ending inventory is (8,000 × $11) + (1,000 × $12) = $100,000, not (a) $113,000, (b) $108,000, or (c) $99,000.

6. (d) Under the average-cost method, total cost of goods available for sale needs to be calculated in order to determine average cost per unit. The total cost of goods available is $430,000 = (5,000 × $8) + (15,000 × $10) + (20,000 × $12). The average cost per unit = ($430,000/40,000 total units available for sale) = $10.75. Therefore, ending inventory is ($10.75 × 7,000) = $75,250, not (a) $84,000, (b) $70,000, or (c) $56,000.

7. (c) In periods of rising prices, LIFO will produce lower net income than FIFO, not (a) higher than FIFO or (b) the same as FIFO. Choice (d) is incorrect because in periods of rising prices, LIFO will produce lower net income than average-cost. LIFO therefore charges the highest inventory cost against revenues in a period of rising prices.

8. (d) Perpetual vs. periodic inventory system is not one of the factors that affect the selection of an inventory costing method. The other choices are incorrect because (a) tax effects, (b) balance sheet effects, and (c) income statement effects all affect the selection of an inventory costing method.

9. (b) Because ending inventory is too low, cost of goods sold will be too high (overstated) and since cost of goods sold (an expense) is too high, net income will be too low (understated). Therefore, the other choices are incorrect.

10. (b) Owner's equity is overstated by $15,000 at December 31, 2016, and is properly stated at December 31, 2017. An ending inventory error in one period will have an equal and opposite effect on cost of goods sold and net income in the next period; after two years, the errors have offset each other. The other choices are incorrect because owner's equity (a) is properly stated, not understated, at December 31,2017; (c) is overstated, not understated, by $15,000 at December 31, 2016, and is properly stated, not understated, at December 31, 2017; and (d) is properly stated at December 31, 2017, not overstated.

11. (d) Under the LCM basis, "market" is defined as the current replacement cost. Therefore, ending inventory would be valued at 200 widgets × $80 each = $16,000, not (a) $91,000, (b) $80,000, or (c) $18,200.

12. (b) Santana's days in inventory = 365/Inventory turnover = 365/[$285,000/ ($80,000 + $110,000)/2)] = 121.7 days, not (a) 73 days, (c) 102.5 days, or (d) 84.5 days.

13. (d) Decreasing the amount of inventory on hand will cause the denominator to decrease, causing inventory turnover to increase. Increasing sales will cause the numerator of the ratio to increase (higher sales means higher COGS), thus causing inventory turnover to increase even more. The other choices are incorrect because (a) increasing the amount of inventory on hand causes the denominator of the ratio to increase while the numerator stays the same, causing inventory turnover to decrease; (b) keeping the amount of inventory on hand constant but increasing sales will cause inventory turnover to increase because the numerator of the ratio will increase (higher sales means higher COGS) while the denominator stays the same, which will result in a lesser inventory increase than decreasing amount of inventory on hand and increasing sales; and (c) keeping the amount of inventory on hand constant but decreasing sales will cause inventory turnover to decrease because the numerator of the ratio will decrease (lower sales means lower COGS) while the denominator stays the same.

***14. (d)** FIFO cost of goods sold is the same under both a periodic and a perpetual inventory system. The other choices are incorrect because (a) LIFO cost of goods sold is not the same under a periodic and a perpetual inventory system; (b) average costs are based on a moving average of unit costs, not an average of unit costs; and (c) a new average is computed under the average-cost method after each purchase, not sale.

***15. (b)** COGS = Sales ($150,000) − Gross profit ($150,000 × 30%) = $105,000. Ending inventory = Cost of goods available for sale ($135,000) − COGS ($105,000) = $30,000, not (a) $15,000, (c) $45,000, or (d) $75,000.

PRACTICE EXERCISES

Determine the correct inventory amount.

(LO 1)

1. Matt Clark, an auditor with Grant CPAs, is performing a review of Parson Company's inventory account. Parson did not have a good year and top management is under pressure to boost reported income. According to its records. the inventory balance at year-end was $600,000. However, the following information was not considered when determining that amount.

1. The physical count did not include goods purchased by Parson with a cost of $30,000 that were shipped FOB destination on December 28 and did not arrive at Parson's warehouse until January 3.
2. Included in the company's count were goods with a cost of $150,000 that the company is holding on consignment. The goods belong to Alvarez Corporation.
3. Included in the inventory account was $21,000 of office supplies that were stored in the warehouse and were to be used by the company's supervisors and managers during the coming year.
4. The company received an order on December 28 that was boxed and was sitting on the loading dock awaiting pick-up on December 31. The shipper picked up the goods on January 1 and delivered them on January 6. The shipping terms were FOB shipping point. The goods had a selling price of $29,000 and a cost of $19,000. The goods were not included in the count because they were sitting on the dock.
5. On December 29, Parson shipped goods with a selling price of $56,000 and a cost of $40,000 to Decco Corporation FOB shipping point. The goods arrived on January 3. Decco had only ordered goods with a selling price of $10,000 and a cost of $6,000. However, a Parson's sales manager had authorized the shipment and said that if Decco wanted to ship the goods back next week, it could.
6. Included in the count was $27,000 of goods that were parts for a machine that the company no longer made. Given the high-tech nature of Parson's products, it was unlikely that these obsolete parts had any other use. However, management would prefer to keep them on the books at cost, "since that is what we paid for them, after all."

Instructions

Prepare a schedule to determine the correct inventory amount. Provide explanations for each item above, saying why you did or did not make an adjustment for each item.

Solution

1. Ending inventory—as reported	$600,000
1. No effect—title does not pass to Parson until goods are received (Jan. 3).	0
2. Subtract from inventory: The goods belong to Alvarez Corporation. Parson is merely holding them as a consignee.	(150,000)
3. Subtract from inventory: Office supplies should be carried in a separate account. They are not considered inventory held for resale.	(21,000)
4. Add to inventory: The goods belong to Parson until they are shipped (Jan. 1).	19,000
5. Add to inventory: Decco ordered goods with a cost of $6,000. Parson should record the corresponding sales revenue of $10,000. Parson's decision to ship extra "unordered" goods does not constitute a sale. The manager's statement that Decco could ship the goods back indicates that Parson knows this over-shipment is not a legitimate sale. The manager acted unethically in an attempt to improve Parson's reported income by overshipping.	34,000
6. Subtract from inventory: GAAP require that inventory be valued at the lower-of-cost-or-market. Obsolete parts should be adjusted from cost to zero if they have no other use.	(27,000)
Correct inventory	$455,000

2. Rhode Software reported cost of goods sold as follows.

Determine effects of inventory errors.

(LO 3)

	2016	2017
Beginning inventory	$ 27,000	$ 40,000
Cost of goods purchased	200,000	235,000
Cost of goods available for sale	227,000	275,000
Ending inventory	40,000	45,000
Cost of goods sold	$187,000	$230,000

Rhode made two errors: (1) 2016 ending inventory was overstated $4,000, and (2) 2017 ending inventory was understated $9,000.

Instructions

Compute the correct cost of goods sold for each year.

Solution

2.

	2016	2017
Beginning inventory	$ 27,000	$ 36,000
Cost of goods purchased	200,000	235,000
Cost of goods available for sale	227,000	271,000
Corrected ending inventory	(36,000)[a]	(54,000)[b]
Cost of goods sold	$191,000	$217,000

[a]$40,000 − $4,000 = $36,000; [b]$45,000 + $9,000 = $54,000

PRACTICE PROBLEMS

1. Gerald D. Englehart Company has the following inventory, purchases, and sales data for the month of March.

Compute inventory and cost of goods sold using three cost flow methods in a periodic inventory system.

(LO 2)

Inventory:	March 1	200 units @ $4.00	$ 800
Purchases:	March 10	500 units @ $4.50	2,250
	March 20	400 units @ $4.75	1,900
	March 30	300 units @ $5.00	1,500
Sales:	March 15	500 units	
	March 25	400 units	

The physical inventory count on March 31 shows 500 units on hand.

Instructions

Under a **periodic inventory system**, determine the cost of inventory on hand at March 31 and the cost of goods sold for March under (a) FIFO, (b) LIFO, and (c) average-cost.

Solution

1. The cost of goods available for sale is $6,450, as follows.

Inventory:		200 units @ $4.00	$ 800
Purchases:	March 10	500 units @ $4.50	2,250
	March 20	400 units @ $4.75	1,900
	March 30	300 units @ $5.00	1,500
Total:		1,400	$6,450

Under a **periodic inventory system**, the cost of goods sold under each cost flow method is as follows.

(a) **FIFO Method**

Ending inventory:

Date	Units	Unit Cost	Total Cost	
March 30	300	$5.00	$1,500	
March 20	200	4.75	950	$2,450

Cost of goods sold: $6,450 − $2,450 = $4,000

(b) **LIFO Method**

Ending inventory:

Date	Units	Unit Cost	Total Cost	
March 1	200	$4.00	$ 800	
March 10	300	4.50	1,350	$2,150

Cost of goods sold: $6,450 − $2,150 = $4,300

(c) **Average-Cost Method**

Average unit cost: $6,450 ÷ 1,400 = $4.607
Ending inventory: 500 × $4.607 = $2,303.50

Cost of goods sold: $6,450 − $2,303.50 = $4,146.50

Compute inventory and cost of goods sold using three cost flow methods in a perpetual inventory system.

(LO 5)

***2. Practice Problem 1** on page 291 showed cost of goods sold computations under a periodic inventory system. Now let's assume that Gerald D. Englehart Company uses a perpetual inventory system. The company has the same inventory, purchases, and sales data for the month of March as shown earlier:

Inventory:	March 1	200 units @ $4.00	$ 800
Purchases:	March 10	500 units @ $4.50	2,250
	March 20	400 units @ $4.75	1,900
	March 30	300 units @ $5.00	1,500
Sales:	March 15	500 units	
	March 25	400 units	

The physical inventory count on March 31 shows 500 units on hand.

Instructions

Under a **perpetual inventory system**, determine the cost of inventory on hand at March 31 and the cost of goods sold for March under (a) FIFO, (b) LIFO, and (c) moving-average cost.

Solution

2. The cost of goods available for sale is $6,450, as follows.

Inventory:		200 units @ $4.00	$ 800
Purchases:	March 10	500 units @ $4.50	2,250
	March 20	400 units @ $4.75	1,900
	March 30	300 units @ $5.00	1,500
Total:		1,400	$6,450

Under a **perpetual inventory system**, the cost of goods sold under each cost flow method is as follows.

(a) **FIFO Method**

Date	Purchases	Cost of Goods Sold	Balance
March 1			(200 @ $4.00) $ 800
March 10	(500 @ $4.50) $2,250		(200 @ $4.00) (500 @ $4.50) } $3,050
March 15		(200 @ $4.00) (300 @ $4.50) $2,150	(200 @ $4.50) $ 900
March 20	(400 @ $4.75) $1,900		(200 @ $4.50) (400 @ $4.75) } $2,800
March 25		(200 @ $4.50) (200 @ $4.75) $1,850	(200 @ $4.75) $ 950
March 30	(300 @ $5.00) $1,500		(200 @ $4.75) (300 @ $5.00) } $2,450

Ending inventory $2,450   Cost of goods sold: $2,150 + $1,850 = $4,000

(b) **LIFO Method**

Date	Purchases		Cost of Goods Sold		Balance	
March 1					(200 @ \$4.00)	\$ 800
March 10	(500 @ \$4.50)	\$2,250			(200 @ \$4.00) (500 @ \$4.50)	\$3,050
March 15			(500 @ \$4.50)	\$2,250	(200 @ \$4.00)	\$ 800
March 20	(400 @ \$4.75)	\$1,900			(200 @ \$4.00) (400 @ \$4.75)	\$2,700
March 25			(400 @ \$4.75)	\$1,900	(200 @ \$4.00)	\$ 800
March 30	(300 @ \$5.00)	\$1,500			(200 @ \$4.00) (300 @ \$5.00)	\$2,300

Ending inventory \$2,300 Cost of goods sold: \$2,250 + \$1,900 = \$4,150

(c) **Moving-Average Cost Method**

Date	Purchases		Cost of Goods Sold		Balance	
March 1					(200 @ \$ 4.00)	\$ 800
March 10	(500 @ \$4.50)	\$2,250			(700 @ \$4.357)	\$3,050
March 15			(500 @ \$4.357)	\$2,179	(200 @ \$4.357)	\$ 871
March 20	(400 @ \$4.75)	\$1,900			(600 @ \$4.618)	\$2,771
March 25			(400 @ \$4.618)	\$1,847	(200 @ \$4.618)	\$ 924
March 30	(300 @ \$5.00)	\$1,500			(500 @ \$4.848)	\$2,424

Ending inventory \$2,424 Cost of goods sold: \$2,179 + \$1,847 = \$4,026

NOTE: All asterisked Questions, Exercises, and Problems relate to material in the appendices to the chapter.

QUESTIONS

1. "The key to successful business operations is effective inventory management." Do you agree? Explain.
2. An item must possess two characteristics to be classified as inventory by a merchandiser. What are these two characteristics?
3. Your friend Ben Johnson has been hired to help take the physical inventory in Pearson Hardware Store. Explain to Ben what this job will entail.
4. (a) Jovad Company ships merchandise to Martin Company on December 30. The merchandise reaches the buyer on January 6. Indicate the terms of sale that will result in the goods being included in (1) Jovad's December 31 inventory, and (2) Martin's December 31 inventory.
   (b) Under what circumstances should Jovad Company include consigned goods in its inventory?
5. Topp Hat Shop received a shipment of hats for which it paid the wholesaler \$2,970. The price of the hats was \$3,000 but Topp was given a \$30 cash discount and required to pay freight charges of \$50. In addition, Topp paid \$130 to cover the travel expenses of an employee who negotiated the purchase of the hats. What amount will Topp record for inventory? Why?
6. Explain the difference between the terms FOB shipping point and FOB destination.
7. Leah Clement believes that the allocation of inventoriable costs should be based on the actual physical flow of the goods. Explain to Leah why this may be both impractical and inappropriate.
8. What is a major advantage and a major disadvantage of the specific identification method of inventory costing?
9. "The selection of an inventory cost flow method is a decision made by accountants." Do you agree? Explain. Once a method has been selected, what accounting requirement applies?
10. Which assumed inventory cost flow method:
    (a) usually parallels the actual physical flow of merchandise?
    (b) assumes that goods available for sale during an accounting period are identical?
    (c) assumes that the latest units purchased are the first to be sold?
11. In a period of rising prices, the inventory reported in Bert Company's balance sheet is close to the current cost of the inventory. Ernie Company's inventory is considerably below its current cost. Identify the inventory cost flow method being used by each company. Which company has probably been reporting the higher gross profit?
12. Oscar Company has been using the FIFO cost flow method during a prolonged period of rising prices. During the same time period, Oscar has been paying out all of its net income as dividends. What adverse effects may result from this policy?
13. Kyle Adams is studying for the next accounting midterm examination. What should Kyle know about (a) departing from the cost basis of accounting for

inventories and (b) the meaning of "market" in the lower-of-cost-or-market method?

14. Hendrix Entertainment Center has 5 televisions on hand at the balance sheet date. Each cost $400. The current replacement cost is $380 per unit. Under the lower-of-cost-or-market basis of accounting for inventories, what value should be reported for the televisions on the balance sheet? Why?
15. Warnke Stores has 20 toasters on hand at the balance sheet date. Each costs $27. The current replacement cost is $30 per unit. Under the lower-of-cost-or-market basis of accounting for inventories, what value should Warnke report for the toasters on the balance sheet? Why?
16. Sayaovang Company discovers in 2017 that its ending inventory at December 31, 2016, was $7,000 understated. What effect will this error have on (a) 2016 net income, (b) 2017 net income, and (c) the combined net income for the 2 years?
17. Dreher Company's balance sheet shows Inventory $162,800. What additional disclosures should be made?
18. Under what circumstances might inventory turnover be too high? That is, what possible negative consequences might occur?
19. What inventory cost flow does Apple use for its inventories? (*Hint:* You will need to examine the notes for Apple's financial statements.)

*20. "When perpetual inventory records are kept, the results under the FIFO and LIFO methods are the same as they would be in a periodic inventory system." Do you agree? Explain.

*21. How does the average-cost method of inventory costing differ between a perpetual inventory system and a periodic inventory system?

*22. When is it necessary to estimate inventories?

*23. Both the gross profit method and the retail inventory method are based on averages. For each method, indicate the average used, how it is determined, and how it is applied.

*24. Pawlowski Company has net sales of $400,000 and cost of goods available for sale of $300,000. If the gross profit rate is 35%, what is the estimated cost of the ending inventory? Show computations.

*25. Cinderella Shoe Shop had goods available for sale in 2017 with a retail price of $120,000. The cost of these goods was $84,000. If sales during the period were $80,000, what is the ending inventory at cost using the retail inventory method?

BRIEF EXERCISES

Identify items to be included in taking a physical inventory.
(LO 1)

BE6-1 Peosta Company identifies the following items for possible inclusion in the taking of a physical inventory. Indicate whether each item should be included or excluded from the inventory taking.

(a) Goods shipped on consignment by Peosta to another company.
(b) Goods in transit from a supplier shipped FOB destination.
(c) Goods sold but being held for customer pickup.
(d) Goods held on consignment from another company.

Determine ending inventory amount.
(LO 1)

BE6-2 Stallman Company took a physical inventory on December 31 and determined that goods costing $200,000 were on hand. Not included in the physical count were $25,000 of goods purchased from Pelzer Corporation, FOB shipping point, and $22,000 of goods sold to Alvarez Company for $30,000, FOB destination. Both the Pelzer purchase and the Alvarez sale were in transit at year-end. What amount should Stallman report as its December 31 inventory?

Compute ending inventory using FIFO and LIFO.
(LO 2)

BE6-3 In its first month of operations, Weatherall Company made three purchases of merchandise in the following sequence: (1) 300 units at $6, (2) 400 units at $7, and (3) 200 units at $8. Assuming there are 380 units on hand, compute the cost of the ending inventory under the (a) FIFO method and (b) LIFO method. Weatherall uses a periodic inventory system.

Compute the ending inventory using average-cost.
(LO 2)

BE6-4 Data for Weatherall Company are presented in BE6-3. Compute the cost of the ending inventory under the average-cost method, assuming there are 380 units on hand.

Explain the financial statement effect of inventory cost flow assumptions.
(LO 2)

BE6-5 The management of Mastronardo Corp. is considering the effects of inventory-costing methods on its financial statements and its income tax expense. Assuming that the price the company pays for inventory is increasing, which method will:

(a) Provide the highest net income?
(b) Provide the highest ending inventory?
(c) Result in the lowest income tax expense?
(d) Result in the most stable earnings over a number of years?

Determine correct income statement amounts.
(LO 3)

BE6-6 Larkin Company reports net income of $90,000 in 2017. However, ending inventory was understated $7,000. What is the correct net income for 2017? What effect, if any, will this error have on total assets as reported in the balance sheet at December 31, 2017?

BE6-7 Cruz Video Center accumulates the following cost and market data at December 31.

Determine the LCM valuation using inventory categories.

(LO 4)

Inventory Categories	Cost Data	Market Data
Cameras	$12,000	$12,300
Camcorders	9,500	9,700
Blu-ray players	14,000	12,900

Compute the lower-of-cost-or-market valuation for the company's total inventory.

BE6-8 At December 31, 2017, the following information was available for E. Hetzel Company: ending inventory $40,000, beginning inventory $56,000, cost of goods sold $270,000, and sales revenue $380,000. Calculate inventory turnover and days in inventory for E. Hetzel Company.

Compute inventory turnover and days in inventory.

(LO 4)

***BE6-9** Rosario Department Store uses a perpetual inventory system. Data for product E2-D2 include the following purchases.

Apply cost flow methods to perpetual inventory records.

(LO 5)

Date	Number of Units	Unit Price
May 7	50	$10
July 28	30	13

On June 1, Rosario sold 26 units, and on August 27, 40 more units. Prepare the perpetual inventory schedule for the above transactions using (a) FIFO, (b) LIFO, and (c) moving-average cost.

***BE6-10** At May 31, Brunet Company has net sales of $340,000 and cost of goods available for sale of $230,000. Compute the estimated cost of the ending inventory, assuming the gross profit rate is 35%.

Apply the gross profit method.

(LO 6)

***BE6-11** On June 30, Joanna Fabrics has the following data pertaining to the retail inventory method. Goods available for sale: at cost $38,000; at retail $50,000; net sales $40,000; and ending inventory at retail $10,000. Compute the estimated cost of the ending inventory using the retail inventory method.

Apply the retail inventory method.

(LO 6)

DO IT! Exercises

DO IT! 6-1 Gresa Company just took its physical inventory. The count of inventory items on hand at the company's business locations resulted in a total inventory cost of $300,000. In reviewing the details of the count and related inventory transactions, you have discovered the following.

Apply rules of ownership to determine inventory cost.

(LO 1)

1. Gresa has sent inventory costing $26,000 on consignment to Alissa Company. All of this inventory was at Alissa's showrooms on December 31.
2. The company did not include in the count inventory (cost, $20,000) that was sold on December 28, terms FOB shipping point. The goods were in transit on December 31.
3. The company did not include in the count inventory (cost, $14,000) that was purchased with terms of FOB shipping point. The goods were in transit on December 31.

Compute the correct December 31 inventory.

DO IT! 6-2 The accounting records of Americo Electronics show the following data.

Compute cost of goods sold under different cost flow methods.

(LO 2)

Beginning inventory	3,000 units at $5
Purchases	8,000 units at $7
Sales	9,400 units at $10

Determine cost of goods sold during the period under a periodic inventory system using (a) the FIFO method, (b) the LIFO method, and (c) the average-cost method. (Round unit cost to nearest tenth of a cent.)

Determine effect of inventory error.

(LO 3)

DO IT! 6-3 Vanida Company understated its 2016 ending inventory by $27,000. Determine the impact this error has on ending inventory, cost of goods sold, and owner's equity in 2016 and 2017.

Compute inventory value under LCM and assess inventory level.

(LO 4)

DO IT! 6-4 (a) Cody Company sells three different categories of tools (small, medium, and large). The cost and market value of its inventory of tools are as follows.

	Cost	Market
Small	$ 64,000	$ 73,000
Medium	290,000	260,000
Large	152,000	171,000

Determine the value of the company's inventory under the lower-of-cost-or-market approach.
(b) Early in 2017, Yeng Company switched to a just-in-time inventory system. Its sales, cost of goods sold, and inventory amounts for 2016 and 2017 are shown below.

	2016	2017
Sales	$3,120,000	$3,713,000
Cost of goods sold	1,200,000	1,425,000
Beginning inventory	180,000	220,000
Ending inventory	220,000	100,000

Determine the inventory turnover and days in inventory for 2016 and 2017. Discuss the changes in the amount of inventory, the inventory turnover and days in inventory, and the amount of sales across the two years.

EXERCISES

Determine the correct inventory amount.

(LO 1)

E6-1 Tri-State Bank and Trust is considering giving Wilfred Company a loan. Before doing so, management decides that further discussions with Wilfred's accountant may be desirable. One area of particular concern is the inventory account, which has a year-end balance of $297,000. Discussions with the accountant reveal the following.

1. Wilfred sold goods costing $38,000 to Lilja Company, FOB shipping point, on December 28. The goods are not expected to arrive at Lilja until January 12. The goods were not included in the physical inventory because they were not in the warehouse.
2. The physical count of the inventory did not include goods costing $95,000 that were shipped to Wilfred FOB destination on December 27 and were still in transit at year-end.
3. Wilfred received goods costing $22,000 on January 2. The goods were shipped FOB shipping point on December 26 by Brent Co. The goods were not included in the physical count.
4. Wilfred sold goods costing $35,000 to Jesse Co., FOB destination, on December 30. The goods were received at Jesse on January 8. They were not included in Wilfred's physical inventory.
5. Wilfred received goods costing $44,000 on January 2 that were shipped FOB destination on December 29. The shipment was a rush order that was supposed to arrive December 31. This purchase was included in the ending inventory of $297,000.

Instructions

Determine the correct inventory amount on December 31.

Determine the correct inventory amount.

(LO 1)

E6-2 Kari Downs, an auditor with Wheeler CPAs, is performing a review of Depue Company's inventory account. Depue did not have a good year, and top management is under pressure to boost reported income. According to its records, the inventory balance at year-end was $740,000. However, the following information was not considered when determining that amount.

1. Included in the company's count were goods with a cost of $250,000 that the company is holding on consignment. The goods belong to Kroeger Corporation.
2. The physical count did not include goods purchased by Depue with a cost of $40,000 that were shipped FOB destination on December 28 and did not arrive at Depue warehouse until January 3.

3. Included in the inventory account was $14,000 of office supplies that were stored in the warehouse and were to be used by the company's supervisors and managers during the coming year.
4. The company received an order on December 29 that was boxed and sitting on the loading dock awaiting pick-up on December 31. The shipper picked up the goods on January 1 and delivered them on January 6. The shipping terms were FOB shipping point. The goods had a selling price of $40,000 and a cost of $28,000. The goods were not included in the count because they were sitting on the dock.
5. On December 29, Depue shipped goods with a selling price of $80,000 and a cost of $60,000 to Macchia Sales Corporation FOB shipping point. The goods arrived on January 3. Macchia had only ordered goods with a selling price of $10,000 and a cost of $8,000. However, a sales manager at Depue had authorized the shipment and said that if Machia wanted to ship the goods back next week, it could.
6. Included in the count was $40,000 of goods that were parts for a machine that the company no longer made. Given the high-tech nature of Depue's products, it was unlikely that these obsolete parts had any other use. However, management would prefer to keep them on the books at cost, "since that is what we paid for them, after all."

Instructions

Prepare a schedule to determine the correct inventory amount. Provide explanations for each item above, saying why you did or did not make an adjustment for each item.

Calculate cost of goods sold using specific identification and FIFO.

(LO 2)

E6-3 On December 1, Kiyak Electronics Ltd. has three DVD players left in stock. All are identical, all are priced to sell at $150. One of the three DVD players left in stock, with serial #1012, was purchased on June 1 at a cost of $100. Another, with serial #1045, was purchased on November 1 for $88. The last player, serial #1056, was purchased on November 30 for $80.

Instructions

(a) Calculate the cost of goods sold using the FIFO periodic inventory method assuming that two of the three players were sold by the end of December, Kiyak Electronics' year-end.

(b) If Kiyak Electronics used the specific identification method instead of the FIFO method, how might it alter its earnings by "selectively choosing" which particular players to sell to the two customers? What would Kiyak's cost of goods sold be if the company wished to minimize earnings? Maximize earnings?

(c) Which of the two inventory methods do you recommend that Kiyak use? Explain why.

Compute inventory and cost of goods sold using FIFO and LIFO.

(LO 2)

E6-4 Elsa's Boards sells a snowboard, Xpert, that is popular with snowboard enthusiasts. Information relating to Elsa's purchases of Xpert snowboards during September is shown below. During the same month, 121 Xpert snowboards were sold. Elsa's uses a periodic inventory system.

Date	Explanation	Units	Unit Cost	Total Cost
Sept. 1	Inventory	26	$ 97	$ 2,522
Sept. 12	Purchases	45	102	4,590
Sept. 19	Purchases	20	104	2,080
Sept. 26	Purchases	50	105	5,250
	Totals	141		$14,442

Instructions

(a) Compute the ending inventory at September 30 and cost of goods sold using the FIFO and LIFO methods. Prove the amount allocated to cost of goods sold under each method.

(b) For both FIFO and LIFO, calculate the sum of ending inventory and cost of goods sold. What do you notice about the answers you found for each method?

Compute inventory and cost of goods sold using FIFO and LIFO.

(LO 2)

E6-5 Ballas Co. uses a periodic inventory system. Its records show the following for the month of May, in which 68 units were sold.

		Units	Unit Cost	Total Cost
May 1	Inventory	30	$ 8	$240
15	Purchases	25	11	275
24	Purchases	35	12	420
	Totals	90		$935

Instructions

Compute the ending inventory at May 31 and cost of goods sold using the FIFO and LIFO methods. Prove the amount allocated to cost of goods sold under each method.

Compute inventory and cost of goods sold using FIFO and LIFO.

(LO 2)

E6-6 Moath Company reports the following for the month of June.

		Units	Unit Cost	Total Cost
June 1	Inventory	200	$5	$1,000
12	Purchase	400	6	2,400
23	Purchase	300	7	2,100
30	Inventory	100		

Instructions

(a) Compute the cost of the ending inventory and the cost of goods sold under (1) FIFO and (2) LIFO.
(b) Which costing method gives the higher ending inventory? Why?
(c) Which method results in the higher cost of goods sold? Why?

Compute inventory under FIFO, LIFO, and average-cost.

(LO 2)

E6-7 Shawn Company had 100 units in beginning inventory at a total cost of $10,000. The company purchased 200 units at a total cost of $26,000. At the end of the year, Shawn had 75 units in ending inventory.

Instructions

(a) Compute the cost of the ending inventory and the cost of goods sold under (1) FIFO, (2) LIFO, and (3) average-cost.
(b) Which cost flow method would result in the highest net income?
(c) Which cost flow method would result in inventories approximating current cost in the balance sheet?
(d) Which cost flow method would result in Shawn paying the least taxes in the first year?

Compute inventory and cost of goods sold using average-cost.

(LO 2)

E6-8 Inventory data for Moath Company are presented in E6-6.

Instructions

(a) Compute the cost of the ending inventory and the cost of goods sold using the average-cost method.
(b) Will the results in (a) be higher or lower than the results under (1) FIFO and (2) LIFO?
(c) Why is the average unit cost not $6?

Determine effects of inventory errors.

(LO 3)

E6-9 Elliott's Hardware reported cost of goods sold as follows.

	2016	2017
Beginning inventory	$ 20,000	$ 30,000
Cost of goods purchased	150,000	175,000
Cost of goods available for sale	170,000	205,000
Ending inventory	30,000	35,000
Cost of goods sold	$140,000	$170,000

Elliott's made two errors: (1) 2016 ending inventory was overstated $3,000, and (2) 2017 ending inventory was understated $5,000.

Instructions

Compute the correct cost of goods sold for each year.

Prepare correct income statements.

(LO 3)

E6-10 Smart Watch Company reported the following income statement data for a 2-year period.

	2016	2017
Sales revenue	$220,000	$250,000
Cost of goods sold		
Beginning inventory	32,000	44,000
Cost of goods purchased	173,000	202,000
Cost of goods available for sale	205,000	246,000
Ending inventory	44,000	52,000
Cost of goods sold	161,000	194,000
Gross profit	$ 59,000	$ 56,000

Smart uses a periodic inventory system. The inventories at January 1, 2016, and December 31, 2017, are correct. However, the ending inventory at December 31, 2016, was overstated $6,000.

Instructions

(a) Prepare correct income statement data for the 2 years.

(b) What is the cumulative effect of the inventory error on total gross profit for the 2 years?

(c) Explain in a letter to the president of Smart Watch Company what has happened, i.e., the nature of the error and its effect on the financial statements.

E6-11 Freeze Frame Camera Shop uses the lower-of-cost-or-market basis for its inventory. The following data are available at December 31.

Determine ending inventory under LCM.

(LO 4)

Item	Units	Unit Cost	Market
Cameras:			
Minolta	5	$170	$156
Canon	6	150	152
Light meters:			
Vivitar	10	125	115
Kodak	14	120	135

Instructions

Determine the amount of the ending inventory by applying the lower-of-cost-or-market basis.

E6-12 Charapata Company applied FIFO to its inventory and got the following results for its ending inventory.

Compute lower-of-cost-or-market

(LO 4)

Cameras	100 units at a cost per unit of $65
Blu-ray players	150 units at a cost per unit of $75
iPods	125 units at a cost per unit of $80

The cost of purchasing units at year-end was cameras $71, Blu-ray players $67, and iPods $78.

Instructions

Determine the amount of ending inventory at lower-of-cost-or-market.

E6-13 This information is available for Abdullah's Photo Corporation for 2015, 2016, and 2017.

Compute inventory turnover, days in inventory, and gross profit rate.

(LO 4)

	2015	2016	2017
Beginning inventory	$ 100,000	$ 300,000	$ 400,000
Ending inventory	300,000	400,000	480,000
Cost of goods sold	900,000	1,152,000	1,300,000
Sales revenue	1,200,000	1,600,000	1,900,000

Instructions

Calculate inventory turnover, days in inventory, and gross profit rate (from Chapter 5) for Abdullah's Photo Corporation for 2015, 2016, and 2017. Comment on any trends.

E6-14 The cost of goods sold computations for Sooner Company and Later Company are shown below.

Compute inventory turnover and days in inventory.

(LO 4)

	Sooner Company	Later Company
Beginning inventory	$ 45,000	$ 71,000
Cost of goods purchased	200,000	290,000
Cost of goods available for sale	245,000	361,000
Ending inventory	55,000	69,000
Cost of goods sold	$190,000	$292,000

Instructions

(a) Compute inventory turnover and days in inventory for each company.

(b) Which company moves its inventory more quickly?

Apply cost flow methods to perpetual records.

(LO 5)

***E6-15** Ehrhart Appliance uses a perpetual inventory system. For its flat-screen television sets, the January 1 inventory was 3 sets at $600 each. On January 10, Ehrhart purchased 6 units at $660 each. The company sold 2 units on January 8 and 5 units on January 15.

Instructions

Compute the ending inventory under (a) FIFO, (b) LIFO, and (c) moving-average cost.

Calculate inventory and cost of goods sold using three cost flow methods in a perpetual inventory system.

(LO 5)

***E6-16** Moath Company reports the following for the month of June.

Date	Explanation	Units	Unit Cost	Total Cost
June 1	Inventory	200	$5	$1,000
12	Purchase	400	6	2,400
23	Purchase	300	7	2,100
30	Inventory	100		

Instructions

(a) Calculate the cost of the ending inventory and the cost of goods sold for each cost flow assumption, using a perpetual inventory system. Assume a sale of 440 units occurred on June 15 for a selling price of $8 and a sale of 360 units on June 27 for $9.

(b) How do the results differ from E6-6 and E6-8?

(c) Why is the average unit cost not $6 [($5 + $6 + $7) ÷ 3 = $6]?

Apply cost flow methods to perpetual records.

(LO 5)

***E6-17** Information about Elsa's Boards is presented in E6-4. Additional data regarding Elsa's sales of Xpert snowboards are provided below. Assume that Elsa's uses a perpetual inventory system.

Date		Units	Unit Price	Total Revenue
Sept. 5	Sale	12	$199	$ 2,388
Sept. 16	Sale	50	199	9,950
Sept. 29	Sale	59	209	12,331
	Totals	121		$24,669

Instructions

(a) Compute ending inventory at September 30 using FIFO, LIFO, and moving-average cost.

(b) Compare ending inventory using a perpetual inventory system to ending inventory using a periodic inventory system (from E6-4).

(c) Which inventory cost flow method (FIFO, LIFO) gives the same ending inventory value under both periodic and perpetual? Which method gives different ending inventory values?

Use the gross profit method to estimate inventory.

(LO 6)

***E6-18** Shereen Company reported the following information for November and December 2017.

	November	December
Cost of goods purchased	$536,000	$ 610,000
Inventory, beginning-of-month	130,000	120,000
Inventory, end-of-month	120,000	?
Sales revenue	840,000	1,000,000

Shereen's ending inventory at December 31 was destroyed in a fire.

Instructions

(a) Compute the gross profit rate for November.

(b) Using the gross profit rate for November, determine the estimated cost of inventory lost in the fire.

Determine merchandise lost using the gross profit method of estimating inventory.

(LO 6)

***E6-19** The inventory of Hang Company was destroyed by fire on March 1. From an examination of the accounting records, the following data for the first 2 months of the year are obtained: Sales Revenue $51,000, Sales Returns and Allowances $1,000, Purchases $31,200, Freight-In $1,200, and Purchase Returns and Allowances $1,400.

Instructions

Determine the merchandise lost by fire, assuming:

(a) A beginning inventory of $20,000 and a gross profit rate of 30% on net sales.

(b) A beginning inventory of $30,000 and a gross profit rate of 40% on net sales.

***E6-20** Kicks Shoe Store uses the retail inventory method for its two departments, Women's Shoes and Men's Shoes. The following information for each department is obtained.

Determine ending inventory at cost using retail method.

(LO 6)

Item	Women's Shoes	Men's Shoes
Beginning inventory at cost	$ 25,000	$ 45,000
Cost of goods purchased at cost	110,000	136,300
Net sales	178,000	185,000
Beginning inventory at retail	46,000	60,000
Cost of goods purchased at retail	179,000	185,000

Instructions

Compute the estimated cost of the ending inventory for each department under the retail inventory method.

EXERCISES: SET B AND CHALLENGE EXERCISES

Visit the book's companion website, at **www.wiley.com/college/weygandt**, and choose the Student Companion site to access Exercises: Set B and Challenge Exercises.

PROBLEMS: SET A

P6-1A Houghton Limited is trying to determine the value of its ending inventory as of February 28, 2017, the company's year-end. The following transactions occurred, and the accountant asked your help in determining whether they should be recorded or not.

Determine items and amounts to be recorded in inventory.

(LO 1)

(a) On February 26, Houghton shipped goods costing $800 to a customer and charged the customer $1,000. The goods were shipped with terms FOB shipping point and the receiving report indicates that the customer received the goods on March 2.
(b) On February 26, Crain Inc. shipped goods to Houghton under terms FOB shipping point. The invoice price was $450 plus $30 for freight. The receiving report indicates that the goods were received by Houghton on March 2.
(c) Houghton had $720 of inventory isolated in the warehouse. The inventory is designated for a customer who has requested that the goods be shipped on March 10.
(d) Also included in Houghton's warehouse is $700 of inventory that Korenic Producers shipped to Houghton on consignment.
(e) On February 26, Houghton issued a purchase order to acquire goods costing $900. The goods were shipped with terms FOB destination on February 27. Houghton received the goods on March 2.
(f) On February 26, Houghton shipped goods to a customer under terms FOB destination. The invoice price was $390; the cost of the items was $240. The receiving report indicates that the goods were received by the customer on March 2.

Instructions

For each of the above transactions, specify whether the item in question should be included in ending inventory, and if so, at what amount.

P6-2A Glee Distribution markets CDs of the performing artist Unique. At the beginning of October, Glee had in beginning inventory 2,000 of Unique's CDs with a unit cost of $7. During October, Glee made the following purchases of Unique's CDs.

Determine cost of goods sold and ending inventory using FIFO, LIFO, and average-cost with analysis.

(LO 2)

Oct. 3	2,500 @ $8	Oct. 19	3,000 @ $10
Oct. 9	3,500 @ $9	Oct. 25	4,000 @ $11

During October, 10,900 units were sold. Glee uses a periodic inventory system.

Instructions

(a) Determine the cost of goods available for sale.
(b) Determine (1) the ending inventory and (2) the cost of goods sold under each of the assumed cost flow methods (FIFO, LIFO, and average-cost). Prove the accuracy of the cost of goods sold under the FIFO and LIFO methods.
(c) Which cost flow method results in (1) the highest inventory amount for the balance sheet and (2) the highest cost of goods sold for the income statement?

(b)(2) Cost of goods sold:

FIFO	$ 94,500
LIFO	$108,700
Average	$101,370

Determine cost of goods sold and ending inventory, using FIFO, LIFO, and average-cost with analysis.

(LO 2)

P6-3A Sekhon Company had a beginning inventory on January 1 of 160 units of Product 4-18-15 at a cost of $20 per unit. During the year, the following purchases were made.

Mar. 15	400 units at $23	Sept. 4	330 units at $26
July 20	250 units at $24	Dec. 2	100 units at $29

1,000 units were sold. Sekhon Company uses a periodic inventory system.

Instructions

(a) Determine the cost of goods available for sale.

(b) Determine (1) the ending inventory, and (2) the cost of goods sold under each of the assumed cost flow methods (FIFO, LIFO, and average-cost). Prove the accuracy of the cost of goods sold under the FIFO and LIFO methods.

(c) Which cost flow method results in (1) the highest inventory amount for the balance sheet, and (2) the highest cost of goods sold for the income statement?

(b)(2) Cost of goods sold:
FIFO $23,340
LIFO $24,840
Average $24,097

Compute ending inventory, prepare income statements, and answer questions using FIFO and LIFO.

(LO 2)

P6-4A The management of Gresa Inc. is reevaluating the appropriateness of using its present inventory cost flow method, which is average-cost. The company requests your help in determining the results of operations for 2017 if either the FIFO or the LIFO method had been used. For 2017, the accounting records show these data:

Inventories		**Purchases and Sales**	
Beginning (7,000 units)	$14,000	Total net sales (180,000 units)	$747,000
Ending (17,000 units)		Total cost of goods purchased (190,000 units)	466,000

Purchases were made quarterly as follows.

Quarter	**Units**	**Unit Cost**	**Total Cost**
1	50,000	$2.20	$110,000
2	40,000	2.35	94,000
3	40,000	2.50	100,000
4	60,000	2.70	162,000
	190,000		$466,000

Operating expenses were $130,000, and the company's income tax rate is 40%.

Instructions

(a) Prepare comparative condensed income statements for 2017 under FIFO and LIFO. (Show computations of ending inventory.)

(b) Answer the following questions for management.

(1) Which cost flow method (FIFO or LIFO) produces the more meaningful inventory amount for the balance sheet? Why?

(2) Which cost flow method (FIFO or LIFO) produces the more meaningful net income? Why?

(3) Which cost flow method (FIFO or LIFO) is more likely to approximate the actual physical flow of goods? Why?

(4) How much more cash will be available for management under LIFO than under FIFO? Why?

(5) Will gross profit under the average-cost method be higher or lower than FIFO? Than LIFO? (*Note:* It is not necessary to quantify your answer.)

(a) Gross profit:
FIFO $312,900
LIFO $303,000

Calculate ending inventory, cost of goods sold, gross profit, and gross profit rate under periodic method; compare results.

(LO 2)

P6-5A You are provided with the following information for Koetteritz Inc. for the month ended June 30, 2017. Koetteritz uses the periodic method for inventory.

Date	**Description**	**Quantity**	**Unit Cost or Selling Price**
June 1	Beginning inventory	40	$40
June 4	Purchase	135	43
June 10	Sale	110	70
June 11	Sale return	15	70
June 18	Purchase	55	46
June 18	Purchase return	10	46
June 25	Sale	65	76
June 28	Purchase	35	50

Instructions

(a) Calculate (i) ending inventory, (ii) cost of goods sold, (iii) gross profit, and (iv) gross profit rate under each of the following methods.
   (1) LIFO. (2) FIFO. (3) Average-cost.
(b) Compare results for the three cost flow assumptions.

(a)(iii) Gross profit:
LIFO $4,330
FIFO $4,830
Average $4,546.90

P6-6A You are provided with the following information for Gobler Inc. Gobler Inc. uses the periodic method of accounting for its inventory transactions.

Compare specific identification, FIFO, and LIFO under periodic method; use cost flow assumption to justify price increase.

(LO 2)

March 1	Beginning inventory 2,000 liters at a cost of 60¢ per liter.
March 3	Purchased 2,500 liters at a cost of 65¢ per liter.
March 5	Sold 2,300 liters for $1.05 per liter.
March 10	Purchased 4,000 liters at a cost of 72¢ per liter.
March 20	Purchased 2,500 liters at a cost of 80¢ per liter.
March 30	Sold 5,200 liters for $1.25 per liter.

Instructions

(a) Prepare partial income statements through gross profit, and calculate the value of ending inventory that would be reported on the balance sheet, under each of the following cost flow assumptions. (Round ending inventory and cost of goods sold to the nearest dollar.)
   (1) Specific identification method assuming:
      (i) The March 5 sale consisted of 1,000 liters from the March 1 beginning inventory and 1,300 liters from the March 3 purchase; and
      (ii) The March 30 sale consisted of the following number of units sold from beginning inventory and each purchase: 450 liters from March 1; 550 liters from March 3; 2,900 liters from March 10; 1,300 liters from March 20.
   (2) FIFO.
   (3) LIFO.
(b) How can companies use a cost flow method to justify price increases? Which cost flow method would best support an argument to increase prices?

(a) Gross profit:
(1) Specific identification $3,715
(2) FIFO $3,930
(3) LIFO $3,385

P6-7A The management of Danica Co. asks your help in determining the comparative effects of the FIFO and LIFO inventory cost flow methods. For 2017, the accounting records provide the following data.

Compute ending inventory, prepare income statements, and answer questions using FIFO and LIFO.

(LO 2)

Inventory, January 1 (10,000 units)	$ 47,000
Cost of 100,000 units purchased	532,000
Selling price of 84,000 units sold	735,000
Operating expenses	140,000

Units purchased consisted of 35,000 units at $5.10 on May 10; 35,000 units at $5.30 on August 15; and 30,000 units at $5.60 on November 20. Income taxes are 30%.

Instructions

(a) Prepare comparative condensed income statements for 2017 under FIFO and LIFO. (Show computations of ending inventory.)
(b) Answer the following questions for management.
   (1) Which inventory cost flow method produces the most meaningful inventory amount for the balance sheet? Why?
   (2) Which inventory cost flow method produces the most meaningful net income? Why?
   (3) Which inventory cost flow method is most likely to approximate actual physical flow of the goods? Why?
   (4) How much additional cash will be available for management under LIFO than under FIFO? Why?
   (5) How much of the gross profit under FIFO is illusory in comparison with the gross profit under LIFO?

(a) Net income
FIFO $113,120
LIFO $101,220

Calculate cost of goods sold and ending inventory under LIFO, FIFO, and moving-average cost under the perpetual system; compare gross profit under each assumption.

(LO 5)

***P6-8A** Dempsey Inc. is a retailer operating in British Columbia. Dempsey uses the perpetual inventory method. All sales returns from customers result in the goods being returned to inventory; the inventory is not damaged. Assume that there are no credit transactions;

all amounts are settled in cash. You are provided with the following information for Dempsey Inc. for the month of January 2017.

Date	Description	Quantity	Unit Cost or Selling Price
January 1	Beginning inventory	100	$15
January 5	Purchase	140	18
January 8	Sale	110	28
January 10	Sale return	10	28
January 15	Purchase	55	20
January 16	Purchase return	5	20
January 20	Sale	90	32
January 25	Purchase	20	22

(a)(iii) Gross profit:
LIFO $2,160
FIFO $2,560
Average $2,421

Instructions

(a) For each of the following cost flow assumptions, calculate (i) cost of goods sold, (ii) ending inventory, and (iii) gross profit.
 (1) LIFO.
 (2) FIFO.
 (3) Moving-average cost. (Round cost per unit to three decimal places.)

(b) Compare results for the three cost flow assumptions.

Determine ending inventory under a perpetual inventory system.

(LO 5)

***P6-9A** Wittmann Co. began operations on July 1. It uses a perpetual inventory system. During July, the company had the following purchases and sales.

	Purchases		
Date	**Units**	**Unit Cost**	**Sales Units**
July 1	5	$122	
July 6			3
July 11	7	$136	
July 14			5
July 21	8	$147	
July 27			5

(a) Ending inventory
FIFO $1,029
Avg. $996
LIFO $957

Instructions

(a) Determine the ending inventory under a perpetual inventory system using (1) FIFO, (2) moving-average cost, and (3) LIFO.

(b) Which costing method produces the highest ending inventory valuation?

Compute gross profit rate and inventory loss using gross profit method.

(LO 6)

XLS

***P6-10A** Bao Company lost all of its inventory in a fire on December 26, 2017. The accounting records showed the following gross profit data for November and December.

	November	December (to 12/26)
Net sales	$600,000	$700,000
Beginning inventory	32,000	36,000
Purchases	389,000	420,000
Purchase returns and allowances	13,300	14,900
Purchase discounts	8,500	9,500
Freight-in	8,800	9,900
Ending inventory	36,000	?

Bao is fully insured for fire losses but must prepare a report for the insurance company.

(a) Gross profit rate 38%

Instructions

(a) Compute the gross profit rate for November.

(b) Using the gross profit rate for November, determine the estimated cost of the inventory lost in the fire.

Compute ending inventory using retail method.

(LO 6)

***P6-11A** Rayre Books uses the retail inventory method to estimate its monthly ending inventories. The following information is available for two of its departments at October 31, 2017.

	Hardcovers		Paperbacks	
	Cost	Retail	Cost	Retail
Beginning inventory	$ 420,000	$ 640,000	$ 280,000	$ 360,000
Purchases	2,135,000	3,200,000	1,155,000	1,540,000
Freight-in	24,000		12,000	
Purchase discounts	44,000		22,000	
Net sales		3,100,000		1,570,000

At December 31, Rayre Books takes a physical inventory at retail. The actual retail values of the inventories in each department are Hardcovers $744,000 and Paperbacks $335,000.

Instructions

(a) Determine the estimated cost of the ending inventory for each department at **October 31**, 2017, using the retail inventory method.

(a) Hardcovers: End. Inv. $488,400

(b) Compute the ending inventory at cost for each department at **December 31**, assuming the cost-to-retail ratios for the year are 65% for Hardcovers and 75% for Paperbacks.

PROBLEMS: SET B AND SET C

Visit the book's companion website, at **www.wiley.com/college/weygandt**, and choose the Student Companion site to access Problems: Set B and Set C.

COMPREHENSIVE PROBLEM

CP6 On December 1, 2017, Annalise Company had the account balances shown below.

	Debit		Credit
Cash	$ 4,800	Accumulated Depreciation—Equipment	$ 1,500
Accounts Receivable	3,900	Accounts Payable	3,000
Inventory	1,800*	Owner's Capital	27,000
Equipment	21,000		$31,500
	$31,500		

*(3,000 × $0.60)

The following transactions occurred during December.

Dec. 3 Purchased 4,000 units of inventory on account at a cost of $0.74 per unit.

5 Sold 4,400 units of inventory on account for $0.90 per unit. (It sold 3,000 of the $0.60 units and 1,400 of the $0.74.)

7 Granted the December 5 customer $180 credit for 200 units of inventory returned costing $120. These units were returned to inventory.

17 Purchased 2,200 units of inventory for cash at $0.80 each.

22 Sold 2,100 units of inventory on account for $0.95 per unit. (It sold 2,100 of the $0.74 units.)

Adjustment data:

1. Accrued salaries payable $400.
2. Depreciation $200 per month.

Instructions

(a) Journalize the December transactions and adjusting entries, assuming Annalise uses the perpetual inventory method.

(b) Enter the December 1 balances in the ledger T-accounts and post the December transactions. In addition to the accounts mentioned above, use the following additional accounts: Cost of Goods Sold, Depreciation Expense, Salaries and Wages Expense, Salaries and Wages Payable, Sales Revenue, and Sales Returns and Allowances.

(c) Prepare an adjusted trial balance as of December 31, 2017.

(d) Prepare an income statement for December 2017 and a classified balance sheet at December 31, 2017.

(e) Compute ending inventory and cost of goods sold under FIFO, assuming Annalise Company uses the periodic inventory system.

(f) Compute ending inventory and cost of goods sold under LIFO, assuming Annalise Company uses the periodic inventory system.

CONTINUING PROBLEM

COOKIE CREATIONS: AN ENTREPRENEURIAL JOURNEY

© leungchopan/ Shutterstock

(*Note:* This is a continuation of the Cookie Creations problem from Chapters 1 through 5.)

CC6 Natalie is busy establishing both divisions of her business (cookie classes and mixer sales) and completing her business degree. Her goals for the next 11 months are to sell one mixer per month and to give two to three classes per week.

The cost of the fine European mixers is expected to increase. Natalie has just negotiated new terms with Kzinski that include shipping costs in the negotiated purchase price (mixers will be shipped FOB destination). Natalie must choose a cost flow assumption for her mixer inventory.

Go to the book's companion website, **www.wiley.com/college/weygandt**, *to see the completion of this problem.*

BROADENING YOUR PERSPECTIVE

FINANCIAL REPORTING AND ANALYSIS

Financial Reporting Problem: Apple Inc.

BYP6-1 The notes that accompany a company's financial statements provide informative details that would clutter the amounts and descriptions presented in the statements. Refer to the financial statements of Apple Inc. in Appendix A as well as its annual report. Instructions for accessing and using the company's complete annual report, including the notes to the financial statements, are also provided in Appendix A.

Instructions

Answer the following questions. Complete the requirements in millions of dollars, as shown in Apple's annual report.

(a) What did Apple report for the amount of inventories in its consolidated balance sheet at September 29, 2012? At September 28, 2013?

(b) Compute the dollar amount of change and the percentage change in inventories between 2012 and 2013. Compute inventory as a percentage of current assets at September 28, 2013.

(c) How does Apple value its inventories? Which inventory cost flow method does Apple use? (See Notes to the Financial Statements.)

(d) What is the cost of sales (cost of goods sold) reported by Apple for 2013, 2012, and 2011? Compute the percentage of cost of sales to net sales in 2013.

Comparative Analysis Problem: PepsiCo, Inc. vs. The Coca-Cola Company

BYP6-2 PepsiCo's financial statements are presented in Appendix B. Financial statements of The Coca-Cola Company are presented in Appendix C. Instructions for accessing and using the complete annual reports of PepsiCo and Coca-Cola, including the notes to the financial statements, are also provided in Appendices B and C, respectively.

Instructions

(a) Based on the information contained in these financial statements, compute the following 2013 ratios for each company.

(1) Inventory turnover.

(2) Days in inventory.

(b) What conclusions concerning the management of the inventory can you draw from these data?

Comparative Analysis Problem: Amazon.com, Inc. vs. Wal-Mart Stores, Inc.

BYP6-3 Amazon.com, Inc.'s financial statements are presented in Appendix D. Financial statements of Wal-Mart Stores, Inc. are presented in Appendix E. Instructions for accessing and using the complete annual reports of Amazon and Wal-Mart, including the notes to the financial statements, are also provided in Appendices D and E, respectively.

Instructions

(a) Based on the information contained in these financial statements, compute the following 2013 ratios for each company.
 (1) Inventory turnover.
 (2) Days in inventory.

(b) What conclusions concerning the management of the inventory can you draw from these data?

Real-World Focus

BYP6-4 A company's annual report usually will identify the inventory method used. Knowing that, you can analyze the effects of the inventory method on the income statement and balance sheet.

Address: **www.cisco.com**, or go to **www.wiley.com/college/weygandt**

Instructions

Answer the following questions based on the current year's annual report on Cisco's website.

(a) At Cisco's fiscal year-end, what was the inventory on the balance sheet?
(b) How has this changed from the previous fiscal year-end?
(c) How much of the inventory was finished goods?
(d) What inventory method does Cisco use?

CRITICAL THINKING

Decision-Making Across the Organization

BYP6-5 On April 10, 2017, fire damaged the office and warehouse of Corvet Company. Most of the accounting records were destroyed, but the following account balances were determined as of March 31, 2017: Inventory (January 1, 2017), $80,000; Sales Revenue (January 1–March 31, 2017), $180,000; Purchases (January 1–March 31, 2017), $94,000.

The company's fiscal year ends on December 31. It uses a periodic inventory system.

From an analysis of the April bank statement, you discover cancelled checks of $4,200 for cash purchases during the period April 1–10. Deposits during the same period totaled $18,500. Of that amount, 60% were collections on accounts receivable, and the balance was cash sales.

Correspondence with the company's principal suppliers revealed $12,400 of purchases on account from April 1 to April 10. Of that amount, $1,600 was for merchandise in transit on April 10 that was shipped FOB destination.

Correspondence with the company's principal customers produced acknowledgments of credit sales totaling $37,000 from April 1 to April 10. It was estimated that $5,600 of credit sales will never be acknowledged or recovered from customers.

Corvet Company reached an agreement with the insurance company that its fire-loss claim should be based on the average of the gross profit rates for the preceding 2 years. The financial statements for 2015 and 2016 showed the following data.

	2016	2015
Net sales	$600,000	$480,000
Cost of goods purchased	404,000	356,000
Beginning inventory	60,000	40,000
Ending inventory	80,000	60,000

Inventory with a cost of $17,000 was salvaged from the fire.

Instructions

With the class divided into groups, answer the following.

(a) Determine the balances in (1) Sales Revenue and (2) Purchases at April 10.

*__(b)__ Determine the average gross profit rate for the years 2015 and 2016. (*Hint:* Find the gross profit rate for each year and divide the sum by 2.)

*__(c)__ Determine the inventory loss as a result of the fire, using the gross profit method.

Communication Activity

BYP6-6 You are the controller of Small Toys Inc. Pamela Bames, the president, recently mentioned to you that she found an error in the 2016 financial statements which she believes has corrected itself.

She determined, in discussions with the Purchasing Department, that 2016 ending inventory was overstated by $1 million. Pamela says that the 2017 ending inventory is correct. Thus, she assumes that 2017 income is correct. Pamela says to you, "What happened has happened—there's no point in worrying about it anymore."

Instructions

You conclude that Pamela is incorrect. Write a brief, tactful memo to Pamela, clarifying the situation.

Ethics Case

BYP6-7 R. J. Graziano Wholesale Corp. uses the LIFO method of inventory costing. In the current year, profit at R. J. Graziano is running unusually high. The corporate tax rate is also high this year, but it is scheduled to decline significantly next year. In an effort to lower the current year's net income and to take advantage of the changing income tax rate, the president of R. J. Graziano Wholesale instructs the plant accountant to recommend to the purchasing department a large purchase of inventory for delivery 3 days before the end of the year. The price of the inventory to be purchased has doubled during the year, and the purchase will represent a major portion of the ending inventory value.

Instructions

(a) What is the effect of this transaction on this year's and next year's income statement and income tax expense? Why?
(b) If R. J. Graziano Wholesale had been using the FIFO method of inventory costing, would the president give the same directive?
(c) Should the plant accountant order the inventory purchase to lower income? What are the ethical implications of this order?

All About You

BYP6-8 Some of the largest business frauds ever perpetrated have involved the misstatement of inventory. Two classics were at Leslie Fay and McKesson Corporation.

Instructions

There is considerable information regarding inventory frauds available on the Internet. Search for information about one of the two cases mentioned above, or inventory fraud at any other company, and prepare a short explanation of the nature of the inventory fraud.

FASB Codification Activity

BYP6-9 If your school has a subscription to the FASB Codification, go to **http://aaahq.org/ascLogin.cfm** to log in and prepare responses to the following.

Instructions

(a) The primary basis for accounting for inventories is cost. How is cost defined in the Codification?
(b) What does the Codification state regarding the use of consistency in the selection or employment of a basis for inventory?

A Look at IFRS

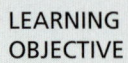

LEARNING OBJECTIVE 7

Compare the accounting for inventories under GAAP and IFRS.

The major IFRS requirements related to accounting and reporting for inventories are the same as GAAP. The major differences are that IFRS prohibits the use of the LIFO cost flow assumption and determines market in the lower-of-cost-or-market inventory valuation differently.

Relevant Facts

Following are the key similarities and differences between GAAP and IFRS related to inventories.

Similarities

- IFRS and GAAP account for inventory acquisitions at historical cost and value inventory at the lower-of-cost-or-market subsequent to acquisition.
- Who owns the goods—goods in transit or consigned goods—as well as the costs to include in inventory are essentially accounted for the same under IFRS and GAAP.

Differences

- The requirements for accounting for and reporting inventories are more principles-based under IFRS. That is, GAAP provides more detailed guidelines in inventory accounting.
- A major difference between IFRS and GAAP relates to the LIFO cost flow assumption. GAAP permits the use of LIFO for inventory valuation. IFRS prohibits its use. FIFO and average-cost are the only two acceptable cost flow assumptions permitted under IFRS. Both sets of standards permit specific identification where appropriate.
- In the lower-of-cost-or-market test for inventory valuation, IFRS defines market as net realizable value. GAAP, on the other hand, defines market as replacement cost.

Looking to the Future

One convergence issue that will be difficult to resolve relates to the use of the LIFO cost flow assumption. As indicated, IFRS specifically prohibits its use. Conversely, the LIFO cost flow assumption is widely used in the United States because of its favorable tax advantages. In addition, many argue that LIFO from a financial reporting point of view provides a better matching of current costs against revenue and, therefore, enables companies to compute a more realistic income.

IFRS Practice

IFRS Self-Test Questions

1. Which of the following should **not** be included in the inventory of a company using IFRS?
   (a) Goods held on consignment from another company.
   (b) Goods shipped on consignment to another company.
   (c) Goods in transit from another company shipped FOB shipping point.
   (d) None of the above.
2. Which method of inventory costing is prohibited under IFRS?
   (a) Specific identification. (c) FIFO.
   (b) LIFO. (d) Average-cost.

IFRS Exercises

IFRS6-1 Briefly describe some of the similarities and differences between GAAP and IFRS with respect to the accounting for inventories.

IFRS6-2 LaTour Inc. is based in France and prepares its financial statements (in euros) in accordance with IFRS. In 2017, it reported cost of goods sold of €578 million and average inventory of €154 million. Briefly discuss how analysis of LaTour's inventory turnover (and comparisons to a company using GAAP) might be affected by differences in inventory accounting between IFRS and GAAP.

International Financial Reporting Problem: Louis Vuitton

IFRS6-3 The financial statements of Louis Vuitton are presented in Appendix F. Instructions for accessing and using the company's complete annual report, including the notes to its financial statements, are also provided in Appendix F.

Instructions

Using the notes to the company's financial statements, answer the following questions.

(a) What cost flow assumption does the company use to value inventory?
(b) What amount of goods purchased for retail and finished products did the company report at December 31, 2013?

Answers to IFRS Self-Test Questions

1. a **2.** b

7 Accounting Information Systems

CHAPTER PREVIEW As the Feature Story below demonstrates, a reliable information system is a necessity for any company. Whether companies use pen, pencil, or computers in maintaining accounting records, certain principles and procedures apply. The purpose of this chapter is to explain and illustrate these features.

FEATURE STORY

QuickBooks® Helps This Retailer Sell Guitars

Starting a small business requires many decisions. For example, you have to decide where to locate, how much space you need, how much inventory to have, how many employees to hire, and where to advertise. Small business owners are typically so concerned about the product and sales side of their business that they often do not give enough thought to something that is also critical to their success—how to keep track of financial results.

Small business owners today can choose either manual or computerized accounting systems. For example, Paul and Laura West were the owners of the first independent dealership of Carvin guitars and professional audio equipment. When they founded their company in Sacramento, California, they decided to purchase a computerized accounting system that would integrate many aspects of their retail operations. They wanted to use their accounting software to manage their inventory of guitars and amplifiers, enter sales, record and report financial data, and process credit card and debit card transactions. They evaluated a number of options and chose QuickBooks® by Intuit Inc.

QuickBooks®, like most other popular software packages, has programs designed for the needs of a specific type of business, which in this case is retailing. This QuickBooks® retailing package automatically collects sales information from its point-of-sale scanning devices. It also keeps track of inventory levels and automatically generates purchase orders for popular items when re-order points are reached. It even supports specialized advertising campaigns.

For example, QuickBooks® compiled a customer database from which the Wests sent out targeted direct mailings to potential customers. The computerized system also enabled data files to be emailed to the company's accountant. This kept down costs and made it easier and more efficient for the Wests to generate financial reports as needed. The Wests believed that the investment in the computerized system saved them time and money, and allowed them to spend more time on other aspects of their business.

Source: Intuit Inc., "QuickBooks® and ProAdvisor® Help Make Guitar Store a Hit," *Journal of Accountancy* (May 2006), p. 101.

Terra Images/Age Fotostock America, Inc.

CHAPTER OUTLINE

Learning Objectives

	Learning Objective	Topics	DO IT!
1	Explain the basic concepts of an accounting information system.	• Computerized accounting systems • Manual accounting systems	DO IT! 1 Basic AIS Concepts
2	Describe the nature and purpose of a subsidiary ledger.	• Subsidiary ledger example • Advantages of subsidiary ledgers	DO IT! 2 Subsidiary Ledgers
3	Record transactions in special journals.	• Sales journal • Cash receipts journal • Purchases journal • Cash payments journal • Effects of special journals • Cyber security	DO IT! 3 Special Journals

Go to the ***REVIEW AND PRACTICE*** section at the end of the chapter for a review of key concepts and practice applications with solutions.

Visit **WileyPLUS with ORION** for additional tutorials and practice opportunities.

LEARNING OBJECTIVE 1

Explain the basic concepts of an accounting information system.

The **accounting information system** collects and processes transaction data and communicates financial information to decision-makers. It includes each of the steps in the accounting cycle that you studied in earlier chapters. It also includes the documents that provide evidence of the transactions, and the records, trial balances, worksheets, and financial statements that result. An **accounting system** may be either manual or computerized. Most businesses use some sort of computerized accounting system, whether it is an off-the-shelf system for small businesses, like QuickBooks® or Sage 50, or a more complex custom-made system.

Efficient and effective accounting information systems are based on certain basic principles. These principles, as described in Illustration 7-1, are (1) cost-effectiveness, (2) usefulness, and (3) flexibility. If the accounting system is cost-effective, provides useful output, and has the flexibility to meet future needs, it can contribute to both individual and organizational goals.

Illustration 7-1
Principles of an efficient and effective accounting information system

Cost-Effectiveness
The accounting system must be cost-effective. Benefits of information must outweigh the costs of providing it.

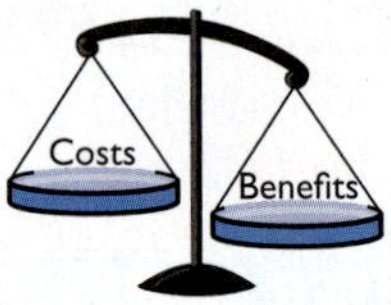

Useful Output
To be useful, information must be understandable, relevant, reliable, timely, and accurate. Designers of accounting systems must consider the needs and knowledge of various users.

Flexibility
The accounting system should accommodate a variety of users and changing information needs. The system should be sufficiently flexible to meet the resulting changes in the demands made upon it.

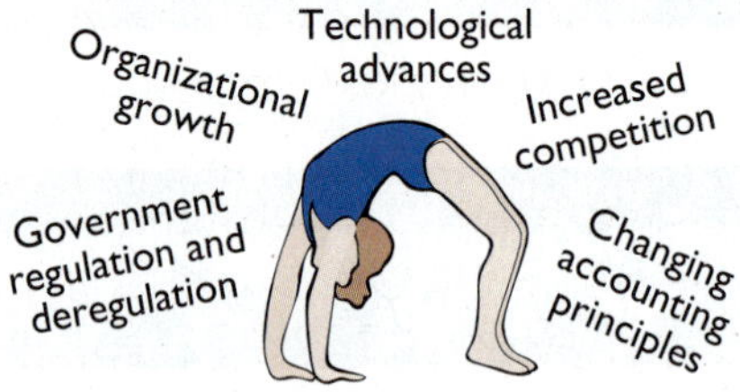

Computerized Accounting Systems

Many small businesses use a computerized general ledger accounting system. **General ledger accounting systems** are software programs that integrate the various accounting functions related to sales, purchases, receivables, payables, cash receipts and disbursements, and payroll. They also generate financial statements. Computerized systems have a number of advantages over manual systems. First, the company typically enters data only once in a computerized system. Second, because the computer does most steps automatically, it eliminates many errors resulting from human intervention in a manual system, such as errors in posting or preparation of financial statements. Computerized systems also provide up-to-the-minute information. More timely information often results in better business decisions. Many different general ledger software packages are available.

CHOOSING A SOFTWARE PACKAGE

To identify the right software for your business, you must understand your company's operations. For example, consider its needs with regard to inventory, billing, payroll, and cash management. In addition, the company might have specific needs that are not supported by all software systems. For example, you might want to track employees' hours on individual jobs or to extract information for determining sales commissions. Choosing the right system is critical because installation of even a basic system is time-consuming, and learning a new system will require many hours of employee time.

ENTRY-LEVEL SOFTWARE

Software publishers tend to classify businesses into groups based on revenue and the number of employees. Companies with revenues of less than $5 million and up to 20 employees generally use **entry-level programs**. The two leading entry-level programs are Intuit's QuickBooks® and The Sage Group's Sage 50. These programs control more than 90% of the market. Each of these entry-level programs comes in many different industry-specific versions. For example, some are designed for very specific industry applications such as restaurants, retailing, construction, manufacturing, or nonprofit.

Quality entry-level packages typically involve more than recording transactions and preparing financial statements. Here are some common features and benefits:

- **Easy data access and report preparation.** Users can easily access information related to specific customers or suppliers. For example, you can view all transactions, invoices, payments, as well as contact information for a specific client.
- **Audit trail.** As a result of the Sarbanes-Oxley Act, companies are now far more concerned that their accounting system minimizes opportunities for fraud. Many programs provide an "audit trail" that enables the tracking of all transactions.
- **Internal controls.** Some systems have an internal accounting review that identifies suspicious transactions or likely mistakes such as wrong account numbers or duplicate transactions.
- **Customization.** This feature enables the company to create data fields specific to the needs of its business.
- **Network-compatibility.** Multiple users in the company can access the system at the same time.

ETHICS NOTE

Entire books and movies have used cyber attacks as a major theme. Most programmers would agree that ensuring cyber security is the most difficult and time-consuming phase of their jobs.

ENTERPRISE RESOURCE PLANNING SYSTEMS

Enterprise resource planning (ERP) systems are typically used by manufacturing companies with more than 500 employees and $500 million in sales. The best-known of these systems are SAP AG's SAP ERP (the most widely used) and Oracle's ERP. ERP systems go far beyond the functions of an entry-level general ledger package. They integrate all aspects of the organization, including accounting, sales, human resource management, and manufacturing. Because of the complexity of an ERP system, implementation can take three years and cost five times as much as the purchase price of the system. Purchase and implementation of ERP systems can cost from $250,000 to as much as $50 million for the largest multinational corporations.

Ethics Insight

© Sean Locke/iStockphoto

Curbing Fraudulent Activity with Software

The Sarbanes-Oxley Act (SOX) requires that companies demonstrate that they have adequate controls in place to detect significant fraudulent behavior by employees. The SOX requirements have created a huge market for software that can monitor and trace every recorded transaction and adjusting entry. This enables companies to pinpoint who used the accounting system and when they used it. These systems also require "electronic signatures" by employees for all significant transactions. Such signatures verify that employees have followed all required procedures, and that all actions are properly authorized. One firm that specializes in compliance software had 10 clients prior to SOX and 250 after SOX.

Note that small businesses have no standards like SOX and often do not have the resources to implement a fraud–prevention system. As a result, small businesses lose nearly $630 billion to fraud each year. To address this problem, more sophisticated software is being designed for small business fraud prevention.

Sources: W. M. Bulkeley and C. Forelle, "Anti-Crime Program: How Corporate Scandals Gave Tech Firms a New Business Line," *Wall Street Journal* (December 9, 2005), p. A1; and "New Software Fights Small Business Fraud," *FOX Business* (August 9, 2013).

Why might this software help reduce fraudulent activity by employees? (Go to **WileyPLUS** for this answer and additional questions.)

Manual Accounting Systems

In **manual accounting systems**, someone performs each of the steps in the accounting cycle by hand. For example, someone manually enters each accounting transaction in the journal and manually posts each to the ledger. Other manual computations must be made to obtain ledger account balances and to prepare a trial balance and financial statements. In the remainder of this chapter, we illustrate the use of a manual system.

You might be wondering, "Why cover manual accounting systems if the real world uses computerized systems?" First, small businesses still abound. Most of them begin operations with manual accounting systems and convert to computerized systems as the business grows. You may work in a small business or start your own someday, so it is useful to know how a manual system works. Second, to understand what computerized accounting systems do, you also need to understand manual accounting systems.

The manual accounting system represented in the first six chapters of this textbook is satisfactory in a company with a low volume of transactions. However, in most companies, it is necessary to add additional ledgers and journals to the accounting system to record transaction data efficiently.

DO IT! 1 Basic AIS Concepts

Indicate whether the following statements are true or false.

1. An accounting information system collects and processes transaction data and communicates financial information to decision-makers.
2. A company typically enters data only once in a manual accounting system.
3. Enterprise resource planning (ERP) systems are typically used by companies with revenues of less than $5 million and up to 20 employees.

Action Plan

✔ Understand the principles of an effective accounting information system.

✔ Recognize the types of available general ledger software packages.

Solution

1. True. **2.** False. A company typically enters data only once in a computerized accounting system. **3.** False. Enterprise resource planning (ERP) systems are typically used by manufacturing companies with more than 500 employees and $500 million in sales.

Related exercise material: **BE7-1, BE7-2, BE7-3, and DO IT! 7-1.**

LEARNING OBJECTIVE 2

Describe the nature and purpose of a subsidiary ledger.

Imagine a business that has several thousand charge (credit) customers and shows the transactions with these customers in only one general ledger account—Accounts Receivable. It would be nearly impossible to determine the balance owed by an individual customer at any specific time. Similarly, the amount payable to one creditor would be difficult to locate quickly from a single Accounts Payable account in the general ledger.

Instead, companies use subsidiary ledgers to keep track of individual balances. A **subsidiary ledger** is a group of accounts with a common characteristic (for example, all accounts receivable). It is an addition to and an expansion of the general ledger. The subsidiary ledger frees the general ledger from the details of individual balances.

Two common subsidiary ledgers are as follows.

1. The **accounts receivable** (or **customers'**) **subsidiary ledger**, which collects transaction data of individual customers.
2. The **accounts payable** (or **creditors'**) **subsidiary ledger**, which collects transaction data of individual creditors.

In each of these subsidiary ledgers, companies usually arrange individual accounts in alphabetical order.

A general ledger account summarizes the detailed data from a subsidiary ledger. For example, the detailed data from the accounts receivable subsidiary ledger are summarized in Accounts Receivable in the general ledger. The general ledger account that summarizes subsidiary ledger data is called a **control account**. Illustration 7-2 presents an overview of the relationship of subsidiary ledgers to the general ledger. There, the general ledger control accounts and subsidiary ledger accounts are in green. Note that Cash and Owner's Capital in this illustration are not control accounts because there are no subsidiary ledger accounts related to these accounts.

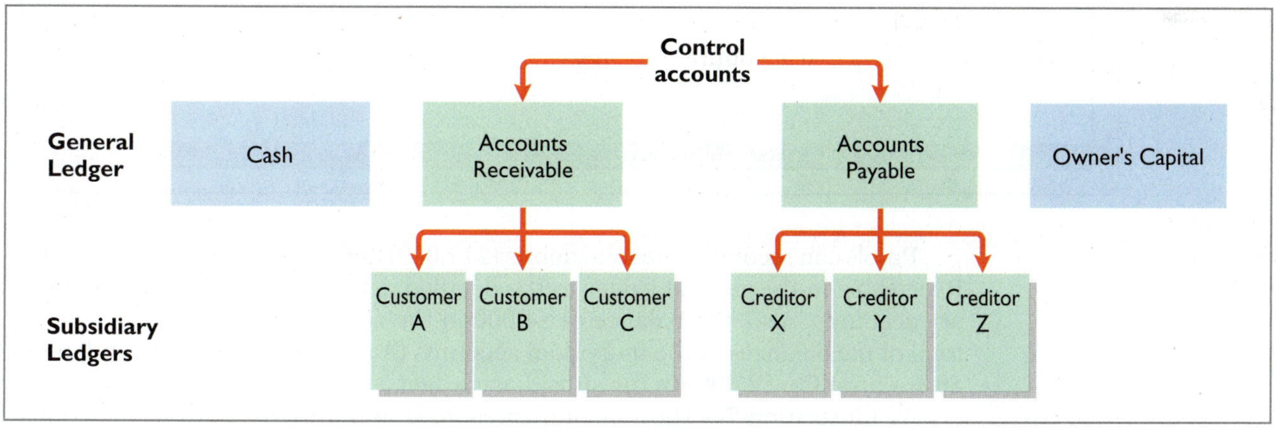

Illustration 7-2
Relationship of general ledger and subsidiary ledgers

At the end of an accounting period, each general ledger control account balance must equal the composite balance of the individual accounts in the related subsidiary ledger. For example, the balance in Accounts Payable in Illustration 7-2 must equal the total of the subsidiary balances of Creditors X + Y + Z.

Subsidiary Ledger Example

Illustration 7-3 (page 316) lists credit sales and collections on account for Pujols Company.

Illustration 7-3
Sales and collection transactions

Credit Sales			Collections on Account		
Jan. 10	Aaron Co.	$ 6,000	Jan. 19	Aaron Co.	$4,000
12	Branden Inc.	3,000	21	Branden Inc.	3,000
20	Caron Co.	3,000	29	Caron Co.	1,000
		$12,000			$8,000

Illustration 7-4 provides an example of a control account and subsidiary ledger for Pujols Company. (Due to space considerations, the explanation column in these accounts is not shown in this and subsequent illustrations.) Illustration 7-4 is based on the transactions listed in Illustration 7-3.

Illustration 7-4
Relationship between general and subsidiary ledgers

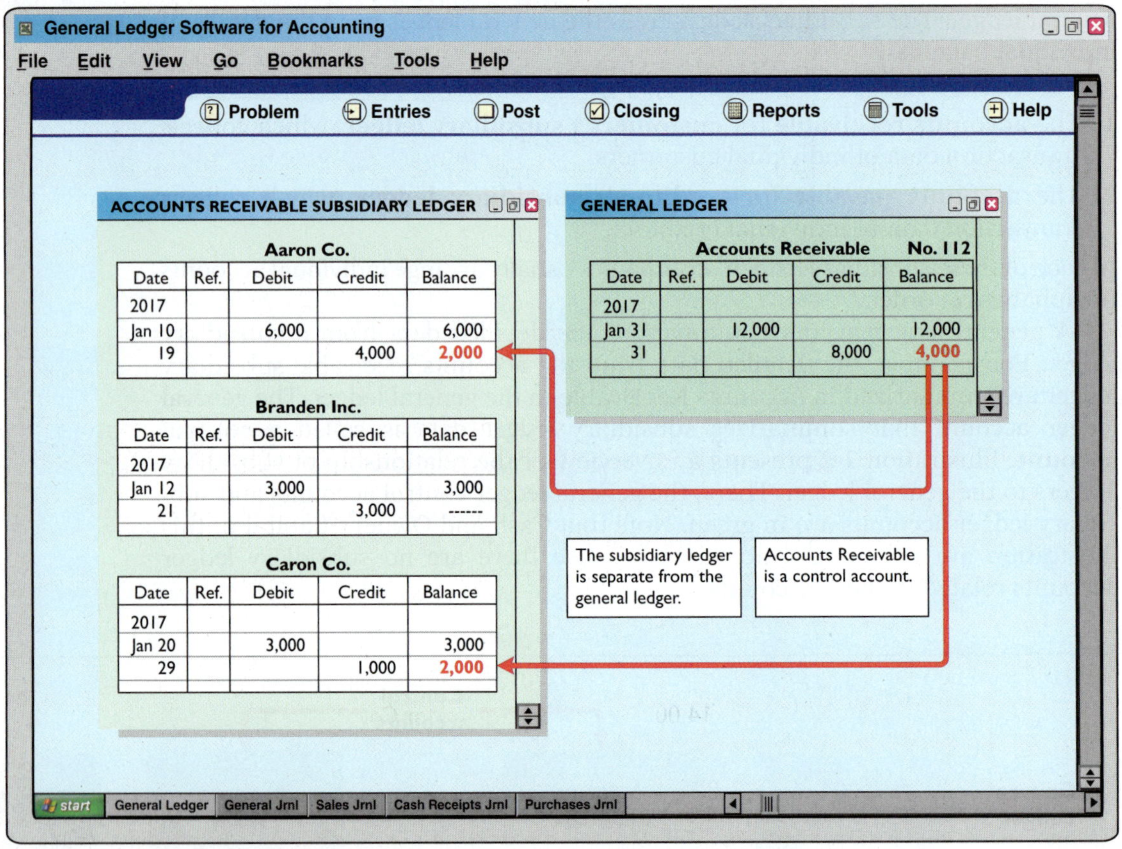

Aaron Co.

Date	Ref.	Debit	Credit	Balance
2017				
Jan 10		6,000		6,000
19			4,000	2,000

Branden Inc.

Date	Ref.	Debit	Credit	Balance
2017				
Jan 12		3,000		3,000
21			3,000	------

Caron Co.

Date	Ref.	Debit	Credit	Balance
2017				
Jan 20		3,000		3,000
29			1,000	2,000

Accounts Receivable **No. 112**

Date	Ref.	Debit	Credit	Balance
2017				
Jan 31		12,000		12,000
31			8,000	4,000

Pujols can reconcile the total debits ($12,000) and credits ($8,000) in Accounts Receivable in the general ledger to the detailed debits and credits in the subsidiary accounts. Also, the balance of $4,000 in the control account agrees with the total of the balances in the individual accounts (Aaron Co. $2,000 + Branden Inc. $0 + Caron Co. $2,000) in the subsidiary ledger.

As Illustration 7-4 shows, companies make monthly postings to the control accounts in the general ledger. This practice allows them to prepare monthly financial statements. Companies post to the individual accounts in the subsidiary ledger daily. Daily posting ensures that account information is current. This enables the company to monitor credit limits, bill customers, and answer inquiries from customers about their account balances.

Advantages of Subsidiary Ledgers

Subsidiary ledgers have several advantages:

1. **They show in a single account transactions affecting one customer or one creditor,** thus providing up-to-date information on specific account balances.

2. **They free the general ledger of excessive details.** As a result, a trial balance of the general ledger does not contain vast numbers of individual account balances.
3. **They help locate errors in individual accounts** by reducing the number of accounts in one ledger and by using control accounts.
4. **They make possible a division of labor** in posting. One employee can post to the general ledger while someone else posts to the subsidiary ledgers.

Accounting Across the Organization

© Niels Laan/iStockphoto

"I'm John Smith, a.k.a. 13695071642"

Rather than relying on customer or creditor names in a subsidiary ledger, a computerized system expands the account number of the control account in a prespecified manner. For example, if the control account Accounts Receivable was numbered 10010, the first account in the accounts receivable subsidiary ledger might be numbered 10010–0001. Most systems allow inquiries about specific accounts in the subsidiary ledger (by account number) or about the control account. With the latter, the system would automatically total all the subsidiary accounts whenever an inquiry to the control account was made.

Why use numbers to identify names in a computerized system? (Go to **WileyPLUS** for this answer and additional questions.)

DO IT! 2 Subsidiary Ledgers

Presented below is information related to Sims Company for its first month of operations. Determine the balances that appear in the accounts payable subsidiary ledger. What Accounts Payable balance appears in the general ledger at the end of January?

Credit Purchases			Cash Paid		
Jan. 5	Devon Co.	$11,000	Jan. 9	Devon Co.	$7,000
11	Shelby Co.	7,000	14	Shelby Co.	2,000
22	Taylor Co.	14,000	27	Taylor Co.	9,000

Solution

Subsidiary ledger balances:

Devon Co.: $4,000 ($11,000 − $7,000)

Shelby Co.: $5,000 ($7,000 − $2,000)

Taylor Co.: $5,000 ($14,000 − $9,000)

General ledger Accounts Payable balance: $14,000 ($4,000 + $5,000 + $5,000)

Related exercise material: **BE7-4, BE7-5, E7-1, E7-2, E7-3, E7-4, E7-5, and DO IT! 7-2.**

Action Plan

✔ Subtract cash paid from credit purchases to determine the balances in the accounts payable subsidiary ledger.

✔ Sum the individual balances to determine the Accounts Payable balance.

LEARNING OBJECTIVE 3 Record transactions in special journals.

So far, you have learned to journalize transactions in a two-column general journal and post each entry to the general ledger. This procedure is satisfactory in only very small companies. To expedite journalizing and posting, most companies use special journals **in addition to the general journal**.

Companies use **special journals** to record similar types of transactions. Examples are all sales of merchandise on account or all cash receipts. The types of transactions that occur frequently in a company determine what special journals the company uses. Most merchandising companies record daily transactions using the journals shown in Illustration 7-5.

Illustration 7-5
Use of special journals and the general journal

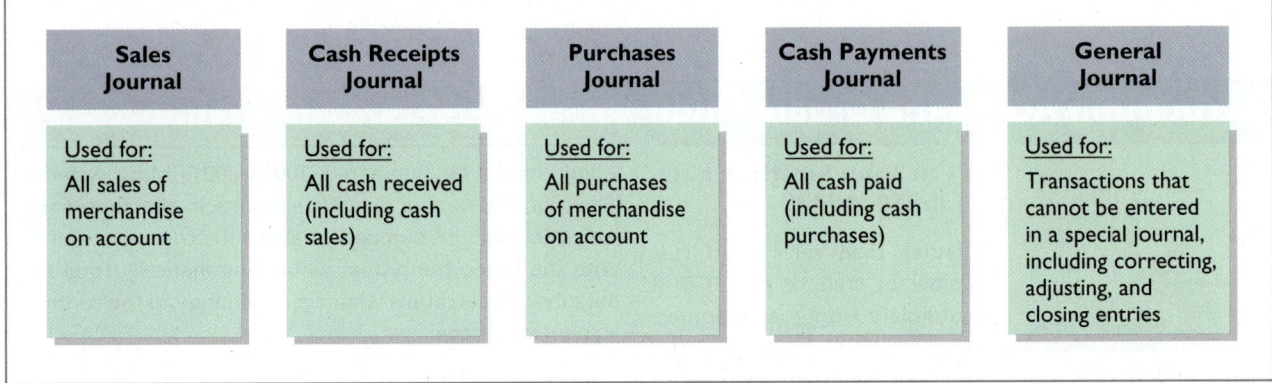

Sales Journal	Cash Receipts Journal	Purchases Journal	Cash Payments Journal	General Journal
Used for: All sales of merchandise on account	Used for: All cash received (including cash sales)	Used for: All purchases of merchandise on account	Used for: All cash paid (including cash purchases)	Used for: Transactions that cannot be entered in a special journal, including correcting, adjusting, and closing entries

If a transaction cannot be recorded in a special journal, the company records it in the general journal. For example, if a company had special journals for only the four types of transactions listed above, it would record purchase returns and allowances that do not affect cash in the general journal. Similarly, **correcting, adjusting, and closing entries are recorded in the general journal.** In some situations, companies might use special journals other than those listed above. For example, when sales returns and allowances that do not affect cash are frequent, a company might use a special journal to record these transactions.

Helpful Hint
Postings are also made daily to individual ledger accounts in the inventory subsidiary ledger to maintain a perpetual inventory.

Special journals **permit greater division of labor** because several people can record entries in different journals at the same time. For example, one employee may journalize all cash receipts, and another may journalize all credit sales. Also, the use of special journals **reduces the time needed to complete the posting process.** With special journals, companies may post some accounts monthly instead of daily, as we will illustrate later in the chapter. On the following pages, we discuss the four special journals shown in Illustration 7-5.

Sales Journal

In the **sales journal**, companies record **sales of merchandise on account**. Cash sales of merchandise go in the cash receipts journal. Credit sales of assets other than merchandise go in the general journal.

JOURNALIZING CREDIT SALES

To demonstrate use of a sales journal, we will use data for Karns Wholesale Supply, which uses a **perpetual inventory system**. Under this system, each entry in the sales journal results in one entry **at selling price** and another entry **at cost**. The entry at selling price is a debit to Accounts Receivable (a control account) and a credit of equal amount to Sales Revenue. The entry at cost is a debit to Cost of Goods Sold and a credit of equal amount to Inventory (a control account). Using a sales journal with two amount columns, the company can show on only one line a sales transaction at both selling price and cost. Illustration 7-6 shows this two-column sales journal of Karns Wholesale Supply, using assumed credit sales transactions (for sales invoices 101–107).

Note that, unlike the general journal, an explanation is not required for each entry in a special journal. Also, the use of prenumbered invoices ensures that all invoices are journalized and no invoices are duplicated. Finally, the reference

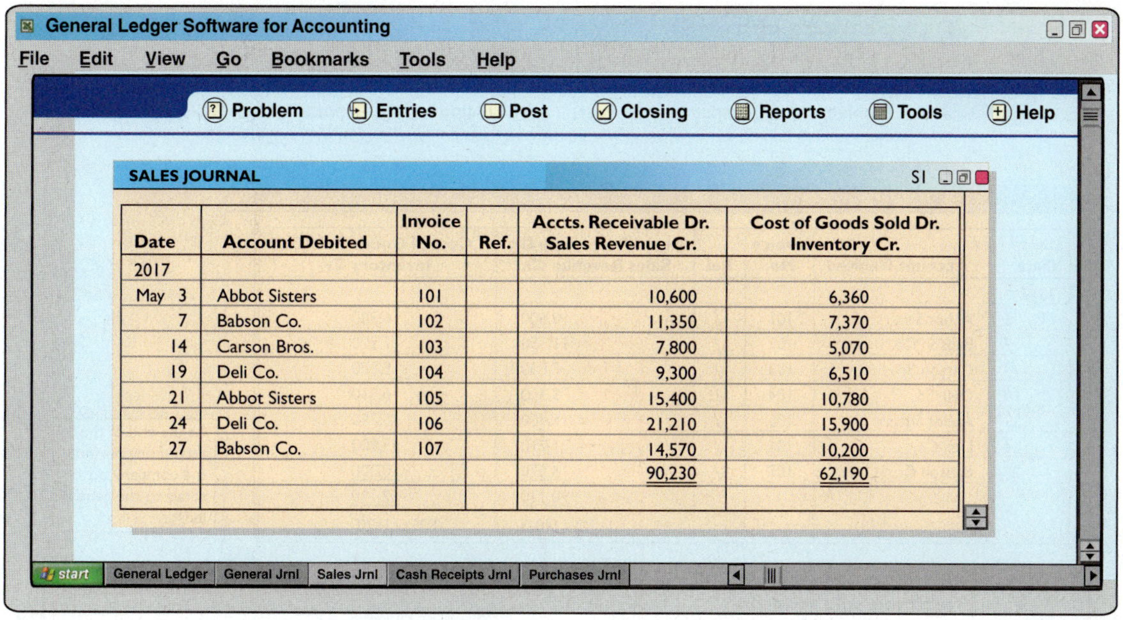

SALES JOURNAL S1

Date	Account Debited	Invoice No.	Ref.	Accts. Receivable Dr. Sales Revenue Cr.	Cost of Goods Sold Dr. Inventory Cr.
2017					
May 3	Abbot Sisters	101		10,600	6,360
7	Babson Co.	102		11,350	7,370
14	Carson Bros.	103		7,800	5,070
19	Deli Co.	104		9,300	6,510
21	Abbot Sisters	105		15,400	10,780
24	Deli Co.	106		21,210	15,900
27	Babson Co.	107		14,570	10,200
				90,230	62,190

Illustration 7-6
Journalizing the sales journal—perpetual inventory system

(Ref.) column is not used in journalizing. It is used in posting the sales journal, as explained in the next section.

POSTING THE SALES JOURNAL

Companies make daily postings from the sales journal **to the individual accounts receivable** in the subsidiary ledger. Posting **to the general ledger** is done **monthly**. Illustration 7-7 (page 320) shows both the daily and monthly postings.

A check mark (✓) is inserted in the reference column to indicate that the daily posting to the customer's account has been made. If the subsidiary ledger accounts were numbered, the account number would be entered in place of the check mark. At the end of the month, Karns posts the column totals of the sales journal to the general ledger. Here, the column totals are as follows. From the selling-price column, a debit of $90,230 to Accounts Receivable (account No. 112), and a credit of $90,230 to Sales Revenue (account No. 401). From the cost column, a debit of $62,190 to Cost of Goods Sold (account No. 505), and a credit of $62,190 to Inventory (account No. 120). Karns inserts the account numbers below the column totals to indicate that the postings have been made. In both the general ledger and subsidiary ledger accounts, the reference **S1** indicates that the posting came from page 1 of the sales journal.

PROVING THE LEDGERS

The next step is to "prove" the ledgers. To do so, Karns must determine two things: (1) The total of the general ledger debit balances must equal the total of the general ledger credit balances. (2) The sum of the subsidiary ledger balances must equal the balance in the control account. Illustration 7-8 (page 321) shows the proof of the postings from the sales journal to the general and subsidiary ledgers.

ADVANTAGES OF THE SALES JOURNAL

The use of a special journal to record sales on account has a number of advantages. First, the one-line entry for each sales transaction saves time. In the sales journal, it is not necessary to write out the four account titles for each transaction. Second, only totals, rather than individual entries, are posted to the general ledger. This saves posting time and reduces the possibilities of errors in posting. Finally, a division of labor results because one individual can take responsibility for the sales journal.

General Ledger Software for Accounting

File Edit View Go Bookmarks Tools Help

Problem Entries Post Closing Reports Tools Help

SALES JOURNAL S1

Date	Account Debited	Invoice No.	Ref.	Accts. Receivable Dr. Sales Revenue Cr.	Cost of Goods Sold Dr. Inventory Cr.
2017					
May 3	Abbot Sisters	101	√	10,600	6,360
7	Babson Co.	102	√	11,350	7,370
14	Carson Bros.	103	√	7,800	5,070
19	Deli Co.	104	√	9,300	6,510
21	Abbot Sisters	105	√	15,400	10,780
24	Deli Co.	106	√	21,210	15,900
27	Babson Co.	107	√	14,570	10,200
				90,230	62,190
				(112) / (401)	(505) / (120)

At the end of the accounting period, the company posts totals to the general ledger.

The company posts individual amounts to the subsidiary ledger daily.

ACCOUNTS RECEIVABLE SUBSIDIARY LEDGER

Abbot Sisters

Date	Ref.	Debit	Credit	Balance
2017				
May 3	S1	10,600		10,600
21	S1	15,400		26,000

Babson Co.

Date	Ref.	Debit	Credit	Balance
2017				
May 7	S1	11,350		11,350
27	S1	14,570		25,920

Carson Bros.

Date	Ref.	Debit	Credit	Balance
2017				
May 14	S1	7,800		7,800

Deli Co.

Date	Ref.	Debit	Credit	Balance
2017				
May 19	S1	9,300		9,300
24	S1	21,210		30,510

GENERAL LEDGER

Accounts Receivable No. 112

Date	Ref.	Debit	Credit	Balance
2017				
May 31	S1	90,230		90,230

Inventory No. 120

Date	Ref.	Debit	Credit	Balance
2017				
May 31	S1		62,190	62,190[1]

Sales Revenue No. 401

Date	Ref.	Debit	Credit	Balance
2017				
May 31	S1		90,230	90,230

Cost of Goods Sold No. 505

Date	Ref.	Debit	Credit	Balance
2017				
May 31	S1	62,190		62,190

The subsidiary ledger is separate from the general ledger.

Accounts Receivable is a control account.

[1]The normal balance for Inventory is a debit. But because of the sequence in which we have posted the special journals, with the sales journal first, the credits to Inventory are posted before the debits. This posting sequence explains the credit balance in Inventory, which exists only until the other journals are posted.

start General Ledger General Jrnl Sales Jrnl Cash Receipts Jrnl Purchases Jrnl

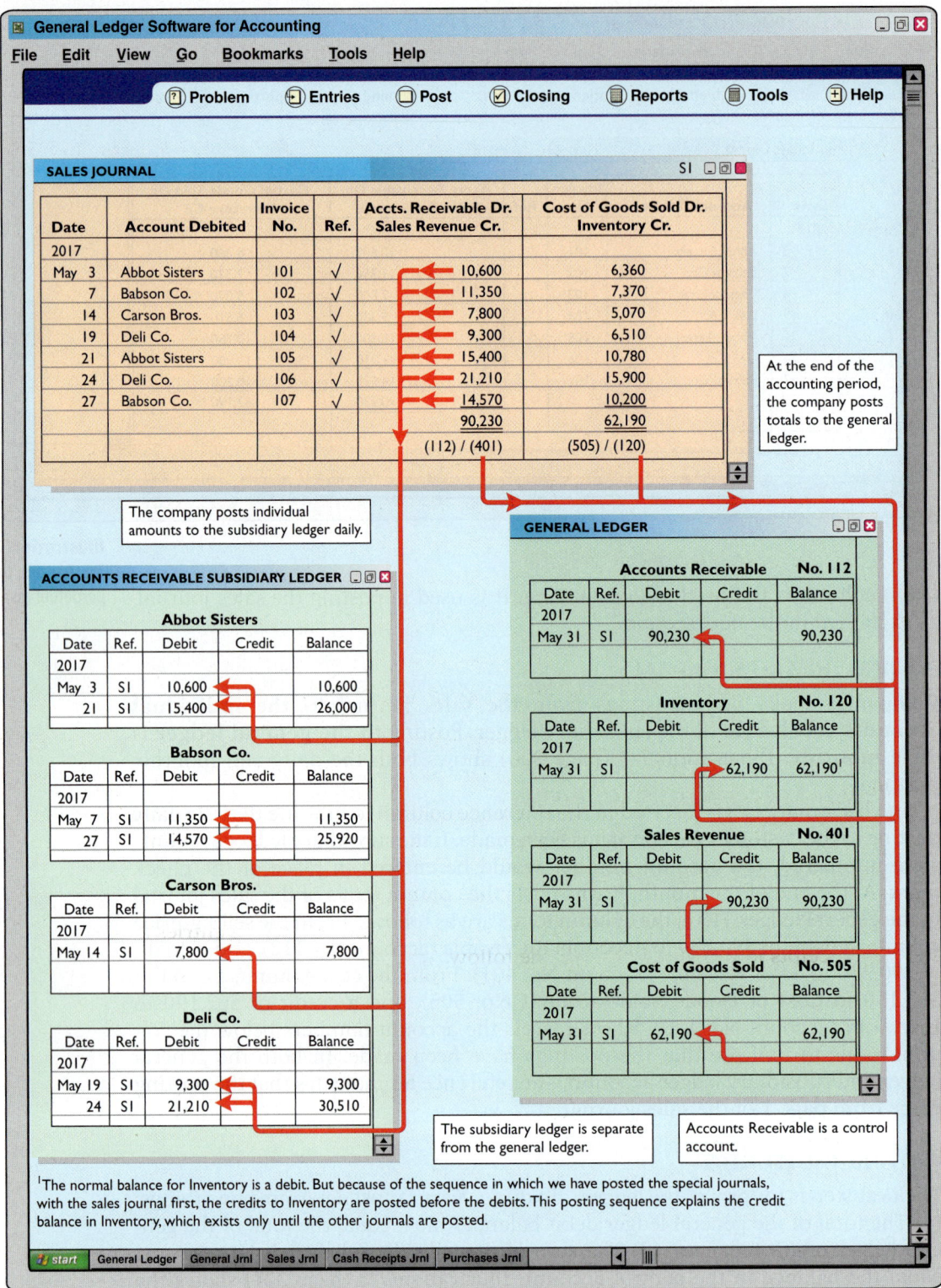

Illustration 7-7
Posting the sales journal

Cash Receipts Journal

In the **cash receipts journal**, companies record all receipts of cash. The most common types of cash receipts are cash sales of merchandise and collections of accounts receivable. Many other possibilities exist, such as receipt of money from bank loans and cash proceeds from disposal of equipment. A one- or two-column cash receipts journal would not have space enough for all possible cash receipt transactions. Therefore, companies use a multiple-column cash receipts journal.

Illustration 7-8
Proving the equality of the postings from the sales journal

Postings to General Ledger

General Ledger

Credits	
Inventory	$62,190
Sales Revenue	90,230
	$152,420

Debits	
Accounts Receivable	$90,230
Cost of Goods Sold	62,190
	$152,420

Debit Postings to the Accounts Receivable Subsidiary Ledger

Subsidiary Ledger

Abbot Sisters	$26,000
Babson Co.	25,920
Carson Bros.	7,800
Deli Co.	30,510
	$90,230

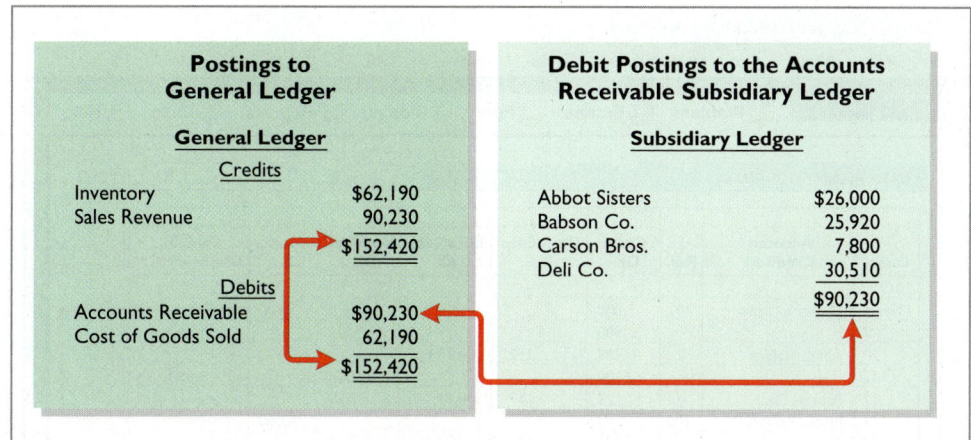

Generally, a cash receipts journal includes the following columns: debit columns for Cash and Sales Discounts, and credit columns for Accounts Receivable, Sales Revenue, and "Other Accounts." Companies use the Other Accounts category when the cash receipt does not involve a cash sale or a collection of accounts receivable. Under a perpetual inventory system, each sales entry also is accompanied by an entry that debits Cost of Goods Sold and credits Inventory for the cost of the merchandise sold. Illustration 7-9 (page 322) shows a six-column cash receipts journal.

Companies may use additional credit columns if these columns significantly reduce postings to a specific account. For example, a loan company such as **Household International** receives thousands of cash collections from customers. Using separate credit columns for Loans Receivable and Interest Revenue, rather than the Other Accounts credit column, would reduce postings.

JOURNALIZING CASH RECEIPTS TRANSACTIONS

To illustrate the journalizing of cash receipts transactions, we will continue with the May transactions of Karns Wholesale Supply. Collections from customers relate to the entries recorded in the sales journal in Illustration 7-6. The entries in the cash receipts journal are based on the following cash receipts.

May	1	D. A. Karns makes an investment of $5,000 in the business.
	7	Cash sales of merchandise total $1,900 (cost, $1,240).
	10	Received a check for $10,388 from Abbot Sisters in payment of invoice No. 101 for $10,600 less a 2% discount.
	12	Cash sales of merchandise total $2,600 (cost, $1,690).
	17	Received a check for $11,123 from Babson Co. in payment of invoice No. 102 for $11,350 less a 2% discount.
	22	Received cash by signing a note for $6,000.
	23	Received a check for $7,644 from Carson Bros. in full for invoice No. 103 for $7,800 less a 2% discount.
	28	Received a check for $9,114 from Deli Co. in full for invoice No. 104 for $9,300 less a 2% discount.

Further information about the columns in the cash receipts journal is listed below and on page 323.

Debit Columns:

1. **Cash.** Karns enters in this column the amount of cash actually received in each transaction. The column total indicates the total cash receipts for the month.
2. **Sales Discounts.** Karns includes a Sales Discounts column in its cash receipts journal. By doing so, it does not need to enter sales discount items in the general journal. As a result, the cash receipts journal shows on one line the collection of an account receivable within the discount period.

Illustration 7-9
Journalizing and posting the cash receipts journal

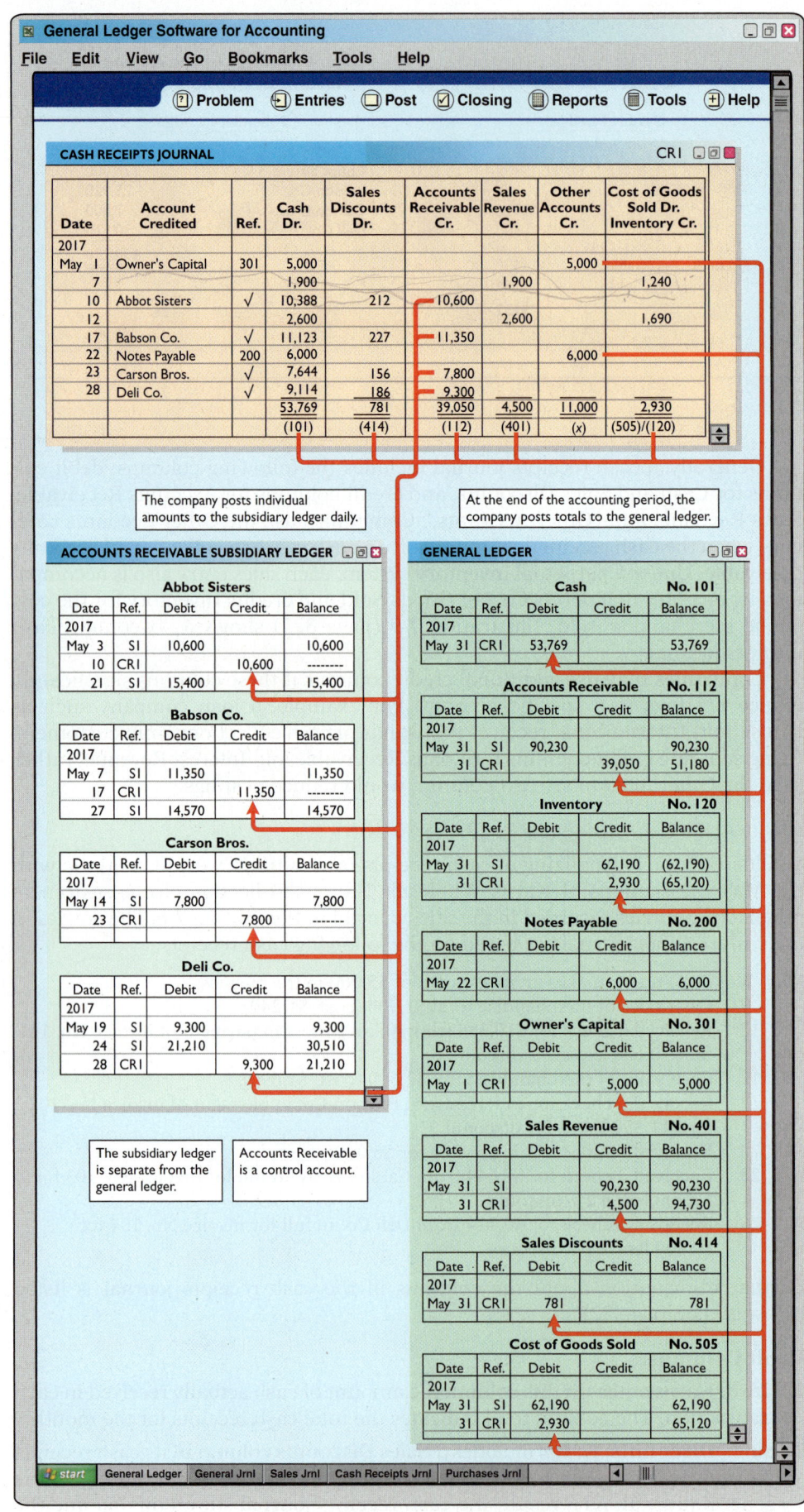

General Ledger Software for Accounting

File Edit View Go Bookmarks Tools Help

Problem Entries Post Closing Reports Tools Help

CASH RECEIPTS JOURNAL CR1

Date	Account Credited	Ref.	Cash Dr.	Sales Discounts Dr.	Accounts Receivable Cr.	Sales Revenue Cr.	Other Accounts Cr.	Cost of Goods Sold Dr. Inventory Cr.
2017								
May 1	Owner's Capital	301	5,000				5,000	
7			1,900			1,900		1,240
10	Abbot Sisters	√	10,388	212	10,600			
12			2,600			2,600		1,690
17	Babson Co.	√	11,123	227	11,350			
22	Notes Payable	200	6,000				6,000	
23	Carson Bros.	√	7,644	156	7,800			
28	Deli Co.	√	9,114	186	9,300			
			53,769	781	39,050	4,500	11,000	2,930
			(101)	(414)	(112)	(401)	(x)	(505)/(120)

The company posts individual amounts to the subsidiary ledger daily.

At the end of the accounting period, the company posts totals to the general ledger.

ACCOUNTS RECEIVABLE SUBSIDIARY LEDGER

Abbot Sisters

Date	Ref.	Debit	Credit	Balance
2017				
May 3	S1	10,600		10,600
10	CR1		10,600	--------
21	S1	15,400		15,400

Babson Co.

Date	Ref.	Debit	Credit	Balance
2017				
May 7	S1	11,350		11,350
17	CR1		11,350	--------
27	S1	14,570		14,570

Carson Bros.

Date	Ref.	Debit	Credit	Balance
2017				
May 14	S1	7,800		7,800
23	CR1		7,800	-------

Deli Co.

Date	Ref.	Debit	Credit	Balance
2017				
May 19	S1	9,300		9,300
24	S1	21,210		30,510
28	CR1		9,300	21,210

The subsidiary ledger is separate from the general ledger.

Accounts Receivable is a control account.

GENERAL LEDGER

Cash No. 101

Date	Ref.	Debit	Credit	Balance
2017				
May 31	CR1	53,769		53,769

Accounts Receivable No. 112

Date	Ref.	Debit	Credit	Balance
2017				
May 31	S1	90,230		90,230
31	CR1		39,050	51,180

Inventory No. 120

Date	Ref.	Debit	Credit	Balance
2017				
May 31	S1		62,190	(62,190)
31	CR1		2,930	(65,120)

Notes Payable No. 200

Date	Ref.	Debit	Credit	Balance
2017				
May 22	CR1		6,000	6,000

Owner's Capital No. 301

Date	Ref.	Debit	Credit	Balance
2017				
May 1	CR1		5,000	5,000

Sales Revenue No. 401

Date	Ref.	Debit	Credit	Balance
2017				
May 31	S1		90,230	90,230
31	CR1		4,500	94,730

Sales Discounts No. 414

Date	Ref.	Debit	Credit	Balance
2017				
May 31	CR1	781		781

Cost of Goods Sold No. 505

Date	Ref.	Debit	Credit	Balance
2017				
May 31	S1	62,190		62,190
31	CR1	2,930		65,120

start General Ledger General Jrnl Sales Jrnl Cash Receipts Jrnl Purchases Jrnl

Credit Columns:

3. **Accounts Receivable.** Karns uses the Accounts Receivable column to record cash collections on account. The amount entered here is the amount to be credited to the individual customer's account.
4. **Sales Revenue.** The Sales Revenue column records all cash sales of merchandise. Cash sales of other assets (plant assets, for example) are not reported in this column.
5. **Other Accounts.** Karns uses the Other Accounts column whenever the credit is other than to Accounts Receivable or Sales Revenue. For example, in the first entry, Karns enters $5,000 as a credit to Owner's Capital. This column is often referred to as the sundry accounts column.

Helpful Hint
A *subsidiary ledger* account is credited when the entry involves a collection of accounts receivable. A *general ledger* account is credited when the account is not shown in a special column (and an amount must be entered in the Other Accounts column). Otherwise, no account is shown in the "Account Credited" column.

Debit and Credit Column:

6. **Cost of Goods Sold and Inventory.** This column records debits to Cost of Goods Sold and credits to Inventory.

In a multi-column journal, generally only one line is needed for each entry. Debit and credit amounts for each line must be equal. When Karns journalizes the collection from Abbot Sisters on May 10, for example, three amounts are indicated. Note also that the Account Credited column identifies both general ledger and subsidiary ledger account titles. General ledger accounts are illustrated in the May 1 and May 22 entries. A subsidiary account is illustrated in the May 10 entry for the collection from Abbot Sisters.

When Karns has finished journalizing a multi-column journal, it totals the amount columns and compares the totals to prove the equality of debits and credits. Illustration 7-10 shows the proof of the equality of Karns's cash receipts journal.

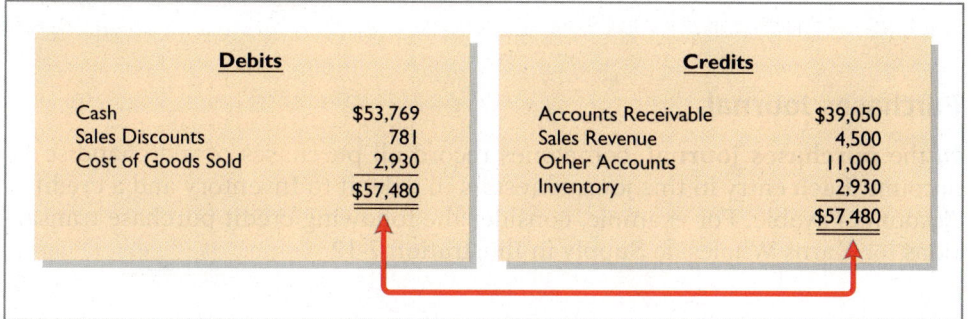

Illustration 7-10
Proving the equality of the cash receipts journal

Debits	
Cash	$53,769
Sales Discounts	781
Cost of Goods Sold	2,930
	$57,480

Credits	
Accounts Receivable	$39,050
Sales Revenue	4,500
Other Accounts	11,000
Inventory	2,930
	$57,480

Totaling the columns of a journal and proving the equality of the totals is called **footing** and **cross-footing** a journal.

POSTING THE CASH RECEIPTS JOURNAL

Posting a multi-column journal (Illustration 7-9, page 322) involves the following steps.

1. **At the end of the month**, the company posts all column totals, except for the Other Accounts total, to the account title(s) specified in the column heading (such as Cash or Accounts Receivable). The company then enters account numbers below the column totals to show that they have been posted. For example, Karns has posted Cash to account No. 101, Accounts Receivable to account No. 112, Inventory to account No. 120, Sales Revenue to account No. 401, Sales Discounts to account No. 414, and Cost of Goods Sold to account No. 505.
2. The company **separately posts the individual amounts comprising the Other Accounts total** to the general ledger accounts specified in the Account Credited column. See, for example, the credit posting to Owner's Capital. The total amount of this column has not been posted. The symbol (X) is inserted below the total to this column to indicate that the amount has not been posted.

3. The individual amounts in a column, posted in total to a control account (Accounts Receivable, in this case), are posted **daily to the subsidiary ledger** account specified in the Account Credited column. See, for example, the credit posting of $10,600 to Abbot Sisters.

The symbol **CR**, used in both the subsidiary and general ledgers, identifies postings from the cash receipts journal.

PROVING THE LEDGERS

After posting of the cash receipts journal is completed, Karns proves the ledgers. As shown in Illustration 7-11, the general ledger totals agree. Also, the sum of the subsidiary ledger balances equals the control account balance.

Illustration 7-11
Proving the ledgers after posting the sales and the cash receipts journals

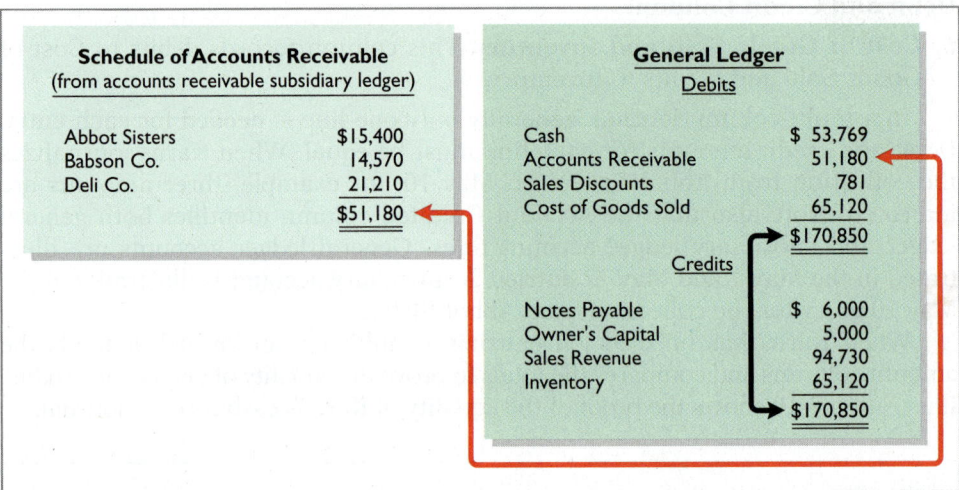

Schedule of Accounts Receivable
(from accounts receivable subsidiary ledger)

Abbot Sisters	$15,400
Babson Co.	14,570
Deli Co.	21,210
	$51,180

General Ledger

Debits	
Cash	$ 53,769
Accounts Receivable	51,180
Sales Discounts	781
Cost of Goods Sold	65,120
	$170,850
Credits	
Notes Payable	$ 6,000
Owner's Capital	5,000
Sales Revenue	94,730
Inventory	65,120
	$170,850

Purchases Journal

In the **purchases journal**, companies record all purchases of merchandise on account. Each entry in this journal results in a debit to Inventory and a credit to Accounts Payable. For example, consider the following credit purchase transactions for Karns Wholesale Supply in Illustration 7-12.

Illustration 7-12
Credit purchase transactions

Date	Supplier	Amount
5/6	Jasper Manufacturing Inc.	$11,000
5/10	Eaton and Howe Inc.	7,200
5/14	Fabor and Son	6,900
5/19	Jasper Manufacturing Inc.	17,500
5/26	Fabor and Son	8,700
5/29	Eaton and Howe Inc.	12,600

Illustration 7-13 shows the purchases journal for Karns Wholesale Supply. When using a one-column purchases journal (as in Illustration 7-13), a company cannot journalize other types of purchases on account or cash purchases in it. For example, if the company used the purchases journal in Illustration 7-13, Karns would have to record credit purchases of equipment or supplies in the general journal. Likewise, all cash purchases would be entered in the cash payments journal.

JOURNALIZING CREDIT PURCHASES OF MERCHANDISE

The journalizing procedure is similar to that for a sales journal. Companies make entries in the purchases journal from purchase invoices. In contrast to the sales journal, the purchases journal may not have an invoice number column because

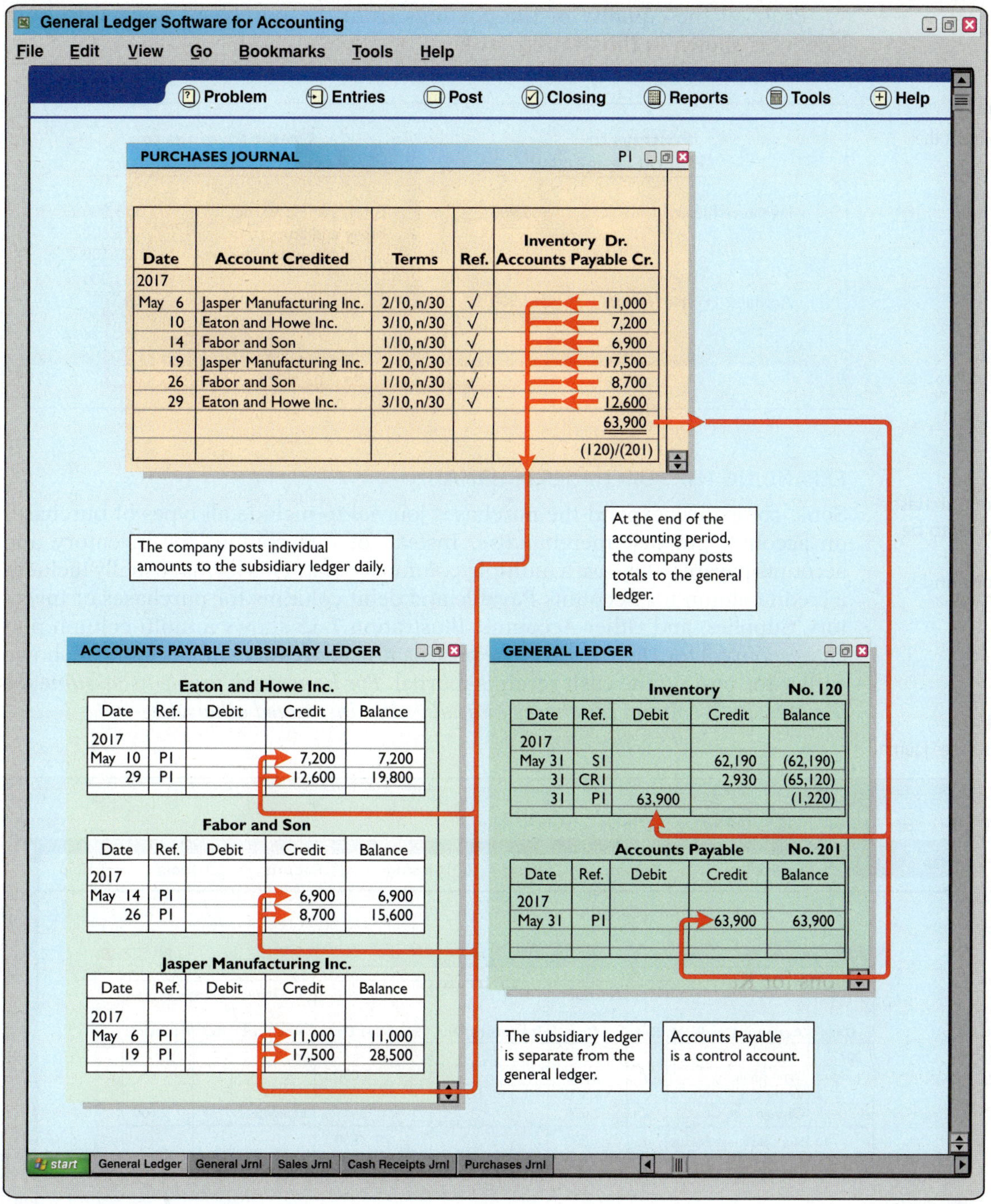

Illustration 7-13
Journalizing and posting the purchases journal

invoices received from different suppliers will not be in numerical sequence. To ensure that they record all purchase invoices, some companies consecutively number each invoice upon receipt and then use an internal document number column in the purchases journal. The entries for Karns Wholesale Supply are based on the assumed credit purchases listed in Illustration 7-12.

POSTING THE PURCHASES JOURNAL

The procedures for posting the purchases journal are similar to those for the sales journal. In this case, Karns makes **daily** postings to the **accounts payable ledger**. It makes **monthly** postings to Inventory and Accounts Payable in the general ledger. In both ledgers, Karns uses **P1** in the reference column to show that the postings are from page 1 of the purchases journal.

Helpful Hint
Postings to subsidiary ledger accounts are done daily because it is often necessary to know a current balance for the subsidiary accounts.

Proof of the equality of the postings from the purchases journal to both ledgers is shown in Illustration 7-14.

Illustration 7-14
Proving the equality of the purchases journal

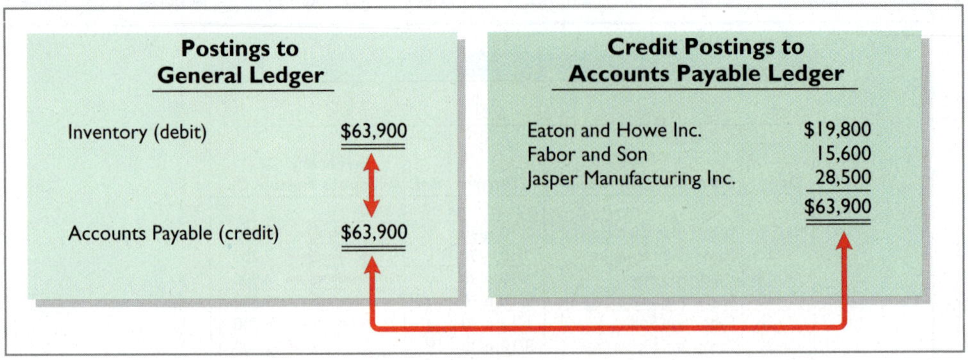

Helpful Hint
A single-column purchases journal needs only to be footed to prove the equality of debits and credits.

EXPANDING THE PURCHASES JOURNAL

Some companies expand the purchases journal to include all types of purchases on account, not just merchandise. Instead of one column for inventory and accounts payable, they use a multiple-column format. This format usually includes a credit column for Accounts Payable and debit columns for purchases of Inventory, Supplies, and Other Accounts. Illustration 7-15 shows a multi-column purchases journal for Hanover Co. The posting procedures are similar to those shown earlier for posting the cash receipts journal. *For homework problems, assume the use of a single-column purchases journal unless instructed otherwise.*

Illustration 7-15
Multi-column purchases journal

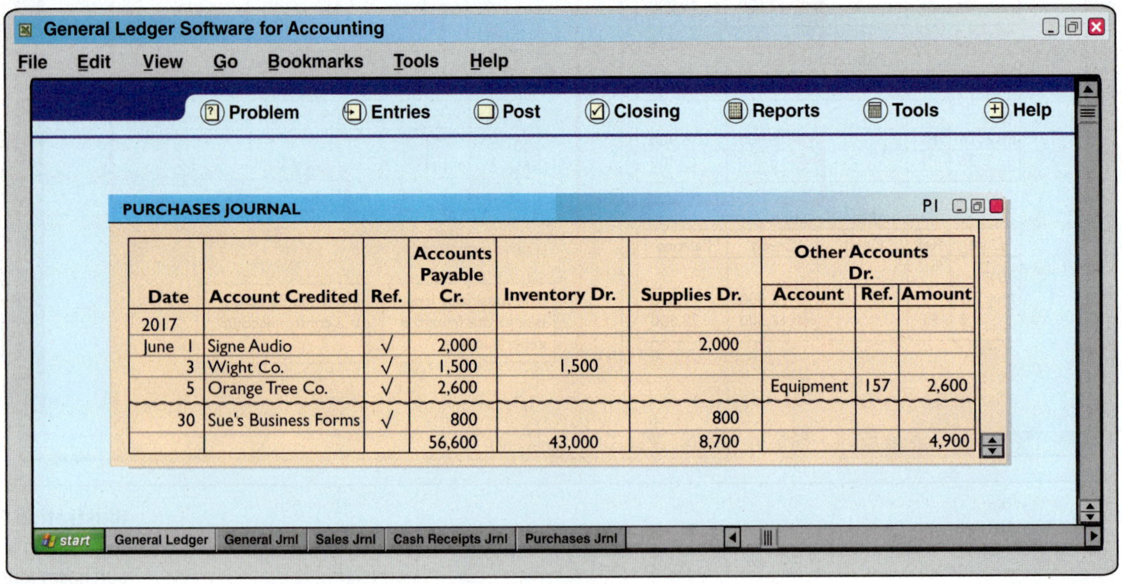

Date	Account Credited	Ref.	Accounts Payable Cr.	Inventory Dr.	Supplies Dr.	Other Accounts Dr. Account	Ref.	Amount
2017								
June 1	Signe Audio	√	2,000		2,000			
3	Wight Co.	√	1,500	1,500				
5	Orange Tree Co.	√	2,600			Equipment	157	2,600
30	Sue's Business Forms	√	800		800			
			56,600	43,000	8,700			4,900

Cash Payments Journal

In a **cash payments (cash disbursements) journal**, companies record all disbursements of cash. Entries are made from prenumbered checks. Because companies make cash payments for various purposes, the cash payments journal has multiple columns. Illustration 7-16 shows a four-column journal.

JOURNALIZING CASH PAYMENTS TRANSACTIONS

The procedures for journalizing transactions in this journal are similar to those for the cash receipts journal. Karns records each transaction on one line, and for each line there must be equal debit and credit amounts. The entries in the cash

General Ledger Software for Accounting

File Edit View Go Bookmarks Tools Help

Problem Entries Post Closing Reports Tools Help

CASH PAYMENTS JOURNAL CP1

Date	Ck. No.	Account Debited	Ref.	Other Accounts Dr.	Accounts Payable Dr.	Inventory Cr.	Cash Cr.
2017							
May 1	101	Prepaid Insurance	130	1,200			1,200
3	102	Inventory	120	100			100
8	103	Inventory	120	4,400			4,400
10	104	Jasper Manuf. Inc.	√		11,000	220	10,780
19	105	Eaton & Howe Inc.	√		7,200	216	6,984
23	106	Fabor and Son	√		6,900	69	6,831
28	107	Jasper Manuf. Inc.	√		17,500	350	17,150
30	108	Owner's Drawings	306	500			500
				6,200	42,600	855	47,945
				(x)	(201)	(120)	(101)

The company posts individual amounts to the subsidiary ledger daily.

At the end of the accounting period, the company posts totals to the general ledger.

ACCOUNTS PAYABLE SUBSIDIARY LEDGER

Eaton and Howe Inc.

Date	Ref.	Debit	Credit	Balance
2017				
May 10	P1		7,200	7,200
19	CP1	7,200		-------
29	P1		12,600	12,600

Fabor and Son

Date	Ref.	Debit	Credit	Balance
2017				
May 14	P1		6,900	6,900
23	CP1	6,900		-------
26	P1		8,700	8,700

Jasper Manufacturing Inc.

Date	Ref.	Debit	Credit	Balance
2017				
May 6	P1		11,000	11,000
10	CP1	11,000		--------
19	P1		17,500	17,500
28	CP1	17,500		--------

GENERAL LEDGER

Cash No. 101

Date	Ref.	Debit	Credit	Balance
2017				
May 31	CR1	53,769		53,769
31	CP1		47,945	5,824

Inventory No. 120

Date	Ref.	Debit	Credit	Balance
2017				
May 3	CP1	100		100
8	CP1	4,400		4,500
31	S1		62,190	57,690
31	CR1		2,930	60,620
31	P1	63,900		3,280
31	CP1		855	2,425

Prepaid Insurance No. 130

Date	Ref.	Debit	Credit	Balance
2017				
May 1	CP1	1,200		1,200

Accounts Payable No. 201

Date	Ref.	Debit	Credit	Balance
2017				
May 31	P1		63,900	63,900
31	CP1	42,600		21,300

Owner's Drawings No. 306

Date	Ref.	Debit	Credit	Balance
2017				
May 30	CP1	500		500

The subsidiary ledger is separate from the general ledger.

Accounts Payable is a control account.

start | General Ledger | General Jrnl | Sales Jrnl | Cash Receipts Jrnl | Purchases Jrnl

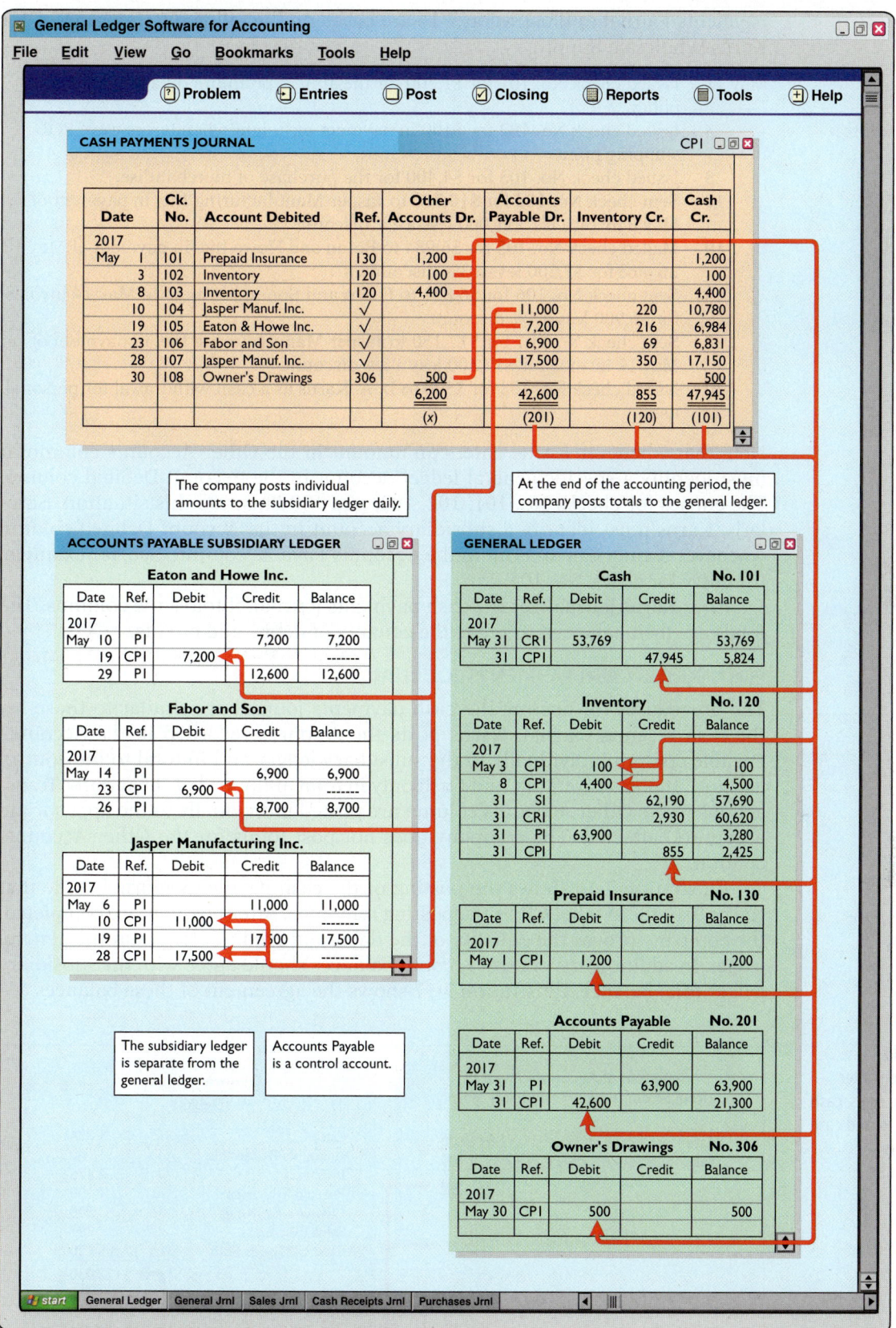

Illustration 7-16
Journalizing and posting the cash payments journal

payments journal in Illustration 7-16 are based on the following transactions for Karns Wholesale Supply.

May	1	Issued check No. 101 for $1,200 for the annual premium on a fire insurance policy.
	3	Issued check No. 102 for $100 in payment of freight when terms were FOB shipping point.
	8	Issued check No. 103 for $4,400 for the purchase of merchandise.
	10	Sent check No. 104 for $10,780 to Jasper Manufacturing Inc. in payment of May 6 invoice for $11,000 less a 2% discount.
	19	Mailed check No. 105 for $6,984 to Eaton and Howe Inc. in payment of May 10 invoice for $7,200 less a 3% discount.
	23	Sent check No. 106 for $6,831 to Fabor and Son in payment of May 14 invoice for $6,900 less a 1% discount.
	28	Sent check No. 107 for $17,150 to Jasper Manufacturing Inc. in payment of May 19 invoice for $17,500 less a 2% discount.
	30	Issued check No. 108 for $500 to D. A. Karns as a cash withdrawal for personal use.

Note that whenever Karns enters an amount in the Other Accounts column, it must identify a specific general ledger account in the Account Debited column. The entries for checks No. 101, 102, 103, and 108 illustrate this situation. Similarly, Karns must identify a subsidiary account in the Account Debited column whenever it enters an amount in the Accounts Payable column. See, for example, the entry for check No. 104.

After Karns journalizes the cash payments journal, it totals the columns. The totals are then balanced to prove the equality of debits and credits.

POSTING THE CASH PAYMENTS JOURNAL

The procedures for posting the cash payments journal are similar to those for the cash receipts journal. Karns posts the amounts recorded in the Accounts Payable column individually to the subsidiary ledger and in total to the control account. It posts Inventory and Cash only in total at the end of the month. Transactions in the Other Accounts column are posted individually to the appropriate account(s) affected. The company does not post totals for the Other Accounts column.

Illustration 7-16 shows the posting of the cash payments journal. Note that Karns uses the symbol **CP** as the posting reference. After postings are completed, the company proves the equality of the debit and credit balances in the general ledger. In addition, the control account balances should agree with the subsidiary ledger total balance. Illustration 7-17 shows the agreement of these balances.

Illustration 7-17
Proving the ledgers after postings from the sales, cash receipts, purchases, and cash payments journals

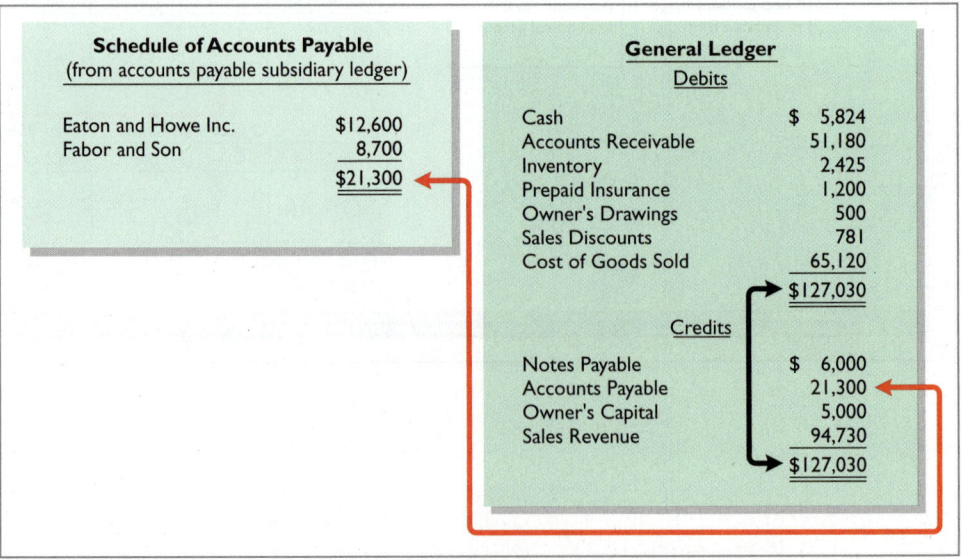

Schedule of Accounts Payable
(from accounts payable subsidiary ledger)

Eaton and Howe Inc.	$12,600
Fabor and Son	8,700
	$21,300

General Ledger

Debits	
Cash	$ 5,824
Accounts Receivable	51,180
Inventory	2,425
Prepaid Insurance	1,200
Owner's Drawings	500
Sales Discounts	781
Cost of Goods Sold	65,120
	$127,030
Credits	
Notes Payable	$ 6,000
Accounts Payable	21,300
Owner's Capital	5,000
Sales Revenue	94,730
	$127,030

Effects of Special Journals on the General Journal

Special journals for sales, purchases, and cash substantially reduce the number of entries that companies make in the general journal. **Only transactions that cannot be entered in a special journal are recorded in the general journal.** For example, a company may use the general journal to record such transactions as granting of credit to a customer for a sales return or allowance, granting of credit from a supplier for purchases returned, acceptance of a note receivable from a customer, and purchase of equipment by issuing a note payable. Also, **correcting, adjusting, and closing entries are made in the general journal**.

The general journal has columns for date, account title and explanation, reference, and debit and credit amounts. When control and subsidiary accounts are not involved, the procedures for journalizing and posting of transactions are the same as those described in earlier chapters. When control and subsidiary accounts are involved, companies make two changes from the earlier procedures:

1. In **journalizing**, they identify both the control and the subsidiary accounts.
2. In **posting**, there must be a **dual posting**: once to the control account and once to the subsidiary account.

To illustrate, assume that on May 31, Karns Wholesale Supply returns $500 of merchandise for credit to Fabor and Son. Illustration 7-18 shows the entry in the general journal and the posting of the entry.

Illustration 7-18
Journalizing and posting the general journal

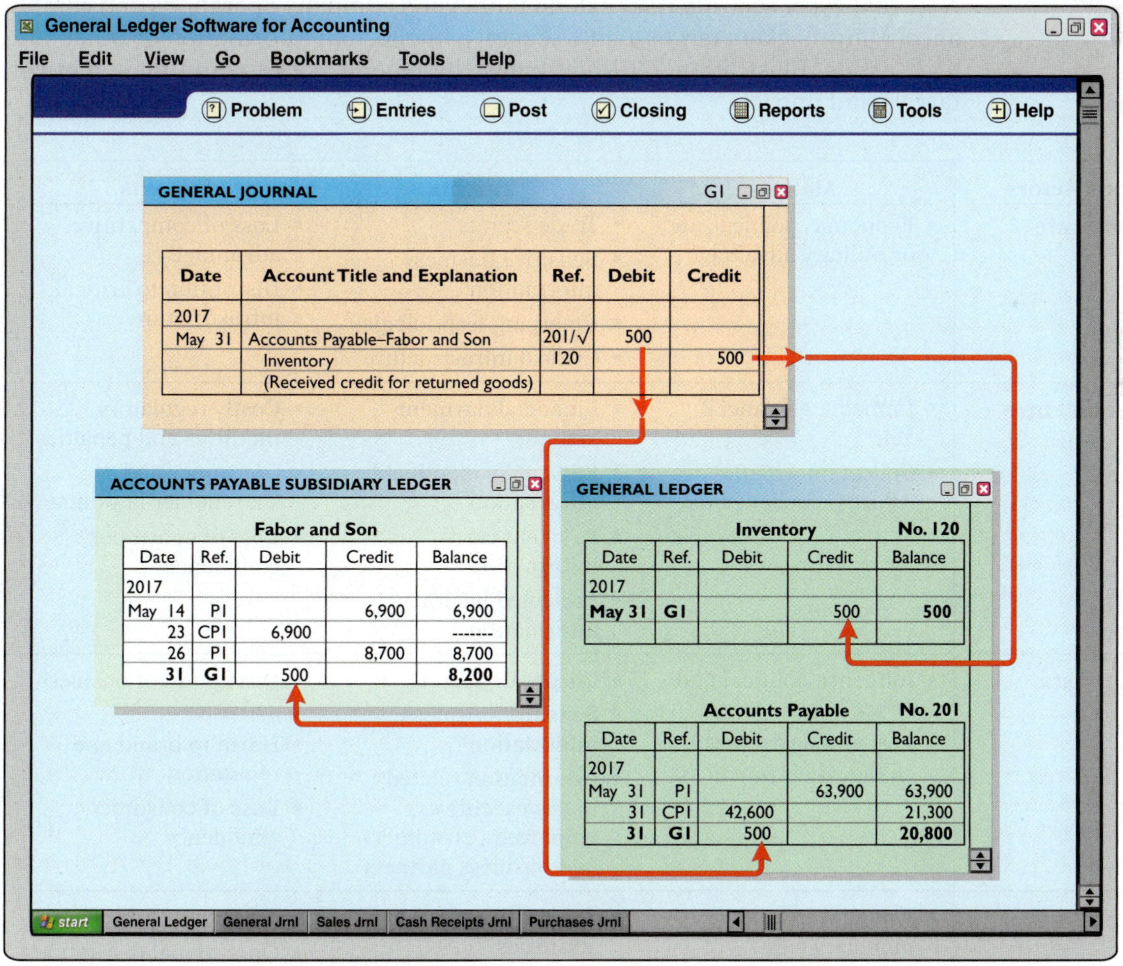

GENERAL JOURNAL — G1

Date	Account Title and Explanation	Ref.	Debit	Credit
2017				
May 31	Accounts Payable–Fabor and Son	201/✓	500	
	Inventory	120		500
	(Received credit for returned goods)			

ACCOUNTS PAYABLE SUBSIDIARY LEDGER — Fabor and Son

Date	Ref.	Debit	Credit	Balance
2017				
May 14	P1		6,900	6,900
23	CP1	6,900		-------
26	P1		8,700	8,700
31	**G1**	500		**8,200**

GENERAL LEDGER — Inventory, No. 120

Date	Ref.	Debit	Credit	Balance
2017				
May 31	**G1**		500	**500**

GENERAL LEDGER — Accounts Payable, No. 201

Date	Ref.	Debit	Credit	Balance
2017				
May 31	P1		63,900	63,900
31	CP1	42,600		21,300
31	**G1**	500		**20,800**

Note that the general journal indicates two accounts (Accounts Payable, and Fabor and Son) for the debit, and two postings ("201/✓") in the reference column. One debit is posted to the control account and another debit is posted to the creditor's account in the subsidiary ledger. If Karns receives cash instead of credit on this return, then it would record the transaction in the cash receipts journal.

Cyber Security: A Final Comment

Have you ever been hacked? With the increasing use of cell phones, tablets, and other social media outlets, a real risk exists that your confidential information may be stolen and used illegally. Companies, individuals, and even nations have all been victims of **cybercrime**—a crime that involves the Internet, a computer system, or computer technology.

For companies, cybercrime is clearly a major threat as the hacking of employees' or customers' records related to cybercrime can cost millions of dollars. Unfortunately, the numbers of security breaches are increasing. A security breach at Target, for example, cost the company a minimum of $20 million, the CEO lost his job, and sales plummeted.

Here are three reasons for the rise in the successful hacks of corporate computer records.

1. Companies and their employees continue to increase their activity on the Internet, primarily due to the use of mobile devices and cloud computing.
2. Companies today collect and store unprecedented amounts of personal data on customers and employees.
3. Companies often take measures to protect themselves from cyber security attacks but then fail to check if employees are carrying out the proper security guidelines.

Note that cyber security risks extend far beyond company operations and compliance. Many hackers target highly sensitive intellectual information or other strategic assets. Illustration 7-19 highlights the type of hackers and their motives, targets and impacts.

Illustration 7-19
Profiles of hackers

Malicious Actors	Motives	Targets	Impacts
Nation-state	• Economic, political, and/or military advantage	• Trade secrets • Sensitive business information • Emerging technologies • Critical infrastructure	• Loss of competitive advantage • Disruption to critical infrastructure
Organized crime	• Immediate financial gain • Collect information for future financial gains	• Financial/payment systems • Personally identifiable information • Payment card information • Protected health information	• Costly regulatory inquiries and penalties • Consumer and shareholder lawsuits • Loss of consumer confidence
Hacktivists	• Influence political and/or social change • Pressure businesses to change their practices	• Corporate secrets • Sensitive business information • Information related to key executives, employees, customers, and business partners	• Disruption of business activities • Harm to brand and reputation • Loss of consumer confidence
Insiders	• Personal advantage, monetary gain • Professional revenge • Patriotism	• Sales, deals, market strategies • Corporate secrets, intellectual property • Business operations • Personnel information	• Trade secret disclosure • Operational disruption • Harm to brand and reputation • National security impact

Source: PriceWaterhouseCoopers, "Answering Your Cybersecurity Questions" (January 2014).

Companies now recognize that cyber security systems that protect confidential data must be implemented. It follows that companies (and nations and individuals) must continually verify that their cyber security defenses are sound and uncompromised.

DO IT! 3 Special Journals

Swisher Company had the following transactions during March.

1. Collected cash on account from Oakland Company.
2. Purchased equipment by signing a note payable.
3. Sold merchandise on account.
4. Purchased merchandise on account.
5. Paid $2,400 for a 2-year insurance policy.

Identify the journal in which each of the transactions above is recorded. The company uses the special journals described in the chapter plus a general journal.

Action Plan

✔ Determine if the transaction involves the receipt of cash (cash receipts journal) or the payment of cash (cash payments journal).

✔ Determine if the transaction is a sale of merchandise on account (sales journal) or a purchase of merchandise on account (purchases journal).

✔ All other transactions are recorded in the general journal.

Solution

1. Collected cash on account from Oakland Company.	Cash receipts journal
2. Purchased equipment by signing a note payable.	General journal
3. Sold merchandise on account.	Sales journal
4. Purchased merchandise on account.	Purchases journal
5. Paid $2,400 for a 2-year insurance policy.	Cash payments journal

Related exercise material: **BE7-6, BE7-7, BE7-8, BE7-9, BE7-10, E7-6, E7-7, E7-8, E7-10, and DO IT! 7-3.**

REVIEW AND PRACTICE

LEARNING OBJECTIVES REVIEW

1 Explain the basic concepts of an accounting information system. The basic principles in developing an accounting information system are cost-effectiveness, useful output, and flexibility. Most companies use a computerized accounting system. Smaller companies use entry-level software such as QuickBooks® or Sage 50. Larger companies use custom-made software packages, which often integrate all aspects of the organization.

2 Describe the nature and purpose of a subsidiary ledger. A subsidiary ledger is a group of accounts with a common characteristic. It facilitates the recording process by freeing the general ledger from details of individual balances.

3 Record transactions in special journals. Companies use special journals to group similar types of transactions. In a special journal, generally only one line is used to record a complete transaction.

GLOSSARY REVIEW

Accounting information system A system that collects and processes transaction data and communicates financial information to decision-makers. (p. 312).

Accounts payable (creditors') subsidiary ledger A subsidiary ledger that collects transaction data of individual creditors. (p. 315).

Accounts receivable (customers') subsidiary ledger A subsidiary ledger that collects transaction data of individual customers. (p. 315).

Cash payments (cash disbursements) journal A special journal that records all disbursements of cash. (p. 326).

Cash receipts journal A special journal that records all cash received. (p. 320).

Control account An account in the general ledger that summarizes subsidiary ledger data. (p. 315).

Cybercrime A crime that involves the Internet, a computer system, or computer technology. (p. 330).

Manual accounting system A system in which someone performs each of the steps in the accounting cycle by hand. (p. 314).

Purchases journal A special journal that records all purchases of merchandise on account. (p. 324).

Sales journal A special journal that records all sales of merchandise on account. (p. 318).

Special journals Journals that record similar types of transactions, such as all credit sales. (p. 318).

Subsidiary ledger A group of accounts with a common characteristic. (p. 315).

PRACTICE MULTIPLE-CHOICE QUESTIONS

(LO 1) 1. The basic principles of an accounting information system include all of the following **except**:
(a) cost-effectiveness. (c) useful output.
(b) flexibility. (d) periodicity.

(LO 1) 2. Which of the following is **not** an advantage of computerized accounting systems?
(a) Data is entered only once in computerized accounting systems.
(b) Computerized accounting systems provide up-to-date information.
(c) Computerized accounting systems eliminate entering of transaction information.
(d) Computerized accounting systems eliminate many errors resulting from human intervention.

(LO 2) 3. Which of the following is **incorrect** concerning subsidiary ledgers?
(a) The purchases ledger is a common subsidiary ledger for creditor accounts.
(b) The accounts receivable ledger is a subsidiary ledger.
(c) A subsidiary ledger is a group of accounts with a common characteristic.
(d) An advantage of the subsidiary ledger is that it permits a division of labor in posting.

(LO 2) 4. Two common subsidiary ledgers are:
(a) accounts receivable and cash receipts.
(b) accounts payable and cash payments.
(c) accounts receivable and accounts payable.
(d) sales and cost of goods sold.

(LO 2) 5. At the beginning of the month, the accounts receivable subsidiary ledger showed balances for Apple Company $5,000 and Berry Company $7,000. During the month, credit sales were made to Apple $6,000, Berry $4,500, and Cantaloupe $8,500. Cash was collected on account from Berry $11,500 and Cantaloupe $3,000. At the end of the month, the control account Accounts Receivable in the general ledger should have a balance of:
(a) $11,000. (c) $16,500.
(b) $12,000. (d) $31,000.

(LO 3) 6. A sales journal will be used for:

	Credit Sales	Cash Sales	Sales Discounts
(a)	no	yes	yes
(b)	yes	no	yes
(c)	yes	no	no
(d)	yes	yes	no

7. A purchase of equipment on account is recorded in the: (LO 3)
(a) cash receipts journal. (c) cash payments journal.
(b) purchases journal. (d) general journal.

8. A purchase of equipment using cash is recorded in the: (LO 3)
(a) cash receipts journal. (c) cash payments journal.
(b) purchases journal. (d) general journal.

9. Which of the following statements is **correct**? (LO 3)
(a) The sales discount column is included in the cash receipts journal.
(b) The purchases journal records all purchases of merchandise whether for cash or on account.
(c) The cash receipts journal records sales on account.
(d) Merchandise returned by the buyer is recorded by the seller in the purchases journal.

10. Dotel Company's cash receipts journal includes an Accounts Receivable column and an Other Accounts column. At the end of the month, these columns are posted to the general ledger as: (LO 3)

	Accounts Receivable	Other Accounts
(a)	a column total	a column total
(b)	individual amounts	a column total
(c)	individual amounts	individual amounts
(d)	a column total	individual amounts

11. Which of the following is **incorrect** concerning the posting of the cash receipts journal? (LO 3)
(a) The total of the Other Accounts column is not posted.
(b) All column totals except the total for the Other Accounts column are posted once at the end of the month to the account title(s) specified in the column heading.
(c) The totals of all columns are posted daily to the accounts specified in the column heading.
(d) The individual amounts in a column posted in total to a control account are posted daily to the subsidiary ledger account specified in the Account Credited column.

12. Postings from the purchases journal to the subsidiary ledger are generally made: (LO 3)
(a) yearly. (c) weekly.
(b) monthly. (d) daily.

13. Which statement is **incorrect** regarding the general journal? (LO 3)
(a) Only transactions that cannot be entered in a special journal are recorded in the general journal.

(b) Dual postings are always required in the general journal.
(c) The general journal may be used to record acceptance of a note receivable in payment of an account receivable.
(d) Correcting, adjusting, and closing entries are made in the general journal.

(LO 3) 14. When companies use special journals:
(a) they record all purchase transactions in the purchases journal.
(b) they record all cash received, except from cash sales, in the cash receipts journal.
(c) they record all cash disbursements in the cash payments journal.
(d) a general journal is not necessary.

15. If a customer returns goods for credit, the selling company normally makes an entry in the: (LO 3)
(a) cash payments journal. (c) general journal.
(b) sales journal. (d) cash receipts journal.

Solutions

1. (d) Periodicity is not one of the basic principles of accounting information systems. The other choices are true statements.

2. (c) Computerized accounting systems do not eliminate the entering of transaction information. The other choices are advantages of computerized accounting systems.

3. (a) The accounts payable ledger, not the purchases ledger, is a common subsidiary ledger for creditor accounts. The other choices are true statements.

4. (c) Accounts receivable and accounts payable are two common subsidiary ledgers. The other choices are incorrect because (a) cash receipts, (b) cash payments, and (d) sales revenue and cost of goods sold are not subsidiary ledgers.

5. (c) The accounts receivable subsidiary ledger balances are the following: Apple Company \$11,000 (beginning balance \$5,000 + credit sales \$6,000), Berry Company \$0 (beginning balance \$7,000 + credit sales \$4,500 − cash collected on account \$11,500), and Cantaloupe \$5,500 (credit sales \$8,500 − cash collected on account \$3,000). The Accounts Receivable control account in the general ledger therefore has a balance of \$16,500 (\$11,000 + \$0 + \$5,500), not (a) \$11,000, (b) \$12,000, or (d) \$31,000.

6. (c) The sales journal is used for credit sales. The cash receipts journal is used for cash sales and sales discounts. Therefore, choices (a), (b), and (d) are incorrect.

7. (d) Unless the company uses a multi-column purchases journal, the general journal is used to record the purchase of equipment **on account**. The other choices are incorrect because (a) the cash receipts journal would be used only if cash is received, (b) a one-column purchases journal cannot be used to record a purchase of equipment on account, and (c) the cash payments journal would be used only if this is a cash purchase.

8. (c) The cash payments journal includes all cash paid, including all **cash** purchases. The other choices are incorrect because (a) the cash receipts journal includes all cash received, including cash sales, not cash purchases; (b) the purchases journal includes only purchases of inventory on account, not cash purchases; and (d) the general journal is only used if a transaction cannot be entered in a special journal. In this case, this transaction can be entered into the cash payments journal.

9. (a) The sales discount column is included in the cash receipts journal. The other choices are incorrect because (b) the purchases journal only records purchases of inventory on account, not for cash; (c) the sales journal, not the cash receipts journal, records sales on account; and (d) when merchandise is returned by a buyer, the seller records this sales return in the general journal.

10. (d) The Accounts Receivable column would be posted to the general ledger as a column total, and the Other Accounts column would be posted as individual amounts. Therefore, the other choices are incorrect.

11. (c) The totals of all columns are not posted daily to the accounts specified in the column heading. Instead, all column totals except the total for the Other Accounts column (which is never posted) are posted once at the end of the month to the account title(s) specified in the column heading. The other choices are true statements.

12. (d) Postings from the purchases journal to the subsidiary ledger are usually made daily, not (a) yearly, (b) monthly, or (c) weekly.

13. (b) Dual postings are not always required in the general journal. Only when control and subsidiary accounts are involved are companies required to dual post: once to the control account and once to the subsidiary account. The other choices are true statements.

14. (c) When special journals are used, companies record all cash disbursements in the cash payments journal. The other choices are incorrect because when special journals are used, (a) companies record only purchases of inventory on account in the purchases journal; (b) companies record all cash receipts, including cash sales, in the cash receipts journal; and (d) a general journal is still needed.

15. (c) When a customer returns goods for **credit** (i.e., no cash is involved), the selling company records the transaction in the general journal, not the (a) cash payments journal, (b) sales journal, or (d) cash receipts journal.

PRACTICE EXERCISES

Post various journals to control and subsidiary accounts.
(LO 2, 3)

1. On June 1, the balance of the Accounts Receivable control account in the general ledger of Rath Company was \$13,620. The customers' subsidiary ledger contained account balances as follows: Wilson \$2,000, Sanchez \$3,140, Roberts \$2,560, and Marks \$5,920. At the end of June, the various journals contained the following information.

Sales journal: Sales to Roberts $900, to Wilson $1,400, to Hardy $1,500, and to Marks $1,200.
Cash receipts journal: Cash received from Roberts $1,610, from Marks $2,600, from Hardy $580, from Sanchez $2,100, and from Wilson $1,540.
General journal: An allowance is granted to Marks $325.

Instructions

(a) Set up control and subsidiary accounts and enter the beginning balances. Do not construct the journals.
(b) Post the various journals. Post the items as individual items or as totals, whichever would be the appropriate procedure. (No sales discounts given.)
(c) Prepare a schedule of accounts receivable and prove the agreement of the control account with the subsidiary ledger at June 30, 2017.

Solution

1. (a) and (b)

GENERAL LEDGER

Accounts Receivable

Date	Explanation	Ref.	Debit	Credit	Balance
June 1	Balance	✓			13,620
		S	5,000		18,620
		CR		8,430	10,190
		G		325	9,865

ACCOUNTS RECEIVABLE SUBSIDIARY LEDGER

Hardy

Date	Explanation	Ref.	Debit	Credit	Balance
June 1					0
		S	1,500		1,500
		CR		580	920

Marks

Date	Explanation	Ref.	Debit	Credit	Balance
June 1	Balance	✓			5,920
		S	1,200		7,120
		CR		2,600	4,520
		G		325	4,195

Roberts

Date	Explanation	Ref.	Debit	Credit	Balance
June 1	Balance	✓			2,560
		S	900		3,460
		CR		1,610	1,850

Sanchez

Date	Explanation	Ref.	Debit	Credit	Balance
June 1	Balance	✓			3,140
		CR		2,100	1,040

Wilson

Date	Explanation	Ref.	Debit	Credit	Balance
June 1	Balance	✓			2,000
		S	1,400		3,400
		CR		1,540	1,860

(c)

RATH COMPANY
Schedule of Accounts Receivable
As of June 30, 2017

Hardy	$ 920
Marks	4,195
Roberts	1,850
Sanchez	1,040
Wilson	1,860
Total	$9,865
Accounts Receivable	$9,865

Indicate use of special journals.
(LO 3)

2. Below are some typical transactions incurred by Brimmer Company.

1. Received credit for merchandise purchased on credit.
2. Payment of employee wages.
3. Sales discount taken on goods sold.
4. Income summary closed to owner's capital.
5. Purchase of office supplies for cash.
6. Depreciation on building.
7. Purchase of merchandise on account.
8. Return of merchandise sold for credit.
9. Payment of creditors on account.
10. Collection on account from customers.
11. Sale of merchandise on account.
12. Sale of land for cash.
13. Sale of merchandise for cash.

Instructions

For each transaction, indicate whether it would normally be recorded in a cash receipts journal, cash payments journal, sales journal, single-column purchases journal, or general journal.

Solution

2.
1. General journal
2. Cash payments journal
3. Cash receipts journal
4. General journal
5. Cash payments journal
6. General journal
7. Purchases journal
8. General journal
9. Cash payments journal
10. Cash receipts journal
11. Sales journal
12. Cash receipts journal
13. Cash receipts journal

PRACTICE PROBLEM

Journalize transactions in cash receipts journal and explain posting procedure.
(LO 3)

Cassandra Wilson Company uses a six-column cash receipts journal with the following columns.

Cash (Dr.)
Sales Discounts (Dr.)
Accounts Receivable (Cr.)
Sales Revenue (Cr.)
Other Accounts (Cr.)
Cost of Goods Sold (Dr.) and Inventory (Cr.)

Cash receipts transactions for the month of July 2017 are as follows.

July	3	Cash sales total $5,800 (cost, $3,480).
	5	Received a check for $6,370 from Jeltz Company in payment of an invoice dated June 26 for $6,500, terms 2/10, n/30.
	9	Cassandra Wilson, the proprietor, made an additional investment of $5,000 in cash in the business.
	10	Cash sales total $12,519 (cost, $7,511).
	12	Received a check for $7,275 from R. Eliot & Co. in payment of a $7,500 invoice dated July 3, terms 3/10, n/30.
	15	Received an advance of $700 cash for future services.
	20	Cash sales total $15,472 (cost, $9,283).
	22	Received a check for $5,880 from Beck Company in payment of $6,000 invoice dated July 13, terms 2/10, n/30.
	29	Cash sales total $17,660 (cost, $10,596).
	31	Received cash of $200 for interest earned for July.

Instructions

(a) Journalize the transactions in the cash receipts journal.

(b) Contrast the posting of the Accounts Receivable and Other Accounts columns.

Solution

(a)

CASSANDRA WILSON COMPANY
Cash Receipts Journal
CR1

Date	Account Credited	Ref.	Cash Dr.	Sales Discounts Dr.	Accounts Receivable Cr.	Sales Revenue Cr.	Other Accounts Cr.	Cost of Goods Sold Dr. Inventory Cr.
2017								
7/3			5,800			5,800		3,480
5	Jeltz Company		6,370	130	6,500			
9	Owner's Capital		5,000				5,000	
10			12,519			12,519		7,511
12	R. Eliot & Co.		7,275	225	7,500			
15	Unearned Service Revenue		700				700	
20			15,472			15,472		9,283
22	Beck Company		5,880	120	6,000			
29			17,660			17,660		10,596
31	Interest Revenue		200				200	
			76,876	475	20,000	51,451	5,900	30,870

(b) The Accounts Receivable column total is posted as a credit to Accounts Receivable. The individual amounts are credited to the customers' accounts identified in the Account Credited column, which are maintained in the accounts receivable subsidiary ledger. The amounts in the Other Accounts column are posted individually. They are credited to the account titles identified in the Account Credited column.

WileyPLUS Brief Exercises, Exercises, DO IT! Exercises, and Problems and many additional resources are available for practice in WileyPLUS

QUESTIONS

1. (a) What is an accounting information system? (b) "An accounting information system applies only to a manual system." Do you agree? Explain.
2. Certain principles should be followed in the development of an accounting information system. Identify and explain each of the principles.
3. What are common features of computerized accounting packages beyond recording transactions and preparing financial statements?
4. How does an enterprise resource planning (ERP) system differ from an entry-level computerized accounting system?
5. What are the advantages of using subsidiary ledgers?
6. (a) When do companies normally post to (1) the subsidiary accounts and (2) the general ledger control accounts? (b) Describe the relationship between a control account and a subsidiary ledger.
7. Identify and explain the four special journals discussed in the chapter. List an advantage of using each of these journals rather than using only a general journal.
8. Kensington Company uses special journals. It recorded in a sales journal a sale made on account to R. Stiner for $435. A few days later, R. Stiner returns $70 worth of merchandise for credit. Where should Kensington Company record the sales return? Why?
9. A $500 purchase of merchandise on account from Lore Company was properly recorded in the purchases journal. When posted, however, the amount recorded in the subsidiary ledger was $50. How might this error be discovered?
10. Why would special journals used in different businesses not be identical in format? What type of business would maintain a cash receipts journal but not include a column for accounts receivable?
11. The cash and the accounts receivable columns in the cash receipts journal were mistakenly over-added by $4,000 at the end of the month. (a) Will the customers' ledger agree with the Accounts Receivable control account? (b) Assuming no other errors, will the trial balance totals be equal?

12. One column total of a special journal is posted at month-end to only two general ledger accounts. One of these two accounts is Accounts Receivable. What is the name of this special journal? What is the other general ledger account to which that same month-end total is posted?
13. In what journal would the following transactions be recorded? (Assume that a two-column sales journal and a single-column purchases journal are used.)
    (a) Recording of depreciation expense for the year.
    (b) Credit given to a customer for merchandise purchased on credit and returned.
    (c) Sales of merchandise for cash.
    (d) Sales of merchandise on account.
    (e) Collection of cash on account from a customer.
    (f) Purchase of office supplies on account.
14. In what journal would the following transactions be recorded? (Assume that a two-column sales journal and a single-column purchases journal are used.)
    (a) Cash received from signing a note payable.
    (b) Investment of cash by the owner of the business.
    (c) Closing of the expense accounts at the end of the year.
    (d) Purchase of merchandise on account.
    (e) Credit received for merchandise purchased and returned to supplier.
    (f) Payment of cash on account due a supplier.
15. What transactions might be included in a multiple-column purchases journal that would not be included in a single-column purchases journal?
16. Give an example of a transaction in the general journal that causes an entry to be posted twice (i.e., to two accounts), one in the general ledger, the other in the subsidiary ledger. Does this affect the debit/credit equality of the general ledger?
17. Give some examples of appropriate general journal transactions for an organization using special journals.

BRIEF EXERCISES

Explain basic concepts of an accounting information system. (LO 1)

BE7-1 Indicate whether each of the following statements is true or false.

1. When designing an accounting system, we need to think about the needs and knowledge of both the top managers and various other users.
2. When the environment changes as a result of technological advances, increased competition, or government regulation, an accounting system does not have to be sufficiently flexible to meet the changes in order to save money.
3. In developing an accounting system, cost is relevant. The benefits obtained from the information disseminated must outweigh the cost of providing it.

Explain basic concepts of an accounting information system. (LO 1)

BE7-2 Here is a list of words or phrases related to computerized accounting systems.

1. Entry-level software.
2. Enterprise resource planning systems.
3. Network-compatible.
4. Audit trail.
5. Internal control.

Instructions

Match each word or phrase with the best description of it.

_______ (a) Allows multiple users to access the system at the same time.
_______ (b) Enables the tracking of all transactions.
_______ (c) Identifies suspicious transactions or likely mistakes such as wrong account numbers or duplicate transactions.
_______ (d) Large-scale computer systems that integrate all aspects of the organization including accounting, sales, human resource management, and manufacturing.
_______ (e) System for companies with revenues of less than $5 million and up to 20 employees.

Explain basic concepts of an accounting information system. (LO 1)

BE7-3 Benji Borke has prepared the following list of statements about accounting information systems.

1. The accounting information system includes each of the steps of the accounting cycle, the documents that provide evidence of transactions that have occurred, and the accounting records.
2. The benefits obtained from information provided by the accounting information system need not outweigh the cost of providing that information.
3. Designers of accounting systems must consider the needs and knowledge of various users.
4. If an accounting information system is cost-effective and provides useful output, it does not need to be flexible.

Instructions

Identify each statement as true or false. If false, indicate how to correct the statement.

Identify subsidiary ledger balances.
(LO 2)

BE7-4 Presented below is information related to Gantner Company for its first month of operations. Identify the balances that appear in the accounts receivable subsidiary ledger and the accounts receivable balance that appears in the general ledger at the end of January.

Credit Sales			Cash Collections		
Jan. 7	Austin Co.	$10,000	Jan. 17	Austin Co.	$7,000
15	Diaz Co.	8,000	24	Diaz Co.	4,000
23	Noble Co.	9,000	29	Noble Co.	9,000

Identify subsidiary ledger accounts.
(LO 2)

BE7-5 Identify in what ledger (general or subsidiary) each of the following accounts is shown.
(a) Rent Expense.
(b) Accounts Receivable—Cabrera.
(c) Notes Payable.
(d) Accounts Payable—Pacheco.

Identify special journals.
(LO 3)

BE7-6 Identify the journal in which each of the following transactions is recorded.
(a) Cash sales.
(b) Owner withdrawal of cash.
(c) Cash purchase of land.
(d) Credit sales.
(e) Purchase of merchandise on account.
(f) Receipt of cash for services performed.

Identify entries to cash receipts journal.
(LO 3)

BE7-7 Indicate whether each of the following debits and credits is included in the cash receipts journal. (Use "Yes" or "No" to answer this question.)
(a) Debit to Sales Revenue.
(b) Credit to Inventory.
(c) Credit to Accounts Receivable.
(d) Debit to Accounts Payable.

Identify transactions for special journals.
(LO 3)

BE7-8 Villar Co. uses special journals and a general journal. Identify the journal in which each of the following transactions is recorded.
(a) Purchased equipment on account.
(b) Purchased merchandise on account.
(c) Paid utility expense in cash.
(d) Sold merchandise on account.

Identify transactions for special journals.
(LO 3)

BE7-9 Identify the special journal(s) in which the following column headings appear.
(a) Sales Discounts Dr.
(b) Accounts Receivable Cr.
(c) Cash Dr.
(d) Sales Revenue Cr.
(e) Inventory Dr.

Indicate postings for cash receipts journal.
(LO 3)

BE7-10 Rauch Computer Components Inc. uses a multi-column cash receipts journal. Indicate which column(s) is/are posted only in total, only daily, or both in total and daily.
(a) Accounts Receivable.
(b) Sales Discounts.
(c) Cash.
(d) Other Accounts.

DO IT! Exercises

Explain basic concepts of an accounting information system.
(LO 1)

DO IT! 7-1 Indicate whether the following statements are true or false.
1. A computerized accounting system must be customized to meet a company's needs.
2. Companies with revenues of less than $5 million and up to 20 employees generally use entry-level programs rather than ERP systems.
3. A manual accounting system provides more timely financial information than a computerized system.

Determine subsidiary and general ledger balances.
(LO 2)

DO IT! 7-2 Presented below is information related to Rizzo Company for its first month of operations. Determine the balances that appear in the accounts payable subsidiary ledger. What Accounts Payable balance appears in the general ledger at the end of January?

Credit Purchases			Cash Paid		
Jan. 6	Gorst Company	$11,000	Jan. 11	Gorst Company	$ 6,500
Jan. 10	Tian Company	12,000	Jan. 16	Tian Company	12,000
Jan. 23	Maddox Company	10,000	Jan. 29	Maddox Company	7,700

DO IT! 7-3 Hinske Company had the following transactions during April.

Identify special journals.
(LO 3)

1. Sold merchandise on account.
2. Purchased merchandise on account.
3. Collected cash from a sale to Renfro Company.
4. Recorded accrued interest on a note payable.
5. Paid $2,000 for supplies.

Identify the journal in which each of the transactions above is recorded.

EXERCISES

Determine control account balances, and explain posting of special journals.
(LO 2, 3)

E7-1 Nex Company uses both special journals and a general journal as described in this chapter. On June 30, after all monthly postings had been completed, the Accounts Receivable control account in the general ledger had a debit balance of $340,000; the Accounts Payable control account had a credit balance of $77,000.

The July transactions recorded in the special journals are summarized below. No entries affecting accounts receivable and accounts payable were recorded in the general journal for July.

Sales journal	Total sales $161,400
Purchases journal	Total purchases $66,400
Cash receipts journal	Accounts receivable column total $131,000
Cash payments journal	Accounts payable column total $47,500

Instructions

(a) What is the balance of the Accounts Receivable control account after the monthly postings on July 31?
(b) What is the balance of the Accounts Payable control account after the monthly postings on July 31?
(c) To what account(s) is the column total of $161,400 in the sales journal posted?
(d) To what account(s) is the accounts receivable column total of $131,000 in the cash receipts journal posted?

Explain postings to subsidiary ledger.
(LO 2)

E7-2 Presented below is the subsidiary accounts receivable account of Jill Longley.

Date	Ref.	Debit	Credit	Balance
2017				
Sept. 2	S31	61,000		61,000
9	G4		14,000	47,000
27	CR8		47,000	—

Instructions

Write a memo to Sara Fogelman, chief financial officer, that explains each transaction.

Post various journals to control and subsidiary accounts.
(LO 2, 3)

E7-3 On September 1, the balance of the Accounts Receivable control account in the general ledger of Montgomery Company was $10,960. The customers' subsidiary ledger contained account balances as follows: Hurley $1,440, Andino $2,640, Fowler $2,060, and Sogard $4,820. At the end of September, the various journals contained the following information.

Sales journal: Sales to Sogard $800, to Hurley $1,260, to Giambi $1,330, and to Fowler $1,600.
Cash receipts journal: Cash received from Fowler $1,310, from Sogard $3,300, from Giambi $380, from Andino $1,800, and from Hurley $1,240.
General journal: An allowance is granted to Sogard $220.

Instructions

(a) Set up control and subsidiary accounts and enter the beginning balances. Do not construct the journals.
(b) Post the various journals. Post the items as individual items or as totals, whichever would be the appropriate procedure. (No sales discounts given.)
(c) Prepare a schedule of accounts receivable and prove the agreement of the controlling account with the subsidiary ledger at September 30, 2017.

Determine control and subsidiary ledger balances for accounts receivable.

(LO 2)

E7-4 Kieschnick Company has a balance in its Accounts Receivable control account of $10,000 on January 1, 2017. The subsidiary ledger contains three accounts: Bixler Company, balance $4,000; Cuddyer Company, balance $2,500; and Freeze Company. During January, the following receivable-related transactions occurred.

	Credit Sales	Collections	Returns
Bixler Company	$9,000	$8,000	$ -0-
Cuddyer Company	7,000	2,500	3,000
Freeze Company	8,500	9,000	-0-

Instructions

(a) What is the January 1 balance in the Freeze Company subsidiary account?
(b) What is the January 31 balance in the control account?
(c) Compute the balances in the subsidiary accounts at the end of the month.
(d) Which January transaction would not be recorded in a special journal?

Determine control and subsidiary ledger balances for accounts payable.

(LO 2)

E7-5 Pennington Company has a balance in its Accounts Payable control account of $9,250 on January 1, 2017. The subsidiary ledger contains three accounts: Hale Company, balance $3,000; Janish Company, balance $1,875; and Valdez Company. During January, the following payable-related transactions occurred.

	Purchases	Payments	Returns
Hale Company	$6,750	$6,000	$ -0-
Janish Company	5,250	1,875	2,250
Valdez Company	6,375	6,750	-0-

Instructions

(a) What is the January 1 balance in the Valdez Company subsidiary account?
(b) What is the January 31 balance in the control account?
(c) Compute the balances in the subsidiary accounts at the end of the month.
(d) Which January transaction would not be recorded in a special journal?

Record transactions in sales and purchases journal.

(LO 3)

E7-6 Gomes Company uses special journals and a general journal. The following transactions occurred during September 2017.

Sept. 2 Sold merchandise on account to H. Drew, invoice no. 101, $620, terms n/30. The cost of the merchandise sold was $420.
10 Purchased merchandise on account from A. Pagan $650, terms 2/10, n/30.
12 Purchased office equipment on account from R. Cairo $6,500.
21 Sold merchandise on account to G. Holliday, invoice no. 102 for $800, terms 2/10, n/30. The cost of the merchandise sold was $480.
25 Purchased merchandise on account from D. Downs $860, terms n/30.
27 Sold merchandise to S. Miller for $700 cash. The cost of the merchandise sold was $400.

Instructions

(a) Prepare a sales journal (see Illustration 7-7) and a single-column purchases journal (see Illustration 7-13). (Use page 1 for each journal.)
(b) Record the transaction(s) for September that should be journalized in the sales journal and the purchases journal.

Record transactions in cash receipts and cash payments journal.

(LO 3)

E7-7 R. Santiago Co. uses special journals and a general journal. The following transactions occurred during May 2017.

May 1 R. Santiago invested $40,000 cash in the business.
2 Sold merchandise to Lawrie Co. for $6,300 cash. The cost of the merchandise sold was $4,200.
3 Purchased merchandise for $7,700 from J. Moskos using check no. 101.
14 Paid salary to H. Rivera $700 by issuing check no. 102.
16 Sold merchandise on account to K. Stanton for $900, terms n/30. The cost of the merchandise sold was $630.
22 A check of $9,000 is received from M. Mangini in full for invoice 101; no discount given.

Instructions

(a) Prepare a multiple-column cash receipts journal (see Illustration 7-9) and a multiple-column cash payments journal (see Illustration 7-16). (Use page 1 for each journal.)

(b) Record the transaction(s) for May that should be journalized in the cash receipts journal and cash payments journal.

E7-8 Francisco Company uses the columnar cash journals illustrated in the textbook. In April, the following selected cash transactions occurred.

Explain journalizing in cash journals.

(LO 3)

1. Made a refund to a customer as an allowance for damaged goods.
2. Received collection from customer within the 3% discount period.
3. Purchased merchandise for cash.
4. Paid a creditor within the 3% discount period.
5. Received collection from customer after the 3% discount period had expired.
6. Paid freight on merchandise purchased.
7. Paid cash for office equipment.
8. Received cash refund from supplier for merchandise returned.
9. Withdrew cash for personal use of owner.
10. Made cash sales.

Instructions

Indicate (a) the journal, and (b) the columns in the journal that should be used in recording each transaction.

E7-9 Hasselback Company has the following selected transactions during March.

Journalize transactions in general journal and explain postings.

(LO 3)

Mar. 2 Purchased equipment costing $7,400 from Bole Company on account.

5 Received credit of $410 from Carwell Company for merchandise damaged in shipment to Hasselback.

7 Issued credit of $400 to Dempsey Company for merchandise the customer returned. The returned merchandise had a cost of $260.

Hasselback Company uses a one-column purchases journal, a sales journal, the columnar cash journals used in the text, and a general journal.

Instructions

(a) Journalize the transactions in the general journal.

(b) In a brief memo to the president of Hasselback Company, explain the postings to the control and subsidiary accounts from each type of journal.

E7-10 Below are some typical transactions incurred by Ricketts Company.

Indicate journalizing in special journals.

(LO 3)

1. Payment of creditors on account.
2. Return of merchandise sold for credit.
3. Collection on account from customers.
4. Sale of land for cash.
5. Sale of merchandise on account.
6. Sale of merchandise for cash.
7. Received credit for merchandise purchased on credit.
8. Sales discount taken on goods sold.
9. Payment of employee wages.
10. Income summary closed to owner's capital.
11. Depreciation on building.
12. Purchase of office supplies for cash.
13. Purchase of merchandise on account.

Instructions

For each transaction, indicate whether it would normally be recorded in a cash receipts journal, cash payments journal, sales journal, single-column purchases journal, or general journal.

E7-11 The general ledger of Hensley Company contained the following Accounts Payable control account (in T-account form). Also shown is the related subsidiary ledger.

Explain posting to control account and subsidiary ledger.

(LO 2, 3)

GENERAL LEDGER

Accounts Payable

Feb. 15	General journal	1,400	Feb. 1	Balance	26,025
28	?	?	5	General journal	265
			11	General journal	550
			28	Purchases	13,400
			Feb. 28	Balance	10,500

ACCOUNTS PAYABLE LEDGER

Benton

	Feb. 28	Bal. 4,600

Parks

	Feb. 28	Bal. ?

Dooley

	Feb. 28	Bal. 2,300

Instructions

(a) Indicate the missing posting reference and amount in the control account, and the missing ending balance in the subsidiary ledger.

(b) Indicate the amounts in the control account that were dual-posted (i.e., posted to the control account and the subsidiary accounts).

Prepare purchases and general journals.
(LO 2, 3)

E7-12 Selected accounts from the ledgers of Youngblood Company at July 31 showed the following.

GENERAL LEDGER

Equipment No. 157

Date	Explanation	Ref.	Debit	Credit	Balance
July 1		G1	3,900		3,900

Inventory No. 120

Date	Explanation	Ref.	Debit	Credit	Balance
July 15		G1	400		400
18		G1		100	300
25		G1		200	100
31		P1	9,300		9,400

Accounts Payable No. 201

Date	Explanation	Ref.	Debit	Credit	Balance
July 1		G1		3,900	3,900
15		G1		400	4,300
18		G1	100		4,200
25		G1	200		4,000
31		P1		9,300	13,300

ACCOUNTS PAYABLE LEDGER

Flaherty Equipment Co.

Date	Explanation	Ref.	Debit	Credit	Balance
July 1		G1		3,900	3,900

Weller Co.

Date	Explanation	Ref.	Debit	Credit	Balance
July 14		P1		1,100	1,100
25		G1	200		900

Marsh Co.

Date	Explanation	Ref.	Debit	Credit	Balance
July 3		P1		2,400	2,400
20		P1		1,700	4,100

Yates Co.

Date	Explanation	Ref.	Debit	Credit	Balance
July 12		P1		500	500
21		P1		600	1,100

Lange Corp

Date	Explanation	Ref.	Debit	Credit	Balance
July 17		P1		1,400	1,400
18		G1	100		1,300
29		P1		1,600	2,900

Bernardo Inc.

Date	Explanation	Ref.	Debit	Credit	Balance
July 15		G1		400	400

Instructions

From the data prepare:

(a) The single-column purchases journal for July.
(b) The general journal entries for July.

E7-13 Tresh Products uses both special journals and a general journal as described in this chapter. Tresh also posts customers' accounts in the accounts receivable subsidiary ledger. The postings for the most recent month are included in the subsidiary T-accounts below.

Determine correct posting amount to control account.

(LO 2, 3)

Estes

Bal.	340	250
	200	

Gehrke

Bal.	150	150
	290	

Truong

Bal.	–0–	145
	145	

Weiser

Bal.	120	120
	190	
	150	

Instructions

Determine the correct amount of the end-of-month posting from the sales journal to the Accounts Receivable control account.

E7-14 Selected account balances for Hulse Company at January 1, 2017, are presented below.

Compute balances in various accounts.

(LO 3)

Accounts Payable	$14,000
Accounts Receivable	22,000
Cash	17,000
Inventory	13,500

Hulse's sales journal for January shows a total of $110,000 in the selling price column, and its one-column purchases journal for January shows a total of $77,000.

The column totals in Hulse's cash receipts journal are Cash Dr. $61,000, Sales Discounts Dr. $1,100, Accounts Receivable Cr. $45,000, Sales Revenue Cr. $6,000, and Other Accounts Cr. $11,100.

The column totals in Hulse's cash payments journal for January are Cash Cr. $55,000, Inventory Cr. $1,000, Accounts Payable Dr. $46,000, and Other Accounts Dr. $10,000. Hulse's total cost of goods sold for January is $63,600.

Accounts Payable, Accounts Receivable, Cash, Inventory, and Sales Revenue are not involved in the Other Accounts column in either the cash receipts or cash payments journal, and are not involved in any general journal entries.

Instructions

Compute the January 31 balance for Hulse in the following accounts.

(a) Accounts Payable.
(b) Accounts Receivable.
(c) Cash.
(d) Inventory.
(e) Sales Revenue.

EXERCISES: SET B AND CHALLENGE EXERCISES

Visit the book's companion website, at **www.wiley.com/college/weygandt**, and choose the Student Companion site to access Exercises: Set B and Challenge Exercises.

PROBLEMS: SET A

P7-1A Kozma Company's chart of accounts includes the following selected accounts.

Journalize transactions in cash receipts journal; post to control account and subsidiary ledger.

(LO 2, 3) GLS

101 Cash	401 Sales Revenue
112 Accounts Receivable	414 Sales Discounts
120 Inventory	505 Cost of Goods Sold
301 Owner's Capital	

On April 1, the accounts receivable ledger of Kozma Company showed the following balances: Morrow $1,550, Rose $1,200, Jennings Co. $2,900, and Dent $2,200. The April transactions involving the receipt of cash were as follows.

Apr.	1	The owner, T. Kozma, invested additional cash in the business $7,200.
	4	Received check for payment of account from Dent less 2% cash discount.
	5	Received check for $920 in payment of invoice no. 307 from Jennings Co.
	8	Made cash sales of merchandise totaling $7,245. The cost of the merchandise sold was $4,347.
	10	Received check for $600 in payment of invoice no. 309 from Morrow.
	11	Received cash refund from a supplier for damaged merchandise $740.
	23	Received check for $1,000 in payment of invoice no. 310 from Jennings Co.
	29	Received check for payment of account from Rose (no cash discount allowed).

Instructions

(a) Balancing totals $25,452

(a) Journalize the transactions above in a six-column cash receipts journal with columns for Cash Dr., Sales Discounts Dr., Accounts Receivable Cr., Sales Revenue Cr., Other Accounts Cr., and Cost of Goods Sold Dr./Inventory Cr. Foot and cross-foot the journal.

(b) Insert the beginning balances in the Accounts Receivable control and subsidiary accounts, and post the April transactions to these accounts.

(c) Accounts Receivable $1,930

(c) Prove the agreement of the control account and subsidiary account balances.

Journalize transactions in cash payments journal; post to control account and subsidiary ledgers.

(LO 2, 3)

GLS

P7-2A Reineke Company's chart of accounts includes the following selected accounts.

101 Cash	201 Accounts Payable
120 Inventory	306 Owner's Drawings
130 Prepaid Insurance	505 Cost of Goods Sold
157 Equipment	

On October 1, the accounts payable ledger of Reineke Company showed the following balances: Uggla Company $2,700, Orr Co. $2,500, Rosenthal Co. $1,800, and Clevenger Company $3,700. The October transactions involving the payment of cash were as follows.

Oct.	1	Purchased merchandise, check no. 63, $300.
	3	Purchased equipment, check no. 64, $800.
	5	Paid Uggla Company balance due of $2,700, less 2% discount, check no. 65, $2,646.
	10	Purchased merchandise, check no. 66, $2,550.
	15	Paid Rosenthal Co. balance due of $1,800, check no. 67.
	16	C. Reineke, the owner, pays his personal insurance premium of $400, check no. 68.
	19	Paid Orr Co. in full for invoice no. 610, $2,000 less 2% cash discount, check no. 69, $1,960.
	29	Paid Clevenger Company in full for invoice no. 264, $2,500, check no. 70.

Instructions

(a) Balancing totals $13,050

(a) Journalize the transactions above in a four-column cash payments journal with columns for Other Accounts Dr., Accounts Payable Dr., Inventory Cr., and Cash Cr. Foot and cross-foot the journal.

(b) Insert the beginning balances in the Accounts Payable control and subsidiary accounts, and post the October transactions to these accounts.

(c) Accounts Payable $1,700

(c) Prove the agreement of the control account and the subsidiary account balances.

Journalize transactions in multi-column purchases journal and sales journal; post to the general and subsidiary ledgers.

(LO 2, 3)

GLS

P7-3A The chart of accounts of LR Company includes the following selected accounts.

112 Accounts Receivable	401 Sales Revenue
120 Inventory	412 Sales Returns and Allowances
126 Supplies	505 Cost of Goods Sold
157 Equipment	610 Advertising Expense
201 Accounts Payable	

In July, the following transactions were completed. All purchases and sales were on account. The cost of all merchandise sold was 70% of the sales price.

July	1	Purchased merchandise from Eby Company $8,000.
	2	Received freight bill from Shaw Shipping on Eby purchase $400.
	3	Made sales to Fort Company $1,300 and to Hefner Bros. $1,500.

5 Purchased merchandise from Getz Company $3,200.
8 Received credit on merchandise returned to Getz Company $300.
13 Purchased store supplies from Dayne Supply $720.
15 Purchased merchandise from Eby Company $3,600 and from Bosco Company $4,300.
16 Made sales to Aybar Company $3,450 and to Hefner Bros. $1,870.
18 Received bill for advertising from Welton Advertisements $600.
21 Sales were made to Fort Company $310 and to Duncan Company $2,800.
22 Granted allowance to Fort Company for merchandise damaged in shipment $40.
24 Purchased merchandise from Getz Company $3,000.
26 Purchased equipment from Dayne Supply $900.
28 Received freight bill from Shaw Shipping on Getz purchase of July 24, $380.
30 Sales were made to Aybar Company $5,600.

Instructions

(a) Journalize the transactions above in a purchases journal, a sales journal, and a general journal. The purchases journal should have the following column headings: Date, Account Credited (Debited), Ref., Accounts Payable Cr., Inventory Dr., and Other Accounts Dr.
(b) Post to both the general and subsidiary ledger accounts. (Assume that all accounts have zero beginning balances.)
(c) Prove the agreement of the control and subsidiary accounts.

(a) Purchases journal—Accounts Payable $25,100
Sales journal—Sales Revenue $16,830
(c) Accounts Receivable $16,790
Accounts Payable $24,800

P7-4A Selected accounts from the chart of accounts of Mercer Company are shown below.

Journalize transactions in special journals.

(LO 2, 3)

GLS

101	Cash	401	Sales Revenue
112	Accounts Receivable	412	Sales Returns and Allowances
120	Inventory	414	Sales Discounts
126	Supplies	505	Cost of Goods Sold
157	Equipment	726	Salaries and Wages Expense
201	Accounts Payable		

The cost of all merchandise sold was 60% of the sales price. During January, Mercer completed the following transactions.

Jan. 3 Purchased merchandise on account from Gallagher Co. $9,000.
4 Purchased supplies for cash $80.
4 Sold merchandise on account to Wheeler $5,250, invoice no. 371, terms 1/10, n/30.
5 Returned $300 worth of damaged goods purchased on account from Gallagher Co. on January 3.
6 Made cash sales for the week totaling $3,150.
8 Purchased merchandise on account from Phegley Co. $4,500.
9 Sold merchandise on account to Linton Corp. $5,400, invoice no. 372, terms 1/10, n/30.
11 Purchased merchandise on account from Cora Co. $3,700.
13 Paid in full Gallagher Co. on account less a 2% discount.
13 Made cash sales for the week totaling $6,260.
15 Received payment from Linton Corp. for invoice no. 372.
15 Paid semi-monthly salaries of $14,300 to employees.
17 Received payment from Wheeler for invoice no. 371.
17 Sold merchandise on account to Delaney Co. $1,200, invoice no. 373, terms 1/10, n/30.
19 Purchased equipment on account from Dozier Corp. $5,500.
20 Cash sales for the week totaled $3,200.
20 Paid in full Phegley Co. on account less a 2% discount.
23 Purchased merchandise on account from Gallagher Co. $7,800.
24 Purchased merchandise on account from Atchison Corp. $5,100.
27 Made cash sales for the week totaling $4,230.
30 Received payment from Delaney Co. for invoice no. 373.
31 Paid semi-monthly salaries of $13,200 to employees.
31 Sold merchandise on account to Wheeler $9,330, invoice no. 374, terms 1/10, n/30.

Mercer Company uses the following journals.

1. Sales journal.
2. Single-column purchases journal.
3. Cash receipts journal with columns for Cash Dr., Sales Discounts Dr., Accounts Receivable Cr., Sales Revenue Cr., Other Accounts Cr., and Cost of Goods Sold Dr./Inventory Cr.
4. Cash payments journal with columns for Other Accounts Dr., Accounts Payable Dr., Inventory Cr., and Cash Cr.
5. General journal.

(a) Sales journal $21,180
Purchases journal $30,100
Cash receipts journal balancing total $38,794
Cash payments journal balancing total $40,780

Instructions

Using the selected accounts provided:

(a) Record the January transactions in the appropriate journal noted.
(b) Foot and cross-foot all special journals.
(c) Show how postings would be made by placing ledger account numbers and check-marks as needed in the journals. (Actual posting to ledger accounts is not required.)

Journalize in sales and cash receipts journals; post; prepare a trial balance; prove control to subsidiary; prepare adjusting entries; prepare an adjusted trial balance.

(LO 2, 3)

GLS

P7-5A Presented below are the purchases and cash payments journals for Fornelli Co. for its first month of operations.

PURCHASES JOURNAL **P1**

Date	Account Credited	Ref.	Inventory Dr. Accounts Payable Cr.
July 4	N. Alvarado		6,800
5	F. Rees		8,100
11	J. Gallup		5,920
13	C. Werly		15,300
20	M. Mangus		7,900
			44,020

CASH PAYMENTS JOURNAL **CP1**

Date	Account Debited	Ref.	Other Accounts Dr.	Accounts Payable Dr.	Inventory Cr.	Cash Cr.
July 4	Supplies		600			600
10	F. Rees			8,100	81	8,019
11	Prepaid Rent		6,000			6,000
15	N. Alvarado			6,800		6,800
19	Owner's Drawings		2,500			2,500
21	C. Werly			15,300	153	15,147
			9,100	30,200	234	39,066

In addition, the following transactions have not been journalized for July. The cost of all merchandise sold was 65% of the sales price.

July	1	The founder, N. Fornelli, invests $80,000 in cash.
	6	Sell merchandise on account to Dow Co. $6,200 terms 1/10, n/30.
	7	Make cash sales totaling $8,000.
	8	Sell merchandise on account to S. Goebel $4,600, terms 1/10, n/30.
	10	Sell merchandise on account to W. Leiss $4,900, terms 1/10, n/30.
	13	Receive payment in full from S. Goebel.
	16	Receive payment in full from W. Leiss.
	20	Receive payment in full from Dow Co.
	21	Sell merchandise on account to H. Kenney $5,000, terms 1/10, n/30.
	29	Returned damaged goods to N. Alvarado and received cash refund of $420.

Instructions

(a) Open the following accounts in the general ledger.

101 Cash	306 Owner's Drawings
112 Accounts Receivable	401 Sales Revenue
120 Inventory	414 Sales Discounts
126 Supplies	505 Cost of Goods Sold
131 Prepaid Rent	631 Supplies Expense
201 Accounts Payable	729 Rent Expense
301 Owner's Capital	

(b) Journalize the transactions that have not been journalized in the sales journal and the cash receipts journal (see Illustration 7-9).

(c) Post to the accounts receivable and accounts payable subsidiary ledgers. Follow the sequence of transactions as shown in the problem.

(d) Post the individual entries and totals to the general ledger.

(e) Prepare a trial balance at July 31, 2017.

(f) Determine whether the subsidiary ledgers agree with the control accounts in the general ledger.

(g) The following adjustments at the end of July are necessary.
  (1) A count of supplies indicates that $140 is still on hand.
  (2) Recognize rent expense for July, $500.
  Prepare the necessary entries in the general journal. Post the entries to the general ledger.

(h) Prepare an adjusted trial balance at July 31, 2017.

(b) Sales journal total $20,700
Cash receipts journal balancing totals $104,120
(e) Totals $122,520
(f) Accounts Receivable $5,000
Accounts Payable $13,820

(h) Totals $122,520

Journalize in special journals; post; prepare a trial balance.

(LO 2, 3)

GLS

P7-6A The post-closing trial balance for Horner Co. is shown below.

HORNER CO.
Post-Closing Trial Balance
December 31, 2017

	Debit	Credit
Cash	$ 41,500	
Accounts Receivable	15,000	
Notes Receivable	45,000	
Inventory	23,000	
Equipment	6,450	
Accumulated Depreciation—Equipment		$ 1,500
Accounts Payable		43,000
Owner's Capital		86,450
	$130,950	$130,950

The subsidiary ledgers contain the following information: (1) accounts receivable—B. Hannigan $2,500, I. Kirk $7,500, and T. Hodges $5,000; (2) accounts payable—T. Igawa $12,000, D. Danford $18,000, and K. Thayer $13,000. The cost of all merchandise sold was 60% of the sales price.

The transactions for January 2018 are as follows.

Jan.	3	Sell merchandise to M. Ziesmer $8,000, terms 2/10, n/30.
	5	Purchase merchandise from E. Pheatt $2,000, terms 2/10, n/30.
	7	Receive a check from T. Hodges $3,500.
	11	Pay freight on merchandise purchased $300.
	12	Pay rent of $1,000 for January.
	13	Receive payment in full from M. Ziesmer.
	14	Post all entries to the subsidiary ledgers. Issued credit of $300 to B. Hannigan for returned merchandise.
	15	Send K. Thayer a check for $12,870 in full payment of account, discount $130.
	17	Purchase merchandise from G. Roland $1,600, terms 2/10, n/30.
	18	Pay sales salaries of $2,800 and office salaries $2,000.
	20	Give D. Danford a 60-day note for $18,000 in full payment of account payable.
	23	Total cash sales amount to $9,100.

Jan. 24 Post all entries to the subsidiary ledgers. Sell merchandise on account to I. Kirk $7,400, terms 1/10, n/30.
27 Send E. Pheatt a check for $950.
29 Receive payment on a note of $40,000 from B. Stout.
30 Post all entries to the subsidiary ledgers. Return merchandise of $300 to G. Roland for credit.

Instructions

(a) Open general and subsidiary ledger accounts for the following.

101 Cash	301 Owner's Capital
112 Accounts Receivable	401 Sales Revenue
115 Notes Receivable	412 Sales Returns and Allowances
120 Inventory	414 Sales Discounts
157 Equipment	505 Cost of Goods Sold
158 Accumulated Depreciation—Equipment	726 Salaries and Wages Expense
200 Notes Payable	729 Rent Expense
201 Accounts Payable	

(b) Sales journal $15,400
Purchases journal $3,600
Cash receipts journal (balancing) $66,060
Cash payments journal (balancing) $20,050
(d) Totals $144,800
(e) Accounts Receivable $18,600
Accounts Payable $14,350

(b) Record the January transactions in a sales journal, a single-column purchases journal, a cash receipts journal (see Illustration 7-9), a cash payments journal (see Illustration 7-16), and a general journal.
(c) Post the appropriate amounts to the general ledger.
(d) Prepare a trial balance at January 31, 2018.
(e) Determine whether the subsidiary ledgers agree with controlling accounts in the general ledger.

PROBLEMS: SET B AND SET C

Visit the book's companion website, at **www.wiley.com/college/weygandt**, and choose the Student Companion site to access Problems: Set B and Set C.

COMPREHENSIVE PROBLEMS: CHAPTERS 3 TO 7

CP7-1 (Perpetual Method) Jeter Co. uses a perpetual inventory system and both an accounts receivable and an accounts payable subsidiary ledger. Balances related to both the general ledger and the subsidiary ledgers for Jeter are indicated in the working papers presented below. Also following are a series of transactions for Jeter Co. for the month of January. Credit sales terms are 2/10, n/30. The cost of all merchandise sold was 60% of the sales price.

GENERAL LEDGER

Account Number	Account Title	January 1 Opening Balance
101	Cash	$35,750
112	Accounts Receivable	13,000
115	Notes Receivable	39,000
120	Inventory	18,000
126	Supplies	1,000
130	Prepaid Insurance	2,000
157	Equipment	6,450
158	Accumulated Depreciation—Equip.	1,500
201	Accounts Payable	35,000
301	Owner's Capital	78,700

Schedule of Accounts Receivable (from accounts receivable subsidiary ledger)

Customer	January 1 Opening Balance
R. Beltre	$1,500
B. Santos	7,500
S. Mahay	4,000

Schedule of Accounts Payable (from accounts payable subsidiary ledger)

Creditor	January 1 Opening Balance
S. Meek	$ 9,000
R. Moses	15,000
D. Saito	11,000

Jan.	3	Sell merchandise on account to B. Corpas $3,600, invoice no. 510, and to J. Revere $1,800, invoice no. 511.
	5	Purchase merchandise from S. Gamel $5,000 and D. Posey $2,200, terms n/30.
	7	Receive checks from S. Mahay $4,000 and B. Santos $2,000 after discount period has lapsed.
	8	Pay freight on merchandise purchased $235.
	9	Send checks to S. Meek for $9,000 less 2% cash discount, and to D. Saito for $11,000 less 1% cash discount.
	9	Issue credit of $300 to J. Revere for merchandise returned.
	10	Daily cash sales from January 1 to January 10 total $15,500. Make one journal entry for these sales.
	11	Sell merchandise on account to R. Beltre $1,600, invoice no. 512, and to S. Mahay $900, invoice no. 513.
	12	Pay rent of $1,000 for January.
	13	Receive payment in full from B. Corpas and J. Revere less cash discounts.
	15	Withdraw $800 cash by M. Jeter for personal use.
	15	Post all entries to the subsidiary ledgers.
	16	Purchase merchandise from D. Saito $15,000, terms 1/10, n/30; S. Meek $14,200, terms 2/10, n/30; and S. Gamel $1,500, terms n/30.
	17	Pay $400 cash for office supplies.
	18	Return $200 of merchandise to S. Meek and receive credit.
	20	Daily cash sales from January 11 to January 20 total $20,100. Make one journal entry for these sales.
	21	Issue $15,000 note, maturing in 90 days, to R. Moses in payment of balance due.
	21	Receive payment in full from S. Mahay less cash discount.
	22	Sell merchandise on account to B. Corpas $2,700, invoice no. 514, and to R. Beltre $2,300, invoice no. 515.
	22	Post all entries to the subsidiary ledgers.
	23	Send checks to D. Saito and S. Meek for full payment less cash discounts.
	25	Sell merchandise on account to B. Santos $3,500, invoice no. 516, and to J. Revere $6,100, invoice no. 517.
	27	Purchase merchandise from D. Saito $14,500, terms 1/10, n/30; D. Posey $3,200, terms n/30; and S. Gamel $5,400, terms n/30.
	27	Post all entries to the subsidiary ledgers.
	28	Pay $200 cash for office supplies.
	31	Daily cash sales from January 21 to January 31 total $21,300. Make one journal entry for these sales.
	31	Pay sales salaries $4,300 and office salaries $3,800.

Instructions

(a) Record the January transactions in a sales journal, a single-column purchases journal, a cash receipts journal as shown in Illustration 7-9, a cash payments journal as shown in Illustration 7-16, and a two-column general journal.

(b) Post the journals to the general ledger.

(c) Prepare a trial balance at January 31, 2017, in the trial balance columns of the worksheet. Complete the worksheet using the following additional information.
  (1) Office supplies at January 31 total $900.
  (2) Insurance coverage expires on October 31, 2017.
  (3) Annual depreciation on the equipment is $1,500.
  (4) Interest of $50 has accrued on the note payable.

(d) Prepare a multiple-step income statement and an owner's equity statement for January and a classified balance sheet at the end of January.

(e) Prepare and post adjusting and closing entries.

(f) Prepare a post-closing trial balance, and determine whether the subsidiary ledgers agree with the control accounts in the general ledger.

CP7-2 (Periodic Inventory) McBride Company has the following opening account balances in its general and subsidiary ledgers on January 1 and uses the periodic inventory system. All accounts have normal debit and credit balances.

GENERAL LEDGER

Account Number	Account Title	January 1 Opening Balance
101	Cash	$33,750
112	Accounts Receivable	13,000
115	Notes Receivable	39,000
120	Inventory	20,000
126	Supplies	1,000
130	Prepaid Insurance	2,000
157	Equipment	6,450
158	Accumulated Depreciation—Equip.	1,500
201	Accounts Payable	35,000
301	Owner's Capital	78,700

Schedule of Accounts Receivable
(from accounts receivable subsidiary ledger)

Customer	January 1 Opening Balance
R. Kotsay	$1,500
B. Boxberger	7,500
S. Andrus	4,000

Schedule of Accounts Payable
(from accounts payable subsidiary ledger)

Creditor	January 1 Opening Balance
S. Otero	$ 9,000
R. Rasmus	15,000
D. Baroni	11,000

In addition, the following transactions have not been journalized for January 2017.

Jan. 3 Sell merchandise on account to B. Berg $3,600, invoice no. 510, and J. Lutz $1,800, invoice no. 511.

5 Purchase merchandise on account from S. Colt $5,000 and D. Kahn $2,700.

7 Receive checks for $4,000 from S. Andrus and $2,000 from B. Boxberger.

8 Pay freight on merchandise purchased $180.

9 Send checks to S. Otero for $9,000 and D. Baroni for $11,000.

9 Issue credit of $300 to J. Lutz for merchandise returned.

10 Cash sales from January 1 to January 10 total $15,500. Make one journal entry for these sales.

11 Sell merchandise on account to R. Kotsay for $2,900, invoice no. 512, and to S. Andrus $900, invoice no. 513.
Post all entries to the subsidiary ledgers.

12 Pay rent of $1,000 for January.

13 Receive payment in full from B. Berg and J. Lutz.

15 Withdraw $800 cash by I. McBride for personal use.

16 Purchase merchandise on account from D. Baroni for $12,000, from S. Otero for $13,900, and from S. Colt for $1,500.

17 Pay $400 cash for supplies.

18 Return $200 of merchandise to S. Otero and receive credit.

20 Cash sales from January 11 to January 20 total $17,500. Make one journal entry for these sales.

21 Issue $15,000 note to R. Rasmus in payment of balance due.

21 Receive payment in full from S. Andrus.
Post all entries to the subsidiary ledgers.

22 Sell merchandise on account to B. Berg for $3,700, invoice no. 514, and to R. Kotsay for $800, invoice no. 515.

23 Send checks to D. Baroni and S. Otero in full payment.

25 Sell merchandise on account to B. Boxberger for $3,500, invoice no. 516, and to J. Lutz for $6,100, invoice no. 517.

27 Purchase merchandise on account from D. Baroni for $12,500, from D. Kahn for $1,200, and from S. Colt for $2,800.
28 Pay $200 cash for office supplies.
31 Cash sales from January 21 to January 31 total $22,920. Make one journal entry for these sales.
31 Pay sales salaries of $4,300 and office salaries of $3,600.

Instructions

(a) Record the January transactions in the appropriate journal—sales, purchases, cash receipts, cash payments, and general.
(b) Post the journals to the general and subsidiary ledgers. Add and number new accounts in an orderly fashion as needed.
(c) Prepare a trial balance at January 31, 2017, using a worksheet. Complete the worksheet using the following additional information.
  (1) Supplies at January 31 total $700.
  (2) Insurance coverage expires on October 31, 2017.
  (3) Annual depreciation on the equipment is $1,500.
  (4) Interest of $30 has accrued on the note payable.
  (5) Inventory at January 31 is $15,000.
(d) Prepare a multiple-step income statement and an owner's equity statement for January and a classified balance sheet at the end of January.
(e) Prepare and post the adjusting and closing entries.
(f) Prepare a post-closing trial balance, and determine whether the subsidiary ledgers agree with the control accounts in the general ledger.

BROADENING YOUR PERSPECTIVE

FINANCIAL REPORTING AND ANALYSIS

Real-World Focus

BYP7-1 Intuit provides some of the leading accounting software packages. Information related to its products is found at its website.

***Address:* http://quickbooks.intuit.com** or go to **www.wiley.com/college/weygandt**

Instructions

Look under product and services for the product QuickBooks for Accountants. Be ready to discuss its new features with the class.

CRITICAL THINKING

Decision-Making Across the Organization

BYP7-2 Ermler & Trump is a wholesaler of small appliances and parts. Ermler & Trump is operated by two owners, Jack Ermler and Andrea Trump. In addition, the company has one employee, a repair specialist, who is on a fixed salary. Revenues are earned through the sale of appliances to retailers (approximately 75% of total revenues), appliance parts to do-it-yourselfers (10%), and the repair of appliances brought to the store (15%). Appliance sales are made on both a credit and cash basis. Customers are billed on prenumbered sales invoices. Credit terms are always net/30 days. All parts sales and repair work are cash only.

Merchandise is purchased on account from the manufacturers of both the appliances and the parts. Practically all suppliers offer cash discounts for prompt payments, and it is company policy to take all discounts. Most cash payments are made by check. Checks are most frequently issued to suppliers, to trucking companies for freight on merchandise purchases, and to newspapers, radio, and TV stations for advertising. All advertising bills are paid as received. Jack and Andrea each make a monthly drawing in cash for personal living expenses. The salaried repairman is paid twice monthly. Ermler & Trump currently has a manual accounting system.

Instructions

With the class divided into groups, answer the following.

(a) Identify the special journals that Ermler & Trump should have in its manual accounting system. List the column headings appropriate for each of the special journals.

(b) What control and subsidiary accounts should be included in Ermler & Trump's manual accounting system? Why?

Communication Activity

BYP7-3 Jill Locey, a classmate, has a part-time bookkeeping job. She is concerned about the inefficiencies in journalizing and posting transactions. Ben Newell is the owner of the company where Jill works. In response to numerous complaints from Jill and others, Ben hired two additional bookkeepers a month ago. However, the inefficiencies have continued at an even higher rate. The accounting information system for the company has only a general journal and a general ledger. Ben refuses to install a computerized accounting system.

Instructions

Now that Jill is an expert in manual accounting information systems, she decides to send a letter to Ben Newell explaining (1) why the additional personnel did not help and (2) what changes should be made to improve the efficiency of the accounting department. Write the letter that you think Jill should send.

Ethics Case

BYP7-4 Wiemers Products Company operates three divisions, each with its own manufacturing plant and marketing/sales force. The corporate headquarters and central accounting office are in Wiemers, and the plants are in Freeport, Rockport, and Bayport, all within 50 miles of Wiemers. Corporate management treats each division as an independent profit center and encourages competition among them. They each have similar but different product lines. As a competitive incentive, bonuses are awarded each year to the employees of the fastest-growing and most-profitable division.

Indy Grover is the manager of Wiemers's centralized computerized accounting operation that enters the sales transactions and maintains the accounts receivable for all three divisions. Indy came up in the accounting ranks from the Bayport division where his wife, several relatives, and many friends still work.

As sales documents are entered into the computer, the originating division is identified by code. Most sales documents (95%) are coded, but some (5%) are not coded or are coded incorrectly. As the manager, Indy has instructed the data-entry personnel to assign the Bayport code to all uncoded and incorrectly coded sales documents. This is done, he says, "in order to expedite processing and to keep the computer files current since they are updated daily." All receivables and cash collections for all three divisions are handled by Wiemers as one subsidiary accounts receivable ledger.

Instructions

(a) Who are the stakeholders in this situation?

(b) What are the ethical issues in this case?

(c) How might the system be improved to prevent this situation?

All About You

BYP7-5 In this chapter, you learned about a basic manual accounting information system. Computerized accounting systems range from the very basic and inexpensive to the very elaborate and expensive. However, even the most sophisticated systems are based on the fundamental structures and relationships that you learned in this chapter.

Instructions

Go to the book's companion site, **www.wiley.com/college/weygandt**, and review the demonstration that is provided for the general ledger software package that is used with this textbook. Prepare a brief explanation of how the general ledger system works—that is, how it is used and what information it provides.

A Look at IFRS

LEARNING OBJECTIVE 4 **Compare accounting information systems under GAAP and IFRS.**

As discussed in Chapter 1, IFRS is growing in acceptance around the world. For example, recent statistics indicate a substantial number of the Global Fortune 500 companies use IFRS. And the chairman of the IASB predicts that IFRS adoption will grow from its current level of 115 countries to nearly 150 countries in the near future.

When countries accept IFRS for use as accepted accounting policies, companies need guidance to ensure that their first IFRS financial statements contain high-quality information. Specifically, *IFRS 1* requires that information in a company's first IFRS statements (1) be transparent, (2) provide a suitable starting point, and (3) have a cost that does not exceed the benefits.

Relevant Facts

Following are the key similarities and differences between GAAP and IFRS related to accounting information systems.

Similarities

- The basic concepts related to an accounting information system are the same under GAAP and IFRS.
- The use of subsidiary ledgers and control accounts, as well as the system used for recording transactions, are the same under GAAP and IFRS.

Differences

- Many companies will be going through a substantial conversion process to switch from their current reporting standards to IFRS.
- Upon first-time adoption of IFRS, a company must present at least one year of comparative information under IFRS.

Looking to the Future

The basic recording process shown in this textbook is followed by companies around the globe. It is unlikely to change in the future. The definitional structure of assets, liabilities, equity, revenues, and expenses may change over time as the IASB and FASB evaluate their overall conceptual framework for establishing accounting standards. In addition, high-quality international accounting requires both high-quality accounting standards and high-quality auditing. Similar to the convergence of GAAP and IFRS, there is a movement to improve international auditing standards.

8 Fraud, Internal Control, and Cash

CHAPTER PREVIEW As the Feature Story about recording cash sales at Barriques indicates below, control of cash is important to ensure that fraud does not occur. Companies also need controls to safeguard other types of assets. For example, Barriques undoubtedly has controls to prevent the theft of food and supplies, and controls to prevent the theft of tableware and dishes from its kitchen.

In this chapter, we explain the essential features of an internal control system and how it prevents fraud. We also describe how those controls apply to a specific asset—cash. The applications include some controls with which you may be already familiar, such as the use of a bank.

FEATURE STORY

Minding the Money in Madison

For many years, Barriques in Madison, Wisconsin, has been named the city's favorite coffeehouse. Barriques not only does a booming business in coffee but also has wonderful baked goods, delicious sandwiches, and a fine selection of wines.

"Our customer base ranges from college students to neighborhood residents as well as visitors to our capital city," says bookkeeper Kerry Stoppleworth, who joined the company shortly after it was founded in 1998. "We are unique because we have customers who come in early on their way to work for a cup of coffee and then will stop back after work to pick up a bottle of wine for dinner. We stay very busy throughout all three parts of the day."

Like most businesses where purchases are low-cost and high-volume, cash control has to be simple. "We use a computerized point-of-sale (POS) system to keep track of our inventory and allow us to efficiently ring through an order for a customer," explains Stoppleworth. "You can either scan a barcode for an item or enter in a code for items that don't have a barcode such as cups of coffee or bakery items." The POS system also automatically tracks sales by department and maintains an electronic journal of all the sales transactions that occur during the day.

"There are two POS stations at each store, and throughout the day any of the staff may operate them," says Stoppleworth. At the end of the day, each POS station is reconciled separately. The staff counts the cash in the drawer and enters this amount into the closing totals in the POS system. The POS system then compares the cash and credit amounts, less the cash being carried forward to the next day (the float), to the shift total in the electronic journal. If there are discrepancies, a recount is done and the journal is reviewed transaction by transaction to identify the problem. The staff then creates a deposit ticket for the cash less the float and puts this in a drop safe with the electronic journal summary report for the manager to review and take to the bank the next day. Ultimately, the bookkeeper reviews all of these documents as well as the deposit receipt that the bank produces to make sure they are all in agreement.

As Stoppleworth concludes, "We keep the closing process and accounting simple so that our staff can concentrate on taking care of our customers and making great coffee and food."

© James Pauls/iStockphoto

CHAPTER OUTLINE

Learning Objectives

Learning Objectives	Topics	DO IT!
1 Discuss fraud and the principles of internal control.	• Fraud • The Sarbanes-Oxley Act • Internal control • Principles of internal control activities • Limitations of internal control	DO IT! 1 Control Activities
2 Apply internal control principles to cash.	• Cash receipts controls • Cash disbursements controls • Petty cash fund	DO IT! 2a Control over Cash Receipts 2b Petty Cash Fund
3 Identify the control features of a bank account.	• Making bank deposits • Writing checks • Bank statements • Reconciling the bank account • EFT system	DO IT! 3 Bank Reconciliation
4 Explain the reporting of cash.	• Cash equivalents • Restricted cash	DO IT! 4 Reporting Cash

io to the ***REVIEW AND PRACTICE*** section at the end of the chapter for a review of key concepts and practice applications with solutions.

'isit **WileyPLUS with ORION** for additional tutorials and practice opportunities.

LEARNING OBJECTIVE 1

Discuss fraud and the principles of internal control.

The Feature Story describes many of the internal control procedures used by **Barriques**. These procedures are necessary to discourage employees from fraudulent activities.

Fraud

A **fraud** is a dishonest act by an employee that results in personal benefit to the employee at a cost to the employer. Examples of fraud reported in the financial press include the following.

- A bookkeeper in a small company diverted $750,000 of bill payments to a personal bank account over a three-year period.
- A shipping clerk with 28 years of service shipped $125,000 of merchandise to himself.
- A computer operator embezzled $21 million from **Wells Fargo Bank** over a two-year period.
- A church treasurer "borrowed" $150,000 of church funds to finance a friend's business dealings.

Why does fraud occur? The three main factors that contribute to fraudulent activity are depicted by the **fraud triangle** in Illustration 8-1 (in the margin).

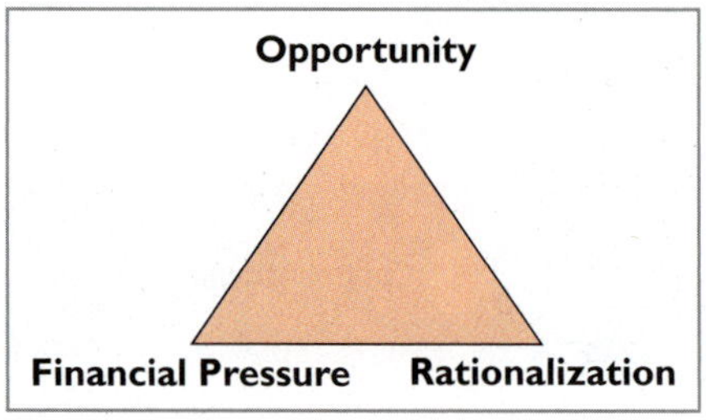

Illustration 8-1
Fraud triangle

The most important element of the fraud triangle is **opportunity**. For an employee to commit fraud, the workplace environment must provide opportunities that an employee can take advantage of. Opportunities occur when the workplace lacks sufficient controls to deter and detect fraud. For example, inadequate monitoring of employee actions can create opportunities for theft and can embolden employees because they believe they will not be caught.

A second factor that contributes to fraud is **financial pressure**. Employees sometimes commit fraud because of personal financial problems caused by too much debt. Or, they might commit fraud because they want to lead a lifestyle that they cannot afford on their current salary.

The third factor that contributes to fraud is **rationalization**. In order to justify their fraud, employees rationalize their dishonest actions. For example, employees sometimes justify fraud because they believe they are underpaid while the employer is making lots of money. Employees feel justified in stealing because they believe they deserve to be paid more.

The Sarbanes-Oxley Act

What can be done to prevent or to detect fraud? After numerous corporate scandals came to light in the early 2000s, Congress addressed this issue by passing the **Sarbanes-Oxley Act (SOX)**. Under SOX, all publicly traded U.S. corporations are required to maintain an adequate system of internal control. Corporate executives and boards of directors must ensure that these controls are reliable and effective. In addition, independent outside auditors must attest to the adequacy of the internal control system. Companies that fail to comply are subject to fines, and company officers can be imprisoned. SOX also created the Public Company Accounting Oversight Board (PCAOB) to establish auditing standards and regulate auditor activity.

One poll found that 60% of investors believe that SOX helps safeguard their stock investments. Many say they would be unlikely to invest in a company that fails to follow SOX requirements. Although some corporate executives have criticized the time and expense involved in following the SOX requirements, SOX appears to be working well. For example, the chief accounting officer of Eli Lily noted that SOX triggered a comprehensive review of how the company documents its controls. This review uncovered redundancies and pointed out controls that needed to be added. In short, it added up to time and money well spent.

Internal Control

Internal control is a process designed to provide reasonable assurance regarding the achievement of objectives related to operations, reporting, and compliance. In more detail, it consists of all the related methods and measures adopted within an organization to safeguard assets, enhance the reliability of accounting records, increase efficiency of operations, and ensure compliance with laws and regulations. Internal control systems have five primary components as listed below.[1]

- **A control environment.** It is the responsibility of top management to make it clear that the organization values integrity and that unethical activity will not be tolerated. This component is often referred to as the "tone at the top."
- **Risk assessment.** Companies must identify and analyze the various factors that create risk for the business and must determine how to manage these risks.
- **Control activities.** To reduce the occurrence of fraud, management must design policies and procedures to address the specific risks faced by the company.
- **Information and communication.** The internal control system must capture and communicate all pertinent information both down and up the organization, as well as communicate information to appropriate external parties.
- **Monitoring.** Internal control systems must be monitored periodically for their adequacy. Significant deficiencies need to be reported to top management and/or the board of directors.

People, Planet, and Profit Insight

© Karl Dolenc/iStockphoto

And the Controls Are . . .

Internal controls are important for an effective financial reporting system. The same is true for sustainability reporting. An effective system of internal controls for sustainability reporting will help in the following ways: (1) prevent the unauthorized use of data; (2) provide reasonable assurance that the information is accurate, valid, and complete; and (3) report information that is consistent with overall sustainability accounting policies. With these types of controls, users will have the confidence that they can use the sustainability information effectively.

Some regulators are calling for even more assurance through audits of this information. Companies that potentially can cause environmental damage through greenhouse gases, as well as companies in the mining and extractive industries, are subject to reporting requirements. And, as demand for more information in the sustainability area expands, the need for audits of this information will grow.

Why is sustainability information important to investors? (Go to **WileyPLUS** for this answer and additional questions.)

[1]The Committee of Sponsoring Organizations of the Treadway Commission, "Internal Control—Integrated Framework," *www.coso.org/documents/990025P_executive_summary_final_May20_e.pdf.*

Principles of Internal Control Activities

Each of the five components of an internal control system is important. Here, we will focus on one component, the control activities. The reason? These activities are the backbone of the company's efforts to address the risks it faces, such as fraud. The specific control activities used by a company will vary, depending on management's assessment of the risks faced. This assessment is heavily influenced by the size and nature of the company.

The six principles of control activities are as follows.

- Establishment of responsibility
- Segregation of duties
- Documentation procedures
- Physical controls
- Independent internal verification
- Human resource controls

We explain these principles in the following sections. You should recognize that they apply to most companies and are relevant to both manual and computerized accounting systems.

ESTABLISHMENT OF RESPONSIBILITY

It's your shift now. I'm turning in my cash drawer and heading home.

Transfer of cash drawers

An essential principle of internal control is to assign responsibility to specific employees. **Control is most effective when only one person is responsible for a given task.**

To illustrate, assume that the cash on hand at the end of the day in a Safeway supermarket is $10 short of the cash entered in the cash register. If only one person has operated the register, the shift manager can quickly determine responsibility for the shortage. If two or more individuals have worked the register, it may be impossible to determine who is responsible for the error.

Many retailers solve this problem by having registers with multiple drawers. This makes it possible for more than one person to operate a register but still allows identification of a particular employee with a specific drawer. Only the signed-in cashier has access to his or her drawer.

Establishing responsibility often requires limiting access only to authorized personnel, and then identifying those personnel. For example, the automated systems used by many companies have mechanisms such as identifying passcodes that keep track of who made a journal entry, who entered a sale, or who went into an inventory storeroom at a particular time. Use of identifying passcodes enables the company to establish responsibility by identifying the particular employee who carried out the activity.

ANATOMY OF A FRAUD

Maureen Frugali was a training supervisor for claims processing at Colossal Healthcare. As a standard part of the claims-processing training program, Maureen created fictitious claims for use by trainees. These fictitious claims were then sent to the accounts payable department. After the training claims had been processed, she was to notify Accounts Payable of all fictitious claims, so that they would not be paid. However, she did not inform Accounts Payable about every fictitious claim. She created some fictitious claims for entities that she controlled (that is, she would receive the payment), and she let Accounts Payable pay her.

Total take: $11 million

THE MISSING CONTROL

Establishment of responsibility. The healthcare company did not adequately restrict the responsibility for authorizing and approving claims transactions. The training supervisor should not have been authorized to create claims in the company's "live" system.

Source: Adapted from Wells, *Fraud Casebook* (2007), pp. 61–70.

SEGREGATION OF DUTIES

Segregation of duties is indispensable in an internal control system. There are two common applications of this principle:

1. Different individuals should be responsible for related activities.
2. The responsibility for recordkeeping for an asset should be separate from the physical custody of that asset.

The rationale for segregation of duties is this: **The work of one employee should, without a duplication of effort, provide a reliable basis for evaluating the work of another employee.** For example, the personnel that design and program computerized systems should not be assigned duties related to day-to-day use of the system. Otherwise, they could design the system to benefit them personally and conceal the fraud through day-to-day use.

SEGREGATION OF RELATED ACTIVITIES **Making one individual responsible for related activities increases the potential for errors and irregularities.** Instead, companies should, for example, assign related **purchasing activities** to different individuals. Related purchasing activities include ordering merchandise, order approval, receiving goods, authorizing payment, and paying for goods or services. Various frauds are possible when one person handles related purchasing activities:

- If a purchasing agent is allowed to order goods without obtaining supervisory approval, the likelihood of the purchasing agent receiving kickbacks from suppliers increases.
- If an employee who orders goods also handles the invoice and receipt of the goods, as well as payment authorization, he or she might authorize payment for a fictitious invoice.

These abuses are less likely to occur when companies divide the purchasing tasks.

Similarly, companies should assign related **sales activities** to different individuals. Related selling activities include making a sale, shipping (or delivering) the goods to the customer, billing the customer, and receiving payment. Various frauds are possible when one person handles related sales activities:

- If a salesperson can make a sale without obtaining supervisory approval, he or she might make sales at unauthorized prices to increase sales commissions.
- A shipping clerk who also has access to accounting records could ship goods to himself.
- A billing clerk who handles billing and receipt could understate the amount billed for sales made to friends and relatives.

These abuses are less likely to occur when companies divide the sales tasks. The salespeople make the sale, the shipping department ships the goods on the basis of the sales order, and the billing department prepares the sales invoice after comparing the sales order with the report of goods shipped.

ANATOMY OF A FRAUD

Lawrence Fairbanks, the assistant vice-chancellor of communications at Aesop University, was allowed to make purchases of under $2,500 for his department without external approval. Unfortunately, he also sometimes bought items for himself, such as expensive antiques and other collectibles. How did he do it? He replaced the vendor invoices he received with fake vendor invoices that he created. The fake invoices had descriptions that were more consistent with the communications department's purchases. He submitted these fake invoices to the accounting department as the basis for their journal entries and to the accounts payable department as the basis for payment.

Total take: $475,000

THE MISSING CONTROL

Segregation of duties. The university had not properly segregated related purchasing activities. Lawrence was ordering items, receiving the items, and receiving the invoice. By receiving the invoice, he had control over the documents that were used to account for the purchase and thus was able to substitute a fake invoice.

Source: Adapted from Wells, *Fraud Casebook* (2007), pp. 3–15.

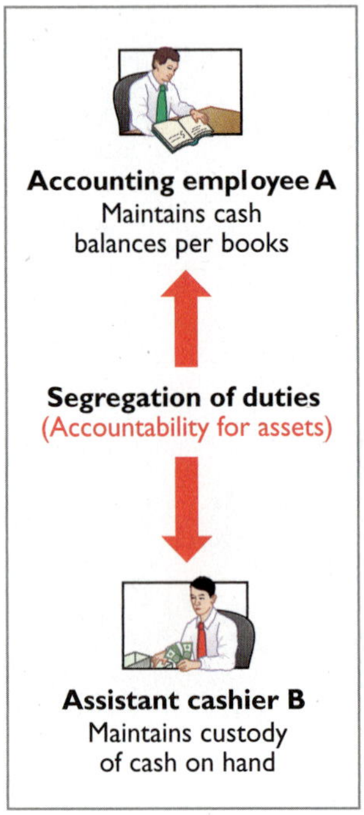

SEGREGATION OF RECORDKEEPING FROM PHYSICAL CUSTODY The accountant should have neither physical custody of the asset nor access to it. Likewise, the custodian of the asset should not maintain or have access to the accounting records. **The custodian of the asset is not likely to convert the asset to personal use when one employee maintains the record of the asset, and a different employee has physical custody of the asset.** The separation of accounting responsibility from the custody of assets is especially important for cash and inventories because these assets are very vulnerable to fraud.

ANATOMY OF A FRAUD

Angela Bauer was an accounts payable clerk for Aggasiz Construction Company. Angela prepared and issued checks to vendors and reconciled bank statements. She perpetrated a fraud in this way: She wrote checks for costs that the company had not actually incurred (e.g., fake taxes). A supervisor then approved and signed the checks. Before issuing the check, though, Angela would "white-out" the payee line on the check and change it to personal accounts that she controlled. She was able to conceal the theft because she also reconciled the bank account. That is, nobody else ever saw that the checks had been altered.

Total take: $570,000

THE MISSING CONTROL

Segregation of duties. Aggasiz Construction Company did not properly segregate recordkeeping from physical custody. Angela had physical custody of the checks, which essentially was control of the cash. She also had recordkeeping responsibility because she prepared the bank reconciliation.

Source: Adapted from Wells, *Fraud Casebook* (2007), pp. 100–107.

DOCUMENTATION PROCEDURES

Documents provide evidence that transactions and events have occurred. For example, Barriques' point-of-sale terminals are networked with the company's computing and accounting records, which results in direct documentation.

Similarly, a shipping document indicates that the goods have been shipped, and a sales invoice indicates that the company has billed the customer for the goods. By requiring signatures (or initials) on the documents, the company can identify the individual(s) responsible for the transaction or event. Companies should document transactions when they occur.

Companies should establish procedures for documents. First, whenever possible, companies should use **prenumbered documents, and all documents should be accounted for.** Prenumbering helps to prevent a transaction from being recorded more than once, or conversely, from not being recorded at all. Second, the control system should require that employees **promptly forward source documents for accounting entries to the accounting department. This control measure helps to ensure timely recording of the transaction** and contributes directly to the accuracy and reliability of the accounting records.

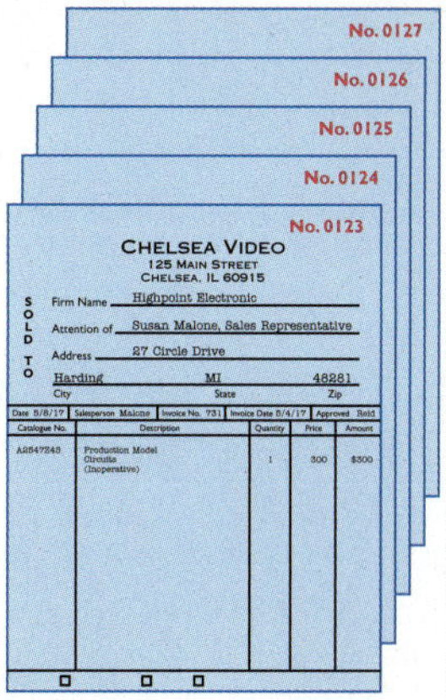

Prenumbered invoices

ANATOMY OF A FRAUD

To support their reimbursement requests for travel costs incurred, employees at Mod Fashions Corporation's design center were required to submit receipts. The receipts could include the detailed bill provided for a meal, the credit card receipt provided when the credit card payment is made, or a copy of the employee's monthly credit card bill that listed the item. A number of the designers who frequently traveled together came up with a fraud scheme: They submitted claims for the same expenses. For example, if they had a meal together that cost $200, one person submitted the detailed meal bill, another submitted the credit card receipt, and a third submitted a monthly credit card bill showing the meal as a line item. Thus, all three received a $200 reimbursement.

Total take: $75,000

THE MISSING CONTROL

Documentation procedures. Mod Fashions should require the original, detailed receipt. It should not accept photocopies, and it should not accept credit card statements. In addition, documentation procedures could be further improved by requiring the use of a corporate credit card (rather than a personal credit card) for all business expenses.

Source: Adapted from Wells, *Fraud Casebook* (2007), pp. 79–90.

PHYSICAL CONTROLS

Use of physical controls is essential. **Physical controls** relate to the safeguarding of assets and enhance the accuracy and reliability of the accounting records. Illustration 8-2 shows examples of these controls.

Illustration 8-2
Physical controls

Physical Controls

Safes, vaults, and safety deposit boxes for cash and business papers

Locked warehouses and storage cabinets for inventories and records

Computer facilities with pass key access or fingerprint or eyeball scans

Alarms to prevent break-ins

Television monitors and garment sensors to deter theft

Time clocks for recording time worked

ANATOMY OF A FRAUD

At Centerstone Health, a large insurance company, the mailroom each day received insurance applications from prospective customers. Mailroom employees scanned the applications into electronic documents before the applications were processed. Once the applications were scanned, they could be accessed online by authorized employees.

Insurance agents at Centerstone Health earn commissions based upon successful applications. The sales agent's name is listed on the application. However, roughly 15% of the applications are from customers who did not work with a sales agent. Two friends—Alex, an employee in recordkeeping, and Parviz, a sales agent—thought up a way to perpetrate a fraud. Alex identified scanned applications that did not list a sales agent. After business hours, he entered the mailroom and found the hard-copy applications that did not show a sales agent. He wrote in Parviz's name as the sales agent and then rescanned the application for processing. Parviz received the commission, which the friends then split.

Total take: $240,000

THE MISSING CONTROL

Physical controls. Centerstone Health lacked two basic physical controls that could have prevented this fraud. First, the mailroom should have been locked during non-business hours, and access during business hours should have been tightly controlled. Second, the scanned applications supposedly could be accessed only by authorized employees using their passwords. However, the password for each employee was the same as the employee's user ID. Since employee user-ID numbers were available to all other employees, all employees knew all other employees' passwords. Unauthorized employees could access the scanned applications. Thus, Alex could enter the system using another employee's password and access the scanned applications.

Source: Adapted from Wells, *Fraud Casebook* (2007), pp. 316–326.

INDEPENDENT INTERNAL VERIFICATION

Most internal control systems provide for **independent internal verification**. This principle involves the review of data prepared by employees. To obtain maximum benefit from independent internal verification:

1. Companies should verify records periodically or on a surprise basis.
2. An employee who is independent of the personnel responsible for the information should make the verification.
3. Discrepancies and exceptions should be reported to a management level that can take appropriate corrective action.

Independent internal verification is especially useful in comparing recorded accountability with existing assets. The reconciliation of the electronic journal with the cash in the point-of-sale terminal at **Barriques** is an example of this internal control principle. Other common examples are the reconciliation of a company's cash balance per books with the cash balance per bank, and the verification of the perpetual inventory records through a count of physical inventory. Illustration 8-3 shows the relationship between this principle and the segregation of duties principle.

ANATOMY OF A FRAUD

Bobbi Jean Donnelly, the office manager for Mod Fashions Corporation's design center, was responsible for preparing the design center budget and reviewing expense reports submitted by design center employees. Her desire to upgrade her wardrobe got the better of her, and she enacted a fraud that involved filing expense-reimbursement requests for her own personal clothing purchases. Bobbi Jean was able to conceal the fraud because she was responsible for reviewing all expense reports, including her

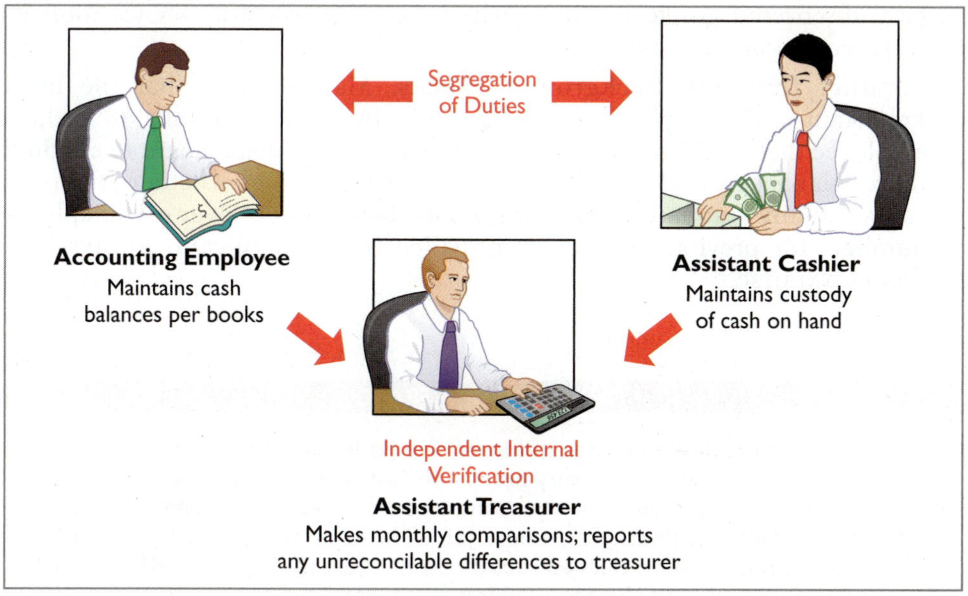

Illustration 8-3
Comparison of segregation of duties principle with independent internal verification principle

own. In addition, she sometimes was given ultimate responsibility for signing off on the expense reports when her boss was "too busy." Also, because she controlled the budget, when she submitted her expenses, she coded them to budget items that she knew were running under budget, so that they would not catch anyone's attention.

Total take: $275,000

THE MISSING CONTROL

Independent internal verification. Bobbi Jean's boss should have verified her expense reports. When asked what he thought her expenses for a year were, the boss said about $10,000. At $115,000 per year, her actual expenses were more than 10 times what would have been expected. However, because he was "too busy" to verify her expense reports or to review the budget, he never noticed.

Source: Adapted from Wells, *Fraud Casebook* (2007), pp. 79–90.

Large companies often assign independent internal verification to internal auditors. **Internal auditors** are company employees who continuously evaluate the effectiveness of the company's internal control systems. They review the activities of departments and individuals to determine whether prescribed internal controls are being followed. They also recommend improvements when needed. For example, **WorldCom** was at one time the second largest U.S. telecommunications company. The fraud that caused its bankruptcy (the largest ever when it occurred) involved billions of dollars. It was uncovered by an internal auditor.

HUMAN RESOURCE CONTROLS

Human resource control activities include the following.

1. **Bond employees who handle cash. Bonding** involves obtaining insurance protection against theft by employees. It contributes to the safeguarding of cash in two ways. First, the insurance company carefully screens all individuals before adding them to the policy and may reject risky applicants. Second, bonded employees know that the insurance company will vigorously prosecute all offenders.
2. **Rotate employees' duties and require employees to take vacations.** These measures deter employees from attempting thefts since they will not be able to permanently conceal their improper actions. Many banks, for example,

have discovered employee thefts when the employee was on vacation or assigned to a new position.

3. **Conduct thorough background checks.** Many believe that the most important and inexpensive measure any business can take to reduce employee theft and fraud is for the human resources department to conduct thorough background checks. Two tips: (1) Check to see whether job applicants actually graduated from the schools they list. (2) Never use telephone numbers for previous employers provided by the applicant. Always look them up yourself.

ANATOMY OF A FRAUD

Ellen Lowry was the desk manager and Josephine Rodriguez was the head of housekeeping at the Excelsior Inn, a luxury hotel. The two best friends were so dedicated to their jobs that they never took vacations, and they frequently filled in for other employees. In fact, Ms. Rodriguez, whose job as head of housekeeping did not include cleaning rooms, often cleaned rooms herself, "just to help the staff keep up." These two "dedicated" employees, working as a team, found a way to earn a little more cash. Ellen, the desk manager, provided significant discounts to guests who paid with cash. She kept the cash and did not register the guest in the hotel's computerized system. Instead, she took the room out of circulation "due to routine maintenance." Because the room did not show up as being used, it did not receive a normal housekeeping assignment. Instead, Josephine, the head of housekeeping, cleaned the rooms during the guests' stay.

Total take: $95,000

THE MISSING CONTROL

Human resource controls. Ellen, the desk manager, had been fired by a previous employer after being accused of fraud. If the Excelsior Inn had conducted a thorough background check, it would not have hired her. The hotel fraud was detected when Ellen missed work for a few days due to illness. A system of mandatory vacations and rotating days off would have increased the chances of detecting the fraud before it became so large.

Source: Adapted from Wells, *Fraud Casebook* (2007), pp. 145–155.

Accounting Across the Organization

Stockbyte/Getty Images, Inc.

SOX Boosts the Role of Human Resources

Under SOX, a company needs to keep track of employees' degrees and certifications to ensure that employees continue to meet the specified requirements of a job. Also, to ensure proper employee supervision and proper separation of duties, companies must develop and monitor an organizational chart. When one corporation went through this exercise, it found that out of 17,000 employees, there were 400 people who did not report to anyone. The corporation also had 35 people who reported to each other. In addition, if an employee complains of an unfair firing and mentions financial issues at the company, HR should refer the case to the company audit committee and possibly to its legal counsel.

Why would unsupervised employees or employees who report to each other represent potential internal control threats? (Go to **WileyPLUS** for this answer and additional questions.)

Limitations of Internal Control

Companies generally design their systems of internal control to provide **reasonable assurance** of proper safeguarding of assets and reliability of the accounting records. The concept of reasonable assurance rests on the premise that the costs of establishing control procedures should not exceed their expected benefit.

To illustrate, consider shoplifting losses in retail stores. Stores could eliminate such losses by having a security guard stop and search customers as they leave the store. But store managers have concluded that the negative effects of such a procedure cannot be justified. Instead, they have attempted to control shoplifting losses by less costly procedures. They post signs saying, "We reserve the right to inspect all packages" and "All shoplifters will be prosecuted." They use hidden cameras and store detectives to monitor customer activity, and they install sensor equipment at exits.

Helpful Hint
Controls may vary with the risk level of the activity. For example, management may consider cash to be high risk and maintaining inventories in the stockroom as low risk. Thus, management would have stricter controls for cash.

The **human element** is an important factor in every system of internal control. A good system can become ineffective as a result of employee fatigue, carelessness, or indifference. For example, a receiving clerk may not bother to count goods received and may just "fudge" the counts. Occasionally, two or more individuals may work together to get around prescribed controls. Such **collusion** can significantly reduce the effectiveness of a system, eliminating the protection offered by segregation of duties. No system of internal control is perfect.

The **size of the business** also may impose limitations on internal control. Small companies often find it difficult to segregate duties or to provide for independent internal verification. A study by the Association of Certified Fraud Examiners (*Report to the Nation on Occupational Fraud and Abuse*) indicates that businesses with fewer than 100 employees are most at risk for employee theft. In fact, 29% of frauds occurred at companies with fewer than 100 employees. The median loss at small companies was $154,000, which was close to the median fraud at companies with more than 10,000 employees ($160,000). A $154,000 loss can threaten the very existence of a small company.

DO IT! 1 Control Activities

Identify which control activity is violated in each of the following situations, and explain how the situation creates an opportunity for a fraud.

1. The person with primary responsibility for reconciling the bank account and making all bank deposits is also the company's accountant.
2. Wellstone Company's treasurer received an award for distinguished service because he had not taken a vacation in 30 years.
3. In order to save money spent on order slips and to reduce time spent keeping track of order slips, a local bar/restaurant does not buy prenumbered order slips.

Solution

1. Violates the control activity of segregation of duties. Recordkeeping should be separate from physical custody. As a consequence, the employee could embezzle cash and make journal entries to hide the theft.
2. Violates the control activity of human resource controls. Key employees must take vacations. Otherwise, the treasurer, who manages the company's cash, might embezzle cash and use his position to conceal the theft.
3. Violates the control activity of documentation procedures. If prenumbered documents are not used, then it is virtually impossible to account for the documents. As a consequence, an employee could write up a dinner sale, receive the cash from the customer, and then throw away the order slip and keep the cash.

Action Plan

✔ Familiarize yourself with each of the control activities summarized on page 358.

✔ Understand the nature of the frauds that each control activity is intended to address.

Related exercise material: **BE8-1, BE8-2, BE8-3, BE8-4, E8-1, and DO IT! 8-1.**

LEARNING OBJECTIVE 2

Apply internal control principles to cash.

Cash is the one asset that is readily convertible into any other type of asset. It also is easily concealed and transported, and is highly desired. Because of these characteristics, **cash is the asset most susceptible to fraudulent activities**. In addition, because of the large volume of cash transactions, numerous errors may occur in executing and recording them. To safeguard cash and to ensure the accuracy of the accounting records for cash, effective internal control over cash is critical.

Cash Receipts Controls

Illustration 8-4 shows how the internal control principles explained earlier apply to cash receipts transactions. As you might expect, companies vary considerably in how they apply these principles. To illustrate internal control over cash receipts, we will examine control activities for a retail store with both over-the-counter and mail receipts.

Illustration 8-4
Application of internal control principles to cash receipts

Cash Receipts Controls

Establishment of Responsibility
Only designated personnel are authorized to handle cash receipts (cashiers)

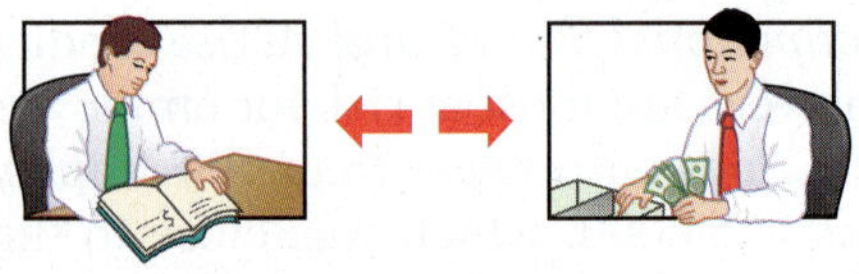

Segregation of Duties
Different individuals receive cash, record cash receipts, and hold the cash

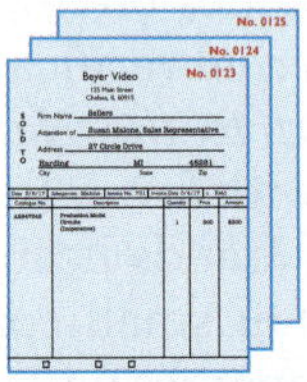

Documentation Procedures
Use remittance advice (mail receipts), cash register tapes or computer records, and deposit slips

Physical Controls
Store cash in safes and bank vaults; limit access to storage areas; use cash registers

Independent Internal Verification
Supervisors count cash receipts daily; assistant treasurer compares total receipts to bank deposits daily

Human Resource Controls
Bond personnel who handle cash; require employees to take vacations; conduct background checks

OVER-THE-COUNTER RECEIPTS

In retail businesses, control of over-the-counter receipts centers on cash registers that are visible to customers. A cash sale is entered in a cash register (or point-of-sale terminal), with the amount clearly visible to the customer. This activity prevents the sales clerk from entering a lower amount and pocketing the difference. The customer receives an itemized cash register receipt slip and is expected to count the change received. (One weakness at Barriques in the Feature Story is that customers are only given a receipt if requested.) The cash register's tape is locked in the register until a supervisor removes it. This tape accumulates the daily transactions and totals.

At the end of the clerk's shift, the clerk counts the cash and sends the cash and the count to the cashier. The cashier counts the cash, prepares a deposit slip, and deposits the cash at the bank. The cashier also sends a duplicate of the deposit slip to the accounting department to indicate cash received. The supervisor removes the cash register tape and sends it to the accounting department as the basis for a journal entry to record the cash received. (For point-of-sale systems, the accounting department receives information on daily transactions and totals through the computer network.) Illustration 8-5 summarizes this process.

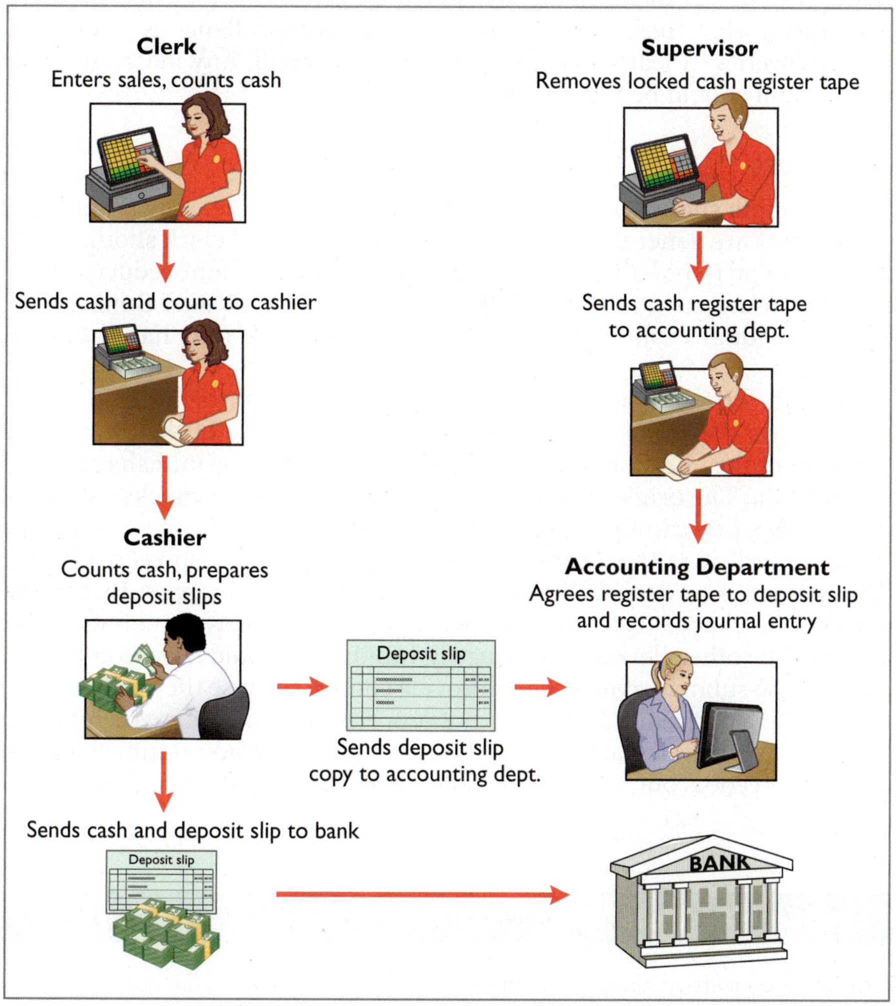

Illustration 8-5
Control of over-the-counter receipts

Helpful Hint
Flowcharts such as this one enhance the understanding of the flow of documents, the processing steps, and the internal control procedures.

This system for handling cash receipts uses an important internal control principle—segregation of recordkeeping from physical custody. The supervisor has access to the cash register tape but **not** to the cash. The clerk and the cashier have access to the cash but **not** to the register tape. In addition, the cash register tape provides documentation and enables independent internal verification. Use of these three principles of internal control (segregation of recordkeeping from physical custody, documentation, and independent internal verification) provides an effective system of internal control. Any attempt at fraudulent activity should be detected unless there is collusion among the employees.

In some instances, the amount deposited at the bank will not agree with the cash recorded in the accounting records based on the cash register tape. These differences often result because the clerk hands incorrect change back to the retail customer. In this case, the difference between the actual cash and the amount reported on the cash register tape is reported in a Cash Over and Short account. For example, suppose that the cash register tape indicated sales of $6,956.20 but the amount of cash was only $6,946.10. A cash shortfall of $10.10 exists. To account for this cash shortfall and related cash, the company makes the following entry.

A	=	L	+	OE
+6,946.10				
				−10.10
				+6,956.20

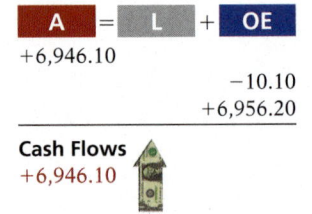

Cash Flows
+6,946.10

Cash	6,946.10	
Cash Over and Short	10.10	
Sales Revenue		6,956.20
(To record cash shortfall)		

Cash Over and Short is an income statement item. It is reported as miscellaneous expense when there is a cash shortfall, and as miscellaneous revenue when there is an overage. Clearly, the amount should be small. Any material amounts in this account should be investigated.

MAIL RECEIPTS

All mail receipts should be opened in the presence of at least two mail clerks. These receipts are generally in the form of checks. A mail clerk should endorse each check "For Deposit Only." This restrictive endorsement reduces the likelihood that someone could divert the check to personal use. Banks will not give an individual cash when presented with a check that has this type of endorsement.

The mail clerks prepare, in triplicate, a list of the checks received each day. This list shows the name of the check issuer, the purpose of the payment, and the amount of the check. Each mail clerk signs the list to establish responsibility for the data. The original copy of the list, along with the checks, is then sent to the cashier's department. A copy of the list is sent to the accounting department for recording in the accounting records. The clerks also keep a copy.

This process provides excellent internal control for the company. By employing two clerks, the chance of fraud is reduced. Each clerk knows he or she is being observed by the other clerk(s). To engage in fraud, they would have to collude. The customers who submit payments also provide control because they will contact the company with a complaint if they are not properly credited for payment. Because the cashier has access to cash but not the records, and the accounting department has access to records but not cash, neither can engage in undetected fraud.

DO IT! 2a Control over Cash Receipts

L. R. Cortez is concerned about the control over cash receipts in his fast-food restaurant, Big Cheese. The restaurant has two cash registers. At no time do more than two employees take customer orders and enter sales. Work shifts for employees range from 4 to 8 hours. Cortez asks your help in installing a good system of internal control over cash receipts.

Action Plan

✔ Differentiate among the internal control principles of (1) establishing responsibility, (2) using physical controls, and (3) independent internal verification.

✔ Design an effective system of internal control over cash receipts.

Solution

Cortez should assign a separate cash register drawer to each employee at the start of each work shift, with register totals set at zero. Each employee should have access to only the assigned register drawer to enter all sales. Each customer should be given a receipt. At the end of the shift, the employee should do a cash count. A separate employee should compare the cash count with the register tape to be sure they agree. In addition, Cortez should install an automated system that would enable the company to compare orders entered in the register to orders processed by the kitchen.

Related exercise material: BE8-5, BE8-6, BE8-7, E8-2, and DO IT! 8-2a.

Cash Disbursements Controls

Companies disburse cash for a variety of reasons, such as to pay expenses and liabilities or to purchase assets. **Generally, internal control over cash disbursements is more effective when companies pay by check or electronic funds transfer (EFT) rather than by cash.** One exception is **payments for incidental amounts that are paid out of petty cash.**[2]

Companies generally issue checks only after following specified control procedures. Illustration 8-6 shows how principles of internal control apply to cash disbursements.

Cash Disbursements Controls

Establishment of Responsibility
Only designated personnel are authorized to sign checks (treasurer) and approve vendors

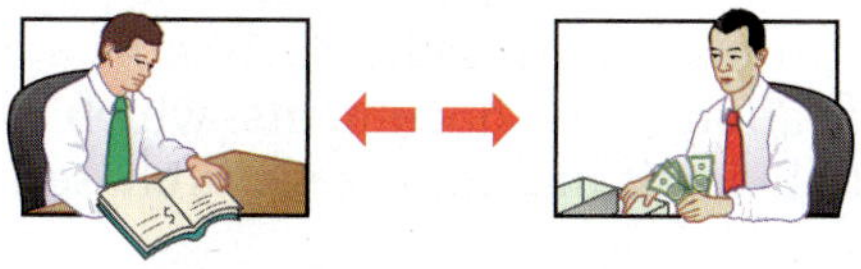

Segregation of Duties
Different individuals approve and make payments; check-signers do not record disbursements

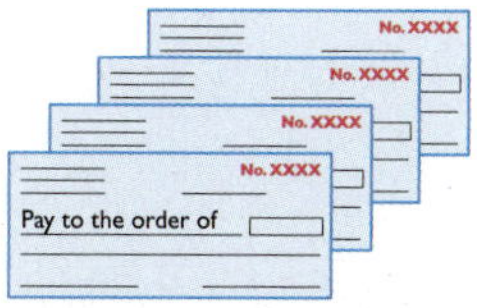

Documentation Procedures
Use prenumbered checks and account for them in sequence; each check must have an approved invoice; require employees to use corporate credit cards for reimbursable expenses; stamp invoices "paid"

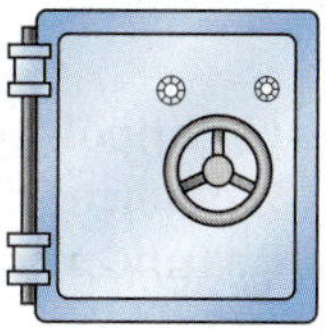

Physical Controls
Store blank checks in safes, with limited access; print check amounts by machine in indelible ink

Independent Internal Verification
Compare checks to invoices; reconcile bank statement monthly

Human Resource Controls
Bond personnel who handle cash; require employees to take vacations; conduct background checks

Illustration 8-6
Application of internal control principles to cash disbursements

VOUCHER SYSTEM CONTROLS

Most medium and large companies use vouchers as part of their internal control over cash disbursements. A **voucher system** is a network of approvals by authorized individuals, acting independently, to ensure that all disbursements by check are proper.

The system begins with the authorization to incur a cost or expense. It ends with the issuance of a check for the liability incurred. A **voucher** is an authorization form prepared for each expenditure. Companies require vouchers for all types of cash disbursements except those from petty cash.

[2]We explain the operation of a petty cash fund on pages 370–372.

The starting point in preparing a voucher is to fill in the appropriate information about the liability on the face of the voucher. The vendor's invoice provides most of the needed information. Then, an employee in accounts payable records the voucher (in a journal called a **voucher register**) and files it according to the date on which it is to be paid. The company issues and sends a check on that date, and stamps the voucher "paid." The paid voucher is sent to the accounting department for recording (in a journal called the **check register**). A voucher system involves two journal entries, one to record the liability when the voucher is issued and a second to pay the liability that relates to the voucher.

The use of a voucher system, whether done manually or electronically, improves internal control over cash disbursements. First, the authorization process inherent in a voucher system establishes responsibility. Each individual has responsibility to review the underlying documentation to ensure that it is correct. In addition, the voucher system keeps track of the documents that back up each transaction. By keeping these documents in one place, a supervisor can independently verify the authenticity of each transaction. Consider, for example, the case of Aesop University presented on page 360. Aesop did not use a voucher system for transactions under $2,500. As a consequence, there was no independent verification of the documents, which enabled the employee to submit fake invoices to hide his unauthorized purchases.

Petty Cash Fund

As you just learned, better internal control over cash disbursements is possible when companies make payments by check. However, using checks to pay small amounts is both impractical and a nuisance. For instance, a company would not want to write checks to pay for postage due, working lunches, or taxi fares. A common way of handling such payments, while maintaining satisfactory control, is to use a **petty cash fund** to pay relatively small amounts. The operation of a petty cash fund, often called an **imprest system**, involves (1) establishing the fund, (2) making payments from the fund, and (3) replenishing the fund.[3]

ESTABLISHING THE PETTY CASH FUND

Two essential steps in establishing a petty cash fund are (1) appointing a petty cash custodian who will be responsible for the fund, and (2) determining the size of the fund. Ordinarily, a company expects the amount in the fund to cover anticipated disbursements for a three- to four-week period.

To establish the fund, a company issues a check payable to the petty cash custodian for the stipulated amount. For example, if Laird Company decides to establish a $100 fund on March 1, the general journal entry is:

A	=	L	+	OE
+100				
−100				

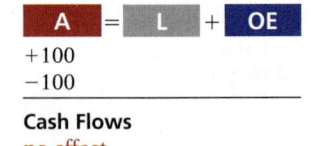

Cash Flows
no effect

Mar. 1	Petty Cash	100	
	Cash		100
	(To establish a petty cash fund)		

The fund custodian cashes the check and places the proceeds in a locked petty cash box or drawer. Most petty cash funds are established on a fixed-amount basis. The company will make no additional entries to the Petty Cash account unless management changes the stipulated amount of the fund. For example, if Laird Company decides on July 1 to increase the size of the fund to $250, it would debit Petty Cash $150 and credit Cash $150.

ETHICS NOTE

Petty cash funds are authorized and legitimate. In contrast, "slush" funds are unauthorized and hidden (under the table).

MAKING PAYMENTS FROM THE PETTY CASH FUND

The petty cash custodian has the authority to make payments from the fund that conform to prescribed management policies. Usually, management limits the size of

[3]The term "imprest" means an advance of money for a designated purpose.

expenditures that come from petty cash. Likewise, it may not permit use of the fund for certain types of transactions (such as making short-term loans to employees).

Each payment from the fund must be documented on a prenumbered petty cash receipt (or petty cash voucher), as shown in Illustration 8-7. The signatures of both the fund custodian and the person receiving payment are required on the receipt. If other supporting documents such as a freight bill or invoice are available, they should be attached to the petty cash receipt.

Helpful Hint
The petty cash receipt satisfies two internal control procedures: (1) establishing responsibility (signature of custodian), and (2) documentation procedures.

Illustration 8-7
Petty cash receipt

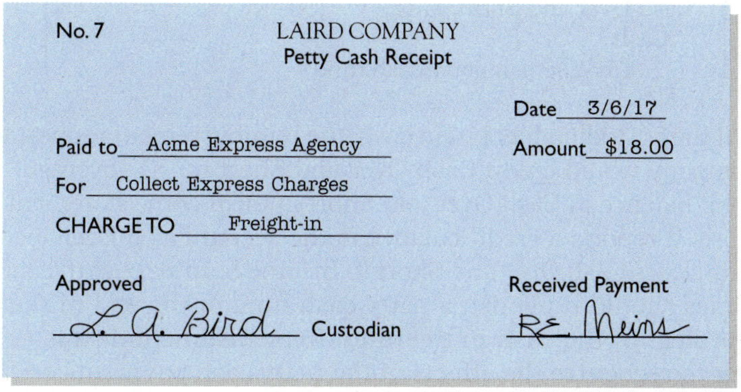
No. 7
LAIRD COMPANY
Petty Cash Receipt
Date 3/6/17
Paid to Acme Express Agency
Amount $18.00
For Collect Express Charges
CHARGE TO Freight-in
Approved
L. A. Bird Custodian
Received Payment
R. E. Meins

The petty cash custodian keeps the receipts in the petty cash box until the fund is replenished. The sum of the petty cash receipts and the money in the fund should equal the established total at all times. Management can (and should) make surprise counts at any time to determine whether the fund is being maintained correctly.

The company does not make an accounting entry to record a payment when it is made from petty cash. It is considered both inexpedient and unnecessary to do so. Instead, the company recognizes the accounting effects of each payment when it replenishes the fund.

ETHICS NOTE
Internal control over a petty cash fund is strengthened by (1) having a supervisor make surprise counts of the fund to confirm whether the paid petty cash receipts and fund cash equal the impress amount, and (2) canceling or mutilating the paid petty cash receipts so they cannot be resubmitted for reimbursement.

REPLENISHING THE PETTY CASH FUND

When the money in the petty cash fund reaches a minimum level, the company replenishes the fund. The petty cash custodian initiates a request for reimbursement. The individual prepares a schedule (or summary) of the payments that have been made and sends the schedule, supported by petty cash receipts and other documentation, to the treasurer's office. The treasurer's office examines the receipts and supporting documents to verify that proper payments from the fund were made. The treasurer then approves the request and issues a check to restore the fund to its established amount. At the same time, all supporting documentation is stamped "paid" so that it cannot be submitted again for payment.

To illustrate, assume that on March 15 Laird's petty cash custodian requests a check for $87. The fund contains $13 cash and petty cash receipts for postage $44, freight-out $38, and miscellaneous expenses $5. The general journal entry to record the check is as follows.

Mar. 15	Postage Expense	44	
	Freight-Out	38	
	Miscellaneous Expense	5	
	Cash		87
	(To replenish petty cash fund)		

A	=	L	+	OE
				−44 Exp
				−38 Exp
				−5 Exp
−87				

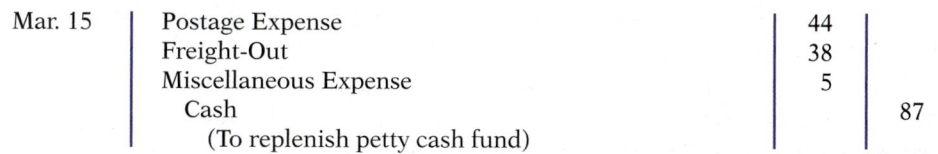

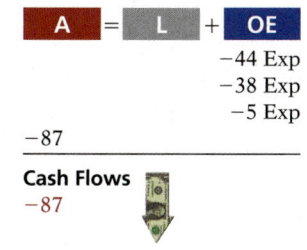

Cash Flows
−87

Note that the reimbursement entry does not affect the Petty Cash account. Replenishment changes the composition of the fund by replacing the petty cash receipts with cash. It does not change the balance in the fund.

Occasionally, in replenishing a petty cash fund, the company may need to recognize a cash shortage or overage. This results when the total of the cash plus receipts in the petty cash box does not equal the established amount of the petty cash fund. To illustrate, assume that Laird's petty cash custodian has only $12 in cash in the fund plus the receipts as listed. The request for reimbursement would therefore be for $88, and Laird would make the following entry.

A	=	L	+	OE
				−44 Exp
				−38 Exp
				−5 Exp
				−1 Exp
−88				

Cash Flows
−88

Mar. 15	Postage Expense	44	
	Freight-Out	38	
	Miscellaneous Expense	5	
	Cash Over and Short	1	
	Cash		88
	(To replenish petty cash fund)		

Conversely, if the custodian has $14 in cash, the reimbursement request would be for $86. The company would credit Cash Over and Short for $1 (overage). A company reports a debit balance in Cash Over and Short in the income statement as miscellaneous expense. It reports a credit balance in the account as miscellaneous revenue. The company closes Cash Over and Short to Income Summary at the end of the year.

Companies should replenish a petty cash fund at the end of the accounting period, regardless of the cash in the fund. Replenishment at this time is necessary in order to recognize the effects of the petty cash payments on the financial statements.

Helpful Hint
Cash over and short situations result from mathematical errors or from failure to keep accurate records.

Ethics Insight

© Chris Fernig/iStockphoto

How Employees Steal

Occupational fraud is using your own occupation for personal gain through the misuse or misapplication of the company's resources or assets. This type of fraud is one of three types:

1. **Asset misappropriation**, such as theft of cash on hand, fraudulent disbursements, false refunds, ghost employees, personal purchases, and fictitious employees. This fraud is the most common but the least costly.
2. **Corruption**, such as bribery, illegal gratuities, and economic extortion. This fraud generally falls in the middle between asset misappropriation and financial statement fraud as regards frequency and cost.
3. **Financial statement fraud**, such as fictitious revenues, concealed liabilities and expenses, improper disclosures, and improper asset values. This fraud occurs less frequently than other types of fraud but it is the most costly.

The graph below shows the frequency and the median loss for each type of occupational fraud.

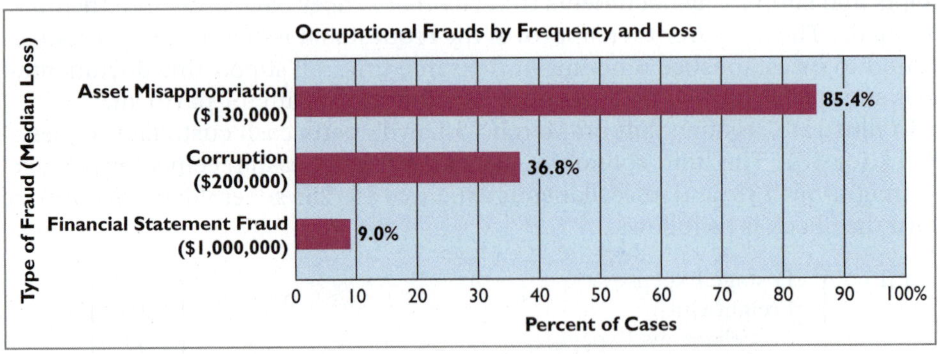

Source: 2014 Report to the Nations on Occupational Fraud and Abuse, Association of Certified Fraud Examiners, pp. 10–12.

How can companies reduce the likelihood of occupational fraud? (Go to **WileyPLUS** for this answer and additional questions.)

DO IT! 2b Petty Cash Fund

Bateer Company established a $50 petty cash fund on July 1. On July 30, the fund had $12 cash remaining and petty cash receipts for postage $14, office supplies $10, and delivery expense $15. Prepare journal entries to establish the fund on July 1 and to replenish the fund on July 30.

Solution

July 1	Petty Cash	50	
	Cash		50
	(To establish petty cash fund)		
30	Postage Expense	14	
	Supplies	10	
	Delivery Expense	15	
	Cash Over and Short		1
	Cash ($50 − $12)		38
	(To replenish petty cash)		

Related exercise material: **BE8-9, E8-7, E8-8, and DO IT! 8-2b.**

Action Plan

- ✔ To establish the fund, set up a separate general ledger account.
- ✔ Determine how much cash is needed to replenish the fund: subtract the cash remaining from the petty cash fund balance.
- ✔ Total the petty cash receipts. Determine any cash over or short—the difference between the cash needed to replenish the fund and the total of the petty cash receipts.
- ✔ Record the expenses incurred according to the petty cash receipts when replenishing the fund.

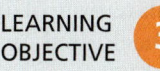

LEARNING OBJECTIVE 3 Identify the control features of a bank account.

The use of a bank contributes significantly to good internal control over cash. A company can safeguard its cash by using a bank as a depository and as a clearinghouse for checks received and written. Use of a bank minimizes the amount of currency that a company must keep on hand. Also, use of a bank facilitates the control of cash because it creates a double record of all bank transactions—one by the company and the other by the bank. The asset account Cash maintained by the company should have the same balance as the bank's liability account for that company. A **bank reconciliation** compares the bank's balance with the company's balance and explains any differences to make them agree.

Many companies have more than one bank account. For efficiency of operations and better control, national retailers like Wal-Mart Stores, Inc. and Target may have regional bank accounts. Large companies, with tens of thousands of employees, may have a payroll bank account, as well as one or more general bank accounts. Also, a company may maintain several bank accounts in order to have more than one source for short-term loans when needed.

Making Bank Deposits

An authorized employee, such as the head cashier, should make a company's bank deposits. Each deposit must be documented by a deposit slip (ticket), as shown in Illustration 8-8 (page 374).

Deposit slips are prepared in duplicate. The bank retains the original; the depositor keeps the duplicate, machine-stamped by the bank to establish its authenticity.

Illustration 8-8
Deposit slip

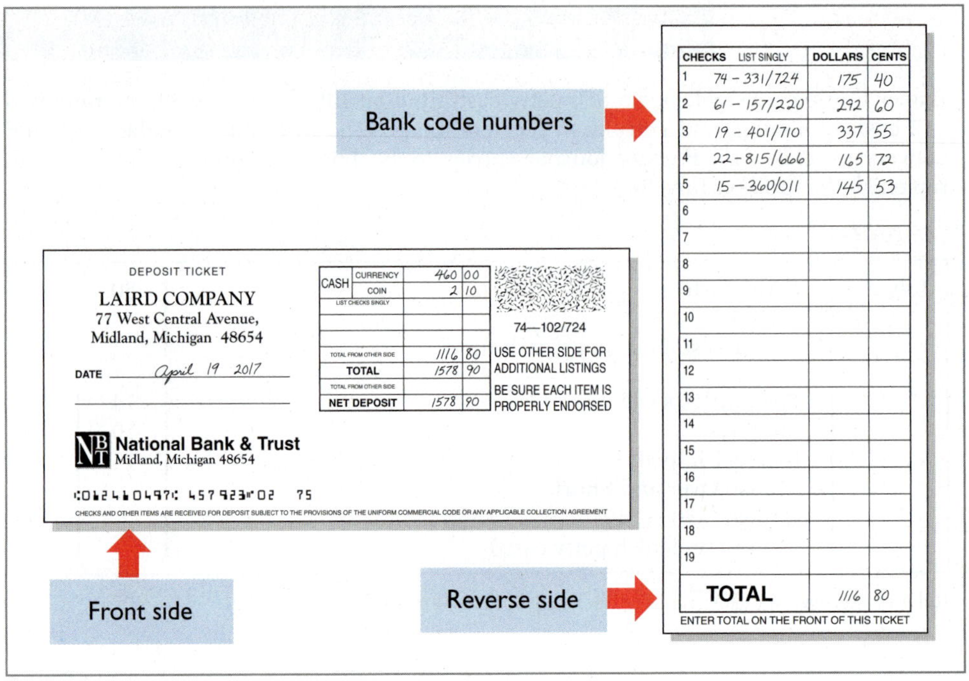

Writing Checks

A **check** is a written order signed by the depositor directing the bank to pay a specified sum of money to a designated recipient. There are three parties to a check: (1) the **maker** (or drawer) who issues the check, (2) the **bank** (or payer) on which the check is drawn, and (3) the **payee** to whom the check is payable. A check is a **negotiable instrument** that one party can transfer to another party by endorsement. Each check should be accompanied by an explanation of its purpose. In many companies, a remittance advice attached to the check, as shown in Illustration 8-9, explains the check's purpose.

Illustration 8-9
Check with remittance advice

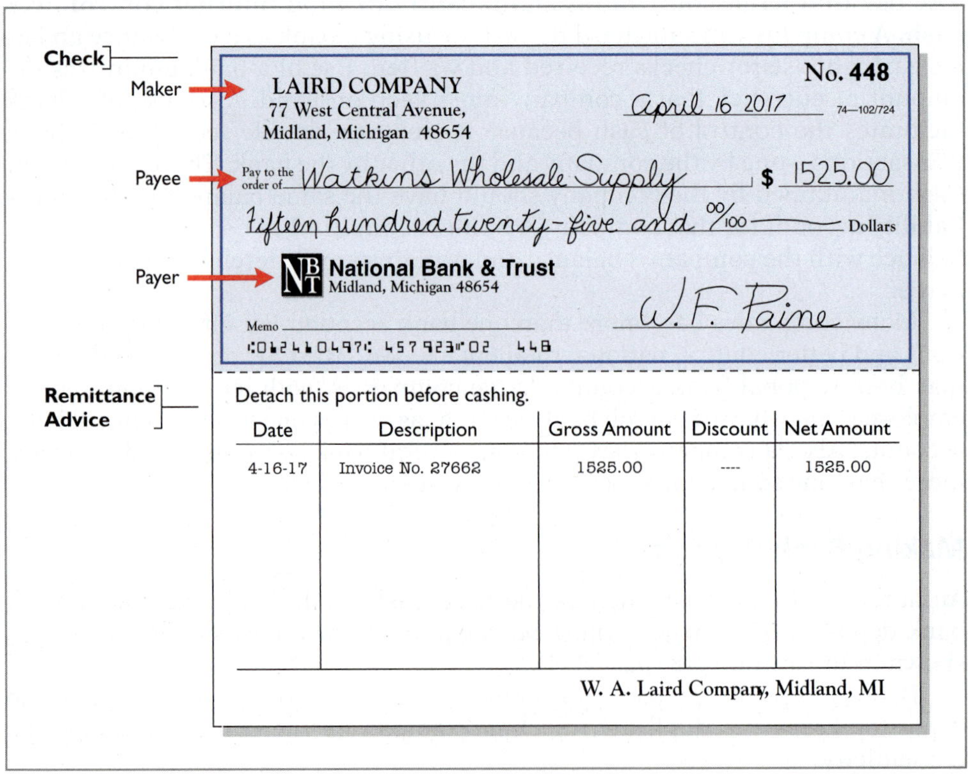

It is important to know the balance in the checking account at all times. To keep the balance current, the depositor should enter each deposit and check on running-balance memo forms (or online statements) provided by the bank or on the check stubs in the checkbook.

Bank Statements

If you have a personal checking account, you are probably familiar with bank statements. A **bank statement** shows the depositor's bank transactions and balances.[4] Each month, a depositor receives a statement from the bank. Illustration 8-10 presents a typical bank statement for Laird Company. It shows (1) checks paid and other debits (such as debit card transactions or direct withdrawals for bill payments) that reduce the balance in the depositor's account, (2) deposits and other credits that increase the balance in the depositor's account, and (3) the account balance after each day's transactions.

Helpful Hint
Essentially, the bank statement is a copy of the bank's records sent to the customer (or available online) for review.

Illustration 8-10
Bank statement

National Bank & Trust
Midland, Michigan 48654 Member FDIC

ACCOUNT STATEMENT

LAIRD COMPANY
77 WEST CENTRAL AVENUE
MIDLAND, MICHIGAN 48654

Statement Date/Credit Line Closing Date: April 30, 2017

457923
ACCOUNT NUMBER

Balance Last Statement	Deposits and Credits		Checks and Debits		Balance This Statement
	No.	Total Amount	No.	Total Amount	
13,256.90	20	34,805.10	26	32,154.55	15,907.45

CHECKS AND DEBITS			DEPOSITS AND CREDITS		DAILY BALANCE	
Date	No.	Amount	Date	Amount	Date	Amount
4-2	435	644.95	4-2	4,276.85	4-2	16,888.80
4-5	436	3,260.00	4-3	2,137.50	4-3	18,249.65
4-4	437	1,185.79	4-5	1,350.47	4-4	17,063.86
4-3	438	776.65	4-7	982.46	4-5	15,154.33
4-8	439	1,781.70	4-8	1,320.28	4-7	14,648.89
4-7	440	1,487.90	4-9 CM	1,035.00	4-8	11,767.47
4-8	441	2,420.00	4-11	2,720.00	4-9	12,802.47
4-11	442	1,585.60	4-12	757.41	4-11	13,936.87
4-12	443	1,226.00	4-13	1,218.56	4-12	13,468.28
4-29	NSF	425.60	4-27	1,545.57	4-27	13,005.45
4-29	459	1,080.30	4-29	2,929.45	4-29	14,429.00
4-30	DM	30.00	4-30	2,128.60	4-30	15,907.45
4-30	461	620.15				

Symbols: **CM** Credit Memo **DM** Debit Memo **EC** Error Correction **INT** Interest Earned **NSF** Not Sufficient Funds **SC** Service Charge

Reconcile Your Account Promptly

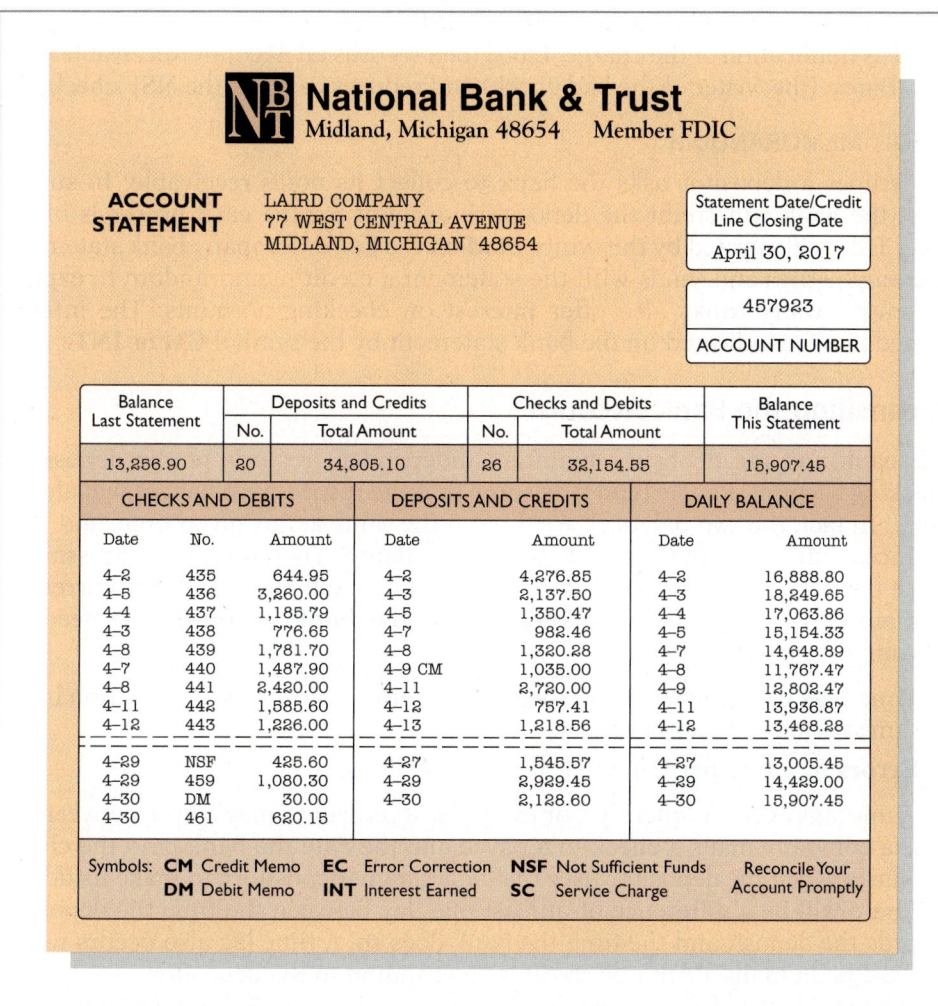

Helpful Hint
The bank *credits* to the customer's account every deposit it receives. The reverse occurs when the bank "pays" a check issued by a company on its checking account balance. Payment reduces the bank's liability. Thus, the bank *debits* check payments to the customer's account with the bank.

The bank statement lists in numerical sequence all "paid" checks, along with the date the check was paid and its amount. Upon paying a check, the bank stamps the check "paid"; a paid check is sometimes referred to as a **canceled** check. On the statement, the bank also includes memoranda explaining other debits and credits it made to the depositor's account.

[4]Our presentation assumes that the depositor makes all adjustments at the end of the month. In practice, a company may also make journal entries during the month as it reviews information from the bank regarding its account.

DEBIT MEMORANDUM

Some banks charge a monthly fee for their services. Often, they charge this fee only when the average monthly balance in a checking account falls below a specified amount. They identify the fee, called a **bank service charge**, on the bank statement by a symbol such as **SC**. The bank also sends with the statement a debit memorandum explaining the charge noted on the statement. Other debit memoranda may also be issued for other bank services such as the cost of printing checks, issuing traveler's checks, and wiring funds to other locations. The symbol **DM** is often used for such charges.

Banks also use a debit memorandum when a deposited check from a customer "bounces" because of insufficient funds. For example, assume that J. R. Baron, a customer of Laird Company, sends a check for $425.60 to Laird Company for services performed. Unfortunately, Baron does not have sufficient funds at its bank to pay for these services. In such a case, Baron's bank marks the check **NSF** (not sufficient funds) and returns it to Laird's (the depositor's) bank. Laird's bank then debits Laird's account, as shown by the symbol NSF on the bank statement in Illustration 8-10. The bank sends the NSF check and debit memorandum to Laird as notification of the charge. Laird then records an Account Receivable from J. R. Baron (the writer of the bad check) and reduces cash for the NSF check.

CREDIT MEMORANDUM

Sometimes a depositor asks the bank to collect its notes receivable. In such a case, the bank will credit the depositor's account for the cash proceeds of the note. This is illustrated by the symbol **CM** on the Laird Company bank statement. The bank issues and sends with the statement a credit memorandum to explain the entry. Many banks also offer interest on checking accounts. The interest earned may be indicated on the bank statement by the symbol **CM** or **INT**.

Reconciling the Bank Account

The bank and the depositor maintain independent records of the depositor's checking account. People tend to assume that the respective balances will always agree. In fact, the two balances are seldom the same at any given time, and both balances differ from the "correct" or "true" balance. Therefore, it is necessary to make the balance per books and the balance per bank agree with the correct or true amount—a process called **reconciling the bank account**. The need for agreement has two causes:

1. **Time lags** that prevent one of the parties from recording the transaction in the same period as the other party.
2. **Errors** by either party in recording transactions.

Time lags occur frequently. For example, several days may elapse between the time a company mails a check to a payee and the date the bank pays the check. Similarly, when the depositor uses the bank's night depository to make its deposits, there will be a difference of at least one day between the time the depositor records the deposit and the time the bank does so. A time lag also occurs whenever the bank mails a debit or credit memorandum to the depositor.

The incidence of errors depends on the effectiveness of the internal controls maintained by the company and the bank. Bank errors are infrequent. However, either party could accidentally record a $450 check as $45 or $540. In addition, the bank might mistakenly charge a check drawn by C. D. Berg to the account of C. D. Burg.

RECONCILIATION PROCEDURE

The bank reconciliation should be prepared by an employee who has no other responsibilities pertaining to cash. If a company fails to follow this internal control principle of independent internal verification, cash embezzlements may go unnoticed. For example, a cashier who prepares the reconciliation can embezzle cash and conceal the embezzlement by misstating the reconciliation. Thus, the bank accounts would reconcile, and the embezzlement would not be detected.

In reconciling the bank account, it is customary to reconcile the balance per books and balance per bank to their adjusted (correct or true) cash balances. The starting point in preparing the reconciliation is to enter the balance per bank statement and balance per books on the reconciliation schedule. The company then makes various adjustments, as shown in Illustration 8-11.

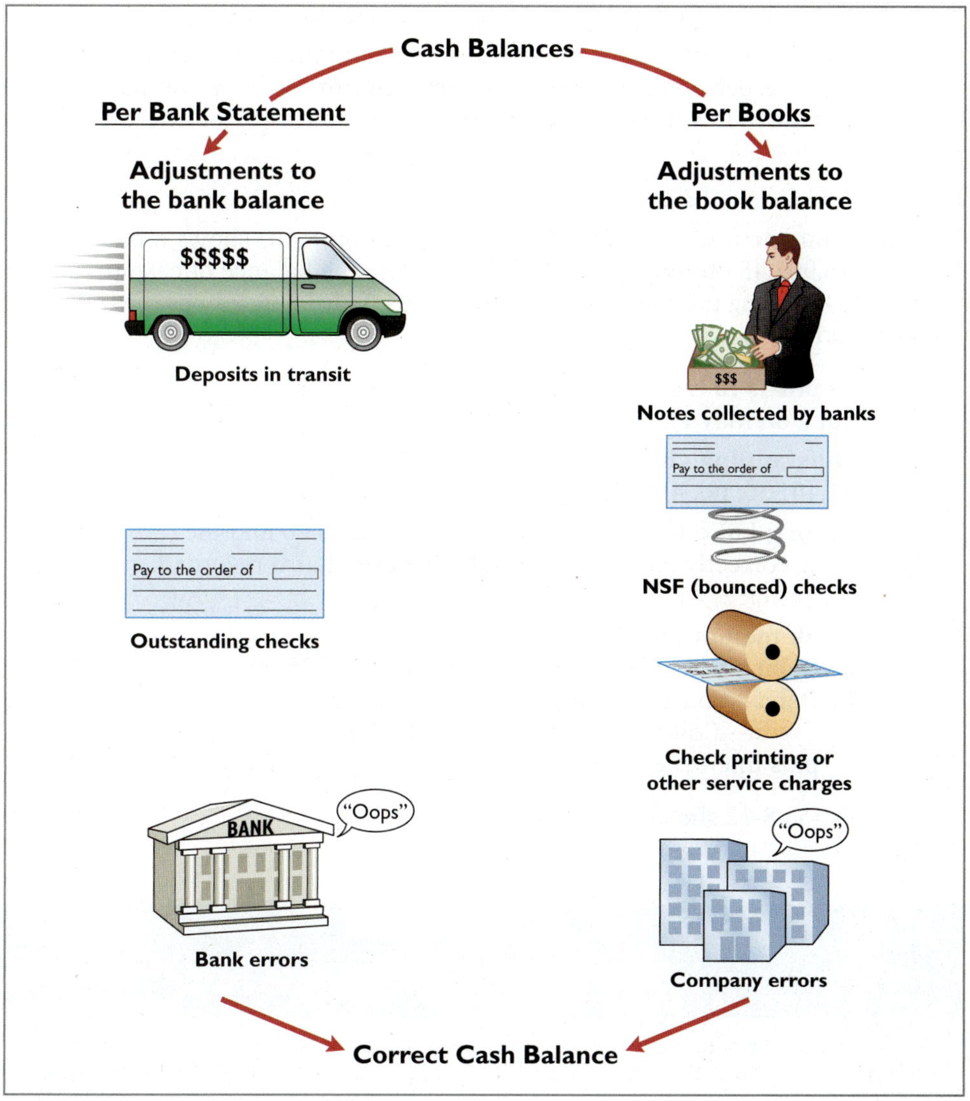

Illustration 8-11
Bank reconciliation adjustments

The following steps should reveal all the reconciling items that cause the difference between the two balances.

Step 1. Deposits in transit. Compare the individual deposits listed on the bank statement with deposits in transit from the preceding bank reconciliation and with the deposits per company records or duplicate deposit slips. Deposits recorded by the depositor that have not been recorded by the bank are the **deposits in transit**. Add these deposits to the balance per bank.

Helpful Hint
Deposits in transit and outstanding checks are reconciling items because of time lags.

Step 2. Outstanding checks. Compare the paid checks shown on the bank statement with (a) checks outstanding from the previous bank reconciliation, and (b) checks issued by the company as recorded in the cash payments journal (or in the check register in your personal checkbook). Issued checks recorded by the company but that have not yet been paid by the bank are **outstanding checks**. Deduct outstanding checks from the balance per bank.

Step 3. Errors. Note any errors discovered in the foregoing steps and list them in the appropriate section of the reconciliation schedule. For example, if the company mistakenly recorded as $169 a paid check correctly written for $196, it would deduct the error of $27 from the balance per books. All errors made by the depositor are reconciling items in determining the adjusted cash balance per books. In contrast, all errors made by the bank are reconciling items in determining the adjusted cash balance per bank.

Step 4. Bank memoranda. Trace bank memoranda to the depositor's records. List in the appropriate section of the reconciliation schedule any unrecorded memoranda. For example, the company would deduct from the balance per books a $5 debit memorandum for bank service charges. Similarly, it would add to the balance per books $32 of interest earned.

BANK RECONCILIATION ILLUSTRATED

Helpful Hint
Note in the bank statement in Illustration 8-10 that checks no. 459 and 461 have been paid but check no. 460 is not listed. Thus, this check is outstanding. If a complete bank statement were provided, checks no. 453 and 457 would also not be listed. The amounts for these three checks are obtained from the company's cash payments records.

The bank statement for Laird Company (Illustration 8-10) shows a balance per bank of $15,907.45 on April 30, 2017. On this date the balance of cash per books is $11,589.45. Using the four reconciliation steps, Laird determines the following reconciling items.

Step 1.	**Deposits in transit:** April 30 deposit (received by bank on May 1).	$2,201.40
Step 2.	**Outstanding checks:** No. 453, $3,000.00; no. 457, $1,401.30; no. 460, $1,502.70.	5,904.00
Step 3.	**Errors:** Laird wrote check no. 443 for $1,226.00 and the bank correctly paid that amount. However, Laird recorded the check as $1,262.00.	36.00
Step 4.	**Bank memoranda:**	
	a. Debit—NSF check from J. R. Baron for $425.60.	425.60
	b. Debit—Charge for printing company checks $30.00.	30.00
	c. Credit—Collection of note receivable for $1,000 plus interest earned $50, less bank collection fee $15.00.	1,035.00

Illustration 8-12 shows Laird's bank reconciliation.

Illustration 8-12
Bank reconciliation

LAIRD COMPANY
Bank Reconciliation
April 30, 2017

Cash balance per bank statement		$ 15,907.45
Add: Deposits in transit		2,201.40
		18,108.85
Less: Outstanding checks		
No. 453	$3,000.00	
No. 457	1,401.30	
No. 460	1,502.70	5,904.00
Adjusted cash balance per bank		**$12,204.85**
Cash balance per books		$ 11,589.45
Add: Collection of note receivable $1,000, plus interest earned $50, less collection fee $15	$1,035.00	
Error in recording check no. 443	36.00	1,071.00
		12,660.45
Less: NSF check	425.60	
Bank service charge	30.00	455.60
Adjusted cash balance per books		**$12,204.85**

Alternative Terminology
The terms *adjusted cash balance, true cash balance,* and *correct cash balance* are used interchangeably.

ENTRIES FROM BANK RECONCILIATION

The company records each reconciling item used to determine the **adjusted cash balance per books. If the company does not journalize and post these items, the Cash account will not show the correct balance.** Laird Company would make the following entries on April 30.

Helpful Hint
The entries that follow are adjusting entries. In prior chapters, Cash was an account that did not require adjustment. That was a simplifying assumption for learning purposes because we had not yet explained a bank reconciliation.

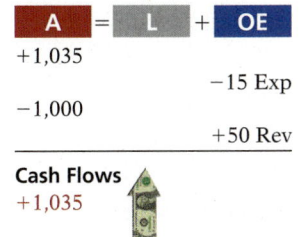

COLLECTION OF NOTE RECEIVABLE This entry involves four accounts. Assuming that the interest of $50 has not been accrued and the collection fee is charged to Miscellaneous Expense, the entry is:

Apr. 30	Cash	1,035.00	
	Miscellaneous Expense	15.00	
	Notes Receivable		1,000.00
	Interest Revenue		50.00
	(To record collection of note receivable by bank)		

A = L + OE
+1,035 (A)
−15 Exp (OE)
−1,000 (A)
+50 Rev (OE)
Cash Flows
+1,035

BOOK ERROR The cash disbursements journal shows that check no. 443 was a payment on account to Andrea Company, a supplier. The correcting entry is:

Apr. 30	Cash	36.00	
	Accounts Payable—Andrea Company		36.00
	(To correct error in recording check no. 443)		

A = L + OE
+36 (A)
+36 (L)
Cash Flows
+36

NSF CHECK As indicated earlier, an NSF check becomes an account receivable to the depositor. The entry is:

Apr. 30	Accounts Receivable—J. R. Baron	425.60	
	Cash		425.60
	(To record NSF check)		

A = L + OE
+425.60
−425.60
Cash Flows
−425.60

BANK SERVICE CHARGES Depositors debit check printing charges (DM) and other bank service charges (SC) to Miscellaneous Expense because they are usually nominal in amount. The entry is:

Apr. 30	Miscellaneous Expense	30.00	
	Cash		30.00
	(To record charge for printing company checks)		

A = L + OE
−30 Exp (OE)
−30 (A)
Cash Flows
−30

Instead of making four separate entries, Laird could combine them into one compound entry.

After Laird has posted the entries, the Cash account will show the following.

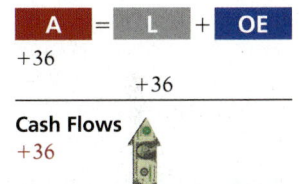

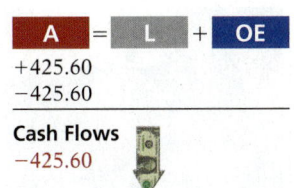

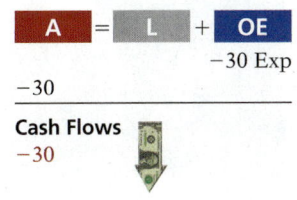

Illustration 8-13
Adjusted balance in Cash account

Cash			
Apr. 30 Bal.	11,589.45	Apr. 30	425.60
30	1,035.00	30	30.00
30	36.00		
Apr. 30 Bal.	**12,204.85**		

The adjusted cash balance in the ledger should agree with the adjusted cash balance per books in the bank reconciliation in Illustration 8-12 (page 378).

What entries does the bank make? If the company discovers any bank errors in preparing the reconciliation, it should notify the bank. The bank then can make the necessary corrections in its records. The bank does not make any entries for deposits in transit or outstanding checks. Only when these items reach the bank will the bank record these items.

Electronic Funds Transfer (EFT) System

It is not surprising that companies and banks have developed approaches to transfer funds among parties without the use of paper (deposit tickets, checks, etc.). Such procedures, called **electronic funds transfers (EFT)**, are disbursement systems that use wire, telephone, or computers to transfer cash balances from one location to another. Use of EFT is quite common. For example, many employees receive no formal payroll checks from their employers. Instead, employers send electronic payroll data to the appropriate banks. Also, individuals and companies now frequently make regular payments such as those for house, car, and utilities by EFT.

EFT transactions normally result in better internal control since no cash or checks are handled by company employees. This does not mean that opportunities for fraud are eliminated. In fact, the same basic principles related to internal control apply to EFT transfers. For example, without proper segregation of duties and authorizations, an employee might be able to redirect electronic payments into a personal bank account and conceal the theft with fraudulent accounting entries.

Investor Insight

Mary Altaffer/©AP/Wide World Photos

Madoff's Ponzi Scheme

No recent fraud has generated more interest and rage than the one perpetrated by Bernard Madoff. Madoff was an elite New York investment fund manager who was highly regarded by securities regulators. Investors flocked to him because he delivered very steady returns of between 10% and 15%, no matter whether the market was going up or going down. However, for many years, Madoff did not actually invest the cash that people gave to him. Instead, he was running a Ponzi scheme: He paid returns to existing investors using cash received from new investors. As long as the size of his investment fund continued to grow from new investments at a rate that exceeded the amounts that he needed to pay out in returns, Madoff was able to operate his fraud smoothly.

To conceal his misdeeds, Madoff fabricated false investment statements that were provided to investors. In addition, Madoff hired an auditor that never verified the accuracy of the investment records but automatically issued unqualified opinions each year. Although a competing fund manager warned the SEC a number of times over a nearly 10-year period that he thought Madoff was engaged in fraud, the SEC never aggressively investigated the allegations. Investors, many of which were charitable organizations, lost more than $18 billion. Madoff was sentenced to a jail term of 150 years.

How was Madoff able to conceal such a giant fraud? (Go to **WileyPLUS** for this answer and additional questions.)

DO IT! 3 Bank Reconciliation

Sally Kist owns Linen Kist Fabrics. Sally asks you to explain how she should treat the following reconciling items when reconciling the company's bank account: (1) a debit memorandum for an NSF check, (2) a credit memorandum for a note collected by the bank, (3) outstanding checks, and (4) a deposit in transit.

Solution

Sally should treat the reconciling items as follows.
(1) NSF check: Deduct from balance per books.
(2) Collection of note: Add to balance per books.
(3) Outstanding checks: Deduct from balance per bank.
(4) Deposit in transit: Add to balance per bank.

Related exercise material: **BE8-11, BE8-12, BE8-13, BE8-14, E8-9, E8-10, E8-11, E8-12, E8-13, and DO IT! 8-3.**

Action Plan

✔ Understand the purpose of a bank reconciliation.

✔ Identify time lags and explain how they cause reconciling items.

LEARNING OBJECTIVE 4

Explain the reporting of cash.

Cash consists of coins, currency (paper money), checks, money orders, and money on hand or on deposit in a bank or similar depository. Companies report cash in two different statements: the balance sheet and the statement of cash flows. The balance sheet reports the amount of cash available at a given point in time. The statement of cash flows shows the sources and uses of cash during a period of time. The statement of cash flows was introduced in Chapter 1 and will be discussed in much detail in Chapter 17. In this section, we discuss some important points regarding the presentation of cash in the balance sheet.

When presented in a balance sheet, cash on hand, cash in banks, and petty cash are often combined and reported simply as **Cash**. Because it is the most liquid asset owned by the company, cash is listed first in the current assets section of the balance sheet.

Cash Equivalents

Many companies use the designation "Cash and cash equivalents" in reporting cash. (See Illustration 8-14 for an example.) **Cash equivalents** are short-term, highly liquid investments that are both:

1. Readily convertible to known amounts of cash, and
2. So near their maturity that their market value is relatively insensitive to changes in interest rates. Generally, only investments with original maturities of three months or less qualify under this definition.

Real World

DELTA AIR LINES, INC.
Balance Sheet (partial)
December 31, 2013 (in millions)

Assets	
Current assets	
Cash and cash equivalents	**$2,844**
Short-term investments	959
Restricted cash	**122**

Illustration 8-14
Balance sheet presentation of cash

Examples of cash equivalents are Treasury bills, commercial paper (short-term corporate notes), and money market funds. All typically are purchased with cash that is in excess of immediate needs.

ETHICS NOTE

Recently, some companies were forced to restate their financial statements because they had too broadly interpreted which types of investments could be treated as cash equivalents. By reporting these items as cash equivalents, the companies made themselves look more liquid.

Occasionally, a company will have a net negative balance in its bank account. In this case, the company should report the negative balance among current liabilities. For example, farm equipment manufacturer Ag-Chem recently reported "Checks outstanding in excess of cash balances" of $2,145,000 among its current liabilities.

Restricted Cash

A company may have **restricted cash**, cash that is not available for general use but rather is restricted for a special purpose. For example, landfill companies are often required to maintain a fund of restricted cash to ensure they will have adequate resources to cover closing and clean-up costs at the end of a landfill site's useful life. McKesson Corp. recently reported restricted cash of $962 million to be paid out as the result of investor lawsuits.

Cash restricted in use should be reported separately on the balance sheet as restricted cash. If the company expects to use the restricted cash within the next year, it reports the amount as a current asset. When this is not the case, it reports the restricted funds as a noncurrent asset.

Illustration 8-14 shows restricted cash reported in the financial statements of Delta Air Lines. The company is required to maintain restricted cash as collateral to support insurance obligations related to workers' compensation claims. Delta does not have access to these funds for general use, and so it must report them separately, rather than as part of cash and cash equivalents.

DO IT! 4 Reporting Cash

Indicate whether each of the following statements is true or false.

1. Cash and cash equivalents are comprised of coins, currency (paper money), money orders, and NSF checks.
2. Restricted cash is classified as either a current asset or noncurrent asset, depending on the circumstances.
3. A company may have a negative balance in its bank account. In this case, it should offset this negative balance against cash and cash equivalents on the balance sheet.
4. Because cash and cash equivalents often includes short-term investments, accounts receivable should be reported as the first item on the balance sheet.

Action Plan

✔ Understand how companies present cash and restricted cash on the balance sheet.

✔ Review the designations of cash equivalents and restricted cash, and how companies typically handle them.

Solution

1. False. NSF checks should be reported as receivables, not cash and cash equivalents. **2.** True. **3.** False. Companies that have a negative balance in their bank accounts should report the negative balance as a current liability. **4.** False. Cash equivalents are readily convertible to known amounts of cash, and so near maturity (less than 3 months) that they are considered more liquid than accounts receivable and therefore are reported before accounts receivable on the balance sheet.

Related exercise material: **E8-14, E8-15, and DO IT! 8-4.**

REVIEW AND PRACTICE

LEARNING OBJECTIVES REVIEW

1 Discuss fraud and the principles of internal control. A fraud is a dishonest act by an employee that results in personal benefit to the employee at a cost to the employer. The fraud triangle refers to the three factors that contribute to fraudulent activity by employees: opportunity, financial pressure, and rationalization. Internal control consists of all the related methods and measures adopted within an organization to safeguard its assets, enhance the reliability of its accounting records, increase efficiency of operations, and ensure compliance with laws and regulations.

The principles of internal control are establishment of responsibility, segregation of duties, documentation procedures, physical controls, independent internal verification, and human resource controls such as bonding and requiring employees to take vacations.

2 Apply internal control principles to cash. Internal controls over cash receipts include (a) designating specific personnel to handle cash; (b) assigning different individuals to receive cash, record cash, and maintain custody of cash; (c) using remittance advices for mail receipts, cash register tapes for over-the-counter receipts, and deposit slips for bank deposits; (d) using company safes and bank vaults to store cash with access limited to authorized personnel, and using cash registers in executing over-the-counter receipts; (e) making independent daily counts of register receipts and daily comparison of total receipts with total deposits; and (f) bonding personnel that handle cash and requiring them to take vacations.

Internal controls over cash disbursements include (a) having specific individuals such as the treasurer authorized to sign checks and approve vendors; (b) assigning different individuals to approve items for payment, make the payment, and record the payment; (c) using prenumbered checks and accounting for all checks, with each check supported by an approved invoice; (d) storing blank checks in a safe or vault with access restricted to authorized personnel, and using a check-writing machine to imprint amounts on checks; (e) comparing each check with the approved invoice before issuing the check, and making monthly reconciliations of bank and book balances; and (f) bonding personnel who handle cash, requiring employees to take vacations, and conducting background checks.

Companies operate a petty cash fund to pay relatively small amounts of cash. They must establish the fund, make payments from the fund, and replenish the fund when the cash in the fund reaches a minimum level.

3 Identify the control features of a bank account. A bank account contributes to good internal control by providing physical controls for the storage of cash. It minimizes the amount of currency that a company must keep on hand, and it creates a double record of a depositor's bank transactions. It is customary to reconcile the balance per books and balance per bank to their adjusted balances. The steps in the reconciling process are to determine deposits in transit, outstanding checks, errors by the depositor or the bank, and unrecorded bank memoranda.

4 Explain the reporting of cash. Companies list cash first in the current assets section of the balance sheet. In some cases, they report cash together with cash equivalents. Cash restricted for a special purpose is reported separately as a current asset or as a noncurrent asset, depending on when the cash is expected to be used.

GLOSSARY REVIEW

Bank reconciliation The process of comparing the bank's balance of an account with the company's balance and explaining any differences to make them agree. (p. 373).

Bank service charge A fee charged by a bank for the use of its services. (p. 376).

Bank statement A monthly statement from the bank that shows the depositor's bank transactions and balances. (p. 375).

Bonding Obtaining insurance protection against theft by employees. (p. 363).

Cash Resources that consist of coins, currency, checks, money orders, and money on hand or on deposit in a bank or similar depository. (p. 381).

Cash equivalents Short-term, highly liquid investments that can be converted to a specific amount of cash. (p. 381).

Check A written order signed by a bank depositor, directing the bank to pay a specified sum of money to a designated recipient. (p. 374).

Deposits in transit Deposits recorded by the depositor but not yet recorded by the bank. (p. 377).

Electronic funds transfer (EFT) A disbursement system that uses wire, telephone, or computers to transfer funds from one location to another. (p. 380).

Fraud A dishonest act by an employee that results in personal benefit to the employee at a cost to the employer. (p. 356).

Fraud triangle The three factors that contribute to fraudulent activity by employees: opportunity, financial pressure, and rationalization. (p. 356).

Internal auditors Company employees who continuously evaluate the effectiveness of the company's internal control system. (p. 363).

Internal control A process designed to provide reasonable assurance regarding the achievement of objectives related to operations, reporting, and compliance. (p. 357).

NSF check A check that is not paid by a bank because of insufficient funds in a customer's bank account. (p. 376).

Outstanding checks Checks issued and recorded by a company but not yet paid by the bank. (p. 377).

Petty cash fund A cash fund used to pay relatively small amounts. (p. 370).

Restricted cash Cash that must be used for a special purpose. (p. 382).

Sarbanes-Oxley Act (SOX) Regulations passed by Congress to try to reduce unethical corporate behavior. (p. 356).

Voucher An authorization form prepared for each payment in a voucher system. (p. 369).

Voucher system A network of approvals by authorized individuals acting independently to ensure that all disbursements by check are proper. (p. 369).

PRACTICE MULTIPLE-CHOICE QUESTIONS

(LO 1) **1.** Which of the following is **not** an element of the fraud triangle?
(a) Rationalization.
(b) Financial pressure.
(c) Segregation of duties.
(d) Opportunity.

(LO 1) **2.** An organization uses internal control to enhance the accuracy and reliability of accounting records and to:
(a) safeguard assets.
(b) prevent fraud.
(c) produce correct financial statements.
(d) deter employee dishonesty.

(LO 1) **3.** Which of the following was **not** a result of the Sarbanes-Oxley Act?
(a) Companies must file financial statements with the Internal Revenue Service.
(b) All publicly traded companies must maintain adequate internal controls.
(c) The Public Company Accounting Oversight Board was created to establish auditing standards and regulate auditor activity.
(d) Corporate executives and board of directors must ensure that controls are reliable and effective, and they can be fined or imprisoned for failure to do so.

(LO 1) **4.** The principles of internal control do **not** include:
(a) establishment of responsibility.
(b) documentation procedures.
(c) management responsibility.
(d) independent internal verification.

(LO 1) **5.** Physical controls do **not** include:
(a) safes and vaults to store cash.
(b) independent bank reconciliations.
(c) locked warehouses for inventories.
(d) bank safety deposit boxes for important papers.

(LO 1) **6.** Which of the following control activities is **not** relevant when a company uses a computerized (rather than manual) accounting system?
(a) Establishment of responsibility.
(b) Segregation of duties.
(c) Independent internal verification.
(d) All of these control activities are relevant to a computerized system.

(LO 2) **7.** Permitting only designated personnel to handle cash receipts is an application of the principle of:
(a) segregation of duties.
(b) establishment of responsibility.
(c) independent internal verification.
(d) human resource controls.

8. The use of prenumbered checks in disbursing cash is an application of the principle of: (LO 2)
(a) establishment of responsibility.
(b) segregation of duties.
(c) physical controls.
(d) documentation procedures.

9. A company writes a check to replenish a $100 petty cash fund when the fund contains receipts of $94 and $4 in cash. In recording the check, the company should: (LO 2)
(a) debit Cash Over and Short for $2.
(b) debit Petty Cash for $94.
(c) credit Cash for $94.
(d) credit Petty Cash for $2.

10. The control features of a bank account do **not** include: (LO 3)
(a) having bank auditors verify the correctness of the bank balance per books.
(b) minimizing the amount of cash that must be kept on hand.
(c) providing a double record of all bank transactions.
(d) safeguarding cash by using a bank as a depository.

11. In a bank reconciliation, deposits in transit are: (LO 3)
(a) deducted from the book balance.
(b) added to the book balance.
(c) added to the bank balance.
(d) deducted from the bank balance.

12. The reconciling item in a bank reconciliation that will result in an adjusting entry by the depositor is: (LO 3)
(a) outstanding checks.
(b) deposit in transit.
(c) a bank error.
(d) bank service charges.

13. Which of the following items in a cash drawer at November 30 is **not** cash? (LO 4)
(a) Money orders.
(b) Coins and currency.
(c) An NSF check.
(d) A customer check dated November 28.

14. Which of the following statements correctly describes the reporting of cash? (LO 4)
(a) Cash cannot be combined with cash equivalents.
(b) Restricted cash funds may be combined with cash.
(c) Cash is listed first in the current assets section.
(d) Restricted cash funds cannot be reported as a current asset.

Solutions

1. (c) Segregation of duties is not an element of the fraud triangle. The other choices are fraud triangle elements.

2. (a) Safeguarding assets is one of the purposes of using internal control. The other choices are incorrect because while internal control can help to (b) prevent fraud, (c) produce correct financial statements, and (d) deter employee dishonesty, it is not one of the main purposes of using it.

3. (a) Filing financial statements with the IRS is not a result of the Sarbanes-Oxley Act (SOX); SOX focuses on the prevention or detection of fraud. The other choices are results of SOX.

4. (c) Management responsibility is not one of the principles of internal control. The other choices are true statements.

5. (b) Independent bank reconciliations are not a physical control. The other choices are true statements.

6. (d) Establishment of responsibility, segregation of duties and independent internal verification are all relevant to a computerized system.

7. (b) Permitting only designated personnel to handle cash receipts is an application of the principle of establishment of responsibility, not (a) segregation of duties, (c) independent internal verification, or (d) human resource controls.

8. (d) The use of prenumbered checks in disbursing cash is an application of the principle of documentation procedures, not (a) establishment of responsibility, (b) segregation of duties, or (c) physical controls.

9. (a) When this check is recorded, the company should debit Cash Over and Short for the shortage of $2 (total of the receipts plus cash in the drawer ($98) versus $100), not (b) debit Petty Cash for $94, (c) credit Cash for $94, or (d) credit Petty Cash for $2.

10. (a) Having bank auditors verify the correctness of the bank balance per books is not one of the control features of a bank account. The other choices are true statements.

11. (c) Deposits in transit are added to the bank balance on a bank reconciliation, not (a) deducted from the book balance, (b) added to the book balance, or (d) deducted from the bank balance.

12. (d) Because the depositor does not know the amount of the bank service charges until the bank statements is received, an adjusting entry must be made when the statement is received. The other choices are incorrect because (a) outstanding checks do not require an adjusting entry by the depositor because the checks have already been recorded in the depositor's books, (b) deposits in transit do not require an adjusting entry by the depositor because the deposits have already been recorded in the depositor's books, and (c) bank errors do not require an adjusting entry by the depositor, but the depositor does need to inform the bank of the error so it can be corrected.

13. (c) An NSF check should not be considered cash. The other choices are true statements.

14. (c) Cash is listed first in the current assets section. The other choices are incorrect because (a) cash and cash equivalents can be appropriately combined when reporting cash on the balance sheet, (b) restricted cash is not to be combined with cash when reporting cash on the balance sheet, and (d) restricted funds can be reported as current assets if they will be used within one year.

PRACTICE EXERCISES

Indicate good or weak internal control procedures.

(LO 1, 2)

1. Listed below are five procedures followed by Viel Company.

1. Total cash receipts are compared to bank deposits daily by Vonda Marshall, who receives cash over the counter.
2. Employees write down hours worked and turn in the sheet to the cashier's office.
3. As a cost-saving measure, employees do not take vacations.
4. Only the sales manager can approve credit sales.
5. Three different employees are assigned one task each related to inventory: ship goods to customers, bill customers, and receive payment from customers.

Instructions

Indicate whether each procedure is an example of good internal control or of weak internal control. If it is an example of good internal control, indicate which internal control principle is being followed. If it is an example of weak internal control, indicate which internal control principles is violated. Use the table below.

Procedure	IC Good or Weak?	Related Internal Control Principle
1.		
2.		
3.		
4.		
5.		

Solution

1. Procedure	IC Good or Weak?	Related Internal Control Principle
1.	Weak	Independent internal verification
2.	Weak	Physical controls
3.	Weak	Human resource controls
4.	Good	Establishment of responsibility
5.	Good	Segregation of duties

Prepare bank reconciliation and adjusting entries.

(LO 3)

2. The information below relates to the Cash account in the ledger of Hillfarms Company.

Balance June 1—$9,947; Cash deposited—$37,120.
Balance June 30—$10,094; Checks written—$36,973.

The June bank statement shows a balance of $9,525 on June 30 and the following memoranda.

Credits		Debits	
Collection of $850 note plus interest $34	$884	NSF check: R. Doll	$245
Interest earned on checking accounts	$26	Safety deposit box rent	$35

At June 30, deposits in transit were $2,581, and outstanding checks totaled $1,382.

Instructions

(a) Prepare the bank reconciliation at June 30.

(b) Prepare the adjusting entries at June 30, assuming (1) the NFS check was from a customer on account, and (2) no interest had been accrued on the note.

Solution

2. (a)

HILLFARMS COMPANY
Bank Reconciliation
June 30

Cash balance per bank statement		$ 9,525
Add: Deposits in transit		2,581
		12,106
Less: Outstanding checks		1,382
Adjusted cash balance per bank		$10,724
Cash balance per books		$10,094
Add: Collection of note receivable ($850 + $34)	$884	
Interest earned	26	910
		11,004
Less: NSF check	245	
Safety deposit box rent	35	280
Adjusted cash balance per books		$10,724

(b)

Date	Account	Debit	Credit
June 30	Cash	884	
	Notes Receivable		850
	Interest Revenue		34
30	Cash	26	
	Interest Revenue		26
30	Miscellaneous Expense	35	
	Cash		35
30	Accounts Receivable (R. Doll)	245	
	Cash		245

PRACTICE PROBLEM

Prepare bank reconciliation and journalize entries.

(LO 3)

Poorten Company's bank statement for May 2017 shows the following data.

Balance 5/1	$12,650	Balance 5/31	$14,280
Debit memorandum:		Credit memorandum:	
NSF check	$175	Collection of note receivable	$505

The cash balance per books at May 31 is $13,319. Your review of the data reveals the following.

1. The NSF check was from Copple Co., a customer.
2. The note collected by the bank was a $500, 3-month, 12% note. The bank charged a $10 collection fee. No interest has been accrued.
3. Outstanding checks at May 31 total $2,410.
4. Deposits in transit at May 31 total $1,752.
5. A Poorten Company check for $352, dated May 10, cleared the bank on May 25. The company recorded this check, which was a payment on account, for $325.

Instructions

(a) Prepare a bank reconciliation at May 31.

(b) Journalize the entries required by the reconciliation.

Solution

(a)

POORTEN COMPANY
Bank Reconciliation
May 31, 2017

Cash balance per bank statement		$14,280
Add: Deposits in transit		1,752
		16,032
Less: Outstanding checks		2,410
Adjusted cash balance per bank		$13,622
Cash balance per books		$13,319
Add: Collection of note receivable $500, plus $15 interest, less collection fee $10		505
		13,824
Less: NSF check	$175	
Error in recording check	27	202
Adjusted cash balance per books		$13,622

(b)

Date	Account	Debit	Credit
May 31	Cash	505	
	Miscellaneous Expense	10	
	Notes Receivable		500
	Interest Revenue		15
	(To record collection of note by bank)		
31	Accounts Receivable—Copple Co.	175	
	Cash		175
	(To record NSF check from Copple Co.)		
31	Accounts Payable	27	
	Cash		27
	(To correct error in recording check)		

WileyPLUS Brief Exercises, Exercises, DO IT! Exercises, and Problems and many additional resources are available for practice in WileyPLUS

QUESTIONS

1. A local bank reported that it lost $150,000 as the result of an employee fraud. Edward Jasso is not clear on what is meant by an "employee fraud." Explain the meaning of fraud to Edward and give an example of frauds that might occur at a bank.
2. Fraud experts often say that there are three primary factors that contribute to employee fraud. Identify the three factors and explain what is meant by each.
3. Identify and describe the five components of a good internal control system.
4. "Internal control is concerned only with enhancing the accuracy of the accounting records." Do you agree? Explain.
5. What principles of internal control apply to most organizations?
6. At the corner grocery store, all sales clerks make change out of one cash register drawer. Is this a violation of internal control? Why?
7. Liz Kelso is reviewing the principle of segregation of duties. What are the two common applications of this principle?
8. How do documentation procedures contribute to good internal control?
9. What internal control objectives are met by physical controls?
10. (a) Explain the control principle of independent internal verification. (b) What practices are important in applying this principle?
11. The management of Nickle Company asks you, as the company accountant, to explain (a) the concept of reasonable assurance in internal control and (b) the importance of the human factor in internal control.
12. Riverside Fertilizer Co. owns the following assets at the balance sheet date.

Cash in bank savings account	$ 8,000
Cash on hand	850
Cash refund due from the IRS	1,000
Checking account balance	14,000
Postdated checks	500

What amount should Riverside report as cash in the balance sheet?

13. What principle(s) of internal control is (are) involved in making daily cash counts of over-the-counter receipts?
14. Seaton Department Stores has just installed new electronic cash registers in its stores. How do cash registers improve internal control over cash receipts?
15. At Kellum Wholesale Company, two mail clerks open all mail receipts. How does this strengthen internal control?
16. "To have maximum effective internal control over cash disbursements, all payments should be made by check." Is this true? Explain.
17. Ken Deangelo Company's internal controls over cash disbursements provide for the treasurer to sign checks imprinted by a check-writing machine in indelible ink after comparing the check with the approved invoice. Identify the internal control principles that are present in these controls.
18. How do the principles of (a) physical controls and (b) documentation controls apply to cash disbursements?
19. (a) What is a voucher system? (b) What principles of internal control apply to a voucher system?
20. What is the essential feature of an electronic funds transfer (EFT) procedure?
21. (a) Identify the three activities that pertain to a petty cash fund, and indicate an internal control principle that is applicable to each activity. (b) When are journal entries required in the operation of a petty cash fund?
22. "The use of a bank contributes significantly to good internal control over cash." Is this true? Why or why not?
23. Anna Korte is confused about the lack of agreement between the cash balance per books and the balance per bank. Explain the causes for the lack of agreement to Anna, and give an example of each cause.
24. What are the four steps involved in finding differences between the balance per books and balance per bank?
25. Heather Kemp asks your help concerning an NSF check. Explain to Heather (a) what an NSF check is, (b) how it is treated in a bank reconciliation, and (c) whether it will require an adjusting entry.
26. (a) "Cash equivalents are the same as cash." Do you agree? Explain. (b) How should restricted cash funds be reported on the balance sheet?
27. At what amount does **Apple** report cash and cash equivalents in its 2013 consolidated balance sheet?

BRIEF EXERCISES

Identify fraud triangle concepts.

(LO 1)

BE8-1 Match each situation with the fraud triangle factor—opportunity, financial pressure, or rationalization—that best describes it.

1. An employee's monthly credit card payments are nearly 75% of his or her monthly earnings.
2. An employee earns minimum wage at a firm that has reported record earnings for each of the last five years.

3. An employee has an expensive gambling habit.
4. An employee has check-writing and signing responsibilities for a small company, as well as reconciling the bank account.

BE8-2 Shelly Eckert has prepared the following list of statements about internal control.

Indicate internal control concepts.

(LO 1)

1. One of the objectives of internal control is to safeguard assets from employee theft, robbery, and unauthorized use.
2. One of the objectives of internal control is to enhance the accuracy and reliability of the accounting records.
3. No laws require U.S. corporations to maintain an adequate system of internal control.

Identify each statement as true or false. If false, indicate how to correct the statement.

BE8-3 Jessica Mahan is the new owner of Penny Parking. She has heard about internal control but is not clear about its importance for her business. Explain to Jessica the four purposes of internal control and give her one application of each purpose for Penny Parking.

Explain the importance of internal control.

(LO 1)

BE8-4 The internal control procedures in Valentine Company provide that:

Identify internal control principles.

(LO 1)

1. Employees who have physical custody of assets do not have access to the accounting records.
2. Each month, the assets on hand are compared to the accounting records by an internal auditor.
3. A prenumbered shipping document is prepared for each shipment of goods to customers.

Identify the principles of internal control that are being followed.

BE8-5 Rosenquist Company has the following internal control procedures over cash receipts. Identify the internal control principle that is applicable to each procedure.

Identify the internal control principles applicable to cash receipts.

(LO 2)

1. All over-the-counter receipts are entered in cash registers.
2. All cashiers are bonded.
3. Daily cash counts are made by cashier department supervisors.
4. The duties of receiving cash, recording cash, and custody of cash are assigned to different individuals.
5. Only cashiers may operate cash registers.

BE8-6 The cash register tape for Bluestem Industries reported sales of $6,871.50. Record the journal entry that would be necessary for each of the following situations. (a) Cash to be accounted for exceeds cash on hand by $50.75. (b) Cash on hand exceeds cash to be accounted for by $28.32.

Make journal entries for cash overage and shortfall.

(LO 2)

BE8-7 While examining cash receipts information, the accounting department determined the following information: opening cash balance $160, cash on hand $1,125.74, and cash sales per register tape $980.83. Prepare the required journal entry based upon the cash count sheet.

Make journal entry using cash count sheet.

(LO 2)

BE8-8 Pennington Company has the following internal control procedures over cash disbursements. Identify the internal control principle that is applicable to each procedure.

Identify the internal control principles applicable to cash disbursements.

(LO 2)

1. Company checks are prenumbered.
2. The bank statement is reconciled monthly by an internal auditor.
3. Blank checks are stored in a safe in the treasurer's office.
4. Only the treasurer or assistant treasurer may sign checks.
5. Check-signers are not allowed to record cash disbursement transactions.

BE8-9 On March 20, Dody's petty cash fund of $100 is replenished when the fund contains $9 in cash and receipts for postage $52, freight-out $26, and travel expense $10. Prepare the journal entry to record the replenishment of the petty cash fund.

Prepare entry to replenish a petty cash fund.

(LO 2)

BE8-10 Lance Bachman is uncertain about the control features of a bank account. Explain the control benefits of (a) a check and (b) a bank statement.

Identify the control features of a bank account.

(LO 3)

Indicate location of reconciling items in a bank reconciliation.
(LO 3)

BE8-11 The following reconciling items are applicable to the bank reconciliation for Ellington Company: (1) outstanding checks, (2) bank debit memorandum for service charge, (3) bank credit memorandum for collecting a note for the depositor, and (4) deposits in transit. Indicate how each item should be shown on a bank reconciliation.

Identify reconciling items that require adjusting entries.
(LO 3)

BE8-12 Using the data in BE8-11, indicate (a) the items that will result in an adjustment to the depositor's records and (b) why the other items do not require adjustment.

Prepare partial bank reconciliation.
(LO 3)

BE8-13 At July 31, Ramirez Company has the following bank information: cash balance per bank $7,420, outstanding checks $762, deposits in transit $1,620, and a bank service charge $20. Determine the adjusted cash balance per bank at July 31.

Prepare partial bank reconciliation.
(LO 3)

BE8-14 At August 31, Pratt Company has a cash balance per books of $9,500 and the following additional data from the bank statement: charge for printing Pratt Company checks $35, interest earned on checking account balance $40, and outstanding checks $800. Determine the adjusted cash balance per books at August 31.

Explain the statement presentation of cash balances.
(LO 4)

BE8-15 Zhang Company has the following cash balances: Cash in Bank $15,742, Payroll Bank Account $6,000, and Plant Expansion Fund Cash $25,000 to be used two years from now. Explain how each balance should be reported on the balance sheet.

DO IT! Exercises

Identify violations of control activities.
(LO 1)

DO IT! 8-1 Identify which control activity is violated in each of the following situations, and explain how the situation creates an opportunity for fraud or inappropriate accounting practices.

1. Once a month, the sales department sends sales invoices to the accounting department to be recorded.
2. Leah Hutcherson orders merchandise for Rice Lake Company; she also receives merchandise and authorizes payment for merchandise.
3. Several clerks at Great Foods use the same cash register drawer.

Design system of internal control over cash receipts.
(LO 2)

DO IT! 8-2a Gary Stanten is concerned with control over mail receipts at Gary's Sporting Goods. All mail receipts are opened by Al Krane. Al sends the checks to the accounting department, where they are stamped "For Deposit Only." The accounting department records and deposits the mail receipts weekly. Gary asks for your help in installing a good system of internal control over mail receipts.

Make journal entries for petty cash fund.
(LO 2)

DO IT! 8-2b Wilkinson Company established a $100 petty cash fund on August 1. On August 31, the fund had $7 cash remaining and petty cash receipts for postage $31, office supplies $42, and miscellaneous expense $16. Prepare journal entries to establish the fund on August 1 and replenish the fund on August 31.

Explain treatment of items in bank reconciliation.
(LO 3)

DO IT! 8-3 Roger Richman owns Richman Blankets. He asks you to explain how he should treat the following reconciling items when reconciling the company's bank account.

1. Outstanding checks.
2. A deposit in transit.
3. The bank charged to the company account a check written by another company.
4. A debit memorandum for a bank service charge.

Analyze statements about the reporting of cash.
(LO 4)

DO IT! 8-4 Indicate whether each of the following statements is true or false.

1. A company has the following assets at the end of the year: cash on hand $40,000, cash refund due from customer $30,000, and checking account balance $22,000. Cash and cash equivalents is therefore $62,000.
2. A company that has received NSF checks should report these checks as a current liability on the balance sheet.
3. Restricted cash that is a current asset is reported as part of cash and cash equivalents.
4. A company has cash in the bank of $50,000, petty cash of $400, and stock investments of $100,000. Total cash and cash equivalents is therefore $50,400.

EXERCISES

E8-1 Eve Herschel is the owner of Herschel's Pizza. Herschel's is operated strictly on a carryout basis. Customers pick up their orders at a counter where a clerk exchanges the pizza for cash. While at the counter, the customer can see other employees making the pizzas and the large ovens in which the pizzas are baked.

Identify the principles of internal control.

(LO 1)

Instructions

Identify the six principles of internal control and give an example of each principle that you might observe when picking up your pizza. (*Note:* It may not be possible to observe all the principles.)

E8-2 The following control procedures are used at Torres Company for over-the-counter cash receipts.

Identify internal control weaknesses over cash receipts and suggest improvements.

(LO 1, 2)

1. To minimize the risk of robbery, cash in excess of $100 is stored in an unlocked attaché case in the stock room until it is deposited in the bank.
2. All over-the-counter receipts are processed by three clerks who use a cash register with a single cash drawer.
3. The company accountant makes the bank deposit and then records the day's receipts.
4. At the end of each day, the total receipts are counted by the cashier on duty and reconciled to the cash register total.
5. Cashiers are experienced; they are not bonded.

Instructions

(a) For each procedure, explain the weakness in internal control, and identify the control principle that is violated.

(b) For each weakness, suggest a change in procedure that will result in good internal control.

E8-3 The following control procedures are used in Mendy Lang's Boutique Shoppe for cash disbursements.

Identify internal control weaknesses over cash disbursements and suggest improvements.

(LO 1, 2)

1. The company accountant prepares the bank reconciliation and reports any discrepancies to the owner.
2. The store manager personally approves all payments before signing and issuing checks.
3. Each week, 100 company checks are left in an unmarked envelope on a shelf behind the cash register.
4. After payment, bills are filed in a paid invoice folder.
5. The company checks are unnumbered.

Instructions

(a) For each procedure, explain the weakness in internal control, and identify the internal control principle that is violated.

(b) For each weakness, suggest a change in the procedure that will result in good internal control.

E8-4 At Danner Company, checks are not prenumbered because both the purchasing agent and the treasurer are authorized to issue checks. Each signer has access to unissued checks kept in an unlocked file cabinet. The purchasing agent pays all bills pertaining to goods purchased for resale. Prior to payment, the purchasing agent determines that the goods have been received and verifies the mathematical accuracy of the vendor's invoice. After payment, the invoice is filed by the vendor name, and the purchasing agent records the payment in the cash disbursements journal. The treasurer pays all other bills following approval by authorized employees. After payment, the treasurer stamps all bills PAID, files them by payment date, and records the checks in the cash disbursements journal. Danner Company maintains one checking account that is reconciled by the treasurer.

Identify internal control weaknesses for cash disbursements and suggest improvements.

(LO 2)

Instructions

(a) List the weaknesses in internal control over cash disbursements.

(b) Write a memo to the company treasurer indicating your recommendations for improvement.

Indicate whether procedure is good or weak internal control.

(LO 1, 2)

E8-5 Listed below are five procedures followed by Eikenberry Company.

1. Several individuals operate the cash register using the same register drawer.
2. A monthly bank reconciliation is prepared by someone who has no other cash responsibilities.
3. Joe Cockrell writes checks and also records cash payment journal entries.
4. One individual orders inventory, while a different individual authorizes payments.
5. Unnumbered sales invoices from credit sales are forwarded to the accounting department every four weeks for recording.

Instructions

Indicate whether each procedure is an example of good internal control or of weak internal control. If it is an example of good internal control, indicate which internal control principle is being followed. If it is an example of weak internal control, indicate which internal control principle is violated. Use the table below.

Procedure	IC Good or Weak?	Related Internal Control Principle
1.		
2.		
3.		
4.		
5.		

Indicate whether procedure is good or weak internal control.

(LO 1, 2)

E8-6 Listed below are five procedures followed by Gilmore Company.

1. Employees are required to take vacations.
2. Any member of the sales department can approve credit sales.
3. Paul Jaggard ships goods to customers, bills customers, and receives payment from customers.
4. Total cash receipts are compared to bank deposits daily by someone who has no other cash responsibilities.
5. Time clocks are used for recording time worked by employees.

Instructions

Indicate whether each procedure is an example of good internal control or of weak internal control. If it is an example of good internal control, indicate which internal control principle is being followed. If it is an example of weak internal control, indicate which internal control principle is violated. Use the table below.

Procedure	IC Good or Weak?	Related Internal Control Principle
1.		
2.		
3.		
4.		
5.		

Prepare journal entries for a petty cash fund.

(LO 2)

E8-7 Setterstrom Company established a petty cash fund on May 1, cashing a check for \$100. The company reimbursed the fund on June 1 and July 1 with the following results.

June 1: Cash in fund \$1.75. Receipts: delivery expense \$31.25, postage expense \$39.00, and miscellaneous expense \$25.00.
July 1: Cash in fund \$3.25. Receipts: delivery expense \$21.00, entertainment expense \$51.00, and miscellaneous expense \$24.75.

On July 10, Setterstrom increased the fund from \$100 to \$130.

Instructions

Prepare journal entries for Setterstrom Company for May 1, June 1, July 1, and July 10.

Prepare journal entries for a petty cash fund.

(LO 2)

E8-8 Horvath Company uses an imprest petty cash system. The fund was established on March 1 with a balance of \$100. During March, the following petty cash receipts were found in the petty cash box.

Date	Receipt No.	For	Amount
3/5	1	Stamp Inventory	$39
7	2	Freight-Out	21
9	3	Miscellaneous Expense	6
11	4	Travel Expense	24
14	5	Miscellaneous Expense	5

The fund was replenished on March 15 when the fund contained $2 in cash. On March 20, the amount in the fund was increased to $175.

Instructions

Journalize the entries in March that pertain to the operation of the petty cash fund.

Prepare bank reconciliation and adjusting entries.

(LO 3)

E8-9 Don Wyatt is unable to reconcile the bank balance at January 31. Don's reconciliation is as follows.

Cash balance per bank	$3,560.20
Add: NSF check	490.00
Less: Bank service charge	25.00
Adjusted balance per bank	$4,025.20
Cash balance per books	$3,875.20
Less: Deposits in transit	530.00
Add: Outstanding checks	730.00
Adjusted balance per books	$4,075.20

Instructions

(a) Prepare a correct bank reconciliation.
(b) Journalize the entries required by the reconciliation.

Determine outstanding checks.

(LO 3)

E8-10 On April 30, the bank reconciliation of Westbrook Company shows three outstanding checks: no. 254, $650; no. 255, $620; and no. 257, $410. The May bank statement and the May cash payments journal show the following.

Bank Statement — Checks Paid

Date	Check No.	Amount
5/4	254	$650
5/2	257	410
5/17	258	159
5/12	259	275
5/20	261	500
5/29	263	480
5/30	262	750

Cash Payments Journal — Checks Issued

Date	Check No.	Amount
5/2	258	$159
5/5	259	275
5/10	260	890
5/15	261	500
5/22	262	750
5/24	263	480
5/29	264	560

Instructions

Using Step 2 in the reconciliation procedure, list the outstanding checks at May 31.

Prepare bank reconciliation and adjusting entries.

(LO 3)

E8-11 The following information pertains to Crane Video Company.

1. Cash balance per bank, July 31, $7,263.
2. July bank service charge not recorded by the depositor $28.
3. Cash balance per books, July 31, $7,284.
4. Deposits in transit, July 31, $1,300.
5. Bank collected $700 note for Crane in July, plus interest $36, less fee $20. The collection has not been recorded by Crane, and no interest has been accrued.
6. Outstanding checks, July 31, $591.

Instructions

(a) Prepare a bank reconciliation at July 31.
(b) Journalize the adjusting entries at July 31 on the books of Crane Video Company.

Prepare bank reconciliation and adjusting entries.

(LO 3)

E8-12 The information below relates to the Cash account in the ledger of Minton Company.

Balance September 1—$17,150; Cash deposited—$64,000.
Balance September 30—$17,404; Checks written—$63,746.

The September bank statement shows a balance of $16,422 on September 30 and the following memoranda.

Credits		Debits	
Collection of $2,500 note plus interest $30	$2,530	NSF check: Richard Nance	$425
Interest earned on checking account	$45	Safety deposit box rent	$65

At September 30, deposits in transit were $5,450, and outstanding checks totaled $2,383.

Instructions

(a) Prepare the bank reconciliation at September 30.
(b) Prepare the adjusting entries at September 30, assuming (1) the NSF check was from a customer on account, and (2) no interest had been accrued on the note.

Compute deposits in transit and outstanding checks for two bank reconciliations.

(LO 3)

E8-13 The cash records of Dawes Company show the following four situations.

1. The June 30 bank reconciliation indicated that deposits in transit total $920. During July, the general ledger account Cash shows deposits of $15,750, but the bank statement indicates that only $15,600 in deposits were received during the month.
2. The June 30 bank reconciliation also reported outstanding checks of $680. During the month of July, Dawes Company's books show that $17,200 of checks were issued. The bank statement showed that $16,400 of checks cleared the bank in July.
3. In September, deposits per the bank statement totaled $26,700, deposits per books were $26,400, and deposits in transit at September 30 were $2,100.
4. In September, cash disbursements per books were $23,700, checks clearing the bank were $25,000, and outstanding checks at September 30 were $2,100.

There were no bank debit or credit memoranda. No errors were made by either the bank or Dawes Company.

Instructions

Answer the following questions.

(a) In situation (1), what were the deposits in transit at July 31?
(b) In situation (2), what were the outstanding checks at July 31?
(c) In situation (3), what were the deposits in transit at August 31?
(d) In situation (4), what were the outstanding checks at August 31?

Show presentation of cash in financial statements.

(LO 4)

E8-14 Wynn Company has recorded the following items in its financial records.

Cash in bank	$ 42,000
Cash in plant expansion fund	100,000
Cash on hand	12,000
Highly liquid investments	34,000
Petty cash	500
Receivables from customers	89,000
Stock investments	61,000

The highly liquid investments had maturities of 3 months or less when they were purchased. The stock investments will be sold in the next 6 to 12 months. The plant expansion project will begin in 3 years.

Instructions

(a) What amount should Wynn report as "Cash and cash equivalents" on its balance sheet?
(b) Where should the items not included in part (a) be reported on the balance sheet?

EXERCISES: SET B AND CHALLENGE EXERCISES

Visit the book's companion website, at **www.wiley.com/college/weygandt**, and choose the Student Companion site to access Exercises: Set B and Challenge Exercises.

PROBLEMS: SET A

Identify internal control principles over cash disbursements.

(LO 1, 2)

P8-1A Bolz Office Supply Company recently changed its system of internal control over cash disbursements. The system includes the following features.

Instead of being unnumbered and manually prepared, all checks must now be prenumbered and prepared by using the new accounts payable software purchased by the company. Before a check can be issued, each invoice must have the approval of Kathy Moon, the purchasing agent, and Robin Self, the receiving department supervisor. Checks must be signed by either Jennifer Edwards, the treasurer, or Rich Woodruff, the assistant treasurer. Before signing a check, the signer is expected to compare the amount of the check with the amount on the invoice.

After signing a check, the signer stamps the invoice PAID and inserts within the stamp, the date, check number, and amount of the check. The "paid" invoice is then sent to the accounting department for recording.

Blank checks are stored in a safe in the treasurer's office. The combination to the safe is known only by the treasurer and assistant treasurer. Each month, the bank statement is reconciled with the bank balance per books by the assistant chief accountant. All employees who handle or account for cash are bonded.

Instructions

Identify the internal control principles and their application to cash disbursements of Bolz Office Supply Company.

Journalize and post petty cash fund transactions.

(LO 2)

GLS

P8-2A Forney Company maintains a petty cash fund for small expenditures. The following transactions occurred over a 2-month period.

July	1	Established petty cash fund by writing a check on Scranton Bank for $200.
	15	Replenished the petty cash fund by writing a check for $196.00. On this date the fund consisted of $4.00 in cash and the following petty cash receipts: freight-out $92.00, postage expense $42.40, entertainment expense $46.60, and miscellaneous expense $11.20.
	31	Replenished the petty cash fund by writing a check for $192.00. At this date, the fund consisted of $8.00 in cash and the following petty cash receipts: freight-out $82.10, charitable contributions expense $45.00, postage expense $25.50, and miscellaneous expense $39.40.
Aug.	15	Replenished the petty cash fund by writing a check for $187.00. On this date, the fund consisted of $13.00 in cash and the following petty cash receipts: freight-out $77.60, entertainment expense $43.00, postage expense $33.00, and miscellaneous expense $37.00.
	16	Increased the amount of the petty cash fund to $300 by writing a check for $100.
	31	Replenished the petty cash fund by writing a check for $284.00. On this date, the fund consisted of $16 in cash and the following petty cash receipts: postage expense $140.00, travel expense $95.60, and freight-out $47.10.

Instructions

(a) Journalize the petty cash transactions.

(b) Post to the Petty Cash account.

(c) What internal control features exist in a petty cash fund?

(a) July 15, Cash short $3.80

(b) Aug. 31 balance $300

Prepare a bank reconciliation and adjusting entries.

(LO 3)

P8-3A On May 31, 2017, Reber Company had a cash balance per books of $6,781.50. The bank statement from New York State Bank on that date showed a balance of $6,404.60. A comparison of the statement with the Cash account revealed the following facts.

1. The statement included a debit memo of $40 for the printing of additional company checks.

2. Cash sales of $836.15 on May 12 were deposited in the bank. The cash receipts journal entry and the deposit slip were incorrectly made for $886.15. The bank credited Reber Company for the correct amount.
3. Outstanding checks at May 31 totaled $576.25. Deposits in transit were $2,416.15.
4. On May 18, the company issued check No. 1181 for $685 to Lynda Carsen on account. The check, which cleared the bank in May, was incorrectly journalized and posted by Reber Company for $658.
5. A $3,000 note receivable was collected by the bank for Reber Company on May 31 plus $80 interest. The bank charged a collection fee of $20. No interest has been accrued on the note.
6. Included with the cancelled checks was a check issued by Stiner Company to Ted Cress for $800 that was incorrectly charged to Reber Company by the bank.
7. On May 31, the bank statement showed an NSF charge of $680 for a check issued by Sue Allison, a customer, to Reber Company on account.

Instructions

(a) Adjusted cash balance per bank $9,044.50

(a) Prepare the bank reconciliation at May 31, 2017.
(b) Prepare the necessary adjusting entries for Reber Company at May 31, 2017.

Prepare a bank reconciliation and adjusting entries from detailed data.

(LO 3)

P8-4A The bank portion of the bank reconciliation for Langer Company at November 30, 2017, was as follows.

LANGER COMPANY
Bank Reconciliation
November 30, 2017

Cash balance per bank			$14,367.90
Add: Deposits in transit			2,530.20
			16,898.10
Less: Outstanding checks			
	Check Number	Check Amount	
	3451	$2,260.40	
	3470	720.10	
	3471	844.50	
	3472	1,426.80	
	3474	1,050.00	6,301.80
Adjusted cash balance per bank			$10,596.30

The adjusted cash balance per bank agreed with the cash balance per books at November 30. The December bank statement showed the following checks and deposits.

Bank Statement

Checks			Deposits	
Date	**Number**	**Amount**	**Date**	**Amount**
12-1	3451	$ 2,260.40	12-1	$ 2,530.20
12-2	3471	844.50	12-4	1,211.60
12-7	3472	1,426.80	12-8	2,365.10
12-4	3475	1,640.70	12-16	2,672.70
12-8	3476	1,300.00	12-21	2,945.00
12-10	3477	2,130.00	12-26	2,567.30
12-15	3479	3,080.00	12-29	2,836.00
12-27	3480	600.00	12-30	1,025.00
12-30	3482	475.50	Total	$18,152.90
12-29	3483	1,140.00		
12-31	3485	540.80		
	Total	$15,438.70		

The cash records per books for December showed the following.

Cash Payments Journal

Date	Number	Amount	Date	Number	Amount
12-1	3475	$1,640.70	12-20	3482	$ 475.50
12-2	3476	1,300.00	12-22	3483	1,140.00
12-2	3477	2,130.00	12-23	3484	798.00
12-4	3478	621.30	12-24	3485	450.80
12-8	3479	3,080.00	12-30	3486	889.50
12-10	3480	600.00	Total		$13,933.20
12-17	3481	807.40			

Cash Receipts Journal

Date	Amount
12-3	$ 1,211.60
12-7	2,365.10
12-15	2,672.70
12-20	2,954.00
12-25	2,567.30
12-28	2,836.00
12-30	1,025.00
12-31	1,690.40
Total	$17,322.10

The bank statement contained two memoranda:

1. A credit of $5,145 for the collection of a $5,000 note for Langer Company plus interest of $160 and less a collection fee of $15. Langer Company has not accrued any interest on the note.
2. A debit of $572.80 for an NSF check written by L. Rees, a customer. At December 31, the check had not been redeposited in the bank.

At December 31, the cash balance per books was $12,485.20, and the cash balance per the bank statement was $20,154.30. The bank did not make any errors, but two errors were made by Langer Company.

Instructions

(a) Using the four steps in the reconciliation procedure, prepare a bank reconciliation at December 31.

(a) Adjusted balance per books $16,958.40

(b) Prepare the adjusting entries based on the reconciliation. (*Hint:* The correction of any errors pertaining to recording checks should be made to Accounts Payable. The correction of any errors relating to recording cash receipts should be made to Accounts Receivable.)

Prepare a bank reconciliation and adjusting entries.

(LO 3)

P8-5A Rodriguez Company maintains a checking account at the Imura Bank. At July 31, selected data from the ledger balance and the bank statement are shown below.

Cash in Bank

	Per Books	Per Bank
Balance, July 1	$17,600	$15,800
July receipts	81,400	
July credits		83,470
July disbursements	77,150	
July debits		74,756
Balance, July 31	$21,850	$24,514

Analysis of the bank data reveals that the credits consist of $79,000 of July deposits and a credit memorandum of $4,470 for the collection of a $4,400 note plus interest revenue of $70. The July debits per bank consist of checks cleared $74,700 and a debit memorandum of $56 for printing additional company checks.

You also discover the following errors involving July checks. (1) A check for $230 to a creditor on account that cleared the bank in July was journalized and posted as $320. (2) A salary check to an employee for $255 was recorded by the bank for $155.

The June 30 bank reconciliation contained only two reconciling items: deposits in transit $8,000 and outstanding checks of $6,200.

Instructions

(a) Prepare a bank reconciliation at July 31, 2017.

(a) Adjusted balance per books $26,354

(b) Journalize the adjusting entries to be made by Rodriguez Company. Assume that interest on the note has not been accrued.

Identify internal control weaknesses in cash receipts and cash disbursements.

(LO 1, 2)

P8-6A Rondelli Middle School wants to raise money for a new sound system for its auditorium. The primary fund-raising event is a dance at which the famous disc jockey D.J. Sound will play classic and not-so-classic dance tunes. Matt Ballester, the music and theater instructor, has been given the responsibility for coordinating the fund-raising efforts. This is Matt's first experience with fund-raising. He decides to put the eighth-grade choir in charge of the event; he will be a relatively passive observer.

Matt had 500 unnumbered tickets printed for the dance. He left the tickets in a box on his desk and told the choir students to take as many tickets as they thought they could sell for $5 each. In order to ensure that no extra tickets would be floating around, he told them to dispose of any unsold tickets. When the students received payment for the tickets, they were to bring the cash back to Matt and he would put it in a locked box in his desk drawer.

Some of the students were responsible for decorating the gymnasium for the dance. Matt gave each of them a key to the money box and told them that if they took money out to purchase materials, they should put a note in the box saying how much they took and what it was used for. After 2 weeks the money box appeared to be getting full, so Matt asked Jeff Kenney to count the money, prepare a deposit slip, and deposit the money in a bank account Matt had opened.

The day of the dance, Matt wrote a check from the account to pay the DJ. D.J. Sound, however, said that he accepted only cash and did not give receipts. So Matt took $200 out of the cash box and gave it to D.J. At the dance, Matt had Sam Copper working at the entrance to the gymnasium, collecting tickets from students, and selling tickets to those who had not prepurchased them. Matt estimated that 400 students attended the dance.

The following day, Matt closed out the bank account, which had $250 in it, and gave that amount plus the $180 in the cash box to Principal Finke. Principal Finke seemed surprised that, after generating roughly $2,000 in sales, the dance netted only $430 in cash. Matt did not know how to respond.

Instructions

Identify as many internal control weaknesses as you can in this scenario, and suggest how each could be addressed.

PROBLEMS: SET B AND SET C

Visit the book's companion website, at **www.wiley.com/college/weygandt**, and choose the Student Companion site to access Problems: Set B and Set C.

COMPREHENSIVE PROBLEM

CP8 On December 1, 2017, Fullerton Company had the following account balances.

	Debit		Credit
Cash	$18,200	Accumulated Depreciation—	
Notes Receivable	2,200	Equipment	$ 3,000
Accounts Receivable	7,500	Accounts Payable	6,100
Inventory	16,000	Owner's Capital	64,400
Prepaid Insurance	1,600		$73,500
Equipment	28,000		
	$73,500		

During December, the company completed the following transactions.

Dec. 7 Received $3,600 cash from customers in payment of account (no discount allowed).
12 Purchased merchandise on account from Vance Co. $12,000, terms 1/10, n/30.
17 Sold merchandise on account $16,000, terms 2/10, n/30. The cost of the merchandise sold was $10,000.
19 Paid salaries $2,200.
22 Paid Vance Co. in full, less discount.
26 Received collections in full, less discounts, from customers billed on December 17.
31 Received $2,700 cash from customers in payment of account (no discount allowed).

Adjustment data:

1. Depreciation $200 per month.
2. Insurance expired $400.

Instructions

(a) Journalize the December transactions. (Assume a perpetual inventory system.)

(b) Enter the December 1 balances in the ledger T-accounts and post the December transactions. Use Cost of Goods Sold, Depreciation Expense, Insurance Expense, Salaries and Wages Expense, Sales Revenue, and Sales Discounts.

(c) The statement from Jackson County Bank on December 31 showed a balance of $26,130. A comparison of the bank statement with the Cash account revealed the following facts.

1. The bank collected a note receivable of $2,200 for Fullerton Company on December 15.
2. The December 31 receipts were deposited in a night deposit vault on December 31. These deposits were recorded by the bank in January.
3. Checks outstanding on December 31 totaled $1,210.
4. On December 31, the bank statement showed an NSF charge of $680 for a check received by the company from L. Bryan, a customer, on account.

Prepare a bank reconciliation as of December 31 based on the available information. (*Hint:* The cash balance per books is $26,100. This can be proven by finding the balance in the Cash account from parts (a) and (b).)

(d) Journalize the adjusting entries resulting from the bank reconciliation and adjustment data.

(e) Post the adjusting entries to the ledger T-accounts.

(f) Prepare an adjusted trial balance.

(g) Prepare an income statement for December and a classified balance sheet at December 31.

CONTINUING PROBLEM

COOKIE CREATIONS: AN ENTREPRENEURIAL JOURNEY

(*Note:* This is a continuation of the Cookie Creations problem from Chapters 1 through 7.)

CC8 Part 1 Natalie is struggling to keep up with the recording of her accounting transactions. She is spending a lot of time marketing and selling mixers and giving her cookie classes. Her friend John is an accounting student who runs his own accounting service. He has asked Natalie if she would like to have him do her accounting. John and Natalie meet and discuss her business.

Part 2 Natalie decides that she cannot afford to hire John to do her accounting. One way that she can ensure that her cash account does not have any errors and is accurate and up-to-date is to prepare a bank reconciliation at the end of each month. Natalie would like you to help her.

© leungchopan/ Shutterstock

Go to the book's companion website, **www.wiley.com/college/weygandt**, *to see the completion of this problem.*

BROADENING YOUR PERSPECTIVE

FINANCIAL REPORTING AND ANALYSIS

Financial Reporting Problem: Apple Inc.

BYP8-1 The financial statements of Apple Inc. are presented in Appendix A at the end of this textbook. Instructions for accessing and using the company's complete annual report, including the notes to the financial statements, are also provided in Appendix A.

Instructions

(a) What comments, if any, are made about cash in the report of the independent registered public accounting firm?

(b) What data about cash and cash equivalents are shown in the consolidated balance sheet?

(c) In its notes to Consolidated Financial Statements, how does Apple define cash equivalents?

(d) In management's Annual Report on Internal Control over Financial Reporting (Item 9A), what does Apple's management say about internal control?

Comparative Analysis Problem: PepsiCo, Inc. vs. The Coca-Cola Company

BYP8-2 PepsiCo's financial statements are presented in Appendix B. Financial statements of The Coca-Cola Company are presented in Appendix C. Instructions for accessing and using the complete annual reports of PepsiCo and Coca-Cola, including the notes to the financial statements, are also provided in Appendices B and C, respectively.

Instructions

(a) Based on the information contained in these financial statements, determine each of the following for each company:
   (1) Cash and cash equivalents balance at December 28, 2013, for PepsiCo and at December 31, 2013, for Coca-Cola.
   (2) Increase (decrease) in cash and cash equivalents from 2012 to 2013.
   (3) Cash provided by operating activities during the year ended December 2013 (from statement of cash flows).

(b) What conclusions concerning the management of cash can be drawn from these data?

Comparative Analysis Problem: Amazon.com, Inc. vs. Wal-Mart Stores, Inc.

BYP8-3 Amazon.com, Inc.'s financial statements are presented in Appendix D. Financial statements of Wal-Mart Stores, Inc. are presented in Appendix E. Instructions for accessing and using the complete annual reports of Amazon and Wal-Mart, including the notes to the financial statements, are also provided in Appendices D and E, respectively.

Instructions

(a) Based on the information contained in these financial statements, determine each of the following for each company:
   (1) Cash and cash equivalents balance at December 31, 2013, for Amazon and at January 31, 2014, for Wal-Mart.
   (2) Increase (decrease) in cash and cash equivalents from 2012 to 2013.
   (3) Net cash provided by operating activities during the year ended December 31, 2013, for Amazon and January 31, 2014, for Wal-Mart from statement of cash flows.

(b) What conclusions concerning the management of cash can be drawn from these data?

Real-World Focus

BYP8-4 All organizations should have systems of internal control. Universities are no exception. This site discusses the basics of internal control in a university setting.

Address: **www.bc.edu/offices/audit/controls**, or go to **www.wiley.com/college/weygandt**

Steps: Go to the site shown above.

Instructions

The home page of this site provides links to pages that answer critical questions. Use these links to answer the following questions.

(a) In a university setting, who has responsibility for evaluating the adequacy of the system of internal control?
(b) What do reconciliations ensure in the university setting? Who should review the reconciliation?
(c) What are some examples of physical controls?
(d) What are two ways to accomplish inventory counts?

CRITICAL THINKING

Decision-Making Across the Organization

BYP8-5 The board of trustees of a local church is concerned about the internal accounting controls for the offering collections made at weekly services. The trustees ask you to serve on a three-person audit team with the internal auditor of a local college and a CPA who has just joined the church.

At a meeting of the audit team and the board of trustees you learn the following.

1. The church's board of trustees has delegated responsibility for the financial management and audit of the financial records to the finance committee. This group prepares the annual budget and approves major disbursements. It is not involved in collections or recordkeeping. No audit has been made in recent years because the same trusted employee has kept church records and served as financial secretary for 15 years. The church does not carry any fidelity insurance.
2. The collection at the weekly service is taken by a team of ushers who volunteer to serve one month. The ushers take the collection plates to a basement office at the rear of the church. They hand their plates to the head usher and return to the church service. After all plates have been turned in, the head usher counts the cash received. The head usher then places the cash in the church safe along with a notation of the amount counted. The head usher volunteers to serve for 3 months.
3. The next morning the financial secretary opens the safe and recounts the collection. The secretary withholds \$150–\$200 in cash, depending on the cash expenditures expected for the week, and deposits the remainder of the collections in the bank. To facilitate the deposit, church members who contribute by check are asked to make their checks payable to "Cash."
4. Each month, the financial secretary reconciles the bank statement and submits a copy of the reconciliation to the board of trustees. The reconciliations have rarely contained any bank errors and have never shown any errors per books.

Instructions

With the class divided into groups, answer the following.

(a) Indicate the weaknesses in internal accounting control over the handling of collections.

(b) List the improvements in internal control procedures that you plan to make at the next meeting of the audit team for (1) the ushers, (2) the head usher, (3) the financial secretary, and (4) the finance committee.

(c) What church policies should be changed to improve internal control?

Communication Activity

BYP8-6 As a new auditor for the CPA firm of Eaton, Quayle, and Hale, you have been assigned to review the internal controls over mail cash receipts of Pritchard Company. Your review reveals the following. Checks are promptly endorsed "For Deposit Only," but no list of the checks is prepared by the person opening the mail. The mail is opened either by the cashier or by the employee who maintains the accounts receivable records. Mail receipts are deposited in the bank weekly by the cashier.

Instructions

Write a letter to Danny Peak, owner of Pritchard Company, explaining the weaknesses in internal control and your recommendations for improving the system.

Ethics Case

BYP8-7 You are the assistant controller in charge of general ledger accounting at Linbarger Bottling Company. Your company has a large loan from an insurance company. The loan agreement requires that the company's cash account balance be maintained at \$200,000 or more, as reported monthly.

At June 30, the cash balance is \$80,000, which you report to Lisa Infante, the financial vice president. Lisa excitedly instructs you to keep the cash receipts book open for one additional day for purposes of the June 30 report to the insurance company. Lisa says, "If we don't get that cash balance over \$200,000, we'll default on our loan agreement. They could close us down, put us all out of our jobs!" Lisa continues, "I talked to Oconto Distributors (one of Linbarger's largest customers) this morning. They said they sent us a check for \$150,000 yesterday. We should receive it tomorrow. If we include just that one check in our cash balance, we'll be in the clear. It's in the mail!"

Instructions

(a) Who will suffer negative effects if you do not comply with Lisa Infante's instructions? Who will suffer if you do comply?

(b) What are the ethical considerations in this case?

(c) What alternatives do you have?

All About You

BYP8-8 The print and electronic media are full of stories about potential security risks that may arise from your computer or smartphone. It is important to keep in mind, however, that there are also many other ways that your identity can be stolen. The federal government provides many resources to help protect you from identity thieves.

Instructions

Go to **http://onguardonline.gov/idtheft.html**, click **Video and Media**, and then click on **ID Theft Faceoff**. Complete the quiz provided there.

FASB Codification Activity

BYP8-9 If your school has a subscription to the FASB Codification, go to **http://aaahq.org/ascLogin.cfm** to log in and prepare responses to the following.

(a) How is cash defined in the Codification?
(b) How are cash equivalents defined in the Codification?
(c) What are the disclosure requirements related to cash and cash equivalents?

A Look at IFRS

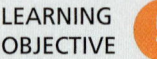

LEARNING OBJECTIVE 5 **Compare the accounting for fraud, internal control, and cash under GAAP and IFRS.**

Fraud can occur anywhere. Because the three main factors that contribute to fraud are universal in nature, the principles of internal control activities are used globally by companies. While Sarbanes-Oxley (SOX) does not apply to international companies, most large international companies have internal controls similar to those indicated in the chapter. IFRS and GAAP are also very similar in accounting for cash. *IAS No. 1 (revised)*, "Presentation of Financial Statements," is the only standard that discusses issues specifically related to cash.

Relevant Facts

Following are the key similarities and differences between GAAP and IFRS related to fraud, internal control, and cash.

Similarities

- The fraud triangle discussed in this chapter is applicable to all international companies. Some of the major frauds on an international basis are Parmalat (Italy), Royal Ahold (the Netherlands), and Satyam Computer Services (India).
- Rising economic crime poses a growing threat to companies, with nearly one-third of all organizations worldwide being victims of fraud in a recent 12-month period.
- Accounting scandals both in the United States and internationally have re-ignited the debate over the relative merits of GAAP, which takes a "rules-based" approach to accounting, versus IFRS, which takes a "principles-based" approach. The FASB announced that it intends to introduce more principles-based standards.
- On a lighter note, at one time the Ig Nobel Prize in Economics went to the CEOs of those companies involved in the corporate accounting scandals of that year for "adapting the mathematical concept of imaginary numbers for use in the business world." A parody of the Nobel Prizes, the Ig Nobel Prizes (read Ignoble, as not noble) are given each year in early October for 10 achievements that "first make people laugh, and then make them think." Organized by the scientific humor magazine *Annals of Improbable Research* (*AIR*), they are presented by a group that includes genuine Nobel laureates at a ceremony at Harvard University's Sanders Theater. (See **en.wikipedia.org/wiki/Ig_Nobel_Prize**.)
- The accounting and internal control procedures related to cash are essentially the same under both IFRS and this textbook. In addition, the definition used for cash equivalents is the same.
- Most companies report cash and cash equivalents together under IFRS, as shown in this textbook. In addition, IFRS follows the same accounting policies related to the reporting of restricted cash.

Differences

- The SOX internal control standards apply only to companies listed on U.S. exchanges. There is continuing debate over whether foreign issuers should have to comply with this extra layer of regulation.

Looking to the Future

Ethics has become a very important aspect of reporting. Different cultures have different perspectives on bribery and other questionable activities, and consequently penalties for engaging in such activities vary considerably across countries.

High-quality international accounting requires both high-quality accounting standards and high-quality auditing. Similar to the convergence of GAAP and IFRS, there is movement to improve international auditing standards. The International Auditing and Assurance Standards Board (IAASB) functions as an independent standard-setting body. It works to establish high-quality auditing and assurance and quality-control standards throughout the world. Whether the IAASB adopts internal control provisions similar to those in SOX remains to be seen. You can follow developments in the international audit arena at **http://www.ifac.org/iaasb/**.

IFRS Practice

IFRS Self-Test Questions

1. Non-U.S companies that follow IFRS:
  (a) do not normally use the principles of internal control activities described in this textbook.
  (b) often offset cash with accounts payable on the balance sheet.
  (c) are not required to follow SOX.
  (d) None of the above.

2. The Sarbanes-Oxley Act applies to:
  (a) all U.S. companies listed on U.S. exchanges.
  (b) all companies that list stock on any stock exchange in any country.
  (c) all European companies listed on European exchanges.
  (d) Both (a) and (c).

3. High-quality international accounting requires both high-quality accounting standards and:
  (a) a reconsideration of SOX to make it less onerous.
  (b) high-quality auditing standards.
  (c) government intervention to ensure that the public interest is protected.
  (d) the development of new principles of internal control activities.

IFRS Exercise

IFRS8-1 Some people argue that the internal control requirements of the Sarbanes-Oxley Act (SOX) put U.S. companies at a competitive disadvantage to companies outside the United States. Discuss the competitive implications (both pros and cons) of SOX.

International Financial Reporting Problem: Louis Vuitton

IFRS8–2 The financial statements of Louis Vuitton are presented in Appendix F. Instructions for accessing and using the company's complete annual report, including the notes to its financial statements, are also provided in Appendix F.

Instructions
Using the notes to the company's financial statements, what are Louis Vuitton's accounting policies related to cash and cash equivalents?

Answers to IFRS Self-Test Questions

1. c **2.** a **3.** b

9 Accounting for Receivables

CHAPTER PREVIEW As indicated in the Feature Story below, receivables are a significant asset for many pharmaceutical companies. Because a large portion of sales in the United States are credit sales, receivables are important to companies in other industries as well. As a consequence, companies must pay close attention to their receivables and manage them carefully. In this chapter, you will learn what journal entries companies make when they sell products, when they collect cash from those sales, and when they write off accounts they cannot collect.

FEATURE STORY

A Dose of Careful Management Keeps Receivables Healthy

"Sometimes you have to know when to be very tough, and sometimes you can give them a bit of a break," said Vivi Su. She wasn't talking about her children but about the customers of a subsidiary of former pharmaceutical company Whitehall-Robins, where she worked as supervisor of credit and collections.

For example, while the company's regular terms were 1/15, n/30 (1% discount if paid within 15 days), a customer might have asked for and received a few days of grace and still got the discount. Or a customer might have placed orders above its credit limit, in which case, depending on its payment history and the circumstances, Ms. Su might have authorized shipment of the goods anyway.

"It's not about drawing a line in the sand, and that's all," she explained. "You want a good relationship with your customers—but you also need to bring in the money."

"The money," in Whitehall-Robins' case, amounted to some $170 million in sales a year. Nearly all of it came in through the credit accounts Ms. Su managed. The process started with the decision to grant a customer an account in the first place. The sales rep gave the customer a credit application. "My department reviews this application very carefully; a customer needs to supply three good references, and we also run a check with a credit firm like Equifax. If we accept them, then based on their size and history, we assign a credit limit," Ms. Su explained.

Once accounts were established, "I get an aging report every single day," said Ms. Su. "The rule of thumb is that we should always have at least 85% of receivables current—meaning they were billed less than 30 days ago," she continued. "But we try to do even better than that—I like to see 90%."

At 15 days overdue, Whitehall-Robins phoned the client. After 45 days, Ms. Su noted, "I send a letter. Then a second notice is sent in writing. After the third and final notice, the client has 10 days to pay, and then I hand it over to a collection agency, and it's out of my hands."

Ms. Su's boss, Terry Norton, recorded an estimate for bad debts every year, based on a percentage of receivables. The percentage depended on the current aging history. He also calculated and monitored the company's accounts receivable turnover, which the company reported in its financial statements.

Ms. Su knew that she and Mr. Norton were crucial to the profitability of Whitehall-Robins. "Receivables are generally the second-largest asset of any company (after its capital assets)," she pointed out. "So it's no wonder we keep a very close eye on them."

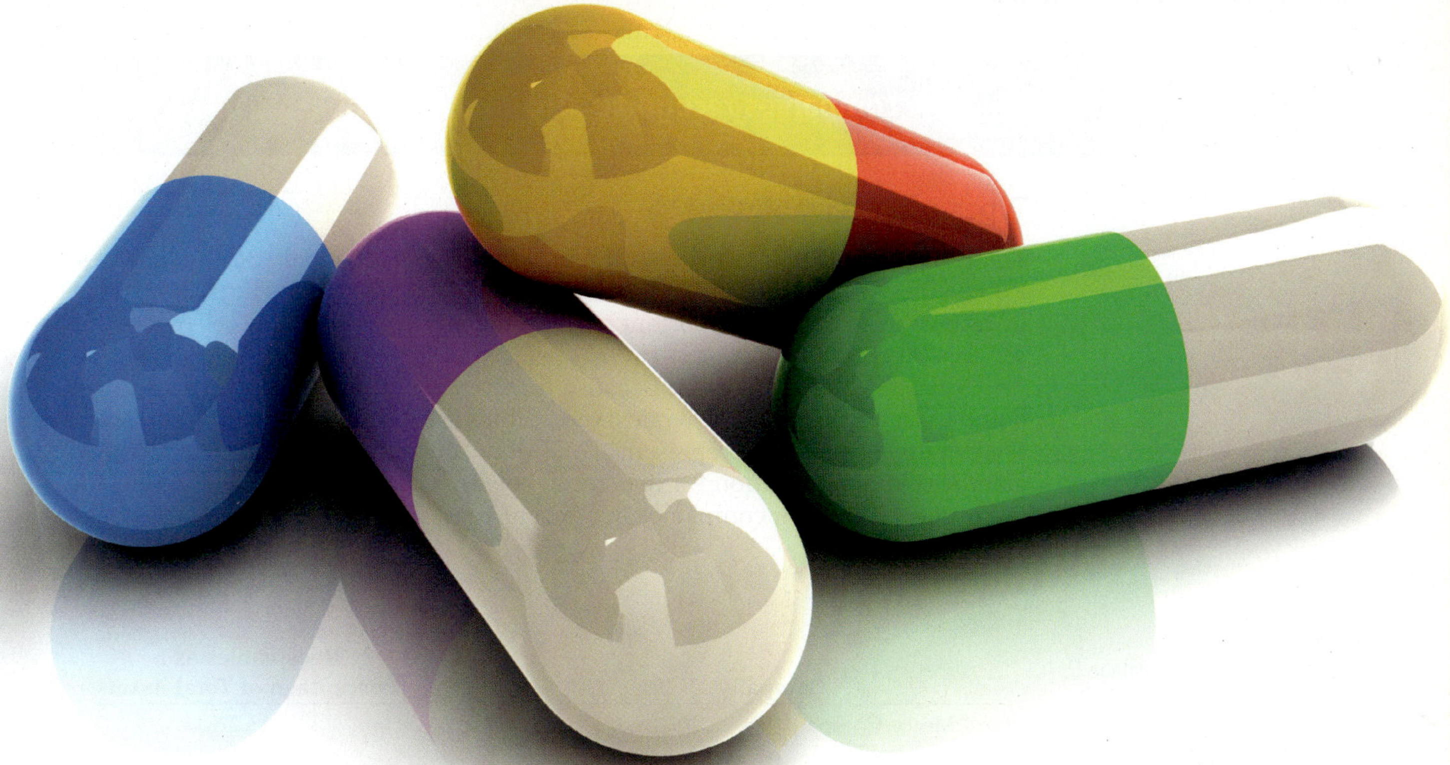

© Cogal/iStockphoto

CHAPTER OUTLINE

Learning Objectives

	Learning Objective	Topics	DO IT!
1	Explain how companies recognize accounts receivable.	• Types of receivables • Recognizing accounts receivable	DO IT! 1 Recognizing Accounts Receivable
2	Describe how companies value accounts receivable and record their disposition.	• Valuing accounts receivable • Disposing of accounts receivable	DO IT! 2 Uncollectible Accounts Receivable
3	Explain how companies recognize notes receivable.	• Determining the maturity date • Computing interest • Recognizing notes receivable	DO IT! 3 Recognizing Notes Receivable
4	Describe how companies value notes receivable, record their disposition, and present and analyze receivables.	• Valuing notes receivable • Disposing of notes receivable • Statement presentation and analysis	DO IT! 4 Analysis of Receivables

io to the ***REVIEW AND PRACTICE*** section at the end of the chapter for a review of key concepts and practice applications with solutions.

'isit **WileyPLUS with ORION** for additional tutorials and practice opportunities.

LEARNING OBJECTIVE 1

Explain how companies recognize accounts receivable.

Types of Receivables

The term **receivables** refers to amounts due from individuals and companies. Receivables are claims that are expected to be collected in cash. The management of receivables is a very important activity for any company that sells goods or services on credit.

Receivables are important because they represent one of a company's most liquid assets. For many companies, receivables are also one of the largest assets. For example, receivables represent 13.7% of the current assets of pharmaceutical giant **Rite Aid**. Illustration 9-1 lists receivables as a percentage of total assets for five other well-known companies in a recent year.

Illustration 9-1
Receivables as a percentage of assets

Company	Receivables as a Percentage of Total Assets
Ford Motor Company	43.2%
General Electric	41.5
Minnesota Mining and Manufacturing Company (3M)	12.7
DuPont Co.	11.7
Intel Corporation	3.9

The relative significance of a company's receivables as a percentage of its assets depends on various factors: its industry, the time of year, whether it extends long-term financing, and its credit policies. To reflect important differences among receivables, they are frequently classified as (1) accounts receivable, (2) notes receivable, and (3) other receivables.

Accounts receivable are amounts customers owe on account. They result from the sale of goods and services. Companies generally expect to collect accounts receivable within 30 to 60 days. They are usually the most significant type of claim held by a company.

ETHICS NOTE

Companies report receivables from employees separately in the financial statements. The reason: Sometimes these receivables are not the result of an "arm's-length" transaction.

Notes receivable are a written promise (as evidenced by a formal instrument) for amounts to be received. The note normally requires the collection of interest and extends for time periods of 60–90 days or longer. Notes and accounts receivable that result from sales transactions are often called **trade receivables**.

Other receivables include nontrade receivables such as interest receivable, loans to company officers, advances to employees, and income taxes refundable. These do not generally result from the operations of the business. Therefore, they are generally classified and reported as separate items in the balance sheet.

Recognizing Accounts Receivable

Recognizing accounts receivable is relatively straightforward. A service organization records a receivable when it performs service on account. A merchandiser records accounts receivable at the point of sale of merchandise on account. When a merchandiser sells goods, it increases (debits) Accounts Receivable and increases (credits) Sales Revenue.

The seller may offer terms that encourage early payment by providing a discount. Sales returns also reduce receivables. The buyer might find some of the goods unacceptable and choose to return the unwanted goods.

To review, assume that Jordache Co. on July 1, 2017, sells merchandise on account to Polo Company for $1,000, terms 2/10, n/30. On July 5, Polo returns merchandise with a sales price of $100 to Jordache Co. On July 11, Jordache receives payment from Polo Company for the balance due. The journal entries to record these transactions on the books of Jordache Co. are as follows. **(Cost of goods sold entries are omitted.)**

July 1	Accounts Receivable—Polo Company	1,000	
	Sales Revenue		1,000
	(To record sales on account)		
July 5	Sales Returns and Allowances	100	
	Accounts Receivable—Polo Company		100
	(To record merchandise returned)		
July 11	Cash ($900 − $18)	882	
	Sales Discounts ($900 × .02)	18	
	Accounts Receivable—Polo Company		900
	(To record collection of accounts receivable)		

ETHICS NOTE

In exchange for lower interest rates, some companies have eliminated the 25-day grace period before finance charges kick in. Be sure you read the fine print in any credit agreement you sign.

Helpful Hint
These entries are the same as those described in Chapter 5. For simplicity, we have omitted inventory and cost of goods sold from this set of journal entries and from end-of-chapter material.

Some retailers issue their own credit cards. When you use a retailer's credit card (**JCPenney**, for example), the retailer charges interest on the balance due if not paid within a specified period (usually 25–30 days).

To illustrate, assume that you use your JCPenney Company credit card to purchase clothing with a sales price of $300 on June 1, 2017. JCPenney will increase (debit) Accounts Receivable for $300 and increase (credit) Sales Revenue for $300 (cost of goods sold entry omitted) as follows.

June 1	Accounts Receivable	300	
	Sales Revenue		300
	(To record sale of merchandise)		

A	=	L	+	OE
+300				+300 Rev

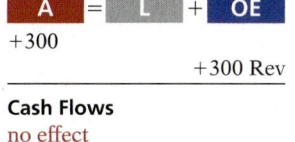

Cash Flows
no effect

Assuming that you owe $300 at the end of the month and JCPenney charges 1.5% per month on the balance due, the adjusting entry that JCPenney makes to record interest revenue of $4.50 ($300 × 1.5%) on June 30 is as follows.

June 30	Accounts Receivable	4.50	
	Interest Revenue		4.50
	(To record interest on amount due)		

A	=	L	+	OE
+4.50				+4.50 Rev

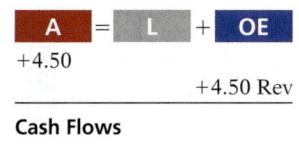

Cash Flows
no effect

Interest revenue is often substantial for many retailers.

ANATOMY OF A FRAUD

Tasanee was the accounts receivable clerk for a large nonprofit foundation that provided performance and exhibition space for the performing and visual arts. Her responsibilities included activities normally assigned to an accounts receivable clerk, such as recording revenues from various sources (donations, facility rental fees, ticket revenue, and bar receipts). However, she was also responsible for handling all cash and checks from the time they were received until the time she deposited them, as well as preparing the bank reconciliation. Tasanee took advantage of her situation by falsifying bank deposits and bank reconciliations so that she could steal cash from the bar receipts. Since nobody else logged the donations or matched the donation receipts to pledges prior to Tasanee receiving them, she was able to offset the cash that was stolen against donations that she received but didn't record. Her crime was made easier by the fact that her boss, the company's controller, only did a very superficial review of the bank reconciliation and thus didn't notice that some numbers had been cut out from other documents and taped onto the bank reconciliation.

Total take: $1.5 million

THE MISSING CONTROLS

Segregation of duties. The foundation should not have allowed an accounts receivable clerk, whose job was to record receivables, to also handle cash, record cash, make deposits, and especially prepare the bank reconciliation.

Independent internal verification. The controller was supposed to perform a thorough review of the bank reconciliation. Because he did not, he was terminated from his position.

Source: Adapted from Wells, *Fraud Casebook* (2007), pp. 183–194.

DO IT! 1 Recognizing Accounts Receivable

On May 1, Wilton sold merchandise on account to Bates for $50,000, terms 3/15, net 45. On May 4, Bates returns merchandise with a sales price of $2,000. On May 16, Wilton receives payment from Bates for the balance due. Prepare journal entries to record the May transactions on Wilton's books. (You may ignore cost of goods sold entries and explanations.)

Action Plan

✔ Prepare entry to record the receivable and related return.

✔ Compute the sales discount and related entry.

Solution

May 1	Accounts Receivable—Bates	50,000	
	Sales Revenue		50,000
May 4	Sales Returns and Allowances	2,000	
	Accounts Receivable—Bates		2,000
May 16	Cash ($48,000 − $1,440)	46,560	
	Sales Discounts ($48,000 × .03)	1,440	
	Accounts Receivable—Bates		48,000

Related exercise material: **BE9-1, BE9-2, E9-1, E9-2, and DO IT! 9-1.**

LEARNING OBJECTIVE 2 Describe how companies value accounts receivable and record their disposition.

Valuing Accounts Receivable

Once companies record receivables in the accounts, the next question is: How should they report receivables in the financial statements? Companies report accounts receivable on the balance sheet as an asset. But determining the **amount** to report is sometimes difficult because some receivables will become uncollectible.

Each customer must satisfy the credit requirements of the seller before the credit sale is approved. Inevitably, though, some accounts receivable become uncollectible. For example, a customer may not be able to pay because of a decline in its sales revenue due to a downturn in the economy. Similarly, individuals may be laid off from their jobs or faced with unexpected hospital bills. Companies record credit losses as **Bad Debt Expense** (or Uncollectible Accounts Expense). Such losses are a normal and necessary risk of doing business on a credit basis.

Alternative Terminology
You will sometimes see *Bad Debt Expense* called *Uncollectible Accounts Expense*.

When U.S. home prices fell, home foreclosures rose, and the economy slowed as a result of the financial crises of 2008, lenders experienced huge increases in their bad debt expense. For example, during one quarter Wachovia (a large U.S. bank now owned by Wells Fargo) increased bad debt expense from $108 million to $408 million. Similarly, American Express increased its bad debt expense by 70%.

Two methods are used in accounting for uncollectible accounts: (1) the direct write-off method and (2) the allowance method. The following sections explain these methods.

DIRECT WRITE-OFF METHOD FOR UNCOLLECTIBLE ACCOUNTS

Under the **direct write-off method**, when a company determines a particular account to be uncollectible, it charges the loss to Bad Debt Expense. Assume, for example, that Warden Co. writes off as uncollectible M. E. Doran's $200 balance on December 12. Warden's entry is as follows.

Dec. 12	Bad Debt Expense	200	
	Accounts Receivable—M. E. Doran		200
	(To record write-off of M. E. Doran account)		

A	=	L	+	OE
				−200 Exp
−200				

Cash Flows
no effect

Under this method, Bad Debt Expense will show only **actual losses** from uncollectibles. The company will report accounts receivable at its gross amount.

Although this method is simple, its use can reduce the usefulness of both the income statement and balance sheet. Consider the following example. Assume that in 2017, Quick Buck Computer Company decided it could increase its revenues by offering computers to college students without requiring any money down and with no credit-approval process. On campuses across the country, it distributed one million computers with a selling price of $800 each. This increased Quick Buck's revenues and receivables by $800 million. The promotion was a huge success! The 2017 balance sheet and income statement looked great. Unfortunately, during 2018, nearly 40% of the customers defaulted on their loans. This made the 2018 income statement and balance sheet look terrible. Illustration 9-2 shows the effect of these events on the financial statements if the direct write-off method is used.

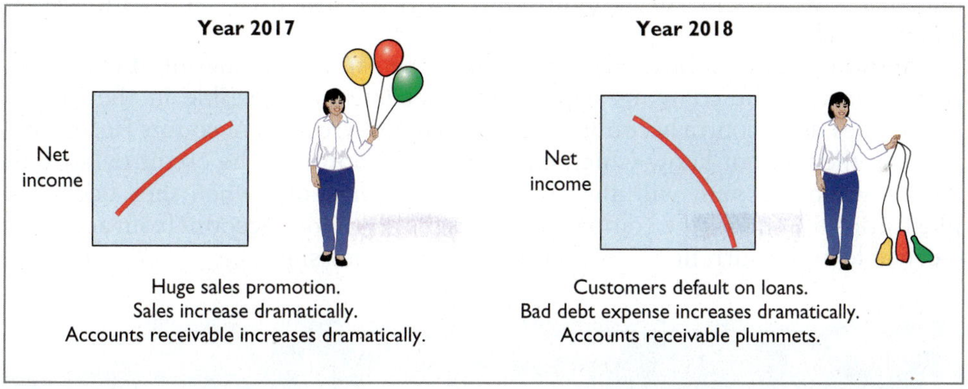

Illustration 9-2
Effects of direct write-off method

Under the direct write-off method, companies often record bad debt expense in a period different from the period in which they record the revenue. The method does not attempt to match bad debt expense to sales revenue in the income statement. Nor does the direct write-off method show accounts receivable in the balance sheet at the amount the company actually expects to receive. **Consequently, unless bad debt losses are insignificant, the direct write-off method is not acceptable for financial reporting purposes.**

ALLOWANCE METHOD FOR UNCOLLECTIBLE ACCOUNTS

The **allowance method** of accounting for bad debts involves estimating uncollectible accounts at the end of each period. This provides better matching on the income statement. It also ensures that companies state receivables on the balance sheet at their cash (net) realizable value. **Cash (net) realizable value** is the net amount the company expects to receive in cash. It excludes amounts that the company estimates it will not collect. Thus, this method reduces receivables in the balance sheet by the amount of estimated uncollectible receivables.

GAAP requires the allowance method for financial reporting purposes when bad debts are material in amount. This method has three essential features:

Helpful Hint
In this context, *material* means significant or important to financial statement users.

1. Companies **estimate** uncollectible accounts receivable. They match this estimated expense **against revenues** in the same accounting period in which they record the revenues.
2. Companies debit estimated uncollectibles to Bad Debt Expense and credit them to Allowance for Doubtful Accounts through an adjusting entry at the end of each period. Allowance for Doubtful Accounts is a contra account to Accounts Receivable.
3. When companies write off a specific account, they debit actual uncollectibles to Allowance for Doubtful Accounts and credit that amount to Accounts Receivable.

RECORDING ESTIMATED UNCOLLECTIBLES To illustrate the allowance method, assume that Hampson Furniture has credit sales of $1,200,000 in 2017. Of this amount, $200,000 remains uncollected at December 31. The credit manager estimates that $12,000 of these sales will be uncollectible. The adjusting entry to record the estimated uncollectibles increases (debits) Bad Debt Expense and increases (credits) Allowance for Doubtful Accounts, as follows.

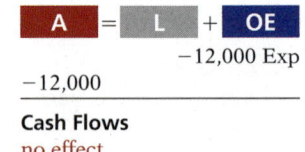

A	=	L	+	OE
				−12,000 Exp
−12,000				

Cash Flows
no effect

Dec. 31	Bad Debt Expense	12,000	
	Allowance for Doubtful Accounts		12,000
	(To record estimate of uncollectible accounts)		

Hampson reports Bad Debt Expense in the income statement as an operating expense (usually as a selling expense). Thus, the estimated uncollectibles are matched with sales in 2017. Hampson records the expense in the same year it made the sales.

Allowance for Doubtful Accounts shows the estimated amount of claims on customers that the company expects will become uncollectible in the future. Companies use a contra account instead of a direct credit to Accounts Receivable because they do not know which customers will not pay. The credit balance in the allowance account will absorb the specific write-offs when they occur. As Illustration 9-3 shows, the company deducts the allowance account from accounts receivable in the current assets section of the balance sheet.

Illustration 9-3
Presentation of allowance for doubtful accounts

HAMPSON FURNITURE
Balance Sheet (partial)

Current assets		
Cash		$ 14,800
Accounts receivable	**$200,000**	
Less: Allowance for doubtful accounts	**12,000**	**188,000**
Inventory		310,000
Supplies		25,000
Total current assets		$537,800

Helpful Hint
Cash realizable value is sometimes referred to as *accounts receivable (net).*

The amount of $188,000 in Illustration 9-3 represents the expected **cash realizable value** of the accounts receivable at the statement date. **Companies do not close Allowance for Doubtful Accounts at the end of the fiscal year.**

RECORDING THE WRITE-OFF OF AN UNCOLLECTIBLE ACCOUNT As described in the Feature Story, companies use various methods of collecting past-due accounts, such as letters, calls, and legal action. When they have exhausted all means of collecting a past-due account and collection appears impossible, the company writes off the account. In the credit card industry, for example, it is standard practice to write off accounts that are 210 days past due. To prevent premature or unauthorized write-offs, authorized management personnel should formally approve each write-off. To maintain segregation of duties, the employee authorized to write off accounts should not have daily responsibilities related to cash or receivables.

To illustrate a receivables write-off, assume that the financial vice president of Hampson Furniture authorizes a write-off of the $500 balance owed by R. A. Ware on March 1, 2018. The entry to record the write-off is as follows.

Mar. 1	Allowance for Doubtful Accounts	500	
	Accounts Receivable—R. A. Ware		500
	(Write-off of R. A. Ware account)		

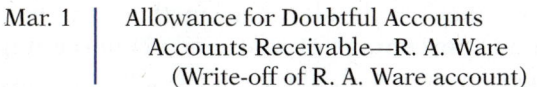

A = L + OE
+500
−500
Cash Flows
no effect

Bad Debt Expense does not increase when the write-off occurs. **Under the allowance method, companies debit every bad debt write-off to the allowance account rather than to Bad Debt Expense.** A debit to Bad Debt Expense would be incorrect because the company has already recognized the expense when it made the adjusting entry for estimated bad debts. Instead, the entry to record the write-off of an uncollectible account reduces both Accounts Receivable and Allowance for Doubtful Accounts. After posting, the general ledger accounts appear as shown in Illustration 9-4.

Illustration 9-4
General ledger balances after write-off

Accounts Receivable				Allowance for Doubtful Accounts			
Jan. 1 Bal.	200,000	Mar. 1	**500**	Mar. 1	**500**	Jan. 1 Bal.	12,000
Mar. 1 Bal.	199,500					Mar. 1 Bal.	11,500

A write-off affects **only balance sheet accounts**—not income statement accounts. The write-off of the account reduces both Accounts Receivable and Allowance for Doubtful Accounts. Cash realizable value in the balance sheet, therefore, remains the same, as Illustration 9-5 shows.

Illustration 9-5
Cash realizable value comparison

	Before Write-Off	After Write-Off
Accounts receivable	$ 200,000	$ 199,500
Allowance for doubtful accounts	12,000	11,500
Cash realizable value	**$188,000**	**$188,000**

RECOVERY OF AN UNCOLLECTIBLE ACCOUNT Occasionally, a company collects from a customer after it has written off the account as uncollectible. The company makes two entries to record the recovery of a bad debt. (1) It reverses the entry made in writing off the account. This reinstates the customer's account. (2) It journalizes the collection in the usual manner.

To illustrate, assume that on July 1, R. A. Ware pays the $500 amount that Hampson had written off on March 1. Hampson makes the following entries.

(1)

July 1	Accounts Receivable—R. A. Ware	500	
	Allowance for Doubtful Accounts		500
	(To reverse write-off of R. A. Ware account)		

A = L + OE
+500
−500
Cash Flows
no effect

(2)

July 1	Cash	500	
	Accounts Receivable—R. A. Ware		500
	(To record collection from R. A. Ware)		

A = L + OE
+500
−500
Cash Flows
+500

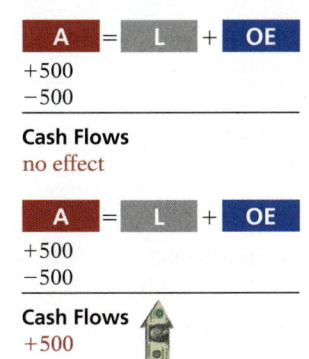

Note that the recovery of a bad debt, like the write-off of a bad debt, affects **only balance sheet accounts**. The net effect of the two entries above is a debit to Cash and a credit to Allowance for Doubtful Accounts for $500. Accounts Receivable and Allowance for Doubtful Accounts both increase in entry (1) for two reasons. First, the company made an error in judgment when it wrote off the account receivable. Second, after R. A. Ware did pay, Accounts Receivable in the general ledger and Ware's account in the subsidiary ledger should show the collection for possible future credit purposes.

ESTIMATING THE ALLOWANCE For Hampson Furniture in Illustration 9-3, the amount of the expected uncollectibles was given. However, in "real life," companies must estimate that amount when they use the allowance method. Two bases are used to determine this amount: **(1) percentage of sales** and **(2) percentage of receivables**. Both bases are generally accepted. The choice is a management decision. It depends on the relative emphasis that management wishes to give to expenses and revenues on the one hand or to cash realizable value of the accounts receivable on the other. The choice is whether to emphasize income statement or balance sheet relationships. Illustration 9-6 compares the two bases.

Illustration 9-6
Comparison of bases for estimating uncollectibles

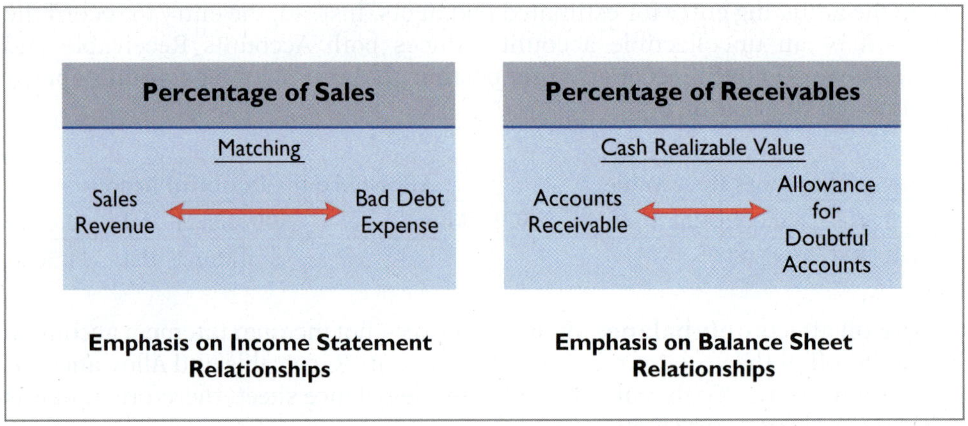

The percentage-of-sales basis results in a better matching of expenses with revenues—an income statement viewpoint. The percentage-of-receivables basis produces the better estimate of cash realizable value—a balance sheet viewpoint. Under both bases, the company must determine its past experience with bad debt losses.

Percentage-of-Sales In the **percentage-of-sales basis**, management estimates what percentage of credit sales will be uncollectible. This percentage is based on past experience and anticipated credit policy.

The company applies this percentage to either total credit sales or net credit sales of the current year. To illustrate, assume that Gonzalez Company elects to use the percentage-of-sales basis. It concludes that 1% of net credit sales will become uncollectible. If net credit sales for 2017 are $800,000, the estimated bad debt expense is $8,000 (1% × $800,000). The adjusting entry is as follows.

A	=	L	+	OE
				−8,000 Exp
−8,000				

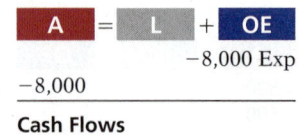

Cash Flows
no effect

Dec. 31	Bad Debt Expense	8,000	
	Allowance for Doubtful Accounts		8,000
	(To record estimated bad debts for year)		

After the adjusting entry is posted, assuming the allowance account already has a credit balance of $1,723, the accounts of Gonzalez Company will show the following.

Illustration 9-7
Bad debt accounts after posting

Bad Debt Expense		Allowance for Doubtful Accounts	
Dec. 31 Adj. **8,000**			Jan. 1 Bal. 1,723
			Dec. 31 Adj. **8,000**
			Dec. 31 Bal. 9,723

This basis of estimating uncollectibles emphasizes the matching of expenses with revenues. As a result, Bad Debt Expense will show a direct percentage relationship to the sales base on which it is computed. **When the company makes the adjusting entry, it disregards the existing balance in Allowance for Doubtful Accounts.** The adjusted balance in this account should be a reasonable approximation of the realizable value of the receivables. If actual write-offs differ significantly from the amount estimated, the company should modify the percentage for future years.

Percentage-of-Receivables Under the **percentage-of-receivables basis**, management estimates what percentage of receivables will result in losses from uncollectible accounts. The company prepares an **aging schedule**, in which it classifies customer balances by the length of time they have been unpaid. Because of its emphasis on time, the analysis is often called **aging the accounts receivable**. In the Feature Story, **Whitehall-Robins** prepared an aging report daily.

After the company arranges the accounts by age, it determines the expected bad debt losses. It applies percentages based on past experience to the totals in each category. The longer a receivable is past due, the less likely it is to be collected. Thus, the estimated percentage of uncollectible debts increases as the number of days past due increases. Illustration 9-8 shows an aging schedule for Dart Company. Note that the estimated percentage uncollectible increases from 2% to 40% as the number of days past due increases.

Helpful Hint
Where appropriate, companies may use only a single percentage rate.

Illustration 9-8
Aging schedule

Worksheet.xls

			Number of Days Past Due			
Customer	Total	Not Yet Due	1–30	31–60	61–90	Over 90
T. E. Adert	$ 600		$ 300		$ 200	$ 100
R. C. Bortz	300	$ 300				
B. A. Carl	450		200	$ 250		
O. L. Diker	700	500			200	
T. O. Ebbet	600			300		300
Others	36,950	26,200	5,200	2,450	1,600	1,500
	$39,600	$27,000	$5,700	$3,000	$2,000	$1,900
Estimated Percentage Uncollectible		2%	4%	10%	20%	40%
Total Estimated Bad Debts	$ 2,228	$ 540	$ 228	$ 300	$ 400	$ 760

Helpful Hint
The older categories have higher percentages because the longer an account is past due, the less likely it is to be collected.

Total estimated bad debts for Dart Company ($2,228) represent the amount of existing customer claims the company expects will become uncollectible in the future. This amount represents the **required balance** in Allowance for Doubtful Accounts at the balance sheet date. **The amount of the bad debt adjusting entry is the difference between the required balance and the existing balance in the allowance account.** If the trial balance shows Allowance for Doubtful Accounts with a credit balance of $528, the company will make an adjusting entry for $1,700 ($2,228 − $528), as shown here.

Dec. 31	Bad Debt Expense	1,700	
	Allowance for Doubtful Accounts		1,700
	(To adjust allowance account to total estimated uncollectibles)		

A	=	L	+	OE
				−1,700 Exp
−1,700				

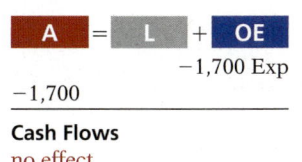

Cash Flows
no effect

After Dart posts its adjusting entry, its accounts will appear as follows.

Illustration 9-9
Bad debt accounts after posting

Bad Debt Expense		Allowance for Doubtful Accounts	
Dec. 31 Adj. **1,700**			Bal. 528
			Dec. 31 Adj. **1,700**
			Bal. 2,228

Allowance for Doubtful Accounts	
Dec. 31 **Unadj.** Bal. 500	Dec. 31 **Adj.** 2,728
	Dec. 31 Bal. 2,228

Occasionally, the allowance account will have a **debit balance** prior to adjustment. This occurs when write-offs during the year have exceeded previous provisions for bad debts. In such a case, the company **adds the debit balance to the required balance** when it makes the adjusting entry. Thus, if there had been a $500 debit balance in the allowance account before adjustment, the adjusting entry would have been for $2,728 ($2,228 + $500) to arrive at a credit balance of $2,228 (see T-account in margin). The percentage-of-receivables basis will normally result in the better approximation of cash realizable value.

Ethics Insight

© Christy Thompson/Shutterstock

Cookie Jar Allowances

There are many pressures on companies to achieve earnings targets. For managers, poor earnings can lead to dismissal or lack of promotion. It is not surprising then that management may be tempted to look for ways to boost their earnings number.

One way a company can achieve greater earnings is to lower its estimate of what is needed in its Allowance for Doubtful Accounts (sometimes referred to as "tapping the cooking jar"). For example, suppose a company has an Allowance for Doubtful Accounts of $10 million and decides to reduce this balance to $9 million. As a result of this change, Bad Debt Expense decreases by $1 million and earnings increase by $1 million.

Large banks such as JP Morgan Chase, Wells Fargo, and Bank of America recently decreased their Allowance for Doubtful Accounts by over $4 billion. These reductions came at a time when these big banks were still suffering from lower mortgage lending and trading activity, both of which lead to lower earnings. They justified these reductions in the allowance balances by noting that credit quality and economic conditions had improved. This may be so, but it sure is great to have a cookie jar that might be tapped when a boost in earnings is needed.

How might investors determine that a company is managing its earnings? (See **WileyPLUS** for this answer and additional questions.)

Disposing of Accounts Receivable

In the normal course of events, companies collect accounts receivable in cash and remove the receivables from the books. However, as credit sales and receivables have grown in significance, the "normal course of events" has changed. Companies now frequently sell their receivables to another company for cash, thereby shortening the cash-to-cash operating cycle.

Companies sell receivables for two major reasons. First, **they may be the only reasonable source of cash**. When money is tight, companies may not be able to borrow money in the usual credit markets. Or if money is available, the cost of borrowing may be prohibitive.

A second reason for selling receivables is that **billing and collection are often time-consuming and costly**. It is often easier for a retailer to sell the receivables to another party with expertise in billing and collection matters. Credit card companies such as MasterCard, Visa, and Discover specialize in billing and collecting accounts receivable.

SALE OF RECEIVABLES

A common sale of receivables is a sale to a factor. A **factor** is a finance company or bank that buys receivables from businesses and then collects the payments directly from the customers. Factoring is a multibillion dollar business.

Factoring arrangements vary widely. Typically, the factor charges a commission to the company that is selling the receivables. This fee ranges from 1–3% of the amount of receivables purchased. To illustrate, assume that Hendredon Furniture factors $600,000 of receivables to Federal Factors. Federal Factors assesses a service charge of 2% of the amount of receivables sold. The journal entry to record the sale by Hendredon Furniture on April 2, 2017, is as follows.

Apr. 2	Cash	588,000	
	Service Charge Expense (2% × $600,000)	12,000	
	Accounts Receivable		600,000
	(To record the sale of accounts receivable)		

A	=	L	+	OE
+588,000				
				−12,000 Exp
−600,000				

Cash Flows
+588,000

If Hendredon often sells its receivables, it records the service charge expense as a selling expense. If the company infrequently sells receivables, it may report this amount in the "Other expenses and losses" section of the income statement.

CREDIT CARD SALES

Over one billion credit cards are in use in the United States—more than three credit cards for every man, woman, and child in this country. Visa, MasterCard, and American Express are the national credit cards that most individuals use. Three parties are involved when national credit cards are used in retail sales: (1) the credit card issuer, who is independent of the retailer; (2) the retailer; and (3) the customer. A retailer's acceptance of a national credit card is another form of selling (factoring) the receivable.

Illustration 9-10 shows the major advantages of national credit cards to the retailer. In exchange for these advantages, the retailer pays the credit card issuer a fee of 2–6% of the invoice price for its services.

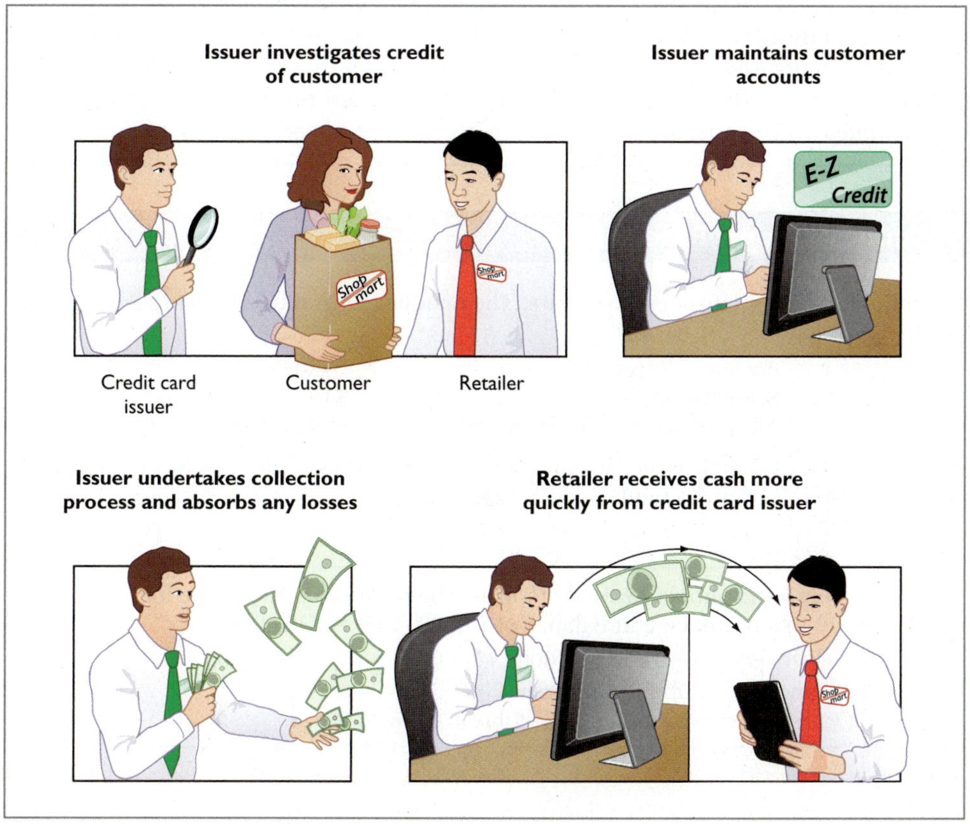

Illustration 9-10
Advantages of credit cards to the retailer

ACCOUNTING FOR CREDIT CARD SALES The retailer generally considers sales from the use of national credit card sales as **cash sales**. The retailer must pay to the bank that issues the card a fee for processing the transactions. The retailer records the credit card slips in a similar manner as checks deposited from a cash sale.

To illustrate, Anita Ferreri purchases $1,000 of compact discs for her restaurant from Karen Kerr Music Co., using her Visa First Bank Card. First Bank charges a service fee of 3%. The entry to record this transaction by Karen Kerr Music on March 22, 2017, is as follows.

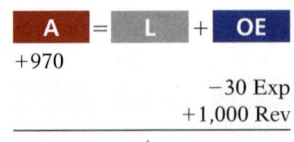

A	=	L	+	OE
+970				
				−30 Exp
				+1,000 Rev

Cash Flows
+970

Mar. 22	Cash	970	
	Service Charge Expense	30	
	Sales Revenue		1,000
	(To record Visa credit card sales)		

Accounting Across the Organization — Nordstrom

© Michael Braun/iStockphoto

How Does a Credit Card Work?

Most of you know how to use a credit card, but do you know what happens in the transaction and how the transaction is processed? Suppose that you use a Visa card to purchase some new ties at Nordstrom. The salesperson swipes your card, which allows the information on the magnetic strip on the back of the card to be read. The salesperson then enters in the amount of the purchase. The machine contacts the Visa computer, which routes the call back to the bank that issued your Visa card. The issuing bank verifies that the account exists, that the card is not stolen, and that you have not exceeded your credit limit. At this point, the slip is printed, which you sign.

Visa acts as the clearing agent for the transaction. It transfers funds from the issuing bank to Nordstrom's bank account. Generally this transfer of funds, from sale to the receipt of funds in the merchant's account, takes two to three days.

In the meantime, Visa puts a pending charge on your account for the amount of the tie purchase; that amount counts immediately against your available credit limit. At the end of the billing period, Visa sends you an invoice (your credit card bill) which shows the various charges you made, and the amounts that Visa expended on your behalf, for the month. You then must "pay the piper" for your stylish new ties.

Assume that Nordstrom prepares a bank reconciliation at the end of each month. If some credit card sales have not been processed by the bank, how should Nordstrom treat these transactions on its bank reconciliation? (Go to **WileyPLUS** for this answer and additional questions.)

DO IT! 2 Uncollectible Accounts Receivable

Brule Co. has been in business five years. The unadjusted trial balance at the end of the current year shows:

Accounts Receivable	$30,000 Dr.
Sales Revenue	$180,000 Cr.
Allowance for Doubtful Accounts	$2,000 Dr.

Brule estimates bad debts to be 10% of receivables. Prepare the entry necessary to adjust Allowance for Doubtful Accounts.

Action Plan

- ✔ Estimate the amount the company does not expect to collect.
- ✔ Consider the existing balance in the allowance account when using the percentage-of-receivables basis.
- ✔ Report receivables at their cash (net) realizable value.

Solution

The following entry should be made to bring the balance in Allowance for Doubtful Accounts up to a normal credit balance of $3,000 (10% × $30,000):

Bad Debt Expense [(10% × $30,000) + $2,000]	5,000	
Allowance for Doubtful Accounts		5,000
(To record estimate of uncollectible accounts)		

Related exercise material: **BE9-3, BE9-4, BE9-5, BE9-6, BE9-7, E9-3, E9-4, E9-5, E9-6, and DO IT! 9-2.**

LEARNING OBJECTIVE 3

Explain how companies recognize notes receivable.

Companies may also grant credit in exchange for a formal credit instrument known as a promissory note. A **promissory note** is a written promise to pay a specified amount of money on demand or at a definite time. Promissory notes may be used (1) when individuals and companies lend or borrow money, (2) when the amount of the transaction and the credit period exceed normal limits, or (3) in settlement of accounts receivable.

In a promissory note, the party making the promise to pay is called the **maker**. The party to whom payment is to be made is called the **payee**. The note may specifically identify the payee by name or may designate the payee simply as the bearer of the note.

In the note shown in Illustration 9-11, Calhoun Company is the maker and Wilma Company is the payee. To Wilma Company, the promissory note is a note receivable. To Calhoun Company, it is a note payable.

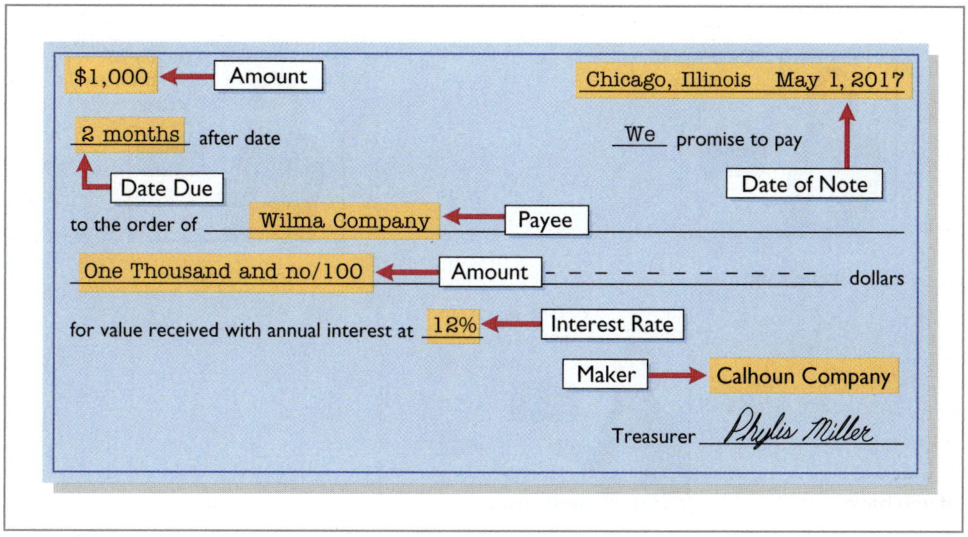

Illustration 9-11
Promissory note

Helpful Hint
For this note, the maker, Calhoun Company, debits Cash and credits Notes Payable. The payee, Wilma Company, debits Notes Receivable and credits Cash.

Notes receivable give the holder a stronger legal claim to assets than do accounts receivable. Like accounts receivable, notes receivable can be readily sold to another party. Promissory notes are negotiable instruments (as are checks), which means that they can be transferred to another party by endorsement.

Companies frequently accept notes receivable from customers who need to extend the payment of an outstanding account receivable. They often require such notes from high-risk customers. In some industries (such as the pleasure and sport boat industry), all credit sales are supported by notes. The majority of notes, however, originate from loans.

The basic issues in accounting for notes receivable are the same as those for accounts receivable. On the following pages, we look at these issues. Before we do, however, we need to consider two issues that do not apply to accounts receivable: determining the maturity date and computing interest.

Determining the Maturity Date

When the life of a note is expressed in terms of months, you find the date when it matures by counting the months from the date of issue. For example, the maturity date of a three-month note dated May 1 is August 1. A note drawn on the last day of a month matures on the last day of a subsequent month. That is, a July 31 note due in two months matures on September 30.

When the due date is stated in terms of days, you need to count the exact number of days to determine the maturity date. In counting, **omit the date the note is issued but include the due date**. For example, the maturity date of a 60-day note dated July 17 is September 15, computed as follows.

Illustration 9-12
Computation of maturity date

Term of note		60 days
July (31−17)	14	
August	31	45
Maturity date: September		**15**

Illustration 9-13 shows three ways of stating the maturity date of a promissory note.

Illustration 9-13
Maturity date of different notes

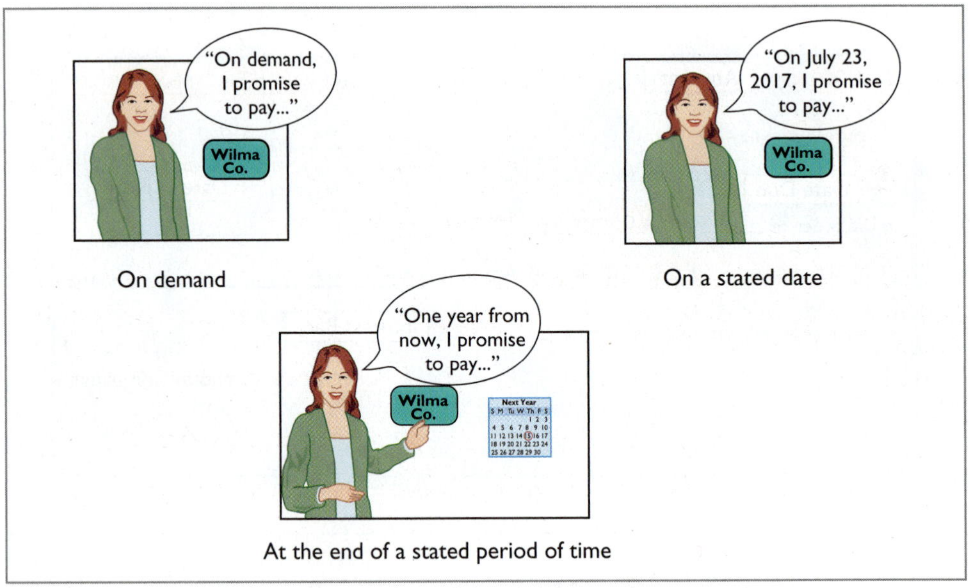

Computing Interest

Illustration 9-14 gives the basic formula for computing interest on an interest-bearing note.

Illustration 9-14
Formula for computing interest

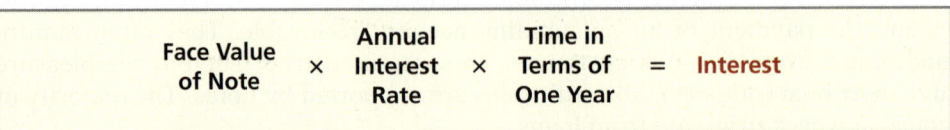

$$\text{Face Value of Note} \times \text{Annual Interest Rate} \times \text{Time in Terms of One Year} = \text{Interest}$$

Helpful Hint
The interest rate specified is the *annual* rate.

The interest rate specified in a note is an **annual** rate of interest. The time factor in the formula in Illustration 9-14 expresses the fraction of a year that the note is outstanding. When the maturity date is stated in days, the time factor is often the number of days divided by 360. When counting days, omit the date that the note is issued but include the due date. When the due date is stated in months, the time factor is the number of months divided by 12. Illustration 9-15 shows computation of interest for various time periods.

Terms of Note	Face	× Rate ×	Time	= Interest
$ 730, 12%, 120 days	$ 730 ×	12% ×	**120/360**	= $ 29.20
$1,000, 9%, 6 months	$1,000 ×	9% ×	**6/12**	= $ 45.00
$2,000, 6%, 1 year	$2,000 ×	6% ×	**1/1**	= $120.00

Illustration 9-15
Computation of interest

There are different ways to calculate interest. For example, the computation in Illustration 9-15 assumes 360 days for the length of the year. Most financial instruments use 365 days to compute interest. *For homework problems, assume 360 days to simplify computations.*

Recognizing Notes Receivable

To illustrate the basic entry for notes receivable, we will use Calhoun Company's $1,000, two-month, 12% promissory note dated May 1. Assuming that Calhoun Company wrote the note to settle an open account, Wilma Company makes the following entry for the receipt of the note.

May 1	Notes Receivable	1,000	
	Accounts Receivable—Calhoun Company		1,000
	(To record acceptance of Calhoun Company note)		

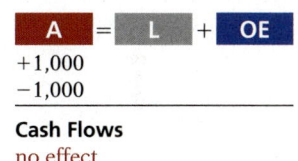

A = L + OE
+1,000
−1,000

Cash Flows
no effect

The company records the note receivable at its **face value**, the amount shown on the face of the note. No interest revenue is reported when the note is accepted because the revenue recognition principle does not recognize revenue until the performance obligation is satisfied. Interest is earned (accrued) as time passes.

If a company lends money using a note, the entry is a debit to Notes Receivable and a credit to Cash in the amount of the loan.

DO IT! 3 Recognizing Notes Receivable

Gambit Stores accepts from Leonard Co. a $3,400, 90-day, 6% note dated May 10 in settlement of Leonard's overdue account. (a) What is the maturity date of the note? (b) What is the interest payable at the maturity date?

Solution

(a) The maturity date is August 8, computed as follows.

Term of note:		90 days
May (31−10)	21	
June	30	
July	31	82
Maturity date: August		8

(b) The interest payable at the maturity date is $51, computed as follows.

Face	× Rate	× Time	= Interest
$3,400	× 6%	× 90/360	= $51

Action Plan

- ✔ Count the exact number of days to determine the maturity date. Omit the date the note is issued, but include the due date.
- ✔ Compute the accrued interest.

Related exercise material: **BE9-9, BE9-10, BE9-11, E9-10, E9-11, and DO IT! 9-3.**

LEARNING OBJECTIVE 4

Describe how companies value notes receivable, record their disposition, and present and analyze receivables.

Valuing Notes Receivable

Valuing short-term notes receivable is the same as valuing accounts receivable. Like accounts receivable, companies report short-term notes receivable at their **cash (net) realizable value**. The notes receivable allowance account is Allowance for Doubtful Accounts. The estimations involved in determining cash realizable value and in recording bad debt expense and the related allowance are done similarly to accounts receivable.

Disposing of Notes Receivable

Notes may be held to their maturity date, at which time the face value plus accrued interest is due. In some situations, the maker of the note defaults, and the payee must make an appropriate adjustment. In other situations, similar to accounts receivable, the holder of the note speeds up the conversion to cash by selling the receivables (as described later in this chapter).

HONOR OF NOTES RECEIVABLE

A note is **honored** when its maker pays in full at its maturity date. For each interest-bearing note, the **amount due at maturity** is the face value of the note plus interest for the length of time specified on the note.

To illustrate, assume that Wolder Co. lends Higley Co. $10,000 on June 1, accepting a five-month, 9% interest note. In this situation, interest is $375 ($\$10,000 \times 9\% \times \frac{5}{12}$). The amount due, **the maturity value**, is $10,375 ($10,000 + $375). To obtain payment, Wolder (the payee) must present the note either to Higley Co. (the maker) or to the maker's agent, such as a bank. If Wolder presents the note to Higley Co. on November 1, the maturity date, Wolder's entry to record the collection is as follows.

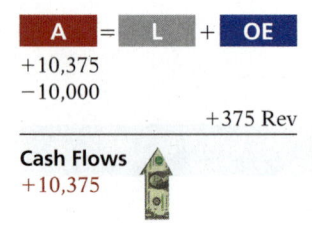

A	= L	+ OE
+10,375		
−10,000		
		+375 Rev

Cash Flows
+10,375

Nov. 1	Cash	10,375	
	Notes Receivable		10,000
	Interest Revenue ($\$10,000 \times 9\% \times \frac{5}{12}$)		375
	(To record collection of Higley note and interest)		

ACCRUAL OF INTEREST RECEIVABLE

Suppose instead that Wolder Co. prepares financial statements as of September 30. The timeline in Illustration 9-16 presents this situation.

Illustration 9-16
Timeline of interest earned

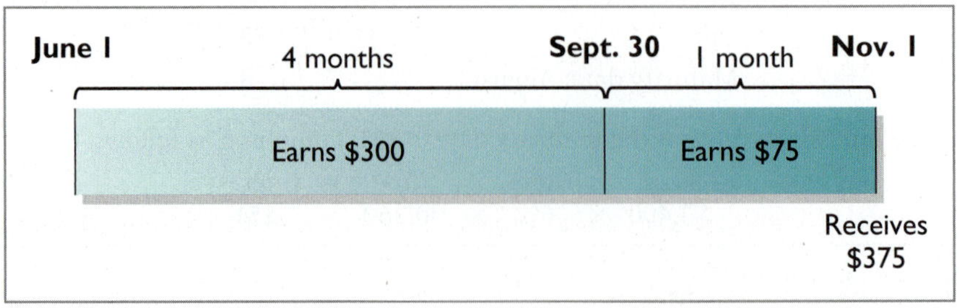

To reflect interest earned but not yet received, Wolder must accrue interest on September 30. In this case, the adjusting entry by Wolder is for four months of interest, or $300, as shown below.

Sept. 30	Interest Receivable ($10,000 × 9% × $\frac{4}{12}$)	300	
	Interest Revenue		300
	(To accrue 4 months' interest on Higley note)		

A	=	L	+	OE
+300				+300 Rev

Cash Flows
no effect

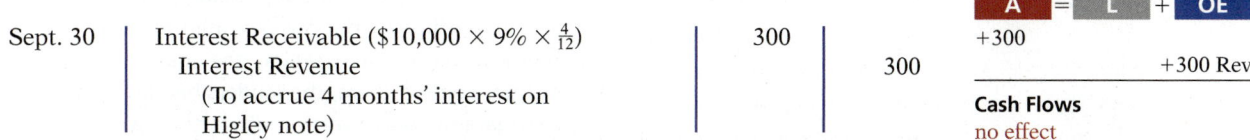

At the note's maturity on November 1, Wolder receives $10,375. This amount represents repayment of the $10,000 note as well as five months of interest, or $375, as shown below. The $375 is comprised of the $300 Interest Receivable accrued on September 30 plus $75 earned during October. Wolder's entry to record the honoring of the Higley note on November 1 is as follows.

Nov. 1	Cash [$10,000 + (10,000 × 9% × $\frac{5}{12}$)]	10,375	
	Notes Receivable		10,000
	Interest Receivable		300
	Interest Revenue (10,000 × 9% × $\frac{1}{12}$)]		75
	(To record collection of Higley note and interest)		

A	=	L	+	OE
+10,375				
−10,000				
−300				+75 Rev

Cash Flows
+10,375

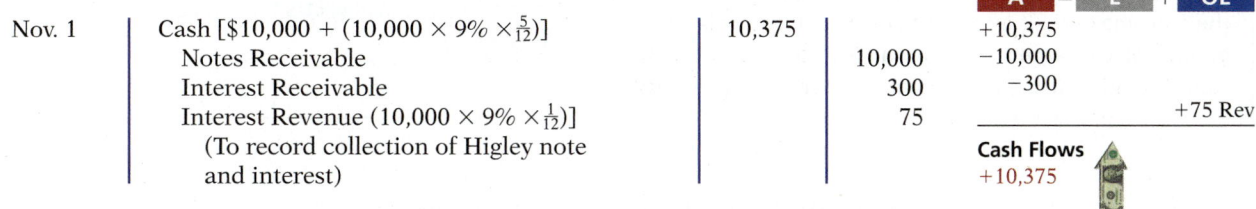

In this case, Wolder credits Interest Receivable because the receivable was established in the adjusting entry on September 30.

DISHONOR OF NOTES RECEIVABLE

A **dishonored (defaulted) note** is a note that is not paid in full at maturity. A dishonored note receivable is no longer negotiable. However, the payee still has a claim against the maker of the note for both the note and the interest. Therefore, the note holder usually transfers the Notes Receivable account to an Accounts Receivable account.

To illustrate, assume that Higley Co. on November 1 indicates that it cannot pay at the present time. The entry to record the dishonor of the note depends on whether Wolder Co. expects eventual collection. If it does expect eventual collection, Wolder Co. debits the amount due (face value and interest) on the note to Accounts Receivable. It would make the following entry at the time the note is dishonored (assuming no previous accrual of interest).

Nov. 1	Accounts Receivable—Higley	10,375	
	Notes Receivable		10,000
	Interest Revenue		375
	(To record the dishonor of Higley note)		

A	=	L	+	OE
+10,375				
−10,000				+375 Rev

Cash Flows
no effect

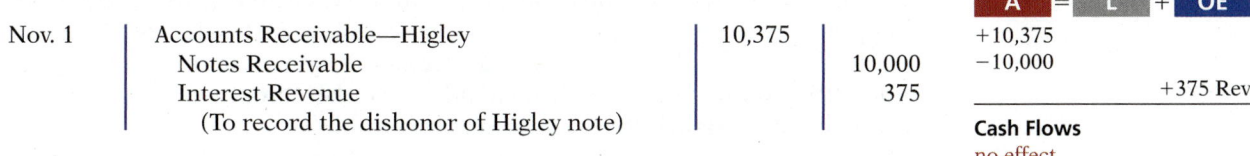

If instead on November 1 there is no hope of collection, the note holder would write off the face value of the note by debiting Allowance for Doubtful Accounts. No interest revenue would be recorded because collection will not occur.

SALE OF NOTES RECEIVABLE

The accounting for the sale of notes receivable is recorded similarly to the sale of accounts receivable. The accounting entries for the sale of notes receivable are left for a more advanced course.

Accounting Across the Organization — Countrywide Financial Corporation

© Andy Dean/iStockphoto

Bad Information Can Lead to Bad Loans

Many factors have contributed to the recent credit crisis. One significant factor that resulted in many bad loans was a failure by lenders to investigate loan customers sufficiently. For example, Countrywide Financial Corporation wrote many loans under its "Fast and Easy" loan program. That program allowed borrowers to provide little or no documentation for their income or their assets. Other lenders had similar programs, which earned the nickname "liars' loans." One study found that in these situations, 60% of applicants overstated their incomes by more than 50% in order to qualify for a loan. Critics of the banking industry say that because loan officers were compensated for loan volume and because banks were selling the loans to investors rather than holding them, the lenders had little incentive to investigate the borrowers' creditworthiness.

Sources: Glenn R. Simpson and James R. Hagerty, "Countrywide Loss Focuses Attention on Underwriting," *Wall Street Journal* (April 30, 2008), p. B1; and Michael Corkery, "Fraud Seen as Driver in Wave of Foreclosures," *Wall Street Journal* (December 21, 2007), p. A1.

What steps should the banks have taken to ensure the accuracy of financial information provided on loan applications? (Go to **WileyPLUS** for this answer and additional questions.)

Statement Presentation and Analysis

PRESENTATION

Companies should identify in the balance sheet or in the notes to the financial statements each of the major types of receivables. Short-term receivables appear in the current assets section of the balance sheet. Short-term investments appear before short-term receivables because these investments are more liquid (nearer to cash). Companies report both the gross amount of receivables and the allowance for doubtful accounts.

In a multiple-step income statement, companies report bad debt expense and service charge expense as selling expenses in the operating expenses section. Interest revenue appears under "Other revenues and gains" in the nonoperating activities section of the income statement.

ANALYSIS

Investors and corporate managers compute financial ratios to evaluate the liquidity of a company's accounts receivable. They use the **accounts receivable turnover** to assess the liquidity of the receivables. This ratio measures the number of times, on average, the company collects accounts receivable during the period. It is computed by dividing net credit sales (net sales less cash sales) by the average net accounts receivable during the year. Unless seasonal factors are significant, average net accounts receivable outstanding can be computed from the beginning and ending balances of net accounts receivable.

For example, in 2013 Cisco Systems had net sales of $38,029 million for the year. It had a beginning accounts receivable (net) balance of $4,369 million and an ending accounts receivable (net) balance of $5,470 million. Assuming that Cisco's sales were all on credit, its accounts receivable turnover is computed as follows.

Illustration 9-17
Accounts receivable turnover and computation

Net Credit Sales	÷	Average Net Accounts Receivable	=	Accounts Receivable Turnover
$38,029	÷	$\frac{\$4,369 + \$5,470}{2}$	=	**7.7 times**

The result indicates an accounts receivable turnover of 7.7 times per year. The higher the turnover, the more liquid the company's receivables.

A variant of the accounts receivable turnover that makes the liquidity even more evident is its conversion into an **average collection period** in terms of days. This is done by dividing the accounts receivable turnover into 365 days. For example, Cisco's turnover of 7.7 times is divided into 365 days, as shown in Illustration 9-18, to obtain approximately 47 days. This means that it takes Cisco 47 days to collect its accounts receivable.

Days in Year	÷	Accounts Receivable Turnover	=	Average Collection Period in Days
365 days	÷	7.7 times	=	**47 days**

Illustration 9-18
Average collection period for receivables formula and computation

Companies frequently use the average collection period to assess the effectiveness of a company's credit and collection policies. The general rule is that the collection period should not greatly exceed the credit term period (that is, the time allowed for payment).

DO IT! 4 Analysis of Receivables

In 2017, Phil Mickelson Company has net credit sales of $923,795 for the year. It had a beginning accounts receivable (net) balance of $38,275 and an ending accounts receivable (net) balance of $35,988. Compute Phil Mickelson Company's (a) accounts receivable turnover and (b) average collection period in days.

Solution

(a)

Net credit sales	÷	Average net accounts receivable	=	Accounts receivable turnover
$923,795	÷	$\frac{\$38{,}275 + \$35{,}988}{2}$	=	24.9 times

(b)

Days in year	÷	Accounts receivable turnover	=	Average collection period in days
365	÷	24.9 times	=	14.7 days

Related exercise material: **BE9-12, E9-14, and DO IT! 9-4.**

Action Plan

- ✔ Review the formula to compute the accounts receivable turnover.
- ✔ Make sure that both the beginning and ending accounts receivable balances are considered in the computation.
- ✔ Review the formula to compute the average collection period in days.

REVIEW AND PRACTICE

LEARNING OBJECTIVES REVIEW

1 Explain how companies recognize accounts receivable. Receivables are frequently classified as (1) accounts, (2) notes, and (3) other. Accounts receivable are amounts customers owe on account. Notes receivable are claims for which lenders issue formal instruments of credit as proof of the debt. Other receivables include nontrade receivables such as interest receivable, loans to company officers, advances to employees, and income taxes refundable.

Companies record accounts receivable when they perform a service on account or at the point of sale of merchandise on account. Accounts receivable are reduced by sales returns and allowances. Cash discounts reduce the amount received on accounts receivable. When interest is charged on a past due receivable, the company adds this interest to the accounts receivable balance and recognizes it as interest revenue.

2 Describe how companies value accounts receivable and record their disposition. There are two methods of accounting for uncollectible accounts: the allowance method and the direct write-off method. Companies may use either the percentage-of-sales or the percentage-of-receivables basis to estimate uncollectible accounts using the allowance method. The percentage-of-sales basis emphasizes the expense recognition (matching) principle. The percentage-of-receivables basis emphasizes the cash realizable value of the accounts receivable. An aging schedule is often used with this basis.

When a company collects an account receivable, it credits Accounts Receivable. When a company sells (factors) an account receivable, a service charge expense reduces the amount received.

3 Explain how companies recognize notes receivable. For a note stated in months, the maturity date is found by counting the months from the date of issue. For a note stated in days, the number of days is counted, omitting the issue date and counting the due date. The formula for computing interest is Face value × Interest rate × Time.

Companies record notes receivable at face value. In some cases, it is necessary to accrue interest prior to maturity. In this case, companies debit Interest Receivable and credit Interest Revenue.

4 Describe how companies value notes receivable, record their disposition, and present and analyze receivables. As with accounts receivable, companies report notes receivable at their cash (net) realizable value. The notes receivable allowance account is Allowance for Doubtful Accounts. The computation and estimations involved in valuing notes receivable at cash realizable value, and in recording the proper amount of bad debt expense and the related allowance, are similar to those for accounts receivable.

Notes can be held to maturity. At that time the face value plus accrued interest is due, and the note is removed from the accounts. In many cases, the holder of the note speeds up the conversion by selling the receivable to another party (a factor). In some situations, the maker of the note dishonors the note (defaults), in which case the company transfers the note and accrued interest to an account receivable or writes off the note.

Companies should identify in the balance sheet or in the notes to the financial statements each major type of receivable. Short-term receivables are considered current assets. Companies report the gross amount of receivables and the allowance for doubtful accounts. They report bad debt and service charge expenses in the multiple-step income statement as operating (selling) expenses. Interest revenue appears under other revenues and gains in the nonoperating activities section of the statement. Managers and investors evaluate accounts receivable for liquidity by computing a turnover ratio and an average collection period.

GLOSSARY REVIEW

Accounts receivable Amounts owed by customers on account. (p. 406).

Accounts receivable turnover A measure of the liquidity of accounts receivable; computed by dividing net credit sales by average net accounts receivable. (p. 422).

Aging the accounts receivable The analysis of customer balances by the length of time they have been unpaid. (p. 413).

Allowance method A method of accounting for bad debts that involves estimating uncollectible accounts at the end of each period. (p. 409).

Average collection period The average amount of time that a receivable is outstanding; calculated by dividing 365 days by the accounts receivable turnover. (p. 423).

Bad Debt Expense An expense account to record uncollectible receivables. (p. 408).

Cash (net) realizable value The net amount a company expects to receive in cash. (p. 409).

Direct write-off method A method of accounting for bad debts that involves expensing accounts at the time they are determined to be uncollectible. (p. 409).

Dishonored (defaulted) note A note that is not paid in full at maturity. (p. 421).

Factor A finance company or bank that buys receivables from businesses and then collects the payments directly from the customers. (p. 415).

Maker The party in a promissory note who is making the promise to pay. (p. 417).

Notes receivable Written promise (as evidenced by a formal instrument) for amounts to be received. (p. 406).

Other receivables Various forms of nontrade receivables, such as interest receivable and income taxes refundable. (p. 406).

Payee The party to whom payment of a promissory note is to be made. (p. 417).

Percentage-of-receivables basis Management estimates what percentage of receivables will result in losses from uncollectible accounts. (p. 413).

Percentage-of-sales basis Management estimates what percentage of credit sales will be uncollectible. (p. 412).

Promissory note A written promise to pay a specified amount of money on demand or at a definite time. (p. 417).

Receivables Amounts due from individuals and other companies. (p. 406).

Trade receivables Notes and accounts receivable that result from sales transactions. (p. 406).

PRACTICE MULTIPLE-CHOICE QUESTIONS

(LO 1) **1.** Receivables are frequently classified as:
(a) accounts receivable, company receivables, and other receivables.
(b) accounts receivable, notes receivable, and employee receivables.
(c) accounts receivable and general receivables.
(d) accounts receivable, notes receivable, and other receivables.

(LO 1) **2.** Buehler Company on June 15 sells merchandise on account to Chaz Co. for $1,000, terms 2/10, n/30. On June 20, Chaz Co. returns merchandise worth $300 to Buehler Company. On June 24, payment is received from Chaz Co. for the balance due. What is the amount of cash received?
(a) $700. (c) $686.
(b) $680. (d) None of the above.

(LO 2) **3.** Which of the following approaches for bad debts is best described as a balance sheet method?
(a) Percentage-of-receivables basis.
(b) Direct write-off method.
(c) Percentage-of-sales basis.
(d) Both percentage-of-receivables basis and direct write-off method.

(LO 2) **4.** Hughes Company has a credit balance of $5,000 in its Allowance for Doubtful Accounts before any adjustments are made at the end of the year. Based on review and aging of its accounts receivable at the end of the year, Hughes estimates that $60,000 of its receivables are uncollectible. The amount of bad debt expense which should be reported for the year is:
(a) $5,000. (c) $60,000.
(b) $55,000. (d) $65,000.

(LO 2) **5.** Use the same information as in Question 4, except that Hughes has a debit balance of $5,000 in its Allowance for Doubtful Accounts before any adjustments are made at the end of the year. In this situation, the amount of bad debt expense that should be reported for the year is:
(a) $5,000. (c) $60,000.
(b) $55,000. (d) $65,000.

(LO 2) **6.** Net sales for the month are $800,000, and bad debts are expected to be 1.5% of net sales. The company uses the percentage-of-sales basis. If Allowance for Doubtful Accounts has a credit balance of $15,000 before adjustment, what is the balance after adjustment?
(a) $15,000. (c) $23,000.
(b) $27,000. (d) $31,000.

(LO 2) **7.** In 2017, Roso Carlson Company had net credit sales of $750,000. On January 1, 2017, Allowance for Doubtful Accounts had a credit balance of $18,000. During 2017, $30,000 of uncollectible accounts receivable were written off. Past experience indicates that 3% of net credit sales become uncollectible. What should be the adjusted balance of Allowance for Doubtful Accounts at December 31, 2017?
(a) $10,050. (c) $22,500.
(b) $10,500. (d) $40,500.

8. An analysis and aging of the accounts receivable of Prince Company at December 31 reveals the following data. (LO 2)

Accounts receivable	$800,000
Allowance for doubtful accounts per books before adjustment	50,000
Amounts expected to become uncollectible	65,000

The cash realizable value of the accounts receivable at December 31, after adjustment, is:
(a) $685,000. (c) $800,000.
(b) $750,000. (d) $735,000.

9. Which of the following statements about Visa credit card sales is **incorrect**? (LO 2)
(a) The credit card issuer makes the credit investigation of the customer.
(b) The retailer is not involved in the collection process.
(c) Two parties are involved.
(d) The retailer receives cash more quickly than it would from individual customers on account.

10. Blinka Retailers accepted $50,000 of Citibank Visa credit card charges for merchandise sold on July 1. Citibank charges 4% for its credit card use. The entry to record this transaction by Blinka Retailers will include a credit to Sales Revenue of $50,000 and a debit(s) to: (LO 2)

(a) Cash	$48,000
and Service Charge Expense	$2,000
(b) Accounts Receivable	$48,000
and Service Charge Expense	$2,000
(c) Cash	$50,000
(d) Accounts Receivable	$50,000

11. One of the following statements about promissory notes is incorrect. The **incorrect** statement is: (LO 3)
(a) The party making the promise to pay is called the maker.
(b) The party to whom payment is to be made is called the payee.
(c) A promissory note is not a negotiable instrument.
(d) A promissory note is often required from high-risk customers.

12. Foti Co. accepts a $1,000, 3-month, 6% promissory note in settlement of an account with Bartelt Co. The entry to record this transaction is as follows. (LO 3)

(a) Notes Receivable	1,015	
Accounts Receivable		1,015
(b) Notes Receivable	1,000	
Accounts Receivable		1,000
(c) Notes Receivable	1,000	
Sales Revenue		1,000
(d) Notes Receivable	1,030	
Accounts Receivable		1,030

13. Ginter Co. holds Kolar Inc.'s $10,000, 120-day, 9% note. The entry made by Ginter Co. when the note is collected, assuming no interest has been previously accrued, is: (LO 4)

(a) Cash	10,300	
Notes Receivable		10,300

(b) Cash	10,000	
Notes Receivable		10,000
(c) Accounts Receivable	10,300	
Notes Receivable		10,000
Interest Revenue		300
(d) Cash	10,300	
Notes Receivable		10,000
Interest Revenue		300

(LO 4) 14. Accounts and notes receivable are reported in the current assets section of the balance sheet at:
(a) cash (net) realizable value.
(b) net book value.
(c) lower-of-cost-or-net realizable value.
(d) invoice cost.

15. Oliveras Company had net credit sales during the year of $800,000 and cost of goods sold of $500,000. The balance in accounts receivable at the beginning of the year was $100,000, and the end of the year it was $150,000. What were the accounts receivable turnover and the average collection period in days? (LO 4)
(a) 4.0 and 91.3 days.
(b) 5.3 and 68.9 days.
(c) 6.4 and 57 days.
(d) 8.0 and 45.6 days.

Solutions

1. (d) Receivables are frequently classified as accounts receivable, notes receivable, and other receivables. The other choices are incorrect because receivables are not frequently classified as (a) company receivables, (b), employee receivables, or (c) general receivables.

2. (c) Because payment is received within 10 days of the purchase, the cash received is $686 {[$1,000 – $300] – [($1,000 – $300) × 2%)]}. The other choices are incorrect because (a) $700 does not consider the 2% discount; (b) the amount of the discount is based upon the amount after the return is granted ($700 × 2%), not the amount before the return of merchandise ($1,000 × 2%); and (d) there is a correct answer.

3. (a) The percentage-of-receivables basis is a balance sheet method because it emphasizes the cash (net) realizable value of accounts receivable. The other choices are incorrect because (b) the direct write-off method is neither a balance sheet nor an income statement method for accounting for bad debts, (c) the percentage-of-sales basis is an income statement method because it results in a better matching of expenses with revenues, and (d) only the percentage-of-receivables basis is a balance sheet method, not the direct write-off method.

4. (b) By crediting Allowance for Doubtful Accounts for $55,000, the new balance will be the required balance of $60,000. This adjusting entry debits Bad Debt Expense for $55,000 and credits Allowance for Doubtful Accounts for $55,000, not (a) $5,000, (c) $60,000, or (d) $65,000.

5. (d) By crediting Allowance for Doubtful Accounts for $65,000, the new balance will be the required balance of $60,000. This adjusting entry debits Bad Debt Expense for $65,000 and credits Allowance for Doubtful Accounts for $65,000, not (a) $5,000, (b) $55,000, or (c) $60,000.

6. (b) Net sales times the percentage expected to default equals the amount of bad debt expense for the year ($800,000 × 1.5% = $12,000). Because this adjusting entry credits Allowance for Doubtful Accounts, the balance after adjustment is $27,000 ($15,000 + $12,000), not (a) $15,000, (c) $23,000, or (d) $31,000.

7. (b) The accounts written off during the year will result in a $30,000 debit to Allowance for Doubtful Accounts. The adjusting entry for bad debts will include a $22,500 credit ($750,000 × 3%) to Allowance for Doubtful Accounts. Combining the beginning balance of $ 18,000 credit, the $30,000 debit, and the $22,500 credit leaves a credit balance of $10,500 in the allowance account, not (a) $10,050, (c) $22,500, or (d) $40,500.

8. (d) Accounts Receivable less the expected uncollectible amount equals the cash realizable value of $735,000 ($800,000 – $65,000), not (a) $685,000, (b) $750,000, or (c) $800,000.

9. (c) There are three parties, not two, involved in Visa credit card sales: the credit card company, the retailer, and the customer. The other choices are true statements.

10. (a) Credit card sales are considered cash sales. Cash is debited $48,000 for the net amount received ($50,000 – $2,000 for credit card use fee), and Service Charge Expense is debited $2,000 for the 4% credit card use fee ($50,000 × 4%). The other choices are therefore incorrect.

11. (c) A promissory note is a negotiable instrument. The other choices are true statements.

12. (b) Notes Receivable is recorded at face value ($1,000). No interest on the note is recorded until it is earned. Accounts Receivable is credited because no new sales have been made. The other choices are therefore incorrect.

13. (d) Cash is debited for its maturity value [$10,000 + interest earned ($10,000 × 1/3 × 9%)], Notes Receivable credited for its face value, and Interest Revenue credited for the amount of interest earned. The other choices are therefore incorrect.

14. (a) Accounts Receivable is reported in the current assets section of the balance sheet at the gross amount less the allowance for doubtful accounts, not at (b) net book value, (c) lower-of-cost-or-net realizable value, or (d) invoice cost.

15. (c) The accounts receivable turnover is 6.4 [$800,000/($100,000 + $150,000)/2)]. The average collection period in days is 57 days (365/6.4). The other choices are therefore incorrect.

PRACTICE EXERCISES

1. The ledger of Nuro Company at the end of the current year shows Accounts Receivable $180,000, Sales Revenue $1,800,000, and Sales Returns and Allowances $60,000.

Journalize entries to record allowance for doubtful accounts using two different bases.

(LO 2)

Instructions

(a) If Nuro uses the direct write-off method to account for uncollectible accounts, journalize the adjusting entry at December 31, assuming Nuro determines that Willie's $2,900 balance is uncollectible.

(b) If Allowance for Doubtful Accounts has a credit balance of $4,300 in the trial balance, journalize the adjusting entry at December 31, assuming bad debts are expected to be (1) 1 % of net sales, and (2) 10% of accounts receivable.

(c) If Allowance for Doubtful Accounts has a debit balance of $410 in the trial balance, journalize the adjusting entry at December 31, assuming bad debts are expected to be (1) 0.75% of net sales and (2) 6% of accounts receivable.

Solution

1. (a)	Dec. 31	Bad Debt Expense	2,900	
		Accounts Receivable—Willie's		2,900
(b) (1)	Dec. 31	Bad Debt Expense		
		[($1,800,000 − $60,000) × 1%]	17,400	
		Allowance for Doubtful Accounts		17,400
(2)	Dec. 31	Bad Debt Expense	13,700	
		Allowance for Doubtful		
		Accounts [($180,000 × 10%) − $4,300]		13,700
(c) (1)	Dec. 31	Bad Debt Expense		
		[($1,800,000 − $60,000) × 0.75%]	13,050	
		Allowance for Doubtful Accounts		13,050
(2)	Dec. 31	Bad Debt Expense	11,210	
		Allowance for Doubtful		
		Accounts [($180,000 × 6%) + $410]		11,210

2. Sargeant Supply Co. has the following transactions related to notes receivable during the last 2 months of 2017.

Journalize entries for notes receivable transactions.

(LO 3, 4)

Nov.	1	Loaned $20,000 cash to Mary Hawkins on a 1-year, 12% note.
Dec.	11	Sold goods to Eminem, Inc., receiving a $9,000. 90-day, 8% note.
	16	Received a $8,000, 6-month, 9% note in exchange for Rick DeLong's outstanding accounts receivable.
	31	Accrued interest revenue on all notes receivable.

Instructions

(a) Journalize the transactions for Sargeant Supply Co.

(b) Record the collection of the Hawkins note at its maturity in 2018.

Solution

2. (a)

2017			
Nov. 1	Notes Receivable	20,000	
	Cash		20,000
Dec. 11	Notes Receivable	9,000	
	Sales Revenue		9,000
16	Notes Receivable	8,000	
	Accounts Receivable—DeLong		8,000
31	Interest Receivable	470	
	Interest Revenue*		470

*Calculation of interest revenue:

Hawkins' note:	$20,000 × 12% × 2/12 = $400
Eminem's note:	9,000 × 8% × 20/360 = 40
DeLong's note:	8,000 × 9% × 15/360 = 30
Total accrued interest	$470

(b)	2018		
Nov. 1	Cash	22,400	
	Interest Receivable		400
	Interest Revenue**		2,000
	Notes Receivable		20,000

**($20,000 × 12% × 10/12)

PRACTICE PROBLEM

Prepare entries for various receivables transactions.

(LO 1, 2, 3, 4)

The following selected transactions relate to Dylan Company.

Mar.	1	Sold $20,000 of merchandise to Potter Company, terms 2/10, n/30.
	11	Received payment in full from Potter Company for balance due on existing accounts receivable.
	12	Accepted Juno Company's $20,000, 6-month, 12% note for balance due.
	13	Made Dylan Company credit card sales for $13,200.
	15	Made Visa credit card sales totaling $6,700. A 3% service fee is charged by Visa.
Apr.	11	Sold accounts receivable of $8,000 to Harcot Factor. Harcot Factor assesses a service charge of 2% of the amount of receivables sold.
	13	Received collections of $8,200 on Dylan Company credit card sales and added finance charges of 1.5% to the remaining balances.
May	10	Wrote off as uncollectible $16,000 of accounts receivable. Dylan uses the percentage-of-sales basis to estimate bad debts.
June	30	Credit sales recorded during the first 6 months total $2,000,000. The bad debt percentage is 1% of credit sales. At June 30, the balance in the allowance account is $3,500 before adjustment.
July	16	One of the accounts receivable written off in May was from J. Simon, who pays the amount due, $4,000, in full.

Instructions

Prepare the journal entries for the transactions. (Ignore entries for cost of goods sold.)

Solution

Mar. 1	Accounts Receivable—Potter	20,000	
	Sales Revenue		20,000
	(To record sales on account)		
11	Cash	19,600	
	Sales Discounts (2% × $20,000)	400	
	Accounts Receivable—Potter		20,000
	(To record collection of accounts receivable)		
12	Notes Receivable	20,000	
	Accounts Receivable—Juno		20,000
	(To record acceptance of Juno Company note)		
13	Accounts Receivable	13,200	
	Sales Revenue		13,200
	(To record company credit card sales)		
15	Cash	6,499	
	Service Charge Expense (3% × $6,700)	201	
	Sales Revenue		6,700
	(To record credit card sales)		
Apr. 11	Cash	7,840	
	Service Charge Expense (2% × $8,000)	160	
	Accounts Receivable		8,000
	(To record sale of receivables to factor)		
13	Cash	8,200	
	Accounts Receivable		8,200
	(To record collection of accounts receivable)		
	Accounts Receivable [($13,200 − $8,200) × 1.5%]	75	
	Interest Revenue		75
	(To record interest on amount due)		

May 10	Allowance for Doubtful Accounts	16,000	
	Accounts Receivable		16,000
	(To record write-off of accounts receivable)		
June 30	Bad Debt Expense ($2,000,000 × 1%)	20,000	
	Allowance for Doubtful Accounts		20,000
	(To record estimate of uncollectible accounts)		
July 16	Accounts Receivable—J. Simon	4,000	
	Allowance for Doubtful Accounts		4,000
	(To reverse write-off of accounts receivable)		
	Cash	4,000	
	Accounts Receivable—J. Simon		4,000
	(To record collection of accounts receivable)		

WileyPLUS Brief Exercises, Exercises, DO IT! Exercises, and Problems and many additional resources are available for practice in WileyPLUS

QUESTIONS

1. What is the difference between an account receivable and a note receivable?
2. What are some common types of receivables other than accounts receivable and notes receivable?
3. Texaco Oil Company issues its own credit cards. Assume that Texaco charges you $40 interest on an unpaid balance. Prepare the journal entry that Texaco makes to record this revenue.
4. What are the essential features of the allowance method of accounting for bad debts?
5. Roger Holloway cannot understand why cash realizable value does not decrease when an uncollectible account is written off under the allowance method. Clarify this point for Roger.
6. Distinguish between the two bases that may be used in estimating uncollectible accounts.
7. Borke Company has a credit balance of $3,000 in Allowance for Doubtful Accounts. The estimated bad debt expense under the percentage-of-sales basis is $4,100. The total estimated uncollectibles under the percentage-of-receivables basis is $5,800. Prepare the adjusting entry under each basis.
8. How are bad debts accounted for under the direct write-off method? What are the disadvantages of this method?
9. Freida Company accepts both its own credit cards and national credit cards. What are the advantages of accepting both types of cards?
10. An article recently appeared in the *Wall Street Journal* indicating that companies are selling their receivables at a record rate. Why are companies selling their receivables?
11. Westside Textiles decides to sell $800,000 of its accounts receivable to First Factors Inc. First Factors assesses a service charge of 3% of the amount of receivables sold. Prepare the journal entry that Westside Textiles makes to record this sale.
12. Your roommate is uncertain about the advantages of a promissory note. Compare the advantages of a note receivable with those of an account receivable.
13. How may the maturity date of a promissory note be stated?
14. Indicate the maturity date of each of the following promissory notes:

	Date of Note	Terms
(a)	March 13	one year after date of note
(b)	May 4	3 months after date
(c)	June 20	30 days after date
(d)	July 1	60 days after date

15. Compute the missing amounts for each of the following notes.

	Principal	Annual Interest Rate	Time	Total Interest
(a)	?	9%	120 days	$ 450
(b)	$30,000	10%	3 years	?
(c)	$60,000	?	5 months	$1,500
(d)	$45,000	8%	?	$1,200

16. In determining interest revenue, some financial institutions use 365 days per year and others use 360 days. Why might a financial institution use 360 days?
17. Jana Company dishonors a note at maturity. What are the options available to the lender?
18. General Motors Corporation has accounts receivable and notes receivable. How should the receivables be reported on the balance sheet?
19. The accounts receivable turnover is 8.14, and average net receivables during the period are $400,000. What is the amount of net credit sales for the period?
20. What percentage does Apple's allowance for doubtful accounts represent as a percentage of its gross receivables?

BRIEF EXERCISES

Identify different types of receivables.
(LO 1)

BE9-1 Presented below are three receivables transactions. Indicate whether these receivables are reported as accounts receivable, notes receivable, or other receivables on a balance sheet.

(a) Sold merchandise on account for $64,000 to a customer.
(b) Received a promissory note of $57,000 for services performed.
(c) Advanced $10,000 to an employee.

Record basic accounts receivable transactions.
(LO 1)

BE9-2 Record the following transactions on the books of RAS Co.

(a) On July 1, RAS Co. sold merchandise on account to Waegelein Inc. for $17,200, terms 2/10, n/30.
(b) On July 8, Waegelein Inc. returned merchandise worth $3,800 to RAS Co.
(c) On July 11, Waegelein Inc. paid for the merchandise.

Prepare entry for allowance method and partial balance sheet.
(LO 2, 4)

BE9-3 During its first year of operations, Gavin Company had credit sales of $3,000,000; $600,000 remained uncollected at year-end. The credit manager estimates that $31,000 of these receivables will become uncollectible.

(a) Prepare the journal entry to record the estimated uncollectibles.
(b) Prepare the current assets section of the balance sheet for Gavin Company. Assume that in addition to the receivables it has cash of $90,000, inventory of $130,000, and prepaid insurance of $7,500.

Prepare entry for write-off; determine cash realizable value.
(LO 2)

BE9-4 At the end of 2017, Carpenter Co. has accounts receivable of $700,000 and an allowance for doubtful accounts of $54,000. On January 24, 2018, the company learns that its receivable from Megan Gray is not collectible, and management authorizes a write-off of $6,200.

(a) Prepare the journal entry to record the write-off.
(b) What is the cash realizable value of the accounts receivable (1) before the write-off and (2) after the write-off?

Prepare entries for collection of bad debt write-off.
(LO 2)

BE9-5 Assume the same information as BE9-4. On March 4, 2018, Carpenter Co. receives payment of $6,200 in full from Megan Gray. Prepare the journal entries to record this transaction.

Prepare entry using percentage-of-sales method.
(LO 2)

BE9-6 Farr Co. elects to use the percentage-of-sales basis in 2017 to record bad debt expense. It estimates that 2% of net credit sales will become uncollectible. Sales revenues are $800,000 for 2017, sales returns and allowances are $40,000, and the allowance for doubtful accounts has a credit balance of $9,000. Prepare the adjusting entry to record bad debt expense in 2017.

Prepare entry using percentage-of-receivables method.
(LO 2)

BE9-7 Kingston Co. uses the percentage-of-receivables basis to record bad debt expense. It estimates that 1% of accounts receivable will become uncollectible. Accounts receivable are $420,000 at the end of the year, and the allowance for doubtful accounts has a credit balance of $1,500.

(a) Prepare the adjusting journal entry to record bad debt expense for the year.
(b) If the allowance for doubtful accounts had a debit balance of $800 instead of a credit balance of $1,500, determine the amount to be reported for bad debt expense.

Prepare entries to dispose of accounts receivable.
(LO 2)

BE9-8 Presented below are two independent transactions.

(a) Tony's Restaurant accepted a Visa card in payment of a $175 lunch bill. The bank charges a 4% fee. What entry should Tony's make?
(b) Larkin Company sold its accounts receivable of $60,000. What entry should Larkin make, given a service charge of 3% on the amount of receivables sold?

Compute interest and determine maturity dates on notes.
(LO 3)

BE9-9 Compute interest and find the maturity date for the following notes.

	Date of Note	Principal	Interest Rate (%)	Terms
(a)	June 10	$80,000	6%	60 days
(b)	July 14	$64,000	7%	90 days
(c)	April 27	$12,000	8%	75 days

BE9-10 Presented below are data on three promissory notes. Determine the missing amounts.

Determine maturity dates and compute interest and rates on notes.

(LO 3)

	Date of Note	Terms	Maturity Date	Principal	Annual Interest Rate	Total Interest
(a)	April 1	60 days	?	$600,000	6%	?
(b)	July 2	30 days	?	90,000	?	$600
(c)	March 7	6 months	?	120,000	10%	?

BE9-11 On January 10, 2017, Perez Co. sold merchandise on account to Robertsen Co. for $15,600, n/30. On February 9, Robertsen Co. gave Perez Co. a 10% promissory note in settlement of this account. Prepare the journal entry to record the sale and the settlement of the account receivable.

Prepare entry for notes receivable exchanged for account receivable.

(LO 3)

BE9-12 The financial statements of Minnesota Mining and Manufacturing Company (3M) report net sales of $20.0 billion. Accounts receivable (net) are $2.7 billion at the beginning of the year and $2.8 billion at the end of the year. Compute 3M's accounts receivable turnover. Compute 3M's average collection period for accounts receivable in days.

Compute ratios to analyze receivables.

(LO 4)

DO IT! Exercises

DO IT! 9-1 On March 1, Lincoln sold merchandise on account to Amelia Company for $28,000, terms 1/10, net 45. On March 6, Amelia returns merchandise with a sales price of $1,000. On March 11, Lincoln receives payment from Amelia for the balance due. Prepare journal entries to record the March transactions on Lincoln's books. (You may ignore cost of goods sold entries and explanations.)

Prepare entries to recognize accounts receivable.

(LO 1)

DO IT! 9-2 Gonzalez Company has been in business several years. At the end of the current year, the ledger shows the following:

Prepare entry for uncollectible accounts.

(LO 2)

Accounts Receivable	$ 310,000 Dr.
Sales Revenue	2,200,000 Cr.
Allowance for Doubtful Accounts	6,100 Cr.

Bad debts are estimated to be 5% of accounts receivable. Prepare the entry to adjust Allowance for Doubtful Accounts.

DO IT! 9-3 Gentry Wholesalers accepts from Benton Stores a $6,200, 4-month, 9% note dated May 31 in settlement of Benton's overdue account. (a) What is the maturity date of the note? (b) What is the interest payable at the maturity date?

Compute maturity date and interest on note.

(LO 3)

DO IT! 9-4 In 2017, Wainwright Company has net credit sales of $1,300,000 for the year. It had a beginning accounts receivable (net) balance of $101,000 and an ending accounts receivable (net) balance of $107,000. Compute Wainwright Company's (a) accounts receivable turnover and (b) average collection period in days.

Compute ratios for receivables.

(LO 4)

EXERCISES

E9-1 Presented below are selected transactions of Molina Company. Molina sells in large quantities to other companies and also sells its product in a small retail outlet.

Journalize entries related to accounts receivable.

(LO 1)

March 1 Sold merchandise on account to Dodson Company for $5,000, terms 2/10, n/30.

3 Dodson Company returned merchandise worth $500 to Molina.

9 Molina collected the amount due from Dodson Company from the March 1 sale.

15 Molina sold merchandise for $400 in its retail outlet. The customer used his Molina credit card.

31 Molina added 1.5% monthly interest to the customer's credit card balance.

Instructions

Prepare journal entries for the transactions above.

Journalize entries for recognizing accounts receivable.

(LO 1)

E9-2 Presented below are two independent situations.

(a) On January 6, Brumbaugh Co. sells merchandise on account to Pryor Inc. for $7,000, terms 2/10, n/30. On January 16, Pryor Inc. pays the amount due. Prepare the entries on Brumbaugh's books to record the sale and related collection.

(b) On January 10, Andrew Farley uses his Paltrow Co. credit card to purchase merchandise from Paltrow Co. for $9,000. On February 10, Farley is billed for the amount due of $9,000. On February 12, Farley pays $5,000 on the balance due. On March 10, Farley is billed for the amount due, including interest at 1% per month on the unpaid balance as of February 12. Prepare the entries on Paltrow Co.'s books related to the transactions that occurred on January 10, February 12, and March 10.

Journalize entries to record allowance for doubtful accounts using two different bases.

(LO 2)

E9-3 The ledger of Costello Company at the end of the current year shows Accounts Receivable $110,000, Sales Revenue $840,000, and Sales Returns and Allowances $20,000.

Instructions

(a) If Costello uses the direct write-off method to account for uncollectible accounts, journalize the adjusting entry at December 31, assuming Costello determines that L. Dole's $1,400 balance is uncollectible.

(b) If Allowance for Doubtful Accounts has a credit balance of $2,100 in the trial balance, journalize the adjusting entry at December 31, assuming bad debts are expected to be (1) 1% of net sales, and (2) 10% of accounts receivable.

(c) If Allowance for Doubtful Accounts has a debit balance of $200 in the trial balance, journalize the adjusting entry at December 31, assuming bad debts are expected to be (1) 0.75% of net sales and (2) 6% of accounts receivable.

Determine bad debt expense; prepare the adjusting entry for bad debt expense.

(LO 2)

E9-4 Menge Company has accounts receivable of $93,100 at March 31. Credit terms are 2/10, n/30. At March 31, Allowance for Doubtful Accounts has a credit balance of $1,200 prior to adjustment. The company uses the percentage-of-receivables basis for estimating uncollectible accounts. The company's estimate of bad debts is shown below.

Age of Accounts	Balance, March 31	Estimated Percentage Uncollectible
1–30 days	$60,000	2.0%
31–60 days	17,600	5.0%
61–90 days	8,500	20.0%
Over 90 days	7,000	50.0%
	$93,100	

Instructions

(a) Determine the total estimated uncollectibles.

(b) Prepare the adjusting entry at March 31 to record bad debt expense.

Journalize write-off and recovery.

(LO 2)

E9-5 At December 31, 2016, Finzelberg Company had a credit balance of $15,000 in Allowance for Doubtful Accounts. During 2017, Finzelberg wrote off accounts totaling $11,000. One of those accounts ($1,800) was later collected. At December 31, 2017, an aging schedule indicated that the balance in Allowance for Doubtful Accounts should be $19,000.

Instructions

Prepare journal entries to record the 2017 transactions of Finzelberg Company.

Journalize percentage of sales basis, write-off, recovery.

(LO 2)

E9-6 On December 31, 2017, Ling Co. estimated that 2% of its net sales of $450,000 will become uncollectible. The company recorded this amount as an addition to Allowance for Doubtful Accounts. On May 11, 2018, Ling Co. determined that the Jeff Shoemaker account was uncollectible and wrote off $1,100. On June 12, 2018, Shoemaker paid the amount previously written off.

Instructions

Prepare the journal entries on December 31, 2017, May 11, 2018, and June 12, 2018.

E9-7 Presented below are two independent situations.

Journalize entries for the sale of accounts receivable.

(LO 2)

(a) On March 3, Kitselman Appliances sells $650,000 of its receivables to Ervay Factors Inc. Ervay Factors assesses a finance charge of 3% of the amount of receivables sold. Prepare the entry on Kitselman Appliances' books to record the sale of the receivables.
(b) On May 10, Fillmore Company sold merchandise for $3,000 and accepted the customer's America Bank MasterCard. America Bank charges a 4% service charge for credit card sales. Prepare the entry on Fillmore Company's books to record the sale of merchandise.

E9-8 Presented below are two independent situations.

Journalize entries for credit card sales.

(LO 2)

(a) On April 2, Jennifer Elston uses her JCPenney Company credit card to purchase merchandise from a JCPenney store for $1,500. On May 1, Elston is billed for the $1,500 amount due. Elston pays $500 on the balance due on May 3. Elston receives a bill dated June 1 for the amount due, including interest at 1.0% per month on the unpaid balance as of May 3. Prepare the entries on JCPenney Co.'s books related to the transactions that occurred on April 2, May 3, and June 1.
(b) On July 4, Spangler's Restaurant accepts a Visa card for a $200 dinner bill. Visa charges a 2% service fee. Prepare the entry on Spangler's books related to this transaction.

E9-9 Colaw Stores accepts both its own and national credit cards. During the year, the following selected summary transactions occurred.

Journalize credit card sales, and indicate the statement presentation of financing charges and service charge expense.

(LO 2)

Jan.	15	Made Colaw credit card sales totaling $18,000. (There were no balances prior to January 15.)
	20	Made Visa credit card sales (service charge fee 2%) totaling $4,500.
Feb.	10	Collected $10,000 on Colaw credit card sales.
	15	Added finance charges of 1.5% to Colaw credit card account balances.

Instructions

Journalize the transactions for Colaw Stores.

E9-10 Elburn Supply Co. has the following transactions related to notes receivable during the last 2 months of 2017. The company does not make entries to accrue interest except at December 31.

Journalize entries for notes receivable transactions.

(LO 3)

Nov.	1	Loaned $30,000 cash to Manny Lopez on a 12 month, 10% note.
Dec.	11	Sold goods to Ralph Kremer, Inc., receiving a $6,750, 90-day, 8% note.
	16	Received a $4,000, 180 day, 9% note in exchange for Joe Fernetti's outstanding accounts receivable.
	31	Accrued interest revenue on all notes receivable.

Instructions

(a) Journalize the transactions for Elburn Supply Co.
(b) Record the collection of the Lopez note at its maturity in 2018.

E9-11 Record the following transactions for Redeker Co. in the general journal.

Journalize entries for notes receivable.

(LO 3)

2017

May 1	Received a $9,000, 12-month, 10% note in exchange for Mark Chamber's outstanding accounts receivable.
Dec. 31	Accrued interest on the Chamber note.
Dec. 31	Closed the interest revenue account.

2018

May 1	Received principal plus interest on the Chamber note. (No interest has been accrued in 2018.)

E9-12 Vandiver Company had the following select transactions.

Prepare entries for note receivable transactions.

(LO 3, 4)

Apr. 1, 2017	Accepted Goodwin Company's 12-month, 12% note in settlement of a $30,000 account receivable.
July 1, 2017	Loaned $25,000 cash to Thomas Slocombe on a 9-month, 10% note.
Dec. 31, 2017	Accrued interest on all notes receivable.
Apr. 1, 2018	Received principal plus interest on the Goodwin note.
Apr. 1, 2018	Thomas Slocombe dishonored its note; Vandiver expects it will eventually collect.

Instructions

Prepare journal entries to record the transactions. Vandiver prepares adjusting entries once a year on December 31.

Journalize entries for dishonor of notes receivable.

(LO 3, 4)

E9-13 On May 2, McLain Company lends $9,000 to Chang, Inc., issuing a 6-month, 9% note. At the maturity date, November 2, Chang indicates that it cannot pay.

Instructions

(a) Prepare the entry to record the issuance of the note.
(b) Prepare the entry to record the dishonor of the note, assuming that McLain Company expects collection will occur.
(c) Prepare the entry to record the dishonor of the note, assuming that McLain Company does not expect collection in the future.

Compute accounts receivable turnover and average collection period.

(LO 4)

E9-14 Kerwick Company had accounts receivable of $100,000 on January 1, 2017. The only transactions that affected accounts receivable during 2017 were net credit sales of $1,000,000, cash collections of $920,000, and accounts written off of $30,000.

Instructions

(a) Compute the ending balance of accounts receivable.
(b) Compute the accounts receivable turnover for 2017.
(c) Compute the average collection period in days.

EXERCISES: SET B AND CHALLENGE EXERCISES

Visit the book's companion website, at **www.wiley.com/college/weygandt**, and choose the Student Companion site to access Exercises: Set B and Challenge Exercises.

PROBLEMS: SET A

Prepare journal entries related to bad debt expense.

(LO 1, 2, 4)

P9-1A At December 31, 2016, House Co. reported the following information on its balance sheet.

Accounts receivable	$960,000
Less: Allowance for doubtful accounts	80,000

During 2017, the company had the following transactions related to receivables.

1. Sales on account	$3,700,000
2. Sales returns and allowances	50,000
3. Collections of accounts receivable	2,810,000
4. Write-offs of accounts receivable deemed uncollectible	90,000
5. Recovery of bad debts previously written off as uncollectible	29,000

Instructions

(a) Prepare the journal entries to record each of these five transactions. Assume that no cash discounts were taken on the collections of accounts receivable.
(b) Enter the January 1, 2017, balances in Accounts Receivable and Allowance for Doubtful Accounts, post the entries to the two accounts (use T-accounts), and determine the balances.
(c) Prepare the journal entry to record bad debt expense for 2017, assuming that an aging of accounts receivable indicates that expected bad debts are $115,000.
(d) Compute the accounts receivable turnover for 2017 assuming the expected bad debt information provided in (c).

(b) Accounts receivable $1,710,000
ADA $19,000
(c) Bad debt expense $96,000

Compute bad debt amounts.

(LO 2)

P9-2A Information related to Mingenback Company for 2017 is summarized below.

Total credit sales	$2,500,000
Accounts receivable at December 31	875,000
Bad debts written off	33,000

Instructions

(a) What amount of bad debt expense will Mingenback Company report if it uses the direct write-off method of accounting for bad debts?
(b) Assume that Mingenback Company estimates its bad debt expense to be 2% of credit sales. What amount of bad debt expense will Mingenback record if it has an Allowance for Doubtful Accounts credit balance of $4,000?

(c) Assume that Mingenback Company estimates its bad debt expense based on 6% of accounts receivable. What amount of bad debt expense will Mingenback record if it has an Allowance for Doubtful Accounts credit balance of $3,000?
(d) Assume the same facts as in (c), except that there is a $3,000 debit balance in Allowance for Doubtful Accounts. What amount of bad debt expense will Mingenback record?
(e) What is the weakness of the direct write-off method of reporting bad debt expense?

P9-3A Presented below is an aging schedule for Halleran Company.

Journalize entries to record transactions related to bad debts.

(LO 2)

Worksheet.xls

Home | Insert | Page Layout | Formulas | Data | Review | View

P18 | fx

	A	B	C	D	E	F	G
1				Number of Days Past Due			
2			Not				
3	Customer	Total	Yet Due	1–30	31–60	61–90	Over 90
4	Anders	$ 22,000		$10,000	$12,000		
5	Blake	40,000	$ 40,000				
6	Coulson	57,000	16,000	6,000		$35,000	
7	Deleon	34,000					$34,000
8	Others	132,000	96,000	16,000	14,000		6,000
9		$285,000	$152,000	$32,000	$26,000	$35,000	$40,000
10	Estimated Percentage Uncollectible		3%	6%	13%	25%	50%
11	Total Estimated Bad Debts	$ 38,610	$ 4,560	$ 1,920	$ 3,380	$ 8,750	$20,000
12							

At December 31, 2017, the unadjusted balance in Allowance for Doubtful Accounts is a credit of $12,000.

Instructions

(a) Journalize and post the adjusting entry for bad debts at December 31, 2017.

(a) Bad debt expense $26,610

(b) Journalize and post to the allowance account the following events and transactions in the year 2018.
  (1) On March 31, a $1,000 customer balance originating in 2017 is judged uncollectible.
  (2) On May 31, a check for $1,000 is received from the customer whose account was written off as uncollectible on March 31.
(c) Journalize the adjusting entry for bad debts on December 31, 2018, assuming that the unadjusted balance in Allowance for Doubtful Accounts is a debit of $800 and the aging schedule indicates that total estimated bad debts will be $31,600.

(c) Bad debt expense $32,400

P9-4A Rigney Inc. uses the allowance method to estimate uncollectible accounts receivable. The company produced the following aging of the accounts receivable at year-end.

Journalize transactions related to bad debts.

(LO 2)

Worksheet.xls

Home | Insert | Page Layout | Formulas | Data | Review | View

P18 | fx

	A	B	C	D	E	F	G
1			Number of Days Outstanding				
2							
3		Total	0–30	31–60	61–90	91–120	Over 120
4	Accounts receivable	200,000	77,000	46,000	39,000	23,000	15,000
5	% uncollectible		1%	4%	5%	8%	20%
6	Estimated bad debts						
7							

Instructions

(a) Calculate the total estimated bad debts based on the above information.

(a) Tot. est. bad debts $9,400

(b) Prepare the year-end adjusting journal entry to record the bad debts using the aged uncollectible accounts receivable determined in (a). Assume the current balance in Allowance for Doubtful Accounts is a $8,000 debit.
(c) Of the above accounts, $5,000 is determined to be specifically uncollectible. Prepare the journal entry to write off the uncollectible account.
(d) The company collects $5,000 subsequently on a specific account that had previously been determined to be uncollectible in (c). Prepare the journal entry(ies) necessary to restore the account and record the cash collection.

(e) Comment on how your answers to (a)–(d) would change if Rigney Inc. used 4% of **total** accounts receivable rather than aging the accounts receivable. What are the advantages to the company of aging the accounts receivable rather than applying a percentage to total accounts receivable?

Journalize entries to record transactions related to bad debts.

(LO 2)

P9-5A At December 31, 2017, the trial balance of Darby Company contained the following amounts before adjustment.

	Debit	Credit
Accounts Receivable	$385,000	
Allowance for Doubtful Accounts		$ 1,000
Sales Revenue		970,000

Instructions

(a) Based on the information given, which method of accounting for bad debts is Darby Company using—the direct write-off method or the allowance method? How can you tell?

(b) Prepare the adjusting entry at December 31, 2017, for bad debt expense under each of the following independent assumptions.

(1) An aging schedule indicates that $11,750 of accounts receivable will be uncollectible.

(2) The company estimates that 1% of sales will be uncollectible.

(b) (2) $9,700

(c) Repeat part (b) assuming that instead of a credit balance there is a $1,000 debit balance in Allowance for Doubtful Accounts.

(d) During the next month, January 2018, a $3,000 account receivable is written off as uncollectible. Prepare the journal entry to record the write-off.

(e) Repeat part (d) assuming that Darby uses the direct write-off method instead of the allowance method in accounting for uncollectible accounts receivable.

(f) What type of account is Allowance for Doubtful Accounts? How does it affect how accounts receivable is reported on the balance sheet at the end of the accounting period?

Prepare entries for various notes receivable transactions.

(LO 1, 2, 3, 4)

GLS

P9-6A Farwell Company closes its books monthly. On September 30, selected ledger account balances are:

Notes Receivable	$37,000
Interest Receivable	183

Notes Receivable include the following.

Date	Maker	Face	Term	Interest
Aug. 16	K. Goza Inc.	$12,000	60 days	8%
Aug. 25	Holt Co.	9,000	60 days	7%
Sept. 30	Noblitt Corp.	16,000	6 months	9%

Interest is computed using a 360-day year. During October, the following transactions were completed.

Oct.	7	Made sales of $6,900 on Farwell credit cards.
	12	Made sales of $900 on MasterCard credit cards. The credit card service charge is 3%.
	15	Added $460 to Farwell customer balances for finance charges on unpaid balances.
	15	Received payment in full from K. Goza Inc. on the amount due.
	24	Received notice that the Holt note has been dishonored. (Assume that Holt is expected to pay in the future.)

Instructions

(a) Journalize the October transactions and the October 31 adjusting entry for accrued interest receivable.

(b) Enter the balances at October 1 in the receivable accounts. Post the entries to all of the receivable accounts. There was no opening balance in accounts receivable.

(c) Show the balance sheet presentation of the receivable accounts at October 31.

(b) Accounts receivable $16,465

(c) Total receivables $32,585

Prepare entries for various receivable transactions.

(LO 1, 2, 3, 4)

P9-7A On January 1, 2017, Harter Company had Accounts Receivable $139,000, Notes Receivable $25,000, and Allowance for Doubtful Accounts $13,200. The note receivable is from Willingham Company. It is a 4-month, 9% note dated December 31, 2016. Harter Company prepares financial statements annually at December 31. During the year, the following selected transactions occurred.

Jan.	5	Sold $20,000 of merchandise to Sheldon Company, terms n/15.
	20	Accepted Sheldon Company's $20,000, 3-month, 8% note for balance due.
Feb.	18	Sold $8,000 of merchandise to Patwary Company and accepted Patwary's $8,000, 6-month, 9% note for the amount due.
Apr.	20	Collected Sheldon Company note in full.
	30	Received payment in full from Willingham Company on the amount due.
May	25	Accepted Potter Inc.'s $6,000, 3-month, 7% note in settlement of a past-due balance on account.
Aug.	18	Received payment in full from Patwary Company on note due.
	25	The Potter Inc. note was dishonored. Potter Inc. is not bankrupt; future payment is anticipated.
Sept.	1	Sold $12,000 of merchandise to Stanbrough Company and accepted a $12,000, 6-month, 10% note for the amount due.

Instructions

Journalize the transactions.

PROBLEMS: SET B AND SET C

Visit the book's companion website, at **www.wiley.com/college/weygandt**, and choose the Student Companion site to access Problems: Set B and Set C.

COMPREHENSIVE PROBLEM

CP9 Winter Company's balance sheet at December 31, 2016, is presented below.

WINTER COMPANY
Balance Sheet
December 31, 2016

Cash	$13,100	Accounts payable	$ 8,750
Accounts receivable	19,780	Owner's capital	32,730
Allowance for doubtful accounts	(800)		$41,480
Inventory	9,400		
	$41,480		

During January 2017, the following transactions occurred. Winter uses the perpetual inventory method.

Jan.	1	Winter accepted a 4-month, 8% note from Merando Company in payment of Merando's $1,200 account.
	3	Winter wrote off as uncollectible the accounts of Inwood Corporation ($450) and Goza Company ($280).
	8	Winter purchased $17,200 of inventory on account.
	11	Winter sold for $28,000 on account inventory that cost $19,600.
	15	Winter sold inventory that cost $700 to Mark Lauber for $1,000. Lauber charged this amount on his Visa First Bank card. The service fee charged Winter by First Bank is 3%.
	17	Winter collected $22,900 from customers on account.
	21	Winter paid $14,300 on accounts payable.
	24	Winter received payment in full ($280) from Goza Company on the account written off on January 3.
	27	Winter purchased supplies for $1,400 cash.
	31	Winter paid other operating expenses, $3,718.

Adjustment data:

1. Interest is recorded for the month on the note from January 1.
2. Bad debts are expected to be 6% of the January 31, 2017, accounts receivable.
3. A count of supplies on January 31, 2017, reveals that $560 remains unused.

Instructions

(You may want to set up T-accounts to determine ending balances.)

(a) Prepare journal entries for the transactions listed above and adjusting entries. (Include entries for cost of goods sold using the perpetual system.)

(b) Prepare an adjusted trial balance at January 31, 2017.

(c) Prepare an income statement and an owner's equity statement for the month ending January 31, 2017, and a classified balance sheet as of January 31, 2017.

(b) Totals $74,765

(c) Tot. assets $47,473

CONTINUING PROBLEM

© leungchopan/ Shutterstock

COOKIE CREATIONS: AN ENTREPRENEURIAL JOURNEY

(*Note:* This is a continuation of the Cookie Creations problem from Chapters 1 through 8.)

CC9 One of Natalie's friends, Curtis Lesperance, runs a coffee shop where he sells specialty coffees and prepares and sells muffins and cookies. He is eager to buy one of Natalie's fine European mixers, which would enable him to make larger batches of muffins and cookies. However, Curtis cannot afford to pay for the mixer for at least 30 days. He asks Natalie if she would be willing to sell him the mixer on credit. Natalie comes to you for advice.

Go to the book's companion website, **www.wiley.com/college/weygandt**, *to see the completion of this problem.*

BROADENING YOUR PERSPECTIVE

FINANCIAL REPORTING AND ANALYSIS

Financial Reporting Problem: RLF Company

BYP9-1 RLF Company sells office equipment and supplies to many organizations in the city and surrounding area on contract terms of 2/10, n/30. In the past, over 75% of the credit customers have taken advantage of the discount by paying within 10 days of the invoice date.

The number of customers taking the full 30 days to pay has increased within the last year. Current indications are that less than 60% of the customers are now taking the discount. Bad debts as a percentage of gross credit sales have risen from the 2.5% provided in past years to about 4.5% in the current year.

The company's Finance Committee has requested more information on the collections of accounts receivable. The controller responded to this request with the report reproduced below.

RLF COMPANY
Accounts Receivable Collections
May 31, 2017

The fact that some credit accounts will prove uncollectible is normal. Annual bad debt write-offs have been 2.5% of gross credit sales over the past 5 years. During the last fiscal year, this percentage increased to slightly less than 4.5%. The current Accounts Receivable balance is $1,400,000. The condition of this balance in terms of age and probability of collection is as follows.

Proportion of Total	Age Categories	Probability of Collection
60%	not yet due	98%
22%	less than 30 days past due	96%
9%	30 to 60 days past due	94%
5%	61 to 120 days past due	91%
$2\frac{1}{2}$%	121 to 180 days past due	75%
$1\frac{1}{2}$%	over 180 days past due	30%

Allowance for Doubtful Accounts had a credit balance of $29,500 on June 1, 2016. RLF has provided for a monthly bad debt expense accrual during the current fiscal year based on the assumption that 4.5% of gross credit sales will be uncollectible. Total gross credit sales for the 2016–2017 fiscal year amounted to $2,900,000. Write-offs of bad accounts during the year totaled $102,000.

Instructions

(a) Prepare an accounts receivable aging schedule for RLF Company using the age categories identified in the controller's report to the Finance Committee showing the following.
  (1) The amount of accounts receivable outstanding for each age category and in total.
  (2) The estimated amount that is uncollectible for each category and in total.

(b) Compute the amount of the year-end adjustment necessary to bring Allowance for Doubtful Accounts to the balance indicated by the age analysis. Then prepare the necessary journal entry to adjust the accounting records.

(c) In a recessionary environment with tight credit and high interest rates:
  (1) Identify steps RLF Company might consider to improve the accounts receivable situation.
  (2) Then evaluate each step identified in terms of the risks and costs involved.

Comparative Analysis Problem: PepsiCo, Inc. vs. The Coca-Cola Company

BYP9-2 PepsiCo, Inc.'s financial statements are presented in Appendix B. Financial statements of The Coca-Cola Company are presented in Appendix C. Instructions for accessing and using the complete annual reports of PepsiCo and Coca-Cola, including the notes to the financial statements, are also provided in Appendices B and C, respectively.

Instructions

(a) Based on the information in these financial statements, compute the following 2013 ratios for each company. (Assume all sales are credit sales and that PepsiCo's receivables on its balance sheet are all trade receivables.)
   (1) Accounts receivable turnover.
   (2) Average collection period for receivables.
(b) What conclusions about managing accounts receivable can you draw from these data?

Comparative Analysis Problem: Amazon.com, Inc. vs. Wal-Mart Stores, Inc.

BYP9-3 Amazon.com, Inc.'s financial statements are presented in Appendix D. Financial statements of Wal-Mart Stores, Inc. are presented in Appendix E. Instructions for accessing and using the complete annual reports of Amazon and Wal-Mart, including the notes to the financial statements, are also provided in Appendices D and E, respectively.

Instructions

(a) Based on the information in these financial statements, compute the following ratios for each company (for the most recent year shown). (Assume all sales are credit sales.)
   (1) Accounts receivable turnover.
   (2) Average collection period for receivables.
(b) What conclusions about managing accounts receivable can you draw from these data?

Real-World Focus

BYP9-4 **Purpose:** To learn more about factoring.

Address: **www.comcapfactoring.com**, or go to **www.wiley.com/college/weygandt**

Steps: Go to the website, click on **Invoice Factoring**, and answer the following questions.
(a) What are some of the benefits of factoring?
(b) What is the range of the percentages of the typical discount rate?
(c) If a company factors its receivables, what percentage of the value of the receivables can it expect to receive from the factor in the form of cash, and how quickly will it receive the cash?

CRITICAL THINKING

Decision-Making Across the Organization

BYP9-5 Carol and Sam Foyle own Campus Fashions. From its inception Campus Fashions has sold merchandise on either a cash or credit basis, but no credit cards have been accepted. During the past several months, the Foyles have begun to question their sales policies. First, they have lost some sales because of refusing to accept credit cards. Second, representatives of two metropolitan banks have been persuasive in almost convincing them to accept their national credit cards. One bank, City National Bank, has stated that its credit card fee is 4%.

The Foyles decide that they should determine the cost of carrying their own credit sales. From the accounting records of the past 3 years, they accumulate the following data.

	2018	2017	2016
Net credit sales	$500,000	$550,000	$400,000
Collection agency fees for slow-paying customers	2,450	2,500	2,300
Salary of part-time accounts receivable clerk	4,100	4,100	4,100

Uncollectible account expense is 1.6% of net credit sales, billing and mailing costs 0.5%, and credit investigation fee on new customers is 0.15%.

Carol and Sam also determine that the average accounts receivable balance outstanding during the year is 5% of net credit sales. The Foyles estimate that they could earn an average of 8% annually on cash invested in other business opportunities.

Instructions

With the class divided into groups, answer the following.

(a) Prepare a table showing, for each year, total credit and collection expenses in dollars and as a percentage of net credit sales.

(b) Determine the net credit and collection expense in dollars and as a percentage of sales after considering the revenue not earned from other investment opportunities.

(c) Discuss both the financial and nonfinancial factors that are relevant to the decision.

Communication Activity

BYP9-6 Jill Epp, a friend of yours, overheard a discussion at work about changes her employer wants to make in accounting for uncollectible accounts. Jill knows little about accounting, and she asks you to help make sense of what she heard. Specifically, she asks you to explain the differences between the percentage-of-sales, percentage-of-receivables, and the direct write-off methods for uncollectible accounts.

Instructions

In a letter of one page (or less), explain to Jill the three methods of accounting for uncollectibles. Be sure to discuss differences among these methods.

Ethics Case

BYP9-7 The controller of Diaz Co. believes that the yearly allowance for doubtful accounts for Diaz Co. should be 2% of net credit sales. The president of Diaz Co., nervous that the owners might expect the company to sustain its 10% growth rate, suggests that the controller increase the allowance for doubtful accounts to 4%. The president thinks that the lower net income, which reflects a 6% growth rate, will be a more sustainable rate for Diaz Co.

Instructions

(a) Who are the stakeholders in this case?

(b) Does the president's request pose an ethical dilemma for the controller?

(c) Should the controller be concerned with Diaz Co.'s growth rate? Explain your answer.

FASB Codification Activity

BYP9-8 If your school has a subscription to the FASB Codification, go to **http://aaahq.org/ascLogin.cfm** to log in and prepare responses to the following.

(a) How are receivables defined in the Codification?

(b) What are the conditions under which losses from uncollectible receivables (Bad Debt Expense) should be reported?

A Look at IFRS

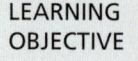

LEARNING OBJECTIVE 5 **Compare the accounting for receivables under GAAP and IFRS.**

The basic accounting and reporting issues related to the recognition, measurement, and disposition of receivables are essentially the same between IFRS and GAAP.

Key Points

Following are the key similarities and differences between GAAP and IFRS as related to the accounting for receivables.

Similarities

- The recording of receivables, recognition of sales returns and allowances and sales discounts, and the allowance method to record bad debts are the same between IFRS and GAAP.
- Both IFRS and GAAP often use the term impairment to indicate that a receivable may not be collected.
- The FASB and IASB have worked to implement fair value measurement (the amount they currently could be sold for) for financial instruments, such as receivables. Both Boards have faced bitter opposition from various factions.

Differences

- Although IFRS implies that receivables with different characteristics should be reported separately, there is no standard that mandates this segregation.
- IFRS and GAAP differ in the criteria used to determine how to record a factoring transaction. IFRS uses a combination approach focused on risks and rewards and loss of control. GAAP uses loss of control as the primary criterion. In addition, IFRS permits partial derecognition of receivables; GAAP does not.

Looking to the Future

The question of recording fair values for financial instruments will continue to be an important issue to resolve as the Boards work toward convergence. Both the IASB and the FASB have indicated that they believe that financial statements would be more transparent and understandable if companies recorded and reported all financial instruments at fair value.

IFRS Practice

IFRS Self-Test Questions

1. Which of the following statements is **false**?
   (a) Receivables include equity securities purchased by the company.
   (b) Receivables include credit card receivables.
   (c) Receivables include amounts owed by employees as a result of company loans to employees.
   (d) Receivables include amounts resulting from transactions with customers.
2. Under IFRS:
   (a) the entry to record estimated uncollected accounts is the same as GAAP.
   (b) it is always acceptable to use the direct write-off method.
   (c) all financial instruments are recorded at fair value.
   (d) None of the above.

International Financial Reporting Problem: Louis Vuitton

IFRS9-1 The financial statements of Louis Vuitton are presented in Appendix F. Instructions for accessing and using the company's complete annual report, including the notes to its financial statements, are also provided in Appendix F.

Instructions
Use the company's annual report to answer the following questions.

(a) What is the accounting policy related to accounting for trade accounts receivable?
(b) According to the notes to the financial statements, what accounted for the difference between gross trade accounts receivable and net accounts receivable?
(c) According to the notes to the financial statements, what was the major reason why the balance in receivables increased relative to the previous year?
(d) Using information in the notes to the financial statements, determine what percentage the provision for impairment of receivables was as a percentage of total trade receivables for 2013 and 2012. How did the ratio change from 2012 to 2013, and what does this suggest about the company's receivables?

Answers to IFRS Self-Test Questions

1. a **2.** a

10 Plant Assets, Natural Resources, and Intangible Assets

CHAPTER PREVIEW The accounting for long-term assets has important implications for a company's reported results. In this chapter, we explain the application of the historical cost principle of accounting to property, plant, and equipment, such as Rent-A-Wreck vehicles, as well as to natural resources and intangible assets, such as the "Rent-A-Wreck" trademark. We also describe the methods that companies may use to allocate an asset's cost over its useful life. In addition, we discuss the accounting for expenditures incurred during the useful life of assets, such as the cost of replacing tires and brake pads on rental cars.

FEATURE STORY

How Much for a Ride to the Beach?

It's spring break. Your plane has landed, you've finally found your bags, and you're dying to hit the beach—but first you need a "vehicular unit" to get you there. As you turn away from baggage claim, you see a long row of rental agency booths. Many are names that you know—Hertz, Avis, and Budget. But a booth at the far end catches your eye—Rent-A-Wreck. Now there's a company making a clear statement!

Any company that relies on equipment to generate revenues must make decisions about what kind of equipment to buy, how long to keep it, and how vigorously to maintain it. Rent-A-Wreck has decided to rent used rather than new cars and trucks. It rents these vehicles across the United States, Europe, and Asia. While the big-name agencies push vehicles with that "new car smell," Rent-A-Wreck competes on price.

Rent-A-Wreck's message is simple: Rent a used car and save some cash. It's not a message that appeals to everyone. If you're a marketing executive wanting to impress a big client, you probably don't want to pull up in a Rent-A-Wreck car. But if you want to get from point A to point B for the minimum cash per mile, then Rent-A-Wreck is playing your tune. The company's message seems to be getting across to the right clientele. Revenues have increased significantly.

When you rent a car from Rent-A-Wreck, you are renting from an independent businessperson. This owner has paid a "franchise fee" for the right to use the Rent-A-Wreck name. In order to gain a franchise, he or she must meet financial and other criteria, and must agree to run the rental agency according to rules prescribed by Rent-A-Wreck. Some of these rules require that each franchise maintain its cars in a reasonable fashion. This ensures that, though you won't be cruising down Daytona Beach's Atlantic Avenue in a Mercedes convertible, you can be reasonably assured that you won't be calling a towtruck.

David Trood/Getty Images, Inc.

CHAPTER OUTLINE

Learning Objectives

Learning Objectives	Topics	DO IT!
1 Explain the accounting for plant asset expenditures.	• Determining the cost of plant assets • Expenditures during useful life	DO IT! **1** Cost of Plant Assets
2 Apply depreciation methods to plant assets.	• Factors in computing depreciation • Depreciation methods • Depreciation and income taxes • Revising periodic depreciation	DO IT! **2a** Straight-Line Depreciation **2b** Revised Depreciation
3 Explain how to account for the disposal of plant assets.	• Retirement of plant assets • Sale of plant assets	DO IT! **3** Plant Asset Disposal
4 Describe how to account for natural resources and intangible assets.	• Natural resources • Depletion • Intangible assets • Accounting for intangible assets • Research and development costs	DO IT! **4** Classification Concepts
5 Discuss how plant assets, natural resources, and intangible assets are reported and analyzed.	• Presentation • Analysis	DO IT! **5** Asset Turnover

o to the ***REVIEW AND PRACTICE*** section at the end of the chapter for a review of key concepts and practice applications with solutions.

isit **WileyPLUS with ORION** for additional tutorials and practice opportunities.

LEARNING OBJECTIVE 1

Explain the accounting for plant asset expenditures.

Plant assets are resources that have three characteristics. They have a physical substance (a definite size and shape), are used in the operations of a business, and are not intended for sale to customers. They are also called **property, plant, and equipment**; **plant and equipment**; and **fixed assets**. These assets are expected to be of use to the company for a number of years. Except for land, plant assets decline in service potential over their useful lives.

Because plant assets play a key role in ongoing operations, companies keep plant assets in good operating condition. They also replace worn-out or outdated plant assets, and expand productive resources as needed. Many companies have substantial investments in plant assets. Illustration 10-1 shows the percentages of plant assets in relation to total assets of companies in a number of industries.

Illustration 10-1
Percentages of plant assets in relation to total assets

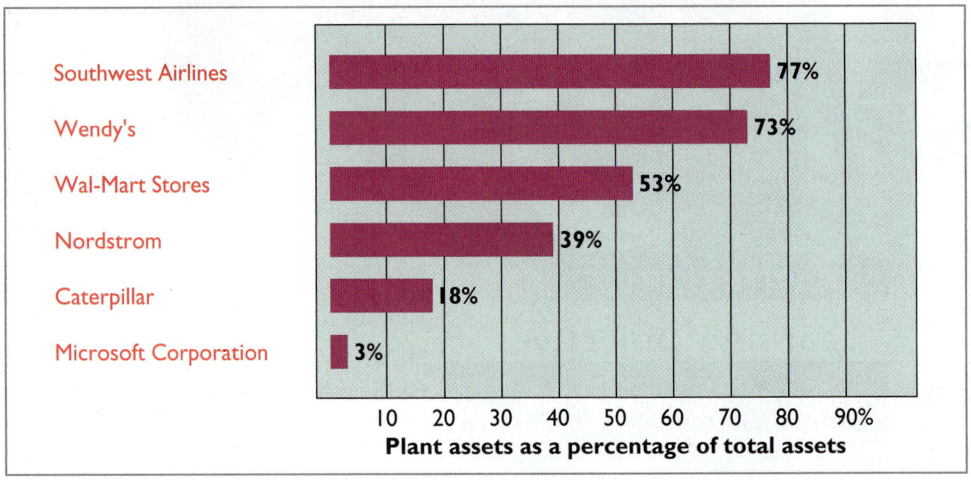

Determining the Cost of Plant Assets

The historical cost principle requires that companies record plant assets at cost. Thus, Rent-A-Wreck records its vehicles at cost. **Cost consists of all expenditures necessary to acquire the asset and make it ready for its intended use.** For example, the cost of factory machinery includes the purchase price, freight costs paid by the purchaser, and installation costs. Once cost is established, the company uses that amount as the basis of accounting for the plant asset over its useful life.

In the following sections, we explain the application of the historical cost principle to each of the major classes of plant assets.

LAND

Companies often use **land** as a building site for a manufacturing plant or office building. The cost of land includes (1) the cash purchase price, (2) closing costs such as title and attorney's fees, (3) real estate brokers' commissions, and (4) accrued property taxes and other liens assumed by the purchaser. For example, if the cash price is $50,000 and the purchaser agrees to pay accrued taxes of $5,000, the cost of the land is $55,000.

Helpful Hint
Management's intended use is important in applying the historical cost principle.

Companies record as debits (increases) to the Land account all necessary costs incurred to make land **ready for its intended use**. When a company acquires vacant land, these costs include expenditures for clearing, draining, filling, and grading. Sometimes the land has a building on it that must be removed before construction of a new building. In this case, the company debits to the

Land account all demolition and removal costs, less any proceeds from salvaged materials.

To illustrate, assume that Hayes Company acquires real estate at a cash cost of $100,000. The property contains an old warehouse that is razed at a net cost of $6,000 ($7,500 in costs less $1,500 proceeds from salvaged materials). Additional expenditures are the attorney's fee, $1,000, and the real estate broker's commission, $8,000. The cost of the land is $115,000, computed as shown in Illustration 10-2.

Illustration 10-2
Computation of cost of land

Land	
Cash price of property	$ 100,000
Net removal cost of warehouse ($7,500 − $1,500)	6,000
Attorney's fee	1,000
Real estate broker's commission	8,000
Cost of land	**$115,000**

Hayes makes the following entry to record the acquisition of the land.

Land	115,000	
Cash		115,000
(To record purchase of land)		

A	=	L	+	OE
+115,000				
−115,000				

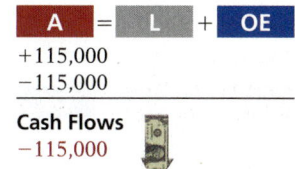

Cash Flows
−115,000

LAND IMPROVEMENTS

Land improvements are structural additions made to land. Examples are driveways, parking lots, fences, landscaping, and underground sprinklers. The cost of land improvements includes all expenditures necessary to make the improvements ready for their intended use. For example, the cost of a new parking lot for Home Depot includes the amount paid for paving, fencing, and lighting. Thus, Home Depot debits to Land Improvements the total of all of these costs.

Land improvements have limited useful lives, and their maintenance and replacement are the responsibility of the company. As a result, companies expense (depreciate) the cost of land improvements over their useful lives.

BUILDINGS

Buildings are facilities used in operations, such as stores, offices, factories, warehouses, and airplane hangars. Companies debit to the Buildings account all necessary expenditures related to the purchase or construction of a building. When a building is **purchased**, such costs include the purchase price, closing costs (attorney's fees, title insurance, etc.), and real estate broker's commission. Costs to make the building ready for its intended use include expenditures for remodeling and replacing or repairing the roof, floors, electrical wiring, and plumbing. When a new building is **constructed**, cost consists of the contract price plus payments for architects' fees, building permits, and excavation costs.

In addition, companies charge certain interest costs to the Buildings account. Interest costs incurred to finance the project are included in the cost of the building when a significant period of time is required to get the building ready for use. In these circumstances, interest costs are considered as necessary as materials and labor. However, the inclusion of interest costs in the cost of a constructed building is **limited to the construction period**. When construction has been completed, the company records subsequent interest payments on funds borrowed to finance the construction as debits (increases) to Interest Expense.

EQUIPMENT

Equipment includes assets used in operations, such as store check-out counters, office furniture, factory machinery, delivery trucks, and airplanes. The cost of equipment, such as Rent-A-Wreck vehicles, consists of the cash purchase price, sales taxes, freight charges, and insurance during transit paid by the purchaser. It also includes expenditures required in assembling, installing, and testing the unit. However, Rent-A-Wreck does not include motor vehicle licenses and accident insurance on company vehicles in the cost of equipment. These costs represent annual recurring expenditures and do not benefit future periods. Thus, they are treated as **expenses** as they are incurred.

To illustrate, assume Merten Company purchases factory machinery at a cash price of $50,000. Related expenditures are for sales taxes $3,000, insurance during shipping $500, and installation and testing $1,000. The cost of the factory machinery is $54,500, as computed in Illustration 10-3.

Illustration 10-3
Computation of cost of factory machinery

Factory Machinery	
Cash price	$ 50,000
Sales taxes	3,000
Insurance during shipping	500
Installation and testing	1,000
Cost of factory machinery	**$54,500**

Merten makes the following summary entry to record the purchase and related expenditures.

A = L + OE	
+54,500	
−54,500	

Cash Flows
−54,500

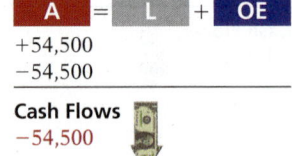

Equipment	54,500	
Cash		54,500
(To record purchase of factory machinery)		

For another example, assume that Lenard Company purchases a delivery truck at a cash price of $22,000. Related expenditures consist of sales taxes $1,320, painting and lettering $500, motor vehicle license $80, and a three-year accident insurance policy $1,600. The cost of the delivery truck is $23,820, computed as follows.

Illustration 10-4
Computation of cost of delivery truck

Delivery Truck	
Cash price	$ 22,000
Sales taxes	1,320
Painting and lettering	500
Cost of delivery truck	**$23,820**

Lenard treats the cost of the motor vehicle license as an expense and the cost of the insurance policy as a prepaid asset. Thus, Lenard makes the following entry to record the purchase of the truck and related expenditures:

A = L + OE	
+23,820	
	−80 Exp
+ 1,600	
−25,500	

Cash Flows
−25,500

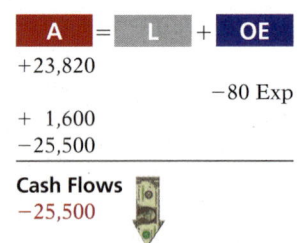

Equipment	23,820	
License Expense	80	
Prepaid Insurance	1,600	
Cash		25,500
(To record purchase of delivery truck and related expenditures)		

Expenditures During Useful Life

During the useful life of a plant asset, a company may incur costs for ordinary repairs, additions, or improvements. **Ordinary repairs** are expenditures to **maintain** the operating efficiency and productive life of the unit. They usually are small amounts that occur frequently. Examples are motor tune-ups and oil changes, the painting of buildings, and the replacing of worn-out gears on machinery. Companies record such repairs as debits to Maintenance and Repairs Expense as they are incurred. Because they are immediately charged as an expense against revenues, these costs are often referred to as **revenue expenditures**.

In contrast, **additions and improvements** are costs incurred to **increase** the operating efficiency, productive capacity, or useful life of a plant asset. They are usually material in amount and occur infrequently. Additions and improvements increase the company's investment in productive facilities. Companies generally debit these amounts to the plant asset affected. They are often referred to as **capital expenditures**.

Companies must use good judgment in deciding between a revenue expenditure and capital expenditure. For example, assume that Rodriguez Co. purchases a number of wastepaper baskets. The proper accounting would appear to be to capitalize and then depreciate these wastepaper baskets over their useful life. However, Rodriguez will generally expense these wastepaper baskets immediately. This practice is justified on the basis of **materiality**. Materiality refers to the impact of an item's size on a company's financial operations. The **materiality concept** states that if an item would not make a difference in decision-making, the company does not have to follow GAAP in reporting that item.

ANATOMY OF A FRAUD

Bernie Ebbers was the founder and CEO of the phone company WorldCom. The company engaged in a series of increasingly large, debt-financed acquisitions of other companies. These acquisitions made the company grow quickly, which made the stock price increase dramatically. However, because the acquired companies all had different accounting systems, WorldCom's financial records were a mess. When WorldCom's performance started to flatten out, Bernie coerced WorldCom's accountants to engage in a number of fraudulent activities to make net income look better than it really was and thus prop up the stock price. One of these frauds involved treating $7 billion of line costs as capital expenditures. The line costs, which were rental fees paid to other phone companies to use their phone lines, had always been properly expensed in previous years. Capitalization delayed expense recognition to future periods and thus boosted current-period profits.

Total take: $7 billion

THE MISSING CONTROLS

Documentation procedures. The company's accounting system was a disorganized collection of non-integrated systems, which resulted from a series of corporate acquisitions. Top management took advantage of this disorganization to conceal its fraudulent activities.

Independent internal verification. A fraud of this size should have been detected by a routine comparison of the actual physical assets with the list of physical assets shown in the accounting records.

Accounting Across the Organization

© Brian Raisbeck/iStockphoto

Many U.S. Firms Use Leases

Leasing is big business for U.S. companies. For example, business investment in equipment in a recent year totaled $800 billion. Leasing accounted for about 33% of all business investments ($264 billion).

Who does the most leasing? Interestingly, major banks such as Continental Bank, J.P. Morgan Leasing, and US Bancorp Equipment Finance are the major lessors. Also, many companies have established separate leasing companies, such as Boeing Capital Corporation, Dell Financial Services, and John Deere Capital Corporation. And, as an excellent example of the magnitude of leasing, leased planes account for nearly 40% of the U.S. fleet of commercial airlines. Leasing is also becoming more common in the hotel industry. Marriott, Hilton, and InterContinental are increasingly choosing to lease hotels that are owned by someone else.

Why might airline managers choose to lease rather than purchase their planes? (Go to **WileyPLUS** for this answer and additional questions.)

DO IT! 1 Cost of Plant Assets

Assume that Drummond Heating and Cooling Co. purchases a delivery truck for $15,000 cash, plus sales taxes of $900 and delivery costs of $500. The buyer also pays $200 for painting and lettering, $600 for an annual insurance policy, and $80 for a motor vehicle license. Explain how each of these costs would be accounted for.

Action Plan

✔ Identify expenditures made in order to get delivery equipment ready for its intended use.

✔ Treat operating costs as expenses.

Solution

The first four payments ($15,000, $900, $500, and $200) are expenditures necessary to make the truck ready for its intended use. Thus, the cost of the truck is $16,600. The payments for insurance and the license are operating costs and therefore are expensed.

Related exercise material: **BE10-1, BE10-2, BE10-3, E10-1, E10-2, E10-3, and DO IT! 10-1.**

LEARNING OBJECTIVE 2 Apply depreciation methods to plant assets.

As explained in Chapter 3, **depreciation is the process of allocating to expense the cost of a plant asset over its useful (service) life in a rational and systematic manner**. Cost allocation enables companies to properly match expenses with revenues in accordance with the expense recognition principle, as shown in Illustration 10-5.

Illustration 10-5
Depreciation as a cost allocation concept

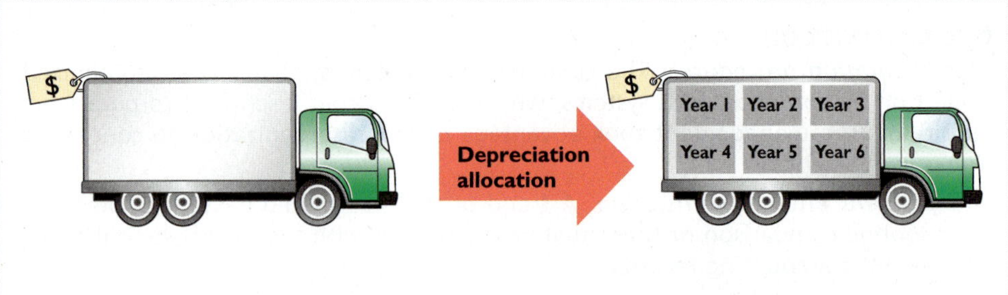

ETHICS NOTE

When a business is acquired, proper allocation of the purchase price to various asset classes is important since different depreciation treatments can materially affect income. For example, buildings are depreciated, but land is not.

It is important to understand that **depreciation is a process of cost allocation. It is not a process of asset valuation.** No attempt is made to measure the change in an asset's fair value during ownership. So, the **book value** (cost less accumulated depreciation) of a plant asset may be quite different from its fair value. In fact, if an asset is fully depreciated, it can have a zero book value but still have a fair value.

Depreciation applies to three classes of plant assets: land improvements, buildings, and equipment. Each asset in these classes is considered to be a **depreciable asset**. Why? Because the usefulness to the company and revenue-producing ability of each asset will decline over the asset's useful life. Depreciation **does not apply to land** because its usefulness and revenue-producing ability generally remain intact over time. In fact, in many cases, the usefulness of land is greater over time because of the scarcity of good land sites. Thus, **land is not a depreciable asset**.

During a depreciable asset's useful life, its revenue-producing ability declines because of **wear and tear**. A delivery truck that has been driven 100,000 miles will be less useful to a company than one driven only 800 miles.

Revenue-producing ability may also decline because of obsolescence. **Obsolescence** is the process of becoming out of date before the asset physically wears out. For example, major airlines moved from Chicago's Midway Airport to Chicago-O'Hare International Airport because Midway's runways were too short for jumbo jets. Similarly, many companies replace their computers long before they originally planned to do so because improvements in new computing technology make the old computers obsolete.

Recognizing depreciation on an asset does not result in an accumulation of cash for replacement of the asset. The balance in Accumulated Depreciation represents the total amount of the asset's cost that the company has charged to expense. It is not a cash fund.

Note that the concept of depreciation is consistent with the going concern assumption. The **going concern assumption** states that the company will continue in operation for the foreseeable future. If a company does not use a going concern assumption, then plant assets should be stated at their fair value. In that case, depreciation of these assets is not needed.

Factors in Computing Depreciation

Three factors affect the computation of depreciation, as shown in Illustration 10-6.

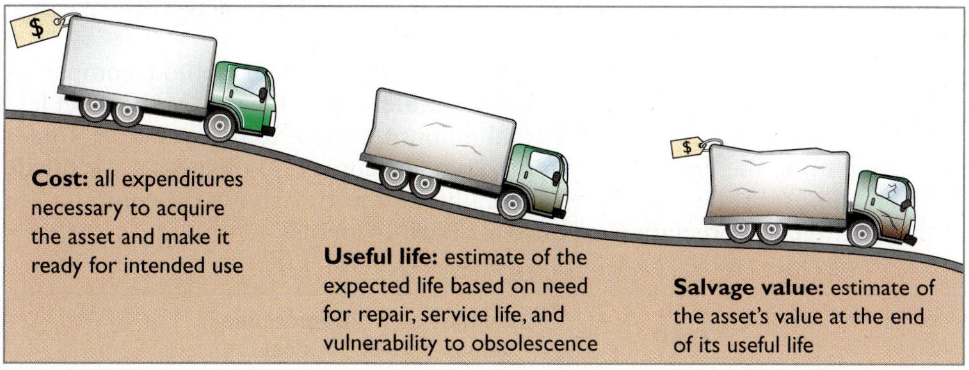

$
$
Cost: all expenditures necessary to acquire the asset and make it ready for intended use
Useful life: estimate of the expected life based on need for repair, service life, and vulnerability to obsolescence
Salvage value: estimate of the asset's value at the end of its useful life

Illustration 10-6
Three factors in computing depreciation

Helpful Hint
Depreciation expense is reported on the income statement. Accumulated depreciation is reported on the balance sheet as a deduction from plant assets.

1. **Cost.** Earlier, we explained the issues affecting the cost of a depreciable asset. Recall that companies record plant assets at cost, in accordance with the historical cost principle.
2. **Useful life.** **Useful life** is an estimate of the expected productive life, also called service life, of the asset for its owner. Useful life may be expressed in terms of time, units of activity (such as machine hours), or units of output. Useful life is an estimate. In making the estimate, management considers such factors as the intended use of the asset, its expected repair and maintenance, and its vulnerability to obsolescence. Past experience with similar assets is often helpful in deciding on expected useful life. We might reasonably expect Rent-A-Wreck and Avis to use different estimated useful lives for their vehicles.
3. **Salvage value.** **Salvage value** is an estimate of the asset's value at the end of its useful life. This value may be based on the asset's worth as scrap or on its expected trade-in value. Like useful life, salvage value is an estimate. In making the estimate, management considers how it plans to dispose of the asset and its experience with similar assets.

Alternative Terminology
Another term sometimes used for salvage value is *residual value*.

Depreciation Methods

Depreciation is generally computed using one of the following methods:

1. Straight-line
2. Units-of-activity
3. Declining-balance

Each method is acceptable under generally accepted accounting principles. Management selects the method(s) it believes to be appropriate. The objective is to select the method that best measures an asset's contribution to revenue over its useful life. Once a company chooses a method, it should apply it consistently over the useful life of the asset. Consistency enhances the comparability of financial statements. Depreciation affects the balance sheet through accumulated depreciation and the income statement through depreciation expense.

We will compare the three depreciation methods using the following data for a small delivery truck purchased by Barb's Florists on January 1, 2017.

Illustration 10-7
Delivery truck data

Cost	$13,000
Expected salvage value	$ 1,000
Estimated useful life in years	5
Estimated useful life in miles	100,000

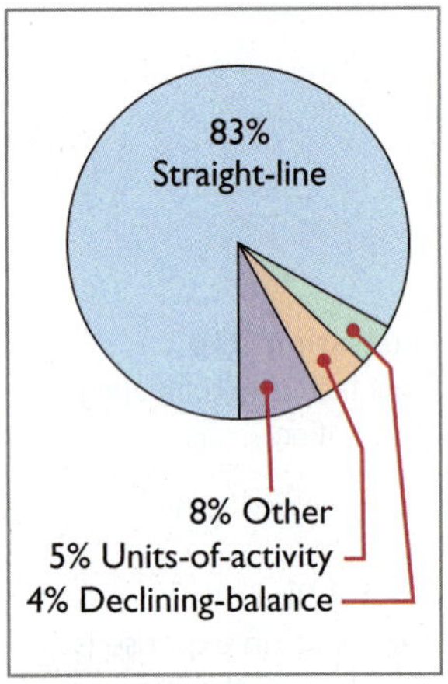

Illustration 10-8
Use of depreciation methods in large U.S. companies

Illustration 10-8 (in the margin) shows the use of the primary depreciation methods in a sample of the largest companies in the United States.

STRAIGHT-LINE METHOD

Under the **straight-line method**, companies expense the same amount of depreciation for each year of the asset's useful life. It is measured solely by the passage of time.

To compute depreciation expense under the straight-line method, companies need to determine depreciable cost. **Depreciable cost** is the cost of the asset less its salvage value. It represents the total amount subject to depreciation. Under the straight-line method, to determine annual depreciation expense, we divide depreciable cost by the asset's useful life. Illustration 10-9 shows the computation of the first year's depreciation expense for Barb's Florists.

Illustration 10-9
Formula for straight-line method

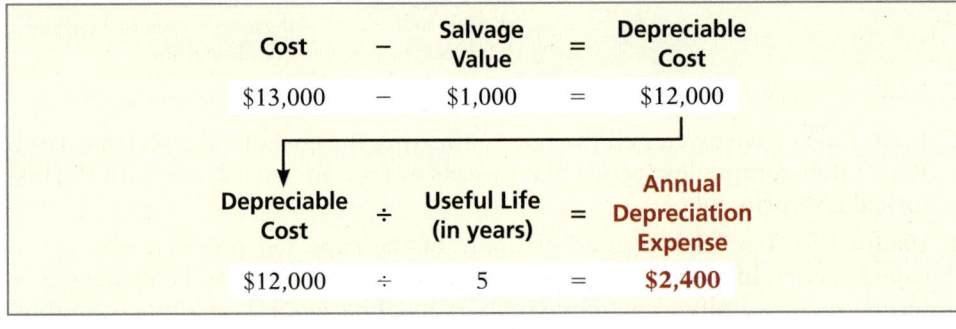

Cost	−	Salvage Value	=	Depreciable Cost
$13,000	−	$1,000	=	$12,000

Depreciable Cost	÷	Useful Life (in years)	=	Annual Depreciation Expense
$12,000	÷	5	=	**$2,400**

Alternatively, we also can compute an annual **rate** of depreciation. In this case, the rate is 20% (100% ÷ 5 years). When a company uses an annual straight-line rate, it applies the percentage rate to the depreciable cost of the asset. Illustration 10-10 shows a **depreciation schedule** using an annual rate.

Illustration 10-10
Straight-line depreciation schedule

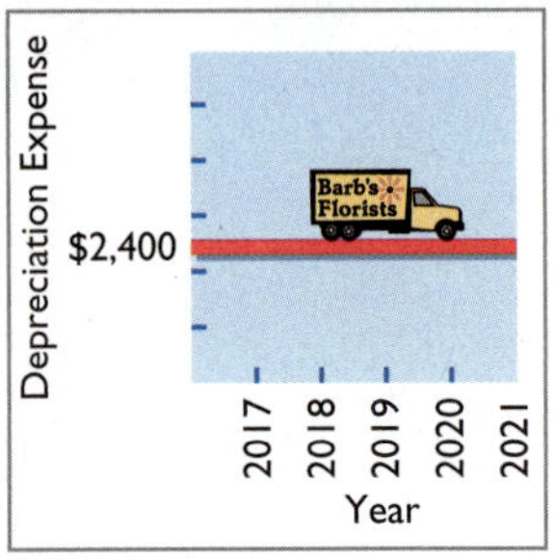

BARB'S FLORISTS

	Computation				Annual	End of Year	
Year	Depreciable Cost	×	Depreciation Rate	=	Depreciation Expense	Accumulated Depreciation	Book Value
2017	$12,000		20%		**$2,400**	$ 2,400	$10,600*
2018	12,000		20		**2,400**	4,800	8,200
2019	12,000		20		**2,400**	7,200	5,800
2020	12,000		20		**2,400**	9,600	3,400
2021	12,000		20		**2,400**	12,000	**1,000**

*Book value = Cost − Accumulated depreciation = ($13,000 − $2,400).

Note that the depreciation expense of $2,400 is the same each year. The book value (computed as cost minus accumulated depreciation) at the end of the useful life is equal to the expected $1,000 salvage value.

What happens to these computations for an asset purchased **during** the year, rather than on January 1? In that case, it is necessary to **prorate the annual depreciation** on a time basis. If Barb's Florists had purchased the delivery truck on April 1, 2017, the company would own the truck for nine months of the first year (April–December). Thus, depreciation for 2017 would be $1,800 ($12,000 × 20% × 9/12 of a year).

The straight-line method predominates in practice. Such large companies as **Campbell Soup**, **Marriott**, and **General Mills** use the straight-line method. It is simple to apply, and it matches expenses with revenues when the use of the asset is reasonably uniform throughout the service life.

DO IT! 2a Straight-Line Depreciation

On January 1, 2017, Iron Mountain Ski Corporation purchased a new snow-grooming machine for $50,000. The machine is estimated to have a 10-year life with a $2,000 salvage value. What journal entry would Iron Mountain Ski Corporation make at December 31, 2017, if it uses the straight-line method of depreciation?

Solution

$$\text{Depreciation expense} = \frac{\text{Cost} - \text{Salvage value}}{\text{Useful life}} = \frac{\$50{,}000 - \$2{,}000}{10} = \$4{,}800$$

The entry to record the first year's depreciation would be:

Dec. 31	Depreciation Expense	4,800	
	Accumulated Depreciation—Equipment		4,800
	(To record annual depreciation on snow-grooming machine)		

Action Plan

✔ Calculate depreciable cost (Cost − Salvage value).

✔ Divide the depreciable cost by the asset's estimated useful life.

Related exercise material: **BE10-4, BE10-5, E10-4, and DO IT! 10-2a.**

UNITS-OF-ACTIVITY METHOD

Under the **units-of-activity method**, useful life is expressed in terms of the total units of production or use expected from the asset, rather than as a time period. The units-of-activity method is ideally suited to factory machinery. Manufacturing companies can measure production in units of output or in machine hours. This method can also be used for such assets as delivery equipment (miles driven) and airplanes (hours in use). The units-of-activity method is generally not suitable for buildings or furniture because depreciation for these assets is more a function of time than of use.

Alternative Terminology
Another term often used is the *units-of-production method.*

To use this method, companies estimate the total units of activity for the entire useful life, and then divide these units into depreciable cost. The resulting number represents the depreciable cost per unit. The depreciable cost per unit is then applied to the units of activity during the year to determine the annual depreciation expense.

Helpful Hint
Under any method, depreciation stops when the asset's book value equals expected salvage value.

To illustrate, assume that Barb's Florists drives its delivery truck 15,000 miles in the first year. Illustration 10-11 (page 452) shows the units-of-activity formula and the computation of the first year's depreciation expense.

Illustration 10-11
Formula for units-of-activity method

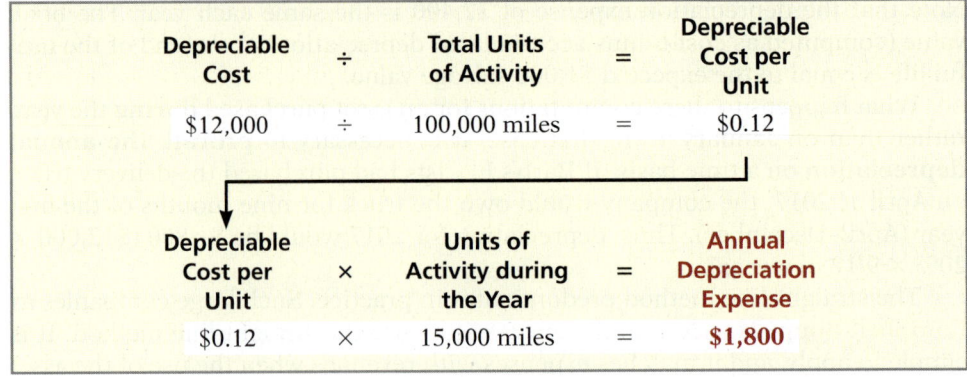

Depreciable Cost	÷	Total Units of Activity	=	Depreciable Cost per Unit
$12,000	÷	100,000 miles	=	$0.12

Depreciable Cost per Unit	×	Units of Activity during the Year	=	Annual Depreciation Expense
$0.12	×	15,000 miles	=	$1,800

The units-of-activity depreciation schedule, using assumed mileage, is as follows.

Illustration 10-12
Units-of-activity depreciation schedule

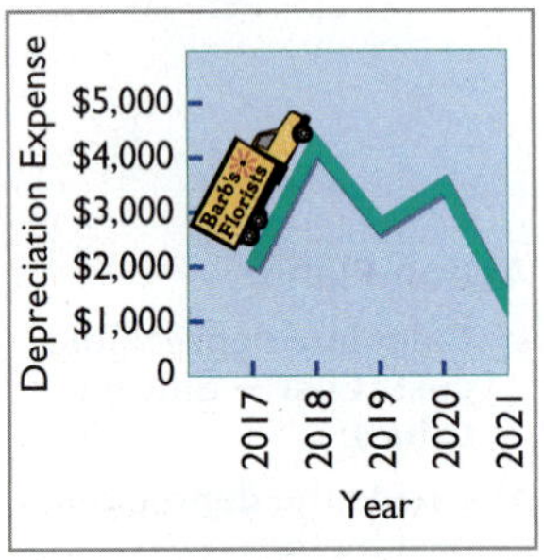

BARB'S FLORISTS

	Computation					End of Year	
Year	Units of Activity	×	Depreciable Cost/Unit	=	Annual Depreciation Expense	Accumulated Depreciation	Book Value
2017	15,000		$0.12		$1,800	$ 1,800	$11,200*
2018	30,000		0.12		3,600	5,400	7,600
2019	20,000		0.12		2,400	7,800	5,200
2020	25,000		0.12		3,000	10,800	2,200
2021	10,000		0.12		1,200	12,000	1,000

*($13,000 − $1,800).

This method is easy to apply for assets purchased mid-year. In such a case, the company computes the depreciation using the productivity of the asset for the partial year.

The units-of-activity method is not nearly as popular as the straight-line method (see Illustration 10-8, page 450) primarily because it is often difficult for companies to reasonably estimate total activity. However, some very large companies, such as Chevron and Boise Cascade (a forestry company), do use this method. When the productivity of an asset varies significantly from one period to another, the units-of-activity method results in the best matching of expenses with revenues.

DECLINING-BALANCE METHOD

The **declining-balance method** produces a decreasing annual depreciation expense over the asset's useful life. The method is so named because the periodic depreciation is based on a **declining book value** (cost less accumulated depreciation) of the asset. With this method, companies compute annual depreciation expense by multiplying the book value at the beginning of the year by the declining-balance depreciation rate. **The depreciation rate remains constant from year to year, but the book value to which the rate is applied declines each year.**

At the beginning of the first year, book value is the cost of the asset. This is because the balance in accumulated depreciation at the beginning of the asset's useful life is zero. In subsequent years, book value is the difference between cost and accumulated depreciation to date. Unlike the other depreciation methods, the declining-balance method does not use depreciable cost in computing annual depreciation expense. That is, **it ignores salvage value in determining the amount to which the declining-balance rate is applied**. Salvage value, however, does limit the total depreciation that can be taken. Depreciation stops when the asset's book value equals expected salvage value.

A common declining-balance rate is double the straight-line rate. The method is often called the **double-declining-balance method**. If Barb's Florists uses the double-declining-balance method, it uses a depreciation rate of 40% (2 × the straight-line rate of 20%). Illustration 10-13 shows the declining-balance formula and the computation of the first year's depreciation on the delivery truck.

Illustration 10-13
Formula for declining-balance method

Book Value at Beginning of Year	×	Declining-Balance Rate	=	Annual Depreciation Expense
$13,000	×	40%	=	**$5,200**

The depreciation schedule under this method is as follows.

Illustration 10-14
Double-declining-balance depreciation schedule

BARB'S FLORISTS

	Computation					End of Year	
Year	**Book Value Beginning of Year**	×	**Depreciation Rate**	=	**Annual Depreciation Expense**	**Accumulated Depreciation**	**Book Value**
2017	$13,000		40%		**$5,200**	$ 5,200	$7,800
2018	7,800		40		**3,120**	8,320	4,680
2019	4,680		40		**1,872**	10,192	2,808
2020	2,808		40		**1,123**	11,315	1,685
2021	1,685		40		**685***	12,000	**1,000**

*Computation of $674 ($1,685 × 40%) is adjusted to $685 in order for book value to equal salvage value.

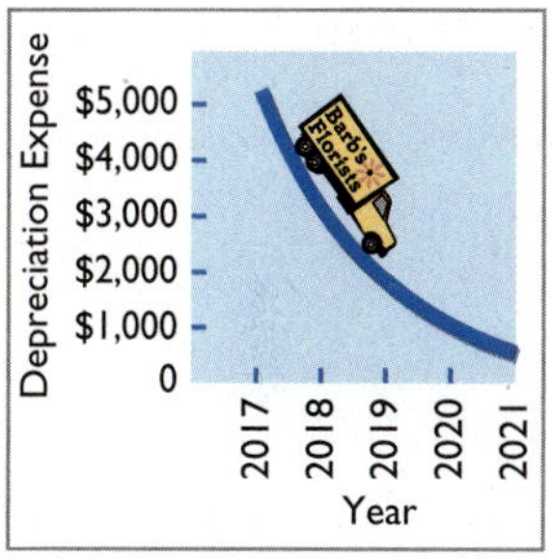

The delivery equipment is 69% depreciated ($8,320 ÷ $12,000) at the end of the second year. Under the straight-line method, the truck would be depreciated 40% ($4,800 ÷ $12,000) at that time. Because the declining-balance method produces higher depreciation expense in the early years than in the later years, it is considered an **accelerated-depreciation method**. The declining-balance method is compatible with the expense recognition principle. It matches the higher depreciation expense in early years with the higher benefits received in these years. It also recognizes lower depreciation expense in later years, when the asset's contribution to revenue is less. Some assets lose usefulness rapidly because of obsolescence. In these cases, the declining-balance method provides the most appropriate depreciation amount.

Helpful Hint
The method recommended for an asset that is expected to be significantly more productive in the first half of its useful life is the declining-balance method.

When a company purchases an asset during the year, it must prorate the first year's declining-balance depreciation on a time basis. For example, if Barb's Florists had purchased the truck on April 1, 2017, depreciation for 2017 would become $3,900 ($13,000 × 40% × 9/12). The book value at the beginning of 2018 is then $9,100 ($13,000 − $3,900), and the 2018 depreciation is $3,640 ($9,100 × 40%). Subsequent computations would follow from those amounts.

COMPARISON OF METHODS

Illustration 10-15 compares annual and total depreciation expense under each of the three methods for Barb's Florists.

Illustration 10-15
Comparison of depreciation methods

Year	Straight-Line	Units-of-Activity	Declining-Balance
2017	$ 2,400	$ 1,800	$ 5,200
2018	2,400	3,600	3,120
2019	2,400	2,400	1,872
2020	2,400	3,000	1,123
2021	2,400	1,200	685
	$12,000	**$12,000**	**$12,000**

Annual depreciation varies considerably among the methods, but **total depreciation expense is the same ($12,000) for the five-year period** under all three methods. Each method is acceptable in accounting because each recognizes in a rational and systematic manner the decline in service potential of the asset. Illustration 10-16 graphs the depreciation expense pattern under each method.

Illustration 10-16
Patterns of depreciation

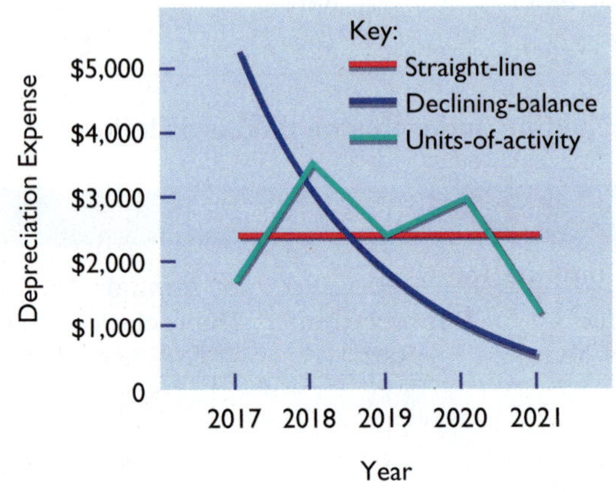

Depreciation and Income Taxes

The Internal Revenue Service (IRS) allows taxpayers to deduct depreciation expense when they compute taxable income. However, the IRS does not require taxpayers to use the same depreciation method on the tax return that is used in preparing financial statements.

Many corporations use straight-line in their financial statements to maximize net income. At the same time, they use a special accelerated-depreciation method on their tax returns to minimize their income taxes. Taxpayers must use on their tax returns either the straight-line method or a special accelerated-depreciation method called the **Modified Accelerated Cost Recovery System** (MACRS).

Revising Periodic Depreciation

Depreciation is one example of the use of estimation in the accounting process. Management should periodically review annual depreciation expense. If wear and tear or obsolescence indicate that annual depreciation estimates are inadequate or excessive, the company should change the amount of depreciation expense.

When a change in an estimate is required, the company makes the change in **current and future years. It does not change depreciation in prior periods.** The rationale is that continual restatement of prior periods would adversely affect confidence in financial statements.

Helpful Hint
Use a step-by-step approach: (1) determine new depreciable cost; (2) divide by remaining useful life.

To determine the new annual depreciation expense, the company first computes the asset's depreciable cost at the time of the revision. It then allocates the revised depreciable cost to the remaining useful life.

To illustrate, assume that Barb's Florists decides on January 1, 2020, to extend the useful life of the truck one year (a total life of six years) and increase its salvage value to $2,200. The company has used the straight-line method to depreciate the asset to date. Depreciation per year was $2,400 [($13,000 − $1,000) ÷ 5]. Accumulated depreciation after three years (2017–2019) is $7,200 ($2,400 × 3), and book value is $5,800 ($13,000 − $7,200). The new annual depreciation is $1,200, computed as shown in Illustration 10-17.

Book value, 1/1/20	$ 5,800	
Less: Salvage value	2,200	
Depreciable cost	$ 3,600	
Remaining useful life	3 years	(2020–2022)
Revised annual depreciation ($3,600 ÷ 3)	**$ 1,200**	

Illustration 10-17
Revised depreciation computation

Barb's Florists makes no entry for the change in estimate. On December 31, 2020, during the preparation of adjusting entries, it records depreciation expense of $1,200. Companies must describe in the financial statements significant changes in estimates.

DO IT! 2b Revised Depreciation

Chambers Corporation purchased a piece of equipment for $36,000. It estimated a 6-year life and $6,000 salvage value. Thus, straight-line depreciation was $5,000 per year [($36,000 − $6,000) ÷ 6]. At the end of year three (before the depreciation adjustment), it estimated the new total life to be 10 years and the new salvage value to be $2,000. Compute the revised depreciation.

Solution

Original depreciation expense = [($36,000 − $6,000) ÷ 6] = $5,000
Accumulated depreciation after 2 years = 2 × $5,000 = $10,000
Book value = $36,000 − $10,000 = $26,000

Book value after 2 years of depreciation	$26,000
Less: New salvage value	2,000
Depreciable cost	$24,000
Remaining useful life	8 years
Revised annual depreciation ($24,000 ÷ 8)	$ 3,000

Action Plan

✔ Calculate depreciable cost.

✔ Divide depreciable cost by new remaining life.

Related exercise material: **BE10-8, E10-8, and DO IT! 10-2b.**

LEARNING OBJECTIVE 3 Explain how to account for the disposal of plant assets.

Companies dispose of plant assets that are no longer useful to them. Illustration 10-18 shows the three ways in which companies make plant asset disposals.

Illustration 10-18
Methods of plant asset disposal

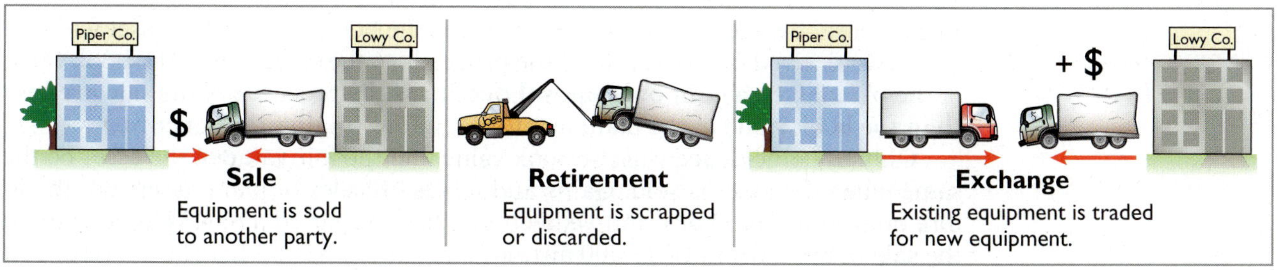
Piper Co.
Lowy Co.
$
Sale
Equipment is sold to another party.
Retirement
Equipment is scrapped or discarded.
Piper Co.
Lowy Co.
+ $
Exchange
Existing equipment is traded for new equipment.

Whatever the disposal method, the company must determine the book value of the plant asset at the disposal date to determine the gain or loss. Recall that the book value is the difference between the cost of the plant asset and the accumulated depreciation to date. If the disposal does not occur on the first day of the year, the company must record depreciation for the fraction of the year to the date of disposal. The company then eliminates the book value by reducing (debiting) Accumulated Depreciation for the total depreciation associated with that asset to the date of disposal and reducing (crediting) the asset account for the cost of the asset.

In this chapter, we examine the accounting for the retirement and sale of plant assets. In the appendix to the chapter, we discuss and illustrate the accounting for exchanges of plant assets.

Retirement of Plant Assets

To illustrate the retirement of plant assets, assume that Hobart Company retires its computer printers, which cost $32,000. The accumulated depreciation on these printers is $32,000. The equipment, therefore, is fully depreciated (zero book value). The entry to record this retirement is as follows.

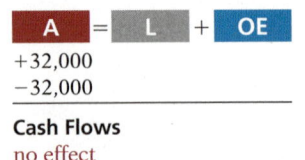

A	= L	+ OE
+32,000		
−32,000		

Cash Flows
no effect

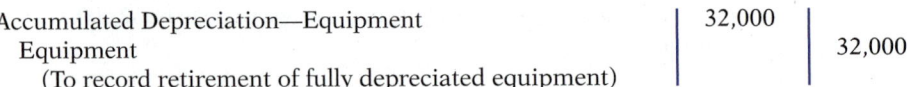

Accumulated Depreciation—Equipment	32,000	
Equipment		32,000
(To record retirement of fully depreciated equipment)		

Helpful Hint
When disposing of a plant asset, a company removes from the accounts all amounts related to the asset. This includes the original cost and the total depreciation to date in the accumulated depreciation account.

What happens if a fully depreciated plant asset is still useful to the company? In this case, the asset and its accumulated depreciation continue to be reported on the balance sheet, without further depreciation adjustment, until the company retires the asset. Reporting the asset and related accumulated depreciation on the balance sheet informs the financial statement reader that the asset is still in use. Once fully depreciated, no additional depreciation should be taken, even if an asset is still being used. In no situation can the accumulated depreciation on a plant asset exceed its cost.

If a company retires a plant asset before it is fully depreciated and no cash is received for scrap or salvage value, a loss on disposal occurs. For example, assume that Sunset Company discards delivery equipment that cost $18,000 and has accumulated depreciation of $14,000. The entry is as follows.

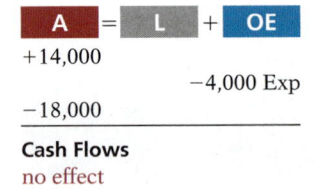

A	= L	+ OE
+14,000		
		−4,000 Exp
−18,000		

Cash Flows
no effect

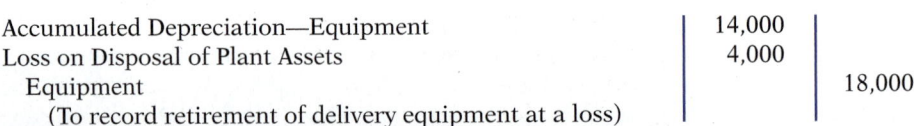

Accumulated Depreciation—Equipment	14,000	
Loss on Disposal of Plant Assets	4,000	
Equipment		18,000
(To record retirement of delivery equipment at a loss)		

Companies report a loss on disposal of plant assets in the "Other expenses and losses" section of the income statement.

Sale of Plant Assets

In a disposal by sale, the company compares the book value of the asset with the proceeds received from the sale. If the proceeds of the sale **exceed** the book value of the plant asset, **a gain on disposal occurs**. If the proceeds of the sale **are less than** the book value of the plant asset sold, **a loss on disposal occurs**.

Only by coincidence will the book value and the fair value of the asset be the same when the asset is sold. Gains and losses on sales of plant assets are therefore quite common. For example, Delta Airlines reported a $94,343,000 gain on the sale of five Boeing B727-200 aircraft and five Lockheed L-1011-1 aircraft.

GAIN ON SALE

To illustrate a gain on sale of plant assets, assume that on July 1, 2017, Wright Company sells office furniture for $16,000 cash. The office furniture originally cost $60,000. As of January 1, 2017, it had accumulated depreciation of $41,000. Depreciation for the first six months of 2017 is $8,000. Wright records depreciation expense and updates accumulated depreciation to July 1 with the following entry.

July 1	Depreciation Expense	8,000	
	Accumulated Depreciation—Equipment		8,000
	(To record depreciation expense for the first 6 months of 2017)		

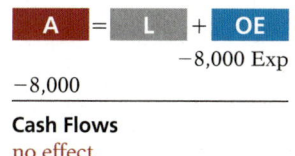

A = L + OE
−8,000 Exp
−8,000

Cash Flows
no effect

After the accumulated depreciation balance is updated, the company computes the gain or loss. The gain or loss is the difference between the proceeds from the sale and the book value at the date of disposal. Illustration 10-19 shows this computation for Wright Company, which has a gain on disposal of $5,000.

Cost of office furniture	$60,000
Less: Accumulated depreciation ($41,000 + $8,000)	49,000
Book value at date of disposal	11,000
Proceeds from sale	16,000
Gain on disposal of plant asset	**$ 5,000**

Illustration 10-19
Computation of gain on disposal

Wright records the sale and the gain on disposal of the plant asset as follows.

July 1	Cash	16,000	
	Accumulated Depreciation—Equipment	49,000	
	Equipment		60,000
	Gain on Disposal of Plant Assets		5,000
	(To record sale of office furniture at a gain)		

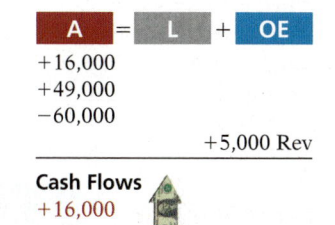

A = L + OE
+16,000
+49,000
−60,000
+5,000 Rev

Cash Flows
+16,000

Companies report a gain on disposal of plant assets in the "Other revenues and gains" section of the income statement.

LOSS ON SALE

Assume that instead of selling the office furniture for $16,000, Wright sells it for $9,000. In this case, Wright computes a loss of $2,000 as follows.

Cost of office furniture	$60,000
Less: Accumulated depreciation	49,000
Book value at date of disposal	11,000
Proceeds from sale	9,000
Loss on disposal of plant asset	**$ 2,000**

Illustration 10-20
Computation of loss on disposal

Wright records the sale and the loss on disposal of the plant asset as follows.

July 1	Cash	9,000	
	Accumulated Depreciation—Equipment	49,000	
	Loss on Disposal of Plant Assets	2,000	
	Equipment		60,000
	(To record sale of office furniture at a loss)		

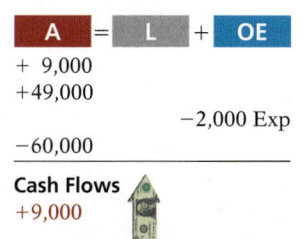

A = L + OE
+ 9,000
+49,000
−2,000 Exp
−60,000

Cash Flows
+9,000

Companies report a loss on disposal of plant assets in the "Other expenses and losses" section of the income statement.

DO IT! 3 Plant Asset Disposal

Overland Trucking has an old truck that cost $30,000, and it has accumulated depreciation of $16,000 on this truck. Overland has decided to sell the truck. (a) What entry would Overland Trucking make to record the sale of the truck for $17,000 cash? (b) What entry would Overland Trucking make to record the sale of the truck for $10,000 cash?

Action Plan

✔ At the time of disposal, determine the book value of the asset.

✔ Compare the asset's book value with the proceeds received to determine whether a gain or loss has occurred.

Solution

(a) Sale of truck for cash at a gain:		
Cash	17,000	
Accumulated Depreciation—Equipment	16,000	
Equipment		30,000
Gain on Disposal of Plant Assets		
[$17,000 – ($30,000 – $16,000)]		3,000
(To record sale of truck at a gain)		
(b) Sale of truck for cash at a loss:		
Cash	10,000	
Accumulated Depreciation—Equipment	16,000	
Loss on Disposal of Plant Assets		
[$10,000 – ($30,000 – $16,000)]	4,000	
Equipment		30,000
(To record sale of truck at a loss)		

Related exercise material: **BE10-9, BE10-10, E10-9, E10-10, and DO IT! 10-3.**

LEARNING OBJECTIVE 4 Describe how to account for natural resources and intangible assets.

Natural Resources

Helpful Hint
On a balance sheet, natural resources may be described more specifically as *timberlands, mineral deposits, oil reserves*, and so on.

Natural resources consist of standing timber and underground deposits of oil, gas, and minerals. These long-lived productive assets have two distinguishing characteristics: (1) they are physically extracted in operations (such as mining, cutting, or pumping), and (2) they are replaceable only by an act of nature.

The acquisition cost of a natural resource is the price needed to acquire the resource **and** prepare it for its intended use. For an already-discovered resource, such as an existing coal mine, cost is the price paid for the property.

Depletion

The allocation of the cost of natural resources in a rational and systematic manner over the resource's useful life is called **depletion**. (That is, depletion is to natural resources as depreciation is to plant assets.) **Companies generally use the units-of-activity method** (learned earlier in the chapter) **to compute depletion**. The reason is that **depletion generally is a function of the units extracted during the year**.

Under the units-of-activity method, companies divide the total cost of the natural resource minus salvage value by the number of units estimated to be in the resource. The result is a **depletion cost per unit**. To compute depletion, the cost per unit is then multiplied by the number of units extracted.

To illustrate, assume that Lane Coal Company invests \$5 million in a mine estimated to have 1 million tons of coal and no salvage value. Illustration 10-21 shows the computation of the depletion cost per unit.

Total Cost − Salvage Value / Total Estimated Units Available	=	Depletion Cost per Unit
\$5,000,000 / \$1,000,000	=	\$5.00 per ton

Illustration 10-21
Computation of depletion cost per unit

If Lane extracts 250,000 tons in the first year, then the depletion for the year is \$1,250,000 (250,000 tons × \$5). It records the depletion as follows.

Inventory (coal)	1,250,000	
Accumulated Depletion		1,250,000

A = L + OE
+1,250,000
−1,250,000

Cash Flows
no effect

Lane debits Inventory for the total depletion for the year and credits Accumulated Depletion to reduce the carrying value of the natural resource. Accumulated Depletion is a contra asset similar to Accumulated Depreciation. Lane credits Inventory when it sells the inventory and debits Cost of Goods Sold. The amount not sold remains in inventory and is reported in the current assets section of the balance sheet.

Some companies do not use an Accumulated Depletion account. In such cases, the company credits the amount of depletion directly to the natural resources account.

ETHICS NOTE

Investors were stunned at news that Royal Dutch/Shell Group had significantly overstated its reported oil reserves—and perhaps had done so intentionally.

People, Planet, and Profit Insight — BHP Billiton

© Christian Uhrig/iStockphoto

Sustainability Report Please

Sustainability reports identify how the company is meeting its corporate social responsibilities. Many companies, both large and small, are now issuing these reports. For example, companies such as Disney, Best Buy, Microsoft, Ford, and ConocoPhilips issue these reports. Presented below is an adapted section of a recent BHP Billiton (a global mining, oil, and gas company) sustainability report on its environmental policies. These policies are to (1) take action to address the challenges of climate change, (2) set and achieve targets that reduce pollution, and (3) enhance biodiversity by assessing and considering ecological values and land-use aspects. Here is how BHP Billiton measures the success or failure of some of these policies:

Environment	Commentary	Target Date
We will maintain total greenhouse gas emissions below FY2006 levels.	FY2013 greenhouse gas emissions were lower than the FY2006 baseline.	30 June 2017
All operations to offset impacts to biodiversity and the related benefits derived from ecosystems.	Land and Biodiversity Management Plans were developed at all our operations.	Annual
We will finance the conservation and continuing management of areas of high biodiversity and ecosystem value.	Two projects of international conservation significance were established—the Five Rivers Conservation Project, in Australia, and the Valdivian Coastal Reserve Conservation Project, in Chile.	30 June 2017

In addition to the environment, BHP Billiton has sections in its sustainability report which discuss people, safety, health, and community.

Why do you believe companies issue sustainability reports? (Go to **WileyPLUS** for this answer and additional questions.)

Intangible Assets

Intangible assets are rights, privileges, and competitive advantages that result from the ownership of long-lived assets that do not possess physical substance. Evidence of intangibles may exist in the form of contracts or licenses. Intangibles may arise from the following sources:

1. Government grants, such as patents, copyrights, licenses, trademarks, and trade names.
2. Acquisition of another business, in which the purchase price includes a payment for **goodwill**.
3. Private monopolistic arrangements arising from contractual agreements, such as franchises and leases.

Some widely known intangibles are **Microsoft**'s patents, **McDonald's** franchises, **Apple**'s trade name iPod, J.K. Rowling's copyrights on the *Harry Potter* books, and the trademark **Rent-A-Wreck** in the Feature Story.

Accounting for Intangible Assets

Companies record intangible assets at cost. Intangibles are categorized as having either a limited life or an indefinite life. If an intangible has a **limited life**, the company allocates its cost over the asset's useful life using a process similar to depreciation. The process of allocating the cost of intangibles is referred to as **amortization**. The cost of intangible assets with **indefinite lives should not be amortized.**

Helpful Hint
Amortization is to intangibles what *depreciation* is to plant assets and *depletion* is to natural resources.

To record amortization of an intangible asset, a company increases (debits) Amortization Expense, and decreases (credits) the specific intangible asset. (Unlike depreciation, no contra account, such as Accumulated Amortization, is usually used.)

Intangible assets are typically amortized on a straight-line basis. For example, the legal life of a patent is 20 years. Companies **amortize the cost of a patent over its 20-year life or its useful life, whichever is shorter**. To illustrate the computation of patent amortization, assume that National Labs purchases a patent at a cost of $60,000. If National estimates the useful life of the patent to be eight years, the annual amortization expense is $7,500 ($60,000 ÷ 8). National records the annual amortization as follows.

A	=	L	+	OE
				−7,500 Exp
−7,500				

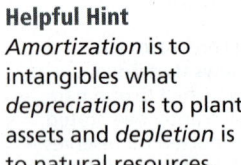

Cash Flows
no effect

Dec. 31	Amortization Expense	7,500	
	Patents		7,500
	(To record patent amortization)		

Companies classify Amortization Expense as an operating expense in the income statement.

There is a difference between intangible assets and plant assets in determining cost. For plant assets, cost includes both the purchase price of the asset and the costs incurred in designing and constructing the asset. In contrast, the initial cost for an intangible asset includes **only the purchase price**. Companies expense any costs incurred in developing an intangible asset.

PATENTS

A **patent** is an exclusive right issued by the U.S. Patent Office that enables the recipient to manufacture, sell, or otherwise control an invention for a period of 20 years from the date of the grant. A patent is nonrenewable. But, companies can extend the legal life of a patent by obtaining new patents for improvements or other changes in the basic design. **The initial cost of a patent is the cash or cash equivalent price paid to acquire the patent.**

The saying, "A patent is only as good as the money you're prepared to spend defending it," is very true. Many patents are subject to litigation by competitors. Any legal costs an owner incurs in successfully defending a patent in an infringement suit are considered necessary to establish the patent's validity. **The owner adds those costs to the Patents account and amortizes them over the remaining life of the patent.**

The patent holder amortizes the cost of a patent over its 20-year legal life or its useful life, whichever is shorter. Companies consider obsolescence and inadequacy in determining useful life. These factors may cause a patent to become economically ineffective before the end of its legal life.

COPYRIGHTS

The federal government grants **copyrights**, which give the owner the exclusive right to reproduce and sell an artistic or published work. Copyrights extend for the life of the creator plus 70 years. The cost of a copyright is the **cost of acquiring and defending it**. The cost may be only the small fee paid to the U.S. Copyright Office. Or, it may amount to much more if an infringement suit is involved.

The useful life of a copyright generally is significantly shorter than its legal life. Therefore, copyrights usually are amortized over a relatively short period of time.

TRADEMARKS AND TRADE NAMES

A **trademark** or **trade name** is a word, phrase, jingle, or symbol that identifies a particular enterprise or product. Trade names like Wheaties, Monopoly, Big Mac, Kleenex, Coca-Cola, and Jeep create immediate product identification. They also generally enhance the sale of the product. The creator or original user may obtain exclusive legal right to the trademark or trade name by registering it with the U.S. Patent Office. Such registration provides 20 years of protection. The registration may be renewed indefinitely as long as the trademark or trade name is in use.

If a company purchases the trademark or trade name, its cost is the purchase price. If a company develops and maintains the trademark or trade name, any costs related to these activities are expensed as incurred. Because trademarks and trade names have indefinite lives, they are not amortized.

FRANCHISES

When you fill up your tank at the corner **Shell** station, eat lunch at **Subway**, or rent a car from **Rent-A-Wreck**, you are dealing with franchises. A **franchise** is a contractual arrangement between a franchisor and a franchisee. The franchisor grants the franchisee the right to sell certain products, perform specific services, or use certain trademarks or trade names, usually within a designated geographic area.

Another type of franchise is a **license**. A license granted by a governmental body permits a company to use public property in performing its services. Examples are the use of city streets for a bus line or taxi service, the use of public land for telephone and electric lines, and the use of airwaves for radio or TV broadcasting. In a recent license agreement, **FOX**, **CBS**, and **NBC** agreed to pay $27.9 billion for the right to broadcast **NFL** football games over an eight-year period. Franchises and licenses may by granted for a definite period of time, an indefinite period, or perpetually.

When a company can identify costs with the purchase of a franchise or license, it should recognize an intangible asset. Companies should amortize the cost of a limited-life franchise (or license) over its useful life. If the life is indefinite, the cost is not amortized. Annual payments made under a franchise agreement are recorded as **operating expenses** in the period in which they are incurred.

GOODWILL

Usually, the largest intangible asset that appears on a company's balance sheet is goodwill. **Goodwill** represents the value of all favorable attributes that relate to a company that are not attributable to any other specific asset. These include exceptional management, desirable location, good customer relations, skilled employees, high-quality products, and harmonious relations with labor unions. Goodwill is unique. Unlike assets such as investments and plant assets, which can be sold **individually** in the marketplace, goodwill can be identified only with the business **as a whole**.

If goodwill can be identified only with the business as a whole, how can its amount be determined? One could try to put a dollar value on the factors listed above (exceptional management, desirable location, and so on). But, the results would be very subjective, and such subjective valuations would not contribute to the reliability of financial statements. **Therefore, companies record goodwill only when an entire business is purchased. In that case, goodwill is the excess of cost over the fair value of the net assets (assets less liabilities) acquired.**

In recording the purchase of a business, the company debits (increases) the identifiable acquired assets, credits liabilities at their fair values, credits cash for the purchase price, and records the difference as goodwill. **Goodwill is not amortized** because it is considered to have an indefinite life. Companies report goodwill in the balance sheet under intangible assets.

Accounting Across the Organization | Google

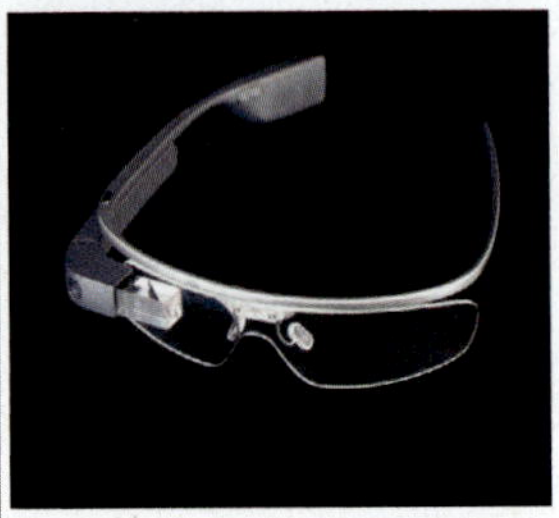

© Hattanas Kumchai/Shutterstock

We Want to Own Glass

Google, which has trademarked the term "Google Glass," now wants to trademark the term "Glass." Why? Because the simple word Glass has marketing advantages over the term Google Glass. It is easy to remember and is more universal. Regulators, however, are balking at Google's request. They say that the possible trademark is too similar to other existing or pending software trademarks that contain the word "glass." Also, regulators suggest that the term Glass is merely descriptive and therefore lacks trademark protection. For example, regulators note that a company that makes salsa could not trademark the term "Spicy Salsa."

BorderStylo LLC, which developed a Web-browser extension called Write on Glass, has filed a notice of opposition to Google's request. Google is fighting back and has sent the trademark examiner a 1,928-page application defense.

Source: Jacob Gershman, "Google Wants to Own 'Glass'," *Wall Street Journal* (April 4, 2014), p. B5.

If Google is successful in registering the term Glass, where will this trademark be reported on its financial statements? (Go to **WileyPLUS** for this answer and additional questions.)

Research and Development Costs

Helpful Hint
Research and development (R&D) costs are not intangible assets. But because they may lead to patents and copyrights, we discuss them in this section.

Research and development costs are expenditures that may lead to patents, copyrights, new processes, and new products. Many companies spend considerable sums of money on research and development (R&D). For example, in a recent year, IBM spent over $5.1 billion on R&D.

Research and development costs present accounting problems. For one thing, it is sometimes difficult to assign the costs to specific projects. Also, there are uncertainties in identifying the extent and timing of future benefits. As a result, companies usually record R&D costs **as an expense when incurred**, whether the research and development is successful or not.

To illustrate, assume that Laser Scanner Company spent $3 million on R&D that resulted in two highly successful patents. It spent $20,000 on legal fees for the patents. The company would add the lawyers' fees to the Patents account. The R&D costs, however, cannot be included in the cost of the patents. Instead, the company would record the R&D costs as an expense when incurred.

Many disagree with this accounting approach. They argue that expensing R&D costs leads to understated assets and net income. Others, however, argue that capitalizing these costs will lead to highly speculative assets on the balance sheet. Who is right is difficult to determine.

DO IT! 4 Classification Concepts

Match the statement with the term most directly associated with it.

Copyrights | Depletion
Intangible assets | Franchises
Research and development costs

1. _______ The allocation of the cost of a natural resource to expense in a rational and systematic manner.

2. _______ Rights, privileges, and competitive advantages that result from the ownership of long-lived assets that do not possess physical substance.

3. _______ An exclusive right granted by the federal government to reproduce and sell an artistic or published work.

4. _______ A right to sell certain products or services or to use certain trademarks or trade names within a designated geographic area.

5. _______ Costs incurred by a company that often lead to patents or new products. These costs must be expensed as incurred.

Action Plan

✔ Know that the accounting for intangibles often depends on whether the item has a finite or indefinite life.

✔ Recognize the many similarities and differences between the accounting for natural resources, plant assets, and intangible assets.

Solution

1. Depletion
2. Intangible assets
3. Copyrights
4. Franchises
5. Research and development costs

Related exercise material: **BE10-11, BE10-12, E10-11, E10-12, E10-13, and DO IT! 10-4.**

LEARNING OBJECTIVE 5 Discuss how plant assets, natural resources, and intangible assets are reported and analyzed.

Presentation

Usually, companies combine plant assets and natural resources under "Property, plant, and equipment" in the balance sheet. They show intangibles separately. Companies disclose either in the balance sheet or the notes the balances of the major classes of assets, such as land, buildings, and equipment, and accumulated depreciation by major classes or in total. In addition, they should describe the depreciation and amortization methods that were used, as well as disclose the amount of depreciation and amortization expense for the period.

Illustration 10-22 (page 464) shows a typical financial statement presentation of property, plant, and equipment and intangibles for **The Procter & Gamble Company (P&G)** in its 2013 balance sheet. The notes to P&G's financial statements present greater details about the accounting for its long-term tangible and intangible assets.

Illustration 10-22
P&G's presentation of property, plant, and equipment, and intangible assets

Real World

THE PROCTER & GAMBLE COMPANY
Balance Sheet (partial)
(in millions)

	June 30	
	2013	**2012**
Property, plant, and equipment		
Buildings	$ 7,829	$ 7,324
Machinery and equipment	34,305	32,029
Land	878	880
	43,012	40,233
Accumulated depreciation	(21,346)	(19,856)
Net property, plant, and equipment	21,666	20,377
Goodwill and other intangible assets		
Goodwill	55,188	53,773
Trademarks and other intangible assets, net	31,572	30,988
Net goodwill and other intangible assets	$86,760	$84,761

Illustration 10-23 shows another comprehensive presentation of property, plant, and equipment from the balance sheet of Owens-Illinois. The notes to the financial statements of Owens-Illinois identify the major classes of property, plant, and equipment. They also indicate that depreciation and amortization are by the straight-line method, and depletion is by the units-of-activity method.

Illustration 10-23
Owens-Illinois' presentation of property, plant, and equipment, and intangible assets

Real World

OWENS-ILLINOIS, INC.
Balance Sheet (partial)
(in millions)

Property, plant, and equipment			
Timberlands, at cost, less accumulated depletion		$ 95.4	
Buildings and equipment, at cost	$2,207.1		
Less: Accumulated depreciation	1,229.0	978.1	
Total property, plant, and equipment			$1,073.5
Intangibles			
Patents			410.0
Total			$1,483.5

Analysis

Using ratios, we can analyze how efficiently a company uses its assets to generate sales. The **asset turnover** analyzes the productivity of a company's assets. It tells us how many dollars of sales a company generates for each dollar invested in assets. This ratio is computed by dividing net sales by average total assets for the period. Illustration 10-24 shows the computation of the asset turnover for The Procter & Gamble Company. P&G's net sales for 2013 were $84,167 million. Its total ending assets were $139,263 million, and beginning assets were $132,244 million.

Illustration 10-24
Asset turnover formula and computation

Net Sales	÷	Average Total Assets	=	Asset Turnover
$84,167	÷	$\frac{\$132,244 + \$139,263}{2}$	=	**.62 times**

Thus, each dollar invested in assets produced $0.62 in sales for P&G. If a company is using its assets efficiently, each dollar of assets will create a high amount of sales. This ratio varies greatly among different industries—from those that are asset-intensive (utilities) to those that are not (services).

DO IT! 5 Asset Turnover

Paramour Company reported net income of $180,000, net sales of $420,000, and had total assets of $460,000 on January 1, 2017, and total assets on December 31, 2017, of $540,000 billion. Determine Paramour's asset turnover for 2017.

Solution

The asset turnover for Paramour Company is computed as follows.

Net Sales ÷ Average Total Assets = Asset Turnover

$$\$420{,}000 \div \frac{\$460{,}000 + \$540{,}000}{2} = .84$$

Related Exercise material: **BE10-14, E10-14, and DO IT! 10-5.**

Action Plan

✔ Recognize that the asset turnover analyzes the productivity of a company's assets.

✔ Know the formula Net sales ÷ Average total assets equals Asset turnover.

LEARNING OBJECTIVE *6

APPENDIX 10A: Explain how to account for the exchange of plant assets.

Ordinarily, companies record a gain or loss on the exchange of plant assets. The rationale for recognizing a gain or loss is that most exchanges have **commercial substance**. An exchange has commercial substance if the future cash flows change as a result of the exchange.

To illustrate, Ramos Co. exchanges some of its equipment for land held by Brodhead Inc. It is likely that the timing and amount of the cash flows arising from the land will differ significantly from the cash flows arising from the equipment. As a result, both Ramos and Brodhead are in different economic positions. Therefore, **the exchange has commercial substance**, and the companies recognize a gain or loss in the exchange. Because most exchanges have commercial substance (even when similar assets are exchanged), we illustrate only this type of situation for both a loss and a gain.

Loss Treatment

To illustrate an exchange that results in a loss, assume that Roland Company exchanged a set of used trucks plus cash for a new semi-truck. The used trucks have a combined book value of $42,000 (cost $64,000 less $22,000 accumulated depreciation). Roland's purchasing agent, experienced in the secondhand market, indicates that the used trucks have a fair value of $26,000. In addition to the trucks, Roland must pay $17,000 for the semi-truck. Roland computes the cost of the semi-truck as follows.

Fair value of used trucks	$26,000
Cash paid	17,000
Cost of semi-truck	$43,000

Illustration 10A-1
Cost of semi-truck

Roland incurs a loss on disposal of plant assets of $16,000 on this exchange. The reason is that the book value of the used trucks is greater than the fair value of these trucks. The computation is as follows.

Illustration 10A-2
Computation of loss on disposal

Book value of used trucks ($64,000 − $22,000)	$ 42,000
Fair value of used trucks	26,000
Loss on disposal of plant assets	**$16,000**

In recording an exchange at a loss, three steps are required: (1) eliminate the book value of the asset given up, (2) record the cost of the asset acquired, and (3) recognize the loss on disposal of plant assets. Roland Company thus records the exchange on the loss as follows.

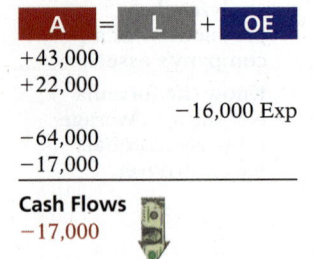

A	=	L	+	OE
+43,000				
+22,000				
				−16,000 Exp
−64,000				
−17,000				

Cash Flows
−17,000

Equipment (new)	43,000	
Accumulated Depreciation—Equipment	22,000	
Loss on Disposal of Plant Assets	16,000	
Equipment (old)		64,000
Cash		17,000
(To record exchange of used trucks for semi-truck)		

Gain Treatment

To illustrate a gain situation, assume that Mark Express Delivery decides to exchange its old delivery equipment plus cash of $3,000 for new delivery equipment. The book value of the old delivery equipment is $12,000 (cost $40,000 less accumulated depreciation $28,000). The fair value of the old delivery equipment is $19,000.

The cost of the new asset is the fair value of the old asset exchanged plus any cash paid (or other consideration given up). The cost of the new delivery equipment is $22,000, computed as follows.

Illustration 10A-3
Cost of new delivery equipment

Fair value of old delivery equipment	$ 19,000
Cash paid	3,000
Cost of new delivery equipment	**$22,000**

A gain results when the fair value of the old delivery equipment is greater than its book value. For Mark Express, there is a gain of $7,000 on disposal of plant assets, computed as follows.

Illustration 10A-4
Computation of gain on disposal

Fair value of old delivery equipment	$19,000
Book value of old delivery equipment ($40,000 − $28,000)	12,000
Gain on disposal of plant assets	**$ 7,000**

Mark Express Delivery records the exchange as follows.

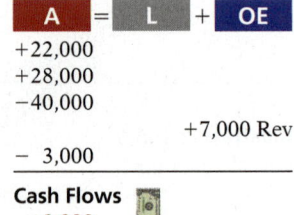

A	=	L	+	OE
+22,000				
+28,000				
−40,000				
				+7,000 Rev
− 3,000				

Cash Flows
− 3,000

Equipment (new)	22,000	
Accumulated Depreciation—Equipment (old)	28,000	
Equipment (old)		40,000
Gain on Disposal of Plant Assets		7,000
Cash		3,000
(To record exchange of old delivery equipment for new delivery equipment)		

In recording an exchange at a gain, the following three steps are involved: (1) eliminate the book value of the asset given up, (2) record the cost of the asset acquired, and (3) recognize the gain on disposal of plant assets. Accounting for exchanges of plant assets becomes more complex if the transaction does not have commercial substance. This issue is discussed in more advanced accounting classes.

REVIEW AND PRACTICE

LEARNING OBJECTIVES REVIEW

1 Explain the accounting for plant asset expenditures. The cost of plant assets includes all expenditures necessary to acquire the asset and make it ready for its intended use. Once cost is established, the company uses that amount as the basis of accounting for the plant assets over its useful life.

Companies incur revenue expenditures to maintain the operating efficiency and productive life of an asset. They debit these expenditures to Maintenance and Repairs Expense as incurred. Capital expenditures increase the operating efficiency, productive capacity, or expected useful life of the asset. Companies generally debit these expenditures to the plant asset affected.

2 Apply depreciation methods to plant assets. Depreciation is the allocation of the cost of a plant asset to expense over its useful (service) life in a rational and systematic manner. Depreciation is not a process of valuation, nor is it a process that results in an accumulation of cash.

Three depreciation methods are:

Method	Effect on Annual Depreciation	Formula
Straight-line	Constant amount	Depreciable cost ÷ Useful life (in years)
Units-of-activity	Varying amount	Depreciable cost per unit × Units of activity during the year
Declining-balance	Decreasing amount	Book value at beginning of year × Declining-balance rate

Companies make revisions of periodic depreciation in present and future periods, not retroactively. They determine the new annual depreciation by dividing the depreciable cost at the time of the revision by the remaining useful life.

3 Explain how to account for the disposal of plant assets. The accounting for disposal of a plant asset through retirement or sale is as follows. (a) Eliminate the book value of the plant asset at the date of disposal. (b) Record cash proceeds, if any. (c) Account for the difference between the book value and the cash proceeds as a gain or loss on disposal.

4 Describe how to account for natural resources and intangible assets. Companies compute depletion cost per unit by dividing the total cost of the natural resource minus salvage value by the number of units estimated to be in the resource. They then multiply the depletion cost per unit by the number of units extracted.

The process of allocating the cost of an intangible asset is referred to as amortization. The cost of intangible assets with indefinite lives is not amortized. Companies normally use the straight-line method for amortizing intangible assets.

5 Discuss how plant assets, natural resources, and intangible assets are reported and analyzed. Companies usually combine plant assets and natural resources under property, plant, and equipment. They show intangibles separately under intangible assets. Either within the balance sheet or in the notes, companies should disclose the balances of the major classes of assets, such as land, buildings, and equipment, and accumulated depreciation by major classes or in total. They also should describe the depreciation and amortization methods used, and should disclose the amount of depreciation and amortization expense for the period. The asset turnover measures the productivity of a company's assets in generating sales.

***6 Explain how to account for the exchange of plant assets.** Ordinarily, companies record a gain or loss on the exchange of plant assets. The rationale for recognizing a gain or loss is that most exchanges have commercial substance. An exchange has commercial substance if the future cash flows change as a result of the exchange.

GLOSSARY REVIEW

Accelerated-depreciation method Depreciation method that produces higher depreciation expense in the early years than in the later years. (p. 453).

Additions and improvements Costs incurred to increase the operating efficiency, productive capacity, or useful life of a plant asset. (p. 447).

Amortization The allocation of the cost of an intangible asset to expense over its useful life in a systematic and rational manner. (p. 460).

Asset turnover A measure of how efficiently a company uses its assets to generate sales; calculated as net sales divided by average total assets. (p. 464).

Capital expenditures Expenditures that increase the company's investment in productive facilities. (p. 447).

Copyrights Exclusive grant from the federal government that allows the owner to reproduce and sell an artistic or published work. (p. 461).

Declining-balance method Depreciation method that applies a constant rate to the declining book value of the asset and produces a decreasing annual depreciation expense over the useful life of the asset. (p. 452).

Depletion The allocation of the cost of a natural resource to expense in a rational and systematic manner over the resource's useful life. (p. 458).

Depreciable cost The cost of a plant asset less its salvage value. (p. 450).

Depreciation The process of allocating to expense the cost of a plant asset over its useful (service) life in a rational and systematic manner. (p. 448).

Franchise (license) A contractual arrangement under which the franchisor grants the franchisee the right to sell certain products, perform specific services, or use certain trademarks or trade names, usually within a designated geographic area. (p. 461).

Going concern assumption States that the company will continue in operation for the foreseeable future. (p. 449).

Goodwill The value of all favorable attributes that relate to a company that is not attributable to any other specific asset. (p. 462).

Intangible assets Rights, privileges, and competitive advantages that result from the ownership of long-lived assets that do not possess physical substance. (p. 460).

Materiality concept If an item would not make a difference in decision-making, a company does not have to follow GAAP in reporting it. (p. 447).

Natural resources Assets that consist of standing timber and underground deposits of oil, gas, and minerals. (p. 458).

Ordinary repairs Expenditures to maintain the operating efficiency and productive life of the unit. (p. 446).

Patent An exclusive right issued by the U.S. Patent Office that enables the recipient to manufacture, sell, or otherwise control an invention for a period of 20 years from the date of the grant. (p. 460).

Plant assets Tangible resources that are used in the operations of the business and are not intended for sale to customers. (p. 444).

Research and development (R&D) costs Expenditures that may lead to patents, copyrights, new processes, or new products. (p. 462).

Revenue expenditures Expenditures that are immediately charged against revenues as an expense. (p. 446).

Salvage value An estimate of an asset's value at the end of its useful life. (p. 449).

Straight-line method Depreciation method in which periodic depreciation is the same for each year of the asset's useful life. (p. 450).

Trademark (trade name) A word, phrase, jingle, or symbol that identifies a particular enterprise or product. (p. 461).

Units-of-activity method Depreciation method in which useful life is expressed in terms of the total units of production or use expected from an asset. (p. 451).

Useful life An estimate of the expected productive life, also called service life, of an asset. (p. 449).

PRACTICE MULTIPLE-CHOICE QUESTIONS

(LO 1) 1. Erin Danielle Company purchased equipment and incurred the following costs.

Cash price	$24,000
Sales taxes	1,200
Insurance during transit	200
Installation and testing	400
Total costs	$25,800

What amount should be recorded as the cost of the equipment?
(a) $24,000. (c) $25,400.
(b) $25,200. (d) $25,800.

(LO 1) 2. Additions to plant assets are:
(a) revenue expenditures.
(b) debited to the Maintenance and Repairs Expense account.
(c) debited to the Purchases account.
(d) capital expenditures.

3. Depreciation is a process of: (LO 2)
(a) valuation. (c) cash accumulation.
(b) cost allocation. (d) appraisal.

4. Micah Bartlett Company purchased equipment on January 1, 2016, at a total invoice cost of $400,000. The equipment has an estimated salvage value of $10,000 and an estimated useful life of 5 years. The amount of accumulated depreciation at December 31, 2017, if the straight-line method of depreciation is used, is: (LO 2)
(a) $80,000. (c) $78,000.
(b) $160,000. (d) $156,000.

5. Ann Torbert purchased a truck for $11,000 on January 1, 2016. The truck will have an estimated salvage value of $1,000 at the end of 5 years. Using the units-of-activity method, the balance in accumulated depreciation at December 31, 2017, can be computed by the following formula: (LO 2)
(a) ($11,000 ÷ Total estimated activity) × Units of activity for 2017.

(b) ($10,000 ÷ Total estimated activity) × Units of activity for 2017.
(c) ($11,000 ÷ Total estimated activity) × Units of activity for 2016 and 2017.
(d) ($10,000 ÷ Total estimated activity) × Units of activity for 2016 and 2017.

(LO 2) **6.** Jefferson Company purchased a piece of equipment on January 1, 2017. The equipment cost $60,000 and has an estimated life of 8 years and a salvage value of $8,000. What was the depreciation expense for the asset for 2018 under the double-declining-balance method?
(a) $6,500. (c) $15,000.
(b) $11,250. (d) $6,562.

(LO 2) **7.** When there is a change in estimated depreciation:
(a) previous depreciation should be corrected.
(b) current and future years' depreciation should be revised.
(c) only future years' depreciation should be revised.
(d) None of the above.

(LO 2) **8.** Able Towing Company purchased a tow truck for $60,000 on January 1, 2015. It was originally depreciated on a straight-line basis over 10 years with an assumed salvage value of $12,000. On December 31, 2017, before adjusting entries had been made, the company decided to change the remaining estimated life to 4 years (including 2017) and the salvage value to $2,000. What was the depreciation expense for 2017?
(a) $6,000. (c) $15,000.
(b) $4,800. (d) $12,100.

(LO 3) **9.** Bennie Razor Company has decided to sell one of its old manufacturing machines on June 30, 2017. The machine was purchased for $80,000 on January 1, 2013, and was depreciated on a straight-line basis for 10 years assuming no salvage value. If the machine was sold for $26,000, what was the amount of the gain or loss recorded at the time of the sale?
(a) $18,000. (c) $22,000.
(b) $54,000. (d) $46,000.

(LO 4) **10.** Maggie Sharrer Company expects to extract 20 million tons of coal from a mine that cost $12 million. If no salvage value is expected and 2 million tons are mined in the first year, the entry to record depletion will include a:
(a) debit to Accumulated Depletion of $2,000,000.
(b) credit to Depletion Expense of $1,200,000.
(c) debit to Inventory of $1,200,000.
(d) credit to Accumulated Depletion of $2,000,000.

(LO 4) **11.** Which of the following statements is **false**?
(a) If an intangible asset has a finite life, it should be amortized.
(b) The amortization period of an intangible asset can exceed 20 years.
(c) Goodwill is recorded only when a business is purchased.
(d) Research and development costs are expensed when incurred, except when the research and development expenditures result in a successful patent.

12. Martha Beyerlein Company incurred $150,000 of research and development costs in its laboratory to develop a patent granted on January 2, 2017. On July 31, 2017, Beyerlein paid $35,000 for legal fees in a successful defense of the patent. The total amount debited to Patents through July 31, 2017, should be: (LO 4)
(a) $150,000. (c) $185,000.
(b) $35,000. (d) $170,000.

13. Indicate which of the following statements is **true**. (LO 5)
(a) Since intangible assets lack physical substance, they need be disclosed only in the notes to the financial statements.
(b) Goodwill should be reported as a contra account in the owner's equity section.
(c) Totals of major classes of assets can be shown in the balance sheet, with asset details disclosed in the notes to the financial statements.
(d) Intangible assets are typically combined with plant assets and natural resources and shown in the property, plant, and equipment section.

14. Lake Coffee Company reported net sales of $180,000, net income of $54,000, beginning total assets of $200,000, and ending total assets of $300,000. What was the company's asset turnover? (LO 5)
(a) 0.90. (c) 0.72.
(b) 0.20. (d) 1.39.

***15.** Schopenhauer Company exchanged an old machine, with a book value of $39,000 and a fair value of $35,000, and paid $10,000 cash for a similar new machine. The transaction has commercial substance. At what amount should the machine acquired in the exchange be recorded on Schopenhauer's books? (LO 6)
(a) $45,000.
(b) $46,000.
(c) $49,000.
(d) $50,000.

***16.** In exchanges of assets in which the exchange has commercial substance: (LO 6)
(a) neither gains nor losses are recognized immediately.
(b) gains, but not losses, are recognized immediately.
(c) losses, but not gains, are recognized immediately.
(d) both gains and losses are recognized immediately.

Solutions

1. (d) All of the costs ($1,200 + $200 + $400) in addition to the cash price ($24,000) should be included in the cost of the equipment because they were necessary expenditures to acquire the asset and make it ready for its intended use. The other choices are therefore incorrect.

2. (d) When an addition is made to plant assets, it is intended to increase productive capacity, increase the assets' useful life, or increase the efficiency of the assets. This is called a capital expenditure. The other choices are incorrect because (a) additions to plant assets are not revenue expenditures because the additions will have a long-term useful life whereas revenue expenditures are minor repairs and maintenance that do not prolong the life of the assets; (b) additions to plant assets are debited to Plant Assets, not Maintenance and Repairs Expense, because the Maintenance and Repairs Expense account is used to record expenditures not intended to increase the life of the assets; and (c) additions to plant assets are debited to Plant Assets, not Purchases, because the Purchases account is used to record assets intended for resale (inventory).

3. (b) Depreciation is a process of allocating the cost of an asset over its useful life, not a process of (a) valuation, (c) cash accumulation, or (d) appraisal.

4. (d) Accumulated depreciation will be the sum of 2 years of depreciation expense. Annual depreciation for this asset is ($400,000 − $10,000)/5 = $78,000. The sum of 2 years' depreciation is therefore $156,000 ($78,000 + $78,000), not (a) $80,000, (b) $160,000, or (c) $78,000.

5. (d) The units-of-activity method takes salvage value into consideration; therefore, the depreciable cost is $10,000. This amount is divided by total estimated activity. The resulting number is multiplied by the units of activity used in 2016 and 2017 to compute the accumulated depreciation at the end of 2017, the second year of the asset's use. The other choices are therefore incorrect.

6. (b) For the double-declining method, the depreciation rate would be 25% or (1/8 × 2). For 2017, annual depreciation expense is $15,000 ($60,000 book value × 25%); for 2018, annual depreciation expense is $11,250 [($60,000 − $15,000) × 25%], not (a) $6,500, (c) $15,000, or (d) $6,562.

7. (b) When there is a change in estimated depreciation, the current and future years' depreciation computation should reflect the new estimates. The other choices are incorrect because (a) previous years' depreciation should not be adjusted when new estimates are made for depreciation, and (c) when there is a change in estimated depreciation, the current and future years' depreciation computation should reflect the new estimates. Choice (d) is wrong because there is a correct answer.

8. (d) First, calculate accumulated depreciation from January 1, 2015, through December 31, 2016, which is $9,600 {[($60,000 − $12,000)/10 years] × 2 years}. Next, calculate the revised depreciable cost, which is $48,400 ($60,000 − $9,600 − $2,000). Thus, the depreciation expense for 2017 is $12,100 ($48,400/4), not (a) $6,000, (b) $4,800, or (c) $15,000.

9. (a) First, the book value needs to be determined. The accumulated depreciation as of June 30, 2017, is $36,000 [($80,000/10) × 4.5 years]. Thus, the cost of the machine less accumulated depreciation equals $44,000 ($80,000 − $36,000). The loss recorded at the time of sale is $18,000 ($26,000 − $44,000), not (b) $54,000, (c) $22,000, or (d) $46,000.

10. (c) The amount of depletion is determined by computing the depletion per unit ($12 million/20 million tons = $0.60 per ton) and then multiplying that amount times the number of units extracted during the year (2 million tons × $0.60 = $1,200,000). This amount is debited to Inventory and credited to Accumulated Depletion. The other choices are therefore incorrect.

11. (d) Research and development (R&D) costs are expensed when incurred, regardless of whether the research and development expenditures result in a successful patent or not. The other choices are true statements.

12. (b) Because the $150,000 was spent developing the patent rather than buying it from another firm, it is debited to Research and Development Expense. Only the $35,000 spent on the successful defense can be debited to Patents, not (a) $150,000, (c) $185,000, or (d) $170,000.

13. (c) Reporting only totals of major classes of assets in the balance sheet is appropriate. Additional details can be shown in the notes to the financial statements. The other choices are false statements.

14. (c) Asset turnover = Net sales ($180,000)/Average total assets [($200,000 + $300,000)/2] = 0.72 times, not (a) 0.90, (b) 0.20, or (d) 1.39 times.

***15. (a)** When an exchange has commercial substance, the debit to the new asset is equal to the fair value of the old asset plus the cash paid ($35,000 + $10,000 = $45,000), not (b) $46,000, (c) $49,000, or (d) $50,000.

***16. (d)** Both gains and losses are recognized immediately when an exchange of assets has commercial substance. The other choices are therefore incorrect.

PRACTICE EXERCISES

Determine depreciation for partial periods

(LO 2)

1. Numo Company purchased a new machine on October 1, 2017, at a cost of $145,000. The company estimated that the machine will have a salvage value of $25,000.The machine is expected to be used for 20,000 working hours during its 5-year life.

Instructions

Compute the depreciation expense under the following methods for the year indicated.

(a) Straight-line for 2017.

(b) Units-of-activity for 2017, assuming machine usage was 3,400 hours.

(c) Declining-balance using double the straight-line rate for 2017 and 2018.

Solution

1. (a) Straight-line method:

$$\left(\frac{\$145{,}000 - \$25{,}000}{5}\right) = \$24{,}000 \text{ per year}$$

2017 depreciation = $24,000 × 3/12 = $6,000

(b) Units-of-activity method:

$$\left(\frac{\$145{,}000 - \$25{,}000}{20{,}000}\right) = \$6.00 \text{ per hour}$$

2017 depreciation = 3,400 hours × $6.00 = $20,400

(c) Declining-balance method:
2017 depreciation = $145,000 × 40% × 3/12 = $14,500

Book value January 1, 2018 = $145,000 − $14,500 = $130,500

2018 depreciation = $130,500 × 40% = $52,200

Prepare entries to set up appropriate accounts for different intangibles; amortize intangible assets.

(LO 4)

2. Henning Company, organized in 2017, has the following transactions related to intangible assets.

1/2/17	Purchased patent (7-year life)	$840,000
4/1/17	Goodwill purchased (indefinite life)	450,000
7/1/17	10-year franchise: expiration date 7/1/2027	330,000
9/1/17	Research and development costs	210,000

Instructions

Prepare the necessary entries to record these intangibles. All costs incurred were for cash. Make the adjusting entries as of December 31, 2017, recording any necessary amortization and reflecting all balances accurately as of that date.

Solution

2. 1/2/17	Patents	840,000	
	Cash		840,000
4/1/17	Goodwill	450,000	
	Cash		450,000
	(Part of the entry to record purchase of another company)		
7/1/17	Franchises	330,000	
	Cash		330,000
9/1/17	Research and Development Expense	210,000	
	Cash		210,000
12/31/17	Amortization Expense ($840,000 ÷ 7) + [($330,000 ÷ 10) × 1/2]	136,500	
	Patents		120,000
	Franchises		16,500

Ending balances, 12/31/17:
Patents = $720,000 ($840,000 − $120,000)
Goodwill = $450,000
Franchises = $313,500 ($330,000 − $16,500)
R&D expense = $210,000

PRACTICE PROBLEMS

Compute depreciation under different methods.

(LO 2)

1. DuPage Company purchases a factory machine at a cost of $18,000 on January 1, 2017. DuPage expects the machine to have a salvage value of $2,000 at the end of its 4-year useful life.

During its useful life, the machine is expected to be used 160,000 hours. Actual annual hourly use was 2017, 40,000; 2018, 60,000; 2019, 35,000; and 2020, 25,000.

Instructions

Prepare depreciation schedules for the following methods: (a) straight-line, (b) units-of-activity, and (c) declining-balance using double the straight-line rate.

Solution

1. (a)

Straight-Line Method

	Computation					End of Year	
Year	Depreciable Cost*	×	Depreciation Rate	=	Annual Depreciation Expense	Accumulated Depreciation	Book Value
2017	$16,000		25%		$4,000	$ 4,000	$14,000**
2018	16,000		25%		4,000	8,000	10,000
2019	16,000		25%		4,000	12,000	6,000
2020	16,000		25%		4,000	16,000	2,000

*$18,000 − $2,000.
**$18,000 − $4,000.

(b)

Units-of-Activity Method

	Computation					End of Year	
Year	Units of Activity	×	Depreciable Cost/Unit	=	Annual Depreciation Expense	Accumulated Depreciation	Book Value
2017	40,000		$0.10*		$4,000	$ 4,000	$14,000
2018	60,000		0.10		6,000	10,000	8,000
2019	35,000		0.10		3,500	13,500	4,500
2020	25,000		0.10		2,500	16,000	2,000

*($18,000 − $2,000) ÷ 160,000.

(c)

Declining-Balance Method

	Computation					End of Year	
Year	Book Value Beginning of Year	×	Depreciation Rate*	=	Annual Depreciation Expense	Accumulated Depreciation	Book Value
2017	$18,000		50%		$9,000	$ 9,000	$9,000
2018	9,000		50%		4,500	13,500	4,500
2019	4,500		50%		2,250	15,750	2,250
2020	2,250		50%		250**	16,000	2,000

*¼ × 2.
**Adjusted to $250 because ending book value should not be less than expected salvage value.

Record disposal of plant asset.

(LO 3)

2. On January 1, 2017, Skyline Limousine Co. purchased a limo at an acquisition cost of $28,000. The vehicle has been depreciated by the straight-line method using a 4-year service life and a $4,000 salvage value. The company's fiscal year ends on December 31.

Instructions

Prepare the journal entry or entries to record the disposal of the limousine assuming that it was:

(a) Retired and scrapped with no salvage value on January 1, 2021.

(b) Sold for $5,000 on July 1, 2020.

Solution

2. (a) 1/1/21	Accumulated Depreciation—Equipment	24,000	
	Loss on Disposal of Plant Assets	4,000	
	Equipment		28,000
	(To record retirement of limousine)		

(b) 7/1/20	Depreciation Expense*	3,000	
	Accumulated Depreciation—Equipment		3,000
	(To record depreciation to date of disposal)		
	Cash	5,000	
	Accumulated Depreciation—Equipment**	21,000	
	Loss on Disposal of Plant Assets	2,000	
	Equipment		28,000
	(To record sale of limousine)		

*[($28,000 − $4,000) ÷ 4] × $\frac{1}{2}$.
**[($28,000 − $4,000) ÷ 4] × 3 = $18,000; $18,000 + $3,000.

WileyPLUS Brief Exercises, Exercises, DO IT! Exercises, and Problems and many additional resources are available for practice in WileyPLUS

NOTE: All asterisked Questions, Exercises, and Problems relate to material in the appendix to the chapter.

QUESTIONS

1. Sid Watney is uncertain about the applicability of the historical cost principle to plant assets. Explain the principle to Sid.
2. What are some examples of land improvements?
3. Lynn Company acquires the land and building owned by Noble Company. What types of costs may be incurred to make the asset ready for its intended use if Lynn Company wants to use (a) only the land, and (b) both the land and the building?
4. In a recent newspaper release, the president of Downs Company asserted that something has to be done about depreciation. The president said, "Depreciation does not come close to accumulating the cash needed to replace the asset at the end of its useful life." What is your response to the president?
5. Andrew is studying for the next accounting examination. He asks your help on two questions: (a) What is salvage value? (b) Is salvage value used in determining periodic depreciation under each depreciation method? Answer Andrew's questions.
6. Contrast the straight-line method and the units-of-activity method as to (a) useful life, and (b) the pattern of periodic depreciation over useful life.
7. Contrast the effects of the three depreciation methods on annual depreciation expense.
8. In the fourth year of an asset's 5-year useful life, the company decides that the asset will have a 6-year service life. How should the revision of depreciation be recorded? Why?
9. Distinguish between revenue expenditures and capital expenditures during useful life.
10. How is a gain or loss on the sale of a plant asset computed?
11. Romero Corporation owns a machine that is fully depreciated but is still being used. How should Romero account for this asset and report it in the financial statements?
12. What are natural resources, and what are their distinguishing characteristics?
13. Explain the concept of depletion and how it is computed.
14. What are the similarities and differences between the terms depreciation, depletion, and amortization?
15. Rowand Company hires an accounting intern who says that intangible assets should always be amortized over their legal lives. Is the intern correct? Explain.
16. Goodwill has been defined as the value of all favorable attributes that relate to a business. What types of attributes could result in goodwill?
17. Jimmy West, a business major, is working on a case problem for one of his classes. In the case problem, the company needs to raise cash to market a new product it developed. Ron Thayer, an engineering major, takes one look at the company's balance sheet and says, "This company has an awful lot of goodwill. Why don't you recommend that they sell some of it to raise cash?" How should Jimmy respond to Ron?
18. Under what conditions is goodwill recorded?
19. Often, research and development costs provide companies with benefits that last a number of years. (For example, these costs can lead to the development of a patent that will increase the company's income for many years.) However, generally accepted accounting principles require that such costs be recorded as an expense when incurred. Why?
20. McDonald's Corporation reports total average assets of $28.9 billion and net sales of $20.5 billion. What is the company's asset turnover?
21. Stark Corporation and Zuber Corporation operate in the same industry. Stark uses the straight-line method to account for depreciation; Zuber uses an accelerated method. Explain what complications might

arise in trying to compare the results of these two companies.

22. Gomez Corporation uses straight-line depreciation for financial reporting purposes but an accelerated method for tax purposes. Is it acceptable to use different methods for the two purposes? What is Gomez's motivation for doing this?
23. You are comparing two companies in the same industry. You have determined that Ace Corp. depreciates its plant assets over a 40-year life, whereas Liu Corp. depreciates its plant assets over a 20-year life. Discuss the implications this has for comparing the results of the two companies.
24. Sosa Company is doing significant work to revitalize its warehouses. It is not sure whether it should capitalize these costs or expense them. What are the implications for current-year net income and future net income of expensing versus capitalizing these costs?

*25. When assets are exchanged in a transaction involving commercial substance, how is the gain or loss on disposal of plant assets computed?

*26. Unruh Refrigeration Company trades in an old machine on a new model when the fair value of the old machine is greater than its book value. The transaction has commercial substance. Should Unruh recognize a gain on disposal of plant assets? If the fair value of the old machine is less than its book value, should Unruh recognize a loss on disposal of plant assets?

BRIEF EXERCISES

Determine the cost of land.
(LO 1)

BE10-1 The following expenditures were incurred by McCoy Company in purchasing land: cash price $50,000, accrued taxes $3,000, attorneys' fees $2,500, real estate broker's commission $2,000, and clearing and grading $3,500. What is the cost of the land?

Determine the cost of a truck.
(LO 1)

BE10-2 Rich Castillo Company incurs the following expenditures in purchasing a truck: cash price $30,000, accident insurance $2,000, sales taxes $2,100, motor vehicle license $100, and painting and lettering $400. What is the cost of the truck?

Prepare entries for delivery truck costs.
(LO 1)

BE10-3 Flaherty Company had the following two transactions related to its delivery truck.

1. Paid $45 for an oil change.
2. Paid $400 to install special gear unit, which increases the operating efficiency of the truck.

Prepare Flaherty's journal entries to record these two transactions.

Compute straight-line depreciation.
(LO 2)

BE10-4 Corales Company acquires a delivery truck at a cost of $38,000. The truck is expected to have a salvage value of $6,000 at the end of its 4-year useful life. Compute annual depreciation expense for the first and second years using the straight-line method.

Compute depreciation and evaluate treatment.
(LO 2)

BE10-5 Chisenhall Company purchased land and a building on January 1, 2017. Management's best estimate of the value of the land was $100,000 and of the building $200,000. However, management told the accounting department to record the land at $220,000 and the building at $80,000. The building is being depreciated on a straight-line basis over 15 years with no salvage value. Why do you suppose management requested this accounting treatment? Is it ethical?

Compute declining-balance depreciation.
(LO 2)

BE10-6 Depreciation information for Corales Company is given in BE10-4. Assuming the declining-balance depreciation rate is double the straight-line rate, compute annual depreciation for the first and second years under the declining-balance method.

Compute depreciation using the units-of-activity method.
(LO 2)

BE10-7 Rosco Taxi Service uses the units-of-activity method in computing depreciation on its taxicabs. Each cab is expected to be driven 150,000 miles. Taxi no. 10 cost $39,500 and is expected to have a salvage value of $500. Taxi no. 10 is driven 30,000 miles in year 1 and 20,000 miles in year 2. Compute the depreciation for each year.

Compute revised depreciation.
(LO 2)

BE10-8 On January 1, 2017, the Morgantown Company ledger shows Equipment $32,000 and Accumulated Depreciation—Equipment $9,000. The depreciation resulted from using the straight-line method with a useful life of 10 years and salvage value of $2,000. On this date, the company concludes that the equipment has a remaining useful life of only 4 years with the same salvage value. Compute the revised annual depreciation.

BE10-9 Prepare journal entries to record the following.

Prepare entries for disposal by retirement.

(LO 3)

(a) Sound Tracker Company retires its delivery equipment, which cost $41,000. Accumulated depreciation is also $41,000 on this delivery equipment. No salvage value is received.
(b) Assume the same information as (a), except that accumulated depreciation is $37,000, instead of $41,000, on the delivery equipment.

BE10-10 Gunkelson Company sells equipment on September 30, 2017, for $18,000 cash. The equipment originally cost $72,000 and as of January 1, 2017, had accumulated depreciation of $42,000. Depreciation for the first 9 months of 2017 is $5,250. Prepare the journal entries to (a) update depreciation to September 30, 2017, and (b) record the sale of the equipment.

Prepare entries for disposal by sale.

(LO 3)

BE10-11 Franceour Mining Co. purchased for $7 million a mine that is estimated to have 35 million tons of ore and no salvage value. In the first year, 5 million tons of ore are extracted.

Prepare depletion entry and balance sheet presentation for natural resources.

(LO 4)

(a) Prepare the journal entry to record depletion for the first year.
(b) Show how this mine is reported on the balance sheet at the end of the first year.

BE10-12 Campanez Company purchases a patent for $140,000 on January 2, 2017. Its estimated useful life is 10 years.

Prepare amortization expense entry and balance sheet presentation for intangibles.

(LO 4)

(a) Prepare the journal entry to record amortization expense for the first year.
(b) Show how this patent is reported on the balance sheet at the end of the first year.

BE10-13 Information related to plant assets, natural resources, and intangibles at the end of 2017 for Dent Company is as follows: buildings $1,100,000, accumulated depreciation—buildings $600,000, goodwill $410,000, coal mine $500,000, and accumulated depletion—coal mine $108,000. Prepare a partial balance sheet of Dent Company for these items.

Classify long-lived assets on balance sheet.

(LO 5)

BE10-14 In a recent annual report, Target reported beginning total assets of $44.1 billion, ending total assets of $44.5 billion, and net sales of $63.4 billion. Compute Target's asset turnover.

Calculate asset turnover.

(LO 5)

***BE10-15** Olathe Company exchanges old delivery equipment for new delivery equipment. The book value of the old delivery equipment is $31,000 (cost $61,000 less accumulated depreciation $30,000). Its fair value is $24,000, and cash of $5,000 is paid. Prepare the entry to record the exchange, assuming the transaction has commercial substance.

Prepare entry for disposal by exchange.

(LO 6)

***BE10-16** Assume the same information as BE10-15, except that the fair value of the old delivery equipment is $33,000. Prepare the entry to record the exchange.

Prepare entry for disposal by exchange.

(LO 6)

DO IT! Exercises

DO IT! 10-1 Lofton Company purchased a delivery truck. The total cash payment was $27,900, including the following items.

Explain accounting for cost of plant assets.

(LO 1)

Negotiated purchase price	$24,000
Installation of special shelving	1,100
Painting and lettering	900
Motor vehicle license	100
Annual insurance policy	500
Sales tax	1,300
Total paid	$27,900

Explain how each of these costs would be accounted for.

DO IT! 10-2a On January 1, 2017, Emporia Country Club purchased a new riding mower for $15,000. The mower is expected to have an 8-year life with a $3,000 salvage value. What journal entry would Emporia make at December 31, 2017, if it uses straight-line depreciation?

Calculate depreciation expense and make journal entry.

(LO 2)

Calculate revised depreciation
(LO 2)

DO IT! 10-2b Pinewood Corporation purchased a piece of equipment for $70,000. It estimated an 8-year life and $2,000 salvage value. At the end of year four (before the depreciation adjustment), it estimated the new total life to be 10 years and the new salvage value to be $6,000. Compute the revised depreciation.

Make journal entries to record plant asset disposal.
(LO 3)

DO IT! 10-3 Napoli Manufacturing has old equipment that cost $52,000. The equipment has accumulated depreciation of $28,000. Napoli has decided to sell the equipment.

(a) What entry would Napoli make to record the sale of the equipment for $26,000 cash?
(b) What entry would Napoli make to record the sale of the equipment for $15,000 cash?

Match intangibles classifications concepts.
(LO 4, 5)

DO IT! 10-4 Match the statement with the term most directly associated with it.

Goodwill	Amortization
Intangible assets	Franchises
Research and development costs	

1. _______ Rights, privileges, and competitive advantages that result from the ownership of long-lived assets that do not possess physical substance.
2. _______ The allocation of the cost of an intangible asset to expense in a rational and systematic manner.
3. _______ A right to sell certain products or services, or use certain trademarks or trade names, within a designated geographic area.
4. _______ Costs incurred by a company that often lead to patents or new products. These costs must be expensed as incurred.
5. _______ The excess of the cost of a company over the fair value of the net assets acquired.

Calculate asset turnover.
(LO 5)

DO IT! 10-5 For 2017, Sale Company reported beginning total assets of $300,000 and ending total assets of $340,000. Its net income for this period was $50,000, and its net sales were $400,000. Compute the company's asset turnover for 2017.

EXERCISES

Determine cost of plant acquisitions.
(LO 1)

E10-1 The following expenditures relating to plant assets were made by Prather Company during the first 2 months of 2017.

1. Paid $5,000 of accrued taxes at time plant site was acquired.
2. Paid $200 insurance to cover possible accident loss on new factory machinery while the machinery was in transit.
3. Paid $850 sales taxes on new delivery truck.
4. Paid $17,500 for parking lots and driveways on new plant site.
5. Paid $250 to have company name and advertising slogan painted on new delivery truck.
6. Paid $8,000 for installation of new factory machinery.
7. Paid $900 for one-year accident insurance policy on new delivery truck.
8. Paid $75 motor vehicle license fee on the new truck.

Instructions

(a) Explain the application of the historical cost principle in determining the acquisition cost of plant assets.
(b) List the numbers of the foregoing transactions, and opposite each indicate the account title to which each expenditure should be debited.

Determine property, plant, and equipment costs.
(LO 1)

E10-2 Benedict Company incurred the following costs.

1. Sales tax on factory machinery purchased	$ 5,000
2. Painting of and lettering on truck immediately upon purchase	700
3. Installation and testing of factory machinery	2,000
4. Real estate broker's commission on land purchased	3,500
5. Insurance premium paid for first year's insurance on new truck	880
6. Cost of landscaping on property purchased	7,200
7. Cost of paving parking lot for new building constructed	17,900
8. Cost of clearing, draining, and filling land	13,300
9. Architect's fees on self-constructed building	10,000

Instructions
Indicate to which account Benedict would debit each of the costs.

Determine acquisition costs of land.
(LO 1)

E10-3 On March 1, 2017, Westmorlan Company acquired real estate on which it planned to construct a small office building. The company paid $75,000 in cash. An old warehouse on the property was razed at a cost of $8,600; the salvaged materials were sold for $1,700. Additional expenditures before construction began included $1,100 attorney's fee for work concerning the land purchase, $5,000 real estate broker's fee, $7,800 architect's fee, and $14,000 to put in driveways and a parking lot.

Instructions
(a) Determine the amount to be reported as the cost of the land.
(b) For each cost not used in part (a), indicate the account to be debited.

Understand depreciation concepts.
(LO 2)

E10-4 Tom Parkey has prepared the following list of statements about depreciation.

1. Depreciation is a process of asset valuation, not cost allocation.
2. Depreciation provides for the proper matching of expenses with revenues.
3. The book value of a plant asset should approximate its fair value.
4. Depreciation applies to three classes of plant assets: land, buildings, and equipment.
5. Depreciation does not apply to a building because its usefulness and revenue-producing ability generally remain intact over time.
6. The revenue-producing ability of a depreciable asset will decline due to wear and tear and to obsolescence.
7. Recognizing depreciation on an asset results in an accumulation of cash for replacement of the asset.
8. The balance in accumulated depreciation represents the total cost that has been charged to expense.
9. Depreciation expense and accumulated depreciation are reported on the income statement.
10. Four factors affect the computation of depreciation: cost, useful life, salvage value, and residual value.

Instructions
Identify each statement as true or false. If false, indicate how to correct the statement.

Compute depreciation under units-of-activity method.
(LO 2)

E10-5 Yello Bus Lines uses the units-of-activity method in depreciating its buses. One bus was purchased on January 1, 2017, at a cost of $148,000. Over its 4-year useful life, the bus is expected to be driven 100,000 miles. Salvage value is expected to be $8,000.

Instructions
(a) Compute the depreciable cost per unit.
(b) Prepare a depreciation schedule assuming actual mileage was: 2017, 26,000; 2018, 32,000; 2019, 25,000; and 2020, 17,000.

Determine depreciation for partial periods.
(LO 2)

E10-6 Rottino Company purchased a new machine on October 1, 2017, at a cost of $150,000. The company estimated that the machine will have a salvage value of $12,000. The machine is expected to be used for 10,000 working hours during its 5-year life.

Instructions
Compute the depreciation expense under the following methods for the year indicated.
(a) Straight-line for 2017.
(b) Units-of-activity for 2017, assuming machine usage was 1,700 hours.
(c) Declining-balance using double the straight-line rate for 2017 and 2018.

Compute depreciation using different methods.
(LO 2)

E10-7 Linton Company purchased a delivery truck for $34,000 on January 1, 2017. The truck has an expected salvage value of $2,000, and is expected to be driven 100,000 miles over its estimated useful life of 8 years. Actual miles driven were 15,000 in 2017 and 12,000 in 2018.

Instructions

(a) Compute depreciation expense for 2017 and 2018 using (1) the straight-line method, (2) the units-of-activity method, and (3) the double-declining-balance method.

(b) Assume that Linton uses the straight-line method.

(1) Prepare the journal entry to record 2017 depreciation.

(2) Show how the truck would be reported in the December 31, 2017, balance sheet.

Compute revised annual depreciation.

(LO 2)

E10-8 Terry Wade, the new controller of Hellickson Company, has reviewed the expected useful lives and salvage values of selected depreciable assets at the beginning of 2017. His findings are as follows.

Type of Asset	Date Acquired	Cost	Accumulated Depreciation 1/1/17	Useful Life in Years		Salvage Value	
				Old	Proposed	Old	Proposed
Building	1/1/11	$800,000	$114,000	40	50	$40,000	$26,000
Warehouse	1/1/12	100,000	19,000	25	20	5,000	6,000

All assets are depreciated by the straight-line method. Hellickson Company uses a calendar year in preparing annual financial statements. After discussion, management has agreed to accept Terry's proposed changes.

Instructions

(a) Compute the revised annual depreciation on each asset in 2017. (Show computations.)

(b) Prepare the entry (or entries) to record depreciation on the building in 2017.

Journalize entries for disposal of plant assets.

(LO 3)

E10-9 Presented below are selected transactions at Ridge Company for 2017.

Jan. 1 Retired a piece of machinery that was purchased on January 1, 2007. The machine cost $62,000 on that date. It had a useful life of 10 years with no salvage value.

June 30 Sold a computer that was purchased on January 1, 2014. The computer cost $45,000. It had a useful life of 5 years with no salvage value. The computer was sold for $14,000.

Dec. 31 Discarded a delivery truck that was purchased on January 1, 2013. The truck cost $33,000. It was depreciated based on a 6-year useful life with a $3,000 salvage value.

Instructions

Journalize all entries required on the above dates, including entries to update depreciation, where applicable, on assets disposed of. Ridge Company uses straight-line depreciation. (Assume depreciation is up to date as of December 31, 2016.)

Journalize entries for disposal of equipment.

(LO 3)

E10-10 Pryce Company owns equipment that cost $65,000 when purchased on January 1, 2014. It has been depreciated using the straight-line method based on estimated salvage value of $5,000 and an estimated useful life of 5 years.

Instructions

Prepare Pryce Company's journal entries to record the sale of the equipment in these four independent situations.

(a) Sold for $31,000 on January 1, 2017.

(b) Sold for $31,000 on May 1, 2017.

(c) Sold for $11,000 on January 1, 2017.

(d) Sold for $11,000 on October 1, 2017.

Journalize entries for natural resources depletion.

(LO 4)

E10-11 On July 1, 2017, Friedman Inc. invested $720,000 in a mine estimated to have 900,000 tons of ore of uniform grade. During the last 6 months of 2017, 100,000 tons of ore were mined.

Instructions

(a) Prepare the journal entry to record depletion.

(b) Assume that the 100,000 tons of ore were mined, but only 80,000 units were sold. How are the costs applicable to the 20,000 unsold units reported?

E10-12 The following are selected 2017 transactions of Pedigo Corporation.

Prepare adjusting entries for amortization.

(LO 4)

Jan. 1 Purchased a small company and recorded goodwill of $150,000. Its useful life is indefinite.

May 1 Purchased for $75,000 a patent with an estimated useful life of 5 years and a legal life of 20 years.

Instructions

Prepare necessary adjusting entries at December 31 to record amortization required by the events above.

E10-13 Gill Company, organized in 2017, has the following transactions related to intangible assets.

Prepare entries to set up appropriate accounts for different intangibles; amortize intangible assets.

(LO 4)

1/2/17	Purchased patent (7-year life)	$595,000
4/1/17	Goodwill purchased (indefinite life)	360,000
7/1/17	10-year franchise; expiration date 7/1/2027	480,000
9/1/17	Research and development costs	185,000

Instructions

Prepare the necessary entries to record these intangibles. All costs incurred were for cash. Make the adjusting entries as of December 31, 2017, recording any necessary amortization and reflecting all balances accurately as of that date.

E10-14 During 2017, Paola Corporation reported net sales of $3,500,000 and net income of $1,500,000. Its balance sheet reported average total assets of $1,400,000.

Calculate asset turnover.

(LO 5)

Instructions

Calculate the asset turnover.

***E10-15** Presented below are two independent transactions. Both transactions have commercial substance.

Journalize entries for exchanges.

(LO 6)

1. Mercy Co. exchanged old trucks (cost $64,000 less $22,000 accumulated depreciation) plus cash of $17,000 for new trucks. The old trucks had a fair value of $38,000.
2. Pence Inc. trades its used machine (cost $12,000 less $4,000 accumulated depreciation) for a new machine. In addition to exchanging the old machine (which had a fair value of $11,000), Pence also paid cash of $3,000.

Instructions

(a) Prepare the entry to record the exchange of assets by Mercy Co.

(b) Prepare the entry to record the exchange of assets by Pence Inc.

***E10-16** Rizzo's Delivery Company and Overland's Express Delivery exchanged delivery trucks on January 1, 2017. Rizzo's truck cost $22,000. It has accumulated depreciation of $15,000 and a fair value of $3,000. Overland's truck cost $10,000. It has accumulated depreciation of $8,000 and a fair value of $3,000. The transaction has commercial substance.

Journalize entries for the exchange of plant assets.

(LO 6)

Instructions

(a) Journalize the exchange for Rizzo's Delivery Company.

(b) Journalize the exchange for Overland's Express Delivery.

EXERCISES: SET B AND CHALLENGE EXERCISES

Visit the book's companion website, at **www.wiley.com/college/weygandt**, and choose the Student Companion site to access Exercises: Set B and Challenge Exercises.

PROBLEMS: SET A

Determine acquisition costs of land and building.

(LO 1)

XLS

P10-1A Venable Company was organized on January 1. During the first year of operations, the following plant asset expenditures and receipts were recorded in random order.

	Debit
1. Cost of filling and grading the land	$ 4,000
2. Full payment to building contractor	690,000
3. Real estate taxes on land paid for the current year	5,000
4. Cost of real estate purchased as a plant site (land $100,000 and building $45,000)	145,000
5. Excavation costs for new building	35,000
6. Architect's fees on building plans	10,000
7. Accrued real estate taxes paid at time of purchase of real estate	2,000
8. Cost of parking lots and driveways	14,000
9. Cost of demolishing building to make land suitable for construction of new building	25,000
	$930,000

	Credit
10. Proceeds from salvage of demolished building	$ 3,500

Totals
Land $172,500
Buildings $735,000

Instructions

Analyze the foregoing transactions using the following column headings. Insert the number of each transaction in the Item space, and insert the amounts in the appropriate columns. For amounts entered in the Other Accounts column, also indicate the account titles.

Item	**Land**	**Buildings**	**Other Accounts**

Compute depreciation under different methods.

(LO 2)

P10-2A In recent years, Avery Transportation purchased three used buses. Because of frequent turnover in the accounting department, a different accountant selected the depreciation method for each bus, and various methods were selected. Information concerning the buses is summarized as follows.

Bus	**Acquired**	**Cost**	**Salvage Value**	**Useful Life in Years**	**Depreciation Method**
1	1/1/15	$ 96,000	$ 6,000	5	Straight-line
2	1/1/15	110,000	10,000	4	Declining-balance
3	1/1/16	92,000	8,000	5	Units-of-activity

For the declining-balance method, the company uses the double-declining rate. For the units-of-activity method, total miles are expected to be 120,000. Actual miles of use in the first 3 years were 2016, 24,000; 2017, 34,000; and 2018, 30,000.

Instructions

(a) Bus 2, 2016, $82,500

(a) Compute the amount of accumulated depreciation on each bus at December 31, 2017.

(b) If Bus 2 was purchased on April 1 instead of January 1, what is the depreciation expense for this bus in (1) 2015 and (2) 2016?

Compute depreciation under different methods.

(LO 2)

P10-3A On January 1, 2017, Evers Company purchased the following two machines for use in its production process.

Machine A: The cash price of this machine was $48,000. Related expenditures included: sales tax $1,700, shipping costs $150, insurance during shipping $80, installation and testing costs $70, and $100 of oil and lubricants to be used with the machinery during its first year of operations. Evers estimates that the useful life of the machine is 5 years with a $5,000 salvage value remaining at the end of that time period. Assume that the straight-line method of depreciation is used.

Machine B: The recorded cost of this machine was $180,000. Evers estimates that the useful life of the machine is 4 years with a $10,000 salvage value remaining at the end of that time period.

Instructions

(a) Prepare the following for Machine A.
   (1) The journal entry to record its purchase on January 1, 2017.
   (2) The journal entry to record annual depreciation at December 31, 2017.

(b) Calculate the amount of depreciation expense that Evers should record for Machine B each year of its useful life under the following assumptions.
   (1) Evers uses the straight-line method of depreciation.
   (2) Evers uses the declining-balance method. The rate used is twice the straight-line rate.
   (3) Evers uses the units-of-activity method and estimates that the useful life of the machine is 125,000 units. Actual usage is as follows: 2017, 45,000 units; 2018, 35,000 units; 2019, 25,000 units; 2020, 20,000 units.

(b) (2) 2017 DDB depreciation $90,000

(c) Which method used to calculate depreciation on Machine B reports the highest amount of depreciation expense in year 1 (2017)? The highest amount in year 4 (2020)? The highest total amount over the 4-year period?

Calculate revisions to depreciation expense.

(LO 2)

P10-4A At the beginning of 2015, Mazzaro Company acquired equipment costing $120,000. It was estimated that this equipment would have a useful life of 6 years and a salvage value of $12,000 at that time. The straight-line method of depreciation was considered the most appropriate to use with this type of equipment. Depreciation is to be recorded at the end of each year.

During 2017 (the third year of the equipment's life), the company's engineers reconsidered their expectations, and estimated that the equipment's useful life would probably be 7 years (in total) instead of 6 years. The estimated salvage value was not changed at that time. However, during 2020 the estimated salvage value was reduced to $5,000.

Instructions

Indicate how much depreciation expense should be recorded each year for this equipment, by completing the following table.

Year	Depreciation Expense	Accumulated Depreciation
2015		
2016		
2017		
2018		
2019		
2020		
2021		

2021 depreciation expense $17,900

Journalize a series of equipment transactions related to purchase, sale, retirement, and depreciation.

(LO 2, 3, 5)

P10-5A At December 31, 2017, Grand Company reported the following as plant assets.

Land		$ 4,000,000
Buildings	$28,500,000	
Less: Accumulated depreciation—buildings	12,100,000	16,400,000
Equipment	48,000,000	
Less: Accumulated depreciation—equipment	5,000,000	43,000,000
Total plant assets		$63,400,000

During 2018, the following selected cash transactions occurred.

April 1	Purchased land for $2,130,000.
May 1	Sold equipment that cost $750,000 when purchased on January 1, 2014. The equipment was sold for $450,000.
June 1	Sold land purchased on June 1, 2008 for $1,500,000. The land cost $400,000.
July 1	Purchased equipment for $2,500,000.
Dec. 31	Retired equipment that cost $500,000 when purchased on December 31, 2008. The company received no proceeds related to salvage.

Instructions

(a) Journalize the above transactions. The company uses straight-line depreciation for buildings and equipment. The buildings are estimated to have a 50-year life and no salvage value. The equipment is estimated to have a 10-year useful life and no salvage value. Update depreciation on assets disposed of at the time of sale or retirement.

(b) Record adjusting entries for depreciation for 2018.

(c) Prepare the plant assets section of Grand's balance sheet at December 31, 2018.

(b) Depreciation Expense—Buildings $570,000; Equipment $4,800,000

(c) Total plant assets $61,760,000

Record disposals.

(LO 3)

(b) $9,000 loss

P10-6A Ceda Co. has equipment that cost $80,000 and that has been depreciated $50,000.

Instructions

Record the disposal under the following assumptions.

(a) It was scrapped as having no value.
(b) It was sold for $21,000.
(c) It was sold for $31,000.

Prepare entries to record transactions related to acquisition and amortization of intangibles; prepare the intangible assets section.

(LO 4, 5)

(b) Amortization Expense (patents) $10,000
Amortization Expense (franchises) $5,500

(c) Total intangible assets $243,300

P10-7A The intangible assets section of Sappelt Company at December 31, 2017, is presented below.

Patents ($70,000 cost less $7,000 amortization)	$63,000
Franchises ($48,000 cost less $19,200 amortization)	28,800
Total	$91,800

The patent was acquired in January 2017 and has a useful life of 10 years. The franchise was acquired in January 2014 and also has a useful life of 10 years. The following cash transactions may have affected intangible assets during 2018.

Jan. 2	Paid $27,000 legal costs to successfully defend the patent against infringement by another company.
Jan.–June	Developed a new product, incurring $140,000 in research and development costs. A patent was granted for the product on July 1. Its useful life is equal to its legal life.
Sept. 1	Paid $50,000 to an extremely large defensive lineman to appear in commercials advertising the company's products. The commercials will air in September and October.
Oct. 1	Acquired a franchise for $140,000. The franchise has a useful life of 50 years.

Instructions

(a) Prepare journal entries to record the transactions above.
(b) Prepare journal entries to record the 2018 amortization expense.
(c) Prepare the intangible assets section of the balance sheet at December 31, 2018.

Prepare entries to correct errors made in recording and amortizing intangible assets.

(LO 4)

1. R&D Exp. $136,000

P10-8A Due to rapid turnover in the accounting department, a number of transactions involving intangible assets were improperly recorded by Goins Company in 2017.

1. Goins developed a new manufacturing process, incurring research and development costs of $136,000. The company also purchased a patent for $60,000. In early January, Goins capitalized $196,000 as the cost of the patents. Patent amortization expense of $19,600 was recorded based on a 10-year useful life.
2. On July 1, 2017, Goins purchased a small company and as a result acquired goodwill of $92,000. Goins recorded a half-year's amortization in 2017, based on a 50-year life ($920 amortization). The goodwill has an indefinite life.

Instructions

Prepare all journal entries necessary to correct any errors made during 2017. Assume the books have not yet been closed for 2017.

Calculate and comment on asset turnover.

(LO 5)

P10-9A LaPorta Company and Lott Corporation, two corporations of roughly the same size, are both involved in the manufacture of in-line skates. Each company depreciates its plant assets using the straight-line approach. An investigation of their financial statements reveals the following information.

	LaPorta Co.	**Lott Corp.**
Net income	$ 800,000	$1,000,000
Sales revenue	1,300,000	1,180,000
Average total assets	2,500,000	2,000,000
Average plant assets	1,800,000	1,000,000

Instructions

(a) For each company, calculate the asset turnover.
(b) Based on your calculations in part (a), comment on the relative effectiveness of the two companies in using their assets to generate sales and produce net income.

PROBLEMS: SET B AND SET C

Visit the book's companion website, at **www.wiley.com/college/weygandt**, and choose the Student Companion site to access Problems: Set B and Set C.

COMPREHENSIVE PROBLEM: CHAPTERS 3 TO 10

CP10 Hassellhouf Company's trial balance at December 31, 2017, is presented below. All 2017 transactions have been recorded except for the items described as unrecorded transactions.

	Debit	Credit
Cash	$ 28,000	
Accounts Receivable	36,800	
Notes Receivable	10,000	
Interest Receivable	–0–	
Inventory	36,200	
Prepaid Insurance	3,600	
Land	20,000	
Buildings	150,000	
Equipment	60,000	
Patents	9,000	
Allowance for Doubtful Accounts		$ 500
Accumulated Depreciation—Buildings		50,000
Accumulated Depreciation—Equipment		24,000
Accounts Payable		27,300
Salaries and Wages Payable		–0–
Unearned Rent Revenue		6,000
Notes Payable (due in 2018)		11,000
Interest Payable		–0–
Notes Payable (due after 2018)		30,000
Owner's Capital		113,600
Owner's Drawings	12,000	
Sales Revenue		905,000
Interest Revenue		–0–
Rent Revenue		–0–
Gain on Disposal of Plant Assets		–0–
Bad Debt Expense	–0–	
Cost of Goods Sold	630,000	
Depreciation Expense	–0–	
Insurance Expense	–0–	
Interest Expense	–0–	
Other Operating Expenses	61,800	
Amortization Expense	–0–	
Salaries and Wages Expense	110,000	
Total	$1,167,400	$1,167,400

Unrecorded transactions:

1. On May 1, 2017, Hassellhouf purchased equipment for $21,200 plus sales taxes of $1,600 (all paid in cash).
2. On July 1, 2017, Hassellhouf sold for $3,500 equipment which originally cost $5,000. Accumulated depreciation on this equipment at January 1, 2017, was $1,800; 2017 depreciation prior to the sale of the equipment was $450.
3. On December 31, 2017, Hassellhouf sold on account $9,000 of inventory that cost $6,300.
4. Hassellhouf estimates that uncollectible accounts receivable at year-end is $3,500.
5. The note receivable is a one-year, 8% note dated April 1, 2017. No interest has been recorded.
6. The balance in prepaid insurance represents payment of a $3,600 6-month premium on September 1, 2017.
7. The building is being depreciated using the straight-line method over 30 years. The salvage value is $30,000.

8. The equipment owned prior to this year is being depreciated using the straight-line method over 5 years. The salvage value is 10% of cost.
9. The equipment purchased on May 1, 2017, is being depreciated using the straight-line method over 5 years, with a salvage value of $1,800.
10. The patent was acquired on January 1, 2017, and has a useful life of 10 years from that date.
11. Unpaid salaries and wages at December 31, 2017, total $5,200.
12. The unearned rent revenue of $6,000 was received on December 1, 2017, for 3 months' rent.
13. Both the short-term and long-term notes payable are dated January 1, 2017, and carry a 9% interest rate. All interest is payable in the next 12 months.

Instructions

(b) Totals $1,205,040
(d) Total assets $259,200

(a) Prepare journal entries for the transactions listed above.
(b) Prepare an updated December 31, 2017, trial balance.
(c) Prepare a 2017 income statement and an owner's equity statement.
(d) Prepare a December 31, 2017, classified balance sheet.

CONTINUING PROBLEM

© leungchopan/ Shutterstock

COOKIE CREATIONS: AN ENTREPRENEURIAL JOURNEY

(*Note:* This is a continuation of the Cookie Creations problem from Chapters 1 through 9.)

CC10 Natalie is also thinking of buying a van that will be used only for business. Natalie is concerned about the impact of the van's cost on her income statement and balance sheet. She has come to you for advice on calculating the van's depreciation.

Go to the book's companion website, **www.wiley.com/college/weygandt**, *to see the completion of this problem.*

BROADENING YOUR PERSPECTIVE

FINANCIAL REPORTING AND ANALYSIS

Financial Reporting Problem: Apple Inc.

BYP10-1 The financial statements of Apple Inc. are presented in Appendix A. Instructions for accessing and using the company's complete annual report, including the notes to the financial statements, are also provided in Appendix A.

Instructions

Refer to Apple's financial statements and answer the following questions.

(a) What was the total cost and book value of property, plant, and equipment at September 28, 2013?
(b) What was the amount of depreciation and amortization expense for each of the three years 2011–2013?
(c) Using the statement of cash flows, what is the amount of capital spending in 2013 and 2012?
(d) Where does the company disclose its intangible assets, and what types of intangibles did it have at September 28, 2013?

Comparative Analysis Problem: PepsiCo, Inc. vs. The Coca-Cola Company

BYP10-2 PepsiCo, Inc.'s financial statements are presented in Appendix B. Financial statements of The Coca-Cola Company are presented in Appendix C. Instructions for accessing and using the complete annual reports of PepsiCo and Coca-Cola, including the notes to the financial statements, are also provided in Appendices B and C, respectively.

Instructions
(a) Compute the asset turnover for each company for 2013.
(b) What conclusions concerning the efficiency of assets can be drawn from these data?

Comparative Analysis Problem: Amazon.com, Inc. vs. Wal-Mart Stores, Inc.

BYP10-3 Amazon.com, Inc.'s financial statements are presented in Appendix D. Financial statements of Wal-Mart Stores, Inc. are presented in Appendix E. Instructions for accessing and using the complete annual reports of Amazon and Wal-Mart, including the notes to the financial statements, are also provided in Appendices D and E, respectively.

Instructions
(a) Compute the asset turnover for each company for 2013.
(b) What conclusions concerning the efficiency of assets can be drawn from these data?

Real-World Focus

BYP10-4 A company's annual report identifies the amount of its plant assets and the depreciation method used.

Address: **www.annualreports.com**, or go to **www.wiley.com/college/weygandt**

Steps
1. Select a particular company.
2. Search by company name.
3. Follow instructions below.

Instructions
Answer the following questions.
(a) What is the name of the company?
(b) What is the Internet address of the annual report?
(c) At fiscal year-end, what is the net amount of its plant assets?
(d) What is the accumulated depreciation?
(e) Which method of depreciation does the company use?

CRITICAL THINKING

Decision-Making Across the Organization

BYP10-5 Pinson Company and Estes Company are two proprietorships that are similar in many respects. One difference is that Pinson Company uses the straight-line method and Estes Company uses the declining-balance method at double the straight-line rate. On January 2, 2015, both companies acquired the depreciable assets shown below.

Asset	Cost	Salvage Value	Useful Life
Buildings	$360,000	$20,000	40 years
Equipment	130,000	10,000	10 years

Including the appropriate depreciation charges, annual net income for the companies in the years 2015, 2016, and 2017 and total income for the 3 years were as follows.

	2015	2016	2017	Total
Pinson Company	$84,000	$88,400	$90,000	$262,400
Estes Company	68,000	76,000	85,000	229,000

At December 31, 2017, the balance sheets of the two companies are similar except that Estes Company has more cash than Pinson Company.

Lynda Peace is interested in buying one of the companies. She comes to you for advice.

Instructions

With the class divided into groups, answer the following.

(a) Determine the annual and total depreciation recorded by each company during the 3 years.
(b) Assuming that Estes Company also uses the straight-line method of depreciation instead of the declining-balance method as in (a), prepare comparative income data for the 3 years.
(c) Which company should Lynda Peace buy? Why?

Communication Activity

BYP10-6 The following was published with the financial statements to American Exploration Company.

AMERICAN EXPLORATION COMPANY
Notes to the Financial Statements

Property, Plant, and Equipment—The Company accounts for its oil and gas exploration and production activities using the successful efforts method of accounting. Under this method, acquisition costs for proved and unproved properties are capitalized when incurred.... The costs of drilling exploratory wells are capitalized pending determination of whether each well has discovered proved reserves. If proved reserves are not discovered, such drilling costs are charged to expense.... Depletion of the cost of producing oil and gas properties is computed on the units-of-activity method.

Instructions

Write a brief memo to your instructor discussing American Exploration Company's note regarding property, plant, and equipment. Your memo should address what is meant by the "successful efforts method" and "units-of-activity method."

Ethics Case

BYP10-7 Turner Container Company is suffering declining sales of its principal product, nonbiodegradeable plastic cartons. The president, Robert Griffin, instructs his controller, Alexis Landrum, to lengthen asset lives to reduce depreciation expense. A processing line of automated plastic extruding equipment, purchased for $3.5 million in January 2017, was originally estimated to have a useful life of 8 years and a salvage value of $300,000. Depreciation has been recorded for 2 years on that basis. Robert wants the estimated life changed to 12 years total, and the straight-line method continued. Alexis is hesitant to make the change, believing it is unethical to increase net income in this manner. Robert says, "Hey, the life is only an estimate, and I've heard that our competition uses a 12-year life on their production equipment."

Instructions

(a) Who are the stakeholders in this situation?
(b) Is the change in asset life unethical, or is it simply a good business practice by an astute president?
(c) What is the effect of Robert Griffin's proposed change on income before taxes in the year of change?

All About You

BYP10-8 The Feature Story at the beginning of the chapter discussed the company Rent-A-Wreck. Note that the trade name Rent-A-Wreck is a very important asset to the company, as it creates immediate product identification. As indicated in the chapter, companies invest substantial sums to ensure that their product is well-known to the consumer. Test your knowledge of who owns some famous brands and their impact on the financial statements.

Instructions

(a) Provide an answer to the four multiple-choice questions below.
  (1) Which company owns both Taco Bell and Pizza Hut?
    (a) McDonald's.
    (b) CKE.
    (c) Yum Brands.
    (d) Wendy's.

(2) Dairy Queen belongs to:
(a) Breyer. (c) GE.
(b) Berkshire Hathaway. (d) The Coca-Cola Company.
(3) Philip Morris, the cigarette maker, is owned by:
(a) Altria. (c) Boeing.
(b) GE. (d) ExxonMobil.
(4) AOL, a major Internet provider, belongs to:
(a) Microsoft. (c) NBC.
(b) Cisco. (d) Time Warner.

(b) How do you think the value of these brands is reported on the appropriate company's balance sheet?

FASB Codification Activity

BYP10-9 If your school has a subscription to the FASB Codification, go to **http://aaahq.org/ascLogin.cfm** to log in and prepare responses to the following.

(a) What does it mean to capitalize an item?
(b) What is the definition provided for an intangible asset?
(c) Your great-uncle, who is a CPA, is impressed that you are taking an accounting class. Based on his experience, he believes that depreciation is something that companies do based on past practice, not on the basis of authoritative guidance. Provide the authoritative literature to support the practice of fixed-asset depreciation.

A Look at IFRS

LEARNING OBJECTIVE 7 **Compare the accounting for long-lived assets under GAAP and IFRS.**

IFRS follows most of the same principles as GAAP in the accounting for property, plant, and equipment. There are, however, some significant differences in the implementation. IFRS allows the use of revaluation of property, plant, and equipment, and it also requires the use of component depreciation. In addition, there are some significant differences in the accounting for both intangible assets and impairments.

Key Points

The following are the key similarities and differences between GAAP and IFRS as related to the recording process for long-lived assets.

Similarities

- The definition for plant assets for both IFRS and GAAP is essentially the same.
- Both IFRS and GAAP follow the historical cost principle when accounting for property, plant, and equipment at date of acquisition. Cost consists of all expenditures necessary to acquire the asset and make it ready for its intended use.
- Under both IFRS and GAAP, interest costs incurred during construction are capitalized. Recently, IFRS converged to GAAP requirements in this area.
- IFRS also views depreciation as an allocation of cost over an asset's useful life. IFRS permits the same depreciation methods (e.g., straight-line, accelerated, and units-of-activity) as GAAP.
- Under both GAAP and IFRS, changes in the depreciation method used and changes in useful life are handled in current and future periods. Prior periods are not affected. GAAP recently conformed to international standards in the accounting for changes in depreciation methods.

- The accounting for subsequent expenditures (such as ordinary repairs and additions) are essentially the same under IFRS and GAAP.
- The accounting for plant asset disposals is essentially the same under IFRS and GAAP.
- Initial costs to acquire natural resources are essentially the same under IFRS and GAAP.
- The definition of intangible assets is essentially the same under IFRS and GAAP.
- The accounting for exchanges of nonmonetary assets has recently converged between IFRS and GAAP. GAAP now requires that gains on exchanges of nonmonetary assets be recognized if the exchange has commercial substance. This is the same framework used in IFRS.

Differences

- IFRS uses the term **residual value** rather than salvage value to refer to an owner's estimate of an asset's value at the end of its useful life for that owner.
- IFRS allows companies to revalue plant assets to fair value at the reporting date. Companies that choose to use the revaluation framework must follow revaluation procedures. If revaluation is used, it must be applied to all assets in a class of assets. Assets that are experiencing rapid price changes must be revalued on an annual basis, otherwise less frequent revaluation is acceptable.
- IFRS requires component depreciation. **Component depreciation** specifies that any significant parts of a depreciable asset that have different estimated useful lives should be separately depreciated. Component depreciation is allowed under GAAP but is seldom used.
- As in GAAP, under IFRS the costs associated with research and development are segregated into the two components. Costs in the research phase are always expensed under both IFRS and GAAP. Under IFRS, however, costs in the development phase are capitalized as Development Costs once technological feasibility is achieved.
- IFRS permits revaluation of intangible assets (except for goodwill). GAAP prohibits revaluation of intangible assets.

Looking to the Future

The IASB and FASB have identified a project that would consider expanded recognition of internally generated intangible assets. IFRS permits more recognition of intangibles compared to GAAP.

IFRS Practice

IFRS Self-Test Questions

1. Which of the following statements is **correct**?
   (a) Both IFRS and GAAP permit revaluation of property, plant, and equipment and intangible assets (except for goodwill).
   (b) IFRS permits revaluation of property, plant, and equipment and intangible assets (except for goodwill).
   (c) Both IFRS and GAAP permit revaluation of property, plant, and equipment but not intangible assets.
   (d) GAAP permits revaluation of property, plant, and equipment but not intangible assets.
2. Research and development costs are:
   (a) expensed under GAAP.
   (b) expensed under IFRS.
   (c) expensed under both GAAP and IFRS.
   (d) None of the above.

IFRS Exercises

IFRS10-1 What is component depreciation, and when must it be used?

IFRS10-2 What is revaluation of plant assets? When should revaluation be applied?

IFRS10-3 Some product development expenditures are recorded as development expenses and others as development costs. Explain the difference between these accounts and how a company decides which classification is appropriate.

International Financial Statement Analysis: Louis Vuitton

IFRS10-4 The financial statements of Louis Vuitton are presented in Appendix F. Instructions for accessing and using the company's complete annual report, including the notes to its financial statements, are also provided in Appendix F.

Instructions

Use the company's annual report to answer the following questions.

(a) According to the notes to the financial statements, what method or methods does the company use to depreciate "property, plant, and equipment?" What rate(s) does it use to depreciate property, plant, and equipment?

(b) Using the notes to the financial statements, identify the brands and trade names that are most significant to the company.

(c) Using the notes to the financial statements, determine (1) the balance in Accumulated Amortization and Impairment for intangible assets (other the goodwill), and (2) the balance in Accumulated Depreciation for property, plant, and equipment. (Round your amounts to the nearest thousand.)

Answers to IFRS Self-Test Questions

1. b **2.** a

11 Current Liabilities and Payroll Accounting

CHAPTER PREVIEW Inventor-entrepreneur Wilbert Murdock, as the Feature Story below notes, had to use multiple credit cards to finance his business ventures. Murdock's credit card debts would be classified as **current liabilities** because they are due every month. Yet, by making minimal payments and paying high interest each month, Murdock used this credit source long-term. Some credit card balances remain outstanding for years as they accumulate interest.

FEATURE STORY

Financing His Dreams

What would you do if you had a great idea for a new product but couldn't come up with the cash to get the business off the ground? Small businesses often cannot attract investors. Nor can they obtain traditional debt financing through bank loans or bond issuances. Instead, they often resort to unusual, and costly, forms of nontraditional financing.

Such was the case for Wilbert Murdock. Murdock grew up in a New York housing project and always had great ambitions. His entrepreneurial spirit led him into some business ventures that failed: a medical diagnostic tool, a device to eliminate carpal tunnel syndrome, custom-designed sneakers, and a device to keep people from falling asleep while driving.

Another idea was computerized golf clubs that analyze a golfer's swing and provide immediate feedback. Murdock saw great potential in the idea. Many golfers are willing to shell out considerable sums of money for devices that might improve their game. But Murdock had no cash to develop his product, and banks and other lenders had shied away. Rather than give up, Murdock resorted to credit cards—in a big way. He quickly owed $25,000 to credit card companies.

While funding a business with credit cards might sound unusual, it isn't. A recent study found that one-third of businesses with fewer than 20 employees financed at least part of their operations with credit cards. As Murdock explained, credit cards are an appealing way to finance a start-up because "credit-card companies don't care how the money is spent." However, they do care how they are paid. And so Murdock faced high interest charges and a barrage of credit card collection letters.

Murdock's debt forced him to sacrifice nearly everything in order to keep his business afloat. His car stopped running, he barely had enough money to buy food, and he lived and worked out of a dimly lit apartment in his mother's basement. Through it all he tried to maintain a positive spirit, joking that, if he becomes successful, he might some day get to appear in an American Express commercial.

Source: Rodney Ho, "Banking on Plastic: To Finance a Dream, Many Entrepreneurs Binge on Credit Cards," *Wall Street Journal* (March 9, 1998), p. A1.

Cary Westfall/iStockphoto

CHAPTER OUTLINE

Learning Objectives

1 Explain how to account for current liabilities.
- What is a current liability?
- Notes payable
- Sales taxes payable
- Unearned revenues
- Current maturities of long-term debt

DO IT! **1** Current Liabilities

2 Discuss how current liabilities are reported and analyzed.
- Reporting uncertainty
- Reporting of current liabilities
- Analysis of current liabilities

DO IT! **2** Reporting and Analyzing

3 Explain how to account for payroll.
- Determining the payroll
- Recording the payroll
- Employer payroll taxes
- Filing and remitting payroll taxes
- Internal control for payroll

DO IT! **3a** Payroll
3b Employer's Payroll Taxes

Go to the ***REVIEW AND PRACTICE*** section at the end of the chapter for a review of key concepts and practice applications with solutions.

Visit **WileyPLUS with ORION** for additional tutorials and practice opportunities.

LEARNING OBJECTIVE 1 **Explain how to account for current liabilities.**

What Is a Current Liability?

You have learned that liabilities are defined as "creditors' claims on total assets" and as "existing debts and obligations." Companies must settle or pay these claims, debts, and obligations at some time in the future by transferring assets or services. The future date on which they are due or payable (the maturity date) is a significant feature of liabilities.

As explained in Chapter 4, a **current liability** is a debt that a company expects to pay within one year or the operating cycle, whichever is longer. Debts that do not meet this criterion are **long-term liabilities.**

Financial statement users want to know whether a company's obligations are current or long-term. A company that has more current liabilities than current assets often lacks liquidity, or short-term debt-paying ability. In addition, users want to know the types of liabilities a company has. If a company declares bankruptcy, a specific, predetermined order of payment to creditors exists. Thus, the amount and type of liabilities are of critical importance.

Helpful Hint
In previous chapters, we explained the entries for accounts payable and the adjusting entries for some current liabilities.

The different types of current liabilities include notes payable, accounts payable, unearned revenues, and accrued liabilities such as taxes, salaries and wages, and interest payable. In the sections that follow, we discuss common types of current liabilities.

Notes Payable

Companies record obligations in the form of written notes as **notes payable**. Notes payable are often used instead of accounts payable because they give the lender formal proof of the obligation in case legal remedies are needed to collect the debt. Companies frequently issue notes payable to meet short-term financing needs. Notes payable usually require the borrower to pay interest.

Notes are issued for varying periods of time. **Those due for payment within one year of the balance sheet date are usually classified as current liabilities.**

To illustrate the accounting for notes payable, assume that First National Bank agrees to lend $100,000 on September 1, 2017, if Cole Williams Co. signs a $100,000, 12%, four-month note maturing on January 1. When a company issues an interest-bearing note, the amount of assets it receives upon issuance of the note generally equals the note's face value. Cole Williams therefore will receive $100,000 cash and will make the following journal entry.

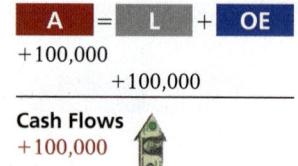

A	=	L	+	OE
+100,000				
		+100,000		

Cash Flows
+100,000

Sept. 1	Cash	100,000	
	Notes Payable		100,000
	(To record issuance of 12%, 4-month note to First National Bank)		

Interest accrues over the life of the note, and the company must periodically record that accrual. If Cole Williams prepares financial statements annually, it makes an adjusting entry at December 31 to recognize interest expense and interest payable of $4,000 ($100,000 × 12% × 4/12). Illustration 11-1 shows the formula for computing interest and its application to Cole Williams' note.

Illustration 11-1
Formula for computing interest

Face Value of Note	×	Annual Interest Rate	×	Time in Terms of One Year	=	Interest
$100,000	×	12%	×	4/12	=	**$4,000**

Cole Williams makes an adjusting entry as follows.

Dec. 31	Interest Expense	4,000	
	Interest Payable		4,000
	(To accrue interest for 4 months on First National Bank note)		

A	=	L	+	OE
				−4,000 Exp
		+4,000		

Cash Flows
no effect

In the December 31 financial statements, the current liabilities section of the balance sheet will show notes payable $100,000 and interest payable $4,000. In addition, the company will report interest expense of $4,000 under "Other expenses and losses" in the income statement. If Cole Williams prepared financial statements monthly, the adjusting entry at the end of each month would be $1,000 ($100,000 × 12% × 1/12).

At maturity (January 1, 2018), Cole Williams must pay the face value of the note ($100,000) plus $4,000 interest ($100,000 × 12% × 4/12). It records payment of the note and accrued interest as follows.

Jan. 1	Notes Payable	100,000	
	Interest Payable	4,000	
	Cash		104,000
	(To record payment of First National Bank interest-bearing note and accrued interest at maturity)		

A	=	L	+	OE
		−100,000		
		−4,000		
−104,000				

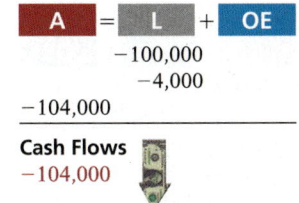

Cash Flows
−104,000

Sales Taxes Payable

Many of the products we purchase at retail stores are subject to sales taxes. Many states also are now collecting sales taxes on purchases made on the Internet as well. Sales taxes are expressed as a percentage of the sales price. The selling company collects the tax from the customer when the sale occurs. Periodically (usually monthly), the retailer remits the collections to the state's department of revenue. Collecting sales taxes is important. For example, the State of New York recently sued Sprint Corporation for $300 million for its alleged failure to collect sales taxes on phone calls.

Under most state sales tax laws, the selling company must enter separately in the cash register the amount of the sale and the amount of the sales tax collected. (Gasoline sales are a major exception.) The company then uses the cash register readings to credit Sales Revenue and Sales Taxes Payable. For example, if the March 25 cash register reading for Cooley Grocery shows sales of $10,000 and sales taxes of $600 (sales tax rate of 6%), the journal entry is as follows.

Mar. 25	Cash	10,600	
	Sales Revenue		10,000
	Sales Taxes Payable		600
	(To record daily sales and sales taxes)		

A	=	L	+	OE
+10,600				
				+10,000 Rev
		+600		

Cash Flows
+10,600

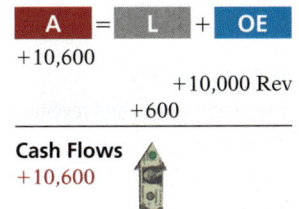

When the company remits the taxes to the taxing agency, it debits Sales Taxes Payable and credits Cash. The company does not report sales taxes as an expense. It simply forwards to the government the amount paid by the customers. Thus, Cooley Grocery serves only as a **collection agent** for the taxing authority.

Sometimes companies do not enter sales taxes separately in the cash register. To determine the amount of sales in such cases, divide total receipts by 100% plus the sales tax percentage. For example, assume that Cooley Grocery enters total receipts of $10,600. The receipts from the sales are equal to the sales price (100%) plus the tax percentage (6% of sales), or 1.06 times the sales total. We can compute the sales amount as follows.

$$\$10{,}600 \div 1.06 = \$10{,}000$$

Thus, we can find the sales tax amount of $600 by either (1) subtracting sales from total receipts ($10,600 − $10,000) or (2) multiplying sales by the sales tax rate ($10,000 × 6%).

Unearned Revenues

A magazine publisher, such as **Sports Illustrated**, receives customers' checks when they order magazines. An airline company, such as **American Airlines**, often receives cash when it sells tickets for future flights. Season tickets for concerts, sporting events, and theater programs are also paid for in advance. How do companies account for unearned revenues that are received before goods are delivered or services are performed?

1. When a company receives the advance payment, it debits Cash and credits a current liability account identifying the source of the unearned revenue.
2. When the company recognizes revenue, it debits an unearned revenue account and credits a revenue account.

To illustrate, assume that Superior University sells 10,000 season football tickets at $50 each for its five-game home schedule. The university makes the following entry for the sale of season tickets.

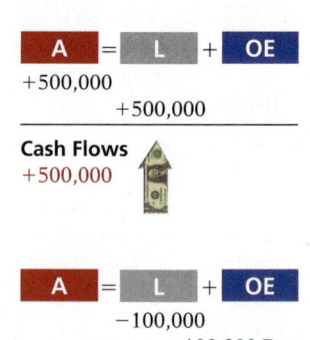

A	=	L	+	OE
+500,000				
		+500,000		

Cash Flows
+500,000

Aug. 6	Cash	500,000	
	Unearned Ticket Revenue		500,000
	(To record sale of 10,000 season tickets)		

As each game is completed, Superior records the recognition of revenue with the following entry.

A	=	L	+	OE
		−100,000		
				+100,000 Rev

Cash Flows
no effect

Sept. 7	Unearned Ticket Revenue	100,000	
	Ticket Revenue		100,000
	(To record football ticket revenue)		

The account Unearned Ticket Revenue represents unearned revenue, and Superior reports it as a current liability. As the school recognizes revenue, it reclassifies the amount from unearned revenue to Ticket Revenue. Unearned revenue is material for some companies. In the airline industry, for example, tickets sold for future flights represent almost 50% of total current liabilities. At **United Air Lines**, unearned ticket revenue is its largest current liability, recently amounting to over $1 billion.

Illustration 11-2 shows specific unearned revenue and revenue accounts used in selected types of businesses.

Illustration 11-2
Unearned revenue and revenue accounts

	Account Title	
Type of Business	**Unearned Revenue**	**Revenue**
Airline	Unearned Ticket Revenue	Ticket Revenue
Magazine publisher	Unearned Subscription Revenue	Subscription Revenue
Hotel	Unearned Rent Revenue	Rent Revenue

Current Maturities of Long-Term Debt

Companies often have a portion of long-term debt that comes due in the current year. That amount is considered a current liability. As an example, assume that Wendy Construction issues a five-year, interest-bearing $25,000 note on January 1, 2016. This note specifies that each January 1, starting January 1, 2017, Wendy should pay $5,000 of the note. When the company prepares financial statements on December 31, 2016, it should report $5,000 as a current liability and $20,000 as a long-term liability. (The $5,000 amount is the portion of the note that is due to be paid within the next 12 months.) Companies often identify current maturities of long-term debt on the balance sheet as **long-term debt due within one year**. In a recent year, General Motors had $724 million of such debt.

It is not necessary to prepare an adjusting entry to recognize the current maturity of long-term debt. At the balance sheet date, all obligations due within one year are classified as current, and all other obligations as long-term.

DO IT! 1 Current Liabilities

You and several classmates are studying for the next accounting exam. They ask you to answer the following questions.

1. If cash is borrowed on a $50,000, 6-month, 12% note on September 1, how much interest expense would be incurred by December 31?
2. How is the sales tax amount determined when the cash register total includes sales taxes?
3. If $15,000 is collected in advance on November 1 for 3 months' rent, what amount of rent revenue should be recognized by December 31?

Solution

1. $50,000 × 12% × 4/12 = $2,000
2. First, divide the total cash register receipts by 100% plus the sales tax percentage to find the sales revenue amount. Second, subtract the sales revenue amount from the total cash register receipts to determine the sales taxes.
3. $15,000 × 2/3 = $10,000

Related exercise material: **BE11-1, BE11-2, BE11-3, BE11-4, E11-1, E11-2, E11-3, E11-4, and DO IT! 11-1.**

Action Plan

✔ Use the interest formula: Face value of note × Annual interest rate × Time in terms of one year.

✔ Divide total receipts by 100% plus the tax rate to determine sales revenue, then subtract sales revenue from the total receipts.

✔ Determine what fraction of the total unearned rent should be recognized this year.

LEARNING OBJECTIVE 2 **Discuss how current liabilities are reported and analyzed.**

Reporting Uncertainty

With notes payable, interest payable, accounts payable, and sales taxes payable, we know that an obligation to make a payment exists. But, suppose that your company is involved in a dispute with the Internal Revenue Service (IRS) over the amount of its income tax liability. Should you report the disputed amount as a liability on the balance sheet? Or, suppose your company is involved in a lawsuit which, if you lose, might result in bankruptcy. How should you report this major contingency? The answers to these questions are difficult because these liabilities are dependent—contingent—upon some future event. In other words, a **contingent liability** is a potential liability that may become an actual liability in the future.

How should companies report contingent liabilities? They use the following guidelines:

1. If the contingency is **probable** (if it is likely to occur) **and** the amount can be **reasonably estimated**, the liability should be recorded in the accounts.
2. If the contingency is only **reasonably possible** (if it could happen), then it needs to be disclosed only in the notes that accompany the financial statements.
3. If the contingency is **remote** (if it is unlikely to occur), it need not be recorded or disclosed.

Accounting Across the Organization — Manville Corp.

Jeffrey Layton/iStockphoto

Contingencies: How Big Are They?

Contingent liabilities abound in the real world. Consider Manville Corp., which filed for bankruptcy when it was hit by billions of dollars in asbestos product-liability claims. Companies having multiple toxic waste sites are faced with cleanup costs that average $10 to $30 million and can reach as high as $500 million depending on the type of waste. For life and health insurance companies and their stockholders, the cost of diseases such as diabetes, Alzheimer's, and AIDS is like an iceberg: Everyone wonders how big such costs really are and what damage they might do in the future. And frequent-flyer programs are so popular that airlines at one time owed participants more than 3 million round-trip domestic tickets. That's enough to fly at least 5.4 billion miles—free for the passengers, but at what future cost to the airlines?

Why do you think most companies disclose, but do not record, contingent liabilities? (Go to **WileyPLUS** for this answer and additional questions.)

REPORTING A CONTINGENT LIABILITY

Product warranties are an example of a contingent liability that companies should record in the accounts. Warranty contracts result in future costs that companies may incur in replacing defective units or repairing malfunctioning units. Generally, a manufacturer, such as Stanley Black & Decker, knows that it will incur some warranty costs. From prior experience with the product, the company usually can reasonably estimate the anticipated cost of servicing (honoring) the warranty.

The accounting for warranty costs is based on the expense recognition principle. **The estimated cost of honoring product warranty contracts should be recognized as an expense in the period in which the sale occurs.** To illustrate, assume that in 2017 Denson Manufacturing Company sells 10,000 washers and dryers at an average price of $600 each. The selling price includes a one-year warranty on parts. Denson expects that 500 units (5%) will be defective and that warranty repair costs will average $80 per unit. In 2017, the company honors warranty contracts on 300 units, at a total cost of $24,000.

At December 31, it is necessary to accrue the estimated warranty costs on the 2017 sales. Denson computes the estimated warranty liability as follows.

Illustration 11-3
Computation of estimated warranty liability

Number of units sold	10,000
Estimated rate of defective units	× 5%
Total estimated defective units	500
Average warranty repair cost	× $80
Estimated warranty liability	**$40,000**

The company makes the following adjusting entry.

A = L + OE
−40,000 Exp
+40,000
Cash Flows
no effect

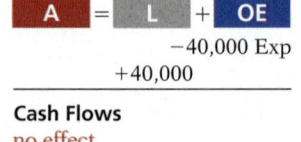

Dec. 31	Warranty Expense	40,000	
	Warranty Liability		40,000
	(To accrue estimated warranty costs)		

Denson records those repair costs incurred in 2017 to honor warranty contracts on 2017 sales as shown below.

A = L + OE
−24,000
−24,000
Cash Flows
no effect

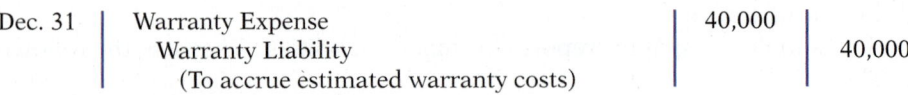

Jan. 1–	Warranty Liability	24,000	
Dec. 31	Repair Parts		24,000
	(To record honoring of 300 warranty contracts on 2017 sales)		

The company reports warranty expense of $40,000 under selling expenses in the income statement. It classifies warranty liability of $16,000 ($40,000 − $24,000) as a current liability on the balance sheet, assuming the warranty is estimated to be honored in the next year.

In the following year, Denson should debit to Warranty Liability all expenses incurred in honoring warranty contracts on 2017 sales. To illustrate, assume that the company replaces 20 defective units in January 2018, at an average cost of $80 in parts and labor. The summary entry for the month of January 2018 is as follows.

Jan. 31	Warranty Liability	1,600	
	Repair Parts		1,600
	(To record honoring of 20 warranty contracts on 2017 sales)		

A	=	L	+	OE
		−1,600		
−1,600				

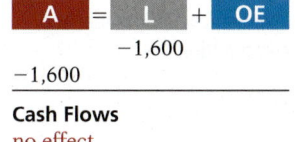

Cash Flows
no effect

Reporting of Current Liabilities

Current liabilities are the first category under liabilities on the balance sheet. Each of the principal types of current liabilities is listed separately. In addition, companies disclose the terms of notes payable and other key information about the individual items in the notes to the financial statements.

Companies seldom list current liabilities in the order of liquidity. The reason is that varying maturity dates may exist for specific obligations such as notes payable. As a matter of custom, many companies show notes payable first and then accounts payable, regardless of amount. The current maturity of long-term debt is often shown last in the current liabilities section. Illustration 11-4 provides an excerpt from Evan Company's balance sheet, which is a common order of presentation among companies.

Illustration 11-4
Balance sheet reporting of current liabilities

EVAN COMPANY
Balance Sheet
December 31, 2017

Assets	
Current assets	$ 500,000
Property, plant and equipment (net)	150,000
Other long-term assets	520,000
Total assets	$1,170,000
Liabilities and Owner's Equity	
Current liabilities	
Notes payable	**$ 40,000**
Accounts payable	**110,000**
Unearned revenue	**30,000**
Salaries and wages payable	**90,000**
Warranty liability	**25,000**
Current maturities of long-term debt	**65,000**
Total current liabilities	**360,000**
Noncurrent liabilities	620,000
Total liabilities	980,000
Owner's equity	190,000
Total liabilities and owner's equity	$1,170,000

Helpful Hint
For examples of real-world current liabilities sections, refer to the PepsiCo and Coca-Cola balance sheets in Appendices B and C.

Analysis of Current Liabilities

Use of current and noncurrent classifications makes it possible to analyze a company's liquidity. **Liquidity** refers to the ability to pay maturing obligations and meet unexpected needs for cash. The relationship of current assets to current liabilities is critical in analyzing liquidity. We can express this relationship as a dollar amount (working capital) and as a ratio (the current ratio).

The excess of current assets over current liabilities is **working capital**. Illustration 11-5 shows the formula for the computation of Evan Company's working capital.

Illustration 11-5
Working capital formula and computation

Current Assets	–	Current Liabilities	=	Working Capital
$500,000	–	$360,000	=	$140,000

As an absolute dollar amount, working capital offers limited informational value. For example, $1 million of working capital may be more than needed for a small company but inadequate for a large corporation. Also, $1 million of working capital may be adequate for a company at one time but inadequate at another time.

The **current ratio** permits us to compare the liquidity of different-sized companies and of a single company at different times. The current ratio is calculated as current assets divided by current liabilities. Illustration 11-6 shows the formula for this ratio, along with its computation using Evan's current asset and current liability data.

Illustration 11-6
Current ratio formula and computation

Current Assets	÷	Current Liabilities	=	Current Ratio
$500,000	÷	$360,000	=	1.39:1

Historically, companies and analysts considered a current ratio of 2:1 to be the standard for a good credit rating. In recent years, however, many healthy companies have maintained ratios well below 2:1 by improving management of their current assets and liabilities. Evan's ratio of 1.39:1 is adequate but certainly below the standard of 2:1.

DO IT! 2 Reporting and Analyzing

Lepid Company has the following account balances at December 31, 2017.

Notes payable ($80,000 due after 12/31/18)	$200,000
Unearned service revenue	75,000
Other long-term debt ($30,000 due in 2018)	150,000
Salaries and wages payable	22,000
Other accrued expenses	15,000
Accounts payable	100,000

In addition, Lepid is involved in a lawsuit. Legal counsel feels it is probable Lepid will pay damages of $38,000 in 2018.

(a) Prepare the current liabilities section of Lepid's December 31, 2017, balance sheet.

(b) Lepid's current assets are $504,000. Compute Lepid's working capital and current ratio.

Action Plan

✔ Determine which liabilities will be paid within one year or the operating cycle and include those as current liabilities.

Solution

(a) Current liabilities

Notes payable	$120,000
Accounts payable	100,000
Unearned service revenue	75,000
Lawsuit liability	38,000
Salaries and wages payable	22,000
Other accrued expenses	15,000
Long-term debt due within one year	30,000
Total current liabilities	$400,000

(b) Working capital = Current assets − Current liabilities = $504,000 − $400,000 = $104,000
Current ratio = Current assets ÷ Current liabilities = $504,000 ÷ $400,000 = 1.26:1

Related exercise material: **BE11-5, E11-7, E11-8, and DO IT! 11-2.**

Action Plan (cont'd)

✔ If the contingent liability is probable and reasonably estimable, include it as a current liability.

✔ Use the formula for working capital: Current assets − Current liabilities.

✔ Use the formula for the current ratio: Current assets ÷ Current liabilities.

LEARNING OBJECTIVE 3

Explain how to account for payroll.

Payroll and related fringe benefits often make up a large percentage of current liabilities. Employee compensation is often the most significant expense that a company incurs. For example, Costco recently reported total employees of 103,000 and labor and fringe benefits costs which approximated 70% of the company's total cost of operations.

Payroll accounting involves more than paying employees' wages. Companies are required by law to maintain payroll records for each employee, to file and pay payroll taxes, and to comply with state and federal tax laws related to employee compensation.

The term "payroll" **pertains to both salaries and wages of employees.** Managerial, administrative, and sales personnel are generally paid **salaries**. Salaries are often expressed in terms of a specified amount per month or per year rather than an hourly rate. Store clerks, factory employees, and manual laborers are normally paid **wages**. Wages are based on a rate per hour or on a piecework basis (such as per unit of product). Frequently, people use the terms "salaries" and "wages" interchangeably.

The term "payroll" **does not apply to payments made for services of professionals** such as certified public accountants, attorneys, and architects. Such professionals are independent contractors rather than salaried employees. Payments to them are called **fees**. This distinction is important because government regulations relating to the payment and reporting of payroll taxes apply only to employees.

Determining the Payroll

Determining the payroll involves computing three amounts: (1) gross earnings, (2) payroll deductions, and (3) net pay.

GROSS EARNINGS

Gross earnings is the total compensation earned by an employee. It consists of wages or salaries, plus any bonuses and commissions.

Companies determine total **wages** for an employee by multiplying the hours worked by the hourly rate of pay. In addition to the hourly pay rate, most companies are required by law to pay hourly workers a minimum of 1½ times the regular hourly rate for overtime work in excess of eight hours per day or 40 hours per week. In addition, many employers pay overtime rates for work done at night, on weekends, and on holidays.

For example, assume that Michael Jordan, an employee of Academy Company, worked 44 hours for the weekly pay period ending January 14. His regular wage is $12 per hour. For any hours in excess of 40, the company pays at one-and-a-half times the regular rate. Academy computes Jordan's gross earnings (total wages) as follows.

Illustration 11-7
Computation of total wages

Type of Pay	Hours	×	Rate	=	Gross Earnings
Regular	40	×	$12	=	$480
Overtime	4	×	18	=	72
Total wages					**$552**

This computation assumes that Jordan receives 1½ times his regular hourly rate ($12 × 1.5) for his overtime hours. Union contracts often require that overtime rates be as much as twice the regular rates.

An employee's **salary** is generally based on a monthly or yearly rate. The company then prorates these rates to its payroll periods (e.g., biweekly or monthly). Most executive and administrative positions are salaried. Federal law does not require overtime pay for employees in such positions.

Many companies have **bonus** agreements for employees. One survey found that over 94% of the largest U.S. manufacturing companies offer annual bonuses to key executives. Bonus arrangements may be based on such factors as increased sales or net income. Companies may pay bonuses in cash and/or by granting employees the opportunity to acquire shares of company stock at favorable prices (called stock option plans).

ETHICS NOTE

Bonuses often reward outstanding individual performance, but successful corporations also need considerable teamwork. A challenge is to motivate individuals while preventing an unethical employee from taking another's idea for his or her own advantage.

PAYROLL DEDUCTIONS

As anyone who has received a paycheck knows, gross earnings are usually very different from the amount actually received. The difference is due to **payroll deductions**.

Payroll deductions may be mandatory or voluntary. **Mandatory deductions are required by law and consist of FICA taxes and income taxes.** Voluntary deductions are at the option of the employee. Illustration 11-8 summarizes common types of payroll deductions. Such deductions do not result in payroll tax expense to the employer. The employer is merely a collection agent, and subsequently transfers the deducted amounts to the government and designated recipients.

Illustration 11-8
Payroll deductions

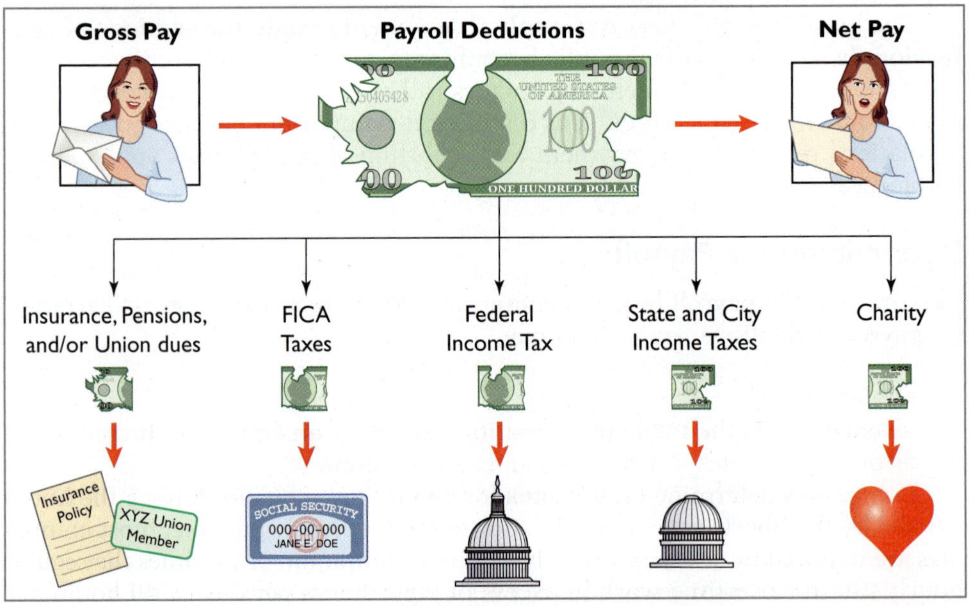

FICA TAXES In 1937, Congress enacted the Federal Insurance Contribution Act (FICA). **FICA taxes are designed to provide workers with supplemental retirement, employment disability, and medical benefits.** In 1965, Congress extended benefits to include Medicare for individuals over 65 years of age. The benefits are financed by a tax levied on employees' earnings.

FICA taxes consist of a Social Security tax and a Medicare tax. They are paid by both employee and employer. The FICA tax rate is 7.65% (6.2% Social Security tax up to $117,000 plus 1.45% Medicare tax) of salary and wages for each employee.[1] In addition, the Medicare tax of 1.45% continues for an employee's salary and wages in excess of $117,000. These tax rate and tax base requirements are shown in Illustration 11-9.

Illustration 11-9
FICA tax rate and tax base

Social Security taxes	
Employee and employer	**6.2%** on salary and wages up to **$117,000**
Medicare taxes	
Employee and employer	**1.45%** on all salary and wages without limitation

To illustrate the computation of FICA taxes, assume that Mario Ruez has total wages for the year of $100,000. In this case, Mario pays FICA taxes of $7,650 ($100,000 × 7.65%). If Mario has total wages of $124,000, Mario pays FICA taxes of $9,052, as shown in Illustration 11-10.

Illustration 11-10
FICA tax computation

Social Security tax	($117,000 × 6.2%)	$ 7,254
Medicare tax	($124,000 × 1.45%)	1,798
Total FICA taxes		**$9,052**

Mario's employer is also required to pay $9,052.

INCOME TAXES Under the U.S. pay-as-you-go system of federal income taxes, employers are required to withhold income taxes from employees each pay period. Four variables determine the amount to be withheld: (1) the employee's gross earnings, (2) marital status, (3) the number of allowances claimed by the employee, and (4) the length of the pay period. The number of allowances claimed typically includes the employee, his or her spouse, and other dependents.

Withholding tables furnished by the Internal Revenue Service indicate the amount of income tax to be withheld. Withholding amounts are based on gross wages and the number of allowances claimed. Separate tables are provided for weekly, biweekly, semimonthly, and monthly pay periods. Illustration 11-11 (page 502) shows the withholding tax table for Michael Jordan (assuming he earns $552 per week, is married, and claims two allowances). For a weekly salary of $552 with two allowances, the income tax to be withheld is $24 (highlighted in red).

In addition, most states (and some cities) require **employers** to withhold income taxes from employees' earnings. As a rule, the amounts withheld are a percentage (specified in the state revenue code) of the amount withheld for the federal income tax. Or they may be a specified percentage of the employee's earnings. For the sake of simplicity, we have assumed that Jordan's wages are subject to state income taxes of 2%, or $11.04 (2% × $552) per week.

There is no limit on the amount of gross earnings subject to income tax withholdings. In fact, under our progressive system of taxation, the higher the earnings, the higher the percentage of income withheld for taxes.

OTHER DEDUCTIONS Employees may voluntarily authorize withholdings for charitable organizations, retirement, and other purposes. All voluntary deductions

[1]The $117,000 limit is based upon 2014 guidelines set by the Social Security Administration.

Illustration 11-11
Withholding tax table

MARRIED Persons — **WEEKLY** Payroll Period
(For Wages Paid through December 2017)

If the wages are —		And the number of withholding allowances claimed is —										
At least	But less than	0	1	2	3	4	5	6	7	8	9	10
		The amount of income tax to be withheld is —										
500	**510**	34	27	19	11	4	0	0	0	0	0	0
510	**520**	35	28	20	12	5	0	0	0	0	0	0
520	**530**	37	29	21	13	6	0	0	0	0	0	0
530	**540**	38	30	22	14	7	0	0	0	0	0	0
540	**550**	40	31	23	15	8	0	0	0	0	0	0
550	**560**	41	32	24	16	9	1	0	0	0	0	0
560	**570**	43	33	25	17	10	2	0	0	0	0	0
570	**580**	44	34	26	18	11	3	0	0	0	0	0
580	**590**	46	35	27	19	12	4	0	0	0	0	0
590	**600**	47	36	28	20	13	5	0	0	0	0	0
600	**610**	49	38	29	21	14	6	0	0	0	0	0
610	**620**	50	39	30	22	15	7	0	0	0	0	0
620	**630**	52	41	31	23	16	8	1	0	0	0	0
630	**640**	53	42	32	24	17	9	2	0	0	0	0
640	**650**	55	44	33	25	18	10	3	0	0	0	0
650	**660**	56	45	34	26	19	11	4	0	0	0	0
660	**670**	58	47	35	27	20	12	5	0	0	0	0
670	**680**	59	48	37	28	21	13	6	0	0	0	0
680	**690**	61	50	38	29	22	14	7	0	0	0	0
690	**700**	62	51	40	30	23	15	8	0	0	0	0

from gross earnings should be authorized in writing by the employee. The authorization(s) may be made individually or as part of a group plan. Deductions for charitable organizations, such as the United Fund, or for financial arrangements, such as U.S. savings bonds and repayment of loans from company credit unions, are made individually. Deductions for union dues, health and life insurance, and pension plans are often made on a group basis. We assume that Jordan has weekly voluntary deductions of $10 for the United Fund and $5 for union dues.

NET PAY

Alternative Terminology
Net pay is also called *take-home pay.*

Academy Company determines **net pay** by subtracting payroll deductions from gross earnings. Illustration 11-12 shows the computation of Jordan's net pay for the pay period.

Illustration 11-12
Computation of net pay

Gross earnings		$ 552.00
Payroll deductions:		
FICA taxes	$42.23	
Federal income taxes	24.00	
State income taxes	11.04	
United Fund	10.00	
Union dues	5.00	92.27
Net pay		**$459.73**

Assuming that Michael Jordan's wages for each week during the year are $552, total wages for the year are $28,704 (52 × $552). Thus, all of Jordan's wages are subject to FICA tax during the year. In comparison, let's assume that Jordan's department head earns $3,000 per week, or $156,000 for the year. Since only the first $117,000 is subject to Social Security taxes, the maximum FICA withholdings on the department head's earnings would be $9,516 [($117,000 × 6.20%) + ($156,000 × 1.45%)].

Recording the Payroll

Recording the payroll involves maintaining payroll department records, recognizing payroll expenses and liabilities, and recording payment of the payroll.

MAINTAINING PAYROLL DEPARTMENT RECORDS

To comply with state and federal laws, an employer must keep a cumulative record of each employee's gross earnings, deductions, and net pay during the year. The record that provides this information is the **employee earnings record**. Illustration 11-13 shows Michael Jordan's employee earnings record.

Academy Company.xls

Home Insert Page Layout Formulas Data Review View

P18 fx

ACADEMY COMPANY
Employee Earnings Record
For the Year 2017

Name	Michael Jordan	**Address**	2345 Mifflin Ave.
Social Security Number	329-35-9547		Hampton, Michigan 48292
Date of Birth	December 24, 1994	**Telephone**	555-238-9051
Date Employed	September 1, 2015	**Date Employment Ended**	
Sex	Male	**Exemptions**	2
Single		**Married**	x

2017 Period Ending	Total Hours	Gross Earnings: Regular	Overtime	Total	Cumulative	Deductions: FICA	Fed. Inc. Tax	State Inc. Tax	United Fund	Union Dues	Total	Payment: Net Amount	Check No.
1/7	42	480.00	36.00	516.00	516.00	39.47	20.00	10.32	10.00	5.00	84.79	431.21	974
1/14	44	480.00	72.00	552.00	1,068.00	42.23	24.00	11.04	10.00	5.00	92.27	459.73	1028
1/21	43	480.00	54.00	534.00	1,602.00	40.85	22.00	10.68	10.00	5.00	88.53	445.47	1077
1/28	42	480.00	36.00	516.00	2,118.00	39.47	20.00	10.32	10.00	5.00	84.79	431.21	1133
Jan. Total		1,920.00	198.00	2,118.00		162.02	86.00	42.36	40.00	20.00	350.38	1,767.62	

Illustration 11-13
Employee earnings record

Companies keep a separate earnings record for each employee and update these records after each pay period. The employer uses the cumulative payroll data on the earnings record to (1) determine when an employee has earned the maximum earnings subject to FICA taxes, (2) file state and federal payroll tax returns (as explained later), and (3) provide each employee with a statement of gross earnings and tax withholdings for the year. Illustration 11-17 (page 509) shows this statement.

In addition to employee earnings records, many companies find it useful to prepare a **payroll register**. This record accumulates the gross earnings, deductions, and net pay by employee for each pay period. Illustration 11-14 (page 504) presents Academy Company's payroll register. It provides the documentation for preparing a paycheck for each employee. For example, it shows the data for Michael Jordan in the wages section. In this example, Academy's total weekly payroll is $17,210, as shown in the salaries and wages expense column (column N, row 31).

Note that this record is a listing of each employee's payroll data for the pay period. In some companies, a payroll register is a journal or book of original entry. Postings are made from it directly to ledger accounts. In other companies, the payroll register is a memorandum record that provides the data for a general journal entry and subsequent posting to the ledger accounts. Academy follows the latter procedure.

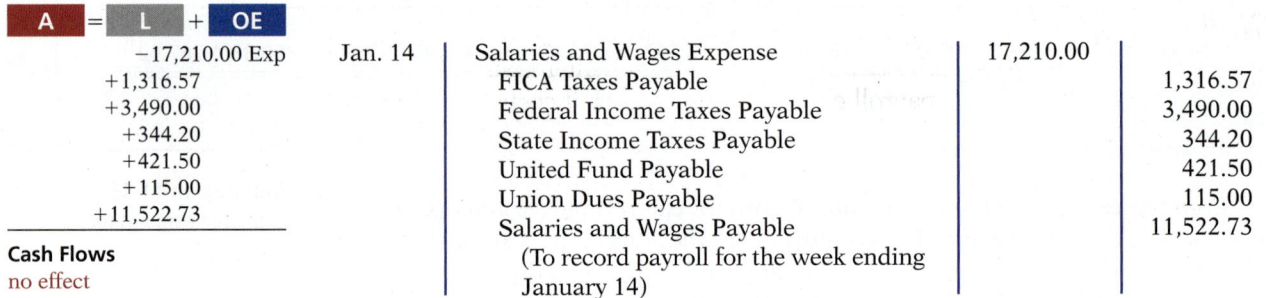

Academy Company.xls

ACADEMY COMPANY
Payroll Register
For the Week Ending January 14, 2017

		Earnings			Deductions						Paid		Account Debited
Employee	Total Hours	Regular	Over-time	Gross	FICA	Federal Income Tax	State Income Tax	United Fund	Union Dues	Total	Net Pay	Check No.	Salaries and Wages Expense
Arnold, Patricia	40	580.00		580.00	44.37	61.00	11.60	15.00		131.97	448.03	998	580.00
Canton, Matthew	40	590.00		590.00	45.14	63.00	11.80	20.00		139.94	450.06	999	590.00
Mueller, William	40	530.00		530.00	40.55	54.00	10.60	11.00		116.15	413.85	1000	530.00
Bennett, Robin	42	480.00	36.00	516.00	39.47	35.00	10.32	18.00	5.00	107.79	408.21	1025	516.00
Jordan, Michael	**44**	**480.00**	**72.00**	**552.00**	**42.23**	**24.00**	**11.04**	**10.00**	**5.00**	**92.27**	**459.73**	**1028**	**552.00**
Milroy, Lee	43	480.00	54.00	534.00	40.85	46.00	10.68	10.00	5.00	112.53	421.47	1029	534.00
Total		16,200.00	1,010.00	17,210.00	1,316.57	3,490.00	344.20	421.50	115.00	5,687.27	11,522.73		17,210.00

Illustration 11-14
Payroll register

RECOGNIZING PAYROLL EXPENSES AND LIABILITIES

From the payroll register in Illustration 11-14, Academy Company makes a journal entry to record the payroll. For the week ending January 14, the entry is as follows.

A	=	L	+	OE
				−17,210.00 Exp
		+1,316.57		
		+3,490.00		
		+344.20		
		+421.50		
		+115.00		
		+11,522.73		

Cash Flows
no effect

Jan. 14	Salaries and Wages Expense	17,210.00	
	FICA Taxes Payable		1,316.57
	Federal Income Taxes Payable		3,490.00
	State Income Taxes Payable		344.20
	United Fund Payable		421.50
	Union Dues Payable		115.00
	Salaries and Wages Payable		11,522.73
	(To record payroll for the week ending January 14)		

The company credits specific liability accounts for the mandatory and voluntary deductions made during the pay period. In the example, Academy debits Salaries and Wages Expense for the gross earnings of its employees. The amount credited to Salaries and Wages Payable is the sum of the individual checks the employees will receive.

RECORDING PAYMENT OF THE PAYROLL

A company makes payments by check (or electronic funds transfer) either from its regular bank account or a payroll bank account. Each paycheck is usually accompanied by a detachable **statement of earnings** document. This shows the employee's gross earnings, payroll deductions, and net pay, both for the period and for the year-to-date. Academy Company uses its regular bank account for payroll checks. Illustration 11-15 shows the paycheck and statement of earnings for Michael Jordan.

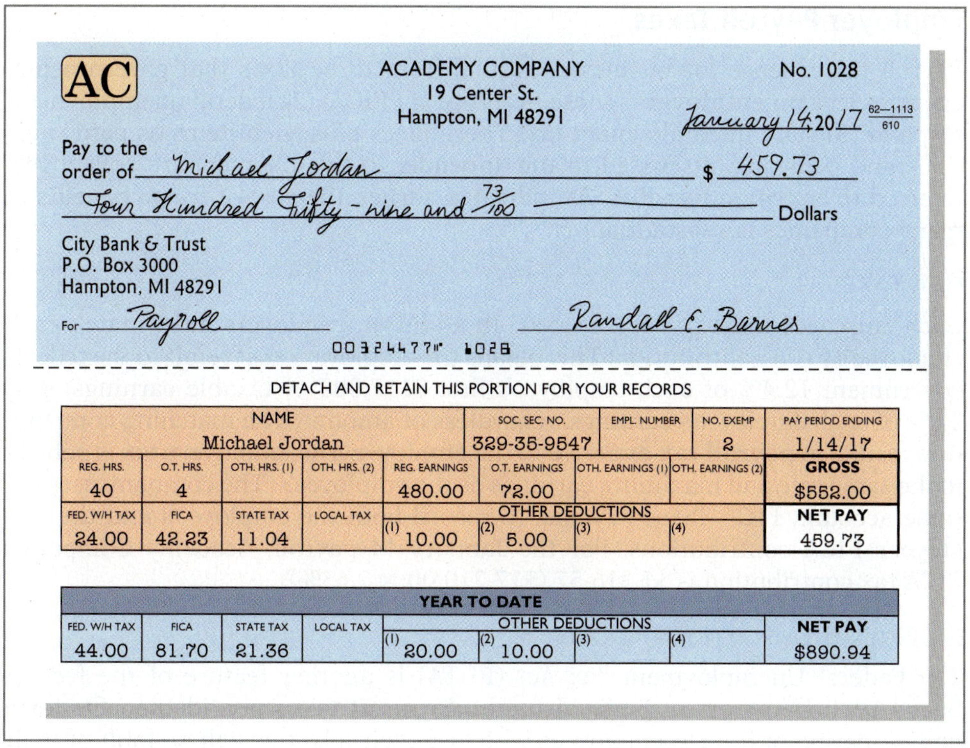

AC ACADEMY COMPANY
19 Center St.
Hampton, MI 48291

No. 1028

January 14, 2017 62—1113/610

Pay to the order of Michael Jordan $ 459.73

Four Hundred Fifty-nine and 73/100 Dollars

City Bank & Trust
P.O. Box 3000
Hampton, MI 48291

For Payroll Randall E. Barnes

DETACH AND RETAIN THIS PORTION FOR YOUR RECORDS

NAME	SOC. SEC. NO.	EMPL. NUMBER	NO. EXEMP	PAY PERIOD ENDING
Michael Jordan	329-35-9547		2	1/14/17

REG. HRS.	O.T. HRS.	OTH. HRS. (1)	OTH. HRS. (2)	REG. EARNINGS	O.T. EARNINGS	OTH. EARNINGS (1)	OTH. EARNINGS (2)	GROSS
40	4			480.00	72.00			$552.00

FED. W/H TAX	FICA	STATE TAX	LOCAL TAX	OTHER DEDUCTIONS (1)	(2)	(3)	(4)	NET PAY
24.00	42.23	11.04		10.00	5.00			459.73

YEAR TO DATE

FED. W/H TAX	FICA	STATE TAX	LOCAL TAX	OTHER DEDUCTIONS (1)	(2)	(3)	(4)	NET PAY
44.00	81.70	21.36		20.00	10.00			$890.94

Illustration 11-15
Paycheck and statement of earnings

Helpful Hint
None of the income tax liabilities result in payroll tax expense for the employer because the employer is acting only as a collection agent for the government.

Following payment of the payroll, the company enters the check numbers in the payroll register. Academy records payment of the payroll as follows.

Jan. 14	Salaries and Wages Payable	11,522.73	
	Cash		11,522.73
	(To record payment of payroll)		

A	=	L	+	OE
		−11,522.73		
−11,522.73				

Cash Flows
−11,522.73

Many medium- and large-size companies use a payroll processing center that performs payroll recordkeeping services. Companies send the center payroll information about employee pay rates and hours worked. The center maintains the payroll records and prepares the payroll checks. In most cases, it costs less to process the payroll through the center (outsource) than if the company did so internally.

DO IT! 3a Payroll

In January, gross earnings in Ramirez Company were $40,000. All earnings are subject to 7.65% FICA taxes. Federal income tax withheld was $9,000, and state income tax withheld was $1,000. (a) Calculate net pay for January, and (b) record the payroll.

Solution

(a) Net pay: $40,000 − (7.65% × $40,000) − $9,000 − $1,000 = $26,940

(b) Salaries and Wages Expense	40,000	
FICA Taxes Payable		3,060
Federal Income Taxes Payable		9,000
State Income Taxes Payable		1,000
Salaries and Wages Payable		26,940
(To record payroll)		

Related exercise material: **BE11-7, BE11-8, E11-9, E11-10, E11-11, E11-12, and DO IT! 11-3a.**

Action Plan

✔ Determine net pay by subtracting payroll deductions from gross earnings.

✔ Record gross earnings as Salaries and Wages Expense, record payroll deductions as liabilities, and record net pay as Salaries and Wages Payable.

Employer Payroll Taxes

Payroll tax expense for businesses results from three taxes that governmental agencies levy **on employers**. These taxes are (1) FICA, (2) federal unemployment tax, and (3) state unemployment tax. These taxes plus such items as paid vacations and pensions (discussed in the appendix to this chapter) are collectively referred to as **fringe benefits**. As indicated earlier, the cost of fringe benefits in many companies is substantial.

FICA TAXES

Each employee must pay FICA taxes. In addition, employers must match each employee's FICA contribution. This means the employer must remit to the federal government 12.4% of each employee's first $117,000 of taxable earnings, plus 2.9% of each employee's earnings, regardless of amount. The matching contribution results in **payroll tax expense** to the employer. The employer's tax is subject to the same rate and maximum earnings as the employee's. The company uses the same account, FICA Taxes Payable, to record both the employee's and the employer's FICA contributions. For the January 14 payroll, Academy Company's FICA tax contribution is $1,316.57 ($17,210.00 × 7.65%).

FEDERAL UNEMPLOYMENT TAXES

Helpful Hint
Both the employer and employee pay FICA taxes. Federal unemployment taxes and (in most states) the state unemployment taxes are borne entirely by the employer.

The Federal Unemployment Tax Act (FUTA) is another feature of the federal Social Security program. **Federal unemployment taxes** provide benefits for a limited period of time to employees who lose their jobs through no fault of their own. The FUTA tax rate is currently 6.2% of taxable wages. The taxable wage base is the first $7,000 of wages paid to each employee in a calendar year. Employers who pay the state unemployment tax on a timely basis will receive an offset credit of up to 5.4%. Therefore, the net federal tax rate is generally 0.8% (6.2% − 5.4%). This rate would equate to a maximum of $56 of federal tax per employee per year (0.8% × $7,000). State tax rates are based on state law.

The **employer** bears the entire federal unemployment tax. There is no deduction or withholding from employees. Companies use the account Federal Unemployment Taxes Payable to recognize this liability. The federal unemployment tax for Academy Company for the January 14 payroll is $137.68 ($17,210.00 × 0.8%).

STATE UNEMPLOYMENT TAXES

All states have unemployment compensation programs under state unemployment tax acts (SUTA). Like federal unemployment taxes, **state unemployment taxes** provide benefits to employees who lose their jobs. These taxes are levied on employers.[2] The basic rate is usually 5.4% on the first $7,000 of wages paid to an employee during the year. The state adjusts the basic rate according to the employer's experience rating. Companies with a history of stable employment may pay less than 5.4%. Companies with a history of unstable employment may pay more than the basic rate. Regardless of the rate paid, the company's credit on the federal unemployment tax is still 5.4%.

Companies use the account State Unemployment Taxes Payable for this liability. The state unemployment tax for Academy Company for the January 14 payroll is $929.34 ($17,210.00 × 5.4%). Illustration 11-16 summarizes the types of employer payroll taxes.

RECORDING EMPLOYER PAYROLL TAXES

Companies usually record employer payroll taxes at the same time they record the payroll. The entire amount of gross pay ($17,210.00) shown in the payroll register in Illustration 11-14 is subject to each of the three taxes mentioned above.

---

[2]In a few states, the employee is also required to make a contribution. *In this textbook, including the homework, we will assume that the tax is only on the employer.*

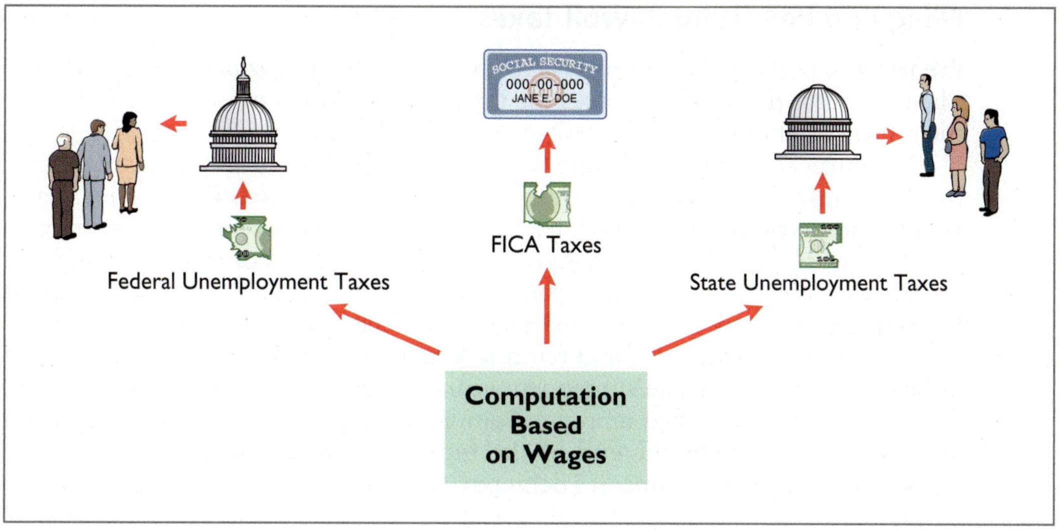

Illustration 11-16
Employer payroll taxes

Accordingly, Academy records the payroll tax expense associated with the January 14 payroll with the following entry.

Jan. 14	Payroll Tax Expense	2,383.59	
	FICA Taxes Payable		1,316.57
	Federal Unemployment Taxes Payable		137.68
	State Unemployment Taxes Payable		929.34
	(To record employer's payroll taxes on January 14 payroll)		

A	=	L	+	OE
				−2,383.59 Exp
		+1,316.57		
		+137.68		
		+929.34		

Cash Flows
no effect

Note that Academy uses separate liability accounts instead of a single credit to Payroll Taxes Payable. Why? Because these liabilities are payable to different taxing authorities at different dates. Companies classify the liability accounts in the balance sheet as current liabilities since they will be paid within the next year. They classify Payroll Tax Expense on the income statement as an operating expense.

Accounting Across the Organization — Bogan Communications

© svetikd/iStockphoto

It Costs $74,000 to Put $44,000 in Sally's Pocket

Sally works for Bogan Communications, a small company in New Jersey that provides audio systems. She makes $59,000 a year but only nets $44,000. What happened to the other $15,000? Well, $2,376 goes for Sally's share of the medical and dental insurance that Bogan provides, $126 for state unemployment insurance, $149 for disability insurance, and $856 for Medicare. New Jersey takes $1,893 in income taxes, and the federal government gets $3,658 for Social Security and another $6,250 for income tax withholding. All of this adds up to some 22% of Sally's gross pay going to Washington or Trenton.

Employing Sally costs Bogan plenty too. Bogan has to write checks for $74,000 so Sally can receive her $59,000 in base pay. Health insurance is the biggest cost. While Sally pays nearly $2,400 for coverage, Bogan pays the rest—$9,561. Then, the federal and state governments take $56 for federal unemployment coverage, $149 for disability insurance, $300 for workers' comp, and $505 for state unemployment insurance. Finally, the government requires Bogan to pay $856 for Sally's Medicare and $3,658 for her Social Security.

When you add it all up, it costs $74,000 to put $44,000 in Sally's pocket and to give her $12,000 in benefits.

Source: Michael P. Fleischer, "Why I'm Not Hiring," *Wall Street Journal* (August 9, 2010), p. A17.

How are the Social Security and Medicare taxes computed for Sally's salary? (Go to **WileyPLUS** for this answer and additional questions.)

Filing and Remitting Payroll Taxes

Preparation of payroll tax returns is the responsibility of the payroll department. The treasurer's department makes the tax payment. Much of the information for the returns is obtained from employee earnings records.

For purposes of reporting and remitting to the IRS, the company combines the FICA taxes and federal income taxes that it withheld. **Companies must report the taxes quarterly**, no later than one month following the close of each quarter. The remitting requirements depend on the amount of taxes withheld and the length of the pay period. Companies remit funds through deposits in either a Federal Reserve bank or an authorized commercial bank.

Companies generally file and remit federal unemployment taxes **annually** on or before January 31 of the subsequent year. Earlier payments are required when the tax exceeds a specified amount. Companies usually must file and pay state unemployment taxes by the **end of the month following each quarter**. When payroll taxes are paid, companies debit payroll liability accounts, and credit Cash.

ANATOMY OF A FRAUD

Art was a custodial supervisor for a large school district. The district was supposed to employ between 35 and 40 regular custodians, as well as 3 or 4 substitute custodians to fill in when regular custodians were absent. Instead, in addition to the regular custodians, Art "hired" 77 substitutes. In fact, almost none of these people worked for the district. Instead, Art submitted time cards for these people, collected their checks at the district office, and personally distributed the checks to the "employees." If a substitute's check was for $1,200, that person would cash the check, keep $200, and pay Art $1,000.

Total take: $150,000

THE MISSING CONTROLS

Human resource controls. Thorough background checks should be performed. No employees should begin work until they have been approved by the Board of Education and entered into the payroll system. No employees should be entered into the payroll system until they have been approved by a supervisor. All paychecks should be distributed directly to employees at the official school locations by designated employees.

Independent internal verification. Budgets should be reviewed monthly to identify situations where actual costs significantly exceed budgeted amounts.

Source: Adapted from Wells, *Fraud Casebook* (2007), pp. 164–171.

Employers also must provide each employee with a **Wage and Tax Statement (Form W-2)** by January 31 following the end of a calendar year. This statement shows gross earnings, FICA taxes withheld, and income taxes withheld for the year. The required W-2 form for Michael Jordan, using assumed annual data, is shown in Illustration 11-17. The employer must send a copy of each employee's Wage and Tax Statement (Form W-2) to the Social Security Administration. This agency subsequently furnishes the Internal Revenue Service with the income data required.

Internal Control for Payroll

Chapter 8 introduced internal control. As applied to payrolls, the objectives of internal control are (1) to safeguard company assets against unauthorized payments of payrolls, and (2) to ensure the accuracy and reliability of the accounting records pertaining to payrolls.

Irregularities often result if internal control is lax. Frauds involving payroll include overstating hours, using unauthorized pay rates, adding fictitious employees to the payroll, continuing terminated employees on the payroll, and

22222	Void ☐	a Employee's social security number 329-35-9547	For Official Use Only ► OMB No. 1545-0008

b Employer identification number (EIN) 36-2167852	1 Wages, tips, other compensation 26,300.00	2 Federal income tax withheld 2,248.00
c Employer's name, address, and ZIP code Academy Company 19 Center St. Hampton, MI 48291	3 Social security wages 26,300.00	4 Social security tax withheld 1,630.60
	5 Medicare wages and tips 26,300.00	6 Medicare tax withheld 381.35
	7 Social security tips	8 Allocated tips
d Control number	9 Advance EIC payment	10 Dependent care benefits
e Employee's first name and initial: Michael · Last name: Jordan · Suff.	11 Nonqualified plans	12a See instructions for box 12 Code
2345 Mifflin Ave. Hampton, MI 48292	13 Statutory employee ☐ Retirement plan ☐ Third-party sick pay ☐	12b Code
	14 Other	12c Code
f Employee's address and ZIP code		12d Code

15 State	Employer's state ID number	16 State wages, tips, etc.	17 State income tax	18 Local wages, tips, etc.	19 Local income tax	20 Locality name
MI	423-1466-3	26,300.00	526.00			

Form **W-2** **Wage and Tax Statement** **2017**

Department of the Treasury—Internal Revenue Service

For Privacy Act and Paperwork Reduction Act Notice, see back of Copy D.

Copy A For Social Security Administration — Send this entire page with Form W-3 to the Social Security Administration; photocopies are **not** acceptable.

Cat. No. 10134D

Illustration 11-17
W-2 form

distributing duplicate payroll checks. Moreover, inaccurate records will result in incorrect paychecks, financial statements, and payroll tax returns.

Payroll activities involve four functions: hiring employees, timekeeping, preparing the payroll, and paying the payroll. For effective internal control, companies should assign these four functions to different departments or individuals. Illustration 11-18 highlights these functions and illustrates their internal control features.

Illustration 11-18
Internal control for payroll

Payroll Function

Hiring Employees

Internal control feature: Human Resources department documents and authorizes employment.

Fraud prevented: Fictitious employees are not added to payroll.

Timekeeping

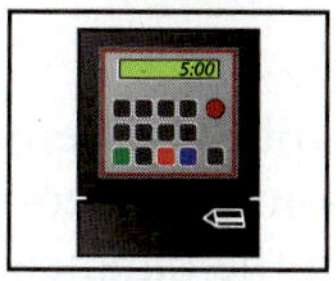

Internal control feature: Supervisors monitor hours worked through time cards and time reports.

Fraud prevented: Employee not paid for hours not worked.

Payroll Function

Preparing the Payroll

Internal control feature: Two (or more) employees verify payroll amounts; supervisor approves.

Fraud prevented: Payroll calculations are accurate and relevant.

Paying the Payroll

Internal control feature: Treasurer signs and distributes prenumbered checks.

Fraud prevented: Checks are not lost, misappropriated, or unavailable for proof of payment; endorsed check provides proof of payment.

DO IT! 3b Employer's Payroll Taxes

In January, the payroll supervisor determines that gross earnings for Halo Company are \$70,000. All earnings are subject to 7.65% FICA taxes, 5.4% state unemployment taxes, and 0.8% federal unemployment taxes. Halo asks you to record the employer's payroll taxes.

Action Plan

- ✔ Compute the employer's payroll taxes on the period's gross earnings.
- ✔ Identify the expense account(s) to be debited.
- ✔ Identify the liability account(s) to be credited.

Solution

The entry to record the employer's payroll taxes is:

Payroll Tax Expense	9,695	
FICA Taxes Payable (\$70,000 × 7.65%)		5,355
Federal Unemployment Taxes Payable (\$70,000 × 0.8%)		560
State Unemployment Taxes Payable (\$70,000 × 5.4%)		3,780
(To record employer's payroll taxes on January payroll)		

Related exercise material: **BE11-9, E11-11, E11-13, and DO IT! 11-3b.**

LEARNING OBJECTIVE *4

APPENDIX 11A: Discuss additional fringe benefits associated with employee compensation.

In addition to the traditional payroll-tax fringe benefits (Social Security taxes, Medicare taxes, and state and federal unemployment taxes), employers incur other substantial fringe benefit costs. Two of the most important are paid absences and postretirement benefits.

Paid Absences

Employees often are given rights to receive compensation for absences when they meet certain conditions of employment. The compensation may be for paid vacations, sick pay benefits, and paid holidays. When the payment for such absences is **probable** and the amount can be **reasonably estimated**, the company should accrue a liability for paid future absences. When the amount cannot be reasonably estimated, the company should instead disclose the potential liability. Ordinarily, vacation pay is the only paid absence that is accrued. The other types of paid absences are only disclosed.

To illustrate, assume that Academy Company employees are entitled to one day's vacation for each month worked. If 30 employees earn an average of \$110 per day in a given month, the accrual for vacation benefits in one month is \$3,300. Academy records the liability at the end of the month by the following adjusting entry.

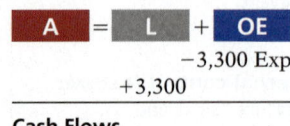

A	=	L	+	OE
				−3,300 Exp
		+3,300		

Cash Flows
no effect

Jan. 31	Vacation Benefits Expense	3,300	
	Vacation Benefits Payable		3,300
	(To accrue vacation benefits expense)		

This accrual is required by the expense recognition principle. Academy would report Vacation Benefits Expense as an operating expense in the income statement, and Vacation Benefits Payable as a current liability in the balance sheet.

Later, when Academy pays vacation benefits, it debits Vacation Benefits Payable and credits Cash. For example, if employees take 10 days of vacation in July, the entry is as follows.

July 31	Vacation Benefits Payable	1,100	
	Cash		1,100
	(To record payment of vacation benefits)		

A	=	L	+	OE
		−1,100		
−1,100				

Cash Flows
−1,100

The magnitude of unpaid absences has gained employers' attention. Consider the case of an assistant superintendent of schools who worked for 20 years and rarely took a vacation or sick day. A month or so before she retired, the school district discovered that she was due nearly $30,000 in accrued benefits. Yet the school district had never accrued the liability.

Postretirement Benefits

Postretirement benefits are benefits that employers provide to retired employees for (1) pensions and (2) healthcare and life insurance. Companies account for both types of postretirement benefits on the accrual basis. The cost of postretirement benefits is getting steep. For example, states and localities must deal with a $1 trillion deficit in public employees' retirement benefit funds. This shortfall amounts to more than $8,800 for every household in the nation.

Average Americans have debt of approximately $10,000 (not counting the mortgage on their home) and little in the way of savings. What will happen at retirement for these people? The picture is not pretty—people are living longer, the future of Social Security is unclear, and companies are cutting back on postretirement benefits. This situation may lead to one of the great social and moral dilemmas this country faces in the next 40 years. The more you know about postretirement benefits, the better you will understand the issues involved in this dilemma.

POSTRETIREMENT HEALTHCARE AND LIFE INSURANCE BENEFITS

Providing medical and related healthcare benefits for retirees was at one time an inexpensive and highly effective way of generating employee goodwill. This practice has now turned into one of corporate America's most worrisome financial problems. Runaway medical costs, early retirement, and increased longevity are sending the liability for retiree health plans through the roof.

Companies estimate and expense postretirement costs during the working years of the employee because the company benefits from the employee's services during this period. However, the company rarely sets up funds to meet the cost of the future benefits. It follows a pay-as-you-go basis for these costs. The major reason is that the company does not receive a tax deduction until it actually pays the medical bill.

PENSION PLANS

A **pension plan** is an agreement whereby an employer provides benefits (payments) to employees after they retire. The need for good accounting for pension plans becomes apparent when we consider the size of existing pension funds. Over 50 million workers currently participate in pension plans in the United States. Most pension plans are subject to the provisions of ERISA (Employee Retirement Income Security Act), a law enacted to curb abuses in the administration and funding of such plans.

Three parties are generally involved in a pension plan. The **employer** (company) sponsors the pension plan. The **plan administrator** receives the contributions from the employer, invests the pension assets, and makes the benefit payments to the **pension recipients** (retired employees). Illustration 11A-1 (page 512) indicates the flow of cash among the three parties involved in a pension plan.

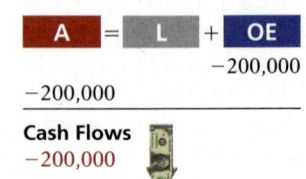

Illustration 11A-1
Parties in a pension plan

An employer-financed pension is part of the employees' compensation. ERISA establishes the minimum contribution that a company must make each year toward employee pensions. The most popular type of pension plan used is the 401(k) plan. A 401(k) plan works as follows. As an employee, you can contribute up to a certain percentage of your pay into a 401(k) plan, and your employer will match a percentage of your contribution. These contributions are then generally invested in stocks and bonds through mutual funds. These funds will grow without being taxed and can be withdrawn beginning at age 59-1/2. If you must access the funds earlier, you may be able to do so, but a penalty usually occurs along with a payment of tax on the proceeds. Any time you have the opportunity to be involved in a 401(k) plan, you should avail yourself of this benefit!

Companies record pension costs as an expense while the employees are working because that is when the company receives benefits from the employees' services. Generally, the pension expense is reported as an operating expense in the company's income statement. Frequently, the amount contributed by the company to the pension plan is different from the amount of the pension expense. A **liability** is recognized when the pension expense to date is **more than** the company's contributions to date. An **asset** is recognized when the pension expense to date is **less than** the company's contributions to date. Further consideration of the accounting for pension plans is left for more advanced courses.

The two most common types of pension arrangements for providing benefits to employees after they retire are defined-contribution plans and defined-benefit plans.

DEFINED-CONTRIBUTION PLAN In a **defined-contribution plan**, the plan defines the employer's contribution but not the benefit that the employee will receive at retirement. That is, the employer agrees to contribute a certain sum each period based on a formula. A 401(k) plan is typically a defined-contribution plan.

The accounting for a defined-contribution plan is straightforward. The employer simply makes a contribution each year based on the formula established in the plan. As a result, the employer's obligation is easily determined. It follows that the company reports **the amount of the contribution required each period as pension expense. The employer reports a liability only if it has not made the contribution in full.**

To illustrate, assume that Alba Office Interiors has a defined-contribution plan in which it contributes $200,000 each year to the pension fund for its employees. The entry to record this transaction is:

A	=	L	+	OE
				−200,000
−200,000				

Cash Flows
−200,000

Pension Expense	200,000	
Cash		200,000
(To record pension expense and contribution to pension fund)		

To the extent that Alba did not contribute the $200,000 defined contribution, it would record a liability. Pension payments to retired employees are made from the pension fund by the plan administrator.

DEFINED-BENEFIT PLAN In a **defined-benefit plan**, the **benefits** that the employee will receive at the time of retirement are defined by the terms of the plan. Benefits are typically calculated using a formula that considers an employee's compensation level when he or she nears retirement and the employee's years of service. Because the benefits in this plan are defined in terms of uncertain future variables, an appropriate funding pattern is established to ensure that enough funds are available at retirement to meet the benefits promised. This funding level depends on a number of factors such as employee turnover, length of service, mortality, compensation levels, and investment earnings. **The proper accounting for these plans is complex and is considered in more advanced accounting courses.**

POSTRETIREMENT BENEFITS AS LONG-TERM LIABILITIES

While part of the liability associated with (1) postretirement healthcare and life insurance benefits and (2) pension plans is generally a current liability, the greater portion of these liabilities extends many years into the future. Therefore, many companies are required to report significant amounts as long-term liabilities for postretirement benefits.

REVIEW AND PRACTICE

LEARNING OBJECTIVES REVIEW

1 Explain how to account for current liabilities. A current liability is a debt that a company expects to pay within one year or the operating cycle, whichever is longer. The major types of current liabilities are notes payable, accounts payable, sales taxes payable, unearned revenues, and accrued liabilities such as taxes, salaries and wages, and interest payable.

When a promissory note is interest-bearing, the amount of assets received upon the issuance of the note is generally equal to the face value of the note. Interest expense accrues over the life of the note. At maturity, the amount paid equals the face value of the note plus accrued interest.

Companies record sales taxes payable at the time the related sales occur. The company serves as a collection agent for the taxing authority. Sales taxes are not an expense to the company. Companies initially record unearned revenues in an Unearned Revenue account. As a company recognizes revenue, a transfer from unearned revenue to revenue occurs. Companies report the current maturities of long-term debt as a current liability in the balance sheet.

2 Discuss how current liabilities are reported and analyzed. With notes payable, interest payable, accounts payable, and sales taxes payable, an obligation to make a payment exists. In some cases, it is difficult to determine whether a liability exists. These situations are called contingent liabilities. If the contingency is **probable** (likely to occur) and the amount is reasonably estimable, the company should record the liability in the accounts. If the contingency is only **reasonably possible** (it could happen), then it should be disclosed only in the notes to the financial statements. If the possibility that the contingency will happen is **remote** (unlikely to occur), it need not be recorded or disclosed.

Companies should report the nature and amount of each current liability in the balance sheet or in schedules in the notes accompanying the statements. The liquidity of a company may be analyzed by computing working capital and the current ratio.

3 Explain how to account for payroll. The computation of the payroll involves gross earnings, payroll deductions, and net pay. In recording the payroll, companies debit Salaries and Wages Expense for gross earnings, credit individual tax and other liability accounts for payroll deductions, and credit Salaries and Wages Payable for net pay. When the payroll is paid, companies debit Salaries and Wages Payable and credit Cash.

Employer payroll taxes consist of FICA, federal unemployment taxes, and state unemployment taxes. The taxes are usually accrued at the time the company records the payroll, by debiting Payroll Tax Expense and crediting separate liability accounts for each type of tax.

The objectives of internal control for payroll are (1) to safeguard company assets against unauthorized payments of payrolls, and (2) to ensure the accuracy of the accounting records pertaining to payrolls.

*4 **Discuss additional fringe benefits associated with employee compensation.** Additional fringe benefits associated with wages are paid absences (paid vacations, sick pay benefits, and paid holidays), and postretirement benefits (pensions, healthcare, and life insurance).

GLOSSARY REVIEW

Bonus Compensation to management and other personnel, based on factors such as increased sales or the amount of net income. (p. 500).

Contingent liability A potential liability that may become an actual liability in the future. (p. 495).

Current ratio A measure of a company's liquidity; computed as current assets divided by current liabilities. (p. 498).

***Defined-benefit plan** A pension plan in which the benefits that the employee will receive at retirement are defined by the terms of the plan. (p. 513).

***Defined-contribution plan** A pension plan in which the employer's contribution to the plan is defined by the terms of the plan. (p. 512).

Employee earnings record A cumulative record of each employee's gross earnings, deductions, and net pay during the year. (p. 503).

Federal unemployment taxes Taxes imposed on the employer by the federal government that provide benefits for a limited time period to employees who lose their jobs through no fault of their own. (p. 506).

Fees Payments made for the services of professionals. (p. 499).

FICA taxes Taxes designed to provide workers with supplemental retirement, employment disability, and medical benefits. (p. 501).

Gross earnings Total compensation earned by an employee. (p. 499).

Net pay Gross earnings less payroll deductions. (p. 502).

Notes payable Obligations in the form of written notes. (p. 492).

Payroll deductions Deductions from gross earnings to determine the amount of a paycheck. (p. 500).

Payroll register A payroll record that accumulates the gross earnings, deductions, and net pay by employee for each pay period. (p. 503).

***Pension plan** An agreement whereby an employer provides benefits to employees after they retire. (p. 511).

***Postretirement benefits** Payments by employers to retired employees for healthcare, life insurance, and pensions. (p. 511).

Salaries Employee pay based on a specified amount rather than an hourly rate. (p. 499).

Statement of earnings A document attached to a paycheck that indicates the employee's gross earnings, payroll deductions, and net pay. (p. 504).

State unemployment taxes Taxes imposed on the employer by states that provide benefits to employees who lose their jobs. (p. 506).

Wage and Tax Statement (Form W-2) A form showing gross earnings, FICA taxes withheld, and income taxes withheld, prepared annually by an employer for each employee. (p. 508).

Wages Amounts paid to employees based on a rate per hour or on a piecework basis. (p. 499).

Working capital A measure of a company's liquidity; computed as current assets minus current liabilities. (p. 498).

PRACTICE MULTIPLE-CHOICE QUESTIONS

(LO 1) 1. The time period for classifying a liability as current is one year or the operating cycle, whichever is:
(a) longer.
(b) shorter.
(c) probable.
(d) possible.

(LO 1) 2. To be classified as a current liability, a debt must be expected to be paid within:
(a) one year.
(b) the operating cycle.
(c) 2 years.
(d) (a) or (b), whichever is longer.

3. Maggie Sharrer Company borrows $88,500 on September 1, 2017, from Sandwich State Bank by signing an $88,500, 12%, one-year note. What is the accrued interest at December 31, 2017? (LO 1)
(a) $2,655.
(b) $3,540.
(c) $4,425.
(d) $10,620.

4. RS Company borrowed $70,000 on December 1 on a 6-month, 6% note. At December 31: (LO 1)
(a) neither the note payable nor the interest payable is a current liability.

(b) the note payable is a current liability, but the interest payable is not.
(c) the interest payable is a current liability but the note payable is not.
(d) both the note payable and the interest payable are current liabilities.

(LO 1) **5.** Becky Sherrick Company has total proceeds from sales of $4,515. If the proceeds include sales taxes of 5%, the amount to be credited to Sales Revenue is:
(a) $4,000.
(b) $4,300.
(c) $4,289.25.
(d) No correct answer given.

(LO 1) **6.** Sensible Insurance Company collected a premium of $18,000 for a 1-year insurance policy on April 1. What amount should Sensible report as a current liability for Unearned Service Revenue at December 31?
(a) $0.
(b) $4,500.
(c) $13,500.
(d) $18,000.

(LO 2) **7.** Working capital is calculated as:
(a) current assets minus current liabilities.
(b) total assets minus total liabilities.
(c) long-term liabilities minus current liabilities.
(d) Both (b) and (c).

(LO 2) **8.** The current ratio is computed as:
(a) total assets divided by total liabilities.
(b) total assets divided by current liabilities.
(c) current assets divided by total liabilities.
(d) current assets divided by current liabilities.

(LO 2) **9.** A contingent liability should be recorded in the accounts when:
(a) it is probable the contingency will happen, but the amount cannot be reasonably estimated.
(b) it is reasonably possible the contingency will happen, and the amount can be reasonably estimated.
(c) it is probable the contingency will happen, and the amount can be reasonably estimated.
(d) it is reasonably possible the contingency will happen, but the amount cannot be reasonably estimated.

10. At December 31, Hanes Company prepares an adjusting entry for a product warranty contract. Which of the following accounts is/are included in the entry? (LO 2)
(a) Miscellaneous Expense.
(b) Warranty Liability.
(c) Repair Parts.
(d) Both (a) and (b).

11. Andy Manion earns $14 per hour for a 40-hour week and $21 per hour for any overtime work. If Manion works 45 hours in a week, gross earnings are: (LO 3)
(a) $560.
(b) $630.
(c) $650.
(d) $665.

12. When recording payroll: (LO 3)
(a) gross earnings are recorded as salaries and wages payable.
(b) net pay is recorded as salaries and wages expense.
(c) payroll deductions are recorded as liabilities.
(d) More than one of the above.

13. Employer payroll taxes do **not** include: (LO 3)
(a) federal unemployment taxes.
(b) state unemployment taxes.
(c) federal income taxes.
(d) FICA taxes.

14. FICA Taxes Payable was credited for $7,500 in the entry when Antonio Company recorded payroll. When Antonio Company records employer's payroll taxes, FICA Taxes Payable should be credited for: (LO 3)
(a) $0.
(b) $7,500.
(c) $15,000.
(d) Some other amount.

15. The department that should pay the payroll is the: (LO 3)
(a) timekeeping department.
(b) human resources department.
(c) payroll department.
(d) treasurer's department.

***16.** Which of the following is **not** an additional fringe benefit? (LO 4)
(a) Postretirement pensions.
(b) Paid absences.
(c) Paid vacations.
(d) Salaries.

Solutions

1. (a) The time period for classifying a liability as current is one year or the operating cycle, whichever is longer, not (b) shorter, (c) probable, or (d) possible.

2. (d) To be classified as a current liability, a debt must be expected to be paid within one year or the operating cycle. Choices (a) and (b) are both correct, but (d) is the better answer. Choice (c) is incorrect.

3. (b) Accrued interest at December 31, 2017, is computed as the face value ($88,500) times the interest rate (12%) times the portion of the year the debt was outstanding (4 months out of 12), or $3,540 ($88,500 × 12% × 4/12), not (a) $2,655, (c) $4,425, or (d) $10,620.

4. (d) Both the note payable and interest payable are current liabilities. Notes due for payment within one year of the balance sheet date are usually classified as current liabilities. The other choices are therefore incorrect.

5. (b) Dividing the total proceeds ($4,515) by one plus the sales tax rate (1.05) will result in the amount of sales to be credited to the Sales Revenue account of $4,300 ($4,515 ÷ 1.05). The other choices are therefore incorrect.

6. (b) The monthly premium is $1,500 or $18,000 divided by 12. Because Sensible has recognized 9 months of insurance revenue (April 1–December 31), 3 months' insurance premium is still unearned. The amount that Sensible should report as Unearned Service Revenue is therefore $4,500 (3 months × $1,500), not (a) $0, (c) $13,500, or (d) $18,000.

7. (a) Working capital is defined as current assets minus current liabilities. The other choices are therefore incorrect.

8. (d) The current ratio is defined as current assets divided by current liabilities. The other choices are therefore incorrect.

9. (c) A contingent liability is recorded when the amount can be reasonably estimated and the likelihood of the contingency is probable. The other choices are therefore incorrect.

10. (b) The adjusting entry for product warranties includes a debit to Warranty Liability, not (a) Miscellaneous Expense, (c) Repair Parts, or (d) both Miscellaneous Expense and Warranty Liability.

11. (d) Gross earnings are computed as (40 hours × $14 per hour) + (5 hours × $21 per hour) = $665, not (a) $560, (b) $630, or (c) $650.

12. (c) When recording payroll, payroll deductions are recorded as liabilities. The other choices are incorrect because (a) gross earnings are recorded as salaries and wages expense, (b) net pay is recorded as salaries and wages payable, and (d) only one of the answer choices is true concerning payroll.

13. (c) Federal income taxes are a payroll deduction, not an employer payroll tax. The employer is merely a collection agent. The other choices are all included in employer payroll taxes.

14. (b) Each employee pays FICA taxes, but the employer must match each employee's FICA contribution. Because the employer's tax is subject to the same rate and maximum earnings as the employee's, FICA Taxes Payable would also be $7,500. The other choices are therefore incorrect.

15. (d) The treasurer's department pays or distributes the payroll checks. The other choices are incorrect because (a) the timekeeping department monitors hours worked by employees, (b) the human resources department documents and authorizes employment, and (c) the payroll department prepares the payroll checks.

***16. (d)** Salaries are not an additional fringe benefit. The other choices are true statements.

PRACTICE EXERCISES

Prepare entries for interest-bearing notes.

(LO 1)

1. On June 1, Streamsong Company borrows $150,000 from First Bank on a 6-month, $150,000, 8% note.

Instructions

(a) Prepare the entry on June 1.

(b) Prepare the adjusting entry on June 30.

(c) Prepare the entry at maturity (December 1), assuming monthly adjusting entries have been made through November 30.

(d) What was the total financing cost (interest expense)?

Solution

1. (a) June 1	Cash	150,000	
	Notes Payable		150,000
(b) June 30	Interest Expense	1,000	
	Interest Payable		
	($150,000 × 8% × 1/12)		1,000
(c) Dec. 1	Notes Payable	150,000	
	Interest Payable		
	($150,000 × 8% × 6/12)	6,000	
	Cash		156,000
(d) $6,000			

Prepare current liabilities section of the balance sheet and evaluate liquidity.

(LO 2)

2. Fun App Company has the following liability accounts after posting adjusting entries: Accounts Payable $77,000, Unearned Ticket Revenue $36,000, Warranty Liability $25,000, Interest Payable $10,000, Mortgage Payable $150,000, Notes Payable $100,000, and Sales Taxes Payable $14,000. Assume the company's operating cycle is less than 1 year, ticket revenue will be recognized within 1 year, warranty costs are expected to be incurred within 1 year, and the notes mature in 3 years.

Instructions

(a) Prepare the current liabilities section of the balance sheet, assuming $40,000 of the mortgage is payable next year.

(b) Comment on Fun App Company's liquidity, assuming total current assets are $350,000.

Solution

2. (a)

FUN APP COMPANY
Partial Balance Sheet

Current liabilities	
Long-term debt due within one year	$ 40,000
Accounts payable	77,000
Unearned ticket revenue	36,000
Warranty liability	25,000
Sales taxes payable	14,000
Interest payable	10,000
Total current liabilities	$202,000

(b) Fun App Company's working capital is $148,000 ($350,000 − $202,000), and its current ratio is 1.73:1 ($350,000 ÷ $202,000). Although a current ratio of 2:1 has been considered the standard for a good credit rating, many companies operate successfully with a current ratio well below 2:1.

3. Erin Berge's regular hourly wage rate is $18, and she receives a wage of 1½ times the regular hourly rate for work in excess of 40 hours. During a March weekly pay period, Erin worked 42 hours. Her gross earnings prior to the current week were $6,000. Erin is married and claims three withholding allowances. Her only voluntary deduction is for group hospitalization insurance at $20 per week. Assume federal income tax withheld is $76.

Compute net pay and record pay for one employee.

(LO 3)

Instructions

(a) Compute the following amounts for Erin's wages for the current week.
  (1) Gross earnings.
  (2) FICA taxes (based on a 7.65% rate).
  (3) State income taxes withheld (based on a 3% rate).
  (4) Net pay.

(b) Record Erin's pay.

Solution

3. (a) (1) Regular 40 hours × $18 = $720
Overtime 2 hours × $27 = 54
Gross earnings $774

(2) FICA taxes: ($774 × 7.65%) = $59.21
(3) State income taxes: ($774 × 3%) = $23.22
(4) Net Pay: ($774.00 − $59.21 − $76.00 − $23.22 −$20.00) = $595.57

(b)

Salaries and Wages Expense	774.00	
FICA Taxes Payable		59.21
Federal Income Taxes Payable		76.00
State Income Taxes Payable		23.22
Health Insurance Payable		20.00
Salaries and Wages Payable		595.57

PRACTICE PROBLEM

Indiana Jones Company had the following selected transactions.

Feb. 1 Signs a $50,000, 6-month, 9%-interest-bearing note payable to CitiBank and receives $50,000 in cash.

10 Cash register sales total $43,200, which includes an 8% sales tax.

28 The payroll for the month consists of salaries and wages of $50,000. All wages are subject to 7.65% FICA taxes. A total of $8,900 federal income taxes are withheld. The salaries are paid on March 1.

28 The company develops the following adjustment data.

1. Interest expense of $375 has been incurred on the note.
2. Employer payroll taxes include 7.65% FICA taxes, a 5.4% state unemployment tax, and a 0.8% federal unemployment tax.
3. Some sales were made under warranty. Of the units sold under warranty, 350 are expected to become defective. Repair costs are estimated to be $40 per unit.

Instructions

(a) Journalize the February transactions.

(b) Journalize the adjusting entries at February 28.

Solution

(a) Feb. 1	Cash	50,000	
	Notes Payable		50,000
	(Issued 6-month, 9%-interest-bearing note to CitiBank)		
10	Cash	43,200	
	Sales Revenue ($43,200 ÷ 1.08)		40,000
	Sales Taxes Payable ($40,000 × 8%)		3,200
	(To record sales revenue and sales taxes payable)		
28	Salaries and Wages Expense	50,000	
	FICA Taxes Payable (7.65% × $50,000)		3,825
	Federal Income Taxes Payable		8,900
	Salaries and Wages Payable		37,275
	(To record February salaries)		
(b) Feb. 28	Interest Expense	375	
	Interest Payable		375
	(To record accrued interest for February)		
28	Payroll Tax Expense	6,925	
	FICA Taxes Payable		3,825
	Federal Unemployment Taxes Payable (0.8% × $50,000)		400
	State Unemployment Taxes Payable (5.4% × $50,000)		2,700
	(To record employer's payroll taxes on February payroll)		
28	Warranty Expense (350 × $40)	14,000	
	Warranty Liability		14,000
	(To record estimated warranty liability)		

WileyPLUS Brief Exercises, Exercises, DO IT! Exercises, and Problems and many additional resources are available for practice in WileyPLUS

NOTE: All asterisked Questions, Exercises, and Problems relate to material in the appendix to the chapter.

QUESTIONS

1. Lori Randle believes a current liability is a debt that can be expected to be paid in one year. Is Lori correct? Explain.

2. Petrocelli Company obtains $40,000 in cash by signing a 7%, 6-month, $40,000 note payable to First Bank on July 1. Petrocelli's fiscal year ends on September 30.

What information should be reported for the note payable in the annual financial statements?

3. (a) Your roommate says, "Sales taxes are reported as an expense in the income statement." Do you agree? Explain.
   (b) Jensen Company has cash proceeds from sales of $8,400. This amount includes $400 of sales taxes. Give the entry to record the proceeds.
4. Ottawa University sold 15,000 season football tickets at $80 each for its six-game home schedule. What entries should be made (a) when the tickets were sold, and (b) after each game?
5. What is liquidity? What are two measures of liquidity?
6. What is a contingent liability? Give an example of a contingent liability that is usually recorded in the accounts.
7. Under what circumstances is a contingent liability disclosed only in the notes to the financial statements? Under what circumstances is a contingent liability not recorded in the accounts nor disclosed in the notes to the financial statements?
8. What is the difference between gross pay and net pay? Which amount should a company record as wages and salaries expense?
9. Which payroll tax is levied on both employers and employees?
10. Are the federal and state income taxes withheld from employee paychecks a payroll tax expense for the employer? Explain your answer.
11. What do the following acronyms stand for: FICA, FUTA, and SUTA?
12. What information is shown in a W-2 statement?
13. Distinguish between the two types of payroll deductions and give examples of each.
14. What are the primary uses of the employee earnings record?
15. (a) Identify the three types of employer payroll taxes.
    (b) How are tax liability accounts and payroll tax expense accounts classified in the financial statements?
16. You are a newly hired accountant with Nolasco Company. On your first day, the controller asks you to identify the main internal control objectives related to payroll accounting. How would you respond?
17. What are the four functions associated with payroll activities?

*18. Identify two additional types of fringe benefits associated with employees' compensation.

*19. Often during job interviews, the candidate asks the potential employer about the firm's paid absences policy. What are paid absences? How are they accounted for?

*20. What are two types of postretirement benefits?

*21. Explain how a 401(k) plan works.

*22. What is the principal difference between a defined-contribution pension plan and a defined-benefit pension plan?

BRIEF EXERCISES

BE11-1 Jamison Company has the following obligations at December 31: (a) a note payable for $100,000 due in 2 years, (b) a 10-year mortgage payable of $300,000 payable in ten $30,000 annual payments, (c) interest payable of $15,000 on the mortgage, and (d) accounts payable of $60,000. For each obligation, indicate whether it should be classified as a current liability. (Assume an operating cycle of less than one year.)

Identify whether obligations are current liabilities.

(LO 1)

BE11-2 Peralta Company borrows $60,000 on July 1 from the bank by signing a $60,000, 10%, one-year note payable.

(a) Prepare the journal entry to record the proceeds of the note.

(b) Prepare the journal entry to record accrued interest at December 31, assuming adjusting entries are made only at the end of the year.

Prepare entries for an interest-bearing note payable.

(LO 1)

BE11-3 Coghlan Auto Supply does not segregate sales and sales taxes at the time of sale. The register total for March 16 is $16,380. All sales are subject to a 5% sales tax. Compute sales taxes payable, and make the entry to record sales taxes payable and sales revenue.

Compute and record sales taxes payable.

(LO 1)

BE11-4 Derby University sells 4,000 season basketball tickets at $210 each for its 12-game home schedule. Give the entry to record (a) the sale of the season tickets and (b) the revenue recognized by playing the first home game.

Prepare entries for unearned revenues.

(LO 1)

BE11-5 Yahoo! Inc.'s recent financial statements contain the following selected data (in thousands).

Current assets	$ 4,594,772	Current liabilities	$1,717,728
Total assets	14,936,030	Total liabilities	2,417,394

Compute (a) working capital and (b) current ratio.

Analyze liquidity.

(LO 2)

BE11-6 On December 1, Bruney Company introduces a new product that includes a one-year warranty on parts. In December, 1,000 units are sold. Management believes that 5% of the units will be defective and that the average warranty costs will be $90 per unit. Prepare the adjusting entry at December 31 to accrue the estimated warranty cost.

Prepare adjusting entry for warranty costs.

(LO 2)

Compute gross earnings and net pay.
(LO 3)

BE11-7 Beth Corbin's regular hourly wage rate is $16, and she receives an hourly rate of $24 for work in excess of 40 hours. During a January pay period, Beth works 45 hours. Beth's federal income tax withholding is $95, she has no voluntary deductions, and the FICA tax rate is 7.65%. Compute Beth Corbin's gross earnings and net pay for the pay period.

Record a payroll and the payment of wages.
(LO 3)

BE11-8 Data for Beth Corbin are presented in BE11-7. Prepare the journal entries to record (a) Beth's pay for the period and (b) the payment of Beth's wages. Use January 15 for the end of the pay period and the payment date.

Record employer payroll taxes.
(LO 3)

BE11-9 In January, gross earnings in Lugo Company totaled $80,000. All earnings are subject to 7.65% FICA taxes, 5.4% state unemployment taxes, and 0.8% federal unemployment taxes. Prepare the entry to record January payroll tax expense.

Identify payroll functions.
(LO 3)

BE11-10 Swenson Company has the following payroll procedures.

(a) Supervisor approves overtime work.
(b) The human resources department prepares hiring authorization forms for new hires.
(c) A second payroll department employee verifies payroll calculations.
(d) The treasurer's department pays employees.

Identify the payroll function to which each procedure pertains.

Record estimated vacation benefits.
(LO 4)

***BE11-11** At Ward Company, employees are entitled to one day's vacation for each month worked. In January, 70 employees worked the full month. Record the vacation pay liability for January, assuming the average daily pay for each employee is $120.

DO IT! Exercises

Answer questions about current liabilities.
(LO 1)

DO IT! 11-1 You and several classmates are studying for the next accounting exam. They ask you to answer the following questions:

1. If cash is borrowed on a $70,000, 9-month, 6% note on August 1, how much interest expense would be incurred by December 31?
2. The cash register total including sales taxes is $42,000, and the sales tax rate is 5%. What is the sales taxes payable?
3. If $45,000 is collected in advance on November 1 for 6-month magazine subscriptions, what amount of subscription revenue should be recognized by December 31?

Prepare current liabilities section and compute liquidity measures.
(LO 2)

DO IT! 11-2 Medlen Company, has the following account balances at December 31, 2017.

Notes payable ($60,000 due after 12/31/18)	$100,000
Unearned service revenue	70,000
Other long-term debt ($90,000 due in 2018)	250,000
Salaries and wages payable	32,000
Accounts payable	63,000

In addition, Medlen is involved in a lawsuit. Legal counsel feels it is probable Medlen will pay damages of $25,000 in 2018.

(a) Prepare the current liabilities section of Medlen's December 31, 2017, balance sheet.
(b) Medlen's current assets are $570,000. Compute Medlen's working capital and current ratio.

Calculate net pay and record payroll.
(LO 3)

DO IT! 11-3a In January, gross earnings in Burrell Company were $80,000. All earnings are subject to 7.65% FICA taxes. Federal income tax withheld was $14,000, and state income tax withheld was $1,600. (a) Calculate net pay for January, and (b) record the payroll.

Record employer's payroll taxes.
(LO 3)

DO IT! 11-3b In January, the payroll supervisor determines that gross earnings for Carlyle Company are $120,000. All earnings are subject to 7.65% FICA taxes, 5.4% state unemployment taxes, and 0.8% federal unemployment taxes. Record the employer's payroll taxes.

EXERCISES

E11-1 C.S. Lewis Company had the following transactions involving notes payable.

Prepare entries for interest-bearing notes.

(LO 1)

July 1, 2017	Borrows $50,000 from First National Bank by signing a 9-month, 8% note.
Nov. 1, 2017	Borrows $60,000 from Lyon County State Bank by signing a 3-month, 6% note.
Dec. 31, 2017	Prepares adjusting entries.
Feb. 1, 2018	Pays principal and interest to Lyon County State Bank.
Apr. 1, 2018	Pays principal and interest to First National Bank.

Instructions

Prepare journal entries for each of the transactions.

E11-2 On June 1, Merando Company borrows $90,000 from First Bank on a 6-month, $90,000, 8% note.

Prepare entries for interest-bearing notes.

(LO 1)

Instructions

(a) Prepare the entry on June 1.
(b) Prepare the adjusting entry on June 30.
(c) Prepare the entry at maturity (December 1), assuming monthly adjusting entries have been made through November 30.
(d) What was the total financing cost (interest expense)?

E11-3 In performing accounting services for small businesses, you encounter the following situations pertaining to cash sales.

Journalize sales and related taxes.

(LO 1)

1. Poole Company enters sales and sales taxes separately on its cash register. On April 10, the register totals are sales $30,000 and sales taxes $1,500.
2. Waterman Company does not segregate sales and sales taxes. Its register total for April 15 is $25,680, which includes a 7% sales tax.

Instructions

Prepare the entry to record the sales transactions and related taxes for each client.

E11-4 Moreno Company publishes a monthly sports magazine, *Fishing Preview*. Subscriptions to the magazine cost $20 per year. During November 2017, Moreno sells 15,000 subscriptions beginning with the December issue. Moreno prepares financial statements quarterly and recognizes subscription revenue at the end of the quarter. The company uses the accounts Unearned Subscription Revenue and Subscription Revenue.

Journalize unearned subscription revenue.

(LO 1)

Instructions

(a) Prepare the entry in November for the receipt of the subscriptions.
(b) Prepare the adjusting entry at December 31, 2017, to record sales revenue recognized in December 2017.
(c) Prepare the adjusting entry at March 31, 2018, to record sales revenue recognized in the first quarter of 2018.

E11-5 Betancourt Company sells automatic can openers under a 75-day warranty for defective merchandise. Based on past experience, Betancourt estimates that 3% of the units sold will become defective during the warranty period. Management estimates that the average cost of replacing or repairing a defective unit is $15. The units sold and units defective that occurred during the last 2 months of 2017 are as follows.

Record estimated liability and expense for warranties.

(LO 2)

Month	Units Sold	Units Defective Prior to December 31
November	30,000	600
December	32,000	400

Instructions

(a) Prepare the journal entries to record the estimated liability for warranties and the costs incurred in honoring 1,000 warranty claims. (Assume actual costs of $15,000.)
(b) Determine the estimated warranty liability at December 31 for the units sold in November and December.
(c) Give the entry to record the honoring of 500 warranty contracts in January at an average cost of $15.

Record and disclose contingent liabilities.

(LO 2)

E11-6 Gallardo Co. is involved in a lawsuit as a result of an accident that took place September 5, 2017. The lawsuit was filed on November 1, 2017, and claims damages of $1,000,000.

Instructions

(a) At December 31, 2017, Gallardo's attorneys feel it is remote that Gallardo will lose the lawsuit. How should the company account for the effects of the lawsuit?

(b) Assume instead that at December 31, 2017, Gallardo's attorneys feel it is probable that Gallardo will lose the lawsuit and be required to pay $1,000,000. How should the company account for this lawsuit?

(c) Assume instead that at December 31, 2017, Gallardo's attorneys feel it is reasonably possible that Gallardo could lose the lawsuit and be required to pay $1,000,000. How should the company account for this lawsuit?

Prepare the current liabilities section of the balance sheet.

(LO 2)

E11-7 Younger Online Company has the following liability accounts after posting adjusting entries: Accounts Payable $73,000, Unearned Ticket Revenue $24,000, Warranty Liability $18,000, Interest Payable $8,000, Mortgage Payable $120,000, Notes Payable $80,000, and Sales Taxes Payable $10,000. Assume the company's operating cycle is less than 1 year, ticket revenue will be recognized within 1 year, warranty costs are expected to be incurred within 1 year, and the notes mature in 3 years.

Instructions

(a) Prepare the current liabilities section of the balance sheet, assuming $30,000 of the mortgage is payable next year.

(b) Comment on Younger Online Company's liquidity, assuming total current assets are $300,000.

Calculate current ratio and working capital before and after paying accounts payable.

(LO 2)

E11-8 Suppose the following financial data were reported by 3M Company for 2016 and 2017 (dollars in millions).

3M COMPANY
Balance Sheets (partial)

	2017	**2016**
Current assets		
Cash and cash equivalents	$ 3,040	$1,849
Accounts receivable, net	3,250	3,195
Inventories	2,639	3,013
Other current assets	1,866	1,541
Total current assets	$10,795	$9,598
Current liabilities	$ 4,897	$5,839

Instructions

(a) Calculate the current ratio and working capital for 3M for 2016 and 2017.

(b) Suppose that at the end of 2017, 3M management used $200 million cash to pay off $200 million of accounts payable. How would its current ratio and working capital have changed?

Compute net pay and record pay for one employee.

(LO 3)

E11-9 Maria Garza's regular hourly wage rate is $16, and she receives a wage of 1½ times the regular hourly rate for work in excess of 40 hours. During a March weekly pay period, Maria worked 42 hours. Her gross earnings prior to the current week were $6,000. Maria is married and claims three withholding allowances. Her only voluntary deduction is for group hospitalization insurance at $25 per week.

Instructions

(a) Compute the following amounts for Maria's wages for the current week.
   (1) Gross earnings.
   (2) FICA taxes. (Assume a 7.65% rate on maximum of $117,000.)
   (3) Federal income taxes withheld. (Use the withholding table in the text, page 502.)
   (4) State income taxes withheld. (Assume a 2.0% rate.)
   (5) Net pay.

(b) Record Maria's pay.

Compute maximum FICA deductions. (LO 3)

E11-10 Employee earnings records for Slaymaker Company reveal the following gross earnings for four employees through the pay period of December 15.

J. Seligman	$93,500	L. Marshall	$115,100
R. Eby	$113,600	T. Olson	$120,000

For the pay period ending December 31, each employee's gross earnings is $4,500. The FICA tax rate is 7.65% on gross earnings of $117,000.

Instructions

Compute the FICA withholdings that should be made for each employee for the December 31 pay period. (Show computations.)

Prepare payroll register and record payroll and payroll tax expense. (LO 3)

E11-11 Ramirez Company has the following data for the weekly payroll ending January 31.

	Hours							Federal	
Employee	**M**	**T**	**W**	**T**	**F**	**S**	**Hourly Rate**	**Income Tax Withholding**	**Health Insurance**
L. Helton	8	8	9	8	10	3	$12	$34	$10
R. Kenseth	8	8	8	8	8	2	14	37	25
D. Tavaras	9	10	8	8	9	0	15	58	25

Employees are paid 1½ times the regular hourly rate for all hours worked in excess of 40 hours per week. FICA taxes are 7.65% on the first $117,000 of gross earnings. Ramirez Company is subject to 5.4% state unemployment taxes and 0.8% federal unemployment taxes on the first $7,000 of gross earnings.

Instructions

(a) Prepare the payroll register for the weekly payroll.
(b) Prepare the journal entries to record the payroll and Ramirez's payroll tax expense.

Compute missing payroll amounts and record payroll. (LO 3)

E11-12 Selected data from a February payroll register for Sutton Company are presented below. Some amounts are intentionally omitted.

Gross earnings:		State income taxes	$ (3)
Regular	$9,100	Union dues	100
Overtime	(1)	Total deductions	(4)
Total	(2)	Net pay	$7,595
Deductions:		Account debited:	
FICA taxes	$ 765	Salaries and wages expense	(5)
Federal income taxes	1,140		

FICA taxes are 7.65%. State income taxes are 4% of gross earnings.

Instructions

(a) Fill in the missing amounts.
(b) Journalize the February payroll and the payment of the payroll.

Determine employer's payroll taxes; record payroll tax expense. (LO 3)

E11-13 According to a payroll register summary of Frederickson Company, the amount of employees' gross pay in December was $850,000, of which $80,000 was not subject to Social Security taxes of 6.2% and $750,000 was not subject to state and federal unemployment taxes.

Instructions

(a) Determine the employer's payroll tax expense for the month, using the following rates: FICA 7.65%, state unemployment 5.4%, and federal unemployment 0.8%.
(b) Prepare the journal entry to record December payroll tax expense.

Prepare adjusting entries for fringe benefits. (LO 4)

***E11-14** Mayberry Company has two fringe benefit plans for its employees:

1. It grants employees 2 days' vacation for each month worked. Ten employees worked the entire month of March at an average daily wage of $140 per employee.
2. In its pension plan, the company recognizes 10% of gross earnings as a pension expense. Gross earnings in March were $40,000. No contribution has been made to the pension fund.

Instructions

Prepare the adjusting entries at March 31.

Prepare journal entries for fringe benefits.

(LO 4)

***E11-15** Podsednik Corporation has 20 employees who each earn $140 a day. The following information is available.

1. At December 31, Podsednik recorded vacation benefits. Each employee earned 5 vacation days during the year.
2. At December 31, Podsednik recorded pension expense of $100,000, and made a contribution of $70,000 to the pension plan.
3. In January, 18 employees used one vacation day each.

Instructions

Prepare Podsednik's journal entries to record these transactions.

EXERCISES: SET B AND CHALLENGE EXERCISES

Visit the book's companion website, at **www.wiley.com/college/weygandt**, and choose the Student Companion site to access Exercises: Set B and Challenge Exercises.

PROBLEMS: SET A

Prepare current liability entries, adjusting entries, and current liabilities section.

(LO 1, 2)

GLS

P11-1A On January 1, 2017, the ledger of Accardo Company contains the following liability accounts.

Accounts Payable	$52,000
Sales Taxes Payable	7,700
Unearned Service Revenue	16,000

During January, the following selected transactions occurred.

Jan. 5 Sold merchandise for cash totaling $20,520, which includes 8% sales taxes.

12 Performed services for customers who had made advance payments of $10,000. (Credit Service Revenue.)

14 Paid state revenue department for sales taxes collected in December 2016 ($7,700).

20 Sold 900 units of a new product on credit at $50 per unit, plus 8% sales tax. This new product is subject to a 1-year warranty.

21 Borrowed $27,000 from Girard Bank on a 3-month, 8%, $27,000 note.

25 Sold merchandise for cash totaling $12,420, which includes 8% sales taxes.

Instructions

(a) Journalize the January transactions.

(b) Journalize the adjusting entries at January 31 for (1) the outstanding notes payable, and (2) estimated warranty liability, assuming warranty costs are expected to equal 7% of sales of the new product. (*Hint:* Use one-third of a month for the Girard Bank note.)

(c) Prepare the current liabilities section of the balance sheet at January 31, 2017. Assume no change in accounts payable.

(c) Current liability total $94,250

Journalize and post note transactions; show balance sheet presentation.

(LO 1)

P11-2A The following are selected transactions of Blanco Company. Blanco prepares financial statements **quarterly**.

Jan. 2 Purchased merchandise on account from Nunez Company, $30,000, terms 2/10, n/30. (Blanco uses the perpetual inventory system.)

Feb. 1 Issued a 9%, 2-month, $30,000 note to Nunez in payment of account.

Mar. 31 Accrued interest for 2 months on Nunez note.

Apr. 1 Paid face value and interest on Nunez note.

July 1 Purchased equipment from Marson Equipment paying $11,000 in cash and signing a 10%, 3-month, $60,000 note.

Sept. 30 Accrued interest for 3 months on Marson note.

Oct. 1 Paid face value and interest on Marson note.

Dec. 1 Borrowed $24,000 from the Paola Bank by issuing a 3-month, 8% note with a face value of $24,000.

Dec. 31 Recognized interest expense for 1 month on Paola Bank note.

The owner of Cunningham Processing, Carol Holt, asks you, as the company's accountant, to prepare a report on the expenses that are pertinent to the decision. If the Banister plan is adopted, Carol will terminate the employment of two permanent employees and will keep two permanent employees. At the moment, each employee earns an annual income of $22,000. Cunningham pays 7.65% FICA taxes, 0.8% federal unemployment taxes, and 5.4% state unemployment taxes. The unemployment taxes apply to only the first $7,000 of gross earnings. In addition, Cunningham pays $40 per month for each employee for medical and dental insurance. Carol indicates that if the Banister Services plan is accepted, her needs for temporary workers will be as follows.

Months	Number of Employees	Working Days per Month
January–March	2	20
April–May	3	25
June–October	2	18
November–December	3	23

Instructions
With the class divided into groups, answer the following.

(a) Prepare a report showing the comparative payroll expense of continuing to employ permanent workers compared to adopting the Banister Services Inc. plan.
(b) What other factors should Carol consider before finalizing her decision?

Communication Activity

BYP11-6 Mike Falcon, president of the Brownlee Company, has recently hired a number of additional employees. He recognizes that additional payroll taxes will be due as a result of this hiring, and that the company will serve as the collection agent for other taxes.

Instructions
In a memorandum to Mike Falcon, explain each of the taxes, and identify the taxes that result in payroll tax expense to Brownlee Company.

Ethics Case

BYP11-7 Robert Eberle owns and manages Robert's Restaurant, a 24-hour restaurant near the city's medical complex. Robert employs 9 full-time employees and 16 part-time employees. He pays all of the full-time employees by check, the amounts of which are determined by Robert's public accountant, Anne Farr. Robert pays all of his part-time employees in currency. He computes their wages and withdraws the cash directly from his cash register.

Anne has repeatedly urged Robert to pay all employees by check. But as Robert has told his competitor and friend, Danny Gall, who owns the Greasy Diner, "My part-time employees prefer the currency over a check. Also, I don't withhold or pay any taxes or worker's compensation insurance on those cash wages because they go totally unrecorded and unnoticed."

Instructions

(a) Who are the stakeholders in this situation?
(b) What are the legal and ethical considerations regarding Robert's handling of his payroll?
(c) Anne Farr is aware of Robert's payment of the part-time payroll in currency. What are her ethical responsibilities in this case?
(d) What internal control principle is violated in this payroll process?

All About You

BYP11-8 Medical costs are substantial and rising. But will they be the most substantial expense over your lifetime? Not likely. Will it be housing or food? Again, not likely. The answer is taxes. On average, Americans work 107 days to afford their taxes. Companies, too, have large tax burdens. They look very hard at tax issues in deciding where to build their plants and where to locate their administrative headquarters.

Instructions

(a) Determine what your state income taxes are if your taxable income is $60,000 and you file as a single taxpayer in the state in which you live.
(b) Assume that you own a home worth $200,000 in your community and the tax rate is 2.1%. Compute the property taxes you would pay.

(c) Assume that the total gasoline bill for your automobile is $1,200 a year (300 gallons at $4 per gallon). What are the amounts of state and federal taxes that you pay on the $1,200?

(d) Assume that your purchases for the year total $9,000. Of this amount, $5,000 was for food and prescription drugs. What is the amount of sales tax you would pay on these purchases? (Many states do not levy a sales tax on food or prescription drugs. Does yours?)

(e) Determine what your Social Security taxes are if your income is $60,000.

(f) Determine what your federal income taxes are if your taxable income is $60,000 and you file as a single taxpayer.

(g) Determine your total taxes paid based on the above calculations, and determine the percentage of income that you would pay in taxes based on the following formula: Total taxes paid ÷ Total income.

FASB Codification Activity

BYP11-9 If your school has a subscription to the FASB Codification, go to **http://aaahq.org/ascLogin.cfm** to log in and prepare responses to the following.

(a) What is the definition of current liabilities?

(b) What is the definition of a contingent liability?

(c) What guidance does the Codification provide for the disclosure of contingent liabilities?

A Look at IFRS

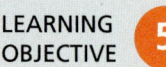

LEARNING OBJECTIVE 5 **Compare the accounting for payroll under GAAP and IFRS.**

IFRS and GAAP have similar definitions of liabilities. The general recording procedures for payroll are similar, although differences occur depending on the types of benefits that are provided in different countries. For example, companies in other countries often have different forms of pensions, unemployment benefits, welfare payments, and so on.

Key Points

Following are the key similarities and differences between GAAP and IFRS related to current liabilities and payroll.

Similarities

- The basic definition of a liability under GAAP and IFRS is very similar. In a more technical way, liabilities are defined by the IASB as a present obligation of the entity arising from past events, the settlement of which is expected to result in an outflow from the entity of resources embodying economic benefits.
- The accounting for current liabilities such as notes payable, unearned revenue, and payroll taxes payable are similar between IFRS and GAAP.
- Under IFRS, liabilities are classified as current if they are expected to be paid within 12 months.

Differences

- Companies using IFRS sometimes show liabilities before assets. Also, they will sometimes show long-term liabilities before current liabilities.
- Under IFRS, companies sometimes will net current liabilities against current assets to show working capital on the face of the statement of financial position.
- Under GAAP, some contingent liabilities are recorded in the financial statements, others are disclosed, and in some cases no disclosure is required. Unlike GAAP, IFRS reserves the use of the term **contingent liability** to refer only to possible obligations that are **not** recognized in the financial statements but may be disclosed if certain criteria are met.

- For those items that GAAP would treat as recordable contingent liabilities, IFRS instead uses the term provisions. **Provisions** are defined as liabilities of uncertain timing or amount. Examples of provisions would be provisions for warranties, employee vacation pay, or anticipated losses. Under IFRS, the measurement of a provision related to an uncertain obligation is based on the best estimate of the expenditure required to settle the obligation.

Looking to the Future

The FASB and IASB are currently involved in two projects, each of which has implications for the accounting for liabilities. One project is investigating approaches to differentiate between debt and equity instruments. The other project, the elements phase of the conceptual framework project, will evaluate the definitions of the fundamental building blocks of accounting. The results of these projects could change the classification of many debt and equity securities.

IFRS Practice

IFRS Self-Test Questions

1. Which of the following is **false**?
   (a) Under IFRS, current liabilities must always be presented before noncurrent liabilities.
   (b) Under IFRS, an item is a current liability if it will be paid within the next 12 months.
   (c) Under IFRS, current liabilities are sometimes netted against current assets on the statement of financial position.
   (d) Under IFRS, a liability is only recognized if it is a present obligation.
2. Under IFRS, a contingent liability is:
   (a) disclosed in the notes if certain criteria are met.
   (b) reported on the face of the financial statements if certain criteria are met.
   (c) the same as a provision.
   (d) not covered by IFRS.
3. Under IFRS, obligations related to warranties are considered:
   (a) contingent liabilities.
   (b) provisions.
   (c) possible obligations.
   (d) None of these.
4. The joint projects of the FASB and IASB could potentially:
   (a) change the definition of liabilities.
   (b) change the definition of equity.
   (c) change the definition of assets.
   (d) All of the above.

IFRS Exercises

IFRS11-1 Define a provision and give an example.

IFRS11-2 Briefly describe some of the similarities and differences between GAAP and IFRS with respect to the accounting for liabilities.

International Financial Statement Analysis: Louis Vuitton

IFRS11-3 The financial statements of Louis Vuitton are presented in Appendix F. Instructions for accessing and using the company's complete annual report, including the notes to the financial statements, are also provided in Appendix F.

Instructions

(a) What were the total current liabilities for the company as of December 31, 2013? What portion of these current liabilities related to provisions?
(b) What is the company's accounting policies related to provisions?

Answers to IFRS Self-Test Questions

1. a **2.** a **3.** b **4.** d

12 Accounting for Partnerships

CHAPTER PREVIEW It is not surprising that when Cliff Chenfeld and Craig Balsam began Razor & Tie (see the Feature Story below), they decided to use the partnership form of organization. Both saw the need for hands-on control of their product and its promotion. In this chapter, we discuss reasons why businesses select the partnership form of organization. We also explain the major issues in accounting for partnerships.

FEATURE STORY

From Trials to the Top Ten

In 1990, Cliff Chenfeld and Craig Balsam gave up the razors, ties, and six-figure salaries they had become accustomed to as New York lawyers. Instead, they set up a partnership, Razor & Tie Music, in Cliff's living room. Ten years later, it became the only record company in the country that had achieved success in selling music both on television and in stores. Razor & Tie's entertaining and effective TV commercials have yielded unprecedented sales for multi-artist music compilations. At the same time, its hot retail label has been behind some of the most recent original, progressive releases from artists such as Norma Jean, For Today, Chelsea Grin, and Starset.

Razor & Tie got its start with its first TV release, *Those Fabulous '70s* (100,000 copies sold), followed by *Disco Fever* (over 300,000 sold). After restoring the respectability of the oft-maligned music of the 1970s, the partners forged into the musical '80s with the same zeal that elicited success with their first releases. In 1993, Razor & Tie released *Totally '80s*, a collection of Top-10 singles from the 1980s that has sold over 450,000 units.

In 1995, Razor & Tie broke into the contemporary music world with *Living in the '90s*, the most successful record in the history of the company. Featuring a number of songs that were still hits on the radio at the time the package initially aired, *Living in the '90s* was a blockbuster. It received Gold certification in less than nine months and rewrote the rules on direct-response albums. For the first time, contemporary music was available through an album offered only through direct-response spots.

In fact, Razor & Tie is now a vertically integrated business that includes a music company with major label distribution, a music publishing business, a media buying company, a home video company, a direct marketing operation, and a growing database of entertainment consumers.

Razor & Tie has carved out a sizable piece of the market through the complementary talents of the two partners. Their imagination and savvy, along with exciting new releases planned for the coming years, ensure Razor & Tie's continued growth.

Ollyy/Shutterstoc

CHAPTER OUTLINE

Learning Objectives

Learning Objective	Topics	DO IT!
1 Discuss and account for the formation of a partnership.	• Characteristics of partnerships • Organizations with partnership characteristics • Advantages and disadvantages of partnerships • The partnership agreement • Accounting for a partnership formation	DO IT! 1 Partnership Organization
2 Explain how to account for net income or net loss of a partnership.	• Dividing net income or net loss • Partnership financial statements	DO IT! 2 Division of Net Income
3 Explain how to account for the liquidation of a partnership.	• No capital deficiency • Capital deficiency	DO IT! 3a Partnership Liquidation—No Capital Deficiency 3b Partnership Liquidation—Capital Deficiency

Go to the ***REVIEW AND PRACTICE*** section at the end of the chapter for a review of key concepts and practice applications with solutions.

Visit **WileyPLUS with ORION** for additional tutorials and practice opportunities.

LEARNING OBJECTIVE 1

Discuss and account for the formation of a partnership.

A **partnership** is an association of two or more persons to carry on as co-owners of a business for profit. Partnerships are sometimes used in small retail, service, or manufacturing companies. Accountants, lawyers, and doctors also find it desirable to form partnerships with other professionals in the field.

Characteristics of Partnerships

Partnerships are fairly easy to form. People form partnerships simply by a verbal agreement or more formally by written agreement. We explain the principal characteristics of partnerships in the following sections.

ASSOCIATION OF INDIVIDUALS

Association of Individuals

A partnership is a legal entity. A partnership can own property (land, buildings, equipment) and can sue or be sued. **A partnership also is an accounting entity.** Thus, the personal assets, liabilities, and transactions of the partners are excluded from the accounting records of the partnership, just as they are in a proprietorship.

The net income of a partnership is not taxed as a separate entity. But, a partnership must file an information tax return showing partnership net income and each partner's share of that net income. Each partner's share is taxable at **personal tax rates**, regardless of the amount of net income each withdraws from the business during the year.

MUTUAL AGENCY

Mutual Agency

Mutual agency means that each partner acts on behalf of the partnership when engaging in partnership business. The act of any partner is binding on all other partners. This is true even when partners act beyond the scope of their authority, so long as the act appears to be appropriate for the partnership. For example, a partner of a grocery store who purchases a delivery truck creates a binding contract in the name of the partnership, even if the partnership agreement denies this authority. On the other hand, if a partner in a law firm purchased a snowmobile for the partnership, such an act would not be binding on the partnership. The purchase is clearly outside the scope of partnership business.

LIMITED LIFE

Limited Life

Corporations have unlimited life. Partnerships do not. A partnership may be ended voluntarily at any time through the acceptance of a new partner or the withdrawal of a partner. It may be ended involuntarily by the death or incapacity of a partner. **Partnership dissolution** occurs whenever a partner withdraws or a new partner is admitted. Dissolution does not necessarily mean that the business ends. If the continuing partners agree, operations can continue without interruption by forming a new partnership.

UNLIMITED LIABILITY

Unlimited Liability

Each partner is **personally and individually liable** for all partnership liabilities. Creditors' claims attach first to partnership assets. If these are insufficient, the claims then attach to the personal resources of any partner, irrespective of that partner's equity in the partnership. Because each partner is responsible for all the debts of the partnership, each partner is said to have **unlimited liability**.

CO-OWNERSHIP OF PROPERTY

Partners jointly own partnership assets. If the partnership is dissolved, each partner has a claim on total assets equal to the balance in his or her respective capital account. This claim does not attach to **specific assets** that an individual partner contributed to the firm. Similarly, if a partner invests a building in the partnership valued at $100,000 and the building is later sold at a gain of $20,000, the partners all share in the gain.

Partnership net income (or net loss) is also co-owned. **If the partnership contract does not specify to the contrary, all net income or net loss is shared equally by the partners.** As you will see later, though, partners may agree to unequal sharing of net income or net loss.

Co-Ownership of Property

Organizations with Partnership Characteristics

If you are starting a business with a friend and each of you has little capital and your business is not risky, you probably want to use a partnership. As indicated above, the partnership is easy to establish and its cost is minimal. These types of partnerships are often called **regular partnerships**. However if your business is risky—say, roof repair or performing some type of professional service—you will want to limit your liability and not use a regular partnership. As a result, special forms of business organizations with partnership characteristics are now often used to provide protection from unlimited liability for people who wish to work together in some activity.

The special partnership forms are limited partnerships, limited liability partnerships, and limited liability companies. These special forms use the same accounting procedures as those described for a regular partnership. In addition, for taxation purposes, all the profits and losses pass through these organizations (similar to the regular partnership) to the owners, who report their share of partnership net income or losses on their personal tax returns.

LIMITED PARTNERSHIPS

In a **limited partnership**, one or more partners have **unlimited liability** and one or more partners have **limited liability** for the debts of the firm. Those with unlimited liability are **general partners**. Those with limited liability are **limited partners**. Limited partners are responsible for the debts of the partnership up to the limit of their investment in the firm.

The words "Limited Partnership," "Ltd.," or "LP" identify this type of organization. For the privilege of limited liability, the limited partner usually accepts less compensation than a general partner and exercises less influence in the affairs of the firm. If the limited partners get involved in management, they risk their liability protection.

International Note

Much of the funding for successful new U.S. businesses comes from "venture capital" firms, which are organized as limited partnerships. To develop its own venture capital industry, China has taken steps to model its partnership laws to allow for limited partnerships like those in the United States.

LIMITED LIABILITY PARTNERSHIP

Most states allow professionals such as lawyers, doctors, and accountants to form a **limited liability partnership** or "LLP." The LLP is designed to protect innocent partners from malpractice or negligence claims resulting from the acts of another partner. LLPs generally carry large insurance policies as protection against malpractice suits. These professional partnerships vary in size from a medical partnership of three to five doctors, to 150 to 200 partners in a large law firm, to more than 2,000 partners in an international accounting firm.

Helpful Hint
In an LLP, *all* partners have limited liability. There are no general partners.

LIMITED LIABILITY COMPANIES

A hybrid form of business organization with certain features like a corporation and others like a limited partnership is the **limited liability company** or "LLC." An LLC usually has a limited life. The owners, called **members**, have limited liability like owners of a corporation. Whereas limited partners do not actively participate in the management of a limited partnership (LP), the members of a limited liability company (LLC) can assume an active management role. For income tax purposes, the IRS usually classifies an LLC as a partnership.

Accounting Across the Organization

© Daniel Laflor/iStockphoto

Limited Liability Companies Gain in Popularity

The proprietorship form of business organization is still the most popular, followed by the corporate form. But whenever a group of individuals wants to form a partnership, the limited liability company is usually the popular choice.

One other form of business organization is a **subchapter S corporation**. A subchapter S corporation has many of the characteristics of a partnership—especially taxation as a partnership—but it is losing its popularity. The reason: It involves more paperwork and expense than a limited liability company, which in most cases offers similar advantages.

Why do you think that the use of the limited liability company is gaining in popularity? (Go to **WileyPLUS** for this answer and additional questions.)

Illustration 12-1 summarizes different forms of organizations that have partnership characteristics.

Illustration 12-1
Different forms of organizations with partnership characteristics

	Major Advantages	**Major Disadvantages**
Regular Partnership  General Partners	Simple and inexpensive to create and operate.	Owners (partners) personally liable for business debts.
Limited Partnership  General Partner / Limited Partners	Limited partners have limited personal liability for business debts as long as they do not participate in management. General partners can raise cash without involving outside investors in management of business.	General partners personally liable for business debts. More expensive to create than regular partnership. Suitable mainly for companies that invest in real estate.
Limited Liability Partnership 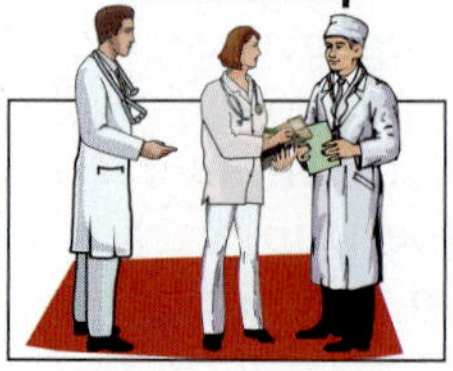	Mostly of interest to partners in old-line professions such as law, medicine, and accounting. Owners (partners) are not personally liable for the malpractice of other partners.	Unlike a limited liability company, owners (partners) remain personally liable for many types of obligations owed to business creditors, lenders, and landlords. Often limited to a short list of professions.
Limited Liability Company 	Owners have limited personal liability for business debts even if they participate in management.	More expensive to create than regular partnership.

Source: www.nolo.com.

Advantages and Disadvantages of Partnerships

Why do people choose partnerships? One major advantage of a partnership is to combine the skills and resources of two or more individuals. In addition, partnerships are easily formed and are relatively free from government regulations and restrictions. A partnership does not have to contend with the "red tape" that a corporation must face. Also, partners generally can make decisions quickly on substantive business matters without having to consult a board of directors.

On the other hand, partnerships also have some major disadvantages. **Unlimited liability** is particularly troublesome. Many individuals fear they may lose not only their initial investment but also their personal assets if those assets are needed to pay partnership creditors.

Illustration 12-2 summarizes the advantages and disadvantages of the regular partnership form of business organization. As indicated previously, different types of partnership forms have evolved to reduce some of the disadvantages.

Advantages	Disadvantages
Combining skills and resources of two or more individuals	Mutual agency
Ease of formation	Limited life
Freedom from governmental regulations and restrictions	Unlimited liability
Ease of decision-making	

Illustration 12-2
Advantages and disadvantages of a partnership

The Partnership Agreement

Ideally, the agreement of two or more individuals to form a partnership should be expressed in a written contract, called the **partnership agreement** or **articles of co-partnership**. The partnership agreement contains such basic information as the name and principal location of the firm, the purpose of the business, and date of inception. In addition, it should specify relationships among the partners, such as:

1. Names and capital contributions of partners.
2. Rights and duties of partners.
3. Basis for sharing net income or net loss.
4. Provision for withdrawals of assets.
5. Procedures for submitting disputes to arbitration.
6. Procedures for the withdrawal or addition of a partner.
7. Rights and duties of surviving partners in the event of a partner's death.

We cannot overemphasize the importance of a written contract. The agreement should attempt to anticipate all possible situations, contingencies, and disagreements. The help of a lawyer is highly desirable in preparing the agreement.

ETHICS NOTE

A well-developed partnership agreement specifies in clear and concise language the process by which the partners will resolve ethical and legal problems. This issue is especially significant when the partnership experiences financial distress.

Accounting Across the Organization

PhotoDisc/Getty Images, Inc.

Dividing Up the Pie

What should you do when you and your business partner disagree to the point where you are no longer on speaking terms? Given how heated business situations can get, this is not an unusual occurrence. Unfortunately, in many instances the partners do everything they can to undermine each other, eventually destroying the business. In some cases, people even steal from the partnership because they either feel that they "deserve it" or they assume that the other partners are stealing from them.

It would be much better to follow the example of Jennifer Appel and her partner. They found that after opening a successful bakery and writing a cookbook, they couldn't agree on how the business should be run. The other partner bought out Ms. Appel's share of the business. Ms. Appel went on to start her own style of bakery, which she ultimately franchised.

Source: Paulette Thomas, "As Partnership Sours, Parting Is Sweet," *Wall Street Journal*, (July 6, 2004), p. A20.

How can partnership conflicts be minimized and more easily resolved? (Go to **WileyPLUS** for this answer and additional questions.)

Accounting for a Partnership Formation

We now turn to the basic accounting for partnerships. The major accounting issues relate to forming the partnership, dividing income or loss, and preparing financial statements.

When forming a partnership, each partner's initial investment in a partnership is entered in the partnership records. The partnership should record these investments at the **fair value of the assets at the date of their transfer to the partnership**. All partners must agree to the values assigned.

To illustrate, assume that A. Rolfe and T. Shea combine their proprietorships to start a partnership named U.S. Software. The firm will specialize in developing financial modeling software. Rolfe and Shea have the following assets prior to the formation of the partnership.

Illustration 12-3
Book and fair values of assets invested

	Book Value		Fair Value	
	A. Rolfe	T. Shea	A. Rolfe	T. Shea
Cash	$ 8,000	$ 9,000	**$ 8,000**	**$ 9,000**
Equipment	5,000		**4,000**	
Accumulated depreciation—equipment	(2,000)			
Accounts receivable		4,000		**4,000**
Allowance for doubtful accounts		(700)		**(1,000)**
	$11,000	$12,300	**$12,000**	**$12,000**

Items under ***owners' equity (OE)*** *in the accounting equation analyses are not labeled in this partnership chapter. Nearly all affect partners'* ***capital*** *accounts.*

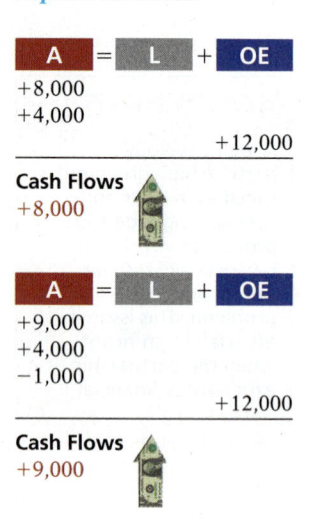

The partnership records the investments as follows.

A	= L +	OE
+8,000		
+4,000		
		+12,000

Cash Flows
+8,000

Investment of A. Rolfe

Cash	8,000	
Equipment	4,000	
A. Rolfe, Capital		12,000
(To record investment of Rolfe)		

A	= L +	OE
+9,000		
+4,000		
−1,000		
		+12,000

Cash Flows
+9,000

Investment of T. Shea

Cash	9,000	
Accounts Receivable	4,000	
Allowance for Doubtful Accounts		1,000
T. Shea, Capital		12,000
(To record investment of Shea)		

Note that the partnership records neither the original cost of the equipment ($5,000) nor its book value ($5,000 − $2,000). It records the equipment at its fair value, $4,000. The partnership does not carry forward any accumulated depreciation from the books of previous entities (in this case, the two proprietorships).

In contrast, the gross claims on customers ($4,000) are carried forward to the partnership. The partnership adjusts the allowance for doubtful accounts to $1,000, to arrive at a cash (net) realizable value of $3,000. A partnership may start with an allowance for doubtful accounts because it will continue to collect existing accounts receivable, some of which are expected to be uncollectible. In addition, this procedure maintains the control and subsidiary relationship between Accounts Receivable and the accounts receivable subsidiary ledger.

After formation of the partnership, the accounting for transactions is similar to any other type of business organization. For example, the partners record all transactions with outside parties, such as the purchase or sale of inventory and the payment or receipt of cash, the same as would a sole proprietor.

The steps in the accounting cycle described in Chapter 4 for a proprietorship also apply to a partnership. For example, the partnership prepares a trial balance and journalizes and posts adjusting entries. A worksheet may be used. There are minor differences in journalizing and posting closing entries and in preparing financial statements, as we explain in the following sections. The differences occur because there is more than one owner.

DO IT! 1 Partnership Organization

Indicate whether each of the following statements is true or false.

_______ **1.** Partnerships have unlimited life. Corporations do not.

_______ **2.** Partners jointly own partnership assets. A partner's claim on partnership assets does not attach to specific assets.

_______ **3.** In a limited partnership, the general partners have unlimited liability.

_______ **4.** The members of a limited liability company have limited liability, like shareholders of a corporation, and they are taxed like corporate shareholders.

_______ **5.** Because of mutual agency, the act of any partner is binding on all other partners.

Solution

1. False. Corporations have unlimited life. Partnerships do not. **2.** True. **3.** True. **4.** False. The members of a limited liability company are taxed like partners in a partnership. **5.** True.

Related exercise material: **E12-1 and DO IT! 12-1.**

Action Plan

✔ When forming a business, carefully consider what type of organization would best suit the needs of the business.

✔ Keep in mind the new, "hybrid" organizational forms that have many of the best characteristics of partnerships and corporations.

LEARNING OBJECTIVE 2 **Explain how to account for net income or net loss of a partnership.**

Dividing Net Income or Net Loss

Partners equally share partnership net income or net loss unless the partnership contract indicates otherwise. The same basis of division usually applies to both net income and net loss. It is customary to refer to this basis as the **income ratio**, the **income and loss ratio**, or the **profit and loss (P&L) ratio**. Because of its wide acceptance, we use the term **income ratio** to identify the basis for dividing net income and net loss. The partnership recognizes a partner's share of net income or net loss in the accounts through closing entries.

CLOSING ENTRIES

As in the case of a proprietorship, a partnership must make four entries in preparing closing entries. The entries are:

1. Debit each revenue account for its balance, and credit Income Summary for total revenues.
2. Debit Income Summary for total expenses, and credit each expense account for its balance.
3. Debit Income Summary for its balance, and credit each partner's capital account for his or her share of net income. Or, credit Income Summary, and debit each partner's capital account for his or her share of net loss.
4. Debit each partner's capital account for the balance in that partner's drawings account, and credit each partner's drawings account for the same amount.

The first two entries are the same as in a proprietorship. The last two entries are different because (1) there are two or more owners' capital and drawings accounts, and (2) it is necessary to divide net income (or net loss) among the partners.

To illustrate the last two closing entries, assume that AB Company has net income of $32,000 for 2017. The partners, L. Arbor and D. Barnett, share net income and net loss equally. Drawings for the year were Arbor $8,000 and Barnett $6,000. The last two closing entries are as follows.

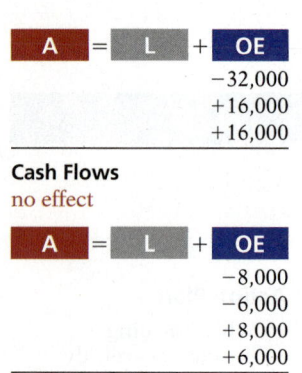

A = L + OE				
−32,000 +16,000 +16,000	Dec. 31	Income Summary L. Arbor, Capital ($32,000 × 50%) D. Barnett, Capital ($32,000 × 50%) (To transfer net income to partners' capital accounts)	32,000	 16,000 16,000

Cash Flows
no effect

A = L + OE				
−8,000 −6,000 +8,000 +6,000	Dec. 31	L. Arbor, Capital D. Barnett, Capital L. Arbor, Drawings D. Barnett, Drawings (To close drawings accounts to capital accounts)	8,000 6,000	 8,000 6,000

Cash Flows
no effect

Assume that the beginning capital balance is $47,000 for Arbor and $36,000 for Barnett. After posting the closing entries, the capital and drawings accounts will appear as shown in Illustration 12-4.

Illustration 12-4
Partners' capital and drawings accounts after closing

L. Arbor, Capital

Debit			Credit		
12/31	**Clos.**	**8,000**	1/1	Bal.	47,000
			12/31	**Clos.**	**16,000**
			12/31	Bal.	55,000

D. Barnett, Capital

Debit			Credit		
12/31	**Clos.**	**6,000**	1/1	Bal.	36,000
			12/31	**Clos.**	**16,000**
			12/31	Bal.	46,000

L. Arbor, Drawings

Debit			Credit		
12/31	Bal.	8,000	12/31	**Clos.**	**8,000**

D. Barnett, Drawings

Debit			Credit		
12/31	Bal.	6,000	12/31	**Clos.**	**6,000**

As in a proprietorship, the partners' capital accounts are permanent accounts. Their drawings accounts are temporary accounts. Normally, the capital accounts will have credit balances, and the drawings accounts will have debit balances. Drawings accounts are debited when partners withdraw cash or other assets from the partnership for personal use.

INCOME RATIOS

Helpful Hint
A proportion such as 4:4:2 has a denominator of 10 (4 + 4 + 2). Thus, the basis for sharing net income or loss is 4/10, 4/10, and 2/10.

As noted earlier, the partnership agreement should specify the basis for sharing net income or net loss. The following are typical income ratios.

1. A fixed ratio, expressed as a proportion (6:4), a percentage (70% and 30%), or a fraction (2/3 and 1/3).
2. A ratio based either on capital balances at the beginning of the year or on average capital balances during the year.
3. Salaries to partners and the remainder on a fixed ratio.
4. Interest on partners' capital balances and the remainder on a fixed ratio.
5. Salaries to partners, interest on partners' capital, and the remainder on a fixed ratio.

The objective is to settle on a basis that will equitably reflect the partners' capital investment and service to the partnership.

A **fixed ratio** is easy to apply, and it may be an equitable basis in some circumstances. Assume, for example, that Hughes and Lane are partners. Each contributes the same amount of capital, but Hughes expects to work full-time in the partnership and Lane expects to work only half-time. Accordingly, the partners agree to a fixed ratio of 2/3 to Hughes and 1/3 to Lane.

A **ratio based on capital balances** may be appropriate when the funds invested in the partnership are considered the critical factor. Capital ratios may also be equitable when the partners hire a manager to run the business and do not plan to take an active role in daily operations.

The three remaining ratios (items 3, 4, and 5) give specific recognition to differences among partners. These ratios provide salary allowances for time worked and interest allowances for capital invested. Then, the partnership allocates any remaining net income or net loss on a fixed ratio.

Salaries to partners and interest on partners' capital are not expenses of the partnership. Therefore, these items do not enter into the matching of expenses with revenues and the determination of net income or net loss. For a partnership, as for other entities, salaries and wages expense pertains to the cost of services performed by employees. Likewise, interest expense relates to the cost of borrowing from creditors. But partners, as owners, are not considered either **employees** or **creditors**. When the partnership agreement permits the partners to make monthly withdrawals of cash based on their "salary," the partnership debits these withdrawals to the partner's drawings account.

SALARIES, INTEREST, AND REMAINDER ON A FIXED RATIO

Under income ratio (5) in the list above, the partnership must apply salaries and interest **before** it allocates the remainder on the specified fixed ratio. **This is true even if the provisions exceed net income. It is also true even if the partnership has suffered a net loss for the year.** The partnership's income statement should show, below net income, detailed information concerning the division of net income or net loss.

To illustrate, assume that Sara King and Ray Lee are co-partners in the Kingslee Company. The partnership agreement provides for (1) salary allowances of $8,400 to King and $6,000 to Lee, (2) interest allowances of 10% on capital balances at the beginning of the year, and (3) the remaining income to be divided equally. Capital balances on January 1 were King $28,000, and Lee $24,000. In 2017, partnership net income is $22,000. The division of net income is as shown in Illustration 12-5.

Illustration 12-5
Division of net income schedule

KINGSLEE COMPANY
Division of Net Income
For the Year Ended December 31, 2017

Net income	$ 22,000		
Division of Net Income			
	Sara King	**Ray Lee**	**Total**
Salary allowance	$ 8,400	$6,000	$14,400
Interest allowance on partners' capital			
Sara King ($28,000 × 10%)	2,800		
Ray Lee ($24,000 × 10%)		2,400	
Total interest allowance			5,200
Total salaries and interest	11,200	8,400	19,600
Remaining income, $2,400 ($22,000 − $19,600)			
Sara King ($2,400 × 50%)	1,200		
Ray Lee ($2,400 × 50%)		1,200	
Total remainder			2,400
Total division of net income	**$12,400**	**$9,600**	**$22,000**

Kingslee records the division of net income as follows.

Dec. 31	Income Summary	22,000	
	Sara King, Capital		12,400
	Ray Lee, Capital		9,600
	(To close net income to partners' capital)		

A	=	L	+	OE
				−22,000
				+12,000
				+9,600

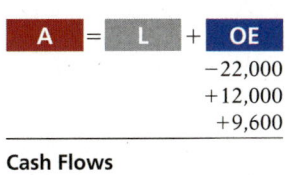

Cash Flows
no effect

Now let's look at a situation in which the salary and interest allowances **exceed** net income. Assume that Kingslee Company's net income is only $18,000. In this case, the salary and interest allowances will create a deficiency of $1,600 ($18,000 − $19,600). The computations of the allowances are the same as those in the preceding example. Beginning with total salaries and interest, we complete the division of net income as shown in Illustration 12-6.

Illustration 12-6
Division of net income—income deficiency

	Sara King	Ray Lee	Total
Total salaries and interest	$11,200	$8,400	$19,600
Remaining deficiency ($1,600)			
($18,000 − $19,600)			
Sara King ($1,600 × 50%)	(800)		
Ray Lee ($1,600 × 50%)		(800)	
Total remainder			(1,600)
Total division	**$10,400**	**$7,600**	**$18,000**

Partnership Financial Statements

The financial statements of a partnership are similar to those of a proprietorship. The differences are due to the number of owners involved. The income statement for a partnership is identical to the income statement for a proprietorship except for the division of net income, as shown earlier.

The owners' equity statement for a partnership is called the **partners' capital statement**. It explains the changes in each partner's capital account and in total partnership capital during the year. Illustration 12-7 shows the partners' capital statement for Kingslee Company. It is based on the division of $22,000 of net income in Illustration 12-5 (page 541). The statement includes assumed data for the additional investment and drawings. The partnership prepares the partners' capital statement from the income statement and the partners' capital and drawings accounts.

Illustration 12-7
Partners' capital statement

KINGSLEE COMPANY
Partners' Capital Statement
For the Year Ended December 31, 2017

	Sara King	Ray Lee	Total
Capital, January 1	$28,000	$24,000	$52,000
Add: Additional investment	2,000		2,000
Net income	12,400	9,600	22,000
	42,400	33,600	76,000
Less: Drawings	7,000	5,000	12,000
Capital, December 31	**$35,400**	**$28,600**	**$64,000**

Helpful Hint
As in a proprietorship, partners' capital may change due to (1) additional investment, (2) drawings, and (3) net income or net loss.

The balance sheet for a partnership is the same as for a proprietorship except for the owners' equity section. For a partnership, the balance sheet shows the capital balances of each partner. Illustration 12-8 shows the owners' equity section for Kingslee Company.

KINGSLEE COMPANY Balance Sheet (partial) December 31, 2017		
Total liabilities (assumed amount)		$115,000
Owners' equity		
Sara King, capital	$35,400	
Ray Lee, capital	28,600	
Total owners' equity		64,000
Total liabilities and owners' equity		$179,000

Illustration 12-8
Owners' equity section of a partnership balance sheet

DO IT! 2 Division of Net Income

LeeMay Company reports net income of $57,000. The partnership agreement provides for salaries of $15,000 to L. Lee and $12,000 to R. May. They will share the remainder on a 60:40 basis (60% to Lee). L. Lee asks your help to divide the net income between the partners and to prepare the closing entry.

Solution

The division of net income is as follows.

	L. Lee	R. May	Total
Salary allowance	$15,000	$12,000	$27,000
Remaining income $30,000 ($57,000 − $27,000)			
L. Lee (60% × $30,000)	18,000		
R. May (40% × $30,000)		12,000	
Total remaining income			30,000
Total division of net income	$33,000	$24,000	$57,000

The closing entry for net income therefore is:

Income Summary	57,000	
L. Lee, Capital		33,000
R. May, Capital		24,000
(To close net income to partners' capital accounts)		

Action Plan

✔ Compute net income exclusive of any salaries to partners and interest on partners' capital.

✔ Deduct salaries to partners from net income.

✔ Apply the partners' income ratios to the remaining net income.

✔ Prepare the closing entry distributing net income or net loss among the partners' capital accounts.

Related exercise material: **BE12-3, BE12-4, BE12-5, E12-4, E12-5, and DO IT! 12-2.**

LEARNING OBJECTIVE 3 Explain how to account for the liquidation of a partnership.

Liquidation of a business involves selling the assets of the firm, paying liabilities, and distributing any remaining assets. Liquidation may result from the sale of the business by mutual agreement of the partners, from the death of a partner, or from bankruptcy. **Partnership liquidation** ends both the legal and economic life of the entity.

From an accounting standpoint, the partnership should complete the accounting cycle for the final operating period prior to liquidation. This includes preparing adjusting entries and financial statements. It also involves preparing closing entries and a post-closing trial balance. Thus, only balance sheet accounts should be open as the liquidation process begins.

In liquidation, the sale of noncash assets for cash is called **realization**. Any difference between book value and the cash proceeds is called the **gain or loss on realization**. To liquidate a partnership, it is necessary to:

ETHICS NOTE

The process of selling noncash assets and then distributing the cash reduces the likelihood of partner disputes. If instead the partnership distributes noncash assets to partners to liquidate the firm, the partners would need to agree on the value of the noncash assets, which can be very difficult to determine.

1. Sell noncash assets for cash and recognize a gain or loss on realization.
2. Allocate gain/loss on realization to the partners based on their income ratios.
3. Pay partnership liabilities in cash.
4. Distribute remaining cash to partners on the basis of their **capital balances**.

Each of the steps must be performed in sequence. The partnership must pay creditors **before** partners receive any cash distributions. Also, an accounting entry must record each step.

When a partnership is liquidated, all partners may have credit balances in their capital accounts. This situation is called **no capital deficiency**. Or, one or more partners may have a debit balance in the capital account. This situation is termed a **capital deficiency**. To illustrate each of these conditions, assume that Ace Company is liquidated when its ledger shows the following assets, liabilities, and owners' equity accounts.

Illustration 12-9
Account balances prior to liquidation

Assets		Liabilities and Owners' Equity	
Cash	$ 5,000	Notes Payable	$15,000
Accounts Receivable	15,000	Accounts Payable	16,000
Inventory	18,000	R. Arnet, Capital	15,000
Equipment	35,000	P. Carey, Capital	17,800
Accum. Depr.—Equipment	(8,000)	W. Eaton, Capital	1,200
	$65,000		$65,000

No Capital Deficiency

Helpful Hint
The income ratios' denominator for Ace Company is 6 (3 + 2 + 1).

The partners of Ace Company agree to liquidate the partnership on the following terms. (1) The partnership will sell its noncash assets to Jackson Enterprises for $75,000 cash. (2) The partnership will pay its partnership liabilities. The income ratios of the partners are 3:2:1, respectively. The steps in the liquidation process are as follows.

1. Ace sells the noncash assets (accounts receivable, inventory, and equipment) for $75,000. The book value of these assets is $60,000 ($15,000 + $18,000 + $35,000 − $8,000). Thus, Ace realizes a gain of $15,000 on the sale. The entry is:

A	= L +	OE
+75,000		
+8,000		
−15,000		
−18,000		
−35,000		
		+15,000

Cash Flows
+75,000

(1)

Cash	75,000	
Accumulated Depreciation–Equipment	8,000	
Accounts Receivable		15,000
Inventory		18,000
Equipment		35,000
Gain on Realization		15,000
(To record realization of noncash assets)		

2. Ace allocates the $15,000 gain on realization to the partners based on their income ratios, which are 3:2:1. The entry is:

A	= L +	OE
		−15,000
		+7,500
		+5,000
		+2,500

Cash Flows
no effect

(2)

Gain on Realization	15,000	
R. Arnet, Capital ($15,000 × 3/6)		7,500
P. Carey, Capital ($15,000 × 2/6)		5,000
W. Eaton, Capital ($15,000 × 1/6)		2,500
(To allocate gain to partners' capital accounts)		

3. Partnership liabilities consist of Notes Payable $15,000 and Accounts Payable $16,000. Ace pays creditors in full by a cash payment of $31,000. The entry is:

(3)

Notes Payable	15,000	
Accounts Payable	16,000	
Cash		31,000
(To record payment of partnership liabilities)		

A	=	L	+	OE
		−15,000		
		−16,000		
−31,000				

Cash Flows
−31,000

4. Ace distributes the remaining cash to the partners on the basis of **their capital balances**. After posting the entries in the first three steps, all partnership accounts, including Gain on Realization, will have zero balances except for four accounts: Cash $49,000; R. Arnet, Capital $22,500; P. Carey, Capital $22,800; and W. Eaton, Capital $3,700, as shown below.

Illustration 12-10
Ledger balances before distribution of cash

Cash		R. Arnet, Capital		P. Carey, Capital		W. Eaton, Capital	
Bal. 5,000	(3) 31,000		Bal. 15,000		Bal. 17,800		Bal. 1,200
(1) 75,000			(2) 7,500		(2) 5,000		(2) 2,500
Bal. 49,000			**Bal. 22,500**		**Bal. 22,800**		**Bal. 3,700**

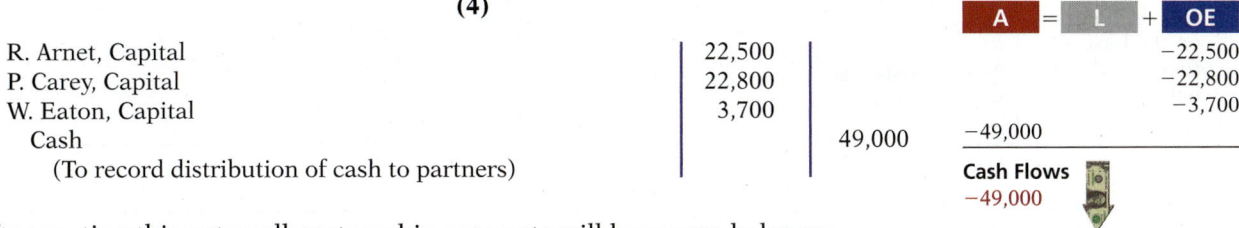

Ace records the distribution of cash as follows.

(4)

R. Arnet, Capital	22,500	
P. Carey, Capital	22,800	
W. Eaton, Capital	3,700	
Cash		49,000
(To record distribution of cash to partners)		

A	=	L	+	OE
				−22,500
				−22,800
				−3,700
−49,000				

Cash Flows
−49,000

After posting this entry, all partnership accounts will have zero balances.

A word of caution: **Partnerships should not distribute remaining cash to partners on the basis of their income-sharing ratios.** On this basis, Arnet would receive three-sixths, or $24,500, which would produce an erroneous debit balance of $2,000. The income ratio is the proper basis for allocating net income or loss. **It is not a proper basis for making the final distribution of cash to the partners.**

Alternative Terminology
The schedule of cash payments is sometimes called a *safe cash payments schedule*.

SCHEDULE OF CASH PAYMENTS

The **schedule of cash payments** shows the distribution of cash to the partners in a partnership liquidation. The schedule of cash payments is organized around the basic accounting equation. Illustration 12-11 shows the schedule for Ace

Illustration 12-11
Schedule of cash payments, no capital deficiency

ACE Company.xls

Home Insert Page Layout Formulas Data Review View

P18 fx

	A	B	C	D	E	F	G	H	I	J	K	L	M
1	**ACE COMPANY Schedule of Cash Payments**												
2	Item		Cash	+	Noncash Assets	=	Liabilities	+	R. Arnet, Capital	+	P. Carey, Capital	+	W. Eaton, Capital
3	Balances before liquidation		5,000	+	60,000	=	31,000	+	15,000	+	17,800	+	1,200
4	Sale of noncash assets and allocation of gain	(1)&(2)	75,000	+	(60,000)	=			7,500	+	5,000	+	2,500
5	New balances		80,000	+	−0−	=	31,000	+	22,500	+	22,800	+	3,700
6	Pay liabilities		(31,000)			=	(31,000)						
7	New balances	(3)	49,000	+	−0−	=	−0−	+	22,500	+	22,800	+	3,700
8	Cash distribution to partners	(4)	(49,000)			=			(22,500)	+	(22,800)	+	(3,700)
9	Final balances		−0−		−0−		−0−		−0−		−0−		−0−
10													
11													

Company. The numbers in parentheses in column B refer to the four required steps in the liquidation of a partnership. They also identify the accounting entries that Ace must make. The cash payments schedule is especially useful when the liquidation process extends over a period of time.

DO IT! 3a Partnership Liquidation—No Capital Deficiency

The partners of Grafton Company have decided to liquidate their business. Noncash assets were sold for $115,000. The income ratios of the partners Kale D., Croix D., and Marais K. are 2:3:3, respectively. Complete the following schedule of cash payments for Grafton Company.

Action Plan

- ✔ First, sell the noncash assets and determine the gain.
- ✔ Allocate the gain to the partners based on their income ratios.
- ✔ Use cash to pay off liabilities.
- ✔ Distribute remaining cash on the basis of their capital balances.

GRAFTON Company.xls

Home Insert Page Layout Formulas Data Review View

P18 fx

	A	B	C	D	E	F	G	H	I	J	K	L
1	Item	Cash	+	Noncash Assets	=	Liabilities	+	Kale D., Capital	+	Croix D., Capital	+	Marais K., Capital
2	Balances before liquidation	10,000		85,000		40,000		15,000		35,000		5,000
3	Sale of noncash assets and allocation of gain											
4	New balances											
5	Pay liabilities											
6	New balances											
7	Cash distribution to partners											
8	Final balances											
9												
10												

Solution

GRAFTON Company.xls

Home Insert Page Layout Formulas Data Review View

P18 fx

	A	B	C	D	E	F	G	H	I	J	K	L
1	Item	Cash	+	Noncash Assets	=	Liabilities	+	Kale D., Capital	+	Croix D., Capital	+	Marais K., Capital
2	Balances before liquidation	10,000		85,000		40,000		15,000		35,000		5,000
3	Sale of noncash assets and allocation of gain	115,000		(85,000)				7,500[a]		11,250[b]		11,250[b]
4	New balances	125,000		–0–		40,000		22,500		46,250		16,250
5	Pay liabilities	(40,000)				(40,000)						
6	New balances	85,000		–0–		–0–		22,500		46,250		16,250
7	Cash distribution to partners	(85,000)						(22,500)		(46,250)		(16,250)
8	Final balances	–0–		–0–		–0–		–0–		–0–		–0–
9												
10	[a]30,000 x 2/8											
11	[b]30,000 x 3/8											

Related exercise material: **BE12-6, E12-8, E12-9, and DO IT! 12-3a.**

Capital Deficiency

A capital deficiency may result from recurring net losses, excessive drawings, or losses from realization suffered during liquidation. To illustrate, assume that Ace Company is on the brink of bankruptcy. The partners decide to liquidate by having a "going-out-of-business" sale. They sell merchandise at substantial discounts, and sell the equipment at auction. Cash proceeds from these sales and collections from customers total only $42,000. Thus, the loss from liquidation is $18,000 ($60,000 − $42,000). The steps in the liquidation process are as follows.

1. The entry for the realization of noncash assets is:

(1)		
Cash	42,000	
Accumulated Depreciation—Equipment	8,000	
Loss on Realization	18,000	
Accounts Receivable		15,000
Inventory		18,000
Equipment		35,000
(To record realization of noncash assets)		

A	= L	+ OE
+42,000		
+8,000		
		−18,000
−15,000		
−18,000		
−35,000		

Cash Flows
+42,000

2. Ace allocates the loss on realization to the partners on the basis of their income ratios. The entry is:

(2)		
R. Arnet, Capital ($18,000 × 3/6)	9,000	
P. Carey, Capital ($18,000 × 2/6)	6,000	
W. Eaton, Capital ($18,000 × 1/6)	3,000	
Loss on Realization		18,000
(To allocate loss on realization to partners)		

A	= L	+ OE
		−9,000
		−6,000
		−3,000
		+18,000

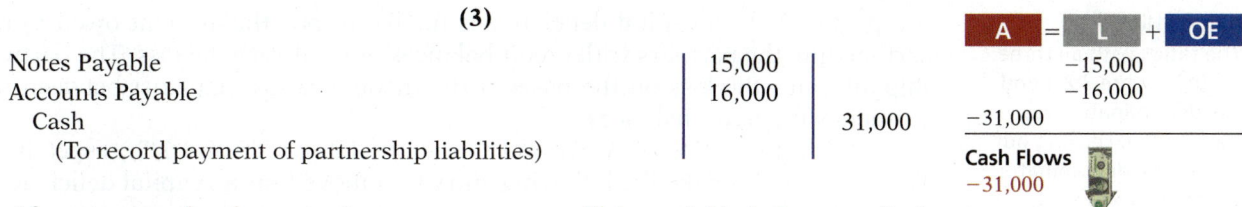

Cash Flows
no effect

3. Ace pays the partnership liabilities. This entry is the same as the previous one.

(3)		
Notes Payable	15,000	
Accounts Payable	16,000	
Cash		31,000
(To record payment of partnership liabilities)		

A	= L	+ OE
	−15,000	
	−16,000	
−31,000		

Cash Flows
−31,000

4. After posting the three entries, two accounts will have debit balances—Cash $16,000 and W. Eaton, Capital $1,800. Two accounts will have credit balances—R. Arnet, Capital $6,000 and P. Carey, Capital $11,800. All four accounts are shown below.

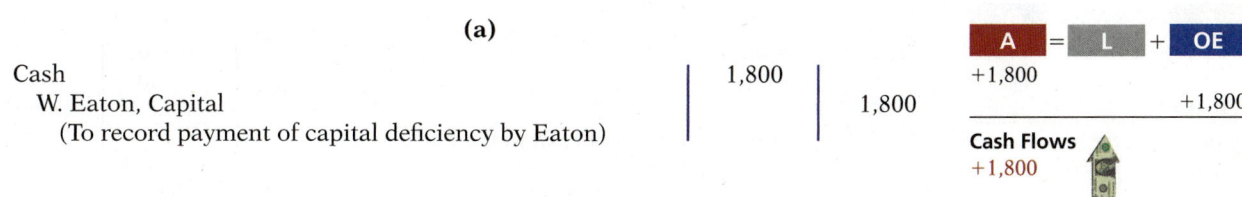

Cash (Dr.)	Cash (Cr.)	R. Arnet, Capital (Dr.)	R. Arnet, Capital (Cr.)	P. Carey, Capital (Dr.)	P. Carey, Capital (Cr.)	W. Eaton, Capital (Dr.)	W. Eaton, Capital (Cr.)
Bal. 5,000	(3) 31,000	(2) 9,000	Bal. 15,000	(2) 6,000	Bal. 17,800	(2) 3,000	Bal. 1,200
(1) 42,000			**Bal. 6,000**		**Bal. 11,800**	**Bal. 1,800**	
Bal. 16,000							

Illustration 12-12
Ledger balances before distribution of cash

Eaton has a capital deficiency of $1,800 and so owes the partnership $1,800. Arnet and Carey have a legally enforceable claim for that amount against Eaton's personal assets. Note that the distribution of cash is still made on the basis of capital balances. But, the amount will vary depending on how Eaton settles the deficiency. Two alternatives are presented in the following sections.

PAYMENT OF DEFICIENCY

If the partner with the capital deficiency pays the amount owed the partnership, the deficiency is eliminated. To illustrate, assume that Eaton pays $1,800 to the partnership. The entry is:

(a)		
Cash	1,800	
W. Eaton, Capital		1,800
(To record payment of capital deficiency by Eaton)		

A	= L	+ OE
+1,800		
		+1,800

Cash Flows
+1,800

After posting this entry, account balances are as follows.

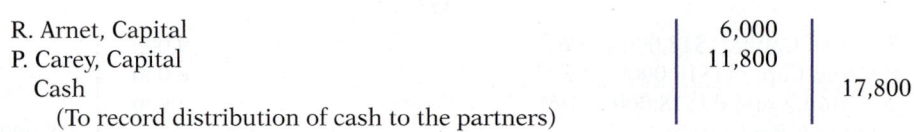

Cash		R. Arnet, Capital		P. Carey, Capital		W. Eaton, Capital	
Bal. 5,000	(3) 31,000	(2) 9,000	Bal. 15,000	(2) 6,000	Bal. 17,800	(2) 3,000	Bal. 1,200
(1) 42,000			**Bal. 6,000**		**Bal. 11,800**		(a) 1,800
(a) 1,800							**Bal. -0-**
Bal. 17,800							

Illustration 12-13
Ledger balances after paying capital deficiency

The cash balance of $17,800 is now equal to the credit balances in the capital accounts (Arnet $6,000 + Carey $11,800). Ace now distributes cash on the basis of these balances. The entry is:

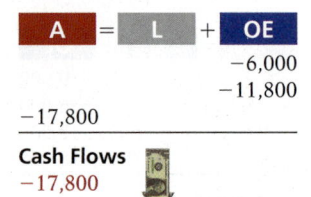

A	= L +	OE
		−6,000
		−11,800
−17,800		

Cash Flows
−17,800

R. Arnet, Capital	6,000	
P. Carey, Capital	11,800	
Cash		17,800
(To record distribution of cash to the partners)		

After posting this entry, all accounts will have zero balances.

NONPAYMENT OF DEFICIENCY

Helpful Hint
The ratios with all three partners were 3:2:1 and the denominator was therefore 6. Leaving out Eaton, the denominator changes to 5 (3 + 2).

If a partner with a capital deficiency is unable to pay the amount owed to the partnership, the partners with credit balances must absorb the loss. The partnership allocates the loss on the basis of the income ratios that exist between the partners with credit balances.

The income ratios of Arnet and Carey are 3:2, or 3/5 and 2/5, respectively. Thus, Ace would make the following entry to remove Eaton's capital deficiency.

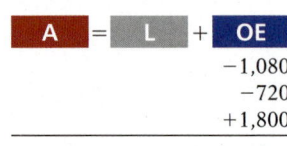

A	= L +	OE
		−1,080
		−720
		+1,800

Cash Flows
no effect

(a)

R. Arnet, Capital ($1,800 × 3/5)	1,080	
P. Carey, Capital ($1,800 × 2/5)	720	
W. Eaton, Capital		1,800
(To record write-off of capital deficiency)		

After posting this entry, the cash and capital accounts will have the following balances.

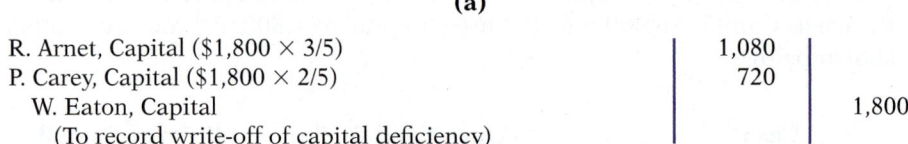

Cash		R. Arnet, Capital		P. Carey, Capital		W. Eaton, Capital	
Bal. 5,000	(3) 31,000	(2) 9,000	Bal. 15,000	(2) 6,000	Bal. 17,800	(2) 3,000	Bal. 1,200
(1) 42,000		(a) 1,080		(a) 720			(a) 1,800
Bal. 16,000			**Bal. 4,920**		**Bal. 11,080**		**Bal. -0-**

Illustration 12-14
Ledger balances after nonpayment of capital deficiency

The cash balance ($16,000) now equals the sum of the credit balances in the capital accounts (Arnet $4,920 + Carey $11,080). Ace records the distribution of cash as:

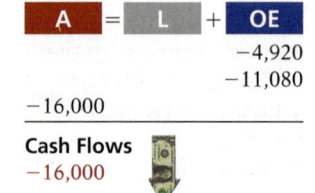

A	= L +	OE
		−4,920
		−11,080
−16,000		

Cash Flows
−16,000

R. Arnet, Capital	4,920	
P. Carey, Capital	11,080	
Cash		16,000
(To record distribution of cash to the partners)		

After posting this entry, all accounts will have zero balances.

DO IT! 3b Partnership Liquidation—Capital Deficiency

Kessington Company wishes to liquidate the firm by distributing the company's cash to the three partners. Prior to the distribution of cash, the company's balances are Cash \$45,000; Rollings, Capital (Cr.) \$28,000; Havens, Capital (Dr.) \$12,000; and Ostergard, Capital (Cr.) \$29,000. The income ratios of the three partners are 4:4:2, respectively. Prepare the entry to record the absorption of Havens' capital deficiency by the other partners and the distribution of cash to the partners with credit balances.

Solution

Rollings, Capital (\$12,000 × 4/6)	8,000	
Ostergard, Capital (\$12,000 × 2/6)	4,000	
Havens, Capital		12,000
(To record write-off of capital deficiency)		
Rollings, Capital (\$28,000 − \$8,000)	20,000	
Ostergard, Capital (\$29,000 − \$4,000)	25,000	
Cash		45,000
(To record distribution of cash to partners)		

Related exercise material: **E12-10 and DO IT! 12-3b.**

Action Plan

- ✔ Allocate any unpaid capital deficiency to the partners with credit balances, based on their income ratios.
- ✔ After distribution of the deficiency, distribute cash to the remaining partners, based on their capital balances.

LEARNING OBJECTIVE *4

APPENDIX 12A: Prepare journal entries when a partner is either admitted or withdraws.

The chapter explained how the basic accounting for a partnership works. We now look at how to account for a common occurrence in partnerships—the addition or withdrawal of a partner.

Admission of a Partner

The admission of a new partner results in the **legal dissolution** of the existing partnership and the beginning of a new one. From an economic standpoint, however, the admission of a new partner (or partners) may be of minor significance in the continuity of the business. For example, in large public accounting or law firms, partners are admitted annually without any change in operating policies. **To recognize the economic effects, it is necessary only to open a capital account for each new partner.** In the entries illustrated in this appendix, we assume that the accounting records of the predecessor firm will continue to be used by the new partnership.

A new partner may be admitted either by (1) purchasing the interest of one or more existing partners or (2) investing assets in the partnership. The former affects only the capital accounts of the partners who are parties to the transaction. The latter increases both net assets and total capital of the partnership.

PURCHASE OF A PARTNER'S INTEREST

The **admission** of a partner **by purchase of an interest** is a personal transaction between one or more existing partners and the new partner. Each party acts as an individual separate from the partnership entity. The individuals involved negotiate the price paid. It may be equal to or different from the capital equity acquired. The purchase price passes directly from the new partner to the partners who are giving up part or all of their ownership claims.

Helpful Hint
In a purchase of an interest, the partnership is not a participant in the transaction. In this transaction, the new partner contributes *no* cash to the partnership.

Any money or other consideration exchanged is the personal property of the participants and **not** the property of the partnership. Upon purchase of an interest, the new partner acquires each selling partner's capital interest and income ratio.

Accounting for the purchase of an interest is straightforward. The partnership records only the changes in partners' capital. **Partners' capital accounts are debited for any ownership claims sold.** At the same time, the new partner's capital account is credited for the capital equity purchased. Total assets, total liabilities, and total capital remain unchanged, as do all individual asset and liability accounts.

To illustrate, assume that L. Carson agrees to pay $10,000 each to C. Ames and D. Barker for $33^1/_3$% (one-third) of their interest in the Ames–Barker partnership. At the time of the admission of Carson, each partner has a $30,000 capital balance. Both partners, therefore, give up $10,000 of their capital equity. The entry to record the admission of Carson is:

C. Ames, Capital	10,000	
D. Barker, Capital	10,000	
L. Carson, Capital		20,000
(To record admission of Carson by purchase)		

The effect of this transaction on net assets and partners' capital is shown below.

Net Assets		C. Ames, Capital		D. Barker, Capital		L. Carson, Capital	
60,000		10,000	30,000	10,000	30,000		20,000
			Bal. 20,000		Bal. 20,000		

Illustration 12A-1
Ledger balances after purchase of a partner's interest

Note that net assets remain unchanged at $60,000, and each partner has a $20,000 capital balance. Ames and Barker continue as partners in the firm, but the capital interest of each has changed. The cash paid by Carson goes directly to the individual partners and not to the partnership.

Regardless of the amount paid by Carson for the one-third interest, the entry is exactly the same. If Carson pays $12,000 each to Ames and Barker for one-third of the partnership, the partnership still makes the entry shown above.

INVESTMENT OF ASSETS IN A PARTNERSHIP

The admission of a partner by an investment of assets is a transaction between the new partner and the partnership. Often referred to simply as **admission by investment**, the transaction **increases both the net assets and total capital of the partnership**.

Assume, for example, that instead of purchasing an interest, Carson invests $30,000 in cash in the Ames-Barker partnership for a $33^1/_3$% capital interest. In such a case, the entry is:

Cash	30,000	
L. Carson, Capital		30,000
(To record admission of Carson by investment)		

Illustration 12A-2 shows the effects of this transaction on the partnership accounts.

Net Assets		C. Ames, Capital		D. Barker, Capital		L. Carson, Capital	
60,000			30,000		30,000		30,000
30,000							
Bal. 90,000							

Illustration 12A-2
Ledger balances after investment of assets

Note that both net assets and total capital have increased by $30,000.

Remember that Carson's one-third capital interest might not result in a one-third income ratio. The new partnership agreement should specify Carson's income ratio, and it may or may not be equal to the one-third capital interest.

The comparison of the net assets and capital balances in Illustration 12A-3 shows the different effects of the purchase of an interest and admission by investment.

Illustration 12A-3
Comparison of purchase of an interest and admission by investment

Purchase of an Interest		Admission by Investment	
Net assets	**$60,000**	**Net assets**	**$90,000**
Capital		Capital	
C. Ames	$20,000	C. Ames	$30,000
D. Barker	20,000	D. Barker	30,000
L. Carson	20,000	L. Carson	30,000
Total capital	**$60,000**	**Total capital**	**$90,000**

When a new partner purchases an interest, the total net assets and total capital of the partnership **do not change**. When a partner is admitted by investment, both the total net assets and the total capital **change** by the amount of the new investment.

In the case of admission by investment, further complications occur when the new partner's investment differs from the capital equity acquired. When those amounts are not the same, the difference is considered a **bonus** either to (1) the existing (old) partners or (2) the new partner.

BONUS TO OLD PARTNERS For both personal and business reasons, the existing partners may be unwilling to admit a new partner without receiving a bonus. In an established firm, existing partners may insist on a bonus as compensation for the work they have put into the company over the years. Two accounting factors underlie the business reason. First, total partners' capital equals the **book value** of the recorded net assets of the partnership. When the new partner is admitted, the fair values of assets such as land and buildings may be higher than their book values. The bonus will help make up the difference between fair value and book value. Second, when the partnership has been profitable, goodwill may exist. But, the partnership balance sheet does not report goodwill. The new partner is usually willing to pay the bonus to become a partner.

A bonus to old partners results when the new partner's investment in the firm is greater than the capital credit on the date of admittance. The bonus results in **an increase in the capital balances of the old partners. The partnership allocates the bonus to them on the basis of their income ratios before the admission of the new partner.** To illustrate, assume that the Bart-Cohen partnership, owned by Sam Bart and Tom Cohen, has total capital of $120,000. Lea Eden acquires a 25% ownership (capital) interest in the partnership by making a cash investment of $80,000. The procedure for determining Eden's capital credit and the bonus to the old partners is as follows.

1. **Determine the total capital of the new partnership.** Add the new partner's investment to the total capital of the old partnership. In this case, the total capital of the new firm is $200,000, computed as follows.

Total capital of existing partnership	$120,000
Investment by new partner, Eden	80,000
Total capital of new partnership	$200,000

2. **Determine the new partner's capital credit.** Multiply the total capital of the new partnership by the new partner's ownership interest. Eden's capital credit is $50,000 ($200,000 × 25%).
3. **Determine the amount of bonus.** Subtract the new partner's capital credit from the new partner's investment. The bonus in this case is $30,000 ($80,000 − $50,000).

4. **Allocate the bonus to the old partners on the basis of their income ratios.** Assuming the ratios are Bart 60%, and Cohen 40%, the allocation is Bart \$18,000 (\$30,000 × 60%) and Cohen \$12,000 (\$30,000 × 40%).

The entry to record the admission of Eden is:

A	=	L	+	OE
+80,000				
				+18,000
				+12,000
				+50,000

Cash Flows
+80,000

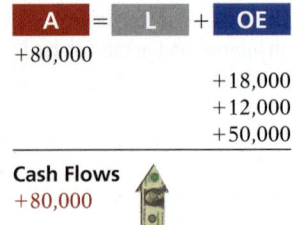

Cash	80,000	
Sam Bart, Capital		18,000
Tom Cohen, Capital		12,000
Lea Eden, Capital		50,000
(To record admission of Eden and bonus to old partners)		

BONUS TO NEW PARTNER A bonus to a new partner results when the new partner's investment in the firm is less than his or her capital credit. This may occur when the new partner possesses special attributes that the partnership wants. For example, the new partner may be able to supply cash that the firm needs for expansion or to meet maturing debts. Or the new partner may be a recognized expert in a relevant field. Thus, an engineering firm may be willing to give a renowned engineer a bonus to join the firm. The partners of a restaurant may offer a bonus to a sports celebrity in order to add the athlete's name to the partnership. A bonus to a new partner may also result when recorded book values on the partnership books are higher than their fair values.

A bonus to a new partner results in a **decrease in the capital balances of the old partners. The amount of the decrease for each partner is based on the income ratios before the admission of the new partner.** To illustrate, assume that Lea Eden invests \$20,000 in cash for a 25% ownership interest in the Bart–Cohen partnership. The computations for Eden's capital credit and the bonus are as follows, using the four procedures described in the preceding section.

Illustration 12A-4
Computation of capital credit and bonus to new partner

1. Total capital of Bart–Cohen partnership		\$120,000
Investment by new partner, Eden		20,000
Total capital of new partnership		\$140,000
2. **Eden's capital credit** (25% × \$140,000)		**\$ 35,000**
3. **Bonus to Eden** (\$35,000 − \$20,000)		**\$ 15,000**
4. Allocation of bonus to old partners:		
Bart (\$15,000 × 60%)	\$9,000	
Cohen (\$15,000 × 40%)	6,000	\$ 15,000

The partnership records the admission of Eden as follows.

A	=	L	+	OE
+20,000				
				−9,000
				−6,000
				+35,000

Cash Flows
+20,000

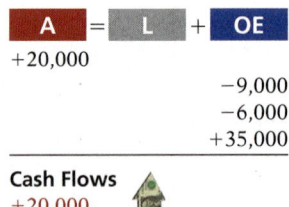

Cash	20,000	
Sam Bart, Capital	9,000	
Tom Cohen, Capital	6,000	
Lea Eden, Capital		35,000
(To record Eden's admission and bonus)		

Withdrawal of a Partner

Now let's look at the opposite situation–the withdrawal of a partner. A partner may withdraw from a partnership **voluntarily**, by selling his or her equity in the firm. Or, he or she may withdraw **involuntarily**, by reaching mandatory retirement age or by dying. The withdrawal of a partner, like the admission of a partner, legally dissolves the partnership. The legal effects may be recognized by dissolving the firm. However, it is customary to record only the economic effects of the partner's withdrawal, while the firm continues to operate and reorganizes itself legally.

As indicated earlier, the partnership agreement should specify the terms of withdrawal. The withdrawal of a partner may be accomplished by (1) payment from partners' personal assets or (2) payment from partnership assets. The former affects only the partners' capital accounts. The latter decreases total net assets and total capital of the partnership.

PAYMENT FROM PARTNERS' PERSONAL ASSETS

Withdrawal by payment from partners' personal assets is a personal transaction between the partners. **It is the direct opposite of admitting a new partner who purchases a partner's interest.** The remaining partners pay the retiring partner directly from their personal assets. **Partnership assets are not involved in any way, and total capital does not change.** The effect on the partnership is limited to changes in the partners' capital balances.

To illustrate, assume that partners Morz, Nead, and Odom have capital balances of $25,000, $15,000, and $10,000, respectively. Morz and Nead agree to buy out Odom's interest. Each of them agrees to pay Odom $8,000 in exchange for one-half of Odom's total interest of $10,000. The entry to record the withdrawal is:

J. Odom, Capital	10,000	
A. Morz, Capital		5,000
M. Nead, Capital		5,000
(To record purchase of Odom's interest)		

A	=	L	+	OE
				−10,000
				+5,000
				+5,000

Cash Flows
no effect

The effect of this entry on the partnership accounts is shown below.

Net Assets		A. Morz, Capital		M. Nead, Capital		J. Odom, Capital	
50,000			25,000		15,000	10,000	10,000
			5,000		5,000		Bal. -0-
			Bal. 30,000		Bal. 20,000		

Illustration 12A-5
Ledger balances after payment from partners' personal assets

Note that net assets and total capital remain the same at $50,000.

What about the $16,000 paid to Odom? You've probably noted that it is not recorded. The entry debited Odom's capital only for $10,000, not for the $16,000 that she received. Similarly, both Morz and Nead credit their capital accounts for only $5,000, not for the $8,000 they each paid.

After Odom's withdrawal, Morz and Nead will share net income or net loss equally unless they indicate another income ratio in the partnership agreement.

PAYMENT FROM PARTNERSHIP ASSETS

Withdrawal by payment from partnership assets is a transaction that involves the partnership. **Both partnership net assets and total capital decrease as a result.** Using partnership assets to pay for a withdrawing partner's interest is the **reverse** of admitting a partner through the investment of assets in the partnership.

Many partnership agreements provide that the amount paid should be based on the fair value of the assets at the time of the partner's withdrawal. When this basis is required, some maintain that any differences between recorded asset balances and their fair values should be (1) recorded by an adjusting entry, and (2) allocated to all partners on the basis of their income ratios. This position has serious flaws. Recording the revaluations violates the historical cost principle, which requires that assets be stated at original cost. It also violates the going-concern assumption, which assumes the entity will continue indefinitely. The terms of the partnership contract should not dictate the accounting for this event.

In accounting for a withdrawal by payment from partnership assets, the partnership should not record asset revaluations. Instead, it should consider any difference between the amount paid and the withdrawing partner's capital balance as **a bonus** to the retiring partner or to the remaining partners.

BONUS TO RETIRING PARTNER A partnership may pay a bonus to a retiring partner when:

1. The fair value of partnership assets is more than their book value,
2. There is unrecorded goodwill resulting from the partnership's superior earnings record, or
3. The remaining partners are eager to remove the partner from the firm.

The partnership deducts the bonus from the remaining partners' capital balances on the basis of their income ratios at the time of the withdrawal.

To illustrate, assume that the following capital balances exist in the RST partnership: Roman $50,000, Sand $30,000, and Terk $20,000. The partners share income in the ratio of 3:2:1, respectively. Terk retires from the partnership and receives a cash payment of $25,000 from the firm. The procedure for determining the bonus to the retiring partner and the allocation of the bonus to the remaining partners is as follows.

1. **Determine the amount of the bonus.** Subtract the retiring partner's capital balance from the cash paid by the partnership. The bonus in this case is $5,000 ($25,000 − $20,000).
2. **Allocate the bonus to the remaining partners on the basis of their income ratios.** The ratios of Roman and Sand are 3:2. Thus, the allocation of the $5,000 bonus is: Roman $3,000 ($5,000 × 3/5) and Sand $2,000 ($5,000 × 2/5).

Helpful Hint
Compare this entry to the one at the bottom of the page.

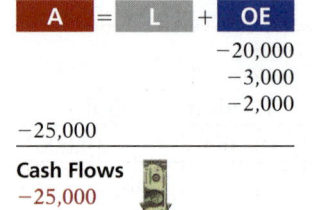

A	= L +	OE
		−20,000
		−3,000
		−2,000
−25,000		

Cash Flows
−25,000

The partnership records the withdrawal of Terk as follows.

B. Terk, Capital	20,000	
F. Roman, Capital	3,000	
D. Sand, Capital	2,000	
Cash		25,000
(To record withdrawal of and bonus to Terk)		

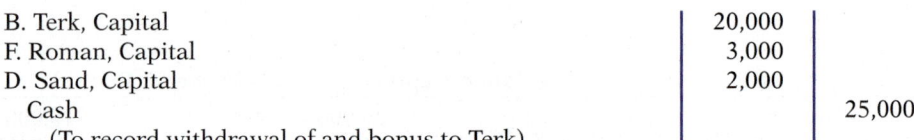

The remaining partners, Roman and Sand, will recover the bonus given to Terk as the partnership sells or uses the undervalued assets.

BONUS TO REMAINING PARTNERS The retiring partner may give a bonus to the remaining partners when:

1. Recorded assets are overvalued.
2. The partnership has a poor earnings record.
3. The partner is eager to leave the partnership.

In such cases, the cash paid to the retiring partner will be less than the retiring partner's capital balance. **The partnership allocates (credits) the bonus to the capital accounts of the remaining partners on the basis of their income ratios.**

To illustrate, assume instead that the partnership pays Terk only $16,000 for her $20,000 equity when she withdraws from the partnership. In that case:

1. The bonus to remaining partners is $4,000 ($20,000 − $16,000).
2. The allocation of the $4,000 bonus is Roman $2,400 ($4,000 × 3/5) and Sand $1,600 ($4,000 × 2/5).

Helpful Hint
Compare this entry to the one above.

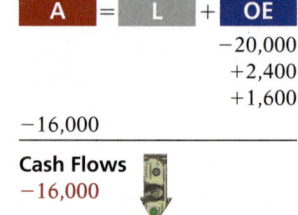

A	= L +	OE
		−20,000
		+2,400
		+1,600
−16,000		

Cash Flows
−16,000

Under these circumstances, the entry to record the withdrawal is as follows.

B. Terk, Capital	20,000	
F. Roman, Capital		2,400
D. Sand, Capital		1,600
Cash		16,000
(To record withdrawal of Terk and bonus to remaining partners)		

Note that if Sand had withdrawn from the partnership, Roman and Terk would divide any bonus on the basis of their income ratio, which is 3:1 or 75% and 25%.

DEATH OF A PARTNER

The death of a partner dissolves the partnership. However, partnership agreements usually contain a provision for the surviving partners to continue operations. When a partner dies, it usually is necessary to determine the partner's equity at the date of death. This is done by (1) determining the net income or loss for the year to date, (2) closing the books, and (3) preparing financial statements. The partnership agreement may also require an independent audit and a revaluation of assets.

The surviving partners may agree to purchase the deceased partner's equity from their personal assets. Or they may use partnership assets to settle with the deceased partner's estate. In both instances, the entries to record the withdrawal of the partner are similar to those presented earlier.

To facilitate payment from partnership assets, some partnerships obtain life insurance policies on each partner, with the partnership named as the beneficiary. The partnership then uses the proceeds from the insurance policy on the deceased partner to settle with the estate.

REVIEW AND PRACTICE

LEARNING OBJECTIVES REVIEW

1 Discuss and account for the formation of a partnership. The principal characteristics of a partnership are (a) association of individuals, (b) mutual agency, (c) limited life, (d) unlimited liability, and (e) co-ownership of property. When formed, a partnership records each partner's initial investment at the fair value of the assets at the date of their transfer to the partnership.

2 Explain how to account for net income or net loss of a partnership. Partnerships divide net income or net loss on the basis of the income ratio, which may be (a) a fixed ratio, (b) a ratio based on beginning or average capital balances, (c) salaries to partners and the remainder on a fixed ratio, (d) interest on partners' capital and the remainder on a fixed ratio, and (e) salaries to partners, interest on partners' capital, and the remainder on a fixed ratio.

The financial statements of a partnership are similar to those of a proprietorship. The principal differences are as follows. (a) The partnership shows the division of net income on the income statement. (b) The owners' equity statement is called a partners' capital statement. (c) The partnership reports each partner's capital on the balance sheet.

3 Explain how to account for the liquidation of a partnership. When a partnership is liquidated, it is necessary to record the (a) sale of noncash assets, (b) allocation of the gain or loss on realization, (c) payment of partnership liabilities, and (d) distribution of cash to the partners on the basis of their capital balances.

***4 Prepare journal entries when a partner is either admitted or withdraws.** The entry to record the admittance of a new partner by purchase of a partner's interest affects only partners' capital accounts. The entries to record the admittance by investment of assets in the partnership (a) increase both net assets and total capital and (b) may result in recognition of a bonus to either the old partners or the new partner.

The entry to record a withdrawal from the firm when the partners pay from their personal assets affects only partners' capital accounts. The entry to record a withdrawal when payment is made from partnership assets (a) decreases net assets and total capital and (b) may result in recognizing a bonus either to the retiring partner or the remaining partners.

GLOSSARY REVIEW

***Admission by investment** Admission of a partner by investing assets in the partnership, causing both partnership net assets and total capital to increase. (p. 550).

***Admission by purchase of an interest** Admission of a partner in a personal transaction between one or more existing partners and the new partner; does not change total partnership assets or total capital. (p. 549).

Capital deficiency A debit balance in a partner's capital account after allocation of gain or loss. (p. 544).

General partners Partners who have unlimited liability for the debts of the firm. (p. 535).

Income ratio The basis for dividing net income and net loss in a partnership. (p. 539).

Limited liability company A form of business organization, usually classified as a partnership for tax purposes and usually with limited life, in which partners, who are called members, have limited liability. (p. 535).

Limited liability partnership A partnership of professionals in which partners are given limited liability and the public is protected from malpractice by insurance carried by the partnership. (p. 535).

Limited partners Partners whose liability for the debts of the firm is limited to their investment in the firm. (p. 535).

Limited partnership A partnership in which one or more general partners have unlimited liability and one or more partners have limited liability for the obligations of the firm. (p. 535).

No capital deficiency All partners have credit balances after allocation of gain or loss. (p. 544).

Partners' capital statement The owners' equity statement for a partnership which shows the changes in each partner's capital account and in total partnership capital during the year. (p. 542).

Partnership An association of two or more persons to carry on as co-owners of a business for profit. (p. 534).

Partnership agreement A written contract expressing the voluntary agreement of two or more individuals in a partnership. (p. 537).

Partnership dissolution A change in partners due to withdrawal or admission, which does not necessarily terminate the business. (p. 534).

Partnership liquidation An event that ends both the legal and economic life of a partnership. (p. 543).

Schedule of cash payments A schedule showing the distribution of cash to the partners in a partnership liquidation. (p. 545).

***Withdrawal by payment from partners' personal assets** Withdrawal of a partner in a personal transaction between partners; does not change total partnership assets or total capital. (p. 553).

***Withdrawal by payment from partnership assets** Withdrawal of a partner in a transaction involving the partnership, causing both partnership net assets and total capital to decrease. (p. 553).

PRACTICE MULTIPLE-CHOICE QUESTIONS

(LO 1) 1. Which of the following is **not** a characteristic of a partnership?
(a) Taxable entity. (c) Mutual agency.
(b) Co-ownership of property. (d) Limited life.

(LO 1) 2. A partnership agreement should include each of the following **except:**
(a) names and capital contributions of partners.
(b) rights and duties of partners as well as basis for sharing net income or loss.
(c) basis for splitting partnership income taxes.
(d) provision for withdrawal of assets.

(LO 1) 3. The advantages of a partnership do **not** include:
(a) ease of formation.
(b) unlimited liability.
(c) freedom from government regulation.
(d) ease of decision-making.

(LO 1) 4. Upon formation of a partnership, each partner's initial investment of assets should be recorded at their:
(a) book values. (c) fair values.
(b) cost. (d) appraised values.

(LO 1) 5. Ben and Sam Jenkins formed a partnership. Ben contributed $8,000 cash and a used truck that originally cost $35,000 and had accumulated depreciation of $15,000. The truck's fair value was $16,000. Sam, a builder, contributed a new storage garage. His cost of construction was $40,000. The garage has a fair value of $55,000. What is the combined total capital that would be recorded on the partnership books for the two partners?
(a) $79,000. (c) $75,000.
(b) $60,000. (d) $90,000.

6. The NBC Company reports net income of $60,000. If partners N, B, and C have an income ratio of 50%, 30%, and 20%, respectively, C's share of the net income is: (LO 2)
(a) $30,000. (c) $18,000.
(b) $12,000. (d) No correct answer is given.

7. Using the data in Practice Multiple-Choice Question 6, what is B's share of net income if the percentages are applicable after each partner receives a $10,000 salary allowance? (LO 2)
(a) $12,000. (c) $19,000.
(b) $20,000. (d) $21,000.

8. To close a partner's drawings account, an entry must be made that: (LO 2)
(a) debits that partner's drawings account and credits Income Summary.
(b) debits that partner's drawings account and credits that partner's capital account.
(c) credits that partner's drawings account and debits that partner's capital account.
(d) credits that partner's drawings account and debits the firm's dividend account.

9. Which of the following statements about partnership financial statements is **true**? (LO 2)
(a) Details of the distribution of net income are shown in the owners' equity statement.
(b) The distribution of net income is shown on the balance sheet.
(c) Only the total of all partner capital balances is shown in the balance sheet.
(d) The owners' equity statement is called the partners' capital statement.

(LO 3) **10.** In the liquidation of a partnership, it is necessary to (1) distribute cash to the partners, (2) sell noncash assets, (3) allocate any gain or loss on realization to the partners, and (4) pay liabilities. These steps should be performed in the following order:
(a) (2), (3), (4), (1).
(b) (2), (3), (1), (4).
(c) (3), (2), (1), (4).
(d) (3), (2), (4), (1).

Use the following account balance information for Creekville Partnership to answer Practice Multiple-Choice Questions 11 and 12. Income ratios are 2:4:4 for Harriet, Mike, and Elly, respectively.

Assets		Liabilities and Owners' Equity	
Cash	$ 9,000	Accounts payable	$ 21,000
Accounts receivable	22,000	Harriet, capital	23,000
		Mike, capital	8,000
Inventory	73,000	Elly, capital	52,000
	$104,000		$104,000

(LO 3) **11.** Assume that as part of liquidation proceedings, Creekville sells its noncash assets for $85,000. The amount of cash that would ultimately be distributed to Elly would be:
(a) $52,000. (c) $34,000.
(b) $48,000. (d) $86,000.

(LO 3) **12.** Assume that as part of liquidation proceedings, Creekville sells its noncash assets for $60,000. As a result, one of the partners has a capital deficiency which that partner decides not to repay. The amount of cash that would ultimately be distributed to Elly would be:
(a) $52,000. (c) $24,000.
(b) $38,000. (d) $34,000.

***13.** Louisa Santiago purchases 50% of Leo Lemon's capital interest in the K & L partnership for $22,000. If the capital balance of Kate Kildare and Leo Lemon are $40,000 and $30,000, respectively, Santiago's capital balance following the purchase is: (LO 4)
(a) $22,000. (c) $20,000.
(b) $35,000. (d) $15,000.

***14.** Capital balances in the MEM partnership are Mary, Capital $60,000; Ellen, Capital $50,000; and Mills, Capital $40,000, and income ratios are 5:3:2, respectively. The MEMO partnership is formed by admitting Oleg to the firm with a cash investment of $60,000 for a 25% capital interest. The bonus to be credited to Mills, Capital in admitting Oleg is: (LO 4)
(a) $10,000. (c) $3,750.
(b) $7,500. (d) $1,500.

***15.** Capital balances in the MURF partnership are Molly, Capital $50,000; Ursula, Capital $40,000; Ray, Capital $30,000; and Fred, Capital $20,000, and income ratios are 4:3:2:1, respectively. Fred withdraws from the firm following payment of $29,000 in cash from the partnership. Ursula's capital balance after recording the withdrawal of Fred is: (LO 4)
(a) $36,000. (c) $38,000.
(b) $37,000. (d) $40,000.

Solutions

1. (a) A partnership is not a taxable entity. Rather, the partnership income is taxed on the individual tax returns of the partners. The other choices are characteristics of a partnership.

2. (c) A partnership is not a taxable entity; therefore, the partnership agreement should not include the basis for splitting partnership income taxes. The other choices should be included in a partnership agreement.

3. (b) Unlimited liability is a disadvantage of a partnership. The other choices are advantages of a partnership.

4. (c) Upon formation of a partnership, each partner's initial investment of assets should be recorded at their fair values, not (a) book values, (b) cost, or (d) appraised values.

5. (a) When a partnership is formed, assets invested by the partners are recorded at their fair values. Thus, the combined total capital is $8,000 (cash) + $16,000 (fair value of truck) + $55,000 (fair value of the new storage garage) = $79,000, not (b) $60,000, (c) $75,000, or (d) $90,000.

6. (b) C's income is computed by multiplying the partnership income ($60,000) by partner C's income ratio (20%) = $12,000. The other choices are incorrect because (a) is the amount of income that would be allocated to partner N ($60,000 × 50% = $30,000), (c) is the amount of income that would be allocated to partner B ($60,000 × 30% = $18,000), and (d) there is a correct answer.

7. (c) After allocating the salary allowance to each partner, $30,000 will be available to divide according to the income ratio [$60,000 − ($10,000 × 3)]. Partner B's share of the remainder is $9,000 ($30,000 × 30%). Partner B's total share of income is equal to $19,000 (salary allowance of $10,000 + B's share of the remainder $9,000), not (a) $12,000, (b) $20,000, or (d) $21,000.

8. (c) To close a partner's drawings account, an entry must be made that credits the partner's drawings account and debits that partner's capital account. The other choices are therefore incorrect because a partner's drawings account or a dividend account is not debited.

9. (d) The owners' equity statement for a partnership is called the partners' capital statement. The other choices are incorrect because (a) the total amount, not the details, of the distribution of net income is shown in the partners' capital statement; (b) the distribution of net income is not shown on the balance sheet but on the partners' capital statement; and (c) each individual partner's capital balance is shown in the balance sheet.

10. (a) The order of events in the liquidation of a partnership is (2) sell noncash assets, (3) allocate gain/loss, (4) pay partnership liabilities, and (1) distribute remaining cash. The other choices are therefore incorrect.

11. (b) The book value of the noncash assets is $95,000 ($22,000 + $73,000). When Creekville sells its noncash assets for $85,000, Creekville realizes a loss of $10,000 on the sale. The income ratio for Elly is 40% (4/10). When allocating the $10,000 loss on realization to the partners, Elly's capital account will be debited for $4,000 ($10,000 × 4/10). The amount of cash that would ultimately be distributed to Elly would be $48,000 ($52,000 − $4,000), not (a) $52,000, (c) $34,000, or (d) $86,000.

12. (d) The loss on realization is $35,000 ($22,000 + $73,000 − $60,000). When allocating the $35,000 loss on realization to the partners, Harriet's, Mike's, and Elly's capital accounts will be debited $7,000, $14,000, and $14,000, respectively, as per their income ratios. Mike will now have a capital deficiency of $6,000 ($8,000 − $14,000). Elly's share of this deficiency is $4,000 ($6,000 × 4/6). The amount of cash that would ultimately be distributed to Elly would be $34,000 ($52,000 − $14,000 − $4,000), not (a) $52,000, (b) $38,000, or (c) $24,000.

***13. (d)** Because this is a purchase of a partner's interest, Santiago's capital account will be equal to half of the interest she is purchasing, or $15,000 ($30,000/2). The $22,000 paid by Santiago to Lemon is irrelevant in this question. The other choices are therefore incorrect.

***14. (d)** Total partnership capital after the investment by Oleg is $210,000 ($60,000 + $50,000 + $40,000 + $60,000). Oleg's share of partnership capital is $52,500 ($210,000 × 25%). The total bonus to the old partners related to Oleg's admission is $7,500 [$60,000 (Oleg's investment) − $52,500 (Oleg's share of partnership capital)]. Mills' share of the total bonus is equal to the total bonus ($7,500) times Mills' income ratio (20%) or $1,500 ($7,500 × 20%), not (a) $10,000, (b) $7,500, or (c) $3,750.

***15. (b)** The total bonus to Fred from the partnership is $9,000 ($29,000 − $20,000). Because Fred has withdrawn, the income ratio must be restated as 4:3:2. Ursula's share of the bonus paid to Fred is $3,000 [$9,000 × [3/(4 + 3 + 2)]]. Because the bonus is being paid to Fred, Ursula's capital account must be reduced by her share of the bonus. After Fred's withdrawal, Ursula's capital account will have a balance of $37,000 ($40,000 − $3,000), not (a) $36,000, (c) $38,000, or (d) $40,000.

PRACTICE EXERCISES

Prepare journal entries to record allocation of net income.

(LO 2)

1. M. Gomez (beginning capital $50,000) and I. Inez (beginning capital $80,000) are partners. During 2017 the partnership earned net income of $60,000, and Gomez made drawings of $15,000 while Inez made drawings of $20,000.

Instructions

(a) Assume the partnership income-sharing agreement calls for income to be divided 55% to Gomez and 45% to Inez. Prepare the journal entry to record the allocation of net income.

(b) Assume the partnership income-sharing agreement calls for income to be divided with a salary of $30,000 to Gomez and $20,000 to Inez with the remainder divided 55% to Gomez and 45% to Inez. Prepare the journal entry to record the allocation of net income.

(c) Assume the partnership income-sharing agreement calls for income to be divided with a salary of $40,000 to Gomez and $30,000 to Inez, interest of 10% on beginning capital, and the remainder divided 50%–50%. Prepare the journal entry to record the allocation of net income.

(d) Compute the partners' ending capital balances under the assumption in part (c).

Solution

1. (a) Income Summary	60,000	
M. Gomez, Capital ($60,000 × 55%)		33,000
I. Inez, Capital ($60,000 × 45%)		27,000
(b) Income Summary	60,000	
M. Gomez, Capital [$30,000 + ($10,000 × 55%)]		35,500
I. Inez, Capital [$20,000 + ($10,000 × 45%)]		24,500
(c) Income Summary	60,000	
M. Gomez, Capital [$40,000 + $5,000 − ($23,000 × 50%)]		33,500
I. Inez, Capital [$30,000 + $8,000 − ($23,000 × 50%)]		26,500

(d) Gomez: $50,000 + $33,500 − $15,000 = $68,500

Inez: $80,000 + $26,500 − $20,000 = $86,500

2. The Braun Company at December 31 has cash $15,000, noncash assets $110,000, liabilities $60,000, and the following capital balances: Ho $40,000 and Li $25,000. The firm is liquidated, and $90,000 in cash is received for the noncash assets. Ho's and Li's income ratios are 60% and 40%, respectively.

Prepare cash distribution schedule and journalize transactions in a liquidation.

(LO 2, 3)

Instructions

(a) Prepare a cash distribution schedule.

(b) Prepare the entries to record the following, assuming that The Braun Company decides to liquidate the company.
(1) The sale of noncash assets.
(2) The allocation of the gain or loss on liquidation to the partners.
(3) Payment of creditors.
(4) Distribution of cash to the partners.

Solution

2. (a)

THE BRAUN COMPANY
Schedule of Cash Payments

Item	Cash	+	Noncash Assets	=	Liabilities	+	Ho, Capital	+	Li, Capital
Balances before liquidation	$ 15,000		$110,000		$60,000		$40,000		$25,000
Sale of noncash assets and allocation of gain	90,000		(110,000)				(12,000)		(8,000)
New balances	105,000		0		60,000		28,000		17,000
Pay liabilities	(60,000)				(60,000)				
New balances	45,000		0		0		28,000		17,000
Cash distribution to partners	(45,000)						(28,000)		(17,000)
Final balances	$ 0		$ 0		$ 0		$ 0		$ 0

(b)

(1) Loss of Realization	20,000	
Cash	90,000	
Noncash Assets		110,000
(2) Ho, Capital	12,000	
Li, Capital	8,000	
Loss on Realization		20,000
(3) Accounts Payable	60,000	
Cash		60,000
(4) Ho, Capital	28,000	
Li, Capital	17,000	
Cash		45,000

PRACTICE PROBLEM

On January 1, 2017, the capital balances in Hollingsworth Company are Lois Holly $26,000 and Jim Worth $24,000. In 2017 the partnership reports net income of $30,000. The income ratio provides for salary allowances of $12,000 for Holly and $10,000 to Worth and the remainder to be shared equally. Neither partner had any drawings in 2017.

Journalize and prepare a schedule showing distribution of net income.

(LO 2)

Instructions

(a) Prepare a schedule showing the distribution of net income in 2017.

(b) Journalize the division of 2017 net income to the partners.

Solution

(a) Net income $30,000

Division of Net Income

	Lois Holly	Jim Worth	Total
Salary allowance	$12,000	$10,000	$22,000
Remaining income $8,000 ($30,000 − $22,000)			
Lois Holly ($8,000 × 50%)	4,000		
Jim Worth ($8,000 × 50%)		4,000	
Total remainder			8,000
Total division of net income	$16,000	$14,000	$30,000

(b)

12/31/17	Income Summary	30,000	
	Lois Holly, Capital		16,000
	Jim Worth, Capital		14,000
	(To close net income to partners' capital)		

WileyPLUS Brief Exercises, Exercises, DO IT! Exercises, and Problems and many additional resources are available for practice in WileyPLUS

NOTE: All asterisked Questions, Exercises, and Problems relate to material in the appendix to the chapter.

QUESTIONS

1. The characteristics of a partnership include the following: (a) association of individuals, (b) limited life, and (c) co-ownership of property. Explain each of these terms.
2. Kevin Mathis is confused about the partnership characteristics of (a) mutual agency and (b) unlimited liability. Explain these two characteristics for Kevin.
3. Lance Kosinski and Matt Morrisen are considering a business venture. They ask you to explain the advantages and disadvantages of the partnership form of organization.
4. Why might a company choose to use a limited partnership?
5. Newland and Palermo form a partnership. Newland contributes land with a book value of $50,000 and a fair value of $60,000. Newland also contributes equipment with a book value of $52,000 and a fair value of $57,000. The partnership assumes a $20,000 mortgage on the land. What should be the balance in Newland's capital account upon formation of the partnership?
6. W. Jenson, N. Emch, and W. Gilligan have a partnership called Outlaws. A dispute has arisen among the partners. Jenson has invested twice as much in assets as the other two partners, and he believes net income and net losses should be shared in accordance with the capital ratios. The partnership agreement does not specify the division of profits and losses. How will net income and net loss be divided?
7. Mutt and Jeff are discussing how income and losses should be divided in a partnership they plan to form. What factors should be considered in determining the division of net income or net loss?
8. M. Elston and R. Ogle have partnership capital balances of $40,000 and $80,000, respectively. The partnership agreement indicates that net income or net loss should be shared equally. If net income for the partnership is $42,000, how should the net income be divided?
9. S. Pletcher and F. Holt share net income and net loss equally. (a) Which account(s) is (are) debited and credited to record the division of net income between the partners? (b) If S. Pletcher withdraws $30,000 in cash for personal use instead of salary, which account is debited and which is credited?
10. Partners T. Greer and R. Parks are provided salary allowances of $30,000 and $25,000, respectively. They divide the remainder of the partnership income in a ratio of 3:2. If partnership net income is $40,000, how much is allocated to Greer and Parks?
11. Are the financial statements of a partnership similar to those of a proprietorship? Discuss.
12. How does the liquidation of a partnership differ from the dissolution of a partnership?
13. Roger Fuller and Mike Rangel are discussing the liquidation of a partnership. Roger maintains that all cash should be distributed to partners on the basis of their income ratios. Is he correct? Explain.
14. In continuing their discussion from Question 13, Mike says that even in the case of a capital deficiency, all cash should still be distributed on the basis of capital balances. Is Mike correct? Explain.
15. Norris, Madson, and Howell have income ratios of 5:3:2 and capital balances of $34,000, $31,000, and $28,000, respectively. Noncash assets are sold at a

gain and allocated to the partners. After creditors are paid, $103,000 of cash is available for distribution to the partners. How much cash should be paid to Madson?

16. Before the final distribution of cash, account balances are Cash $27,000; S. Shea, Capital $19,000 (Cr.); L. Seastrom, Capital $12,000 (Cr.); and M. Luthi, Capital $4,000 (Dr.). Luthi is unable to pay any of the capital deficiency. If the income-sharing ratios are 5:3:2, respectively, how much cash should be paid to L. Seastrom?

17. Why is Apple not a partnership?

*18. Susan Turnbull decides to purchase from an existing partner for $50,000 a one-third interest in a partnership. What effect does this transaction have on partnership net assets?

*19. Jerry Park decides to invest $25,000 in a partnership for a one-sixth capital interest. How much do the partnership's net assets increase? Does Park also acquire a one-sixth income ratio through this investment?

*20. Jill Parsons purchases for $72,000 Jamar's interest in the Tholen-Jamar partnership. Assuming that Jamar has a $68,000 capital balance in the partnership, what journal entry is made by the partnership to record this transaction?

*21. Jaime Keller has a $41,000 capital balance in a partnership. She sells her interest to Sam Parmenter for $45,000 cash. What entry is made by the partnership for this transaction?

*22. Andrea Riley retires from the partnership of Jaggard, Pester, and Riley. She receives $85,000 of partnership assets in settlement of her capital balance of $81,000. Assuming that the income-sharing ratios are 5:3:2, respectively, how much of Riley's bonus is debited to Pester's capital account?

*23. Your roommate argues that partnership assets should be revalued in situations like those in Question 21. Why is this generally not done?

*24. How is a deceased partner's equity determined?

BRIEF EXERCISES

BE12-1 Barbara Ripley and Fred Nichols decide to organize the ALL-Star partnership. Ripley invests $15,000 cash, and Nichols contributes $10,000 cash and equipment having a book value of $3,500. Prepare the entry to record Nichols's investment in the partnership, assuming the equipment has a fair value of $4,000.

Journalize entries in forming a partnership.

(LO 1)

BE12-2 Penner and Torres decide to merge their proprietorships into a partnership called Pentor Company. The balance sheet of Torres Co. shows:

Prepare portion of opening balance sheet for partnership.

(LO 1)

Accounts receivable	$16,000	
Less: Allowance for doubtful accounts	1,200	$14,800
Equipment	20,000	
Less: Accumulated depreciation—equip.	7,000	13,000

The partners agree that the net realizable value of the receivables is $14,500 and that the fair value of the equipment is $11,000. Indicate how the accounts should appear in the opening balance sheet of the partnership.

BE12-3 Rod Dall Co. reports net income of $75,000. The income ratios are Rod 60% and Dall 40%. Indicate the division of net income to each partner, and prepare the entry to distribute the net income.

Journalize the division of net income using fixed income ratios.

(LO 2)

BE12-4 PFW Co. reports net income of $45,000. Partner salary allowances are Pitts $15,000, Filbert $5,000, and Witten $5,000. Indicate the division of net income to each partner, assuming the income ratio is 50:30:20, respectively.

Compute division of net income with a salary allowance and fixed ratios.

(LO 2)

BE12-5 Nabb & Fry Co. reports net income of $31,000. Interest allowances are Nabb $7,000 and Fry $5,000, salary allowances are Nabb $15,000 and Fry $10,000, and the remainder is shared equally. Show the distribution of income.

Show division of net income when allowances exceed net income.

(LO 2)

BE12-6 After liquidating noncash assets and paying creditors, account balances in the Mann Co. are Cash $21,000; A, Capital (Cr.) $8,000; B, Capital (Cr.) $9,000; and C, Capital (Cr.) $4,000. The partners share income equally. Journalize the final distribution of cash to the partners.

Journalize final cash distribution in liquidation.

(LO 3)

***BE12-7** Gamma Co. capital balances are Barr $30,000, Croy $25,000, and Eubank $22,000. The partners share income equally. Tovar is admitted to the firm by purchasing one-half of Eubank's interest for $13,000. Journalize the admission of Tovar to the partnership.

Journalize admission by purchase of an interest.

(LO 4)

Journalize admission by investment.
(LO 4)

***BE12-8** In Eastwood Co., capital balances are Irey $40,000 and Pedigo $50,000. The partners share income equally. Vernon is admitted to the firm with a 45% interest by an investment of cash of $58,000. Journalize the admission of Vernon.

Journalize withdrawal paid by personal assets.
(LO 4)

***BE12-9** Capital balances in Pelmar Co. are Lango $40,000, Oslo $30,000, and Fernetti $20,000. Lango and Oslo each agree to pay Fernetti $12,000 from their personal assets. Lango and Oslo each receive 50% of Fernetti's equity. The partners share income equally. Journalize the withdrawal of Fernetti.

Journalize withdrawal paid by partnership assets.
(LO 4)

***BE12-10** Data pertaining to Pelmar Co. are presented in BE12-9. Instead of payment from personal assets, assume that Fernetti receives $24,000 from partnership assets in withdrawing from the firm. Journalize the withdrawal of Fernetti.

DO IT! Exercises

Analyze statements about partnership organization.
(LO 1)

DO IT! 12-1 Indicate whether each of the following statements is true or false.

_______ 1. Each partner is personally and individually liable for all partnership liabilities.
_______ 2. If a partnership dissolves, each partner has a claim to the specific assets he/she contributed to the firm.
_______ 3. In a limited partnership, all partners have limited liability.
_______ 4. A major advantage of regular partnership is that it is simple and inexpensive to create and operate.
_______ 5. Members of a limited liability company can take an active management role.

Divide net income and prepare closing entry.
(LO 2)

DO IT! 12-2 Frontenac Company reported net income of $75,000. The partnership agreement provides for salaries of $25,000 to Miley and $18,000 to Guthrie. They divide the remainder 40% to Miley and 60% to Guthrie. Miley asks your help to divide the net income between the partners and to prepare the closing entry.

Complete schedule of partnership liquidation payments.
(LO 3)

DO IT! 12-3a The partners of LR Company have decided to liquidate their business. Noncash assets were sold for $125,000. The income ratios of the partners Cisneros, Gunselman, and Forren are 3:2:3, respectively. Complete the following schedule of cash payments for LR Company.

LR Company.xls

Home | Insert | Page Layout | Formulas | Data | Review | View

P18 fx

	A	B	C	D	E	F	G	H	I	J	K	L
1	Item	Cash	+	Noncash Assets	=	Liabilities	+	Cisneros, Capital	+	Gunselman, Capital	+	Forren, Capital
2	Balances before liquidation	15,000		90,000		40,000		20,000		32,000		13,000
3	Sale of noncash assets and allocation of gain											
4	New balances											
5	Pay liabilities											
6	New balances											
7	Cash distribution to partners											
8	Final balances											
9												
10												

Prepare entries to record absorption of capital deficiency and distribution of cash.
(LO 3)

DO IT! 12-3b Parsons Company wishes to liquidate the firm by distributing the company's cash to the three partners. Prior to the distribution of cash, the company's balances are Cash $73,000; Oakley, Capital (Cr.) $47,000; Quaney, Capital (Dr.) $14,000; and Ellis, Capital (Cr.) $40,000. The income ratios of the three partners are 3:3:4, respectively. Prepare the entry to record the absorption of Quaney's capital deficiency by the other partners and the distribution of cash to the partners with credit balances.

EXERCISES

E12-1 Mark Rensing has prepared the following list of statements about partnerships.

Identify characteristics of partnership.

(LO 1)

1. A partnership is an association of three or more persons to carry on as co-owners of a business for profit.
2. The legal requirements for forming a partnership can be quite burdensome.
3. A partnership is not an entity for financial reporting purposes.
4. The net income of a partnership is taxed as a separate entity.
5. The act of any partner is binding on all other partners, even when partners perform business acts beyond the scope of their authority.
6. Each partner is personally and individually liable for all partnership liabilities.
7. When a partnership is dissolved, the assets legally revert to the original contributor.
8. In a limited partnership, one or more partners have unlimited liability and one or more partners have limited liability for the debts of the firm.
9. Mutual agency is a major advantage of the partnership form of business.

Instructions

Identify each statement as true or false. If false, indicate how to correct the statement.

E12-2 K. Decker, S. Rosen, and E. Toso are forming a partnership. Decker is transferring $50,000 of personal cash to the partnership. Rosen owns land worth $15,000 and a small building worth $80,000, which she transfers to the partnership. Toso transfers to the partnership cash of $9,000, accounts receivable of $32,000, and equipment worth $39,000. The partnership expects to collect $29,000 of the accounts receivable.

Journalize entry for formation of a partnership.

(LO 1)

Instructions

(a) Prepare the journal entries to record each of the partners' investments.

(b) What amount would be reported as total owners' equity immediately after the investments?

E12-3 Suzy Vopat has owned and operated a proprietorship for several years. On January 1, she decides to terminate this business and become a partner in the firm of Vopat and Sigma. Vopat's investment in the partnership consists of $12,000 in cash, and the following assets of the proprietorship: accounts receivable $14,000 less allowance for doubtful accounts of $2,000, and equipment $30,000 less accumulated depreciation of $4,000. It is agreed that the allowance for doubtful accounts should be $3,000 for the partnership. The fair value of the equipment is $23,500.

Journalize entry for formation of a partnership.

(LO 1)

Instructions

Journalize Vopat's admission to the firm of Vopat and Sigma.

E12-4 McGill and Smyth have capital balances on January 1 of $50,000 and $40,000, respectively. The partnership income-sharing agreement provides for (1) annual salaries of $22,000 for McGill and $13,000 for Smyth, (2) interest at 10% on beginning capital balances, and (3) remaining income or loss to be shared 60% by McGill and 40% by Smyth.

Prepare schedule showing distribution of net income and closing entry.

(LO 2)

XLS

Instructions

(a) Prepare a schedule showing the distribution of net income, assuming net income is (1) $50,000 and (2) $36,000.

(b) Journalize the allocation of net income in each of the situations above.

E12-5 Coburn (beginning capital, $60,000) and Webb (beginning capital $90,000) are partners. During 2017, the partnership earned net income of $80,000, and Coburn made drawings of $18,000 while Webb made drawings of $24,000.

Prepare journal entries to record allocation of net income.

(LO 2)

Instructions

(a) Assume the partnership income-sharing agreement calls for income to be divided 45% to Coburn and 55% to Webb. Prepare the journal entry to record the allocation of net income.

(b) Assume the partnership income-sharing agreement calls for income to be divided with a salary of $30,000 to Coburn and $25,000 to Webb, with the remainder divided 45% to Coburn and 55% to Webb. Prepare the journal entry to record the allocation of net income.

(c) Assume the partnership income-sharing agreement calls for income to be divided with a salary of $40,000 to Coburn and $35,000 to Webb, interest of 10% on beginning capital, and the remainder divided 50%–50%. Prepare the journal entry to record the allocation of net income.

(d) Compute the partners' ending capital balances under the assumption in part (c).

Prepare partners' capital statement and partial balance sheet.

(LO 2)

E12-6 For National Co., beginning capital balances on January 1, 2017, are Nancy Payne $20,000 and Ann Dody $18,000. During the year, drawings were Payne $8,000 and Dody $5,000. Net income was $40,000, and the partners share income equally.

Instructions

(a) Prepare the partners' capital statement for the year.

(b) Prepare the owners' equity section of the balance sheet at December 31, 2017.

Prepare a classified balance sheet of a partnership.

(LO 2)

E12-7 Terry, Nick, and Frank are forming The Doctor Partnership. Terry is transferring $30,000 of personal cash and equipment worth $25,000 to the partnership. Nick owns land worth $28,000 and a small building worth $75,000, which he transfers to the partnership. There is a long-term mortgage of $20,000 on the land and building, which the partnership assumes. Frank transfers cash of $7,000, accounts receivable of $36,000, supplies worth $3,000, and equipment worth $27,000 to the partnership. The partnership expects to collect $32,000 of the accounts receivable.

Instructions

Prepare a classified balance sheet for the partnership after the partners' investments on December 31, 2017.

Prepare cash payments schedule.

(LO 3)

E12-8 Sedgwick Company at December 31 has cash $20,000, noncash assets $100,000, liabilities $55,000, and the following capital balances: Floyd $45,000 and DeWitt $20,000. The firm is liquidated, and $105,000 in cash is received for the noncash assets. Floyd and DeWitt income ratios are 60% and 40%, respectively.

Instructions

Prepare a schedule of cash payments.

Journalize transactions in a liquidation.

(LO 3)

E12-9 Data for Sedgwick Company are presented in E12-8. Sedgwick Company now decides to liquidate the partnership.

Instructions

Prepare the entries to record:

(a) The sale of noncash assets.

(b) The allocation of the gain or loss on realization to the partners.

(c) Payment of creditors.

(d) Distribution of cash to the partners.

Journalize transactions with a capital deficiency.

(LO 3)

E12-10 Prior to the distribution of cash to the partners, the accounts in the VUP Company are Cash $24,000; Vogel, Capital (Cr.) $17,000; Utech, Capital (Cr.) $15,000; and Pena, Capital (Dr.) $8,000. The income ratios are 5:3:2, respectively. VUP Company decides to liquidate the company.

Instructions

(a) Prepare the entry to record (1) Pena's payment of $8,000 in cash to the partnership and (2) the distribution of cash to the partners with credit balances.

(b) Prepare the entry to record (1) the absorption of Pena's capital deficiency by the other partners and (2) the distribution of cash to the partners with credit balances.

Journalize admission of a new partner by purchase of an interest.

(LO 4)

***E12-11** K. Kolmer, C. Eidman, and C. Ryno share income on a 5:3:2 basis. They have capital balances of $34,000, $26,000, and $21,000, respectively, when Don Jernigan is admitted to the partnership.

Instructions

Prepare the journal entry to record the admission of Don Jernigan under each of the following assumptions.

(a) Purchase of 50% of Kolmer's equity for $19,000.
(b) Purchase of 50% of Eidman's equity for $12,000.
(c) Purchase of $33^1/_3$% of Ryno's equity for $9,000.

***E12-12** S. Pagan and T. Tabor share income on a 6:4 basis. They have capital balances of $100,000 and $60,000, respectively, when W. Wolford is admitted to the partnership.

Journalize admission of a new partner by investment.

(LO 4)

Instructions
Prepare the journal entry to record the admission of W. Wolford under each of the following assumptions.

(a) Investment of $90,000 cash for a 30% ownership interest with bonuses to the existing partners.
(b) Investment of $50,000 cash for a 30% ownership interest with a bonus to the new partner.

***E12-13** N. Essex, C. Gilmore, and C. Heganbart have capital balances of $50,000, $40,000, and $30,000, respectively. Their income ratios are 4:4:2. Heganbart withdraws from the partnership under each of the following independent conditions.

Journalize withdrawal of a partner with payment from partners' personal assets.

(LO 4)

1. Essex and Gilmore agree to purchase Heganbart's equity by paying $17,000 each from their personal assets. Each purchaser receives 50% of Heganbart's equity.
2. Gilmore agrees to purchase all of Heganbart's equity by paying $22,000 cash from her personal assets.
3. Essex agrees to purchase all of Heganbart's equity by paying $26,000 cash from his personal assets.

Instructions
Journalize the withdrawal of Heganbart under each of the assumptions above.

***E12-14** B. Higgins, J. Mayo, and N. Rice have capital balances of $95,000, $75,000, and $60,000, respectively. They share income or loss on a 5:3:2 basis. Rice withdraws from the partnership under each of the following conditions.

Journalize withdrawal of a partner with payment from partnership assets.

(LO 4)

1. Rice is paid $64,000 in cash from partnership assets, and a bonus is granted to the retiring partner.
2. Rice is paid $52,000 in cash from partnership assets, and bonuses are granted to the remaining partners.

Instructions
Journalize the withdrawal of Rice under each of the assumptions above.

***E12-15** Foss, Albertson, and Espinosa are partners who share profits and losses 50%, 30%, and 20%, respectively. Their capital balances are $100,000, $60,000, and $40,000, respectively.

Journalize entry for admission and withdrawal of partners.

(LO 4)

Instructions
(a) Assume Garrett joins the partnership by investing $88,000 for a 25% interest with bonuses to the existing partners. Prepare the journal entry to record his investment.
(b) Assume instead that Foss leaves the partnership. Foss is paid $110,000 with a bonus to the retiring partner. Prepare the journal entry to record Foss's withdrawal.

EXERCISES: SET B AND CHALLENGE EXERCISES

Visit the book's companion website, at **www.wiley.com/college/weygandt**, and choose the Student Companion site to access Exercises: Set B and Challenge Exercises.

PROBLEMS: SET A

Prepare entries for formation of a partnership and a balance sheet.

(LO 1, 2)

GLS

P12-1A The post-closing trial balances of two proprietorships on January 1, 2017, are presented below.

	Sorensen Company Dr.	Sorensen Company Cr.	Lucas Company Dr.	Lucas Company Cr.
Cash	$ 14,000		$12,000	
Accounts receivable	17,500		26,000	
Allowance for doubtful accounts		$ 3,000		$ 4,400
Inventory	26,500		18,400	
Equipment	45,000		29,000	
Accumulated depreciation—equipment		24,000		11,000
Notes payable		18,000		15,000
Accounts payable		22,000		31,000
Sorensen, capital		36,000		
Lucas, capital				24,000
	$103,000	$103,000	$85,400	$85,400

Sorensen and Lucas decide to form a partnership, Solu Company, with the following agreed upon valuations for noncash assets.

	Sorensen Company	Lucas Company
Accounts receivable	$17,500	$26,000
Allowance for doubtful accounts	4,500	4,000
Inventory	28,000	20,000
Equipment	25,000	15,000

All cash will be transferred to the partnership, and the partnership will assume all the liabilities of the two proprietorships. Further, it is agreed that Sorensen will invest an additional $5,000 in cash, and Lucas will invest an additional $19,000 in cash.

Instructions

(a) Sorensen, Capital $40,000
Lucas, Capital $23,000

(c) Total assets $173,000

(a) Prepare separate journal entries to record the transfer of each proprietorship's assets and liabilities to the partnership.
(b) Journalize the additional cash investment by each partner.
(c) Prepare a classified balance sheet for the partnership on January 1, 2017.

Journalize divisions of net income and prepare a partners' capital statement.

(LO 2)

P12-2A At the end of its first year of operations on December 31, 2017, NBS Company's accounts show the following.

Partner	Drawings	Capital
Art Niensted	$23,000	$48,000
Greg Bolen	14,000	30,000
Krista Sayler	10,000	25,000

The capital balance represents each partner's initial capital investment. Therefore, net income or net loss for 2017 has not been closed to the partners' capital accounts.

Instructions

(a) (1) Niensted $18,000
(2) Niensted $20,000
(3) Niensted $17,700

(c) Niensted $42,700

(a) Journalize the entry to record the division of net income for the year 2017 under each of the following independent assumptions.
  (1) Net income is $30,000. Income is shared 6:3:1.
  (2) Net income is $40,000. Niensted and Bolen are given salary allowances of $15,000 and $10,000, respectively. The remainder is shared equally.
  (3) Net income is $19,000. Each partner is allowed interest of 10% on beginning capital balances. Niensted is given a $15,000 salary allowance. The remainder is shared equally.
(b) Prepare a schedule showing the division of net income under assumption (3) above.
(c) Prepare a partners' capital statement for the year under assumption (3) above.

P12-3A The partners in Crawford Company decide to liquidate the firm when the balance sheet shows the following.

Prepare entries with a capital deficiency in liquidation of a partnership.

(LO 3)

GLS

CRAWFORD COMPANY
Balance Sheet
May 31, 2017

Assets		Liabilities and Owners' Equity	
Cash	$ 27,500	Notes payable	$ 13,500
Accounts receivable	25,000	Accounts payable	27,000
Allowance for doubtful accounts	(1,000)	Salaries and wages payable	4,000
Inventory	34,500	A. Jamison, capital	33,000
Equipment	21,000	S. Moyer, capital	21,000
Accumulated depreciation—equipment	(5,500)	P. Roper, capital	3,000
	$101,500		$101,500

The partners share income and loss 5:3:2. During the process of liquidation, the following transactions were completed in the following sequence.

1. A total of $51,000 was received from converting noncash assets into cash.
2. Gain or loss on realization was allocated to partners.
3. Liabilities were paid in full.
4. P. Roper paid his capital deficiency.
5. Cash was paid to the partners with credit balances.

Instructions

(a) Prepare the entries to record the transactions.
(b) Post to the cash and capital accounts.
(c) Assume that Roper is unable to pay the capital deficiency.
  (1) Prepare the entry to allocate Roper's debit balance to Jamison and Moyer.
  (2) Prepare the entry to record the final distribution of cash.

(a) Loss on realization $23,000
Cash paid: to Jamison $21,500; to Moyer $14,100

***P12-4A** At April 30, partners' capital balances in PDL Company are G. Donley $52,000, C. Lamar $48,000, and J. Pinkston $18,000. The income sharing ratios are 5:4:1, respectively. On May 1, the PDLT Company is formed by admitting J. Terrell to the firm as a partner.

Journalize admission of a partner under different assumptions.

(LO 4)

Instructions

(a) Journalize the admission of Terrell under each of the following independent assumptions.
  (1) Terrell purchases 50% of Pinkston's ownership interest by paying Pinkston $16,000 in cash.
  (2) Terrell purchases 33 1/3% of Lamar's ownership interest by paying Lamar $15,000 in cash.
  (3) Terrell invests $62,000 for a 30% ownership interest, and bonuses are given to the old partners.
  (4) Terrell invests $42,000 for a 30% ownership interest, which includes a bonus to the new partner.
(b) Lamar's capital balance is $32,000 after admitting Terrell to the partnership by investment. If Lamar's ownership interest is 20% of total partnership capital, what were (1) Terrell's cash investment and (2) the bonus to the new partner?

(a) (1) Terrell $9,000
(2) Terrell $16,000
(3) Terrell $54,000
(4) Terrell $48,000

***P12-5A** On December 31, the capital balances and income ratios in TEP Company are as follows.

Journalize withdrawal of a partner under different assumptions.

(LO 4)

Partner	Capital Balance	Income Ratio
Trayer	$60,000	50%
Emig	40,000	30%
Posada	30,000	20%

Instructions

(a) Journalize the withdrawal of Posada under each of the following assumptions.
  (1) Each of the continuing partners agrees to pay $18,000 in cash from personal funds to purchase Posada's ownership equity. Each receives 50% of Posada's equity.
  (2) Emig agrees to purchase Posada's ownership interest for $25,000 cash.

(a) (1) Emig, Capital $15,000
(2) Emig, Capital $30,000

(3) Bonus $4,000 (3) Posada is paid $34,000 from partnership assets, which includes a bonus to the retiring partner.

(4) Bonus $8,000 (4) Posada is paid $22,000 from partnership assets, and bonuses to the remaining partners are recognized.

(b) If Emig's capital balance after Posada's withdrawal is $43,600, what were (1) the total bonus to the remaining partners and (2) the cash paid by the partnership to Posada?

PROBLEMS: SET B AND SET C

Visit the book's companion website, at **www.wiley.com/college/weygandt**, and choose the Student Companion site to access Problems: Set B and Set C.

CONTINUING PROBLEM

© leungchopan/ Shutterstock

COOKIE CREATIONS: AN ENTREPRENEURIAL JOURNEY

(*Note:* This is a continuation of the Cookie Creations problem from Chapters 1 through 11.)

CC12 Natalie's high school friend, Katy Peterson, has been operating a bakery for approximately 18 months. Because Natalie has been so successful operating Cookie Creations, Katy would like to have Natalie become her partner. Katy believes that together they will create a thriving cookie-making business. Natalie is quite happy with her current business set-up. Up until now, she had not considered joining forces with anyone. However, Natalie thinks that it may be a good idea to establish a partnership with Katy, and decides to look into it.

Go to the book's companion website, **www.wiley.com/college/weygandt**, *to see the completion of this problem.*

BROADENING YOUR PERSPECTIVE

FINANCIAL REPORTING AND ANALYSIS

Real-World Focus

BYP12-1 This exercise is an introduction to the Big Four accounting firms, all of which are partnerships.

Addresses

Deloitte & Touche	**www.deloitte.com/**
Ernst & Young	**www.ey.com/**
KPMG	**www.us.kpmg.com/**
PricewaterhouseCoopers	**www.pwc.com/**

or go to **www.wiley.com/college/weygandt**

Steps

1. Select a firm that is of interest to you.
2. Go to the firm's homepage.

Instructions

(a) Name two services performed by the firm.
(b) What is the firm's total annual revenue?
(c) How many clients does it service?
(d) How many people are employed by the firm?
(e) How many partners are there in the firm?

Decision-Making Across the Organization

BYP12-2 Stephen Wadson and Mary Shively, two professionals in the finance area, have worked for Morrisen Leasing for a number of years. Morrisen Leasing is a company that leases high-tech medical equipment to hospitals. Stephen and Mary have decided that, with their financial expertise, they might start their own company to perform consulting services for individuals interested in leasing equipment. One form of organization they are considering is a partnership.

If they start a partnership, each individual plans to contribute $50,000 in cash. In addition, Stephen has a used IBM computer that originally cost $3,700, which he intends to invest in the partnership. The computer has a present fair value of $1,500.

Although both Stephen and Mary are financial wizards, they do not know a great deal about how a partnership operates. As a result, they have come to you for advice.

Instructions

With the class divided into groups, answer the following.

(a) What are the major disadvantages of starting a partnership?
(b) What type of document is needed for a partnership, and what should this document contain?
(c) Both Stephen and Mary plan to work full-time in the new partnership. They believe that net income or net loss should be shared equally. However, they are wondering how to provide compensation to Stephen Wadson for his investment of the computer. What would you tell them?
(d) Stephen is not sure how the computer equipment should be reported on his tax return. What would you tell him?
(e) As indicated above, Stephen and Mary have worked together for a number of years. Stephen's skills complement Mary's and vice versa. If one of them dies, it will be very difficult for the other to maintain the business, not to mention the difficulty of paying the deceased partner's estate for his or her partnership interest. What would you advise them to do?

Communication Activity

BYP12-3 You are an expert in the field of forming partnerships. Ronald Hrabik and Meg Percival want to establish a partnership to start "Pasta Shop," and they are going to meet with you to discuss their plans. Prior to the meeting, you will send them a memo discussing the issues they need to consider.

Instructions

Write a memo in good form to be sent to Hrabik and Percival.

Ethics Case

BYP12-4 Alexandra and Kellie operate a beauty salon as partners who share profits and losses equally. The success of their business has exceeded their expectations; the salon is operating quite profitably. Kellie is anxious to maximize profits and schedules appointments from 8 a.m. to 6 p.m. daily, even sacrificing some lunch hours to accommodate regular customers. Alexandra schedules her appointments from 9 a.m. to 5 p.m. and takes long lunch hours. Alexandra regularly makes significantly larger withdrawals of cash than Kellie does, but, she says, "Kellie, you needn't worry, I never make a withdrawal without you knowing about it, so it is properly recorded in my drawings account and charged against my capital at the end of the year." Alexandra's withdrawals to date are double Kellie's.

Instructions

(a) Who are the stakeholders in this situation?
(b) Identify the problems with Alexandra's actions and discuss the ethical considerations involved.
(c) How might the partnership agreement be revised to accommodate the differences in Alexandra's and Kellie's work and withdrawal habits?

All About You

BYP12-5 As this chapter indicates, the partnership form of organization has advantages and disadvantages. The chapter noted that different types of partnerships have been developed to minimize some of these disadvantages. Alternatively, an individual or company can choose the proprietorship or corporate form of organization.

Instructions

Go to two local businesses that are different, such as a restaurant, a retailer, a construction company, or a professional office (dentist, doctor, etc.), and find the answers to the following questions.

(a) What form of organization do you use in your business?
(b) What do you believe are the two major advantages of this form of organization for your business?
(c) What do you believe are the two major disadvantages of this form of organization for your business?
(d) Do you believe that eventually you may choose another form of organization?
(e) Did you have someone help you form this organization (attorney, accountant, relative, etc.)?

As partnership accounting is essentially the same under GAAP and IFRS, there is no A Look at IFRS *section in this chapter.*

13 Corporations: Organization and Capital Stock Transactions

CHAPTER PREVIEW Corporations like Nike and adidas have substantial resources at their disposal. In fact, the corporation is the dominant form of business organization in the United States in terms of sales, earnings, and number of employees. All of the 500 largest companies in the United States are corporations. In this chapter, we will explain the essential features of a corporation and the accounting for a corporation's capital stock transactions. In Chapter 14, we will look at other issues related to accounting for corporations.

FEATURE STORY

What's Cooking?

What major U.S. corporation got its start 41 years ago with a waffle iron? *Hint:* It doesn't sell food. *Second hint:* Swoosh. *Third hint:* "Just do it." That's right, Nike. In 1971, Nike co-founder Bill Bowerman put a piece of rubber into a kitchen waffle iron, and its trademark sole was born. It seems fair to say that at Nike, "They don't make 'em like they used to."

Nike was co-founded by Bowerman and Phil Knight, a member of Bowerman's University of Oregon track team. Each began in the shoe business independently during the early 1960s. Bowerman got his start by making hand-crafted running shoes for his University of Oregon track team. Knight, after completing graduate school, started a small business importing low-cost, high-quality shoes from Japan. In 1964, the two joined forces, each contributing $500, and formed Blue Ribbon Sports, a partnership that marketed Japanese shoes.

It wasn't until 1971 that the company began manufacturing its own line of shoes. With the new shoes came a new corporate name–Nike–the Greek goddess of victory. It is hard to imagine that the company that now boasts a stable full of world-class athletes as promoters at one time had part-time employees selling shoes out of car trunks at track meets. Nike has achieved its success through relentless innovation combined with unbridled promotion.

By 1980, Nike was sufficiently established and issued its first stock to the public. That same year, it created a stock ownership program for its employees, allowing them to share in the company's success. Since then, Nike has enjoyed phenomenal growth, with 2014 sales reaching $27.8 billion and total dividends paid of $799 million.

Nike is not alone in its quest for the top of the sport shoe world. Reebok used to be Nike's arch rival (get it? "arch"), but then Reebok was acquired by the German company adidas. Now adidas pushes Nike every step of the way.

The shoe market is fickle, with new styles becoming popular almost daily and vast international markets still lying untapped. Whether one of these two giants does eventually take control of the pedi-planet remains to be seen. Meanwhile, the shareholders sit anxiously in the stands as this Olympic-size drama unfolds.

Franck Fife/AFP/Getty Images, Inc.

CHAPTER OUTLINE

Learning Objectives

1 Discuss the major characteristics of a corporation.

- Characteristics of a corporation
- Forming a corporation
- Stockholder rights
- Stock issue considerations
- Corporate capital

DO IT! 1a Corporate Organization; 1b Corporate Capital

2 Explain how to account for the issuance of common and preferred stock.

- Issuing par value common stock for cash
- Issuing no-par common stock for cash
- Issuing common stock for services or noncash assets
- Accounting for preferred stock

DO IT! 2 Issuance of Stock

3 Explain how to account for treasury stock.

- Purchase of treasury stock
- Disposal of treasury stock

DO IT! 3 Treasury Stock

4 Prepare a stockholders' equity section.

- Capital stock
- Additional paid-in capital

DO IT! 4 Stockholders' Equity Section

o to the ***REVIEW AND PRACTICE*** section at the end of the chapter for a review of key concepts and practice applications with solutions.

sit **WileyPLUS with ORION** for additional tutorials and practice opportunities.

LEARNING OBJECTIVE 1

Discuss the major characteristics of a corporation.

In 1819, Chief Justice John Marshall defined a corporation as "an artificial being, invisible, intangible, and existing only in contemplation of law." This definition is the foundation for the prevailing legal interpretation that a **corporation** is an **entity separate and distinct from its owners**.

A corporation is created by law, and its continued existence depends upon the statutes of the state in which it is incorporated. As a legal entity, a corporation has most of the rights and privileges of a person. The major exceptions relate to privileges that only a living person can exercise, such as the right to vote or to hold public office. A corporation is subject to the same duties and responsibilities as a person. For example, it must abide by the laws, and it must pay taxes.

Two common ways to classify corporations are by **purpose** and by **ownership**. A corporation may be organized for the purpose of making a profit, or it may be not-for-profit. For-profit corporations include such well-known companies as McDonald's, Nike, PepsiCo, and Google. Not-for-profit corporations are organized for charitable, medical, or educational purposes. Examples are the Salvation Army and the American Cancer Society.

Classification by ownership differentiates publicly held and privately held corporations. A **publicly held corporation** may have thousands of stockholders. Its stock is regularly traded on a national securities exchange such as the New York Stock Exchange or NASDAQ. Examples are IBM, Caterpillar, and Apple.

In contrast, a **privately held corporation** usually has only a few stockholders, and does not offer its stock for sale to the general public. Privately held companies are generally much smaller than publicly held companies, although some notable exceptions exist. Cargill Inc., a private corporation that trades in grain and other commodities, is one of the largest companies in the United States.

Alternative Terminology
Privately held corporations are also referred to as *closely held corporations*.

Characteristics of a Corporation

In 1964, when Nike's founders Phil Knight and Bill Bowerman were just getting started in the running shoe business, they formed their original organization as a partnership. In 1968, they reorganized the company as a corporation. A number of characteristics distinguish corporations from proprietorships and partnerships. We explain the most important of these characteristics below.

Legal existence separate from owners

SEPARATE LEGAL EXISTENCE

As an entity separate and distinct from its owners, the corporation acts under its own name rather than in the name of its stockholders. Nike may buy, own, and sell property. It may borrow money, and it may enter into legally binding contracts in its own name. It may also sue or be sued, and it pays its own taxes.

In a partnership, the acts of the owners (partners) bind the partnership. In contrast, the acts of its owners (stockholders) do not bind the corporation unless such owners are **agents** of the corporation. For example, if you owned shares of Nike stock, you would not have the right to purchase inventory for the company unless you were designated as an agent of the corporation.

Limited liability of stockholders

LIMITED LIABILITY OF STOCKHOLDERS

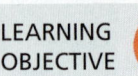

Since a corporation is a separate legal entity, creditors have recourse only to corporate assets to satisfy their claims. The liability of stockholders is normally limited to their investment in the corporation. Creditors have no legal claim on the personal assets of the owners unless fraud has occurred. Even in the event of bankruptcy, stockholders' losses are generally limited to their capital investment in the corporation.

TRANSFERABLE OWNERSHIP RIGHTS

Shares of capital stock give ownership in a corporation. These shares are transferable units. Stockholders may dispose of part or all of their interest in a corporation simply by selling their stock. The transfer of an ownership interest in a partnership requires the consent of each owner. In contrast, the transfer of stock is entirely at the discretion of the stockholder. It does not require the approval of either the corporation or other stockholders.

The transfer of ownership rights between stockholders normally has no effect on the daily operating activities of the corporation. Nor does it affect the corporation's assets, liabilities, and total ownership equity. The transfer of these ownership rights is a transaction between individual owners. The company does not participate in the transfer of these ownership rights after the original sale of the capital stock.

ABILITY TO ACQUIRE CAPITAL

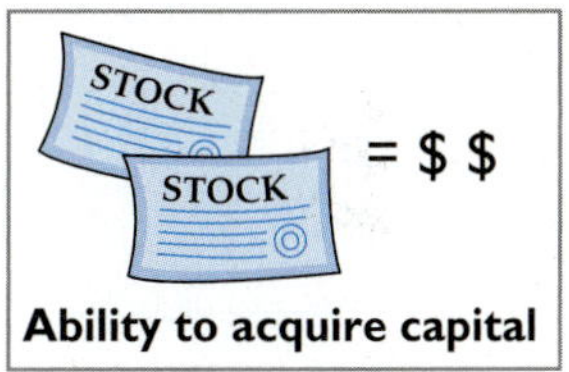

It is relatively easy for a corporation to obtain capital through the issuance of stock. Buying stock in a corporation is often attractive to an investor because a stockholder has limited liability and shares of stock are readily transferable. Also, numerous individuals can become stockholders by investing relatively small amounts of money.

CONTINUOUS LIFE

The life of a corporation is stated in its charter. The life may be perpetual, or it may be limited to a specific number of years. If it is limited, the company can extend the life through renewal of the charter. Since a corporation is a separate legal entity, its continuance as a going concern is not affected by the withdrawal, death, or incapacity of a stockholder, employee, or officer. As a result, a successful company can have a continuous and perpetual life.

CORPORATION MANAGEMENT

Stockholders legally own the corporation. However, they manage the corporation indirectly through a board of directors they elect. Philip Knight is the chairman of Nike. The board, in turn, formulates the operating policies for the company. The board also selects officers, such as a president and one or more vice presidents, to execute policy and to perform daily management functions. As a result of the Sarbanes-Oxley Act, the board is now required to monitor management's actions more closely. Many feel that the failures of Enron, WorldCom, and more recently MF Global could have been avoided by more diligent boards.

Illustration 13-1 (page 574) presents a typical organization chart showing the delegation of responsibility. The chief executive officer (CEO) has overall responsibility for managing the business. As the organization chart shows, the CEO delegates responsibility to other officers. The chief accounting officer is the **controller**. The controller's responsibilities include (1) maintaining the accounting records, (2) ensuring an adequate system of internal control, and (3) preparing financial statements, tax returns, and internal reports. The **treasurer** has custody of the corporation's funds and is responsible for maintaining the company's cash position.

> **ETHICS NOTE**
>
> Managers who are not owners are often compensated based on the performance of the firm. They thus may be tempted to exaggerate firm performance by inflating income figures.

The organizational structure of a corporation enables a company to hire professional managers to run the business. On the other hand, the separation of ownership and management often reduces an owner's ability to actively manage the company.

Illustration 13-1
Corporation organization chart

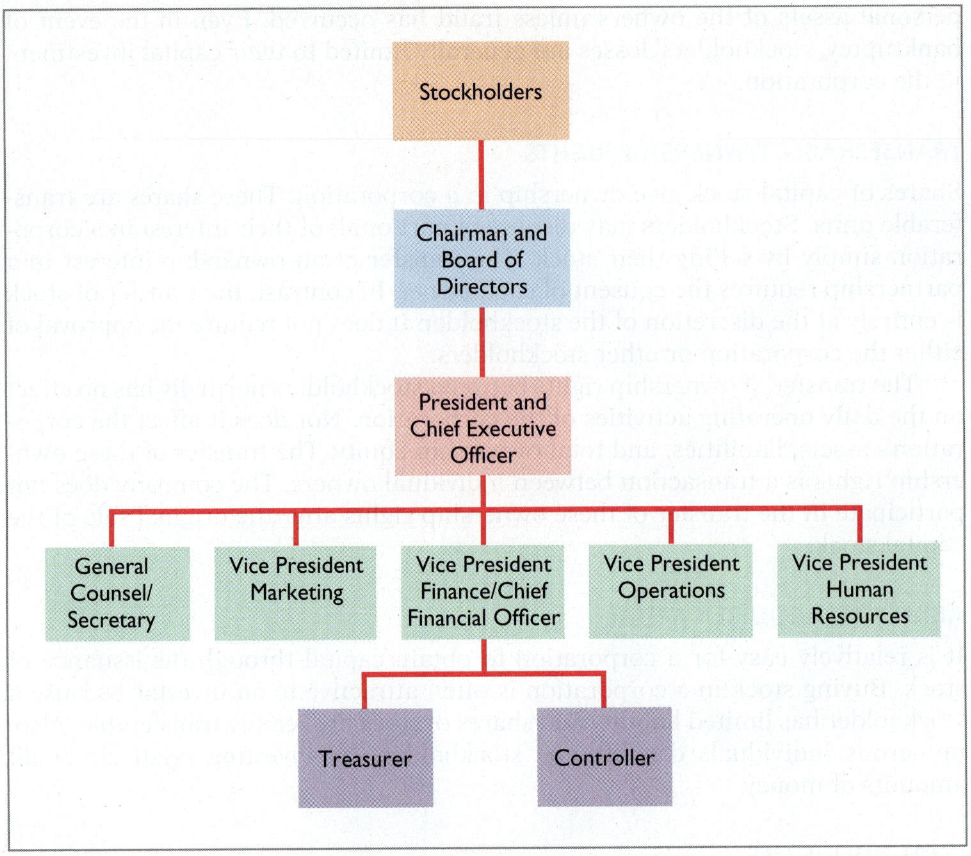

GOVERNMENT REGULATIONS

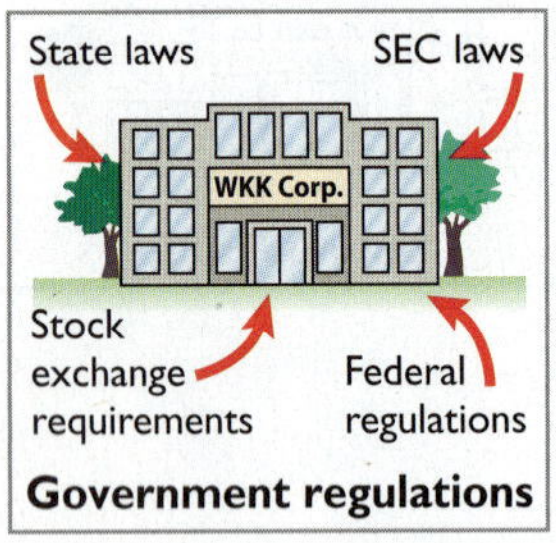

A corporation is subject to numerous state and federal regulations. For example, state laws usually prescribe the requirements for issuing stock, the distributions of earnings permitted to stockholders, and the acceptable methods for buying back and retiring stock. Federal securities laws govern the sale of capital stock to the general public. Also, most publicly held corporations are required to make extensive disclosure of their financial affairs to the Securities and Exchange Commission (SEC) through quarterly and annual reports (Forms 10Q and 10K). In addition, when a corporation lists its stock on organized securities exchanges, it must comply with the reporting requirements of these exchanges. Government regulations are designed to protect the owners of the corporation.

ADDITIONAL TAXES

Owners of proprietorships and partnerships report their share of earnings on their personal income tax returns. The individual owner then pays taxes on this amount. Corporations, on the other hand, must pay federal and state income taxes **as a separate legal entity**. These taxes can be substantial. They can amount to as much as 40% of taxable income.

In addition, stockholders must pay taxes on cash dividends (pro rata distributions of net income). Thus, many argue that the government taxes corporate income **twice (double taxation)**—once at the corporate level and again at the individual level.

In summary, Illustration 13-2 shows the advantages and disadvantages of a corporation compared to a proprietorship and a partnership.

Forming a Corporation

A corporation is formed by grant of a state **charter**. The charter is a document that describes the name and purpose of the corporation, the types and number of shares of stock that are authorized to be issued, the names of the individuals that

Advantages	Disadvantages
Separate legal existence	Corporation management—separation of ownership and management
Limited liability of stockholders	Government regulations
Transferable ownership rights	Additional taxes
Ability to acquire capital	
Continuous life	
Corporation management—professional managers	

Illustration 13-2
Advantages and disadvantages of a corporation

formed the company, and the number of shares that these individuals agreed to purchase. Regardless of the number of states in which a corporation has operating divisions, it is incorporated in only one state.

Alternative Terminology
The charter is often referred to as the *articles of incorporation.*

It is to the company's advantage to incorporate in a state whose laws are favorable to the corporate form of business organization. For example, although General Motors has its headquarters in Michigan, it is incorporated in New Jersey. In fact, more and more corporations have been incorporating in states with rules that favor existing management. For example, Gulf Oil changed its state of incorporation to Delaware to thwart possible unfriendly takeovers. There, certain defensive tactics against takeovers can be approved by the board of directors alone, without a vote by shareholders.

Upon receipt of its charter from the state of incorporation, the corporation establishes **by-laws**. The by-laws establish the internal rules and procedures for conducting the affairs of the corporation. Corporations engaged in interstate commerce must also obtain a **license** from each state in which they do business. The license subjects the corporation's operating activities to the general corporation laws of the state.

Costs incurred in the formation of a corporation are called **organization costs**. These costs include legal and state fees, and promotional expenditures involved in the organization of the business. **Corporations expense organization costs as incurred.** Determining the amount and timing of future benefits is so difficult that it is standard procedure to take a conservative approach of expensing these costs immediately.

Accounting Across the Organization — Facebook

Jeff Chiu/AP/Wide World Photos

A Thousand Millionaires!

Traveling to space or embarking on an expedition to excavate lost Mayan ruins are normally the stuff of adventure novels. But for employees of Facebook, these and other lavish dreams moved closer to reality when the world's No. 1 online social network went public through an initial public offering (IPO) that may have created at least a thousand millionaires. The IPO was the largest in Internet history, valuing Facebook at over $104 billion.

With all these riches to be had, why did Mark Zuckerberg, the founder of Facebook, delay taking his company public? Consider that the main motivation for issuing shares to the public is to raise money so you can grow your business. However, unlike a manufacturer or even an online retailer, Facebook doesn't need major physical resources, it doesn't have inventory, and it doesn't really need much money for marketing. So in the past, the company hasn't had much need for additional cash beyond what it was already generating on its own. Finally, as head of a closely held, nonpublic company, Zuckerberg was subject to far fewer regulations than a public company.

Source: "Status Update: I'm Rich! Facebook Flotation to Create 1,000 Millionaires Among Company's Rank and File," *Daily Mail Reporter* (February 1, 2012).

Why did Mark Zuckerberg, the CEO and founder of Facebook, delay taking his company's shares public through an initial public offering (IPO)? (Go to **WileyPLUS** for this answer and additional questions.)

Stockholder Rights

When chartered, the corporation may begin selling shares of stock. When a corporation has only one class of stock, it is **common stock**. Each share of common stock gives the stockholder the ownership rights pictured in Illustration 13-3. The articles of incorporation or the by-laws state the ownership rights of a share of stock.

Illustration 13-3
Ownership rights of stockholders

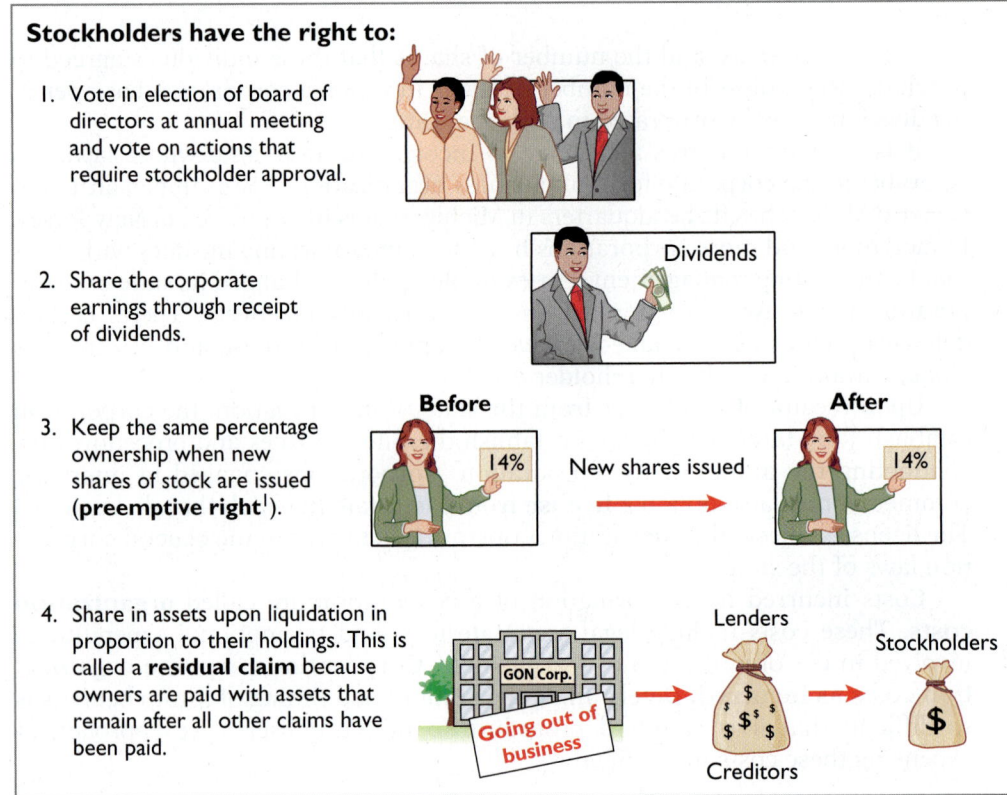

Stockholders have the right to:

1. Vote in election of board of directors at annual meeting and vote on actions that require stockholder approval.

2. Share the corporate earnings through receipt of dividends.

3. Keep the same percentage ownership when new shares of stock are issued (**preemptive right**[1]).

4. Share in assets upon liquidation in proportion to their holdings. This is called a **residual claim** because owners are paid with assets that remain after all other claims have been paid.

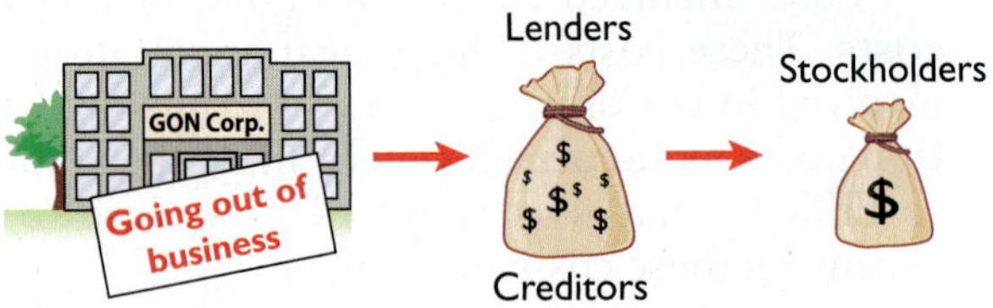

Proof of stock ownership is evidenced by a form known as a **stock certificate**. As Illustration 13-4 shows, the face of the certificate shows the name of the corporation, the stockholder's name, the class and special features of the stock, the number of shares owned, and the signatures of authorized corporate officials. Prenumbered certificates facilitate accountability. They may be issued for any quantity of shares.

Stock Issue Considerations

Although Nike incorporated in 1968, it did not sell stock to the public until 1980. At that time, Nike evidently decided it would benefit from the infusion of cash that a public sale would bring. When a corporation decides to issue stock, it must resolve a number of basic questions: How many shares should it authorize for sale? How should it issue the stock? What value should the corporation assign to the stock? We address these questions in the following sections.

[1]A number of companies have eliminated the preemptive right because they believe it makes an unnecessary and cumbersome demand on management. For example, by stockholder approval, IBM has dropped its preemptive right for stockholders.

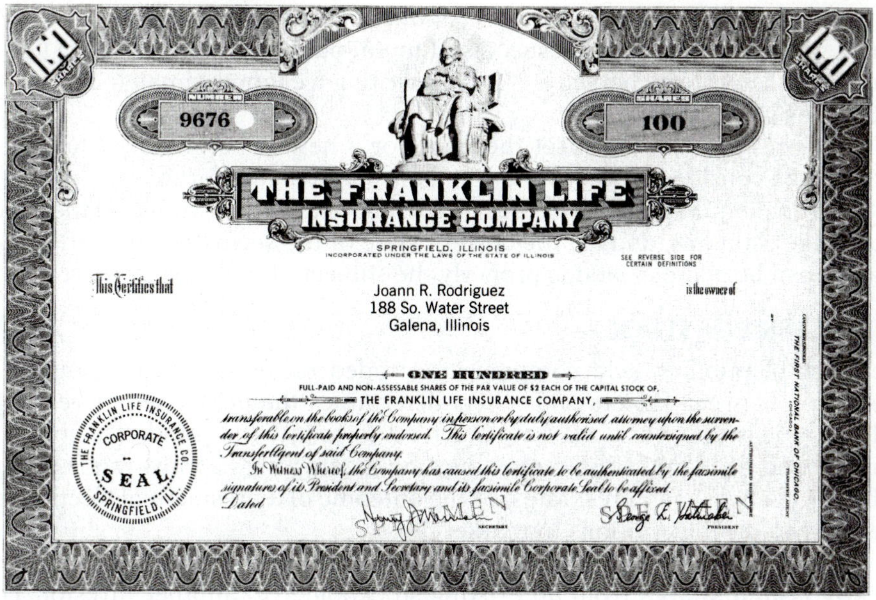

Illustration 13-4
A stock certificate

AUTHORIZED STOCK

The charter indicates the amount of stock that a corporation is **authorized** to sell. The total amount of **authorized stock** at the time of incorporation normally anticipates both initial and subsequent capital needs. As a result, the number of shares authorized generally exceeds the number initially sold. If it sells all authorized stock, a corporation must obtain consent of the state to amend its charter before it can issue additional shares.

The authorization of capital stock does not result in a formal accounting entry. The reason is that the event has no immediate effect on either corporate assets or stockholders' equity. However, the number of authorized shares is often reported in the stockholders' equity section. It is then simple to determine the number of unissued shares that the corporation can issue without amending the charter: subtract the total shares issued from the total authorized. For example, if Advanced Micro was authorized to sell 100,000 shares of common stock and issued 80,000 shares, 20,000 shares would remain unissued.

Indirect issuance

ISSUANCE OF STOCK

A corporation can issue common stock **directly** to investors. Alternatively, it can issue the stock **indirectly** through an investment banking firm that specializes in bringing securities to the attention of prospective investors. Direct issue is typical in closely held companies. Indirect issue is customary for a publicly held corporation.

In an indirect issue, the investment banking firm may agree to **underwrite** the entire stock issue. In this arrangement, the investment banker buys the stock from the corporation at a stipulated price and resells the shares to investors. The corporation thus avoids any risk of being unable to sell the shares. Also, it obtains immediate use of the cash received from the underwriter. The investment banking firm, in turn, assumes the risk of reselling the shares, in return for an underwriting fee.[2]

[2]Alternatively, the investment banking firm may agree only to enter into a **best-efforts contract** with the corporation. In such cases, the banker agrees to sell as many shares as possible at a specified price. The corporation bears the risk of unsold stock. Under a best-efforts arrangement, the banking firm is paid a fee or commission for its services.

For example, Google (the world's number-one Internet search engine) used underwriters when it issued a highly successful initial public offering, raising $1.67 billion. The underwriters charged a 3% underwriting fee (approximately $50 million) on Google's stock offering.

How does a corporation set the price for a new issue of stock? Among the factors to be considered are (1) the company's anticipated future earnings, (2) its expected dividend rate per share, (3) its current financial position, (4) the current state of the economy, and (5) the current state of the securities market. The calculation can be complex and is properly the subject of a finance course.

MARKET PRICE OF STOCK

The stock of publicly held companies is traded on organized exchanges. The interaction between buyers and sellers determines the prices per share. In general, the prices set by the marketplace tend to follow the trend of a company's earnings and dividends. But, factors beyond a company's control, such as an oil embargo, changes in interest rates, or the outcome of a presidential election, may cause day-to-day fluctuations in market prices.

The trading of capital stock on securities exchanges involves the transfer of **already issued shares** from an existing stockholder to another investor. These transactions have **no impact** on a corporation's stockholders' equity.

Investor Insight Nike

Joe Robbins/Getty Images, Inc.

How to Read Stock Quotes

Organized exchanges trade the stock of publicly held companies at dollar prices per share established by the interaction between buyers and sellers. For each listed security, the financial press reports the high and low prices of the stock during the year, the total volume of stock traded on a given day, the high and low prices for the day, and the closing market price, with the net change for the day. Nike is listed on the New York Stock Exchange. Here is a listing for Nike:

	52 Weeks						
Stock	High	Low	Volume	High	Low	Close	Net Change
Nike	79.64	62.81	2,912,866	77.25	76.39	76.78	−0.35

These numbers indicate the following. The high and low market prices for the last 52 weeks have been $79.64 and $62.81. The trading volume for the day was 2,912,866 shares. The high, low, and closing prices for that date were $77.25, $76.39, and $76.78, respectively. The net change for the day was a decrease of $0.35 per share.

For stocks traded on organized exchanges, how are the dollar prices per share established? What factors might influence the price of shares in the marketplace? (Go to **WileyPLUS** for this answer and additional questions.)

PAR AND NO-PAR VALUE STOCKS

Par value stock is capital stock to which the charter has assigned a value per share. Years ago, par value determined the **legal capital** per share that a company must retain in the business for the protection of corporate creditors. That amount was not available for withdrawal by stockholders. Thus, in the past, most states required the corporation to sell its shares at par or above.

However, par value was often immaterial relative to the value of the company's stock—even at the time of issue. Thus, its usefulness as a protective device to creditors was questionable. For example, Loews Corporation's par value is $0.01 per share, yet a new issue in 2014 would have sold at a **market price** in the $44 per share range. Thus, par has no relationship with market price. In the vast majority of cases, it is an immaterial amount. As a consequence, today many states do not require a par value. Instead, they use other means to protect creditors.

No-par value stock is capital stock to which the charter has not assigned a value. No-par value stock is fairly common today. For example, Nike and Procter & Gamble both have no-par stock. In many states, the board of directors assigns a **stated value** to no-par shares.

DO IT! 1a Corporate Organization

Indicate whether each of the following statements is true or false.

_____ **1.** Similar to partners in a partnership, stockholders of a corporation have unlimited liability.

_____ **2.** It is relatively easy for a corporation to obtain capital through the issuance of stock.

_____ **3.** The separation of ownership and management is an advantage of the corporate form of business.

_____ **4.** The journal entry to record the authorization of capital stock includes a credit to the appropriate capital stock account.

_____ **5.** All states require a par value per share for capital stock.

Action Plan

✔ Review the characteristics of a corporation and understand which are advantages and which are disadvantages.

✔ Understand that corporations raise capital through the issuance of stock, which can be par or no-par.

Solution

1. False. The liability of stockholders is normally limited to their investment in the corporation. **2.** True. **3.** False. The separation of ownership and management is a disadvantage of the corporate form of business. **4.** False. The authorization of capital stock does not result in a formal accounting entry. **5.** False. Many states do not require a par value.

Related exercise material: **BE13-1, E13-1, E13-2, and DO IT! 13-1a.**

Corporate Capital

Owners' equity is identified by various names: **stockholders' equity**, **shareholders' equity**, or **corporate capital**. The stockholders' equity section of a corporation's balance sheet consists of two parts: (1) paid-in (contributed) capital and (2) retained earnings (earned capital).

The distinction between **paid-in capital** and **retained earnings** is important from both a legal and a financial point of view. Legally, corporations can make distributions of earnings (declare dividends) out of retained earnings in all states. However, in many states they cannot declare dividends out of paid-in capital. Management, stockholders, and others often look to retained earnings for the continued existence and growth of the corporation.

PAID-IN CAPITAL

Paid-in capital is the total amount of cash and other assets paid in to the corporation by stockholders in exchange for capital stock. As noted earlier, when a corporation has only one class of stock, it is **common stock**.

RETAINED EARNINGS

Retained earnings is net income that a corporation retains for future use. Net income is recorded in Retained Earnings by a closing entry that debits Income Summary and credits Retained Earnings. For example, assuming that net income for Delta Robotics in its first year of operations is $130,000, the closing entry is:

Income Summary	130,000	
Retained Earnings		130,000
(To close Income Summary and transfer net income to Retained Earnings)		

A	=	L	+	SE
				−130,000 Inc
				+130,000 RE

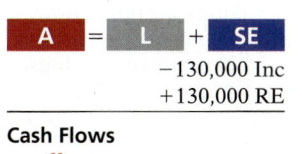

Cash Flows
no effect

If Delta Robotics has a balance of $800,000 in common stock at the end of its first year, its stockholders' equity section is as follows.

Illustration 13-5
Stockholders' equity section

DELTA ROBOTICS Balance Sheet (partial)		
Stockholders' equity		
Paid-in capital		
Common stock	$800,000	
Retained earnings	130,000	
Total stockholders' equity		**$930,000**

Illustration 13-6 compares the owners' equity (stockholders' equity) accounts reported on a balance sheet for a proprietorship, a partnership, and a corporation.

Illustration 13-6
Comparison of owners' equity accounts

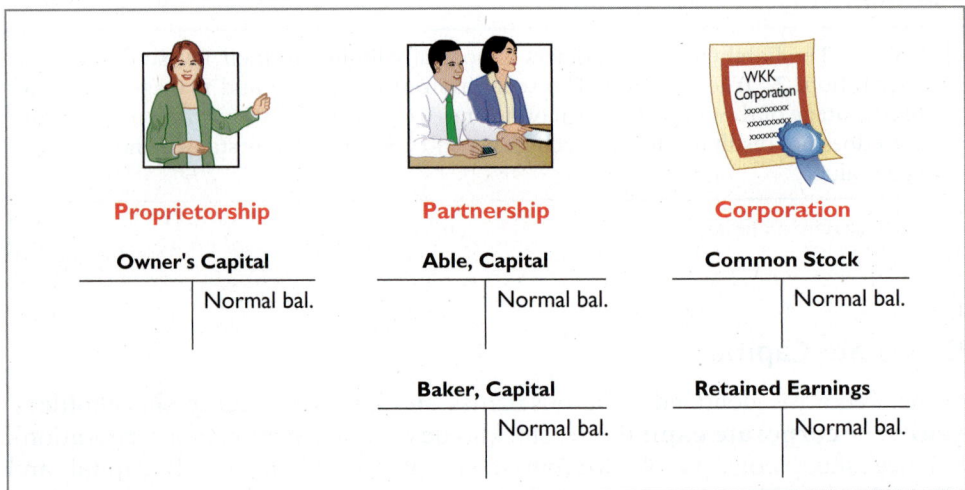

Proprietorship

Owner's Capital — Normal bal. (credit side)

Partnership

Able, Capital — Normal bal. (credit side)

Baker, Capital — Normal bal. (credit side)

Corporation

Common Stock — Normal bal. (credit side)

Retained Earnings — Normal bal. (credit side)

DO IT! 1b Corporate Capital

At the end of its first year of operation, Doral Corporation has $750,000 of common stock and net income of $122,000. Prepare (a) the closing entry for net income and (b) the stockholders' equity section at year-end.

Action Plan

✔ Record net income in Retained Earnings by a closing entry in which Income Summary is debited and Retained Earnings is credited.

✔ In the stockholders' equity section, show (1) paid-in capital and (2) retained earnings.

Solution

(a) Income Summary	122,000	
Retained Earnings		122,000
(To close Income Summary and transfer net income to Retained Earnings)		

(b) Stockholders' equity		
Paid-in capital		
Common stock	$750,000	
Retained earnings	122,000	
Total stockholders' equity		$872,000

Related exercise material: **BE13-2 and DO IT! 13-1b.**

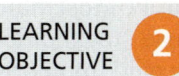

LEARNING OBJECTIVE **2**

Explain how to account for the issuance of common and preferred stock.

Let's now look at how to account for issues of common stock. The primary objectives in accounting for the issuance of common stock are (1) to identify the specific sources of paid-in capital, and (2) to maintain the distinction between paid-in capital and retained earnings. **The issuance of common stock affects only paid-in capital accounts.**

Issuing Par Value Common Stock for Cash

As discussed earlier, par value does not indicate a stock's market price. Therefore, the cash proceeds from issuing par value stock may be equal to, greater than, or less than par value. When the company records issuance of common stock for cash, it credits the par value of the shares to Common Stock. It also records in a separate paid-in capital account the portion of the proceeds that is above or below par value.

To illustrate, assume that Hydro-Slide, Inc. issues 1,000 shares of $1 par value common stock at par for cash. The entry to record this transaction is:

Cash	1,000	
Common Stock		1,000
(To record issuance of 1,000 shares of $1 par common stock at par)		

A	=	L	+	SE
+1,000				
				+1,000 CS

Cash Flows
+1,000

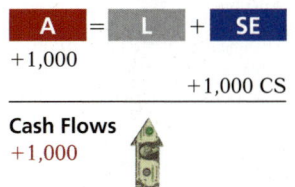

Now assume that Hydro-Slide issues an additional 1,000 shares of the $1 par value common stock for cash at $5 per share. The amount received above the par value, in this case $4 ($5 − $1), is credited to Paid-in Capital in Excess of Par—Common Stock. The entry is:

Cash	5,000	
Common Stock		1,000
Paid-in Capital in Excess of Par—Common Stock		4,000
(To record issuance of 1,000 shares of $1 par common stock)		

A	=	L	+	SE
+5,000				
				+1,000 CS
				+4,000 CS

Cash Flows
+5,000

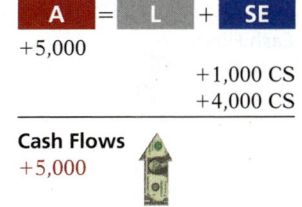

The total paid-in capital from these two transactions is $6,000, and the legal capital is $2,000. Assuming Hydro-Slide, Inc. has retained earnings of $27,000, Illustration 13-7 shows the company's stockholders' equity section.

Illustration 13-7
Stockholders' equity—paid-in capital in excess of par

HYDRO-SLIDE, INC.
Balance Sheet (partial)

Stockholders' equity	
Paid-in capital	
Common stock	$ 2,000
Paid-in capital in excess of par—common stock	**4,000**
Total paid-in capital	6,000
Retained earnings	27,000
Total stockholders' equity	$33,000

Alternative Terminology
Paid-in Capital in Excess of Par is also called *Premium on Stock.*

When a corporation issues stock for less than par value, it debits the account Paid-in Capital in Excess of Par—Common Stock if a credit balance exists in this account. If a credit balance does not exist, then the corporation debits to Retained

Earnings the amount less than par. This situation occurs only rarely. Most states do not permit the sale of common stock below par value because stockholders may be held personally liable for the difference between the price paid upon original sale and par value.

Issuing No-Par Common Stock for Cash

When no-par common stock has a stated value, the entries are similar to those illustrated for par value stock. The corporation credits the stated value to Common Stock. Also, when the selling price of no-par stock exceeds stated value, the corporation credits the excess to Paid-in Capital in Excess of Stated Value—Common Stock.

For example, assume that instead of $1 par value stock, Hydro-Slide, Inc. has $5 stated value no-par stock and the company issues 5,000 shares at $8 per share for cash. The entry is as follows.

A	= L +	SE
+40,000		
		+25,000 CS
		+15,000 CS

Cash Flows
+40,000

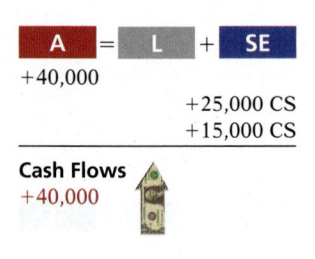

Cash	40,000	
Common Stock		25,000
Paid-in Capital in Excess of Stated Value—Common Stock		15,000
(To record issue of 5,000 shares of $5 stated value no-par stock)		

Hydro-Slide, Inc. reports Paid-in Capital in Excess of Stated Value—Common Stock as part of paid-in capital in the stockholders' equity section.

What happens when no-par stock does not have a stated value? In that case, the corporation credits the entire proceeds to Common Stock. Thus, if Hydro-Slide does not assign a stated value to its no-par stock, it records the issuance of the 5,000 shares at $8 per share for cash as follows.

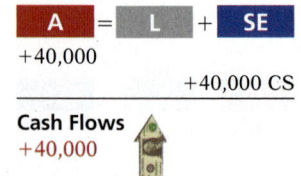

A	= L +	SE
+40,000		
		+40,000 CS

Cash Flows
+40,000

Cash	40,000	
Common Stock		40,000
(To record issue of 5,000 shares of no-par stock)		

Issuing Common Stock for Services or Noncash Assets

Corporations also may issue stock for services (compensation to attorneys or consultants) or for noncash assets (land, buildings, and equipment). In such cases, what cost should be recognized in the exchange transaction? To comply with the **historical cost principle**, in a noncash transaction **cost is the cash equivalent price**. Thus, **cost is either the fair value of the consideration given up or the fair value of the consideration received**, whichever is more clearly determinable.

To illustrate, assume that attorneys have helped Jordan Company incorporate. They have billed the company $5,000 for their services. They agree to accept 4,000 shares of $1 par value common stock in payment of their bill. At the time of the exchange, there is no established market price for the stock. In this case, the fair value of the consideration received, $5,000, is more clearly evident. Accordingly, Jordan Company makes the following entry.

A	= L +	SE
		−5,000 Exp
		+4,000 CS
		+1,000 CS

Cash Flows
no effect

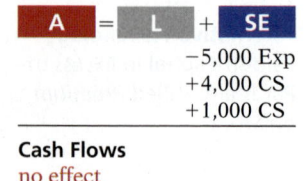

Organization Expense	5,000	
Common Stock		4,000
Paid-in Capital in Excess of Par—Common Stock		1,000
(To record issuance of 4,000 shares of $1 par value stock to attorneys)		

As explained on page 575, organization costs are expensed as incurred.

In contrast, assume that Athletic Research Inc. is an existing publicly held corporation. Its $5 par value stock is actively traded at $8 per share. The company issues 10,000 shares of stock to acquire land recently advertised for sale at $90,000.

The most clearly evident value in this noncash transaction is the market price of the consideration given, $80,000. The company records the transaction as follows.

Land	80,000	
Common Stock		50,000
Paid-in Capital in Excess of Par—Common Stock		30,000
(To record issuance of 10,000 shares of $5 par value stock for land)		

A	=	L	+	SE
+80,000				
				+50,000 CS
				+30,000 CS

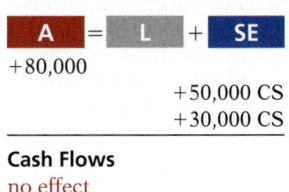

Cash Flows
no effect

As illustrated in these examples, **the par value of the stock is never a factor in determining the cost of the assets or services received in noncash transactions**. This is also true of the stated value of no-par stock.

Accounting for Preferred Stock

To appeal to a larger segment of potential investors, a corporation may issue an additional class of stock, called preferred stock. **Preferred stock** has contractual provisions that give it some preference or priority over common stock. Typically, preferred stockholders have a priority as to (1) distributions of earnings (dividends) and (2) assets in the event of liquidation. However, they generally do not have voting rights.

Like common stock, corporations may issue preferred stock for cash or for noncash assets. The entries for these transactions are similar to the entries for common stock. When a corporation has more than one class of stock, each paid-in capital account title should identify the stock to which it relates. A company might have the following accounts: Preferred Stock, Common Stock, Paid-in Capital in Excess of Par—Preferred Stock, and Paid-in Capital in Excess of Par—Common Stock.

For example, if Stine Corporation issues 10,000 shares of $10 par value preferred stock for $12 cash per share, the entry to record the issuance is as follows.

Cash	120,000	
Preferred Stock		100,000
Paid-in Capital in Excess of Par—Preferred Stock		20,000
(To record the issuance of 10,000 shares of $10 par value preferred stock)		

A	=	L	+	SE
+120,000				
				+100,000 PS
				+20,000 PS

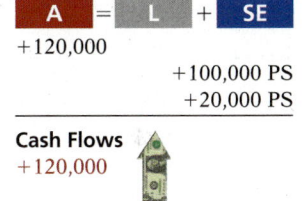

Cash Flows
+120,000

Preferred stock may have either a par value or no-par value. In the stockholders' equity section of the balance sheet, companies list preferred stock first because of its dividend and liquidation preferences over common stock.

DO IT! 2 Issuance of Stock

Cayman Corporation begins operations on March 1 by issuing 100,000 shares of $1 par value common stock for cash at $12 per share. On March 15, it issues 5,000 shares of common stock to attorneys in settlement of their bill of $50,000 for organization costs. On March 28, Cayman Corporation issues 1,500 shares of $10 par value preferred stock for cash at $30 per share. Journalize the issuance of the common and preferred shares, assuming the shares are not publicly traded.

Action Plan

- ✔ In issuing shares for cash, credit Common Stock for par value per share.
- ✔ Credit any additional proceeds in excess of par to a separate paid-in capital account.
- ✔ When stock is issued for services, use the cash equivalent price.

Solution

Mar. 1	Cash	1,200,000	
	Common Stock (100,000 × $1)		100,000
	Paid-in Capital in Excess of Par—Common Stock		1,100,000
	(To record issuance of 100,000 shares at $12 per share)		

Action Plan (cont'd)

✔ For the cash equivalent price, use either the fair value of what is given up or the fair value of what is received, whichever is more clearly determinable.

Mar. 15	Organization Expense	50,000	
	Common Stock (5,000 × $1)		5,000
	Paid-in Capital in Excess of Par—Common Stock		45,000
	(To record issuance of 5,000 shares for attorneys' fees)		
Mar. 28	Cash	45,000	
	Preferred Stock (1,500 × $10)		15,000
	Paid-in Capital in Excess of Par—Preferred Stock		30,000
	(To record issuance of 1,500 shares at $30 per share)		

Related exercise material: **BE13-3, BE13-4, BE13-5, BE13-6, E13-3, E13-4, E13-6, and DO IT! 13-2.**

LEARNING OBJECTIVE 3

Explain how to account for treasury stock.

Treasury stock is a corporation's own stock that it has issued and subsequently reacquired from shareholders but not retired. A corporation may acquire treasury stock for various reasons:

Helpful Hint
Treasury shares do not have dividend rights or voting rights.

1. To reissue the shares to officers and employees under bonus and stock compensation plans.
2. To increase trading of the company's stock in the securities market. Companies expect that buying their own stock will signal that management believes the stock is underpriced, which they hope will enhance its market price.
3. To have additional shares available for use in the acquisition of other companies.
4. To reduce the number of shares outstanding and thereby increase earnings per share.

Another infrequent reason for purchasing shares is that management may want to eliminate hostile shareholders by buying them out.

Many corporations have treasury stock. For example, approximately 65% of U.S. companies have treasury stock. In a recent year, Nike purchased more than 6 million treasury shares.

Purchase of Treasury Stock

Companies generally account for treasury stock by **the cost method**. This method uses the cost of the shares purchased to value the treasury stock. Under the cost method, the company debits **Treasury Stock** for the **price paid to reacquire the shares**. When the company disposes of the shares, it credits to Treasury Stock **the same amount** it paid to reacquire the shares.

To illustrate, assume that on January 1, 2017, the stockholders' equity section of Mead, Inc. has 400,000 shares authorized and 100,000 shares of $5 par value common stock outstanding (all issued at par value) and Retained Earnings of $200,000. The stockholders' equity section before purchase of treasury stock is as follows.

Illustration 13-8
Stockholders' equity with no treasury stock

MEAD, INC.
Balance Sheet (partial)

Stockholders' equity	
Paid-in capital	
Common stock, $5 par value, 400,000 shares authorized, 100,000 shares issued and outstanding	$500,000
Retained earnings	200,000
Total stockholders' equity	$700,000

On February 1, 2017, Mead acquires 4,000 shares of its stock at $8 per share. The entry is as follows.

Feb. 1	Treasury Stock	32,000	
	Cash		32,000
	(To record purchase of 4,000 shares of treasury stock at $8 per share)		

A	=	L	+	SE
				−32,000 TS
−32,000				

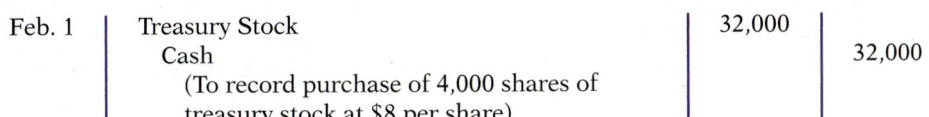

Cash Flows
−32,000

Mead debits Treasury Stock for the cost of the shares purchased ($32,000). Is the original paid-in capital account, Common Stock, affected? No, because the number of issued shares does not change.

In the stockholders' equity section of the balance sheet, Mead deducts treasury stock from total paid-in capital and retained earnings. Treasury Stock is a **contra stockholders' equity account**. Thus, the acquisition of treasury stock reduces stockholders' equity. The stockholders' equity section of Mead, Inc. after purchase of treasury stock is as follows.

Illustration 13-9
Stockholders' equity with treasury stock

MEAD, INC.
Balance Sheet (partial)

Stockholders' equity	
Paid-in capital	
Common stock, $5 par value, 400,000 shares authorized, 100,000 shares issued, and 96,000 shares outstanding	$500,000
Retained earnings	200,000
Total paid-in capital and retained earnings	700,000
Less: Treasury stock (4,000 shares)	**32,000**
Total stockholders' equity	$668,000

Mead discloses in the balance sheet both the number of shares issued (100,000) and the number in the treasury (4,000). The difference is the number of shares of stock outstanding (96,000). The term **outstanding stock** means the number of shares of issued stock that are being held by stockholders.

Some maintain that companies should report treasury stock as an asset because it can be sold for cash. But under this reasoning, companies would also show unissued stock as an asset, which is clearly incorrect. Rather than being an asset, treasury stock reduces stockholder claims on corporate assets. This effect is correctly shown by reporting treasury stock as a deduction from total paid-in capital and retained earnings.

ETHICS NOTE

The purchase of treasury stock reduces the cushion (cash available) for creditors and preferred stockholders. A restriction for the cost of treasury stock purchased is often required. The restriction is usually applied to retained earnings.

Disposal of Treasury Stock

Treasury stock is usually sold or retired. The accounting for its sale differs when treasury stock is sold above cost than when it is sold below cost.

SALE OF TREASURY STOCK ABOVE COST

If the selling price of the treasury shares is equal to their cost, the company records the sale of the shares by a debit to Cash and a credit to Treasury Stock. When the selling price of the shares is greater than their cost, the company credits the difference to Paid-in Capital from Treasury Stock.

To illustrate, assume that on July 1, Mead, Inc. sells for $10 per share 1,000 of the 4,000 shares of its treasury stock previously acquired at $8 per share. The entry is as follows.

Helpful Hint
Treasury stock transactions are classified as capital stock transactions. As in the case when stock is issued, the income statement is not involved.

July 1	Cash	10,000	
	Treasury Stock		8,000
	Paid-in Capital from Treasury Stock		2,000
	(To record sale of 1,000 shares of treasury stock above cost)		

A	=	L	+	SE
+10,000				
				+8,000 TS
				+2,000 TS

Cash Flows
+10,000

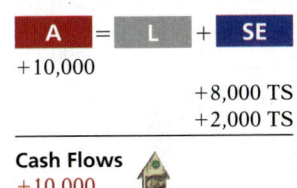

Mead does not record a $2,000 gain on sale of treasury stock for two reasons. (1) Gains on sales occur when **assets** are sold, and treasury stock is not an asset. (2) A corporation does not realize a gain or suffer a loss from stock transactions with its own stockholders. Thus, companies should **not** include in net income any paid-in capital arising from the sale of treasury stock. Instead, they report Paid-in Capital from Treasury Stock separately on the balance sheet, as a part of paid-in capital.

SALE OF TREASURY STOCK BELOW COST

When a company sells treasury stock below its cost, it usually debits to Paid-in Capital from Treasury Stock the excess of cost over selling price. Thus, if Mead, Inc. sells an additional 800 shares of treasury stock on October 1 at $7 per share, it makes the following entry.

A	=	L	+	SE
+5,600				
				−800 TS
				+6,400 TS

Cash Flows
+5,600

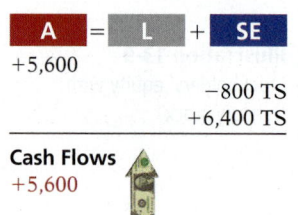

Oct. 1	Cash	5,600	
	Paid-in Capital from Treasury Stock	800	
	Treasury Stock		6,400
	(To record sale of 800 shares of treasury stock below cost)		

Observe the following from the two sales entries. (1) Mead credits Treasury Stock at cost in each entry. (2) Mead uses Paid-in Capital from Treasury Stock for the difference between cost and the resale price of the shares. (3) The original paid-in capital account, Common Stock, is not affected. **The sale of treasury stock increases both total assets and total stockholders' equity.**

After posting the foregoing entries, the treasury stock accounts will show the following balances on October 1.

Illustration 13-10
Treasury stock accounts

Treasury Stock				Paid-in Capital from Treasury Stock			
Feb. 1	32,000	July 1	8,000	Oct. 1	800	July 1	2,000
		Oct. 1	6,400			Oct. 1 Bal.	1,200
Oct. 1 Bal.	17,600						

When a company fully depletes the credit balance in Paid-in Capital from Treasury Stock, it debits to Retained Earnings any additional excess of cost over selling price. To illustrate, assume that Mead, Inc. sells its remaining 2,200 shares at $7 per share on December 1. The excess of cost over selling price is $2,200 [2,200 × ($8 − $7)]. In this case, Mead debits $1,200 of the excess to Paid-in Capital from Treasury Stock. It debits the remainder to Retained Earnings. The entry is as follows.

A	=	L	+	SE
+15,400				
				−1,200 TS
				−1,000 RE
				+17,600 TS

Cash Flows
+15,400

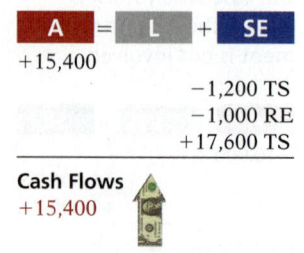

Dec. 1	Cash	15,400	
	Paid-in Capital from Treasury Stock	1,200	
	Retained Earnings	1,000	
	Treasury Stock		17,600
	(To record sale of 2,200 shares of treasury stock at $7 per share)		

Accounting Across the Organization — Reebok

Han Myung-Gu/WireImage/Getty Images, Inc

Why Did Reebok Buy Its Own Stock?

In a bold (and some would say risky) move, Reebok at one time bought back nearly a third of its shares. This repurchase of shares dramatically reduced Reebok's available cash. In fact, the company borrowed significant funds to accomplish the repurchase. In a press release, management stated that it was repurchasing the shares because it believed its stock was severely underpriced. The repurchase of so many shares was meant to signal management's belief in good future earnings.

Skeptics, however, suggested that Reebok's management was repurchasing shares to make it less likely that another company would acquire Reebok (in which case Reebok's top managers would likely lose their jobs). By depleting its cash, Reebok became a less attractive acquisition target. Acquiring companies like to purchase companies with large cash balances so they can pay off debt used in the acquisition.

What signal might a large stock repurchase send to investors regarding management's belief about the company's growth opportunities? (Go to **WileyPLUS** for this answer and additional questions.)

DO IT! 3 Treasury Stock

Santa Anita Inc. purchases 3,000 shares of its $50 par value common stock for $180,000 cash on July 1. It will hold the shares in the treasury until resold. On November 1, the corporation sells 1,000 shares of treasury stock for cash at $70 per share. Journalize the treasury stock transactions.

Solution

July 1	Treasury Stock	180,000	
	Cash		180,000
	(To record the purchase of 3,000 shares at $60 per share)		
Nov. 1	Cash	70,000	
	Treasury Stock		60,000
	Paid-in Capital from Treasury Stock		10,000
	(To record the sale of 1,000 shares at $70 per share)		

Related exercise material: **BE13-7, E13-5, E13-7, E13-8, and DO IT! 13-3.**

Action Plan

- ✔ Record the purchase of treasury stock at cost.
- ✔ When treasury stock is sold above its cost, credit the excess of the selling price over cost to Paid-in Capital from Treasury Stock.
- ✔ When treasury stock is sold below its cost, debit the excess of cost over selling price to Paid-in Capital from Treasury Stock.

LEARNING OBJECTIVE 4 Prepare a stockholders' equity section.

Companies report paid-in capital and retained earnings in the stockholders' equity section of the balance sheet. They identify the specific sources of paid-in capital, using the following classifications.

Alternative Terminology Paid-in capital is sometimes called *contributed capital*.

1. **Capital stock.** This category consists of preferred and common stock. Preferred stock appears before common stock because of its preferential rights. Companies report par value, shares authorized, shares issued, and shares outstanding for each class of stock.
2. **Additional paid-in capital.** This category includes the excess of amounts paid in over par or stated value and paid-in capital from treasury stock.

The stockholders' equity section of Connally Inc. in Illustration 13-11 includes most of the accounts discussed in this chapter. The disclosures pertaining to Connally's common stock indicate that the company issued 400,000 shares; 100,000 shares are unissued (500,000 authorized less 400,000 issued); and 390,000 shares are outstanding (400,000 issued less 10,000 shares in treasury).

Illustration 13-11
Stockholders' equity section

CONNALLY INC.
Balance Sheet (partial)

Stockholders' equity		
Paid-in capital		
Capital stock		
9% preferred stock, $100 par value, 10,000 shares authorized, 6,000 shares issued and outstanding		$ 600,000
Common stock, no par, $5 stated value, 500,000 shares authorized, 400,000 shares issued, and 390,000 shares outstanding		2,000,000
Total capital stock		2,600,000
Additional paid-in capital		
In excess of par—preferred stock	$ 30,000	
In excess of stated value—common stock	860,000	
From treasury stock	140,000	
Total additional paid-in capital		1,030,000
Total paid-in capital		3,630,000
Retained earnings		1,058,000
Total paid-in capital and retained earnings		4,688,000
Less: Treasury stock (10,000 common shares) (at cost)		80,000
Total stockholders' equity		$4,608,000

ANATOMY OF A FRAUD

The president, chief operating officer, and chief financial officer of SafeNet, a software encryption company, were each awarded employee stock options by the company's board of directors as part of their compensation package. Stock options enable an employee to buy a company's stock sometime in the future at the price that existed when the stock option was awarded. For example, suppose that you received stock options today, when the stock price of your company was $30. Three years later, if the stock price rose to $100, you could "exercise" your options and buy the stock for $30 per share, thereby making $70 per share. After being awarded their stock options, the three employees changed the award dates in the company's records to dates in the past, when the company's stock was trading at historical lows. For example, using the previous example, they would choose a past date when the stock was selling for $10 per share, rather than the $30 price on the actual award date. In our example, this would increase the profit from exercising the options to $90 per share.

Total take: $1.7 million

THE MISSING CONTROL

Independent internal verification. The company's board of directors should have ensured that the awards were properly administered. For example, the date on the minutes from the board meeting could be compared to the dates that were recorded for the awards. In addition, the dates should again be confirmed upon exercise.

DO IT! 4 Stockholders' Equity Section

Jennifer Corporation has issued 300,000 shares of $3 par value common stock. It authorized 600,000 shares. The paid-in capital in excess of par on the common stock is $380,000. The corporation has reacquired 15,000 shares at a cost of $50,000 and is currently holding those shares. Treasury stock was reissued in prior years for $72,000 more than its cost.

The corporation also has 4,000 shares issued and outstanding of 8%, $100 par value preferred stock. It authorized 10,000 shares. The paid-in capital in excess of par on the preferred stock is $25,000. Retained earnings is $610,000.

Prepare the stockholders' equity section of the balance sheet.

Solution

JENNIFER CORPORATION
Balance Sheet (partial)

Stockholders' equity		
Paid-in capital		
Capital stock		
8% preferred stock, $100 par value, 10,000 shares authorized, 4,000 shares issued and outstanding		$ 400,000
Common stock, $3 par value, 600,000 shares authorized, 300,000 shares issued, and 285,000 shares outstanding		900,000
Total capital stock		1,300,000
Additional paid-in capital		
In excess of par—preferred stock	$ 25,000	
In excess of par—common stock	380,000	
From treasury stock	72,000	
Total additional paid-in capital		477,000
Total paid-in capital		1,777,000
Retained earnings		610,000
Total paid-in capital and retained earnings		2,387,000
Less: Treasury stock (15,000 common shares) (at cost)		50,000
Total stockholders' equity		$2,337,000

Action Plan

- ✔ Present capital stock first; list preferred stock before common stock.
- ✔ Present additional paid-in capital after capital stock.
- ✔ Report retained earnings after capital stock and additional paid-in capital.
- ✔ Deduct treasury stock from total paid-in capital and retained earnings.

Related exercise material: **BE13-8, E13-9, E13-11, E13-12, E13-13, E13-14, and DO IT! 13-4.**

REVIEW AND PRACTICE

LEARNING OBJECTIVES REVIEW

1 Discuss the major characteristics of a corporation. The major characteristics of a corporation are separate legal existence, limited liability of stockholders, transferable ownership rights, ability to acquire capital, continuous life, corporation management, government regulations, and additional taxes.

Paid-in capital is the total amount paid in on capital stock. It is often called contributed capital. Retained earnings is net income retained in a corporation. It is often called earned capital.

2 Explain how to account for the issuance of common and preferred stock. When companies record the issuance of common stock for cash, they credit the par value of the shares to Common Stock. They record in a separate paid-in capital account the portion of the proceeds that is above or below par value. When no-par common stock has a stated value, the entries are similar to those for par value stock. When no-par stock does not have a stated value, companies credit the entire proceeds to Common Stock.

Preferred stock has contractual provisions that give it priority over common stock in certain areas. Typically, preferred stockholders have preferences (1) to dividends and (2) to assets in liquidation. They usually do not have voting rights.

3 Explain how to account for treasury stock. The cost method is generally used in accounting for treasury stock. Under this approach, companies debit Treasury Stock at the price paid to reacquire the shares. They credit the same amount to Treasury Stock when they sell the shares. The difference between the sales price and cost is recorded in stockholders' equity accounts, not in income statement accounts.

4 Prepare a stockholders' equity section. In the stockholders' equity section, companies report paid-in capital and retained earnings and identify specific sources of paid-in capital. Within paid-in capital, two classifications are shown: capital stock and additional paid-in capital. If a corporation has treasury stock, it deducts the cost of treasury stock from total paid-in capital and retained earnings to obtain total stockholders' equity.

GLOSSARY REVIEW

Authorized stock The amount of stock that a corporation is authorized to sell as indicated in its charter. (p. 577).

Charter A document that is issued by the state to set forth important terms and features regarding the creation of a corporation. (p. 574).

Corporation A business organized as a legal entity separate and distinct from its owners under state corporation law. (p. 572).

No-par value stock Capital stock that has not been assigned a value in the corporate charter. (p. 579).

Organization costs Costs incurred in the formation of a corporation. (p. 575).

Outstanding stock Capital stock that has been issued and is being held by stockholders. (p. 585).

Paid-in capital Total amount of cash and other assets paid in to the corporation by stockholders in exchange for capital stock. (p. 579).

Par value stock Capital stock that has been assigned a value per share in the corporate charter. (p. 578).

Preferred stock Capital stock that has some preferences over common stock. (p. 583).

Privately held corporation A corporation that has only a few stockholders and whose stock is not available for sale to the general public. (p. 572).

Publicly held corporation A corporation that may have thousands of stockholders and whose stock is regularly traded on a national securities exchange. (p. 572).

Retained earnings Net income that the corporation retains for future use. (p. 579).

Stated value The amount per share assigned by the board of directors to no-par value stock. (p. 579).

Treasury stock A corporation's own stock that has been issued and subsequently reacquired from shareholders by the corporation but not retired. (p. 584).

PRACTICE MULTIPLE-CHOICE QUESTIONS

(LO 1) 1. Which of the following is **not** a major advantage of a corporate form of organization?
(a) Separate legal existence.
(b) Continuous life.
(c) Government regulations.
(d) Transferable ownership rights.

(LO 1) 2. A major disadvantage of a corporation is:
(a) limited liability of stockholders.
(b) additional taxes.
(c) transferable ownership rights.
(d) separate legal existence.

(LO 1) 3. Costs incurred in the formation of a corporation:
(a) do not include legal fees.
(b) are expensed as incurred.
(c) are recorded as an asset.
(d) provide future benefits whose amounts and timing are easily determined.

(LO 1) 4. Which of the following statements is **false**?
(a) Ownership of common stock gives the owner a voting right.
(b) The stockholders' equity section begins with paid-in capital.
(c) The authorization of capital stock does not result in a formal accounting entry.
(d) Legal capital per share applies to par value stock but not to no-par value stock.

5. Total stockholders' equity (in the absence of treasury stock) equals: (LO 1)
(a) Total paid-in capital + Retained earnings.
(b) Paid-in capital + Capital stock + Retained earnings.
(c) Capital stock + Additional paid-in capital − Retained earnings.
(d) Common stock + Retained earnings.

6. The account Retained Earnings is: (LO 1)
(a) a subdivision of paid-in capital.
(b) net income retained in the corporation.
(c) reported as an expense in the income statement.
(d) closed to capital stock.

7. A-Team Corporation issued 1,000 shares of $5 par value stock for land. The stock is actively traded at $9 per share. The land was advertised for sale at $10,500. The land should be recorded at: (LO 2)
(a) $4,000.
(b) $5,000.
(c) $9,000.
(d) $10,500.

(LO 2) **8.** ABC Corporation issues 1,000 shares of $10 par value common stock at $13 per share. In recording the transaction, credits are made to:
(a) Common Stock $10,000 and Paid-in Capital in Excess of Stated Value $3,000.
(b) Common Stock $13,000.
(c) Common Stock $10,000 and Paid-in Capital in Excess of Par $3,000.
(d) Common Stock $10,000 and Retained Earnings $3,000.

(LO 2) **9.** Lucroy Corporation issues 100 shares of $10 par value preferred stock at $12 per share. In recording the transaction, credits are made to:
(a) Preferred Stock $1,200.
(b) Preferred Stock $1,000 and Retained Earnings $200.
(c) Preferred Stock $1,000 and Paid-in Capital in Excess of Preferred Value $200.
(d) Preferred Stock $1,000 and Paid-in Capital in Excess of Par—Preferred Stock $200.

(LO 3) **10.** Treasury stock may be repurchased:
(a) to reissue the shares to officers and employees under bonus and stock compensation plans.
(b) to signal to the stock market that management believes the stock is underpriced.
(c) to have additional shares available for use in the acquisition of other companies.
(d) More than one of the above.

11. XYZ, Inc. sells 100 shares of $5 par value treasury stock at $13 per share. If the cost of acquiring the shares was $10 per share, the entry for the sale should include credits to: (LO 3)
(a) Treasury Stock $1,000 and Paid-in Capital from Treasury Stock $300.
(b) Treasury Stock $500 and Paid-in Capital from Treasury Stock $800.
(c) Treasury Stock $1,000 and Retained Earnings $300.
(d) Treasury Stock $500 and Paid-in Capital in Excess of Par $800.

12. In the stockholders' equity section, the cost of treasury stock is deducted from: (LO 3)
(a) total paid-in capital and retained earnings.
(b) retained earnings.
(c) total stockholders' equity.
(d) common stock in paid-in capital.

13. Which of the following is **not** reported under additional paid-in capital? (LO 4)
(a) Paid-in capital in excess of par.
(b) Common stock.
(c) Paid-in capital in excess of stated value.
(d) Paid-in capital from treasury stock.

14. In the stockholders' equity section of the balance sheet, common stock: (LO 4)
(a) is listed before preferred stock.
(b) is added to total capital stock.
(c) is part of paid-in capital.
(d) is part of additional paid-in capital.

Solutions

1. (c) Government regulations are a disadvantage of a corporation. The other choices are advantages of a corporation.

2. (b) Additional taxes are a disadvantage of a corporation. The other choices are advantages of a corporation.

3. (b) Costs incurred in the formation of a corporation are expensed as incurred. The other choices are incorrect because costs incurred in the formation of a corporation (a) do include legal fees; (c) are recorded as an expense, not an asset; and (d) provide future benefits whose amounts and timing are difficult to determine. As a result, these costs are immediately expensed.

4. (d) Legal capital per share applies to both par value stock and no-par value stock. Many states no longer require a par value and therefore use other means to determine legal capital. The other choices are true statements.

5. (a) Total stockholders' equity = Total paid-in capital + Retained earnings. The other choices are incorrect because (b) capital stock and (d) common stock are included under paid-in capital. Choice (c) is incorrect because retained earnings is generally not subtracted in arriving at total stockholders' equity.

6. (b) Retained Earnings is net income retained in the corporation. The other choices are incorrect because the Retained Earnings account (a) is earned capital, not paid-in capital; (c) is reported in the statement of retained earnings and on the balance sheet, but not on the income statement; and (d) is a permanent or real account and is never closed.

7. (c) Cost is either the fair value of the consideration given up or the fair value of the consideration received, whichever is more clearly determinable. The most clearly determinable value in this noncash transaction is the fair value of the consideration given up of $9,000 ($9 per share × 1,000). The other choices are therefore incorrect.

8. (c) Common Stock should be credited for $10,000 and Paid-in Capital in Excess of Par should be credited for $3,000. The stock is par value stock, not stated value stock, and this excess is contributed, not earned, capital. The other choices are therefore incorrect.

9. (d) Preferred Stock should be credited for $1,000 and Paid-In Capital in Excess of Par—Preferred Stock should be credited for $200. The other choices are incorrect because (a) a total credit for the entire proceeds to Preferred Stock is incorrect because Preferred Stock has a total par value that is different than total proceeds; (b) this is contributed capital, not earned capital, so a credit to Retained Earnings is not correct; and (c) the account Paid-in Capital in Excess of Preferred Value is not an appropriate account title.

10. (d) Corporations repurchase treasury stock to have additional shares available for use in acquisition, to reissue shares under bonus and stock compensation plans, and to signal to the stock market that management believes the stock is underpriced. Although the other choices are true statements, choice (d) is the better answer.

11. (a) Treasury Stock should be credited for $1,000 (100 shares × $10, the acquisition price). Paid-in Capital from Treasury Stock should be credited for the difference between the $1,000 and the cash received of $1,300 (100 shares × $13), or $300. The other choices are therefore incorrect.

12. (a) The cost of treasury stock is deducted from total paid-in capital and retained earnings. The other choices are therefore incorrect.

13. (b) Common stock is reported in the capital stock section of paid-in capital, not in the additional paid-in capital section. The other choices are true statements.

14. (c) Common stock is part of paid-in capital. The other choices are incorrect because common stock (a) is listed after preferred stock, (b) is not added to total capital stock but is part of capital stock, and (d) is part of capital stock, not additional paid-in capital.

PRACTICE EXERCISES

Journalize issuance of common and preferred stock and purchase of treasury stock.

(LO 2, 3)

1. Bostick Co. had the following transactions during the current period.

Mar. 2	Issued 4,000 shares of $1 par value common stock to attorneys in payment of a bill for $35,000 for services performed in helping the company to incorporate.
June 12	Issued 50,000 shares of $1 par value common stock for cash of $360,000.
July 11	Issued 2,000 shares of $100 par value preferred stock for cash at $120 per share.
Nov. 28	Purchased 2,000 shares of treasury stock for $70,000.

Instructions

Journalize the transactions.

Solution

1. Mar. 2	Organization Expense	35,000	
	Common Stock (4,000 × $1)		4,000
	Paid-in Capital in Excess of Par—Common Stock		31,000
June 12	Cash	360,000	
	Common Stock (50,000 × $1)		50,000
	Paid-in Capital in Excess of Par—Common Stock		310,000
July 11	Cash (2,000 × $120)	240,000	
	Preferred Stock (2,000 × $100)		200,000
	Paid-in Capital in Excess of Par—Preferred Stock (2,000 × $20)		40,000
Nov. 28	Treasury Stock	70,000	
	Cash		70,000

Journalize treasury stock transactions.

(LO 3)

2. Star Corporation purchased from its stockholders 5,000 shares of its own previously issued stock for $250,000. It later resold 2,000 shares for $53 per share, then 2,000 more shares for $48 per share, and finally 1,000 shares for $43 per share.

Instructions

Prepare journal entries for the purchase of the treasury stock and the three sales of treasury stock.

Solution

2. Treasury Stock	250,000	
Cash		250,000
Cash (2,000 × $53)	106,000	
Treasury Stock (2,000 × $50)		100,000
Paid-in Capital from Treasury Stock		6,000
Cash (2,000 × $48)	96,000	
Paid-in Capital from Treasury Stock	4,000	
Treasury Stock (2,000 × $50)		100,000
Cash (1,000 × $43)	43,000	
Paid-in Capital from Treasury Stock ($6,000 − $4,000)	2,000	
Retained Earnings	5,000	
Treasury Stock (1,000 × $50)		50,000

PRACTICE PROBLEM

Journalize transactions and prepare stockholders' equity section.

(LO 2, 3, 4)

Rolman Corporation is authorized to issue 1,000,000 shares of $5 par value common stock. In its first year, the company has the following stock transactions.

Jan. 10	Issued 400,000 shares of stock at $8 per share.
July 1	Issued 100,000 shares of stock for land. The land had an asking price of $900,000. The stock is currently selling on a national exchange at $8.25 per share.
Sept. 1	Purchased 10,000 shares of common stock for the treasury at $9 per share.
Dec. 1	Sold 4,000 shares of the treasury stock at $10 per share.

Instructions

(a) Journalize the transactions.

(b) Prepare the stockholders' equity section assuming the company had retained earnings of $200,000 at December 31.

Solution

(a) Jan. 10	Cash	3,200,000	
	Common Stock		2,000,000
	Paid-in Capital in Excess of Par—Common Stock		1,200,000
	(To record issuance of 400,000 shares of $5 par value stock)		
July 1	Land	825,000	
	Common Stock		500,000
	Paid-in Capital in Excess of Par—Common Stock		325,000
	(To record issuance of 100,000 shares of $5 par value stock for land)		
Sept. 1	Treasury Stock	90,000	
	Cash		90,000
	(To record purchase of 10,000 shares of treasury stock at cost)		
Dec. 1	Cash	40,000	
	Treasury Stock		36,000
	Paid-in Capital from Treasury Stock		4,000
	(To record sale of 4,000 shares of treasury stock above cost)		

(b)

ROLMAN CORPORATION
Balance Sheet (partial)

Stockholders' equity		
Paid-in capital		
Capital stock		
Common stock, $5 par value, 1,000,000 shares authorized, 500,000 shares issued, 494,000 shares outstanding		$2,500,000
Additional paid-in capital		
In excess of par—common stock	$1,525,000	
From treasury stock	4,000	
Total additional paid-in capital		1,529,000
Total paid-in capital		4,029,000
Retained earnings		200,000
Total paid-in capital and retained earnings		4,229,000
Less: Treasury stock (6,000 shares)		54,000
Total stockholders' equity		$4,175,000

WileyPLUS Brief Exercises, Exercises, DO IT! Exercises, and Problems and many additional resources are available for practice in WileyPLUS

QUESTIONS

1. Mark Kemp, a student, asks your help in understanding the following characteristics of a corporation: (a) separate legal existence, (b) limited liability of stockholders, and (c) transferable ownership rights. Explain these characteristics to Mark.
2. (a) Your friend Katie Fehr cannot understand how the characteristic of corporation management is both an advantage and a disadvantage. Clarify this problem for Katie.
   (b) Identify and explain two other disadvantages of a corporation.
3. (a) The following terms pertain to the forming of a corporation: (1) charter, (2) by-laws, and (3) organization costs. Explain the terms.
   (b) Donna Fleming believes a corporation must be incorporated in the state in which its headquarters' office is located. Is Donna correct? Explain.
4. What are the basic ownership rights of common stockholders in the absence of restrictive provisions?
5. (a) What are the two principal components of stockholders' equity?
   (b) What is paid-in capital? Give three examples.
6. How does the balance sheet for a corporation differ from the balance sheet for a proprietorship?
7. The corporate charter of Luney Corporation allows the issuance of a maximum of 100,000 shares of common stock. During its first two years of operations, Luney sold 70,000 shares to shareholders and reacquired 7,000 of these shares. After these transactions, how many shares are authorized, issued, and outstanding?
8. Which is the better investment—common stock with a par value of $5 per share, or common stock with a par value of $20 per share? Why?
9. What factors help determine the market price of stock?
10. What effect does the issuance of stock at a price above par value have on the issuer's net income? Explain.
11. Why is common stock usually not issued at a price that is less than par value?
12. Land appraised at $80,000 is purchased by issuing 1,000 shares of $20 par value common stock. The market price of the shares at the time of the exchange, based on active trading in the securities market, is $95 per share. Should the land be recorded at $20,000, $80,000, or $95,000? Explain.
13. For what reasons might a company like IBM repurchase some of its stock (treasury stock)?
14. Meng, Inc. purchases 1,000 shares of its own previously issued $5 par common stock for $12,000. Assuming the shares are held in the treasury, what effect does this transaction have on (a) net income, (b) total assets, (c) total paid-in capital, and (d) total stockholders' equity?
15. The treasury stock purchased in Question 14 is resold by Meng, Inc. for $16,000. What effect does this transaction have on (a) net income, (b) total assets, (c) total paid-in capital, and (d) total stockholders' equity?
16. Diaz Inc.'s common stock has a par value of $1 and a current market price of $15. Explain why these amounts are different.
17. Indicate how each of the following accounts should be classified in the stockholders' equity section.
    (a) Common stock.
    (b) Paid-in capital in excess of par—common stock.
    (c) Retained earnings.
    (d) Treasury stock.
    (e) Paid-in capital from treasury stock.
    (f) Paid-in capital in excess of stated value—common stock.
    (g) Preferred stock.
18. How many shares of common stock did Apple have outstanding at September 28, 2013, and at September 29, 2012?

BRIEF EXERCISES

List the advantages and disadvantages of a corporation.
(LO 1)

BE13-1 Angie Baden is studying for her accounting midterm examination. Identify for Angie the advantages and disadvantages of the corporate form of business organization.

Prepare closing entries.
(LO 1)

BE13-2 At December 31, Ortiz Corporation reports net income of $480,000. Prepare the entry to close net income.

Prepare entries for issuance of par value common stock.
(LO 2)

BE13-3 On May 10, Jack Corporation issues 2,000 shares of $10 par value common stock for cash at $18 per share. Journalize the issuance of the stock.

Prepare entries for issuance of no-par value common stock.
(LO 2)

BE13-4 On June 1, Noonan Inc. issues 4,000 shares of no-par common stock at a cash price of $6 per share. Journalize the issuance of the shares assuming the stock has a stated value of $1 per share.

Prepare entries for issuance of stock in a noncash transaction.
(LO 2)

BE13-5 Lei Inc.'s $10 par value common stock is actively traded at a market price of $15 per share. Lei issues 5,000 shares to purchase land advertised for sale at $85,000. Journalize the issuance of the stock in acquiring the land.

BE13-6 Garb Inc. issues 5,000 shares of $100 par value preferred stock for cash at $130 per share. Journalize the issuance of the preferred stock.

Prepare entries for issuance of preferred stock.
(LO 2)

BE13-7 On July 1, Raney Corporation purchases 500 shares of its $5 par value common stock for the treasury at a cash price of $9 per share. On September 1, it sells 300 shares of the treasury stock for cash at $11 per share. Journalize the two treasury stock transactions.

Prepare entries for treasury stock transactions.
(LO 3)

BE13-8 Pine Corporation has the following accounts at December 31: Common Stock, $10 par, 5,000 shares issued, $50,000; Paid-in Capital in Excess of Par—Common Stock $30,000; Retained Earnings $45,000; and Treasury Stock, 500 shares, $11,000. Prepare the stockholders' equity section of the balance sheet.

Prepare stockholders' equity section.
(LO 4)

DO IT! Exercises

DO IT! 13-1a Indicate whether each of the following statements is true or false.

_____ 1. The corporation is an entity separate and distinct from its owners.
_____ 2. The liability of stockholders is normally limited to their investment in the corporation.
_____ 3. The relative lack of government regulation is an advantage of the corporate form of business.
_____ 4. There is no journal entry to record the authorization of capital stock.
_____ 5. No-par value stock is quite rare today.

Analyze statements about corporate organization.
(LO 1)

DO IT! 13-1b At the end of its first year of operation, Goss Corporation has $1,000,000 of common stock and net income of $236,000. Prepare (a) the closing entry for net income and (b) the stockholders' equity section at year-end.

Close net income and prepare stockholders' equity section.
(LO 1)

DO IT! 13-2 Beauty Island Corporation began operations on April 1 by issuing 60,000 shares of $5 par value common stock for cash at $13 per share. On April 19, it issued 2,000 shares of common stock to attorneys in settlement of their bill of $27,500 for organization costs. In addition, Beauty Island issued 1,000 shares of $1 par value preferred stock for $6 cash per share. Journalize the issuance of the common and preferred shares, assuming the shares are not publicly traded.

Journalize issuance of stock.
(LO 2)

DO IT! 13-3 Fouts Corporation purchased 2,000 shares of its $10 par value common stock for $130,000 on August 1. It will hold these shares in the treasury until resold. On December 1, the corporation sold 1,200 shares of treasury stock for cash at $72 per share. Journalize the treasury stock transactions.

Journalize treasury stock transactions.
(LO 3)

DO IT! 13-4 Anders Corporation has issued 100,000 shares of $5 par value common stock. It authorized 500,000 shares. The paid-in capital in excess of par on the common stock is $240,000. The corporation has reacquired 7,000 shares at a cost of $46,000 and is currently holding those shares. Treasury stock was reissued in prior years for $47,000 more than its cost.

The corporation also has 2,000 shares issued and outstanding of 7%, $100 par value preferred stock. It authorized 10,000 shares. The paid-in capital in excess of par on the preferred stock is $23,000. Retained earnings is $372,000.

Prepare the stockholders' equity section of the balance sheet.

Prepare stockholders' equity section.
(LO 4)

EXERCISES

E13-1 Andrea has prepared the following list of statements about corporations.

Identify characteristics of a corporation.
(LO 1)

1. A corporation is an entity separate and distinct from its owners.
2. As a legal entity, a corporation has most of the rights and privileges of a person.
3. Most of the largest U.S. corporations are privately held corporations.
4. Corporations may buy, own, and sell property; borrow money; enter into legally binding contracts; and sue and be sued.
5. The net income of a corporation is not taxed as a separate entity.

6. Creditors have a legal claim on the personal assets of the owners of a corporation if the corporation does not pay its debts.
7. The transfer of stock from one owner to another requires the approval of either the corporation or other stockholders.
8. The board of directors of a corporation legally owns the corporation.
9. The chief accounting officer of a corporation is the controller.
10. Corporations are subject to fewer state and federal regulations than partnerships or proprietorships.

Instructions

Identify each statement as true or false. If false, indicate how to correct the statement.

Identify characteristics of a corporation.

(LO 1)

E13-2 Andrea (see E13-1) has studied the information you gave her in that exercise and has come to you with more statements about corporations.

1. Corporation management is both an advantage and a disadvantage of a corporation compared to a proprietorship or a partnership.
2. Limited liability of stockholders, government regulations, and additional taxes are the major disadvantages of a corporation.
3. When a corporation is formed, organization costs are recorded as an asset.
4. Each share of common stock gives the stockholder the ownership rights to vote at stockholder meetings, share in corporate earnings, keep the same percentage ownership when new shares of stock are issued, and share in assets upon liquidation.
5. The number of issued shares is always greater than or equal to the number of authorized shares.
6. A journal entry is required for the authorization of capital stock.
7. Publicly held corporations usually issue stock directly to investors.
8. The trading of capital stock on a securities exchange involves the transfer of already issued shares from an existing stockholder to another investor.
9. The market price of common stock is usually the same as its par value.
10. Retained earnings is the total amount of cash and other assets paid in to the corporation by stockholders in exchange for capital stock.

Instructions

Identify each statement as true or false. If false, indicate how to correct the statement.

Journalize issuance of common stock.

(LO 2)

E13-3 During its first year of operations, Foyle Corporation had the following transactions pertaining to its common stock.

Jan. 10 Issued 70,000 shares for cash at $5 per share.
July 1 Issued 40,000 shares for cash at $7 per share.

Instructions

(a) Journalize the transactions, assuming that the common stock has a par value of $5 per share.
(b) Journalize the transactions, assuming that the common stock is no-par with a stated value of $1 per share.

Journalize issuance of common stock.

(LO 2)

E13-4 Osage Corporation issued 2,000 shares of stock.

Instructions

Prepare the entry for the issuance under the following assumptions.

(a) The stock had a par value of $5 per share and was issued for a total of $52,000.
(b) The stock had a stated value of $5 per share and was issued for a total of $52,000.
(c) The stock had no par or stated value and was issued for a total of $52,000.
(d) The stock had a par value of $5 per share and was issued to attorneys for services during incorporation valued at $52,000.
(e) The stock had a par value of $5 per share and was issued for land worth $52,000.

Journalize issuance of common and preferred stock and purchase of treasury stock.

(LO 2, 3)

E13-5 Quay Co. had the following transactions during the current period.

Mar. 2 Issued 5,000 shares of $5 par value common stock to attorneys in payment of a bill for $30,000 for services performed in helping the company to incorporate.
June 12 Issued 60,000 shares of $5 par value common stock for cash of $375,000.
July 11 Issued 1,000 shares of $100 par value preferred stock for cash at $110 per share.
Nov. 28 Purchased 2,000 shares of treasury stock for $80,000.

Instructions
Journalize the transactions.

E13-6 As an auditor for the CPA firm of Hinkson and Calvert, you encounter the following situations in auditing different clients.

Journalize noncash common stock transactions.

(LO 2)

1. LR Corporation is a closely held corporation whose stock is not publicly traded. On December 5, the corporation acquired land by issuing 5,000 shares of its $20 par value common stock. The owners' asking price for the land was $120,000, and the fair value of the land was $110,000.
2. Vera Corporation is a publicly held corporation whose common stock is traded on the securities markets. On June 1, it acquired land by issuing 20,000 shares of its $10 par value stock. At the time of the exchange, the land was advertised for sale at $250,000. The stock was selling at $11 per share.

Instructions
Prepare the journal entries for each of the situations above.

E13-7 On January 1, 2017, the stockholders' equity section of Newlin Corporation shows common stock ($5 par value) $1,500,000; paid-in capital in excess of par $1,000,000; and retained earnings $1,200,000. During the year, the following treasury stock transactions occurred.

Journalize treasury stock transactions.

(LO 3)

Mar. 1	Purchased 50,000 shares for cash at $15 per share.
July 1	Sold 10,000 treasury shares for cash at $17 per share.
Sept. 1	Sold 8,000 treasury shares for cash at $14 per share.

Instructions
(a) Journalize the treasury stock transactions.
(b) Restate the entry for September 1, assuming the treasury shares were sold at $12 per share.

E13-8 Rinehart Corporation purchased from its stockholders 5,000 shares of its own previously issued stock for $255,000. It later resold 2,000 shares for $54 per share, then 2,000 more shares for $49 per share, and finally 1,000 shares for $43 per share.

Journalize treasury stock transactions.

(LO 3)

Instructions
Prepare journal entries for the purchase of the treasury stock and the three sales of treasury stock.

E13-9 Tran Corporation is authorized to issue both preferred and common stock. The par value of the preferred is $50. During the first year of operations, the company had the following events and transactions pertaining to its preferred stock.

Journalize preferred stock transactions and indicate statement presentation.

(LO 2, 4)

Feb. 1	Issued 20,000 shares for cash at $53 per share.
July 1	Issued 12,000 shares for cash at $57 per share.

Instructions
(a) Journalize the transactions.
(b) Post to the stockholders' equity accounts.
(c) Indicate the financial statement presentation of the related accounts.

E13-10 Gilliam Corporation recently hired a new accountant with extensive experience in accounting for partnerships. Because of the pressure of the new job, the accountant was unable to review his textbooks on the topic of corporation accounting. During the first month, the accountant made the following entries for the corporation's capital stock.

Prepare correct entries for capital stock transactions.

(LO 2, 3)

May 2	Cash	130,000	
	Capital Stock		130,000
	(Issued 10,000 shares of $10 par value common stock at $13 per share)		
10	Cash	600,000	
	Capital Stock		600,000
	(Issued 10,000 shares of $50 par value preferred stock at $60 per share)		

15	Capital Stock	15,000	
	Cash		15,000
	(Purchased 1,000 shares of common stock for the treasury at $15 per share)		
31	Cash	8,000	
	Capital Stock		5,000
	Gain on Sale of Stock		3,000
	(Sold 500 shares of treasury stock at $16 per share)		

Instructions

On the basis of the explanation for each entry, prepare the entry that should have been made for the capital stock transactions.

Prepare a stockholders' equity section.

(LO 4)

E13-11 The following stockholders' equity accounts, arranged alphabetically, are in the ledger of Eudaley Corporation at December 31, 2017.

Common Stock ($5 stated value)	$1,500,000
Paid-in Capital in Excess of Par—Preferred Stock	280,000
Paid-in Capital in Excess of Stated Value—Common Stock	900,000
Preferred Stock (8%, $100 par)	500,000
Retained Earnings	1,234,000
Treasury Stock (10,000 common shares)	120,000

Instructions

Prepare the stockholders' equity section of the balance sheet at December 31, 2017.

Answer questions about stockholders' equity section.

(LO 2, 3, 4)

E13-12 The stockholders' equity section of Haley Corporation at December 31 is as follows.

HALEY CORPORATION
Balance Sheet (partial)

Paid-in capital	
Preferred stock, 10,000 shares authorized, 6,000 shares issued and outstanding	$ 300,000
Common stock, no par, 750,000 shares authorized, 600,000 shares issued	1,200,000
Total paid-in capital	1,500,000
Retained earnings	1,858,000
Total paid-in capital and retained earnings	3,358,000
Less: Treasury stock (10,000 common shares)	64,000
Total stockholders' equity	$3,294,000

Instructions

From a review of the stockholders' equity section, as chief accountant, write a memo to the president of the company answering the following questions.

(a) How many shares of common stock are outstanding?
(b) Assuming there is a stated value, what is the stated value of the common stock?
(c) What is the par value of the preferred stock?

Prepare a stockholders' equity section.

(LO 4)

E13-13 The stockholders' equity section of Aluminum Company of America (Alcoa) showed the following (in alphabetical order): additional paid-in capital $6,101, common stock $925, preferred stock $56, retained earnings $7,428, and treasury stock 2,828. All dollar data are in millions.

The preferred stock has 557,740 shares authorized, with a par value of $100. At December 31 of the current year, 557,649 shares of preferred are issued and 546,024 shares are outstanding. There are 1.8 billion shares of $1 par value common stock authorized, of which 924.6 million are issued and 844.8 million are outstanding at December 31.

Instructions
Prepare the stockholders' equity section of the current year, including disclosure of all relevant data.

E13-14 The ledger of Rolling Hills Corporation contains the following accounts: Common Stock, Preferred Stock, Treasury Stock, Paid-in Capital in Excess of Par—Preferred Stock, Paid-in Capital in Excess of Stated Value—Common Stock, Paid-in Capital from Treasury Stock, and Retained Earnings.

Classify stockholders' equity accounts.

(LO 4)

Instructions
Classify each account using the following table headings.

	Paid-in Capital			
Account	**Capital Stock**	**Additional**	**Retained Earnings**	**Other**

EXERCISES: SET B AND CHALLENGE EXERCISES

Visit the book's companion website, at **www.wiley.com/college/weygandt**, and choose the Student Companion site to access Exercises: Set B and Challenge Exercises.

PROBLEMS: SET A

P13-1A DeLong Corporation was organized on January 1, 2017. It is authorized to issue 10,000 shares of 8%, $100 par value preferred stock, and 500,000 shares of no-par common stock with a stated value of $2 per share. The following stock transactions were completed during the first year.

Journalize stock transactions, post, and prepare paid-in capital section.

(LO 2, 4)

GLS

Jan. 10	Issued 80,000 shares of common stock for cash at $4 per share.
Mar. 1	Issued 5,000 shares of preferred stock for cash at $105 per share.
Apr. 1	Issued 24,000 shares of common stock for land. The asking price of the land was $90,000. The fair value of the land was $85,000.
May 1	Issued 80,000 shares of common stock for cash at $4.50 per share.
Aug. 1	Issued 10,000 shares of common stock to attorneys in payment of their bill of $30,000 for services performed in helping the company organize.
Sept. 1	Issued 10,000 shares of common stock for cash at $5 per share.
Nov. 1	Issued 1,000 shares of preferred stock for cash at $109 per share.

Instructions
(a) Journalize the transactions.
(b) Post to the stockholders' equity accounts. (Use J5 as the posting reference.)
(c) Prepare the paid-in capital section of stockholders' equity at December 31, 2017.

(c) Total paid-in capital $1,479,000

P13-2A Fechter Corporation had the following stockholders' equity accounts on January 1, 2017: Common Stock ($5 par) $500,000, Paid-in Capital in Excess of Par—Common Stock $200,000, and Retained Earnings $100,000. In 2017, the company had the following treasury stock transactions.

Journalize and post treasury stock transactions, and prepare stockholders' equity section.

(LO 3, 4)

Mar. 1	Purchased 5,000 shares at $8 per share.
June 1	Sold 1,000 shares at $12 per share.
Sept. 1	Sold 2,000 shares at $10 per share.
Dec. 1	Sold 1,000 shares at $7 per share.

Fechter Corporation uses the cost method of accounting for treasury stock. In 2017, the company reported net income of $30,000.

Instructions
(a) Journalize the treasury stock transactions, and prepare the closing entry at December 31, 2017, for net income.

(b) Treasury Stock $8,000

(c) Total stockholders' equity $829,000

(b) Open accounts for (1) Paid-in Capital from Treasury Stock, (2) Treasury Stock, and (3) Retained Earnings. Post to these accounts using J10 as the posting reference.
(c) Prepare the stockholders' equity section for Fechter Corporation at December 31, 2017.

Journalize and post transactions, and prepare stockholders' equity section.

(LO 1, 2, 3, 4)

GLS

P13-3A The stockholders' equity accounts of Castle Corporation on January 1, 2017, were as follows.

Preferred Stock (8%, $50 par, 10,000 shares authorized)	$ 400,000
Common Stock ($1 stated value, 2,000,000 shares authorized)	1,000,000
Paid-in Capital in Excess of Par—Preferred Stock	100,000
Paid-in Capital in Excess of Stated Value—Common Stock	1,450,000
Retained Earnings	1,816,000
Treasury Stock (10,000 common shares)	50,000

During 2017, the corporation had the following transactions and events pertaining to its stockholders' equity.

Feb. 1	Issued 25,000 shares of common stock for $120,000.
Apr. 14	Sold 6,000 shares of treasury stock—common for $33,000.
Sept. 3	Issued 5,000 shares of common stock for a patent valued at $35,000.
Nov. 10	Purchased 1,000 shares of common stock for the treasury at a cost of $6,000.
Dec. 31	Determined that net income for the year was $452,000.

No dividends were declared during the year.

Instructions

(a) Journalize the transactions and the closing entry for net income.
(b) Enter the beginning balances in the accounts, and post the journal entries to the stockholders' equity accounts. (Use J5 for the posting reference.)
(c) Prepare a stockholders' equity section at December 31, 2017.

(c) Total stockholders' equity $5,350,000

Journalize and post stock transactions, and prepare stockholders' equity section.

(LO 1, 2, 4)

GLS

P13-4A Peck Corporation is authorized to issue 20,000 shares of $50 par value, 10% preferred stock and 125,000 shares of $5 par value common stock. On January 1, 2017, the ledger contained the following stockholders' equity balances.

Preferred Stock (10,000 shares)	$500,000
Paid-in Capital in Excess of Par—Preferred Stock	75,000
Common Stock (70,000 shares)	350,000
Paid-in Capital in Excess of Par—Common Stock	700,000
Retained Earnings	300,000

During 2017, the following transactions occurred.

Feb. 1	Issued 2,000 shares of preferred stock for land having a fair value of $120,000.
Mar. 1	Issued 1,000 shares of preferred stock for cash at $65 per share.
July 1	Issued 16,000 shares of common stock for cash at $7 per share.
Sept. 1	Issued 400 shares of preferred stock for a patent. The asking price of the patent was $30,000. Market price for the preferred stock was $70 and the fair value for the patent was indeterminable.
Dec. 1	Issued 8,000 shares of common stock for cash at $7.50 per share.
Dec. 31	Net income for the year was $260,000. No dividends were declared.

Instructions

(a) Journalize the transactions and the closing entry for net income.
(b) Enter the beginning balances in the accounts, and post the journal entries to the stockholders' equity accounts. (Use J2 for the posting reference.)
(c) Prepare a stockholders' equity section at December 31, 2017.

(c) Total stockholders' equity $2,570,000

Prepare stockholders' equity section.

(LO 4)

XLS

P13-5A The following stockholders' equity accounts arranged alphabetically are in the ledger of Galindo Corporation at December 31, 2017.

Common Stock ($5 stated value)	$2,000,000
Paid-in Capital from Treasury Stock	10,000
Paid-in Capital in Excess of Par—Preferred Stock	679,000
Paid-in Capital in Excess of Stated Value—Common Stock	1,600,000
Preferred Stock (8%, $50 par)	800,000
Retained Earnings	1,748,000
Treasury Stock (10,000 common shares)	130,000

Instructions

Prepare a stockholders' equity section at December 31, 2017.

Total stockholders' equity $6,707,000

P13-6A Irwin Corporation has been authorized to issue 20,000 shares of $100 par value, 10%, preferred stock and 1,000,000 shares of no-par common stock. The corporation assigned a $2.50 stated value to the common stock. At December 31, 2017, the ledger contained the following balances pertaining to stockholders' equity.

Prepare entries for stock transactions and prepare stockholders' equity section.

(LO 2, 3, 4)

Preferred Stock	$ 120,000
Paid-in Capital in Excess of Par—Preferred Stock	20,000
Common Stock	1,000,000
Paid-in Capital in Excess of Stated Value—Common Stock	1,800,000
Treasury Stock (1,000 common shares)	11,000
Paid-in Capital from Treasury Stock	1,500
Retained Earnings	82,000

The preferred stock was issued for land having a fair value of $140,000. All common stock issued was for cash. In November, 1,500 shares of common stock were purchased for the treasury at a per share cost of $11. In December, 500 shares of treasury stock were sold for $14 per share. No dividends were declared in 2017.

Instructions

(a) Prepare the journal entries for the:
 (1) Issuance of preferred stock for land.
 (2) Issuance of common stock for cash.
 (3) Purchase of common treasury stock for cash.
 (4) Sale of treasury stock for cash.
(b) Prepare the stockholders' equity section at December 31, 2017.

(b) Total stockholders' equity $3,012,500

PROBLEMS: SET B AND SET C

Visit the book's companion website, at **www.wiley.com/college/weygandt**, and choose the Student Companion site to access Problems: Set B and Set C.

CONTINUING PROBLEM

COOKIE CREATIONS: AN ENTREPRENEURIAL JOURNEY

(*Note:* This is a continuation of the Cookie Creations problem from Chapters 1 through 12.)

© leungchopan/ Shutterstock

CC13 Natalie's friend, Curtis Lesperance, decides to meet with Natalie after hearing that her discussions about a possible business partnership with her friend Katy Peterson have failed. Because Natalie has been so successful with Cookie Creations and Curtis has been just as successful with his coffee shop, they both conclude that they could benefit from each other's business expertise. Curtis and Natalie next evaluate the different types of business organization. Because of the advantage of limited personal liability, they decide to form a corporation. Natalie and Curtis are very excited about this new business venture. They come to you with information about their businesses and with a number of questions.

Go to the book's companion website, **www.wiley.com/college/weygandt**, *to see the completion of this problem.*

BROADENING YOUR PERSPECTIVE

FINANCIAL REPORTING AND ANALYSIS

Financial Reporting Problem: Apple Inc.

BYP13-1 The stockholders' equity section for Apple Inc. is shown in Appendix A. Instructions for accessing and using the company's complete annual report, including the notes to the financial statements, are also provided in Appendix A.

Instructions

(a) What is the par or stated value per share of Apple's common stock?
(b) What percentage of Apple's authorized common stock was issued at September 28, 2013?

Comparative Analysis Problem: PepsiCo, Inc. vs. The Coca-Cola Company

BYP13-2 PepsiCo, Inc.'s financial statements are presented in Appendix B. Financial statements of The Coca-Cola Company are presented in Appendix C. Instructions for accessing and using the complete annual reports of PepsiCo and Coca-Cola, including the notes to the financial statements, are also provided in Appendices B and C, respectively.

Instructions

(a) What is the par or stated value of Coca-Cola's and PepsiCo's common stock?
(b) What percentage of authorized shares was issued by Coca-Cola at December 31, 2013, and by PepsiCo at December 28, 2013?
(c) How many shares are held as treasury stock by Coca-Cola at December 31, 2013, and by PepsiCo at December 28, 2013?
(d) How many Coca-Cola common shares are outstanding at December 31, 2013? How many PepsiCo shares of common stock are outstanding at December 28, 2013?

Comparative Analysis Problem: Amazon.com, Inc. vs. Wal-Mart Stores, Inc.

BYP13-3 Amazon.com, Inc.'s financial statements are presented in Appendix D. Financial statements of Wal-Mart Stores, Inc. are presented in Appendix E. Instructions for accessing and using the complete annual reports of Amazon and Wal-Mart, including the notes to the financial statements, are also provided in Appendices D and E, respectively. Wal-Mart has 11,000 million shares authorized.

Instructions

(a) What is the par or stated value of Amazon's and Wal-Mart's common stock?
(b) What percentage of authorized shares was issued by Amazon at December 31, 2013, and by Wal-Mart at January 31, 2014?
(c) How many shares are held as treasury stock by Amazon at December 31, 2013, and by Wal-Mart at January 31, 2014?
(d) How many Amazon common shares are outstanding at December 31, 2013? How many Wal-Mart shares of common stock are outstanding at January 31, 2014?

Real-World Focus

BYP13-4 SEC filings of publicly traded companies are available to view online.

Address: **http://biz.yahoo.com/i**, or go to **www.wiley.com/college/weygandt**

Steps

1. Pick a company and type in the company's name.
2. Choose **Quote**.

Instructions
Answer the following questions.

(a) What company did you select?
(b) What is its stock symbol?
(c) What was the stock's trading range today?
(d) What was the stock's trading range for the year?

CRITICAL THINKING

Decision-Making Across the Organization

BYP13-5 The stockholders' meeting for Percival Corporation has been in progress for some time. The chief financial officer for Percival is presently reviewing the company's financial statements and is explaining the items that comprise the stockholders' equity section of the balance sheet for the current year. The stockholders' equity section of Percival Corporation at December 31, 2017, is as follows.

PERCIVAL CORPORATION
Balance Sheet (partial)
December 31, 2017

Paid-in capital		
Capital stock		
Preferred stock, authorized 1,000,000 shares, $100 par value, 6,000 shares issued and outstanding		$ 600,000
Common stock, authorized 5,000,000 shares, $1 par value, 3,000,000 shares issued, and 2,700,000 outstanding		3,000,000
Total capital stock		3,600,000
Additional paid-in capital		
In excess of par—preferred stock	$ 50,000	
In excess of par—common stock	25,000,000	
Total additional paid-in capital		25,050,000
Total paid-in capital		28,650,000
Retained earnings		900,000
Total paid-in capital and retained earnings		29,550,000
Less: Treasury stock (300,000 common shares)		9,300,000
Total stockholders' equity		$20,250,000

At the meeting, stockholders have raised a number of questions regarding the stockholders' equity section.

Instructions
With the class divided into groups, answer the following questions as if you were the chief financial officer for Percival Corporation.

(a) "I thought the common stock was presently selling at $29.75, but the company has the stock stated at $1 per share. How can that be?"
(b) "Why is the company buying back its common stock? Furthermore, the treasury stock has a debit balance because it is subtracted from stockholders' equity. Why is treasury stock not reported as an asset if it has a debit balance?"

Communication Activity

BYP13-6 Joe Moyer, your uncle, is an inventor who has decided to incorporate. Uncle Joe knows that you are an accounting major at U.N.O. In a recent letter to you, he ends with the question, "I'm filling out a state incorporation application. Can you tell me the difference in the following terms: (1) authorized stock, (2) issued stock, (3) outstanding stock, and (4) preferred stock?"

Instructions

In a brief note, differentiate for Uncle Joe among the four different stock terms. Write the letter to be friendly, yet professional.

Ethics Case

BYP13-7 The R&D division of Piqua Chemical Corp. has just developed a chemical for sterilizing the vicious Brazilian "killer bees" which are invading Mexico and the southern United States. The president of the company is anxious to get the chemical on the market to boost the company's profits. He believes his job is in jeopardy because of decreasing sales and profits. The company has an opportunity to sell this chemical in Central American countries, where the laws are much more relaxed than in the United States.

The director of Piqua's R&D division strongly recommends further testing in the laboratory for side-effects of this chemical on other insects, birds, animals, plants, and even humans. He cautions the president, "We could be sued from all sides if the chemical has tragic side-effects that we didn't even test for in the labs." The president answers, "We can't wait an additional year for your lab tests. We can avoid losses from such lawsuits by establishing a separate wholly owned corporation to shield Piqua Corp. from such lawsuits. We can't lose any more than our investment in the new corporation, and we'll invest in just the patent covering this chemical. We'll reap the benefits if the chemical works and is safe, and avoid the losses from lawsuits if it's a disaster." The following week, Piqua creates a new wholly owned corporation called Finlay Inc., sells the chemical patent to it for $10, and watches the spraying begin.

Instructions

(a) Who are the stakeholders in this situation?
(b) Are the president's motives and actions ethical?
(c) Can Piqua shield itself against losses of Finlay Inc.?

All About You

BYP13-8 A high percentage of Americans own stock in corporations. As a shareholder in a corporation, you will receive an annual report. One of the goals of this course is for you to learn how to navigate your way around an annual report.

Instructions

Use Apple's 2013 annual report provided in Appendix A to answer the following questions.

(a) What CPA firm performed the audit of Apple's financial statements?
(b) What was the amount of Apple's earnings per share in 2013?
(c) What were net sales in 2013?
(d) How much cash did Apple spend on capital expenditures in 2013?
(e) Over what life does the company depreciate its buildings?
(f) What were the proceeds from issuance of common stock in 2013?

FASB Codification Activity

BYP13-9 If your school has a subscription to the FASB Codification, go to **http://aaahq.org/ascLogin.cfm** to log in and prepare responses to the following.

(a) How is common stock defined?
(b) How is preferred stock defined?
(c) What is the meaning of the term shares?

A Look at IFRS

LEARNING OBJECTIVE 5

Compare the accounting for stockholders' equity under GAAP and IFRS.

The accounting for transactions related to stockholders' equity, such as issuance of shares and purchase of treasury stock, are similar under both IFRS and GAAP. Major differences relate to terminology used, introduction of items such as revaluation surplus, and presentation of stockholders' equity information.

Key Points

Following are the key similarities and differences between GAAP and IFRS as related to stockholders' equity.

Similarities

- Aside from terminology used, the accounting transactions for the issuance of shares and the purchase of treasury stocks are similar.
- Like GAAP, IFRS does not allow a company to record gains or losses on purchases of its own shares.

Differences

- Under IFRS, the term **reserves** is used to describe all equity accounts other than those arising from contributed (paid-in) capital. This would include, for example, reserves related to retained earnings, asset revaluations, and fair value differences.
- Many countries have a different mix of investor groups than in the United States. For example, in Germany, financial institutions like banks are not only major creditors of corporations but often are the largest corporate stockholders as well. In the United States, Asia, and the United Kingdom, many companies rely on substantial investment from private investors.
- There are often terminology differences for equity accounts. The following summarizes some of the common differences in terminology.

GAAP	IFRS
Common stock	Share capital—ordinary
Stockholders	Shareholders
Par value	Nominal or face value
Authorized stock	Authorized share capital
Preferred stock	Share capital—preference
Paid-in capital	Issued/allocated share capital
Paid-in capital in excess of par—common stock	Share premium—ordinary
Paid-in capital in excess of par—preferred stock	Share premium—preference
Retained earnings	Retained earnings or Retained profits
Retained earnings deficit	Accumulated losses
Accumulated other comprehensive income	General reserve and other reserve accounts

As an example of how similar transactions use different terminology under IFRS, consider the accounting for the issuance of 1,000 shares of $1 par value common stock for $5 per share. Under IFRS, the entry is as follows.

Cash	5,000	
Share Capital—Ordinary		1,000
Share Premium—Ordinary		4,000

- A major difference between IFRS and GAAP relates to the account Revaluation Surplus. Revaluation surplus arises under IFRS because companies are permitted to revalue their property, plant, and equipment to fair value under certain circumstances. This account is part of general reserves under IFRS and is not considered contributed capital.

- IFRS often uses terms such as **retained profits** or **accumulated profit or loss** to describe retained earnings. The term **retained earnings** is also often used.
- Equity is given various descriptions under IFRS, such as shareholders' equity, owners' equity, capital and reserves, and shareholders' funds.

Looking to the Future

As indicated in earlier discussions, the IASB and the FASB are currently working on a project related to financial statement presentation. An important part of this study is to determine whether certain line items, subtotals, and totals should be clearly defined and required to be displayed in the financial statements.

IFRS Practice

IFRS Self-Test Questions

1. Which of the following is **true**?
   (a) In the United States, the primary corporate stockholders are financial institutions.
   (b) Share capital means total assets under IFRS.
   (c) The IASB and FASB are presently studying how financial statement information should be presented.
   (d) The accounting for treasury stock differs extensively between GAAP and IFRS.
2. Under IFRS, the amount of capital received in excess of par value would be credited to:
   (a) Retained Earnings.
   (b) Contributed Capital.
   (c) Share Premium.
   (d) Par value is not used under IFRS.
3. Which of the following is **false**?
   (a) Under GAAP, companies cannot record gains on transactions involving their own shares.
   (b) Under IFRS, companies cannot record gains on transactions involving their own shares.
   (c) Under IFRS, the statement of stockholders' equity is a required statement.
   (d) Under IFRS, a company records a revaluation surplus when it experiences an increase in the price of its common stock.
4. Which of the following does **not** represent a pair of GAAP/IFRS-comparable terms?
   (a) Additional paid-in capital/Share premium.
   (b) Treasury stock/Repurchase reserve.
   (c) Common stock/Share capital.
   (d) Preferred stock/Preference shares.

IFRS Exercises

IFRS13-1 On May 10, Jaurez Corporation issues 1,000 shares of $10 par value ordinary shares for cash at $18 per share. Journalize the issuance of the shares.

IFRS13-2 Meenen Corporation has the following accounts at December 31 (in euros): Share Capital—Ordinary, €10 par, 5,000 shares issued, €50,000; Share Premium—Ordinary €10,000; Retained Earnings €45,000; and Treasury Shares—Ordinary, 500 shares, €11,000. Prepare the equity section of the statement of financial position.

IFRS13-3 Overton Co. had the following transactions during the current period.

Mar. 2	Issued 5,000 shares of $1 par value ordinary shares to attorneys in payment of a bill for $30,000 for services performed in helping the company to incorporate.
June 12	Issued 60,000 shares of $1 par value ordinary shares for cash of $375,000.
July 11	Issued 1,000 shares of $100 par value preference shares for cash at $110 per share.
Nov. 28	Purchased 2,000 treasury shares for $80,000.

Instructions

Journalize the above transactions.

International Financial Reporting Problem: Louis Vuitton

IFRS13-4 The financial statements of Louis Vuitton are presented in Appendix F. Instructions for accessing and using the company's complete annual report, including the notes to its financial statements, are also provided in Appendix F.

Instructions

Use the company's annual report to answer the following questions.

(a) Determine the following amounts at December 31, 2013: (1) total equity, (2) total revaluation reserve, and (3) number of treasury shares.

(b) Examine the equity section of the company's balance sheet. For each of the following, provide the comparable label that would be used under GAAP: (1) share capital, (2) share premium, and (3) net profit, group share.

Answers to IFRS Self-Test Questions

1. c **2.** c **3.** d **4.** b

14 Corporations: Dividends, Retained Earnings, and Income Reporting

CHAPTER PREVIEW As indicated in the Feature Story below, a profitable corporation like Van Meter Inc. can provide real benefits to employees through its stock bonus plan. And as employees learn more about the role of dividends, retained earnings, and earnings per share, they develop an understanding and appreciation for what the company is providing to them.

FEATURE STORY

Owning a Piece of the Action

Van Meter Inc., an electrical-parts distributor in Cedar Rapids, Iowa, is 100% employee-owned. For many years, the company has issued bonuses in the form of shares of company stock to all of its employees. These bonus distributions typically have a value equal to several weeks of pay. Top management always thought that this was a great program. Therefore, it came as quite a surprise a few years ago when an employee stood up at a company-wide meeting and said that he did not see any real value in receiving the company's shares. Instead, he wanted "a few hundred extra bucks for beer and cigarettes."

As it turned out, many of the company's 340 employees felt this way. Rather than end the stock bonus program, however, the company decided to educate its employees on the value of share ownership. The employees are now taught how to determine the worth of their shares, the rights that come with share ownership, and what they can do to help increase the value of those shares.

As part of the education program, management developed a slogan, "Work ten, get five free." The idea is that after working 10 years, an employee's shares would be worth the equivalent of about five years' worth of salary. For example, a person earning a $30,000 salary would earn $300,000 in wages over a 10-year period. During that same 10-year period, it was likely that the value of the employee's shares would accumulate to about $150,000 (five years' worth of salary). This demonstrates in more concrete terms why employees should be excited about share ownership.

A 12-member employee committee has the responsibility of educating new employees about the program. The committee also runs training programs so that employees understand how their cost-saving actions improve the company's results—and its stock price. It appears that the company's education program to encourage employees to act like owners is working. Profitability has increased rapidly, and employee turnover has fallen from 18% to 8%. Given Van Meter's success, many of the 10,000 other employee-owned companies in the United States might want to investigate whether their employees understand the benefits of share ownership.

Source: Adapted from Simona Covel, "How to Get Workers to Think and Act Like Owners," *Wall Street Journal Online* (February 15, 2008).

Daisy Daisy/Photographer's Choice/Getty Images, Inc.

CHAPTER OUTLINE

Learning Objectives

Learning Objective	Topics	DO IT!
1 Explain how to account for cash dividends.	• Cash dividends • Dividend preferences	DO IT! 1 Dividends on Preferred and Common Stock
2 Explain how to account for stock dividends and splits.	• Stock dividends • Stock splits	DO IT! 2 Stock Dividends and Stock Splits
3 Prepare and analyze a comprehensive stockholders' equity section.	• Retained earnings • Statement presentation and analysis	DO IT! 3 Retained Earnings Statement
4 Describe the form and content of corporation income statements.	• Income statement presentation • Income statement analysis	DO IT! 4 Stockholders' Equity and EPS

Go to the ***REVIEW AND PRACTICE*** section at the end of the chapter for a review of key concepts and practice applications with solutions.

Visit **WileyPLUS with ORION** for additional tutorials and practice opportunities.

LEARNING OBJECTIVE 1

Explain how to account for cash dividends.

A **dividend is a corporation's distribution of cash or stock to its stockholders on a pro rata (proportional to ownership) basis.** Pro rata means that if you own 10% of the common shares, you will receive 10% of the dividend. Dividends can take four forms: cash, property, scrip (a promissory note to pay cash), or stock. Cash dividends predominate in practice although companies also declare stock dividends with some frequency. These two forms of dividends are therefore the focus of discussion in this chapter.

Investors are very interested in a company's dividend practices. In the financial press, **dividends are generally reported quarterly as a dollar amount per share**. (Sometimes they are reported on an annual basis.) For example, Nike's **quarterly** dividend rate in the fourth quarter of 2013 was 24 cents per share. The dividend rate for the fourth quarter of 2013 for GE was 22 cents, and for ConAgra Foods it was 25 cents.

Cash Dividends

A **cash dividend** is a pro rata distribution of cash to stockholders. Cash dividends are not paid on treasury shares. For a corporation to pay a cash dividend, it must have the following.

1. **Retained earnings.** The legality of a cash dividend depends on the laws of the state in which the company is incorporated. Payment of cash dividends from retained earnings is legal in all states. In general, cash dividend distributions from only the balance in common stock (legal capital) are illegal.

   A dividend declared out of paid-in capital is termed a **liquidating dividend**. Such a dividend reduces or "liquidates" the amount originally paid in by stockholders. Statutes vary considerably with respect to cash dividends based on paid-in capital in excess of par or stated value. Many states permit such dividends.

2. **Adequate cash.** The legality of a dividend and the ability to pay a dividend are two different things. For example, Nike, with retained earnings of over $5.6 billion, could legally declare a dividend of at least $5.6 billion. But Nike's cash balance is only $3.3 billion.

   Before declaring a cash dividend, a company's board of directors must carefully consider both current and future demands on the company's cash resources. In some cases, current liabilities may make a cash dividend inappropriate. In other cases, a major plant expansion program may warrant only a relatively small dividend.

3. **Declared dividends.** A company does not pay dividends unless its board of directors decides to do so, at which point the board "declares" the dividend. The board of directors has full authority to determine the amount of income to distribute in the form of a dividend and the amount to retain in the business. Dividends do not accrue like interest on a note payable, and they are not a liability until declared.

The amount and timing of a dividend are important issues for management to consider. The payment of a large cash dividend could lead to liquidity problems for the company. On the other hand, a small dividend or a missed dividend may cause unhappiness among stockholders. Many stockholders expect to receive a reasonable cash payment from the company on a periodic basis. Many companies declare and pay cash dividends quarterly. On the other hand, a number of high-growth companies pay no dividends, preferring to conserve cash to finance future capital expenditures.

ENTRIES FOR CASH DIVIDENDS

Three dates are important in connection with dividends: (1) the declaration date, (2) the record date, and (3) the payment date. Normally, there are two to four weeks between each date. Companies make accounting entries on the declaration date and the payment date.

On the **declaration date**, the board of directors formally declares (authorizes) the cash dividend and announces it to stockholders. The declaration of a cash dividend **commits the corporation to a legal obligation**. The company must make an entry to recognize the increase in Cash Dividends and the increase in the liability Dividends Payable.

To illustrate, assume that on December 1, 2017, the directors of Media General declare a 50 cents per share cash dividend on 100,000 shares of $10 par value common stock. The dividend is $50,000 (100,000 × $0.50). The entry to record the declaration is as follows.

Declaration Date

Dec. 1	Cash Dividends	50,000	
	Dividends Payable		50,000
	(To record declaration of cash dividend)		

A	=	L	+	SE
				−50,000 Div
		+50,000		

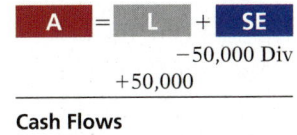

Cash Flows
no effect

Media General debits the account Cash Dividends. Cash dividends decrease retained earnings. We use the specific title Cash Dividends to differentiate it from other types of dividends, such as stock dividends. Dividends Payable is a current liability. It will normally be paid within the next several months. *For homework problems, you should use the Cash Dividends account for recording dividend declarations.*

At the **record date**, the company determines ownership of the outstanding shares for dividend purposes. The stockholders' records maintained by the corporation supply this information. In the interval between the declaration date and the record date, the corporation updates its stock ownership records. For Media General, the record date is December 22. No entry is required on this date because the corporation's liability recognized on the declaration date is unchanged.

Helpful Hint
The purpose of the record date is to identify the persons or entities that will receive the dividend, not to determine the amount of the dividend liability.

Record Date

Dec. 22	No entry		

On the **payment date**, the company makes cash dividend payments to the stockholders of record (as of December 22) and records the payment of the dividend. If January 20 is the payment date for Media General, the entry on that date is as follows.

Payment Date

Jan. 20	Dividends Payable	50,000	
	Cash		50,000
	(To record payment of cash dividend)		

A	=	L	+	SE
		−50,000		
−50,000				

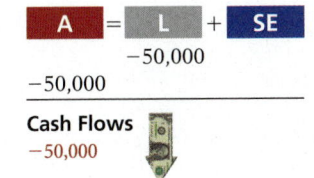

Cash Flows
−50,000

Note that payment of the dividend reduces both current assets and current liabilities. It has no effect on stockholders' equity. The cumulative effect of the declaration and payment of a cash dividend is to **decrease both stockholders' equity and total assets**. Illustration 14-1 (page 612) summarizes the three important dates associated with dividends for Media General.

Illustration 14-1
Key dividend dates

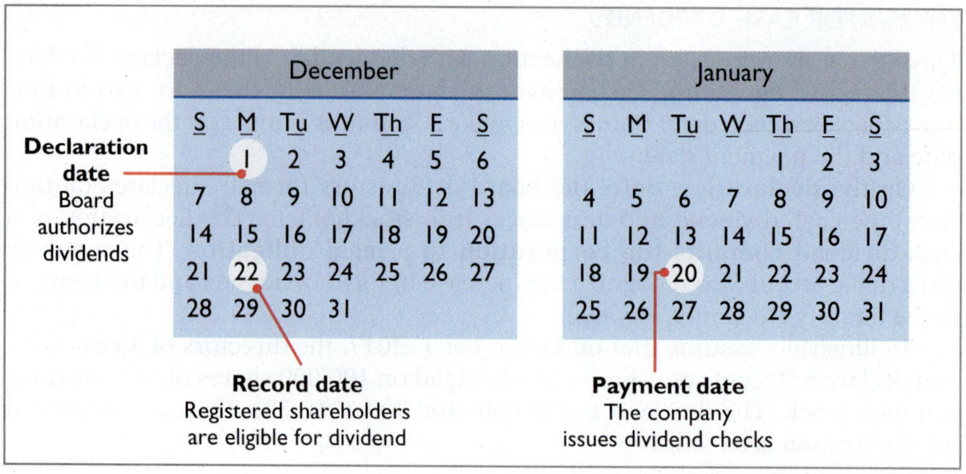

When using a Cash Dividends account, Media General should transfer the balance of that account to Retained Earnings at the end of the year by a closing entry. The entry for Media General at closing is as follows.

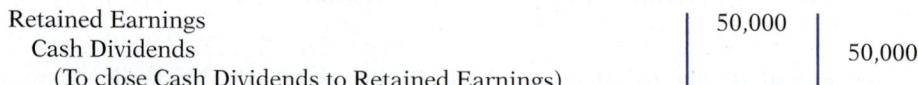

Retained Earnings	50,000	
Cash Dividends		50,000
(To close Cash Dividends to Retained Earnings)		

Dividend Preferences

Preferred stockholders have the right to receive dividends before common stockholders. For example, if the dividend rate on preferred stock is $5 per share, common shareholders cannot receive any dividends in the current year until preferred stockholders have received $5 per share. The first claim to dividends does not, however, **guarantee** the payment of dividends. Dividends depend on many factors, such as adequate retained earnings and availability of cash. If a company does not pay dividends to preferred stockholders, it cannot pay dividends to common stockholders.

For preferred stock, companies state the per share dividend amount as a percentage of the par value or as a specified amount. For example, **Earthlink** specifies a 3% dividend on its $100 par value preferred. **PepsiCo** pays $4.56 per share on its no-par value stock.

Most preferred stocks also have a preference on corporate assets if the corporation fails. This feature provides security for the preferred stockholder. The preference to assets may be for the par value of the shares or for a specified liquidating value. For example, **Commonwealth Edison**'s preferred stock entitles its holders to receive $31.80 per share, plus accrued and unpaid dividends, in the event of liquidation. The liquidation preference establishes the respective claims of creditors and preferred stockholders in litigation involving bankruptcy lawsuits.

CUMULATIVE DIVIDEND

Preferred stock often contains a **cumulative dividend** feature. This feature stipulates that preferred stockholders must be paid both current-year dividends and any unpaid prior-year dividends before common stockholders are paid dividends. When preferred stock is cumulative, preferred dividends not declared in a given period are called **dividends in arrears**.

To illustrate, assume that Scientific Leasing has 5,000 shares of 7%, $100 par value, cumulative preferred stock outstanding. Each $100 share pays a $7 dividend (.07 × $100). The annual dividend is $35,000 (5,000 × $7 per share). If dividends are two years in arrears, preferred stockholders are entitled to receive the dividends shown in Illustration 14-2.

Dividends in arrears ($35,000 × 2)	$ 70,000
Current-year dividends	35,000
Total preferred dividends	**$105,000**

Illustration 14-2
Computation of total dividends to preferred stock

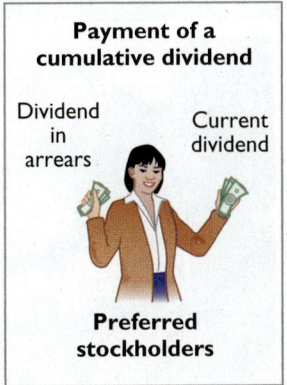

Payment of a cumulative dividend

Preferred stockholders

The company cannot pay dividends to common stockholders until it pays the entire preferred dividend. In other words, companies cannot pay dividends to common stockholders while any preferred dividends are in arrears.

Dividends in arrears are not considered a liability. **No obligation exists until the board of directors formally declares that the corporation will pay a dividend.** However, companies should disclose in the notes to the financial statements the amount of dividends in arrears. Doing so enables investors to assess the potential impact of this commitment on the corporation's financial position.

The investment community does not look favorably on companies that are unable to meet their dividend obligations. As a financial officer noted in discussing one company's failure to pay its cumulative preferred dividend for a period of time, "Not meeting your obligations on something like that is a major black mark on your record."

ALLOCATING CASH DIVIDENDS BETWEEN PREFERRED AND COMMON STOCK

As indicated, preferred stock has priority over common stock in regard to dividends. Holders of cumulative preferred stock must be paid any unpaid prior-year dividends and their current year's dividend before common stockholders receive dividends.

To illustrate, assume that at December 31, 2017, IBR Inc. has 1,000 shares of 8%, $100 par value cumulative preferred stock. It also has 50,000 shares of $10 par value common stock outstanding. The dividend per share for preferred stock is $8 ($100 par value × 8%). The required annual dividend for preferred stock is therefore $8,000 (1,000 shares × $8). At December 31, 2017, the directors declare a $6,000 cash dividend. In this case, the entire dividend amount goes to preferred stockholders because of their dividend preference. The entry to record the declaration of the dividend is as follows.

Dec. 31	Cash Dividends	6,000	
	Dividends Payable		6,000
	(To record $6 per share cash dividend to preferred stockholders)		

A	=	L	+	SE
				−6,000 Div
		+6,000		

Cash Flows
no effect

Because of the cumulative feature, dividends of $2 ($8 − $6) per share are in arrears on preferred stock for 2017. IBR must pay these dividends to preferred stockholders before it can pay any future dividends to common stockholders. IBR should disclose dividends in arrears in the financial statements.

At December 31, 2018, IBR declares a $50,000 cash dividend. The allocation of the dividend to the two classes of stock is as follows.

Total dividend		$50,000
Allocated to preferred stock		
Dividends in arrears, 2017 (1,000 × $2)	**$2,000**	
2018 dividend (1,000 × $8)	**8,000**	10,000
Remainder allocated to common stock		$40,000

Illustration 14-3
Allocating dividends to preferred and common stock

The entry to record the declaration of the dividend is as follows.

Dec. 31	Cash Dividends	50,000	
	Dividends Payable		50,000
	(To record declaration of cash dividends of $10,000 to preferred stock and $40,000 to common stock)		

A	=	L	+	SE
				−50,000 Div
		+50,000		

Cash Flows
no effect

If IBR's preferred stock is not cumulative, preferred stockholders receive only $8,000 in dividends in 2018. Common stockholders receive $42,000.

Investor Insight

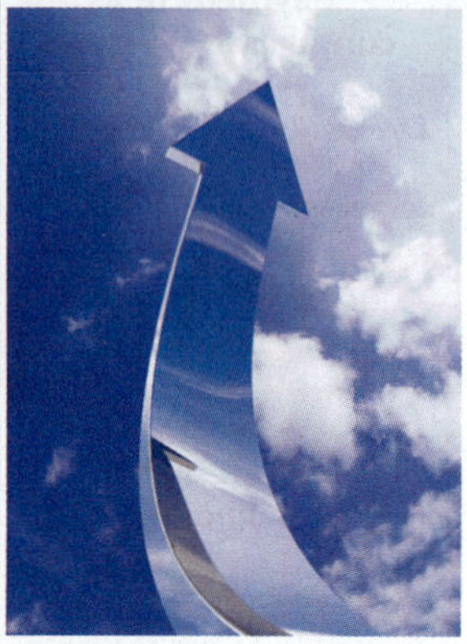

Palto/iStockphoto

Dividends in Demand

Investors seeking dividend income enjoyed a great year in 2013. A total of 418 companies in the Standard & Poor's 500 index paid a dividend, matching the highest total since 1998. As shown in the following chart, dividend growth since 2008 more than doubled.

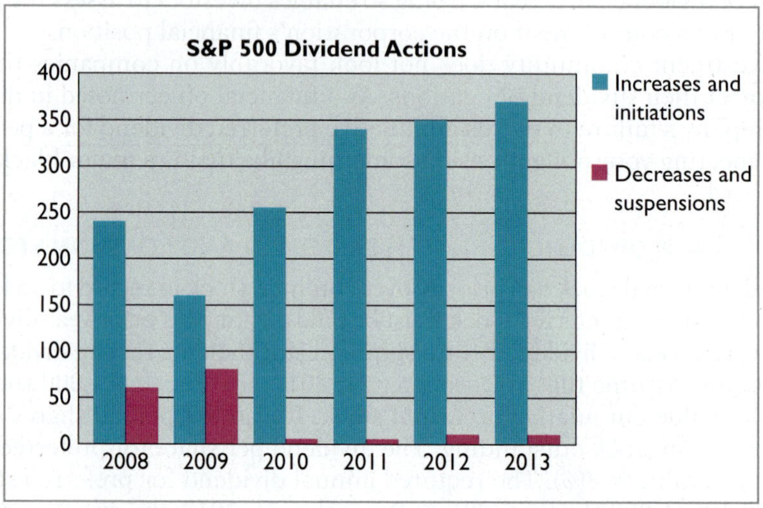

And for holders of dividend-paying stocks, corporate America may continue to sweeten the pot. One reason for optimism is that the average dividend payout—the percentage of corporate profits paid out as dividends—remains low at 36%. The historical average is 52%.

Source: Trevor Delaney and Jenni Sohn, "Dividends in Demand" *Naples Daily News* (January 8, 2014), p. 5B.

What factors must management consider in deciding how large a dividend to pay? (Go to **WileyPLUS** for this answer and additional questions.)

DO IT! 1 Dividends on Preferred and Common Stock

MasterMind Corporation has 2,000 shares of 6%, $100 par value preferred stock outstanding at December 31, 2017. At December 31, 2017, the company declared a $60,000 cash dividend. Determine the dividend paid to preferred stockholders and common stockholders under each of the following scenarios.

1. The preferred stock is noncumulative, and the company has not missed any dividends in previous years.
2. The preferred stock is noncumulative, and the company did not pay a dividend in each of the two previous years.
3. The preferred stock is cumulative, and the company did not pay a dividend in each of the two previous years.

Action Plan

✔ Determine dividends on preferred shares by multiplying the dividend rate times the par value of the stock times the number of preferred shares.

Solution

1. The company has not missed past dividends and the preferred stock is noncumulative. Thus, the preferred stockholders are paid only this year's dividend. The dividend paid to preferred stockholders would be $12,000 (2,000 × .06 × $100). The dividend paid to common stockholders would be $48,000 ($60,000 − $12,000).

2. The preferred stock is noncumulative. Thus, past unpaid dividends do not have to be paid. The dividend paid to preferred stockholders would be $12,000 (2,000 × .06 × $100). The dividend paid to common stockholders would be $48,000 ($60,000 − $12,000).
3. The preferred stock is cumulative. Thus, dividends that have been missed (dividends in arrears) must be paid. The dividend paid to preferred stockholders would be $36,000 (3 × 2,000 × .06 × $100). Of the $36,000, $24,000 relates to dividends in arrears and $12,000 relates to the current dividend on preferred stock. The dividend paid to common stockholders would be $24,000 ($60,000 − $36,000).

Related exercise material: **BE14-2, E14-2 and DO IT! 14-1.**

Action Plan (cont'd)

✔ **Understand the cumulative feature. If preferred stock is cumulative, then any missed dividends (dividends in arrears) and the current year's dividend must be paid to preferred stockholders before dividends are paid to common stockholders.**

LEARNING OBJECTIVE 2 **Explain how to account for stock dividends and splits.**

Stock Dividends

A **stock dividend** is a pro rata (proportional to ownership) distribution of the corporation's own stock to stockholders. Whereas a company pays cash in a cash dividend, a company issues shares of stock in a stock dividend. **A stock dividend results in a decrease in retained earnings and an increase in paid-in capital.** Unlike a cash dividend, a stock dividend does not decrease total stockholders' equity or total assets.

To illustrate, assume that you have a 2% ownership interest in Cetus Inc. That is, you own 20 of its 1,000 shares of common stock. If Cetus declares a 10% stock dividend, it would issue 100 shares (1,000 × 10%) of stock. You would receive two shares (2% × 100). Would your ownership interest change? No, it would remain at 2% (22 ÷ 1,100). **You now own more shares of stock, but your ownership interest has not changed.**

Cetus has disbursed no cash and has assumed no liabilities. What, then, are the purposes and benefits of a stock dividend? Corporations issue stock dividends generally for one or more of the following reasons.

1. To satisfy stockholders' dividend expectations without spending cash.
2. To increase the marketability of the corporation's stock. When the number of shares outstanding increases, the market price per share decreases. Decreasing the market price of the stock makes it easier for smaller investors to purchase the shares.
3. To emphasize that a company has permanently reinvested in the business a portion of stockholders' equity, which therefore is unavailable for cash dividends.

When the dividend is declared, the board of directors determines the size of the stock dividend and the value assigned to each dividend.

Generally, if the company issues a **small stock dividend** (less than 20–25% of the corporation's issued stock), the value assigned to the dividend is the fair value (market price) per share. This treatment is based on the assumption that a small stock dividend will have little effect on the market price of the shares previously outstanding. Thus, many stockholders consider small stock dividends to be distributions of earnings equal to the market price of the shares distributed. If a company issues a **large stock dividend** (greater than 20–25%), the price assigned to the dividend is the par or stated value. Small stock dividends predominate in practice. Thus, we will illustrate only entries for small stock dividends.

ENTRIES FOR STOCK DIVIDENDS

To illustrate the accounting for small stock dividends, assume that Medland Corporation has a balance of $300,000 in retained earnings. It declares a 10% stock dividend on its 50,000 shares of $10 par value common stock. The current market price of its stock is $15 per share. The number of shares to be issued is 5,000 (10% × 50,000). Therefore, the total amount to be debited to Stock Dividends is $75,000 (5,000 × $15). The entry to record the declaration of the stock dividend is as follows.

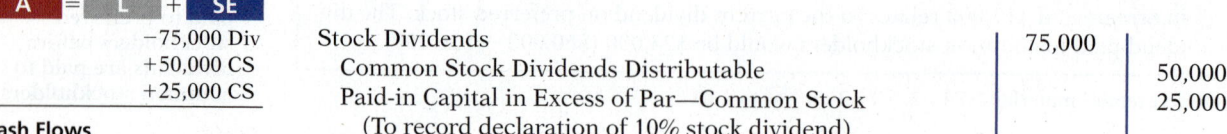

A = L + SE	
−75,000 Div	
+50,000 CS	
+25,000 CS	

Cash Flows
no effect

	Debit	Credit
Stock Dividends	75,000	
Common Stock Dividends Distributable		50,000
Paid-in Capital in Excess of Par—Common Stock		25,000
(To record declaration of 10% stock dividend)		

Medland debits Stock Dividends for the market price of the stock issued ($15 × 5,000). (Similar to Cash Dividends, Stock Dividends decrease retained earnings.) Medland also credits Common Stock Dividends Distributable for the par value of the dividend shares ($10 × 5,000) and credits Paid-in Capital in Excess of Par—Common Stock for the excess of the market price over par ($5 × 5,000).

Common Stock Dividends Distributable is a **stockholders' equity account.** It is not a liability because assets will not be used to pay the dividend. If the company prepares a balance sheet before it issues the dividend shares, it reports the distributable account under paid-in capital as shown in Illustration 14-4.

Illustration 14-4
Statement presentation of common stock dividends distributable

Paid-in capital	
Common stock	$500,000
Common stock dividends distributable	**50,000**
Paid-in capital in excess of par—common stock	25,000
Total paid-in capital	$575,000

When Medland issues the dividend shares, it debits Common Stock Dividends Distributable and credits Common Stock, as follows.

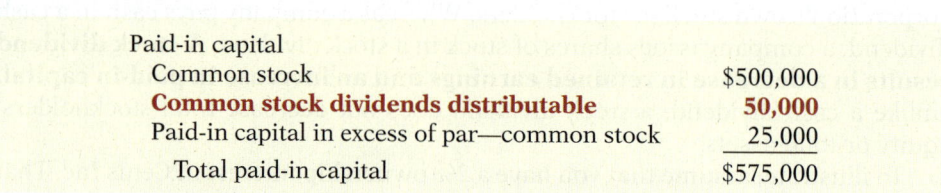

A = L + SE	
−50,000 CS	
+50,000 CS	

Cash Flows
no effect

	Debit	Credit
Common Stock Dividends Distributable	50,000	
Common Stock		50,000
(To record issuance of 5,000 shares in a stock dividend)		

EFFECTS OF STOCK DIVIDENDS

How do stock dividends affect stockholders' equity? They **change the composition of stockholders' equity** because they transfer a portion of retained earnings to paid-in capital. However, **total stockholders' equity remains the same.** Stock dividends also have no effect on the par or stated value per share, but the number of shares outstanding increases. Illustration 14-5 shows these effects for Medland.

Illustration 14-5
Stock dividend effects

	Before Dividend	Change	After Dividend
Stockholders' equity			
Paid-in capital			
Common stock, $10 par	$ 500,000	$ 50,000	$ 550,000
Paid-in capital in excess of par	—	25,000	25,000
Total paid-in capital	500,000	+75,000	575,000
Retained earnings	300,000	−75,000	225,000
Total stockholders' equity	**$800,000**	**$ 0**	**$800,000**
Outstanding shares	**50,000**	**+5,000**	**55,000**
Par value per share	**$10.00**	**$ 0**	**$10.00**

In this example, total paid-in capital increases by $75,000 (50,000 shares × 10% × $15) and retained earnings decreases by the same amount. Note also that total stockholders' equity remains unchanged at $800,000. The number of shares increases by 5,000 (50,000 × 10%).

Stock Splits

A **stock split**, like a stock dividend, involves issuance of additional shares to stockholders according to their percentage ownership. **However, a stock split results in a reduction in the par or stated value per share.** The purpose of a stock split is to increase the marketability of the stock by lowering its market price per share. This, in turn, makes it easier for the corporation to issue additional stock.

Helpful Hint
A stock split changes the par value per share but does not affect any balances in stockholders' equity.

The effect of a split on market price is generally **inversely proportional** to the size of the split. For example, after a 2-for-1 stock split, the market price of Nike's stock fell from $111 to approximately $55. The lower market price stimulated market activity. Within one year, the stock was trading above $100 again. Illustration 14-6 shows the effect of a 4-for-1 stock split for stockholders.

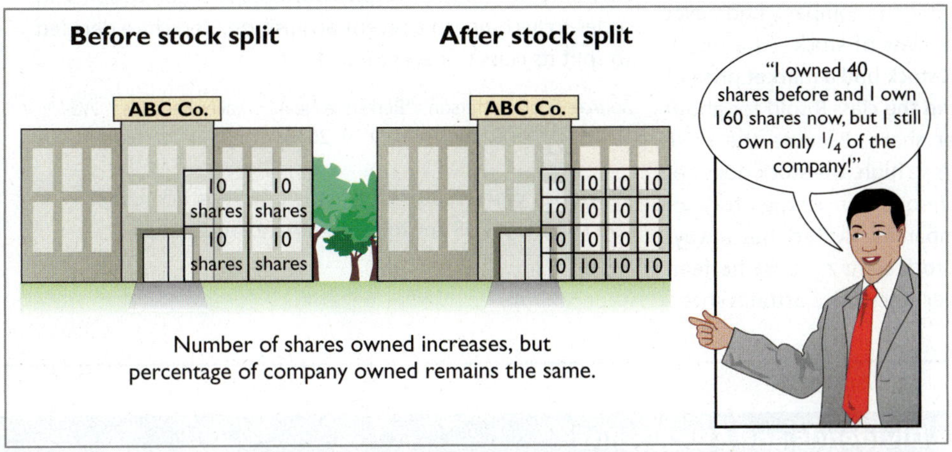

Illustration 14-6
Effect of stock split for stockholders

In a stock split, the company increases the number of shares in the same proportion that par or stated value per share decreases. For example, in a 2-for-1 split, the company exchanges one share of $10 par value stock for two shares of $5 par value stock. **A stock split does not have any effect on total paid-in capital, retained earnings, or total stockholders' equity.** However, the number of shares outstanding increases, and par value per share decreases. Illustration 14-7 shows these effects for Medland Corporation, assuming that it splits its 50,000 shares of common stock on a 2-for-1 basis.

Illustration 14-7
Stock split effects

	Before Stock Split	Change	After Stock Split
Stockholders' equity			
Paid-in capital			
Common stock	$ 500,000		$ 500,000
Paid-in capital in excess of par	–0–		–0–
Total paid-in capital	500,000	$ 0	500,000
Retained earnings	300,000	0	300,000
Total stockholders' equity	**$800,000**	**$ 0**	**$800,000**
Outstanding shares	**50,000**	**+50,000**	**100,000**
Par value per share	**$10.00**	**−$5.00**	**$5.00**

A stock split does not affect the balances in any stockholders' equity accounts. Therefore, **a company does not need to journalize a stock split.**

Illustration 14-8 summarizes the differences between stock dividends and stock splits.

Illustration 14-8
Differences between the effects of stock dividends and stock splits

Item	Stock Dividend	Stock Split
Total paid-in capital	Increase	No change
Total retained earnings	Decrease	No change
Total par value (common stock)	Increase	No change
Par value per share	No change	Decrease
Outstanding shares	Increase	Increase
Total stockholders' equity	No change	No change

Investor Insight Berkshire Hathaway

Dietmar Klement/ iStockphoto

A No-Split Philosophy

Warren Buffett's company, Berkshire Hathaway, has two classes of shares. Until recently, the company had never split either class of stock. As a result, the class A stock had a market price of $97,000 and the class B sold for about $3,200 per share. Because the price per share is so high, the stock does not trade as frequently as the stock of other companies. Buffett has always opposed stock splits because he feels that a lower stock price attracts short-term investors. He appears to be correct. For example, while more than 6 million shares of IBM are exchanged on the average day, only about 1,000 class A shares of Berkshire are traded. Despite Buffett's aversion to splits, in order to accomplish a recent acquisition, Berkshire decided to split its class B shares 50 to 1.

Source: Scott Patterson, "Berkshire Nears Smaller Baby B's," *Wall Street Journal Online* (January 19, 2010).

Why does Warren Buffett usually oppose stock splits? (Go to **WileyPLUS** for this answer and additional questions.)

DO IT! 2 Stock Dividends and Stock Splits

Sing CD Company has had five years of record earnings. Due to this success, the market price of its 500,000 shares of $2 par value common stock has tripled from $15 per share to $45. During this period, paid-in capital remained the same at $2,000,000. Retained earnings increased from $1,500,000 to $10,000,000. President Joan Elbert is considering either a 10% stock dividend or a 2-for-1 stock split. She asks you to show the before-and-after effects of each option on retained earnings, total stockholders' equity, shares outstanding, and par value per share.

Action Plan

- ✔ Calculate the stock dividend's effect on retained earnings by multiplying the number of new shares times the market price of the stock (or par value for a large stock dividend).
- ✔ Recall that a stock dividend increases the number of shares without affecting total stockholders' equity.
- ✔ Recall that a stock split only increases the number of shares outstanding and decreases the par value per share.

Solution

The stock dividend amount is $2,250,000 [(500,000 × 10%) × $45]. The new balance in retained earnings is $7,750,000 ($10,000,000 − $2,250,000). The retained earnings balance after the stock split is the same as it was before the split: $10,000,000. Total stockholders' equity does not change. The effects on the stockholders' equity accounts are as follows.

	Original Balances	After Dividend	After Split
Paid-in capital	$ 2,000,000	$ 4,250,000	$ 2,000,000
Retained earnings	10,000,000	7,750,000	10,000,000
Total stockholders' equity	$12,000,000	$12,000,000	$12,000,000
Shares outstanding	500,000	550,000	1,000,000
Par value per share	$2.00	$2.00	$1.00

Related exercise material: **BE14-3, BE14-4, E14-4, E14-5, E14-6, E14-7, and DO IT! 14-2.**

LEARNING OBJECTIVE 3 **Prepare and analyze a comprehensive stockholders' equity section.**

Retained Earnings

Retained earnings is net income that a company retains in the business. The balance in retained earnings is part of the stockholders' claim on the total assets of the corporation. It does not, however, represent a claim on any specific asset. Nor can the amount of retained earnings be associated with the balance of any asset account. For example, a $100,000 balance in retained earnings does not mean that there should be $100,000 in cash. The reason is that the company may have used the cash resulting from the excess of revenues over expenses to purchase buildings, equipment, and other assets.

To demonstrate that retained earnings and cash may be quite different, Illustration 14-9 shows recent amounts of retained earnings and cash in selected companies.

Illustration 14-9
Retained earnings and cash balances

	(in millions)	
Company	**Retained Earnings**	**Cash**
Facebook	$ 3,159	$3,323
Google	61,262	8,989
Nike, Inc.	5,695	3,337
Starbucks	4,130	2,576
Amazon.com	2,190	8,658

Remember from Chapter 13 that when a company has net income, it closes net income to retained earnings. The closing entry is a debit to Income Summary and a credit to Retained Earnings.

Helpful Hint
Remember that Retained Earnings is a stockholders' equity account, whose normal balance is a credit.

When a company has a **net loss** (expenses exceed revenues), it also closes this amount to retained earnings. The closing entry is a debit to Retained Earnings and a credit to Income Summary. To illustrate, assume that Rendle Corporation has a net loss of $400,000 in 2017. The closing entry to record this loss is as follows.

Retained Earnings	400,000	
Income Summary		400,000
(To close net loss to Retained Earnings)		

This closing entry is done even if it results in a debit balance in Retained Earnings. **Companies do not debit net losses to paid-in capital accounts.** To do so would destroy the distinction between paid-in and earned capital. If cumulative losses exceed cumulative income over a company's life, a debit balance in Retained Earnings results. A debit balance in Retained Earnings is identified as a **deficit**. A company reports a deficit as a deduction in the stockholders' equity section, as shown in Illustration 14-10.

Illustration 14-10
Stockholders' equity with deficit

Balance Sheet (partial)

Stockholders' equity	
Paid-in capital	
Common stock	$800,000
Retained earnings (deficit)	**(50,000)**
Total stockholders' equity	$750,000

RETAINED EARNINGS RESTRICTIONS

The balance in retained earnings is generally available for dividend declarations. In some cases, however, there may be **retained earnings restrictions**. These make a portion of the retained earnings balance currently unavailable for dividends. Restrictions result from one or more of the following causes.

1. **Legal restrictions.** Many states require a corporation to restrict retained earnings for the cost of treasury stock purchased. The restriction keeps intact the corporation's legal capital that is being temporarily held as treasury stock. When the company sells the treasury stock, the restriction is lifted.
2. **Contractual restrictions.** Long-term debt contracts may restrict retained earnings as a condition for the loan. The restriction limits the use of corporate assets for payment of dividends. Thus, it increases the likelihood that the corporation will be able to meet required loan payments.
3. **Voluntary restrictions.** The board of directors may voluntarily create retained earnings restrictions for specific purposes. For example, the board may authorize a restriction for future plant expansion. By reducing the amount of retained earnings available for dividends, the company makes more cash available for the planned expansion.

Companies generally disclose **retained earnings restrictions** in the notes to the financial statements. For example, as shown in Illustration 14-11, Tektronix Inc., a manufacturer of electronic measurement devices, had total retained earnings of $774 million, but the unrestricted portion was only $223.8 million.

Illustration 14-11
Disclosure of restriction

Real World

TEKTRONIX INC.
Notes to the Financial Statements

Certain of the Company's debt agreements require compliance with debt covenants. Management believes that the Company is in compliance with such requirements. The Company had unrestricted retained earnings of $223.8 million after meeting those requirements.

PRIOR PERIOD ADJUSTMENTS

Suppose that a corporation has closed its books and issued financial statements. The corporation then discovers that it made a material error in reporting net income of a prior year. How should the company record this situation in the accounts and report it in the financial statements?

The correction of an error in previously issued financial statements is known as a **prior period adjustment**. The company makes the correction directly to Retained Earnings because the effect of the error is now in this account. The net income for the prior period has been recorded in retained earnings through the journalizing and posting of closing entries.

To illustrate, assume that General Microwave discovers in 2017 that it understated depreciation expense on equipment in 2016 by $300,000 due to computational errors. These errors overstated both net income for 2016 and the current balance in retained earnings. The entry for the prior period adjustment, ignoring all tax effects, is as follows.

A	=	L	+	SE
				−300,000 RE
−300,000				

Cash Flows
no effect

Retained Earnings	300,000	
Accumulated Depreciation—Equipment		300,000
(To adjust for understatement of depreciation in a prior period)		

A debit to an income statement account in 2017 is incorrect because the error pertains to a prior year.

Companies report prior period adjustments in the retained earnings statement. They add (or deduct, as the case may be) these adjustments from the beginning retained earnings balance. This results in an adjusted beginning balance. For example, assuming a beginning balance of $800,000 in retained earnings, General Microwave reports the prior period adjustment as follows.

Illustration 14-12
Statement presentation of prior period adjustments

GENERAL MICROWAVE Retained Earnings Statement (partial)	
Balance, January 1, as reported	$ 800,000
Correction for overstatement of net income in prior period (depreciation error)	**(300,000)**
Balance, January 1, as adjusted	$ 500,000

Again, reporting the correction in the current year's income statement would be incorrect because it applies to a prior year's income statement.

RETAINED EARNINGS STATEMENT

The **retained earnings statement** shows the changes in retained earnings during the year. The company prepares the statement from the Retained Earnings account. Illustration 14-13 shows (in T-account form) transactions that affect retained earnings.

Illustration 14-13
Debits and credits to retained earnings

Retained Earnings	
1. Net loss	1. Net income
2. Prior period adjustments for overstatement of net income	2. Prior period adjustments for understatement of net income
3. Cash dividends and stock dividends	
4. Some disposals of treasury stock	

As indicated, net income increases retained earnings, and a net loss decreases retained earnings. Prior period adjustments may either increase or decrease retained earnings. Both cash dividends and stock dividends decrease retained earnings. The circumstances under which treasury stock transactions decrease retained earnings are explained in Chapter 13, page 586.

A complete retained earnings statement for Graber Inc., based on assumed data, is shown in Illustration 14-14.

Illustration 14-14
Retained earnings statement

GRABER INC. Retained Earnings Statement For the Year Ended December 31, 2017		
Balance, January 1, as reported		$1,050,000
Correction for understatement of net income in prior period (inventory error)		50,000
Balance, January 1, as adjusted		1,100,000
Add: Net income		360,000
		1,460,000
Less: Cash dividends	$100,000	
Stock dividends	200,000	300,000
Balance, December 31		$1,160,000

Statement Presentation and Analysis

PRESENTATION

Illustration 14-15 presents the stockholders' equity section of Graber Inc.'s balance sheet. Note the following: (1) "Common stock dividends distributable" is shown under "Capital stock" in "Paid-in capital" and (2) a note (Note R) discloses a retained earnings restriction.

Illustration 14-15
Comprehensive stockholders' equity section

GRABER INC.
Balance Sheet (partial)

Stockholders' equity		
Paid-in capital		
Capital stock		
9% Preferred stock, $100 par value, cumulative, callable at $120, 10,000 shares authorized, 6,000 shares issued and outstanding		$ 600,000
Common stock, no par, $5 stated value, 500,000 shares authorized, 400,000 shares issued and 390,000 shares outstanding	$2,000,000	
Common stock dividends distributable	**50,000**	2,050,000
Total capital stock		2,650,000
Additional paid-in capital		
In excess of par—preferred stock	30,000	
In excess of stated value—common stock	1,050,000	
Total additional paid-in capital		1,080,000
Total paid-in capital		3,730,000
Retained earnings **(see Note R)**		1,160,000
Total paid-in capital and retained earnings		4,890,000
Less: Treasury stock (10,000 common shares)		80,000
Total stockholders' equity		$4,810,000

Note R: Retained earnings is restricted for the cost of treasury stock, $80,000.

Instead of presenting a detailed stockholders' equity section in the balance sheet and a retained earnings statement, many companies prepare a **stockholders' equity statement**. This statement shows the changes (1) in each stockholders' equity account and (2) in total that occurred during the year. An example of a stockholders' equity statement appears in Apple's financial statements in Appendix A.

ANALYSIS

Investors and analysts can measure profitability from the viewpoint of the common stockholder by the **return on common stockholders' equity**. This ratio, as shown in Illustration 14-16, indicates how many dollars of net income the company earned for each dollar invested by the common stockholders. It is computed by dividing **net income available to common stockholders** (which is net income minus preferred stock dividends) by average common stockholders' equity.

To illustrate, Walt Disney Company's beginning-of-the-year and end-of-the-year common stockholders' equity were $31,820 and $30,753 million, respectively. Its net income was $4,687 million, and no preferred stock was outstanding. The return on common stockholders' equity is computed as follows.

Net Income minus Preferred Dividends	÷	Average Common Stockholders' Equity	=	Return on Common Stockholders' Equity
($4,687 − $0)	÷	$\frac{(\$31,820 + \$30,753)}{2}$	=	**15.0%**

Illustration 14-16
Return on common stockholders' equity and computation

As shown above, if a company has preferred stock, we would deduct the amount of **preferred dividends** from the company's net income to compute income available to common stockholders. Also, the par value of preferred stock is deducted from total stockholders' equity when computing the average common stockholders' equity.

DO IT! 3 Retained Earnings Statement

Vega Corporation has retained earnings of $5,130,000 on January 1, 2017. During the year, Vega earned $2,000,000 of net income. It declared and paid a $250,000 cash dividend. In 2017, Vega recorded an adjustment of $180,000 due to the understatement (from a mathematical error) of 2016 depreciation expense. Prepare a retained earnings statement for 2017.

Solution

VEGA CORPORATION
Retained Earnings Statement
For the Year Ended December 31, 2017

Balance, January 1, as reported	$5,130,000
Correction for overstatement of net income in prior period (depreciation error)	(180,000)
Balance, January 1, as adjusted	4,950,000
Add: Net income	2,000,000
	6,950,000
Less: Cash dividends	250,000
Balance, December 31	$6,700,000

Related exercise material: **BE14-5, BE14-6, E14-8, E14-9, and DO IT! 14-3.**

Action Plan

- ✔ Recall that a retained earnings statement begins with retained earnings, as reported at the end of the previous year.
- ✔ Add or subtract any prior period adjustments to arrive at the adjusted beginning figure.
- ✔ Add net income and subtract dividends declared to arrive at the ending balance in retained earnings.

LEARNING OBJECTIVE 4 **Describe the form and content of corporation income statements.**

Income Statement Presentation

Income statements for **corporations are the same as the statements for proprietorships or partnerships except for one thing: the reporting of income taxes**. For income tax purposes, corporations are a separate legal entity. As a result, corporations report **income tax expense** in a separate section of the corporation income statement, before net income. The condensed income statement for Leads Inc. in Illustration 14-17 (page 624) shows a typical presentation. Note that the corporation reports income before income taxes as one line item and income tax expense as another.

Illustration 14-17
Income statement with income taxes

LEADS INC. Income Statement For the Year Ended December 31, 2017	
Sales revenue	$800,000
Cost of goods sold	600,000
Gross profit	200,000
Operating expenses	50,000
Income from operations	150,000
Other revenues and gains	10,000
Other expenses and losses	(4,000)
Income before income taxes	**156,000**
Income tax expense	**46,800**
Net income	$109,200

Companies record income tax expense and the related liability for income taxes payable as part of the adjusting process. Using the data for Leads Inc., in Illustration 14-17, the adjusting entry for income tax expense at December 31, 2017, is as follows.

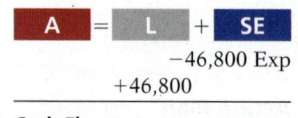

A	=	L	+	SE
				−46,800 Exp
		+46,800		

Cash Flows
no effect

Income Tax Expense	46,800	
Income Taxes Payable		46,800
(To record income taxes for 2017)		

The income statement of Apple (in Appendix A) presents another illustration of income taxes.

Income Statement Analysis

The financial press frequently reports earnings data. Stockholders and potential investors widely use these data in evaluating the profitability of a company. A convenient measure of earnings is **earnings per share (EPS)**, which indicates the net income earned by each share of outstanding **common stock**.

EPS AND PREFERRED DIVIDENDS

The existence of preferred dividends slightly complicates the calculation of EPS. When a corporation has both preferred and common stock, we must subtract the current year's preferred dividend from net income, to arrive at **income available to common stockholders**. Illustration 14-18 shows the formula for computing EPS.

Illustration 14-18
Formula for earnings per share

Net Income minus Preferred Dividends	÷	Weighted-Average Common Shares Outstanding	=	Earnings per Share

ETHICS NOTE

In order to meet market expectations for EPS, some managers engage in elaborate treasury stock transactions. These transactions can be very costly for the remaining shareholders.

To illustrate, assume that Rally Inc. reports net income of $211,000 on its 102,500 weighted-average common shares.[1] During the year, it also declares a $6,000 dividend on its preferred stock. Therefore, the amount Rally has available for common stock dividends is $205,000 ($211,000 − $6,000). Earnings per share is $2 ($205,000 ÷ 102,500). If the preferred stock is cumulative, Rally deducts the dividend for the current year, whether or not it is declared. Remember that companies report **earnings per share only for common stock**.

[1]The calculation of the weighted average of common shares outstanding is discussed in advanced accounting courses.

Investors often attempt to link earnings per share to the market price per share of a company's stock.[2] Because of the importance of earnings per share, most companies must report it on the face of the income statement. Generally, companies simply report this amount below net income on the statement. For Rally Inc., the presentation is as follows.

Illustration 14-19
Basic earnings per share disclosure

RALLY INC.
Income Statement (partial)

Net income	$211,000
Earnings per share	**$2.00**

People, Planet, and Profit Insight

© Robert Churchill/iStockphoto

The Impact of Corporate Social Responsibility

A recent survey conducted by Institutional Shareholder Services, a proxy advisory firm, shows that 83% of investors now believe environmental and social factors can significantly impact shareholder value over the long term. This belief is clearly visible in the rising level of support for shareholder proposals requesting action related to social and environmental issues.

The following table shows that the number of corporate social responsibility (CSR)-related shareholder proposals rose from 150 in 2000 to 191 in 2010. Moreover, those proposals received average voting support of 18.4% of votes cast versus just 7.5% a decade earlier.

Trends in Shareholder Proposals on Corporate Responsibility

	2000	2005	2010
Number of proposals voted	150	155	191
Average voting support	7.5%	9.9%	18.4%
Percent proposals receiving >10% support	16.7%	31.2%	52.1%

Source: Investor Responsibility Research Center, Ernst & Young, *Seven Questions CEOs and Boards Should Ask About: "Triple Bottom Line" Reporting.*

Why are CSR-related shareholder proposals increasing? (Go to **WileyPLUS** for this answer and additional questions.)

DO IT! 4 Stockholders' Equity and EPS

On January 1, 2017, Siena Corporation purchased 2,000 shares of treasury stock. Other information regarding Siena Corporation is provided below.

	2016	**2017**
Net income	$110,000	$110,000
Dividends on preferred stock	$10,000	$10,000
Dividends on common stock	$2,000	$1,600
Weighted-average number of shares outstanding	10,000	8,000*
Common stockholders' equity, beginning of year	$500,000	$400,000*
Common stockholders' equity, end of year	$500,000	$400,000

*Adjusted for purchase of treasury stock.

Compute (a) return on common stockholders' equity for each year and (b) earnings per share for each year, and (c) discuss the changes in each.

[2]The ratio of the market price per share to the earnings per share is called the **price/earnings (P/E) ratio**. The financial media report this ratio for common stocks listed on major stock exchanges.

Action Plan

✔ Determine return on common stockholders' equity by dividing net income available to common stockholders by the average common stockholders' equity.

✔ Determine earnings per share by dividing net income available to common stockholders by the weighted-average number of common shares outstanding.

Solution

(a)

	2016		2017	
Return on common stock-holders' equity	$\frac{(\$110,000 - \$10,000)}{(\$500,000 + \$500,000)/2}$	= 20%	$\frac{(\$110,000 - \$10,000)}{(\$400,000 + \$400,000)/2}$	= 25%

(b)

Earnings per share	$\frac{(\$110,000 - \$10,000)}{10,000}$	= \$10	$\frac{(\$110,000 - \$10,000)}{8,000}$	= \$12.50

(c) Between 2016 and 2017, return on common stockholders' equity improved from 20% to 25%. Earnings per share increased from \$10 to \$12.50. While this would appear to be good news for the company's common stockholders, these increases should be carefully evaluated. It is important to note that net income did not change during this period. The increase in both ratios was due to the purchase of treasury shares, which reduced the denominator of each ratio. As the company repurchases its own shares, it becomes more reliant on debt and thus increases its risk.

Related exercise material: **BE14-10, BE14-11, E14-12, E14-13, E14-14, E14-15, E14-16, E14-17, and DO IT! 14-4.**

REVIEW AND PRACTICE

LEARNING OBJECTIVES REVIEW

1 Explain how to account for cash dividends. Companies make entries for cash dividends at the declaration date and at the payment date. At the **declaration date**, the entry is debit Cash Dividends and credit Dividends Payable. At the **payment date**, the entry is debit Dividends Payable and credit Cash.

2 Explain how to account for stock dividends and splits. At the declaration date, the entry for a small stock dividend is debit Stock Dividends, credit Paid-in Capital in Excess of Par (or Stated Value)—Common Stock, and credit Common Stock Dividends Distributable.

At the payment date, the entry for a small stock dividend is debit Common Stock Dividends Distributable and credit Common Stock. A stock split reduces the par or stated value per share and increases the number of shares but does not affect balances in stockholders' equity accounts.

3 Prepare and analyze a comprehensive stockholders' equity section. Companies report each of the individual debits and credits to retained earnings in the retained earnings statement. Additions consist of net income and prior period adjustments to correct understatements of prior years' net income. Deductions consist of net loss, prior period adjustments to correct overstatements of prior years' net income, cash and stock dividends, and some disposals of treasury stock.

A comprehensive stockholders' equity section includes all stockholders' equity accounts. It consists of two sections: paid-in capital and retained earnings. It should also include notes to the financial statements that explain any restrictions on retained earnings and any dividends in arrears. One measure of profitability is the return on common stockholders' equity. It is calculated by dividing net income minus preferred stock dividends by average common stockholders' equity.

4 Describe the form and content of corporation income statements. The form and content of corporation income statements are similar to the statements of proprietorships and partnerships with one exception: Corporations must report income taxes or income tax expense in a separate section before net income in the income statement.

Companies compute earnings per share by dividing net income by the weighted-average number of common shares outstanding during the period. When preferred stock dividends exist, they must be deducted from net income in order to calculate EPS.

GLOSSARY REVIEW

Cash dividend A pro rata distribution of cash to stockholders. (p. 610).

Cumulative dividend A feature of preferred stock entitling the stockholder to receive current-year and any unpaid prior-year dividends before common stockholders are paid dividends. (p. 612).

Declaration date The date the board of directors formally declares (authorizes) a dividend and announces it to stockholders. (p. 611).

Deficit A debit balance in retained earnings. (p. 619).

Dividend A corporation's distribution of cash or stock to its stockholders on a pro rata (proportional) basis. (p. 610).

Earnings per share The net income earned by each share of outstanding common stock. (p. 624).

Liquidating dividend A dividend declared out of paid-in capital. (p. 610).

Payment date The date dividends are transferred to stockholders. (p. 611).

Prior period adjustment The correction of an error in previously issued financial statements. (p. 620).

Record date The date when ownership of outstanding shares is determined for dividend purposes. (p. 611).

Retained earnings Net income that a company retains in the business. (p. 619).

Retained earnings restrictions Circumstances that make a portion of retained earnings currently unavailable for dividends. (p. 620).

Retained earnings statement A financial statement that shows the changes in retained earnings during the year. (p. 621).

Return on common stockholders' equity A measure of profitability that shows how many dollars of net income were earned for each dollar invested by the owners; computed as net income minus preferred dividends divided by average common stockholders' equity. (p. 622).

Stock dividend A pro rata distribution to stockholders of the corporation's own stock. (p. 615).

Stockholders' equity statement A statement that shows the changes in each stockholders' equity account and in total stockholders' equity during the year. (p. 622).

Stock split The issuance of additional shares of stock to stockholders according to their percentage ownership. It is accompanied by a reduction in the par or stated value per share. (p. 617).

PRACTICE MULTIPLE-CHOICE QUESTIONS

(LO 1) **1.** Entries for cash dividends are required on the:
(a) declaration date and the payment date.
(b) record date and the payment date.
(c) declaration date, record date, and payment date.
(d) declaration date and the record date.

(LO 1) **2.** Preferred stock may have priority over common stock **except** in:
(a) dividends.
(b) assets in the event of liquidation.
(c) cumulative dividend features.
(d) voting.

(LO 1) **3.** Encore Inc. declared an $80,000 cash dividend. It currently has 3,000 shares of 7%, $100 par value cumulative preferred stock outstanding. It is one year in arrears on its preferred stock. How much cash will Encore distribute to the common stockholders?
(a) $38,000. (c) $59,000.
(b) $42,000. (d) None.

(LO 2) **4.** Which of the following statements about small stock dividends is **true**?
(a) A debit to Retained Earnings for the par value of the shares issued should be made.
(b) A small stock dividend decreases total stockholders' equity.
(c) Market price per share should be assigned to the dividend shares.
(d) A small stock dividend ordinarily will have an effect on par value per share of stock.

5. Which of the following statements about a 3-for-1 stock split is **true**? (LO 2)
(a) It will triple the market price of the stock.
(b) It will triple the amount of total stockholders' equity.
(c) It will have no effect on total stockholders' equity.
(d) It requires the company to distribute cash.

6. Raptor Inc. has retained earnings of $500,000 and total stockholders' equity of $2,000,000. It has 100,000 shares of $8 par value common stock outstanding, which is currently selling for $30 per share. If Raptor declares a 10% stock dividend on its common stock: (LO 2)
(a) net income will decrease by $80,000.
(b) retained earnings will decrease by $80,000 and total stockholders' equity will increase by $80,000.
(c) retained earnings will decrease by $300,000 and total stockholders' equity will increase by $300,000.
(d) retained earnings will decrease by $300,000 and total paid-in capital will increase by $300,000.

7. Which of the following can cause a restriction in retained earnings? (LO 3)
(a) State laws regarding treasury stock.
(b) Long-term debt contract terms.
(c) Authorizations by the board of directors in light of planned expansion of corporate facilities.
(d) All of these answer choices are correct.

(LO 3) 8. All **but one** of the following is reported in a retained earnings statement. The exception is:
(a) cash and stock dividends.
(b) net income and net loss.
(c) sales revenue.
(d) prior period adjustments.

(LO 3) 9. A prior period adjustment is:
(a) reported in the income statement as a nontypical item.
(b) a correction of an error that is recorded directly to retained earnings.
(c) reported directly in the stockholders' equity section.
(d) reported in the retained earnings statement as an adjustment of the ending balance of retained earnings.

(LO 3) 10. In the stockholders' equity section, Common Stock Dividends Distributable is reported as a(n):
(a) deduction from total paid-in capital and retained earnings.
(b) addition to additional paid-in capital.
(c) deduction from retained earnings.
(d) addition to capital stock.

(LO 3) 11. The return on common stockholders' equity is defined as:
(a) net income divided by total assets.
(b) cash dividends divided by average common stockholders' equity.
(c) income available to common stockholders divided by average common stockholders' equity.
(d) None of these is correct.

(LO 3) 12. Katie Inc. reported net income of $186,000 during 2017 and paid dividends of $26,000 on common stock. It also has 10,000 shares of 6%, $100 par value, noncumulative preferred stock outstanding and paid dividends of $60,000 on preferred stock. Common stockholders' equity was $1,200,000 on January 1, 2017, and $1,600,000 on December 31, 2017. The company's return on common stockholders' equity for 2017 is:
(a) 10.0%. (c) 7.1%.
(b) 9.0%. (d) 13.3%.

13. During 2017, Talon Inc. had sales revenue $376,000, gross profit $176,000, operating expenses $66,000, cash dividends $30,000, other expenses and losses $20,000. Its corporate tax rate is 30%. What was Talon's income tax expense for the year? (LO 4)
(a) $18,000. (c) $112,800.
(b) $52,800. (d) $27,000.

14. Corporation income statements may be the same as the income statements for unincorporated companies **except** for: (LO 4)
(a) gross profit. (c) operating income.
(b) income tax expense. (d) net sales.

15. If everything else is held constant, earnings per share is increased by: (LO 4)
(a) the payment of a cash dividend to common shareholders.
(b) the payment of a cash dividend to preferred shareholders.
(c) the issuance of new shares of common stock.
(d) the purchase of treasury stock.

16. The income statement for Nadeen, Inc. shows income before income taxes $700,000, income tax expense $210,000, and net income $490,000. If Nadeen has 100,000 shares of common stock outstanding throughout the year, earnings per share is: (LO 4)
(a) $7.00. (c) $2.10.
(b) $4.90. (d) No correct answer is given.

Solutions

1. (a) Entries are required for dividends on the declaration date and the payment date, but not the record date. The other choices are therefore incorrect.

2. (d) Preferred stock usually does not have voting rights and therefore does not have priority over common stock on this issue. The other choices are true statements.

3. (a) The preferred stockholders will receive a total of $42,000 in dividends (3,000 × .07 × $100 × 2 years). The common stockholders will receive $38,000 ($80,000 − $42,000), not (b) $42,000, (c) $59,000, or (d) none.

4. (c) Because the stock dividend is considered small, the fair value (market price), not the par value, is assigned to the shares. The other choices are incorrect because (a) a debit to Retained Earnings for the fair value of the shares issued should be made; (b) a small stock dividend changes the composition of total stockholders' equity, but does not change the total; and (d) a small stock dividend will have no effect on par value per share.

5. (c) Stock splits have no effect on total paid-in capital, retained earnings, or total stockholders' equity. The other choices are incorrect because (a) stock splits reduce the market price per share of stock, (b) stock splits have no effect on total stockholders' equity, and (d) the company will distribute additional shares of stock, not cash.

6. (d) Retained earnings will decrease by $300,000 and total paid-in capital will increase by $300,000. The other choices are therefore incorrect because (a) net income is not affected, (b) retained earnings decreases by $300,000, and (c) total stockholders' equity does not change.

7. (d) All of the answer choices are correct. Although choices (a), (b), and (c) are true statements, choice (d) is the better answer.

8. (c) Sales revenue is not reported on the retained earnings statement. The other choices are true statements.

9. (b) A prior period adjustment is a correction of an error that is recorded directly to retained earnings. The other choices are incorrect because a prior period adjustment is reported in the retained earnings statement, not in the (a) income statement or (c) stockholders' equity section of the balance sheet. Choice (d) is incorrect because the prior period adjustment is an adjustment of the beginning, not the ending, balance of retained earnings.

10. (d) Common Stock Dividends Distributable is reported as an addition to capital stock, not (a) as a deduction from total paid-in capital and retained earnings, (b) as an addition to additional paid-in capital, or (c) as a deduction from retained earnings.

11. (c) Return on common stockholders' equity equals Net income less Preferred dividends (income available to common stockholders) divided by Average common stockholders' equity. The other choices are therefore incorrect.

12. (b) Return on common stockholders' equity is Net income available to common stockholders divided by Average common stockholders' equity. Net income available to common stockholders is Net income less Preferred dividends = $126,000 [$186,000 − (10,000 × .06 × $100)]. The company's return on common stockholders' equity for the year is therefore 9.0% [$126,000/ ($1,200,000 + $1,600,000)/2)], not (a) 10.0%, (c) 7.1%, or (d) 13.3%.

13. (d) Income before income taxes = Gross profit ($176,000) − Operating expenses ($66,000) − Other expenses and losses ($20,000) = $90,000. Talon's income tax expense therefore = $27,000 ($90,000 × .30), not (a) $18,000, (b) $52,800, or (c) $112,800.

14. (b) Corporation income statements report income tax expense but income statements for unincorporated firms do not. The other choices are true statements.

15. (d) Earnings per share is increased by the purchase of treasury stock because the denominator (the weighted-average common shares outstanding) would decrease with this transaction. The other choices are incorrect because (a) earnings per share is unchanged by the payment of a cash dividend to common shareholders; (b) earnings per share is decreased, not increased, by the payment of a cash dividend to preferred shareholders; and (c) earnings per share is decreased by the issuance of new shares of common stock.

16. (b) Earnings per share equals Net income ($700,000 − $210,000) less Preferred dividends ($0) divided by Weighted-average common shares outstanding (100,000) = $4.90 per share. The other choices are therefore incorrect.

PRACTICE EXERCISES

Allocate cash dividends to preferred and common stock.

(LO 1)

1. At December 31, 2017, Lebron Company distributes $50,000 of cash dividends. Its outstanding common stock has a par value of $400,000, and its 6% preferred stock has a par value of $100,000 at December 31, 2017.

Instructions

(a) Show the allocation of dividends to each class of stock, assuming that the preferred stock dividend is 6% and not cumulative.

(b) Show the allocation of the dividends to each class of stock, assuming the preferred stock dividend of 6% is cumulative and Lebron Company did not pay any dividends on the preferred stock in the preceding 2 years.

(c) Journalize the declaration of the cash dividend at December 31, 2017, assuming the requirements in part (b).

Solution

1. (a)

	2017
Total dividend declaration	$50,000
Allocation to preferred stock (6% × $100,000)	(6,000)
Remainder to common stock	$44,000

(b)

	2017
Total dividend declaration	$50,000
Allocation to preferred stock (6% × $100,000 × 3)	(18,000)
Remainder to common stock	$32,000

(c)

Dec. 31	Cash Dividends	50,000	
	Dividends Payable		50,000

Journalize cash dividends; indicate statement presentation.

(LO 1, 3)

2. On January 1, Michelle Corporation had 95,000 shares of no-par common stock issued and outstanding. The stock has a stated value of $5 per share. During the year, the following occurred.

Apr. 1	Issued 55,000 additional shares of common stock for $17 per share.
June 15	Declared a cash dividend of $1 per share to stockholders of record on June 30.
July 10	Paid the $1 cash dividend.
Dec. 1	Issued 2,000 additional shares of common stock for $19 per share.
15	Declared a cash dividend on outstanding shares of $1.20 per share to stockholders of record on December 31.

Instructions

(a) Prepare the entries, if any, on each of the three dividend dates.

(b) How are dividends and dividends payable reported in the financial statements prepared at December 31?

Solution

2. (a) June 15	Cash Dividends (150,000 × $1)	150,000	
	Dividends Payable		150,000
July 10	Dividends Payable	150,000	
	Cash		150,000
Dec. 15	Cash Dividends (152,000 × $1.20)	182,400	
	Dividends Payable		182,400

(b) In the retained earnings statement, dividends of $332,400 will be deducted. In the balance sheet, Dividends Payable of $182,400 will be reported as a current liability.

Prepare a retained earnings statement.

(LO 3)

3. Oswald Company reported retained earnings at December 31, 2016, of $400,000. Oswald had 200,000 shares of common stock outstanding throughout 2017.

The following transactions occurred during 2017.

1. An error was discovered; in 2015, insurance expense was recorded at $90,000, but the correct amount was $60,000.
2. A cash dividend of $0.50 per share was declared and paid.
3. A 5% stock dividend was declared and distributed when the market price per share was $18 per share.
4. Net income was $310,000.

Instruction

Prepare a retained earnings statement for 2017.

Solution

OSWALD COMPANY
Retained Earnings Statement
For the Year Ended December 31, 2017

Balance, January 1, as reported		$400,000
Correction for understatement of 2015 net income		30,000
Balance, January 1, as adjusted		430,000
Add: Net income		310,000
		740,000
Less: Cash dividends	$100,000*	
Stock dividends	180,000**	280,000
Balance, December 31		$460,000

*(200,000 × $.50/sh); **(200,000 × .05 × $18/sh)

PRACTICE PROBLEM

Prepare dividend entries and stockholders' equity section.

(LO 1, 2, 3)

On January 1, 2017, Hayslett Corporation had the following stockholders' equity accounts.

Common Stock ($10 par value, 260,000 shares issued and outstanding)	$2,600,000
Paid-in Capital in Excess of Par—Common Stock	1,500,000
Retained Earnings	3,200,000

During the year, the following transactions occurred.

April	1	Declared a $1.50 cash dividend per share to stockholders of record on April 15, payable May 1.
May	1	Paid the dividend declared in April.
June	1	Announced a 2-for-1 stock split. Prior to the split, the market price per share was $24.
Aug.	1	Declared a 10% stock dividend to stockholders of record on August 15, distributable August 31. On August 1, the market price of the stock was $10 per share.
	31	Issued the shares for the stock dividend.
Dec.	1	Declared a $1.50 per share dividend to stockholders of record on December 15, payable January 5, 2018.
	31	Determined that net income for the year was $600,000.

Instructions

(a) Journalize the transactions and the closing entries for net income, stock dividends, and cash dividends.

(b) Prepare a stockholders' equity section at December 31.

Solution

(a)

Date		Account	Debit	Credit
Apr.	1	Cash Dividends (260,000 × $1.50)	390,000	
		Dividends Payable		390,000
May	1	Dividends Payable	390,000	
		Cash		390,000
June	1	No journal entry needed for stock split		
Aug.	1	Stock Dividends (52,000* × $10)	520,000	
		Common Stock Dividends Distributable (52,000 × $5)		260,000
		Paid-in Capital in Excess of Par—Common Stock (52,000 × $5)		260,000
		*520,000 × .10		
	31	Common Stock Dividends Distributable	260,000	
		Common Stock		260,000
Dec.	1	Cash Dividends (572,000** × $1.50)	858,000	
		Dividends Payable		858,000
		**(260,000 × 2) + 52,000		
	31	Income Summary	600,000	
		Retained Earnings		600,000
	31	Retained Earnings	1,768,000	
		Stock Dividends		520,000
		Cash Dividends ($390,000 + $858,000)		1,248,000

(b)

HAYSLETT CORPORATION
Balance Sheet (Partial)

Stockholders' equity	
Paid-in capital	
Capital stock	
Common stock, $5 par value, 572,000 shares issued and outstanding	$2,860,000
Paid-in capital in excess of par—common stock	1,760,000
Total paid-in capital	4,620,000
Retained earnings	2,032,000*
Total stockholders' equity	$6,652,000

*$3,200,000 + $600,000 − $390,000 − $520,000 − $858,000

QUESTIONS

1. (a) What is a dividend? (b) "Dividends must be paid in cash." Do you agree? Explain.
2. Jan Kimler maintains that adequate cash is the only requirement for the declaration of a cash dividend. Is Jan correct? Explain.
3. (a) Three dates are important in connection with cash dividends. Identify these dates, and explain their significance to the corporation and its stockholders.
   (b) Identify the accounting entries that are made for a cash dividend and the date of each entry.
4. Farley Inc. declares a $55,000 cash dividend on December 31, 2017. The required annual dividend on preferred stock is $10,000. Determine the allocation of the dividend to preferred and common stockholders assuming the preferred stock is cumulative and dividends are 1 year in arrears.
5. Contrast the effects of a cash dividend and a stock dividend on a corporation's balance sheet.
6. Rich Mordica asks, "Since stock dividends don't change anything, why declare them?" What is your answer to Rich?
7. Gorton Corporation has 30,000 shares of $10 par value common stock outstanding when it announces a 2-for-1 stock split. Before the split, the stock had a market price of $120 per share. After the split, how many shares of stock will be outstanding? What will be the approximate market price per share?
8. The board of directors is considering either a stock split or a stock dividend. They understand that total stockholders' equity will remain the same under either action. However, they are not sure of the different effects of the two types of actions on other aspects of stockholders' equity. Explain the differences to the directors.
9. What is a prior period adjustment, and how is it reported in the financial statements?
10. NAJ Corporation has a retained earnings balance of $230,000 on January 1. During the year, a prior period adjustment of $50,000 is recorded because of the understatement of depreciation in the prior period. Show the retained earnings statement presentation of these data.
11. What is the purpose of a retained earnings restriction? Identify the possible causes of retained earnings restrictions.
12. How are retained earnings restrictions generally reported in the financial statements?
13. Identify the events that result in debits and credits to retained earnings.
14. Rafy Furcal believes that both the beginning and ending balances in retained earnings are shown in the stockholders' equity section. Is Rafy correct? Discuss.
15. Dean Percival, who owns many investments in common stock, says, "I don't care what a company's net income is. The stock price tells me everything I need to know!" How do you respond to Dean?
16. What is the unique feature of a corporation income statement? Illustrate this feature, using assumed data.
17. Why must preferred stock dividends be subtracted from net income in computing earnings per share?
18. What were the amounts of basic earnings per share of common stock that Apple reported in the years 2009 to 2013?

BRIEF EXERCISES

Prepare entries for a cash dividend. (LO 1)

BE14-1 Greenwood Corporation has 80,000 shares of common stock outstanding. It declares a $1 per share cash dividend on November 1 to stockholders of record on December 1. The dividend is paid on December 31. Prepare the entries on the appropriate dates to record the declaration and payment of the cash dividend.

Determine dividends paid to common stockholders. (LO 1)

BE14-2 M. Bot Corporation has 10,000 shares of 8%, $100 par value, cumulative preferred stock outstanding at December 31, 2017. No dividends were declared in 2015 or 2016. If M. Bot wants to pay $375,000 of dividends in 2017, what amount of dividends will common stockholders receive?

Prepare entries for a stock dividend. (LO 2)

BE14-3 Langley Corporation has 50,000 shares of $10 par value common stock outstanding. It declares a 15% stock dividend on December 1 when the market price per share is $16. The dividend shares are issued on December 31. Prepare the entries for the declaration and issuance of the stock dividend.

Show before-and-after effects of a stock dividend. (LO 2)

BE14-4 The stockholders' equity section of Pretzer Corporation consists of common stock ($10 par) $2,000,000 and retained earnings $500,000. A 10% stock dividend (20,000 shares) is declared when the market price per share is $14. Show the before-and-after effects of the dividend on the following.

(a) The components of stockholders' equity.
(b) Shares outstanding.
(c) Par value per share.

Prepare a retained earnings statement.
(LO 3)

BE14-5 For the year ending December 31, 2017, Soto Inc. reports net income $170,000 and dividends $85,000. Prepare the retained earnings statement for the year assuming the balance in retained earnings on January 1, 2017, was $220,000.

Prepare a retained earnings statement.
(LO 3)

BE14-6 The balance in retained earnings on January 1, 2017, for Palmer Inc. was $800,000. During the year, the corporation paid cash dividends of $90,000 and distributed a stock dividend of $8,000. In addition, the company determined that it had understated its insurance expense in prior years by $50,000. Net income for 2017 was $120,000. Prepare the retained earnings statement for 2017.

Calculate the return on common stockholders' equity.
(LO 3)

BE14-7 SUPERVALU, one of the largest grocery retailers in the United States, is headquartered in Minneapolis. Suppose the following financial information (in millions) was taken from the company's 2017 annual report: net sales $40,597, net income $393, beginning common stockholders' equity $2,581, and ending common stockholders' equity $2,887. Compute the return on common stockholders' equity.

Compute the return on common stockholders' equity.
(LO 3)

BE14-8 Whetzel Corporation reported net income of $152,000, declared dividends on common stock of $50,000, and had an ending balance in retained earnings of $360,000. Common stockholders' equity was $700,000 at the beginning of the year and $820,000 at the end of the year. Compute the return on common stockholders' equity.

Prepare a corporate income statement.
(LO 4)

BE14-9 The following information is available for Reinsch Corporation for the year ended December 31, 2017: cost of goods sold $205,000, sales revenue $350,000, other revenues and gains $50,000, and operating expenses $75,000. Assuming a corporate tax rate of 30%, prepare an income statement for the company.

Compute earnings per share.
(LO 4)

BE14-10 Ziegler Corporation reports net income of $380,000 and a weighted-average of 200,000 shares of common stock outstanding for the year. Compute the earnings per share of common stock.

Compute earnings per share with cumulative preferred stock.
(LO 4)

BE14-11 Income and common stock data for Ziegler Corporation are presented in BE14-10. Assume also that Ziegler has cumulative preferred stock dividends for the current year of $30,000 that were declared and paid. Compute the earnings per share of common stock.

DO IT! Exercises

Determine dividends paid to preferred and common stockholders.
(LO 1)

DO IT! 14-1 Herr Corporation has 3,000 shares of 7%, $100 par value preferred stock outstanding at December 31, 2017. At December 31, 2017, the company declared a $105,000 cash dividend. Determine the dividend paid to preferred stockholders and common stockholders under each of the following scenarios.

1. The preferred stock is noncumulative, and the company has not missed any dividends in previous years.
2. The preferred stock is noncumulative, and the company did not pay a dividend in each of the two previous years.
3. The preferred stock is cumulative, and the company did not pay a dividend in each of the two previous years.

Determine effects of stock dividend and stock split.
(LO 2)

DO IT! 14-2 Jurgens Company has had 4 years of net income. Due to this success, the market price of its 400,000 shares of $3 par value common stock has increased from $12 per share to $46. During this period, paid-in capital remained the same at $2,800,000. Retained earnings increased from $1,800,000 to $12,000,000. President E. Rife is considering either a 15% stock dividend or a 2-for-1 stock split. He asks you to show the before-and-after effects of each option on (a) retained earnings and (b) total stockholders' equity.

Prepare a retained earnings statement.
(LO 3)

DO IT! 14-3 Foley Corporation has retained earnings of $3,100,000 on January 1, 2017. During the year, Foley earned $1,200,000 of net income. It declared and paid a $150,000 cash dividend. In 2017, Foley recorded an adjustment of $110,000 due to the overstatement (from mathematical error) of 2016 depreciation expense. Prepare a retained earnings statement for 2017.

Compute return on stockholders' equity and EPS and discuss changes in each.

(LO 4)

DO IT! 14-4 On January 1, 2017, Vahsholtz Corporation purchased 5,000 shares of treasury stock. Other information regarding Vahsholtz Corporation is provided as follows.

	2016	2017
Net income	$100,000	$110,000
Dividends on preferred stock	$30,000	$30,000
Dividends on common stock	$20,000	$25,000
Weighted-average number of common shares outstanding	50,000	45,000
Common stockholders' equity beginning of year	$600,000	$750,000
Common stockholders' equity end of year	$750,000	$830,000

Compute (a) return on common stockholders' equity for each year and (b) earnings per share for each year, and (c) discuss the changes in each.

EXERCISES

Journalize cash dividends; indicate statement presentation.

(LO 1)

E14-1 On January 1, Guillen Corporation had 95,000 shares of no-par common stock issued and outstanding. The stock has a stated value of $5 per share. During the year, the following occurred.

Apr.	1	Issued 25,000 additional shares of common stock for $17 per share.
June	15	Declared a cash dividend of $1 per share to stockholders of record on June 30.
July	10	Paid the $1 cash dividend.
Dec.	1	Issued 2,000 additional shares of common stock for $19 per share.
	15	Declared a cash dividend on outstanding shares of $1.20 per share to stockholders of record on December 31.

Instructions

(a) Prepare the entries to record these transactions.

(b) How are dividends and dividends payable reported in the financial statements prepared at December 31?

Allocate cash dividends to preferred and common stock.

(LO 1)

E14-2 Knudsen Corporation was organized on January 1, 2016. During its first year, the corporation issued 2,000 shares of $50 par value preferred stock and 100,000 shares of $10 par value common stock. At December 31, the company declared the following cash dividends: 2016, $5,000; 2017, $12,000; and 2018, $28,000.

Instructions

(a) Show the allocation of dividends to each class of stock, assuming the preferred stock dividend is 6% and noncumulative.

(b) Show the allocation of dividends to each class of stock, assuming the preferred stock dividend is 7% and cumulative.

(c) Journalize the declaration of the cash dividend at December 31, 2018, under part (b).

Journalize stock dividends.

(LO 2)

E14-3 On January 1, 2017, Frontier Corporation had $1,000,000 of common stock outstanding that was issued at par. It also had retained earnings of $750,000. The company issued 40,000 shares of common stock at par on July 1 and earned net income of $400,000 for the year.

Instructions

Journalize the declaration of a 15% stock dividend on December 10, 2017, for the following independent assumptions.

(a) Par value is $10, and market price is $18.

(b) Par value is $5, and market price is $20.

Compare effects of a stock dividend and a stock split.

(LO 2)

E14-4 On October 31, the stockholders' equity section of Heins Company consists of common stock $500,000 and retained earnings $900,000. Heins is considering the following two courses of action: (1) declaring a 5% stock dividend on the 50,000, $10 par value shares outstanding, or (2) effecting a 2-for-1 stock split that will reduce par value to $5 per share. The current market price is $14 per share.

Instructions
Prepare a tabular summary of the effects of the alternative actions on the components of stockholders' equity, outstanding shares, and par value per share. Use the following column headings: Before Action, After Stock Dividend, and After Stock Split.

E14-5 On October 1, Little Bobby Corporation's stockholders' equity is as follows.

Indicate account balances after a stock dividend.

(LO 2)

Common stock, $5 par value	$400,000
Paid-in capital in excess of par—common stock	25,000
Retained earnings	155,000
Total stockholders' equity	$580,000

On October 1, Little Bobby declares and distributes a 10% stock dividend when the market price of the stock is $15 per share.

Instructions
(a) Compute the par value per share (1) before the stock dividend and (2) after the stock dividend.
(b) Indicate the balances in the three stockholders' equity accounts after the stock dividend shares have been distributed.

E14-6 During 2017, Roblez Corporation had the following transactions and events.

Indicate the effects on stockholders' equity components.

(LO 1, 2, 3)

1. Declared a cash dividend.
2. Issued par value common stock for cash at par value.
3. Completed a 2-for-1 stock split in which $10 par value stock was changed to $5 par value stock.
4. Declared a small stock dividend when the market price was higher than par value.
5. Made a prior period adjustment for overstatement of net income.
6. Issued the shares of common stock required by the stock dividend declaration in item no. 4 above.
7. Paid the cash dividend in item no. 1 above.
8. Issued par value common stock for cash above par value.

Instructions
Indicate the effect(s) of each of the foregoing items on the subdivisions of stockholders' equity. Present your answer in tabular form with the following columns. Use (I) for increase, (D) for decrease, and (NE) for no effect. Item no. 1 is given as an example.

	Paid-in Capital		
Item	**Capital Stock**	**Additional**	**Retained Earnings**
1	NE	NE	D

E14-7 Before preparing financial statements for the current year, the chief accountant for Toso Company discovered the following errors in the accounts.

Prepare correcting entries for dividends and a stock split.

(LO 2)

1. The declaration and payment of $50,000 cash dividend was recorded as a debit to Interest Expense $50,000 and a credit to Cash $50,000.
2. A 10% stock dividend (1,000 shares) was declared on the $10 par value stock when the market price per share was $18. The only entry made was Stock Dividends (Dr.) $10,000 and Dividend Payable (Cr.) $10,000. The shares have not been issued.
3. A 4-for-1 stock split involving the issue of 400,000 shares of $5 par value common stock for 100,000 shares of $20 par value common stock was recorded as a debit to Retained Earnings $2,000,000 and a credit to Common Stock $2,000,000.

Instructions
Prepare the correcting entries at December 31.

E14-8 On January 1, 2017, Eddy Corporation had retained earnings of $650,000. During the year, Eddy had the following selected transactions.

Prepare a retained earnings statement.

(LO 3)

1. Declared cash dividends $120,000.
2. Corrected overstatement of 2016 net income because of inventory error $40,000.
3. Earned net income $350,000.
4. Declared stock dividends $90,000.

Instructions
Prepare a retained earnings statement for the year.

Prepare a retained earnings statement.

(LO 3)

E14-9 Newland Company reported retained earnings at December 31, 2016, of $310,000. Newland had 200,000 shares of common stock outstanding at the beginning of 2017.

The following transactions occurred during 2017.

1. An error was discovered. In 2015, depreciation expense was recorded at $70,000, but the correct amount was $50,000.
2. A cash dividend of $0.50 per share was declared and paid.
3. A 5% stock dividend was declared and distributed when the market price per share was $15 per share.
4. Net income was $285,000.

Instructions

Prepare a retained earnings statement for 2017.

Prepare a stockholders' equity section.

(LO 3)

E14-10 Dirk Company reported the following balances at December 31, 2016: common stock $500,000, paid-in capital in excess of par value—common stock $100,000, and retained earnings $250,000. During 2017, the following transactions affected stockholders' equity.

1. Issued preferred stock with a par value of $125,000 for $200,000.
2. Purchased treasury stock (common) for $40,000.
3. Earned net income of $180,000.
4. Declared and paid cash dividends of $56,000.

Instructions

Prepare the stockholders' equity section of Dirk Company's December 31, 2017, balance sheet.

Prepare a stockholders' equity section.

(LO 3)

E14-11 The following accounts appear in the ledger of Horner Inc. after the books are closed at December 31.

Common Stock, no par, $1 stated value, 400,000 shares authorized; 300,000 shares issued	$ 300,000
Common Stock Dividends Distributable	30,000
Paid-in Capital in Excess of Stated Value—Common Stock	1,200,000
Preferred Stock, $5 par value, 8%, 40,000 shares authorized; 30,000 shares issued	150,000
Retained Earnings	800,000
Treasury Stock (10,000 common shares)	74,000
Paid-in Capital in Excess of Par—Preferred Stock	344,000

Instructions

Prepare the stockholders' equity section at December 31, assuming retained earnings is restricted for plant expansion in the amount of $100,000.

Prepare an income statement and compute earnings per share.

(LO 4)

E14-12 The following information is available for Norman Corporation for the year ended December 31, 2017: sales revenue $700,000, other revenues and gains $92,000, operating expenses $110,000, cost of goods sold $465,000, other expenses and losses $32,000, and preferred stock dividends $30,000. The company's tax rate was 30%, and it had 50,000 shares outstanding during the entire year.

Instructions

(a) Prepare a corporate income statement.
(b) Calculate earnings per share.

Prepare an income statement and compute return on equity.

(LO 3, 4)

E14-13 In 2017, Pennington Corporation had net sales of $600,000 and cost of goods sold of $360,000. Operating expenses were $153,000, and interest expense was $7,500. The corporation's tax rate is 30%. The corporation declared preferred dividends of $15,000 in 2017, and its average common stockholders' equity during the year was $200,000.

Instructions

(a) Prepare an income statement for Pennington Corporation.
(b) Compute Pennington Corporation's return on common stockholders' equity for 2017.

Compute EPS.

(LO 4)

E14-14 Ringgold Corporation has outstanding at December 31, 2017, 50,000 shares of $20 par value, cumulative, 6% preferred stock and 200,000 shares of $5 par value common stock. All shares were outstanding the entire year. During 2017, Ringgold earned total revenues of $2,000,000 and incurred total expenses (except income taxes) of $1,300,000. Ringgold's income tax rate is 30%.

Instructions
Compute Ringgold's 2017 earnings per share.

E14-15 The following financial information is available for Plummer Corporation.

Calculate ratios to evaluate earnings performance.
(LO 3, 4)

	2017	2016
Average common stockholders' equity	$1,200,000	$900,000
Dividends paid to common stockholders	50,000	30,000
Dividends paid to preferred stockholders	20,000	20,000
Net income	290,000	200,000
Market price of common stock	20	15

The weighted-average number of shares of common stock outstanding was 80,000 for 2016 and 100,000 for 2017.

Instructions
Calculate earnings per share and return on common stockholders' equity for 2017 and 2016.

E14-16 This financial information is available for Klinger Corporation.

Calculate ratios to evaluate earnings performance.
(LO 3, 4)

	2017	2016
Average common stockholders' equity	$1,800,000	$1,900,000
Dividends paid to common stockholders	90,000	70,000
Dividends paid to preferred stockholders	20,000	20,000
Net income	200,000	191,000
Market price of common stock	20	25

The weighted-average number of shares of common stock outstanding was 180,000 for 2016 and 150,000 for 2017.

Instructions
Calculate earnings per share and return on common stockholders' equity for 2017 and 2016.

E14-17 At December 31, 2017, Millwood Corporation has 2,000 shares of $100 par value, 8%, preferred stock outstanding and 100,000 shares of $10 par value common stock issued. Millwood's net income for the year is $241,000.

Compute earnings per share under different assumptions.
(LO 4)

XLS

Instructions
Compute the earnings per share of common stock under the following independent situations. (Round to two decimals.)

(a) The dividend to preferred stockholders was declared. There has been no change in the number of shares of common stock outstanding during the year.
(b) The dividend to preferred stockholders was not declared. The preferred stock is cumulative. Millwood held 10,000 shares of common treasury stock throughout the year.

EXERCISES: SET B AND CHALLENGE EXERCISES

Visit the book's companion website, at **www.wiley.com/college/weygandt**, and choose the Student Companion site to access Exercises: Set B and Challenge Exercises.

PROBLEMS: SET A

P14-1A On January 1, 2017, Geffrey Corporation had the following stockholders' equity accounts.

Prepare dividend entries and stockholders' equity section.
(LO 1, 2, 3)

GLS

Common Stock ($20 par value, 60,000 shares issued and outstanding)	$1,200,000
Paid-in Capital in Excess of Par—Common Stock	200,000
Retained Earnings	600,000

During the year, the following transactions occurred.

Feb. 1	Declared a $1 cash dividend per share to stockholders of record on February 15, payable March 1.
Mar. 1	Paid the dividend declared in February.
Apr. 1	Announced a 2-for-1 stock split. Prior to the split, the market price per share was $36.
July 1	Declared a 10% stock dividend to stockholders of record on July 15, distributable July 31. On July 1, the market price of the stock was $13 per share.
31	Issued the shares for the stock dividend.
Dec. 1	Declared a $0.50 per share dividend to stockholders of record on December 15, payable January 5, 2018.
31	Determined that net income for the year was $350,000.

Instructions

(a) Journalize the transactions and the closing entries for net income and dividends.

(b) Enter the beginning balances, and post the entries to the stockholders' equity accounts. (*Note:* Open additional stockholders' equity accounts as needed.)

(c) Prepare a stockholders' equity section at December 31.

(c) Total stockholders' equity $2,224,000

Journalize and post transactions; prepare retained earnings statement and stockholders' equity section.

(LO 1, 2, 3)

GLS

P14-2A The stockholders' equity accounts of Karp Company at January 1, 2017, are as follows.

Preferred Stock, 6%, $50 par	$600,000
Common Stock, $5 par	800,000
Paid-in Capital in Excess of Par—Preferred Stock	200,000
Paid-in Capital in Excess of Par—Common Stock	300,000
Retained Earnings	800,000

There were no dividends in arrears on preferred stock. During 2017, the company had the following transactions and events.

July 1	Declared a $0.60 cash dividend per share on common stock.
Aug. 1	Discovered $25,000 understatement of depreciation expense in 2016. (Ignore income taxes.)
Sept. 1	Paid the cash dividend declared on July 1.
Dec. 1	Declared a 15% stock dividend on common stock when the market price of the stock was $18 per share.
15	Declared a 6% cash dividend on preferred stock payable January 15, 2018.
31	Determined that net income for the year was $355,000.
31	Recognized a $200,000 restriction of retained earnings for plant expansion.

Instructions

(a) Journalize the transactions, events, and closing entries for net income and dividends.

(b) Enter the beginning balances in the accounts, and post to the stockholders' equity accounts. (*Note:* Open additional stockholders' equity accounts as needed.)

(c) Prepare a retained earnings statement for the year.

(d) Prepare a stockholders' equity section at December 31, 2017.

(c) Ending balance $566,000
(d) Total stockholders' equity $2,898,000

Prepare retained earnings statement and stockholders' equity section, and compute allocation of dividends and earnings per share.

(LO 1, 2, 3, 4)

P14-3A The post-closing trial balance of Storey Corporation at December 31, 2017, contains the following stockholders' equity accounts.

Preferred Stock (15,000 shares issued)	$ 750,000
Common Stock (250,000 shares issued)	2,500,000
Paid-in Capital in Excess of Par—Preferred Stock	250,000
Paid-in Capital in Excess of Par—Common Stock	400,000
Common Stock Dividends Distributable	250,000
Retained Earnings	1,042,000

A review of the accounting records reveals the following.

1. No errors have been made in recording 2017 transactions or in preparing the closing entry for net income.
2. Preferred stock is $50 par, 6%, and cumulative; 15,000 shares have been outstanding since January 1, 2016.
3. Authorized stock is 20,000 shares of preferred, 500,000 shares of common with a $10 par value.

4. The January 1 balance in Retained Earnings was $1,170,000.
5. On July 1, 20,000 shares of common stock were issued for cash at $16 per share.
6. On September 1, the company discovered an understatement error of $90,000 in computing salaries and wages expense in 2016. The net of tax effect of $63,000 was properly debited directly to Retained Earnings.
7. A cash dividend of $250,000 was declared and properly allocated to preferred and common stock on October 1. No dividends were paid to preferred stockholders in 2016.
8. On December 31, a 10% common stock dividend was declared out of retained earnings on common stock when the market price per share was $16.
9. Net income for the year was $585,000.
10. On December 31, 2017, the directors authorized disclosure of a $200,000 restriction of retained earnings for plant expansion. (Use Note X.)

Instructions

(a) Reproduce the Retained Earnings account (T-account) for 2017.
(b) Prepare a retained earnings statement for 2017.
(c) Prepare a stockholders' equity section at December 31, 2017.
(d) Compute the allocation of the cash dividend to preferred and common stock.

(c) Total stockholders' equity $5,192,000

P14-4A On January 1, 2017, Ven Corporation had the following stockholders' equity accounts.

Prepare the stockholders' equity section, reflecting dividends and stock split.

(LO 1, 2, 3)

Common Stock (no par value, 90,000 shares issued and outstanding)	$1,600,000
Retained Earnings	500,000

During the year, the following transactions occurred.

Feb. 1	Declared a $1 cash dividend per share to stockholders of record on February 15, payable March 1.
Mar. 1	Paid the dividend declared in February.
Apr. 1	Announced a 3-for-1 stock split. Prior to the split, the market price per share was $36.
July 1	Declared a 5% stock dividend to stockholders of record on July 15, distributable July 31. On July 1, the market price of the stock was $16 per share.
31	Issued the shares for the stock dividend.
Dec. 1	Declared a $0.50 per share dividend to stockholders of record on December 15, payable January 5, 2018.
31	Determined that net income for the year was $350,000.

Instructions

Prepare the stockholders' equity section of the balance sheet at (a) March 31, (b) June 30, (c) September 30, and (d) December 31, 2017.

(d) Total stockholders' equity $2,218,250

P14-5A On January 1, 2017, Shellenburger Inc. had the following stockholders' equity account balances.

Prepare the stockholders' equity section, reflecting various events.

(LO 1, 2, 3)

Common Stock, no-par value (500,000 shares issued)	$1,500,000
Common Stock Dividends Distributable	200,000
Retained Earnings	600,000

During 2017, the following transactions and events occurred.

1. Issued 50,000 shares of common stock as a result of a 10% stock dividend declared on December 15, 2016.
2. Issued 30,000 shares of common stock for cash at $6 per share.
3. Corrected an error that had understated the net income for 2015 by $70,000.
4. Declared and paid a cash dividend of $80,000.
5. Earned net income of $300,000.

Instructions

Prepare the stockholders' equity section of the balance sheet at December 31, 2017.

Total stockholders' equity $2,770,000

PROBLEMS: SET B AND SET C

Visit the book's companion website, at **www.wiley.com/college/weygandt**, and choose the Student Companion site to access Problems: Set B and Set C.

CONTINUING PROBLEM

© leungchopan/ Shutterstock

COOKIE CREATIONS: AN ENTREPRENEURIAL JOURNEY

(*Note:* This is a continuation of the Cookie Creations problem from Chapters 1 through 13.)

CC14 After establishing their company's fiscal year-end to be October 31, Natalie and Curtis began operating Cookie & Coffee Creations Inc. on November 1, 2017. On that date, they issued both preferred and common stock. After the first year of operations, Natalie and Curtis want to prepare financial information for the year.

Go to the book's companion website, **www.wiley.com/college/weygandt***, to see the completion of this problem.*

BROADENING YOUR PERSPECTIVE

FINANCIAL REPORTING AND ANALYSIS

Financial Reporting Problem: Apple Inc.

BYP14-1 The financial statements of Apple Inc. are presented in Appendix A. Instructions for accessing and using the company's complete annual report, including the notes to the financial statements, are also provided in Appendix A.

Instructions

Refer to Apple's financial statements and answer the following question.

What amount, if any, did Apple declare in dividends on common stock in the year ended September 28, 2013?

Comparative Analysis Problem: PepsiCo, Inc. vs. The Coca-Cola Company

BYP14-2 PepsiCo's financial statements are presented in Appendix B. Financial statements of The Coca-Cola Company are presented in Appendix C. Instructions for accessing and using the complete annual reports of PepsiCo and Coca-Cola, including the notes to the financial statements, are also provided in Appendices B and C, respectively.

Instructions

(a) Compute earnings per share and return on common stockholders' equity for both companies for 2013. Assume PepsiCo's weighted-average shares were 1,541 million and Coca-Cola's weighted-average shares were 4,568 million. Can these measures be used to compare the profitability of the two companies? Why or why not?

(b) What was the total amount of dividends paid by each company in 2013?

Comparative Analysis Problem: Amazon.com, Inc. vs. Wal-Mart Stores, Inc.

BYP14-3 Amazon.com, Inc.'s financial statements are presented in Appendix D. Financial statements of Wal-Mart Stores, Inc. are presented in Appendix E. Instructions for accessing and using the complete annual reports of Amazon and Wal-Mart, including the notes to the financial statements, are also provided in Appendices D and E, respectively.

Instructions

(a) What are the basic earnings per share for both Amazon and Wal-Mart as of December 31, 2013, and January 31, 2014, respectively?

(b) What was the total amount of dividends, if any, paid by Amazon for the year ending December 31, 2013? What was the total dividends paid by Wal-Mart for the year ending January 31, 2014?

Real-World Focus

BYP14-4 Use the stockholders' equity section of an annual report and identify the major components.

Address: **www.annualreports.com**, or go to **www.wiley.com/college/weygandt**

Steps

1. From the Annual Reports Homepage, choose **Search by Alphabet**, and choose a letter.
2. Select a particular company.
3. Choose Annual Report.
4. Follow instructions below.

Instructions

Answer the following questions.

(a) What is the company's name?
(b) What classes of capital stock has the company issued?
(c) For each class of stock:
 (1) How many shares are authorized, issued, and/or outstanding?
 (2) What is the par value?
(d) What are the company's retained earnings?
(e) Has the company acquired treasury stock? How many shares?

CRITICAL THINKING

Decision-Making Across the Organization

BYP14-5 The stockholders' equity accounts of Gonzalez, Inc., at January 1, 2017, are as follows.

Preferred Stock, no par, 4,000 shares issued	$400,000
Common Stock, no par, 140,000 shares issued	700,000
Retained Earnings	550,000

During 2017, the company had the following transactions and events.

July 1	Declared a $0.50 cash dividend per share on common stock.
Aug. 1	Discovered a $72,000 overstatement of 2016 depreciation expense. (Ignore income taxes.)
Sept. 1	Paid the cash dividend declared on July 1.
Dec. 1	Declared a 10% stock dividend on common stock when the market price of the stock was $12 per share.
15	Declared a $6 per share cash dividend on preferred stock, payable January 31, 2018.
31	Determined that net income for the year was $320,000.

Instructions

With the class divided into groups, answer the following questions.

(a) Prepare a retained earnings statement for the year. There are no preferred dividends in arrears.
(b) Discuss why the overstatement of 2016 depreciation expense is not treated as an adjustment of the current year's income.
(c) Discuss the reasons why a company might decide to issue a stock dividend rather than a cash dividend.

Communication Activity

BYP14-6 In the past year, Gosser Corporation declared a 10% stock dividend, and Jenks, Inc. announced a 2-for-1 stock split. Your parents own 100 shares of each company's $50 par value common stock. During a recent phone call, your parents ask you, as an accounting student, to explain the differences between the two events.

Instructions

Write a letter to your parents that explains the effects of the two events on them as stockholders and the effects of each event on the financial statements of each corporation.

Ethics Case

BYP14-7 Molina Corporation has paid 60 consecutive quarterly cash dividends (15 years). The last 6 months, however, have been a cash drain on the company, as profit margins have been greatly narrowed by increasing competition. With a cash balance sufficient to meet only day-to-day operating needs, the president, Rob Lowery, has decided that a stock dividend instead of a cash dividend should be declared. He tells Molina's financial vice president, Debbie Oler, to issue a press release stating that the company is extending its consecutive dividend record with the issuance of a 5% stock dividend. "Write the press release convincing the stockholders that the stock dividend is just as good as a cash dividend," he orders. "Just watch our stock rise when we announce the stock dividend. It must be a good thing if that happens."

Instructions

(a) Who are the stakeholders in this situation?
(b) Is there anything unethical about Lowery's intentions or actions?
(c) What is the effect of a stock dividend on a corporation's stockholders' equity accounts? Which would you rather receive as a stockholder—a cash dividend or a stock dividend? Why?

All About You

BYP14-8 In this textbook, you learned that in response to the Sarbanes-Oxley Act, many companies have implemented formal ethics codes. Many other organizations also have ethics codes.

Instructions

Obtain the ethics code from an organization that you belong to (e.g., student organization, business school, employer, or a volunteer organization). Evaluate the ethics code based on how clearly it identifies proper and improper behavior. Discuss its strengths, and how it might be improved.

FASB Codification Activity

BYP14-9 If your school has a subscription to the FASB Codification, go to **http://aaahq.org/ascLogin.cfm** to log in and prepare responses to the following.

(a) What is the stock dividend?
(b) What is a stock split?
(c) At what percentage point does the issuance of additional shares qualify as a stock dividend, as opposed to a stock split?

A Look at IFRS

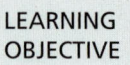

LEARNING OBJECTIVE 5 **Compare the accounting for dividends, retained earnings, and income reporting under GAAP and IFRS.**

The basic accounting for cash and stock dividends is essentially the same under both GAAP and IFRS although IFRS terminology may differ.

Key Points

Following are the key similarities and differences between GAAP and IFRS as related to dividends, retained earnings, and income reporting.

Similarities

- The accounting related to prior period adjustment is essentially the same under IFRS and GAAP.
- The stockholders' equity section is essentially the same under IFRS and GAAP. However, terminology used to describe certain components is often different. These differences are discussed in Chapter 13.
- The income statement using IFRS is called the **statement of comprehensive income**. A statement of comprehensive income is presented in a one- or two-statement format. The single-statement approach includes all items of income and expense, as well as each component of other comprehensive income or loss by its individual characteristic. In the two-statement approach, a traditional income statement is prepared. It is then followed by a statement of comprehensive income, which starts with net income or loss and then adds other comprehensive income or loss items. Regardless of which approach is reported, income tax expense is required to be reported.
- The computations related to earnings per share are essentially the same under IFRS and GAAP.

Differences

- The term **reserves** is used in IFRS to indicate all non–contributed (non–paid-in) capital. Reserves include retained earnings and other comprehensive income items, such as revaluation surplus and unrealized gains or losses on available-for-sale securities.
- IFRS often uses terms such as **retained profits** or **accumulated profit or loss** to describe retained earnings. The term retained earnings is also often used.

- Equity is given various descriptions under IFRS, such as shareholders' equity, owners' equity, capital and reserves, and shareholders' funds.

Looking to the Future

The IASB and the FASB are currently working on a project related to financial statement presentation. An important part of this study is to determine whether certain line items, subtotals, and totals should be clearly defined and required to be displayed in the financial statements. For example, it is likely that the statement of stockholders' equity and its presentation will be examined closely.

Both the IASB and FASB are working toward convergence of any remaining differences related to earnings per share computations. This convergence will deal with highly technical changes beyond the scope of this textbook.

IFRS Practice

IFRS Self-Test Questions

1. The basic accounting for cash dividends and stock dividends:
   (a) is different under IFRS versus GAAP.
   (b) is the same under IFRS and GAAP.
   (c) differs only for the accounting for cash dividends between GAAP and IFRS.
   (d) differs only for the accounting for stock dividends between GAAP and IFRS.
2. Which item is **not** considered part of reserves?
   (a) Unrealized loss on available-for-sale investments.
   (b) Revaluation surplus.
   (c) Retained earnings.
   (d) Issued shares.
3. Under IFRS, a statement of comprehensive income must include:
   (a) accounts payable.
   (b) retained earnings.
   (c) income tax expense.
   (d) preference stock.
4. Which set of terms can be used to describe total stockholders' equity under IFRS?
   (a) Shareholders' equity, capital and reserves, other comprehensive income.
   (b) Capital and reserves, shareholders' equity, shareholders' funds.
   (c) Capital and reserves, retained earnings, shareholders' equity.
   (d) All of the answer choices are correct.
5. Earnings per share computations related to IFRS and GAAP:
   (a) are essentially similar.
   (b) result in an amount referred to as earnings per share.
   (c) must deduct preferred (preference) dividends when computing earnings per share.
   (d) All of the answer choices are correct.

International Financial Reporting Problem: Louis Vuitton

IFRS14-1 The financial statements of Louis Vuitton are presented in Appendix F. Instructions for accessing and using the company's complete annual report, including the notes to its financial statements, are also provided in Appendix F.

Instructions
Use the company's annual report to answer the following questions.

(a) Did the company declare and pay any dividends for the year ended December 31, 2013?
(b) Compute the company's return on ordinary shareholders' equity for the year ended December 31, 2013.
(c) What was Louis Vuitton's earnings per share for the year ended December 31, 2013?

Answers to IFRS Self-Test Questions

1. b **2.** d **3.** c **4.** b **5.** d

15 Long-Term Liabilities

CHAPTER PREVIEW As you can see from the Feature Story below, having liabilities can be dangerous in difficult economic times. In this chapter, we will explain the accounting for the major types of long-term liabilities reported on the balance sheet. Long-term liabilities are obligations that are expected to be paid more than one year in the future. These liabilities may be bonds, long-term notes, or lease obligations.

FEATURE STORY

And Then There Were Two

Debt can help a company acquire the things it needs to grow, but it is often the very thing that kills a company. A brief history of Maxwell Car Company illustrates the role of debt in the U.S. auto industry. In 1920, Maxwell Car Company was on the brink of financial ruin. Because it was unable to pay its bills, its creditors stepped in and took over. They hired a former General Motors (GM) executive named Walter Chrysler to reorganize the company. By 1925, he had taken over the company and renamed it Chrysler. By 1933, Chrysler was booming, with sales surpassing even those of Ford.

But the next few decades saw Chrysler make a series of blunders. By 1980, with its creditors pounding at the gates, Chrysler was again on the brink of financial ruin.

At that point, Chrysler brought in a former Ford executive named Lee Iacocca to save the company. Iacocca argued that the United States could not afford to let Chrysler fail because of the loss of jobs. He convinced the federal government to grant loan guarantees—promises that if Chrysler failed to pay its creditors, the government would pay them. Iacocca then streamlined operations and brought out some profitable products. Chrysler repaid all of its government-guaranteed loans by 1983, seven years ahead of the scheduled final payment.

To compete in today's global vehicle market, you must be big—really big. So in 1998, Chrysler merged with German automaker Daimler-Benz to form DaimlerChrysler. For a time, this left just two U.S.-based auto manufacturers—GM and Ford. But in 2007, DaimlerChrysler sold 81% of Chrysler to Cerberus, an investment group, to provide much-needed cash infusions to the automaker. In 2009, Daimler turned over its remaining stake to Cerberus. Three days later, Chrysler filed for bankruptcy. But by 2010, it was beginning to show signs of a turnaround.

The car companies are giants. GM and Ford typically rank among the top five U.S. firms in total assets. But GM and Ford accumulated truckloads of debt on their way to getting big. Although debt made it possible to get so big, the Chrysler story, and GM's recent bankruptcy, make it clear that debt can also threaten a company's survival.

© Henrik Jonsson/iStockphoto

CHAPTER OUTLINE

Learning Objectives

Learning Objective	Topics	DO IT!
1 Describe the major characteristics of bonds.	• Types of bonds • Issuing procedures • Determining the market price of a bond	DO IT! 1 Bond Terminology
2 Explain how to account for bond transactions.	• Issuing bonds at face value • Discount or premium on bonds • Issuing bonds at a discount • Issuing bonds at a premium • Redeeming and converting bonds	DO IT! 2a Bond Issuance 2b Bond Redemption
3 Explain how to account for long-term notes payable.	• Long-term notes payable • Mortgage notes payable	DO IT! 3 Long-Term Notes
4 Discuss how long-term liabilities are reported and analyzed.	• Presentation • Use of ratios • Debt and equity financing • Lease liabilities and off-balance-sheet financing	DO IT! 4 Lease Liability; Analysis of Long-Term Liabilities

o to the ***REVIEW AND PRACTICE*** section at the end of the chapter for a review of key concepts and practice applications with solutions.

sit **WileyPLUS with ORION** for additional tutorials and practice opportunities.

LEARNING OBJECTIVE **1**

Describe the major characteristics of bonds.

Long-term liabilities are obligations that a company expects to pay more than one year in the future. In this chapter, we explain the accounting for the principal types of obligations reported in the long-term liabilities section of the balance sheet. These obligations often are in the form of bonds or long-term notes.

Bonds are a form of interest-bearing note payable issued by corporations, universities, and governmental agencies. Bonds, like common stock, are sold in small denominations (usually $1,000 or multiples of $1,000). As a result, bonds attract many investors. When a corporation issues bonds, it is borrowing money. The person who buys the bonds (the bondholder) is investing in bonds.

Secured Bonds

Unsecured Bonds

Types of Bonds

Bonds may have many different features. In the following sections, we describe the types of bonds commonly issued.

SECURED AND UNSECURED BONDS

Secured bonds have specific assets of the issuer pledged as collateral for the bonds. A bond secured by real estate, for example, is called a **mortgage bond**. A bond secured by specific assets set aside to redeem (retire) the bonds is called a **sinking fund bond**.

Unsecured bonds, also called **debenture bonds**, are issued against the general credit of the borrower. Companies with good credit ratings use these bonds extensively. For example, at one time DuPont reported over $2 billion of debenture bonds outstanding.

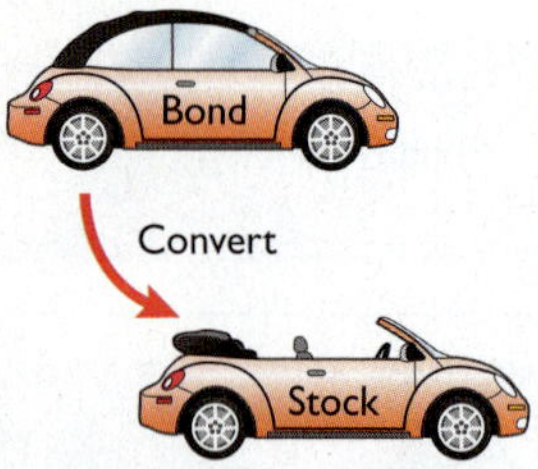

Convertible Bonds

Callable Bonds

CONVERTIBLE AND CALLABLE BONDS

Bonds that can be converted into common stock at the bondholder's option are **convertible bonds**. The conversion feature generally is attractive to bond buyers. Bonds that the issuing company can redeem (buy back) at a stated dollar amount prior to maturity are **callable bonds**. A call feature is included in nearly all corporate bond issues.

Issuing Procedures

State laws grant corporations the power to issue bonds. Both the board of directors and stockholders usually must approve bond issues. **In authorizing the bond issue, the board of directors must stipulate the number of bonds to be authorized, total face value, and contractual interest rate.** The total bond authorization often exceeds the number of bonds the company originally issues. This gives the corporation the flexibility to issue more bonds, if needed, to meet future cash requirements.

The **face value** is the amount of principal due at the maturity date. The **maturity date** is the date that the final payment is due to the investor from the issuing company. The **contractual interest rate**, often referred to as the **stated rate**, is the rate used to determine the amount of cash interest the borrower pays and the investor receives. Usually, the contractual rate is stated as an annual rate.

The terms of the bond issue are set forth in a legal document called a **bond indenture**. The indenture shows the terms and summarizes the rights of the bondholders and their trustees, and the obligations of the issuing company. The **trustee** (usually a financial institution) keeps records of each bondholder, maintains custody of unissued bonds, and holds conditional title to pledged property.

In addition, the issuing company arranges for the printing of **bond certificates**. The indenture and the certificate are separate documents. As shown in Illustration 15-1, a bond certificate provides the following information: name of the issuer, face value, contractual interest rate, and maturity date. An investment company that specializes in selling securities generally sells the bonds for the issuing company.

ETHICS NOTE

Some companies try to minimize the amount of debt reported on their balance sheet by not reporting certain types of commitments as liabilities. This subject is of intense interest in the financial community.

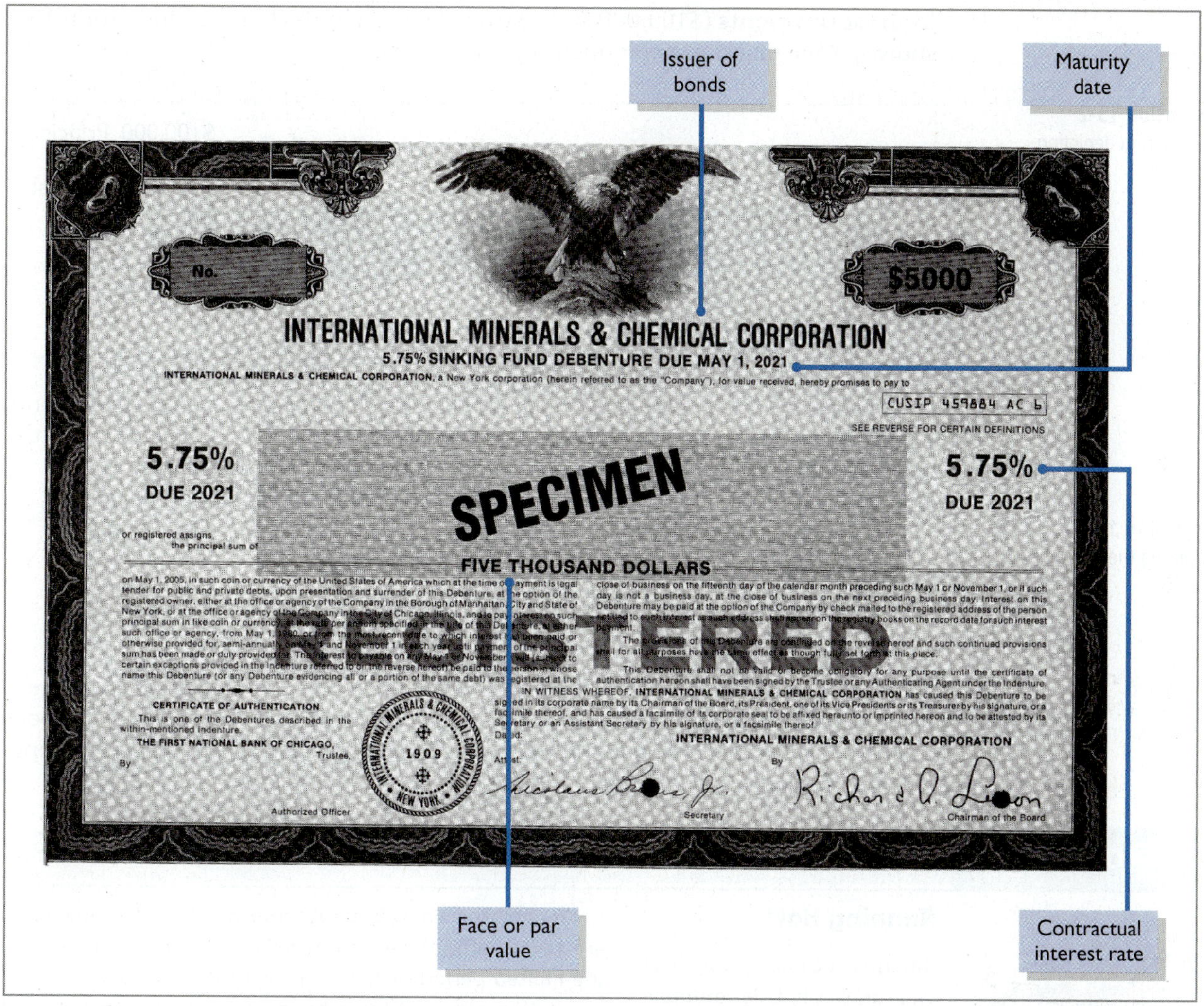

Illustration 15-1
Bond certificate

Determining the Market Price of a Bond

If you were an investor wanting to purchase a bond, how would you determine how much to pay? To be more specific, assume that Coronet, Inc. issues a **zero-interest bond** (pays no interest) with a face value of $1,000,000 due in 20 years. For this bond, the only cash you receive is a million dollars at the end of 20 years. Would you pay a million dollars for this bond? We hope not! A million dollars received 20 years from now is not the same as a million dollars received today.

Same dollars at different times are not equal.

The term **time value of money** is used to indicate the relationship between time and money—that a dollar received today is worth more than a dollar promised at some time in the future. If you had $1 million today, you would invest it. From that investment, you would earn interest such that at the end of 20 years, you would have much more than $1 million. Thus, if someone is going to pay you $1 million 20 years from now, you would want to find its equivalent today, or its present value. In other words, you would want to determine the value today of the amount to be received in the future after taking into account current interest rates.

The current market price (present value) of a bond is the value at which it should sell in the marketplace. Market price therefore is a function of the three factors that determine present value: (1) the dollar amounts to be received, (2) the length of time until the amounts are received, and (3) the market rate of interest. The **market interest rate** is the rate investors demand for loaning funds.

To illustrate, assume that Acropolis Company on January 1, 2017, issues $100,000 of 9% bonds, due in five years, with interest payable annually at year-end. The purchaser of the bonds would receive the following two types of cash payments: (1) **principal** of $100,000 to be paid at maturity, and (2) five $9,000

interest payments ($100,000 × 9%) over the term of the bonds. Illustration 15-2 shows a time diagram depicting both cash flows.

Illustration 15-2
Time diagram depicting cash flows

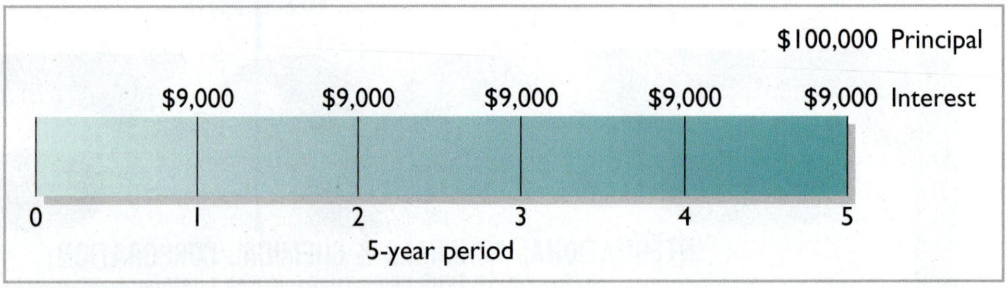

The current market price of a bond is equal to the present value of all the future cash payments promised by the bond. Illustration 15-3 lists and totals the present values of these amounts, assuming the market rate of interest is 9%.

Illustration 15-3
Computing the market price of bonds

Present value of $100,000 received in 5 years	$ 64,993
Present value of $9,000 received annually for 5 years	35,007
Market price of bonds	**$100,000**

Tables are available to provide the present value numbers to be used, or these values can be determined mathematically or with financial calculators.[1] Appendix G, near the end of the textbook, provides further discussion of the concepts and the mechanics of the time value of money computations.

Investor Insight

© alphaspirit/Shutterstock

Running Hot!

Recently, the market for bonds was running hot. For example, consider these two large deals: Apple Inc. sold $17 billion of debt, which at the time was the largest corporate bond ever sold. But shortly thereafter, it was beat by Verizon Communications Inc., which sold $49 billion of debt. The following chart highlights the increased issuance of bonds.

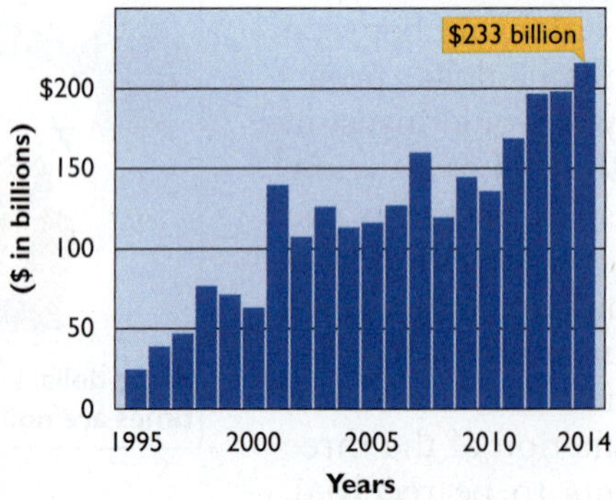

Note: Data reflect each year through March 7.
Source: Thomson Reuters.

As one expert noted about these increases, "Companies are taking advantage of this lower-rate environment in the limited period of time it is going to be around." An interesting aspect of these bond issuances is that companies, like Philip Morris International, Medtronic, Inc., and Simon Properties, are even selling 30-year bonds. These bond issuers are benefitting from "a massive sentiment shift," says one bond expert. The belief that the economy will recover is making investors more comfortable holding longer-term bonds, as they search for investments that offer better returns than U.S. Treasury bonds.

Sources: Vipal Monga, "The Big Number," *Wall Street Journal* (March 20, 2012), p. B5; and Mike Cherney, "Renewed Embrace of Bonds Sparks Boom," *Wall Street Journal* (March 8–9, 2014), p. B5.

What are the advantages for companies of issuing 30-year bonds instead of 5-year bonds? (Go to **WileyPLUS** for this answer and additional questions.)

[1]For those knowledgeable in the use of present value tables, the computations in the example shown in Illustration 15-3 are $100,000 × .64993 = $64,993, and $9,000 × 3.88965 = 35,007 (rounded).

DO IT! 1 Bond Terminology

State whether each of the following statements is true or false.

_______ **1.** Mortgage bonds and sinking fund bonds are both examples of secured bonds.

_______ **2.** Unsecured bonds are also known as debenture bonds.

_______ **3.** The stated rate is the rate investors demand for loaning funds.

_______ **4.** The face value is the amount of principal the issuing company must pay at the maturity date.

_______ **5.** The market price of a bond is equal to its maturity value.

Solution

Action Plan

✔ Review the types of bonds and the basic terms associated with bonds.

1. True. **2.** True. **3.** False. The stated rate is the contractual interest rate used to determine the amount of cash interest the borrower pays. **4.** True. **5.** False. The market price of a bond is the value at which it should sell in the marketplace. As a result, the market price of the bond and its maturity value are often different.

Related exercise material: **E15-1 and DO IT! 15-1.**

LEARNING OBJECTIVE 2 Explain how to account for bond transactions.

A corporation records bond transactions when it issues (sells) or redeems (buys back) bonds and when bondholders convert bonds into common stock. If bondholders sell their bond investments to other investors, the issuing firm receives no further money on the transaction, **nor does the issuing corporation journalize the transaction** (although it does keep records of the names of bondholders in some cases).

Bonds may be issued at face value, below face value (discount), or above face value (premium). Bond prices for both new issues and existing bonds are quoted as **a percentage of the face value of the bond. Face value is usually $1,000.** Thus, a $1,000 bond with a quoted price of 97 means that the selling price of the bond is 97% of face value, or $970.

Issuing Bonds at Face Value

To illustrate the accounting for bonds issued at face value, assume that on January 1, 2017, Candlestick, Inc. issues $100,000, five-year, 10% bonds at 100 (100% of face value). The entry to record the sale is as follows.

Jan. 1	Cash	100,000	
	Bonds Payable		100,000
	(To record sale of bonds at face value)		

A	=	L	+	SE
+100,000				
		+100,000		

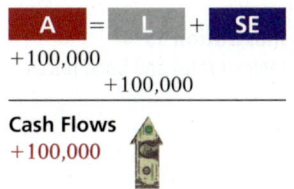

Cash Flows
+100,000

Candlestick reports bonds payable in the long-term liabilities section of the balance sheet because the maturity date is January 1, 2022 (more than one year away).

Over the term (life) of the bonds, companies make entries to record bond interest. Interest on bonds payable is computed in the same manner as interest on notes payable, as explained in Chapter 11 (page 492). Assume that interest is payable annually on January 1 on the Candlestick bonds. In that case, Candlestick accrues interest of $10,000 ($100,000 × 10%) on December 31. At December 31,

Candlestick recognizes the $10,000 of interest expense incurred with the following adjusting entry.

A	=	L	+	SE
				−10,000 Exp
		+10,000		

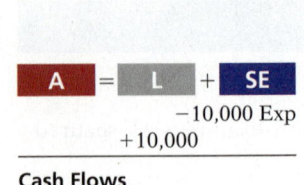

Cash Flows
no effect

Dec. 31	Interest Expense	10,000	
	Interest Payable		10,000
	(To accrue bond interest)		

The company classifies interest payable as a current liability because it is scheduled for payment within the next year. When Candlestick pays the interest on January 1, 2018, it debits (decreases) Interest Payable and credits (decreases) Cash for $10,000.

Candlestick records the payment on January 1 as follows.

A	=	L	+	SE
		−10,000		
−10,000				

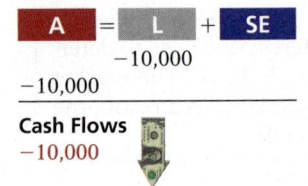

Cash Flows
−10,000

Jan. 1	Interest Payable	10,000	
	Cash		10,000
	(To record payment of bond interest)		

Discount or Premium on Bonds

The previous example assumed that the contractual (stated) interest rate and the market (effective) interest rate paid on the bonds were the same. Recall that the **contractual interest rate** is the rate applied to the face (par) value to arrive at the interest paid in a year. The **market interest rate** is the rate investors demand for loaning funds to the corporation. When the contractual interest rate and the market interest rate are the same, bonds sell **at face value (par value)**.

However, market interest rates change daily. The type of bond issued, the state of the economy, current industry conditions, and the company's performance all affect market interest rates. As a result, contractual and market interest rates often differ. To make bonds salable when the two rates differ, bonds sell below or above face value.

To illustrate, suppose that a company issues 10% bonds at a time when other bonds of similar risk are paying 12%. Investors will not be interested in buying the 10% bonds, so their value will fall below their face value. When a bond is sold for less than its face value, the difference between the face value of a bond and its selling price is called a **discount**. As a result of the decline in the bonds' selling price, the actual interest rate incurred by the company increases to the level of the current market interest rate.

Conversely, if the market rate of interest is **lower than** the contractual interest rate, investors will have to pay more than face value for the bonds. That is, if the market rate of interest is 8% but the contractual interest rate on the bonds is 10%, the price of the bonds will be bid up. When a bond is sold for more than its face value, the difference between the face value and its selling price is called a **premium**. Illustration 15-4 shows these relationships.

Illustration 15-4
Interest rates and bond prices

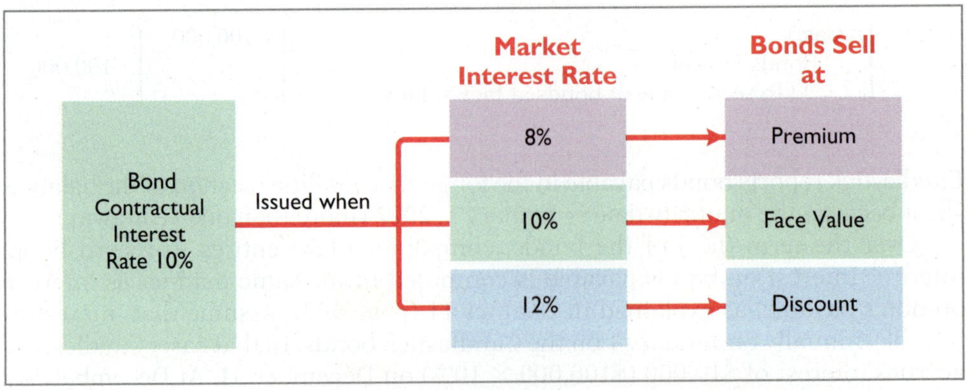

Issuance of bonds at an amount different from face value is quite common. By the time a company prints the bond certificates and markets the bonds, it will be a coincidence if the market rate and the contractual rate are the same. Thus, the issuance of bonds at a discount does not mean that the issuer's financial strength is suspect. Conversely, the sale of bonds at a premium does not indicate that the financial strength of the issuer is exceptional.

Helpful Hint

Discount on Bonds Payable	
Increase Debit ↓ Normal Balance	Decrease Credit

Issuing Bonds at a Discount

To illustrate issuance of bonds at a discount, assume that on January 1, 2017, Candlestick, Inc. sells $100,000, five-year, 10% bonds for $98,000 (98% of face value). Interest is payable annually on January 1. The entry to record the issuance is as follows.

Jan. 1	Cash	98,000	
	Discount on Bonds Payable	2,000	
	Bonds Payable		100,000
	(To record sale of bonds at a discount)		

A	=	L	+	SE
+98,000				
		−2,000		
		+100,000		

Cash Flows
+98,000

Although Discount on Bonds Payable has a debit balance, **it is not an asset.** Rather, it is a **contra account**. This account is **deducted from bonds payable** on the balance sheet, as shown in Illustration 15-5.

Illustration 15-5
Statement presentation of discount on bonds payable

CANDLESTICK, INC.
Balance Sheet (partial)

Long-term liabilities		
Bonds payable	$100,000	
Less: Discount on bonds payable	**2,000**	$98,000

The $98,000 represents the **carrying (or book) value** of the bonds. On the date of issue, this amount equals the market price of the bonds.

The issuance of bonds below face value—at a discount—causes the total cost of borrowing to differ from the bond interest paid. That is, the issuing corporation must pay not only the contractual interest rate over the term of the bonds but also the face value (rather than the issuance price) at maturity. Therefore, the difference between the issuance price and face value of the bonds—the discount—is an **additional cost of borrowing**. The company records this additional cost as **interest expense** over the life of the bonds. The total cost of borrowing $98,000 for Candlestick, Inc. is therefore $52,000, computed as follows.

Helpful Hint
Carrying value (book value) of bonds issued at a discount is determined by subtracting the balance of the discount account from the balance of the Bonds Payable account.

Illustration 15-6
Total cost of borrowing—bonds issued at a discount

Bonds Issued at a Discount

Annual interest payments	
($100,000 × 10% = $10,000; $10,000 × 5)	$ 50,000
Add: Bond discount ($100,000 − $98,000)	2,000
Total cost of borrowing	**$52,000**

Alternatively, we can compute the total cost of borrowing as follows.

Illustration 15-7
Alternative computation of total cost of borrowing—bonds issued at a discount

Bonds Issued at a Discount

Principal at maturity	$100,000
Annual interest payments ($10,000 × 5)	50,000
Cash to be paid to bondholders	150,000
Less: Cash received from bondholders	98,000
Total cost of borrowing	**$ 52,000**

To follow the expense recognition principle, companies allocate bond discount to expense in each period in which the bonds are outstanding. This is referred to as **amortizing the discount**. Amortization of the discount **increases** the amount of interest expense reported each period. That is, after the company amortizes the discount, the amount of interest expense it reports in a period will exceed the contractual amount. As shown in Illustration 15-6, for the bonds issued by Candlestick, Inc., total interest expense will exceed the contractual interest by $2,000 over the life of the bonds.

As the discount is amortized, its balance declines. As a consequence, the carrying value of the bonds will increase, until at maturity the carrying value of the bonds equals their face amount. This is shown in Illustration 15-8. Appendices 15A and 15B at the end of this chapter discuss procedures for amortizing bond discount.

Illustration 15-8
Amortization of bond discount

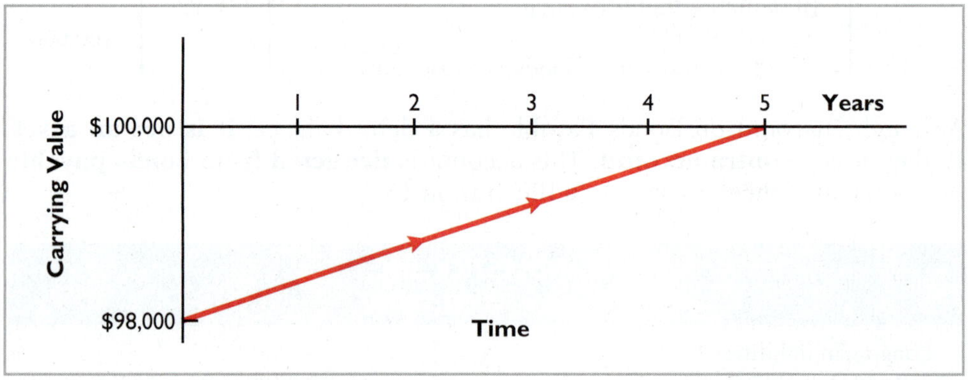

Issuing Bonds at a Premium

To illustrate the issuance of bonds at a premium, we now assume the Candlestick, Inc. bonds described above sell for $102,000 (102% of face value) rather than for $98,000. The entry to record the sale is as follows.

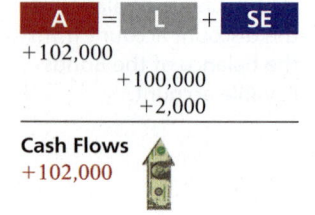

A	=	L	+	SE
+102,000				
		+100,000		
		+2,000		

Cash Flows
+102,000

Jan. 1	Cash	102,000	
	Bonds Payable		100,000
	Premium on Bonds Payable		2,000
	(To record sale of bonds at a premium)		

Candlestick adds the premium on bonds payable **to the bonds payable amount** on the balance sheet, as shown in Illustration 15-9.

Illustration 15-9
Statement presentation of bond premium

CANDLESTICK, INC.
Balance Sheet (partial)

Long-term liabilities		
Bonds payable	$100,000	
Add: Premium on bonds payable	2,000	**$102,000**

Helpful Hint

Premium on Bonds Payable	
Decrease Debit	Increase Credit ↓ Normal Balance

The sale of bonds above face value causes the total cost of borrowing to be **less than the bond interest paid**. The reason: The borrower is not required to pay the bond premium at the maturity date of the bonds. Thus, the bond premium is considered to be **a reduction in the cost of borrowing** that reduces bond interest over the life of the bonds. The total cost of borrowing $102,000 for Candlestick, Inc. is computed as follows.

Illustration 15-10
Total cost of borrowing—bonds issued at a premium

Bonds Issued at a Premium	
Annual interest payments ($100,000 × 10% = $10,000; $10,000 × 5)	$ 50,000
Less: Bond premium ($102,000 − $100,000)	2,000
Total cost of borrowing	**$48,000**

Alternatively, we can compute the cost of borrowing as follows.

Illustration 15-11
Alternative computation of total cost of borrowing—bonds issued at a premium

Bonds Issued at a Premium	
Principal at maturity	$100,000
Annual interest payments ($10,000 × 5)	50,000
Cash to be paid to bondholders	150,000
Less: Cash received from bondholders	102,000
Total cost of borrowing	**$ 48,000**

Similar to bond discount, companies allocate bond premium to expense in each period in which the bonds are outstanding. This is referred to as **amortizing the premium**. Amortization of the premium **decreases** the amount of interest expense reported each period. That is, after the company amortizes the premium, the amount of interest expense it reports in a period will be less than the contractual amount. As shown in Illustration 15-10, for the bonds issued by Candlestick, Inc., contractual interest will exceed the interest expense by $2,000 over the life of the bonds.

As the premium is amortized, its balance declines. As a consequence, the carrying value of the bonds will decrease, until at maturity the carrying value of the bonds equals their face amount. This is shown in Illustration 15-12. Appendices 15A and 15B at the end of this chapter discuss procedures for amortizing bond premium.

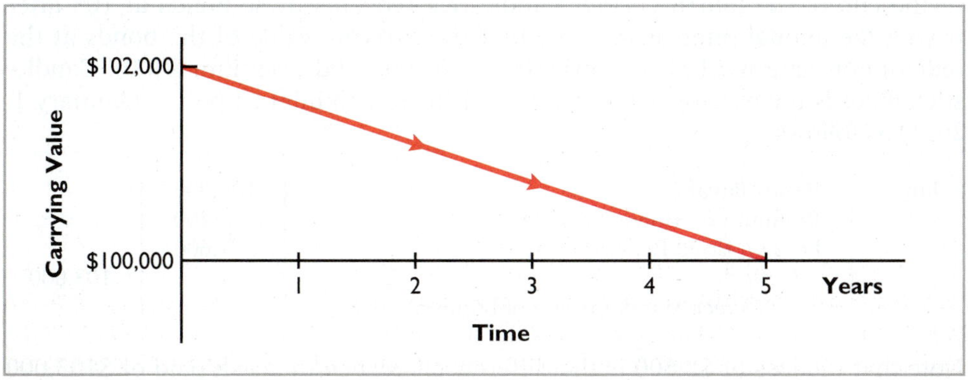

Illustration 15-12
Amortization of bond premium

DO IT! 2a Bond Issuance

Giant Corporation issues $200,000 of bonds for $189,000. (a) Prepare the journal entry to record the issuance of the bonds, and (b) show how the bonds would be reported on the balance sheet at the date of issuance.

Action Plan

- ✔ Record cash received, bonds payable at face value, and the difference as a discount or premium.
- ✔ Report discount as a deduction from bonds payable and premium as an addition to bonds payable.

Solution

(a)

Cash	189,000	
Discount on Bonds Payable	11,000	
Bonds Payable		200,000
(To record sale of bonds at a discount)		

(b)

Long-term liabilities		
Bonds payable	$200,000	
Less: Discount on bonds payable	11,000	$189,000

Related exercise material: **BE15-1, BE15-2, BE15-3, BE15-4, BE15-5, E15-2, E15-3, E15-4, E15-6, and DO IT! 15-2a.**

Redeeming and Converting Bonds

REDEEMING BONDS AT MATURITY

Regardless of the issue price of bonds, the book value of the bonds at maturity will equal their face value. Assuming that the company pays and records separately the interest for the last interest period, Candlestick records the redemption of its bonds at maturity as follows.

A = L + SE
−100,000 (L)
−100,000 (A)
Cash Flows
−100,000

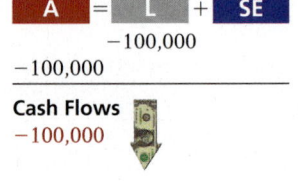

Jan. 1	Bonds Payable	100,000	
	Cash		100,000
	(To record redemption of bonds at maturity)		

REDEEMING BONDS BEFORE MATURITY

Helpful Hint
If a bond is redeemed prior to its maturity date and its carrying value exceeds its redemption price, this results in a gain.

Bonds may be redeemed before maturity. A company may decide to redeem bonds before maturity to reduce interest cost and to remove debt from its balance sheet. A company should redeem debt early only if it has sufficient cash resources.

When a company redeems bonds before maturity, it is necessary to (1) eliminate the carrying value of the bonds at the redemption date, (2) record the cash paid, and (3) recognize the gain or loss on redemption. The **carrying value** of the bonds is the face value of the bonds less any remaining bond discount or plus any remaining bond premium at the redemption date.

To illustrate, assume that Candlestick, Inc. has sold its bonds at a premium. At the end of the fourth period, Candlestick redeems these bonds at 103 after paying the annual interest. Assume that the carrying value of the bonds at the redemption date is $100,400 (principal $100,000 and premium $400). Candlestick records the redemption at the end of the fourth interest period (January 1, 2021) as follows.

A = L + SE
−100,000 (L)
−400 (L)
−2,600 Exp (SE)
−103,000 (A)
Cash Flows
−103,000

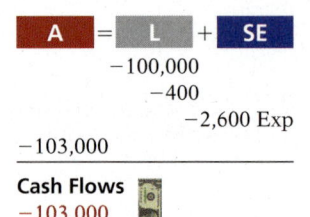

Jan. 1	Bonds Payable	100,000	
	Premium on Bonds Payable	400	
	Loss on Bond Redemption	2,600	
	Cash		103,000
	(To record redemption of bonds at 103)		

Note that the loss of $2,600 is the difference between the cash paid of $103,000 and the carrying value of the bonds of $100,400.

CONVERTING BONDS INTO COMMON STOCK

Convertible bonds have features that are attractive both to bondholders and to the issuer. The conversion often gives bondholders an opportunity to benefit if the market price of the common stock increases substantially. Until conversion, though, the bondholder receives interest on the bond. For the issuer of convertible bonds, the bonds sell at a higher price and pay a lower rate of interest than comparable debt securities without the conversion option. Many corporations, such as Intel, Ford, and Wells Fargo, have convertible bonds outstanding.

When the issuing company records a conversion, the company ignores the current market prices of the bonds and stock. Instead, the company transfers the **carrying value** of the bonds to paid-in capital accounts. **No gain or loss is recognized.**

To illustrate, assume that on July 1, Saunders Associates converts $100,000 bonds sold at face value into 2,000 shares of $10 par value common stock. Both the bonds and the common stock have a market value of $130,000. Saunders makes the following entry to record the conversion.

July 1	Bonds Payable	100,000	
	Common Stock		20,000
	Paid-in Capital in Excess of Par—Common Stock		80,000
	(To record bond conversion)		

A	=	L	+	SE
		−100,000		
				+20,000 CS
				+80,000 CS

Cash Flows
no effect

Note that the company does not consider the current market value of the bonds and stock ($130,000) in making the entry. This method of recording the bond conversion is often referred to as the **carrying (or book) value method**.

People, Planet, and Profit Insight — Unilever

© CarpathianPrince/Shutterstock

How About Some Green Bonds?

Unilever recently began producing popular frozen treats such as Magnums and Cornettos, funded by green bonds. Green bonds are debt used to fund activities such as renewable-energy projects. In Unilever's case, the proceeds from the sale of green bonds are used to clean up the company's manufacturing operations and cut waste (such as related to energy consumption).

The use of green bonds has taken off as companies now have guidelines as to how to disclose and report on these green-bond proceeds. These standardized disclosures provide transparency as to how these bonds are used and their effect on overall profitability.

Investors are taking a strong interest in these bonds. Investing companies are installing socially responsible investing teams and have started to integrate sustainability into their investment processes. The disclosures of how companies are using the bond proceeds help investors to make better financial decisions.

Source: Ben Edwards, "Green Bonds Catch On," *Wall Street Journal* (April 3, 2014), p. C5.

Why might standardized disclosure help investors to better understand how proceeds from the sale or issuance of bonds are used? (Go to **WileyPLUS** for this answer and additional questions.)

DO IT! 2b Bond Redemption

R & B Inc. issued $500,000, 10-year bonds at a discount. Prior to maturity, when the carrying value of the bonds is $496,000, the company redeems the bonds at 98. Prepare the entry to record the redemption of the bonds.

Action Plan

- ✔ Determine and eliminate the carrying value of the bonds.
- ✔ Record the cash paid.
- ✔ Compute and record the gain or loss (the difference between the first two items).

Solution

There is a gain on redemption. The cash paid, \$490,000 (\$500,000 × 98%), is less than the carrying value of \$496,000. The entry is:

Bonds Payable	500,000	
Discount on Bonds Payable		4,000
Gain on Bond Redemption		6,000
Cash		490,000
(To record redemption of bonds at 98)		

Related exercise material: BE15-6, E15-5, E15-7, E15-8, and DO IT! 15-2b.

LEARNING OBJECTIVE 3

Explain how to account for long-term notes payable.

Other common types of long-term obligations are notes payable and lease liabilities. We discuss notes payable next.

Long-Term Notes Payable

The use of notes payable in long-term debt financing is quite common. **Long-term notes payable** are similar to short-term interest-bearing notes payable except that the term of the notes exceeds one year. In periods of unstable interest rates, lenders may tie the interest rate on long-term notes to changes in the market rate for comparable loans.

A long-term note may be secured by a **mortgage** that pledges title to specific assets as security for a loan. Individuals widely use **mortgage notes payable** to purchase homes, and many small and some large companies use them to acquire plant assets. At one time, approximately 18% of McDonald's long-term debt related to mortgage notes on land, buildings, and improvements.

Like other long-term notes payable, the mortgage loan terms may stipulate either a **fixed** or an **adjustable** interest rate. The interest rate on a fixed-rate mortgage remains the same over the life of the mortgage. The interest rate on an adjustable-rate mortgage is adjusted periodically to reflect changes in the market rate of interest. Typically, the terms require the borrower to make equal installment payments over the term of the loan. Each payment consists of (1) interest on the unpaid balance of the loan and (2) a reduction of loan principal. While the total amount of the payment remains constant, the interest decreases each period, while the portion applied to the loan principal increases.

Companies initially record mortgage notes payable at face value. They subsequently make entries for each installment payment. To illustrate, assume that Porter Technology Inc. issues a \$500,000, 8%, 20-year mortgage note on December 31, 2017, to obtain needed financing for a new research laboratory. The terms provide for annual installment payments of \$50,926 (not including real estate taxes and insurance). The installment payment schedule for the first four years is as follows.

Illustration 15-13 Mortgage installment payment schedule

Interest Period	(A) Cash Payment	(B) Interest Expense (D) × 8%	(C) Reduction of Principal (A) − (B)	(D) Principal Balance (D) − (C)
Issue date				\$500,000
1	\$50,926	\$40,000	\$10,926	489,074
2	50,926	39,126	11,800	477,274
3	50,926	38,182	12,744	464,530
4	50,926	37,162	13,764	450,766

Porter records the mortgage loan on December 31, 2017, as follows.

Dec. 31	Cash	500,000	
	Mortgage Payable		500,000
	(To record mortgage loan)		

A	=	L	+	SE
+500,000				
		+500,000		

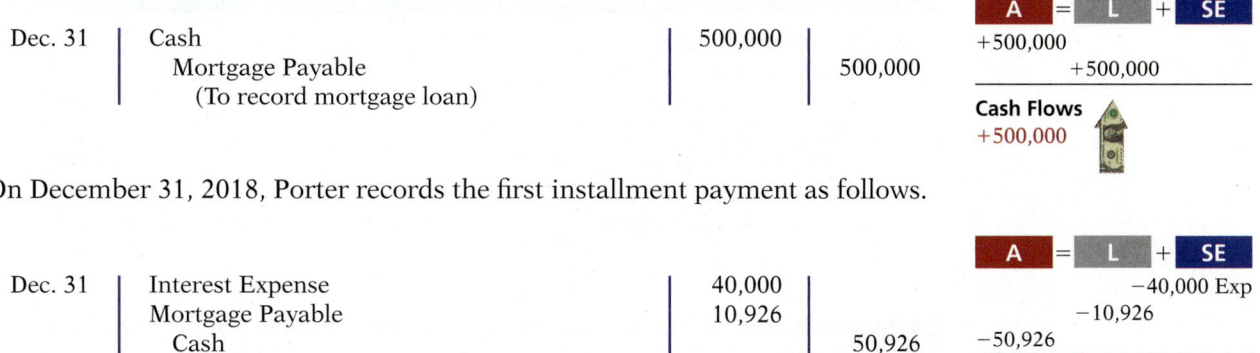

Cash Flows
+500,000

On December 31, 2018, Porter records the first installment payment as follows.

Dec. 31	Interest Expense	40,000	
	Mortgage Payable	10,926	
	Cash		50,926
	(To record annual payment on mortgage)		

A	=	L	+	SE
				−40,000 Exp
		−10,926		
−50,926				

Cash Flows
−50,926

In the balance sheet, the company reports the reduction in principal for the next year as a current liability, and it classifies the remaining unpaid principal balance as a long-term liability. At December 31, 2018, the total liability is $489,074. Of that amount, $11,800 is current and $477,274 ($489,074 − $11,800) is long-term.

DO IT! 3 Long-Term Notes

Cole Research issues a $250,000, 6%, 20-year mortgage note to obtain needed financing for a new lab. The terms call for annual payments of $21,796 each. Prepare the entries to record the mortgage loan and the first payment.

Solution

Cash	250,000	
Mortgage Payable		250,000
(To record mortgage loan)		
Interest Expense	15,000*	
Mortgage Payable	6,796	
Cash		21,796
(To record annual payment on mortgage)		

*Interest expense = $250,000 × 6% = $15,000.

Action Plan

- ✔ Record the issuance of the note as a cash receipt and a liability.
- ✔ Each installment payment consists of interest and payment of principal.

Related exercise material: **BE15-7, E15-9, E15-10, and DO IT! 15-3.**

LEARNING OBJECTIVE 4 Discuss how long-term liabilities are reported and analyzed.

Presentation

Companies report long-term liabilities in a separate section of the balance sheet immediately following current liabilities, as shown in Illustration 15-14 (page 658). Alternatively, companies may present summary data in the balance sheet, with detailed data (interest rates, maturity dates, conversion privileges, and assets pledged as collateral) shown in a supporting schedule.

Illustration 15-14
Balance sheet presentation of long-term liabilities

LAX CORPORATION Balance Sheet (partial)		
Long-term liabilities		
Bonds payable 10% due in 2022	$1,000,000	
Less: Discount on bonds payable	80,000	$ 920,000
Mortgage payable, 11%, due in 2028 and secured by plant assets		500,000
Lease liability		440,000
Total long-term liabilities		$1,860,000

Companies report the current maturities of long-term debt under current liabilities if they are to be paid within one year or the operating cycle, whichever is longer.

Use of Ratios

Two ratios are helpful in better understanding a company's debt-paying ability and long-term solvency. Long-term creditors and stockholders are interested in a company's long-run solvency. Of particular interest is the company's ability to pay interest as it comes due and to repay the face value of the debt at maturity.

The **debt to assets ratio** measures the percentage of the total assets provided by creditors. It is computed by dividing total liabilities (both current and long-term liabilities) by total assets. To illustrate, we use data from a recent Kellogg Company annual report. The company reported total liabilities of $8,925 million, total assets of $11,200 million, interest expense of $295 million, income taxes of $476 million, and net income of $1,208 million. As shown in Illustration 15-15, Kellogg's debt to assets ratio is 79.7%. The higher the percentage of debt to assets, the greater the risk that the company may be unable to meet its maturing obligation.

Illustration 15-15
Debt to assets ratio

Total Liabilities	÷	Total Assets	=	Debt to Assets Ratio
$8,925	÷	$11,200	=	**79.7%**

Times interest earned indicates the company's ability to meet interest payments as they come due. It is computed by dividing the sum of net income, interest expense, and income tax expense by interest expense. As shown in Illustration 15-16, Kellogg's times interest earned is 6.71 times. This interest coverage is considered safe.

Illustration 15-16
Times interest earned

Net Income + Interest Expense + Income Tax Expense	÷	Interest Expense	=	Times Interest Earned
$1,208 + $295 + $476	÷	$295	=	**6.71 times**

Debt and Equity Financing

To obtain large amounts of long-term capital, corporate management has to decide whether to issue additional common stock (equity financing), bonds or notes (debt financing), or a combination of the two. This decision is important to both the company and to investors and creditors. The capital structure of a company provides clues as to the potential profit that can be achieved and the risks taken by the company. Debt financing offers these advantages over common stock, as shown in Illustration 15-17.

Illustration 15-17
Advantages of bond financing over common stock

Bond Financing	Advantages
	1. **Stockholder control is not affected.** Bondholders do not have voting rights, so current owners (stockholders) retain full control of the company.
	2. **Tax savings result.** Bond interest is deductible for tax purposes; dividends on stock are not.
Income statement / **EPS**	3. **Earning per share (EPS) may be higher.** Although bond interest expense reduces net income, earning per share is higher under bond financing because no additional shares of common stock are issued.

As Illustration 15-17 shows, one reason to issue bonds is that they do not affect stockholder control. Because bondholders do not have voting rights, owners can raise capital with bonds and still maintain corporate control. In addition, bonds are attractive to corporations because the cost of bond interest is tax-deductible. As a result of this tax treatment, which stock dividends do not offer, bonds may result in lower cost of capital than equity financing.

To illustrate another advantage of bond financing, assume that Microsystems, Inc. is considering two plans for financing the construction of a new \$5 million plant. Plan A involves issuance of 200,000 shares of common stock at the current market price of \$25 per share. Plan B involves issuance of \$5 million, 8% bonds at face value. Income before interest and taxes on the new plant will be \$1.5 million. Income taxes are expected to be 30%. Microsystems currently has 100,000 shares of common stock outstanding. Illustration 15-18 shows the alternative effects on earnings per share.

Illustration 15-18
Effects on earnings per share—stocks vs. bonds

	Plan A Issue Stock	Plan B Issue Bonds
Income before interest and taxes	\$1,500,000	\$1,500,000
Interest (8% × \$5,000,000)	—	400,000
Income before income taxes	1,500,000	1,100,000
Income tax expense (30%)	450,000	330,000
Net income	\$1,050,000	\$ 770,000
Outstanding shares	300,000	100,000
Earnings per share	**\$3.50**	**\$7.70**

Note that net income is \$280,000 less (\$1,050,000 − \$770,000) with long-term debt financing (bonds). However, earnings per share is higher because there are 200,000 fewer shares of common stock outstanding.

A major disadvantage of using debt financing is that a company must pay interest on a periodic basis. In addition, the company must also repay principal at the due date. A company with fluctuating earnings and a relatively weak cash position may have great difficulty making interest payments when earnings are low. Furthermore, when the economy, stock market, or a company's revenues stagnate, debt payments can gobble up cash quickly and limit a company's ability to meet its financial obligations.

Lease Liabilities and Off-Balance-Sheet Financing

A lease is a contractual arrangement between a lessor (owner of the property) and a lessee (renter of the property). It grants the right to use specific property for a period of time in return for cash payments. Leasing is big business. The global leasing market for capital equipment has recently been over \$850 billion. This represents approximately one-third of equipment financed in a year. The two most common types of leases are operating leases and capital leases.

OPERATING LEASES

The renting of an apartment and the rental of a car at an airport are examples of **operating leases. In an operating lease, the intent is temporary use of the property by the lessee, while the lessor continues to own the property.**

In an operating lease, the lessee records the lease (or rental) payments as an expense. The lessor records the payments as revenue. For example, assume that a sales representative for Western Inc. leases a car from Hertz Car Rental at the Los Angeles airport and that Hertz charges a total of $275. Western, the lessee, records the rental as follows.

A	=	L	+	SE
				−275 Exp
−275				

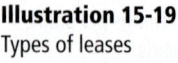

Cash Flows
−275

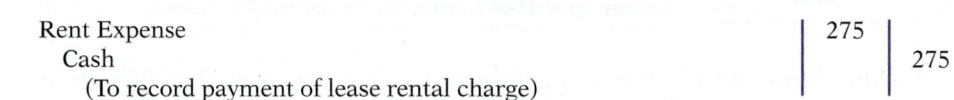

Rent Expense	275	
Cash		275
(To record payment of lease rental charge)		

The lessee may incur other costs during the lease period. For example, in the case above, Western will generally incur costs for gas. Western would report these costs as an expense.

CAPITAL LEASES

In most lease contracts, the lessee makes a periodic payment and records that payment in the income statement as rent expense. In some cases, however, the lease contract transfers to the lessee substantially all the benefits and risks of ownership. Such a lease is in effect a purchase of the property. This type of lease is a **capital lease**. Its name comes from the fact that the company capitalizes the present value of the cash payments for the lease and records that amount as an asset. Illustration 15-19 indicates the major difference between operating and capital leases.

Illustration 15-19
Types of leases

Helpful Hint
A capital lease situation is one that, although legally a rental case, is *in substance* an installment purchase by the lessee. Accounting standards require that substance over form be used in such a situation.

If **any one** of the following conditions exists, the lessee must record a lease **as an asset**—that is, as a capital lease:

1. **The lease transfers ownership of the property to the lessee.** *Rationale:* If during the lease term the lessee receives ownership of the asset, the lessee should report the leased item as an asset on its books.
2. **The lease contains a bargain purchase option.** *Rationale:* If during the term of the lease the lessee can purchase the asset at a price substantially below its

fair value, the lessee will exercise this option. Thus, the lessee should report the leased item as an asset on its books.

3. **The lease term is equal to 75% or more of the economic life of the leased property.** *Rationale:* If the lease term is for much of the asset's useful life, the lessee should report the leased item as an asset on its books.
4. **The present value of the lease payments equals or exceeds 90% of the fair value of the leased property.** *Rationale:* If the present value of the lease payments is equal to or almost equal to the fair value of the asset, the lessee has essentially purchased the asset. As a result, the lessee should report the leased item as an asset on its books.

To illustrate, assume that Gonzalez Company decides to lease new equipment. The lease period is four years. The economic life of the leased equipment is estimated to be five years. The present value of the lease payments is $190,000, which is equal to the fair value of the equipment. There is no transfer of ownership during the lease term, nor is there any bargain purchase option.

In this example, Gonzalez has essentially purchased the equipment. Conditions 3 and 4 have been met. First, the lease term is 75% or more of the economic life of the asset. Second, the present value of cash payments is equal to the equipment's fair value. Gonzalez records the transaction as follows.

Leased Asset—Equipment	190,000	
Lease Liability		190,000
(To record leased asset and lease liability)		

A	=	L	+	SE
+190,000				
		+190,000		

Cash Flows
no effect

The lessee reports a leased asset on the balance sheet under plant assets. It reports the lease liability on the balance sheet as a liability. **The portion of the lease liability expected to be paid in the next year is a current liability. The remainder is classified as a long-term liability.**

Most lessees do not like to report leases on their balance sheets. Why? Because the lease liability increases the company's total liabilities. This, in turn, may make it more difficult for the company to obtain needed funds from lenders. As a result, companies attempt to keep leased assets and lease liabilities off the balance sheet by structuring leases so as not to meet any of the four conditions discussed earlier. The practice of keeping liabilities off the balance sheet is referred to as **off-balance-sheet financing**.

ETHICS NOTE

Accounting standard-setters are attempting to rewrite rules on lease accounting because of concerns that abuse of the current standards is reducing the usefulness of financial statements.

Investor Insight "Covenant-Lite" Debt

Paul Fleet/Alamy

In many corporate loans and bond issuances, the lending agreement specifies debt covenants. These covenants typically are specific financial measures, such as minimum levels of retained earnings, cash flows, times interest earned, or other measures that a company must maintain during the life of the loan. If the company violates a covenant, it is considered to have violated the loan agreement. The creditors can then demand immediate repayment, or they can renegotiate the loan's terms. Covenants protect lenders because they enable lenders to step in and try to get their money back before the borrower gets too deeply into trouble.

During the 1990s, most traditional loans specified between three to six covenants or "triggers." In more recent years, when lots of cash was available, lenders began reducing or completely eliminating covenants from loan agreements in order to be more competitive with other lenders. Lending to weaker companies on easy terms is now common as investors' appetite for higher-yielding debt grows stronger and the Federal Reserve keeps money flowing at ultralow rates. Since the 2008 financial crisis, companies have been able to borrow more without offering investors what were once considered standard protections against possible losses.

Sources: Cynthia Koons, "Risky Business: Growth of 'Covenant-Lite' Debt," *Wall Street Journal* (June 18, 2007), p. C2; and Katy Burne, "More Loans Come with Few Strings Attached," *Wall Street Journal* (June 12, 2014).

How can financial ratios such as those covered in this chapter provide protection for creditors? (Go to **WileyPLUS** for this answer and additional questions.)

DO IT! 4 Lease Liability; Analysis of Long-Term Liabilities

FX Corporation leases new equipment on December 31, 2017. The lease transfers ownership to FX at the end of the lease. The present value of the lease payments is $240,000. After recording this lease, FX has assets of $2,000,000, liabilities of $1,200,000, and stockholders' equity of $800,000. (a) Prepare the entry to record the lease, and (b) compute and discuss the debt to assets ratio at year-end.

Action Plan

✔ Record the present value of the lease payments as an asset and a liability.

✔ Use the formula for the debt to assets ratio (Total liabilities divided by Total assets).

Solution

(a)

Leased Asset—Equipment	240,000	
Lease Liability		240,000
(To record leased asset and lease liability)		

(b) The debt to assets ratio = $1,200,000 ÷ $2,000,000 = 60%. This means that 60% of its assets were provided by creditors. The higher the percentage of debt to assets, the greater the risk that the company may be unable to meet its maturing obligations.

Related exercise material: **BE15-10, E15-13, E15-14, and DO IT! 15-4.**

LEARNING OBJECTIVE *5

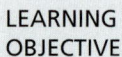

APPENDIX 15A: Apply the straight-line method of amortizing bond discount and bond premium.

Amortizing Bond Discount

To follow the expense recognition principle, companies allocate bond discount to expense in each period in which the bonds are outstanding. The **straight-line method of amortization** allocates the same amount to interest expense in each interest period. The calculation is presented in Illustration 15A-1.

Illustration 15A-1
Formula for straight-line method of bond discount amortization

Bond Discount	÷	Number of Interest Periods	=	Bond Discount Amortization

In the Candlestick, Inc. example (page 651), the company sold $100,000, five-year, 10% bonds on January 1, 2017, for $98,000. This resulted in a $2,000 bond discount ($100,000 − $98,000). The bond discount amortization is $400 ($2,000 ÷ 5) for each of the five amortization periods. Candlestick records the first accrual of bond interest and the amortization of bond discount on December 31 as follows.

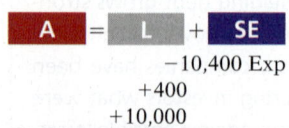

A	=	L	+	SE
				−10,400 Exp
		+400		
		+10,000		

Cash Flows
no effect

Dec. 31	Interest Expense	10,400	
	Discount on Bonds Payable		400
	Interest Payable		10,000
	(To record accrued bond interest and amortization of bond discount)		

Alternative Terminology
The amount in the Discount on Bonds Payable account is often referred to as *Unamortized Discount on Bonds Payable.*

Over the term of the bonds, the balance in Discount on Bonds Payable will decrease annually by the same amount until it has a zero balance at the maturity date of the bonds. Thus, the carrying value of the bonds at maturity will be equal to the face value of the bonds.

Preparing a bond discount amortization schedule, as shown in Illustration 15A-2, is useful to determine interest expense, discount amortization, and the carrying value of the bond. As indicated, the interest expense recorded each period is $10,400. Also note that the carrying value of the bond increases $400 each period until it reaches its face value of $100,000 at the end of period 5.

Candlestick Inc.xls

CANDLESTICK, INC.
Bond Discount Amortization Schedule
Straight-Line Method—Annual Interest Payments
$100,000 of 10%, 5-Year Bonds

Interest Periods	(A) Interest to Be Paid (10% × $100,000)	(B) Interest Expense to Be Recorded (A) + (C)	(C) Discount Amortization ($2,000 ÷ 5)	(D) Unamortized Discount (D) – (C)	(E) Bond Carrying Value ($100,000 – D)
Issue date				$2,000	$ 98,000
1	$10,000	$10,400	$ 400	1,600	98,400
2	10,000	10,400	400	1,200	98,800
3	10,000	10,400	400	800	99,200
4	10,000	10,400	400	400	99,600
5	10,000	10,400	400	0	100,000
	$50,000	$52,000	$2,000		

Column **(A)** remains constant because the face value of the bonds ($100,000) is multiplied by the annual contractual interest rate (10%) each period.
Column **(B)** is computed as the interest paid (Column A) plus the discount amortization (Column C).
Column **(C)** indicates the discount amortization each period.
Column **(D)** decreases each period by the same amount until it reaches zero at maturity.
Column **(E)** increases each period by the amount of discount amortization until it equals the face value at maturity.

Illustration 15A-2
Bond discount amortization schedule

Amortizing Bond Premium

The amortization of bond premium parallels that of bond discount. Illustration 15A-3 presents the formula for determining bond premium amortization under the straight-line method.

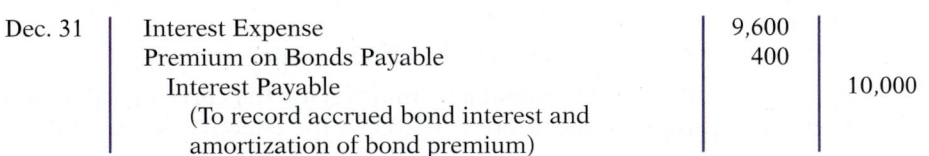

Bond Premium	÷	Number of Interest Periods	=	Bond Premium Amortization

Illustration 15A-3
Formula for straight-line method of bond premium amortization

Continuing our example, assume Candlestick, Inc., sells the bonds described above for $102,000, rather than $98,000 (see page 652). This results in a bond premium of $2,000 ($102,000 − $100,000). The premium amortization for each interest period is $400 ($2,000 ÷ 5). Candlestick records the first accrual of interest on December 31 as follows.

Dec. 31	Interest Expense	9,600	
	Premium on Bonds Payable	400	
	Interest Payable		10,000
	(To record accrued bond interest and amortization of bond premium)		

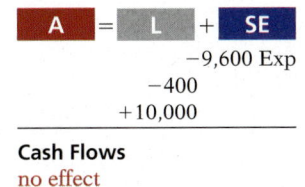

A = L + SE
−9,600 Exp
−400
+10,000

Cash Flows
no effect

A bond premium amortization schedule, as shown in Illustration 15A-4 (page 664), is useful to determine interest expense, premium amortization, and the carrying value of the bond. As indicated, the interest expense Candlestick records

Illustration 15A-4
Bond premium amortization schedule

each period is $9,600. Note that the carrying value of the bond decreases $400 each period until it reaches its face value of $100,000 at the end of period 5.

Candlestick Inc.xls

CANDLESTICK, INC.
Bond Premium Amortization Schedule
Straight-Line Method—Annual Interest Payments
$100,000 of 10%, 5-Year Bonds

Interest Periods	(A) Interest to Be Paid (10% × $100,000)	(B) Interest Expense to Be Recorded (A) – (C)	(C) Premium Amortization ($2,000 ÷ 5)	(D) Unamortized Premium (D) – (C)	(E) Bond Carrying Value ($100,000 + D)
Issue date				$2,000	$102,000
1	$10,000	$ 9,600	$ 400	1,600	101,600
2	10,000	9,600	400	1,200	101,200
3	10,000	9,600	400	800	100,800
4	10,000	9,600	400	400	100,400
5	10,000	9,600	400	0	100,000
	$50,000	$48,000	$2,000		

Column **(A)** remains constant because the face value of the bonds ($100,000) is multiplied by the annual contractual interest rate (10%) each period.
Column **(B)** is computed as the interest paid (Column A) less the premium amortization (Column C).
Column **(C)** indicates the premium amortization each period.
Column **(D)** decreases each period by the same amount until it reaches zero at maturity.
Column **(E)** decreases each period by the amount of premium amortization until it equals the face value at maturity.

LEARNING OBJECTIVE *6

APPENDIX 15B: Apply the effective-interest method of amortizing bond discount and bond premium.

To follow the expense recognition principle, companies allocate bond discount to expense in each period in which the bonds are outstanding. However, to completely comply with the expense recognition principle, interest expense as a percentage of carrying value should not change over the life of the bonds.

This percentage, referred to as the **effective-interest rate**, is established when the bonds are issued and remains constant in each interest period. Unlike the straight-line method, the effective-interest method of amortization accomplishes this result.

Under the **effective-interest method of amortization**, the amortization of bond discount or bond premium results in periodic interest expense equal to a constant percentage of the carrying value of the bonds. The effective-interest method results in **varying amounts** of amortization and interest expense per period but a **constant percentage rate**. In contrast, the straight-line method results in constant amounts of amortization and interest expense per period but a varying percentage rate.

Companies follow three steps under the effective-interest method:

1. Compute the **bond interest expense** by multiplying the carrying value of the bonds at the beginning of the interest period by the effective-interest rate.
2. Compute the **bond interest paid** (or accrued) by multiplying the face value of the bonds by the contractual interest rate.
3. Compute the **amortization amount** by determining the difference between the amounts computed in steps (1) and (2).

Illustration 15B-1 depicts these steps.

(1) Bond Interest Expense		(2) Bond Interest Paid		(3)
[Carrying Value of Bonds at Beginning of Period × Effective-Interest Rate]	−	[Face Amount of Bond × Contractual Interest Rate]	=	**Amortization Amount**

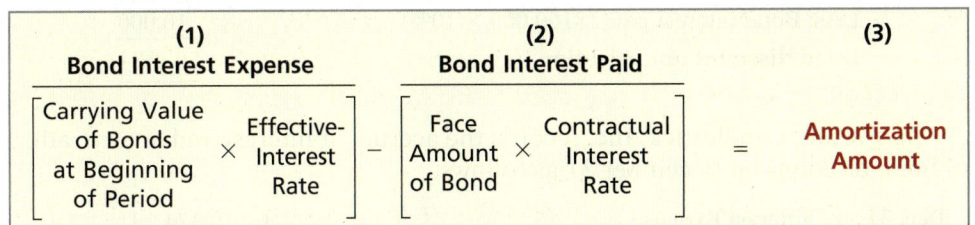

Illustration 15B-1
Computation of amortization using effective-interest method

Both the straight-line and effective-interest methods of amortization result in the same total amount of interest expense over the term of the bonds. Furthermore, interest expense each interest period is generally comparable in amount. However, **when the amounts are materially different, generally accepted accounting principles (GAAP) require use of the effective-interest method.**

Helpful Hint
Note that the amount of periodic interest expense increases over the life of the bonds when the effective-interest method is used for bonds issued at a discount. The reason is that a constant percentage is applied to an increasing bond carrying value to compute interest expense. The carrying value is increasing because of the amortization of the discount.

Amortizing Bond Discount

In the Candlestick, Inc. example (page 651), the company sold $100,000, five-year, 10% bonds on January 1, 2017, for $98,000. This resulted in a $2,000 bond discount ($100,000 − $98,000). This discount results in an effective-interest rate of approximately 10.5348%. (The effective-interest rate can be computed using the techniques shown in Appendix G near the end of this textbook.)

Preparing a bond discount amortization schedule as shown in Illustration 15B-2 facilitates the recording of interest expense and the discount amortization. Note that interest expense as a percentage of carrying value remains constant at 10.5348%.

Candlestick Inc.xls

Home Insert Page Layout Formulas Data Review View

P18 fx

CANDLESTICK, INC.
Bond Discount Amortization Schedule
Effective-Interest Method—Annual Interest Payments
10% Bonds Issued at 10.5348%

Interest Periods	(A) Interest to Be Paid (10% × $100,000)	(B) Interest Expense to Be Recorded (10.5348% × Preceding Bond Carrying Value)		(C) Discount Amortization (B) − (A)	(D) Unamortized Discount (D) − (C)	(E) Bond Carrying Value ($100,000 − D)
Issue date					$2,000	$ 98,000
1	$10,000	$10,324	(10.5348% × $98,000)	$ 324	1,676	98,324
2	10,000	10,358	(10.5348% × $98,324)	358	1,318	98,682
3	10,000	10,396	(10.5348% × $98,682)	396	922	99,078
4	10,000	10,438	(10.5348% × $99,078)	438	484	99,516
5	10,000	10,484	(10.5348% × $99,516)	484	-0-	100,000
	$50,000	$52,000		$2,000		

Column **(A)** remains constant because the face value of the bonds ($100,000) is multiplied by the annual contractual interest rate (10%) each period.
Column **(B)** is computed as the preceding bond carrying value times the annual effective-interest rate (10.5348%).
Column **(C)** indicates the discount amortization each period.
Column **(D)** decreases each period until it reaches zero at maturity.
Column **(E)** increases each period until it equals face value at maturity.

Illustration 15B-2
Bond discount amortization schedule

For the first interest period, the computations of bond interest expense and the bond discount amortization are as follows.

Illustration 15B-3
Computation of bond discount amortization

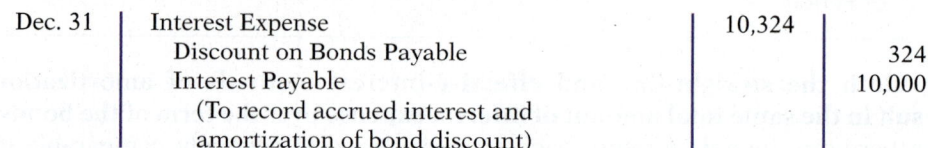

Bond interest expense ($98,000 × 10.5348%)	$10,324
Less: Bond interest paid ($100,000 × 10%)	10,000
Bond discount amortization	**$ 324**

As a result, Candlestick, Inc. records the accrual of interest and amortization of bond discount on December 31 as follows.

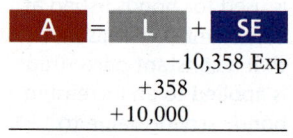

A	=	L	+	SE
				−10,324 Exp
		+324		
		+10,000		

Cash Flows
no effect

Dec. 31	Interest Expense	10,324	
	Discount on Bonds Payable		324
	Interest Payable		10,000
	(To record accrued interest and amortization of bond discount)		

For the second interest period, bond interest expense will be $10,358 ($98,324 × 10.5348%), and the discount amortization will be $358. At December 31, Candlestick makes the following adjusting entry.

A	=	L	+	SE
				−10,358 Exp
		+358		
		+10,000		

Cash Flows
no effect

Dec. 31	Interest Expense	10,358	
	Discount on Bonds Payable		358
	Interest Payable		10,000
	(To record accrued interest and amortization of bond discount)		

Amortizing Bond Premium

Continuing our example, assume Candlestick, Inc. sells the bonds described above for $102,000 rather than $98,000 (see page 652). This would result in a bond premium of $2,000 ($102,000 − $100,000). This premium results in an effective-interest rate of approximately 9.4794%. (The effective-interest rate can be solved for using the techniques shown in Appendix G near the end of this textbook.) Illustration 15B-4 shows the bond premium amortization schedule.

Illustration 15B-4
Bond premium amortization schedule

Candlestick Inc.xls

CANDLESTICK, INC.
Bond Premium Amortization Schedule
Effective-Interest Method—Annual Interest Payments
10% Bonds Issued at 9.4794%

Interest Periods	(A) Interest to Be Paid (10% × $100,000)	(B) Interest Expense to Be Recorded (9.4794% × Preceding Bond Carrying Value)	(C) Premium Amortization (A) − (B)	(D) Unamortized Premium (D) − (C)	(E) Bond Carrying Value ($100,000 + D)
Issue date				$2,000	$102,000
1	$10,000	$ 9,669 (9.4794% × $102,000)	$ 331	1,669	101,669
2	10,000	9,638 (9.4794% × $101,669)	362	1,307	101,307
3	10,000	9,603 (9.4794% × $101,307)	397	910	100,910
4	10,000	9,566 (9.4794% × $100,910)	434	476	100,476
5	10,000	9,524* (9.4794% × $100,476)	476*	−0−	100,000
	$50,000	$48,000	$2,000		

Column **(A)** remains constant because the face value of the bonds ($100,000) is multiplied by the contractual interest rate (10%) each period.
Column **(B)** is computed as the carrying value of the bonds times the annual effective-interest rate (9.4794%).
Column **(C)** indicates the premium amortization each period.
Column **(D)** decreases each period until it reaches zero at maturity.
Column **(E)** decreases each period until it equals face value at maturity.

*Rounded to eliminate remaining discount resulting from rounding the effective rate.

For the first interest period, the computations of bond interest expense and the bond premium amortization are as follows.

Bond interest paid ($100,000 × 10%)	$10,000
Less: Bond interest expense ($102,000 × 9.4794%)	9,669
Bond premium amortization	**$ 331**

Illustration 15B-5
Computation of bond premium amortization

Dec. 31	Interest Expense	9,669	
	Premium on Bonds Payable	331	
	Interest Payable		10,000
	(To record accrued interest and amortization of bond premium)		

A = L + SE
−9,669 Exp
−331
+10,000

Cash Flows
no effect

For the second interest period, interest expense will be $9,638, and the premium amortization will be $362. Note that the amount of periodic interest expense decreases over the life of the bond when companies apply the effective-interest method to bonds issued at a premium. The reason is that a constant percentage is applied to a decreasing bond carrying value to compute interest expense. The carrying value is decreasing because of the amortization of the premium.

REVIEW AND PRACTICE

LEARNING OBJECTIVES REVIEW

1 Describe the major characteristics of bonds. Bonds can have many different features and may be secured, unsecured, convertible, or callable. The terms of the bond issue are set forth in a bond indenture, and a bond certificate provides the specific information about the bond itself.

2 Explain how to account for bond transactions. When companies issue bonds, they debit Cash for the cash proceeds and credit Bonds Payable for the face value of the bonds. The account Premium on Bonds Payable shows a bond premium. Discount on Bonds Payable shows a bond discount.

When bondholders redeem bonds at maturity, the issuing company credits Cash and debits Bonds Payable for the face value of the bonds. When bonds are redeemed before maturity, the issuing company (a) eliminates the carrying value of the bonds at the redemption date, (b) records the cash paid, and (c) recognizes the gain or loss on redemption. When bonds are converted to common stock, the issuing company transfers the carrying (or book) value of the bonds to appropriate paid-in capital accounts. No gain or loss is recognized.

3 Explain how to account for long-term notes payable. Each payment consists of (1) interest on the unpaid balance of the loan and (2) a reduction of loan principal. The interest decreases each period, while the portion applied to the loan principal increases.

4 Discuss how long-term liabilities are reported and analyzed. Companies should report the nature and amount of each long-term debt in the balance sheet or in the notes accompanying the financial statements. Companies may sell bonds to investors to raise long-term capital. Bonds offer the following advantages over common stock: (a) stockholder control is not affected, (b) tax savings result, and (c) earnings per share of common stock may be higher.

Stockholders and long-term creditors are interested in a company's long-run solvency. Debt to assets and times interest earned are two ratios that provide information about debt-paying ability and long-run solvency.

A lease grants the right to use specific property for a period of time in return for cash payments. For an operating lease, the lessee (renter) records lease (rental) payments as an expense. For a capital lease, the lessee records the asset and related obligation at the present value of the future lease payments.

***5 Apply the straight-line method of amortizing bond discount and bond premium.** The straight-line method of amortization results in a constant amount of amortization and interest expense per period.

***6 Apply the effective-interest method of amortizing bond discount and bond premium.** The effective-interest method results in varying amounts of amortization and interest expense per period but a constant percentage rate of interest. When the difference between the straight-line and effective-interest method is material, GAAP requires use of the effective-interest method.

GLOSSARY REVIEW

Bond certificate A legal document that indicates the name of the issuer, the face value of the bonds, the contractual interest rate, and maturity date of the bonds. (p. 646).

Bond indenture A legal document that sets forth the terms of the bond issue. (p. 646).

Bonds A form of interest-bearing notes payable issued by corporations, universities, and governmental entities. (p. 646).

Callable bonds Bonds that are subject to redemption (buy back) at a stated dollar amount prior to maturity at the option of the issuer. (p. 646).

Capital lease A contractual arrangement that transfers substantially all the benefits and risks of ownership to the lessee so that the lease is in effect a purchase of the property. (p. 660).

Contractual interest rate Rate used to determine the amount of cash interest the borrower pays and the investor receives. (p. 646).

Convertible bonds Bonds that permit bondholders to convert them into common stock at the bondholders' option. (p. 646).

Debenture bonds Bonds issued against the general credit of the borrower. Also called unsecured bonds. (p. 646).

Debt to assets ratio A solvency measure that indicates the percentage of total assets provided by creditors; computed as total liabilities divided by total assets. (p. 658).

Discount (on a bond) The difference between the face value of a bond and its selling price, when the bond is sold for less than its face value. (p. 650).

***Effective-interest method of amortization** Amortization of bond discount or bond premium which results in periodic interest expense equal to a constant percentage of the carrying value of the bonds. (p. 664).

***Effective-interest rate** Rate established when bonds are issued that maintains a constant value for interest expense as a percentage of bond carrying value in each interest period. (p. 664).

Face value Amount of principal due at the maturity date of the bond. (p. 646).

Long-term liabilities Obligations expected to be paid more than one year in the future. (p. 646).

Market interest rate The rate investors demand for loaning funds to the corporation. (p. 647).

Maturity date The date on which the final payment on the bond is due from the bond issuer to the investor. (p. 646).

Mortgage bond A bond secured by real estate. (p. 646).

Mortgage notes payable A long-term note secured by a mortgage that pledges title to specific assets as security for a loan. (p. 656).

Operating lease A contractual arrangement giving the lessee temporary use of the property, with continued ownership of the property by the lessor. (p. 660).

Premium (on a bond) The difference between the selling price and the face value of a bond, when the bond is sold for more than its face value. (p. 650).

Secured bonds Bonds that have specific assets of the issuer pledged as collateral. (p. 646).

Sinking fund bonds Bonds secured by specific assets set aside to redeem them. (p. 646).

***Straight-line method of amortization** Allocates the same amount to interest expense in each interest period. (p. 662).

Times interest earned A solvency measure that indicates a company's ability to meet interest payments; computed by dividing the sum of net income, interest expense, and income tax expense by interest expense. (p. 658).

Time value of money The relationship between time and money. A dollar received today is worth more than a dollar promised at some time in the future. (p. 647).

Unsecured bonds Bonds issued against the general credit of the borrower. Also called debenture bonds. (p. 646).

PRACTICE MULTIPLE-CHOICE QUESTIONS

(LO 1) **1.** The term used for bonds that are unsecured is:
(a) callable bonds. (c) debenture bonds.
(b) U.S. Treasury bonds. (d) convertible bonds.

(LO 1) **2.** The market interest rate:
(a) is the contractual interest rate used to determine the amount of cash interest paid by the borrower.
(b) is listed in the bond indenture.
(c) is the rate investors demand for loaning funds.
(d) More than one of the above is true.

(LO 2) **3.** Karson Inc. issues 10-year bonds with a maturity value of $200,000. If the bonds are issued at a premium, this indicates that:
(a) the contractual interest rate exceeds the market interest rate.
(b) the market interest rate exceeds the contractual interest rate.
(c) the contractual interest rate and the market interest rate are the same.
(d) no relationship exists between the two rates.

4. Four-Nine Corporation issued bonds that pay interest every January 1. The entry to accrue bond interest at December 31 includes a: (LO 2)
(a) debit to Interest Payable.
(b) credit to Cash.

(c) credit to Interest Expense.
(d) credit to Interest Payable.

(LO 2) 5. Gester Corporation redeems its $100,000 face value bonds at 105 on January 1, following the payment of annual interest. The carrying value of the bonds at the redemption date is $103,745. The entry to record the redemption will include a:
(a) credit of $3,745 to Loss on Bond Redemption.
(b) debit of $3,745 to Premium on Bonds Payable.
(c) credit of $1,255 to Gain on Bond Redemption.
(d) debit of $5,000 to Premium on Bonds Payable.

(LO 2) 6. Colson Inc. converts $600,000 of bonds sold at face value into 10,000 shares of common stock, par value $1. Both the bonds and the stock have a market value of $760,000. What amount should be credited to Paid-in Capital in Excess of Par—Common Stock as a result of the conversion?
(a) $10,000. (c) $600,000.
(b) $160,000. (d) $590,000.

(LO 3) 7. Howard Corporation issued a 20-year mortgage note payable on January 1, 2017. At December 31, 2017, the unpaid principal balance will be reported as:
(a) a current liability.
(b) a long-term liability.
(c) part current and part long-term liability.
(d) interest payable.

(LO 3) 8. Andrews Inc. issues a $497,000, 10% 3-year mortgage note on January 1. The note will be paid in three annual installments of $200,000, each payable at the end of the year. What is the amount of interest expense that should be recognized by Andrews Inc. in the second year?
(a) $16,567. (c) $34,670.
(b) $49,700. (d) $346,700.

(LO 4) 9. For 2017, Corn Flake Corporation reported net income of $300,000. Interest expense was $40,000 and income taxes were $100,000. The times interest earned was:
(a) 3 times. (c) 7.5 times.
(b) 4.4 times. (d) 11 times.

(LO 4) 10. Lease A does not contain a bargain purchase option, but the lease term is equal to 90% of the estimated economic life of the leased property. Lease B does not transfer ownership of the property to the lessee by the end of the lease term, but the lease term is equal to 75% of the estimated economic life of the leased property. How should the lessee classify these leases?

	Lease A	Lease B
(a)	Operating lease	Capital lease
(b)	Operating lease	Operating lease
(c)	Capital lease	Operating lease
(d)	Capital lease	Capital lease

*11. On December 31, Hurley Corporation issues $500,000, 5-year, 12% bonds at 96 with interest payable on December 31, 2017. The entry on December 31, 2018, to record payment of bond interest and the amortization of bond discount using the straight-line method will include a: (LO 5)
(a) debit to Interest Expense $30,000.
(b) debit to Interest Expense $60,000.
(c) credit to Discount on Bonds Payable $4,000.
(d) credit to Discount on Bonds Payable $2,000.

*12. For the bonds issued in Question 11, what is the carrying value of the bonds at the end of the third interest period? (LO 5)
(a) $492,000. (c) $486,000.
(b) $488,000. (d) $464,000.

*13. On January 1, Besalius Inc. issued $1,000,000, 9% bonds for $938,554. The market rate of interest for these bonds is 10%. Interest is payable annually on December 31. Besalius uses the effective-interest method of amortizing bond discount. At the end of the first year, Besalius should report unamortized bond discount of: (LO 6)
(a) $54,900. (c) $51,610.
(b) $57,591. (d) $51,000.

*14. On December 31, Dias Corporation issued $1,000,000, 14%, 5-year bonds with interest payable annually on December 31. The bonds sold for $1,072,096. The market rate of interest for these bonds was 12%. On the first interest date, using the effective-interest method, the debit entry to Interest Expense is for: (LO 6)
(a) $120,000. (c) $128,652.
(b) $125,581. (d) $140,000.

Solutions

1. (c) Debenture bonds are not secured by any collateral. The other choices are incorrect because (a) callable bonds can be paid off or retired by the issuer before they reach their maturity date, (b) U.S. Treasury bonds are secured by the federal government, and (d) convertible bonds permit bondholders to convert them into common stock at the bondholders' option.

2. (c) Market interest rate is the rate investors demand for loaning funds. The other choices are incorrect because (a) market interest rate is the same as contractual interest rate only if bonds sell at face value (par value) and (b) the contractual interest rate, not the market interest rate, is listed in the bond indenture. Choice (d) is wrong as there is only one correct answer.

3. (a) When bonds are issued at a premium, this indicates that the contractual interest rate is higher than the market interest rate. The other choices are incorrect because (b) when the market interest rate exceeds the contractual interest rate, bonds are sold at a discount; (c) when the contractual interest rate and the market interest rate are the same, bonds will be issued at par; and (d) the relationship between the market rate of interest and the contractual rate of interest determines whether bonds are issued at par, a discount, or a premium.

4. (d) The adjusting entry to accrue bond interest at December 31 includes a debit to Interest Expense and credit to Interest Payable. The other choices are therefore incorrect.

5. (b) The entry to record the retirement of bonds will include a debit to Bonds Payable of $100,000, a debit to Premium on Bonds Payable of $3,745 ($103,745 − $100,000), a credit to Cash of $105,000 ($100,000 × 1.05) and a debit to Loss on Bond Redemption of $1,255 ($105,000 − $103,745). The other choices are therefore incorrect.

6. (d) First, the market value in this transaction is ignored. Bonds Payable will be debited for $600,000; Common Stock will be credited for $10,000 since this account is always credited for shares issued (10,000) times par value ($1). The remaining amount, $590,000 ($600,000 − $10,000) is credited to Paid-in Capital in Excess of Par–Common Stock, not (a) $10,000, (b) $160,000, or (c) $600,000.

7. (c) Howard Corporation reports the reduction in principal for the next year as a current liability, and it classifies the remaining unpaid principal balance as a long-term liability. The other choices are therefore incorrect.

8. (c) In the first year, Andrews will recognize $49,700 of interest expense ($497,000 × 10%). After the first payment is made, the amount remaining on the note will be $346,700 [$497,000 principal − ($200,000 payment − $49,700 interest)]. The remaining balance ($346,700) is multiplied by the interest rate (10%) to compute the interest expense to be recognized for the second year, $34,670 ($346,700 × 10%), not (a) $16,567, (b) $49,700, or (d) $346,700.

9. (d) Times interest earned = Net income + Interest expense + Income tax expense ($300,000 + $40,000 + $100,000 = $440,000) divided by Interest expense ($40,000), which equals 11 times, not (a) 3, (b) 4.4, or (c) 7.5 times.

10. (d) Both leases should be classified as capital leases because both lease terms are greater than or equal to 75% of the economic life of the respective assets. The other choices are therefore incorrect.

***11. (c)** [$500,000 − (96% × $500,000)] = $20,000; $20,000 ÷ 5 = $4,000 of discount to amortize annually. As a result, the entry would involve a credit to Discount on Bonds Payable $4,000. The other choices are therefore incorrect.

***12. (a)** The carrying value of bonds increases by the amount of the periodic discount amortization. Discount amortization using the straight-line method is $4,000 each period. Total discount amortization for three periods is $12,000 ($4,000 × 3 periods) which is added to the initial carrying value ($480,000) to arrive at $492,000, the carrying value at the end of the third interest period, not (b) $488,000, (c) $486,000, or (d) $464,000.

***13. (b)** The beginning balance of unamortized discount is $61,446 ($1,000,000 − $938,554). The discount amortization is $3,855, the difference between the cash interest payment of $90,000 ($1,000,000 × 9%) and the interest expense recorded of $93,855 ($938,554 × 10%). This discount amortization ($3,855) is then subtracted from the beginning balance of unamortized discount ($61,446), to arrive at a balance of $57,591 at the end of the first year, not (a) $54,900, (c) $51,610, or (d) $51,000.

***14. (c)** The debit to Interest Expense = $1,072,096 (initial carrying value of bond) × 12% (market rate) = $128,652, not (a) $120,000, (b) $125,581, or (d) $140,000.

PRACTICE EXERCISES

Prepare entries for bonds issued at face value.
(LO 2)

1. North Airlines Company issued $900,000 of 8%, 10-year bonds on January 1, 2017, at face value. Interest is payable annually on January 1.

Instructions

Prepare the journal entries to record the following events.

(a) The issuance of the bonds.

(b) The accrual of interest on December 31.

(c) The payment of interest on January 1, 2018.

(d) The redemption of bonds at maturity, assuming interest for the last interest period has been paid and recorded.

Solution

1. (a)	**January 1, 2017**		
	Cash	900,000	
	Bonds Payable		900,000
(b)	**December 31, 2017**		
	Interest Expense	72,000	
	Interest Payable ($900,000 × 8%)		72,000
(c)	**January 1, 2018**		
	Interest Payable	72,000	
	Cash		72,000
(d)	**January 1, 2027**		
	Bonds Payable	900,000	
	Cash		900,000

2. Hollenbeck Company issued $3,000,000 of bonds on January 1, 2017.

Prepare entries for issuance, retirement, and conversion of bonds.

(LO 2)

Instructions

(a) Prepare the journal entry to record the issuance of the bonds if they are issued at (1) 100, (2) 98, and (3) 103.

(b) Prepare the journal entry to record the retirement of the bonds at maturity, assuming the bonds were issued at 100.

(c) Prepare the journal entry to record the retirement of the bonds before maturity at 98. Assume the balance in Premium on Bonds Payable is $18,000.

(d) Prepare the journal entry to record the conversion of the bonds into 70,000 shares of $1 par value common stock. Assume the bonds were issued at par.

Solution

At 100		
2. (a) (1) Cash ($3,000,000 × 100%)	3,000,000	
Bonds Payable		3,000,000
At 98		
(2) Cash ($3,000,000 × 98%)	2,940,000	
Discount on Bonds Payable	60,000	
Bonds Payable		3,000,000
At 103		
(3) Cash ($3,000,000 × 103%)	3,090,000	
Bonds Payable		3,000,000
Premium on Bonds Payable		90,000
(b) Bonds Payable	3,000,000	
Cash		3,000,000
(c) Bonds Payable	3,000,000	
Premium on Bonds Payable	18,000	
Cash ($3,000,000 × 98%)		2,940,000
Gain on Bond Redemption		78,000
(d) Bonds Payable	3,000,000	
Common Stock (70,000 × $1)		70,000
Paid-in Capital in Excess of Par—Common Stock		2,930,000

3. Clipper Company borrowed $500,000 on December 31, 2017, by issuing a $500,000, 7% mortgage note payable. The terms call for annual installment payments of $80,000 on December 31.

Prepare entries to record mortgage note and installment payments.

(LO 3)

Instructions

(a) Prepare the journal entries to record the mortgage loan and the first two installment payments.

(b) Indicate the amount of mortgage note payable to be reported as a current liability and as a long-term liability at December 31, 2018.

Solution

3. (a) **December 31, 2017**		
Cash	500,000	
Mortgage Payable		500,000
December 31, 2018		
Interest Expense ($500,000 × 7%)	35,000	
Mortgage Payable	45,000	
Cash		80,000
December 31, 2019		
Interest Expense [($500,000 − $45,000) × 7%]	31,850	
Mortgage Payable	48,150	
Cash		80,000

(b) Current: $48,150
Long-term: $406,850 ($500,000 − $45,000 − $48,150)

PRACTICE PROBLEM

Prepare entries to record issuance of bonds and long-term notes, interest accrual, and bond redemption.

(LO 1, 2, 3)

Snyder Software Inc. has successfully developed a new spreadsheet program. To produce and market the program, the company needed $1.9 million of additional financing. On January 1, 2017, Snyder borrowed money as follows.

1. Snyder issued $500,000, 11%, 10-year convertible bonds. The bonds sold at face value and pay annual interest on January 1. Each $1,000 bond is convertible into 30 shares of Snyder's $20 par value common stock.
2. Snyder issued $1 million, 10%, 10-year bonds at face value. Interest is payable on January 1.
3. Snyder also issued a $400,000, 6%, 15-year mortgage payable. The terms provide for annual installment payments of $41,185 on December 31.

Instructions

1. For the convertible bonds, prepare journal entries for:
   (a) The issuance of the bonds on January 1, 2017.
   (b) Interest expense on December 31, 2017.
   (c) The payment of interest on January 1, 2018.
   (d) The conversion of all bonds into common stock on January 1, 2018, when the market price of the common stock was $67 per share.
2. For the 10-year, 10% bonds:
   (a) Journalize the issuance of the bonds on January 1, 2017.
   (b) Prepare the journal entry for interest expense in 2017.
   (c) Prepare the entry for the redemption of the bonds at 101 on January 1, 2020, after paying the interest due on this date.
3. For the mortgage payable:
   (a) Prepare the entry for the issuance of the note on January 1, 2017.
   (b) Prepare a payment schedule for the first four installment payments.
   (c) Indicate the current and noncurrent amounts for the mortgage payable at December 31, 2017.

Solution

1. (a)	**2017**			
	Jan. 1	Cash	500,000	
		Bonds Payable		500,000
		(To record issue of 11%, 10-year convertible bonds at face value)		
(b)	Dec. 31	Interest Expense	55,000	
		Interest Payable ($500,000 × 11%)		55,000
		(To record accrual of annual bond interest)		
(c)	**2018**			
	Jan. 1	Interest Payable	55,000	
		Cash		55,000
		(To record payment of accrued interest)		
(d)	Jan. 1	Bonds Payable	500,000	
		Common Stock		300,000*
		Paid-in Capital in Excess of Par—Common Stock		200,000
		(To record conversion of bonds into common stock)		

*($500,000 ÷ $1,000 = 500 bonds; 500 × 30 = 15,000 shares; 15,000 × $20 = $300,000)

2. (a)	**2017**			
	Jan. 1	Cash	1,000,000	
		Bonds Payable		1,000,000
		(To record issuance of bonds)		

(b) **2017**

		Debit	Credit
Dec. 31	Interest Expense	100,000	
	Interest Payable ($1,000,000 × 10%)		100,000
	(To record accrual of annual interest)		

(c) **2020**

		Debit	Credit
Jan. 1	Bonds Payable	1,000,000	
	Loss on Bond Redemption	10,000*	
	Cash		1,010,000
	(To record redemption of bonds at 101)		

*($1,010,000 − $1,000,000)

3. (a) **2017**

		Debit	Credit
Jan. 1	Cash	400,000	
	Mortgage Payable		400,000
	(To record issuance of mortgage payable)		

(b)

Interest Period	Cash Payment	Interest Expense	Reduction of Principal	Principal Balance
Issue date				$400,000
1	$41,185	$24,000	$17,185	382,815
2	41,185	22,969	18,216	364,599
3	41,185	21,876	19,309	345,290
4	41,185	20,717	20,468	324,822

(c) Current liability: $18,216
Long-term liability: $364,599

WileyPLUS Brief Exercises, Exercises, DO IT! Exercises, and Problems and many additional resources are available for practice in WileyPLUS

NOTE: All asterisked Questions, Exercises, and Problems relate to material in the appendices to the chapter.

QUESTIONS

1. (a) What are long-term liabilities? Give three examples. (b) What is a bond?
2. Contrast the following types of bonds: (a) secured and unsecured, and (b) convertible and callable.
3. The following terms are important in issuing bonds: (a) face value, (b) contractual interest rate, (c) bond indenture, and (d) bond certificate. Explain each of these terms.
4. Describe the two major obligations incurred by a company when bonds are issued.
5. Assume that Remington Inc. sold bonds with a face value of $100,000 for $104,000. Was the market interest rate equal to, less than, or greater than the bonds' contractual interest rate? Explain.
6. If a 7%, 10-year, $800,000 bond is issued at face value and interest is paid annually, what is the amount of the interest payment at the end of the first year period?
7. If the Bonds Payable account has a balance of $900,000 and the Discount on Bonds Payable account has a balance of $120,000, what is the carrying value of the bonds?
8. Which accounts are debited and which are credited if a bond issue originally sold at a premium is redeemed before maturity at 97 immediately following the payment of interest?
9. Rattigan Corporation is considering issuing a convertible bond. What is a convertible bond? Discuss the advantages of a convertible bond from the standpoint of (a) the bondholders and (b) the issuing corporation.
10. Rob Grier, a friend of yours, has recently purchased a home for $125,000, paying $25,000 down and the remainder financed by a 10.5%, 20-year mortgage, payable at $998.38 per month. At the end of the first month, Rob receives a statement from the bank indicating that only $123.38 of principal was paid during the month. At this rate, he calculates that it will take over 67 years to pay off the mortgage. Is he right? Discuss.
11. In general, what are the requirements for the financial statement presentation of long-term liabilities?
12. (a) As a source of long-term financing, what are the major advantages of bonds over common stock? (b) What are the major disadvantages in using bonds for long-term financing?
13. (a) What is a lease agreement? (b) What are the two most common types of leases? (c) Distinguish between the two types of leases.

14. Jhutti Company rents a warehouse on a month-to-month basis for the storage of its excess inventory. The company periodically must rent space when its production greatly exceeds actual sales. What is the nature of this type of lease agreement and what accounting treatment should be used?

15. Benedict Company entered into an agreement to lease 12 computers from Haley Electronics, Inc. The present value of the lease payments is $186,300. Assuming that this is a capital lease, what entry would Benedict Company make on the date of the lease agreement?

16. Did Apple redeem any of its debt during the fiscal year ended September 28, 2013? (*Hint:* Examine Apple's statement of cash flows.)

***17.** Explain the straight-line method of amortizing discount and premium on bonds payable.

***18.** DeWeese Corporation issues $400,000 of 8%, 5-year bonds on January 1, 2017, at 105. Assuming that the straight-line method is used to amortize the premium, what is the total amount of interest expense for 2017?

***19.** Kelli Deane is discussing the advantages of the effective-interest method of bond amortization with her accounting staff. What do you think Kelli is saying?

***20.** Windsor Corporation issues $500,000 of 9%, 5-year bonds on January 1, 2017, at 104. If Windsor uses the effective-interest method in amortizing the premium, will the annual interest expense increase or decrease over the life of the bonds? Explain.

BRIEF EXERCISES

Prepare entry for bonds issued.
(LO 2)

BE15-1 Randle Inc. issues $300,000, 10-year, 8% bonds at 98. Prepare the journal entry to record the sale of these bonds on March 1, 2017.

Prepare entry for bonds issued.
(LO 2)

BE15-2 Price Company issues $400,000, 20-year, 7% bonds at 101. Prepare the journal entry to record the sale of these bonds on June 1, 2017.

Prepare entries for bonds issued at face value.
(LO 2)

BE15-3 Meera Corporation issued 4,000, 8%, 5-year, $1,000 bonds dated January 1, 2017, at 100. Interest is paid each January 1.

(a) Prepare the journal entry to record the sale of these bonds on January 1, 2017.
(b) Prepare the adjusting journal entry on December 31, 2017, to record interest expense.
(c) Prepare the journal entry on January 1, 2018, to record interest paid.

Prepare entries for bonds sold at a discount and a premium.
(LO 2)

BE15-4 Nasreen Company issues $2 million, 10-year, 8% bonds at 97, with interest payable each January 1.

(a) Prepare the journal entry to record the sale of these bonds on January 1, 2017.
(b) Assuming instead that the above bonds sold for 104, prepare the journal entry to record the sale of these bonds on January 1, 2017.

Prepare entries for bonds issued.
(LO 2)

BE15-5 Frankum Company has issued three different bonds during 2017. Interest is payable annually on each of these bonds.

1. On January 1, 2017, 1,000, 8%, 5-year, $1,000 bonds dated January 1, 2017, were issued at face value.
2. On July 1, $900,000, 9%, 5-year bonds dated July 1, 2017, were issued at 102.
3. On September 1, $400,000, 7%, 5-year bonds dated September 1, 2017, were issued at 98.

Prepare the journal entry to record each bond transaction at the date of issuance.

Prepare entry for redemption of bonds.
(LO 2)

BE15-6 The balance sheet for Miley Consulting reports the following information on July 1, 2017.

Long-term liabilities		
Bonds payable	$1,000,000	
Less: Discount on bonds payable	60,000	$940,000

Miley decides to redeem these bonds at 101 after paying annual interest. Prepare the journal entry to record the redemption on July 1, 2017.

Prepare entries for long-term notes payable.
(LO 3)

BE15-7 Hanschu Inc. issues an $800,000, 10%, 10-year mortgage note on December 31, 2017, to obtain financing for a new building. The terms provide for annual installment payments of $130,196. Prepare the entry to record the mortgage loan on December 31, 2017, and the first installment payment on December 31, 2018.

BE15-8 Presented below are long-term liability items for Lind Company at December 31, 2017. Prepare the long-term liabilities section of the balance sheet for Lind Company.

Prepare statement presentation of long-term liabilities.

(LO 4)

Bonds payable, due 2019	$600,000
Lease liability	70,000
Notes payable, due 2022	80,000
Discount on bonds payable	45,000

BE15-9 Moby Inc. is considering two alternatives to finance its construction of a new $2 million plant.

Compare bond versus stock financing.

(LO 4)

(a) Issuance of 200,000 shares of common stock at the market price of $10 per share.
(b) Issuance of $2 million, 8% bonds at face value.

Complete the following table, and indicate which alternative is preferable.

	Issue Stock	Issue Bond
Income before interest and taxes	$700,000	$700,000
Interest expense from bonds	______	______
Income before income taxes		
Income tax expense (30%)	______	______
Net income	$	$
Outstanding shares		500,000
Earnings per share	______	______

BE15-10 Prepare the journal entries that the lessee should make to record the following transactions.

Contrast accounting for operating and capital leases.

(LO 4)

1. The lessee makes a lease payment of $80,000 to the lessor in an operating lease transaction.
2. Imhoff Company leases a new building from Noble Construction, Inc. The present value of the lease payments is $700,000. The lease qualifies as a capital lease.

***BE15-11** Sweetwood Company issues $5 million, 10-year, 9% bonds at 96, with interest payable annually on January 1. The straight-line method is used to amortize bond discount.

Prepare entries for bonds issued at a discount.

(LO 5)

(a) Prepare the journal entry to record the sale of these bonds on January 1, 2017.
(b) Prepare the adjusting journal entry to record interest expense and bond discount amortization on December 31, 2017.

***BE15-12** Golden Inc. issues $4 million, 5-year, 10% bonds at 102, with interest payable annually on January 1. The straight-line method is used to amortize bond premium.

Prepare entries for bonds issued at a premium.

(LO 5)

(a) Prepare the journal entry to record the sale of these bonds on January 1, 2017.
(b) Prepare the adjusting journal entry to record interest expense and bond premium amortization on December 31, 2017.

***BE15-13** Presented below is the partial bond discount amortization schedule for Gomez Corp. Gomez uses the effective-interest method of amortization.

Use effective-interest method of bond amortization.

(LO 2, 6)

Interest Periods	Interest to Be Paid	Interest Expense to Be Recorded	Discount Amortization	Unamortized Discount	Bond Carrying Value
Issue date				$38,609	$961,391
1	$45,000	$48,070	$3,070	35,539	964,461
2	45,000	48,223	3,223	32,316	967,684

(a) Prepare the journal entry to record the payment of interest and the discount amortization at the end of period 1.
(b) Explain why interest expense is greater than interest paid.
(c) Explain why interest expense will increase each period.

DO IT! Exercises

Evaluate statements about bonds.
(LO 1)

DO IT! 15-1 State whether each of the following statements is true or false.

_____ 1. Mortgage bonds and sinking fund bonds are both examples of debenture bonds.
_____ 2. Convertible bonds are also known as callable bonds.
_____ 3. The market rate is the rate investors demand for loaning funds.
_____ 4. Annual interest on bonds is equal to the face value times the stated rate.
_____ 5. The present value of a bond is the value at which it should sell in the market.

Prepare journal entry for bond issuance and show balance sheet presentation.
(LO 2)

DO IT! 15-2a Eubank Corporation issues $500,000 of bonds for $520,000. (a) Prepare the journal entry to record the issuance of the bonds, and (b) show how the bonds would be reported on the balance sheet at the date of issuance.

Prepare entry for bond redemption.
(LO 2)

DO IT! 15-2b Prater Corporation issued $400,000 of 10-year bonds at a discount. Prior to maturity, when the carrying value of the bonds was $390,000, the company redeemed the bonds at 99. Prepare the entry to record the redemption of the bonds.

Prepare entries for mortgage note and installment payment on note.
(LO 3)

DO IT! 15-3 Detwiler Orchard issues a $700,000, 6%, 15-year mortgage note to obtain needed financing for a new lab. The terms call for annual payments of $72,074 each. Prepare the entries to record the mortgage loan and the first installment payment.

Prepare entry for lease, and compute debt to assets ratio.
(LO 4)

DO IT! 15-4 Huebner Corporation leases new equipment on December 31, 2017. The lease transfers ownership of the equipment to Huebner at the end of the lease. The present value of the lease payments is $192,000. After recording this lease, Huebner has assets of $1,800,000, liabilities of $1,100,000, and stockholders' equity of $700,000. (a) Prepare the entry to record the lease, and (b) compute and discuss the debt to assets ratio at year-end.

EXERCISES

Evaluate statements about bonds.
(LO 1)

E15-1 Nick Bosch has prepared the following list of statements about bonds.

1. Bonds are a form of interest-bearing notes payable.
2. Secured bonds have specific assets of the issuer pledged as collateral for the bonds.
3. Secured bonds are also known as debenture bonds.
4. A conversion feature may be added to bonds to make them more attractive to bond buyers.
5. The rate used to determine the amount of cash interest the borrower pays is called the stated rate.
6. Bond prices are usually quoted as a percentage of the face value of the bond.
7. The present value of a bond is the value at which it should sell in the marketplace.

Instructions
Identify each statement as true or false. If false, indicate how to correct the statement.

Prepare entries for issuance of bonds, and payment and accrual of bond interest.
(LO 2)

E15-2 On January 1, 2017, Klosterman Company issued $500,000, 10%, 10-year bonds at face value. Interest is payable annually on January 1.

Instructions
Prepare journal entries to record the following.

(a) The issuance of the bonds.
(b) The accrual of interest on December 31, 2017.
(c) The payment of interest on January 1, 2018.

Prepare entries for bonds issued at face value.
(LO 2)

E15-3 On January 1, 2017, Forrester Company issued $400,000, 8%, 5-year bonds at face value. Interest is payable annually on January 1.

Instructions
Prepare journal entries to record the following.

(a) The issuance of the bonds.
(b) The accrual of interest on December 31, 2017.
(c) The payment of interest on January 1, 2018.

E15-4 Laudie Company issued $400,000 of 9%, 10-year bonds on January 1, 2017, at face value. Interest is payable annually on January 1, 2018.

Prepare entries for bonds issued at face value.

(LO 2)

Instructions

Prepare the journal entries to record the following events.

(a) The issuance of the bonds.
(b) The accrual of interest on December 31, 2017.
(c) The payment of interest on January 1, 2018.
(d) The redemption of bonds at maturity, assuming interest for the last interest period has been paid and recorded.

E15-5 Swisher Company issued $2,000,000 of bonds on January 1, 2017.

Prepare entries for issuance, redemption, and conversion of bonds.

(LO 2)

Instructions

(a) Prepare the journal entry to record the issuance of the bonds if they are issued at (1) 100, (2) 98, and (3) 103.
(b) Prepare the journal entry to record the redemption of the bonds at maturity, assuming the bonds were issued at 100.
(c) Prepare the journal entry to record the redemption of the bonds before maturity at 98. Assume the balance in Premium on Bonds Payable is $9,000.
(d) Prepare the journal entry to record the conversion of the bonds into 60,000 shares of $10 par value common stock. Assume the bonds were issued at par.

E15-6 Whitmore Company issued $500,000 of 5-year, 8% bonds at 97 on January 1, 2017. The bonds pay interest annually.

Prepare entries to record issuance of bonds at discount and premium.

(LO 2)

Instructions

(a) (1) Prepare the journal entry to record the issuance of the bonds.
    (2) Compute the total cost of borrowing for these bonds.
(b) Repeat the requirements from part (a), assuming the bonds were issued at 105.

E15-7 The following section is taken from Ohlman Corp.'s balance sheet at December 31, 2016.

Prepare entries for bond interest and redemption.

(LO 2)

Current liabilities	
Interest payable	$ 112,000
Long-term liabilities	
Bonds payable, 7%, due January 1, 2021	1,600,000

Bond interest is payable annually on January 1. The bonds are callable on any interest date.

Instructions

(a) Journalize the payment of the bond interest on January 1, 2017.
(b) Assume that on January 1, 2017, after paying interest, Ohlman calls bonds having a face value of $600,000. The call price is 103. Record the redemption of the bonds.
(c) Prepare the entry to record the accrual of interest on December 31, 2017.

E15-8 Presented below and on page 678 are three independent situations.

Prepare entries for redemption of bonds and conversion of bonds into common stock.

(LO 2)

1. Longbine Corporation redeemed $130,000 face value, 12% bonds on June 30, 2017, at 102. The carrying value of the bonds at the redemption date was $117,500. The bonds pay annual interest, and the interest payment due on June 30, 2017, has been made and recorded.
2. Tastove Inc. redeemed $150,000 face value, 12.5% bonds on June 30, 2017, at 98. The carrying value of the bonds at the redemption date was $151,000. The bonds pay annual interest, and the interest payment due on June 30, 2017, has been made and recorded.
3. Precision Company has $80,000, 8%, 12-year convertible bonds outstanding. These bonds were sold at face value and pay annual interest on December 31 of each year. The bonds are convertible into 30 shares of Precision $5 par value common stock for each

$1,000 worth of bonds. On December 31, 2017, after the bond interest has been paid, $20,000 face value bonds were converted. The market price of Precision common stock was $44 per share on December 31, 2017.

Instructions
For each independent situation above, prepare the appropriate journal entry for the redemption or conversion of the bonds.

Prepare entries to record mortgage note and payments.
(LO 3)

E15-9 Jernigan Co. receives $300,000 when it issues a $300,000, 10%, mortgage note payable to finance the construction of a building at December 31, 2017. The terms provide for annual installment payments of $50,000 on December 31.

Instructions
Prepare the journal entries to record the mortgage loan and the first two payments.

Prepare entries to record mortgage note and installment payments.
(LO 3)

E15-10 Dreiling Company borrowed $300,000 on January 1, 2017, by issuing a $300,000, 8% mortgage note payable. The terms call for annual installment payments of $40,000 on December 31.

Instructions
(a) Prepare the journal entries to record the mortgage loan and the first two installment payments.
(b) Indicate the amount of mortgage note payable to be reported as a current liability and as a long-term liability at December 31, 2017.

Prepare long-term liabilities section.
(LO 4)

E15-11 The adjusted trial balance for Karr Farm Corporation at the end of the current year contained the following accounts.

Interest Payable	$ 9,000
Lease Liability	89,500
Bonds Payable, due 2022	180,000
Premium on Bonds Payable	32,000

Instructions
Prepare the long-term liabilities section of the balance sheet.

Compare two alternatives of financing—issuance of common stock vs. issuance of bonds.
(LO 4)

E15-12 Gilliland Airlines is considering two alternatives for the financing of a purchase of a fleet of airplanes. These two alternatives are:

1. Issue 90,000 shares of common stock at $30 per share. (Cash dividends have not been paid nor is the payment of any contemplated.)
2. Issue 10%, 10-year bonds at face value for $2,700,000.

It is estimated that the company will earn $800,000 before interest and taxes as a result of this purchase. The company has an estimated tax rate of 30% and has 120,000 shares of common stock outstanding prior to the new financing.

Instructions
Determine the effect on net income and earnings per share for these two methods of financing.

Compute debt to assets ratio and times interest earned.
(LO 4)

E15-13 Hatfield Corporation reports the following amounts in its 2017 financial statements:

	At December 31, 2017	For the Year 2017
Total assets	$1,000,000	
Total liabilities	580,000	
Total stockholders' equity	?	
Interest expense		$ 20,000
Income tax expense		100,000
Net income		150,000

Instructions
(a) Compute the December 31, 2017, balance in stockholders' equity.
(b) Compute the debt to assets ratio at December 31, 2017.
(c) Compute times interest earned for 2017.

E15-14 Presented below are two independent situations.

Prepare entries for operating lease and capital lease.

(LO 4)

1. Flinthills Car Rental leased a car to Jayhawk Company for one year. Terms of the operating lease agreement call for monthly payments of $500.
2. On January 1, 2017, Throm Inc. entered into an agreement to lease 20 computers from Drummond Electronics. The terms of the lease agreement require three annual rental payments of $20,000 (including 10% interest) beginning December 31, 2017. The present value of the three rental payments is $49,735. Throm considers this a capital lease.

Instructions

(a) Prepare the appropriate journal entry to be made by Jayhawk Company for the first lease payment.
(b) Prepare the journal entry to record the lease agreement on the books of Throm Inc. on January 1, 2017.

***E15-15** Adcock Company issued $600,000, 9%, 20-year bonds on January 1, 2017, at 103. Interest is payable annually on January 1. Adcock uses straight-line amortization for bond premium or discount.

Prepare entries to record issuance of bonds, payment of interest, amortization of premium, and redemption at maturity.

(LO 5)

Instructions

Prepare the journal entries to record the following.

(a) The issuance of the bonds.
(b) The accrual of interest and the premium amortization on December 31, 2017.
(c) The payment of interest on January 1, 2018.
(d) The redemption of the bonds at maturity, assuming interest for the last interest period has been paid and recorded.

***E15-16** Gridley Company issued $800,000, 11%, 10-year bonds on December 31, 2016, for $730,000. Interest is payable annually on December 31. Gridley Company uses the straight-line method to amortize bond premium or discount.

Prepare entries to record issuance of bonds, payment of interest, amortization of discount, and redemption at maturity.

(LO 5)

Instructions

Prepare the journal entries to record the following.

(a) The issuance of the bonds.
(b) The payment of interest and the discount amortization on December 31, 2017.
(c) The redemption of the bonds at maturity, assuming interest for the last interest period has been paid and recorded.

***E15-17** Lorance Corporation issued $400,000, 7%, 20-year bonds on January 1, 2017, for $360,727. This price resulted in an effective-interest rate of 8% on the bonds. Interest is payable annually on January 1. Lorance uses the effective-interest method to amortize bond premium or discount.

Prepare entries for issuance of bonds, payment of interest, and amortization of discount using effective-interest method.

(LO 6)

Instructions

Prepare the journal entries to record the following. (Round to the nearest dollar.)

(a) The issuance of the bonds.
(b) The accrual of interest and the discount amortization on December 31, 2017.
(c) The payment of interest on January 1, 2018.

***E15-18** LRNA Company issued $380,000, 7%, 10-year bonds on January 1, 2017, for $407,968. This price resulted in an effective-interest rate of 6% on the bonds. Interest is payable annually on January 1. LRNA uses the effective-interest method to amortize bond premium or discount.

Prepare entries for issuance of bonds, payment of interest, and amortization of premium using effective-interest method.

(LO 6)

Instructions

Prepare the journal entries to record the following. (Round to the nearest dollar.)

(a) The issuance of the bonds.
(b) The accrual of interest and the premium amortization on December 31, 2017.
(c) The payment of interest on January 1, 2018.

EXERCISES: SET B AND CHALLENGE EXERCISES

Visit the book's companion website, at **www.wiley.com/college/weygandt**, and choose the Student Companion site to access Exercises: Set B and Challenge Exercises.

PROBLEMS: SET A

Prepare entries to record issuance of bonds, interest accrual, and bond redemption.

(LO 2, 4)

P15-1A On May 1, 2017, Herron Corp. issued $600,000, 9%, 5-year bonds at face value. The bonds were dated May 1, 2017, and pay interest annually on May 1. Financial statements are prepared annually on December 31.

Instructions

(a) Prepare the journal entry to record the issuance of the bonds.
(b) Prepare the adjusting entry to record the accrual of interest on December 31, 2017.
(c) Show the balance sheet presentation on December 31, 2017.
(d) Prepare the journal entry to record payment of interest on May 1, 2018.
(e) Prepare the adjusting entry to record the accrual of interest on December 31, 2018.
(f) Assume that on January 1, 2019, Herron pays the accrual bond interest and calls the bonds. The call price is 102. Record the payment of interest and redemption of the bonds.

(d) Int. exp. $18,000

Prepare entries to record issuance of bonds, interest accrual, and bond redemption.

(LO 2, 4)

P15-2A Kershaw Electric sold $6,000,000, 10%, 10-year bonds on January 1, 2017. The bonds were dated January 1, 2017, and paid interest on January 1. The bonds were sold at 98.

Instructions

(a) Prepare the journal entry to record the issuance of the bonds on January 1, 2017.
(b) At December 31, 2017, $8,000 of the Discount on Bonds Payable account has been amortized. Show the balance sheet presentation of the long-term liability at December 31, 2017.
(c) On January 1, 2019, when the carrying value of the bonds was $5,896,000, the company redeemed the bonds at 102. Record the redemption of the bonds assuming that interest for the period has already been paid.

(c) Loss $224,000

Prepare entries for interest payment, bond redemption, and interest accrual.

(LO 2)

P15-3A The following section is taken from Mareska's balance sheet at December 31, 2017.

Current liabilities	
Interest payable	$ 40,000
Long-term liabilities	
Bonds payable (8%, due January 1, 2021)	500,000

Interest is payable annually on January 1. The bonds are callable on any annual interest date.

Instructions

(a) Journalize the payment of the bond interest on January 1, 2018.
(b) Assume that on January 1, 2018, after paying interest, Mareska calls bonds having a face value of $200,000. The call price is 103. Record the redemption of the bonds.
(c) Prepare the adjusting entry on December 31, 2018, to accrue the interest on the remaining bonds.

Prepare installment payments schedule and journal entries for a mortgage note payable.

(LO 3, 4)

P15-4A Talkington Electronics issues a $400,000, 8%, 15-year mortgage note on December 31, 2016. The proceeds from the note are to be used in financing a new research laboratory. The terms of the note provide for annual installment payments, exclusive of real estate taxes and insurance, of $59,612. Payments are due on December 31.

Instructions

(a) Prepare an installment payments schedule for the first 4 years.
(b) Prepare the entries for (1) the loan and (2) the first installment payment.

(b) December 31 debit Mortgage Payable $27,612

(c) Show how the total mortgage liability should be reported on the balance sheet at December 31, 2017.

(c) Current liability—2017 $29,821

P15-5A Presented below are three different lease transactions that occurred for Ruggiero Inc. in 2017. Assume that all lease contracts start on January 1, 2017. In no case does Ruggiero receive title to the properties leased during or at the end of the lease term.

Analyze three different lease situations and prepare journal entries.

(LO 4)

	Lessor		
	Judson Delivery	**Hester Co.**	**Gunselman Auto**
Type of property	Computer	Delivery equipment	Automobile
Yearly rental	$ 5,000	$ 4,200	$ 3,700
Lease term	6 years	4 years	2 years
Estimated economic life	7 years	7 years	5 years
Fair value of lease asset	$27,500	$19,000	$11,000
Present value of the lease rental payments	$26,000	$13,000	$ 6,400
Bargain purchase option	None	None	None

Instructions

(a) Which of the leases are operating leases and which are capital leases? Explain.
(b) How should the lease transaction for Hester Co. be recorded in 2017?
(c) How should the lease transaction for Judson Delivery be recorded on January 1, 2017?

***P15-6A** Paris Electric sold $3,000,000, 10%, 10-year bonds on January 1, 2017. The bonds were dated January 1 and pay interest annually on January 1. Paris Electric uses the straight-line method to amortize bond premium or discount. The bonds were sold at 104.

Prepare entries to record issuance of bonds, interest accrual, and straight-line amortization for 2 years.

(LO 4, 5)

Instructions

(a) Prepare the journal entry to record the issuance of the bonds on January 1, 2017.
(b) Prepare a bond premium amortization schedule for the first 4 interest periods.
(c) Prepare the journal entries for interest and the amortization of the premium in 2017 and 2018.
(d) Show the balance sheet presentation of the bond liability at December 31, 2018.

(b) Amortization $12,000

(d) Premium on bonds payable $96,000

***P15-7A** Saberhagen Company sold $3,500,000, 8%, 10-year bonds on January 1, 2017. The bonds were dated January 1, 2017 and pay interest annually on January 1. Saberhagen Company uses the straight-line method to amortize bond premium or discount.

Prepare entries to record issuance of bonds, interest, and straight-line amortization of bond premium and discount.

(LO 4, 5)

Instructions

(a) Prepare all the necessary journal entries to record the issuance of the bonds and bond interest expense for 2017, assuming that the bonds sold at 104.
(b) Prepare journal entries as in part (a) assuming that the bonds sold at 98.
(c) Show balance sheet presentation for the bonds at December 31, 2017, for both the requirements in (a) and (b).

(a) Amortization $14,000

(b) Amortization $7,000

(c) Premium on bonds payable $126,000
Discount on bonds payable $63,000

***P15-8A** The following is taken from the Colaw Company balance sheet.

Prepare entries to record interest payments, straight-line premium amortization, and redemption of bonds.

(LO 5)

COLAW COMPANY
Balance Sheet (partial)
December 31, 2017

Current liabilities		
Interest payable (for 12 months from January 1 to December 31)		$ 210,000
Long-term liabilities		
Bonds payable, 7% due January 1, 2028	$3,000,000	
Add: Premium on bonds payable	200,000	3,200,000

Interest is payable annually on January 1. The bonds are callable on any annual interest date. Colaw uses straight-line amortization for any bond premium or discount. From December 31, 2017, the bonds will be outstanding for an additional 10 years (120 months).

Instructions

(a) Journalize the payment of bond interest on January 1, 2018.

(b) Amortization $20,000

(b) Prepare the entry to amortize bond premium and to accrue the interest due on December 31, 2018.

(c) Gain $60,000

(c) Assume that on January 1, 2019, after paying interest, Colaw Company calls bonds having a face value of $1,200,000. The call price is 101. Record the redemption of the bonds.

(d) Amortization $12,000

(d) Prepare the adjusting entry at December 31, 2019, to amortize bond premium and to accrue interest on the remaining bonds.

Prepare journal entries to record issuance of bonds, payment of interest, and amortization of bond discount using effective-interest method.

(LO 6)

***P15-9A** On January 1, 2017, Lock Corporation issued $1,800,000 face value, 5%, 10-year bonds at $1,667,518. This price resulted in an effective-interest rate of 6% on the bonds. Lock uses the efective-interest method to amortize bond premium or discount. The bonds pay annual interest January 1.

Instructions

(Round all computations to the nearest dollar.)

(a) Prepare the journal entry to record the issuance of the bonds on January 1, 2017.

(b) Prepare an amortization table through December 31, 2019 (three interest periods) for this bond issue.

(c) Interest Expense $100,051

(c) Prepare the journal entry to record the accrual of interest and the amortization of the discount on December 31, 2017.

(d) Prepare the journal entry to record the payment of interest on January 1, 2018.

(e) Prepare the journal entry to record the accrual of interest and the amortization of the discount on December 31, 2018.

Prepare journal entries to record issuance of bonds, payment of interest, and effective-interest amortization, and balance sheet presentation.

(LO 4, 6)

***P15-10A** On January 1, 2017, Jade Company issued $2,000,000 face value, 7%, 10-year bonds at $2,147,202. This price resulted in a 6% effective-interest rate on the bonds. Jade uses the effective-interest method to amortize bond premium or discount. The bonds pay annual interest on each January 1.

Instructions

(a) Prepare the journal entries to record the following transactions.
   (1) The issuance of the bonds on January 1, 2017.
   (2) Accrual of interest and amortization of the premium on December 31, 2017.
   (3) The payment of interest on January 1, 2018.
   (4) Accrual of interest and amortization of the premium on December 31, 2018.

(a) (4) Interest Expense $128,162

(b) Show the proper long-term liabilities balance sheet presentation for the liability for bonds payable at December 31, 2018.

(c) Provide the answers to the following questions in narrative form.
   (1) What amount of interest expense is reported for 2018?
   (2) Would the bond interest expense reported in 2018 be the same as, greater than, or less than the amount that would be reported if the straight-line method of amortization were used?

PROBLEMS: SET B AND SET C

Visit the book's companion website, at **www.wiley.com/college/weygandt**, and choose the Student Companion site to access Problems: Set B and Set C.

COMPREHENSIVE PROBLEM: CHAPTERS 13 TO 15

CP15 Quigley Corporation's trial balance at December 31, 2017, is presented below. All 2017 transactions have been recorded except for the items described below.

	Debit	Credit
Cash	$ 25,500	
Accounts Receivable	51,000	
Inventory	22,700	
Land	65,000	
Buildings	95,000	
Equipment	40,000	
Allowance for Doubtful Accounts		$ 450
Accumulated Depreciation—Buildings		30,000
Accumulated Depreciation—Equipment		14,400
Accounts Payable		19,300
Interest Payable		–0–
Dividends Payable		–0–
Unearned Rent Revenue		8,000
Bonds Payable (10%)		50,000
Common Stock ($10 par)		30,000
Paid-in Capital in Excess of Par—Common Stock		6,000
Preferred Stock ($20 par)		–0–
Paid-in Capital in Excess of Par—Preferred Stock		–0–
Retained Earnings		75,050
Treasury Stock	–0–	
Cash Dividends	–0–	
Sales Revenue		570,000
Rent Revenue		–0–
Bad Debt Expense	–0–	
Interest Expense	–0–	
Cost of Goods Sold	400,000	
Depreciation Expense	–0–	
Other Operating Expenses	39,000	
Salaries and Wages Expense	65,000	
Total	$803,200	$803,200

Unrecorded transactions and adjustments:

1. On January 1, 2017, Quigley issued 1,000 shares of $20 par, 6% preferred stock for $22,000.
2. On January 1, 2017, Quigley also issued 1,000 shares of common stock for $23,000.
3. Quigley reacquired 300 shares of its common stock on July 1, 2017, for $49 per share.
4. On December 31, 2017, Quigley declared the annual cash dividend on the preferred stock and a $1.50 per share dividend on the outstanding common stock, all payable on January 15, 2018.
5. Quigley estimates that uncollectible accounts receivable at year-end is $5,100.
6. The building is being depreciated using the straight-line method over 30 years. The salvage value is $5,000.
7. The equipment is being depreciated using the straight-line method over 10 years. The salvage value is $4,000.
8. The unearned rent was collected on October 1, 2017. It was the receipt of 4 months' rent in advance (October 1, 2017 through January 31, 2018).
9. The 10% bonds payable pay interest every January 1. The interest for the 12 months ended December 31, 2017, has not been paid or recorded.

Instructions

(Ignore income taxes.)

(a) Prepare journal entries for the transactions and adjustment listed above.

(b) Prepare an updated December 31, 2017, trial balance, reflecting the journal entries in (a). (b) Total $871,200

(c) Prepare a multiple-step income statement for the year ending December 31, 2017.

(d) Prepare a retained earnings statement for the year ending December 31, 2017.

(e) Prepare a classified balance sheet as of December 31, 2017. (e) Total assets $273,400

CONTINUING PROBLEM

© leungchopan/ Shutterstock

COOKIE CREATIONS: AN ENTREPRENEURIAL JOURNEY

(*Note:* This is a continuation of the Cookie Creations problem from Chapters 1 through 14.)

CC15 Natalie and Curtis have been experiencing great demand for their cookies and muffins. As a result, they are now thinking about buying a commercial oven. They know which oven they want and how much it will cost. They have some cash set aside for the purchase and will need to borrow the rest. They met with a bank manager to discuss their options.

Go to the book's companion website, **www.wiley.com/college/weygandt**, *to see the completion of this problem.*

BROADENING YOUR PERSPECTIVE

FINANCIAL REPORTING AND ANALYSIS

Financial Reporting Problem: Apple Inc.

BYP15-1 The financial statements of Apple Inc. are presented in Appendix A. Instructions for accessing and using the company's complete annual report, including the notes to the financial statements, are also provided in Appendix A.

Instructions

(a) What were Apple's total long-term liabilities at September 28, 2013? What was the increase/decrease in total long-term liabilities from the prior year?

(b) Determine whether Apple redeemed (bought back) any long-term liabilities during the fiscal year ended September 28, 2013.

Comparative Analysis Problem: PepsiCo, Inc. vs. The Coca-Cola Company

BYP15-2 PepsiCo's financial statements are presented in Appendix B. Financial statements of The Coca-Cola Company are presented in Appendix C. Instructions for accessing and using the complete annual reports of PepsiCo and Coca-Cola, including the notes to the financial statements, are also provided in Appendices B and C, respectively.

Instructions

(a) Based on the information contained in these financial statements, compute the following 2013 ratios for each company.
   (1) Debt to assets.
   (2) Times interest earned.

(b) What conclusions concerning the companies' long-run solvency can be drawn from these ratios?

Comparative Analysis Problem: Amazon.com, Inc. vs. Wal-Mart Stores, Inc.

BYP15-3 Amazon.com, Inc.'s financial statements are presented in Appendix D. Financial statements of Wal-Mart Stores, Inc. are presented in Appendix E. Instructions for accessing and using the complete annual reports of Amazon and Wal-Mart, including the notes to the financial statements, are also provided in Appendices D and E, respectively.

Instructions

(a) Based on the information contained in these financial statements, compute the following 2013 ratios for Amazon and 2014 ratios for Wal-Mart.
   (1) Debt to assets.
   (2) Times interest earned.

(b) What conclusions concerning the companies' long-run solvency can be drawn from these ratios?

Real-World Focus

BYP15-4 Bond or debt securities pay a stated rate of interest. This rate of interest is dependent on the risk associated with the investment. Also, bond prices change when the risks associated with those bonds change. Standard & Poor's provides ratings for companies that issue debt securities.

Address: **www.standardandpoors.com/ratings/definitions-and-faqs/en/us**, or go to **www.wiley.com/college/weygandt**

Instructions

Go to the website shown and answer the following questions.

(a) Explain the meaning of an "A" rating. Explain the meaning of a "C" rating.

(b) What types of things can cause a change in a company's credit rating?

(c) Explain the relationship between a company's credit rating and the merit of an investment in that company's bonds.

CRITICAL THINKING

Decision-Making Across the Organization

***BYP15-5** On January 1, 2015, Glover Corporation issued $2,400,000 of 5-year, 8% bonds at 95. The bonds pay interest annually on January 1. By January 1, 2017, the market rate of interest for bonds of risk similar to those of Glover Corporation had risen. As a result, the market value of these bonds was $2,000,000 on January 1, 2017—below their carrying value. Joanna Glover, president of the company, suggests repurchasing all of these bonds in the open market at the $2,000,000 price. To do so, the company will have to issue $2,000,000 (face value) of new 10-year, 11% bonds at par. The president asks you, as controller, "What is the feasibility of my proposed repurchase plan?"

Instructions

With the class divided into groups, answer the following.

(a) What is the carrying value of the outstanding Glover Corporation 5-year bonds on January 1, 2017? (Assume straight-line amortization.)

(b) Prepare the journal entry to redeem the 5-year bonds on January 1, 2017. Prepare the journal entry to issue the new 10-year bonds.

(c) Prepare a short memo to the president in response to her request for advice. List the economic factors that you believe should be considered for her repurchase proposal.

Communication Activity

BYP15-6 Sam Masasi, president of Masasi Corporation, is considering the issuance of bonds to finance an expansion of his business. He has asked you to (1) discuss the advantages of bonds over common stock financing, (2) indicate the types of bonds he might issue, and (3) explain the issuing procedures used in bond transactions.

Instructions

Write a memo to the president, answering his request.

Ethics Case

BYP15-7 Ken Iwig is the president, founder, and majority owner of Olathe Medical Corporation, an emerging medical technology products company. Olathe is in dire need of additional capital to keep operating and to bring several promising products to final development, testing, and production. Ken, as owner of 51% of the outstanding stock, manages the company's operations. He places heavy emphasis on research and development and on long-term growth. The other principal stockholder is Barb Lowery who, as a nonemployee investor, owns 40% of the stock. Barb would like to deemphasize the R&D functions and emphasize the marketing function, to maximize short-run sales and profits from existing products. She believes this strategy would raise the market price of Olathe's stock.

All of Ken's personal capital and borrowing power is tied up in his 51% stock ownership. He knows that any offering of additional shares of stock will dilute his controlling interest because he won't be able to participate in such an issuance. But, Barb has money and would likely buy enough shares to gain control of Olathe. She then would dictate the company's future direction, even if it meant replacing Ken as president and CEO.

The company already has considerable debt. Raising additional debt will be costly, will adversely affect Olathe's credit rating, and will increase the company's reported losses due to the growth in interest expense. Barb and the other minority stockholders express opposition to the assumption of additional debt, fearing the company will be pushed to the brink of bankruptcy. Wanting to maintain his control and to preserve the direction of "his" company, Ken is doing everything to avoid a stock issuance. He is contemplating a large issuance of bonds, even if it means the bonds are issued with a high effective-interest rate.

Instructions

(a) Who are the stakeholders in this situation?
(b) What are the ethical issues in this case?
(c) What would you do if you were Ken?

All About You

BYP15-8 Numerous articles have been written that identify early warning signs that you might be getting into trouble with your personal debt load. You can find many good articles on this topic on the Internet.

Instructions

Find an article that identifies early warning signs of personal debt trouble. Write a summary of the article and bring your summary and the article to class to share.

FASB Codification Activity

BYP15-9 If your school has a subscription to the FASB Codification, go to **http://aaahq.org/ascLogin.cfm** to log in and prepare responses to the following:

(a) What is the definition of long-term obligation?
(b) What guidance does the Codification provide for the disclosure of long-term obligations?

A Look at IFRS

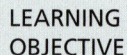

LEARNING OBJECTIVE 7 **Compare the accounting for long-term liabilities under GAAP and IFRS.**

IFRS and GAAP have similar definitions of liabilities but have a different approach for accounting certain long-term liabilities.

Key Points

Following are the key similarities and difference between GAAP and IFRS as related to accounting for long-term liabilities.

Similarities

- As indicated in Chapter 11, in general GAAP and IFRS define liabilities similarly.
- IFRS requires that companies classify liabilities as current or noncurrent on the face of the statement of financial position (balance sheet), except in industries where a **presentation** based on liquidity would be considered to provide more useful information (such as financial institutions). When current liabilities (also called short-term liabilities) are presented, they are generally presented in order of liquidity.
- Under IFRS, liabilities are classified as current if they are expected to be paid within 12 months.
- Similar to GAAP, items are normally reported in order of liquidity. Companies sometimes show liabilities before assets. Also, they will sometimes show noncurrent (long-term) liabilities before current liabilities.
- The basic calculation for bond valuation is the same under GAAP and IFRS. In addition, the accounting for bond liability transactions is essentially the same between GAAP and IFRS.
- IFRS requires use of the effective-interest method for amortization of bond discounts and premiums. GAAP also requires the effective-interest method, except that it allows use of the straight-line method where the difference is not material. Under IFRS, companies do not use a premium or discount account but instead show the bond at its net amount. For example, if a $100,000 bond was issued at 97, under IFRS a company would record:

Cash	97,000	
Bonds Payable		97,000

Differences

- The accounting for convertible bonds differs between IFRS and GAAP. Unlike GAAP, IFRS splits the proceeds from the convertible bond between an equity component and a debt component. The equity conversion rights are reported in equity.

  To illustrate, assume that Harris Corp. issues convertible 7% bonds with a face value of $1,000,000 and receives $1,000,000. Comparable bonds without a conversion feature would have required a 9% rate of interest. To determine how much of the proceeds would be allocated to debt and how much to equity, the promised payments of the bond obligation would be discounted at the market rate of 9%. Suppose that this results in a present value of $850,000. The entry to record the issuance would be:

Cash	1,000,000	
Bonds Payable		850,000
Share Premium—Conversion Equity		150,000

- The IFRS leasing standard is *IAS 17*. Both Boards share the same objective of recording leases by lessees and lessors according to their economic substance—that is, according to the definitions of assets and liabilities. However, GAAP for leases is much more "rules-based" with specific bright-line criteria (such as the "90% of fair value" test) to determine if a lease arrangement transfers the risks and rewards of ownership; IFRS is more conceptual in its provisions. Rather than a 90% cut-off, it asks whether the agreement transfers substantially all of the risks and rewards associated with ownership.

Looking to the Future

The FASB and IASB are currently involved in two projects, each of which has implications for the accounting for liabilities. One project is investigating approaches to differentiate between debt and equity instruments. The other project, the elements phase of the conceptual framework project, will evaluate the definitions of the fundamental building blocks of accounting. The results of these projects could change the classification of many debt and equity securities.

In addition to these projects, the FASB and IASB have also identified leasing as one of the most problematic areas of accounting. A joint project is now focused on lessee accounting. One of the first areas studied is, "What are the assets and liabilities to be recognized related to a lease contract?" Should the focus remain on the leased item or the right to use the leased item? This question is tied to the Boards' joint project on the conceptual framework—defining an "asset" and a "liability."

IFRS Practice

IFRS Self-Test Questions

1. The accounting for bonds payable is:
   (a) essentially the same under IFRS and GAAP.
   (b) differs in that GAAP requires use of the straight-line method for amortization of bond premium and discount.
   (c) the same except that market prices may be different because the present value calculations are different between IFRS and GAAP.
   (d) not covered by IFRS.
2. Stevens Corporation issued 5% convertible bonds with a total face value of $3,000,000 for $3,000,000. If the bonds had not had a conversion feature, they would have sold for $2,600,000. Under IFRS, the entry to record the transaction would require a credit to:
   (a) Bonds Payable for $3,000,000.
   (b) Bonds Payable for $400,000.
   (c) Share Premium—Conversion Equity for $400,000.
   (d) Discount on Bonds Payable for $400,000.
3. The leasing standards employed by IFRS:
   (a) rely more heavily on interpretation of the conceptual meaning of assets and liabilities than GAAP.
   (b) are more "rules based" than those of GAAP.
   (c) employ the same "bright-line test" as GAAP.
   (d) are identical to those of GAAP.
4. The joint projects of the FASB and IASB could potentially:
   (a) change the definition of liabilities.
   (b) change the definition of equity.
   (c) change the definition of assets.
   (d) All of the above.

IFRS Exercises

IFRS15-1 Briefly describe some of the similarities and differences between GAAP and IFRS with respect to the accounting for liabilities.

IFRS15-2 Ratzlaff Company issues (in euros) €2 million, 10-year, 8% bonds at 97, with interest payable annually on January 1.

Instructions

(a) Prepare the journal entry to record the sale of these bonds on January 1, 2017.
(b) Assuming instead that the above bonds sold for 104, prepare the journal entry to record the sale of these bonds on January 1, 2017.

IFRS15-3 Archer Company issued (in pounds) £4,000,000 par value, 7% convertible bonds at 99 for cash. The net present value of the debt without the conversion feature is £3,800,000. Prepare the journal entry to record the issuance of the convertible bonds.

International Financial Statement Analysis: Louis Vuitton

IFRS15-4 The financial statements of Louis Vuitton are presented in Appendix F. Instructions for accessing and using the company's complete annual report, including the notes to its financial statements, are also provided in Appendix F.

Instructions

Use the company's annual report to answer the following questions.

(a) According to the notes to the financial statements, what is the composition of long-term gross borrowings?

(b) According to the accounting policy note to the financial statements, how are borrowings measured?

(c) Determine the amount of fixed-rate and adjustable-rate (floating) borrowings (gross) that the company reports.

(d) Identify where non-current liabilities are reported on the company's balance sheet.

Answers to IFRS Self-Test Questions

1. a **2.** c **3.** a **4.** d

16 Investments

CHAPTER PREVIEW Time Warner's management, as the Feature Story below indicates, believes in aggressive growth through investing in the stock of existing companies. Besides purchasing stock, companies also purchase other securities such as bonds issued by corporations or by governments. Companies can make investments for a short or long period of time, as a passive investment, or with the intent to control another company. As you will see in this chapter, the way in which a company accounts for its investments is determined by a number of factors.

FEATURE STORY

"Is There Anything Else We Can Buy?"

In a rapidly changing world, you must keep up or suffer the consequences. In business, change requires investment.

A case in point is found in the entertainment industry. Technology is bringing about innovations so quickly that it is nearly impossible to guess which technologies will last and which will soon fade away. For example, will both satellite TV and cable TV survive? Or, will both be replaced by something else?

Consider the publishing industry as well. Will paper newspapers and magazines be replaced completely by online news? If you are a publisher, you have to make your best guess about what the future holds and invest accordingly.

Time Warner Inc. lives at the center of this arena. It is not an environment for the timid, and Time Warner's philosophy is anything but that. Instead, it might be characterized as, "If we can't beat you, we will buy you." Its mantra is "invest, invest, invest." A partial list of Time Warner's holdings gives an idea of its reach:

Magazines: *Time, Life, Sports Illustrated,* and *Fortune.*

Book publishers: Time-Life Books; Book-of-the-Month Club; Little, Brown & Co; and Sunset Books.

Television and movies: Warner Bros. ("The Big Bang Theory" and "The Mentalist"), HBO, and movies like *The Hobbit: The Battle of the Five Armies* and *Into the Storm.*

Broadcasting: TNT, CNN news, and Turner's library of thousands of classic movies.

Internet: America Online and AOL Anywhere.

Time Warner owns more information and entertainment copyrights and brands than any other company in the world.

Recently, Rupert Murdoch, chairman and CEO of 21st Century Fox, made an unsolicited $80 billion offer to buy the major media conglomerate. Murdoch's bid put "a positive light on Time Warner's assets," says one analyst. Murdoch eventually withdrew his bid, which resulted in driving down Time Warner's stock price. However, analysts expect the stock to eventually rebound as the long-term institutional investors start taking advantage of the lower price.

Source: Gene Marcial, "Why Time Warner Will Deliver Superb Growth and Valuation Despite Murdoch's Surrender," *Forbes* (August 6, 2014).

Robert Voets/CBS via Getty Images

CHAPTER OUTLINE

Learning Objectives

Learning Objective	Topics	DO IT!
1 Explain how to account for debt investments.	• Why corporations invest • Accounting for debt investments	DO IT! 1 Debt Investments
2 Explain how to account for stock investments.	• Holdings of less than 20% • Holdings between 20% and 50% • Holdings of more than 50%	DO IT! 2 Stock Investments
3 Discuss how debt and stock investments are reported in financial statements.	• Categories of securities • Balance sheet presentation • Presentation of realized and unrealized gain or loss • Classified balance sheet	DO IT! 3a Trading and Available-for-Sale Securities 3b Financial Statement Presentation of Investments

Go to the ***REVIEW AND PRACTICE*** section at the end of the chapter for a review of key concepts and practice applications with solutions.

Visit **WileyPLUS with ORION** for additional tutorials and practice opportunities.

LEARNING OBJECTIVE **1** **Explain how to account for debt investments.**

Why Corporations Invest

Corporations purchase investments in debt or stock securities generally for one of three reasons. First, a corporation may **have excess cash** that it does not need for the immediate purchase of operating assets. For example, many companies experience seasonal fluctuations in sales. A Cape Cod marina has more sales in the spring and summer than in the fall and winter. The reverse is true for an Aspen ski shop. Thus, at the end of an operating cycle, many companies may have cash on hand that is temporarily idle until the start of another operating cycle. These companies may invest the excess funds to earn—through interest and dividends—a greater return than they would get by just holding the funds in the bank. Illustration 16-1 shows the role that temporary investments play in the operating cycle.

Illustration 16-1
Temporary investments and the operating cycle

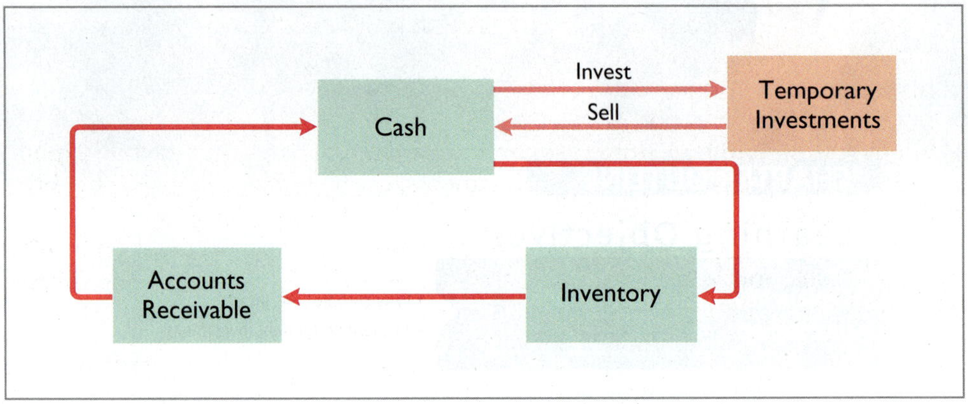

A second reason some companies such as banks purchase investments is to generate **earnings from investment income**. Although banks make most of their earnings by lending money, they also generate earnings by investing primarily in debt securities. Banks purchase investment securities because loan demand varies both seasonally and with changes in the economic climate. Thus, when loan demand is low, a bank must find other uses for its cash.

Some companies attempt to generate investment income through speculative investments. That is, they are speculating that the investment will increase in value and thus result in positive returns. Therefore, they invest mostly in the common stock of other corporations.

Third, companies also invest for **strategic reasons**. A company may purchase a noncontrolling interest in another company in a related industry in which it wishes to establish a presence. Or, a company can exercise some influence over one of its customers or suppliers by purchasing a significant, but not controlling, interest in that company. Another option is for a corporation to purchase a controlling interest in another company in order to enter a new industry without incurring the costs and risks associated with starting from scratch.

In summary, businesses invest in other companies for the reasons shown in Illustration 16-2.

Illustration 16-2
Why corporations invest

Reason	Typical Investment
To house excess cash until needed 	Low-risk, highly liquid, short-term securities such as government-issued securities
To generate earnings 	Debt securities (banks and other financial institutions) and stock securities (mutual funds and pension funds)
To meet strategic goals 	Stocks of companies in a related industry or in an unrelated industry that the company wishes to enter

Accounting for Debt Investments

Debt investments are investments in government and corporation bonds. In accounting for debt investments, companies make entries to record (1) the acquisition, (2) the interest revenue, and (3) the sale.

RECORDING ACQUISITION OF BONDS

At acquisition, debt investments are recorded at cost. Cost includes all expenditures necessary to acquire these investments, such as the price paid plus brokerage fees (commissions), if any.

For example, assume that Kuhl Corporation acquires 50 Doan Inc. 8%, 10-year, $1,000 bonds on January 1, 2017, for $50,000. Kuhl records the investment as:

Jan. 1	Debt Investments (50 × $1,000)	50,000	
	Cash		50,000
	(To record purchase of 50 Doan Inc. bonds)		

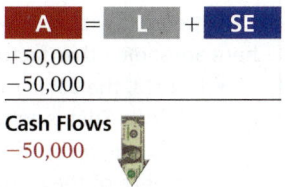

A = L + SE
+50,000
−50,000
Cash Flows
−50,000

RECORDING BOND INTEREST

The Doan Inc. bonds pay interest of $4,000 annually on January 1 ($50,000 × 8%). If Kuhl Corporation's fiscal year ends on December 31, it accrues the interest of $4,000 earned since January 1. The adjusting entry is:

Dec. 31	Interest Receivable	4,000	
	Interest Revenue		4,000
	(To accrue interest on Doan Inc. bonds)		

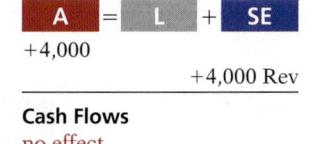

A = L + SE
+4,000
+4,000 Rev
Cash Flows
no effect

Kuhl reports Interest Receivable as a current asset in the balance sheet. It reports Interest Revenue under "Other revenues and gains" in the income statement.

Kuhl reports receipt of the interest on January 1 as follows.

Jan. 1	Cash	4,000	
	Interest Receivable		4,000
	(To record receipt of accrued interest)		

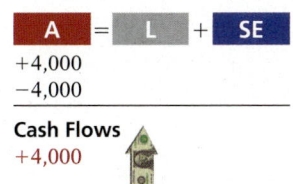

A = L + SE
+4,000
−4,000
Cash Flows
+4,000

A credit to Interest Revenue at this time is incorrect because the company earned and accrued interest revenue in the **preceding** accounting period.

RECORDING SALE OF BONDS

When Kuhl sells the bonds, it credits the investment account for the cost of the bonds. Kuhl records as a gain or loss any difference between the net proceeds from the sale (sales price less brokerage fees) and the cost of the bonds.

Assume, for example, that Kuhl Corporation receives net proceeds of $54,000 on the sale of the Doan Inc. bonds on January 1, 2018, after receiving the interest due. Since the securities cost $50,000, the company realizes a gain of $4,000. It records the sale as:

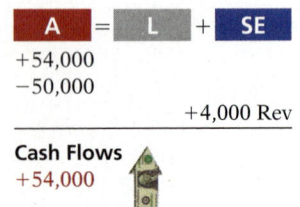

A	=	L	+	SE
+54,000				
−50,000				
				+4,000 Rev

Cash Flows
+54,000

Jan. 1	Cash	54,000	
	Debt Investments		50,000
	Gain on Sale of Debt Investments		4,000
	(To record sale of Doan Inc. bonds)		

Kuhl reports the gain on sale of debt investments under "Other revenues and gains" in the income statement and reports losses under "Other expenses and losses."

Investor Insight

© Jane0606/Shutterstock

Hey, I Thought It Was Safe!

It is often stated that bond investments are safer than stock investments. After all, with an investment in bonds, you are guaranteed return of principal and interest payments over the life of the bonds. However, here are some other factors you may want to consider:

- In 2013, the value of bonds fell by 2% due to interest rate risk. That is, when interest rates rise, it makes the yields paid on existing bonds less attractive. As a result, the price of the existing bond you are holding falls.
- While interest rates are currently low, it is likely that they will increase in the future. If you hold bonds, there is a real possibility that the value of your bonds will be reduced.
- Credit risk also must be considered. Credit risk means that a company may not be able to pay back what it borrowed. Former bondholders in companies like General Motors, United Air Lines, and Eastman Kodak saw their bond values drop substantially when these companies declared bankruptcy.

An advantage of a bond investment over stock is that if you hold it to maturity, you will receive your principal and also interest payments over the life of the bond. But if you have to sell your bond investment before maturity, you may be facing a roller coaster regarding its value.

Why is the fluctuating value of bonds of concern if a company intends to hold them until maturity? (Go to **WileyPLUS** for this answer and additional questions.)

DO IT! 1 Debt Investments

Waldo Corporation had the following transactions pertaining to debt investments.

Jan. 1, 2017	Purchased 30, $1,000 Hillary Co. 10% bonds for $30,000. Interest is payable annually on January 1.
Dec. 31, 2017	Accrued interest on Hillary Co. bonds in 2017.
Jan. 1, 2018	Received interest on Hillary Co. bonds.
Jan. 1, 2018	Sold 15 Hillary Co. bonds for $14,600.
Dec. 31, 2018	Accrued interest on Hillary Co. bonds in 2018.

Journalize the transactions.

Solution

Date	Account Titles and Explanation	Debit	Credit
Jan. 1 (2017)	Debt Investments	30,000	
	Cash		30,000
	(To record purchase of 30 Hillary Co. bonds)		
Dec. 31 (2017)	Interest Receivable	3,000	
	Interest Revenue ($30,000 × 10%)		3,000
	(To accrue interest on Hillary Co. bonds)		
Jan. 1 (2018)	Cash	3,000	
	Interest Receivable		3,000
	(To record receipt of interest on Hillary Co. bonds)		
Jan. 1 (2018)	Cash	14,600	
	Loss on Sale of Debt Investments	400	
	Debt Investments ($30,000 × 15/30)		15,000
	(To record sale of 15 Hillary Co. bonds)		
Dec. 31 (2018)	Interest Receivable	1,500	
	Interest Revenue ($15,000 × 10%)		1,500
	(To accrue interest on Hillary Co. bonds)		

Related exercise material: **BE16-1, E16-2, E16-3, and DO IT! 16-1.**

Action Plan

- ✔ Record bond investments at cost.
- ✔ Record interest when accrued.
- ✔ When bonds are sold, credit the investment account for the cost of the bonds.
- ✔ Record any difference between the cost and the net proceeds as a gain or loss.

LEARNING OBJECTIVE 2 Explain how to account for stock investments.

Stock investments are investments in the capital stock of other corporations. When a company holds stock (and/or debt) of several different corporations, the group of securities is identified as an **investment portfolio**.

The accounting for investments in common stock depends on the extent of the investor's influence over the operating and financial affairs of the issuing corporation (the **investee**). Illustration 16-3 shows the general guidelines.

Investor's Ownership Interest in Investee's Common Stock		Presumed Influence on Investee	Accounting Guidelines
	Less than 20%	Insignificant	Cost method
	Between 20% and 50%	Significant	Equity method
	More than 50%	Controlling	Consolidated financial statements

Illustration 16-3
Accounting guidelines for stock investments

Companies are required to use judgment instead of blindly following the guidelines.[1] We explain the application of each guideline next.

Helpful Hint
The entries for investments in common stock also apply to investments in preferred stock.

Holdings of Less than 20%

In accounting for stock investments of less than 20%, companies use the cost method. Under the **cost method**, companies record the investment at cost, and recognize revenue only when cash dividends are received.

RECORDING ACQUISITION OF STOCK INVESTMENTS

At acquisition, stock investments are recorded at cost. Cost includes all expenditures necessary to acquire these investments, such as the price paid plus any brokerage fees (commissions), if any.

For example, assume that on July 1, 2017, Sanchez Corporation acquires 1,000 shares (10% ownership) of Beal Corporation common stock. Sanchez pays $40 per share. The entry for the purchase is:

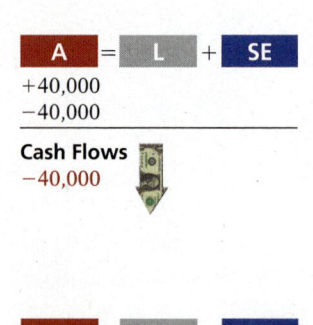

A = L + SE
+40,000
−40,000
Cash Flows
−40,000

July 1	Stock Investments (1,000 × $40)	40,000	
	Cash		40,000
	(To record purchase of 1,000 shares of Beal Corporation common stock)		

RECORDING DIVIDENDS

During the time Sanchez owns the stock, it makes entries for any cash dividends received. If Sanchez receives a $2 per share dividend on December 31, the entry is:

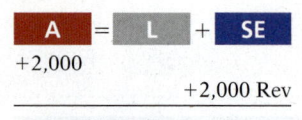

A = L + SE
+2,000
+2,000 Rev
Cash Flows
+2,000

Dec. 31	Cash (1,000 × $2)	2,000	
	Dividend Revenue		2,000
	(To record receipt of a cash dividend)		

Sanchez reports Dividend Revenue under "Other revenues and gains" in the income statement. Unlike interest on notes and bonds, dividends do not accrue. Therefore, companies do not make adjusting entries to accrue dividends.

RECORDING SALE OF STOCK

When a company sells a stock investment, it recognizes as a gain or a loss the difference between the net proceeds from the sale (sales price less brokerage fees) and the cost of the stock.

Assume that Sanchez Corporation receives net proceeds of $39,000 on the sale of its Beal stock on February 10, 2018. Because the stock cost $40,000, Sanchez incurred a loss of $1,000. The entry to record the sale is:

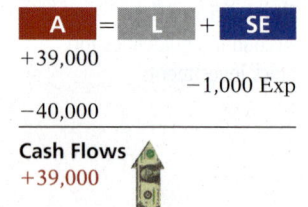

A = L + SE
+39,000
−1,000 Exp
−40,000
Cash Flows
+39,000

Feb. 10	Cash	39,000	
	Loss on Sale of Stock Investments	1,000	
	Stock Investments		40,000
	(To record sale of Beal common stock)		

Sanchez reports the loss under "Other expenses and losses" in the income statement. It would show a gain on sale under "Other revenues and gains."

Holdings Between 20% and 50%

When an investor company owns only a small portion of the shares of stock of another company, the investor cannot exercise control over the investee. But,

[1]Among the questions that are considered in determining an investor's influence are these: (1) Does the investor have representation on the investee's board? (2) Does the investor participate in the investee's policy-making process? (3) Are there material transactions between the investor and investee? (4) Is the common stock held by other stockholders concentrated or dispersed?

when an investor owns between 20% and 50% of the common stock of a corporation, it is presumed that the investor has significant influence over the financial and operating activities of the investee. The investor probably has a representative on the investee's board of directors. Through that representative, the investor may exercise some control over the investee. The investee company in some sense becomes part of the investor company.

For example, even prior to purchasing all of Turner Broadcasting, Time Warner owned 20% of Turner. Because it exercised significant control over major decisions made by Turner, Time Warner used an approach called the equity method. Under the **equity method**, **the investor records its share of the net income of the investee in the year when it is earned.** An alternative might be to delay recognizing the investor's share of net income until the investee declares a cash dividend. But, that approach would ignore the fact that the investor and investee are, in some sense, one company, making the investor better off by the investee's earned income.

Helpful Hint
Under the equity method, the investor recognizes revenue on the accrual basis, i.e., when it is earned by the investee.

Under the equity method, the investor company initially records the investment in common stock at cost. After that, it **adjusts** the investment account annually to show the investor's equity in the investee. Each year, the investor does the following. (1) It increases (debits) the investment account and increases (credits) revenue for its share of the investee's net income.[2] (2) The investor also decreases (credits) the investment account for the amount of dividends received. The investment account is reduced for dividends received because payment of a dividend decreases the net assets of the investee.

RECORDING ACQUISITION OF STOCK

Assume that Milar Corporation acquires 30% of the common stock of Beck Company for $120,000 on January 1, 2017. The entry to record this transaction is:

Jan. 1	Stock Investments	120,000	
	Cash		120,000
	(To record purchase of Beck common stock)		

A = L + SE
+120,000
−120,000
Cash Flows
−120,000

RECORDING REVENUE AND DIVIDENDS

For 2017, Beck reports net income of $100,000. It declares and pays a $40,000 cash dividend. Milar records (1) its share of Beck's income, $30,000 (30% × $100,000) and (2) the reduction in the investment account for the dividends received, $12,000 ($40,000 × 30%). The entries are:

(1)

Dec. 31	Stock Investments	30,000	
	Revenue from Stock Investments		30,000
	(To record 30% equity in Beck's 2017 net income)		

A = L + SE
+30,000 +30,000 Rev
Cash Flows
no effect

(2)

Dec. 31	Cash	12,000	
	Stock Investments		12,000
	(To record dividends received)		

A = L + SE
+12,000
−12,000
Cash Flows
+12,000

After Milar posts the transactions for the year, its investment and revenue accounts will show the following.

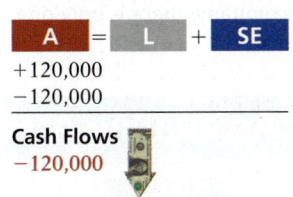

Illustration 16-4
Investment and revenue accounts after posting

Stock Investments

Jan. 1	120,000	Dec. 31	12,000
Dec. 31	30,000		
Dec. 31 Bal.	138,000		

Revenue from Stock Investments

		Dec. 31	30,000

[2]Conversely, the investor increases (debits) a loss account and decreases (credits) the investment account for its share of the investee's net loss.

During the year, the investment account increased $18,000. This increase of $18,000 is explained as follows: (1) Milar records a $30,000 increase in revenue from its stock investment in Beck, and (2) Milar records a $12,000 decrease due to dividends received from its stock investment in Beck.

Note that the difference between reported revenue under the cost method and reported revenue under the equity method can be significant. For example, Milar would report only $12,000 of dividend revenue (30% × $40,000) if it used the cost method.

Holdings of More than 50%

A company that owns more than 50% of the common stock of another entity is known as the **parent company**. The entity whose stock the parent company owns is called the **subsidiary (affiliated) company**. Because of its stock ownership, the parent company has a **controlling interest** in the subsidiary.

When a company owns more than 50% of the common stock of another company, it usually prepares **consolidated financial statements**. These statements present the total assets and liabilities controlled by the parent company. They also present the total revenues and expenses of the subsidiary companies. Companies prepare consolidated statements **in addition to** the financial statements for the parent and individual subsidiary companies.

Helpful Hint
If parent (A) has three wholly owned subsidiaries (B, C, and D), there are four separate legal entities. From the viewpoint of the shareholders of the parent company, there is only one economic entity.

As noted earlier, when Time Warner had a 20% investment in Turner, it reported this investment in a single line item—Other Investments. After the merger, Time Warner instead consolidated Turner's results with its own. Under this approach, Time Warner included Turner's individual assets and liabilities with its own. Its plant and equipment were added to Time Warner's plant and equipment, its receivables were added to Time Warner's receivables, and so on.

Accounting Across the Organization — Procter & Gamble Company

© Stígur Karlsson/iStockphoto

How Procter & Gamble Accounts for Gillette

Several years ago, Procter & Gamble Company acquired Gillette Company for $53.4 billion. The common stockholders of Procter & Gamble elect the board of directors of the company, who in turn select the officers and managers of the company. Procter & Gamble's board of directors controls the property owned by the corporation, which includes the common stock of Gillette. Thus, they are in a position to elect the board of directors of Gillette and, in effect, control its operations. These relationships are graphically illustrated here.

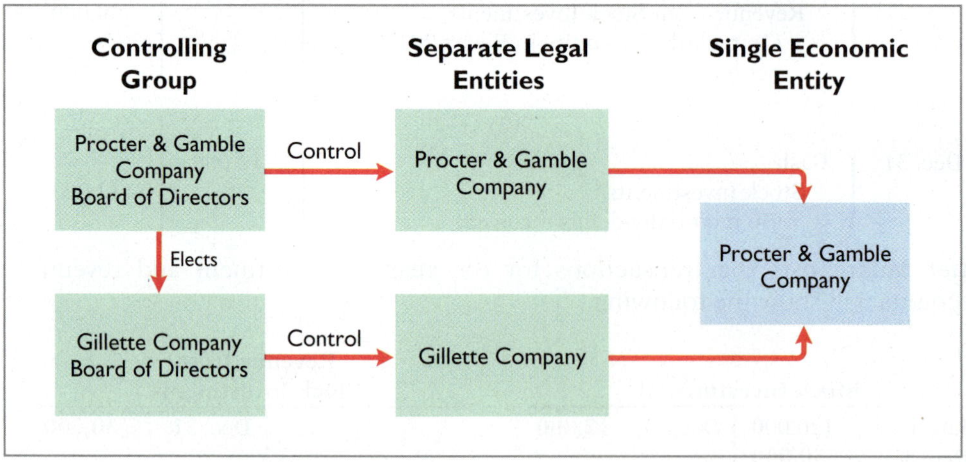

Where on Procter & Gamble's balance sheet will you find its investment in Gillette Company? (Go to **WileyPLUS** for this answer and additional questions.)

Consolidated statements are useful to the stockholders, board of directors, and management of the parent company. These statements indicate the magnitude and scope of operations of the companies under common control. For example, regulators and the courts undoubtedly used the consolidated statements of AT&T to determine whether a breakup of the company was in the public interest. Illustration 16-5 lists three companies that prepare consolidated statements and some of the companies they have owned.

PepsiCo	Cendant	The Disney Company
Frito-Lay	Howard Johnson	Capital Cities/ABC, Inc.
Tropicana	Ramada Inn	Disneyland, Disney World
Quaker Oats	Century 21	Mighty Ducks
Pepsi-Cola	Coldwell Banker	Anaheim Angels
Gatorade	Avis	ESPN

Illustration 16-5
Examples of consolidated companies and their subsidiaries

DO IT! 2 Stock Investments

Presented below are two independent situations.

1. Rho Jean Inc. acquired 5% of the 400,000 shares of common stock of Stillwater Corp. at a total cost of $6 per share on May 18, 2017. On August 30, Stillwater declared and paid a $75,000 dividend. On December 31, Stillwater reported net income of $244,000 for the year.
2. Debbie, Inc. obtained significant influence over North Sails by buying 40% of North Sails' 60,000 outstanding shares of common stock at a cost of $12 per share on January 1, 2017. On April 15, North Sails declared and paid a cash dividend of $45,000. On December 31, North Sails reported net income of $120,000 for the year.

Prepare all necessary journal entries for 2017 for (1) Rho Jean Inc. and (2) Debbie, Inc.

Solution

(1) May 18	Stock Investments (400,000 × 5% × $6)
	  Cash
	    (To record purchase of 20,000 shares of Stillwater Co. stock)
		120,000	
			120,000

Aug. 30	Cash
	  Dividend Revenue ($75,000 × 5%)
	    (To record receipt of cash dividend)
		3,750	
			3,750

(2) Jan. 1	Stock Investments (60,000 × 40% × $12)
	  Cash
	    (To record purchase of 24,000 shares of North Sails' stock)
		288,000	
			288,000

Apr. 15	Cash
	  Stock Investments ($45,000 × 40%)
	    (To record receipt of cash dividend)
		18,000	
			18,000

Dec. 31	Stock Investments ($120,000 × 40%)
	  Revenue from Stock Investments
	    (To record 40% equity in North Sails' net income)
		48,000	
			48,000

Related exercise material: **BE16-2, BE16-3, E16-4, E16-5, E16-6, E16-7, E16-8, and DO IT! 16-2.**

Action Plan

✔ Presume that the investor has relatively little influence over the investee when an investor owns less than 20% of the common stock of another corporation. In this case, net income earned by the investee is not considered a proper basis for recognizing income from the investment by the investor.

✔ Presume significant influence for investments of 20%–50%. Therefore, record the investor's share of the net income of the investee.

LEARNING OBJECTIVE **3**

Discuss how debt and stock investments are reported in financial statements.

The value of debt and stock investments may fluctuate greatly during the time they are held. For example, in one 12-month period, the stock price of Time Warner hit a high of $58.50 and a low of $9. In light of such price fluctuations, how should companies value investments at the balance sheet date? Valuation could be at cost, at fair value, or at the lower-of-cost-or-market value.

Many people argue that fair value offers the best approach because it represents the expected cash realizable value of securities. **Fair value** is the amount for which a security could be sold in a normal market. Others counter that unless a security is going to be sold soon, the fair value is not relevant because the price of the security will likely change again.

Categories of Securities

For purposes of valuation and reporting at a financial statement date, companies classify **debt investments** into three categories:

1. **Trading securities** are bought and held primarily for sale in the near term to generate income on short-term price differences.
2. **Available-for-sale securities** are held with the intent of selling them sometime in the future.
3. **Held-to-maturity securities** are debt securities that the investor has the intent and ability to hold to maturity.[3]

Stock investments are classified into two categories:

1. **Trading securities** (as defined above).
2. **Available-for-sale securities** (as defined above).

Stock investments have no maturity date. Therefore, they are never classified as held-to-maturity securities.

Illustration 16-6 shows the valuation guidelines for these securities. **These guidelines apply to all debt securities and all stock investments in which the holdings are less than 20%.**

Illustration 16-6
Valuation guidelines for securities

TRADING SECURITIES

Companies hold trading securities with the intention of selling them in a short period (generally less than a month). **Trading** means frequent buying and selling.

[3]This category is provided for completeness. The accounting and valuation issues related to held-to-maturity securities are discussed in more advanced accounting courses.

As indicated in Illustration 16-7, companies adjust trading securities to fair value at the end of each period (an approach referred to as mark-to-market accounting). They report changes from cost as part of net income. The changes are reported as **unrealized gains or losses** because the securities have not been sold. The unrealized gain or loss is the difference between the **total cost** of trading securities and their **total fair value**. Companies classify trading securities as current assets.

Illustration 16-7 shows the cost and fair values for investments Pace Corporation classified as trading securities on December 31, 2017. Pace has an unrealized gain of $7,000 because total fair value of $147,000 is $7,000 greater than total cost of $140,000.

Illustration 16-7
Valuation of trading securities

Trading Securities, December 31, 2017

Investments	Cost	Fair Value	Unrealized Gain (Loss)
Yorkville Company bonds	$ 50,000	$ 48,000	$(2,000)
Kodak Company stock	90,000	99,000	9,000
Total	$140,000	$147,000	**$ 7,000**

Pace records fair value and unrealized gain or loss through an adjusting entry at the time it prepares financial statements. In this entry, the company uses a valuation allowance account, Fair Value Adjustment—Trading, to record the difference between the total cost and the total fair value of the securities. The adjusting entry for Pace Corporation is:

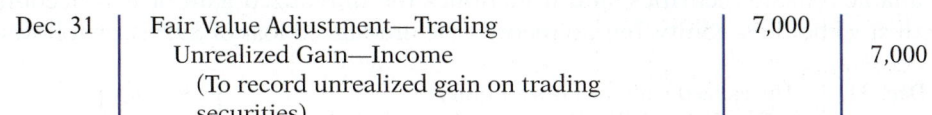

Dec. 31	Fair Value Adjustment—Trading	7,000	
	Unrealized Gain—Income		7,000
	(To record unrealized gain on trading securities)		

A	=	L	+	SE
+7,000				+7,000 Rev

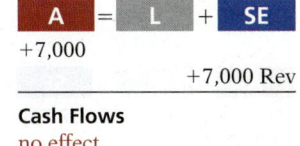

Cash Flows
no effect

The use of a Fair Value Adjustment—Trading account enables Pace to maintain a record of the investment cost. It needs actual cost to determine the gain or loss realized when it sells the securities. Pace adds the debit balance (or subtracts a credit balance) of the Fair Value Adjustment—Trading account to the cost of the investments to arrive at a fair value for the trading securities.

The fair value of the securities is the amount Pace reports on its balance sheet. It reports the unrealized gain in the income statement in the "Other revenues and gains" section. The term "Income" in the account title indicates that the gain affects net income.

If the total cost of the trading securities is greater than total fair value, an unrealized loss has occurred. In such a case, the adjusting entry is a debit to Unrealized Loss—Income and a credit to Fair Value Adjustment—Trading. Companies report the unrealized loss under "Other expenses and losses" in the income statement.

The Fair Value Adjustment—Trading account is carried forward into future accounting periods. The company does not make any entry to the account until the end of each reporting period. At that time, the company adjusts the balance in the account to the difference between cost and fair value. For trading securities, it closes the Unrealized Gain (Loss)—Income account at the end of the reporting period.

ETHICS NOTE

At one time, the SEC accused investment bank Morgan Stanley of overstating the value of certain bond investments by $75 million. The SEC stated that, in applying market value accounting, Morgan Stanley used its own more-optimistic assumptions rather than relying on external pricing sources.

AVAILABLE-FOR-SALE SECURITIES

As indicated earlier, companies hold available-for-sale securities with the intent of selling these investments sometime in the future. If the intent is to sell the securities within the next year or operating cycle, the investor classifies the

> **ETHICS NOTE**
>
> Some managers seem to hold their available-for-sale securities that have experienced losses, while selling those that have gains, thus increasing income. Do you think this is ethical?

securities as current assets in the balance sheet. Otherwise, it classifies them as long-term assets in the investments section of the balance sheet.

Companies report available-for-sale securities at fair value. The procedure for determining fair value and the unrealized gain or loss for these securities is the same as for trading securities. To illustrate, assume that Ingrao Corporation has two securities that it classifies as available-for-sale. Illustration 16-8 provides information on the cost, fair value, and amount of the unrealized gain or loss on December 31, 2017. There is an unrealized loss of $9,537 because total cost of $293,537 is $9,537 more than total fair value of $284,000.

Illustration 16-8
Valuation of available-for-sale securities

Available-for-Sale Securities, December 31, 2017

Investments	Cost	Fair Value	Unrealized Gain (Loss)
Campbell Soup Corporation			
8% bonds	$ 93,537	$103,600	$10,063
Hershey Company stock	200,000	180,400	(19,600)
Total	$293,537	$284,000	$(9,537)

Both the adjusting entry and the reporting of the unrealized gain or loss for Ingrao's available-for-sale securities differ from those illustrated for trading securities. The differences result because Ingrao does not expect to sell these securities in the near term. Thus, prior to actual sale it is more likely that changes in fair value may change either unrealized gains or losses. Therefore, Ingrao does not report an unrealized gain or loss in the income statement. Instead, it reports it as a **separate component of stockholders' equity**.

In the adjusting entry, Ingrao identifies the fair value adjustment account with available-for-sale securities, and it identifies the unrealized gain or loss account with stockholders' equity. Ingrao records the unrealized loss of $9,537 as follows.

A	=	L	+	SE
				−9,537 Exp
−9,537				

Cash Flows
no effect

Dec. 31	Unrealized Gain or Loss—Equity	9,537	
	Fair Value Adjustment—Available-for-Sale		9,537
	(To record unrealized loss on available-for-sale securities)		

If total fair value exceeds total cost, Ingrao debits Fair Value Adjustment—Available-for-Sale and credits Unrealized Gain or Loss—Equity.

For available-for-sale securities, the company carries forward the Unrealized Gain or Loss—Equity account to future periods. At each future balance sheet date, Ingrao adjusts the Fair Value Adjustment—Available-for-Sale account and the Unrealized Gain or Loss—Equity account to show the difference between cost and fair value at that time.

Investor Insight

enciktepstudio/Shutterstock

Can Fair Value Be Unfair?

The FASB is considering proposals for how to account for financial instruments. The FASB has at one time proposed that loans and receivables be accounted for at their fair value (the amount they could currently be sold for), as are most investments. The FASB believes that this would provide a more accurate view of a company's financial position. It might be especially useful as an early warning when a bank is in trouble because of poor-quality loans. But, banks argue that fair values are difficult to estimate accurately. They are also concerned that volatile fair values could cause large swings in a bank's reported net income.

Source: David Reilly, "Banks Face a Mark-to-Market Challenge," *Wall Street Journal Online* (March 15, 2010).

What are the arguments in favor of and against fair value accounting for loans and receivables? (Go to **WileyPLUS** for this answer and additional questions.)

DO IT! 3a Trading and Available-for-Sale Securities

Some of Powderhorn Corporation's investment securities are classified as trading securities and some are classified as available-for-sale. The cost and fair value of each category at December 31, 2017, are shown below.

	Cost	Fair Value	Unrealized Gain (Loss)
Trading securities	$93,600	$94,900	$1,300
Available-for-sale securities	$48,800	$51,400	$2,600

At December 31, 2016, the Fair Value Adjustment—Trading account had a debit balance of $9,200, and the Fair Value Adjustment—Available-for-Sale account had a credit balance of $5,750. Prepare the required journal entries for each group of securities for December 31, 2017.

Solution

Trading securities:

Unrealized Loss—Income	7,900*	
Fair Value Adjustment—Trading		7,900
(To record unrealized loss on trading securities)		

*$9,200 − $1,300

Available-for-sale securities:

Fair Value Adjustment—Available-for-Sale	8,350**	
Unrealized Gain or Loss—Equity		8,350
(To record unrealized gain on available-for-sale securities)		

**$5,750 + $2,600

Action Plan

✔ Mark trading securities to fair value and report the adjustment in current-period income.

✔ Mark available-for-sale securities to fair value and report the adjustment as a separate component of stockholders' equity.

Related exercise material: **BE16-4, BE16-6, E16-10, E16-11, E16-12, and DO IT! 16-3a.**

Balance Sheet Presentation

In the balance sheet, companies classify investments as either short-term or long-term.

SHORT-TERM INVESTMENTS

Short-term investments (also called **marketable securities**) are securities held by a company that are (1) **readily marketable** and (2) **intended to be converted into cash** within the next year or operating cycle, whichever is longer. Investments that do not meet **both criteria** are classified as **long-term investments**.

READILY MARKETABLE An investment is readily marketable when it can be sold easily whenever the need for cash arises. Short-term paper[4] meets this criterion. It can be readily sold to other investors. Stocks and bonds traded on organized securities exchanges, such as the New York Stock Exchange, are readily marketable. They can be bought and sold daily. In contrast, there may be only a limited market for the securities issued by small corporations, and no market for the securities of a privately held company.

Helpful Hint
Trading securities are always classified as short-term. Available-for-sale securities can be either short-term or long-term.

INTENT TO CONVERT Intent to convert means that management intends to sell the investment within the next year or operating cycle, whichever is

[4]**Short-term paper** includes (1) certificates of deposit (CDs) issued by banks, (2) money market certificates issued by banks and savings and loan associations, (3) Treasury bills issued by the U.S. government, and (4) commercial paper (notes) issued by corporations with good credit ratings.

longer. Generally, this criterion is satisfied when the investment is considered a resource that the investor will use whenever the need for cash arises. For example, a ski resort may invest idle cash during the summer months with the intent to sell the securities to buy supplies and equipment shortly before the winter season. This investment is considered short-term even if lack of snow cancels the next ski season and eliminates the need to convert the securities into cash as intended.

Because of their high liquidity, short-term investments appear immediately below Cash in the "Current assets" section of the balance sheet. They are reported at fair value. For example, Pace Corporation would report its trading securities as shown in Illustration 16-9.

Illustration 16-9
Presentation of short-term investments

PACE CORPORATION Balance Sheet (partial)	
Current assets	
Cash	$ 21,000
Short-term investments, at fair value	147,000

LONG-TERM INVESTMENTS

Companies generally report long-term investments in a separate section of the balance sheet immediately below "Current assets," as shown later in Illustration 16-12 (page 706). Long-term investments in available-for-sale securities are reported at fair value. Investments in common stock accounted for under the equity method are reported at equity.

Presentation of Realized and Unrealized Gain or Loss

Companies must present in the financial statements gains and losses on investments, whether realized or unrealized. In the income statement, companies report gains and losses in the nonoperating activities section under the categories listed in Illustration 16-10. Interest and dividend revenue are also reported in that section.

Illustration 16-10
Nonoperating items related to investments

Other Revenues and Gains	Other Expenses and Losses
Interest Revenue	Loss on Sale of Investments
Dividend Revenue	Unrealized Loss—Income
Gain on Sale of Investments	
Unrealized Gain—Income	

As indicated earlier, companies report an unrealized gain or loss on available-for-sale securities as a separate component of stockholders' equity. To illustrate, assume that Dawson Inc. has common stock of $3,000,000, retained earnings of $1,500,000, and an unrealized loss on available-for-sale securities of $100,000. Illustration 16-11 shows the balance sheet presentation of the unrealized loss.

Illustration 16-11
Unrealized loss in stockholders' equity section

DAWSON INC. Balance Sheet (partial)	
Stockholders' equity	
Common stock	$3,000,000
Retained earnings	1,500,000
Total paid-in capital and retained earnings	4,500,000
Less: Unrealized loss on available-for-sale securities	**100,000**
Total stockholders' equity	$4,400,000

Note that the presentation of the loss is similar to the presentation of the cost of treasury stock in the stockholders' equity section (it decreases stockholders' equity). An unrealized gain would be added to this section. Reporting the unrealized gain or loss in the stockholders' equity section serves two purposes. (1) It reduces the volatility of net income due to fluctuations in fair value. (2) It informs the financial statement user of the gain or loss that would occur if the securities were sold at fair value.

Companies must report items such as unrealized gains or losses on available-for-sale securities as part of a more inclusive measure called comprehensive income. Unrealized gains and losses on available-for-sale securities therefore affect comprehensive income (and stockholders' equity) but are not included in the computation of net income. We discuss comprehensive income more fully in Chapter 18.

Classified Balance Sheet

We have presented many sections of classified balance sheets in this and preceding chapters. The classified balance sheet in Illustration 16-12 (page 706) includes, in one place, key topics from previous chapters: the issuance of par value common stock, restrictions of retained earnings, and issuance of long-term bonds. From this chapter, the statement includes (highlighted in red) short-term and long-term investments. The investments in short-term securities are considered trading securities. The long-term investments in stock of less than 20% owned companies are considered available-for-sale securities. Illustration 16-12 also includes a long-term investment reported at equity and descriptive notations within the statement, such as the cost flow method for valuing inventory and one note to the statement.

DO IT! 3b Financial Statement Presentation of Investments

Identify where each of the following items would be reported in the financial statements.

1. Interest earned on investments in bonds.
2. Fair value adjustment—available-for-sale.
3. Unrealized loss on available-for-sale securities.
4. Gain on sale of investments in stock.
5. Unrealized gain on trading securities.

Use the following possible categories:

Balance sheet:

Current assets	Current liabilities
Investments	Long-term liabilities
Property, plant, and equipment	Stockholders' equity
Intangible assets	

Income statement:

Other revenues and gains	Other expenses and losses

Action Plan

✔ Classify investments as current assets if they will be held for less than one year.

✔ Report unrealized gains or losses on trading securities in income.

✔ Report unrealized gains or losses on available-for-sale securities in equity.

✔ Report realized gains and losses on investments in the income statement as "Other revenues and gains" or as "Other expenses and losses."

Solution

Item	Financial Statement	Category
1. Interest earned on investments in bonds.	Income statement	Other revenues and gains
2. Fair value adjustment—available-for-sale	Balance sheet	Investments
3. Unrealized loss on available-for-sale securities	Balance sheet	Stockholders' equity
4. Gain on sale of investments in stock	Income statement	Other revenues and gains
5. Unrealized gain on trading securities	Income statement	Other revenues and gains

Related exercise material: **BE16-5, BE16-7, BE16-8, E16-10, E16-11, E16-12, and DO IT! 16-3b.**

Illustration 16-12
Classified balance sheet

PACE CORPORATION
Balance Sheet
December 31, 2017

Assets

Current assets			
Cash			$ 21,000
Short-term investments, at fair value			**147,000**
Accounts receivable		$ 84,000	
Less: Allowance for doubtful accounts		4,000	80,000
Inventory, at FIFO cost			43,000
Prepaid insurance			23,000
Total current assets			314,000
Investments			
Investments in stock of less than 20% owned companies, at fair value		**50,000**	
Investment in stock of 20–50% owned company, at equity		**150,000**	
Total investments			200,000
Property, plant, and equipment			
Land		200,000	
Buildings	$800,000		
Less: Accumulated depreciation—buildings	200,000	600,000	
Equipment	180,000		
Less: Accumulated depreciation—equipment	54,000	126,000	
Total property, plant, and equipment			926,000
Intangible assets			
Goodwill			270,000
Total assets			$1,710,000

Liabilities and Stockholders' Equity

Current liabilities		
Accounts payable		$ 185,000
Federal income taxes payable		60,000
Interest payable		10,000
Total current liabilities		255,000
Long-term liabilities		
Bonds payable, 10%, due 2024	$ 300,000	
Less: Discount on bonds	10,000	
Total long-term liabilities		290,000
Total liabilities		545,000
Stockholders' equity		
Paid-in capital		
Common stock, $10 par value, 200,000 shares authorized, 80,000 shares issued and outstanding	800,000	
Paid-in capital in excess of par—common stock	100,000	
Total paid-in capital	900,000	
Retained earnings (Note 1)	255,000	
Total paid-in capital and retained earnings	1,155,000	
Add: Unrealized gain on available-for-sale securities	**10,000**	
Total stockholders' equity		1,165,000
Total liabilities and stockholders' equity		$1,710,000

Note 1. Retained earnings of $100,000 is restricted for plant expansion.

REVIEW AND PRACTICE

LEARNING OBJECTIVES REVIEW

1 Explain how to account for debt investments. Companies record investments in debt securities when they purchase bonds, receive or accrue interest, and sell the bonds. They report gains or losses on the sale of bonds in the "Other revenues and gains" or "Other expenses and losses" sections of the income statement.

2 Explain how to account for stock investments. Companies record investments in common stock when they purchase the stock, receive dividends, and sell the stock. When ownership is less than 20%, the cost method is used. When ownership is between 20% and 50%, the equity method should be used. When ownership is more than 50%, companies prepare consolidated financial statements. Consolidated financial statements indicate the magnitude and scope of operations of the companies under common control.

3 Discuss how debt and stock investments are reported in financial statements. Investments in debt securities are classified as trading, available-for-sale, or held-to-maturity securities for valuation and reporting purposes. Stock investments are classified either as trading or available-for-sale securities. Stock investments have no maturity date and therefore are never classified as held-to-maturity securities. Trading securities are reported as current assets at fair value, with changes from cost reported in net income. Available-for-sale securities are also reported at fair value, with the changes from cost reported in stockholders' equity. Available-for-sale securities are classified as short-term or long-term, depending on their expected future sale date.

Short-term investments are securities that are (a) readily marketable and (b) intended to be converted to cash within the next year or operating cycle, whichever is longer. Investments that do not meet both criteria are classified as long-term investments.

GLOSSARY REVIEW

Available-for-sale securities Securities that are held with the intent of selling them sometime in the future. (p. 700).

Consolidated financial statements Financial statements that present the assets and liabilities controlled by the parent company and the total revenues and expenses of the subsidiary companies. (p. 698).

Controlling interest Ownership of more than 50% of the common stock of another entity. (p. 698).

Cost method An accounting method in which the investment in common stock is recorded at cost, and revenue is recognized only when cash dividends are received. (p. 696).

Debt investments Investments in government and corporation bonds. (p. 693).

Equity method An accounting method in which the investment in common stock is initially recorded at cost, and the investment account is then adjusted annually to show the investor's equity in the investee. (p. 697).

Fair value Amount for which a security could be sold in a normal market. (p. 700).

Held-to-maturity securities Debt securities that the investor has the intent and ability to hold to their maturity date. (p. 700).

Investment portfolio A group of stocks and/or debt securities in different corporations held for investment purposes. (p. 695).

Long-term investments Investments that are not readily marketable or that management does not intend to convert into cash within the next year or operating cycle, whichever is longer. (p. 703).

Parent company A company that owns more than 50% of the common stock of another entity. (p. 698).

Short-term investments Investments that are readily marketable and intended to be converted into cash within the next year or operating cycle, whichever is longer. (p. 703).

Stock investments Investments in the capital stock of other corporations. (p. 695).

Subsidiary (affiliated) company A company in which more than 50% of its stock is owned by another company. (p. 698).

Trading securities Securities bought and held primarily for sale in the near term to generate income on short-term price differences. (p. 700).

PRACTICE MULTIPLE-CHOICE QUESTIONS

(LO 1) 1. Which of the following is **not** a primary reason why corporations invest in debt and equity securities?
(a) They wish to gain control of a competitor.
(b) They have excess cash.
(c) They wish to move into a new line of business.
(d) They are required to by law.

(LO 1) 2. Debt investments are initially recorded at:
(a) cost.
(b) cost plus accrued interest.
(c) fair value.
(d) face value.

(LO 1) 3. Hanes Company sells debt investments costing $26,000 for $28,000. In journalizing the sale, credits are to:
(a) Debt Investments and Loss on Sale of Debt Investments.
(b) Debt Investments and Gain on Sale of Debt Investments.
(c) Stock Investments and Gain on Sale of Stock Investments.
(d) No correct answer is given.

(LO 2) 4. Pryor Company receives net proceeds of $42,000 on the sale of stock investments that cost $39,500. This transaction will result in reporting in the income statement a:
(a) loss of $2,500 under "Other expenses and losses."
(b) loss of $2,500 under "Operating expenses."
(c) gain of $2,500 under "Other revenues and gains."
(d) gain of $2,500 under "Operating revenues."

(LO 2) 5. The equity method of accounting for long-term investments in stock should be used when the investor has significant influence over an investee and owns:
(a) between 20% and 50% of the investee's common stock.
(b) 20% or more of the investee's common stock.
(c) more than 50% of the investee's common stock.
(d) less than 20% of the investee's common stock.

(LO 2) 6. Assume that Horicon Corp. acquired 25% of the common stock of Sheboygan Corp. on January 1, 2017, for $300,000. During 2017, Sheboygan Corp. reported net income of $160,000 and paid total dividends of $60,000. If Horicon uses the equity method to account for its investment, the balance in the investment account on December 31, 2017, will be:
(a) $300,000.
(b) $325,000.
(c) $400,000.
(d) $340,000.

(LO 2) 7. Using the information in Question 6, what entry would Horicon make to record the receipt of the dividend from Sheboygan?
(a) Debit Cash and credit Revenue from Stock Investments.
(b) Debit Cash Dividends and credit Revenue from Stock Investments.
(c) Debit Cash and credit Stock Investments.
(d) Debit Cash and credit Dividend Revenue.

(LO 2) 8. You have a controlling interest if:
(a) you own more than 20% of a company's stock.
(b) you are the president of the company.
(c) you use the equity method.
(d) you own more than 50% of a company's stock.

(LO 2) 9. Which of the following statements is **false**? Consolidated financial statements are useful to:
(a) determine the profitability of specific subsidiaries.
(b) determine the total profitability of companies under common control.
(c) determine the breadth of a parent company's operations.
(d) determine the full extent of total obligations of companies under common control.

(LO 3) 10. At the end of the first year of operations, the total cost of the trading securities portfolio is $120,000. Total fair value is $115,000. The financial statements should show:
(a) a reduction of an asset of $5,000 and a realized loss of $5,000.
(b) a reduction of an asset of $5,000 and an unrealized loss of $5,000 in the stockholders' equity section.
(c) a reduction of an asset of $5,000 in the current assets section and an unrealized loss of $5,000 in "Other expenses and losses."
(d) a reduction of an asset of $5,000 in the current assets section and a realized loss of $5,000 in "Other expenses and losses."

(LO 3) 11. At December 31, 2017, the fair value of available-for-sale securities is $41,300 and the cost is $39,800. At January 1, 2017, there was a credit balance of $900 in the Fair Value Adjustment—Available-for-Sale account. The required adjusting entry would be:
(a) Debit Fair Value Adjustment—Available-for-Sale for $1,500 and credit Unrealized Gain or Loss—Equity for $1,500.
(b) Debit Fair Value Adjustment—Available-for-Sale for $600 and credit Unrealized Gain or Loss—Equity for $600.
(c) Debit Fair Value Adjustment—Available-for-Sale for $2,400 and credit Unrealized Gain or Loss—Equity for $2,400.
(d) Debit Unrealized Gain or Loss—Equity for $2,400 and credit Fair Value Adjustment—Available-for-Sale for $2,400.

(LO 3) 12. If a company wants to increase its reported income by manipulating its investment accounts, which should it do?
(a) Sell its "winner" trading securities and hold its "loser" trading securities.
(b) Hold its "winner" trading securities and sell its "loser" trading securities.
(c) Sell its "winner" available-for-sale securities and hold its "loser" available-for-sale securities.
(d) Hold its "winner" available-for-sale securities and sell its "loser" available-for-sale securities.

(LO 3) 13. In the balance sheet, a debit balance in Unrealized Gain or Loss—Equity is reported as a(n):
(a) increase to stockholders' equity.
(b) decrease to stockholders' equity.

(c) loss in the income statement.
(d) loss in the retained earnings statement.

(LO 3) 14. Short-term debt investments must be readily marketable and expected to be sold within:
(a) 3 months from the date of purchase.
(b) the next year or operating cycle, whichever is shorter.
(c) the next year or operating cycle, whichever is longer.
(d) the operating cycle.

Solutions

1. (d) Corporations are not required to by law to invest in debt and equity securities. The other choices are reasons why corporations invest in debt and equity securities.

2. (a) When debt investments are purchased, they are recorded at cost, not (b) cost plus accrued interest, (c) fair value, or (d) face value.

3. (b) Credits are made to Debt Investments $26,000 and Gain on Sale of Debt Investments $2,000 ($28,000 − $26,000). The other choices are therefore incorrect.

4. (c) Because the cash received ($42,000) is greater than the cost ($39,500), this sale results in a gain, not a loss, which will be reported under "Other revenues and gains" in the income statement. The other choices are therefore incorrect.

5. (a) The equity method is used when the investor can exercise significant influence and owns between 20% and 50% of the investee's common stock. The other choices are therefore incorrect.

6. (b) Horicon records the acquisition of the stock investment by debiting Stock Investments $300,000 and crediting Cash $300,000. Then, Horicon records (1) its share in Sheboygan Corp.'s net income ($160,000 × .25) by debiting Stock Investments $40,000 and crediting Revenue from Stock Investments $40,000 and (2) the reduction in the investment account for the dividends received ($60,000 × .25) by debiting Cash $15,000 and crediting Stock Investments $15,000. Thus, the balance in the investment account on December 31 will be $325,000 ($300,000 + $40,000 − $15,000), not (a) $300,000, (c) $400,000, or (d) $340,000.

7. (c) Horicon records the receipt of the dividend from Sheboygan by debiting Cash and crediting Stock Investments. The other choices are therefore incorrect.

8. (d) You have a controlling interest if you own more than 50% of a company's stock, not (a) 20% of a company's stock, (b) are president of the company, or (c) use the equity method.

9. (a) Consolidated financial statements are not useful in determining the profitability of specific subsidiaries (legal entities) because consolidated financial statements represent the results of the single economic entity. The other choices are true statements.

10. (c) The difference between the fair value ($115,000) and total cost ($120,000) of trading securities at the end of the first year would result in a reduction of an asset of $5,000 through the valuation allowance account in the current assets section and an unrealized loss of $5,000 in "Other expenses and losses." The other choices are therefore incorrect.

11. (c) In this case, there is an unrealized gain of $1,500 because total fair value of $41,300 is $1,500 greater than the total cost of $39,800. The desired balance in the market adjustment account is $1,500 debit. The required adjusting entry considers the existing credit balance of $900 and is a debit to Fair Value Adjustment—Available-for-Sale for $2,400 ($1,500 + $900) and a credit to Unrealized Gain or Loss—Equity for $2,400 ($1,500 + $900). The other choices are therefore incorrect.

12. (c) When a company sells its winners as related to available-for-sale securities, it has a realized gain that increases net income. Selling the winners will affect the balance in Unrealized Holding Gain or Loss—Equity, but any change in this balance does not affect net income. Choices (a) and (b) are incorrect because trading securities' gains and losses related to changes in valuation are reported in net income. Thus, when a company sells a trading security, it should have no effect on net income because the value change was recognized in net income previously. Choice (d) is incorrect because selling the losing available-for-sale securities will decrease net income.

13. (b) A debit balance in Unrealized Gain or Loss—Equity is reported on the balance sheet as a separate component of stockholders' equity, decreasing stockholders' equity. The other choices are therefore incorrect.

14. (c) Short-term investments are current assets that are expected to be consumed, sold, or converted to cash within one year or the operating cycle, whichever is longer. The other choices are therefore incorrect.

PRACTICE EXERCISES

Journalize debt investment transactions, accrue interest, and record sale.

(LO 1)

1. Potter Company purchased 50 Quinn Company 6%, 10-year, $1,000 bonds on January 1, 2017, for $50,000. The bonds pay interest annually. On January 1, 2018, after receipt of interest, Potter Company sold 30 of the bonds for $28,100.

Instructions

Prepare the journal entries to record the transactions described above.

Solution

1.	January 1, 2017		
Debt Investments		50,000	
Cash			50,000
	December 31, 2017		
Interest Receivable		3,000	
Interest Revenue ($50,000 × 6%)			3,000
	January 1, 2018		
Cash		3,000	
Interest Receivable			3,000
	January 1, 2018		
Cash		28,100	
Loss on Sale of Debt Investments		1,900	
Debt Investments (30/50 × $50,000)			30,000

Journalize transactions for investments in stocks.

(LO 2)

2. Lucy Inc. had the following transactions in 2017 pertaining to investments in common stock.

Jan. 1	Purchased 4,000 shares of Morgan Corporation common stock (5%) for $180,000 cash.
July 1	Received a cash dividend of $3 per share.
Dec. 1	Sold 600 shares of Morgan Corporation common stock for $32,000 cash.
Dec. 31	Received a cash dividend of $3 per share.

Instructions

Journalize the transactions.

Solution

2.	January 1, 2017		
Stock Investments		180,000	
Cash			180,000
	July 1, 2017		
Cash (4,000 × $3)		12,000	
Dividend Revenue			12,000
	December 1, 2017		
Cash		32,000	
Stock Investments ($180,000 × 600/4,000)			27,000
Gain on Sale of Stock Investments			5,000
	December 31, 2017		
Cash [($4,000 − $600) × $3]		10,200	
Dividend Revenue			10,200

Prepare adjusting entries for fair value, and indicate statement presentation for two classes of securities.

(LO 3)

3. Remy Company started business on January 1, 2017, and has the following data at December 31, 2017.

Securities	Cost	Fair Value
Trading	$120,000	$132,000
Available-for-sale	100,000	86,000

The available-for-sale securities are held as a long-term investment.

Instructions

(a) Prepare the adjusting entries to report each class of securities at fair value.

(b) Indicate the statement presentation of each class of securities and the related unrealized gain (loss) accounts.

Solution

3.	**December 31, 2017**		
(a)	Fair Value Adjustment—Trading ($132,000 − $120,000)	12,000	
	Unrealized Gain—Income		12,000
	Unrealized Gain or Loss—Equity ($100,000 − $86,000)	14,000	
	Fair Value Adjustment—Available-for-Sale		14,000
(b)	**Balance Sheet**		
	Current assets		
	Short-term investments, at fair value	$132,000	
	Investments		
	Investment in stock of less than 20% owned companies, at fair value	86,000	
	Stockholders' equity		
	Less: Unrealized loss on available-for-sale securities	$ (14,000)	
	Income Statement		
	Other revenues and gains		
	Unrealized gain on trading securities	$ 12,000	

PRACTICE PROBLEM

Journalize transactions and prepare adjusting entry to record fair value.

(LO 2, 3)

In its first year of operations, DeMarco Company had the following selected transactions in stock investments that are considered trading securities.

June 1 Purchased for cash 600 shares of Sanburg common stock at $24 per share.
July 1 Purchased for cash 800 shares of Cey Corporation common stock at $33 per share.
Sept. 1 Received a $1 per share cash dividend from Cey Corporation.
Nov. 1 Sold 200 shares of Sanburg common stock for cash at $27 per share.
Dec. 15 Received a $0.50 per share cash dividend on Sanburg common stock.

At December 31, the fair values per share were Sanburg $25 and Cey $30.

Instructions

(a) Journalize the transactions.

(b) Prepare the adjusting entry at December 31 to report the securities at fair value.

Solution

(a)	June 1	Stock Investments	14,400	
		Cash (600 × $24)		14,400
		(To record purchase of 600 shares of Sanburg common stock)		
	July 1	Stock Investments	26,400	
		Cash (800 × $33)		26,400
		(To record purchase of 800 shares of Cey common stock)		
	Sept. 1	Cash (800 × $1.00)	800	
		Dividend Revenue		800
		(To record receipt of $1 per share cash dividend from Cey Corporation)		
	Nov. 1	Cash (200 × $27)	5,400	
		Stock Investments (200 × $24)		4,800
		Gain on Sale of Stock Investments		600
		(To record sale of 200 shares of Sanburg common stock)		
	Dec. 15	Cash [(600 − 200) × $0.50]	200	
		Dividend Revenue		200
		(To record receipt of $0.50 per share dividend from Sanburg)		

(b) Dec. 31	Unrealized Loss—Income	2,000	
	Fair Value Adjustment—Trading		2,000
	(To record unrealized loss on trading securities)		

Investment	Cost	Fair Value	Unrealized Gain (Loss)
Sanburg common stock	$ 9,600[a]	$10,000[b]	$ 400
Cey common stock	26,400[c]	24,000[d]	(2,400)
Totals	$36,000	$34,000	$(2,000)

[a]400 × $24; [b]400 × $25; [c]800 × $33; [d]800 × $30

WileyPLUS Brief Exercises, Exercises, DO IT! Exercises, and Problems and many additional resources are available for practice in WileyPLUS

QUESTIONS

1. What are the reasons that corporations invest in securities?
2. (a) What is the cost of an investment in bonds?
   (b) When is interest on bonds recorded?
3. Alex Ramirez is confused about losses and gains on the sale of debt investments. Explain to Alex (a) how the gain or loss is computed, and (b) the statement presentation of the gains and losses.
4. Seibel Company sells Mayo's bonds costing $40,000 for $45,000, including $500 of accrued interest. Seibel records a $5,000 gain on this sale. Is this correct? Explain.
5. What is the cost of an investment in stock?
6. To acquire Peoples Corporation stock, J. Rich pays $62,000 in cash. What entry should be made for this investment?
7. (a) When should a long-term investment in common stock be accounted for by the equity method? (b) When is revenue recognized under this method?
8. Ling Corporation uses the equity method to account for its ownership of 35% of the common stock of Gorman Packing. During 2017, Gorman reported a net income of $80,000 and declares and pays cash dividends of $10,000. What recognition should Ling Corporation give to these events?
9. What constitutes "significant influence" when an investor's financial interest is below the 50% level?
10. Distinguish between the cost and equity methods of accounting for investments in stocks.
11. What are consolidated financial statements?
12. What are the classification guidelines for investments at a balance sheet date?
13. Jill Hollern is the controller of Chavez Inc. At December 31, the company's investments in trading securities cost $74,000. They have a fair value of $72,000. Indicate how Jill would report these data in the financial statements prepared on December 31.
14. Using the data in Question 13, how would Jill report the data if the investment were long-term and the securities were classified as available-for-sale?
15. Culver Company's investments in available-for-sale securities at December 31 show total cost of $195,000 and total fair value of $205,000. Prepare the adjusting entry.
16. Using the data in Question 15, prepare the adjusting entry assuming the securities are classified as trading securities.
17. What is the proper statement presentation of the account Unrealized Loss—Equity?
18. What purposes are served by reporting Unrealized Gain or Loss—Equity in the stockholders' equity section?
19. Deering Wholesale Supply owns stock in Orr Corporation. Deering intends to hold the stock indefinitely because of some negative tax consequences if sold. Should the investment in Orr be classified as a short-term investment? Why or why not?
20. What does Apple state regarding its accounting policy involving consolidated financial statements?

BRIEF EXERCISES

Journalize entries for debt investments.
(LO 1)

BE16-1 Ownbey Corporation purchased debt investments for $52,000 on January 1, 2017. On July 1, 2017, Ownbey received cash interest of $2,340. Journalize the purchase and the receipt of interest. Assume that no interest has been accrued.

Journalize entries for stock investments.
(LO 2)

BE16-2 On August 1, Shaw Company buys 1,000 shares of Estrada common stock for $37,000 cash. On December 1, Shaw sells the stock investments for $40,000 in cash. Journalize the purchase and sale of the common stock.

BE16-3 Noler Company owns 25% of Lauer Company. For the current year, Lauer reports net income of $180,000 and declares and pays a $50,000 cash dividend. Record Noler's equity in Lauer's net income and the receipt of dividends from Lauer.

Record transactions under the equity method of accounting.

(LO 2)

BE16-4 The cost of the trading securities of Munoz Company at December 31, 2017, is $64,000. At December 31, 2017, the fair value of the securities is $59,000. Prepare the adjusting entry to record the securities at fair value.

Prepare adjusting entry using fair value.

(LO 3)

BE16-5 For the data presented in BE16-4, show the financial statement presentation of the trading securities and related accounts.

Indicate statement presentation using fair value.

(LO 3)

BE16-6 Godfrey Corporation holds, as a long-term investment, available-for-sale securities costing $72,000. At December 31, 2017, the fair value of the securities is $68,000. Prepare the adjusting entry to record the securities at fair value.

Prepare adjusting entry using fair value.

(LO 3)

BE16-7 For the data presented in BE16-6, show the financial statement presentation of the available-for-sale securities and related accounts. Assume the available-for-sale securities are noncurrent.

Indicate statement presentation using fair value.

(LO 3)

BE16-8 Kruger Corporation has the following long-term investments. (1) Common stock of Eidman Co. (10% ownership) held as available-for-sale securities, cost $108,000, fair value $115,000. (2) Common stock of Pickerill Inc. (30% ownership), cost $210,000, equity $260,000. Prepare the investments section of the balance sheet.

Prepare investments section of balance sheet.

(LO 3)

DO IT! Exercises

DO IT! 16-1 Kurtyka Corporation had the following transactions relating to debt investments:

Make journal entry for bond purchase and adjusting entry for interest accrual.

(LO 1)

Jan. 1, 2017	Purchased 50, $1,000, 10% Spiller Company bonds for $50,000. Interest is payable annually on January 1.
Dec. 31, 2017	Accrued interest on Spiller Company bonds.
Jan. 1, 2018	Received interest from Spiller Company bonds.
Jan. 1, 2018	Sold 30 Spiller Company bonds for $29,000.

(a) Journalize the transactions, and (b) prepare the adjusting entry for the accrual of interest on December 31, 2017.

DO IT! 16-2 Presented below are two independent situations:

Make journal entries for stock investments.

(LO 2)

1. Edelman Inc. acquired 10% of the 500,000 shares of common stock of Schuberger Corporation at a total cost of $11 per share on June 17, 2017. On September 3, Schuberger declared and paid a $160,000 dividend. On December 31, Schuberger reported net income of $550,000 for the year.
2. Wen Corporation obtained significant influence over Hunsaker Company by buying 30% of Hunsaker's 100,000 outstanding shares of common stock at a cost of $18 per share on January 1, 2017. On May 15, Hunsaker declared and paid a cash dividend of $150,000. On December 31, Hunsaker reported net income of $270,000 for the year.

Prepare all necessary journal entries for 2017 for (a) Edelman and (b) Wen.

DO IT! 16-3a Some of Tollakson Corporation's investment securities are classified as trading securities and some are classified as available-for-sale. The cost and fair value of each category at December 31, 2017, were as follows.

Make journal entries for trading and available-for-sale securities.

(LO 3)

	Cost	Fair Value	Unrealized Gain (Loss)
Trading securities	$96,300	$84,900	$(11,400)
Available-for-sale securities	$59,000	$63,200	$ 4,200

At December 31, 2016, the Fair Value Adjustment—Trading account had a debit balance of $3,200, and the Fair Value Adjustment—Available-for-Sale account had a credit balance of $5,750. Prepare the required journal entries for each group of securities for December 31, 2017.

Indicate financial statement presentation of investments.
(LO 3)

DO IT! 16-3b Identify where each of the following items would be reported in the financial statements.

1. Loss on sale of investments in stock.
2. Unrealized gain on available-for-sale securities.
3. Fair value adjustment—trading.
4. Interest earned on investments in bonds.
5. Unrealized loss on trading securities.

Use the following possible categories:

Balance sheet:

Current assets	Current liabilities
Investments	Long-term liabilities
Property, plant, and equipment	Stockholders' equity
Intangible assets	

Income statement:

Other revenues and gains	Other expenses and losses

EXERCISES

Understand debt and stock investments.
(LO 1)

E16-1 Mr. Taliaferro is studying for an accounting test and has developed the following questions about investments.

1. What are three reasons why companies purchase investments in debt or stock securities?
2. Why would a corporation have excess cash that it does not need for operations?
3. What is the typical investment when investing cash for short periods of time?
4. What are the typical investments when investing cash to generate earnings?
5. Why would a company invest in securities that provide no current cash flows?
6. What is the typical stock investment when investing cash for strategic reasons?

Instructions
Provide answers for Mr. Taliaferro.

Journalize debt investment transactions and accrue interest.
(LO 1)

E16-2 Jenek Corporation had the following transactions pertaining to debt investments.

1. Purchased 50 9%, $1,000 Leeds Co. bonds for $50,000 cash. Interest is payable annually on January 1, 2017.
2. Accrued interest on Leeds Co. bonds on December 31, 2017.
3. Received interest on Leeds Co. bonds on January 1, 2018.
4. Sold 30 Leeds Co. bonds for $33,000 on January 1, 2018.

Instructions
Journalize the transactions.

Journalize debt investment transactions, accrue interest, and record sale.
(LO 1)

E16-3 Flynn Company purchased 70 Rinehart Company 6%, 10-year, $1,000 bonds on January 1, 2017, for $70,000. The bonds pay interest annually on January 1. On January 1, 2018, after receipt of interest, Flynn Company sold 40 of the bonds for $38,500.

Instructions
Prepare the journal entries to record the transactions described above.

Journalize stock investment transactions.
(LO 2)

E16-4 Hulse Company had the following transactions pertaining to stock investments.

Feb. 1	Purchased 600 shares of Wade common stock (2%) for $7,200 cash.
July 1	Received cash dividends of $1 per share on Wade common stock.
Sept. 1	Sold 300 shares of Wade common stock for $4,300.
Dec. 1	Received cash dividends of $1 per share on Wade common stock.

Instructions
(a) Journalize the transactions.
(b) Explain how dividend revenue and the gain (loss) on sale should be reported in the income statement.

Journalize transactions for investments in stocks.

(LO 2)

E16-5 Nosker Inc. had the following transactions pertaining to investments in common stock.

Jan. 1	Purchased 2,500 shares of Escalante Corporation common stock (5%) for $152,000 cash.
July 1	Received a cash dividend of $3 per share.
Dec. 1	Sold 500 shares of Escalante Corporation common stock for $32,000 cash.
Dec. 31	Received a cash dividend of $3 per share.

Instructions

Journalize the transactions.

Journalize transactions for investments in stocks.

(LO 2)

E16-6 On February 1, Rinehart Company purchased 500 shares (2% ownership) of Givens Company common stock for $32 per share. On March 20, Rinehart Company sold 100 shares of Givens stock for $2,900. Rinehart received a dividend of $1.00 per share on April 25. On June 15, Rinehart sold 200 shares of Givens stock for $7,600. On July 28, Rinehart received a dividend of $1.25 per share.

Instructions

Prepare the journal entries to record the transactions described above.

Journalize and post transactions, under the equity method.

(LO 2)

E16-7 On January 1, Zabel Corporation purchased a 25% equity in Helbert Corporation for $180,000. At December 31, Helbert declared and paid a $60,000 cash dividend and reported net income of $200,000.

Instructions

(a) Journalize the transactions.

(b) Determine the amount to be reported as an investment in Helbert stock at December 31.

Journalize entries under cost and equity methods.

(LO 2, 3)

E16-8 Presented below are two independent situations.

1. Gambino Cosmetics acquired 10% of the 200,000 shares of common stock of Nevins Fashion at a total cost of $13 per share on March 18, 2017. On June 30, Nevins declared and paid a $60,000 dividend. On December 31, Nevins reported net income of $122,000 for the year. At December 31, the market price of Nevins Fashion was $15 per share. The stock is classified as available-for-sale.
2. Kanza, Inc., obtained significant influence over Rogan Corporation by buying 40% of Rogan's 30,000 outstanding shares of common stock at a total cost of $9 per share on January 1, 2017. On June 15, Rogan declared and paid a cash dividend of $30,000. On December 31, Rogan reported a net income of $80,000 for the year.

Instructions

Prepare all the necessary journal entries for 2017 for (a) Gambino Cosmetics and (b) Kanza, Inc.

Understand the usefulness of consolidated statements.

(LO 2)

E16-9 Agee Company purchased 70% of the outstanding common stock of Himes Corporation.

Instructions

(a) Explain the relationship between Agee Company and Himes Corporation.

(b) How should Agee account for its investment in Himes?

(c) Why is the accounting treatment described in (b) useful?

Prepare adjusting entry to record fair value, and indicate statement presentation.

(LO 3)

E16-10 At December 31, 2017, the trading securities for Storrer, Inc. are as follows.

Security	Cost	Fair Value
A	$17,500	$16,000
B	12,500	14,000
C	23,000	21,000
	$53,000	$51,000

Instructions

(a) Prepare the adjusting entry at December 31, 2017, to report the securities at fair value.

(b) Show the balance sheet and income statement presentation at December 31, 2017, after adjustment to fair value.

Prepare adjusting entry to record fair value, and indicate statement presentation.

(LO 3)

E16-11 Data for investments in stock classified as trading securities are presented in E16-10. Assume instead that the investments are classified as available-for-sale securities. They have the same cost and fair value. The securities are considered to be a long-term investment.

Instructions

(a) Prepare the adjusting entry at December 31, 2017, to report the securities at fair value.
(b) Show the statement presentation at December 31, 2017, after adjustment to fair value.
(c) E. Kretsinger, a member of the board of directors, does not understand the reporting of the unrealized gains or losses. Write a letter to Ms. Kretsinger explaining the reporting and the purposes that it serves.

Prepare adjusting entries for fair value, and indicate statement presentation for two classes of securities.

(LO 3)

E16-12 Uttinger Company has the following data at December 31, 2017.

Securities	Cost	Fair Value
Trading	$120,000	$126,000
Available-for-sale	100,000	96,000

The available-for-sale securities are held as a long-term investment.

Instructions

(a) Prepare the adjusting entries to report each class of securities at fair value.
(b) Indicate the statement presentation of each class of securities and the related unrealized gain (loss) accounts.

EXERCISES: SET B AND CHALLENGE EXERCISES

Visit the book's companion website, at **www.wiley.com/college/weygandt**, and choose the Student Companion site to access Exercises: Set B and Challenge Exercises.

PROBLEMS: SET A

Journalize debt investment transactions and show financial statement presentation.

(LO 2, 3)

P16-1A Vilander Carecenters Inc. provides financing and capital to the healthcare industry, with a particular focus on nursing homes for the elderly. The following selected transactions relate to bonds acquired as an investment by Vilander, whose fiscal year ends on December 31.

2017

Jan. 1	Purchased at face value $2,000,000 of Javier Nursing Centers, Inc., 10-year, 8% bonds dated January 1, 2017, directly from Javier.
Dec. 31	Accrual of interest at year-end on the Javier bonds.

(Assume that all intervening transactions and adjustments have been properly recorded and that the number of bonds owned has not changed from December 31, 2017, to December 31, 2019.)

2020

Jan. 1	Received the annual interest on the Javier bonds.
Jan. 1	Sold $1,000,000 Javier bonds at 106.
Dec. 31	Accrual of interest at year-end on the Javier bonds.

Instructions

(a) Gain on sale of debt investment $60,000

(a) Journalize the listed transactions for the years 2017 and 2020.
(b) Assume that the fair value of the bonds at December 31, 2017, was $2,200,000. These bonds are classified as available-for-sale securities. Prepare the adjusting entry to record these bonds at fair value.
(c) Based on your analysis in part (b), show the balance sheet presentation of the bonds and interest receivable at December 31, 2017. Assume the investments are considered long-term. Indicate where any unrealized gain or loss is reported in the financial statements.

P16-2A In January 2017, the management of Kinzie Company concludes that it has sufficient cash to permit some short-term investments in debt and stock securities. During the year, the following transactions occurred.

Journalize investment transactions, prepare adjusting entry, and show statement presentation.

(LO 2, 3)

GLS

Feb.	1	Purchased 600 shares of Muninger common stock for $32,400.
Mar.	1	Purchased 800 shares of Tatman common stock for $20,000.
Apr.	1	Purchased 50 $1,000, 7% Yoakem bonds for $50,000. Interest is payable semiannually on April 1 and October 1.
July	1	Received a cash dividend of $0.60 per share on the Muninger common stock.
Aug.	1	Sold 200 shares of Muninger common stock at $58 per share.
Sept.	1	Received a $1 per share cash dividend on the Tatman common stock.
Oct.	1	Received the semiannual interest on the Yoakem bonds.
Oct.	1	Sold the Yoakem bonds for $49,000.

At December 31, the fair value of the Muninger common stock was $55 per share. The fair value of the Tatman common stock was $24 per share.

Instructions

(a) Journalize the transactions and post to the accounts Debt Investments and Stock Investments. (Use the T-account form.)

(a) Gain on sale of stock investment $800

(b) Prepare the adjusting entry at December 31, 2017, to report the investment securities at fair value. All securities are considered to be trading securities.

(c) Show the balance sheet presentation of investment securities at December 31, 2017.

(d) Identify the income statement accounts and give the statement classification of each account.

P16-3A On December 31, 2017, Turnball Associates owned the following securities, held as a long-term investment. The securities are not held for influence or control of the investee.

Journalize transactions and adjusting entry for stock investments.

(LO 2, 3)

XLS

Common Stock	Shares	Cost
Gehring Co.	2,000	$60,000
Wooderson Co.	5,000	45,000
Kitselton Co.	1,500	30,000

On December 31, 2017, the total fair value of the securities was equal to its cost. In 2018, the following transactions occurred.

Aug.	1	Received $0.50 per share cash dividend on Gehring Co. common stock.
Sept.	1	Sold 1,500 shares of Wooderson Co. common stock for cash at $8 per share.
Oct.	1	Sold 800 shares of Gehring Co. common stock for cash at $33 per share.
Nov.	1	Received $1 per share cash dividend on Kitselton Co. common stock.
Dec.	15	Received $0.50 per share cash dividend on Gehring Co. common stock.
	31	Received $1 per share annual cash dividend on Wooderson Co. common stock.

At December 31, the fair values per share of the common stocks were: Gehring Co. $32, Wooderson Co. $8, and Kitselton Co. $18.

Instructions

(a) Journalize the 2018 transactions and post to the account Stock Investments. (Use the T-account form.)

(b) Prepare the adjusting entry at December 31, 2018, to show the securities at fair value. The stock should be classified as available-for-sale securities.

(b) Unrealized loss $4,100

(c) Show the balance sheet presentation of the investments at December 31, 2018. At this date, Turnball Associates has common stock $1,500,000 and retained earnings $1,000,000.

P16-4A Heidebrecht Design acquired 20% of the outstanding common stock of Quayle Company on January 1, 2017, by paying $800,000 for the 30,000 shares. Quayle declared and paid $0.30 per share cash dividends on March 15, June 15, September 15, and December 15, 2017. Quayle reported net income of $320,000 for the year. At December 31, 2017, the market price of Quayle common stock was $34 per share.

Prepare entries under the cost and equity methods, and tabulate differences.

(LO 2)

Instructions

(a) Total dividend revenue $36,000

(b) Revenue from stock investments $64,000

(a) Prepare the journal entries for Heidebrecht Design for 2017 assuming Heidebrecht Design cannot exercise significant influence over Quayle. (Use the cost method and assume that Quayle common stock should be classified as a trading security.)
(b) Prepare the journal entries for Heidebrecht Design for 2017, assuming Heidebrecht Design can exercise significant influence over Quayle. Use the equity method.
(c) Indicate the balance sheet and income statement account balances at December 31, 2017, under each method of accounting.

Journalize stock investment transactions and show statement presentation.

(LO 2, 3)

P16-5A The following securities are in Frederick Company's portfolio of long-term available-for-sale securities at December 31, 2017.

	Cost
1,000 shares of Willhite Corporation common stock	$52,000
1,400 shares of Hutcherson Corporation common stock	84,000
1,200 shares of Downing Corporation preferred stock	33,600

On December 31, 2017, the total cost of the portfolio equaled total fair value. Frederick had the following transactions related to the securities during 2018.

Jan.	20	Sold all 1,000 shares of Willhite Corporation common stock at $55 per share.
	28	Purchased 400 shares of $70 par value common stock of Liggett Corporation at $78 per share.
	30	Received a cash dividend of $1.15 per share on Hutcherson Corp. common stock.
Feb.	8	Received cash dividends of $0.40 per share on Downing Corp. preferred stock.
	18	Sold all 1,200 shares of Downing Corp. preferred stock at $27 per share.
July	30	Received a cash dividend of $1.00 per share on Hutcherson Corp. common stock.
Sept.	6	Purchased an additional 900 shares of $10 par value common stock of Liggett Corporation at $82 per share.
Dec.	1	Received a cash dividend of $1.50 per share on Liggett Corporation common stock.

At December 31, 2018, the fair values of the securities were:

Hutcherson Corporation common stock	$64 per share
Liggett Corporation common stock	$72 per share

Instructions

(a) Loss on sale of stock investment $1,200

(c) Unrealized loss $5,800

(a) Prepare journal entries to record the transactions.
(b) Post to the investment accounts. (Use T-accounts.)
(c) Prepare the adjusting entry at December 31, 2018 to report the portfolio at fair value.
(d) Show the balance sheet presentation at December 31, 2018, for the investment-related accounts.

Prepare a balance sheet.

(LO 3)

P16-6A The following data, presented in alphabetical order, are taken from the records of Nieto Corporation.

Accounts payable	$ 260,000
Accounts receivable	140,000
Accumulated depreciation—buildings	180,000
Accumulated depreciation—equipment	52,000
Allowance for doubtful accounts	6,000
Bonds payable (10%, due 2025)	500,000
Buildings	950,000
Cash	62,000
Common stock ($10 par value; 500,000 shares authorized, 150,000 shares issued)	1,500,000
Dividends payable	80,000
Equipment	275,000
Fair value adjustment—available-for-sale securities (Dr)	8,000
Goodwill	200,000
Income taxes payable	120,000
Inventory	170,000
Investment in Mara common stock (30% ownership), at equity	380,000

Investment in Sasse common stock (10% ownership), at cost	278,000
Land	390,000
Notes payable (due 2018)	70,000
Paid-in capital in excess of par—common stock	130,000
Premium on bonds payable	40,000
Prepaid insurance	16,000
Retained earnings	103,000
Short-term investments, at fair value (and cost)	180,000
Unrealized gain—available-for-sale securities	8,000

The investment in Sasse common stock is considered to be a long-term available-for-sale security.

Instructions

Prepare a classified balance sheet at December 31, 2017.

Total assets $2,811,000

PROBLEMS: SET B AND SET C

Visit the book's companion website, at **www.wiley.com/college/weygandt**, and choose the Student Companion site to access Problems: Set B and Set C.

COMPREHENSIVE PROBLEM: CHAPTERS 12 TO 16

CP16 Part I Debby Kauffman and her two colleagues, Jamie Hiatt and Ella Rincon, are personal trainers at an upscale health spa/resort in Tampa, Florida. They want to start a health club that specializes in health plans for people in the 50+ age range. The growing population in this age range and strong consumer interest in the health benefits of physical activity have convinced them they can profitably operate their own club. In addition to many other decisions, they need to determine what type of business organization they want. Jamie believes there are more advantages to the corporate form than a partnership, but he hasn't yet convinced Debby and Ella. They have come to you, a small-business consulting specialist, seeking information and advice regarding the choice of starting a partnership versus a corporation.

Instructions

(a) Prepare a memo (dated May 26, 2016) that describes the advantages and disadvantages of both partnerships and corporations. Advise Debby, Jamie, and Ella regarding which organizational form you believe would better serve their purposes. Make sure to include reasons supporting your advice.

Part II After deciding to incorporate, each of the three investors receives 20,000 shares of $2 par common stock on June 12, 2016, in exchange for their co-owned building ($200,000 fair value) and $100,000 total cash they contributed to the business. The next decision that Debby, Jamie, and Ella need to make is how to obtain financing for renovation and equipment. They understand the difference between equity securities and debt securities, but do not understand the tax, net income, and earnings per share consequences of equity versus debt financing on the future of their business.

Instructions

(b) Prepare notes for a discussion with the three entrepreneurs in which you will compare the consequences of using equity versus debt financing. As part of your notes, show the differences in interest and tax expense assuming $1,400,000 is financed with common stock, and then alternatively with debt. Assume that when common stock is used, 140,000 shares will be issued. When debt is used, assume the interest rate on debt is 9%, the tax rate is 32%, and income before interest and taxes is $300,000. (You may want to use an electronic spreadsheet.)

Part III During the discussion about financing, Ella mentions that one of her clients, Timothy Hansen, has approached her about buying a significant interest in the new club. Having an interested investor sways the three to issue equity securities to provide the financing they need. On July 21, 2016, Mr. Hansen buys 90,000 shares at a price of $10 per share.

The club, LifePath Fitness, opens on January 12, 2017, and after a slow start begins to produce the revenue desired by the owners. The owners decide to pay themselves a stock dividend since cash has been less than abundant since they opened their doors. The 10% stock dividend is declared by the owners on July 27, 2017. The market price of the stock is $3 on the declaration date. The date of record is July 31, 2017 (there have been no changes in stock ownership since the initial issuance), and the issue date is August 15, 2017. By the middle of the fourth quarter of 2017, the cash flow of LifePath Fitness has improved to the point that the owners feel ready to pay themselves a cash dividend. They declare a $0.05 cash dividend on December 4, 2017. The record date is December 14, 2017, and the payment date is December 24, 2017.

Instructions

(c) (1) Record all of the transactions related to the common stock of LifePath Fitness during the years 2016 and 2017. (2) Indicate how many shares are issued and outstanding after the stock dividend is issued.

Part IV Since the club opened, a major concern has been the pool facilities. Although the existing pool is adequate, Debby, Jamie, and Ella all desire to make LifePath a cutting-edge facility. Until the end of 2017, financing concerns prevented this improvement. However, because there has been steady growth in clientele, revenue, and income since the third quarter of 2017, the owners have explored possible financing options. They are hesitant to issue stock and change the ownership mix because they have been able to work together as a team with great effectiveness. They have formulated a plan to issue secured term bonds to raise the needed $600,000 for the pool facilities. By the end of December 2017, everything was in place for the bond issue to go ahead. On January 1, 2018, the bonds were issued for $548,000. The bonds pay annual interest of 6% on January 1 of each year. The bonds mature in 10 years, and amortization is computed using the straight-line method.

Instructions

(d) Record (1) the issuance of the secured bonds, (2) the adjusting entry required at December 31, 2018, (3) the interest payment made on January 1, 2019, and (4) the interest accrued on December 31, 2019.

Part V Mr. Hansen's purchase of the stock of LifePath Fitness was done through his business. The stock investment has always been accounted for using the cost method on his firm's books. However, early in 2019 he decided to take his company public. He is preparing an IPO (initial public offering), and he needs to have the firm's financial statements audited. One of the issues to be resolved is to restate the stock investment in LifePath Fitness using the equity method since Mr. Hansen's ownership percentage is greater than 20%.

Instructions

(e) (1) Give the entries that would have been made on Hansen's books if the equity method of accounting for investments had been used from the initial investment through 2018. Assume the following data for LifePath.

	2016	2017	2018
Net income	$30,000	$70,000	$105,000
Total cash dividends	$ 2,100	$20,000	$ 50,000

(2) Compute the balance in the Stock Investment account (as it relates to LifePath Fitness) at the end of 2018.

CONTINUING PROBLEM

© leungchopan/ Shutterstock

COOKIE CREATIONS: AN ENTREPRENEURIAL JOURNEY

(*Note:* This is a continuation of the Cookie Creations problem from Chapters 1 through 15.)

CC16 Natalie has been approached by Ken Thornton, a shareholder of The Beanery Coffee Inc. Ken wants to retire and would like to sell his 1,000 shares in The Beanery Coffee, which represents 30% of all shares issued. The Beanery is currently operated by Ken's twin daughters, who each own 35% of the common shares. The Beanery not only operates a coffee shop but also roasts and sells beans to retailers, under the name "Rocky Mountain Beanery."

Ken has met with Curtis and Natalie to discuss the business operation. All have concluded that there would be many advantages for Cookie & Coffee Creations Inc. to acquire an interest in The Beanery Coffee. Despite the apparent advantages, however, Natalie and Curtis are still not convinced that they should participate in this business venture.

Go to the book's companion website, **www.wiley.com/college/weygandt**, *to see the completion of this problem.*

BROADENING YOUR PERSPECTIVE

FINANCIAL REPORTING AND ANALYSIS

Financial Reporting Problem: Apple Inc.

BYP16-1 The annual report of Apple Inc. is presented in Appendix A. Instructions for accessing and using the company's complete annual report, including the notes to the financial statements, are also provided in Appendix A.

Instructions

(a) Determine the percentage increase for (1) short-term marketable securities from 2012 to 2013, and (2) long-term marketable securities from 2012 to 2013.

(b) Using Apple's consolidated statement of cash flows, determine:
   (1) Purchases of marketable securities during the current year.
   (2) How much was spent for business acquisitions, net of cash acquired during the current year.

Comparative Analysis Problem: PepsiCo, Inc. vs. The Coca-Cola Company

BYP16-2 PepsiCo's financial statements are presented in Appendix B. Financial statements of The Coca-Cola Company are presented in Appendix C. Instructions for accessing and using the complete annual reports of PepsiCo and Coca-Cola, including the notes to the financial statements, are also provided in Appendices B and C, respectively.

Instructions

(a) Based on the information contained in these financial statements, determine the following for each company.
   (1) Net cash used in investing (investment) activities for the current year (from the statement of cash flows).
   (2) Cash used for capital expenditures during the current year.

(b) Each of PepsiCo's financial statements is labeled "consolidated." What has been consolidated? That is, from the contents of PepsiCo's annual report, identify by name the corporations that have been consolidated (parent and subsidiaries).

Comparative Analysis Problem: Amazon.com, Inc. vs. Wal-Mart Stores, Inc.

BYP16-3 Amazon.com, Inc.'s financial statements are presented in Appendix D. Financial statements of Wal-Mart Stores, Inc. are presented in Appendix E. Instructions for accessing and using the complete annual reports of Amazon and Wal-Mart, including the notes to the financial statements, are also provided in Appendices D and E, respectively.

Instructions

(a) Based on the information contained in these financial statements, determine the following for each company.
   (1) Net cash used for investing (investment) activities for the current year (from the statement of cash flows).
   (2) Cash used for business acquisitions, net of cash acquired during the current year.

(b) Each of Amazon's financial statements is labeled "consolidated." What has been consolidated? That is, from the contents of Amazon's annual report, identify by name the corporations that have been consolidated (parent and subsidiaries).

Real-World Focus

BYP16-4 Most publicly traded companies are examined by numerous analysts. These analysts often don't agree about a company's future prospects. In this exercise, you will find analysts' ratings about companies and make comparisons over time and across companies in the same industry. You will also see to what extent the analysts experienced "earnings surprises." Earnings surprises can cause changes in stock prices.

Address: **biz.yahoo.com/i**, or go to **www.wiley.com/college/weygandt**

Steps
1. Choose a company.
2. Use the index to find the company's name.
3. Choose **Research**.

Instructions
(a) How many analysts rated the company?
(b) What percentage rated it a strong buy?
(c) What was the average rating for the week?
(d) Did the average rating improve or decline relative to the previous week?
(e) What was the amount of the earnings surprise percentage during the last quarter?

CRITICAL THINKING

Decision-Making Across the Organization

BYP16-5 At the beginning of the question-and-answer portion of the annual stockholders' meeting of Neosho Corporation, stockholder John Linton asks, "Why did management sell the holdings in JMB Company at a loss when this company has been very profitable during the period Neosho held its stock?"

Since president Tony Cedeno has just concluded his speech on the recent success and bright future of Neosho, he is taken aback by this question and responds, "I remember we paid $1,300,000 for that stock some years ago. I am sure we sold that stock at a much higher price. You must be mistaken."

Linton retorts, "Well, right here in footnote number 7 to the annual report it shows that 240,000 shares, a 30% interest in JMB, were sold on the last day of the year. Also, it states that JMB earned $520,000 this year and paid out $160,000 in cash dividends. Further, a summary statement indicates that in past years, while Neosho held JMB stock, JMB earned $1,240,000 and paid out $440,000 in dividends. Finally, the income statement for this year shows a loss on the sale of JMB stock of $180,000. So, I doubt that I am mistaken."

Red-faced, president Cedeno turns to you.

Instructions
With the class divided into groups, answer the following.

(a) What dollar amount did Neosho receive upon the sale of the JMB stock?
(b) Explain why both stockholder Linton and president Cedeno are correct.

Communication Activity

BYP16-6 Fegan Corporation has purchased two securities for its portfolio. The first is a stock investment in Plummer Corporation, one of its suppliers. Fegan purchased 10% of Plummer with the intention of holding it for a number of years, but has no intention of purchasing more shares. The second investment was a purchase of debt securities. Fegan purchased the debt securities because its analysts believe that changes in market interest rates will cause these securities to increase in value in a short period of time. Fegan intends to sell the securities as soon as they have increased in value.

Instructions
Write a memo to Sam Nichols, the chief financial officer, explaining how to account for each of these investments. Explain what the implications for reported income are from this accounting treatment.

Ethics Case

BYP16-7 Harding Financial Services Company holds a large portfolio of debt and stock securities as an investment. The total fair value of the portfolio at December 31, 2017, is greater than total cost. Some securities have increased in value and others have decreased. Ann Bales, the financial vice president, and Kim Reeble, the controller, are in the process of classifying for the first time the securities in the portfolio.

Bales suggests classifying the securities that have increased in value as trading securities in order to increase net income for the year. She wants to classify the securities that have decreased in value as long-term available-for-sale securities, so that the decreases in value will not affect 2017 net income.

Reeble disagrees. She recommends classifying the securities that have decreased in value as trading securities and those that have increased in value as long-term available-for-sale securities. Reeble argues that the company is having a good earnings year and that recognizing the losses now will help to smooth income for this year. Moreover, for future years, when the company may not be as profitable, the company will have built-in gains.

Instructions

(a) Will classifying the securities as Bales and Reeble suggest actually affect earnings as each says it will?
(b) Is there anything unethical in what Bales and Reeble propose? Who are the stakeholders affected by their proposals?
(c) Assume that Bales and Reeble properly classify the portfolio. At year-end, Bales proposes to sell the securities that will increase 2017 net income, and that Reeble proposes to sell the securities that will decrease 2017 net income. Is this unethical?

All About You

BYP16-8 The Securities and Exchange Commission (SEC) is the primary regulatory agency of U.S. financial markets. Its job is to ensure that the markets remain fair for all investors. The following SEC sites provide useful information for investors.

Address: **www.sec.gov/answers.shtml** and **http://www.sec.gov/investor/tools/quiz.htm**, or go to **www.wiley.com/college/weygandt**.

Instructions

(a) Go to the first SEC site and find the definition of the following terms.
  (i) Ask price.
  (ii) Margin.
  (iii) Prospectus.
  (iv) Index fund.
(b) Go to the second SEC site and take the short quiz.

FASB Codification Activity

BYP16-9 If your school has a subscription to the FASB Codification, go to **http://aaahq.org/ascLogin.cfm** to log in and prepare responses to the following.

(a) What is the definition of a trading security?
(b) What is the definition of an available-for-sale security?
(c) What is definition of a holding gain or loss?

A Look at IFRS

LEARNING OBJECTIVE 4 **Compare the accounting for investments under GAAP and IFRS.**

Until recently, when the IASB issued *IFRS 9*, the accounting and reporting for investments under IFRS and GAAP were for the most part very similar. However, *IFRS 9* introduces a new framework for classifying investments.

Key Points

Following are the similarities and differences between GAAP and IFRS as related to investments.

Similarities

- The basic accounting entries to record the acquisition of debt securities, the receipt of interest, and the sale of debt securities are the same under IFRS and GAAP.
- The basic accounting entries to record the acquisition of stock investments, the receipt of dividends, and the sale of stock securities are the same under IFRS and GAAP.
- Both IFRS and GAAP use the same criteria to determine whether the equity method of accounting should be used—that is, significant influence with a general guide of over 20% ownership. IFRS uses the term **associate investment** rather than equity investment to describe its investment under the equity method.
- Equity investments are generally recorded and reported at fair value under IFRS. Equity investments do not have a fixed interest or principal payment schedule and therefore cannot be accounted for at amortized cost. In general, equity investments are valued at fair value, with all gains and losses reported in income, similar to GAAP.
- Unrealized gains and losses related to available-for-sale securities are reported in other comprehensive income under GAAP and IFRS. These gains and losses that accumulate are then reported in the balance sheet.

Differences

- Under IFRS, both the investor and an associate company should follow the same accounting policies. As a result, in order to prepare financial information, adjustments are made to the associate's policies to conform to the investor's books. GAAP does not have that requirement.
- In general, IFRS requires that companies determine how to measure their financial assets based on two criteria:
  - The company's business model for managing their financial assets; and
  - The contractual cash flow characteristics of the financial asset.

  If a company has (1) a business model whose objective is to hold assets in order to collect contractual cash flows and (2) the contractual terms of the financial asset gives specified dates to cash flows that are solely payments of principal and interest on the principal amount outstanding, then the company should use cost (often referred to as amortized cost).

  For example, assume that Mitsubishi purchases a bond investment that it intends to hold to maturity (held-for-collection). Its business model for this type of investment is to collect interest and then principal at maturity. The payment dates for the interest rate and principal are stated on the bond. In this case, Mitsubishi accounts for the investment at cost. If, on the other hand, Mitsubishi purchased the bonds as part of a trading strategy to speculate on interest rate changes (a trading investment), then the debt investment is reported at fair value. As a result, only debt investments such as receivables, loans, and bond investments that meet the two criteria above are recorded at amortized cost. All other debt investments are recorded and reported at fair value.

Looking to the Future

As indicated earlier, the IASB has issued a new revised IFRS which deals with the accounting issues related to investment securities. The FASB is now in the final process of issuing a new standard in this area. It is likely that some differences will continue to exist between the IFRS and the FASB regarding investments.

IFRS Practice

IFRS Self-Test Questions

1. The following asset is **not** considered a financial asset under IFRS:
   (a) trading securities.
   (b) equity securities.
   (c) held-for-collection securities.
   (d) inventories.

2. Under IFRS, the equity method of accounting for long-term investments in common stock should be used when the investor has significant influence over an investee and owns:
   (a) between 20% and 50% of the investee's common stock.
   (b) 30% or more of the investee's common stock.
   (c) more than 50% of the investee's common stock.
   (d) less than 20% of the investee's common stock.
3. Under IFRS, the unrealized loss on trading investments should be reported:
   (a) as part of other comprehensive loss reducing net income.
   (b) on the income statement reducing net income.
   (c) as part of other comprehensive loss not affecting net income.
   (d) directly to stockholders' equity bypassing the income statement.

Answers to IFRS Self-Test Questions

1. d **2.** a **3.** b

17 Statement of Cash Flows

CHAPTER PREVIEW The balance sheet, income statement, and retained earnings statement do not always show the whole picture of the financial condition of a company or institution. In fact, looking at the financial statements of some well-known companies, a thoughtful investor might ask questions like these: How did Eastman Kodak finance cash dividends of $649 million in a year in which it earned only $17 million? How could United Air Lines purchase new planes that cost $1.9 billion in a year in which it reported a net loss of over $2 billion? How did the companies that spent a combined fantastic $3.4 trillion on mergers and acquisitions in a recent year finance those deals? Answers to these and similar questions can be found in this chapter, which presents the statement of cash flows.

FEATURE STORY

Got Cash?

Companies must be ready to respond to changes quickly in order to survive and thrive. This requires careful management of cash. One company that managed cash successfully in its early years was Microsoft. During those years, the company paid much of its payroll with stock options (rights to purchase company stock in the future at a given price) instead of cash. This conserved cash and turned more than a thousand of its employees into millionaires.

In recent years, Microsoft has had a different kind of cash problem. Now that it has reached a more "mature" stage in life, it generates so much cash—roughly $1 billion per month—that it cannot always figure out what to do with it. At one time, Microsoft had accumulated $60 billion.

The company said it was accumulating cash to invest in new opportunities, buy other companies, and pay off pending lawsuits. Microsoft's stockholders complained that holding all this cash was putting a drag on the company's profitability. Why? Because Microsoft had the cash invested in very low-yielding government securities. Stockholders felt that the company either should find new investment projects that would bring higher returns, or return some of the cash to stockholders.

Finally, Microsoft announced a plan to return cash to stockholders by paying a special one-time $32 billion dividend. This special dividend was so large that, according to the U.S. Commerce Department, it caused total personal income in the United States to rise by 3.7% in one month—the largest increase ever recorded by the agency. (It also made the holiday season brighter, especially for retailers in the Seattle area.) Microsoft also doubled its regular annual dividend to $3.50 per share. Further, it announced that it would spend another $30 billion buying treasury stock.

Apple also has encountered this cash "problem." Recently, Apple had nearly $100 billion in liquid assets (cash, cash equivalents, and investment securities). The company was generating $37 billion of cash per year from its operating activities but spending only about $7 billion on plant assets and purchases of patents. Shareholders pressured Apple to unload some of this cash. In response, Apple announced that it would begin to pay a quarterly dividend of $2.65 per share and it would buy back up to $10 billion of its stock. Analysts noted that the dividend consumes only $10 billion of cash per year. This leaves Apple wallowing in cash. The rest of us should have such problems.

Source: "Business: An End to Growth? Microsoft's Cash Bonanza," *The Economist* (July 23, 2005), p. 61.

Justin Sullivan/Getty Images, Inc.

CHAPTER OUTLINE

Learning Objectives

1 Discuss the usefulness and format of the statement of cash flows.

- Usefulness of the statement of cash flows
- Classification of cash flows
- Significant noncash activities
- Format of the statement of cash flows

DO IT! 1 Classification of Cash Flows

2 Prepare a statement of cash flows using the indirect method.

- Indirect and direct methods
- Indirect method—Computer Services Company
- Step 1: Operating activities
- Summary of conversion to net cash provided by operating activities
- Step 2: Investing and financing activities
- Step 3: Net change in cash

DO IT! 2a Cash from Operating Activities
2b Indirect Method

3 Analyze the statement of cash flows.

- Free cash flow

DO IT! 3 Free Cash Flow

o to the ***REVIEW AND PRACTICE*** section at the end of the chapter for a review of key concepts and practice applications with solutions.

sit **WileyPLUS with ORION** for additional tutorials and practice opportunities.

LEARNING OBJECTIVE 1

Discuss the usefulness and format of the statement of cash flows.

The balance sheet, income statement, and retained earnings statement provide only limited information about a company's cash flows (cash receipts and cash payments). For example, comparative balance sheets show the increase in property, plant, and equipment during the year. But, they do not show how the additions were financed or paid for. The income statement shows net income. But, it does not indicate the amount of cash generated by operating activities. The retained earnings statement shows cash dividends declared but not the cash dividends paid during the year. None of these statements presents a detailed summary of where cash came from and how it was used.

Usefulness of the Statement of Cash Flows

The **statement of cash flows** reports the cash receipts, cash payments, and net change in cash resulting from operating, investing, and financing activities during a period. The information in a statement of cash flows helps investors, creditors, and others assess the following.

1. **The entity's ability to generate future cash flows.** By examining relationships between items in the statement of cash flows, investors can better predict the amounts, timing, and uncertainty of future cash flows than they can from accrual-basis data.
2. **The entity's ability to pay dividends and meet obligations.** If a company does not have adequate cash, it cannot pay employees, settle debts, or pay dividends. Employees, creditors, and stockholders should be particularly interested in this statement because it alone shows the flows of cash in a business.
3. **The reasons for the difference between net income and net cash provided (used) by operating activities.** Net income provides information on the success or failure of a business. However, some financial statement users are critical of accrual-basis net income because it requires many estimates. As a result, users often challenge the reliability of the number. Such is not the case with cash. Many readers of the statement of cash flows want to know the reasons for the difference between net income and net cash provided by operating activities. Then, they can assess for themselves the reliability of the income number.
4. **The cash investing and financing transactions during the period.** By examining a company's investing and financing transactions, a financial statement reader can better understand why assets and liabilities changed during the period.

ETHICS NOTE

Though we discourage reliance on cash flows to the exclusion of accrual accounting, comparing net cash provided by operating activities to net income can reveal important information about the "quality" of reported net income. Such a comparison can reveal the extent to which net income provides a good measure of actual performance.

Classification of Cash Flows

The statement of cash flows classifies cash receipts and cash payments as operating, investing, and financing activities. Transactions and other events characteristic of each kind of activity are as follows.

1. **Operating activities** include the cash effects of transactions that create revenues and expenses. They thus enter into the determination of net income.
2. **Investing activities** include (a) acquiring and disposing of investments and property, plant, and equipment, and (b) lending money and collecting the loans.
3. **Financing activities** include (a) obtaining cash from issuing debt and repaying the amounts borrowed, and (b) obtaining cash from stockholders, repurchasing shares, and paying dividends.

The operating activities category is the most important. It shows the cash provided by company operations. This source of cash is generally considered to be the best measure of a company's ability to generate sufficient cash to continue as a going concern.

Illustration 17-1 lists typical cash receipts and cash payments within each of the three classifications. **Study the list carefully.** It will prove very useful in solving homework exercises and problems.

Illustration 17-1
Typical receipt and payment classifications

TYPES OF CASH INFLOWS AND OUTFLOWS

Operating activities—Income statement items
- Cash inflows:
  - From sale of goods or services.
  - From interest received and dividends received.
- Cash outflows:
  - To suppliers for inventory.
  - To employees for wages.
  - To government for taxes.
  - To lenders for interest.
  - To others for expenses.

Investing activities—Changes in investments and long-term assets
- Cash inflows:
  - From sale of property, plant, and equipment.
  - From sale of investments in debt or equity securities of other entities.
  - From collection of principal on loans to other entities.
- Cash outflows:
  - To purchase property, plant, and equipment.
  - To purchase investments in debt or equity securities of other entities.
  - To make loans to other entities.

Financing activities—Changes in long-term liabilities and stockholders' equity
- Cash inflows:
  - From sale of common stock.
  - From issuance of debt (bonds and notes).
- Cash outflows:
  - To stockholders as dividends.
  - To redeem long-term debt or reacquire capital stock (treasury stock).

Operating activities

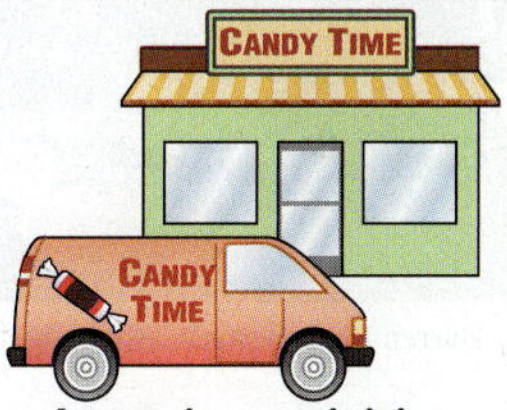

Investing activities

Financing activities

Note the following general guidelines:

1. Operating activities involve income statement items.
2. Investing activities involve cash flows resulting from changes in investments and long-term asset items.
3. Financing activities involve cash flows resulting from changes in long-term liability and stockholders' equity items.

Companies classify as operating activities some cash flows related to investing or financing activities. For example, receipts of investment revenue (interest and dividends) are classified as operating activities. So are payments of interest to lenders. Why are these considered operating activities? **Because companies report these items in the income statement, where results of operations are shown.**

Significant Noncash Activities

Not all of a company's significant activities involve cash. Examples of significant noncash activities are as follows.

1. Direct issuance of common stock to purchase assets.
2. Conversion of bonds into common stock.
3. Direct issuance of debt to purchase assets.
4. Exchanges of plant assets.

Helpful Hint
Do not include noncash investing and financing activities in the body of the statement of cash flows. Report this information in a separate schedule.

Companies do not report in the body of the statement of cash flows significant financing and investing activities that do not affect cash. Instead, they report these activities in either a **separate schedule** at the bottom of the statement of cash flows or in a **separate note or supplementary schedule** to the financial statements. The reporting of these noncash activities in a separate schedule satisfies the **full disclosure principle**.

In solving homework assignments, you should present significant noncash investing and financing activities in a separate schedule at the bottom of the statement of cash flows (see the last entry in Illustration 17-2 below).

Accounting Across the Organization — Target Corporation

Darren McCollester/Getty Images, Inc.

Net *What*?

Net income is not the same as net cash provided by operating activities. Below are some results from recent annual reports (dollars in millions), including Target Corporation. Note how the numbers differ greatly across the list even though all these companies engage in retail merchandising.

Company	Net Income	Net Cash Provided by Operating Activities
Kohl's Corporation	$ 889	$ 1,884
Wal-Mart Stores, Inc.	16,669	25,591
J. C. Penney Company, Inc.	(1,388)	(1,814)
Costco Wholesale Corp.	20,391	3,437
Target Corporation	1,971	6,520

In general, why do differences exist between net income and net cash provided by operating activities? (Go to **WileyPLUS** for this answer and additional questions.)

Format of the Statement of Cash Flows

The general format of the statement of cash flows presents the results of the three activities discussed previously—operating, investing, and financing—plus the significant noncash investing and financing activities. Illustration 17-2 shows a widely used form of the statement of cash flows.

Illustration 17-2
Format of statement of cash flows

COMPANY NAME
Statement of Cash Flows
For the Period Covered

Cash flows from operating activities		
(List of individual items)	XX	
Net cash provided (used) by operating activities		XXX
Cash flows from investing activities		
(List of individual inflows and outflows)	XX	
Net cash provided (used) by investing activities		XXX
Cash flows from financing activities		
(List of individual inflows and outflows)	XX	
Net cash provided (used) by financing activities		XXX
Net increase (decrease) in cash		XXX
Cash at beginning of period		XXX
Cash at end of period		XXX
Noncash investing and financing activities		
(List of individual noncash transactions)		XXX

The cash flows from operating activities section always appears first, followed by the investing activities section and then the financing activities section. The sum of the operating, investing, and financing sections equals the net increase or decrease in cash for the period. This amount is added to the beginning cash balance to arrive at the ending cash balance—the same amount reported on the balance sheet.

DO IT! 1 Classification of Cash Flows

During its first week, Duffy & Stevenson Company had these transactions.

1. Issued 100,000 shares of $5 par value common stock for $800,000 cash.
2. Borrowed $200,000 from Castle Bank, signing a 5-year note bearing 8% interest.
3. Purchased two semi-trailer trucks for $170,000 cash.
4. Paid employees $12,000 for salaries and wages.
5. Collected $20,000 cash for services performed.

Classify each of these transactions by type of cash flow activity.

Action Plan

✔ Identify the three types of activities used to report all cash inflows and outflows.

✔ Report as operating activities the cash effects of transactions that create revenues and expenses and enter into the determination of net income.

✔ Report as investing activities transactions that (a) acquire and dispose of investments and long-term assets and (b) lend money and collect loans.

✔ Report as financing activities transactions that (a) obtain cash from issuing debt and repay the amounts borrowed and (b) obtain cash from stockholders and pay them dividends.

Solution

1. Financing activity.	**4.** Operating activity.
2. Financing activity.	**5.** Operating activity.
3. Investing activity.	

Related exercise material: **BE17-1, BE17-2, BE17-3, E17-1, E17-2, E17-3, and DO IT! 17-1.**

LEARNING OBJECTIVE 2 Prepare a statement of cash flows using the indirect method.

Companies prepare the statement of cash flows differently from the three other basic financial statements. First, it is not prepared from an adjusted trial balance. It requires detailed information concerning the changes in account balances that occurred between two points in time. An adjusted trial balance will not provide the necessary data. Second, the statement of cash flows deals with cash receipts and payments. As a result, the company **adjusts** the effects of the use of accrual accounting **to determine cash flows.**

The information to prepare this statement usually comes from three sources:

- **Comparative balance sheets.** Information in the comparative balance sheets indicates the amount of the changes in assets, liabilities, and stockholders' equities from the beginning to the end of the period.
- **Current income statement.** Information in this statement helps determine the amount of net cash provided or used by operating activities during the period.
- **Additional information.** Such information includes transaction data that are needed to determine how cash was provided or used during the period.

Preparing the statement of cash flows from these data sources involves three major steps, explained in Illustration 17-3.

Illustration 17-3
Three major steps in preparing the statement of cash flows

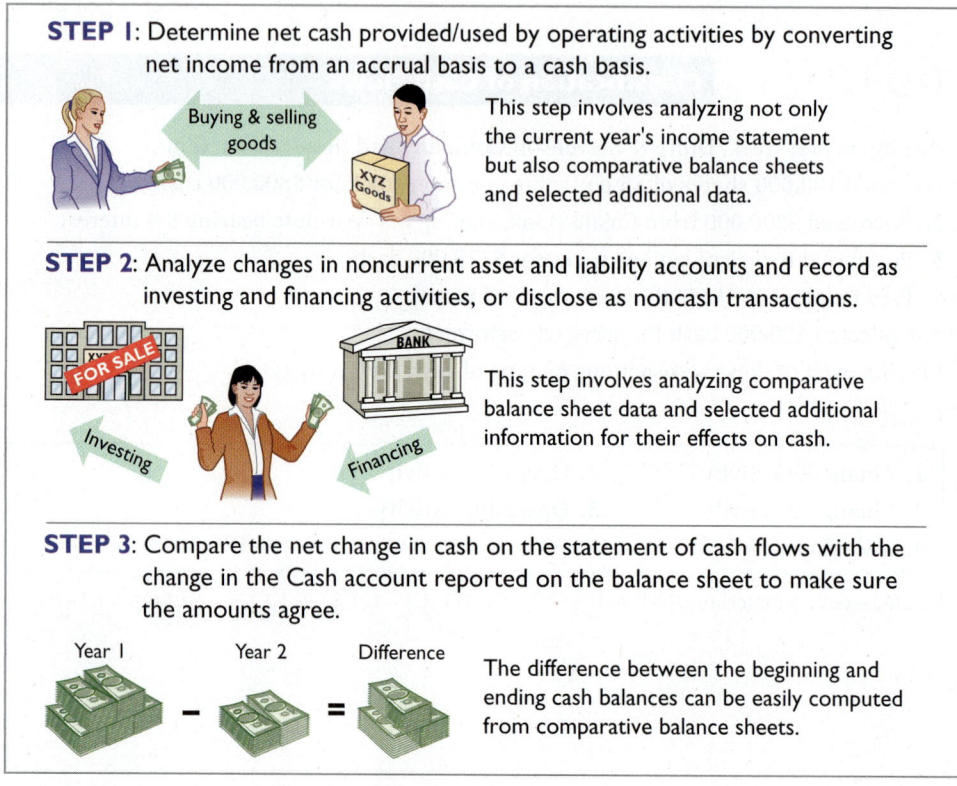

STEP 1: Determine net cash provided/used by operating activities by converting net income from an accrual basis to a cash basis.

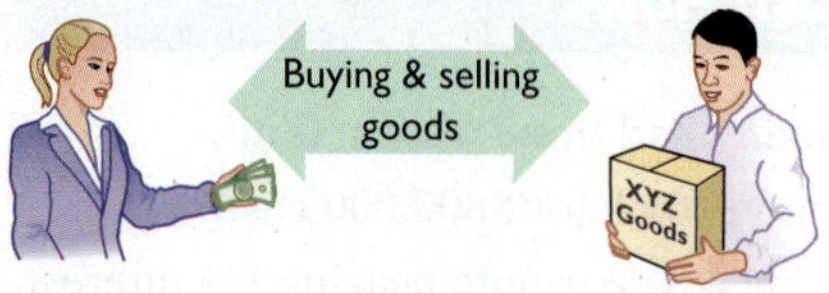

This step involves analyzing not only the current year's income statement but also comparative balance sheets and selected additional data.

STEP 2: Analyze changes in noncurrent asset and liability accounts and record as investing and financing activities, or disclose as noncash transactions.

This step involves analyzing comparative balance sheet data and selected additional information for their effects on cash.

STEP 3: Compare the net change in cash on the statement of cash flows with the change in the Cash account reported on the balance sheet to make sure the amounts agree.

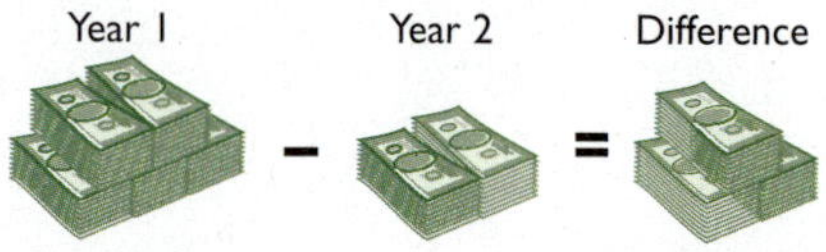

The difference between the beginning and ending cash balances can be easily computed from comparative balance sheets.

Indirect and Direct Methods

In order to perform Step 1, a company **must convert net income from an accrual basis to a cash basis**. This conversion may be done by either of two methods: (1) the indirect method or (2) the direct method. **Both methods arrive at the same amount** for "Net cash provided by operating activities." They differ in **how** they arrive at the amount.

The **indirect method** adjusts net income for items that do not affect cash. A great majority of companies use this method. Companies favor the indirect method for two reasons: (1) it is easier and less costly to prepare, and (2) it focuses on the differences between net income and net cash flow from operating activities.

The **direct method** shows operating cash receipts and payments. It is prepared by adjusting each item in the income statement from the accrual basis to the cash basis. The FASB has expressed a preference for the direct method but allows the use of either method.

The next section illustrates the more popular indirect method. Appendix 17A illustrates the direct method.

Indirect Method—Computer Services Company

To explain how to prepare a statement of cash flows using the indirect method, we use financial information from Computer Services Company. Illustration 17-4 presents Computer Services' current- and previous-year balance sheets, its current-year income statement, and related financial information for the current year.

Illustration 17-4
Comparative balance sheets, income statement, and additional information for Computer Services Company

COMPUTER SERVICES COMPANY
Comparative Balance Sheets
December 31

Assets	**2017**	**2016**	**Change in Account Balance Increase/Decrease**
Current assets			
Cash	$ 55,000	$ 33,000	$ 22,000 Increase
Accounts receivable	20,000	30,000	10,000 Decrease
Inventory	15,000	10,000	5,000 Increase
Prepaid expenses	5,000	1,000	4,000 Increase
Property, plant, and equipment			
Land	130,000	20,000	110,000 Increase
Buildings	160,000	40,000	120,000 Increase
Accumulated depreciation—buildings	(11,000)	(5,000)	6,000 Increase
Equipment	27,000	10,000	17,000 Increase
Accumulated depreciation—equipment	(3,000)	(1,000)	2,000 Increase
Total assets	$398,000	$138,000	
Liabilities and Stockholders' Equity			
Current liabilities			
Accounts payable	$ 28,000	$ 12,000	$ 16,000 Increase
Income taxes payable	6,000	8,000	2,000 Decrease
Long-term liabilities			
Bonds payable	130,000	20,000	110,000 Increase
Stockholders' equity			
Common stock	70,000	50,000	20,000 Increase
Retained earnings	164,000	48,000	116,000 Increase
Total liabilities and stockholders' equity	$398,000	$138,000	

COMPUTER SERVICES COMPANY
Income Statement
For the Year Ended December 31, 2017

Sales revenue		$507,000
Cost of goods sold	$150,000	
Operating expenses (excluding depreciation)	111,000	
Depreciation expense	9,000	
Loss on disposal of equipment	3,000	
Interest expense	42,000	315,000
Income before income tax		192,000
Income tax expense		47,000
Net income		$145,000

Additional information for 2017:

1. Depreciation expense was comprised of $6,000 for building and $3,000 for equipment.
2. The company sold equipment with a book value of $7,000 (cost $8,000, less accumulated depreciation $1,000) for $4,000 cash.
3. Issued $110,000 of long-term bonds in direct exchange for land.
4. A building costing $120,000 was purchased for cash. Equipment costing $25,000 was also purchased for cash.
5. Issued common stock for $20,000 cash.
6. The company declared and paid a $29,000 cash dividend.

We now apply the three steps for preparing a statement of cash flows to the information provided for Computer Services Company.

Step 1: Operating Activities

DETERMINE NET CASH PROVIDED/USED BY OPERATING ACTIVITIES BY CONVERTING NET INCOME FROM AN ACCRUAL BASIS TO A CASH BASIS

To determine net cash provided by operating activities under the indirect method, companies **adjust net income in numerous ways**. A useful starting point is to understand **why** net income must be converted to net cash provided by operating activities.

Under generally accepted accounting principles, most companies use the accrual basis of accounting. This basis requires that companies record revenue when their performance obligation is satisfied and record expenses when incurred. Revenues include credit sales for which the company has not yet collected cash. Expenses incurred include some items that it has not yet paid in cash. Thus, under the accrual basis, net income is not the same as net cash provided by operating activities.

Therefore, under the **indirect method**, companies must adjust net income to convert certain items to the cash basis. The indirect method (or reconciliation method) starts with net income and converts it to net cash provided by operating activities. Illustration 17-5 lists the three types of adjustments.

Illustration 17-5
Three types of adjustments to convert net income to net cash provided by operating activities

Net Income	+/−	Adjustments	=	Net Cash Provided/ Used by Operating Activities
		• **Add back noncash expenses**, such as depreciation expense and amortization expense. • **Deduct gains and add losses** that resulted from investing and financing activities. • **Analyze changes** to noncash current asset and current liability accounts.		

Helpful Hint
Depreciation is similar to any other expense in that it reduces net income. It differs in that it does not involve a current cash outflow. That is why it must be *added back* to net income to arrive at net cash provided by operating activities.

We explain the three types of adjustments in the next three sections.

DEPRECIATION EXPENSE

Computer Services' income statement reports depreciation expense of $9,000. Although depreciation expense reduces net income, it does not reduce cash. In other words, depreciation expense is a noncash charge. The company must add it back to net income to arrive at net cash provided by operating activities. Computer Services reports depreciation expense in the statement of cash flows as shown below.

Illustration 17-6
Adjustment for depreciation

Cash flows from operating activities	
Net income	$145,000
Adjustments to reconcile net income to net cash provided by operating activities:	
Depreciation expense	**9,000**
Net cash provided by operating activities	$154,000

As the first adjustment to net income in the statement of cash flows, companies frequently list depreciation and similar noncash charges such as amortization of intangible assets, depletion expense, and bad debt expense.

LOSS ON DISPOSAL OF EQUIPMENT

Illustration 17-1 states that cash received from the sale (disposal) of plant assets is reported in the investing activities section. Because of this, **companies eliminate**

from net income all gains and losses related to the disposal of plant assets, to arrive at net cash provided by operating activities.

In our example, Computer Services' income statement reports a $3,000 loss on the disposal of equipment (book value $7,000, less $4,000 cash received from disposal of equipment). The company's loss of $3,000 should not be included in the operating activities section of the statement of cash flows. Illustration 17-7 shows that the $3,000 loss is eliminated by adding $3,000 back to net income to arrive at net cash provided by operating activities.

Illustration 17-7
Adjustment for loss on disposal of equipment

Cash flows from operating activities		
Net income		$145,000
Adjustments to reconcile net income to net cash provided by operating activities:		
Depreciation expense	$9,000	
Loss on disposal of equipment	**3,000**	12,000
Net cash provided by operating activities		$157,000

If a gain on disposal occurs, the company deducts the gain from net income in order to determine net cash provided by operating activities. **In the case of either a gain or a loss, companies report as a source of cash in the investing activities section of the statement of cash flows the actual amount of cash received from the sale.**

CHANGES TO NONCASH CURRENT ASSET AND CURRENT LIABILITY ACCOUNTS

A final adjustment in reconciling net income to net cash provided by operating activities involves examining all changes in current asset and current liability accounts. The accrual-accounting process records revenues in the period in which the performance obligation is satisfied and expenses are incurred. For example, Accounts Receivable reflects amounts owed to the company for sales that have been made but for which cash collections have not yet been received. Prepaid Insurance reflects insurance that has been paid for but which has not yet expired (therefore has not been expensed). Similarly, Salaries and Wages Payable reflects salaries and wages expense that has been incurred but has not been paid.

As a result, companies need to adjust net income for these accruals and prepayments to determine net cash provided by operating activities. Thus, they must analyze the change in each current asset and current liability account to determine its impact on net income and cash.

CHANGES IN NONCASH CURRENT ASSETS. The adjustments required for changes in noncash current asset accounts are as follows. **Deduct from net income increases in current asset accounts, and add to net income decreases in current asset accounts, to arrive at net cash provided by operating activities.** We observe these relationships by analyzing the accounts of Computer Services.

DECREASE IN ACCOUNTS RECEIVABLE Computer Services' accounts receivable decreased by $10,000 (from $30,000 to $20,000) during the period. For Computer Services, this means that cash receipts were $10,000 higher than sales revenue. The Accounts Receivable account in Illustration 17-8 shows that Computer Services had $507,000 in sales revenue (as reported on the income statement), but it collected $517,000 in cash.

Illustration 17-8
Analysis of accounts receivable

Accounts Receivable

1/1/17	Balance	30,000	**Receipts from customers**	**517,000**
	Sales revenue	**507,000**		
12/31/17	Balance	20,000		

As shown in Illustration 17-9 (below), to adjust net income to net cash provided by operating activities, the company adds to net income the decrease of $10,000 in accounts receivable. When the Accounts Receivable balance increases, cash receipts are lower than sales revenue earned under the accrual basis. Therefore, the company deducts from net income the amount of the increase in accounts receivable, to arrive at net cash provided by operating activities.

INCREASE IN INVENTORY Computer Services' inventory increased $5,000 (from $10,000 to $15,000) during the period. The change in the Inventory account reflects the difference between the amount of inventory purchased and the amount sold. For Computer Services, this means that the cost of merchandise purchased exceeded the cost of goods sold by $5,000. As a result, cost of goods sold does not reflect $5,000 of cash payments made for merchandise. The company deducts from net income this inventory increase of $5,000 during the period, to arrive at net cash provided by operating activities (see Illustration 17-9). If inventory decreases, the company adds to net income the amount of the change, to arrive at net cash provided by operating activities.

INCREASE IN PREPAID EXPENSES Computer Services' prepaid expenses increased during the period by $4,000. This means that cash paid for expenses is higher than expenses reported on an accrual basis. In other words, the company has made cash payments in the current period but will not charge expenses to income until future periods (as charges to the income statement). To adjust net income to net cash provided by operating activities, the company deducts from net income the $4,000 increase in prepaid expenses (see Illustration 17-9).

Illustration 17-9
Adjustments for changes in current asset accounts

Cash flows from operating activities		
Net income		$145,000
Adjustments to reconcile net income to net cash provided by operating activities:		
Depreciation expense	$ 9,000	
Loss on disposal of equipment	3,000	
Decrease in accounts receivable	**10,000**	
Increase in inventory	**(5,000)**	
Increase in prepaid expenses	**(4,000)**	13,000
Net cash provided by operating activities		$158,000

If prepaid expenses decrease, reported expenses are higher than the expenses paid. Therefore, the company adds to net income the decrease in prepaid expenses, to arrive at net cash provided by operating activities.

CHANGES IN CURRENT LIABILITIES. The adjustments required for changes in current liability accounts are as follows. **Add to net income increases in current liability accounts and deduct from net income decreases in current liability accounts, to arrive at net cash provided by operating activities.**

INCREASE IN ACCOUNTS PAYABLE For Computer Services, Accounts Payable increased by $16,000 (from $12,000 to $28,000) during the period. That means the company received $16,000 more in goods than it actually paid for. As shown in Illustration 17-10, to adjust net income to determine net cash provided by operating activities, the company adds to net income the $16,000 increase in Accounts Payable.

DECREASE IN INCOME TAXES PAYABLE When a company incurs income tax expense but has not yet paid its taxes, it records income taxes payable. A change in the Income Taxes Payable account reflects the difference between income tax expense incurred and income tax actually paid. Computer Services' Income Taxes Payable account decreased by $2,000. That means the $47,000 of income tax expense reported on the income statement was $2,000 less than the amount of taxes paid during the period of $49,000. As shown in Illustration 17-10, to adjust net income to a cash basis, the company must reduce net income by $2,000.

Cash flows from operating activities		
Net income		$145,000
Adjustments to reconcile net income to net cash provided by operating activities:		
Depreciation expense	$ 9,000	
Loss on disposal of equipment	3,000	
Decrease in accounts receivable	10,000	
Increase in inventory	(5,000)	
Increase in prepaid expenses	(4,000)	
Increase in accounts payable	**16,000**	
Decrease in income taxes payable	**(2,000)**	27,000
Net cash provided by operating activities		$172,000

Illustration 17-10
Adjustments for changes in current liability accounts

Illustration 17-10 shows that after starting with net income of $145,000, the sum of all of the adjustments to net income was $27,000. This resulted in net cash provided by operating activities of $172,000.

Summary of Conversion to Net Cash Provided by Operating Activities—Indirect Method

As shown in the previous illustrations, the statement of cash flows prepared by the indirect method starts with net income. It then adds or deducts items to arrive at net cash provided by operating activities. The required adjustments are of three types:

1. Noncash charges such as depreciation and amortization.
2. Gains and losses on the disposal of plant assets.
3. Changes in noncash current asset and current liability accounts.

Illustration 17-11 provides a summary of these changes and required adjustments.

		Adjustments Required to Convert Net Income to Net Cash Provided by Operating Activities
Noncash Charges	Depreciation expense	Add
	Amortization expense	Add
Gains and Losses	Loss on disposal of plant assets	Add
	Gain on disposal of plant assets	Deduct
Changes in Current Assets and Current Liabilities	Increase in current asset account	Deduct
	Decrease in current asset account	Add
	Increase in current liability account	Add
	Decrease in current liability account	Deduct

Illustration 17-11
Adjustments required to convert net income to net cash provided by operating activities

DO IT! 2a Cash from Operating Activities

Josh's PhotoPlus reported net income of $73,000 for 2017. Included in the income statement were depreciation expense of $7,000 and a gain on disposal of equipment of $2,500. Josh's comparative balance sheets show the following balances.

	12/31/16	12/31/17
Accounts receivable	$17,000	$21,000
Accounts payable	6,000	2,200

Calculate net cash provided by operating activities for Josh's PhotoPlus.

Action Plan

✔ Add noncash charges such as depreciation back to net income to compute net cash provided by operating activities.

Action Plan (*cont.*)

✔ Deduct from net income gains on the disposal of plant assets, or add losses back to net income, to compute net cash provided by operating activities.

✔ Use changes in noncash current asset and current liability accounts to compute net cash provided by operating activities.

Solution

Cash flows from operating activities		
Net income		$73,000
Adjustments to reconcile net income to net cash provided by operating activities:		
Depreciation expense	$ 7,000	
Gain on disposal of equipment	(2,500)	
Increase in accounts receivable	(4,000)	
Decrease in accounts payable	(3,800)	(3,300)
Net cash provided by operating activities		$69,700

Related exercise material: **BE17-4, BE17-5, BE17-6, E17-4, E17-5, E17-6, and DO IT! 17-2.**

Step 2: Investing and Financing Activities

ANALYZE CHANGES IN NONCURRENT ASSET AND LIABILITY ACCOUNTS AND RECORD AS INVESTING AND FINANCING ACTIVITIES, OR AS NONCASH INVESTING AND FINANCING ACTIVITIES

INCREASE IN LAND As indicated from the change in the Land account and the additional information, Computer Services purchased land of $110,000 by directly exchanging bonds for land. The issuance of bonds payable for land has no effect on cash. But, it is a significant noncash investing and financing activity that merits disclosure in a separate schedule (see Illustration 17-13).

INCREASE IN BUILDINGS As the additional data indicate, Computer Services acquired an office building for $120,000 cash. This is a cash outflow reported in the investing activities section (see Illustration 17-13).

INCREASE IN EQUIPMENT The Equipment account increased $17,000. The additional information explains that this net increase resulted from two transactions: (1) a purchase of equipment of $25,000, and (2) the sale for $4,000 of equipment costing $8,000. These transactions are investing activities. The company should report each transaction separately. Thus, it reports the purchase of equipment as an outflow of cash for $25,000. It reports the sale as an inflow of cash for $4,000. The T-account below shows the reasons for the change in this account during the year.

Illustration 17-12
Analysis of equipment

Equipment

1/1/17	Balance	10,000	Cost of equipment sold	8,000
	Purchase of equipment	**25,000**		
12/31/17	Balance	27,000		

The following entry shows the details of the equipment sale transaction.

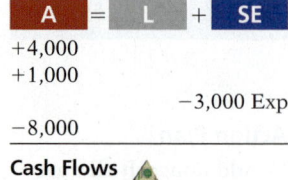

A	= L	+ SE
+4,000		
+1,000		
		−3,000 Exp
−8,000		

Cash Flows
+4,000

	Debit	Credit
Cash	4,000	
Accumulated Depreciation—Equipment	1,000	
Loss on Disposal of Equipment	3,000	
Equipment		8,000

INCREASE IN BONDS PAYABLE The Bonds Payable account increased $110,000. As indicated in the additional information, the company acquired land from the issuance of these bonds. It reports this noncash transaction in a separate schedule at the bottom of the statement.

INCREASE IN COMMON STOCK The balance sheet reports an increase in Common Stock of $20,000. The additional information section notes that this increase resulted from the issuance of new shares of stock. This is a cash inflow reported in the financing activities section.

Helpful Hint
When companies issue stocks or bonds for cash, the actual proceeds will appear in the statement of cash flows as a financing inflow (rather than the par value of the stocks or face value of bonds).

INCREASE IN RETAINED EARNINGS Retained earnings increased $116,000 during the year. This increase can be explained by two factors: (1) net income of $145,000 increased retained earnings, and (2) dividends of $29,000 decreased retained earnings. The company adjusts net income to net cash provided by operating activities in the operating activities section. Payment of the dividends (not the declaration) is a **cash outflow that the company reports as a financing activity**.

STATEMENT OF CASH FLOWS—2017

Using the previous information, we can now prepare a statement of cash flows for 2017 for Computer Services Company as shown in Illustration 17-13.

Illustration 17-13
Statement of cash flows, 2017—indirect method

COMPUTER SERVICES COMPANY
Statement of Cash Flows—Indirect Method
For the Year Ended December 31, 2017

Cash flows from operating activities		
Net income		$145,000
Adjustments to reconcile net income to net cash provided by operating activities:		
Depreciation expense	$ 9,000	
Loss on disposal of equipment	3,000	
Decrease in accounts receivable	10,000	
Increase in inventory	(5,000)	
Increase in prepaid expenses	(4,000)	
Increase in accounts payable	16,000	
Decrease in income taxes payable	(2,000)	27,000
Net cash provided by operating activities		172,000
Cash flows from investing activities		
Purchase of building	(120,000)	
Purchase of equipment	(25,000)	
Sale of equipment	4,000	
Net cash used by investing activities		(141,000)
Cash flows from financing activities		
Issuance of common stock	20,000	
Payment of cash dividends	(29,000)	
Net cash used by financing activities		(9,000)
Net increase in cash		22,000
Cash at beginning of period		33,000
Cash at end of period		$ 55,000
Noncash investing and financing activities		
Issuance of bonds payable to purchase land		$110,000

Helpful Hint
Note that in the investing and financing activities sections, positive numbers indicate cash inflows (receipts), and negative numbers indicate cash outflows (payments).

Step 3: Net Change in Cash

COMPARE THE NET CHANGE IN CASH ON THE STATEMENT OF CASH FLOWS WITH THE CHANGE IN THE CASH ACCOUNT REPORTED ON THE BALANCE SHEET TO MAKE SURE THE AMOUNTS AGREE

Illustration 17-13 indicates that the net change in cash during the period was an increase of $22,000. This agrees with the change in Cash account reported on the balance sheet in Illustration 17-4 (page 733).

Accounting Across the Organization

© Soubrette/iStockphoto

Burning Through Our Cash

Box (cloud storage), Cyan (game creator), Fireeye (cyber security), and Mobile Iron (mobile security of data) are a few of the tech companies that recently have issued or are about to issue stock to the public. Investors now have to determine whether these tech companies have viable products and high chances for success.

An important consideration in evaluating a tech company is determining its financial flexibility—its ability to withstand adversity if an economic setback occurs. One way to measure financial flexibility is to assess a company's cash burn rate, which determines how long its cash will hold out if the company is expending more cash than it is receiving.

Fireeye, for example, burned cash in excess of $50 million in 2013. But the company also had over $150 million as a cash cushion, so it would take over 30 months before it runs out of cash. And even though Box has a much lower cash burn rate than Fireeye, it still has over a year's cushion. Compare that to the tech companies in 2000, when over one-quarter of them were on track to run out of cash within a year. And many did. Fortunately, the tech companies of today seem to be better equipped to withstand an economic setback.

Source: Shira Ovide, "Tech Firms' Cash Hoards Cool Fears of a Meltdown," *Wall Street Journal* (May 14, 2014).

What implications does a company's cash burn rate have for its survival? (See **WileyPLUS** for this answer and additional questions.)

DO IT! 2b Indirect Method

Use the information below and on page 741 to prepare a statement of cash flows using the indirect method.

REYNOLDS COMPANY
Comparative Balance Sheets
December 31

Assets	2017	2016	Change Increase/Decrease
Cash	$ 54,000	$ 37,000	$ 17,000 Increase
Accounts receivable	68,000	26,000	42,000 Increase
Inventory	54,000	–0–	54,000 Increase
Prepaid expenses	4,000	6,000	2,000 Decrease
Land	45,000	70,000	25,000 Decrease
Buildings	200,000	200,000	–0–
Accumulated depreciation—buildings	(21,000)	(11,000)	10,000 Increase
Equipment	193,000	68,000	125,000 Increase
Accumulated depreciation—equipment	(28,000)	(10,000)	18,000 Increase
Totals	$569,000	$386,000	
Liabilities and Stockholders' Equity			
Accounts payable	$ 23,000	$ 40,000	$ 17,000 Decrease
Accrued expenses payable	10,000	–0–	10,000 Increase
Bonds payable	110,000	150,000	40,000 Decrease
Common stock ($1 par)	220,000	60,000	160,000 Increase
Retained earnings	206,000	136,000	70,000 Increase
Totals	$569,000	$386,000	

REYNOLDS COMPANY
Income Statement
For the Year Ended December 31, 2017

Sales revenue		$890,000
Cost of goods sold	$465,000	
Operating expenses	221,000	
Interest expense	12,000	
Loss on disposal of equipment	2,000	700,000
Income before income taxes		190,000
Income tax expense		65,000
Net income		$125,000

Additional information:
1. Operating expenses include depreciation expense of $33,000 and charges from prepaid expenses of $2,000.
2. Land was sold at its book value for cash.
3. Cash dividends of $55,000 were declared and paid in 2017.
4. Interest expense of $12,000 was paid in cash.
5. Equipment with a cost of $166,000 was purchased for cash. Equipment with a cost of $41,000 and a book value of $36,000 was sold for $34,000 cash.
6. Bonds of $10,000 were redeemed at their face value for cash. Bonds of $30,000 were converted into common stock.
7. Common stock ($1 par) of $130,000 was issued for cash.
8. Accounts payable pertain to merchandise suppliers.

Solution

REYNOLDS COMPANY
Statement of Cash Flows—Indirect Method
For the Year Ended December 31, 2017

Cash flows from operating activities		
Net income		$ 125,000
Adjustments to reconcile net income to net cash provided by operating activities:		
Depreciation expense	$ 33,000	
Loss on disposal of equipment	2,000	
Increase in accounts receivable	(42,000)	
Increase in inventory	(54,000)	
Decrease in prepaid expenses	2,000	
Decrease in accounts payable	(17,000)	
Increase in accrued expenses payable	10,000	(66,000)
Net cash provided by operating activities		59,000
Cash flows from investing activities		
Sale of land	25,000	
Sale of equipment	34,000	
Purchase of equipment	(166,000)	
Net cash used by investing activities		(107,000)
Cash flows from financing activities		
Redemption of bonds	(10,000)	
Sale of common stock	130,000	
Payment of dividends	(55,000)	
Net cash provided by financing activities		65,000
Net increase in cash		17,000
Cash at beginning of period		37,000
Cash at end of period		$54,000
Noncash investing and financing activities		
Conversion of bonds into common stock		$30,000

Action Plan

- ✔ Determine net cash provided/used by operating activities by adjusting net income for items that did not affect cash.
- ✔ Determine net cash provided/used by investing activities and financing activities.
- ✔ Determine the net increase/decrease in cash.

Related exercise material: **BE17-4, BE17-5, BE17-6, BE17-7, E17-4, E17-5, E17-6, and E17-8.**

LEARNING OBJECTIVE 3

Analyze the statement of cash flows.

Traditionally, investors and creditors used ratios based on accrual accounting. These days, cash-based ratios are gaining increased acceptance among analysts.

Free Cash Flow

In the statement of cash flows, net cash provided by operating activities is intended to indicate the cash-generating capability of a company. Analysts have noted, however, that **net cash provided by operating activities fails to take into account that a company must invest in new fixed assets** just to maintain its current level of operations. Companies also must at least **maintain dividends at current levels** to satisfy investors. The measurement of free cash flow provides additional insight regarding a company's cash-generating ability. **Free cash flow** describes the net cash provided by operating activities after adjustment for capital expenditures and dividends.

Consider the following example. Suppose that MPC produced and sold 10,000 personal computers this year. It reported $100,000 net cash provided by operating activities. In order to maintain production at 10,000 computers, MPC invested $15,000 in equipment. It chose to pay $5,000 in dividends. Its free cash flow was $80,000 ($100,000 − $15,000 − $5,000). The company could use this $80,000 either to purchase new assets to expand the business or to pay an $80,000 dividend and continue to produce 10,000 computers. In practice, free cash flow is often calculated with the formula in Illustration 17-14. (Alternative definitions also exist.)

Illustration 17-14
Free cash flow

Free Cash Flow = **Net Cash Provided by Operating Activities** − **Capital Expenditures** − **Cash Dividends**

Illustration 17-15 provides basic information (in millions) excerpted from the 2013 statement of cash flows of Microsoft Corporation.

Illustration 17-15
Microsoft's cash flow information ($ in millions)

Real World

MICROSOFT CORPORATION
Statement of Cash Flows (partial)
2013

Cash provided by operating activities		$21,863
Cash flows from investing activities		
Additions to property and equipment	$ (4,257)	
Purchases of investments	(75,396)	
Sales of investments	52,464	
Acquisitions of companies	(1,584)	
Maturities of investments	5,130	
Other	(168)	
Cash used by investing activities		(23,811)
Cash paid for dividends		(7,455)

Microsoft's free cash flow is calculated as shown in Illustration 17-16.

Illustration 17-16
Calculation of Microsoft's free cash flow ($ in millions)

Cash provided by operating activities	$21,863
Less: Expenditures on property, plant, and equipment	4,257
Dividends paid	7,455
Free cash flow	**$10,151**

Microsoft generated approximately $10.15 billion of free cash flow. This is a tremendous amount of cash generated in a single year. It is available for the acquisition of new assets, the retirement of stock or debt, or the payment of dividends. Also note that Microsoft's cash from operations of $21.8 billion is nearly identical to its 2013 net income of $21.9 billion. This lends additional credibility to Microsoft's income number as an indicator of potential future performance.

DO IT! 3 Free Cash Flow

Chicago Corporation issued the following statement of cash flows for 2017.

CHICAGO CORPORATION
Statement of Cash Flows—Indirect Method
For the Year Ended December 31, 2017

Cash flows from operating activities		
Net income		$ 19,000
Adjustments to reconcile net income to net cash provided by operating activities:		
Depreciation expense	$ 8,100	
Loss on disposal of plant assets	1,300	
Decrease in accounts receivable	6,900	
Increase in inventory	(4,000)	
Decrease in accounts payable	(2,000)	10,300
Net cash provided by operating activities		29,300
Cash flows from investing activities		
Sale of investments	1,100	
Purchase of equipment	(19,000)	
Net cash used by investing activities		(17,900)
Cash flows from financing activities		
Issuance of stock	10,000	
Payment on long-term note payable	(5,000)	
Payment for dividends	(9,000)	
Net cash used by financing activities		(4,000)
Net increase in cash		7,400
Cash at beginning of year		10,000
Cash at end of year		$ 17,400

(a) Compute free cash flow for Chicago Corporation. (b) Explain why free cash flow often provides better information than "Net cash provided by operating activities."

Solution

(a) Free cash flow = $29,300 – $19,000 – $9,000 = $1,300

(b) Net cash provided by operating activities fails to take into account that a company must invest in new plant assets just to maintain the current level of operations. Companies must also maintain dividends at current levels to satisfy investors. The measurement of free cash flow provides additional insight regarding a company's cash-generating ability.

Action Plan

✔ Compute free cash flow as Net cash provided by operating activities – Capital expenditures – Cash dividends.

Related exercise material: **BE17-8, BE17-9, BE17-10, BE17-11, E17-7, E17-9, and DO IT! 17-3.**

LEARNING OBJECTIVE *4

APPENDIX 17A: Prepare a statement of cash flows using the direct method.

To explain and illustrate the direct method for preparing a statement of cash flows, we use the transactions of Computer Services Company for 2017. Illustration 17A-1 (page 744) presents information related to 2017 for the company.

Illustration 17A-1
Comparative balance sheets, income statement, and additional information for Computer Services Company

COMPUTER SERVICES COMPANY
Comparative Balance Sheets
December 31

Assets	2017	2016	Change in Account Balance Increase/Decrease
Current assets			
Cash	$ 55,000	$ 33,000	$ 22,000 Increase
Accounts receivable	20,000	30,000	10,000 Decrease
Inventory	15,000	10,000	5,000 Increase
Prepaid expenses	5,000	1,000	4,000 Increase
Property, plant, and equipment			
Land	130,000	20,000	110,000 Increase
Buildings	160,000	40,000	120,000 Increase
Accumulated depreciation—buildings	(11,000)	(5,000)	6,000 Increase
Equipment	27,000	10,000	17,000 Increase
Accumulated depreciation—equipment	(3,000)	(1,000)	2,000 Increase
Total assets	$398,000	$138,000	
Liabilities and Stockholders' Equity			
Current liabilities			
Accounts payable	$ 28,000	$ 12,000	$ 16,000 Increase
Income taxes payable	6,000	8,000	2,000 Decrease
Long-term liabilities			
Bonds payable	130,000	20,000	110,000 Increase
Stockholders' equity			
Common stock	70,000	50,000	20,000 Increase
Retained earnings	164,000	48,000	116,000 Increase
Total liabilities and stockholders' equity	$398,000	$138,000	

COMPUTER SERVICES COMPANY
Income Statement
For the Year Ended December 31, 2017

Sales revenue		$507,000
Cost of goods sold	$150,000	
Operating expenses (excluding depreciation)	111,000	
Depreciation expense	9,000	
Loss on disposal of equipment	3,000	
Interest expense	42,000	315,000
Income before income tax		192,000
Income tax expense		47,000
Net income		$145,000

Additional information for 2017:

1. Depreciation expense was comprised of $6,000 for building and $3,000 for equipment.
2. The company sold equipment with a book value of $7,000 (cost $8,000, less accumulated depreciation $1,000) for $4,000 cash.
3. Issued $110,000 of long-term bonds in direct exchange for land.
4. A building costing $120,000 was purchased for cash. Equipment costing $25,000 was also purchased for cash.
5. Issued common stock for $20,000 cash.
6. The company declared and paid a $29,000 cash dividend.

To prepare a statement of cash flows under the direct approach, we apply the three steps outlined in Illustration 17-3 (page 732).

Step 1: Operating Activities

DETERMINE NET CASH PROVIDED/USED BY OPERATING ACTIVITIES BY CONVERTING NET INCOME FROM AN ACCRUAL BASIS TO A CASH BASIS

Under the **direct method**, companies compute net cash provided by operating activities by **adjusting each item in the income statement** from the accrual basis to the cash basis. To simplify and condense the operating activities section, companies **report only major classes of operating cash receipts and cash payments**. For these major classes, the difference between cash receipts and cash payments is the net cash provided by operating activities. These relationships are as shown in Illustration 17A-2.

Illustration 17A-2
Major classes of cash receipts and payments

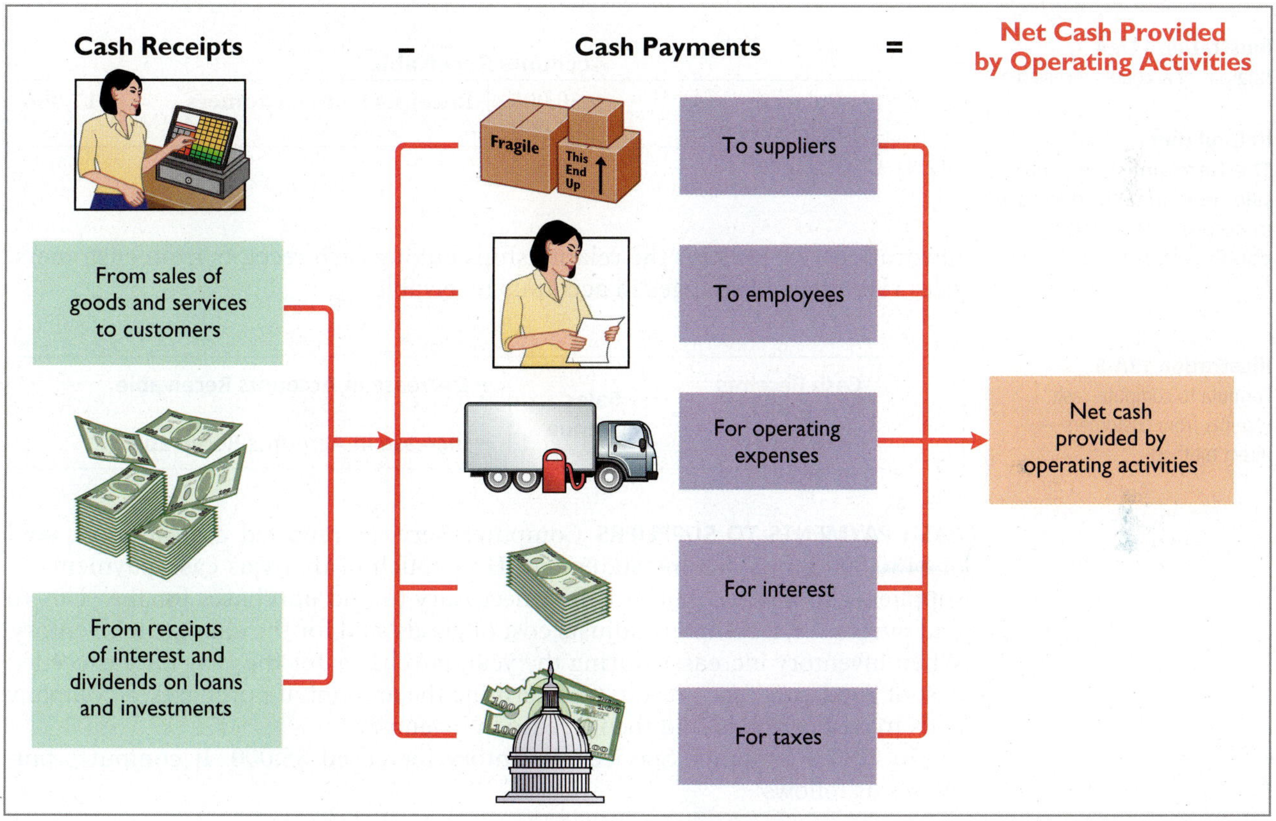

An efficient way to apply the direct method is to analyze the items reported in the income statement in the order in which they are listed. We then determine cash receipts and cash payments related to these revenues and expenses. The following presents the adjustments required to prepare a statement of cash flows for Computer Services Company using the direct approach.

CASH RECEIPTS FROM CUSTOMERS The income statement for Computer Services reported sales revenue from customers of $507,000. How much of that was cash receipts? To answer that, a company considers the change in accounts receivable during the year. When accounts receivable increase during the year, revenues on an accrual basis are higher than cash receipts from customers. Operations led to revenues, but not all of those revenues resulted in cash receipts.

To determine the amount of cash receipts, a company deducts from sales revenue the increase in accounts receivable. On the other hand, there may be a decrease in accounts receivable. That would occur if cash receipts from customers exceeded sales revenue. In that case, a company adds to sales revenue the decrease in accounts receivable. For Computer Services, accounts receivable decreased $10,000. Thus, cash receipts from customers were $517,000, computed as shown in Illustration 17A-3.

Illustration 17A-3
Computation of cash receipts from customers

Sales revenue	$ 507,000
Add: Decrease in accounts receivable	10,000
Cash receipts from customers	**$517,000**

Computer Services can also determine cash receipts from customers from an analysis of the Accounts Receivable account, as shown in Illustration 17A-4.

Illustration 17A-4
Analysis of accounts receivable

Helpful Hint
The T-account shows that sales revenue plus decrease in accounts receivable equals cash receipts.

Accounts Receivable

1/1/17	Balance	30,000	**Receipts from customers**	**517,000**
	Sales revenue	507,000		
12/31/17	Balance	20,000		

Illustration 17A-5 shows the relationships among cash receipts from customers, sales revenue, and changes in accounts receivable.

Illustration 17A-5
Formula to compute cash receipts from customers—direct method

Cash Receipts from Customers	=	**Sales Revenue**	**+ Decrease in Accounts Receivable** or **− Increase in Accounts Receivable**

CASH PAYMENTS TO SUPPLIERS Computer Services reported cost of goods sold of $150,000 on its income statement. How much of that was cash payments to suppliers? To answer that, it is first necessary to find purchases for the year. To find purchases, a company adjusts cost of goods sold for the change in inventory. When inventory increases during the year, purchases for the year have exceeded cost of goods sold. As a result, to determine the amount of purchases, a company adds to cost of goods sold the increase in inventory.

In 2017, Computer Services' inventory increased $5,000. It computes purchases as follows.

Illustration 17A-6
Computation of purchases

Cost of goods sold	$ 150,000
Add: Increase in inventory	5,000
Purchases	**$155,000**

Computer Services can also determine purchases from an analysis of the Inventory account, as shown in Illustration 17A-7.

Illustration 17A-7
Analysis of inventory

Inventory

1/1/17	Balance	10,000	Cost of goods sold	150,000
	Purchases	**155,000**		
12/31/17	Balance	15,000		

After computing purchases, a company can determine cash payments to suppliers. This is done by adjusting purchases for the change in accounts payable. When accounts payable increase during the year, purchases on an accrual basis are higher than they are on a cash basis. As a result, to determine cash payments to suppliers, a company deducts from purchases the increase in accounts payable. On the other hand, if cash payments to suppliers exceed purchases, there will be a decrease in accounts payable. In that case, a company adds to purchases the decrease in accounts payable. For Computer Services, cash payments to suppliers were $139,000, computed as follows.

Illustration 17A-8
Computation of cash payments to suppliers

Purchases	$ 155,000
Deduct: Increase in accounts payable	16,000
Cash payments to suppliers	**$139,000**

Computer Services also can determine cash payments to suppliers from an analysis of the Accounts Payable account, as shown in Illustration 17A-9.

Illustration 17A-9
Analysis of accounts payable

Accounts Payable

Payments to suppliers	**139,000**	1/1/17	Balance	12,000
			Purchases	155,000
		12/31/17	Balance	28,000

Helpful Hint
The T-account shows that purchases less increase in accounts payable equals payments to suppliers.

Illustration 17A-10 shows the relationships among cash payments to suppliers, cost of goods sold, changes in inventory, and changes in accounts payable.

Illustration 17A-10
Formula to compute cash payments to suppliers—direct method

Cash Payments to Suppliers	=	**Cost of Goods Sold**	**+ Increase in Inventory** or **− Decrease in Inventory**	**+ Decrease in Accounts Payable** or **− Increase in Accounts Payable**

CASH PAYMENTS FOR OPERATING EXPENSES Computer Services reported on its income statement operating expenses of $111,000. How much of that amount was cash paid for operating expenses? To answer that, we need to adjust this amount for any changes in prepaid expenses and accrued expenses payable. For example, if prepaid expenses increased during the year, cash paid for operating expenses is higher than operating expenses reported on the income statement. To convert operating expenses to cash payments for operating expenses, a company adds the increase in prepaid expenses to operating expenses. On the other hand, if prepaid expenses decrease during the year, it deducts the decrease from operating expenses.

Companies must also adjust operating expenses for changes in accrued expenses payable. When accrued expenses payable increase during the year, operating expenses on an accrual basis are higher than they are in a cash basis. As a result, to determine cash payments for operating expenses, a company deducts from operating expenses an increase in accrued expenses payable. On the other hand, a company adds to operating expenses a decrease in accrued expenses payable because cash payments exceed operating expenses.

Computer Services' cash payments for operating expenses were $115,000, computed as follows.

Illustration 17A-11
Computation of cash payments for operating expenses

Operating expenses	$ 111,000
Add: Increase in prepaid expenses	4,000
Cash payments for operating expenses	**$115,000**

Illustration 17A-12 shows the relationships among cash payments for operating expenses, changes in prepaid expenses, and changes in accrued expenses payable.

Illustration 17A-12
Formula to compute cash payments for operating expenses—direct method

Cash Payments for Operating Expenses	=	**Operating Expenses**	**+ Increase in Prepaid Expenses** or **− Decrease in Prepaid Expenses**	**+ Decrease in Accrued Expenses Payable** or **− Increase in Accrued Expenses Payable**

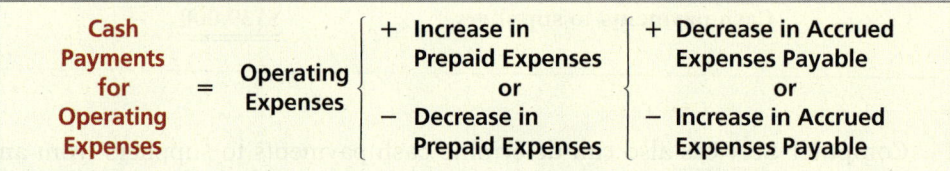

DEPRECIATION EXPENSE AND LOSS ON DISPOSAL OF EQUIPMENT Computer Services' depreciation expense in 2017 was $9,000. Depreciation expense is not shown on a statement of cash flows under the direct method because it is a noncash charge. If the amount for operating expenses includes depreciation expense, operating expenses must be reduced by the amount of depreciation to determine cash payments for operating expenses.

The loss on disposal of equipment of $3,000 is also a noncash charge. The loss on disposal of equipment reduces net income, but it does not reduce cash. Thus, the loss on disposal of equipment is not shown on the statement of cash flows under the direct method.

Other charges to expense that do not require the use of cash, such as the amortization of intangible assets, depletion expense, and bad debt expense, are treated in the same manner as depreciation.

CASH PAYMENTS FOR INTEREST Computer Services reported on the income statement interest expense of $42,000. Since the balance sheet did not include an accrual for interest payable for 2016 or 2017, the amount reported as expense is the same as the amount of interest paid.

CASH PAYMENTS FOR INCOME TAXES Computer Services reported income tax expense of $47,000 on the income statement. Income taxes payable, however, decreased $2,000. This decrease means that income taxes paid were more than income taxes reported in the income statement. Cash payments for income taxes were therefore $49,000 as shown below.

Illustration 17A-13
Computation of cash payments for income taxes

Income tax expense	$ 47,000
Add: Decrease in income taxes payable	2,000
Cash payments for income taxes	**$49,000**

Computer Services can also determine cash payments for income taxes from an analysis of the Income Taxes Payable account, as shown in Illustration 17A-14.

Illustration 17A-14
Analysis of income taxes payable

Income Taxes Payable

		1/1/17	Balance	8,000
Cash payments for income taxes	**49,000**		Income tax expense	47,000
		12/31/17	Balance	6,000

Illustration 17A-15 shows the relationships among cash payments for income taxes, income tax expense, and changes in income taxes payable.

Cash Payments for Income Taxes	=	Income Tax Expense	+	Decrease in Income Taxes Payable
				or
			−	Increase in Income Taxes Payable

Illustration 17A-15
Formula to compute cash payments for income taxes—direct method

The operating activities section of the statement of cash flows of Computer Services is shown in Illustration 17A-16.

Illustration 17A-16
Operating activities section of the statement of cash flows

Cash flows from operating activities		
Cash receipts from customers		$517,000
Less: Cash payments:		
To suppliers	$139,000	
For operating expenses	115,000	
For interest expense	42,000	
For income taxes	49,000	345,000
Net cash provided by operating activities		$172,000

When a company uses the direct method, it must also provide in a **separate schedule** (not shown here) the net cash flows from operating activities as computed under the indirect method.

Step 2: Investing and Financing Activities

ANALYZE CHANGES IN NONCURRENT ASSET AND LIABILITY ACCOUNTS AND RECORD AS INVESTING AND FINANCING ACTIVITIES, OR DISCLOSE AS NONCASH TRANSACTIONS

INCREASE IN LAND As indicated from the change in the Land account and the additional information, Computer Services purchased land of $110,000 by directly exchanging bonds for land. The exchange of bonds payable for land has no effect on cash. But, it is a significant noncash investing and financing activity that merits disclosure in a separate schedule (see Illustration 17A-18).

Helpful Hint
The investing and financing activities are measured and reported the same under both the direct and indirect methods.

INCREASE IN BUILDINGS As the additional data indicate, Computer Services acquired an office building for $120,000 cash. This is a cash outflow reported in the investing activities section (see Illustration 17A-18).

INCREASE IN EQUIPMENT The Equipment account increased $17,000. The additional information explains that this was a net increase that resulted from two transactions: (1) a purchase of equipment of $25,000, and (2) the sale for $4,000 of equipment costing $8,000. These transactions are investing activities. The company should report each transaction separately. The statement in Illustration 17A-18 reports the purchase of equipment as an outflow of cash for $25,000. It reports the sale as an inflow of cash for $4,000. The T-account below shows the reasons for the change in this account during the year.

Illustration 17A-17
Analysis of equipment

Equipment

1/1/17	Balance	10,000	Cost of equipment sold	8,000
	Purchase of equipment	**25,000**		
12/31/17	Balance	27,000		

A	=	L	+	SE
+4,000				
+1,000				
				−3,000 Exp
−8,000				

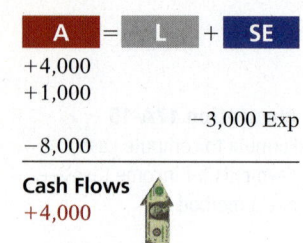

Cash Flows
+4,000

The following entry shows the details of the equipment sale transaction.

Cash	4,000	
Accumulated Depreciation—Equipment	1,000	
Loss on Disposal of Equipment	3,000	
Equipment		8,000

Helpful Hint
When companies issue stocks or bonds for cash, the actual proceeds will appear in the statement of cash flows as a financing inflow (rather than the par value of the stocks or face value of bonds).

INCREASE IN BONDS PAYABLE The Bonds Payable account increased $110,000. As indicated in the additional information, the company acquired land by directly exchanging bonds for land. Illustration 17A-18 reports this noncash transaction in a separate schedule at the bottom of the statement.

INCREASE IN COMMON STOCK The balance sheet reports an increase in Common Stock of $20,000. The additional information section notes that this increase resulted from the issuance of new shares of stock. This is a cash inflow reported in the financing activities section in Illustration 17A-18.

INCREASE IN RETAINED EARNINGS Retained earnings increased $116,000 during the year. This increase can be explained by two factors: (1) net income of $145,000 increased retained earnings, and (2) dividends of $29,000 decreased retained earnings. The company adjusts net income to net cash provided by operating activities in the operating activities section. **Payment** of the dividends (not the declaration) is a **cash outflow that the company reports as a financing activity in Illustration 17A-18.**

STATEMENT OF CASH FLOWS—2017

Illustration 17A-18 shows the statement of cash flows for Computer Services Company.

Illustration 17A-18
Statement of cash flows, 2017—direct method

COMPUTER SERVICES COMPANY
Statement of Cash Flows—Direct Method
For the Year Ended December 31, 2017

Cash flows from operating activities		
Cash receipts from customers		$ 517,000
Less: Cash payments:		
To suppliers	$ 139,000	
For operating expenses	115,000	
For income taxes	49,000	
For interest expense	42,000	345,000
Net cash provided by operating activities		172,000
Cash flows from investing activities		
Sale of equipment	4,000	
Purchase of building	(120,000)	
Purchase of equipment	(25,000)	
Net cash used by investing activities		(141,000)
Cash flows from financing activities		
Issuance of common stock	20,000	
Payment of cash dividends	(29,000)	
Net cash used by financing activities		(9,000)
Net increase in cash		22,000
Cash at beginning of period		33,000
Cash at end of period		$ 55,000
Noncash investing and financing activities		
Issuance of bonds payable to purchase land		$ 110,000

Step 3: Net Change in Cash

COMPARE THE NET CHANGE IN CASH ON THE STATEMENT OF CASH FLOWS WITH THE CHANGE IN THE CASH ACCOUNT REPORTED ON THE BALANCE SHEET TO MAKE SURE THE AMOUNTS AGREE

Illustration 17A-18 indicates that the net change in cash during the period was an increase of $22,000. This agrees with the change in balances in the Cash account reported on the balance sheets in Illustration 17A-1 (page 744).

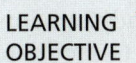

LEARNING OBJECTIVE *5

APPENDIX 17B: Use a worksheet to prepare the statement of cash flows using the indirect method.

When preparing a statement of cash flows, companies may need to make numerous adjustments of net income. In such cases, they often use **a worksheet to assemble and classify the data that will appear on the statement**. The worksheet is merely an aid in preparing the statement. Its use is optional. Illustration 17B-1 shows the skeleton format of the worksheet for preparation of the statement of cash flows.

Illustration 17B-1
Format of worksheet

XYZ Company.xls

Home | Insert | Page Layout | Formulas | Data | Review | View

P18 fx

	A	B	C	D	E
1					
2	**XYZ COMPANY**				
3	**Worksheet**				
4	**Statement of Cash Flows For the Year Ended . . .**				
5					
6		End of			End of
7		Last Year	Reconciling Items		Current Year
8	Balance Sheet Accounts	Balances	Debit	Credit	Balances
9	Debit balance accounts	XX	XX	XX	XX
10		XX	XX	XX	XX
11	Totals	XXX			XXX
12	Credit balance accounts	XX	XX	XX	XX
13		XX	XX	XX	XX
14	Totals	XXX			XXX
15					
16	Statement of Cash				
17	Flows Effects				
18	Operating activities				
19	Net income		XX		
20	Adjustments to net income		XX	XX	
21	Investing activities				
22	Receipts and payments		XX	XX	
23	Financing activities				
24	Receipts and payments		XX	XX	
25	Totals		XXX	XXX	
26	Increase (decrease) in cash		(XX)	XX	
27	Totals		XXX	XXX	
28					

The following guidelines are important in preparing a worksheet.

1. In the balance sheet accounts section, **list accounts with debit balances separately from those with credit balances**. This means, for example, that Accumulated Depreciation appears under credit balances and not as a contra account under debit balances. Enter the beginning and ending balances of each account in the appropriate columns. Enter as reconciling items in the two middle columns the transactions that caused the change in the account balance during the year.

   After all reconciling items have been entered, each line pertaining to a balance sheet account should "foot across." That is, the beginning balance plus or minus the reconciling item(s) must equal the ending balance. When this agreement exists for all balance sheet accounts, all changes in account balances have been reconciled.

2. The bottom portion of the worksheet consists of the operating, investing, and financing activities sections. It provides the information necessary to prepare the formal statement of cash flows. **Enter inflows of cash as debits in the reconciling columns. Enter outflows of cash as credits in the reconciling columns.** Thus, in this section, the sale of equipment for cash at book value appears as a debit under investing activities. Similarly, the purchase of land for cash appears as a credit under investing activities.
3. **The reconciling items shown in the worksheet are not entered in any journal or posted to any account.** They do not represent either adjustments or corrections of the balance sheet accounts. They are used only to facilitate the preparation of the statement of cash flows.

Preparing the Worksheet

As in the case of worksheets illustrated in earlier chapters, preparing a worksheet involves a series of prescribed steps. The steps in this case are:

1. Enter in the balance sheet accounts section the balance sheet accounts and their beginning and ending balances.
2. Enter in the reconciling columns of the worksheet the data that explain the changes in the balance sheet accounts other than cash and their effects on the statement of cash flows.
3. Enter on the cash line and at the bottom of the worksheet the increase or decrease in cash. This entry should enable the totals of the reconciling columns to be in agreement.

To illustrate the preparation of a worksheet, we will use the 2017 data for Computer Services Company. Your familiarity with these data (from the chapter) should help you understand the use of a worksheet. For ease of reference, the comparative balance sheets, income statement, and selected data for 2017 are presented in Illustration 17B-2.

DETERMINING THE RECONCILING ITEMS

Companies can use one of several approaches to determine the reconciling items. For example, they can first complete the changes affecting net cash provided by operating activities, and then can determine the effects of financing and investing transactions. Or, they can analyze the balance sheet accounts in the order in which they are listed on the worksheet. We will follow this latter approach for Computer Services, except for cash. As indicated in Step 3, **cash is handled last**.

ACCOUNTS RECEIVABLE The decrease of $10,000 in accounts receivable means that cash collections from sales revenue are higher than the sales revenue reported in the income statement. To convert net income to net cash provided by operating activities, we add the decrease of $10,000 to net income. The entry in the reconciling columns of the worksheet is:

(a)	Operating—Decrease in Accounts Receivable	10,000	
	Accounts Receivable		10,000

INVENTORY Computer Services Company's inventory balance increases $5,000 during the period. The Inventory account reflects the difference between the amount of inventory that the company purchased and the amount that it sold. For Computer Services, this means that the cost of merchandise purchased exceeds the cost of goods sold by $5,000. As a result, cost of goods sold does not reflect $5,000 of cash payments made for merchandise. We deduct this inventory increase of $5,000 during the period from net income to arrive at net cash provided by operating activities. The worksheet entry is:

(b)	Inventory	5,000	
	Operating—Increase in Inventory		5,000

Illustration 17B-2
Comparative balance sheets, income statement, and additional information for Computer Services Company

Computer Services Company.xls

Home Insert Page Layout Formulas Data Review View

P18 fx

	A	B	C	D
1	**COMPUTER SERVICES COMPANY**			
2	**Comparative Balance Sheets**			
3	**December 31**			
4				Change in
5				Account Balance
6	Assets	2017	2016	Increase/Decrease
7	Current assets			
8	Cash	$ 55,000	$ 33,000	$ 22,000 Increase
9	Accounts receivable	20,000	30,000	10,000 Decrease
10	Inventory	15,000	10,000	5,000 Increase
11	Prepaid expenses	5,000	1,000	4,000 Increase
12	Property, plant, and equipment			
13	Land	130,000	20,000	110,000 Increase
14	Buildings	160,000	40,000	120,000 Increase
15	Accumulated depreciation—buildings	(11,000)	(5,000)	6,000 Increase
16	Equipment	27,000	10,000	17,000 Increase
17	Accumulated depreciation—equipment	(3,000)	(1,000)	2,000 Increase
18	Total assets	$398,000	$138,000	
19				
20	Liabilities and Stockholders' Equity			
21	Current liabilities			
22	Accounts payable	$ 28,000	$ 12,000	$ 16,000 Increase
23	Income taxes payable	6,000	8,000	2,000 Decrease
24	Long-term liabilities			
25	Bonds payable	130,000	20,000	110,000 Increase
26	Stockholders' equity			
27	Common stock	70,000	50,000	20,000 Increase
28	Retained earnings	164,000	48,000	116,000 Increase
29	Total liabilities and stockholders' equity	$398,000	$138,000	

Computer Services Company.xls

Home Insert Page Layout Formulas Data Review View

P18 fx

	A	B	C	D
1				
2	**COMPUTER SERVICES COMPANY**			
3	**Income Statement**			
4	**For the Year Ended December 31, 2017**			
5	Sales revenue			$507,000
6	Cost of goods sold		$150,000	
7	Operating expenses (excluding depreciation)		111,000	
8	Depreciation expense		9,000	
9	Loss on disposal of equipment		3,000	
10	Interest expense		42,000	315,000
11	Income before income tax			192,000
12	Income tax expense			47,000
13	Net income			$145,000
14				

Additional information for 2017:

1. Depreciation expense was comprised of $6,000 for building and $3,000 for equipment.
2. The company sold equipment with a book value of $7,000 (cost $8,000, less accumulated depreciation $1,000) for $4,000 cash.
3. Issued $110,000 of long-term bonds in direct exchange for land.
4. A building costing $120,000 was purchased for cash. Equipment costing $25,000 was also purchased for cash.
5. Issued common stock for $20,000 cash.
6. The company declared and paid a $29,000 cash dividend.

PREPAID EXPENSES An increase of $4,000 in prepaid expenses means that expenses deducted in determining net income are less than expenses that were paid in cash. We deduct the increase of $4,000 from net income in determining net cash provided by operating activities. The worksheet entry is as follows.

(c)	Prepaid Expenses	4,000	
	Operating—Increase in Prepaid Expenses		4,000

Helpful Hint
These amounts are asterisked in the worksheet to indicate that they result from a significant noncash transaction.

LAND The increase in land of $110,000 resulted from a purchase through the issuance of long-term bonds. The company should report this transaction as a significant noncash investing and financing activity. The worksheet entry is:

(d)	Land	110,000	
	Bonds Payable		110,000

BUILDINGS The cash purchase of a building for $120,000 is an investing activity cash outflow. The entry in the reconciling columns of the worksheet is:

(e)	Buildings	120,000	
	Investing—Purchase of Building		120,000

EQUIPMENT The increase in equipment of $17,000 resulted from a cash purchase of $25,000 and the disposal of equipment costing $8,000. The book value of the equipment was $7,000, the cash proceeds were $4,000, and a loss of $3,000 was recorded. The worksheet entries are:

(f)	Equipment	25,000	
	Investing—Purchase of Equipment		25,000
(g)	Investing—Sale of Equipment	4,000	
	Operating—Loss on Disposal of Equipment	3,000	
	Accumulated Depreciation—Equipment	1,000	
	Equipment		8,000

ACCOUNTS PAYABLE We must add the increase of $16,000 in accounts payable to net income to determine net cash provided by operating activities. The worksheet entry is:

(h)	Operating—Increase in Accounts Payable	16,000	
	Accounts Payable		16,000

INCOME TAXES PAYABLE When a company incurs income tax expense but has not yet paid its taxes, it records income taxes payable. A change in the Income Taxes Payable account reflects the difference between income tax expense incurred and income tax actually paid. Computer Services' Income Taxes Payable account decreases by $2,000. That means the $47,000 of income tax expense reported on the income statement was $2,000 less than the amount of taxes paid during the period of $49,000. To adjust net income to a cash basis, we must reduce net income by $2,000. The worksheet entry is:

(i)	Income Taxes Payable	2,000	
	Operating—Decrease in Income Taxes Payable		2,000

BONDS PAYABLE The increase of $110,000 in this account resulted from the issuance of bonds for land. This is a significant noncash investing and financing activity. Worksheet entry (d) above is the only entry necessary.

COMMON STOCK The balance sheet reports an increase in Common Stock of $20,000. The additional information section notes that this increase resulted from the issuance of new shares of stock. This is a cash inflow reported in the financing section. The worksheet entry is:

(j)	Financing—Issuance of Common Stock	20,000	
	Common Stock		20,000

ACCUMULATED DEPRECIATION—BUILDINGS, AND ACCUMULATED DEPRECIATION—EQUIPMENT Increases in these accounts of $6,000 and $3,000, respectively, resulted from depreciation expense. Depreciation expense is a **noncash charge that we must add to net income** to determine net cash provided by operating activities. The worksheet entries are:

(k)	Operating—Depreciation Expense	6,000	
	Accumulated Depreciation—Buildings		6,000
(l)	Operating—Depreciation Expense	3,000	
	Accumulated Depreciation—Equipment		3,000

RETAINED EARNINGS The $116,000 increase in retained earnings resulted from net income of $145,000 and the declaration and payment of a $29,000 cash dividend. Net income is included in net cash provided by operating activities, and the dividends are a financing activity cash outflow. The entries in the reconciling columns of the worksheet are:

(m)	Operating—Net Income	145,000	
	Retained Earnings		145,000
(n)	Retained Earnings	29,000	
	Financing—Payment of Dividends		29,000

DISPOSITION OF CHANGE IN CASH The firm's cash increased $22,000 in 2017. The final entry on the worksheet, therefore, is:

(o)	Cash	22,000	
	Increase in Cash		22,000

As shown in the worksheet, we enter the increase in cash in the reconciling credit column as a **balancing** amount. This entry should complete the reconciliation of the changes in the balance sheet accounts. Also, it should permit the totals of the reconciling columns to be in agreement. When all changes have been explained and the reconciling columns are in agreement, the reconciling columns are ruled to complete the worksheet. The completed worksheet for Computer Services Company is shown in Illustration 17B-3 (page 756).

LEARNING OBJECTIVE *6

APPENDIX 17C: Use the T-account approach to prepare a statement of cash flows.

Many people like to use T-accounts to provide structure to the preparation of a statement of cash flows. The use of T-accounts is based on the accounting equation that you learned in Chapter 1. The basic equation is:

Assets = Liabilities + Equity

Now, let's rewrite the left-hand side as:

Cash + Noncash Assets = Liabilities + Equity

Next, rewrite the equation by subtracting Noncash Assets from each side to isolate Cash on the left-hand side:

Cash = Liabilities + Equity − Noncash Assets

Finally, if we insert the Δ symbol (which means "change in"), we have:

Δ Cash = Δ Liabilities + Δ Equity − Δ Noncash Assets

Illustration 17B-3
Completed worksheet—indirect method

Computer Services Company.xls

Home | Insert | Page Layout | Formulas | Data | Review | View

P18 fx

	A	B	C	D	E
1	**COMPUTER SERVICES COMPANY**				
2	**Worksheet**				
3	**Statement of Cash Flows For the Year Ended December 31, 2017**				
4					
5		Balance	Reconciling Items		Balance
6	Balance Sheet Accounts	12/31/16	Debit	Credit	12/31/17
7	Debits				
8	Cash	33,000	(o) 22,000		55,000
9	Accounts Receivable	30,000		(a) 10,000	20,000
10	Inventory	10,000	(b) 5,000		15,000
11	Prepaid Expenses	1,000	(c) 4,000		5,000
12	Land	20,000	(d) 110,000*		130,000
13	Buildings	40,000	(e) 120,000		160,000
14	Equipment	10,000	(f) 25,000	(g) 8,000	27,000
15	Total	144,000			412,000
16	Credits				
17	Accounts Payable	12,000		(h) 16,000	28,000
18	Income Taxes Payable	8,000	(i) 2,000		6,000
19	Bonds Payable	20,000		(d) 110,000*	130,000
20	Accumulated Depreciation—Buildings	5,000		(k) 6,000	11,000
21	Accumulated Depreciation—Equipment	1,000	(g) 1,000	(l) 3,000	3,000
22	Common Stock	50,000		(j) 20,000	70,000
23	Retained Earnings	48,000	(n) 29,000	(m) 145,000	164,000
24	Total	144,000			412,000
25					
26	Statement of Cash Flows Effects				
27	Operating activities				
28	Net income		(m) 145,000		
29	Decrease in accounts receivable		(a) 10,000		
30	Increase in inventory			(b) 5,000	
31	Increase in prepaid expenses			(c) 4,000	
32	Increase in accounts payable		(h) 16,000		
33	Decrease in income taxes payable			(i) 2,000	
34	Depreciation expense		(k) 6,000		
35			(l) 3,000		
36	Loss on disposal of equipment		(g) 3,000		
37	Investing activities				
38	Purchase of building			(e) 120,000	
39	Purchase of equipment			(f) 25,000	
40	Sale of equipment		(g) 4,000		
41	Financing activities				
42	Issuance of common stock		(j) 20,000		
43	Payment of dividends			(n) 29,000	
44	Totals		525,000	503,000	
45	Increase in cash			(o) 22,000	
46	Totals		525,000	525,000	
47					

* Significant noncash investing and financing activity.

What this means is that the change in cash is equal to the change in all of the other balance sheet accounts. Another way to think about this is that if we analyze the changes in all of the noncash balance sheet accounts, we will explain the change in the Cash account. This, of course, is exactly what we are trying to do with the statement of cash flows.

To implement this approach, first prepare a large Cash T-account with sections for operating, investing, and financing activities. Then, prepare smaller T-accounts for all of the other noncash balance sheet accounts. Insert the beginning and ending balances for each of these accounts. Once you have done this, then walk through the steps outlined in Illustration 17-3 (page 732). As you walk through the steps, enter debit and credit amounts into the affected accounts. When all of the changes in the T-accounts have been explained, you are done. To demonstrate, we apply this approach to the example of Computer Services Company that is presented in the chapter. Each of the adjustments in Illustration 17C-1 is numbered so you can follow them through the T-accounts.

Cash

Operating			
(1) Net income	145,000	5,000	Inventory (5)
(2) Depreciation expense	9,000	4,000	Prepaid expenses (6)
(3) Loss on equipment	3,000	2,000	Income taxes payable (8)
(4) Accounts receivable	10,000		
(7) Accounts payable	16,000		
Net cash provided by operating activities	172,000		
Investing			
(3) Sold equipment	4,000	120,000	Purchased building (10)
		25,000	Purchased equipment (11)
		141,000	Net cash used by investing activities
Financing			
(12) Issued common stock	20,000	29,000	Dividend paid (13)
		9,000	Net cash used by financing activities
	22,000		

Accounts Receivable

30,000	10,000 (4)
20,000	

Inventory

10,000	
(5) 5,000	
15,000	

Prepaid Expenses

1,000	
(6) 4,000	
5,000	

Land

20,000	
(9) 110,000	
130,000	

Buildings

40,000	
(10) 120,000	
160,000	

Accumulated Depreciation—Buildings

	5,000
	6,000 (2)
	11,000

Equipment

10,000	
(11) 25,000	8,000 (3)
27,000	

Accumulated Depreciation—Equipment

	1,000
(3) 1,000	3,000 (2)
	3,000

Accounts Payable

	12,000
	16,000 (7)
	28,000

Income Taxes Payable

	8,000
(8) 2,000	
	6,000

Bonds Payable

	20,000
	110,000 (9)
	130,000

Common Stock

	50,000
	20,000 (12)
	70,000

Retained Earnings

	48,000
	145,000 (1)
(13) 29,000	
	164,000

Illustration 17C-1
T-account approach

1. Post net income as a debit to the operating section of the Cash T-account and a credit to Retained Earnings. Make sure to label all adjustments to the Cash T-account. It also helps to number each adjustment so you can trace all of them if you make an error.
2. Post depreciation expense as a debit to the operating section of Cash and a credit to each of the appropriate accumulated depreciation accounts.
3. Post any gains or losses on the sale of property, plant, and equipment. To do this, it is best to first prepare the journal entry that was recorded at the time of the sale and then post each element of the journal entry. For example, for Computer Services the entry was as follows.

Cash	4,000	
Accumulated Depreciation—Equipment	1,000	
Loss on Disposal of Equipment	3,000	
Equipment		8,000

The $4,000 cash entry is a source of cash in the investing section of the Cash account. Accumulated Depreciation—Equipment is debited for $1,000. The Loss on Disposal of Equipment is a debit to the operating section of the Cash T-account. Finally, Equipment is credited for $8,000.

4–8. Next, post each of the changes to the noncash current asset and current liability accounts. For example, to explain the $10,000 decline in Computer Services' accounts receivable, credit Accounts Receivable for $10,000 and debit the operating section of the Cash T-account for $10,000.

9. Analyze the changes in the noncurrent accounts. Land was purchased by issuing bonds payable. This requires a debit to Land for $110,000 and a credit to Bonds Payable for $110,000. Note that this is a significant noncash event that requires disclosure at the bottom of the statement of cash flows.

10. Buildings is debited for $120,000, and the investing section of the Cash T-account is credited for $120,000 as a use of cash from investing.

11. Equipment is debited for $25,000 and the investing section of the Cash T-account is credited for $25,000 as a use of cash from investing.

12. Common Stock is credited for $20,000 for the issuance of shares of stock, and the financing section of the Cash T-account is debited for $20,000.

13. Retained Earnings is debited to reflect the payment of the $29,000 dividend, and the financing section of the Cash T-account is credited to reflect the use of Cash.

At this point, all of the changes in the noncash accounts have been explained. All that remains is to subtotal each section of the Cash T-account and compare the total change in cash with the change shown on the balance sheet. Once this is done, the information in the Cash T-account can be used to prepare a statement of cash flows.

REVIEW AND PRACTICE

LEARNING OBJECTIVES REVIEW

1 Discuss the usefulness and format of the statement of cash flows. The statement of cash flows provides information about the cash receipts, cash payments, and net change in cash resulting from the operating, investing, and financing activities of a company during the period. Operating activities include the cash effects of transactions that enter into the determination of net income. Investing activities involve cash flows resulting from changes in investments and long-term asset items. Financing activities involve cash flows resulting from changes in long-term liability and stockholders' equity items.

2 Prepare a statement of cash flows using the indirect method. The preparation of a statement of cash flows involves three major steps. (1) Determine net cash provided/used by operating activities by converting net income from an accrual basis to a cash basis. (2) Analyze changes in noncurrent asset and liability accounts and record as investing and financing activities, or disclose as noncash transactions. (3) Compare the net change in cash on the statement of cash flows with the change in the Cash account reported on the balance sheet to make sure the amounts agree.

3 Analyze the statement of cash flows. Free cash flow indicates the amount of cash a company generated during the current year that is available for the payment of additional dividends or for expansion.

***4 Prepare a statement of cash flows using the direct method.** The preparation of the statement of cash flows involves three major steps. (1) Determine net cash provided/used by operating activities by converting net income from an accrual basis to a cash basis. (2) Analyze changes in noncurrent asset and liability accounts and record as investing and financing activities, or disclose as noncash transactions. (3) Compare the net change in cash on the statement of cash flows with the change in the Cash account reported on the balance sheet to make sure the amounts agree. The direct method reports cash receipts less cash payments to arrive at net cash provided by operating activities.

***5 Use a worksheet to prepare the statement of cash flows using the indirect method.** When there are numerous adjustments, a worksheet can be a helpful tool in preparing the statement of cash flows. Key guidelines for using a worksheet are as follows. (1) List accounts with debit balances separately from those with credit balances. (2) In the reconciling columns in the bottom portion of the worksheet, show cash inflows as debits and cash outflows as credits. (3) Do not enter reconciling items in any journal or account, but use them only to help prepare the statement of cash flows.

The steps in preparing the worksheet are as follows. (1) Enter beginning and ending balances of balance sheet accounts. (2) Enter debits and credits in reconciling columns. (3) Enter the increase or decrease in cash in two places as a balancing amount.

*6 **Use the T-account approach to prepare a statement of cash flows.** To use T-accounts to prepare the statement of cash flows: (1) prepare a large Cash T-account with sections for operating, investing, and financing activities; (2) prepare smaller T-accounts for all other noncash accounts; (3) insert beginning and ending balances for all accounts; and (4) follows the steps in Illustration 17-3 (page 732), entering debit and credit amounts as needed.

GLOSSARY REVIEW

***Direct method** A method of preparing a statement of cash flows that shows operating cash receipts and payments, making it more consistent with the objective of the statement of cash flows. (pp. 732, 745).

Financing activities Cash flow activities that include (a) obtaining cash from issuing debt and repaying the amounts borrowed and (b) obtaining cash from stockholders, repurchasing shares, and paying dividends. (p. 728).

Free cash flow Net cash provided by operating activities adjusted for capital expenditures and dividends paid. (p. 742).

Indirect method A method of preparing a statement of cash flows in which net income is adjusted for items that do not affect cash, to determine net cash provided by operating activities. (pp. 732, 734).

Investing activities Cash flow activities that include (a) purchasing and disposing of investments and property, plant, and equipment using cash and (b) lending money and collecting the loans. (p. 728).

Operating activities Cash flow activities that include the cash effects of transactions that create revenues and expenses and thus enter into the determination of net income. (p. 728).

Statement of cash flows A basic financial statement that provides information about the cash receipts, cash payments, and net change in cash during a period, resulting from operating, investing, and financing activities. (p. 728).

PRACTICE MULTIPLE-CHOICE QUESTIONS

(LO 1) 1. Which of the following is **incorrect** about the statement of cash flows?
   (a) It is a fourth basic financial statement.
   (b) It provides information about cash receipts and cash payments of an entity during a period.
   (c) It reconciles the ending Cash account balance to the balance per the bank statement.
   (d) It provides information about the operating, investing, and financing activities of the business.

(LO 1) 2. Which of the following is **not** reported in the statement of cash flows?
   (a) The net change in stockholders' equity during the year.
   (b) Cash payments for plant assets during the year.
   (c) Cash receipts from sales of plant assets during the year.
   (d) How acquisitions of plant assets during the year were financed.

(LO 1) 3. The statement of cash flows classifies cash receipts and cash payments by these activities:
   (a) operating and nonoperating.
   (b) investing, financing, and operating.
   (c) financing, operating, and nonoperating.
   (d) investing, financing, and nonoperating.

(LO 1) 4. Which is an example of a cash flow from an operating activity?
   (a) Payment of cash to lenders for interest.
   (b) Receipt of cash from the sale of common stock.
   (c) Payment of cash dividends to the company's stockholders.
   (d) None of the above.

5. Which is an example of a cash flow from an investing activity? (LO 1)
   (a) Receipt of cash from the issuance of bonds payable.
   (b) Payment of cash to repurchase outstanding common stock.
   (c) Receipt of cash from the sale of equipment.
   (d) Payment of cash to suppliers for inventory.

6. Cash dividends paid to stockholders are classified on the statement of cash flows as: (LO 1)
   (a) an operating activity.
   (b) an investing activity.
   (c) a combination of (a) and (b).
   (d) a financing activity.

7. Which is an example of a cash flow from a financing activity? (LO 1)
   (a) Receipt of cash from sale of land.
   (b) Issuance of debt for cash.
   (c) Purchase of equipment for cash.
   (d) None of the above

8. Which of the following is **incorrect** about the statement of cash flows? (LO 1)
   (a) The direct method may be used to report net cash provided by operating activities.
   (b) The statement shows the net cash provided (used) for three categories of activity.
   (c) The operating section is the last section of the statement.
   (d) The indirect method may be used to report net cash provided by operating activities.

Use the indirect method to solve Questions 9 through 11.

(LO 2) **9.** Net income is $132,000, accounts payable increased $10,000 during the year, inventory decreased $6,000 during the year, and accounts receivable increased $12,000 during the year. Under the indirect method, what is net cash provided by operating activities?
(a) $102,000. (c) $124,000.
(b) $112,000. (d) $136,000.

(LO 2) **10.** Items that are added back to net income in determining net cash provided by operating activities under the indirect method do **not** include:
(a) depreciation expense.
(b) an increase in inventory.
(c) amortization expense.
(d) loss on disposal of equipment.

(LO 2) **11.** The following data are available for Allen Clapp Corporation.

Net income	$200,000
Depreciation expense	40,000
Dividends paid	60,000
Gain on disposal of land	10,000
Decrease in accounts receivable	20,000
Decrease in accounts payable	30,000

Net cash provided by operating activities is:
(a) $160,000. (c) $240,000.
(b) $220,000. (d) $280,000.

(LO 2) **12.** The following data are available for Orange Peels Corporation.

Proceeds from sale of land	$100,000
Proceeds from sale of equipment	50,000
Issuance of common stock	70,000
Purchase of equipment	30,000
Payment of cash dividends	60,000

Net cash provided by investing activities is:
(a) $120,000. (c) $150,000.
(b) $130,000. (d) $190,000.

(LO 2) **13.** The following data are available for Something Strange!

Increase in accounts payable	$ 40,000
Increase in bonds payable	100,000
Sale of investment	50,000
Issuance of common stock	60,000
Payment of cash dividends	30,000

Net cash provided by financing activities is:
(a) $90,000. (c) $160,000.
(b) $130,000. (d) $170,000.

14. The statement of cash flows should **not** be used to evaluate an entity's ability to: (LO 3)
(a) earn net income.
(b) generate future cash flows.
(c) pay dividends.
(d) meet obligations.

15. Free cash flow provides an indication of a company's ability to: (LO 3)
(a) generate net income.
(b) generate cash to pay dividends.
(c) generate cash to invest in new capital expenditures.
(d) Both (b) and (c).

Use the direct method to solve Questions 16 and 17.

***16.** The beginning balance in accounts receivable is $44,000, the ending balance is $42,000, and sales during the period are $129,000. What are cash receipts from customers? (LO 4)
(a) $127,000. (c) $131,000.
(b) $129,000. (d) $141,000.

***17.** Which of the following items is reported on a statement of cash flows prepared by the direct method? (LO 4)
(a) Loss on disposal of building.
(b) Increase in accounts receivable.
(c) Depreciation expense.
(d) Cash payments to suppliers.

***18.** In a worksheet for the statement of cash flows, a decrease in accounts receivable is entered in the reconciling columns as a credit to Accounts Receivable and a debit in the: (LO 5)
(a) investing activities section.
(b) operating activities section.
(c) financing activities section.
(d) None of the above.

***19.** In a worksheet for the statement of cash flows, a worksheet entry that includes a credit to accumulated depreciation will also include a: (LO 5)
(a) credit in the operating activities section and a debit in another section.
(b) debit in the operating activities section.
(c) debit in the investing activities section.
(d) debit in the financing activities section.

Solutions

1. (c) The statement of cash flows does not reconcile the ending cash balance to the balance per the bank statement. The other choices are true statements.

2. (a) The net change in stockholders' equity during the year is not reported in the statement of cash flows. The other choices are true statements.

3. (b) Operating, investing, and financing activities are the three classifications of cash receipts and cash payments used in the statement of cash flows. The other choices are therefore incorrect.

4. (a) Payment of cash to lenders for interest is an operating activity. The other choices are incorrect because (b) receipt of cash from the sale of common stock is a financing activity, (c) payment of cash dividends to the company's stockholders is a financing activity, and (d) there is a correct answer.

5. (c) Receipt of cash from the sale of equipment is an investing activity. The other choices are incorrect because (a) the receipt of cash from the issuance of bonds payable is a financing activity, (b) payment of cash to repurchase outstanding common stock is a financing activity, and (d) payment of cash to suppliers for inventory is an operating activity.

6. (d) Cash dividends paid to stockholders are classified as a financing activity, not (a) an operating activity, (b) an investing activity, or (c) a combination of (a) and (b).

7. (b) Issuance of debt for cash is a financing activity. The other choices are incorrect because (a) the receipt of cash for the sale of land is an investing activity, (c) the purchase of equipment for cash is an investing activity, and (d) there is a correct answer.

8. (c) The operating section of the statement of cash flows is the first, not the last, section of the statement. The other choices are true statements.

9. (d) Net cash provided by operating activities is computed by adjusting net income for the changes in the three current asset/current liability accounts listed. An increase in accounts payable ($10,000) and a decrease in inventory ($6,000) are added to net income ($132,000), while an increase in accounts receivable ($12,000) is subtracted from net income, or $132,000 + $10,000 + $6,000 − $12,000 = $136,000, not (a) $102,000, (b) $112,000, or (c) $124,000.

10. (b) An increase in inventory is subtracted, not added, to net income in determining net cash provided by operating activities. The other choices are incorrect because (a) depreciation expense, (c) amortization expense, and (d) loss on disposal of equipment are all added back to net income in determining net cash provided by operating activities.

11. (b) Net cash provided by operating activities is $220,000 (Net income $200,000 + Depreciation expense $40,000 − Gain on disposal of land $10,000 + Decrease in accounts receivable $20,000 − Decrease in accounts payable $30,000), not (a) $160,000, (c) $240,000, or (d) $280,000.

12. (a) Net cash provided by investing activities is $120,000 (Sale of land $100,000 + Sale of equipment $50,000 − Purchase of equipment $30,000), not (b) $130,000, (c) $150,000, or (d) $190,000. Issuance of common stock and payment of cash dividends are financing activities.

13. (b) Net cash provided by financing activities is $130,000 (Increase in bonds payable $100,000 + Issuance of common stock $60,000 − Payment of cash dividends $30,000), not (a) $90,000, (c) $160,000, or (d) $170,000. Increase in accounts payable is an operating activity and sale of investment is an investing activity.

14. (a) The statement of cash flows is not used to evaluate an entity's ability to earn net income. The other choices are true statements.

15. (d) Free cash flow provides an indication of a company's ability to generate cash to pay dividends and to invest in new capital expenditures. Choice (a) is incorrect because other measures besides free cash flow provide the best measure of a company's ability to earn net income. Choices (b) and (c) are true statements, but (d) is the better answer.

***16. (c)** Cash collections from customers amount to $131,000 ($129,000 + $2,000). The other choices are therefore incorrect.

***17. (d)** Cash payments to suppliers are reported on a statement of cash flows prepared by the direct method. The other choices are incorrect because (a) loss on disposal of building, (b) increase in accounts receivable, and (c) depreciation expense are reported in the operating activities section of the statement of cash flows when the indirect, not direct, method is used.

***18. (b)** Because accounts receivable is a current asset, the debit belongs in the operating activities section of the worksheet, not in the (a) investing activities or (c) financing activities section. Choice (d) is incorrect as there is a right answer.

***19. (b)** A worksheet entry that includes a credit to accumulated depreciation will also include a debit to depreciation expense. This debit in the operating activities section of the statement of cash flows will be added to the net income to determine net cash provided by operating activities. The other choices are therefore incorrect.

PRACTICE EXERCISES

Prepare journal entries to determine effect on statement of cash flows.

(LO 2)

1. Furst Corporation had the following transactions.

1. Paid salaries of $14,000.
2. Issued 1,000 shares of $1 par value common stock for equipment worth $16,000.
3. Sold equipment (cost $10,000, accumulated depreciation $6,000) for $3,000.
4. Sold land (cost $12,000) for $16,000.
5. Issued another 1,000 shares of $1 per value common stock for $18,000.
6. Recorded depreciation of $20,000.

Instructions

For each transaction above, (a) prepare the journal entry, and (b) indicate how it would affect the statement of cash flows. Assume the indirect method.

Solution

1. 1. (a) Salaries and Wages Expense	14,000	
Cash		14,000

(b) Salaries and wages expense is not reported separately on the statement of cash flows. It is part of the computation of net income in the income statement and is included in the net income amount on the statement of cash flows.

2. (a) Equipment	16,000	
Common Stock		1,000
Paid-in Capital in Excess of Par—Common Stock		15,000

(b) The issuance of common stock for equipment ($16,000) is reported as a noncash financing and investing activity at the bottom of the statement of cash flows.

3. (a)

Cash	3,000	
Loss on Disposal of Plant Assets	1,000	
Accumulated Depreciation—Equipment	6,000	
Equipment		10,000

(b) The cash receipt ($3,000) is reported in the investing section. The loss ($1,000) is added to net income in the operating section.

4. (a)

Cash	16,000	
Land		12,000
Gain on Disposal of Plant Assets		4,000

(b) The cash receipt ($16,000) is reported in the investing section. The gain ($4,000) is deducted from net income in the operating section.

5. (a)

Cash	18,000	
Common Stock		1,000
Paid-in Capital in Excess of Par—Common Stock		17,000

(b) The cash receipt ($18,000) is reported in the financing section.

6. (a)

Depreciation Expense	20,000	
Accumulated Depreciation—Equipment		20,000

(b) Depreciation expense ($20,000) is added to net income in the operating section.

Prepare statement of cash flows and compute free cash flow.

(LO 2, 3)

2. Strong Corporation's comparative balance sheets are presented below.

STRONG CORPORATION
Comparative Balance Sheets
December 31

	2017	**2016**
Cash	$ 28,200	$ 17,700
Accounts receivable	24,200	22,300
Investments	23,000	16,000
Equipment	60,000	70,000
Accumulated depreciation—equipment	(14,000)	(10,000)
Total	$121,400	$116,000
Accounts payable	$ 19,600	$ 11,100
Bonds payable	10,000	30,000
Common stock	60,000	45,000
Retained earnings	31,800	29,900
Total	$121,400	$116,000

Additional information:

1. Net income was $28,300. Dividends declared and paid were $26,400.
2. Equipment which cost $10,000 and had accumulated depreciation of $1,200 was sold for $4,300.
3. All other changes in noncurrent account balances had a direct effect on cash flows, except the change in accumulated depreciation.

Instructions

(a) Prepare a statement of cash flows for 2017 using the indirect method.

(b) Compute free cash flow.

Solution

2. (a)

STRONG CORPORATION
Statement of Cash Flows
For the Year Ended December 31, 2017

Cash flows from operating activities	
Net income	$ 28,300
Adjustments to reconcile net income to net cash provided by operating activities:	

Depreciation expense	$ 5,200*	
Loss on sale of equipment	4,500**	
Increase in accounts payable	8,500	
Increase in accounts receivable	(1,900)	16,300
Net cash provided by operating activities		44,600
Cash flows from investing activities		
Sale of equipment	4,300	
Purchase of investments	(7,000)	
Net cash used by investing activities		(2,700)
Cash flows from financing activities		
Issuance of common stock	15,000	
Retirement of bonds	(20,000)	
Payment of dividends	(26,400)	
Net cash used by financing activities		(31,400)
Net increase in cash		10,500
Cash at beginning of period		17,700
Cash at end of period		$ 28,200

*[$14,000 – ($10,000 – $1,200)]; **[$4,300 – ($10,000 – $1,200)]

(b) $44,600 – $0 – $26,400 = $18,200

PRACTICE PROBLEMS

Prepare statement of cash flows using indirect method.

(LO 2)

1. The income statement for the year ended December 31, 2017, for Kosinski Manufacturing Company contains the following condensed information.

KOSINSKI MANUFACTURING COMPANY
Income Statement
For the Year Ended December 31, 2017

Sales revenue		$6,583,000
Operating expenses (excluding depreciation)	$4,920,000	
Depreciation expense	880,000	5,800,000
Income before income taxes		783,000
Income tax expense		353,000
Net income		$ 430,000

Included in operating expenses is a $24,000 loss resulting from the sale of equipment for $270,000 cash. Equipment was purchased at a cost of $750,000.

The following balances are reported on Kosinski's comparative balance sheets at December 31.

KOSINSKI MANUFACTURING COMPANY
Comparative Balance Sheets (partial)

	2017	2016
Cash	$672,000	$130,000
Accounts receivable	775,000	610,000
Inventory	834,000	867,000
Accounts payable	521,000	501,000

Income tax expense of $353,000 represents the amount paid in 2017. Dividends declared and paid in 2017 totaled $200,000.

Instructions

Prepare the statement of cash flows using the indirect method.

Solution

1.

KOSINSKI MANUFACTURING COMPANY
Statement of Cash Flows—Indirect Method
For the Year Ended December 31, 2017

Cash flows from operating activities		
Net income		$ 430,000
Adjustments to reconcile net income to net cash provided by operating activities:		
Depreciation expense	$ 880,000	
Loss on disposal of equipment	24,000	
Increase in accounts receivable	(165,000)	
Decrease in inventory	33,000	
Increase in accounts payable	20,000	792,000
Net cash provided by operating activities		1,222,000
Cash flows from investing activities		
Sale of equipment	270,000	
Purchase of equipment	(750,000)	
Net cash used by investing activities		(480,000)
Cash flows from financing activities		
Payment of cash dividends		(200,000)
Net increase in cash		542,000
Cash at beginning of period		130,000
Cash at end of period		$ 672,000

Prepare statement of cash flows using direct method.

(LO 4)

*2. The income statement for Kosinski Manufacturing Company contains the following condensed information.

KOSINSKI MANUFACTURING COMPANY
Income Statement
For the Year Ended December 31, 2017

Sales revenue		$6,583,000
Operating expenses, excluding depreciation	$4,920,000	
Depreciation expense	880,000	5,800,000
Income before income taxes		783,000
Income tax expense		353,000
Net income		$ 430,000

Included in operating expenses is a $24,000 loss resulting from the sale of equipment for $270,000 cash. Equipment was purchased at a cost of $750,000. The following balances are reported on Kosinski's comparative balance sheet at December 31.

KOSINSKI MANUFACTURING COMPANY
Comparative Balance Sheets (partial)

	2017	2016
Cash	$672,000	$130,000
Accounts receivable	775,000	610,000
Inventory	834,000	867,000
Accounts payable	521,000	501,000

Income tax expense of $353,000 represents the amount paid in 2017. Dividends declared and paid in 2017 totaled $200,000.

Instructions

Prepare the statement of cash flows using the direct method.

Solution

2.

KOSINSKI MANUFACTURING COMPANY
Statement of Cash Flows—Direct Method
For the Year Ended December 31, 2017

Cash flows from operating activities		
Cash collections from customers		$6,418,000*
Cash payments:		
For operating expenses	$4,843,000**	
For income taxes	353,000	5,196,000
Net cash provided by operating activities		1,222,000
Cash flows from investing activities		
Sale of equipment	270,000	
Purchase of equipment	(750,000)	
Net cash used by investing activities		(480,000)
Cash flows from financing activities		
Payment of cash dividends	(200,000)	
Net cash used by financing activities		(200,000)
Net increase in cash		542,000
Cash at beginning of period		130,000
Cash at end of period		$ 672,000

Direct-Method Computations:

*Computation of cash collections from customers:	
Sales revenue	$6,583,000
Deduct: Increase in accounts receivable	(165,000)
Cash collections from customers	$6,418,000
**Computation of cash payments for operating expenses:	
Operating expenses	$4,920,000
Deduct: Loss on disposal of equipment	(24,000)
Deduct: Decrease in inventories	(33,000)
Deduct: Increase in accounts payable	(20,000)
Cash payments for operating expenses	$4,843,000

WileyPLUS Brief Exercises, Exercises, DO IT! Exercises, and Problems and many additional resources are available for practice in WileyPLUS

NOTE: All asterisked Questions, Exercises, and Problems relate to material in the appendices to the chapter.

QUESTIONS

1. (a) What is a statement of cash flows?
   (b) Mark Paxson maintains that the statement of cash flows is an optional financial statement. Do you agree? Explain.
2. What questions about cash are answered by the statement of cash flows?
3. Distinguish among the three types of activities reported in the statement of cash flows.
4. (a) What are the major sources (inflows) of cash in a statement of cash flows?
   (b) What are the major uses (outflows) of cash?
5. Why is it important to disclose certain noncash transactions? How should they be disclosed?
6. Diane Hollowell and Terry Parmenter were discussing the format of the statement of cash flows of Snow Candy Co. At the bottom of Snow Candy's statement

of cash flows was a separate section entitled "Noncash investing and financing activities." Give three examples of significant noncash transactions that would be reported in this section.

7. Why is it necessary to use comparative balance sheets, a current income statement, and certain transaction data in preparing a statement of cash flows?
8. Contrast the advantages and disadvantages of the direct and indirect methods of preparing the statement of cash flows. Are both methods acceptable? Which method is preferred by the FASB? Which method is more popular?
9. When the total cash inflows exceed the total cash outflows in the statement of cash flows, how and where is this excess identified?
10. Describe the indirect method for determining net cash provided (used) by operating activities.
11. Why is it necessary to convert accrual-basis net income to cash-basis income when preparing a statement of cash flows?
12. The president of Merando Company is puzzled. During the last year, the company experienced a net loss of $800,000, yet its cash increased $300,000 during the same period of time. Explain to the president how this could occur.
13. Identify five items that are adjustments to convert net income to net cash provided by operating activities under the indirect method.
14. Why and how is depreciation expense reported in a statement of cash flows prepared using the indirect method?
15. Why is the statement of cash flows useful?
16. During 2017, Doubleday Company converted $1,700,000 of its total $2,000,000 of bonds payable into common stock. Indicate how the transaction would be reported on a statement of cash flows, if at all.
17. In its 2013 statement of cash flows, what amount did Apple report for net cash (a) provided by operating activities, (b) used for investing activities, and (c) used for financing activities?

*18. Describe the direct method for determining net cash provided by operating activities.

*19. Give the formulas under the direct method for computing (a) cash receipts from customers and (b) cash payments to suppliers.

*20. Molino Inc. reported sales revenue of $2 million for 2017. Accounts receivable decreased $200,000 and accounts payable increased $300,000. Compute cash receipts from customers, assuming that the receivable and payable transactions related to operations.

*21. In the direct method, why is depreciation expense not reported in the cash flows from operating activities section?

*22. Why is it advantageous to use a worksheet when preparing a statement of cash flows? Is a worksheet required to prepare a statement of cash flows?

BRIEF EXERCISES

Indicate statement presentation of selected transactions.

(LO 1)

BE17-1 Each of the items below must be considered in preparing a statement of cash flows for Baskerville Co. for the year ended December 31, 2017. For each item, state how it should be shown in the statement of cash flows for 2017.

(a) Issued bonds for $200,000 cash.
(b) Purchased equipment for $150,000 cash.
(c) Sold land costing $20,000 for $20,000 cash.
(d) Declared and paid a $50,000 cash dividend.

Classify items by activities.

(LO 1)

BE17-2 Classify each item as an operating, investing, or financing activity. Assume all items involve cash unless there is information to the contrary and the indirect method is used.

(a) Purchase of equipment.
(b) Proceeds from sale of building.
(c) Redemption of bonds.
(d) Depreciation.
(e) Payment of dividends.
(f) Issuance of common stock.

Identify financing activity transactions.

(LO 1)

BE17-3 The following T-account is a summary of the Cash account of Cuellar Company.

Cash (Summary Form)

Balance, Jan. 1	8,000		
Receipts from customers	364,000	Payments for goods	200,000
Dividends on stock investments	6,000	Payments for operating expenses	140,000
Proceeds from sale of equipment	36,000	Interest paid	10,000
Proceeds from issuance of bonds payable	300,000	Taxes paid	8,000
		Dividends paid	50,000
Balance, Dec. 31	306,000		

What amount of net cash provided (used) by financing activities should be reported in the statement of cash flows?

BE17-4 Telfer, Inc. reported net income of $2.8 million in 2017. Depreciation for the year was $160,000, accounts receivable decreased $350,000, and accounts payable decreased $280,000. Compute net cash provided by operating activities using the indirect method.

Compute net cash provided by operating activities—indirect method.

(LO 2)

BE17-5 The net income for Metz Co. for 2017 was $280,000. For 2017, depreciation on plant assets was $70,000, and the company incurred a loss on disposal of plant assets of $12,000. Compute net cash provided by operating activities under the indirect method.

Compute net cash provided by operating activities—indirect method.

(LO 2)

BE17-6 The comparative balance sheets for Montalvo Company show these changes in noncash current asset accounts: accounts receivable decrease $80,000, prepaid expenses increase $28,000, and inventories increase $30,000. Compute net cash provided by operating activities using the indirect method assuming that net income is $300,000.

Compute net cash provided by operating activities—indirect method.

(LO 2)

BE17-7 The T-accounts for Equipment and the related Accumulated Depreciation—Equipment for Luo Company at the end of 2017 are shown here.

Determine cash received from sale of equipment.

(LO 2)

Equipment			
Beg. bal.	80,000	Disposals	22,000
Acquisitions	41,600		
End. bal.	99,600		

Accumulated Depreciation—Equipment			
Disposals	5,500	Beg. bal.	44,500
		Depr. exp.	12,000
		End. bal.	51,000

In addition, Luo Company's income statement reported a loss on the disposal of equipment of $6,500. What amount was reported on the statement of cash flows as "cash flow from sale of equipment"?

BE17-8 Assume that during 2017, Cypress Semiconductor Corporation reported net cash provided by operating activities of $155,793,000, net cash used in investing activities of $207,826,000 (including cash spent for plant assets of $132,280,000), and net cash used in financing activities of $33,372,000. Dividends of $5,000,000 were paid. Calculate free cash flow.

Calculate free cash flow.

(LO 3)

BE17-9 Hinck Corporation reported net cash provided by operating activities of $360,000, net cash used by investing activities of $250,000 (including cash spent for capital assets of $200,000), and net cash provided by financing activities of $70,000. Dividends of $140,000 were paid. Calculate free cash flow.

Calculate free cash flow.

(LO 3)

BE17-10 Suppose in a recent quarter, Alliance Atlantis Communications Inc. reported net cash provided by operating activities of $45,600,000 and revenues of $264,800,000. Cash spent on plant asset additions during the quarter was $1,600,000. No dividends were paid. Calculate free cash flow.

Calculate free cash flow.

(LO 3)

BE17-11 The management of Morrow Inc. is trying to decide whether it can increase its dividend. During the current year, it reported net income of $875,000. It had net cash provided by operating activities of $734,000, paid cash dividends of $70,000, and had capital expenditures of $280,000. Compute the company's free cash flow, and discuss whether an increase in the dividend appears warranted. What other factors should be considered?

Calculate and analyze free cash flow.

(LO 3)

***BE17-12** Suppose Columbia Sportswear Company had accounts receivable of $206,024,000 at the beginning of a recent year, and $267,653,000 at year-end. Sales revenue was $1,095,307,000 for the year. What is the amount of cash receipts from customers?

Compute receipts from customers—direct method.

(LO 4)

***BE17-13** Howell Corporation reported income tax expense of $340,000,000 on its 2017 income statement and income taxes payable of $297,000,000 at December 31, 2016, and $522,000,000 at December 31, 2017. What amount of cash payments were made for income taxes during 2017?

Compute cash payments for income taxes—direct method.

(LO 4)

***BE17-14** Sisson Corporation reports operating expenses of $80,000 excluding depreciation expense of $15,000 for 2017. During the year, prepaid expenses decreased $6,600 and accrued expenses payable increased $4,400. Compute the cash payments for operating expenses in 2017.

Compute cash payments for operating expenses—direct method.

(LO 4)

Indicate entries in worksheet.
(LO 5)

***BE17-15** During the year, prepaid expenses decreased $5,600, and accrued expenses increased $2,400. Indicate how the changes in prepaid expenses and accrued expenses payable should be entered in the reconciling columns of a worksheet. Assume that beginning balances were prepaid expenses $18,600 and accrued expenses payable $8,200.

DO IT! Exercises

Classify transactions by type of cash flow activity.
(LO 1)

DO IT! 17-1 Ragsdell Corporation had the following transactions.

1. Issued $200,000 of bonds payable.
2. Paid utilities expense.
3. Issued 500 shares of preferred stock for $45,000.
4. Sold land and a building for $250,000.
5. Lent $30,000 to Tegtmeier Corporation, receiving Tegtmeier's 1-year, 12% note.

Classify each of these transactions by type of cash flow activity (operating, investing, or financing).

Calculate net cash from operating activities.
(LO 2)

DO IT! 17-2 Wise Photography reported net income of $130,000 for 2017. Included in the income statement were depreciation expense of $6,000, amortization expense of $2,000, and a gain on disposal of equipment of $3,600. Wise's comparative balance sheets show the following balances.

	12/31/16	12/31/17
Accounts receivable	$27,000	$21,000
Accounts payable	6,000	9,200

Calculate net cash provided by operating activities for Wise Photography.

Compute and discuss free cash flow.
(LO 3)

DO IT! 17-3 Obermeyer Corporation issued the following statement of cash flows for 2017.

OBERMEYER CORPORATION
Statement of Cash Flows—Indirect Method
For the Year Ended December 31, 2017

Cash flows from operating activities		
Net income		$59,000
Adjustments to reconcile net income to net cash provided by operating activities:		
Depreciation expense	$ 9,100	
Loss on disposal of equipment	9,500	
Increase in inventory	(5,000)	
Decrease in accounts receivable	3,300	
Decrease in accounts payable	(2,200)	14,700
Net cash provided by operating activities		73,700
Cash flows from investing activities		
Sale of investments	3,100	
Purchase of equipment	(27,000)	
Net cash used by investing activities		(23,900)
Cash flows from financing activities		
Issuance of stock	20,000	
Payment on long-term note payable	(10,000)	
Payment for dividends	(15,000)	
Net cash used by financing activities		(5,000)
Net increase in cash		44,800
Cash at beginning of year		13,000
Cash at end of year		$57,800

(a) Compute free cash flow for Obermeyer Corporation. (b) Explain why free cash flow often provides better information than "Net cash provided by operating activities."

EXERCISES

E17-1 Tabares Corporation had these transactions during 2017.

Classify transactions by type of activity.
(LO 1)

(a) Issued $50,000 par value common stock for cash.
(b) Purchased a machine for $30,000, giving a long-term note in exchange.
(c) Issued $200,000 par value common stock upon conversion of bonds having a face value of $200,000.
(d) Declared and paid a cash dividend of $18,000.
(e) Sold a long-term investment with a cost of $15,000 for $15,000 cash.
(f) Collected $16,000 of accounts receivable.
(g) Paid $18,000 on accounts payable.

Instructions
Analyze the transactions and indicate whether each transaction resulted in a cash flow from operating activities, investing activities, financing activities, or noncash investing and financing activities.

E17-2 An analysis of comparative balance sheets, the current year's income statement, and the general ledger accounts of Wellman Corp. uncovered the following items. Assume all items involve cash unless there is information to the contrary.

Classify transactions by type of activity.
(LO 1)

(a) Payment of interest on notes payable.
(b) Exchange of land for patent.
(c) Sale of building at book value.
(d) Payment of dividends.
(e) Depreciation.
(f) Receipt of dividends on investment in stock.
(g) Receipt of interest on notes receivable.
(h) Issuance of common stock.
(i) Amortization of patent.
(j) Issuance of bonds for land.
(k) Purchase of land.
(l) Conversion of bonds into common stock.
(m) Sale of land at a loss.
(n) Retirement of bonds.

Instructions
Indicate how each item should be classified in the statement of cash flows using these four major classifications: operating activity (indirect method), investing activity, financing activity, and significant noncash investing and financing activity.

E17-3 Cushenberry Corporation had the following transactions.

Prepare journal entry and determine effect on cash flows.
(LO 1)

1. Sold land (cost $12,000) for $15,000.
2. Issued common stock at par for $20,000.
3. Recorded depreciation on buildings for $17,000.
4. Paid salaries of $9,000.
5. Issued 1,000 shares of $1 par value common stock for equipment worth $8,000.
6. Sold equipment (cost $10,000, accumulated depreciation $7,000) for $1,200.

Instructions
For each transaction above, (a) prepare the journal entry, and (b) indicate how it would affect the statement of cash flows using the indirect method.

E17-4 Gutierrez Company reported net income of $225,000 for 2017. Gutierrez also reported depreciation expense of $45,000 and a loss of $5,000 on the disposal of equipment. The comparative balance sheet shows a decrease in accounts receivable of $15,000 for the year, a $17,000 increase in accounts payable, and a $4,000 decrease in prepaid expenses.

Prepare the operating activities section—indirect method.
(LO 2)

Instructions
Prepare the operating activities section of the statement of cash flows for 2017. Use the indirect method.

E17-5 The current sections of Scoggin Inc.'s balance sheets at December 31, 2016 and 2017, are presented here. Scoggin's net income for 2017 was $153,000. Depreciation expense was $24,000.

Prepare the operating activities section—indirect method.
(LO 2)

	2017	2016
Current assets		
Cash	$105,000	$ 99,000
Accounts receivable	110,000	89,000
Inventory	158,000	172,000
Prepaid expenses	27,000	22,000
Total current assets	$400,000	$382,000
Current liabilities		
Accrued expenses payable	$ 15,000	$ 5,000
Accounts payable	85,000	92,000
Total current liabilities	$100,000	$ 97,000

Instructions

Prepare the net cash provided by operating activities section of the company's statement of cash flows for the year ended December 31, 2017, using the indirect method.

Prepare partial statement of cash flows—indirect method.

(LO 2)

E17-6 The three accounts shown below appear in the general ledger of Herrick Corp. during 2017.

Equipment

Date		Debit	Credit	Balance
Jan. 1	Balance			160,000
July 31	Purchase of equipment	70,000		230,000
Sept. 2	Cost of equipment constructed	53,000		283,000
Nov. 10	Cost of equipment sold		49,000	234,000

Accumulated Depreciation—Equipment

Date		Debit	Credit	Balance
Jan. 1	Balance			71,000
Nov. 10	Accumulated depreciation on equipment sold	30,000		41,000
Dec. 31	Depreciation for year		28,000	69,000

Retained Earnings

Date		Debit	Credit	Balance
Jan. 1	Balance			105,000
Aug. 23	Dividends (cash)	14,000		91,000
Dec. 31	Net income		77,000	168,000

Instructions

From the postings in the accounts, indicate how the information is reported on a statement of cash flows using the indirect method. The loss on disposal of equipment was $7,000. (*Hint:* Cost of equipment constructed is reported in the investing activities section as a decrease in cash of $53,000.)

Prepare statement of cash flows and compute free cash flow.

(LO 2, 3)

E17-7 Rojas Corporation's comparative balance sheets are presented below.

ROJAS CORPORATION
Comparative Balance Sheets
December 31

	2017	2016
Cash	$ 14,300	$ 10,700
Accounts receivable	21,200	23,400
Land	20,000	26,000
Buildings	70,000	70,000
Accumulated depreciation—buildings	(15,000)	(10,000)
Total	$110,500	$120,100

Accounts payable	$ 12,370	$ 31,100
Common stock	75,000	69,000
Retained earnings	23,130	20,000
Total	$110,500	$120,100

Additional information:

1. Net income was $22,630. Dividends declared and paid were $19,500.
2. No noncash investing and financing activities occurred during 2017.
3. The land was sold for cash of $4,900.

Instructions

(a) Prepare a statement of cash flows for 2017 using the indirect method.
(b) Compute free cash flow.

E17-8 Here are comparative balance sheets for Velo Company.

Prepare a statement of cash flows—indirect method.

(LO 2)

VELO COMPANY
Comparative Balance Sheets
December 31

Assets	**2017**	**2016**
Cash	$ 63,000	$ 22,000
Accounts receivable	85,000	76,000
Inventory	170,000	189,000
Land	75,000	100,000
Equipment	270,000	200,000
Accumulated depreciation—equipment	(66,000)	(32,000)
Total	$597,000	$555,000
Liabilities and Stockholders' Equity		
Accounts payable	$ 39,000	$ 47,000
Bonds payable	150,000	200,000
Common stock ($1 par)	216,000	174,000
Retained earnings	192,000	134,000
Total	$597,000	$555,000

Additional information:

1. Net income for 2017 was $93,000.
2. Cash dividends of $35,000 were declared and paid.
3. Bonds payable amounting to $50,000 were redeemed for cash $50,000.
4. Common stock was issued for $42,000 cash.
5. No equipment was sold during 2017, but land was sold at cost.

Instructions

Prepare a statement of cash flows for 2017 using the indirect method.

E17-9 Rodriquez Corporation's comparative balance sheets are presented below.

Prepare statement of cash flows and compute free cash flow.

(LO 2, 3)

RODRIQUEZ CORPORATION
Comparative Balance Sheets
December 31

	2017	**2016**
Cash	$ 15,200	$ 17,700
Accounts receivable	25,200	22,300
Investments	20,000	16,000
Equipment	60,000	70,000
Accumulated depreciation—equipment	(14,000)	(10,000)
Total	$106,400	$116,000

	2017	2016
Accounts payable	$ 14,600	$ 11,100
Bonds payable	10,000	30,000
Common stock	50,000	45,000
Retained earnings	31,800	29,900
Total	$106,400	$116,000

Additional information:

1. Net income was $18,300. Dividends declared and paid were $16,400.
2. Equipment which cost $10,000 and had accumulated depreciation of $1,200 was sold for $3,300.
3. No noncash investing and financing activities occurred during 2017.

Instructions

(a) Prepare a statement of cash flows for 2017 using the indirect method.
(b) Compute free cash flow.

Compute net cash provided by operating activities—direct method.

(LO 4)

***E17-10** Macgregor Company completed its first year of operations on December 31, 2017. Its initial income statement showed that Macgregor had revenues of $192,000 and operating expenses of $78,000. Accounts receivable and accounts payable at year-end were $60,000 and $23,000, respectively. Assume that accounts payable related to operating expenses. Ignore income taxes.

Instructions

Compute net cash provided by operating activities using the direct method.

Compute cash payments—direct method.

(LO 4)

***E17-11** Suppose a recent income statement for **McDonald's Corporation** shows cost of goods sold $4,852.7 million and operating expenses (including depreciation expense of $1,201 million) $10,671.5 million. The comparative balance sheet for the year shows that inventory increased $18.1 million, prepaid expenses increased $56.3 million, accounts payable (merchandise suppliers) increased $136.9 million, and accrued expenses payable increased $160.9 million.

Instructions

Using the direct method, compute (a) cash payments to suppliers and (b) cash payments for operating expenses.

Compute cash flow from operating activities—direct method.

(LO 4)

***E17-12** The 2017 accounting records of Blocker Transport reveal these transactions and events.

Payment of interest	$ 10,000	Collection of accounts receivable	$182,000
Cash sales	48,000	Payment of salaries and wages	53,000
Receipt of dividend revenue	18,000	Depreciation expense	16,000
Payment of income taxes	12,000	Proceeds from sale of vehicles	12,000
Net income	38,000	Purchase of equipment for cash	22,000
Payment of accounts payable		Loss on disposal of vehicles	3,000
for merchandise	115,000	Payment of dividends	14,000
Payment for land	74,000	Payment of operating expenses	28,000

Instructions

Prepare the cash flows from operating activities section using the direct method. (Not all of the items will be used.)

Calculate cash flows—direct method.

(LO 4)

***E17-13** The following information is taken from the 2017 general ledger of Swisher Company.

Rent	Rent expense	$ 48,000
	Prepaid rent, January 1	5,900
	Prepaid rent, December 31	9,000
Salaries	Salaries and wages expense	$ 54,000
	Salaries and wages payable, January 1	10,000
	Salaries and wages payable, December 31	8,000

Sales	Sales revenue	$175,000
	Accounts receivable, January 1	16,000
	Accounts receivable, December 31	7,000

Instructions

In each case, compute the amount that should be reported in the operating activities section of the statement of cash flows under the direct method.

***E17-14** Comparative balance sheets for International Company are presented below.

Prepare a worksheet.

(LO 5)

INTERNATIONAL COMPANY
Comparative Balance Sheets
December 31

Assets	**2017**	**2016**
Cash	$ 73,000	$ 22,000
Accounts receivable	85,000	76,000
Inventory	180,000	189,000
Land	75,000	100,000
Equipment	250,000	200,000
Accumulated depreciation—equipment	(66,000)	(42,000)
Total	$597,000	$545,000
Liabilities and Stockholders' Equity		
Accounts payable	$ 34,000	$ 47,000
Bonds payable	150,000	200,000
Common stock ($1 par)	214,000	164,000
Retained earnings	199,000	134,000
Total	$597,000	$545,000

Additional information:

1. Net income for 2017 was $135,000.
2. Cash dividends of $70,000 were declared and paid.
3. Bonds payable amounting to $50,000 were redeemed for cash $50,000.
4. Common stock was issued for $50,000 cash.
5. Depreciation expense was $24,000.
6. Sales revenue for the year was $978,000.
7. Land was sold at cost, and equipment was purchased for cash.

Instructions

Prepare a worksheet for a statement of cash flows for 2017 using the indirect method. Enter the reconciling items directly on the worksheet, using letters to cross-reference each entry.

EXERCISES: SET B AND CHALLENGE EXERCISES

Visit the book's companion website, at **www.wiley.com/college/weygandt**, and choose the Student Companion site to access Exercises: Set B and Challenge Exercises.

PROBLEMS: SET A

P17-1A You are provided with the following transactions that took place during a recent fiscal year.

Distinguish among operating, investing, and financing activities.

(LO 1)

Transaction	**Statement of Cash Flows Activity Affected**	**Cash Inflow, Outflow, or No Effect?**
(a) Recorded depreciation expense on the plant assets.		
(b) Recorded and paid interest expense.		
(c) Recorded cash proceeds from a disposal of plant assets.		
(d) Acquired land by issuing common stock.		

Transaction	Statement of Cash Flows Activity Affected	Cash Inflow, Outflow, or No Effect?
(e) Paid a cash dividend to preferred stockholders.		
(f) Paid a cash dividend to common stockholders.		
(g) Recorded cash sales.		
(h) Recorded sales on account.		
(i) Purchased inventory for cash.		
(j) Purchased inventory on account.		

Instructions

Complete the table indicating whether each item (1) affects operating (O) activities, investing (I) activities, financing (F) activities, or is a noncash (NC) transaction reported in a separate schedule, and (2) represents a cash inflow or cash outflow or has no cash flow effect. Assume use of the indirect approach.

Determine cash flow effects of changes in equity accounts.

(LO 2)

P17-2A The following account balances relate to the stockholders' equity accounts of Kerbs Corp. at year-end.

	2017	2016
Common stock, 10,500 and 10,000 shares, respectively, for 2017 and 2016	$170,000	$140,000
Preferred stock, 5,000 shares	125,000	125,000
Retained earnings	300,000	250,000

A small stock dividend was declared and issued in 2017. The market value of the shares was $10,500. Cash dividends were $15,000 in both 2017 and 2016. The common stock has no par or stated value.

Instructions

(a) Net income $75,500

(a) What was the amount of net income reported by Kerbs Corp. in 2017?

(b) Determine the amounts of any cash inflows or outflows related to the common stock and dividend accounts in 2017.

(c) Indicate where each of the cash inflows or outflows identified in (b) would be classified on the statement of cash flows.

Prepare the operating activities section—indirect method.

(LO 2)

XLS

P17-3A The income statement of Whitlock Company is presented here.

WHITLOCK COMPANY
Income Statement
For the Year Ended November 30, 2017

Sales revenue		$7,700,000
Cost of goods sold		
Beginning inventory	$1,900,000	
Purchases	4,400,000	
Goods available for sale	6,300,000	
Ending inventory	1,400,000	
Total cost of goods sold		4,900,000
Gross profit		2,800,000
Operating expenses		1,150,000
Net income		$1,650,000

Additional information:

1. Accounts receivable increased $200,000 during the year, and inventory decreased $500,000.
2. Prepaid expenses increased $150,000 during the year.
3. Accounts payable to suppliers of merchandise decreased $340,000 during the year.
4. Accrued expenses payable decreased $100,000 during the year.
5. Operating expenses include depreciation expense of $70,000.

Instructions
Prepare the operating activities section of the statement of cash flows for the year ended November 30, 2017, for Whitlock Company, using the indirect method.

Cash from operations $1,430,000

***P17-4A** Data for Whitlock Company are presented in P17-3A.

Prepare the operating activities section—direct method.

(LO 4)

Instructions
Prepare the operating activities section of the statement of cash flows using the direct method.

Cash from operations $1,430,000

P17-5A Zumbrunn Company's income statement contained the condensed information below.

Prepare the operating activities section—indirect method.

(LO 2)

ZUMBRUNN COMPANY
Income Statement
For the Year Ended December 31, 2017

Service revenue		$970,000
Operating expenses, excluding depreciation	$624,000	
Depreciation expense	60,000	
Loss on disposal of equipment	16,000	700,000
Income before income taxes		270,000
Income tax expense		40,000
Net income		$230,000

Zumbrunn's balance sheet contained the comparative data at December 31, shown below.

	2017	2016
Accounts receivable	$75,000	$65,000
Accounts payable	46,000	28,000
Income taxes payable	11,000	7,000

Accounts payable pertain to operating expenses.

Instructions
Prepare the operating activities section of the statement of cash flows using the indirect method.

Cash from operations $318,000

***P17-6A** Data for Zumbrunn Company are presented in P17-5A.

Prepare the operating activities section—direct method.

(LO 4)

Instructions
Prepare the operating activities section of the statement of cash flows using the direct method.

Cash from operations $318,000

P17-7A The following are the financial statements of Nosker Company.

Prepare a statement of cash flows—indirect method, and compute free cash flow.

(LO 2, 3)

NOSKER COMPANY
Comparative Balance Sheets
December 31

Assets	**2017**	**2016**
Cash	$ 38,000	$ 20,000
Accounts receivable	30,000	14,000
Inventory	27,000	20,000
Equipment	60,000	78,000
Accumulated depreciation—equipment	(29,000)	(24,000)
Total	$126,000	$108,000
Liabilities and Stockholders' Equity		
Accounts payable	$ 24,000	$ 15,000
Income taxes payable	7,000	8,000
Bonds payable	27,000	33,000
Common stock	18,000	14,000
Retained earnings	50,000	38,000
Total	$126,000	$108,000

NOSKER COMPANY
Income Statement
For the Year Ended December 31, 2017

Sales revenue	$242,000
Cost of goods sold	175,000
Gross profit	67,000
Operating expenses	24,000
Income from operations	43,000
Interest expense	3,000
Income before income taxes	40,000
Income tax expense	8,000
Net income	$ 32,000

Additional data:

1. Dividends declared and paid were $20,000.
2. During the year equipment was sold for $8,500 cash. This equipment cost $18,000 originally and had a book value of $8,500 at the time of sale.
3. All depreciation expense, $14,500, is in the operating expenses.
4. All sales and purchases are on account.

Instructions

(a) Cash from operations $31,500

(a) Prepare a statement of cash flows using the indirect method.
(b) Compute free cash flow.

Prepare a statement of cash flows—direct method, and compute free cash flow.

(LO 3, 4)

XLS

***P17-8A** Data for Nosker Company are presented in P17-7A. Further analysis reveals the following.

1. Accounts payable pertain to merchandise suppliers.
2. All operating expenses except for depreciation were paid in cash.

Instructions

(a) Cash from operations $31,500

(a) Prepare a statement of cash flows for Nosker Company using the direct method.
(b) Compute free cash flow.

Prepare a statement of cash flows—indirect method.

(LO 2)

P17-9A Condensed financial data of Cheng Inc. follow.

CHENG INC.
Comparative Balance Sheets
December 31

Assets	**2017**	**2016**
Cash	$ 80,800	$ 48,400
Accounts receivable	92,800	33,000
Inventory	117,500	102,850
Prepaid expenses	28,400	26,000
Investments	143,000	114,000
Equipment	270,000	242,500
Accumulated depreciation—equipment	(50,000)	(52,000)
Total	$682,500	$514,750
Liabilities and Stockholders' Equity		
Accounts payable	$112,000	$ 67,300
Accrued expenses payable	16,500	17,000
Bonds payable	110,000	150,000
Common stock	220,000	175,000
Retained earnings	224,000	105,450
Total	$682,500	$514,750

CHENG INC.
Income Statement
For the Year Ended December 31, 2017

Sales revenue		$392,780
Less:		
Cost of goods sold	$135,460	
Operating expenses, excluding depreciation	12,410	
Depreciation expense	46,500	
Income tax expense	27,280	
Interest expense	4,730	
Loss on disposal of plant assets	7,500	233,880
Net income		$158,900

Additional information:

1. New equipment costing $85,000 was purchased for cash during the year.
2. Old equipment having an original cost of $57,500 was sold for $1,500 cash.
3. Bonds matured and were paid off at face value for cash.
4. A cash dividend of $40,350 was declared and paid during the year.

Instructions

Prepare a statement of cash flows using the indirect method.

Cash from operations $180,250

***P17-10A** Data for Cheng Inc. are presented in P17-9A. Further analysis reveals that accounts payable pertain to merchandise creditors.

Prepare a statement of cash flows—direct method.

(LO 4)

Instructions

Prepare a statement of cash flows for Cheng Inc. using the direct method.

Cash from operations $180,250

P17-11A The comparative balance sheets for Rothlisberger Company as of December 31 are presented below.

Prepare a statement of cash flows—indirect method.

(LO 2)

ROTHLISBERGER COMPANY
Comparative Balance Sheets
December 31

Assets	**2017**	**2016**
Cash	$ 81,000	$ 45,000
Accounts receivable	41,000	62,000
Inventory	151,450	142,000
Prepaid expenses	15,280	21,000
Land	105,000	130,000
Buildings	200,000	200,000
Accumulated depreciation—buildings	(60,000)	(40,000)
Equipment	221,000	155,000
Accumulated depreciation—equipment	(45,000)	(35,000)
Total	$709,730	$680,000
Liabilities and Stockholders' Equity		
Accounts payable	$ 47,730	$ 40,000
Bonds payable	260,000	300,000
Common stock, $1 par	200,000	160,000
Retained earnings	202,000	180,000
Total	$709,730	$680,000

Additional information:

1. Operating expenses include depreciation expense of $42,000 and charges from prepaid expenses of $5,720.
2. Land was sold for cash at book value.
3. Cash dividends of $20,000 were paid.
4. Net income for 2017 was $42,000.

5. Equipment was purchased for $88,000 cash. In addition, equipment costing $22,000 with a book value of $10,000 was sold for $6,000 cash.
6. Bonds were converted at face value by issuing 40,000 shares of $1 par value common stock.

Cash from operations
$113,000

Instructions

Prepare a statement of cash flows for the year ended December 31, 2017, using the indirect method.

Prepare a worksheet—indirect method.
(LO 5)

***P17-12A** Condensed financial data of Oakley Company appear below.

OAKLEY COMPANY
Comparative Balance Sheets
December 31

Assets	**2017**	**2016**
Cash	$ 82,700	$ 47,250
Accounts receivable	90,800	57,000
Inventory	126,900	102,650
Investments	84,500	87,000
Equipment	255,000	205,000
Accumulated depreciation—equipment	(49,500)	(40,000)
	$590,400	$458,900
Liabilities and Stockholders' Equity		
Accounts payable	$ 57,700	$ 48,280
Accrued expenses payable	12,100	18,830
Bonds payable	100,000	70,000
Common stock	250,000	200,000
Retained earnings	170,600	121,790
	$590,400	$458,900

OAKLEY COMPANY
Income Statement
For the Year Ended December 31, 2017

Sales revenue		$297,500
Gain on disposal of equipment		8,750
		306,250
Less:		
Cost of goods sold	$99,460	
Operating expenses (excluding depreciation expense)	14,670	
Depreciation expense	49,700	
Income tax expense	7,270	
Interest expense	2,940	174,040
Net income		$132,210

Additional information:

1. Equipment costing $97,000 was purchased for cash during the year.
2. Investments were sold at cost.
3. Equipment costing $47,000 was sold for $15,550, resulting in gain of $8,750.
4. A cash dividend of $83,400 was declared and paid during the year.

Reconciling items total
$610,210

Instructions

Prepare a worksheet for the statement of cash flows using the indirect method. Enter the reconciling items directly in the worksheet columns, using letters to cross-reference each entry.

PROBLEMS: SET B AND SET C

Visit the book's companion website, at **www.wiley.com/college/weygandt**, and choose the Student Companion site to access Problems: Set B and Set C.

CONTINUING PROBLEM

COOKIE CREATIONS: AN ENTREPRENEURIAL JOURNEY

(*Note:* This is a continuation of the Cookie Creations problem from Chapters 1 through 16.)

CC17 Natalie has prepared the balance sheet and income statement of Cookie & Coffee Creations Inc. and would like you to prepare the statement of cash flows.

Go to the book's companion website, **www.wiley.com/college/weygandt**, *to see the completion of this problem.*

© leungchopan/ Shutterstock

BROADENING YOUR PERSPECTIVE

FINANCIAL REPORTING AND ANALYSIS

Financial Reporting Problem: Apple Inc.

BYP17-1 The financial statements of Apple Inc. are presented in Appendix A. Instructions for accessing and using the company's complete annual report, including the notes to the financial statements, are also provided in Appendix A.

Instructions

(a) What was the amount of net cash provided by operating activities for the year ended September 28, 2013? For the year ended September 29, 2012?
(b) What was the amount of increase or decrease in cash and cash equivalents for the year ended September 28, 2013? For the year ended September 29, 2012?
(c) Which method of computing net cash provided by operating activities does Apple use?
(d) From your analysis of the 2013 statement of cash flows, did the change in accounts and notes receivable require or provide cash? Did the change in inventories require or provide cash? Did the change in accounts payable and other current liabilities require or provide cash?
(e) What was the net outflow or inflow of cash from investing activities for the year ended September 28, 2013?
(f) What was the amount of income taxes paid in the year ended September 28, 2013?

Comparative Analysis Problem: PepsiCo, Inc. vs. The Coca-Cola Company

BYP17-2 PepsiCo's financial statements are presented in Appendix B. Financial statements of The Coca-Cola Company are presented in Appendix C. Instructions for accessing and using the complete annual reports of PepsiCo and Coca-Cola, including the notes to the financial statements, are also provided in Appendices B and C, respectively.

Instructions

(a) Based on the information contained in these financial statements, compute free cash flow for each company.
(b) What conclusions concerning the management of cash can be drawn from these data?

Comparative Analysis Problem: Amazon.com, Inc. vs. Wal-Mart Stores, Inc.

BYP17-3 Amazon.com, Inc.'s financial statements are presented in Appendix D. Financial statements of Wal-Mart Stores, Inc. are presented in Appendix E. Instructions for accessing and using the complete annual reports for Amazon and Wal-Mart, including the notes to the financial statements, are also provided in Appendices D and E, respectively.

Instructions

(a) Based on the information contained in these financial statements, compute free cash flow for each company.
(b) What conclusions concerning the management of cash can be drawn from these data?

Decision-Making Across the Organization

BYP17-4 Tom Epps and Mary Jones are examining the following statement of cash flows for Guthrie Company for the year ended January 31, 2017.

GUTHRIE COMPANY
Statement of Cash Flows
For the Year Ended January 31, 2017

Sources of cash	
From sales of merchandise	$380,000
From sale of capital stock	420,000
From sale of investment (purchased below)	80,000
From depreciation	55,000
From issuance of note for truck	20,000
From interest on investments	6,000
Total sources of cash	961,000
Uses of cash	
For purchase of fixtures and equipment	330,000
For merchandise purchased for resale	258,000
For operating expenses (including depreciation)	160,000
For purchase of investment	75,000
For purchase of truck by issuance of note	20,000
For purchase of treasury stock	10,000
For interest on note payable	3,000
Total uses of cash	856,000
Net increase in cash	$105,000

Tom claims that Guthrie's statement of cash flows is an excellent portrayal of a superb first year with cash increasing $105,000. Mary replies that it was not a superb first year. Rather, she says, the year was an operating failure, that the statement is presented incorrectly, and that $105,000 is not the actual increase in cash. The cash balance at the beginning of the year was $140,000.

Instructions

With the class divided into groups, answer the following.

(a) Using the data provided, prepare a statement of cash flows in proper form using the indirect method. The only noncash items in the income statement are depreciation and the gain from the sale of the investment.

(b) With whom do you agree, Tom or Mary? Explain your position.

Real-World Focus

BYP17-5 Purpose: Learn about the SEC.

Address: **www.sec.gov/index.html**, or go to **www.wiley.com/college/weygandt**

From the SEC homepage, choose **About the SEC**.

Instructions

Answer the following questions.

(a) How many enforcement actions does the SEC take each year against securities law violators? What are typical infractions?

(b) After the Depression, Congress passed the Securities Acts of 1933 and 1934 to improve investor confidence in the markets. What two "common sense" notions are these laws based on?

(c) Who was the President of the United States at the time of the creation of the SEC? Who was the first SEC Chairperson?

BYP17-6 Purpose: Use the Internet to view SEC filings.

Address: **biz.yahoo.com/i**, or go to **www.wiley.com/college/weygandt**

Steps:

1. Type in a company name.
2. Choose **Profile**.
3. Choose **SEC Filings**. (This will take you to Yahoo-Edgar Online.)

Instructions

Answer the following questions.

(a) What company did you select?
(b) Which filing is the most recent? What is the date?
(c) What other recent SEC filings are available for your viewing?

CRITICAL THINKING

Communication Activity

BYP17-7 Will Hardin, the owner-president of Computer Services Company, is unfamiliar with the statement of cash flows that you, as his accountant, prepared. He asks for further explanation.

Instructions
Write him a brief memo explaining the form and content of the statement of cash flows as shown in Illustration 17-13 (page 739).

Ethics Case

BYP17-8 Wesley Corp. is a medium-sized wholesaler of automotive parts. It has 10 stockholders who have been paid a total of $1 million in cash dividends for 8 consecutive years. The board's policy requires that, for this dividend to be declared, net cash provided by operating activities as reported in Wesley's current year's statement of cash flows must exceed $1 million. President and CEO Samuel Gunkle's job is secure so long as he produces annual operating cash flows to support the usual dividend.

At the end of the current year, controller Gerald Rondelli presents president Samuel Gunkle with some disappointing news: The net cash provided by operating activities is calculated by the indirect method to be only $970,000. The president says to Gerald, "We must get that amount above $1 million. Isn't there some way to increase operating cash flow by another $30,000?" Gerald answers, "These figures were prepared by my assistant. I'll go back to my office and see what I can do." The president replies, "I know you won't let me down, Gerald."

Upon close scrutiny of the statement of cash flows, Gerald concludes that he can get the operating cash flows above $1 million by reclassifying a $60,000, 2-year note payable listed in the financing activities section as "Proceeds from bank loan—$60,000." He will report the note instead as "Increase in payables—$60,000" and treat it as an adjustment of net income in the operating activities section. He returns to the president, saying, "You can tell the board to declare their usual dividend. Our net cash flow provided by operating activities is $1,030,000." "Good man, Gerald! I knew I could count on you," exults the president.

Instructions
(a) Who are the stakeholders in this situation?
(b) Was there anything unethical about the president's actions? Was there anything unethical about the controller's actions?
(c) Are the board members or anyone else likely to discover the misclassification?

All About You

BYP17-9 In this chapter, you learned that companies prepare a statement of cash flows in order to keep track of their sources and uses of cash and to help them plan for their future cash needs. Planning for your own short- and long-term cash needs is every bit as important as it is for a company.

Instructions
Read the article ("Financial Uh-Oh? No Problem") provided at **www.fool.com/personal-finance/saving/index.aspx**, and answer the following questions. To access this article, it may be necessary to register at no cost.

(a) Describe the three factors that determine how much money you should set aside for short-term needs.
(b) How many months of living expenses does the article suggest to set aside?
(c) Estimate how much you should set aside based upon your current situation. Are you closer to Cliff's scenario or to Prudence's?

FASB Codification Activity

BYP17-10 If your school has a subscription to the FASB Codification, go to **http://aaahq.org/ascLogin.cfm** to log in and prepare responses to the following. Use the Master Glossary to determine the proper definitions. AP

(a) What are cash equivalents?
(b) What are financing activities?
(c) What are investing activities?
(d) What are operating activities?

(e) What is the primary objective for the statement of cash flow? Is working capital the basis for meeting this objective?

(f) Do companies need to disclose information about investing and financing activities that do not affect cash receipts or cash payments? If so, how should such information be disclosed?

A Look at IFRS

LEARNING OBJECTIVE 7 **Compare the procedures for the statement of cash flows under GAAP and IFRS.**

As in GAAP, the statement of cash flows is a required statement for IFRS. In addition, the content and presentation of an IFRS statement of cash flows is similar to the one used for GAAP. However, the disclosure requirements related to the statement of cash flows are more extensive under GAAP. *IAS 7* ("Cash Flow Statements") provides the overall IFRS requirements for cash flow information.

Relevant Facts

Following are the key similarities and differences between GAAP and IFRS as related to the statement of cash flows.

Similarities

- Companies preparing financial statements under IFRS must also prepare a statement of cash flows as an integral part of the financial statements.
- Both IFRS and GAAP require that the statement of cash flows should have three major sections—operating, investing, and financing activities—along with changes in cash and cash equivalents.
- Similar to GAAP, the statement of cash flows can be prepared using either the indirect or direct method under IFRS. In both U.S. and international settings, companies choose for the most part to use the indirect method for reporting net cash flows from operating activities.
- The definition of cash equivalents used in IFRS is similar to that used in GAAP. A major difference is that in certain situations, bank overdrafts are considered part of cash and cash equivalents under IFRS (which is not the case in GAAP). Under GAAP, bank overdrafts are classified as financing activities in the statement of cash flows and are reported as liabilities on the balance sheet.

Differences

- IFRS requires that noncash investing and financing activities be excluded from the statement of cash flows. Instead, these noncash activities should be reported elsewhere. This requirement is interpreted to mean that noncash investing and financing activities should be disclosed in the notes to the financial statements instead of in the financial statements. Under GAAP, companies may present this information on the face of the statement of cash flows.
- One area where there can be substantial differences between IFRS and GAAP relates to the classification of interest, dividends, and taxes. The following table indicates the differences between the two approaches.

Item	IFRS	GAAP
Interest paid	Operating or financing	Operating
Interest received	Operating or investing	Operating
Dividends paid	Operating or financing	Financing
Dividends received	Operating or investing	Operating
Taxes paid	Operating—unless specific identification with financing or investing activity	Operating

- Under IFRS, some companies present the operating section in a single line item, with a full reconciliation provided in the notes to the financial statements. This presentation is not seen under GAAP.

Looking to the Future

Presently, the FASB and the IASB are involved in a joint project on the presentation and organization of information in the financial statements. One interesting approach, revealed in a published proposal from that project, is that in the future the income statement and balance sheet would adopt headings similar to those of the statement of cash flows. That is, the income statement and balance sheet would be broken into operating, investing, and financing sections.

IFRS Practice

IFRS Self-Test Questions

1. Under IFRS, interest paid can be reported as:
   (a) only a financing activity.
   (b) a financing activity or an investing activity.
   (c) a financing activity or an operating activity.
   (d) only an operating activity.
2. IFRS requires that noncash items:
   (a) be reported in the section to which they relate, that is, a noncash investing activity would be reported in the investing section.
   (b) be disclosed in the notes to the financial statements.
   (c) do not need to be reported.
   (d) be treated in a fashion similar to cash equivalents.
3. In the future, it appears likely that:
   (a) the income statement and balance sheet will have headings of operating, investing, and financing, much like the statement of cash flows.
   (b) cash and cash equivalents will be combined in a single line item.
   (c) the IASB will not allow companies to use the direct approach to the statement of cash flows.
   (d) None of the above.
4. Under IFRS:
   (a) taxes are always treated as an operating activity.
   (b) the income statement uses the headings operating, investing, and financing.
   (c) dividends received can be either an operating or investing activity.
   (d) dividends paid can be either an operating or investing activity.
5. Which of the following is **correct**?
   (a) Under IFRS, the statement of cash flows is optional.
   (b) IFRS requires use of the direct approach in preparing the statement of cash flows.
   (c) The majority of companies following GAAP and the majority following IFRS employ the indirect approach to the statement of cash flows.
   (d) Under IFRS, companies offset financing activities against investing activities.

IFRS Exercises

IFRS17-1 Discuss the differences that exist in the treatment of bank overdrafts under GAAP and IFRS.

IFRS17-2 Describe the treatment of each of the following items under IFRS versus GAAP.

(a) Interest paid.
(b) Interest received.
(c) Dividends paid.
(d) Dividends received.

International Financial Reporting Problem: Louis Vuitton

IFRS17-3 The financial statements of Louis Vuitton are presented in Appendix F. Instructions for accessing and using the company's complete annual report, including the notes to its financial statements, are also provided in Appendix F.

Instructions
Use the company's annual report to answer the following questions.

(a) In which section (operating, investing, or financing) does Louis Vuitton report interest paid (finance costs)?
(b) In which section (operating, investing, or financing) does Louis Vuitton report dividends received?
(c) If Louis Vuitton reported under GAAP rather than IFRS, how would its treatment of bank overdrafts differ?

Answers to IFRS Self-Test Questions

1. c **2.** b **3.** a **4.** c **5.** c

18 Financial Statement Analysis

CHAPTER PREVIEW As the Feature Story below highlights, we can all learn an important lesson from Warren Buffett. Study companies carefully if you wish to invest. Do not get caught up in fads but instead find companies that are financially healthy. Using some of the decision tools presented in this textbook, you can perform a rudimentary analysis on any U.S. company and draw basic conclusions about its financial health. Although it would not be wise for you to bet your life savings on a company's stock relying solely on your current level of knowledge, we strongly encourage you to practice your new skills wherever possible. Only with practice will you improve your ability to interpret financial numbers.

Before unleashing you on the world of high finance, we present a few more important concepts and techniques, as well as provide you with one more comprehensive review of corporate financial statements. We use all of the decision tools presented in this textbook to analyze a single company—Macy's, Inc.—one of the country's oldest and largest retail store chains.

FEATURE STORY

It Pays to Be Patient

A recent issue of *Forbes* magazine listed Warren Buffett as the richest person in the world. His estimated wealth was $62 billion, give or take a few million. How much is $62 billion? If you invested $62 billion in an investment earning just 4%, you could spend $6.8 million per day—every day—forever.

So, how does Buffett spend his money? Basically, he doesn't! He still lives in the same house that he purchased in Omaha, Nebraska, in 1958 for $31,500. He still drives his own car (a Cadillac DTS). And, in case you believe that his kids are riding the road to Easy Street, think again. Buffett has committed to donate virtually all of his money to charity before he dies.

How did Buffett amass this wealth? Through careful investing. He applies the basic techniques he learned in the 1950s from the great value investor Benjamin Graham. Buffett looks for companies that have good long-term potential but are currently underpriced. He invests in companies that have low exposure to debt and that reinvest their earnings for future growth. He does not get caught up in fads or the latest trends.

For example, Buffett sat out on the dot-com mania in the 1990s. When other investors put lots of money into fledgling high-tech firms, Buffett didn't bite because the dot-com companies failed to meet his criteria. He didn't get to enjoy the stock price boom on the way up, but on the other hand, he didn't have to suffer the plummet back down to Earth. When the dot-com bubble burst, everyone else suffered from investment shock. Buffett swooped in and scooped up deals on companies that he had been following for years.

In 2012, when the stock market reached near record highs, Buffett's returns significantly lagged behind the market. Only 26% of his investments at that time were in stock, and he was sitting on $38 billion in cash. One commentator noted that "if the past is any guide, just when Buffett seems to look most like a loser, the party is about to end."

If you think you want to follow Buffett's example and transform your humble nest egg into a mountain of cash, be warned. His techniques have been widely circulated and emulated, but never practiced with the same degree of success. You should probably start by honing your financial analysis skills. A good way for you to begin your career as a successful investor is to master the fundamentals of financial analysis discussed in this chapter.

Source: Jason Zweig, "Buffett Is Out of Step," *Wall Street Journal* (May 7, 2012).

Daniel Acker/Bloomberg/Getty Images, Inc.

CHAPTER OUTLINE

Learning Objectives

Learning Objective	Topics	DO IT!
1 Apply horizontal and vertical analysis to financial statements.	• Need for comparative analysis • Tools of analysis • Horizontal analysis • Vertical analysis	DO IT! 1 Horizontal Analysis
2 Analyze a company's performance using ratio analysis.	• Liquidity ratios • Profitability ratios • Solvency ratios • Summary of ratios	DO IT! 2 Ratio Analysis
3 Apply the concept of sustainable income.	• Discontinued operations • Other comprehensive income	DO IT! 3 Unusual Items

o to the ***REVIEW AND PRACTICE*** section at the end of the chapter for a review of key concepts and practice applications with solutions.

isit **WileyPLUS with ORION** for additional tutorials and practice opportunities.

LEARNING OBJECTIVE 1

Apply horizontal and vertical analysis to financial statements.

Analyzing financial statements involves evaluating three characteristics: a company's liquidity, profitability, and solvency. A **short-term creditor**, such as a bank, is primarily interested in liquidity—the ability of the borrower to pay obligations when they come due. The liquidity of the borrower is extremely important in evaluating the safety of a loan. A **long-term creditor**, such as a bondholder, looks to profitability and solvency measures that indicate the company's ability to survive over a long period of time. Long-term creditors consider such measures as the amount of debt in the company's capital structure and its ability to meet interest payments. Similarly, **stockholders** look at the profitability and solvency of the company. They want to assess the likelihood of dividends and the growth potential of the stock.

Need for Comparative Analysis

Every item reported in a financial statement has significance. When Macy's, Inc. reports cash and cash equivalents of $2.3 billion on its balance sheet, we know the company had that amount of cash on the balance sheet date. But, we do not know whether the amount represents an increase over prior years, or whether it is adequate in relation to the company's need for cash. To obtain such information, we need to compare the amount of cash with other financial statement data.

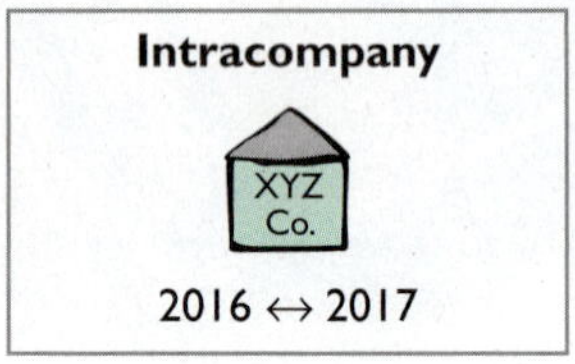

Comparisons can be made on a number of different bases. Three are illustrated in this chapter.

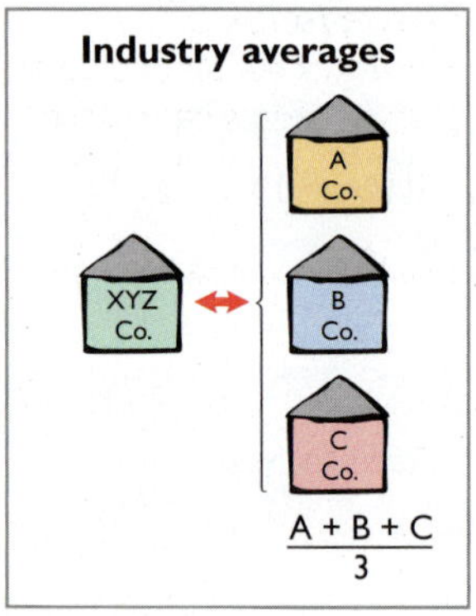

1. **Intracompany basis.** Comparisons within a company are often useful to detect changes in financial relationships and significant trends. For example, a comparison of Macy's current year's cash amount with the prior year's cash amount shows either an increase or a decrease. Likewise, a comparison of Macy's year-end cash amount with the amount of its total assets at year-end shows the proportion of total assets in the form of cash.
2. **Industry averages.** Comparisons with industry averages provide information about a company's relative position within the industry. For example, financial statement readers can compare Macy's financial data with the averages for its industry compiled by financial rating organizations such as Dun & Bradstreet, Moody's, and Standard & Poor's, or with information provided on the Internet by organizations such as Yahoo! on its financial site.

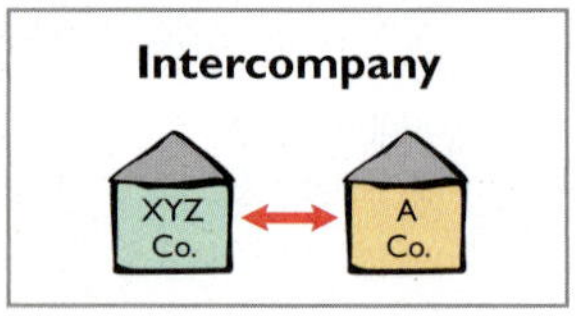

3. **Intercompany basis.** Comparisons with other companies provide insight into a company's competitive position. For example, investors can compare Macy's total sales for the year with the total sales of its competitors in retail, such as J.C. Penney.

Tools of Analysis

We use various tools to evaluate the significance of financial statement data. Three commonly used tools are as follows.

- **Horizontal analysis** evaluates a series of financial statement data over a period of time.
- **Vertical analysis** evaluates financial statement data by expressing each item in a financial statement as a percentage of a base amount.
- **Ratio analysis** expresses the relationship among selected items of financial statement data.

Horizontal analysis is used primarily in intracompany comparisons. Two features in published financial statements and annual report information facilitate this type of comparison. First, each of the basic financial statements presents comparative financial data for a minimum of two years. Second, a summary of selected financial data is presented for a series of five to 10 years or more. Vertical analysis is used in both intra- and intercompany comparisons. Ratio analysis is used in all three types of comparisons. In the following sections, we explain and illustrate each of the three types of analysis.

Horizontal Analysis

Horizontal analysis, also called **trend analysis**, is a technique for evaluating a series of financial statement data over a period of time. Its purpose is to determine the increase or decrease that has taken place. This change may be expressed as either an amount or a percentage. For example, Illustration 18-1 shows recent net sales figures of **Macy's, Inc.**

Illustration 18-1
Macy's, Inc.'s net sales

Real World

MACY'S, INC.
Net Sales (in millions)

2013	2012	2011
$27,931	$27,686	$26,405

If we assume that 2011 is the base year, we can measure all percentage increases or decreases from this base period amount as follows.

Illustration 18-2
Formula for horizontal analysis of changes since base period

$$\text{Change Since Base Period} = \frac{\text{Current Year Amount} - \text{Base Year Amount}}{\text{Base Year Amount}}$$

For example, we can determine that net sales for Macy's increased from 2011 to 2012 approximately 4.9% [($27,686 − $26,405) ÷ $26,405]. Similarly, we can determine that net sales increased from 2011 to 2013 approximately 5.8% [($27,931 − $26,405) ÷ $26,405].

Alternatively, we can express current year sales as a percentage of the base period. We do this by dividing the current year amount by the base year amount, as shown below.

Illustration 18-3
Formula for horizontal analysis of current year in relation to base year

$$\text{Current Results in Relation to Base Period} = \frac{\text{Current Year Amount}}{\text{Base Year Amount}}$$

Illustration 18-4 presents this analysis for Macy's for a three-year period using 2011 as the base period.

Illustration 18-4
Horizontal analysis of Macy's, Inc.'s net sales in relation to base period

Real World

MACY'S, INC.
Net Sales (in millions)
in relation to base period 2011

2013	2012	2011
$27,931	$27,686	$26,405
105.8%	104.9%	100%

BALANCE SHEET

To further illustrate horizontal analysis, we will use the financial statements of Quality Department Store Inc., a fictional retailer. Illustration 18-5 presents a horizontal analysis of its two-year condensed balance sheets, showing dollar and percentage changes.

Illustration 18-5
Horizontal analysis of balance sheets

QUALITY DEPARTMENT STORE INC.
Condensed Balance Sheets
December 31

			Increase or (Decrease) during 2013	
	2013	**2012**	**Amount**	**Percent**
Assets				
Current assets	$1,020,000	$ 945,000	$ 75,000	7.9%
Plant assets (net)	800,000	632,500	167,500	26.5%
Intangible assets	15,000	17,500	(2,500)	(14.3%)
Total assets	$1,835,000	$1,595,000	$240,000	15.0%
Liabilities				
Current liabilities	$ 344,500	$ 303,000	$ 41,500	13.7%
Long-term liabilities	487,500	497,000	(9,500)	(1.9%)
Total liabilities	832,000	800,000	32,000	4.0%
Stockholders' Equity				
Common stock, $1 par	275,400	270,000	5,400	2.0%
Retained earnings	727,600	525,000	202,600	38.6%
Total stockholders' equity	1,003,000	795,000	208,000	26.2%
Total liabilities and stockholders' equity	$1,835,000	$1,595,000	$240,000	15.0%

The comparative balance sheets in Illustration 18-5 show that a number of significant changes have occurred in Quality Department Store's financial structure from 2012 to 2013:

- In the assets section, plant assets (net) increased $167,500, or 26.5%.
- In the liabilities section, current liabilities increased $41,500, or 13.7%.
- In the stockholders' equity section, retained earnings increased $202,600, or 38.6%.

These changes suggest that the company expanded its asset base during 2013 and **financed this expansion primarily by retaining income** rather than assuming additional long-term debt.

INCOME STATEMENT

Illustration 18-6 presents a horizontal analysis of the two-year condensed income statements of Quality Department Store Inc. for the years 2013 and 2012. Horizontal analysis of the income statements shows the following changes:

- Net sales increased $260,000, or 14.2% ($260,000 ÷ $1,837,000).
- Cost of goods sold increased $141,000, or 12.4% ($141,000 ÷ $1,140,000).
- Total operating expenses increased $37,000, or 11.6% ($37,000 ÷ $320,000).

Overall, gross profit and net income were up substantially. Gross profit increased 17.1%, and net income, 26.5%. Quality's profit trend appears favorable.

Illustration 18-6
Horizontal analysis of income statements

QUALITY DEPARTMENT STORE INC.
Condensed Income Statements
For the Years Ended December 31

			Increase or (Decrease) during 2013	
	2013	2012	Amount	Percent
Sales revenue	$2,195,000	$1,960,000	$235,000	12.0%
Sales returns and allowances	98,000	123,000	(25,000)	(20.3%)
Net sales	2,097,000	1,837,000	260,000	14.2%
Cost of goods sold	1,281,000	1,140,000	141,000	12.4%
Gross profit	816,000	697,000	119,000	17.1%
Selling expenses	253,000	211,500	41,500	19.6%
Administrative expenses	104,000	108,500	(4,500)	(4.1%)
Total operating expenses	357,000	320,000	37,000	11.6%
Income from operations	459,000	377,000	82,000	21.8%
Other revenues and gains				
Interest and dividends	9,000	11,000	(2,000)	(18.2%)
Other expenses and losses				
Interest expense	36,000	40,500	(4,500)	(11.1%)
Income before income taxes	432,000	347,500	84,500	24.3%
Income tax expense	168,200	139,000	29,200	21.0%
Net income	$ 263,800	$ 208,500	$ 55,300	26.5%

Helpful Hint
Note that though the amount column is additive (the total is $55,300), the percentage column is not additive (26.5% is not the column total). A separate percentage has been calculated for each item.

RETAINED EARNINGS STATEMENT

Illustration 18-7 presents a horizontal analysis of Quality Department Store's comparative retained earnings statements. Analyzed horizontally, net income increased $55,300, or 26.5%, whereas dividends on the common stock increased only $1,200, or 2%. We saw in the horizontal analysis of the balance sheet that ending retained earnings increased 38.6%. As indicated earlier, the company retained a significant portion of net income to finance additional plant facilities.

Illustration 18-7
Horizontal analysis of retained earnings statements

QUALITY DEPARTMENT STORE INC.
Retained Earnings Statements
For the Years Ended December 31

			Increase or (Decrease) during 2013	
	2013	2012	Amount	Percent
Retained earnings, Jan. 1	$525,000	$376,500	$148,500	39.4%
Add: Net income	263,800	208,500	55,300	26.5%
	788,800	585,000	203,800	
Deduct: Dividends	61,200	60,000	1,200	2.0%
Retained earnings, Dec. 31	$727,600	$525,000	$202,600	38.6%

Horizontal analysis of changes from period to period is relatively straightforward and is quite useful. But, complications can occur in making the computations. If an item has no value in a base year or preceding year but does have a value in the next year, we cannot compute a percentage change. Similarly, if a negative amount appears in the base or preceding period and a positive amount exists the following year (or vice versa), no percentage change can be computed.

Vertical Analysis

Vertical analysis, also called **common-size analysis**, is a technique that expresses each financial statement item as a percentage of a base amount. On a balance sheet, we might say that current assets are 22% of total assets—total assets being the base amount. Or on an income statement, we might say that selling expenses are 16% of net sales—net sales being the base amount.

BALANCE SHEET

Illustration 18-8 presents the vertical analysis of Quality Department Store Inc.'s comparative balance sheets. The base for the asset items is **total assets**. The base for the liability and stockholders' equity items is **total liabilities and stockholders' equity**.

Illustration 18-8
Vertical analysis of balance sheets

QUALITY DEPARTMENT STORE INC.
Condensed Balance Sheets
December 31

	2013		2012	
	Amount	**Percent**	**Amount**	**Percent**
Assets				
Current assets	$1,020,000	55.6%	$ 945,000	59.2%
Plant assets (net)	800,000	43.6%	632,500	39.7%
Intangible assets	15,000	0.8%	17,500	1.1%
Total assets	$1,835,000	100.0%	$1,595,000	100.0%
Liabilities				
Current liabilities	$ 344,500	18.8%	$ 303,000	19.0%
Long-term liabilities	487,500	26.5%	497,000	31.2%
Total liabilities	832,000	45.3%	800,000	50.2%
Stockholders' Equity				
Common stock, $1 par	275,400	15.0%	270,000	16.9%
Retained earnings	727,600	39.7%	525,000	32.9%
Total stockholders' equity	1,003,000	54.7%	795,000	49.8%
Total liabilities and stockholders' equity	$1,835,000	100.0%	$1,595,000	100.0%

Helpful Hint
The formula for calculating these balance sheet percentages is:

$$\frac{\text{Each item on B/S}}{\text{Total assets}} = \%$$

Vertical analysis shows the relative size of each category in the balance sheet. It also can show the **percentage change** in the individual asset, liability, and stockholders' equity items. For example, we can see that current assets decreased from 59.2% of total assets in 2012 to 55.6% in 2013 (even though the absolute dollar amount increased $75,000 in that time). Plant assets (net) have increased from 39.7% to 43.6% of total assets. Retained earnings have increased from 32.9% to 39.7% of total liabilities and stockholders' equity. These results reinforce the earlier observations that **Quality Department Store is choosing to finance its growth through retention of earnings rather than through issuing additional debt**.

INCOME STATEMENT

Illustration 18-9 shows vertical analysis of Quality Department Store's income statements. Cost of goods sold as a percentage of net sales declined 1% (62.1% vs. 61.1%), and total operating expenses declined 0.4% (17.4% vs. 17.0%). As a result,

Illustration 18-9
Vertical analysis of income statements

QUALITY DEPARTMENT STORE INC.
Condensed Income Statements
For the Years Ended December 31

	2013		2012	
	Amount	**Percent**	**Amount**	**Percent**
Sales revenue	$2,195,000	104.7%	$1,960,000	106.7%
Sales returns and allowances	98,000	4.7%	123,000	6.7%
Net sales	2,097,000	100.0%	1,837,000	100.0%
Cost of goods sold	1,281,000	61.1%	1,140,000	62.1%
Gross profit	816,000	38.9%	697,000	37.9%
Selling expenses	253,000	12.0%	211,500	11.5%
Administrative expenses	104,000	5.0%	108,500	5.9%
Total operating expenses	357,000	17.0%	320,000	17.4%
Income from operations	459,000	21.9%	377,000	20.5%
Other revenues and gains				
Interest and dividends	9,000	0.4%	11,000	0.6%
Other expenses and losses				
Interest expense	36,000	1.7%	40,500	2.2%
Income before income taxes	432,000	20.6%	347,500	18.9%
Income tax expense	168,200	8.0%	139,000	7.5%
Net income	$ 263,800	12.6%	$ 208,500	11.4%

Helpful Hint
The formula for calculating these income statement percentages is:

$$\frac{\text{Each item on I/S}}{\text{Net sales}} = \%$$

it is not surprising to see net income as a percentage of net sales increase from 11.4% to 12.6%. Quality Department Store appears to be a profitable business that is becoming even more successful.

An associated benefit of vertical analysis is that it enables you to compare companies of different sizes. For example, suppose Quality Department Store's main competitor is a Macy's store in a nearby town. Using vertical analysis, we can compare the condensed income statements of Quality Department Store Inc. (a small retail company) with **Macy's, Inc.**[1] (a giant international retailer), as shown in Illustration 18-10.

Illustration 18-10
Intercompany income statement comparison

Condensed Income Statements
For the Year Ended December 31, 2013
(in thousands)

	Quality Department Store Inc.		Macy's, Inc.	
	Dollars	**Percent**	**Dollars**	**Percent**
Net sales	$2,097	100.0%	$27,931,000	100.0%
Cost of goods sold	1,281	61.1%	16,725,000	59.9%
Gross profit	816	38.9%	11,206,000	40.1%
Selling and administrative expenses	357	17.0%	8,440,000	30.2%
Income from operations	459	21.9%	2,766,000	9.9%
Other expenses and revenues (including income taxes)	195	9.3%	1,280,000	4.6%
Net income	$ 264	12.6%	$ 1,486,000	5.3%

[1]*2013 Annual Report,* Macy's, Inc. (Cincinnati, Ohio).

Macy's net sales are 13,320 times greater than the net sales of relatively tiny Quality Department Store. But vertical analysis eliminates this difference in size. The percentages show that Quality's and Macy's gross profit rates were comparable at 38.9% and 40.1%, respectively. However, the percentages related to income from operations were significantly different at 21.9% and 9.9%, respectively. This disparity can be attributed to Quality's selling and administrative expense percentage (17%) which is much lower than Macy's (30.2%). Although Macy's earned net income more than 5,629 times larger than Quality's, Macy's net income as a **percentage of each sales dollar** (5.3%) is only 42% of Quality's (12.6%).

DO IT! 1 Horizontal Analysis

Summary financial information for Rosepatch Company is as follows.

	December 31, 2017	December 31, 2016
Current assets	$234,000	$180,000
Plant assets (net)	756,000	420,000
Total assets	$990,000	$600,000

Compute the amount and percentage changes in 2017 using horizontal analysis, assuming 2016 is the base year.

Action Plan

- ✔ Find the percentage change by dividing the amount of the increase by the 2016 amount (base year).

Solution

	Increase in 2017	
	Amount	**Percent**
Current assets	$ 54,000	30% [($234,000 − $180,000) ÷ $180,000]
Plant assets (net)	336,000	80% [($756,000 − $420,000) ÷ $420,000]
Total assets	$390,000	65% [($990,000 − $600,000) ÷ $600,000]

Related exercise material: **BE18-2, BE18-3, BE18-5, BE18-6, BE18-7, E18-1, E18-3, E18-4, and DO IT! 18-1.**

LEARNING OBJECTIVE 2 Analyze a company's performance using ratio analysis.

Ratio analysis expresses the relationship among selected items of financial statement data. A **ratio** expresses the mathematical relationship between one quantity and another. The relationship is expressed in terms of either a percentage, a rate, or a simple proportion. To illustrate, in 2013 **Nike, Inc.** had current assets of $13,626 million and current liabilities of $3,926 million. We can find the relationship between these two measures by dividing current assets by current liabilities. The alternative means of expression are as follows.

Percentage: Current assets are 347% of current liabilities.
Rate: Current assets are 3.47 times current liabilities.
Proportion: The relationship of current assets to liabilities is 3.47:1.

To analyze the primary financial statements, we can use ratios to evaluate liquidity, profitability, and solvency. Illustration 18-11 describes these classifications.

Liquidity Ratios

Measure short-term ability of the company to pay its maturing obligations and to meet unexpected needs for cash

Profitability Ratios

Measure the income or operating success of a company for a given period of time

Solvency Ratios

Measure the ability of the company to survive over a long period of time

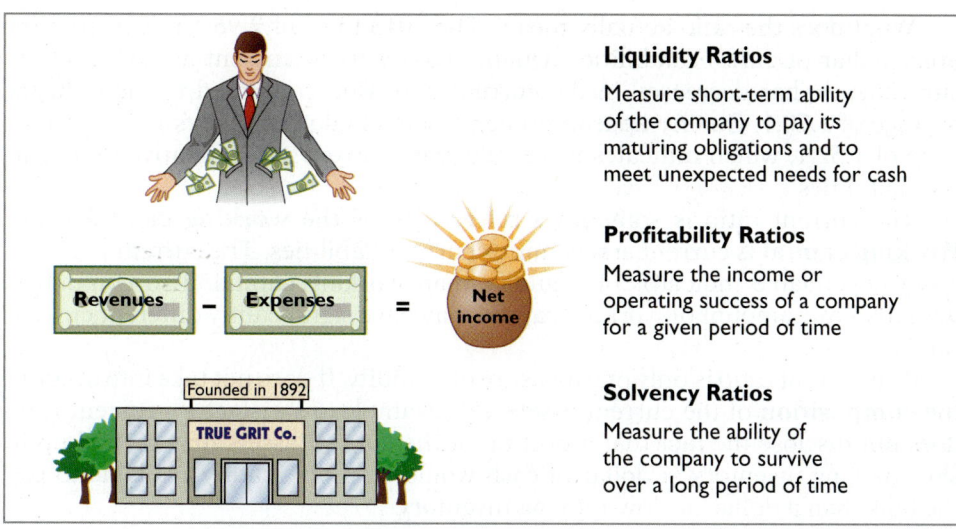

Illustration 18-11
Financial ratio classifications

Ratios can provide clues to underlying conditions that may not be apparent from individual financial statement components. However, a single ratio by itself is not very meaningful. Thus, in the discussion of ratios we will use the following types of comparisons.

1. **Intracompany comparisons** for two years for Quality Department Store.
2. **Industry average comparisons** based on median ratios for department stores.
3. **Intercompany comparisons** based on **Macy's, Inc.** as Quality Department Store's principal competitor.

> **International Note**
>
> As more countries adopt international accounting standards, the ability of analysts to compare companies from different countries should improve. However, international standards are open to widely varying interpretations. In addition, some countries adopt international standards "with modifications." As a consequence, most cross-country comparisons are still not as transparent as within-country comparisons.

Liquidity Ratios

Liquidity ratios measure the short-term ability of the company to pay its maturing obligations and to meet unexpected needs for cash. Short-term creditors such as bankers and suppliers are particularly interested in assessing liquidity. The ratios we can use to determine the company's short-term debt-paying ability are the current ratio, the acid-test ratio, accounts receivable turnover, and inventory turnover.

1. CURRENT RATIO

The **current ratio** is a widely used measure for evaluating a company's liquidity and short-term debt-paying ability. The ratio is computed by dividing current assets by current liabilities. Illustration 18-12 shows the 2013 and 2012 current ratios for Quality Department Store and 2013 comparative data.

$$\text{Current Ratio} = \frac{\text{Current Assets}}{\text{Current Liabilities}}$$

Quality Department Store

2013	2012
$\frac{\$1,020,000}{\$344,500} = 2.96:1$	$\frac{\$945,000}{\$303,000} = 3.12:1$
Industry average	Macy's, Inc.
1.70:1	**1.52:1**

Illustration 18-12
Current ratio

Helpful Hint
Any company can operate successfully without working capital if it has very predictable cash flows and solid earnings. For example, Whirlpool, American Standard, and Campbell's Soup are pursuing this goal as less money tied up in working capital means more money to invest in the business.

What does the ratio actually mean? The 2013 ratio of 2.96:1 means that for every dollar of current liabilities, Quality has $2.96 of current assets. Quality's current ratio has decreased in the current year. But, compared to the industry average of 1.70:1, Quality appears to be reasonably liquid. Macy's has a current ratio of 1.52:1, which indicates it has adequate current assets relative to its current liabilities.

The current ratio is sometimes referred to as the **working capital ratio. Working capital** is current assets minus current liabilities. The current ratio is a more dependable indicator of liquidity than working capital. Two companies with the same amount of working capital may have significantly different current ratios.

The current ratio is only one measure of liquidity. It does not take into account the **composition** of the current assets. For example, a satisfactory current ratio does not disclose the fact that a portion of the current assets may be tied up in slow-moving inventory. A dollar of cash would be more readily available to pay the bills than a dollar of slow-moving inventory.

Investor Insight

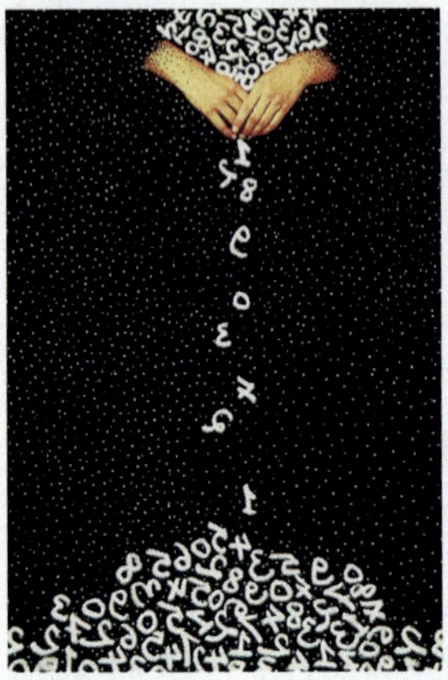
SuperStock

How to Manage the Current Ratio

The apparent simplicity of the current ratio can have real-world limitations because adding equal amounts to both the numerator and the denominator causes the ratio to decrease.

Assume, for example, that a company has $2,000,000 of current assets and $1,000,000 of current liabilities. Thus, its current ratio is 2:1. If the company purchases $1,000,000 of inventory on account, it will have $3,000,000 of current assets and $2,000,000 of current liabilities. Its current ratio therefore decreases to 1.5:1. If, instead, the company pays off $500,000 of its current liabilities, it will have $1,500,000 of current assets and $500,000 of current liabilities. Its current ratio then increases to 3:1. Thus, any trend analysis should be done with care because the ratio is susceptible to quick changes and is easily influenced by management.

How might management influence a company's current ratio? (Go to **WileyPLUS** for this answer and additional questions.)

2. ACID-TEST RATIO

The **acid-test (quick) ratio** is a measure of a company's immediate short-term liquidity. We compute this ratio by dividing the sum of cash, short-term investments, and net accounts receivable by current liabilities. Thus, it is an important complement to the current ratio. For example, assume that the current assets of Quality Department Store for 2013 and 2012 consist of the items shown in Illustration 18-13.

Illustration 18-13
Current assets of Quality Department Store

QUALITY DEPARTMENT STORE INC.
Balance Sheet (partial)

	2013	2012
Current assets		
Cash	**$ 100,000**	**$155,000**
Short-term investments	**20,000**	**70,000**
Accounts receivable (net*)	**230,000**	**180,000**
Inventory	620,000	500,000
Prepaid expenses	50,000	40,000
Total current assets	$1,020,000	$ 945,000

*Allowance for doubtful accounts is $10,000 at the end of each year.

Cash, short-term investments, and accounts receivable (net) are highly liquid compared to inventory and prepaid expenses. The inventory may not be readily saleable, and the prepaid expenses may not be transferable to others. Thus, the acid-test ratio measures **immediate** liquidity. The 2013 and 2012 acid-test ratios for Quality Department Store and 2013 comparative data are as follows.

Illustration 18-14
Acid-test ratio

$$\textbf{Acid-Test Ratio} = \frac{\textbf{Cash + Short-Term Investments + Accounts Receivable (Net)}}{\textbf{Current Liabilities}}$$

Quality Department Store

2013	2012
$\frac{\$100,000 + \$20,000 + \$230,000}{\$344,500} = 1.02:1$	$\frac{\$155,000 + \$70,000 + \$180,000}{\$303,000} = 1.34:1$
Industry average	Macy's, Inc.
0.70:1	**0.47:1**

The ratio has declined in 2013. Is an acid-test ratio of 1.02:1 adequate? This depends on the industry and the economy. When compared with the industry average of 0.70:1 and Macy's of 0.47:1, Quality's acid-test ratio seems adequate.

3. ACCOUNTS RECEIVABLE TURNOVER

We can measure liquidity by how quickly a company can convert certain assets to cash. How liquid, for example, are the accounts receivable? The ratio used to assess the liquidity of the receivables is the **accounts receivable turnover**. It measures the number of times, on average, the company collects receivables during the period. We compute accounts receivable turnover by dividing net credit sales (net sales less cash sales) by the average net accounts receivable. Unless seasonal factors are significant, average net accounts receivable can be computed from the beginning and ending balances of the net accounts receivable.[2]

Assume that all sales are credit sales. The balance of net accounts receivable at the beginning of 2012 is $200,000. Illustration 18-15 shows the accounts receivable turnover for Quality Department Store and 2013 comparative data. Quality's accounts receivable turnover improved in 2013. However, the turnover of 10.2 times is substantially lower than Macy's 69.1 times and is also lower than the department store industry's average of 46.4 times.

Illustration 18-15
Accounts receivable turnover

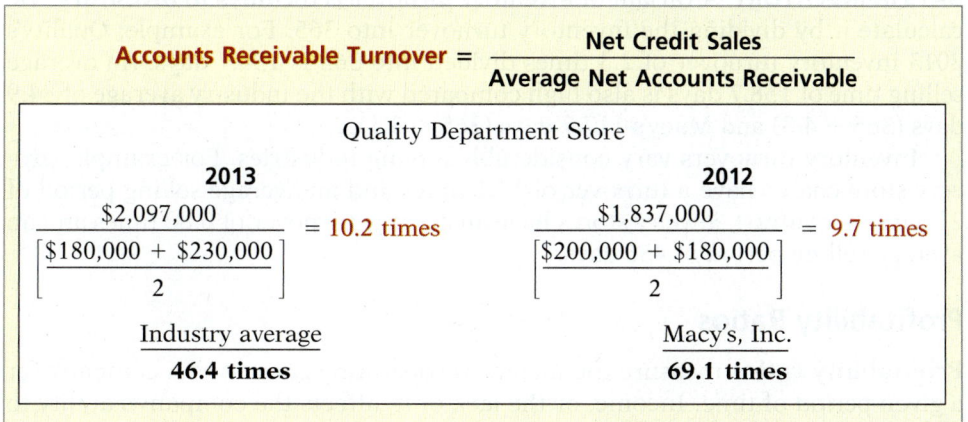

$$\textbf{Accounts Receivable Turnover} = \frac{\textbf{Net Credit Sales}}{\textbf{Average Net Accounts Receivable}}$$

Quality Department Store

2013	2012
$\frac{\$2,097,000}{\left[\frac{\$180,000 + \$230,000}{2}\right]} = 10.2 \text{ times}$	$\frac{\$1,837,000}{\left[\frac{\$200,000 + \$180,000}{2}\right]} = 9.7 \text{ times}$
Industry average	Macy's, Inc.
46.4 times	**69.1 times**

[2]If seasonal factors are significant, the average accounts receivable balance might be determined by using monthly amounts.

AVERAGE COLLECTION PERIOD A popular variant of the accounts receivable turnover is to convert it to an **average collection period** in terms of days. To do so, we divide the accounts receivable turnover into 365 days. For example, the accounts receivable turnover of 10.2 times divided into 365 days gives an average collection period of approximately 36 days. This means that accounts receivable are collected on average every 36 days, or about every 5 weeks. Analysts frequently use the average collection period to assess the effectiveness of a company's credit and collection policies. The general rule is that the collection period should not greatly exceed the credit term period (the time allowed for payment).

4. INVENTORY TURNOVER

Inventory turnover measures the number of times, on average, the inventory is sold during the period. Its purpose is to measure the liquidity of the inventory. We compute the inventory turnover by dividing cost of goods sold by the average inventory. Unless seasonal factors are significant, we can use the beginning and ending inventory balances to compute average inventory.

Assuming that the inventory balance for Quality Department Store at the beginning of 2012 was $450,000, its inventory turnover and 2013 comparative data are as shown in Illustration 18-16. Quality's inventory turnover declined slightly in 2013. The turnover of 2.3 times is low compared with the industry average of 4.3 and Macy's 3.1. Generally, the faster the inventory turnover, the less cash a company has tied up in inventory and the less chance a company has of inventory obsolescence.

Illustration 18-16
Inventory turnover

$$\text{Inventory Turnover} = \frac{\text{Cost of Goods Sold}}{\text{Average Inventory}}$$

Quality Department Store

2013	2012
$\dfrac{\$1,281,000}{\left[\dfrac{\$500,000 + \$620,000}{2}\right]} = 2.3 \text{ times}$	$\dfrac{\$1,140,000}{\left[\dfrac{\$450,000 + \$500,000}{2}\right]} = 2.4 \text{ times}$
Industry average	Macy's, Inc.
4.3 times	**3.1 times**

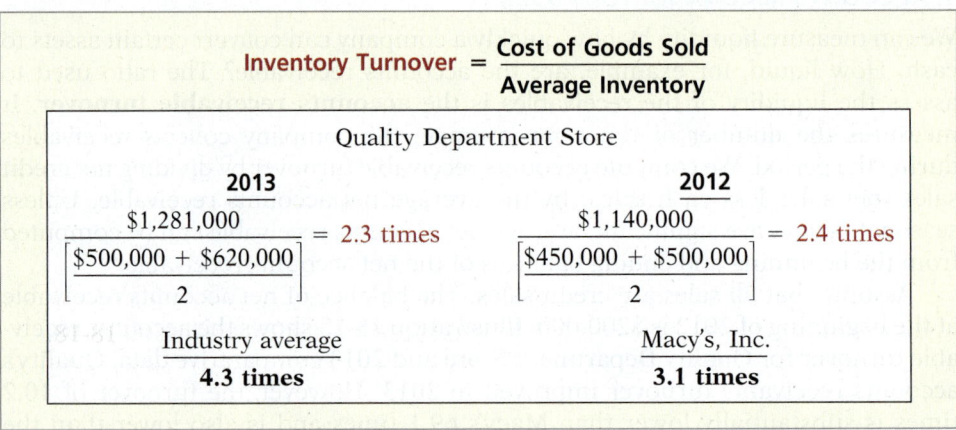

DAYS IN INVENTORY A variant of inventory turnover is the **days in inventory**. We calculate it by dividing the inventory turnover into 365. For example, Quality's 2013 inventory turnover of 2.3 times divided into 365 is 158.7 days. An average selling time of 158.7 days is also high compared with the industry average of 84.9 days (365 ÷ 4.3) and Macy's 117.7 days (365 ÷ 3.1).

Inventory turnovers vary considerably among industries. For example, grocery store chains have a turnover of 17.1 times and an average selling period of 21 days. In contrast, jewelry stores have an average turnover of 0.80 times and an average selling period of 456 days.

Profitability Ratios

Profitability ratios measure the income or operating success of a company for a given period of time. Income, or the lack of it, affects the company's ability to obtain debt and equity financing. It also affects the company's liquidity position and the company's ability to grow. As a consequence, both creditors and investors are interested in evaluating earning power—profitability. Analysts frequently use profitability as the ultimate test of management's operating effectiveness.

5. PROFIT MARGIN

Profit margin is a measure of the percentage of each dollar of sales that results in net income. We can compute it by dividing net income by net sales. Illustration 18-17 shows Quality Department Store's profit margin and 2013 comparative data.

Alternative Terminology
Profit margin is also called the *rate of return on sales.*

Illustration 18-17
Profit margin

$$\text{Profit Margin} = \frac{\text{Net Income}}{\text{Net Sales}}$$

Quality Department Store

2013	2012
$\frac{\$263{,}800}{\$2{,}097{,}000} = 12.6\%$	$\frac{\$208{,}500}{\$1{,}837{,}000} = 11.4\%$
Industry average	Macy's, Inc.
8.0%	**5.3%**

Quality experienced an increase in its profit margin from 2012 to 2013. Its profit margin is unusually high in comparison with the industry average of 8% and Macy's 5.3%.

High-volume (high inventory turnover) businesses, such as grocery stores (Safeway or Kroger) and discount stores (Kmart or Wal-Mart), generally experience low profit margins. In contrast, low-volume businesses, such as jewelry stores (Tiffany & Co.) or airplane manufacturers (Boeing Co.), have high profit margins.

6. ASSET TURNOVER

Asset turnover measures how efficiently a company uses its assets to generate sales. It is determined by dividing net sales by average total assets. The resulting number shows the dollars of sales produced by each dollar invested in assets. Unless seasonal factors are significant, we can use the beginning and ending balance of total assets to determine average total assets. Assuming that total assets at the beginning of 2012 were $1,446,000, the 2013 and 2012 asset turnover for Quality Department Store and 2013 comparative data are shown in Illustration 18-18.

Illustration 18-18
Asset turnover

$$\text{Asset Turnover} = \frac{\text{Net Sales}}{\text{Average Total Assets}}$$

Quality Department Store

2013	2012
$\frac{\$2{,}097{,}000}{\left[\frac{\$1{,}595{,}000 + \$1{,}835{,}000}{2}\right]} = 1.2 \text{ times}$	$\frac{\$1{,}837{,}000}{\left[\frac{\$1{,}446{,}000 + \$1{,}595{,}000}{2}\right]} = 1.2 \text{ times}$
Industry average	Macy's, Inc.
1.4 times	**1.3 times**

Asset turnover shows that in 2013 Quality generated sales of $1.20 for each dollar it had invested in assets. The ratio changed very little from 2012 to 2013. Quality's asset turnover is below the industry average of 1.4 times and Macy's ratio of 1.3 times.

Asset turnovers vary considerably among industries. For example, a large utility company like Consolidated Edison (New York) has a ratio of 0.4 times, and the large grocery chain Kroger Stores has a ratio of 3.4 times.

7. RETURN ON ASSETS

An overall measure of profitability is **return on assets**. We compute this ratio by dividing net income by average total assets. The 2013 and 2012 return on assets for Quality Department Store and 2013 comparative data are shown below.

Illustration 18-19
Return on assets

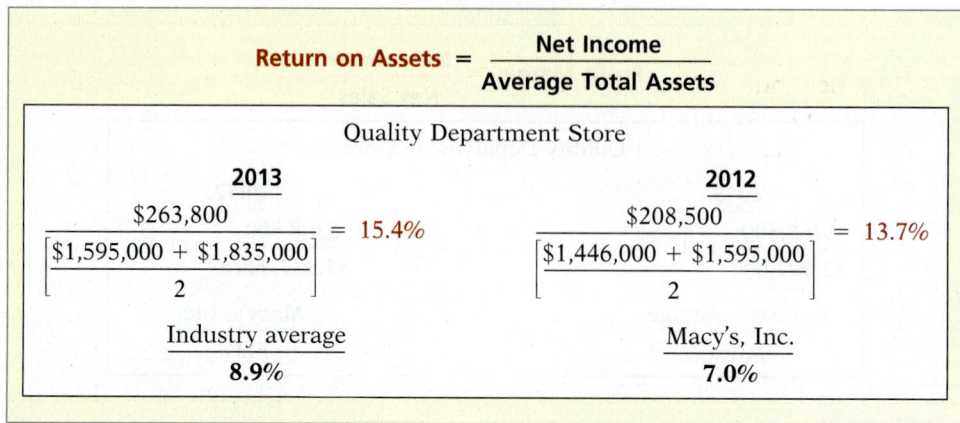

$$\text{Return on Assets} = \frac{\text{Net Income}}{\text{Average Total Assets}}$$

Quality Department Store

2013

$$\frac{\$263{,}800}{\left[\dfrac{\$1{,}595{,}000 + \$1{,}835{,}000}{2}\right]} = 15.4\%$$

2012

$$\frac{\$208{,}500}{\left[\dfrac{\$1{,}446{,}000 + \$1{,}595{,}000}{2}\right]} = 13.7\%$$

Industry average	Macy's, Inc.
8.9%	**7.0%**

Quality's return on assets improved from 2012 to 2013. Its return of 15.4% is very high compared with the department store industry average of 8.9% and Macy's 7.0%.

8. RETURN ON COMMON STOCKHOLDERS' EQUITY

Another widely used profitability ratio is **return on common stockholders' equity**. It measures profitability from the common stockholders' viewpoint. This ratio shows how many dollars of net income the company earned for each dollar invested by the owners. We compute it by dividing net income by average common stockholders' equity. Assuming that common stockholders' equity at the beginning of 2012 was $667,000, Illustration 18-20 shows the 2013 and 2012 ratios for Quality Department Store and 2013 comparative data.

Illustration 18-20
Return on common stockholders' equity

$$\text{Return on Common Stockholders' Equity} = \frac{\text{Net Income}}{\text{Average Common Stockholders' Equity}}$$

Quality Department Store

2013

$$\frac{\$263{,}800}{\left[\dfrac{\$795{,}000 + \$1{,}003{,}000}{2}\right]} = 29.3\%$$

2012

$$\frac{\$208{,}500}{\left[\dfrac{\$667{,}000 + \$795{,}000}{2}\right]} = 28.5\%$$

Industry average	Macy's, Inc.
18.3%	**24.2%**

Quality's rate of return on common stockholders' equity is high at 29.3%, considering an industry average of 18.3% and a rate of 24.2% for Macy's.

WITH PREFERRED STOCK When a company has preferred stock, we must deduct **preferred dividend** requirements from net income to compute income available to common stockholders. Similarly, we deduct the par value of preferred stock (or call price, if applicable) from total stockholders' equity to determine the amount of common stockholders' equity used in this ratio. The ratio then appears as follows.

Illustration 18-21
Return on common stockholders' equity with preferred stock

$$\text{Return on Common Stockholders' Equity} = \frac{\text{Net Income} - \text{Preferred Dividends}}{\text{Average Common Stockholders' Equity}}$$

Note that Quality's rate of return on stockholders' equity (29.3%) is substantially higher than its rate of return on assets (15.4%). The reason is that Quality has made effective use of **leverage**. **Leveraging** or **trading on the equity** at a gain means that the company has borrowed money at a lower rate of interest than it is able to earn by using the borrowed money. Leverage enables Quality to use money supplied by nonowners to increase the return to the owners. A comparison of the rate of return on total assets with the rate of interest paid for borrowed money indicates the profitability of trading on the equity. Quality earns more on its borrowed funds than it has to pay in the form of interest. Thus, the return to stockholders exceeds the return on the assets, due to benefits from the positive leveraging.

9. EARNINGS PER SHARE (EPS)

Earnings per share (EPS) is a measure of the net income earned on each share of common stock. It is computed by dividing net income less preferred dividends by the number of weighted-average common shares outstanding during the year. A measure of net income earned on a per share basis provides a useful perspective for determining profitability. Assuming that there is no change in the number of outstanding shares during 2012 and that the 2013 increase occurred midyear, Illustration 18-22 shows the net income per share for Quality Department Store for 2013 and 2012, assuming no preferred dividends.

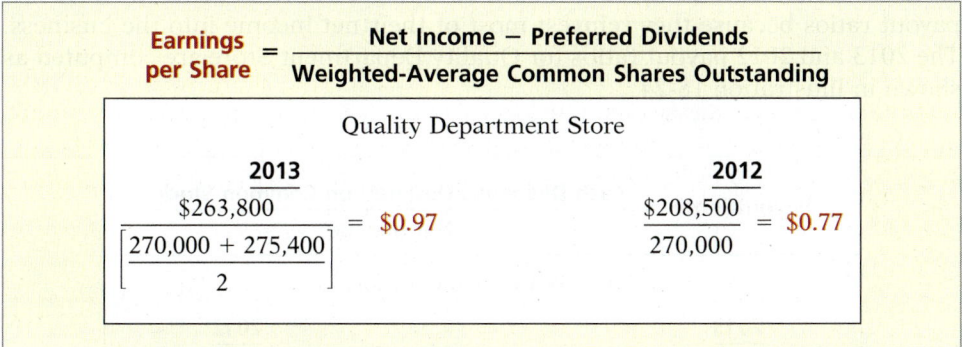

Illustration 18-22
Earnings per share

$$\text{Earnings per Share} = \frac{\text{Net Income} - \text{Preferred Dividends}}{\text{Weighted-Average Common Shares Outstanding}}$$

Quality Department Store

2013	2012
$\dfrac{\$263,800}{\left[\dfrac{270,000 + 275,400}{2}\right]} = \$0.97$	$\dfrac{\$208,500}{270,000} = \$0.77$

Note that no industry or specific competitive data are presented. Such comparisons are not meaningful because of the wide variations in the number of shares of outstanding stock among companies. The only meaningful EPS comparison is an intracompany trend comparison. Here, Quality's earnings per share increased 20 cents per share in 2013. This represents a 26% increase over the 2012 earnings per share of 77 cents.

The terms "earnings per share" and "net income per share" refer to the amount of net income applicable to each share of **common stock**. Therefore, in computing EPS, if there are preferred dividends declared for the period, we must deduct them from net income to determine income available to the common stockholders.

10. PRICE-EARNINGS RATIO

The **price-earnings (P-E) ratio** is a widely used measure of the ratio of the market price of each share of common stock to the earnings per share. The price-earnings (P-E) ratio reflects investors' assessments of a company's future earnings. We compute it by dividing the market price per share of the stock by earnings per share. Assuming that the market price of Quality Department Store stock is $8 in 2012 and $12 in 2013, the price-earnings ratio computation is computed as shown in Illustration 18-23 (page 800).

Illustration 18-23
Price-earnings ratio

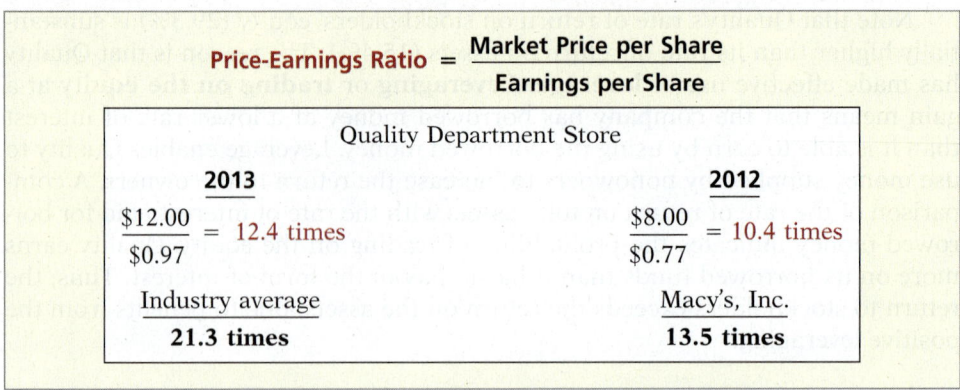

$$\text{Price-Earnings Ratio} = \frac{\text{Market Price per Share}}{\text{Earnings per Share}}$$

Quality Department Store

2013	2012
$\frac{\$12.00}{\$0.97}$ = 12.4 times	$\frac{\$8.00}{\$0.77}$ = 10.4 times
Industry average	Macy's, Inc.
21.3 times	**13.5 times**

In 2013, each share of Quality's stock sold for 12.4 times the amount that the company earned on each share. Quality's price-earnings ratio is lower than the industry average of 21.3 times but much closer to the ratio of 13.5 times for Macy's. For overall comparison to the market, the average price-earnings ratio for the stocks that constitute the Standard and Poor's 500 Index (500 largest U.S. firms) in mid-2014 was approximately 19.6 times.

11. PAYOUT RATIO

The **payout ratio** measures the percentage of earnings distributed in the form of cash dividends. We compute it by dividing cash dividends declared on common stock by net income. Companies that have high growth rates generally have low payout ratios because they reinvest most of their net income into the business. The 2013 and 2012 payout ratios for Quality Department Store are computed as shown in Illustration 18-24.

Illustration 18-24
Payout ratio

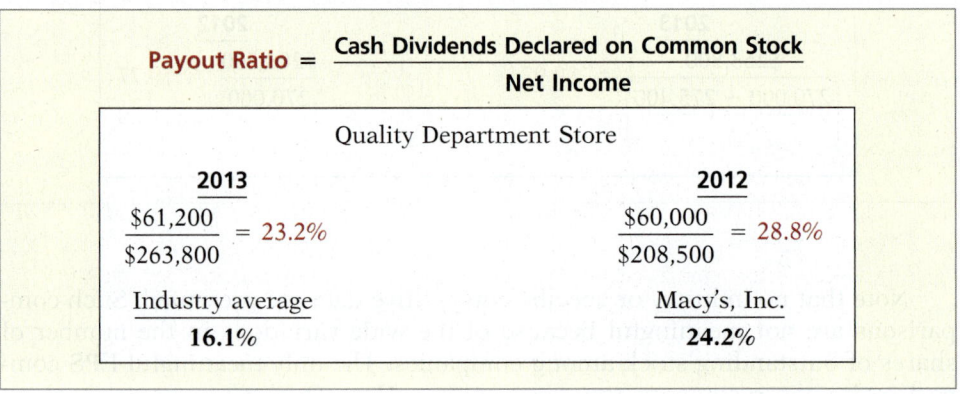

$$\text{Payout Ratio} = \frac{\text{Cash Dividends Declared on Common Stock}}{\text{Net Income}}$$

Quality Department Store

2013	2012
$\frac{\$61,200}{\$263,800}$ = 23.2%	$\frac{\$60,000}{\$208,500}$ = 28.8%
Industry average	Macy's, Inc.
16.1%	**24.2%**

Quality's payout ratio is higher than the industry average payout ratio of 16.1%.

Solvency Ratios

Solvency ratios measure the ability of a company to survive over a long period of time. Long-term creditors and stockholders are particularly interested in a company's ability to pay interest as it comes due and to repay the face value of debt at maturity. Debt to assets and times interest earned are two ratios that provide information about debt-paying ability.

12. DEBT TO ASSETS RATIO

The **debt to assets ratio** measures the percentage of the total assets that creditors provide. We compute it by dividing total liabilities (both current and long-term liabilities) by total assets. This ratio indicates the company's degree of leverage. It also provides some indication of the company's ability to withstand losses without impairing the interests of creditors. The higher the percentage of total liabilities to total assets, the greater the risk that the company may be unable to meet its maturing obligations. The 2013 and 2012 ratios for Quality Department Store and 2013 comparative data are as follows.

Illustration 18-25
Debt to assets ratio

$$\text{Debt to Assets Ratio} = \frac{\text{Total Liabilities}}{\text{Total Assets}}$$

Quality Department Store

2013	2012
$\frac{\$832{,}000}{\$1{,}835{,}000} = 45.3\%$	$\frac{\$800{,}000}{\$1{,}595{,}000} = 50.2\%$
Industry average	Macy's, Inc.
34.2%	**71.1%**

A ratio of 45.3% means that creditors have provided 45.3% of Quality Department Store's total assets. Quality's 45.3% is above the industry average of 34.2%. It is considerably below the high 71.1% ratio of Macy's. The lower the ratio, the more equity "buffer" there is available to the creditors. Thus, from the creditors' point of view, a low ratio of debt to assets is usually desirable.

The adequacy of this ratio is often judged in the light of the company's earnings. Generally, companies with relatively stable earnings (such as public utilities) have higher debt to assets ratios than cyclical companies with widely fluctuating earnings (such as many high-tech companies).

13. TIMES INTEREST EARNED

Times interest earned provides an indication of the company's ability to meet interest payments as they come due. We compute it by dividing the sum of net income, interest expense, and income tax expense by interest expense. Illustration 18-26 shows the 2013 and 2012 ratios for Quality Department Store and 2013 comparative data. Note that times interest earned uses net income before income tax expense and interest expense. This represents the amount available to cover interest. For Quality Department Store, the 2013 amount is computed by taking net income of $263,800 and adding back the $36,000 of interest expense and the $168,200 of income tax expense.

Alternative Terminology
Times interest earned is also called *interest coverage*.

Illustration 18-26
Times interest earned

$$\text{Times Interest Earned} = \frac{\text{Net Income + Interest Expense + Income Tax Expense}}{\text{Interest Expense}}$$

Quality Department Store

2013	2012
$\frac{\$263{,}800 + \$36{,}000 + \$168{,}200}{\$36{,}000} = 13\text{ times}$	$\frac{\$208{,}500 + \$40{,}500 + \$139{,}000}{\$40{,}500} = 9.6\text{ times}$
Industry average	Macy's, Inc.
16.1 times	**6.9 times**

Quality's interest expense is well covered at 13 times. It is less than the industry average of 16.1 times but significantly exceeds Macy's 6.9 times.

Summary of Ratios

Illustration 18-27 summarizes the ratios discussed in this chapter. The summary includes the formula and purpose or use of each ratio.

Ratio	Formula	Purpose or Use
Liquidity Ratios		
1. Current ratio	$\frac{\text{Current assets}}{\text{Current liabilities}}$	Measures short-term debt-paying ability.
2. Acid-test (quick) ratio	$\frac{\text{Cash + Short-term investments + Accounts receivable (net)}}{\text{Current liabilities}}$	Measures immediate short-term liquidity.
3. Accounts receivable turnover	$\frac{\text{Net credit sales}}{\text{Average net accounts receivable}}$	Measures liquidity of accounts receivable.
4. Inventory turnover	$\frac{\text{Cost of goods sold}}{\text{Average inventory}}$	Measures liquidity of inventory.
Profitability Ratios		
5. Profit margin	$\frac{\text{Net income}}{\text{Net sales}}$	Measures net income generated by each dollar of sales.
6. Asset turnover	$\frac{\text{Net sales}}{\text{Average total assets}}$	Measures how efficiently assets are used to generate sales.
7. Return on assets	$\frac{\text{Net income}}{\text{Average total assets}}$	Measures overall profitability of assets.
8. Return on common stockholders' equity	$\frac{\text{Net income − Preferred dividends}}{\text{Average common stockholders' equity}}$	Measures profitability of owners' investment.
9. Earnings per share (EPS)	$\frac{\text{Net income − Preferred dividends}}{\text{Weighted-average common shares outstanding}}$	Measures net income earned on each share of common stock.
10. Price-earnings (P-E) ratio	$\frac{\text{Market price per share}}{\text{Earnings per share}}$	Measures the ratio of the market price per share to earnings per share.
11. Payout ratio	$\frac{\text{Cash dividends declared on common stock}}{\text{Net income}}$	Measures percentage of earnings distributed in the form of cash dividends.
Solvency Ratios		
12. Debt to assets ratio	$\frac{\text{Total liabilities}}{\text{Total assets}}$	Measures the percentage of total assets provided by creditors.
13. Times interest earned	$\frac{\text{Net income + Interest expense + Income tax expense}}{\text{Interest expense}}$	Measures ability to meet interest payments as they come due.

Illustration 18-27
Summary of liquidity, profitability, and solvency ratios

DO IT! 2 Ratio Analysis

The condensed financial statements of John Cully Company, for the years ended June 30, 2017 and 2016, are presented below.

JOHN CULLY COMPANY
Balance Sheets
June 30

	(in thousands)	
Assets	**2017**	**2016**
Current assets		
Cash and cash equivalents	$ 553.3	$ 611.6
Accounts receivable (net)	776.6	664.9
Inventory	768.3	653.5
Prepaid expenses and other current assets	204.4	269.2
Total current assets	2,302.6	2,199.2
Investments	12.3	12.6
Property, plant, and equipment (net)	694.2	647.0
Intangibles and other assets	876.7	849.3
Total assets	$3,885.8	$3,708.1
Liabilities and Stockholders' Equity		
Current liabilities	$1,497.7	$1,322.0
Long-term liabilities	679.5	637.1
Stockholders' equity—common	1,708.6	1,749.0
Total liabilities and stockholders' equity	$3,885.8	$3,708.1

JOHN CULLY COMPANY
Income Statements
For the Year Ended June 30

	(in thousands)	
	2017	**2016**
Sales revenue	$6,336.3	$5,790.4
Costs and expenses		
Cost of goods sold	1,617.4	1,476.3
Selling and administrative expenses	4,007.6	3,679.0
Interest expense	13.9	27.1
Total costs and expenses	5,638.9	5,182.4
Income before income taxes	697.4	608.0
Income tax expense	291.3	232.6
Net income	$ 406.1	$ 375.4

Compute the following ratios for 2017 and 2016.

(a) Current ratio.

(b) Inventory turnover. (Inventory on 6/30/15 was $599.0.)

(c) Profit margin.

(d) Return on assets. (Assets on 6/30/15 were $3,349.9.)

(e) Return on common stockholders' equity. (Stockholders' equity on 6/30/15 was $1,795.9.)

(f) Debt to assets ratio.

(g) Times interest earned.

Action Plan

✔ Remember that the current ratio includes all current assets. The acid-test ratio uses only cash, short-term investments, and net accounts receivable.

✔ Use average balances for turnover ratios like inventory, accounts receivable, and return on assets.

Solution

	2017	2016
(a) Current ratio:		
$2,302.6 ÷ $1,497.7 =	1.5:1	
$2,199.2 ÷ $1,322.0 =		1.7:1
(b) Inventory turnover:		
$1,617.4 ÷ [($768.3 + $653.5) ÷ 2] =	2.3 times	
$1,476.3 ÷ [($653.5 + $599.0) ÷ 2] =		2.4 times
(c) Profit margin:		
$406.1 ÷ $6,336.3 =	6.4%	
$375.4 ÷ $5,790.4 =		6.5%
(d) Return on assets:		
$406.1 ÷ [($3,885.8 + $3,708.1) ÷ 2] =	10.7%	
$375.4 ÷ [($3,708.1 + $3,349.9) ÷ 2] =		10.6%
(e) Return on common stockholders' equity:		
($406.1 − $0) ÷ [($1,708.6 + $1,749.0) ÷ 2] =	23.5%	
($375.4 − $0) ÷ [($1,749.0 + $1,795.9) ÷ 2] =		21.2%
(f) Debt to assets ratio:		
($1,497.7 + $679.5) ÷ $3,885.8 =	56.0%	
($1,322.0 + $637.1) ÷ $3,708.1 =		52.8%
(g) Times interest earned:		
($406.1 + $13.9 + $291.3) ÷ $13.9 =	51.2 times	
($375.4 + $27.1 + $232.6) ÷ $27.1 =		23.4 times

Related exercise material: **BE18-9, BE18-10, BE18-12, BE18-13, E18-5, E18-6, E18-7, E18-8, E18-9, E18-10, E18-11, and DO IT! 18-2.**

LEARNING OBJECTIVE 3

Apply the concept of sustainable income.

The value of a company like **Google** is a function of the amount, timing, and uncertainty of its future cash flows. Google's current and past income statements are particularly useful in helping analysts predict these future cash flows. In using this approach, analysts must make sure that Google's past income numbers reflect its **sustainable income**, that is, do not include unusual (out-of-the-ordinary) revenues, expenses, gains, and losses. **Sustainable income** is, therefore, the most likely level of income to be obtained by a company in the future. Sustainable income differs from actual net income by the amount of unusual revenues, expenses, gains, and losses included in the current year's income. Analysts are interested in sustainable income because it helps them derive an estimate of future earnings without the "noise" of unusual items.

Fortunately, an income statement provides information on sustainable income by separating operating transactions from nonoperating transactions. This statement also highlights intermediate components of income such as income from operations, income before income taxes, and income from continuing operations. In addition, information on unusual items such as gains or losses on discontinued items and components of other comprehensive income are disclosed.

Illustration 18-28 presents a statement of comprehensive income for Cruz Company for the year 2017. A statement of comprehensive income includes not only net income but a broader measure of income called comprehensive income. The two major unusual items in this statement are discontinued operations and other comprehensive income (highlighted in red). When estimating future cash flows, analysts must consider the implications of each of these components.

Illustration 18-28
Statement of comprehensive income

CRUZ COMPANY
Statement of Comprehensive Income
For the year ended 2017

Sales revenue	$900,000
Cost of goods sold	650,000
Gross profit	250,000
Operating expenses	100,000
Income from operations	150,000
Other revenues (expenses) and gains (losses)	20,000
Income before income taxes	170,000
Income tax expense	24,000
Income from continuing operations	146,000
Discontinued operations (net of tax)	**30,000**
Net income	176,000
Other comprehensive income items (net of tax)	**10,000**
Comprehensive income	$186,000

In looking at Illustration 18-28, note that Cruz Company's two major types of unusual items, discontinued operations and other comprehensive income, are reported net of tax. That is, Cruz first calculates income tax expense before income from continuing operations. Then, it calculates income tax expense related to the discontinued operations and other comprehensive income. The general concept is, "Let the tax follow the income or loss." We discuss discontinued operations and other comprehensive income in more detail next.

Discontinued Operations

Discontinued operations refers to the disposal of a **significant component** of a business, such as the elimination of a major class of customers, or an entire activity. For example, to downsize its operations, General Dynamics Corp. sold its missile business to Hughes Aircraft Co. for $450 million. In its statement of comprehensive income, General Dynamics reported the sale in a separate section entitled "Discontinued operations."

Following the disposal of a significant component, the company should report on its statement both income from continuing operations and income (or loss) from discontinued operations. **The income (loss) from discontinued operations consists of two parts: the income (loss) from operations** and **the gain (loss) on disposal of the component.**

To illustrate, assume that during 2017 Acro Energy Inc. has income before income taxes of $800,000. During 2017, Acro discontinued and sold its unprofitable chemical division. The loss in 2017 from chemical operations (net of $60,000 taxes) was $140,000. The loss on disposal of the chemical division (net of $30,000 taxes) was $70,000. Assuming a 30% tax rate on income, Illustration 18-29 (page 806) shows Acro's statement of comprehensive income presentation.

Note that the statement uses the caption "Income from continuing operations" and adds a new section "Discontinued operations." **The new section reports both the operating loss and the loss on disposal net of applicable income taxes.** This presentation clearly indicates the separate effects of continuing operations and discontinued operations on net income.

Other Comprehensive Income

Most revenues, expenses, gains, and losses are included in net income. However, certain gains and losses bypass net income. Instead, companies record these items as direct adjustments to stockholders' equity. The FASB requires companies to report not only net income but also other comprehensive income.

Illustration 18-29
Statement presentation of discontinued operations

Helpful Hint
Observe the dual disclosures: (1) the results of operation of the discontinued division must be eliminated from the results of continuing operations, and (2) the company must also report the disposal of the division.

ACRO ENERGY INC.
Statement of Comprehensive Income (partial)
For the Year Ended December 31, 2017

Income before income taxes		$ 800,000
Income tax expense		240,000
Income from continuing operations		560,000
Discontinued operations		
Loss from operation of chemical division, net of $60,000 income tax savings	**$140,000**	
Loss from disposal of chemical division, net of $30,000 income tax savings	**70,000**	**210,000**
Net income		$ 350,000

Other comprehensive income includes all changes in stockholders' equity during a period except those changes resulting from investments by stockholders and distributions to stockholders.

ILLUSTRATION OF OTHER COMPREHENSIVE INCOME

Accounting standards require that companies adjust most investments in stocks and bonds up or down to their market price at the end of each accounting period. For example, assume that during 2017 Stassi Company purchased IBM stock for $10,000 as an investment. At the end of 2017, Stassi was still holding the investment, but the stock's market price was now $8,000. In this case, Stassi is required to reduce the recorded value of its IBM investment by $2,000. The $2,000 difference is an unrealized loss.

Should Stassi include this $2,000 unrealized loss in net income? It depends on whether Stassi classifies the IBM stock as a trading security or an available-for-sale security. A **trading security** is bought and held primarily for sale in the near term to generate income on short-term price differences. Companies report unrealized losses on trading securities in the "Other expenses and losses" section of the income statement. The rationale: It is likely that the company will realize the unrealized loss (or an unrealized gain), so the company should report the loss (gain) as part of net income.

If Stassi did not purchase the investment for trading purposes, it is classified as available-for-sale. **Available-for-sale securities** are held with the intent of selling them sometime in the future. Companies do not include unrealized gains or losses on available-for-sale securities in net income. Instead, they report them as part of "Other comprehensive income." Other comprehensive income is not included in net income. It bypasses net income and is recorded as a direct adjustment to stockholders' equity.

FORMAT

One format for reporting other comprehensive income is to report a statement of comprehensive income. For example, assuming that Stassi Company has a net income of $300,000, the unrealized loss would be reported below net income as follows.

Illustration 18-30
Lower portion of statement of comprehensive income

STASSI CORPORATION
Statement of Comprehensive Income (partial)
For the Year Ended 2017

Net income	$ 300,000
Unrealized loss on available-for-sale securities (net of tax)	2,000
Comprehensive income	**$298,000**

Companies also report the unrealized loss on available-for-sale securities as a separate component of stockholders' equity. To illustrate, assume Stassi Corporation has common stock of $3,000,000, retained earnings of $1,500,000, and an unrealized loss on available-for-sale securities of $2,000. Illustration 18-31 shows the balance sheet presentation of the unrealized loss.

Illustration 18-31
Unrealized loss in stockholders' equity section

Balance Sheet (partial)	
Stockholders' equity	
Common stock	$3,000,000
Retained earnings	1,500,000
Total paid-in capital and retained earnings	4,500,000
Less: Unrealized loss on available-for-sale securities	**2,000**
Total stockholders' equity	$4,498,000

Note that the presentation of the loss is similar to the presentation of the cost of treasury stock in the stockholders' equity section. (An unrealized gain would be added in this section of the balance sheet.) Reporting the unrealized gain or loss in the stockholders' equity section serves two important purposes: (1) it reduces the volatility of net income due to fluctuations in fair value, and (2) it informs the financial statement user of the gain or loss that would occur if the company sold the securities at fair value.

COMPLETE STATEMENT OF COMPREHENSIVE INCOME

The statement of comprehensive income for Pace Corporation in Illustration 18-32 presents the types of items found on this statement, such as net sales, cost of goods sold, operating expenses, and income taxes. In addition, it shows how companies report discontinued operations and other comprehensive income (highlighted in red).

Illustration 18-32
Complete statement of comprehensive income

PACE CORPORATION
Statement of Comprehensive Income
For the Year Ended December 31, 2017

Net sales		$440,000
Cost of goods sold		260,000
Gross profit		180,000
Operating expenses		110,000
Income from operations		70,000
Other revenues and gains		5,600
Other expenses and losses		9,600
Income before income taxes		66,000
Income tax expense ($66,000 × 30%)		19,800
Income from continuing operations		46,200
Discontinued operations		
Loss from operation of Plastics Division, net of income tax savings $18,000 ($60,000 × 30%)	**$42,000**	
Gain on disposal of Plastics Division, net of $15,000 income taxes ($50,000 × 30%)	**35,000**	**7,000**
Net income		**39,200**
Unrealized gain on available-for-sale securities, net of income taxes ($15,000 × 30%)		**10,500**
Comprehensive income		**$ 49,700**

Investor Insight Cisco Systems

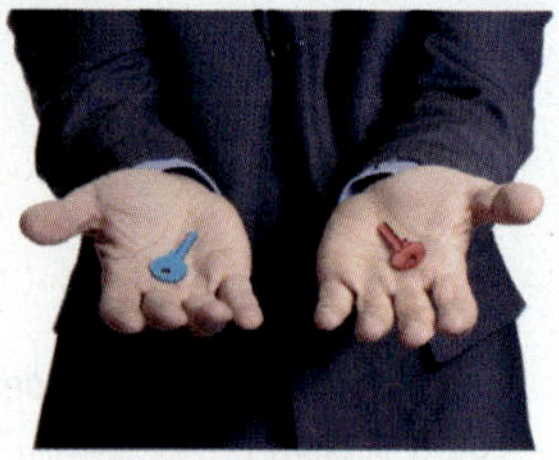

© gosphotodesign/Shutterstock

Another Measure of Sustainable Income?

Companies whose stock is publicly traded are required to present their income statement following GAAP. In recent years, many companies now report a second measure of income, called pro forma income. **Pro forma income** usually excludes items that the company thinks are unusual or nonrecurring. For example, in a recent year, Cisco Systems (a high-tech company) reported a quarterly net loss under GAAP of $2.7 billion. Cisco reported pro forma income for the same quarter as a profit of $230 million. This large difference in profits between GAAP income numbers and pro forma income is not unusual. For example, during one 9-month period, the 100 largest companies on the Nasdaq stock exchange reported a total pro forma income of $19.1 billion but a total loss as measured by GAAP of $82.3 billion—a difference of about $100 billion!

To compute pro forma income, companies generally exclude any items they deem inappropriate for measuring their performance. Many analysts and investors are critical of the practice of using pro forma income because these numbers often make companies look better than they really are. As the financial press noted, pro forma numbers might be called "earnings before bad stuff." Companies, on the other hand, argue that pro forma numbers more clearly indicate sustainable income because they exclude unusual items. "Cisco's technique gives readers of financial statements a clear picture of Cisco's normal business activities," the company said in a statement issued in response to questions about its pro forma income accounting.

Recently, the SEC provided some guidance on how companies should present pro forma information. Stay tuned: Everyone seems to agree that pro forma numbers can be useful if they provide insights into determining a company's sustainable income. However, many companies have abused the flexibility that pro forma numbers allow and have used the measure as a way to put their companies in a more favorable light.

What incentive do companies have to report pro forma income? (Go to **WileyPLUS** for this answer and additional questions.)

DO IT! 3 Unusual Items

In its proposed 2017 income statement, AIR Corporation reports income before income taxes $400,000, unrealized gain on available-for-sale securities $100,000, income taxes $120,000 (not including unusual items), loss from operation of discontinued flower division $50,000, and loss on disposal of discontinued flower division $90,000. The income tax rate is 30%. Prepare a correct statement of comprehensive income, beginning with "Income before income taxes."

Action Plan

✔ Show discontinued operations and other comprehensive income net of tax.

Solution

AIR CORPORATION
Statement of Comprehensive Income (partial)
For the Year Ended December 31, 2017

Income before income taxes		$400,000
Income tax expense		120,000
Income from continuing operations		280,000
Discontinued operations		
Loss from operation of flower division, net of $15,000 income tax savings	$35,000	
Loss on disposal of flower division, net of $27,000 income tax savings	63,000	98,000
Net income		182,000
Unrealized gain on available-for-sale securities, net of $30,000 income taxes		70,000
Comprehensive income		$252,000

Related exercise material: **BE18-14, BE18-15, E18-12, E18-13, and DO IT! 18-3.**

REVIEW AND PRACTICE

LEARNING OBJECTIVES REVIEW

1 Apply horizontal and vertical analysis to financial statements. There are three bases of comparison: (1) intracompany, which compares an item or financial relationship with other data within a company; (2) industry, which compares company data with industry averages; and (3) intercompany, which compares an item or financial relationship of a company with data of one or more competing companies.

Horizontal analysis is a technique for evaluating a series of data over a period of time to determine the increase or decrease that has taken place, expressed as either an amount or a percentage. Vertical analysis is a technique that expresses each item within a financial statement in terms of a percentage of a relevant total or a base amount.

2 Analyze a company's performance using ratio analysis. The formula and purpose of each ratio is presented in Illustration 18-27 (page 802).

3 Apply the concept of sustainable income. Sustainable income analysis is useful in evaluating a company's performance. Sustainable income is the most likely level of income to be obtained by the company in the future. Discontinued operations and other comprehensive income are presented on the statement of comprehensive income to highlight their unusual nature. Items below income from continuing operations must be presented net of tax.

GLOSSARY REVIEW

Accounts receivable turnover A measure of the liquidity of accounts receivable; computed by dividing net credit sales by average net accounts receivable. (p. 795).

Acid-test (quick) ratio A measure of a company's immediate short-term liquidity; computed by dividing the sum of cash, short-term investments, and net accounts receivable by current liabilities. (p. 794).

Asset turnover A measure of how efficiently a company uses its assets to generate sales; computed by dividing net sales by average total assets. (p. 797).

Current ratio A measure used to evaluate a company's liquidity and short-term debt-paying ability; computed by dividing current assets by current liabilities. (p. 793).

Debt to assets ratio Measures the percentage of assets provided by creditors; computed by dividing total liabilities by total assets. (p. 800).

Discontinued operations The disposal of a significant component of a business. (p. 805).

Earnings per share (EPS) The net income earned on each share of common stock; computed by dividing net income minus preferred dividends (if any) by the number of weighted-average common shares outstanding. (p. 799).

Horizontal analysis A technique for evaluating a series of financial statement data over a period of time, to determine the increase (decrease) that has taken place, expressed as either an amount or a percentage. (p. 787).

Inventory turnover A measure of the liquidity of inventory; computed by dividing cost of goods sold by average inventory. (p. 796).

Leveraging See *Trading on the equity*. (p. 799).

Liquidity ratios Measures of the short-term ability of the company to pay its maturing obligations and to meet unexpected needs for cash. (p. 793).

Other comprehensive income Includes all changes in stockholders' equity during a period except those resulting from investments by stockholders and distributions to stockholders. (p. 806).

Payout ratio Measures the percentage of earnings distributed in the form of cash dividends; computed by dividing cash dividends declared on common stock by net income. (p. 800).

Price-earnings (P-E) ratio Measures the ratio of the market price of each share of common stock to the earnings per share; computed by dividing the market price per share by earnings per share. (p. 799).

Profit margin Measures the percentage of each dollar of sales that results in net income; computed by dividing net income by net sales. (p. 797).

Profitability ratios Measures of the income or operating success of a company for a given period of time. (p. 796).

Ratio An expression of the mathematical relationship between one quantity and another. The relationship may be expressed either as a percentage, a rate, or a simple proportion. (p. 792).

Ratio analysis A technique for evaluating financial statements that expresses the relationship between selected financial statement data. (p. 792).

Return on assets An overall measure of profitability; computed by dividing net income by average total assets. (p. 798).

Return on common stockholders' equity Measures the dollars of net income earned for each dollar invested by the owners; computed by dividing net income minus preferred dividends (if any) by average common stockholders' equity. (p. 798).

Solvency ratios Measures of the ability of the company to survive over a long period of time. (p. 800).

Sustainable income The most likely level of income to be obtained by a company in the future. (p. 804).

Times interest earned Measures a company's ability to meet interest payments as they come due; computed by dividing the sum of net income, interest expense, and income tax expense by interest expense. (p. 801).

Trading on the equity Borrowing money at a lower rate of interest than can be earned by using the borrowed money. (p. 799).

Vertical analysis A technique for evaluating financial statement data that expresses each item within a financial statement as a percentage of a base amount. (p. 790).

PRACTICE MULTIPLE-CHOICE QUESTIONS

(LO 1) 1. Comparisons of data within a company are an example of the following comparative basis:
(a) Industry averages. (c) Intercompany.
(b) Intracompany. (d) Both (b) and (c).

(LO 1) 2. In horizontal analysis, each item is expressed as a percentage of the:
(a) net income amount.
(b) stockholders' equity amount.
(c) total assets amount.
(d) base year amount.

(LO 1) 3. Sammy Corporation reported net sales of $300,000, $330,000, and $360,000 in the years, 2015, 2016, and 2017, respectively. If 2015 is the base year, what is the trend percentage for 2017?
(a) 77%. (c) 120%.
(b) 108%. (d) 130%.

(LO 1) 4. The following schedule is a display of what type of analysis?

	Amount	Percent
Current assets	$200,000	25%
Property, plant, and equipment	600,000	75%
Total assets	$800,000	

(a) Horizontal analysis. (c) Vertical analysis.
(b) Differential analysis. (d) Ratio analysis.

(LO 1) 5. In vertical analysis, the base amount for depreciation expense is generally:
(a) net sales.
(b) depreciation expense in a previous year.
(c) gross profit.
(d) fixed assets.

(LO 2) 6. Which of the following measures is an evaluation of a firm's ability to pay current liabilities?
(a) Acid-test ratio. (c) Both (a) and (b).
(b) Current ratio. (d) None of the above.

(LO 2) 7. A measure useful in evaluating the efficiency in managing inventories is:
(a) inventory turnover. (c) Both (a) and (b).
(b) days in inventory. (d) None of the above.

Use the following financial statement information as of the end of each year to answer Questions 8-12.

	2017	2016
Inventory	$ 54,000	$ 48,000
Current assets	81,000	106,000
Total assets	382,000	326,000
Current liabilities	27,000	36,000
Total liabilities	102,000	88,000
Preferred stock	40,000	40,000
Common stockholders' equity	240,000	198,000
Net sales	784,000	697,000
Cost of goods sold	306,000	277,000
Net income	134,000	90,000
Income tax expense	22,000	18,000
Interest expense	12,000	12,000
Dividends paid to preferred stockholders	4,000	4,000
Dividends paid to common stockholders	15,000	10,000

8. Compute the days in inventory for 2017. (LO 2)
(a) 64.4 days. (c) 6 days.
(b) 60.8 days. (d) 24 days.

9. Compute the current ratio for 2017. (LO 2)
(a) 1.26:1. (c) 0.80:1.
(b) 3.0:1. (d) 3.75:1.

10. Compute the profit margin for 2017. (LO 2)
(a) 17.1%. (c) 37.9%.
(b) 18.1%. (d) 5.9%.

11. Compute the return on common stockholders' equity for 2017. (LO 2)
(a) 47.9%. (c) 61.2%.
(b) 51.7%. (d) 59.4%.

12. Compute the times interest earned for 2017. (LO 2)
(a) 11.2 times. (c) 14.0 times.
(b) 65.3 times. (d) 13.0 times.

13. In reporting discontinued operations, the statement of comprehensive income should show in a special section: (LO 3)
(a) gains and losses on the disposal of the discontinued component.
(b) other comprehensive income items.
(c) Both (a) and (b).
(d) None of these answer choices are correct.

14. Scout Corporation has income before taxes of $400,000 and a loss on discontinued operations of $100,000. If the income tax rate is 25% on all items, the statement of comprehensive income should show income from continuing operations and discontinued operations, respectively, of: (LO 3)
(a) $325,000 and $100,000.
(b) $325,000 and $75,000.
(c) $300,000 and $100,000.
(d) $300,000 and $75,000.

Solutions

1. **(b)** Comparisons of data within a company are called intracompany comparisons, not (a) industry averages, (c) intercompany comparisons, or (d) both intracompany and intercompany comparisons. Intercompany comparisons are among companies.

2. **(d)** Horizontal analysis converts each succeeding year's balance to a percentage of the base year amount, not (a) net income amount, (b) stockholders' equity amount, or (c) total assets amount.

3. **(c)** The trend percentage for 2017 is 120% ($360,000/$300,000), not (a) 77%, (b) 108%, or (d) 130%.

4. **(c)** The data in the schedule is a display of vertical analysis because the individual asset items are expressed as a percentage of total assets. The other choices are therefore incorrect. Horizontal analysis is a technique for evaluating a series of data over a period of time.

5. **(a)** In vertical analysis, net sales is used as the base amount for income statement items, not (b) depreciation expense in a previous year, (c) gross profit, or (d) fixed assets.

6. **(c)** Both the acid-test ratio and the current ratio measure a firm's ability to pay current liabilities. Choices (a) and (b) are correct but (c) is the better answer. Choice (d) is incorrect because there is a correct answer.

7. **(c)** Both inventory turnover and days in inventory measure a firm's efficiency in managing inventories. Choices (a) and (b) are correct but (c) is the better answer. Choice (d) is incorrect because there is a correct answer.

8. **(b)** Inventory turnover = Cost of goods sold/Average inventory [$306,000/($54,000 + $48,000)/2] = 6 times. Thus, days in inventory = 60.8 (365/6), not (a) 64.4, (c) 6, or (d) 24 days.

9. **(b)** Current ratio = Current assets/Current liabilities ($81,000/$27,000) = 3.0:1, not (a) 1.26:1, (c) 0.80:1, or (d) 3.75:1.

10. **(a)** Profit margin = Net income/Net sales ($134,000/$784,000) =17.1%, not (b) 18.1%, (c) 37.9%, or (d) 5.9%.

11. **(d)** Return on common stockholders' equity = Net income ($134,000) − Dividends to preferred stockholders ($4,000) /Average common stockholders' equity [($240,000 + $198,000)/2] = 59.4%, not (a) 47.9%, (b) 51.7%, or (c) 61.2%.

12. **(c)** Times interest earned = Net income + Interest expense + Income tax expense divided by Interest expense [($134,000 + $12,000 + $22,000)/$12,000] = 14.0 times, not (a) 11.2, (b) 65.3, or (d) 13.0 times.

13. **(c)** Gains and losses on the disposal of the discontinued segment and gains and losses from operations of the discontinued component are shown in the special section titled discontinued operations. Other comprehensive income items are reported in a separate section after net income on the statement of comprehensive income. Choices (a) and (b) are therefore correct but (c) is the better answer. Choice (d) is incorrect as there is a correct answer.

14. **(d)** Income tax expense = 25% × $400,000 = $100,000; therefore, income from continuing operations = $400,000 − $100,000 = $300,000. The loss on discontinued operations is shown net of tax, $100,000 × 75% = $75,000. The other choices are therefore incorrect.

PRACTICE EXERCISES

1. The comparative condensed balance sheets of Roadway Corporation are presented below.

Prepare horizontal and vertical analysis.

(LO 1)

ROADWAY CORPORATION
Condensed Balance Sheets
December 31

	2017	2016
Assets		
Current assets	$ 76,000	$ 80,000
Property, plant, and equipment (net)	99,000	90,000
Intangibles	25,000	40,000
Total assets	$200,000	$210,000
Liabilities and stockholders' equity		
Current liabilities	$ 40,800	$ 48,000
Long-term liabilities	143,000	150,000
Stockholders' equity	16,200	12,000
Total liabilities and stockholders' equity	$200,000	$210,000

Instructions

(a) Prepare a horizontal analysis of the balance sheet data for Roadway Corporation using 2016 as a base.

(b) Prepare a vertical analysis of the balance sheet data for Roadway Corporation in columnar form for 2017.

Solution

1. (a)

ROADWAY CORPORATION
Condensed Balance Sheets
December 31

	2017	2016	Increase (Decrease)	Percent Change from 2016
Assets				
Current assets	$ 76,000	$ 80,000	$ (4,000)	(5.0%)
Property, plant, and equipment (net)	99,000	90,000	9,000	10.0%
Intangibles	25,000	40,000	(15,000)	(37.5%)
Total assets	$200,000	$210,000	$(10,000)	(4.8%)
Liabilities and stockholders' equity				
Current liabilities	$ 40,800	$ 48,000	$ (7,200)	(15.0%)
Long-term liabilities	143,000	150,000	(7,000)	(4.7%)
Stockholders' equity	16,200	12,000	4,200	35.0%
Total liabilities and stockholders' equity	$200,000	$210,000	$(10,000)	(4.8%)

(b)

ROADWAY CORPORATION
Condensed Balance Sheet
December 31, 2017

	Amount	Percent
Assets		
Current assets	$ 76,000	38.0%
Property, plant, and equipment (net)	99,000	49.5%
Intangibles	25,000	12.5%
Total assets	$200,000	100.0%
Liabilities and stockholders' equity		
Current liabilities	$ 40,800	20.4%
Long-term liabilities	143,000	71.5%
Stockholders' equity	16,200	8.1%
Total liabilities and stockholders' equity	$200,000	100.0%

Compute ratios.
(LO 2)

2. Rondo Corporation's comparative balance sheets are presented below.

RONDO CORPORATION
Balance Sheets
December 31

	2017	2016
Cash	$ 5,300	$ 3,700
Accounts receivable	21,200	23,400
Inventory	9,000	7,000
Land	20,000	26,000
Buildings	70,000	70,000
Accumulated depreciation—buildings	(15,000)	(10,000)
Total	$110,500	$120,100
Accounts payable	$ 10,370	$ 31,100
Common stock	75,000	69,000
Retained earnings	25,130	20,000
Total	$110,500	$120,100

Rondo's 2017 income statement included net sales of $120,000, cost of goods sold of $70,000, and net income of $14,000.

Instructions

Compute the following ratios for 2017.

(a) Current ratio.
(b) Acid-test ratio.
(c) Accounts receivable turnover.
(d) Inventory turnover.

(e) Profit margin.
(f) Asset turnover.
(g) Return on assets.
(h) Return on common stockholders' equity.
(i) Debt to assets ratio.

Solution

2. (a) ($5,300 + $21,200 + $9,000)/$10,370 = 3.42
   (b) ($5,300 + $21,200)/$10,370 = 2.56
   (c) $120,000/[($21,200 + $23,400)/2] = 5.38
   (d) $70,000/[($9,000 + $7,000)/2] = 8.8
   (e) $14,000/$120,000 = 11.7%
   (f) $120,000/[($110,500 + $120,100)/2] = 1.04
   (g) $14,000/[($110,500 + $120,100)/2] = 12.1%
   (h) $14,000/[($100,130 + $89,000)/2] = 14.8%
   (i) $10,370/$110,500 = 9.4%

PRACTICE PROBLEM

Prepare a statement of comprehensive income.

(LO 3)

The events and transactions of Dever Corporation for the year ending December 31, 2017, resulted in the following data.

Cost of goods sold	$2,600,000
Net sales	4,400,000
Other expenses and losses	9,600
Other revenues and gains	5,600
Selling and administrative expenses	1,100,000
Income from operations of plastics division	70,000
Gain from disposal of plastics division	500,000
Unrealized loss on available-for-sale securities	60,000

Analysis reveals the following:

1. All items are before the applicable income tax rate of 30%.
2. The plastics division was sold on July 1.
3. All operating data for the plastics division have been segregated.

Instructions

Prepare a statement of comprehensive income for the year.

Solution

DEVER CORPORATION
Statement of Comprehensive Income
For the Year Ended December 31, 2017

Net sales		$4,400,000
Cost of goods sold		2,600,000
Gross profit		1,800,000
Selling and administrative expenses		1,100,000
Income from operations		700,000
Other revenues and gains		5,600
Other expenses and losses		9,600
Income before income taxes		696,000
Income tax expense ($696,000 × 30%)		208,800
Income from continuing operations		487,200
Discontinued operations		
Income from operation of plastics division, net of $21,000 income taxes ($70,000 × 30%)	49,000	
Gain from disposal of plastics division, net of $150,000 income taxes ($500,000 × 30%)	350,000	399,000
Net income		886,200
Unrealized loss on available-for-sale securities, net of $18,000 income tax savings ($60,000 × 30%)		42,000
Comprehensive income		$ 844,200

WileyPLUS Brief Exercises, Exercises, DO IT! Exercises, and Problems and many additional resources are available for practice in WileyPLUS

QUESTIONS

1. (a) Jose Ramirez believes that the analysis of financial statements is directed at two characteristics of a company: liquidity and profitability. Is Jose correct? Explain.
   (b) Are short-term creditors, long-term creditors, and stockholders interested primarily in the same characteristics of a company? Explain.
2. (a) Distinguish among the following bases of comparison: (1) intracompany, (2) industry averages, and (3) intercompany.
   (b) Give the principal value of using each of the three bases of comparison.
3. Two popular methods of financial statement analysis are horizontal analysis and vertical analysis. Explain the difference between these two methods.
4. (a) If Peoples Company had net income of $390,000 in 2017 and it experienced a 24.5% increase in net income for 2018, what is its net income for 2018?
   (b) If six cents of every dollar of Peoples' revenue is net income in 2017, what is the dollar amount of 2017 revenue?
5. What is a ratio? What are the different ways of expressing the relationship of two amounts? What information does a ratio provide?
6. Name the major ratios useful in assessing (a) liquidity and (b) solvency.
7. Roberto Perez is puzzled. His company had a profit margin of 10% in 2017. He feels that this is an indication that the company is doing well. Julie Beck, his accountant, says that more information is needed to determine the firm's financial well-being. Who is correct? Why?
8. What do the following classes of ratios measure? (a) Liquidity ratios. (b) Profitability ratios. (c) Solvency ratios.
9. What is the difference between the current ratio and the acid-test ratio?
10. Hizar Company, a retail store, has an accounts receivable turnover of 4.5 times. The industry average is 12.5 times. Does Hizar have a collection problem with its accounts receivable?
11. Which ratios should be used to help answer the following questions?
    (a) How efficient is a company in using its assets to produce sales?
    (b) How near to sale is the inventory on hand?
    (c) How many dollars of net income were earned for each dollar invested by the owners?
    (d) How able is a company to meet interest charges as they fall due?
12. The price-earnings ratio of General Motors (automobile builder) was 8, and the price-earnings ratio of Microsoft (computer software) was 38. Which company did the stock market favor? Explain.
13. What is the formula for computing the payout ratio? Would you expect this ratio to be high or low for a growth company?
14. Holding all other factors constant, indicate whether each of the following changes generally signals good or bad news about a company.
    (a) Increase in profit margin.
    (b) Decrease in inventory turnover.
    (c) Increase in the current ratio.
    (d) Decrease in earnings per share.
    (e) Increase in price-earnings ratio.
    (f) Increase in debt to assets ratio.
    (g) Decrease in times interest earned.
15. The return on assets for Zhang Corporation is 7.6%. During the same year, Zhang's return on common stockholders' equity is 12.8%. What is the explanation for the difference in the two rates?
16. Which two ratios do you think should be of greatest interest to:
    (a) A pension fund considering the purchase of 20-year bonds?
    (b) A bank contemplating a short-term loan?
    (c) A common stockholder?
17. Why must preferred dividends be subtracted from net income in computing earnings per share?
18. (a) What is meant by trading on the equity?
    (b) How would you determine the profitability of trading on the equity?
19. Lippert Inc. has net income of $160,000, weighted-average shares of common stock outstanding of 50,000, and preferred dividends for the period of $40,000. What is Lippert's earnings per share of common stock? Kate Lippert, the president of Lippert Inc., believes the computed EPS of the company is high. Comment.
20. Why is it important to report discontinued operations separately from income from continuing operations?
21. You are considering investing in Wingert Transportation. The company reports 2017 earnings per share of $6.50 on income from continuing operations and $4.75 on net income. Which EPS figure would you consider more relevant to your investment decision? Why?
22. RAF Inc. reported 2016 earnings per share of $3.20 and had no discontinued operations items. In 2017, EPS on income from continuing operations was $2.99, and EPS on net income was $3.49. Is this a favorable trend?
23. Identify the specific sections in Apple's 2013 annual report where horizontal and vertical analyses of financial data are presented.

BRIEF EXERCISES

Follow the rounding procedures used in the chapter.

BE18-1 You recently received a letter from your Uncle Sammy. A portion of the letter is presented below.

Discuss need for comparative analysis.

(LO 1)

You know that I have a significant amount of money I saved over the years. I am thinking about starting an investment program. I want to do the investing myself, based on my own research and analysis of financial statements. I know that you are studying accounting, so I have a couple of questions for you. I have heard that different users of financial statements are interested in different characteristics of companies. Is this true and, if so, why? Also, some of my friends who are already investing have told me that comparisons involving a company's financial data can be made on a number of different bases. Can you explain these bases to me?

Instructions

Write a letter to your Uncle Sammy which answers his questions.

BE18-2 Schellhammer Corporation reported the following amounts in 2016, 2017, and 2018.

Identify and use tools of financial statement analysis.

(LO 1, 2)

	2016	2017	2018
Current assets	$200,000	$210,000	$240,000
Current liabilities	150,000	168,000	184,000
Total assets	500,000	600,000	620,000

Instructions

(a) Identify and describe the three tools of financial statement analysis. (b) Perform each of the three types of analysis on Schellhammer's current assets.

BE18-3 Using the following data from the comparative balance sheet of Goody Company, illustrate horizontal analysis.

Prepare horizontal analysis.

(LO 1)

	December 31, 2017	December 31, 2016
Accounts receivable	$ 520,000	$ 400,000
Inventory	840,000	600,000
Total assets	3,000,000	2,500,000

BE18-4 Using the same data presented above in BE18-3 for Goody Company, illustrate vertical analysis.

Prepare vertical analysis.

(LO 1)

BE18-5 Net income was $500,000 in 2016, $450,000 in 2017, and $522,000 in 2018. What is the percentage of change from (a) 2016 to 2017 and (b) 2017 to 2018? Is the change an increase or a decrease?

Calculate percentage of change.

(LO 1)

BE18-6 If Sappington Company had net income of $585,000 in 2017 and it experienced a 20% increase in net income over 2016, what was its 2016 net income?

Calculate net income.

(LO 1)

BE18-7 Horizontal analysis (trend analysis) percentages for Dody Company's sales revenue, cost of goods sold, and expenses are shown below.

Calculate change in net income.

(LO 1)

	2018	2017	2016
Sales revenue	96.2%	106.8%	100.0%
Cost of goods sold	102.0	97.0	100.0
Expenses	109.6	98.4	100.0

Did Dody's net income increase, decrease, or remain unchanged over the 3-year period?

Calculate change in net income.

(LO 1)

BE18-8 Vertical analysis (common size) percentages for Kochheim Company's sales revenue, cost of goods sold, and expenses are shown below.

	2018	2017	2016
Sales revenue	100.0%	100.0%	100.0%
Cost of goods sold	60.2	62.4	63.5
Expenses	25.0	25.6	27.5

Did Kochheim's net income as a percentage of sales increase, decrease, or remain unchanged over the 3-year period? Provide numerical support for your answer.

Calculate liquidity ratios.

(LO 2)

BE18-9 Selected condensed data taken from a recent balance sheet of Heidebrecht Inc. are as follows.

HEIDEBRECHT INC.
Balance Sheet (partial)

Cash	$ 8,041,000
Short-term investments	4,947,000
Accounts receivable	12,545,000
Inventory	14,814,000
Other current assets	5,571,000
Total current assets	$45,918,000
Total current liabilities	$40,644,000

What are the (a) working capital, (b) current ratio, and (c) acid-test ratio?

Calculate profitability ratios.

(LO 2)

BE18-10 Linebarger Corporation has net income of $11.44 million and net revenue of $95 million in 2017. Its assets are $14 million at the beginning of the year and $18 million at the end of the year. What are Linebarger's (a) asset turnover and (b) profit margin?

Evaluate collection of accounts receivable.

(LO 2)

BE18-11 The following data are taken from the financial statements of Rainsberger Company.

	2018	2017
Accounts receivable (net), end of year	$ 550,000	$ 520,000
Net sales on account	3,960,000	3,100,000
Terms for all sales are 1/10, n/60.		

(a) Compute for each year (1) the accounts receivable turnover and (2) the average collection period. At the end of 2016, accounts receivable (net) was $480,000.
(b) What conclusions about the management of accounts receivable can be drawn from these data?

Evaluate management of inventory.

(LO 2)

BE18-12 The following data are from the income statements of Haskin Company.

	2017	2016
Sales revenue	$6,420,000	$6,240,000
Beginning inventory	940,000	860,000
Purchases	4,340,000	4,661,000
Ending inventory	1,020,000	940,000

(a) Compute for each year (1) the inventory turnover and (2) the days in inventory.
(b) What conclusions concerning the management of the inventory can be drawn from these data?

Calculate amounts from profitability ratios.

(LO 2)

BE18-13 Guo Company has stockholders' equity of $400,000 and net income of $66,000. It has a payout ratio of 20% and a return on assets of 15%. How much did Guo pay in cash dividends, and what were its average assets?

BE18-14 An inexperienced accountant for Silva Corporation showed the following in the income statement: income before income taxes $450,000 and unrealized gain on available-for-sale securities (before taxes) $70,000. The unrealized gain on available-for-sale securities and income before income taxes are both subject to a 25% tax rate. Prepare a correct statement of comprehensive income.

Prepare statement of comprehensive income including unusual items.
(LO 3)

BE18-15 On June 30, Holloway Corporation discontinued its operations in Europe. During the year, the operating loss was $300,000 before taxes. On September 1, Holloway disposed of its European facilities at a pretax loss of $120,000. The applicable tax rate is 20%. Show the discontinued operations section of the statement of comprehensive income.

Prepare discontinued operations section of statement of comprehensive income.
(LO 3)

DO IT! Exercises

DO IT! 18-1 Summary financial information for Wolford Company is as follows.

Prepare horizontal analysis.
(LO 1)

	December 31, 2017	December 31, 2016
Current assets	$ 199,000	$ 220,000
Plant assets	821,000	780,000
Total assets	$1,020,000	$1,000,000

Compute the amount and percentage changes in 2017 using horizontal analysis, assuming 2016 is the base year.

DO IT! 18-2 The condensed financial statements of Murawski Company for the years 2016 and 2017 are presented below. (Amounts in thousands.)

Compute ratios.
(LO 2)

MURAWSKI COMPANY
Balance Sheets
December 31

	2017	2016
Current assets		
Cash and cash equivalents	$ 330	$ 360
Accounts receivable (net)	470	400
Inventory	460	390
Prepaid expenses	120	160
Total current assets	1,380	1,310
Investments	10	10
Property, plant, and equipment	420	380
Intangibles and other assets	530	510
Total assets	$2,340	$2,210
Current liabilities	$ 900	$ 790
Long-term liabilities	410	380
Stockholders' equity—common	1,030	1,040
Total liabilities and stockholders' equity	$2,340	$2,210

MURAWSKI COMPANY
Income Statements
For the Years Ended December 31

	2017	2016
Sales revenue	$3,800	$3,460
Costs and expenses		
Cost of goods sold	955	890
Selling & administrative expenses	2,400	2,330
Interest expense	25	20
Total costs and expenses	3,380	3,240
Income before income taxes	420	220
Income tax expense	126	66
Net income	$ 294	$ 154

Compute the following ratios for 2017 and 2016.

(a) Current ratio.
(b) Inventory turnover. (Inventory on 12/31/15 was $340.)
(c) Profit margin.
(d) Return on assets. (Assets on 12/31/15 were $1,900.)
(e) Return on common stockholders' equity. (Stockholders' equity on 12/31/15 was $900.)
(f) Debt to assets ratio.
(g) Times interest earned.

Prepare statement of comprehensive income including unusual items.
(LO 3)

DO IT! 18-3 In its proposed 2017 income statement, Hrabik Corporation reports income before income taxes $500,000, income taxes $100,000 (not including unusual items), loss on operation of discontinued music division $60,000, gain on disposal of discontinued music division $40,000, and unrealized loss on available-for-sale securities $150,000. The income tax rate is 20%. Prepare a correct statement of comprehensive income, beginning with income before income taxes.

EXERCISES

Follow the rounding procedures used in the chapter.

Prepare horizontal analysis.
(LO 1)

E18-1 Financial information for Kurzen Inc. is presented below.

	December 31, 2017	December 31, 2016
Current assets	$125,000	$100,000
Plant assets (net)	396,000	330,000
Current liabilities	91,000	70,000
Long-term liabilities	133,000	95,000
Common stock, $1 par	161,000	115,000
Retained earnings	136,000	150,000

Instructions
Prepare a schedule showing a horizontal analysis for 2017 using 2016 as the base year.

Prepare vertical analysis.
(LO 1)

E18-2 Operating data for Navarro Corporation are presented below.

	2017	2016
Net sales	$750,000	$600,000
Cost of goods sold	465,000	390,000
Selling expenses	105,000	66,000
Administrative expenses	60,000	54,000
Income tax expense	36,000	27,000
Net income	84,000	63,000

Instructions
Prepare a schedule showing a vertical analysis for 2017 and 2016.

Prepare horizontal and vertical analyses.
(LO 1)

E18-3 The comparative condensed balance sheets of Gurley Corporation are presented on page 819.

GURLEY CORPORATION
Comparative Condensed Balance Sheets
December 31

	2017	2016
Assets		
Current assets	$ 74,000	$ 80,000
Property, plant, and equipment (net)	99,000	90,000
Intangibles	27,000	40,000
Total assets	$200,000	$210,000
Liabilities and stockholders' equity		
Current liabilities	$ 42,000	$ 48,000
Long-term liabilities	143,000	150,000
Stockholders' equity	15,000	12,000
Total liabilities and stockholders' equity	$200,000	$210,000

Instructions

(a) Prepare a horizontal analysis of the balance sheet data for Gurley Corporation using 2016 as a base.

(b) Prepare a vertical analysis of the balance sheet data for Gurley Corporation in columnar form for 2017.

E18-4 The comparative condensed income statements of Emley Corporation are shown below.

Prepare horizontal and vertical analyses.

(LO 1)

EMLEY CORPORATION
Comparative Condensed Income Statements
For the Years Ended December 31

	2017	2016
Net sales	$660,000	$600,000
Cost of goods sold	483,000	420,000
Gross profit	177,000	180,000
Operating expenses	125,000	120,000
Net income	$ 52,000	$ 60,000

Instructions

(a) Prepare a horizontal analysis of the income statement data for Emley Corporation using 2016 as a base. (Show the amounts of increase or decrease.)

(b) Prepare a vertical analysis of the income statement data for Emley Corporation in columnar form for both years.

E18-5 Suppose Nordstrom, Inc., which operates department stores in numerous states, has the following selected financial statement data for a recent year.

Compute liquidity ratios and compare results.

(LO 2)

NORDSTROM, INC.
Balance Sheet (partial)

(in millions)	End-of-Year	Beginning-of-Year
Cash and cash equivalents	$ 795	$ 72
Accounts receivable (net)	2,035	1,942
Inventory	898	900
Prepaid expenses	88	93
Other current assets	238	210
Total current assets	$4,054	$3,217
Total current liabilities	$2,014	$1,601

For the year, net sales were $8,258 and cost of goods sold was $5,328 (in millions).

Instructions

(a) Compute the four liquidity ratios at the end of the year.

(b) Using the data in the chapter, compare Nordstrom's liquidity with (1) that of Macy's, Inc., and (2) the industry averages for department stores.

Perform current and acid-test ratio analysis.

(LO 2)

E18-6 Keener Incorporated had the following transactions occur involving current assets and current liabilities during February 2017.

Feb.	3	Accounts receivable of $15,000 are collected.
	7	Equipment is purchased for $28,000 cash.
	11	Paid $3,000 for a 3-year insurance policy.
	14	Accounts payable of $12,000 are paid.
	18	Cash dividends of $5,000 are declared.

Additional information:

1. As of February 1, 2017, current assets were $110,000, and current liabilities were $50,000.
2. As of February 1, 2017, current assets included $15,000 of inventory and $2,000 of prepaid expenses.

Instructions

(a) Compute the current ratio as of the beginning of the month and after each transaction.

(b) Compute the acid-test ratio as of the beginning of the month and after each transaction.

Compute selected ratios.

(LO 2)

E18-7 Frizell Company has the following comparative balance sheet data.

FRIZELL COMPANY
Balance Sheets
December 31

	2017	**2016**
Cash	$ 15,000	$ 30,000
Accounts receivable (net)	70,000	60,000
Inventory	60,000	50,000
Plant assets (net)	200,000	180,000
	$345,000	$320,000
Accounts payable	$ 50,000	$ 60,000
Mortgage payable (6%)	100,000	100,000
Common stock, $10 par	140,000	120,000
Retained earnings	55,000	40,000
	$345,000	$320,000

Additional information for 2017:

1. Net income was $25,000.
2. Sales on account were $410,000. Sales returns and allowances were $20,000.
3. Cost of goods sold was $198,000.

Instructions

Compute the following ratios at December 31, 2017.

(a) Current ratio.
(b) Acid-test ratio.
(c) Accounts receivable turnover.
(d) Inventory turnover.

Compute selected ratios.

(LO 2)

E18-8 Selected comparative statement data for Queen Products Company are presented below. All balance sheet data are as of December 31.

	2017	**2016**
Net sales	$750,000	$720,000
Cost of goods sold	480,000	440,000
Interest expense	7,000	5,000
Net income	45,000	42,000
Accounts receivable	120,000	100,000
Inventory	85,000	75,000
Total assets	580,000	500,000
Total common stockholders' equity	430,000	325,000

Instructions

Compute the following ratios for 2017.

(a) Profit margin.
(b) Asset turnover.
(c) Return on assets.
(d) Return on common stockholders' equity.

E18-9 The income statement for Sutherland, Inc., appears below.

Compute selected ratios.

(LO 2)

SUTHERLAND, INC.
Income Statement
For the Year Ended December 31, 2017

Net sales	$400,000
Cost of goods sold	230,000
Gross profit	170,000
Expenses (including $16,000 interest and $24,000 income taxes)	105,000
Net income	$ 65,000

Additional information:

1. The weighted-average common shares outstanding in 2017 were 30,000 shares.
2. The market price of Sutherland, Inc. stock was $13 in 2017.
3. Cash dividends of $26,000 were paid, $5,000 of which were to preferred stockholders.

Instructions

Compute the following ratios for 2017.

(a) Earnings per share.
(b) Price-earnings ratio.
(c) Payout ratio.
(d) Times interest earned.

E18-10 Lingenfelter Corporation experienced a fire on December 31, 2017, in which its financial records were partially destroyed. It has been able to salvage some of the records and has ascertained the following balances.

Compute amounts from ratios.

(LO 2)

	December 31, 2017	December 31, 2016
Cash	$ 30,000	$ 10,000
Accounts receivable (net)	72,500	126,000
Inventory	200,000	180,000
Accounts payable	50,000	90,000
Notes payable	30,000	60,000
Common stock, $100 par	400,000	400,000
Retained earnings	113,500	101,000

Additional information:

1. The inventory turnover is 4.5 times.
2. The return on common stockholders' equity is 16%. The company had no additional paid-in capital.
3. The accounts receivable turnover is 8.8 times.
4. The return on assets is 12.5%.
5. Total assets at December 31, 2016, were $655,000.

Instructions

Compute the following for Lingenfelter Corporation.

(a) Cost of goods sold for 2017.
(b) Net sales (credit) for 2017.
(c) Net income for 2017.
(d) Total assets at December 31, 2017.

E18-11 Wiemers Corporation's comparative balance sheets are presented on the next page.

Compute ratios.

(LO 2)

WIEMERS CORPORATION
Balance Sheets
December 31

	2017	2016
Cash	$ 4,300	$ 3,700
Accounts receivable (net)	21,200	23,400
Inventory	10,000	7,000
Land	20,000	26,000
Buildings	70,000	70,000
Accumulated depreciation—buildings	(15,000)	(10,000)
Total	$110,500	$120,100
Accounts payable	$ 12,370	$ 31,100
Common stock	75,000	69,000
Retained earnings	23,130	20,000
Total	$110,500	$120,100

Wiemers's 2017 income statement included net sales of $100,000, cost of goods sold of $60,000, and net income of $15,000.

Instructions

Compute the following ratios for 2017.

(a) Current ratio.
(b) Acid-test ratio.
(c) Accounts receivable turnover.
(d) Inventory turnover.
(e) Profit margin.
(f) Asset turnover.
(g) Return on assets.
(h) Return on common stockholders' equity.
(i) Debt to assets ratio.

Prepare a correct statement of comprehensive income.
(LO 3)

E18-12 For its fiscal year ending October 31, 2017, Haas Corporation reports the following partial data shown below.

Income before income taxes	$540,000
Income tax expense (20% × $420,000)	84,000
Income from continuing operations	456,000
Loss on discontinued operations	120,000
Net income	$336,000

The loss on discontinued operations was comprised of a $50,000 loss from operations and a $70,000 loss from disposal. The income tax rate is 20% on all items.

Instructions

(a) Prepare a correct statement of comprehensive income beginning with income before income taxes.
(b) Explain in memo form why the income statement data are misleading.

Prepare statement of comprehensive income.
(LO 3)

E18-13 Trayer Corporation has income from continuing operations of $290,000 for the year ended December 31, 2017. It also has the following items (before considering income taxes).

1. An unrealized loss of $80,000 on available-for-sale securities.
2. A gain of $30,000 on the discontinuance of a division (comprised of a $10,000 loss from operations and a $40,000 gain on disposal).
3. A correction of an error in last year's financial statements that resulted in a $20,000 understatement of 2016 net income.

Assume all items are subject to income taxes at a 20% tax rate.

Instructions

Prepare a statement of comprehensive income, beginning with income from continuing operations.

EXERCISES: SET B AND CHALLENGE EXERCISES

Visit the book's companion website, at **www.wiley.com/college/weygandt**, and choose the Student Companion site to access Exercises: Set B and Challenge Exercises.

PROBLEMS

Follow the rounding procedures used in the chapter.

Prepare vertical analysis and comment on profitability.

(LO 1, 2)

P18-1 Comparative statement data for Farris Company and Ratzlaff Company, two competitors, appear below. All balance sheet data are as of December 31, 2017, and December 31, 2016.

	Farris Company		Ratzlaff Company	
	2017	**2016**	**2017**	**2016**
Net sales	$1,549,035		$339,038	
Cost of goods sold	1,080,490		241,000	
Operating expenses	302,275		79,000	
Interest expense	8,980		2,252	
Income tax expense	54,500		6,650	
Current assets	325,975	$312,410	83,336	$ 79,467
Plant assets (net)	521,310	500,000	139,728	125,812
Current liabilities	65,325	75,815	35,348	30,281
Long-term liabilities	108,500	90,000	29,620	25,000
Common stock, $10 par	500,000	500,000	120,000	120,000
Retained earnings	173,460	146,595	38,096	29,998

Instructions

(a) Prepare a vertical analysis of the 2017 income statement data for Farris Company and Ratzlaff Company in columnar form.

(b) Comment on the relative profitability of the companies by computing the return on assets and the return on common stockholders' equity for both companies.

Compute ratios from balance sheet and income statement.

(LO 2)

P18-2 The comparative statements of Painter Tool Company are presented below and on page 824.

PAINTER TOOL COMPANY
Income Statement
For the Years Ended December 31

	2017	**2016**
Net sales	$1,818,500	$1,750,500
Cost of goods sold	1,011,500	996,000
Gross profit	807,000	754,500
Selling and administrative expenses	499,000	479,000
Income from operations	308,000	275,500
Other expenses and losses		
Interest expense	18,000	14,000
Income before income taxes	290,000	261,500
Income tax expense	87,000	77,000
Net income	$ 203,000	$ 184,500

PAINTER TOOL COMPANY
Balance Sheets
December 31

Assets	**2017**	**2016**
Current assets		
Cash	$ 60,100	$ 64,200
Short-term investments	69,000	50,000
Accounts receivable (net)	107,800	102,800
Inventory	133,000	115,500
Total current assets	369,900	332,500
Plant assets (net)	600,300	520,300
Total assets	$970,200	$852,800
Liabilities and Stockholders' Equity		
Current liabilities		
Accounts payable	$160,000	$145,400
Income taxes payable	43,500	42,000
Total current liabilities	203,500	187,400
Bonds payable	200,000	200,000
Total liabilities	403,500	387,400
Stockholders' equity		
Common stock ($5 par)	280,000	300,000
Retained earnings	286,700	165,400
Total stockholders' equity	566,700	465,400
Total liabilities and stockholders' equity	$970,200	$852,800

All sales were on account.

Instructions

Compute the following ratios for 2017. (Weighted-average common shares in 2017 were 57,000.)

(a) Earnings per share.
(b) Return on common stockholders' equity.
(c) Return on assets.
(d) Current ratio.
(e) Acid-test ratio.
(f) Accounts receivable turnover.
(g) Inventory turnover.
(h) Times interest earned.
(i) Asset turnover.
(j) Debt to assets ratio.

Perform ratio analysis, and evaluate financial position and operating results.

(LO 2)

P18-3 Condensed balance sheet and income statement data for Landwehr Corporation appear below and on page 825.

LANDWEHR CORPORATION
Balance Sheets
December 31

	2018	**2017**	**2016**
Cash	$ 25,000	$ 20,000	$ 18,000
Accounts receivable (net)	50,000	45,000	48,000
Other current assets	90,000	95,000	64,000
Investments	75,000	70,000	45,000
Plant and equipment (net)	400,000	370,000	358,000
	$640,000	$600,000	$533,000
Current liabilities	$ 75,000	$ 80,000	$ 70,000
Long-term debt	80,000	85,000	50,000
Common stock, $10 par	340,000	310,000	300,000
Retained earnings	145,000	125,000	113,000
	$640,000	$600,000	$533,000

LANDWEHR CORPORATION
Income Statement
For the Years Ended December 31

	2018	2017
Sales revenue	$740,000	$700,000
Less: Sales returns and allowances	40,000	50,000
Net sales	700,000	650,000
Cost of goods sold	420,000	400,000
Gross profit	280,000	250,000
Operating expenses (including income taxes)	235,000	220,000
Net income	$ 45,000	$ 30,000

Additional information:

1. The market price of Landwehr's common stock was $4.00, $5.00, and $8.00 for 2016, 2017, and 2018, respectively.
2. All dividends were paid in cash.

Instructions

(a) Compute the following ratios for 2017 and 2018.
  (1) Profit margin.
  (2) Asset turnover.
  (3) Earnings per share. (Weighted-average common shares in 2018 were 32,000 and in 2017 were 31,000.)
  (4) Price-earnings ratio.
  (5) Payout ratio.
  (6) Debt to assets ratio.

(b) Based on the ratios calculated, discuss briefly the improvement or lack thereof in financial position and operating results from 2017 to 2018 of Landwehr Corporation.

P18-4 Financial information for Messersmith Company is presented below and on page 826.

Compute ratios, and comment on overall liquidity and profitability.

(LO 2)

MESSERSMITH COMPANY
Balance Sheets
December 31

Assets	2017	2016
Cash	$ 70,000	$ 65,000
Short-term investments	52,000	40,000
Accounts receivable (net)	98,000	80,000
Inventory	125,000	135,000
Prepaid expenses	29,000	23,000
Land	130,000	130,000
Building and equipment (net)	180,000	175,000
	$684,000	$648,000

Liabilities and Stockholders' Equity		
Notes payable	$100,000	$100,000
Accounts payable	48,000	42,000
Accrued liabilities	50,000	40,000
Bonds payable, due 2020	150,000	150,000
Common stock, $10 par	200,000	200,000
Retained earnings	136,000	116,000
	$684,000	$648,000

MESSERSMITH COMPANY
Income Statement
For the Years Ended December 31

	2017	2016
Net sales	$850,000	$790,000
Cost of goods sold	620,000	575,000
Gross profit	230,000	215,000
Operating expenses	187,000	173,000
Net income	$ 43,000	$ 42,000

Additional information:

1. Inventory at the beginning of 2016 was $118,000.
2. Total assets at the beginning of 2016 were $630,000.
3. No common stock transactions occurred during 2016 or 2017.
4. All sales were on account. Accounts receivable, net at the beginning of 2016, were $88,000.
5. Notes payable are classified as current liabilities.

Instructions

(a) Indicate, by using ratios, the change in liquidity and profitability of Messersmith Company from 2016 to 2017. (*Note:* Not all profitability ratios can be computed.)

(b) Given below are three independent situations and a ratio that may be affected. For each situation, compute the affected ratio (1) as of December 31, 2017, and (2) as of December 31, 2018, after giving effect to the situation. Net income for 2018 was $50,000. Total assets on December 31, 2018, were $700,000.

Situation	Ratio
(1) 18,000 shares of common stock were sold at par on July 1, 2018.	Return on common stockholders' equity
(2) All of the notes payable were paid in 2018. The only change in liabilities was that the notes payable were paid.	Debt to assets ratio
(3) Market price of common stock was $9 on December 31, 2017, and $12.80 on December 31, 2018.	Price-earnings ratio

Compute selected ratios, and compare liquidity, profitability, and solvency for two companies.

(LO 2)

P18-5 Selected financial data of Target Corporation and Wal-Mart Stores, Inc. for a recent year are presented here (in millions).

	Target Corporation	Wal-Mart Stores, Inc.
	Income Statement Data for Year	
Net sales	$61,471	$374,526
Cost of goods sold	41,895	286,515
Selling and administrative expenses	16,200	70,847
Interest expense	647	1,798
Other income (expense)	1,896	4,273
Income tax expense	1,776	6,908
Net income	$ 2,849	$ 12,731
	Balance Sheet Data (End of Year)	
Current assets	$18,906	$ 47,585
Noncurrent assets	25,654	115,929
Total assets	$44,560	$163,514
Current liabilities	$11,782	$ 58,454
Long-term debt	17,471	40,452
Total stockholders' equity	15,307	64,608
Total liabilities and stockholders' equity	$44,560	$163,514

	Target Corporation	Wal-Mart Stores, Inc.
	Beginning-of-Year Balances	
Total assets	$37,349	$151,587
Total stockholders' equity	15,633	61,573
Current liabilities	11,117	52,148
Total liabilities	21,716	90,014
	Other Data	
Average net accounts receivable	$ 7,124	$ 3,247
Average inventory	6,517	34,433
Net cash provided by operating activities	4,125	20,354

Instructions

(a) For each company, compute the following ratios.

(1) Current ratio.
(2) Accounts receivable turnover.
(3) Average collection period.
(4) Inventory turnover.
(5) Days in inventory.
(6) Profit margin.
(7) Asset turnover.
(8) Return on assets.
(9) Return on common stockholders' equity.
(10) Debt to assets ratio.
(11) Times interest earned.

(b) Compare the liquidity, profitability, and solvency of the two companies.

P18-6 The comparative statements of Corbin Company are presented below and on page 828.

Compute numerous ratios.
(LO 2)

CORBIN COMPANY
Income Statement
For the Years Ended December 31

	2017	2016
Net sales (all on account)	$595,000	$520,000
Expenses		
Cost of goods sold	415,000	354,000
Selling and administrative	120,800	114,800
Interest expense	7,800	6,000
Income tax expense	15,000	14,000
Total expenses	558,600	488,800
Net income	$ 36,400	$ 31,200

CORBIN COMPANY
Balance Sheets
December 31

Assets	2017	2016
Current assets		
Cash	$ 21,000	$ 18,000
Short-term investments	18,000	15,000
Accounts receivable (net)	91,000	74,000
Inventory	85,000	70,000
Total current assets	215,000	177,000
Plant assets (net)	423,000	383,000
Total assets	$638,000	$560,000

Liabilities and Stockholders' Equity	**2017**	**2016**
Current liabilities		
Accounts payable	$122,000	$110,000
Income taxes payable	23,000	20,000
Total current liabilities	145,000	130,000
Long-term liabilities		
Bonds payable	120,000	80,000
Total liabilities	265,000	210,000
Stockholders' equity		
Common stock ($5 par)	150,000	150,000
Retained earnings	223,000	200,000
Total stockholders' equity	373,000	350,000
Total liabilities and stockholders' equity	$638,000	$560,000

Additional data:

The common stock recently sold at $19.50 per share.

Instructions

Compute the following ratios for 2017.

(a) Current ratio.
(b) Acid-test ratio.
(c) Accounts receivable turnover.
(d) Inventory turnover.
(e) Profit margin.
(f) Asset turnover.
(g) Return on assets.
(h) Return on common stockholders' equity.
(i) Earnings per share.
(j) Price-earnings ratio.
(k) Payout ratio.
(l) Debt to assets ratio.
(m) Times interest earned.

Compute missing information given a set of ratios.

(LO 2)

P18-7 An incomplete income statement and an incomplete comparative balance sheet of Deines Corporation are presented below and on page 829.

DEINES CORPORATION
Income Statement
For the Year Ended December 31, 2017

Net sales	$11,000,000
Cost of goods sold	?
Gross profit	?
Operating expenses	1,665,000
Income from operations	?
Other expenses and losses	
Interest expense	?
Income before income taxes	?
Income tax expense	560,000
Net income	$?

DEINES CORPORATION
Balance Sheets
December 31

Assets	**2017**	**2016**
Current assets		
Cash	$ 450,000	$ 375,000
Accounts receivable (net)	?	950,000
Inventory	?	1,720,000
Total current assets	?	3,045,000
Plant assets (net)	4,620,000	3,955,000
Total assets	$?	$7,000,000

Liabilities and Stockholders' Equity	2017	2016
Current liabilities	$?	$ 825,000
Long-term notes payable	?	2,800,000
Total liabilities	?	3,625,000
Common stock, $1 par	3,000,000	3,000,000
Retained earnings	400,000	375,000
Total stockholders' equity	3,400,000	3,375,000
Total liabilities and stockholders' equity	$?	$7,000,000

Additional information:

1. The accounts receivable turnover for 2017 is 10 times.
2. All sales are on account.
3. The profit margin for 2017 is 14.5%.
4. Return on assets is 22% for 2017.
5. The current ratio on December 31, 2017, is 3.0.
6. The inventory turnover for 2017 is 4.8 times.

Instructions

Compute the missing information given the ratios above. Show computations. (*Note:* Start with one ratio and derive as much information as possible from it before trying another ratio. List all missing amounts under the ratio used to find the information.)

Prepare a statement of comprehensive income.

(LO 3)

P18-8 Terwilliger Corporation owns a number of cruise ships and a chain of hotels. The hotels, which have not been profitable, were discontinued on September 1, 2017. The 2017 operating results for the company were as follows.

Operating revenues	$12,850,000
Operating expenses	8,700,000
Operating income	$ 4,150,000

Analysis discloses that these data include the operating results of the hotel chain, which were operating revenues $1,500,000 and operating expenses $2,400,000. The hotels were sold at a gain of $200,000 before taxes. This gain is not included in the operating results. During the year, Terwilliger had an unrealized loss on its available-for-sale securities of $600,000 before taxes, which is not included in the operating results. In 2017, the company had other revenues and gains of $100,000, which are not included in the operating results. The corporation is in the 30% income tax bracket.

Instructions

Prepare a statement of comprehensive income.

Prepare a statement of comprehensive income.

(LO 3)

P18-9 The ledger of Jaime Corporation at December 31, 2017, contains the following summary data.

Net sales	$1,700,000	Cost of goods sold	$1,100,000
Selling expenses	120,000	Administrative expenses	150,000
Other revenues and gains	20,000	Other expenses and losses	28,000

Your analysis reveals the following additional information that is not included in the above data.

1. The entire Puzzles Division was discontinued on August 31. The income from operation for this division before income taxes was $20,000. The Puzzles Division was sold at a loss of $90,000 before income taxes.
2. The company had an unrealized gain on available-for-sale securities of $120,000 before income taxes for the year.
3. The income tax rate on all items is 25%.

Instructions

Prepare a statement of comprehensive income for the year ended December 31, 2017.

PROBLEMS: SET B

Visit the book's companion website, at **www.wiley.com/college/weygandt**, and choose the Student Companion site to access Problems: Set B.

CONTINUING PROBLEM

© leungchopan/ Shutterstock

COOKIE CREATIONS: AN ENTREPRENEURIAL JOURNEY

(*Note:* This is a continuation of the Cookie Creations problem from Chapters 1 through 17.)

CC18 Natalie and Curtis have the balance sheet and income statement for the first year of operations for Cookie & Coffee Creations Inc. They have been told that they can use these financial statements to prepare horizontal and vertical analyses, and to calculate financial ratios, to determine how their business is doing and to make some decisions they have been considering.

Go to the book's companion website, **www.wiley.com/college/weygandt**, *to see the completion of this problem.*

BROADENING YOUR PERSPECTIVE

FINANCIAL REPORTING AND ANALYSIS

Financial Reporting Problem: Apple Inc.

BYP18-1 Your parents are considering investing in Apple Inc. common stock. They ask you, as an accounting expert, to make an analysis of the company for them. Apple's financial statements are presented in Appendix A. Instructions for accessing and using the company's complete annual report, including the notes to the financial statements, are also provided in Appendix A.

Instructions

(Follow the approach in the chapter for rounding numbers.)

(a) Make a 3-year trend analysis, using 2011 as the base year, of (1) net sales and (2) net income. Comment on the significance of the trend results.

(b) Compute for 2013 and 2012 the (1) profit margin, (2) asset turnover, (3) return on assets, and (4) return on common stockholders' equity. How would you evaluate Apple's profitability? Total assets at September 24, 2011, were \$116,371 and total stockholders' equity at September 24, 2011, was \$76,615.

(c) Compute for 2013 and 2012 the (1) debt to assets ratio and (2) times interest earned. How would you evaluate Apple's long-term solvency?

(d) What information outside the annual report may also be useful to your parents in making a decision about Apple?

Comparative Analysis Problem: PepsiCo, Inc. vs. The Coca-Cola Company

BYP18-2 PepsiCo's financial statements are presented in Appendix B. Financial statements of The Coca-Cola Company are presented in Appendix C. Instructions for accessing and using the complete annual reports of PepsiCo and Coca-Cola, including the notes to the financial statements, are also provided in Appendices B and C, respectively.

Instructions

(a) Based on the information contained in these financial statements, determine each of the following for each company.

(1) The percentage increase (decrease) in (i) net sales and (ii) net income from 2012 to 2013.

(2) The percentage increase in (i) total assets and (ii) total common stockholders' (shareholders') equity from 2012 to 2013.

(3) The basic earnings per share and price-earnings ratio for 2013. (For both PepsiCo and Coca-Cola, use the basic earnings per share.) Coca-Cola's common stock had a market price of \$41.31 at the end of fiscal-year 2013, and PepsiCo's common stock had a market price of \$82.71.

(b) What conclusions concerning the two companies can be drawn from these data?

Comparative Analysis Problem: Amazon.com, Inc. vs. Wal-Mart Stores, Inc.

BYP18-3 Amazon.com, Inc.'s financial statements are presented in Appendix D. Financial statements of Wal-Mart Stores, Inc. are presented in Appendix E. Instructions for accessing and using the complete annual reports of Amazon and Wal-Mart, including the notes to be financial statements, are also provided in Appendices D and E, respectively.

Instructions

(a) Based on the information contained in these financial statements, determine each of the following for each company.
   (1) The percentage increase (decrease) in (i) net sales and (ii) net income from 2012 to 2013.
   (2) The percentage increase in (i) total assets and (ii) total common stockholders' (shareholders') equity from 2012 to 2013.
   (3) The basic earnings per share and price-earnings ratio for 2013. (For both Amazon and Wal-Mart, use the basic earnings per share.) Amazon's common stock had a market price of $398.79 at the end of fiscal-year 2013, and Wal-Mart's common stock had a market price of $74.68.

(b) What conclusions concerning the two companies can be drawn from these data?

Decision-Making Across the Organization

BYP18-4 As the CPA for Gandara Manufacturing Inc., you have been asked to develop some key ratios from the comparative financial statements. This information is to be used to convince creditors that the company is solvent and will continue as a going concern. The data requested and the computations developed from the financial statements follow.

	2017	2016
Current ratio	3.1 times	2.1 times
Acid-test ratio	.8 times	1.4 times
Asset turnover	2.8 times	2.2 times
Net income	Up 32%	Down 8%
Earnings per share	$3.30	$2.50

Instructions

With the class divided into groups, complete the following.

Gandara Manufacturing Inc. asks you to prepare a list of brief comments stating how each of these items supports the solvency and going-concern potential of the business. The company wishes to use these comments to support its presentation of data to its creditors. You are to prepare the comments as requested, giving the implications and the limitations of each item separately. Then prepare a collective inference that may be drawn from the individual items about Gandara's solvency and going-concern potential.

Real-World Focus

BYP18-5 The Management Discussion and Analysis section of an annual report addresses corporate performance for the year and sometimes uses financial ratios to support its claims.

Address: **www.ibm.com/investor/tools/index.phtml**, or go to **www.wiley.com/college/weygandt**

Steps

1. Choose **How to read annual reports** (in the Guides section).
2. Choose **Anatomy**.

Instructions

Using the information from the above site, answer the following questions.

(a) What are the optional elements that are often included in an annual report?
(b) What are the elements of an annual report that are required by the SEC?
(c) Describe the contents of the Management Discussion.
(d) Describe the contents of the Auditors' Report.
(e) Describe the contents of the Selected Financial Data.

CRITICAL THINKING

Communication Activity

BYP18-6 Abby Landis is the CEO of Pletcher's Electronics. Landis is an expert engineer but a novice in accounting. She asks you to explain the bases for comparison in analyzing Pletcher's financial statements.

Instructions

Write a letter to Abby Landis that explains the bases for comparison.

Ethics Case

BYP18-7 Dave Schonhardt, president of Schonhardt Industries, wishes to issue a press release to bolster his company's image and maybe even its stock price, which has been gradually falling. As controller, you have been asked to provide a list of 20 financial ratios along with some other operating statistics relative to Schonhardt Industries' first quarter financials and operations.

Two days after you provide the ratios and data requested, Steven Verlin, the public relations director of Schonhardt, asks you to prove the accuracy of the financial and operating data contained in the press release written by the president and edited by Steven. In the press release, the president highlights the sales increase of 25% over last year's first quarter and the positive change in the current ratio from 1.5:1 last year to 3:1 this year. He also emphasizes that production was up 50% over the prior year's first quarter.

You note that the press release contains only positive or improved ratios and none of the negative or deteriorated ratios. For instance, no mention is made that the debt to assets ratio has increased from 35% to 55%, that inventories are up 89%, and that while the current ratio improved, the acid-test ratio fell from 1:1 to 0.5:1. Nor is there any mention that the reported profit for the quarter would have been a loss had not the estimated lives of Schonhardt's plant and machinery been increased by 30%. Steven emphasizes, "The prez wants this release by early this afternoon."

Instructions

(a) Who are the stakeholders in this situation?
(b) Is there anything unethical in president Schonhardt's actions?
(c) Should you as controller remain silent? Does Steven have any responsibility?

All About You

BYP18-8 In this chapter, you learned how to use many tools for performing a financial analysis of a company. When making personal investments, however, it is most likely that you won't be buying stocks and bonds in individual companies. Instead, when most people want to invest in stock, they buy mutual funds. By investing in a mutual fund, you reduce your risk because the fund diversifies by buying the stock of a variety of different companies, bonds, and other investments, depending on the stated goals of the fund.

Before you invest in a fund, you will need to decide what type of fund you want. For example, do you want a fund that has the potential of high growth (but also high risk), or are you looking for lower risk and a steady stream of income? Do you want a fund that invests only in U.S. companies, or do you want one that invests globally? Many resources are available to help you with these types of decisions.

Instructions

Go to **http://web.archive.org/web/20050210200843/http://www.cnb1.com/invallocmdl.htm** and complete the investment allocation questionnaire. Add up your total points to determine the type of investment fund that would be appropriate for you.

FASB Codification Activity

BYP18-9 If your school has a subscription to the FASB Codification, go to **http://aaahq.org/ascLogin.cfm** to log in and prepare responses to the following. Use the Master Glossary for determining the proper definitions.

(a) Discontinued operations.
(b) Comprehensive income.

A Look at IFRS

LEARNING OBJECTIVE 4 **Compare financial statement analysis and income statement presentation under GAAP and IFRS.**

The tools of financial statement analysis, covered in the first section of this chapter, are the same throughout the world. Techniques such as vertical and horizontal analysis, for example, are tools used by analysts regardless of whether GAAP- or IFRS-related financial statements are being evaluated. In addition, the ratios provided in the textbook are the same ones that are used internationally.

The latter part of this chapter relates to the income statement and irregular items. As in GAAP, the income statement is a required statement under IFRS. In addition, the content and presentation of an IFRS income statement is similar to the one used for GAAP.

Relevant Facts

Following are the key similarities between GAAP and IFRS as related to financial statement analysis and income statement presentation. There are no significant differences between the two standards.

- The tools of financial statement analysis covered in this chapter are universal and therefore no significant differences exist in the analysis methods used.
- The basic objectives of the income statement are the same under both GAAP and IFRS. A very important objective is to ensure that users of the income statement can evaluate the sustainable income of the company.
- The basic accounting for discontinued operations is the same under IFRS and GAAP.
- The accounting for changes in accounting principles and changes in accounting estimates are the same for both GAAP and IFRS.
- Both GAAP and IFRS follow the same approach in reporting comprehensive income.

Looking to the Future

The FASB and the IASB are working on a project that would rework the structure of financial statements. Recently, the IASB decided to require a statement of comprehensive income, similar to what was required under GAAP.

IFRS Practice

IFRS Self-Test Questions

1. The basic tools of financial analysis are the same under both GAAP and IFRS **except** that:
   (a) horizontal analysis cannot be done because the format of the statements is sometimes different.
   (b) analysis is different because vertical analysis cannot be done under IFRS.
   (c) the current ratio cannot be computed because current liabilities are often reported before current assets in IFRS statements of position.
   (d) None of the above.
2. Presentation of comprehensive income must be reported under IFRS in:
   (a) the statement of stockholders' equity.
   (b) the income statement ending with net income.
   (c) the notes to the financial statements.
   (d) a statement of comprehensive income.
3. In preparing its income statement for 2017, Parmalane assembles the following information.

Sales revenue	$500,000
Cost of goods sold	300,000
Operating expenses	40,000
Loss on discontinued operations	20,000

   Ignoring income taxes, what is Parmalane's income from continuing operations for 2017 under IFRS?
   (a) $260,000.
   (b) $250,000
   (c) $240,000.
   (d) $160,000.

International Financial Reporting Problem: Louis Vuitton

IFRS18-1 The financial statements of Louis Vuitton are presented in Appendix F. Instructions for accessing and using the company's complete annual report, including the notes to its financial statements, are also provided in Appendix F.

Instructions
Use the company's **2013 annual report** to answer the following questions.

(a) What was the company's profit margin for 2013? Has it increased or decreased from 2011?
(b) What was the company's operating profit for 2013?
(c) The company reported comprehensive income of €4,255 billion in 2013. What are the other comprehensive gains and losses recorded in 2013?

Answers to IFRS Self-Test Questions
1. d **2.** d **3.** d

Appendix A Specimen Financial Statements: Apple Inc.

Once each year, a corporation communicates to its stockholders and other interested parties by issuing a complete set of audited financial statements. The **annual report**, as this communication is called, summarizes the financial results of the company's operations for the year and its plans for the future. Many annual reports are attractive, multicolored, glossy public relations pieces, containing pictures of corporate officers and directors as well as photos and descriptions of new products and new buildings. Yet the basic function of every annual report is to report financial information, almost all of which is a product of the corporation's accounting system.

The content and organization of corporate annual reports have become fairly standardized. Excluding the public relations part of the report (pictures, products, etc.), the following are the traditional financial portions of the annual report:

- Financial Highlights
- Letter to the Stockholders
- Management's Discussion and Analysis
- Financial Statements
- Notes to the Financial Statements
- Management's Responsibility for Financial Reporting
- Management's Report on Internal Control over Financial Reporting
- Report of Independent Registered Public Accounting Firm
- Selected Financial Data

The official SEC filing of the annual report is called a **Form 10-K**, which often omits the public relations pieces found in most standard annual reports. On the following pages, we present Apple Inc.'s financial statements taken from the company's 2013 Form 10-K. To access Apple's Form 10-K, including notes to the financial statements, follow these steps:

1. Go to **http://investor.apple.com**.
2. Select the Financial Information tab.
3. Select the 10-K annual report dated September 28, 2013.
4. The Notes to Consolidated Financial Statements begin on page 50.

CONSOLIDATED STATEMENTS OF OPERATIONS

(In millions, except number of shares which are reflected in thousands and per share amounts)

	Years ended		
	September 28, 2013	September 29, 2012	September 24, 2011
Net sales	$ 170,910	$ 156,508	$ 108,249
Cost of sales	106,606	87,846	64,431
Gross margin	64,304	68,662	43,818
Operating expenses:			
Research and development	4,475	3,381	2,429
Selling, general and administrative	10,830	10,040	7,599
Total operating expenses	15,305	13,421	10,028
Operating income	48,999	55,241	33,790
Other income/(expense), net	1,156	522	415
Income before provision for income taxes	50,155	55,763	34,205
Provision for income taxes	13,118	14,030	8,283
Net income	$ 37,037	$ 41,733	$ 25,922
Earnings per share:			
Basic	$ 40.03	$ 44.64	$ 28.05
Diluted	$ 39.75	$ 44.15	$ 27.68
Shares used in computing earnings per share:			
Basic	925,331	934,818	924,258
Diluted	931,662	945,355	936,645
Cash dividends declared per common share	$ 11.40	$ 2.65	$ 0.00

See accompanying Notes to Consolidated Financial Statements.

CONSOLIDATED STATEMENTS OF COMPREHENSIVE INCOME

(In millions)

	Years ended		
	September 28, 2013	September 29, 2012	September 24, 2011
Net income	$37,037	$41,733	$25,922
Other comprehensive income/(loss):			
Change in foreign currency translation, net of tax effects of $35, $13 and $18, respectively	(112)	(15)	(12)
Change in unrecognized gains/losses on derivative instruments:			
Change in fair value of derivatives, net of tax benefit/(expense) of $(351), $73 and $(50), respectively	522	(131)	92
Adjustment for net losses/(gains) realized and included in net income, net of tax expense/(benefit) of $255, $220 and $(250), respectively	(458)	(399)	450
Total change in unrecognized gains/losses on derivative instruments, net of tax	64	(530)	542
Change in unrealized gains/losses on marketable securities:			
Change in fair value of marketable securities, net of tax benefit/(expense) of $458, $(421) and $17, respectively	(791)	715	29
Adjustment for net losses/(gains) realized and included in net income, net of tax expense/(benefit) of $82, $68 and $(40), respectively	(131)	(114)	(70)
Total change in unrealized gains/losses on marketable securities, net of tax	(922)	601	(41)
Total other comprehensive income/(loss)	(970)	56	489
Total comprehensive income	$36,067	$41,789	$26,411

See accompanying Notes to Consolidated Financial Statements.

CONSOLIDATED BALANCE SHEETS

(In millions, except number of shares which are reflected in thousands)

	September 28, 2013	September 29, 2012
ASSETS:		
Current assets:		
Cash and cash equivalents	$ 14,259	$ 10,746
Short-term marketable securities	26,287	18,383
Accounts receivable, less allowances of $99 and $98, respectively	13,102	10,930
Inventories	1,764	791
Deferred tax assets	3,453	2,583
Vendor non-trade receivables	7,539	7,762
Other current assets	6,882	6,458
Total current assets	73,286	57,653
Long-term marketable securities	106,215	92,122
Property, plant and equipment, net	16,597	15,452
Goodwill	1,577	1,135
Acquired intangible assets, net	4,179	4,224
Other assets	5,146	5,478
Total assets	$ 207,000	$ 176,064
LIABILITIES AND SHAREHOLDERS' EQUITY:		
Current liabilities:		
Accounts payable	$ 22,367	$ 21,175
Accrued expenses	13,856	11,414
Deferred revenue	7,435	5,953
Total current liabilities	43,658	38,542
Deferred revenue – non-current	2,625	2,648
Long-term debt	16,960	0
Other non-current liabilities	20,208	16,664
Total liabilities	83,451	57,854
Commitments and contingencies		
Shareholders' equity:		
Common stock, no par value; 1,800,000 shares authorized; 899,213 and 939,208 shares issued and outstanding, respectively	19,764	16,422
Retained earnings	104,256	101,289
Accumulated other comprehensive income/(loss)	(471)	499
Total shareholders' equity	123,549	118,210
Total liabilities and shareholders' equity	$ 207,000	$ 176,064

See accompanying Notes to Consolidated Financial Statements.

CONSOLIDATED STATEMENTS OF SHAREHOLDERS' EQUITY
(In millions, except number of shares which are reflected in thousands)

	Common Stock		Retained Earnings	Accumulated Other Comprehensive Income/(Loss)	Total Shareholders' Equity
	Shares	Amount			
Balances as of September 25, 2010	915,970	$10,668	$ 37,169	$ (46)	$ 47,791
Net income	0	0	25,922	0	25,922
Other comprehensive income/(loss)	0	0	0	489	489
Share-based compensation	0	1,168	0	0	1,168
Common stock issued under stock plans, net of shares withheld for employee taxes	13,307	561	(250)	0	311
Tax benefit from equity awards, including transfer pricing adjustments	0	934	0	0	934
Balances as of September 24, 2011	929,277	13,331	62,841	443	76,615
Net income	0	0	41,733	0	41,733
Other comprehensive income/(loss)	0	0	0	56	56
Dividends and dividend equivalent rights declared	0	0	(2,523)	0	(2,523)
Share-based compensation	0	1,740	0	0	1,740
Common stock issued under stock plans, net of shares withheld for employee taxes	9,931	200	(762)	0	(562)
Tax benefit from equity awards, including transfer pricing adjustments	0	1,151	0	0	1,151
Balances as of September 29, 2012	939,208	16,422	101,289	499	118,210
Net income	0	0	37,037	0	37,037
Other comprehensive income/(loss)	0	0	0	(970)	(970)
Dividends and dividend equivalent rights declared	0	0	(10,676)	0	(10,676)
Repurchase of common stock	(46,976)	0	(22,950)	0	(22,950)
Share-based compensation	0	2,253	0	0	2,253
Common stock issued under stock plans, net of shares withheld for employee taxes	6,981	(143)	(444)	0	(587)
Tax benefit from equity awards, including transfer pricing adjustments	0	1,232	0	0	1,232
Balances as of September 28, 2013	899,213	$19,764	$104,256	$ (471)	$123,549

See accompanying Notes to Consolidated Financial Statements.

CONSOLIDATED STATEMENTS OF CASH FLOWS
(In millions)

	Years ended September 28, 2013	September 29, 2012	September 24, 2011
Cash and cash equivalents, beginning of the year	$ 10,746	$ 9,815	$ 11,261
Operating activities:			
Net income	37,037	41,733	25,922
Adjustments to reconcile net income to cash generated by operating activities:			
Depreciation and amortization	6,757	3,277	1,814
Share-based compensation expense	2,253	1,740	1,168
Deferred income tax expense	1,141	4,405	2,868
Changes in operating assets and liabilities:			
Accounts receivable, net	(2,172)	(5,551)	143
Inventories	(973)	(15)	275
Vendor non-trade receivables	223	(1,414)	(1,934)
Other current and non-current assets	1,080	(3,162)	(1,391)
Accounts payable	2,340	4,467	2,515
Deferred revenue	1,459	2,824	1,654
Other current and non-current liabilities	4,521	2,552	4,495
Cash generated by operating activities	53,666	50,856	37,529
Investing activities:			
Purchases of marketable securities	(148,489)	(151,232)	(102,317)
Proceeds from maturities of marketable securities	20,317	13,035	20,437
Proceeds from sales of marketable securities	104,130	99,770	49,416
Payments made in connection with business acquisitions, net	(496)	(350)	(244)
Payments for acquisition of property, plant and equipment	(8,165)	(8,295)	(4,260)
Payments for acquisition of intangible assets	(911)	(1,107)	(3,192)
Other	(160)	(48)	(259)
Cash used in investing activities	(33,774)	(48,227)	(40,419)
Financing activities:			
Proceeds from issuance of common stock	530	665	831
Excess tax benefits from equity awards	701	1,351	1,133
Taxes paid related to net share settlement of equity awards	(1,082)	(1,226)	(520)
Dividends and dividend equivalent rights paid	(10,564)	(2,488)	0
Repurchase of common stock	(22,860)	0	0
Proceeds from issuance of long-term debt, net	16,896	0	0
Cash generated by/(used in) financing activities	(16,379)	(1,698)	1,444
Increase/(decrease) in cash and cash equivalents	3,513	931	(1,446)
Cash and cash equivalents, end of the year	$ 14,259	$ 10,746	$ 9,815
Supplemental cash flow disclosure:			
Cash paid for income taxes, net	$ 9,128	$ 7,682	$ 3,338

See accompanying Notes to Consolidated Financial Statements.

Appendix B Specimen Financial Statements: PepsiCo, Inc.

PepsiCo, Inc. is a world leader in convenient snacks, foods, and beverages. The following are PepsiCo's financial statements as presented in its 2013 annual report. To access PepsiCo's complete annual report, including notes to the financial statements, follow these steps:

1. Go to **www.pepsico.com**.
2. Select Annual Reports and Proxy Information under the Investors tab.
3. Select the 2013 Annual Report.
4. The Notes to Consolidated Financial Statements begin on page 73.

Consolidated Statement of Income
PepsiCo, Inc. and Subsidiaries
Fiscal years ended December 28, 2013, December 29, 2012 and December 31, 2011
(in millions except per share amounts)

	2013	2012	2011
Net Revenue	**$ 66,415**	$ 65,492	$ 66,504
Cost of sales	**31,243**	31,291	31,593
Selling, general and administrative expenses	**25,357**	24,970	25,145
Amortization of intangible assets	**110**	119	133
Operating Profit	**9,705**	9,112	9,633
Interest expense	**(911)**	(899)	(856)
Interest income and other	**97**	91	57
Income before income taxes	**8,891**	8,304	8,834
Provision for income taxes	**2,104**	2,090	2,372
Net income	**6,787**	6,214	6,462
Less: Net income attributable to noncontrolling interests	**47**	36	19
Net Income Attributable to PepsiCo	**$ 6,740**	$ 6,178	$ 6,443
Net Income Attributable to PepsiCo per Common Share			
Basic	**$ 4.37**	$ 3.96	$ 4.08
Diluted	**$ 4.32**	$ 3.92	$ 4.03
Weighted-average common shares outstanding			
Basic	**1,541**	1,557	1,576
Diluted	**1,560**	1,575	1,597
Cash dividends declared per common share	**$ 2.24**	$ 2.1275	$ 2.025

See accompanying notes to consolidated financial statements.

Consolidated Statement of Comprehensive Income

PepsiCo, Inc. and Subsidiaries
Fiscal years ended December 28, 2013, December 29, 2012 and December 31, 2011
(in millions)

	2013		
	Pre-tax amounts	**Tax amounts**	**After-tax amounts**
Net income			$ 6,787
Other Comprehensive Income			
Currency translation adjustment	$ (1,303)	$ —	(1,303)
Cash flow hedges:			
Reclassification of net losses to net income	45	(17)	28
Net derivative losses	(20)	10	(10)
Pension and retiree medical:			
Net prior service cost	(23)	8	(15)
Net gains	2,540	(895)	1,645
Unrealized gains on securities	57	(28)	29
Other	—	(16)	(16)
Total Other Comprehensive Income	$ 1,296	$ (938)	358
Comprehensive income			7,145
Comprehensive income attributable to noncontrolling interests			(45)
Comprehensive Income Attributable to PepsiCo			$ 7,100

	2012		
	Pre-tax amounts	Tax amounts	After-tax amounts
Net income			$ 6,214
Other Comprehensive Income			
Currency translation adjustment	$ 737	$ —	737
Cash flow hedges:			
Reclassification of net losses to net income	90	(32)	58
Net derivative losses	(50)	10	(40)
Pension and retiree medical:			
Net prior service cost	(32)	12	(20)
Net losses	(41)	(11)	(52)
Unrealized gains on securities	18	—	18
Other	—	36	36
Total Other Comprehensive Income	$ 722	$ 15	737
Comprehensive income			6,951
Comprehensive income attributable to noncontrolling interests			(31)
Comprehensive Income Attributable to PepsiCo			$ 6,920

	2011		
	Pre-tax amounts	Tax amounts	After-tax amounts
Net income			$ 6,462
Other Comprehensive Loss			
Currency translation adjustment	$ (1,464)	$ —	(1,464)
Cash flow hedges:			
Reclassification of net losses to net income	5	4	9
Net derivative losses	(126)	43	(83)
Pension and retiree medical:			
Net prior service cost	(18)	8	(10)
Net losses	(1,468)	501	(967)
Unrealized losses on securities	(27)	19	(8)
Other	(16)	5	(11)
Total Other Comprehensive Loss	$ (3,114)	$ 580	(2,534)
Comprehensive income			3,928
Comprehensive income attributable to noncontrolling interests			(84)
Comprehensive Income Attributable to PepsiCo			$ 3,844

See accompanying notes to consolidated financial statements.

Consolidated Statement of Cash Flows
PepsiCo, Inc. and Subsidiaries
Fiscal years ended December 28, 2013, December 29, 2012 and December 31, 2011
(in millions)

	2013	2012	2011
Operating Activities			
Net income	$ 6,787	$ 6,214	$ 6,462
Depreciation and amortization	2,663	2,689	2,737
Stock-based compensation expense	303	278	326
Merger and integration costs	10	16	329
Cash payments for merger and integration costs	(25)	(83)	(377)
Restructuring and impairment charges	163	279	383
Cash payments for restructuring charges	(133)	(343)	(31)
Restructuring and other charges related to the transaction with Tingyi	—	176	—
Cash payments for restructuring and other charges related to the transaction with Tingyi	(26)	(109)	—
Non-cash foreign exchange loss related to Venezuela devaluation	111	—	—
Excess tax benefits from share-based payment arrangements	(117)	(124)	(70)
Pension and retiree medical plan contributions	(262)	(1,865)	(349)
Pension and retiree medical plan expenses	663	796	571
Deferred income taxes and other tax charges and credits	(1,058)	321	495
Change in accounts and notes receivable	(88)	(250)	(666)
Change in inventories	4	144	(331)
Change in prepaid expenses and other current assets	(51)	89	(27)
Change in accounts payable and other current liabilities	1,007	548	520
Change in income taxes payable	86	(97)	(340)
Other, net	(349)	(200)	(688)
Net Cash Provided by Operating Activities	9,688	8,479	8,944
Investing Activities			
Capital spending	(2,795)	(2,714)	(3,339)
Sales of property, plant and equipment	109	95	84
Acquisition of WBD, net of cash and cash equivalents acquired	—	—	(2,428)
Investment in WBD	—	—	(164)
Cash payments related to the transaction with Tingyi	(3)	(306)	—
Other acquisitions and investments in noncontrolled affiliates	(109)	(121)	(601)
Divestitures	133	(32)	780
Short-term investments, by original maturity			
More than three months – maturities	—	—	21
Three months or less, net	61	61	45
Other investing, net	(21)	12	(16)
Net Cash Used for Investing Activities	(2,625)	(3,005)	(5,618)
Financing Activities			
Proceeds from issuances of long-term debt	$ 4,195	$ 5,999	$ 3,000
Payments of long-term debt	(3,894)	(2,449)	(1,596)
Debt repurchase	—	—	(771)
Short-term borrowings, by original maturity			
More than three months – proceeds	23	549	523
More than three months – payments	(492)	(248)	(559)
Three months or less, net	1,634	(1,762)	339
Cash dividends paid	(3,434)	(3,305)	(3,157)
Share repurchases – common	(3,001)	(3,219)	(2,489)
Share repurchases – preferred	(7)	(7)	(7)
Proceeds from exercises of stock options	1,123	1,122	945
Excess tax benefits from share-based payment arrangements	117	124	70
Acquisition of noncontrolling interests	(20)	(68)	(1,406)
Other financing	(33)	(42)	(27)
Net Cash Used for Financing Activities	(3,789)	(3,306)	(5,135)
Effect of exchange rate changes on cash and cash equivalents	(196)	62	(67)
Net Increase/(Decrease) in Cash and Cash Equivalents	3,078	2,230	(1,876)
Cash and Cash Equivalents, Beginning of Year	6,297	4,067	5,943
Cash and Cash Equivalents, End of Year	$ 9,375	$ 6,297	$ 4,067

See accompanying notes to consolidated financial statements.

Consolidated Balance Sheet
PepsiCo, Inc. and Subsidiaries
December 28, 2013 and December 29, 2012
(in millions except per share amounts)

	2013	2012
ASSETS		
Current Assets		
Cash and cash equivalents	$ 9,375	$ 6,297
Short-term investments	303	322
Accounts and notes receivable, net	6,954	7,041
Inventories	3,409	3,581
Prepaid expenses and other current assets	2,162	1,479
Total Current Assets	22,203	18,720
Property, Plant and Equipment, net	18,575	19,136
Amortizable Intangible Assets, net	1,638	1,781
Goodwill	16,613	16,971
Other nonamortizable intangible assets	14,401	14,744
Nonamortizable Intangible Assets	31,014	31,715
Investments in Noncontrolled Affiliates	1,841	1,633
Other Assets	2,207	1,653
Total Assets	$ 77,478	$ 74,638
LIABILITIES AND EQUITY		
Current Liabilities		
Short-term obligations	$ 5,306	$ 4,815
Accounts payable and other current liabilities	12,533	11,903
Income taxes payable	—	371
Total Current Liabilities	17,839	17,089
Long-Term Debt Obligations	24,333	23,544
Other Liabilities	4,931	6,543
Deferred Income Taxes	5,986	5,063
Total Liabilities	53,089	52,239
Commitments and contingencies		
Preferred Stock, no par value	41	41
Repurchased Preferred Stock	(171)	(164)
PepsiCo Common Shareholders' Equity		
Common stock, par value $1^2/_3$¢ per share (authorized 3,600 shares, issued, net of repurchased common stock at par value: 1,529 and 1,544 shares, respectively)	25	26
Capital in excess of par value	4,095	4,178
Retained earnings	46,420	43,158
Accumulated other comprehensive loss	(5,127)	(5,487)
Repurchased common stock, in excess of par value (337 and 322 shares, respectively)	(21,004)	(19,458)
Total PepsiCo Common Shareholders' Equity	24,409	22,417
Noncontrolling interests	110	105
Total Equity	24,389	22,399
Total Liabilities and Equity	$ 77,478	$ 74,638

See accompanying notes to consolidated financial statements.

Consolidated Statement of Equity

PepsiCo, Inc. and Subsidiaries
Fiscal years ended December 28, 2013, December 29, 2012 and December 31, 2011
(in millions)

	2013		2012		2011	
	Shares	**Amount**	Shares	Amount	Shares	Amount
Preferred Stock	**0.8**	**$ 41**	0.8	$ 41	0.8	$ 41
Repurchased Preferred Stock						
Balance, beginning of year	**(0.6)**	**(164)**	(0.6)	(157)	(0.6)	(150)
Redemptions	**—**	**(7)**	—	(7)	—	(7)
Balance, end of year	**(0.6)**	**(171)**	(0.6)	(164)	(0.6)	(157)
Common Stock						
Balance, beginning of year	**1,544**	**26**	1,565	26	1,582	26
Repurchased common stock	**(15)**	**(1)**	(21)	—	(17)	—
Balance, end of year	**1,529**	**25**	1,544	26	1,565	26
Capital in Excess of Par Value						
Balance, beginning of year		**4,178**		4,461		4,527
Stock-based compensation expense		**303**		278		326
Stock option exercises/RSUs and PEPUnits converted [(a)]		**(287)**		(431)		(361)
Withholding tax on RSUs converted		**(87)**		(70)		(56)
Other		**(12)**		(60)		25
Balance, end of year		**4,095**		4,178		4,461
Retained Earnings						
Balance, beginning of year		**43,158**		40,316		37,090
Net income attributable to PepsiCo		**6,740**		6,178		6,443
Cash dividends declared – common		**(3,451)**		(3,312)		(3,192)
Cash dividends declared – preferred		**(1)**		(1)		(1)
Cash dividends declared – RSUs		**(26)**		(23)		(24)
Balance, end of year		**46,420**		43,158		40,316
Accumulated Other Comprehensive Loss						
Balance, beginning of year		**(5,487)**		(6,229)		(3,630)
Currency translation adjustment		**(1,301)**		742		(1,529)
Cash flow hedges, net of tax:						
Reclassification of net losses to net income		**28**		58		9
Net derivative losses		**(10)**		(40)		(83)
Pension and retiree medical, net of tax:						
Reclassification of net losses to net income		**230**		421		133
Remeasurement of net liabilities and translation		**1,400**		(493)		(1,110)
Unrealized gains/(losses) on securities, net of tax		**29**		18		(8)
Other		**(16)**		36		(11)
Balance, end of year		**(5,127)**		(5,487)		(6,229)
Repurchased Common Stock						
Balance, beginning of year	**(322)**	**(19,458)**	(301)	(17,870)	(284)	(16,740)
Share repurchases	**(37)**	**(3,000)**	(47)	(3,219)	(39)	(2,489)
Stock option exercises	**20**	**1,301**	24	1,488	20	1,251
Other	**2**	**153**	2	143	2	108
Balance, end of year	**(337)**	**(21,004)**	(322)	(19,458)	(301)	(17,870)
Total PepsiCo Common Shareholders' Equity		**24,409**		22,417		20,704
Noncontrolling Interests						
Balance, beginning of year		**105**		311		312
Net income attributable to noncontrolling interests		**47**		36		19
Distributions to noncontrolling interests, net		**(34)**		(37)		(24)
Currency translation adjustment		**(2)**		(5)		65
Acquisitions and divestitures		**(6)**		(200)		(57)
Other, net		**—**		—		(4)
Balance, end of year		**110**		105		311
Total Equity		**$ 24,389**		$ 22,399		$ 20,899

(a) Includes total tax benefits of $45 million in 2013, $84 million in 2012 and $43 million in 2011.

See accompanying notes to consolidated financial statements.

Appendix C Specimen Financial Statements: The Coca-Cola Company

The Coca-Cola Company is a global leader in the beverage industry. It offers hundreds of brands, including soft drinks, fruit juices, sports drinks and other beverages in more than 200 countries. The following are Coca-Cola's financial statements as presented in its 2013 annual report. To access Coca-Cola's complete annual report, including notes to the financial statements, follow these steps:

1. Go to **www.coca-colacompany.com**.
2. Select the Investors link near the bottom of the page, and then select Financial Reports & Information.
3. Select the 2013 Annual Report on Form 10-K.
4. The Notes to Consolidated Financial Statements begin on page 79.

THE COCA-COLA COMPANY AND SUBSIDIARIES

CONSOLIDATED STATEMENTS OF INCOME

Year Ended December 31,	**2013**	2012	2011
(In millions except per share data)			
NET OPERATING REVENUES	**$ 46,854**	$ 48,017	$ 46,542
Cost of goods sold	**18,421**	19,053	18,215
GROSS PROFIT	**28,433**	28,964	28,327
Selling, general and administrative expenses	**17,310**	17,738	17,422
Other operating charges	**895**	447	732
OPERATING INCOME	**10,228**	10,779	10,173
Interest income	**534**	471	483
Interest expense	**463**	397	417
Equity income (loss) — net	**602**	819	690
Other income (loss) — net	**576**	137	529
INCOME BEFORE INCOME TAXES	**11,477**	11,809	11,458
Income taxes	**2,851**	2,723	2,812
CONSOLIDATED NET INCOME	**8,626**	9,086	8,646
Less: Net income attributable to noncontrolling interests	**42**	67	62
NET INCOME ATTRIBUTABLE TO SHAREOWNERS OF THE COCA-COLA COMPANY	**$ 8,584**	$ 9,019	$ 8,584
BASIC NET INCOME PER SHARE[1]	**$ 1.94**	$ 2.00	$ 1.88
DILUTED NET INCOME PER SHARE[1]	**$ 1.90**	$ 1.97	$ 1.85
AVERAGE SHARES OUTSTANDING	**4,434**	4,504	4,568
Effect of dilutive securities	**75**	80	78
AVERAGE SHARES OUTSTANDING ASSUMING DILUTION	**4,509**	4,584	4,646

[1] Calculated based on net income attributable to shareowners of The Coca-Cola Company.

Refer to Notes to Consolidated Financial Statements.

THE COCA-COLA COMPANY AND SUBSIDIARIES
CONSOLIDATED STATEMENTS OF COMPREHENSIVE INCOME

Year Ended December 31,	2013	2012	2011
(In millions)			
CONSOLIDATED NET INCOME	**$ 8,626**	$ 9,086	$ 8,646
Other comprehensive income:			
Net foreign currency translation adjustment	**(1,187)**	(182)	(692)
Net gain (loss) on derivatives	**151**	99	145
Net unrealized gain (loss) on available-for-sale securities	**(80)**	178	(7)
Net change in pension and other benefit liabilities	**1,066**	(668)	(763)
TOTAL COMPREHENSIVE INCOME	**8,576**	8,513	7,329
Less: Comprehensive income (loss) attributable to noncontrolling interests	**39**	105	10
TOTAL COMPREHENSIVE INCOME ATTRIBUTABLE TO SHAREOWNERS OF THE COCA-COLA COMPANY	**$ 8,537**	$ 8,408	$ 7,319

Refer to Notes to Consolidated Financial Statements.

THE COCA-COLA COMPANY AND SUBSIDIARIES
CONSOLIDATED BALANCE SHEETS

December 31,	2013	2012
(In millions except par value)		
ASSETS		
CURRENT ASSETS		
Cash and cash equivalents	**$ 10,414**	$ 8,442
Short-term investments	**6,707**	5,017
TOTAL CASH, CASH EQUIVALENTS AND SHORT-TERM INVESTMENTS	**17,121**	13,459
Marketable securities	**3,147**	3,092
Trade accounts receivable, less allowances of $61 and $53, respectively	**4,873**	4,759
Inventories	**3,277**	3,264
Prepaid expenses and other assets	**2,886**	2,781
Assets held for sale	**—**	2,973
TOTAL CURRENT ASSETS	**31,304**	30,328
EQUITY METHOD INVESTMENTS	**10,393**	9,216
OTHER INVESTMENTS, PRINCIPALLY BOTTLING COMPANIES	**1,119**	1,232
OTHER ASSETS	**4,661**	3,585
PROPERTY, PLANT AND EQUIPMENT — net	**14,967**	14,476
TRADEMARKS WITH INDEFINITE LIVES	**6,744**	6,527
BOTTLERS' FRANCHISE RIGHTS WITH INDEFINITE LIVES	**7,415**	7,405
GOODWILL	**12,312**	12,255
OTHER INTANGIBLE ASSETS	**1,140**	1,150
TOTAL ASSETS	**$ 90,055**	$ 86,174
LIABILITIES AND EQUITY		
CURRENT LIABILITIES		
Accounts payable and accrued expenses	**$ 9,577**	$ 8,680
Loans and notes payable	**16,901**	16,297
Current maturities of long-term debt	**1,024**	1,577
Accrued income taxes	**309**	471
Liabilities held for sale	**—**	796
TOTAL CURRENT LIABILITIES	**27,811**	27,821
LONG-TERM DEBT	**19,154**	14,736
OTHER LIABILITIES	**3,498**	5,468
DEFERRED INCOME TAXES	**6,152**	4,981
THE COCA-COLA COMPANY SHAREOWNERS' EQUITY		
Common stock, $0.25 par value; Authorized — 11,200 shares; Issued — 7,040 and 7,040 shares, respectively	**1,760**	1,760
Capital surplus	**12,276**	11,379
Reinvested earnings	**61,660**	58,045
Accumulated other comprehensive income (loss)	**(3,432)**	(3,385)
Treasury stock, at cost — 2,638 and 2,571 shares, respectively	**(39,091)**	(35,009)
EQUITY ATTRIBUTABLE TO SHAREOWNERS OF THE COCA-COLA COMPANY	**33,173**	32,790
EQUITY ATTRIBUTABLE TO NONCONTROLLING INTERESTS	**267**	378
TOTAL EQUITY	**33,440**	33,168
TOTAL LIABILITIES AND EQUITY	**$ 90,055**	$ 86,174

Refer to Notes to Consolidated Financial Statements.

THE COCA-COLA COMPANY AND SUBSIDIARIES
CONSOLIDATED STATEMENTS OF CASH FLOWS

Year Ended December 31,	2013	2012	2011
(In millions)			
OPERATING ACTIVITIES			
Consolidated net income	**$ 8,626**	$ 9,086	$ 8,646
Depreciation and amortization	**1,977**	1,982	1,954
Stock-based compensation expense	**227**	259	354
Deferred income taxes	**648**	632	1,035
Equity (income) loss — net of dividends	**(201)**	(426)	(269)
Foreign currency adjustments	**168**	(130)	7
Significant (gains) losses on sales of assets — net	**(670)**	(98)	(220)
Other operating charges	**465**	166	214
Other items	**234**	254	(354)
Net change in operating assets and liabilities	**(932)**	(1,080)	(1,893)
Net cash provided by operating activities	**10,542**	10,645	9,474
INVESTING ACTIVITIES			
Purchases of investments	**(14,782)**	(14,824)	(4,798)
Proceeds from disposals of investments	**12,791**	7,791	5,811
Acquisitions of businesses, equity method investments and nonmarketable securities	**(353)**	(1,486)	(971)
Proceeds from disposals of businesses, equity method investments and nonmarketable securities	**872**	20	398
Purchases of property, plant and equipment	**(2,550)**	(2,780)	(2,920)
Proceeds from disposals of property, plant and equipment	**111**	143	101
Other investing activities	**(303)**	(268)	(145)
Net cash provided by (used in) investing activities	**(4,214)**	(11,404)	(2,524)
FINANCING ACTIVITIES			
Issuances of debt	**43,425**	42,791	27,495
Payments of debt	**(38,714)**	(38,573)	(22,530)
Issuances of stock	**1,328**	1,489	1,569
Purchases of stock for treasury	**(4,832)**	(4,559)	(4,513)
Dividends	**(4,969)**	(4,595)	(4,300)
Other financing activities	**17**	100	45
Net cash provided by (used in) financing activities	**(3,745)**	(3,347)	(2,234)
EFFECT OF EXCHANGE RATE CHANGES ON CASH AND CASH EQUIVALENTS	**(611)**	(255)	(430)
CASH AND CASH EQUIVALENTS			
Net increase (decrease) during the year	**1,972**	(4,361)	4,286
Balance at beginning of year	**8,442**	12,803	8,517
Balance at end of year	**$ 10,414**	$ 8,442	$ 12,803

Refer to Notes to Consolidated Financial Statements.

THE COCA-COLA COMPANY AND SUBSIDIARIES
CONSOLIDATED STATEMENTS OF SHAREOWNERS' EQUITY

Year Ended December 31,	2013	2012	2011
(In millions except per share data)			
EQUITY ATTRIBUTABLE TO SHAREOWNERS OF THE COCA-COLA COMPANY			
NUMBER OF COMMON SHARES OUTSTANDING			
Balance at beginning of year	**4,469**	4,526	4,583
Purchases of treasury stock	**(121)**	(121)	(127)
Treasury stock issued to employees related to stock compensation plans	**54**	64	70
Balance at end of year	**4,402**	4,469	4,526
COMMON STOCK	**$ 1,760**	$ 1,760	$ 1,760
CAPITAL SURPLUS			
Balance at beginning of year	**11,379**	10,332	9,177
Stock issued to employees related to stock compensation plans	**569**	640	724
Tax benefit (charge) from stock compensation plans	**144**	144	79
Stock-based compensation	**227**	259	354
Other activities	**(43)**	4	(2)
Balance at end of year	**12,276**	11,379	10,332
REINVESTED EARNINGS			
Balance at beginning of year	**58,045**	53,621	49,337
Net income attributable to shareowners of The Coca-Cola Company	**8,584**	9,019	8,584
Dividends (per share — $1.12, $1.02 and $0.94 in 2013, 2012 and 2011, respectively)	**(4,969)**	(4,595)	(4,300)
Balance at end of year	**61,660**	58,045	53,621
ACCUMULATED OTHER COMPREHENSIVE INCOME (LOSS)			
Balance at beginning of year	**(3,385)**	(2,774)	(1,509)
Net other comprehensive income (loss)	**(47)**	(611)	(1,265)
Balance at end of year	**(3,432)**	(3,385)	(2,774)
TREASURY STOCK			
Balance at beginning of year	**(35,009)**	(31,304)	(27,762)
Stock issued to employees related to stock compensation plans	**745**	786	830
Purchases of treasury stock	**(4,827)**	(4,491)	(4,372)
Balance at end of year	**(39,091)**	(35,009)	(31,304)
TOTAL EQUITY ATTRIBUTABLE TO SHAREOWNERS OF THE COCA-COLA COMPANY	**$ 33,173**	$ 32,790	$ 31,635
EQUITY ATTRIBUTABLE TO NONCONTROLLING INTERESTS			
Balance at beginning of year	**$ 378**	$ 286	$ 314
Net income attributable to noncontrolling interests	**42**	67	62
Net foreign currency translation adjustment	**(3)**	38	(52)
Dividends paid to noncontrolling interests	**(58)**	(48)	(38)
Acquisition of interests held by noncontrolling owners	**(34)**	(15)	—
Contributions by noncontrolling interests	**6**	—	—
Business combinations	**25**	50	—
Deconsolidation of certain entities	**(89)**	—	—
TOTAL EQUITY ATTRIBUTABLE TO NONCONTROLLING INTERESTS	**$ 267**	$ 378	$ 286

Refer to Notes to Consolidated Financial Statements.

Appendix D Specimen Financial Statements: Amazon.com, Inc.

Amazon.com, Inc. is the world's largest online retailer. It also produces consumer electronics—notably the Kindle e-book reader and the Kindle Fire Tablet computer—and is a major provider of cloud computing services. The following are Amazon's financial statements as presented in the company's 2013 annual report. To access Amazon's complete annual report, including notes to the financial statements, follow these steps:

1. Go to **www.amazon.com**.
2. Select the Investor Relations link at the bottom of the page and then select the 2013 Annual Report under Annual Reports and Proxies.
3. The Notes to Consolidated Financial Statements begin on page 40.

AMAZON.COM, INC.

CONSOLIDATED STATEMENTS OF CASH FLOWS
(in millions)

	Year Ended December 31,		
	2013	2012	2011
CASH AND CASH EQUIVALENTS, BEGINNING OF PERIOD	$ 8,084	$ 5,269	$ 3,777
OPERATING ACTIVITIES:			
Net income (loss)	274	(39)	631
Adjustments to reconcile net income (loss) to net cash from operating activities:			
Depreciation of property and equipment, including internal-use software and website development, and other amortization	3,253	2,159	1,083
Stock-based compensation	1,134	833	557
Other operating expense (income), net	114	154	154
Losses (gains) on sales of marketable securities, net	1	(9)	(4)
Other expense (income), net	166	253	(56)
Deferred income taxes	(156)	(265)	136
Excess tax benefits from stock-based compensation	(78)	(429)	(62)
Changes in operating assets and liabilities:			
Inventories	(1,410)	(999)	(1,777)
Accounts receivable, net and other	(846)	(861)	(866)
Accounts payable	1,888	2,070	2,997
Accrued expenses and other	736	1,038	1,067
Additions to unearned revenue	2,691	1,796	1,064
Amortization of previously unearned revenue	(2,292)	(1,521)	(1,021)
Net cash provided by (used in) operating activities	5,475	4,180	3,903
INVESTING ACTIVITIES:			
Purchases of property and equipment, including internal-use software and website development	(3,444)	(3,785)	(1,811)
Acquisitions, net of cash acquired, and other	(312)	(745)	(705)
Sales and maturities of marketable securities and other investments	2,306	4,237	6,843
Purchases of marketable securities and other investments	(2,826)	(3,302)	(6,257)
Net cash provided by (used in) investing activities	(4,276)	(3,595)	(1,930)
FINANCING ACTIVITIES:			
Excess tax benefits from stock-based compensation	78	429	62
Common stock repurchased	—	(960)	(277)
Proceeds from long-term debt and other	394	3,378	177
Repayments of long-term debt, capital lease, and finance lease obligations	(1,011)	(588)	(444)
Net cash provided by (used in) financing activities	(539)	2,259	(482)
Foreign-currency effect on cash and cash equivalents	(86)	(29)	1
Net increase (decrease) in cash and cash equivalents	574	2,815	1,492
CASH AND CASH EQUIVALENTS, END OF PERIOD	$ 8,658	$ 8,084	$ 5,269
SUPPLEMENTAL CASH FLOW INFORMATION:			
Cash paid for interest on long-term debt	$ 97	$ 31	$ 14
Cash paid for income taxes (net of refunds)	169	112	33
Property and equipment acquired under capital leases	1,867	802	753
Property and equipment acquired under build-to-suit leases	877	29	259

See accompanying notes to consolidated financial statements.

AMAZON.COM, INC.
CONSOLIDATED STATEMENTS OF OPERATIONS
(in millions, except per share data)

	Year Ended December 31, 2013	2012	2011
Net product sales	$ 60,903	$ 51,733	$ 42,000
Net services sales	13,549	9,360	6,077
Total net sales	74,452	61,093	48,077
Operating expenses (1):			
Cost of sales	54,181	45,971	37,288
Fulfillment	8,585	6,419	4,576
Marketing	3,133	2,408	1,630
Technology and content	6,565	4,564	2,909
General and administrative	1,129	896	658
Other operating expense (income), net	114	159	154
Total operating expenses	73,707	60,417	47,215
Income from operations	745	676	862
Interest income	38	40	61
Interest expense	(141)	(92)	(65)
Other income (expense), net	(136)	(80)	76
Total non-operating income (expense)	(239)	(132)	72
Income before income taxes	506	544	934
Provision for income taxes	(161)	(428)	(291)
Equity-method investment activity, net of tax	(71)	(155)	(12)
Net income (loss)	$ 274	$ (39)	$ 631
Basic earnings per share	$ 0.60	$ (0.09)	$ 1.39
Diluted earnings per share	$ 0.59	$ (0.09)	$ 1.37
Weighted average shares used in computation of earnings per share:			
Basic	457	453	453
Diluted	465	453	461

(1) Includes stock-based compensation as follows:

	2013	2012	2011
Fulfillment	$ 294	$ 212	$ 133
Marketing	88	61	39
Technology and content	603	434	292
General and administrative	149	126	93

See accompanying notes to consolidated financial statements.

AMAZON.COM, INC.

CONSOLIDATED STATEMENTS OF COMPREHENSIVE INCOME
(in millions)

	Year Ended December 31,		
	2013	2012	2011
Net income (loss)	$ 274	$ (39)	$ 631
Other comprehensive income (loss):			
Foreign currency translation adjustments, net of tax of $(20), $(30), and $20	63	76	(123)
Net change in unrealized gains on available-for-sale securities:			
Unrealized gains (losses), net of tax of $3, $(3), and $1	(10)	8	(1)
Reclassification adjustment for losses (gains) included in "Other income (expense), net," net of tax of $(1), $3, and $1	1	(7)	(2)
Net unrealized gains (losses) on available-for-sale securities	(9)	1	(3)
Total other comprehensive income (loss)	54	77	(126)
Comprehensive income	$ 328	$ 38	$ 505

See accompanying notes to consolidated financial statements.

AMAZON.COM, INC.

CONSOLIDATED BALANCE SHEETS
(in millions, except per share data)

	December 31, 2013	December 31, 2012
ASSETS		
Current assets:		
Cash and cash equivalents	$ 8,658	$ 8,084
Marketable securities	3,789	3,364
Inventories	7,411	6,031
Accounts receivable, net and other	4,767	3,817
Total current assets	24,625	21,296
Property and equipment, net	10,949	7,060
Goodwill	2,655	2,552
Other assets	1,930	1,647
Total assets	$ 40,159	$ 32,555
LIABILITIES AND STOCKHOLDERS' EQUITY		
Current liabilities:		
Accounts payable	$ 15,133	$ 13,318
Accrued expenses and other	6,688	4,892
Unearned revenue	1,159	792
Total current liabilities	22,980	19,002
Long-term debt	3,191	3,084
Other long-term liabilities	4,242	2,277
Commitments and contingencies		
Stockholders' equity:		
Preferred stock, $0.01 par value:		
Authorized shares — 500		
Issued and outstanding shares — none	—	—
Common stock, $0.01 par value:		
Authorized shares — 5,000		
Issued shares — 483 and 478		
Outstanding shares — 459 and 454	5	5
Treasury stock, at cost	(1,837)	(1,837)
Additional paid-in capital	9,573	8,347
Accumulated other comprehensive loss	(185)	(239)
Retained earnings	2,190	1,916
Total stockholders' equity	9,746	8,192
Total liabilities and stockholders' equity	$ 40,159	$ 32,555

See accompanying notes to consolidated financial statements.

AMAZON.COM, INC.

CONSOLIDATED STATEMENTS OF STOCKHOLDERS' EQUITY
(in millions)

	Common Stock						
	Shares	Amount	Treasury Stock	Additional Paid-In Capital	Accumulated Other Comprehensive Income (Loss)	Retained Earnings	Total Stockholders' Equity
Balance as of January 1, 2011	451	$ 5	$ (600)	$ 6,325	$ (190)	$ 1,324	$ 6,864
Net income	—	—	—	—	—	631	631
Other comprehensive income (loss)	—	—	—	—	(126)	—	(126)
Exercise of common stock options	5	—	—	7	—	—	7
Repurchase of common stock	(1)	—	(277)	—	—	—	(277)
Excess tax benefits from stock-based compensation	—	—	—	62	—	—	62
Stock-based compensation and issuance of employee benefit plan stock	—	—	—	569	—	—	569
Issuance of common stock for acquisition activity	—	—	—	27	—	—	27
Balance as of December 31, 2011	455	5	(877)	6,990	(316)	1,955	7,757
Net income (loss)	—	—	—	—	—	(39)	(39)
Other comprehensive income	—	—	—	—	77	—	77
Exercise of common stock options	4	—	—	8	—	—	8
Repurchase of common stock	(5)	—	(960)	—	—	—	(960)
Excess tax benefits from stock-based compensation	—	—	—	429	—	—	429
Stock-based compensation and issuance of employee benefit plan stock	—	—	—	854	—	—	854
Issuance of common stock for acquisition activity	—	—	—	66	—	—	66
Balance as of December 31, 2012	454	5	(1,837)	8,347	(239)	1,916	8,192
Net income	—	—	—	—	—	274	274
Other comprehensive income	—	—	—	—	54	—	54
Exercise of common stock options	5	—	—	4	—	—	4
Repurchase of common stock	—	—	—	—	—	—	—
Excess tax benefits from stock-based compensation	—	—	—	73	—	—	73
Stock-based compensation and issuance of employee benefit plan stock	—	—	—	1,149	—	—	1,149
Balance as of December 31, 2013	459	$ 5	$ (1,837)	$ 9,573	$ (185)	$ 2,190	$ 9,746

See accompanying notes to consolidated financial statements.

Appendix E

Specimen Financial Statements: Wal-Mart Stores, Inc.

The following are **Wal-Mart Stores, Inc.**'s financial statements as presented in the company's 2014 annual report. To access Wal-Mart's complete annual report, including notes to the financial statements, follow these steps:

1. Go to **http://corporate.walmart.com**.
2. Select Annual Reports under the Investors tab.
3. Select the 2014 Annual Report (Wal-Mart's fiscal year ends January 31).
4. The Notes to Consolidated Financial Statements begin on page 40.

Consolidated Statements of Income

	Fiscal Years Ended January 31,		
(Amounts in millions, except per share data)	**2014**	2013	2012
Revenues:			
Net sales	**$473,076**	$465,604	$443,416
Membership and other income	**3,218**	3,047	3,093
Total revenues	**476,294**	468,651	446,509
Costs and expenses:			
Cost of sales	**358,069**	352,297	334,993
Operating, selling, general and administrative expenses	**91,353**	88,629	85,025
Operating income	**26,872**	27,725	26,491
Interest:			
Debt	**2,072**	1,977	2,034
Capital leases	**263**	272	286
Interest income	**(119)**	(186)	(161)
Interest, net	**2,216**	2,063	2,159
Income from continuing operations before income taxes	**24,656**	25,662	24,332
Provision for income taxes:			
Current	**8,619**	7,976	6,722
Deferred	**(514)**	(18)	1,202
Total provision for income taxes	**8,105**	7,958	7,924
Income from continuing operations	**16,551**	17,704	16,408
Income (loss) from discontinued operations, net of income taxes	**144**	52	(21)
Consolidated net income	**16,695**	17,756	16,387
Less consolidated net income attributable to noncontrolling interest	**(673)**	(757)	(688)
Consolidated net income attributable to Walmart	**$ 16,022**	$ 16,999	$ 15,699
Basic net income per common share:			
Basic income per common share from continuing operations attributable to Walmart	**$ 4.87**	$ 5.03	$ 4.55
Basic income (loss) per common share from discontinued operations attributable to Walmart	**0.03**	0.01	(0.01)
Basic net income per common share attributable to Walmart	**$ 4.90**	$ 5.04	$ 4.54
Diluted net income per common share:			
Diluted income per common share from continuing operations attributable to Walmart	**$ 4.85**	$ 5.01	$ 4.53
Diluted income (loss) per common share from discontinued operations attributable to Walmart	**0.03**	0.01	(0.01)
Diluted net income per common share attributable to Walmart	**$ 4.88**	$ 5.02	$ 4.52
Weighted-average common shares outstanding:			
Basic	**3,269**	3,374	3,460
Diluted	**3,283**	3,389	3,474
Dividends declared per common share	**$ 1.88**	$ 1.59	$ 1.46

See accompanying notes.

Consolidated Statements of Comprehensive Income

	Fiscal Years Ended January 31,		
(Amounts in millions)	**2014**	2013	2012
Consolidated net income	**$16,695**	$17,756	$16,387
Less consolidated net income attributable to nonredeemable noncontrolling interest	**(606)**	(684)	(627)
Less consolidated net income attributable to redeemable noncontrolling interest	**(67)**	(73)	(61)
Consolidated net income attributable to Walmart	**16,022**	16,999	15,699
Other comprehensive income (loss), net of income taxes			
Currency translation and other	**(3,146)**	1,042	(2,758)
Derivative instruments	**207**	136	(67)
Minimum pension liability	**153**	(166)	43
Other comprehensive income (loss), net of income taxes	**(2,786)**	1,012	(2,782)
Less other comprehensive income (loss) attributable to nonredeemable noncontrolling interest	**311**	(138)	660
Less other comprehensive income (loss) attributable to redeemable noncontrolling interest	**66**	(51)	66
Other comprehensive income (loss) attributable to Walmart	**(2,409)**	823	(2,056)
Comprehensive income, net of income taxes	**13,909**	18,768	13,605
Less comprehensive income (loss) attributable to nonredeemable noncontrolling interest	**(295)**	(822)	33
Less comprehensive income (loss) attributable to redeemable noncontrolling interest	**(1)**	(124)	5
Comprehensive income attributable to Walmart	**$13,613**	$17,822	$13,643

See accompanying notes.

Consolidated Balance Sheets

	As of January 31,	
(Amounts in millions)	**2014**	2013
ASSETS		
Current assets:		
Cash and cash equivalents	**$ 7,281**	$ 7,781
Receivables, net	**6,677**	6,768
Inventories	**44,858**	43,803
Prepaid expenses and other	**1,909**	1,551
Current assets of discontinued operations	**460**	37
Total current assets	**61,185**	59,940
Property and equipment:		
Property and equipment	**173,089**	165,825
Less accumulated depreciation	**(57,725)**	(51,896)
Property and equipment, net	**115,364**	113,929
Property under capital leases:		
Property under capital leases	**5,589**	5,899
Less accumulated amortization	**(3,046)**	(3,147)
Property under capital leases, net	**2,543**	2,752
Goodwill	**19,510**	20,497
Other assets and deferred charges	**6,149**	5,987
Total assets	**$204,751**	$203,105
LIABILITIES, REDEEMABLE NONCONTROLLING INTEREST AND EQUITY		
Current liabilities:		
Short-term borrowings	**$ 7,670**	$ 6,805
Accounts payable	**37,415**	38,080
Accrued liabilities	**18,793**	18,808
Accrued income taxes	**966**	2,211
Long-term debt due within one year	**4,103**	5,587
Obligations under capital leases due within one year	**309**	327
Current liabilities of discontinued operations	**89**	—
Total current liabilities	**69,345**	71,818
Long-term debt	**41,771**	38,394
Long-term obligations under capital leases	**2,788**	3,023
Deferred income taxes and other	**8,017**	7,613
Redeemable noncontrolling interest	**1,491**	519
Commitments and contingencies		
Equity:		
Common stock	**323**	332
Capital in excess of par value	**2,362**	3,620
Retained earnings	**76,566**	72,978
Accumulated other comprehensive income (loss)	**(2,996)**	(587)
Total Walmart shareholders' equity	**76,255**	76,343
Nonredeemable noncontrolling interest	**5,084**	5,395
Total equity	**81,339**	81,738
Total liabilities, redeemable noncontrolling interest and equity	**$204,751**	$203,105

See accompanying notes.

Consolidated Statements of Shareholders' Equity

(Amounts in millions)	Common Stock Shares	Common Stock Amount	Capital in Excess of Par Value	Retained Earnings	Accumulated Other Comprehensive Income (Loss)	Total Walmart Shareholders' Equity	Nonredeemable Noncontrolling Interest	Total Equity	Redeemable Noncontrolling Interest
Balances as of February 1, 2011	3,516	$352	$ 3,577	$63,967	$ 646	$68,542	$2,705	$71,247	$ 408
Consolidated net income	—	—	—	15,699	—	15,699	627	16,326	61
Other comprehensive loss, net of income taxes	—	—	—	—	(2,056)	(2,056)	(660)	(2,716)	(66)
Cash dividends declared ($1.46 per share)	—	—	—	(5,048)	—	(5,048)	—	(5,048)	—
Purchase of Company stock	(113)	(11)	(229)	(5,930)	—	(6,170)	—	(6,170)	—
Nonredeemable noncontrolling interest of acquired entity	—	—	—	—	—	—	1,988	1,988	—
Other	15	1	344	3	—	348	(214)	134	1
Balances as of January 31, 2012	3,418	342	3,692	68,691	(1,410)	71,315	4,446	75,761	404
Consolidated net income	—	—	—	16,999	—	16,999	684	17,683	73
Other comprehensive income, net of income taxes	—	—	—	—	823	823	138	961	51
Cash dividends declared ($1.59 per share)	—	—	—	(5,361)	—	(5,361)	—	(5,361)	—
Purchase of Company stock	(115)	(11)	(357)	(7,341)	—	(7,709)	—	(7,709)	—
Nonredeemable noncontrolling interest of acquired entity	—	—	—	—	—	—	469	469	—
Other	11	1	285	(10)	—	276	(342)	(66)	(9)
Balances as of January 31, 2013	**3,314**	**332**	**3,620**	**72,978**	**(587)**	**76,343**	**5,395**	**81,738**	**519**
Consolidated net income	**—**	**—**	**—**	**16,022**	**—**	**16,022**	**595**	**16,617**	**78**
Other comprehensive loss, net of income taxes	**—**	**—**	**—**	**—**	**(2,409)**	**(2,409)**	**(311)**	**(2,720)**	**(66)**
Cash dividends declared ($1.88 per share)	**—**	**—**	**—**	**(6,139)**	**—**	**(6,139)**	**—**	**(6,139)**	**—**
Purchase of Company stock	**(87)**	**(9)**	**(294)**	**(6,254)**	**—**	**(6,557)**	**—**	**(6,557)**	**—**
Redemption value adjustment of redeemable noncontrolling interest	**—**	**—**	**(1,019)**	**—**	**—**	**(1,019)**	**—**	**(1,019)**	**1,019**
Other	**6**	**—**	**55**	**(41)**	**—**	**14**	**(595)**	**(581)**	**(59)**
Balances as of January 31, 2014	**3,233**	**$323**	**$ 2,362**	**$76,566**	**$(2,996)**	**$76,255**	**$5,084**	**$81,339**	**$1,491**

Consolidated Statements of Cash Flows

(Amounts in millions)	Fiscal Years Ended January 31, 2014	2013	2012
Cash flows from operating activities:			
Consolidated net income	**$ 16,695**	$ 17,756	$ 16,387
Income (loss) from discontinued operations, net of income taxes	**(144)**	(52)	21
Income from continuing operations	**16,551**	17,704	16,408
Adjustments to reconcile income from continuing operations to net cash provided by operating activities:			
Depreciation and amortization	**8,870**	8,478	8,106
Deferred income taxes	**(279)**	(133)	1,050
Other operating activities	**938**	602	468
Changes in certain assets and liabilities, net of effects of acquisitions:			
Receivables, net	**(566)**	(614)	(796)
Inventories	**(1,667)**	(2,759)	(3,727)
Accounts payable	**531**	1,061	2,687
Accrued liabilities	**103**	271	(935)
Accrued income taxes	**(1,224)**	981	994
Net cash provided by operating activities	**23,257**	25,591	24,255
Cash flows from investing activities:			
Payments for property and equipment	**(13,115)**	(12,898)	(13,510)
Proceeds from the disposal of property and equipment	**727**	532	580
Investments and business acquisitions, net of cash acquired	**(15)**	(316)	(3,548)
Other investing activities	**105**	71	(131)
Net cash used in investing activities	**(12,298)**	(12,611)	(16,609)
Cash flows from financing activities:			
Net change in short-term borrowings	**911**	2,754	3,019
Proceeds from issuance of long-term debt	**7,072**	211	5,050
Payments of long-term debt	**(4,968)**	(1,478)	(4,584)
Dividends paid	**(6,139)**	(5,361)	(5,048)
Dividends paid to and stock purchases of noncontrolling interest	**(722)**	(414)	(526)
Purchase of Company stock	**(6,683)**	(7,600)	(6,298)
Other financing activities	**(488)**	(84)	(71)
Net cash used in financing activities	**(11,017)**	(11,972)	(8,458)
Effect of exchange rates on cash and cash equivalents	**(442)**	223	(33)
Net increase (decrease) in cash and cash equivalents	**(500)**	1,231	(845)
Cash and cash equivalents at beginning of year	**7,781**	6,550	7,395
Cash and cash equivalents at end of year	**$ 7,281**	$ 7,781	$ 6,550
Supplemental disclosure of cash flow information:			
Income taxes paid	**$ 8,641**	$ 7,304	$ 5,899
Interest paid	**2,362**	2,262	2,346

See accompanying notes.

Appendix F

Specimen Financial Statements: Louis Vuitton

Louis Vuitton is a French company and is one of the leading international fashion houses in the world. Louis Vuitton has been named the world's most valuable luxury brand. Note that its financial statements are IFRS-based and are presented in euros (€). To access the company's complete financial statements, follow these steps:

1. Go to **www.lvmh.com/investor-relations**.
2. Select 2013 Annual report, and then select the Finance tab once the Intro has played.
3. Note that the comments (notes) to the financial statements are placed after each corresponding statement.

CONSOLIDATED BALANCE SHEET

ASSETS *(EUR millions)*	2013	2012[1]	2011[1]
Brands and other intangible assets	11,458	11,510	11,482
Goodwill	9,959	7,806	6,957
Property, plant and equipment	9,602	8,769	8,017
Investments in associates	152	163	170
Non-current available for sale financial assets	7,080	6,004	5,982
Other non-current assets	432	519	478
Deferred tax	909	954	760
NON-CURRENT ASSETS	39,592	35,725	33,846
Inventories and work in progress	8,586	8,080	7,510
Trade accounts receivable	2,189	1,985	1,878
Income taxes	235	201	121
Other current assets	1,851	1,811	1,455
Cash and cash equivalents	3,221	2,196	2,303
CURRENT ASSETS	16,082	14,273	13,267
TOTAL ASSETS	55,674	49,998	47,113

(Continued.)

(Continued.)

LIABILITIES AND EQUITY

(EUR millions)	2013	2012[1]	2011[1]
Share capital	152	152	152
Share premium account	3,849	3,848	3,801
Treasury shares and LVMH-share settled derivatives	(451)	(414)	(485)
Cumulative translation adjustment	(8)	342	431
Revaluation reserves	3,900	2,731	2,637
Other reserves	15,817	14,341	12,770
Net profit, Group share	3,436	3,424	3,065
Equity, Group share	26,695	24,424	22,371
Minority interests	1,028	1,084	1,055
TOTAL EQUITY	27,723	25,508	23,426
Long term borrowings	4,159	3,836	4,132
Provisions	1,755	1,756	1,530
Deferred tax	3,934	3,960	3,925
Other non-current liabilities	6,403	5,456	4,506
NON-CURRENT LIABILITIES	16,251	15,008	14,093
Short term borrowings	4,688	2,976	3,134
Trade accounts payable	3,308	3,134	2,952
Income taxes	382	442	443
Provisions	322	335	349
Other current liabilities	3,000	2,595	2,716
CURRENT LIABILITIES	11,700	9,482	9,594
TOTAL LIABILITIES AND EQUITY	55,674	49,998	47,113

(1) The balance sheets as of December 31, 2012 and 2011 have been restated to reflect the retrospective application as of January 1, 2011 of IAS 19 Employee Benefits as amended.

CONSOLIDATED INCOME STATEMENT

(EUR millions, except for earnings per share)	2013	2012	2011
REVENUE	29,149	28,103	23,659
Cost of sales	(10,055)	(9,917)	(8,092)
GROSS MARGIN	19,094	18,186	15,567
Marketing and selling expenses	(10,849)	(10,101)	(8,360)
General and administrative expenses	(2,224)	(2,164)	(1,944)
PROFIT FROM RECURRING OPERATIONS	6,021	5,921	5,263
Other operating income and expenses	(127)	(182)	(109)
OPERATING PROFIT	5,894	5,739	5,154
Cost of net financial debt	(103)	(140)	(151)
Other financial income and expenses	(96)	126	(91)
NET FINANCIAL INCOME (EXPENSE)	(199)	(14)	(242)
Income taxes	(1,755)	(1,820)	(1,453)
Income (loss) from investments in associates	7	4	6
NET PROFIT BEFORE MINORITY INTERESTS	3,947	3,909	3,465
Minority interests	(511)	(485)	(400)
NET PROFIT, GROUP SHARE	3,436	3,424	3,065
BASIC GROUP SHARE OF NET EARNINGS PER SHARE *(EUR)*	6.87	6.86	6.27
Number of shares on which the calculation is based	500,283,414	499,133,643	488,769,286
DILUTED GROUP SHARE OF NET EARNINGS PER SHARE *(EUR)*	6.83	6.82	6.23
Number of shares on which the calculation is based	503,217,497	502,229,952	492,207,492

CONSOLIDATED STATEMENT OF COMPREHENSIVE GAINS AND LOSSES

(EUR millions)	2013	2012[1]	2011[1]
NET PROFIT BEFORE MINORITY INTERESTS	3,947	3,909	3,465
Translation adjustments	(346)	(99)	190
Tax impact	(48)	(18)	47
	(394)	(117)	237
Change in value of available for sale financial assets	963	(27)	1,634
Amounts transferred to income statement	(16)	(14)	(38)
Tax impact	(35)	(6)	(116)
	912	(47)	1,480
Change in value of hedges of future foreign currency cash flows	304	182	95
Amounts transferred to income statement	(265)	13	(168)
Tax impact	(17)	(50)	21
	22	145	(52)
GAINS AND LOSSES RECOGNIZED IN EQUITY, TRANSFERABLE TO INCOME STATEMENT	540	(19)	1,665
Change in value of vineyard land	369	85	25
Tax impact	(127)	(28)	(11)
	242	57	14
Employee benefit commitments: change in value resulting from actuarial gains and losses	80	(101)	(45)
Tax impact	(22)	29	13
	58	(72)	(32)
GAINS AND LOSSES RECOGNIZED IN EQUITY, NOT TRANSFERABLE TO INCOME STATEMENT	300	(15)	(18)
COMPREHENSIVE INCOME	4,787	3,875	5,112
Minority interests	(532)	(470)	(429)
COMPREHENSIVE INCOME, GROUP SHARE	4,255	3,405	4,683

(1) The consolidated statements of comprehensive gains and losses as of December 31, 2012 and 2011 have been restated to reflect the retrospective application as of January 1, 2011 of IAS 19 Employee Benefits as amended.

CONSOLIDATED CASH FLOW STATEMENT

(EUR millions)	2013	2012	2011
I. OPERATING ACTIVITIES AND OPERATING INVESTMENTS			
Operating profit	5,894	5,739	5,154
Net increase in depreciation, amortization and provisions	1,454	1,299	999
Other computed expenses	(29)	(62)	(45)
Dividends received	86	188	61
Other adjustments	(76)	(51)	(32)
CASH FROM OPERATIONS BEFORE CHANGES IN WORKING CAPITAL	7,329	7,113	6,137
Cost of net financial debt: interest paid	(112)	(154)	(152)
Income taxes paid	(1,979)	(1,970)	(1,544)
NET CASH FROM OPERATING ACTIVITIES BEFORE CHANGES IN WORKING CAPITAL	5,238	4,989	4,441
Change in working capital	(617)	(813)	(534)
NET CASH FROM OPERATING ACTIVITIES	4,621	4,176	3,907
Operating investments	(1,663)	(1,702)	(1,730)
NET CASH FROM OPERATING ACTIVITIES AND OPERATING INVESTMENTS (free cash flow)	2,958	2,474	2,177
II. FINANCIAL INVESTMENTS			
Purchase of non-current available for sale financial assets	(197)	(131)	(518)
Proceeds from sale of non-current available for sale financial assets	38	36	17
Impact of purchase and sale of consolidated investments	(2,158)	(45)	(785)[1]
NET CASH FROM (used in) FINANCIAL INVESTMENTS	(2,317)	(140)	(1,286)
III. TRANSACTIONS RELATING TO EQUITY			
Capital increases of LVMH	66	94	94[1]
Capital increases of subsidiaries subscribed by minority interests	7	8	3
Acquisition and disposals of treasury shares and LVMH-share settled derivatives	(113)	5	2
Interim and final dividends paid by LVMH	(1,501)	(1,447)	(1,069)
Interim and final dividends paid to minority interests in consolidated subsidiaries	(220)	(314)	(189)
Purchase and proceeds from sale of minority interests	(150)	(206)	(1,413)
NET CASH FROM (used in) TRANSACTIONS RELATING TO EQUITY	(1,911)	(1,860)	(2,572)
CHANGE IN CASH BEFORE FINANCING ACTIVITIES	(1,270)	474	(1,681)
IV. FINANCING ACTIVITIES			
Proceeds from borrowings	3,145	1,068	2,659
Repayment of borrowings	(1,099)	(1,526)	(1,005)
Purchase and proceeds from sale of current available for sale financial assets	101	(67)	6
NET CASH FROM (used in) FINANCING ACTIVITIES	2,147	(525)	1,660
V. EFFECT OF EXCHANGE RATE CHANGES	46	(42)	60
NET INCREASE (decrease) IN CASH AND CASH EQUIVALENTS (I + II + III + IV + V)	923	(93)	39
CASH AND CASH EQUIVALENTS AT BEGINNING OF PERIOD	1,988	2,081	2,042
CASH AND CASH EQUIVALENTS AT END OF PERIOD	2,911	1,988	2,081
Transactions included in the table above, generating no change in cash:			
– acquisition of assets by means of finance leases	7	5	3

(1) *Not including the impact of the amount attributable to the acquisition of Bulgari remunerated by the capital increase of LVMH SA as of June 30, 2011, which did not generate any cash flows.*

CONSOLIDATED STATEMENT OF CHANGES IN EQUITY

(EUR millions)	Number of shares	Share capital	Share premium account	Treasury shares and LVMH-share settled derivatives	Cumulative translation adjustment	Revaluation reserves				Net profit and other reserves	Total equity		
						Available for sale financial assets	Hedges of future foreign currency cash flows	Vineyard land	Employee benefit commitments		Group share	Minority interests	Total
AS OF DECEMBER 31, 2012 AFTER RESTATEMENT	508,163,349	152	3,848	(414)	342	1,943	118	758	(88)	17,765	24,424	1,084	25,508
Gains and losses recognized in equity					(350)	912	18	188	51		819	21	840
Net profit										3,436	3,436	511	3,947
COMPREHENSIVE INCOME		-	-	-	(350)	912	18	188	51	3,436	4,255	532	4,787
Stock option plan and similar expenses										31	31	3	34
(Acquisition)/disposal of treasury shares and LVMH-share settled derivatives				(103)						(7)	(110)	-	(110)
Exercise of LVMH share subscription options	1,025,418		67								67	-	67
Retirement of LVMH shares	(1,395,106)		(66)	66							-	-	-
Capital increase in subsidiaries											-	8	8
Interim and final dividends paid										(1,500)	(1,500)	(228)	(1,728)
Changes in control of consolidated entities										1	1	50	51
Acquisition and disposal of minority interests' shares										(73)	(73)	(76)	(149)
Purchase commitments for minority interests' shares										(400)	(400)	(345)	(745)
AS OF DECEMBER 31, 2013	507,793,661	152	3,849	(451)	(8)	2,855	136	946	(37)	19,253	26,695	1,028	27,723

Appendix G Time Value of Money

APPENDIX PREVIEW Would you rather receive $1,000 today or a year from now? You should prefer to receive the $1,000 today because you can invest the $1,000 and then earn interest on it. As a result, you will have more than $1,000 a year from now. What this example illustrates is the concept of the **time value of money**. Everyone prefers to receive money today rather than in the future because of the interest factor.

LEARNING OBJECTIVES

1. **Compute interest and future values.**
   - Nature of interest
   - Future value of a single amount
   - Future value of an annuity
2. **Compute present values.**
   - Present value variables
   - Present value of a single amount
   - Present value of an annuity
   - Time periods and discounting
   - Present value of a long-term note or bond
3. **Compute the present value in capital budgeting situations.**
   - Using alternative discount rates
4. **Use a financial calculator to solve time value of money problems.**
   - Present value of a single sum
   - Present value of an annuity
   - Useful financial calculator applications

LEARNING OBJECTIVE 1

Compute interest and future values.

Nature of Interest

Interest is payment for the use of another person's money. It is the difference between the amount borrowed or invested (called the **principal**) and the amount repaid or collected. The amount of interest to be paid or collected is usually stated as a rate over a specific period of time. The rate of interest is generally stated as an annual rate.

The amount of interest involved in any financing transaction is based on three elements:

1. **Principal (p):** The original amount borrowed or invested.
2. **Interest Rate (i):** An annual percentage of the principal.
3. **Time (n):** The number of periods that the principal is borrowed or invested.

SIMPLE INTEREST

Simple interest is computed on the principal amount only. It is the return on the principal for one period. Simple interest is usually expressed as shown in Illustration G-1.

Illustration G-1
Interest computation

$$\text{Interest} = \underset{p}{\text{Principal}} \times \underset{i}{\text{Rate}} \times \underset{n}{\text{Time}}$$

For example, if you borrowed $5,000 for 2 years at a simple interest rate of 12% annually, you would pay $1,200 in total interest, computed as follows.

$$\begin{aligned}\text{Interest} &= p \times i \times n\\ &= \$5{,}000 \times .12 \times 2\\ &= \$1{,}200\end{aligned}$$

COMPOUND INTEREST

Compound interest is computed on principal **and** on any interest earned that has not been paid or withdrawn. It is the return on (or growth of) the principal for two or more time periods. Compounding computes interest not only on the principal but also on the interest earned to date on that principal, assuming the interest is left on deposit.

To illustrate the difference between simple and compound interest, assume that you deposit $1,000 in Bank Two, where it will earn simple interest of 9% per year, and you deposit another $1,000 in Citizens Bank, where it will earn compound interest of 9% per year compounded annually. Also assume that in both cases you will not withdraw any cash until three years from the date of deposit. Illustration G-2 shows the computation of interest to be received and the accumulated year-end balances.

Illustration G-2
Simple versus compound interest

Bank Two

Simple Interest Calculation	Simple Interest	Accumulated Year-End Balance
Year 1 $1,000.00 × 9%	$ 90.00	$1,090.00
Year 2 $1,000.00 × 9%	90.00	$1,180.00
Year 3 $1,000.00 × 9%	90.00	$1,270.00
	$ 270.00	

Citizens Bank

Compound Interest Calculation	Compound Interest	Accumulated Year-End Balance
Year 1 $1,000.00 × 9%	$ 90.00	$1,090.00
Year 2 $1,090.00 × 9%	98.10	$1,188.10
Year 3 $1,188.10 × 9%	106.93	$1,295.03
	$ 295.03	

$25.03 Difference

Note in Illustration G-2 that simple interest uses the initial principal of $1,000 to compute the interest in all three years. Compound interest uses the accumulated balance (principal plus interest to date) at each year-end to compute interest in the succeeding year—which explains why your compound interest account is larger.

Obviously, if you had a choice between investing your money at simple interest or at compound interest, you would choose compound interest, all other things—especially risk—being equal. In the example, compounding provides $25.03 of additional interest income. For practical purposes, compounding assumes that unpaid interest earned becomes a part of the principal, and the accumulated balance at the end of each year becomes the new principal on which interest is earned during the next year.

Illustration G-2 indicates that you should invest your money at the bank that compounds interest. Most business situations use compound interest. Simple interest is generally applicable only to short-term situations of one year or less.

Future Value of a Single Amount

The **future value of a single amount** is the value at a future date of a given amount invested, assuming compound interest. For example, in Illustration G-2, $1,295.03 is the future value of the $1,000 investment earning 9% for three years. The $1,295.03 is determined more easily by using the following formula.

$$FV = p \times (1 + i)^n$$

Illustration G-3
Formula for future value

where:

FV = future value of a single amount
p = principal (or present value; the value today)
i = interest rate for one period
n = number of periods

The $1,295.03 is computed as follows.

$$\begin{aligned} FV &= \quad p \quad \times (1 + i)^n \\ &= \$1{,}000 \times (1 + .09)^3 \\ &= \$1{,}000 \times 1.29503 \\ &= \$1{,}295.03 \end{aligned}$$

The 1.29503 is computed by multiplying (1.09 × 1.09 × 1.09). The amounts in this example can be depicted in the time diagram shown in Illustration G-4.

Illustration G-4
Time diagram

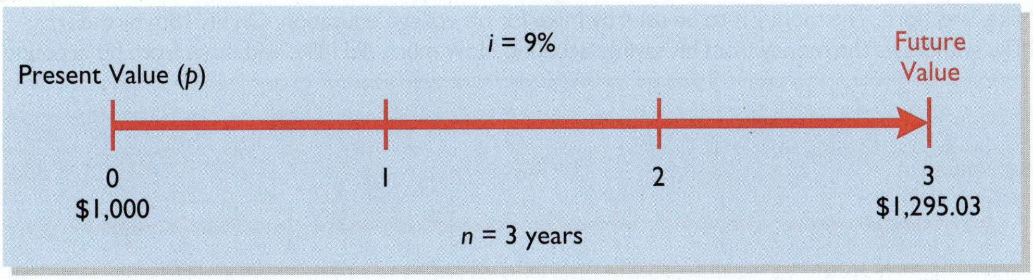

Another method used to compute the future value of a single amount involves a compound interest table. This table shows the future value of 1 for n periods. Table 1 (page G-4) is such a table.

In Table 1, n is the number of compounding periods, the percentages are the periodic interest rates, and the 5-digit decimal numbers in the respective columns are the future value of 1 factors. To use Table 1, you multiply the principal amount by the future value factor for the specified number of periods and interest rate. For example, the future value factor for two periods at 9% is 1.18810. Multiplying this factor by $1,000 equals $1,188.10—which is the accumulated balance at the end of year 2 in the Citizens Bank example in Illustration G-2. The $1,295.03 accumulated balance at the end of the third year is calculated from Table 1 by multiplying the future value factor for three periods (1.29503) by the $1,000.

The demonstration problem in Illustration G-5 shows how to use Table 1.

TABLE 1 Future Value of 1

(*n*) Periods	4%	5%	6%	7%	8%	9%	10%	11%	12%	15%
0	1.00000	1.00000	1.00000	1.00000	1.00000	1.00000	1.00000	1.00000	1.00000	1.00000
1	1.04000	1.05000	1.06000	1.07000	1.08000	1.09000	1.10000	1.11000	1.12000	1.15000
2	1.08160	1.10250	1.12360	1.14490	1.16640	1.18810	1.21000	1.23210	1.25440	1.32250
3	1.12486	1.15763	1.19102	1.22504	1.25971	1.29503	1.33100	1.36763	1.40493	1.52088
4	1.16986	1.21551	1.26248	1.31080	1.36049	1.41158	1.46410	1.51807	1.57352	1.74901
5	1.21665	1.27628	1.33823	1.40255	1.46933	1.53862	1.61051	1.68506	1.76234	2.01136
6	1.26532	1.34010	1.41852	1.50073	1.58687	1.67710	1.77156	1.87041	1.97382	2.31306
7	1.31593	1.40710	1.50363	1.60578	1.71382	1.82804	1.94872	2.07616	2.21068	2.66002
8	1.36857	1.47746	1.59385	1.71819	1.85093	1.99256	2.14359	2.30454	2.47596	3.05902
9	1.42331	1.55133	1.68948	1.83846	1.99900	2.17189	2.35795	2.55803	2.77308	3.51788
10	1.48024	1.62889	1.79085	1.96715	2.15892	2.36736	2.59374	2.83942	3.10585	4.04556
11	1.53945	1.71034	1.89830	2.10485	2.33164	2.58043	2.85312	3.15176	3.47855	4.65239
12	1.60103	1.79586	2.01220	2.25219	2.51817	2.81267	3.13843	3.49845	3.89598	5.35025
13	1.66507	1.88565	2.13293	2.40985	2.71962	3.06581	3.45227	3.88328	4.36349	6.15279
14	1.73168	1.97993	2.26090	2.57853	2.93719	3.34173	3.79750	4.31044	4.88711	7.07571
15	1.80094	2.07893	2.39656	2.75903	3.17217	3.64248	4.17725	4.78459	5.47357	8.13706
16	1.87298	2.18287	2.54035	2.95216	3.42594	3.97031	4.59497	5.31089	6.13039	9.35762
17	1.94790	2.29202	2.69277	3.15882	3.70002	4.32763	5.05447	5.89509	6.86604	10.76126
18	2.02582	2.40662	2.85434	3.37993	3.99602	4.71712	5.55992	6.54355	7.68997	12.37545
19	2.10685	2.52695	3.02560	3.61653	4.31570	5.14166	6.11591	7.26334	8.61276	14.23177
20	2.19112	2.65330	3.20714	3.86968	4.66096	5.60441	6.72750	8.06231	9.64629	16.36654

Illustration G-5
Demonstration problem—
Using Table 1 for *FV* of 1

John and Mary Rich invested $20,000 in a savings account paying 6% interest at the time their son, Mike, was born. The money is to be used by Mike for his college education. On his 18th birthday, Mike withdraws the money from his savings account. How much did Mike withdraw from his account?

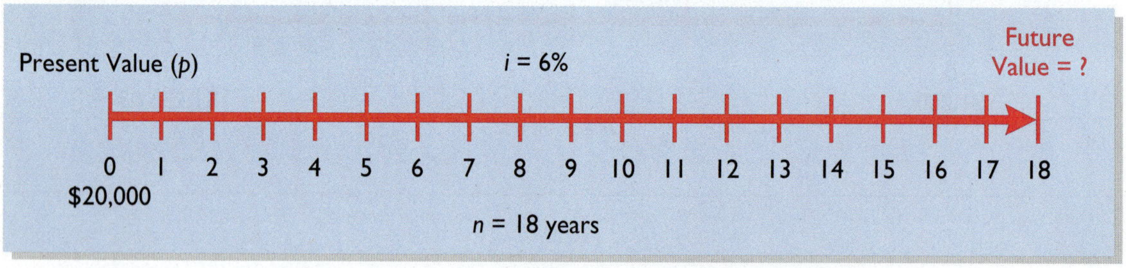

Answer: The future value factor from Table 1 is 2.85434 (18 periods at 6%). The future value of $20,000 earning 6% per year for 18 years is **$57,086.80** ($20,000 × 2.85434).

Future Value of an Annuity

The preceding discussion involved the accumulation of only a single principal sum. Individuals and businesses frequently encounter situations in which a

series of equal dollar amounts are to be paid or received at evenly spaced time intervals (periodically), such as loans or lease (rental) contracts. A series of payments or receipts of equal dollar amounts is referred to as an **annuity**.

The **future value of an annuity** is the sum of all the payments (receipts) plus the accumulated compound interest on them. In computing the future value of an annuity, it is necessary to know (1) the interest rate, (2) the number of payments (receipts), and (3) the amount of the periodic payments (receipts).

To illustrate the computation of the future value of an annuity, assume that you invest $2,000 at the end of each year for three years at 5% interest compounded annually. This situation is depicted in the time diagram in Illustration G-6.

Illustration G-6
Time diagram for a three-year annuity

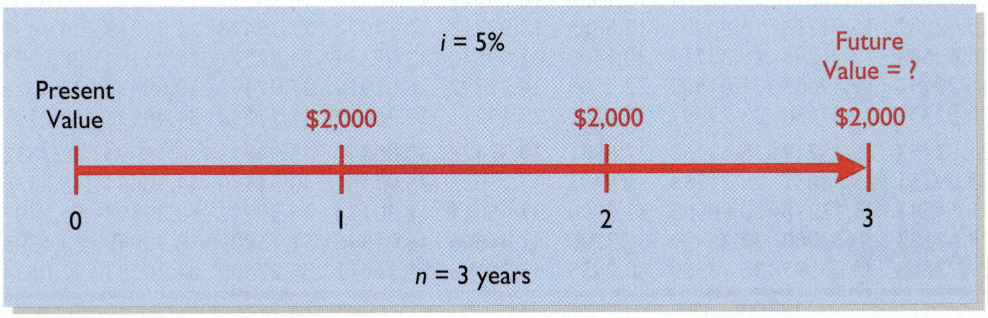

The $2,000 invested at the end of year 1 will earn interest for two years (years 2 and 3), and the $2,000 invested at the end of year 2 will earn interest for one year (year 3). However, the last $2,000 investment (made at the end of year 3) will not earn any interest. Using the future value factors from Table 1, the future value of these periodic payments is computed as shown in Illustration G-7.

Illustration G-7
Future value of periodic payment computation

Invested at End of Year	Number of Compounding Periods	Amount Invested	×	Future Value of 1 Factor at 5%	=	Future Value
1	2	$2,000		1.10250		$ 2,205
2	1	2,000		1.05000		2,100
3	0	2,000		1.00000		2,000
				3.15250		**$6,305**

The first $2,000 investment is multiplied by the future value factor for two periods (1.1025) because two years' interest will accumulate on it (in years 2 and 3). The second $2,000 investment will earn only one year's interest (in year 3) and therefore is multiplied by the future value factor for one year (1.0500). The final $2,000 investment is made at the end of the third year and will not earn any interest. Thus, $n = 0$ and the future value factor is 1.00000. Consequently, the future value of the last $2,000 invested is only $2,000 since it does not accumulate any interest.

Calculating the future value of each individual cash flow is required when the periodic payments or receipts are not equal in each period. However, when the periodic payments (receipts) are **the same in each period**, the future value can be computed by using a future value of an annuity of 1 table. Table 2 (page G-6) is such a table.

TABLE 2 Future Value of an Annuity of 1

(*n*) Payments	4%	5%	6%	7%	8%	9%	10%	11%	12%	15%
1	1.00000	1.00000	1.00000	1.0000	1.00000	1.00000	1.00000	1.00000	1.00000	1.00000
2	2.04000	2.05000	2.06000	2.0700	2.08000	2.09000	2.10000	2.11000	2.12000	2.15000
3	3.12160	3.15250	3.18360	3.2149	3.24640	3.27810	3.31000	3.34210	3.37440	3.47250
4	4.24646	4.31013	4.37462	4.4399	4.50611	4.57313	4.64100	4.70973	4.77933	4.99338
5	5.41632	5.52563	5.63709	5.7507	5.86660	5.98471	6.10510	6.22780	6.35285	6.74238
6	6.63298	6.80191	6.97532	7.1533	7.33592	7.52334	7.71561	7.91286	8.11519	8.75374
7	7.89829	8.14201	8.39384	8.6540	8.92280	9.20044	9.48717	9.78327	10.08901	11.06680
8	9.21423	9.54911	9.89747	10.2598	10.63663	11.02847	11.43589	11.85943	12.29969	13.72682
9	10.58280	11.02656	11.49132	11.9780	12.48756	13.02104	13.57948	14.16397	14.77566	16.78584
10	12.00611	12.57789	13.18079	13.8164	14.48656	15.19293	15.93743	16.72201	17.54874	20.30372
11	13.48635	14.20679	14.97164	15.7836	16.64549	17.56029	18.53117	19.56143	20.65458	24.34928
12	15.02581	15.91713	16.86994	17.8885	18.97713	20.14072	21.38428	22.71319	24.13313	29.00167
13	16.62684	17.71298	18.88214	20.1406	21.49530	22.95339	24.52271	26.21164	28.02911	34.35192
14	18.29191	19.59863	21.01507	22.5505	24.21492	26.01919	27.97498	30.09492	32.39260	40.50471
15	20.02359	21.57856	23.27597	25.1290	27.15211	29.36092	31.77248	34.40536	37.27972	47.58041
16	21.82453	23.65749	25.67253	27.8881	30.32428	33.00340	35.94973	39.18995	42.75328	55.71747
17	23.69751	25.84037	28.21288	30.8402	33.75023	36.97351	40.54470	44.50084	48.88367	65.07509
18	25.64541	28.13238	30.90565	33.9990	37.45024	41.30134	45.59917	50.39593	55.74972	75.83636
19	27.67123	30.53900	33.75999	37.3790	41.44626	46.01846	51.15909	56.93949	63.43968	88.21181
20	29.77808	33.06595	36.78559	40.9955	45.76196	51.16012	57.27500	64.20283	72.05244	102.44358

Table 2 shows the future value of 1 to be received periodically for a given number of payments. It assumes that each payment is made at the **end** of each period. We can see from Table 2 that the future value of an annuity of 1 factor for three payments at 5% is 3.15250. The future value factor is the total of the three individual future value factors as shown in Illustration G-7. Multiplying this amount by the annual investment of $2,000 produces a future value of $6,305.

The demonstration problem in Illustration G-8 shows how to use Table 2.

Illustration G-8
Demonstration problem—Using Table 2 for *FV* of an annuity of 1

John and Char Lewis's daughter, Debra, has just started high school. They decide to start a college fund for her and will invest $2,500 in a savings account at the end of each year she is in high school (4 payments total). The account will earn 6% interest compounded annually. How much will be in the college fund at the time Debra graduates from high school?

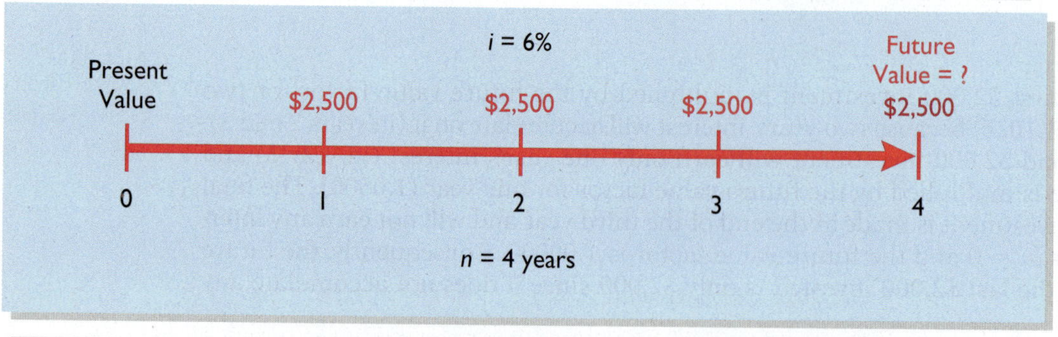

Answer: The future value factor from Table 2 is 4.37462 (4 payments at 6%). The future value of $2,500 invested each year for 4 years at 6% interest is **$10,936.55** ($2,500 × 4.37462).

LEARNING OBJECTIVE 2

Compute present values.

Present Value Variables

The **present value** is the value now of a given amount to be paid or received in the future, assuming compound interest. The present value, like the future value, is based on three variables: (1) the dollar amount to be received (future amount), (2) the length of time until the amount is received (number of periods), and (3) the interest rate (the discount rate). The process of determining the present value is referred to as **discounting the future amount**.

Present value computations are used in measuring many items. For example, the present value of principal and interest payments is used to determine the market price of a bond. Determining the amount to be reported for notes payable and lease liabilities also involves present value computations. In addition, capital budgeting and other investment proposals are evaluated using present value computations. Finally, all rate of return and internal rate of return computations involve present value techniques.

Present Value of a Single Amount

To illustrate present value, assume that you want to invest a sum of money today that will provide $1,000 at the end of one year. What amount would you need to invest today to have $1,000 one year from now? If you want a 10% rate of return, the investment or present value is $909.09 ($1,000 ÷ 1.10). The formula for calculating present value is shown in Illustration G-9.

Present Value (PV) = Future Value (FV) ÷ $(1 + i)^n$

Illustration G-9
Formula for present value

The computation of $1,000 discounted at 10% for one year is as follows.

$$\begin{aligned} PV &= FV \div (1 + i)^n \\ &= \$1{,}000 \div (1 + .10)^1 \\ &= \$1{,}000 \div 1.10 \\ &= \$909.09 \end{aligned}$$

The future amount ($1,000), the discount rate (10%), and the number of periods (1) are known. The variables in this situation are depicted in the time diagram in Illustration G-10.

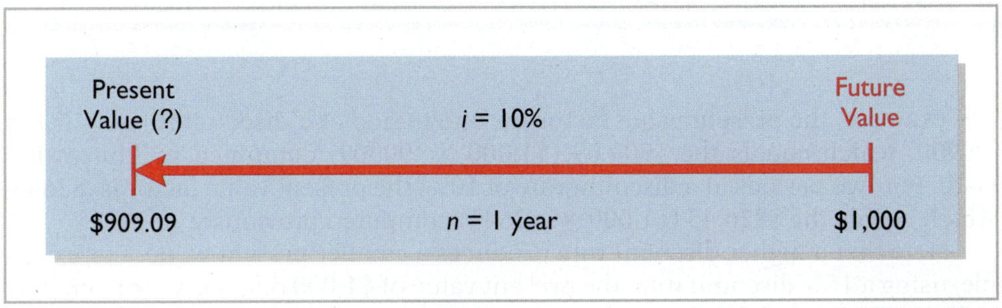

Illustration G-10
Finding present value if discounted for one period

If the single amount of $1,000 is to be received **in two years** and discounted at 10% [$PV = \$1{,}000 \div (1 + .10)^2$], its present value is $826.45 [($1,000 ÷ 1.21), depicted in Illustration G-11 (page G-8).

Illustration G-11
Finding present value if discounted for two periods

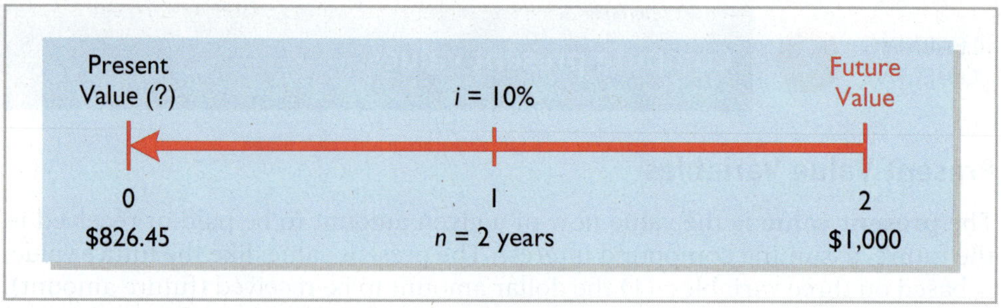

The present value of 1 may also be determined through tables that show the present value of 1 for *n* periods. In Table 3 (see below), *n* is the number of discounting periods involved. The percentages are the periodic interest rates or discount rates, and the 5-digit decimal numbers in the respective columns are the present value of 1 factors.

When using Table 3, the future value is multiplied by the present value factor specified at the intersection of the number of periods and the discount rate.

TABLE 3 Present Value of 1

(*n*) Periods	4%	5%	6%	7%	8%	9%	10%	11%	12%	15%
1	.96154	.95238	.94340	.93458	.92593	.91743	.90909	.90090	.89286	.86957
2	.92456	.90703	.89000	.87344	.85734	.84168	.82645	.81162	.79719	.75614
3	.88900	.86384	.83962	.81630	.79383	.77218	.75132	.73119	.71178	.65752
4	.85480	.82270	.79209	.76290	.73503	.70843	.68301	.65873	.63552	.57175
5	.82193	.78353	.74726	.71299	.68058	.64993	.62092	.59345	.56743	.49718
6	.79031	.74622	.70496	.66634	.63017	.59627	.56447	.53464	.50663	.43233
7	.75992	.71068	.66506	.62275	.58349	.54703	.51316	.48166	.45235	.37594
8	.73069	.67684	.62741	.58201	.54027	.50187	.46651	.43393	.40388	.32690
9	.70259	.64461	.59190	.54393	.50025	.46043	.42410	.39092	.36061	.28426
10	.67556	.61391	.55839	.50835	.46319	.42241	.38554	.35218	.32197	.24719
11	.64958	.58468	.52679	.47509	.42888	.38753	.35049	.31728	.28748	.21494
12	.62460	.55684	.49697	.44401	.39711	.35554	.31863	.28584	.25668	.18691
13	.60057	.53032	.46884	.41496	.36770	.32618	.28966	.25751	.22917	.16253
14	.57748	.50507	.44230	.38782	.34046	.29925	.26333	.23199	.20462	.14133
15	.55526	.48102	.41727	.36245	.31524	.27454	.23939	.20900	.18270	.12289
16	.53391	.45811	.39365	.33873	.29189	.25187	.21763	.18829	.16312	.10687
17	.51337	.43630	.37136	.31657	.27027	.23107	.19785	.16963	.14564	.09293
18	.49363	.41552	.35034	.29586	.25025	.21199	.17986	.15282	.13004	.08081
19	.47464	.39573	.33051	.27615	.23171	.19449	.16351	.13768	.11611	.07027
20	.45639	.37689	.31180	.25842	.21455	.17843	.14864	.12403	.10367	.06110

For example, the present value factor for one period at a discount rate of 10% is .90909, which equals the $909.09 ($1,000 × .90909) computed in Illustration G-10. For two periods at a discount rate of 10%, the present value factor is .82645, which equals the $826.45 ($1,000 × .82645) computed previously.

Note that a higher discount rate produces a smaller present value. For example, using a 15% discount rate, the present value of $1,000 due one year from now is $869.57, versus $909.09 at 10%. Also note that the further removed from the present the future value is, the smaller the present value. For example, using the same discount rate of 10%, the present value of $1,000 due in **five years** is $620.92. The present value of $1,000 due in **one year** is $909.09, a difference of $288.17.

The following two demonstration problems (Illustrations G-12 and G-13) illustrate how to use Table 3.

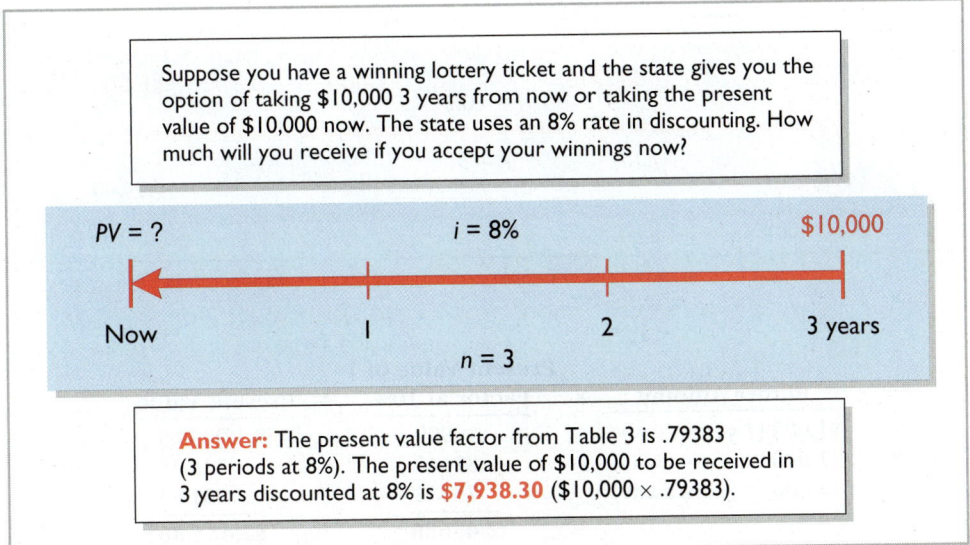

Illustration G-12
Demonstration problem—Using Table 3 for *PV* of 1

Suppose you have a winning lottery ticket and the state gives you the option of taking $10,000 3 years from now or taking the present value of $10,000 now. The state uses an 8% rate in discounting. How much will you receive if you accept your winnings now?

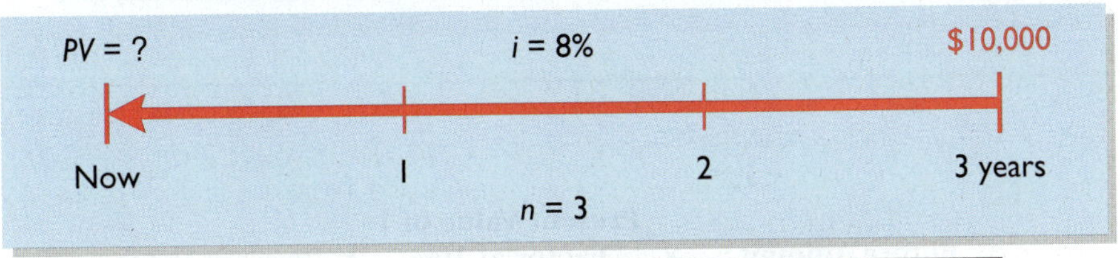

Answer: The present value factor from Table 3 is .79383 (3 periods at 8%). The present value of $10,000 to be received in 3 years discounted at 8% is **$7,938.30** ($10,000 × .79383).

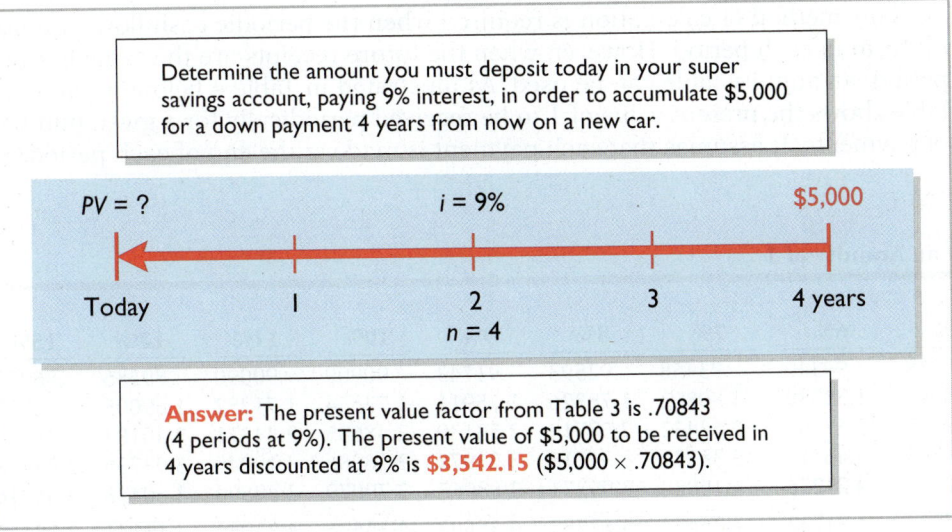

Illustration G-13
Demonstration problem—Using Table 3 for *PV* of 1

Determine the amount you must deposit today in your super savings account, paying 9% interest, in order to accumulate $5,000 for a down payment 4 years from now on a new car.

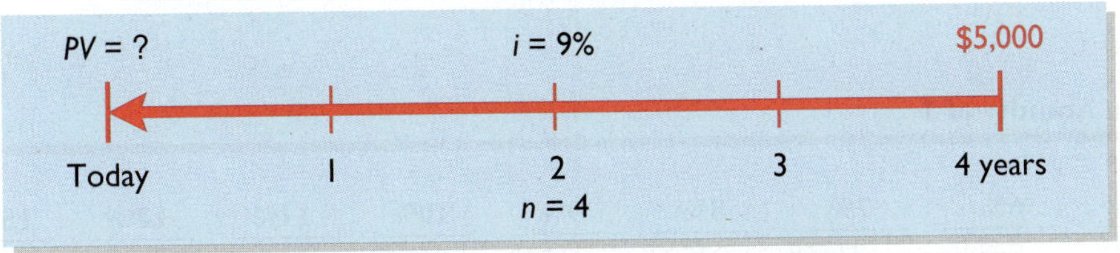

Answer: The present value factor from Table 3 is .70843 (4 periods at 9%). The present value of $5,000 to be received in 4 years discounted at 9% is **$3,542.15** ($5,000 × .70843).

Present Value of an Annuity

The preceding discussion involved the discounting of only a single future amount. Businesses and individuals frequently engage in transactions in which a series of equal dollar amounts are to be received or paid at evenly spaced time intervals (periodically). Examples of a series of periodic receipts or payments are loan agreements, installment sales, mortgage notes, lease (rental) contracts, and pension obligations. As discussed earlier, these periodic receipts or payments are **annuities.**

The **present value of an annuity** is the value now of a series of future receipts or payments, discounted assuming compound interest. In computing the present value of an annuity, it is necessary to know (1) the discount rate, (2) the number of payments (receipts), and (3) the amount of the periodic receipts or payments. To illustrate the computation of the present value of an annuity, assume that you will receive $1,000 cash annually for three years at a time when the discount rate is 10%. This situation is depicted in the time diagram in Illustration G-14. Illustration G-15 shows the computation of its present value in this situation.

Illustration G-14
Time diagram for a three-year annuity

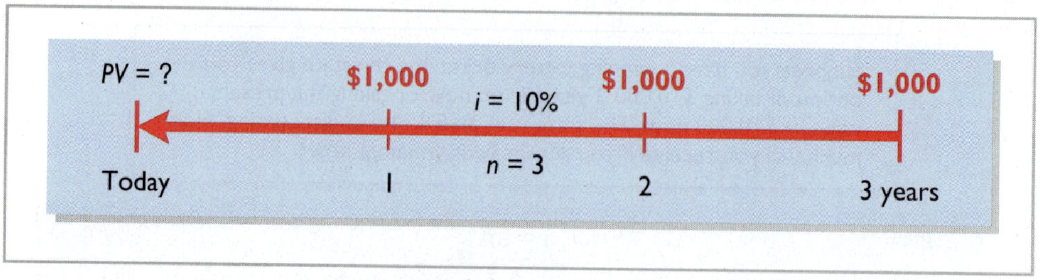

Illustration G-15
Present value of a series of future amounts computation

Future Amount	×	Present Value of 1 Factor at 10%	=	Present Value
$1,000 (1 year away)		.90909		$ 909.09
1,000 (2 years away)		.82645		826.45
1,000 (3 years away)		.75132		751.32
		2.48686		**$2,486.86**

This method of calculation is required when the periodic cash flows are not uniform in each period. However, when the future receipts are the same in each period, an annuity table can be used. As illustrated in Table 4 below, an annuity table shows the present value of 1 to be received periodically for a given number of payments. It assumes that each payment is made at the end of each period.

TABLE 4 Present Value of an Annuity of 1

(*n*) Payments	4%	5%	6%	7%	8%	9%	10%	11%	12%	15%
1	.96154	.95238	.94340	.93458	.92593	.91743	.90909	.90090	.89286	.86957
2	1.88609	1.85941	1.83339	1.80802	1.78326	1.75911	1.73554	1.71252	1.69005	1.62571
3	2.77509	2.72325	2.67301	2.62432	2.57710	2.53130	2.48685	2.44371	2.40183	2.28323
4	3.62990	3.54595	3.46511	3.38721	3.31213	3.23972	3.16986	3.10245	3.03735	2.85498
5	4.45182	4.32948	4.21236	4.10020	3.99271	3.88965	3.79079	3.69590	3.60478	3.35216
6	5.24214	5.07569	4.91732	4.76654	4.62288	4.48592	4.35526	4.23054	4.11141	3.78448
7	6.00205	5.78637	5.58238	5.38929	5.20637	5.03295	4.86842	4.71220	4.56376	4.16042
8	6.73274	6.46321	6.20979	5.97130	5.74664	5.53482	5.33493	5.14612	4.96764	4.48732
9	7.43533	7.10782	6.80169	6.51523	6.24689	5.99525	5.75902	5.53705	5.32825	4.77158
10	8.11090	7.72173	7.36009	7.02358	6.71008	6.41766	6.14457	5.88923	5.65022	5.01877
11	8.76048	8.30641	7.88687	7.49867	7.13896	6.80519	6.49506	6.20652	5.93770	5.23371
12	9.38507	8.86325	8.38384	7.94269	7.53608	7.16073	6.81369	6.49236	6.19437	5.42062
13	9.98565	9.39357	8.85268	8.35765	7.90378	7.48690	7.10336	6.74987	6.42355	5.58315
14	10.56312	9.89864	9.29498	8.74547	8.24424	7.78615	7.36669	6.98187	6.62817	5.72448
15	11.11839	10.37966	9.71225	9.10791	8.55948	8.06069	7.60608	7.19087	6.81086	5.84737
16	11.65230	10.83777	10.10590	9.44665	8.85137	8.31256	7.82371	7.37916	6.97399	5.95424
17	12.16567	11.27407	10.47726	9.76322	9.12164	8.54363	8.02155	7.54879	7.11963	6.04716
18	12.65930	11.68959	10.82760	10.05909	9.37189	8.75563	8.20141	7.70162	7.24967	6.12797
19	13.13394	12.08532	11.15812	10.33560	9.60360	8.95012	8.36492	7.83929	7.36578	6.19823
20	13.59033	12.46221	11.46992	10.59401	9.81815	9.12855	8.51356	7.96333	7.46944	6.25933

Table 4 shows that the present value of an annuity of 1 factor for three payments at 10% is 2.48685.[1] This present value factor is the total of the three individual present value factors, as shown in Illustration G-15. Applying this amount to the annual cash flow of $1,000 produces a present value of $2,486.85.

The following demonstration problem (Illustration G-16) illustrates how to use Table 4.

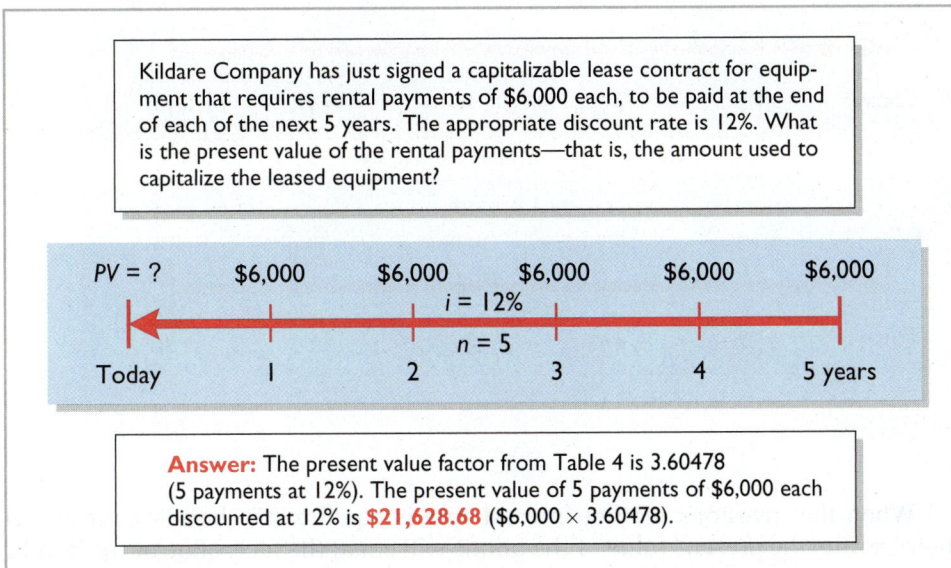

Illustration G-16
Demonstration problem—Using Table 4 for *PV* of an annuity of 1

Kildare Company has just signed a capitalizable lease contract for equipment that requires rental payments of $6,000 each, to be paid at the end of each of the next 5 years. The appropriate discount rate is 12%. What is the present value of the rental payments—that is, the amount used to capitalize the leased equipment?

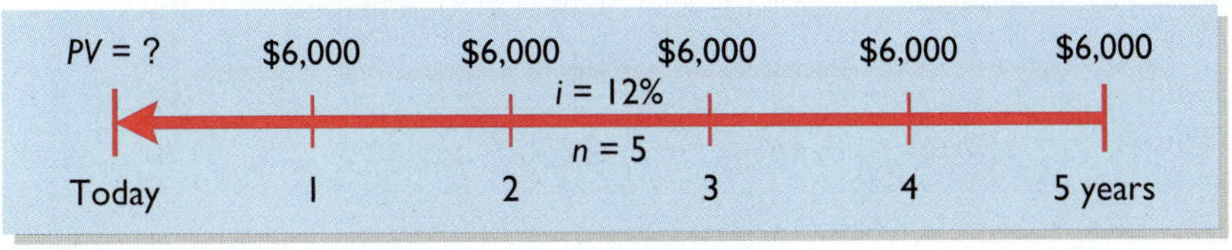

Answer: The present value factor from Table 4 is 3.60478 (5 payments at 12%). The present value of 5 payments of $6,000 each discounted at 12% is **$21,628.68** ($6,000 × 3.60478).

Time Periods and Discounting

In the preceding calculations, the discounting was done on an annual basis using an annual interest rate. Discounting may also be done over shorter periods of time such as monthly, quarterly, or semiannually.

When the time frame is less than one year, it is necessary to convert the annual interest rate to the applicable time frame. Assume, for example, that the investor in Illustration G-14 received $500 **semiannually** for three years instead of $1,000 annually. In this case, the number of periods becomes six (3 × 2), the discount rate is 5% (10% ÷ 2), the present value factor from Table 4 is 5.07569 (6 periods at 5%), and the present value of the future cash flows is $2,537.85 (5.07569 × $500). This amount is slightly higher than the $2,486.86 computed in Illustration G-15 because interest is computed twice during the same year. That is, during the second half of the year, interest is earned on the first half-year's interest.

Present Value of a Long-Term Note or Bond

The present value (or market price) of a long-term note or bond is a function of three variables: (1) the payment amounts, (2) the length of time until the amounts are paid, and (3) the discount rate. Our example uses a five-year bond issue.

The first variable (dollars to be paid) is made up of two elements: (1) a series of interest payments (an annuity) and (2) the principal amount (a single sum). To

[1]The difference of .00001 between 2.48686 and 2.48685 is due to rounding.

compute the present value of the bond, both the interest payments and the principal amount must be discounted—two different computations. The time diagrams for a bond due in five years are shown in Illustration G-17.

Illustration G-17
Time diagrams for the present value of a bond

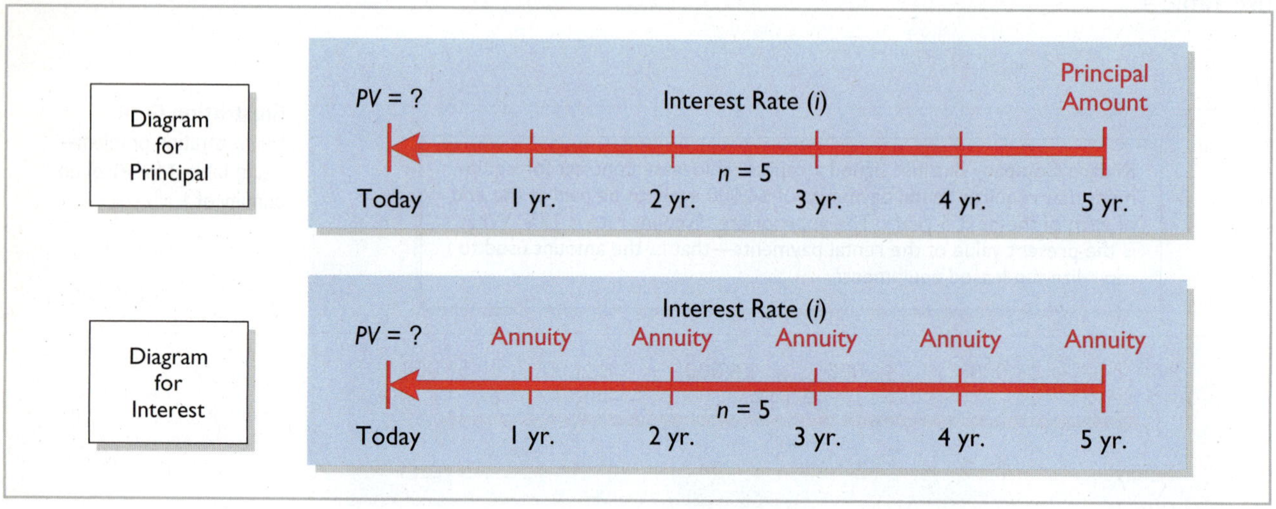

When the investor's market interest rate is equal to the bond's contractual interest rate, the present value of the bonds will equal the face value of the bonds. To illustrate, assume a bond issue of 10%, five-year bonds with a face value of $100,000 with interest payable **semiannually** on January 1 and July 1. If the discount rate is the same as the contractual rate, the bonds will sell at face value. In this case, the investor will receive (1) $100,000 at maturity and (2) a series of ten $5,000 interest payments [($100,000 × 10%) ÷ 2] over the term of the bonds. The length of time is expressed in terms of interest periods—in this case—10, and the discount rate per interest period, 5%. The following time diagram (Illustration G-18) depicts the variables involved in this discounting situation.

Illustration G-18
Time diagram for present value of a 10%, five-year bond paying interest semiannually

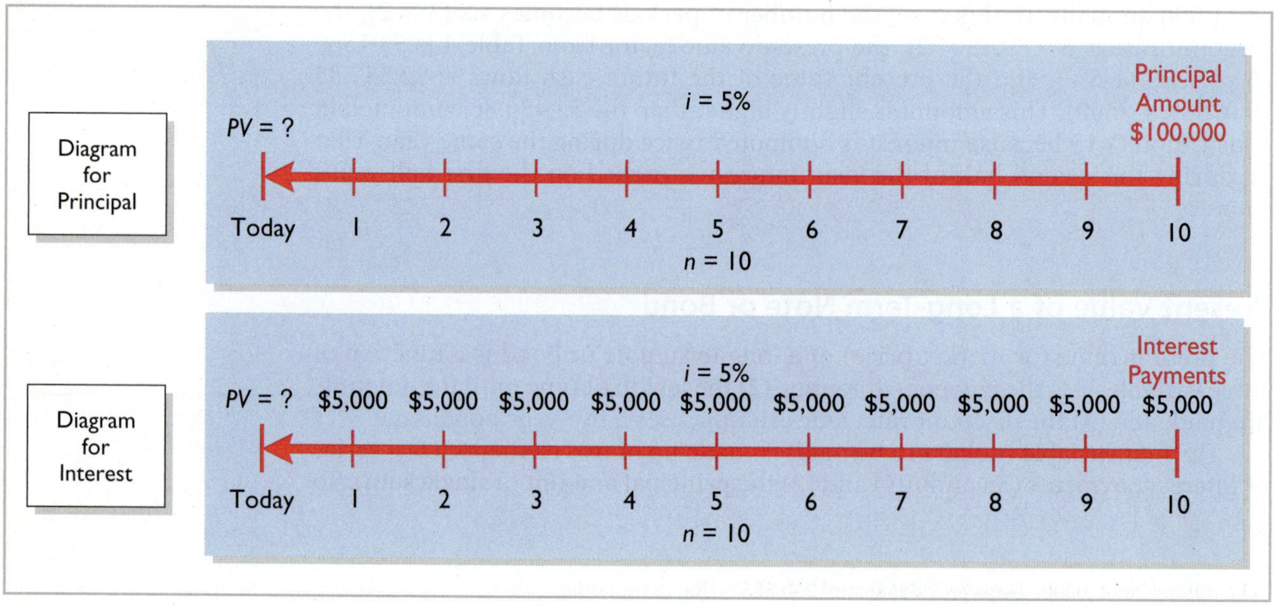

Illustration G-19 shows the computation of the present value of these bonds.

Illustration G-19
Present value of principal and interest—face value

10% Contractual Rate—10% Discount Rate	
Present value of principal to be received at maturity	
$100,000 × *PV* of 1 due in 10 periods at 5%	
$100,000 × .61391 (Table 3)	$ 61,391
Present value of interest to be received periodically over the term of the bonds	
$5,000 × *PV* of 1 due periodically for 10 periods at 5%	
$5,000 × 7.72173 (Table 4)	38,609*
Present value of bonds	**$100,000**

*Rounded

Now assume that the investor's required rate of return is 12%, not 10%. The future amounts are again $100,000 and $5,000, respectively, but now a discount rate of 6% (12% ÷ 2) must be used. The present value of the bonds is $92,639, as computed in Illustration G-20.

Illustration G-20
Present value of principal and interest—discount

10% Contractual Rate—12% Discount Rate	
Present value of principal to be received at maturity	
$100,000 × .55839 (Table 3)	$ 55,839
Present value of interest to be received periodically over the term of the bonds	
$5,000 × 7.36009 (Table 4)	36,800
Present value of bonds	**$92,639**

Conversely, if the discount rate is 8% and the contractual rate is 10%, the present value of the bonds is $108,111, computed as shown in Illustration G-21.

Illustration G-21
Present value of principal and interest—premium

10% Contractual Rate—8% Discount Rate	
Present value of principal to be received at maturity	
$100,000 × .67556 (Table 3)	$ 67,556
Present value of interest to be received periodically over the term of the bonds	
$5,000 × 8.11090 (Table 4)	40,555
Present value of bonds	**$108,111**

The above discussion relied on present value tables in solving present value problems. Calculators may also be used to compute present values without the use of these tables. Many calculators, especially financial calculators, have present value (*PV*) functions that allow you to calculate present values by merely inputting the proper amount, discount rate, periods, and pressing the PV key. We discuss the use of financial calculators in a later section.

LEARNING OBJECTIVE 3

Compute the present value in capital budgeting situations.

The decision to make long-term capital investments is best evaluated using discounting techniques that recognize the time value of money. To do this, many companies calculate the present value of the cash flows involved in a capital investment.

To illustrate, Nagel-Siebert Trucking Company, a cross-country freight carrier in Montgomery, Illinois, is considering adding another truck to its fleet because of a purchasing opportunity. **Navistar Inc.**, Nagel-Siebert's primary supplier of overland rigs, is overstocked and offers to sell its biggest rig for $154,000 cash payable upon delivery. Nagel-Siebert knows that the rig will produce a net cash flow per year of $40,000 for five years (received at the end of each year), at which time it will be sold for an estimated salvage value of $35,000. Nagel-Siebert's discount rate in evaluating capital expenditures is 10%. Should Nagel-Siebert commit to the purchase of this rig?

The cash flows that must be discounted to present value by Nagel-Siebert are as follows.

Cash payable on delivery (today): $154,000.

Net cash flow from operating the rig: $40,000 for 5 years (at the end of each year).

Cash received from sale of rig at the end of 5 years: $35,000.

The time diagrams for the latter two cash flows are shown in Illustration G-22.

Illustration G-22
Time diagrams for Nagel-Siebert Trucking Company

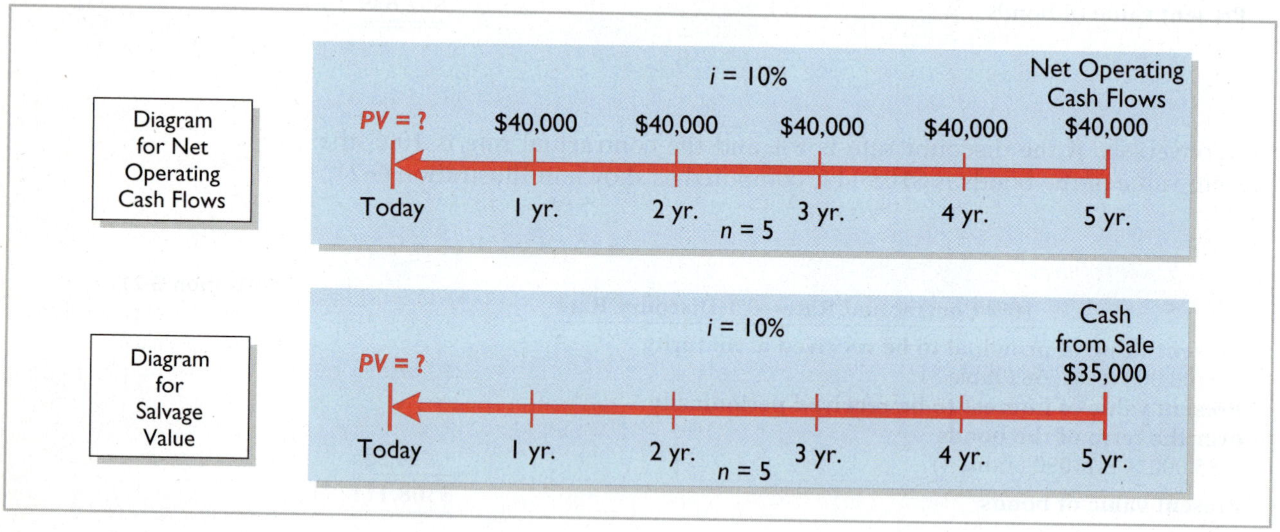

Notice from the diagrams that computing the present value of the net operating cash flows ($40,000 at the end of each year) is **discounting an annuity** (Table 4), while computing the present value of the $35,000 salvage value is **discounting a single sum** (Table 3). The computation of these present values is shown in Illustration G-23.

Illustration G-23
Present value computations at 10%

Present Values Using a 10% Discount Rate	
Present value of net operating cash flows received annually over 5 years	
$40,000 × PV of 1 received annually for 5 years at 10%	
$40,000 × 3.79079 (Table 4)	$ 151,631.60
Present value of salvage value (cash) to be received in 5 years	
$35,000 × PV of 1 received in 5 years at 10%	
$35,000 × .62092 (Table 3)	21,732.20
Present value of cash **inflows**	173,363.80
Present value of cash **outflows** (purchase price due today at 10%)	
$154,000 × PV of 1 due today	
$154,000 × 1.00000	(154,000.00)
Net present value	**$ 19,363.80**

Because the present value of the cash receipts (inflows) of $173,363.80 ($151,631.60 + $21,732.20) exceeds the present value of the cash payments (outflows) of $154,000.00, the net present value of $19,363.80 is positive, and **the decision to invest should be accepted.**

Now assume that Nagle-Siebert uses a discount rate of 15%, not 10%, because it wants a greater return on its investments in capital assets. The cash receipts and cash payments by Nagel-Siebert are the same. The present values of these receipts and cash payments discounted at 15% are shown in Illustration G-24.

Illustration G-24
Present value computations at 15%

Present Values Using a 15% Discount Rate	
Present value of net operating cash flows received annually over 5 years at 15%	
$40,000 × 3.35216 (Table 4)	$ 134,086.40
Present value of salvage value (cash) to be received in 5 years at 15%	
$35,000 × .49718 (Table 3)	17,401.30
Present value of cash **inflows**	151,487.70
Present value of cash **outflows** (purchase price due today at 15%)	
$154,000 × 1.00000	(154,000.00)
Net present value	**$ (2,512.30)**

Because the present value of the cash payments (outflows) of $154,000.00 exceeds the present value of the cash receipts (inflows) of $151,487.70 ($134,086.40 + $17,401.30), the net present value of $2,512.30 is negative, and **the investment should be rejected.**

The above discussion relied on present value tables in solving present value problems. As we show in the next section, calculators may also be used to compute present values without the use of these tables. Financial calculators have present value (PV) functions that allow you to calculate present values by merely identifying the proper amount, discount rate, periods, and pressing the PV key.

LEARNING OBJECTIVE 4

Use a financial calculator to solve time value of money problems.

Business professionals, once they have mastered the underlying time value of money concepts, often use a financial calculator to solve these types of problems. In most cases, they use calculators if interest rates or time periods do not correspond with the information provided in the compound interest tables.

To use financial calculators, you enter the time value of money variables into the calculator. Illustration G-25 shows the five most common keys used to solve time value of money problems.[2]

Illustration G-25
Financial calculator keys

where:

N = number of periods
I = interest rate per period (some calculators use I/YR or i)
PV = present value (occurs at the beginning of the first period)
PMT = payment (all payments are equal, and none are skipped)
FV = future value (occurs at the end of the last period)

In solving time value of money problems in this appendix, you will generally be given three of four variables and will have to solve for the remaining variable. The fifth key (the key not used) is given a value of zero to ensure that this variable is not used in the computation.

Present Value of a Single Sum

To illustrate how to solve a present value problem using a financial calculator, assume that you want to know the present value of $84,253 to be received in five years, discounted at 11% compounded annually. Illustration G-26 depicts this problem.

Illustration G-26
Calculator solution for present value of a single sum

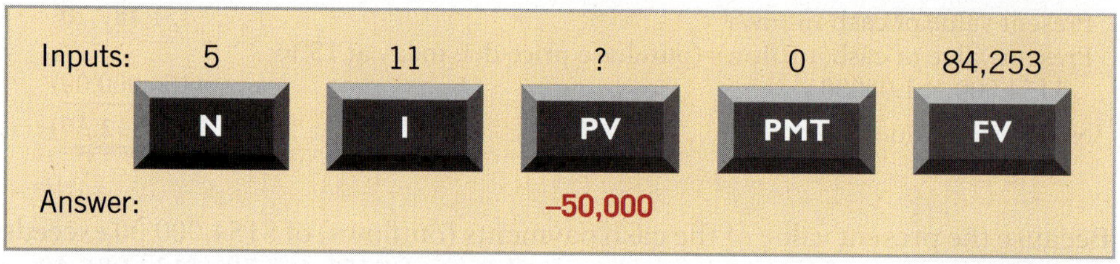

Illustration G-26 shows you the information (inputs) to enter into the calculator: N = 5, I = 11, PMT = 0, and FV = 84,253. You then press PV for the answer: −$50,000. As indicated, the PMT key was given a value of zero because a series of payments did not occur in this problem.

PLUS AND MINUS

The use of plus and minus signs in time value of money problems with a financial calculator can be confusing. Most financial calculators are programmed so that the positive and negative cash flows in any problem offset each other. In the present value problem above, we identified the $84,253 future value initial investment as a positive (inflow); the answer −$50,000 was shown as a negative amount, reflecting a cash outflow. If the 84,253 were entered as a negative, then the final answer would have been reported as a positive 50,000.

Hopefully, the sign convention will not cause confusion. If you understand what is required in a problem, you should be able to interpret a positive or negative amount in determining the solution to a problem.

[2] On many calculators, these keys are actual buttons on the face of the calculator; on others, they appear on the display after the user accesses a present value menu.

COMPOUNDING PERIODS

In the previous problem, we assumed that compounding occurs once a year. Some financial calculators have a default setting, which assumes that compounding occurs 12 times a year. You must determine what default period has been programmed into your calculator and change it as necessary to arrive at the proper compounding period.

ROUNDING

Most financial calculators store and calculate using 12 decimal places. As a result, because compound interest tables generally have factors only up to five decimal places, a slight difference in the final answer can result. In most time value of money problems, the final answer will not include more than two decimal places.

Present Value of an Annuity

To illustrate how to solve a present value of an annuity problem using a financial calculator, assume that you are asked to determine the present value of rental receipts of $6,000 each to be received at the end of each of the next five years, when discounted at 12%, as pictured in Illustration G-27.

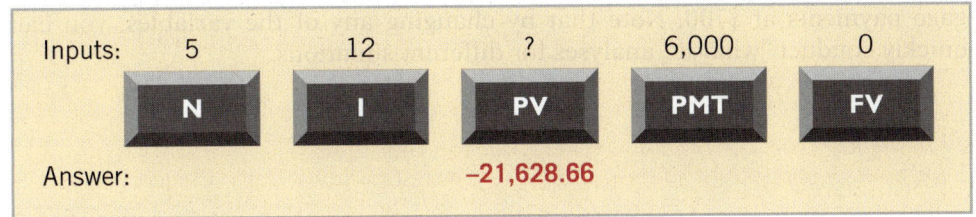

Illustration G-27 Calculator solution for present value of an annuity

Inputs:	5	12	?	6,000	0
	N	**I**	**PV**	**PMT**	**FV**
Answer:			–21,628.66		

In this case, you enter N = 5, I = 12, PMT = 6,000, FV = 0, and then press PV to arrive at the answer of −$21,628.66.

Useful Applications of the Financial Calculator

With a financial calculator, you can solve for any interest rate or for any number of periods in a time value of money problem. Here are some examples of these applications.

AUTO LOAN

Assume you are financing the purchase of a used car with a three-year loan. The loan has a 9.5% stated annual interest rate, compounded monthly. The price of the car is $6,000, and you want to determine the monthly payments, assuming that the payments start one month after the purchase. This problem is pictured in Illustration G-28.

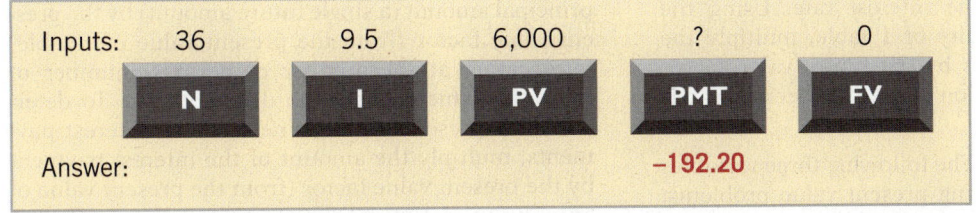

Illustration G-28 Calculator solution for auto loan payments

Inputs:	36	9.5	6,000	?	0
	N	**I**	**PV**	**PMT**	**FV**
Answer:				–192.20	

To solve this problem, you enter N = 36 (12 × 3), I = 9.5, PV = 6,000, FV = 0, and then press PMT. You will find that the monthly payments will be $192.20. Note that the payment key is usually programmed for 12 payments per year. Thus, you must change the default (compounding period) if the payments are other than monthly.

MORTGAGE LOAN AMOUNT

Say you are evaluating financing options for a loan on a house (a mortgage). You decide that the maximum mortgage payment you can afford is $700 per month. The annual interest rate is 8.4%. If you get a mortgage that requires you to make monthly payments over a 15-year period, what is the maximum home loan you can afford? Illustration G-29 depicts this problem.

Illustration G-29
Calculator solution for mortgage amount

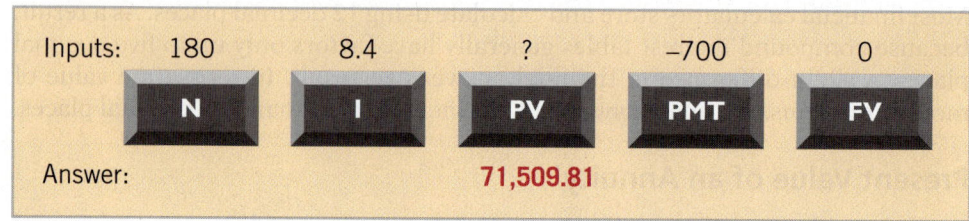

Inputs:	180	8.4	?	–700	0
	N	I	PV	PMT	FV
Answer:			71,509.81		

You enter N = 180 (12 × 15 years), I = 8.4, PMT = −700, FV = 0, and press PV. With the payments-per-year key set at 12, you find a present value of $71,509.81—the maximum home loan you can afford, given that you want to keep your mortgage payments at $700. Note that by changing any of the variables, you can quickly conduct "what-if" analyses for different situations.

REVIEW

LEARNING OBJECTIVES REVIEW

1 Compute interest and future values. Simple interest is computed on the principal only, while compound interest is computed on the principal and any interest earned that has not been withdrawn.

To solve for future value of a single amount, prepare a time diagram of the problem. Identify the principal amount, the number of compounding periods, and the interest rate. Using the future value of 1 table, multiply the principal amount by the future value factor specified at the intersection of the number of periods and the interest rate.

To solve for future value of an annuity, prepare a time diagram of the problem. Identify the amount of the periodic payments (receipts), the number of payments (receipts), and the interest rate. Using the future value of an annuity of 1 table, multiply the amount of the payments by the future value factor specified at the intersection of the number of periods and the interest rate.

2 Compute present value. The following three variables are fundamental to solving present value problems: (1) the future amount, (2) the number of periods, and (3) the interest rate (the discount rate).

To solve for present value of a single amount, prepare a time diagram of the problem. Identify the future amount, the number of discounting periods, and the discount (interest) rate. Using the present value of a single amount table, multiply the future amount by the present value factor specified at the intersection of the number of periods and the discount rate.

To solve for present value of an annuity, prepare a time diagram of the problem. Identify the amount of future periodic receipts or payments (annuities), the number of payments (receipts), and the discount (interest) rate. Using the present value of an annuity of 1 table, multiply the amount of the annuity by the present value factor specified at the intersection of the number of payments and the interest rate.

To compute the present value of notes and bonds, determine the present value of the principal amount and the present value of the interest payments. Multiply the principal amount (a single future amount) by the present value factor (from the present value of 1 table) intersecting at the number of periods (number of interest payments) and the discount rate. To determine the present value of the series of interest payments, multiply the amount of the interest payment by the present value factor (from the present value of an annuity of 1 table) intersecting at the number of periods (number of interest payments) and the discount rate. Add the present value of the principal amount to the present value of the interest payments to arrive at the present value of the note or bond.

3 Compute the present value in capital budgeting situations. Compute the present values of all cash inflows and all cash outflows related to the capital budgeting proposal (an investment-type decision). If the **net** present value is positive, accept the proposal (make the investment). If the **net** present value is negative, reject the proposal (do not make the investment).

4 Use a financial calculator to solve time value of money problems. Financial calculators can be used to solve the same and additional problems as those solved with time value of money tables. Enter into the financial calculator the amounts for all of the known elements of a time value of money problem (periods, interest rate, payments, future or present value), and it solves for the unknown element. Particularly useful situations involve interest rates and compounding periods not presented in the tables.

GLOSSARY REVIEW

Annuity A series of equal dollar amounts to be paid or received at evenly spaced time intervals (periodically). (p. G-5).

Compound interest The interest computed on the principal and any interest earned that has not been paid or withdrawn. (p. G-2).

Discounting the future amount(s) The process of determining present value. (p. G-7).

Future value of an annuity The sum of all the payments (receipts) plus the accumulated compound interest on them. (p. G-5).

Future value of a single amount The value at a future date of a given amount invested, assuming compound interest. (p. G-3).

Interest Payment for the use of another person's money. (p. G-1).

Present value The value now of a given amount to be paid or received in the future, assuming compound interest. (p. G-7).

Present value of an annuity The value now of a series of future receipts or payments, discounted assuming compound interest. (p. G-9).

Principal The amount borrowed or invested. (p. G-1).

Simple interest The interest computed on the principal only. (p. G-2).

BRIEF EXERCISES

(Use tables to solve exercises BEG-1 to BEG-23.)

BEG-1 Jozy Altidore invested $6,000 at 5% annual interest, and left the money invested without withdrawing any of the interest for 12 years. At the end of the 12 years, Jozy withdrew the accumulated amount of money. (a) What amount did Jozy withdraw, assuming the investment earns simple interest? (b) What amount did Jozy withdraw, assuming the investment earns interest compounded annually?

Compute the future value of a single amount.
(LO 1)

BEG-2 For each of the following cases, indicate (a) what interest rate columns and (b) what number of periods you would refer to in looking up the future value factor.

Use future value tables.
(LO 1)

(1) In Table 1 (future value of 1):

	Annual Rate	Number of Years Invested	Compounded
Case A	5%	3	Annually
Case B	12%	4	Semiannually

(2) In Table 2 (future value of an annuity of 1):

	Annual Rate	Number of Years Invested	Compounded
Case A	3%	8	Annually
Case B	8%	6	Semiannually

Compute the future value of a single amount.
(LO 1)

BEG-3 Liam Company signed a lease for an office building for a period of 12 years. Under the lease agreement, a security deposit of $9,600 is made. The deposit will be returned at the expiration of the lease with interest compounded at 4% per year. What amount will Liam receive at the time the lease expires?

Compute the future value of an annuity.
(LO 1)

BEG-4 Bates Company issued $1,000,000, 10-year bonds and agreed to make annual sinking fund deposits of $78,000. The deposits are made at the end of each year into an account paying 6% annual interest. What amount will be in the sinking fund at the end of 10 years?

Compute the future value of a single amount and of an annuity.
(LO 1)

BEG-5 Andrew and Emma Garfield invested $8,000 in a savings account paying 5% annual interest when their daughter, Angela, was born. They also deposited $1,000 on each of her birthdays until she was 18 (including her 18th birthday). How much was in the savings account on her 18th birthday (after the last deposit)?

Compute the future value of a single amount.
(LO 1)

BEG-6 Hugh Curtin borrowed $35,000 on July 1, 2017. This amount plus accrued interest at 8% compounded annually is to be repaid on July 1, 2022. How much will Hugh have to repay on July 1, 2022?

Use present value tables.
(LO 2)

BEG-7 For each of the following cases, indicate (a) what interest rate columns and (b) what number of periods you would refer to in looking up the discount rate.

(1) In Table 3 (present value of 1):

	Annual Rate	Number of Years Involved	Discounts per Year
Case A	12%	7	Annually
Case B	8%	11	Annually
Case C	10%	8	Semiannually

(2) In Table 4 (present value of an annuity of 1):

	Annual Rate	Number of Years Involved	Number of Payments Involved	Frequency of Payments
Case A	10%	20	20	Annually
Case B	10%	7	7	Annually
Case C	6%	5	10	Semiannually

Determine present values.
(LO 2)

BEG-8 (a) What is the present value of $25,000 due 9 periods from now, discounted at 10%?
(b) What is the present value of $25,000 to be received at the end of each of 6 periods, discounted at 9%?

Compute the present value of a single amount investment.
(LO 2)

BEG-9 Messi Company is considering an investment that will return a lump sum of $900,000 6 years from now. What amount should Messi Company pay for this investment to earn an 8% return?

Compute the present value of a single amount investment.
(LO 2)

BEG-10 Lloyd Company earns 6% on an investment that will return $450,000 8 years from now. What is the amount Lloyd should invest now to earn this rate of return?

Compute the present value of an annuity investment.
(LO 2)

BEG-11 Robben Company is considering investing in an annuity contract that will return $40,000 annually at the end of each year for 15 years. What amount should Robben Company pay for this investment if it earns an 8% return?

Compute the present value of an annual investment.
(LO 2)

BEG-12 Kaehler Enterprises earns 5% on an investment that pays back $80,000 at the end of each of the next 6 years. What is the amount Kaehler Enterprises invested to earn the 5% rate of return?

Compute the present value of bonds.
(LO 2)

BEG-13 Dempsey Railroad Co. is about to issue $400,000 of 10-year bonds paying an 11% interest rate, with interest payable semiannually. The discount rate for such securities is 10%. How much can Dempsey expect to receive for the sale of these bonds?

BEG-14 Assume the same information as BEG-13 except that the discount rate is 12% instead of 10%. In this case, how much can Dempsey expect to receive from the sale of these bonds?

Compute the present value of bonds.
(LO 2)

BEG-15 Neymar Taco Company receives a $75,000, 6-year note bearing interest of 4% (paid annually) from a customer at a time when the discount rate is 6%. What is the present value of the note received by Neymar?

Compute the present value of a note.
(LO 2)

BEG-16 Gleason Enterprises issued 6%, 8-year, $2,500,000 par value bonds that pay interest semiannually on October 1 and April 1. The bonds are dated April 1, 2017, and are issued on that date. The discount rate of interest for such bonds on April 1, 2017, is 8%. What cash proceeds did Gleason receive from issuance of the bonds?

Compute the present value of bonds.
(LO 2)

BEG-17 Frazier Company issues a 10%, 5-year mortgage note on January 1, 2017, to obtain financing for new equipment. Land is used as collateral for the note. The terms provide for semiannual installment payments of $48,850. What are the cash proceeds received from the issuance of the note?

Compute the present value of a note.
(LO 2)

BEG-18 If Colleen Mooney invests $4,765.50 now and she will receive $12,000 at the end of 12 years, what annual rate of interest will Colleen earn on her investment? (*Hint:* Use Table 3.)

Compute the interest rate on a single amount.
(LO 2)

BEG-19 Tim Howard has been offered the opportunity of investing $36,125 now. The investment will earn 11% per year and at the end of that time will return Tim $75,000. How many years must Tim wait to receive $75,000? (*Hint:* Use Table 3.)

Compute the number of periods of a single amount.
(LO 2)

BEG-20 Joanne Quick made an investment of $10,271.38. From this investment, she will receive $1,200 annually for the next 15 years starting one year from now. What rate of interest will Joanne's investment be earning for her? (*Hint:* Use Table 4.)

Compute the interest rate on an annuity.
(LO 2)

BEG-21 Kevin Morales invests $7,793.83 now for a series of $1,300 annual returns beginning one year from now. Kevin will earn a return of 9% on the initial investment. How many annual payments of $1,300 will Kevin receive? (*Hint:* Use Table 4.)

Compute the number of periods of an annuity.
(LO 2)

BEG-22 Barney Googal owns a garage and is contemplating purchasing a tire retreading machine for $12,820. After estimating costs and revenues, Barney projects a net cash inflow from the retreading machine of $2,700 annually for 7 years. Barney hopes to earn a return of 9% on such investments. What is the present value of the retreading operation? Should Barney Googal purchase the retreading machine?

Compute the present value of a machine for purposes of making a purchase decision.
(LO 3)

BEG-23 Snyder Company is considering purchasing equipment. The equipment will produce the following cash inflows: Year 1, $25,000; Year 2, $30,000; and Year 3, $40,000. Snyder requires a minimum rate of return of 11%. What is the maximum price Snyder should pay for this equipment?

Compute the maximum price to pay for a machine.
(LO 3)

BEG-24 Carly Simon wishes to invest $18,000 on July 1, 2017, and have it accumulate to $50,000 by July 1, 2027. Use a financial calculator to determine at what exact annual rate of interest Carly must invest the $18,000.

Determine interest rate.
(LO 4)

BEG-25 On July 17, 2016, Keith Urban borrowed $42,000 from his grandfather to open a clothing store. Starting July 17, 2017, Keith has to make 10 equal annual payments of $6,500 each to repay the loan. Use a financial calculator to determine what interest rate Keith is paying.

Determine interest rate.
(LO 4)

BEG-26 As the purchaser of a new house, Carrie Underwood has signed a mortgage note to pay the Nashville National Bank and Trust Co. $8,400 every 6 months for 20 years, at the end of which time she will own the house. At the date the mortgage is signed, the purchase price was $198,000 and Underwood made a down payment of $20,000. The first payment will be made 6 months after the date the mortgage is signed. Using a financial calculator, compute the exact rate of interest earned on the mortgage by the bank.

Determine interest rate.
(LO 4)

Various time value of money situations.

(LO 4)

BEG-27 Using a financial calculator, solve for the unknowns in each of the following situations.

(a) On June 1, 2016, Jennifer Lawrence purchases lakefront property from her neighbor, Josh Hutcherson, and agrees to pay the purchase price in seven payments of $16,000 each, the first payment to be payable June 1, 2017. (Assume that interest compounded at an annual rate of 7.35% is implicit in the payments.) What is the purchase price of the property?

(b) On January 1, 2016, Gerrard Corporation purchased 200 of the $1,000 face value, 8% coupon, 10-year bonds of Sterling Inc. The bonds mature on January 1, 2026, and pay interest annually beginning January 1, 2017. Gerrard purchased the bonds to yield 10.65%. How much did Gerrard pay for the bonds?

Various time value of money situations.

(LO 4)

BEG-28 Using a financial calculator, provide a solution to each of the following situations.

(a) Lynn Anglin owes a debt of $42,000 from the purchase of her new sport utility vehicle. The debt bears annual interest of 7.8% compounded monthly. Lynn wishes to pay the debt and interest in equal monthly payments over 8 years, beginning one month hence. What equal monthly payments will pay off the debt and interest?

(b) On January 1, 2017, Roger Molony offers to buy Dave Feeney's used snowmobile for $8,000, payable in five equal annual installments, which are to include 7.25% interest on the unpaid balance and a portion of the principal. If the first payment is to be made on December 31, 2017, how much will each payment be?

Appendix H Standards of Ethical Conduct for Management Accountants

APPENDIX PREVIEW Management accountants have an obligation to the organizations they serve, their profession, the public, and themselves to maintain the highest standards of ethical conduct. In recognition of this obligation, the **Institute of Management Accountants** has published and promoted the following standards of ethical conduct for management accountants.

IMA Statement of Ethical Professional Practice

Members of IMA shall behave ethically. A commitment to ethical professional practice includes: overarching principles that express our values, and standards that guide our conduct.

Principles

IMA's overarching ethical principles include: Honesty, Fairness, Objectivity, and Responsibility. Members shall act in accordance with these principles and shall encourage others within their organizations to adhere to them.

Standards

A member's failure to comply with the following standards may result in disciplinary action.

I. COMPETENCE

Each member has a responsibility to:

1. Maintain an appropriate level of professional expertise by continually developing knowledge and skills.
2. Perform professional duties in accordance with relevant laws, regulations, and technical standards.
3. Provide decision support information and recommendations that are accurate, clear, concise, and timely.
4. Recognize and communicate professional limitations or other constraints that would preclude responsible judgment or successful performance of an activity.

II. CONFIDENTIALITY

Each member has a responsibility to:

1. Keep information confidential except when disclosure is authorized or legally required.
2. Inform all relevant parties regarding appropriate use of confidential information. Monitor subordinates' activities to ensure compliance.
3. Refrain from using confidential information for unethical or illegal advantage.

III. INTEGRITY

Each member has a responsibility to:

1. Mitigate actual conflicts of interest, regularly communicate with business associates to avoid apparent conflicts of interest. Advise all parties of any potential conflicts.
2. Refrain from engaging in any conduct that would prejudice carrying out duties ethically.
3. Abstain from engaging in or supporting any activity that might discredit the profession.

IV. CREDIBILITY

Each member has a responsibility to:

1. Communicate information fairly and objectively.
2. Disclose all relevant information that could reasonably be expected to influence an intended user's understanding of the reports, analyses, or recommendations.
3. Disclose delays or deficiencies in information, timeliness, processing, or internal controls in conformance with organization policy and/or applicable law.

Resolution of Ethical Conflict

In applying the Standards of Ethical Professional Practice, you may encounter problems identifying unethical behavior or resolving an ethical conflict. When faced with ethical issues, you should follow your organization's established policies on the resolution of such conflict. If these policies do not resolve the ethical conflict, you should consider the following courses of action:

1. Discuss the issue with your immediate supervisor except when it appears that the supervisor is involved. In that case, present the issue to the next level. If you cannot achieve a satisfactory resolution, submit the issue to the next management level. If your immediate superior is the chief executive officer or equivalent, the acceptable reviewing authority may be a group such as the audit committee, executive committee, board of directors, board of trustees, or owners. Contact with levels above the immediate superior should be initiated only with your superior's knowledge, assuming he or she is not involved. Communication of such problems to authorities or individuals not employed or engaged by the organization is not considered appropriate, unless you believe there is a clear violation of the law.
2. Clarify relevant ethical issues by initiating a confidential discussion with an IMA Ethics Counselor or other impartial advisor to obtain a better understanding of possible courses of action.
3. Consult your own attorney as to legal obligations and rights concerning the ethical conflict.

Source: Institute of Management Accountants. Reprinted by permission. Go to *www.imanet.org/about_ima/our_mission.aspx* to learn more about the IMA's commitment to ethical professional practices and its available resources, including an Ethics Helpline.

Company Index

Subject Index